Azizah Abd Manaf   Shamsul Sahibuddin
Rabiah Ahmad   Salwani Mohd Daud
Eyas El-Qawasmeh (Eds.)

Informatics Engineering and Information Science

International Conference, ICIEIS 2011
Kuala Lumpur, Malaysia, November 14-16, 2011
Proceedings, Part III

Springer

Volume Editors

Azizah Abd Manaf
Advanced Informatics School (UTM AIS)
UTM International Campus
Kuala Lumpur, 54100, Malaysia
E-mail: azizah07@ic.utm.my

Shamsul Sahibuddin
Advanced Informatics School (UTM AIS)
UTM International Campus
Kuala Lumpur, 54100, Malaysia
E-mail: shamsul@utm.my

Rabiah Ahmad
Advanced Informatics School (UTM AIS)
UTM International Campus
Kuala Lumpur, 54100, Malaysia
E-mail: rabiah@utem.edu.my

Salwani Mohd Daud
Advanced Informatics School (UTM AIS)
UTM International Campus
Kuala Lumpur, 54100, Malaysia
E-mail: salwani@ic.utm.my

Eyas El-Qawasmeh
King Saud University
Information Systems Department
Riyadh, Saudi Arabia
E-mail: eyasa@usa.net

ISSN 1865-0929
ISSN 1865-0937 (electronic)
ISBN 978-3-642-25461-1
ISBN 978-3-642-25462-8 (eBook)
DOI 10.1007/978-3-642-25462-8
Springer Heidelberg Dordrecht London New York

Library of Congress Control Number: 2011941089

CR Subject Classification (1998): C.2, H.4, I.2, H.3, D.2, H.5

Typesetting: Camera-ready by author, data conversion by Scientific Publishing Services, Chennai, India

Printed on acid-free paper

Springer is part of Springer Science+Business Media (www.springer.com)

Communications
in Computer and Information Science 253

Message from the Chair

The International Conference on Informatics Engineering and Information Science (ICIEIS 2011)—co-sponsored by Springer—was organized and hosted by Universiti Teknologi Malaysia in Kuala Lumpur, Malaysia, during November 14–16, 2011 in association with the Society of Digital Information and Wireless Communications. ICIEIS 2011 was planned as a major event in the computer and information sciences and served as a forum for scientists and engineers to meet and present their latest research results, ideas, and papers in the diverse areas of digital information processing, digital communications, information security, information ethics, and data management, and other related topics.

This scientific conference comprised guest lectures and 210 research papers for presentation over many parallel sessions. This number was selected from more than 600 papers. For each presented paper, a minimum of two reviewers went through each paper and filled a reviewing form. The system involves assigning grades to each paper based on the reviewers' comments. The system that is used is open conference. It assigns grades for each paper that range from 6 to 1. After that, the Scientific Committee re-evaluates the paper and its reviewing and decides on either acceptance or rejection.

This meeting provided a great opportunity to exchange knowledge and experiences for all the participants who joined us from all over the world to discuss new ideas in the areas of data and information management and its applications. We are grateful to Universiti Teknologi Malaysia in Kuala Lumpur for hosting this conference. We use this occasion to express thanks to the Technical Committee and to all the external reviewers. We are grateful to Springer for co-sponsoring the event. Finally, we would like to thank all the participants and sponsors.

Azizah Abd Manaf

Preface

On behalf of the ICIEIS 2011 conference, the Program Committee and Universiti Teknologi Malaysia in Kuala Lumpur, I have the pleasure to present the proceedings of the International Conference on Informatics Engineering and Information Science' (ICIEIS 2011).

The ICIEIS 2011 conference explored new advances in digital information and data communications technologies. It brought together researchers from various areas of computer science, information sciences, and data communications to address both theoretical and applied aspects of digital communications and wireless technology. We hope that the discussions and exchange of ideas will contribute to advancements in the technology in the near future.

The conference received more than 600 papers of which 530 papers were considered for evaluation. The number of accepted papers 210. The accepted papers were authored by researchers from 39 countries covering many significant areas of digital information and data communications. Each paper was evaluated by a minimum of two reviewers.

Organization

General Chair

Azizah Abd Manaf	Universiti Teknologi Malaysia, Malaysia

Program Chair

Ezendu Ariwa	London Metropolitan University, UK
Mazdak Zamani	Universiti Teknologi Malaysia, Malaysia

Program Co-chairs

Yoshiro Imai	Kagawa University, Japan
Jacek Stando	Technical University of Lodz, Poland

Proceedings Chair

Jan Platos	VSB-Technical University of Ostrava, Czech Republic

Publicity Chair

Maitham Safar	Kuwait University, Kuwait
Zuqing Zhu	University of Science and Technology of China, China

International Program Committee

Abdullah Almansur	King Saud University, Saudi Arabia
Akram Zeki	International Islamic University Malaysia, Malaysia
Ali Dehghan Tanha	Asia Pacific University, Malaysia
Ali Sher	American University of Ras Al Khaimah, UAE
Altaf Mukati	Bahria University, Pakistan
Andre Leon S. Gradvohl	State University of Campinas, Brazil
Arash Habibi Lashkari	University Technology Malaysia (UTM), Malaysia
Asadollah Shahbahrami	Delft University of Technology, The Netherlands
Chantal Cherifi	Université de Corse, France
Craig Standing	Edith Cowan University, Australia

D.B. Karron	Computer Aided Surgery and Informatics, USA
Duc T. Pham	Cardiff University, UK
E. George Dharma Prakash Raj	Bharathidasan University, India
Eric Atwell	University of Leeds, UK
Estevam Rafael Hruschka	Carnegie Mellon University, USA
Eyas El-Qawasmeh	King Saud University, Saudi Arabia
Ezendu Ariwa	London Metropolitan University, UK
Fouzi Harrag	UFAS University, Algeria
Genge Bela	University of Targu Mures, Romania
Gianni Fenu	University of Cagliari, Italy
Guo Bin	Institute Telecom & Management SudParis, France
Hamid Jahankhani	University of East London, UK
Hend Al-Khalifa	King Saud University, Saudi Arabia
Hocine Cherifi	Université de Bourgogne, France
Isamu Shioya	Hosei University, Japan
Isao Nakanishi	Tottori University, Japan
Jim Yonazi	The Institute of Finance Management, Tanzania
Jose Filho	University of Grenoble, France
Juan Martinez	Gran Mariscal de Ayacucho University, Venezuela
Khaled A. Mahdi	Kuwait University, Kuwait
Kosuke Numa	The University of Tokyo, Japan
Ladislav Burita	University of Defence, Czech Republic
Laxmisha Rai	Shandong University of Science and Technology, China
Manjaiah D.H.	Mangalore University, India
Majid Haghparast	Islamic Azad University, Shahre-Rey Branch, Iran
Malinka Ivanova	Technical University, Bulgaria
Martin J. Dudziak	Stratford University, USA
Mazdak Zamani	Universiti Teknologi Malaysia, Malaysia
Mirel Cosulschi	University of Craiova, Romania
Mohd Abd Wahab	Universiti Tun Hussein Onn Malaysia, Malaysia
Monica Vladoiu	PG University of Ploiesti, Romania
Nan Zhang	George Washington University, USA
Nazri Mahrin	Universiti Teknologi Malaysia, Malaysia
Noraziah Ahmad	Universiti Malaysia Pahang, Malaysia
Pasquale De Meo	University of Applied Sciences of Porto, Portugal
Paulino Leite da Silva	ISCAP-IPP University, Portugal
Piet Kommers	University of Twente, The Netherlands
Prabhat Mahanti	University of New Brunswick, Canada
Rabiah Ahmad	Universiti Teknologi Malaysia, Malaysia

Radhamani Govindaraju	Damodaran College of Science, India
Ram Palanisamy	St. Francis Xavier University, Canada
Riaza Mohd Rias	University of Technology MARA, Malaysia
Salwani Mohd Daud	Universiti Teknologi Malaysia, Malaysia
Sami Alyazidi	King Saud University, Saudi Arabia
Shamsul Mohd Shahibudin	Universiti Teknologi Malaysia, Malaysia
Talib Mohammad	University of Botswana, Botswana
Valentina Dagiene	Institute of Mathematics and Informatics, Lithuania
Viacheslav Wolfengagen	JurInfoR-MSU Institute, Russia
Waralak V. Siricharoen	University of the Thai Chamber of Commerce, Thailand
Wojciech Mazurczyk	Warsaw University of Technology, Poland
Wojciech Zabierowski	Technical University of Lodz, Poland
Yi Pan	Georgia State University, USA
Zanifa Omary	Dublin Institute of Technology, Ireland
Zuqing Zhu	The University of Science and Technology of China, China
Zuqing Zhu	University of Science and Technology of China, China
Zuraini Ismail	Universiti Teknologi Malaysia, Malaysia

Reviewers

Morteza Gholipour Geshnyani	University of Tehran, Iran
Asadollah Shahbahrami	University of Guilan, Iran
Mohd Faiz Hilmi	Universiti Sains Malaysia, Malaysia
Brij Gupta	Indian Institute of Technology, India
Naeem Shah	Xavor Corporation, Pakistan
Shanmugasundaram Hariharan	B.S. Abdur Rahman University, India
Rajibul Islam	University Technology Malaysia, Malaysia
Luca Mazzola	Università della Svizzera Italiana, Italy
K.P. Yadav	Acme College of Engineering, India
Jesuk Ko	Gwangju University, Korea
Mohd Wahab	Universiti Tun Hussein Onn Malaysia, Malaysia
Luca Mazzola	Università della Svizzera Italiana, Italy
Anirban Kundu	West Bengal University of Technology, India
Hamouid Khaled	Batna University, Algeria
Muhammad Naveed	Iqra University, Pakistan
Yana Hassim	Universiti Tun Hussein Onn Malaysia, Malaysia
Reza Moradi Rad	University of Guilan, Iran
Rahman Attar	University of Guilan, Iran
Zulkefli Bin Mansor	Universiti Teknologi MARA, Malaysia
Mourad Amad	Bejaia University, Algeria
Reza Ebrahimi Atani	University of Guilan, Iran
Vishal Bharti	Dronacharya College of Engineering, India

Kalum P. Udagepola	BBCG, Australia
Muhammad Javed	Dublin City University, Ireland
Partha Sarati Das	Dhaka University of Engineering, Bangladesh
Ainita Ban	Universiti Putra Malaysia, Malaysia
Noridayu Manshor	Universiti Putra Malaysia, Malaysia
Syed Muhammad Noman	Sir Syed University of Engineering and Technology, Pakistan
Zhefu Shi	University of Missouri, USA
Noraini Ibrahim	Universiti Teknologi Malaysia (UTM), Malaysia
Przemyslaw Pawluk	York University, Canada
Kumudha Raimond	Addis Ababa University, Ethiopia
Gurvan Le Guernic	KTH- Royal Institute of Technology, Sweden
Sarma A.D.N	Nagarjuna University, India
Utku Kose	Afyon Kocatepe University, Turkey
Kamal Srivastava	SRMCEM, India
Marzanah A. Jabar	Universiti Putra Malaysia, Malaysia
Eyas ElQawasmeh	King Saud University, Saudi Arabia
Adelina Tang	Sunway University, Malaysia
Samarjeet Borah	Sikkim Manipal Institute of Technology, India
Ayyoub Akbari	Universiti Putra Malaysia, Malaysia
Abbas Mehdizadeh	Universiti Putra Malaysia (UPM), Malaysia
Looi Qin En	Institute for Infocomm Research, Singapore
Krishna Prasad Miyapuram	Università degli Studi di Trento, Italy
M.Hemalatha	Karpagam University, India
Azizi Nabiha	Annaba University of Algeria, Algeria
Mallikarjun Hangarge	Science and Commerce College, India
J. Satheesh Kumar	Bharathiar University, India
Abbas Hanon AlAsadi	Basra University, Iraq
Maythem Abbas	Universiti Teknologi PETRONAS, Malaysia
Mohammad Reza Noruzi	Tarbiat Modarres University, Iran
Santoso Wibowo	CQ University Melbourne, Australia
Ramez Alkhatib	AlBaath University, Syrian Arab Republic
Ashraf Mohammed Iqbal	Dalhousie University, Canada
Hari Shanker Hota	GGV Central University, India
Tamer Beitelmal	Carleton University, Canada
Azlan Iqbal	Universiti Tenaga Nasional, Malaysia
Alias Balamurugan	Thiagarajar College of Engineering, India
Muhammad Sarfraz	Kuwait University, Kuwait
Vuong M. Ngo	HCMC University of Technology, Vietnam
Asad Malik	College of Electrical and Mechincal Engineering, Pakistan
Anju Sharma	Thapar University, India
Mohammad Ali Orumiehchiha	Macquarie University, Australia
Khalid Hussain	University Technology Malaysia, Malaysia

Parvinder Singh	Deenbandhu Chhotu Ram University of Science and Technology, India
Amir Hossein Azadnia	University Technology Malaysia (UTM), Malaysia
Zulkhar Nain	American University, United Arab Emirates
Shashirekha H.L.	Mangalore University, India
Dinesh Hanchate	Vidypratishthan's College Of Engineering, India
Mueen Uddin	Universiti Teknologi Malaysia (UTM), Malaysia
Muhammad Fahim	Kyung Hee University, Korea
Sharifah Mastura Syed Mohamad	Universiti Sains Malaysia, Malaysia
Baisa Gunjal	Amrutvahini College of Engineering, India
Ali Ahmad Alawneh	Philadelphia University, Jordan
Nabhan Hamadneh	Murdoch University, Australia
Vaitheeshwar Ramachandran	Tata Consultancy Services, India
Ahmad Shoara	Farabi Higher Education Institute, Iran
Murtaza Ali Khan	Royal University for Women, Bahrain
Norshidah Katiran	Universiti Teknologi Malaysia, Malaysia
Haniyeh Kazemitabar	Universiti Teknologi PETRONAS, Malaysia
Sharifah Mastura Syed Mohamad	Universiti Sains Malaysia, Malaysia
Somnuk Phon-Amnuaisuk	Universiti Tunku Abdul Rahman, Malaysia
Prasanalakshmi Balaji	Bharathiar University, India
Mueen Uddin	Universiti Teknologi Malaysia, Malaysia
Bhumika Patel	CKPithawalla College of Engineering and Technology, India
Sachin Thanekar	University of Pune, India
Nuzhat Shaikh	MES College of Engineering, India
Safiye Ghasemi	Islamic Azad University, Iran
Nor Laily Hashim	Universiti Utara Malaysia, Malaysia
Joao Pedro Costa	University of Coimbra, Portugal
S. Parthasarathy	Thiagarajar College of Engineering, India
Omar Kareem Jasim	Maaref College University, Iraq
Balasubramanian Thangavelu	SVM Arts and Science College, India
Lee Chai Har	Multimedia University (MMU), Malaysia
Md Asikur Rahman	Memorial University of Newfoundland, Canada
Renatus Michael	The Institute of Finance Management, Tanzania
Shin-ya Nishizaki	Tokyo Institute of Technology, Japan
Sahadeo Padhye	Motilal Nehru National Institute of Technology, India
Faith Shimba	The Institute of Finance Management, Tanzania
Subashini Selvarajan	Annamalai University, India

Valentina Emilia Balas	University of Arad, Romania
Muhammad Imran Khan	Universiti Teknologi PETRONAS, Malaysia
Daniel Koloseni	The Institute of Finance Management, Tanzania
Jacek Stando	Technical University of Lodz, Poland
Yang-Sae Moon	Kangwon National University, Korea
Mohammad Islam	University of Chittagong, Bangladesh
Joseph Ng	University Tunku Abdul Rahman, Malaysia
Umang Singh	ITS Group of Institutions, India
Sim-Hui Tee	Multimedia University, Malaysia
Ahmad Husni Mohd Shapri	Universiti Malaysia Perlis, Malaysia
Syaripah Ruzaini Syed Aris	Universiti Teknologi MARA, Malaysia
Ahmad Pahlavan	Islamic Azad University, Iran
Aaradhana Deshmukh	Pune University, India
Sanjay Singh	Manipal University, India
Subhashini Radhakrishnan	Sathyabama University, India
Binod Kumar	Lakshmi Narain College of Technology, India
Farah Jahan	University of Chittagong, Bangladesh
Masoumeh Bourjandi	Islamic Azad University, Iran
Rainer Schick	University of Siegen, Germany
Zaid Mujaiyid Putra Ahmad	Universiti Teknologi MARA, Malaysia
Abdul Syukor Mohamad Jaya	Universiti Teknikal Malaysia Melaka, Malaysia
Yasir Mahmood	NUST SEECS, Pakistan
Razulaimi Razali	Universiti Teknologi MARA, Malaysia
Anand Sharma	MITS, LAkshmangarh, India
Seung Ho Choi	Seoul National University of Science and Technology, Korea
Safoura Janosepah	Islamic Azad University, Iran
Rosiline Jeetha B	RVS College of Arts and Science, India
Mustafa Man	University Malaysia Terengganu, Malaysia
Intan Najua Kamal Nasir	Universiti Teknologi PETRONAS, Malaysia
Ali Tufail	Ajou University, Korea
Bowen Zhang	Beijing University of Posts and Telecommunications, China
Rekha Labade	Amrutvahini College of Engineering, India
Ariffin Abdul Mutalib	Universiti Utara Malaysia, Malaysia
Mohamed Saleem Haja Nazmudeen	Universiti Tunku Abdul Rahman, Malaysia
Norjihan Abdul Ghani	University of Malaya, Malaysia
Micheal Arockiaraj	Loyola College, India
A. Kannan	K.L.N.College of Engineering, India
Nursalasawati Rusli	Universiti Malaysia Perlis, Malaysia
Ali Dehghantanha	Asia-Pacific University, Malaysia
Kathiresan V.	RVS College of Arts and Science, India
Saeed Ahmed	CIIT,Islamabad, Pakistan
Muhammad Bilal	UET Peshawar, Pakistan

Hanumanthappa J.	University of Mangalore, India
Tomasz Kajdanowicz	Wroclaw University of Technology, Poland
Rehmat Ullah	University of Engineering and Technology, Peshawar, Pakistan
Nur Zuraifah Syazrah Othman	Universiti Teknologi Malaysia, Malaysia
Mourad Daoudi	University of Sciences and Technologies Houari Boumediene, Algeria
Mingyu Lee	Sugnkyunkwan University, Korea
Cyriac Grigorious	Loyola College, India
Sudeep Stephen	Loyola College, India
Amit K. Awasthi	Gautam Buddha University, India
Zaiton Abdul Mutalip	Universiti Teknikal Malaysia Melaka, Malaysia
Abdu Gumaei	King Saud University, Saudi Arabia
E. Martin	University of California, Berkeley, USA
Mareike Dornhöfer	University of Siegen, Germany
Arash Salehpour	University of Nabi Akram, Iran
Mojtaba Seyedzadegan	UPM, Malaysia
Raphael Jackson	Kentucky State University, USA
Abdul Mateen	Federal Urdu University of Science and Technology, Pakistan
Subhashini Ramakrishnan	Dr G.R. Damodaran College of Science, India
Randall Duran	Singapore Management University, Singapore
Yoshiro Imai	Kagawa University, Japan
Syaril Nizam	University Technology Malaysia, Malaysia
Pantea Keikhosrokiani	Universiti Sains Malaysia, Malaysia
Kok Chin Khor	Multimedia University, Malaysia
Salah Bindahman	Universiti Sains Malaysia, Malaysia
Sami Miniaoui	University of Dubai, United Arab Emirates
Intisar A.M. Al Sayed	Al Isra University, Jordan
Teddy Mantoro	International Islamic University Malaysia, Malaysia
Kitsiri Chochiang	PSU University, Thailand
Khadoudja Ghanem	University Mentouri Constantine, Algeria
Rozeha A. Rashid	Universiti Teknologi Malaysia, Malaysia
Redhwan Qasem Shaddad	Taiz University, Yemen
MuhammadAwais Khan	COMSATS Institute of Information and Technology, Pakistan
Noreen Kausar	Universiti Teknologi PETRONAS, Malaysia
Hala Jubara	UTM, Malaysia
Alsaidi Altaher	Universiti Sains Malaysia, Malaysia
Syed Abdul Rahman Al-Haddad	Universiti Putra Malaysia, Malaysia
Norma Alias	Universiti Teknologi Malaysia, Malaysia
Adib M. Monzer Habbal	University Utara Malaysia, Malaysia
Heri Kuswanto	Institut Teknologi Sepuluh Nopember, Indonesia

Table of Contents – Part III

Neural Networks

Social Networks

Grid Computing

Biometric Technologies

Networks

Distributed and Parallel Computing

Wireless Networks

Erratum

Improved Adaptive Neuro-Fuzzy Inference System for HIV/AIDS Time Series Prediction

Purwanto[1,3,*], C. Eswaran[1], and R. Logeswaran[2]

[1] Faculty of Information Technology, Multimedia University, 63100 Cyberjaya, Malaysia
[2] Faculty of Engineering, Multimedia University, 63100 Cyberjaya, Malaysia
[3] Faculty of Computer Science, Dian Nuswantoro University, 50131 Semarang, Indonesia
mypoenk@gmail.com, {eswaran,loges}@mmu.edu.my

Abstract. Improving accuracy in time series prediction has always been a challenging task for researchers. Prediction of time series data in healthcare such as HIV/AIDS data assumes importance in healthcare management. Statistical techniques such as moving average (MA), weighted moving average (WMA) and autoregressive integrated moving average (ARIMA) models have limitations in handling the non-linear relationships among the data. Artificial intelligence (AI) techniques such as neural networks are considered to be better for prediction of non-linear data. In general, for complex healthcare data, it may be difficult to obtain high prediction accuracy rates using the statistical or AI models individually. To solve this problem, a hybrid model such as adaptive neuro-fuzzy inference system (ANFIS) is required. In this paper, we propose an improved ANFIS model to predict HIV/AIDS data. Using two statistical indicators, namely, Root Mean Square Error (RMSE) and Mean Absolute Error (MAE), the prediction accuracy of the proposed model is compared with the accuracies obtained with MA, WMA, ARIMA and Neural Network models based on HIV/AIDS data. The results indicate that the proposed model yields improvements as high as 87.84% compared to the other models.

Keywords: Adaptive Neuro-Fuzzy Inference Systems, Neural Network, ARIMA, Moving Average.

1 Introduction

Human immunodeficiency virus (HIV) / Acquired immune deficiency syndrome (AIDS) has become a serious threat around the world due to lack of affordable effective drugs and vaccines for prevention and cure. This disease also has a long asymptomatic (without symptoms) phase. The number of cases of HIV/ AIDS has increased despite various preventive measures. No country is unaffected by this disease [1].

The spread of HIV / AIDS cases will cause an adverse effect on the development of a country. It not only affects the health sector but also the socio-economic situation. Moreover, this disease is most prevalent in the productive age group.

* Corresponding author.

A. Abd Manaf et al. (Eds.): ICIEIS 2011, Part III, CCIS 253, pp. 1–13, 2011.

Therefore, information about the development and prediction of new HIV / AIDS cases are needed to assess the magnitude of the problem for prevention and mitigation. Good and accurate prediction is very helpful in devising appropriate action plans.

Many models have been applied in time series prediction such as moving average [2] and autoregressive integrated moving average (ARIMA) [3]. Seasonal ARIMA model has been used to predict the AIDS incidence [4]. Box-Jenkins ARIMA model has been used to predict cases of incident HIV infection [5]. However, traditional statistical techniques may not produce satisfactory results for time series prediction. Recent studies have discussed the problem of time series prediction using different concepts, including artificial neural networks that have self learning capabilities, to handle non-linear data and have been used in many applications [6]-[9].

In soft computing, fuzzy logic can tolerate imprecise information, and also can make an approximate reasoning framework. Unfortunately, fuzzy logic lacks self-learning capability. The Adaptive Neuro-Fuzzy Inference System is a combination artificial neural networks and fuzzy logic that has been used to predict observed real world time series [10]-[16]. An issue that has gained much attention with regard to the ANFIS model is how to determine the appropriate input lags for univariate time series.

In this paper, we propose an improved ANFIS model to predict HIV/AIDS time series data. A new procedure is presented to determine the accurate number of input lags in ANFIS model for univariate time series prediction. The proposed model is then tested using the HIV/ AIDS data obtained from the health department of Indonesia. We also compare the proposed model with neural network and statistical models.

2 Model Used

The following is a brief description of the time series prediction models such as moving average (MA) and autoregressive integrated moving average (ARIMA), neural network and adaptive neuro-fuzzy inference systems (ANFIS) models used in this study.

2.1 Moving Average (MA) Model

A moving average model provides an efficient mechanism to obtain the value of a stationary time series prediction. The MA model is one of the most widely used models for time series prediction. In this paper, we use MA and weighted moving average (WMA) model to predict univariate time series data.

The MA model of span m at time t is calculated as [17]:

$$\hat{y}_{t+1} = \frac{1}{m} \sum_{i=t-m+1}^{t} y_i \tag{1}$$

The weighted moving average model uses different weights for the past observations as shown in Eq. (2):

$$\hat{y}_t = w_1 y_{t-1} + w_2 y_{t-2} + w_3 y_{t-3} + \ldots + w_m y_{t-m} \tag{2}$$

where $w_1, w_2, \ldots, w_m$ denote the weights associated with the past observed values.

2.2 Autoregressive Integrated Moving Average (ARIMA) Model

Box and Jenkins [3] have popularized auto regressive moving average (ARMA) and auto regressive integrated moving average (ARIMA) models for time series prediction. An ARMA model assumes that the time series data for prediction is stationary. The ARMA model is made up an AR(*p*) autoregressive part and a MA (*q*) moving average part. The ARMA (*p*,*q*) model is calculated by [18]:

$$x_t = \sum_{i=1}^{p} \phi_i x_{t-i} + e_t + \sum_{j=1}^{q} \theta_j e_{t-j} \tag{3}$$

where e_t is residual at time *t*, ϕ_i (i= 1, 2, …, p) are the parameters of the autoregressive part and θ_j (j= 1, 2, …, q) are the parameters of the moving average part.

The autoregressive integrated moving average (ARIMA) model is an ARMA model employed for time series data that uses ordinary differencing (*d*). General form of the ARIMA (*p, d, q*) model could be computed as [18]:

$$\phi(B)(1-B)^d x_t = \theta(B)e_t \tag{4}$$

where *p* is the number of autoregressive lags, *d* the number of differences, *q* is the number of moving average lags, B is the backward shift operator.

2.3 Neural Network Model

The neural network model used in this study is the Multilayer Perceptron (MLP). There are many fields of application for the MLP model such as classification, pattern recognition and prediction. The MLP model is the most common neural network model used in prediction [19]. It consists of an input layer, one hidden layer and an output layers. The output layer has one neuron and a variable number of neurons or nodes exist in the input and hidden layers. Each neuron has a configurable bias and the strength of each connection of a node to another is determined by a flexible weight on each connection [19]. Processing in each neuron is via the summing of the multiplication results of the connection weights by the input data. The result of the processing of the neuron is transferred to the next neuron through an activation function. There are several kinds of activation functions, such as bipolar sigmoid, sigmoid, and hyperbolic tangent

The time series prediction output, *Y*(*x*), of the MLP is calculated as [19]:

$$Y(x) = \beta_0 + \sum_{j=1}^{H} \beta_j \psi(\gamma_{j0} + \sum_{i=1}^{n} \gamma_{ji} x_i) \tag{5}$$

where (β_0, β_1, …,β_H) and (γ_{10},…, γ_{Hn}) are weights of the MLP, ψ is activation function..

2.4 Adaptive Neuro-Fuzzy Inference System Model

A neuro-fuzzy system is defined as a combination of artificial neural networks and fuzzy inference system (FIS) [21]. The Adaptive Neuro-Fuzzy Inference System or

Adaptive Network-based Fuzzy Inference System (ANFIS) is a new neuro-fuzzy model reported in [22]. In neuro-fuzzy, neural network learning process with pairs of data is used to determine the parameters of fuzzy inference system. The fuzzy reasoning mechanism is shown in Fig. 1 [22].

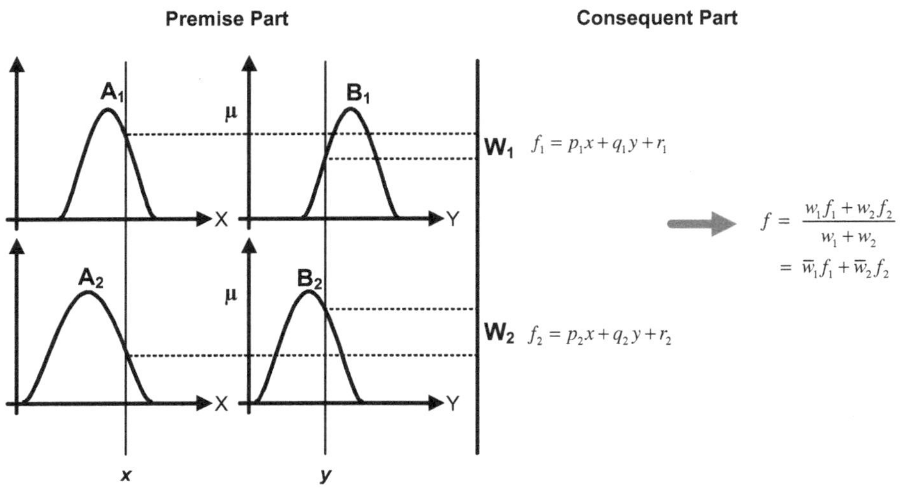

Fig. 1. Fuzzy reasoning mechanism

In Fig.1, it is assumed that the fuzzy inference system has two input variables, namely *x* and *y*, and one output *f*. The FIS also has two fuzzy if-then rules of Takagi and Sugeno's type which are given as [21]:

Rule 1: If x is A_1 and y is B_1 then $f_1 = p_1x + q_1y + r_1$

Rule 2: If x is A_2 and y is B_2 then $f_2 = p_2x + q_2y + r_2$.

where x and y are the input variables, A_1, A_2, B_1 and B_2 are the fuzzy sets, f_1 and f_2 are the output variables and p_1, p_2, q_1, q_2, r_1 and r_2 are the parameters.

Fig. 2 shows the structure of the ANFIS [21]. Different layers of ANFIS have different nodes. The output of each layer is used as input of the next layer.

The five layers with their associated nodes are described below:

Layer 0: The input layer. The input layer has k nodes where k is the number of inputs to the ANFIS.

Layer 1: Each node i in layer 1 is adaptive node with a function of node [21]:

$$O_{1,i} = \mu_{A_i}(x), \text{ where } i = 1, 2 \tag{6}$$

$$O_{1,i} = \mu_{B_{i-2}}(y), \text{ where } i = 3, 4 \tag{7}$$

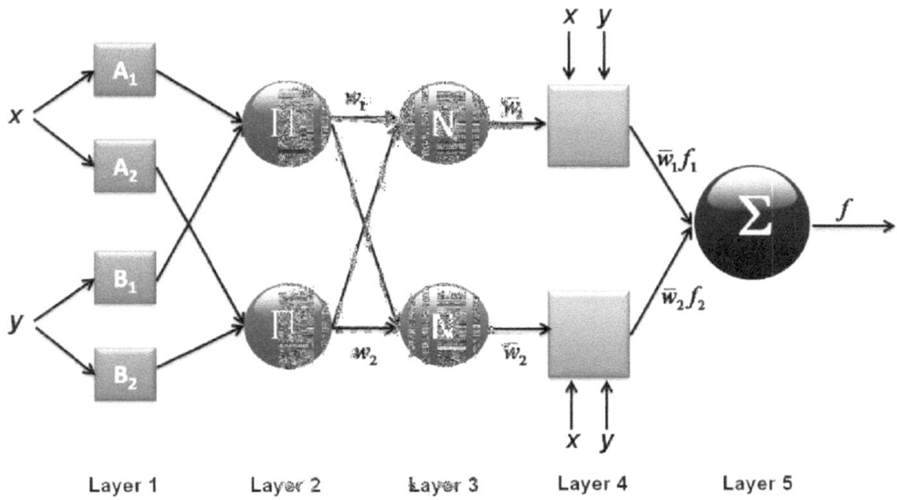

Fig. 2. Adaptive neuro-fuzzy inferences system architecture

where

x (or y) : input to node I,

A_i (or B_{i-2}) : linguistic label (low, high etc) associated with this node function,

$O_{1,i}$: membership function from fuzzy sets (A_1, A_2, B_1, B_2).

The membership function commonly used is the generalized bell [21]:

$$\mu_{A_i} = \frac{1}{1+\left[\left(\frac{x-c_i}{a_i}\right)^2\right]^{b_i}} \tag{8}$$

where $\{a_i, b_i, c_i\}$ are the set of parameters of function. The parameters in this layer are called premise parameters. Their values are adaptive by means of the back-propagation algorithm during the learning state.

Layer 2: Every node in layer 2 is a circle node, which is labeled with Π. Every node calculates the multiplication of the input values and gives the product as output, indicated by the following equation:

$$O_{2,i} = \mu_{A_i}(x)\mu_{B_i}(y), \text{ where } i=1,2 \tag{9}$$

Layer 3: Each node in layer 3 is a circle node, which is labeled with N. The i-th node calculates the ratio of the i-th rules firing strength to the sum of all rules' firing strength according to Eq. (10):

$$O_{3,i} = \overline{w}_i = \frac{w_i}{\sum_{i=1}^{2} w_i} \tag{10}$$

where w_i is firing strength of the i-th rule which is computed in layer 2. The output of this layer will be called normalized firing strength.

Layer 4: Each node i in layer 4 is a square node. The node function is given as [21]:

$$O_{4,i} = \overline{w}_i f_i = \overline{w}_i (p_i x + q_i y + r_i) \tag{11}$$

where $\overline{w}_i$ is the output of layer 3, $\{p_i, q_i, r_i\}$ are the set of parameters. The parameters in layer 4 are referred consequent parameters.

Layer 5: The single node in layer 5 is a circle node, which is labeled with $\sum$. This layer is as the output layer. The value of output is obtained the summation of all incoming signals. The output is calculated as:

$$O_{5,i} = \sum_i \overline{w}_i f_i = \frac{\sum_i w_i f_i}{\sum_i w_i} \tag{12}$$

where $\overline{w}_i f_i$ is the output of node i in layer 4.

The learning algorithm for ANFIS uses a hybrid algorithm in order to train the network, which is a combination of the least-squares estimator (LSE) and error back propagation (EBP) method [21]. Error back-propagation method is used to determine the parameters in layer 1. For training the parameters in layer 4, LSE is used.

2.5 Performance Measures

Two performance measures are used to compare the performances of obtained MA, WMA, ARIMA and ANFIS models. The following statistical indicators are used for this work: Root Mean Square Error (RMSE) and Mean Absolute Error (MAE) [23, 24]:

$$RMSE = \sqrt{\frac{\sum_{t=1}^{n} \left(Y_t - \hat{Y}_t\right)^2}{n}} \tag{13}$$

$$MAE = \frac{\sum_{t=1}^{n} \left|Y_t - \hat{Y}_t\right|}{n} \tag{14}$$

where Y_t and $\hat{Y}_t$ are the observed and predicted values at time t respectively, and n is the number of data.

3 Data Used

The HIV/AIDS data used in this study for evaluating the performance were collected from the Department of Health Republic, Indonesia. The data comprises the number of HIV/AIDS for the years 1990 to 2009. The descriptive statistics of the HIV/AIDS data such as the minimum, maximum, mean and standard deviation are shown in Table. 1.

Table 1. Descriptive statistics of HIV/AIDS data

Name	Min	Max	Mean	Std. Dev.
HIV/AIDS	5.00	4969.00	9.98×10^2	1545.27

From Table 1, it is seen that the HIV/AIDS data have a high value of standard deviation. This indicates that the HIV/AIDS data are spread over a wide range of values.

4 Methodology

The input variables that are used have different patterns. The learning process will be performed based on the number of inputs. The purpose of the learning process is to study the pattern of time series data and get the value of ANFIS parameters (premise and consequent) that is used for time series prediction. In the learning process of ANFIS for univariate time series, data are divided as input and target/ output. Fig. 3 illustrates the division of univariate time series data [25].

From Fig. 3, the pattern of univariate time series data for ANFIS is presented in Table 2 as follows:

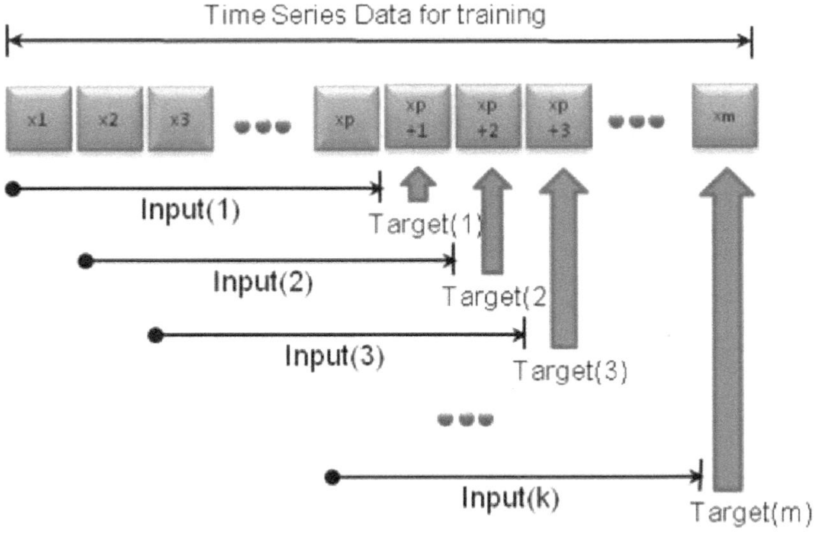

Fig. 3. The division of univariate time series data for ANFIS

Table 2. The pattern of univariate time series data for ANFIS

Pattern	Input lag	Output/ Target
1	$x_1, x_2, x_3, x_4, \ldots, x_p$	x_{p+1}
2	$x_2, x_3, x_4, x_5, \ldots, x_{p+1}$	x_{p+2}
3	$x_3, x_4, x_5, x_6, \ldots, x_{p+2}$	x_{p+3}
...	...	....
m-p	$x_{m-p}, x_{m-p+1}, x_{m-p+2}, \ldots, x_{m-1}$	x_m

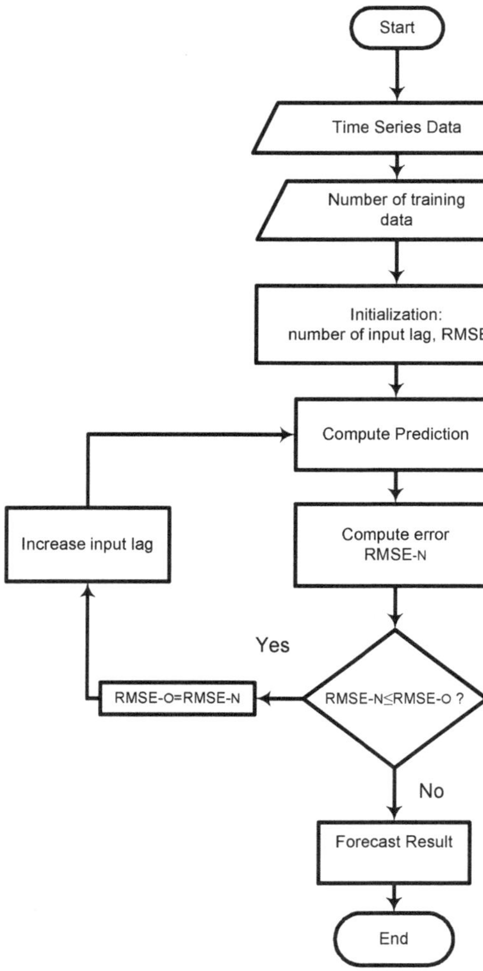

Fig. 4. The proposed procedure of ANFIS model for univariate time series prediction

ANFIS method performs learning process based on the input data that will be trained. The ANFIS algorithm that is used in this work is a hybrid learning algorithm. The algorithm uses a combination of the Least-squares estimator (LSE) method and error back propagation (EBP).

The proposed procedure of ANFIS model for univariate time series prediction in this work is shown in Fig. 4. This procedure is used to determine the optimal number of input for univariate time series prediction. In the first step, training data is applied to the ANFIS model using number of input data and target/ output, as described in Fig. 3. For Initialization, ANFIS model uses a small number of input lag. The values of premises and consequent parameters are obtained from the ANFIS model shown in Fig. 2. Furthermore, we calculate the performance of the prediction using RMSE. The next step is to test the performance of prediction ($RMSE_{-New} \leq RMSE_{-Old}$). The input lags are increased one by one to improve the performance of prediction. If value of $RMSE_{-New}$ is greater than the value of $RMSE_{-Old}$, then the iteration will be stopped. The final step, we calculate the prediction using the best configuration with optimum number of input lags.

5 Experimental Results

The performance of the proposed ANFIS model is compared with MA, WMA, ARIMA and neural network models using the HIV/AIDS data for the period 1990 to 2009 collected in Indonesia.

5.1 Moving Average Model

The moving average consists of MA and WMA models are used for time series prediction. Several numbers of inputs are made to choose the optimal moving average model. The performance measures obtained using different number of inputs (*m*) is shown in Table 3. It is found that MA (2) and WMA (2) perform better than other models with WMA (2) yielding the minimum values of RMSE and MAE.

Table 3. Performance measures using MA and WMA for HIV/ AIDS data

Model	(m)	PERFORMANCE MEASURES	
		RMSE	MAE
MA	**2**	728.028	362.222
	3	853.420	478.431
	5	1193.559	748.613
	7	1497.661	1021.978
	9	1781.642	1319.384
WMA	**2**	**696.274**	**353.741**
	3	773.803	410.745
	5	997.877	604.027
	7	1240.606	832.006
	9	1494.362	1098.236

5.2 ARIMA Model

In this section, the ARIMA models are used to predict HIV/AIDS time series. The ARIMA model with different parameter (*p*, *d*, *q*) values are computed to choose the optimal ARIMA model. It is known that an ARIMA models assume that the data are stationary. If data are not stationary, they are made stationary by performing differencing. We calculate autocorrelation of the HIV/AIDS data to check whether the data are stationary.

Table 4. Performance measures using ARIMA models for HIV/AIDS data

MODELS	PERFORMANCE MEASURES	
	RMSE	MAE
ARIMA(1,1,1)	664.510	432.039
ARIMA(2,1,1)	687.290	420.387
ARIMA(3,1,3)	**642.200**	**364.017**
ARIMA(4,2,3)	680.721	380.767
ARIMA(7,1,3)	767.718	371.315

The result of performance measures with ARIMA model is shown in Table 4. From Table 4, it is seen that the minimum values of RMSE and MAE are obtained for the ARIMA(3,1,3) model.

5.3 Neural Network Model

The MLP model is applied for HIV/AIDS time series prediction. The architecture configurations with different numbers of input and hidden layer neurons are tested to determine the optimum setup. From the experimental results, it is found that the neural network model with 7 input neurons, 12 hidden layer neurons and using hyperbolic tangent activation functions for the hidden and output layers yields the minimum values for RMSE and MAE. The result of performance measures with Neural Network model is shown in Table 5.

Table 5. Performance measures using Neural Network models for HIV/AIDS data

MODELS (input, hidden, output)	PERFORMANCE MEASURES	
	RMSE	MAE
NN(6,10,1)	216.646	125.166
NN(6,11,1)	195.520	118.957
NN(6,12,1)	150.015	88.426
NN(7,12,1)	**143.011**	**87.732**
NN(8,12,1)	181.258	110.169
NN(7,14,1)	162.745	94.508
NN(8,14,1)	145.149	91.938

5.4 ANFIS Model

The proposed ANFIS model to predict HIV/AIDS are tested using the time series of HIV/AIDS data in the period 1990 to 2009. The ANFIS model is constructed using 20 training data. The number of rules used was 2 and the number of epochs used for training was 1000. The proposed ANFIS model is tested using the procedure of Fig.4. It is found that the optimum input lag and the corresponding RMSE were obtained as 2 and 84.698 respectively. And the value of MAE using ANFIS model with optimum input lag and 1output (abbreviated as ANFIS (2, 1)) is 49.265. The values of RMSE and MAE using ANFIS(3,1) model are obtained as 90.972 and 55.456 respectively.

6 Comparison of Models

The proposed ANFIS model is compared with known statistical and artificial intelligence models such as neural network models based on the prediction performances for the HIV/AIDS data. Fig. 5 shows a comparison of RMSE and MAE values obtained using WMA, ARIMA, Neural Network and the proposed ANFIS(2,1) models.

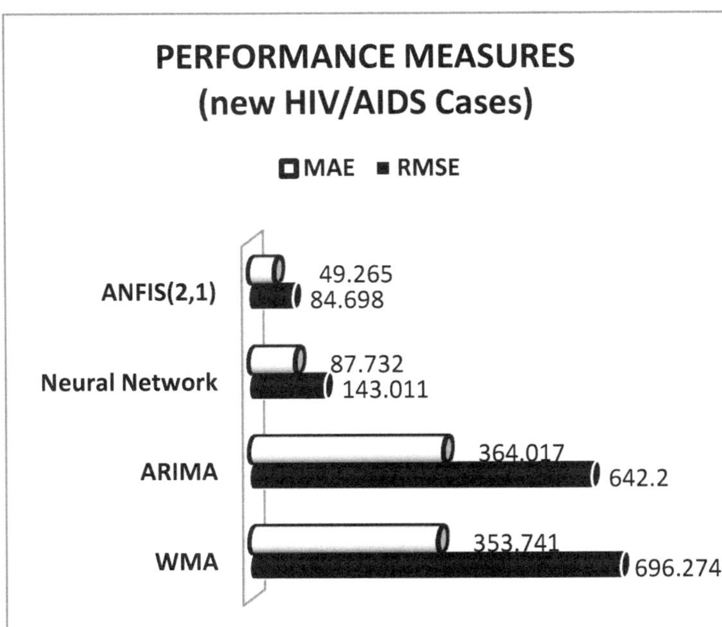

Fig. 5. Comparison of performance measures

We note that the proposed ANFIS model (ANFIS(2,1)) gives the best results compared to all other models.

The percentage improvements achieved by the proposed ANFIS with respect to RMSE and MAE values by the ANFIS model over other models are presented in

Table 6. From this table, the proposed ANFIS model is able to achieve significant performance improvements over other models for HIV/ AIDS time series prediction.

Table 6. Improvement achieved by proposed ANFIS model over the other models for HIV/AIDS data

MODELS	RMSE (%)	MAE (%)
WMA	87.84	86.07
ARIMA	86.81	86.47
Neural Network	40.78	43.85

7 Conclusion

This study has presented an improved ANFIS model for HIV/ AIDS time series prediction. The modified ANFIS model has been tested using HIV/AIDS data for a period of 20 years. The performance of the proposed model has been compared with other models using measures such as RMSE and MAE. The experimental results show that the improved ANFIS model using optimum input lag performs significantly better than MA, WMA, ARIMA and neural network models. It can be concluded that an improved ANFIS model is best suited for HIV/AIDS time series prediction.

References

1. Susilo, B., Kurniasih, N., Manullang, E., Wardah, Anam, M.S.: Istiqomah: HIV / AIDS situation in Indonesia- 1987-2006. Department of Health, Indonesia, Jakarta (2006)
2. Zhuang, Y., Chen, L., Wang, X.S., Lian, J.: A Weighted Moving Average-based Approach for Cleaning Sensor Data. In: 27th International Conference on Distributed Computing Systems, pp. 38–45 (2007)
3. Box, G., Jenkins, G.: Time Series Analysis, Forecasting and Control. Holden-Day, CA (1970)
4. Tabnak, F., Zhou, T., Sun, R., Azari, R.: Time series forecasting of AIDS incidence using mortality series. In: International Conference on AIDS (2000)
5. Aboagye-Sarfo, P., Cross, J., Mueller, U.: Trend analysis and short-term forecast of incident HIV infection in Ghana. African Journal of AIDS Research 9, 165–173 (2010)
6. Jain, B.A., Nag, B.N.: Performance Evaluation of Neural Network Decision Models. Manage Information Systems 14, 201–216 (1997)
7. Niskaa, H., Hiltunena, T., Karppinenb, A., Ruuskanena, J., Kolehmaine, M.: Evolving the Neural Network Model for Forecasting Air Pollution Time Series. Engineering Applications of Artificial Intelligence 17, 159–167 (2004)
8. Georgakarakos, S., Koutsoubas, D., Valavanis, V.: Time Series Analysis and Forecasting Techniques Applied on Loliginid and Ommastrephid Landings in Greek Waters. Fisheries Research 78, 55–71 (2006)
9. Aminian, F., Suarez, E.D., Aminian, M., Walz, D.T.: Forecasting Economic Data with Neural Networks. Computational Economics 28, 71–88 (2006)

10. Chang, F.J., Chang, Y.T.: Adaptive Neuro-Fuzzy Inference System for Prediction of Water Level in Reservoir. Advances in Water Resources 29, 1–10 (2006)
11. Tektas, M.: Weather Forecasting Using ANFIS and ARIMA Models, A Case Study for Istanbul. Environmental Research, Engineering and Management 1(51), 5–10 (2010)
12. Hernandez, S.C.A., Pedraza, M.L.F., Salcedo, P.O.J.: Comparative Analysis of Time Series Techniques ARIMA and ANFIS to Forecast Wimax Traffic. The Online Journal on Electronics and Electrical Engineering (OJEEE) 2(2), 223–228 (2010)
13. Rasit, A.T.A.: An Adaptive Neuro-Fuzzy Inference System Approach for Prediction of Power Factor in Wind Turbines. Journal of Electrical & Electronics Engineering 9(1), 905–912 (2009)
14. Caydas, U., Hascalık, A., Ekici, S.: An Adaptive Neuro-Fuzzy Inference System (ANFIS) Model for Wire-EDM. Expert Systems with Applications 36, 6135–6139 (2009)
15. Firat, M.: Artificial Intelligence Techniques for River Flow Forecasting in the Seyhan River, Catchment, Turkey. Hydrol. Earth Syst. Sci. Discuss 4, 1369–1406 (2007)
16. Atsalakis, G.S., Valavanis, K.P.: Forecasting Stock Market Short-Term Trends Using a Neuro-Fuzzy Based Methodology. Expert Systems with Applications 36, 10696–10707 (2009)
17. Makridakis, S., Wheelwright, S.C., McGee, V.E.: Metode dan aplikasi peramalan. Edisi Revisi, Jilid I, Binarupa Aksara, Jakarta (2009)
18. Brockwell, P.J., Davis, R.A.: Introduction to Time Series and Forecasting. Springer, New York (2002)
19. Suhartono: Feedforward Neural Networks Untuk Pemodelan Runtun Waktu. Gajah Mada University, Indonesia (2008)
20. Dewi, S.K.: Neuro-Fuzzy Integrasi Sistem Fuzzy Dan Jaringan Syaraf. Graha Ilmu, Indonesia, Jogjakarta (2006)
21. Jang, J.S.R., Sun, C.T., Mizutani, E.: Neuro Fuzzy and Soft Computing: A Computational Approach To Learning And Machine Intelligence. Prentice Hall International, Inc., New Jersey (1997)
22. Jang, J.: ANFIS: Adaptive Network based Fuzzy Inference System. IEEE Trans systems, Man and Cybernetics 23(3), 665–684 (1993)
23. Faruk, D.O.: A Hybrid Neural Network and ARIMA Model for Water Quality Time Series Prediction. Engineering Applications of Artificial Intelligence 23, 586–594 (2010)
24. Rojas, I., Valenzuela, O., Rojas, F., Guillen, A., Herrera, L.J., Pomares, H., Marquez, L., Pasadas, M.: Soft-Computing Techniques and ARMA Model for Time Series Prediction. Neurocomputing 71, 519–537 (2008)
25. Fariza, A., Helen, A., Rasyid, A.: Performansi Neuro Fuzzy Untuk Peramalan Data Time Series. Seminar Nasional Aplikasi Teknologi Informasi, D-77-82 (2007)

Design of Experiment to Optimize the Architecture of Wavelet Neural Network for Forecasting the Tourist Arrivals in Indonesia

Bambang W. Otok, Suhartono, Brodjol S.S. Ulama, and Alfonsus J. Endharta

Department of Statistics, Institut Teknologi Sepuluh Nopember,
60111 Surabaya, Indonesia
{bambang_wo,suhartono,brodjol_su}@statistika.its.ac.id,
alfonsus_je@yahoo.com

Abstract. Wavelet Neural Network (WNN) is a method based on the combination of neural network and wavelet theories. The disadvantage of WNN is the lack of structured method to determine the optimum level of WNN factors, which are mostly set by trial and error. The factors affecting the performance of WNN are the level of MODWT decomposition, the wavelet family, the lag inputs, and the number of neurons in the hidden layer. This research presents the use of design of experiments for planning the possible combination of factor levels in order to get the best WNN. The number of tourist arrivals in Indonesia via Soekarno-Hatta airport in Jakarta and via Ngurah Rai airport in Bali is used as case study. The result shows that design of experiments is a practical approach to determine the best combination of WNN factor level. The best WNN for data in Soekarno-Hatta airport is WNN with level 4 of MODWT decomposition, Daubechies wavelet, and 1 neuron in the hidden layer. Whereas, the best WNN for data in Ngurah Rai airport is WNN with MODWT decomposition level 3 and using input proposed by Renaud, Starck, and Murtagh [11] and seasonal lag input addition.

Keywords: wavelet, neural network, design of experiments, tourist arrival.

1 Introduction

In recent years, wavelet method becomes an alternative for time series analysis. Wavelet is a function which mathematically divides the data into different components and learns the components with suitable resolution [4]. The advantage of wavelet method is the ability of modeling and estimating trend data which have autocorrelation [9]. Abramovich, Bailey, and Sapatinas [1] have reviewed the application of the wavelet method in the statistical problems, such as nonparametric regression, density estimation, linear inverse problems, structural change problems, and specific issues in time series analysis such as spectral density estimation. Zhang et al. [17] defined wavelet method as a multiresolution decomposition technique for solving the problems in modeling which gives a local representation signal, both in the time and frequency domain. Renaud, Starck, and Murtagh [11] stated that the other advantage of wavelet method is the ability to separate automatically the trend from the data.

A. Abd Manaf et al. (Eds.): ICIEIS 2011, Part III, CCIS 253, pp. 14–23, 2011.

Neural Network (NN) is one of artificial intelligence method which has been widely used in statistical problems. The flexibility of modeling nonlinear data and the assumption free are the reasons why NN is used. NN consists of some components, i.e. neuron, layer, and transfer function. There are many kinds of NN, such as Feed-Forward Neural Network (FFNN), Recurrent Neural Network (RNN), Radial Basis Function Neural Network (RBFNN), Generalized Regression Neural Network (GRNN), etc.

In time series analysis, the most-used NN is FFNN where the inputs are the lags of the output. In most researches, only the number of neuron in the hidden layer is optimized to find the optimum output. Though, there are also some researches which use more factors to find the optimum output, such as researches proposed by Sukhtomya and Tannock [14], Tortum, Yayla, Çelik, and Gökdağ [15], Lasheras, Vilán, Nieto, and Díaz [6]. The factors are the transformation data, the number of the training data, the number of the neuron in the input layer, the number of the neuron in the hidden layer, and the activation function. Taguchi method is used to find the optimum output in those researches.

The combination of NN and wavelet method is often called Wavelet Neural Network (WNN). The motivation is to make such sensitive model as in the wavelet theories and such flexible model as in NN method. Therefore, the factors of WNN are more than of NN. In the wavelet method, there are factors which can be changed, such as the level of Maximum Overlap Discrete Wavelet Transform (MODWT) decomposition and the wavelet family. WNN has been proposed in researches about electricity demands by Zhang and Dong [18], Benaouda, Murtagh, Starck, and Renaud [2], and Ulagammai, Venkatesh, Kannan, and Padhy [16]. Another research which used WNN is the research done by Mitra and Mitra [8] about exchange rates. Chen, Yang, and Dong [3] used Local Linear Wavelet Neural Network (LLWNN).

In this research, design of experiments is proposed to find the best combination of factors which yield the best WNN for forecasting the tourist arrivals data. WNN is selected due to its good ability in prediction and known as a relatively new hybrid model in forecasting. Moreover, no researcher already applies design of experiments for optimizing the architecture of WNN. In this design, the experimental unit is Root Mean Square Error (RMSE) of out-sample data. Two datasets are used as case study, i.e. the number of foreign tourist arrivals in Indonesia via Soekarno-Hatta airport in Jakarta and via Ngurah Rai airport in Bali. The result shows that design of experiments is a practical approach to determine the best combination of WNN factor level in the case of foreign tourist arrivals in Indonesia. The best WNN for data in Soekarno-Hatta airport is WNN with level 4 of MODWT decomposition, Daubechies wavelet, and 1 neuron in the hidden layer. The best WNN for data in Ngurah Rai airport is WNN with MODWT decomposition level 3 and using input proposed by Renaud, Starck, and Murtagh [11] and seasonal lag input addition.

2 Wavelet Neural Network

In time series analysis, a linear model which is developed from wavelet theories is called Multiscale Autoregressive (MAR) model. This model is similar to linear regression model. Therefore, some assumptions, such as normality of the residual, independent, and identical residual, must be fulfilled.

The input (predictor) of MAR model is the lags of wavelet and scale coefficients which are yielded by MODWT decomposition. Based on Renaud et al. [11], the developed MAR model is shown as follows:

$$\hat{X}_{t+1} = \sum_{j=1}^{J}\sum_{k=1}^{A_j} \hat{a}_{j,k} w_{j,t-2^j(k-1)} + \sum_{k=1}^{A_j} \hat{a}_{J+1,k} v_{J,t-2^J(k-1)} \tag{1}$$

where X_t is the actual data at time t, J is the level of MODWT decomposition, A_j is the order of MAR model, $w_{j,t}$ is the wavelet coefficient for level j at time t, $v_{J,t}$ is the scale coefficient for level J at time t, and $\hat{a}_{j,k}$ is the estimated parameter for the corresponding variable.

A new model is developed by combining computational approach, such as NN, and MAR model in order to produce a nonlinear model. The nonlinear model which made of NN and MAR model is Wavelet Neural Network (WNN). WNN is also called Neural Networks-Multiscale Autoregressive (NN-MAR) or Multiresolution Neural Network (MNN). This combined model is free-of-assumption due to the characteristic of NN. Mathematically, WNN model can be defined as follows:

$$\hat{X}_{t+1} = \sum_{p=1}^{P} \hat{b}_p g\left(\sum_{j=1}^{J}\sum_{k=1}^{A_j} \hat{a}_{j,k,p} w_{j,t-2^j(k-1)} + \sum_{k=1}^{A_j} \hat{a}_{J+1,k,p} v_{J,t-2^J(k-1)} \right) \tag{2}$$

where $g(.)$ is the activation function in the hidden layer, P is the number of neurons in the hidden layer, and the other symbols are the same as in MAR model.

3 Experimental Plan

In this section, the information criteria, which correctly measure the performance of WNN, are determined. With the experimental design, the optimum level of the controllable factors is shown. In this research, RMSE of out-sample data is selected as the information criteria. RMSE of out-sample data is defined as follows:

$$\text{RMSE} = \sqrt{\sum_{t=1}^{n} \frac{e_t^2}{n}} = \sqrt{\sum_{i=1}^{n} \frac{(X_t - \hat{X}_t)^2}{n}} \tag{3}$$

where X_t is the actual out-sample data at time t, $\hat{X}$ is the prediction of out-sample data at time t, n is the number of out-sample data.

Based on the previous study about WNN model, the controllable factors which could affect the performance of WNN and their levels are determined as follows:

(A) *Level of MODWT decomposition.* Maximal Overlap Discrete Wavelet Transform (MODWT) is kind of discrete wavelet transform. MODWT decompose the data into two components, i.e. wavelet and scale coefficients. The number of wavelet and scale coefficients depends on the level of MODWT decomposition. The detail information about MODWT can be seen in Percival and Walden [10].

(B) *Wavelet family.* There are many kinds of wavelet family, such as Haar wavelet, Meyer wavelet, Daubechies wavelet, Mexican Hat wavelet, Coiflet wavelet, and Last Assymetric [4]. In this research, we use only Haar and Daubechies wavelet.

(C) *Input.* The input variables in MAR model are the lags of wavelet and scale coefficients which have been produced by MODWT decomposition. The determination of the amount of the lags is the issue in MAR model. Renaud et al. [9] have introduced a procedure to determine the input (predictors) of MAR model. The inputs proposed by Renaud et al. do not include seasonal lags so that these inputs are not suitable for data which have seasonal pattern. Therefore, the additional input corresponding to the data is seasonal lags, in this case, it is lag 12, 24, 36, and 48 and the plus minus 1 from the seasonal lags.

(D) *The number of neurons in the hidden layer.* The performance of NNs is mostly affected by this factor. Most research using NN find the optimum model based on this factor only. In this research, the number of neuron in the hidden layer varies from 1 to 10.

From these levels of all factors, there will be $3\times2\times2\times10$ combinations or 120 combinations of the levels. The combinations for the experiments are shown in Table 1. Each combination is repeated 3 times.

Table 1. Design of experiments with 4 factors in WNN

Combination No.	Factors and their levels			
	A	B	C	D
1-10	2	Haar	Renaud et al. only	1-10
11-20	2	Haar	Renaud et al. + Seasonal	1-10
21-30	2	Daubechies	Renaud et al. only	1-10
31-40	2	Daubechies	Renaud et al. + Seasonal	1-10
41-50	3	Haar	Renaud et al. only	1-10
51-60	3	Haar	Renaud et al. + Seasonal	1-10
61-70	3	Daubechies	Renaud et al. only	1-10
71-80	3	Daubechies	Renaud et al. + Seasonal	1-10
81-90	4	Haar	Renaud et al. only	1-10
91-100	4	Haar	Renaud et al. + Seasonal	1-10
101-110	4	Daubechies	Renaud et al. only	1-10
111-120	4	Daubechies	Renaud et al. + Seasonal	1-10

The analysis step of WNN based on the proposed design of experiments is as follows:

Step 1. Applying regular (non-seasonal) differencing to the raw data.
Step 2. Applying MODWT decomposition with certain level and wavelet family in order to get the wavelet and scale coefficients.
Step 3. Calculating the lags of the wavelet and scale coefficients and use them as the inputs in the architecture of NN.
Step 4. Running the NN with certain number of neurons in the hidden layer.
Step 5. Repeating step 2 to step 4 for 3 times for each combination of factor level.
Step 6. Calculating RMSE of out-sample data.
Step 7. Using RMSE of out-sample data as the experimental unit (response) in the design of experiments.
Step 8. Evaluating the best WNN based on the smallest RMSE of out-sample data.

There are 2 datasets used in this research, i.e. the number of foreign tourist arrivals in Indonesia via Soekarno-Hatta airport in Jakarta and via Ngurah Rai airport in Denpasar, Bali. The data is monthly data, starting from January 1989 until December 2009. Some previous researches also used these data, such as Ismail, Suhartono, Yahaya, and Efendi [5], and then Lee, Suhartono, and Sanugi [7] that applied intervention model for forecasting these tourist arrivals data.

The plots of the data are shown in Fig. 1 and 2. The in-sample data is taken from January 1989 until December 2008 and the out-sample data is the last year (2009). Based on Suhartono and Subanar [13] and Suhartono, Ulama, and Endharta [12], it is better to use the differencing of the raw data than using the raw data directly in MODWT decomposition when the data have a trend, because this treatment (differencing) yields a model with more accurate forecast.

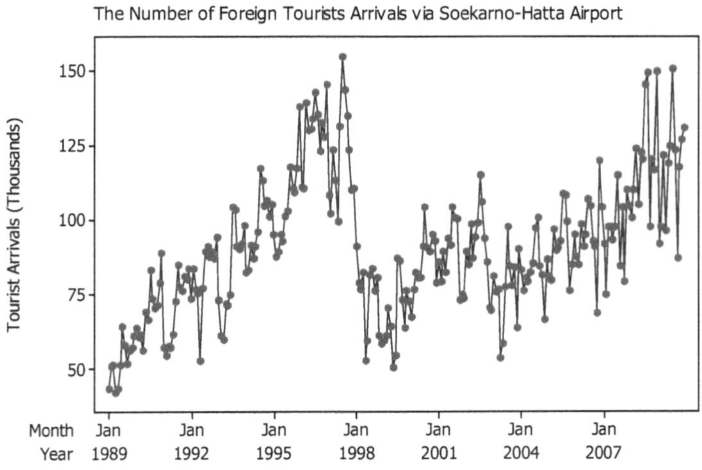

Fig. 1. Plot of the number of foreign tourist arrivals in Indonesia via Soekarno-Hatta airport

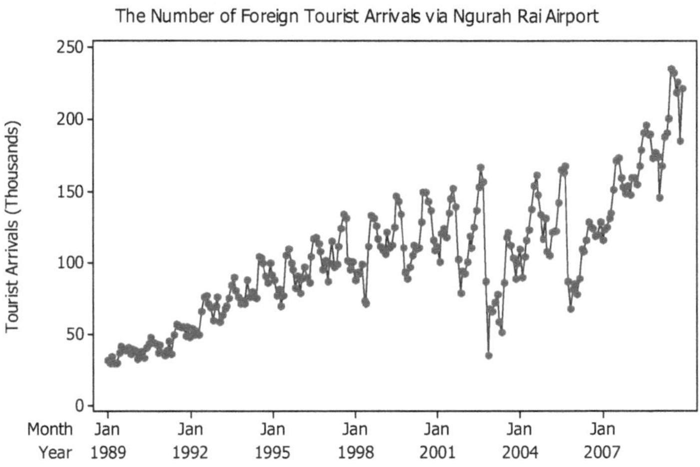

Fig. 2. Plot of the number of foreign tourist arrivals in Indonesia via Ngurah Rai airport

4 Results and Discussion

Based on the number of levels and replications used in the design, there are 360 WNNs. Each WNN brings different RMSE which is used as the observed response in the experimental design. The first dataset, the number of foreign tourists arrivals in Indonesia through Soekarno-Hatta airport, yield 360 RMSEs of out-sample data. The selection of the best WNN based on the design is by comparing the factor level. Fig. 3 shows the comparison between levels per factor.

The graphs at Fig. 3 show that the influence factors are the wavelet family and the level of MODWT decomposition. Based on the level of MODWT decomposition, the effects of using level 2 and level 3 are same. Based on the wavelet family, the use of Haar and Daubechies wavelet brings different effect and the use of Daubechies wavelet brings the smallest RMSE. The use of input proposed by Renaud et al. [11] and the use of those inputs with additional seasonal lags inputs yield the same effect. The plot based on the number of neurons in the hidden layer shows that the use of 1 neuron in the hidden layer yield the smallest RMSE of out-sample data. Therefore, the best WNN based on the evaluation of each WNN factor for forecasting the number of foreign tourist arrivals in Indonesia through Soekarno-Hatta airport is by using MODWT decomposition level 4, Daubechies wavelet, and 1 neuron in the hidden layer.

Fig. 4 shows the average RMSE of out-sample data based on the experimental combination. Based on Fig. 4, the smallest RMSE of out-sample data is at combination number 91, which is the combination of level 4 of MODWT decomposition, Haar wavelet, the input proposed by Renaud et al. [11] and the addition of seasonal lag input, and 1 neuron in the hidden layer (see Table 1).

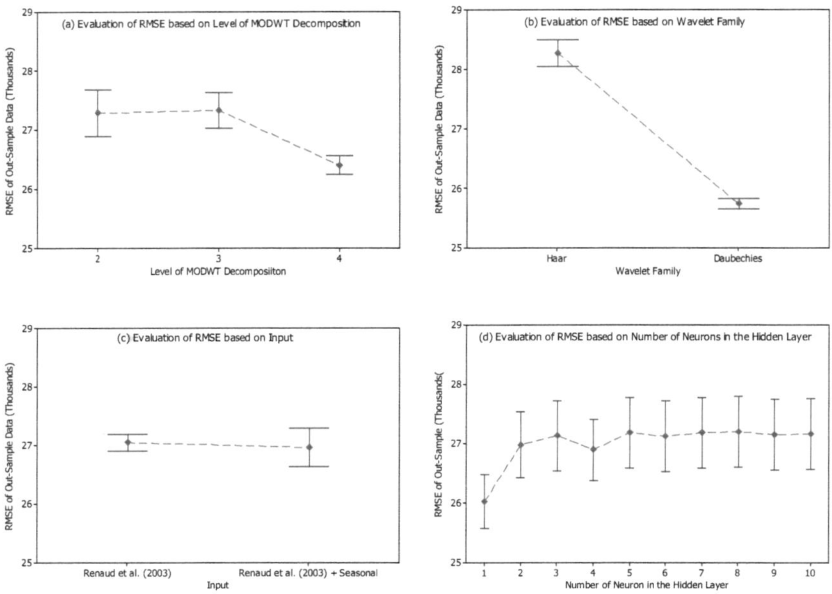

Fig. 3. Visual evaluation of RMSE at out-sample data based on (a) level of MODWT decomposition, (b) wavelet family, (c) input and (d) the number of neurons in the hidden layer for data in Soekarno-Hatta airport

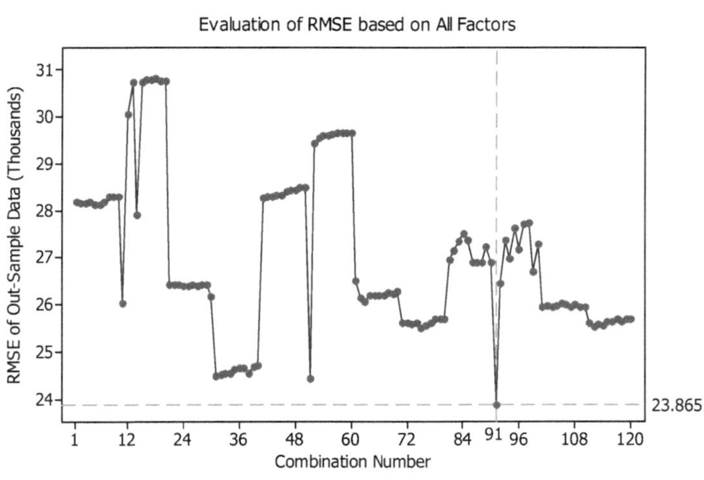

Fig. 4. Visual evaluation of RMSE at out-sample data based on combination of all factors for data in Soekarno-Hatta airport

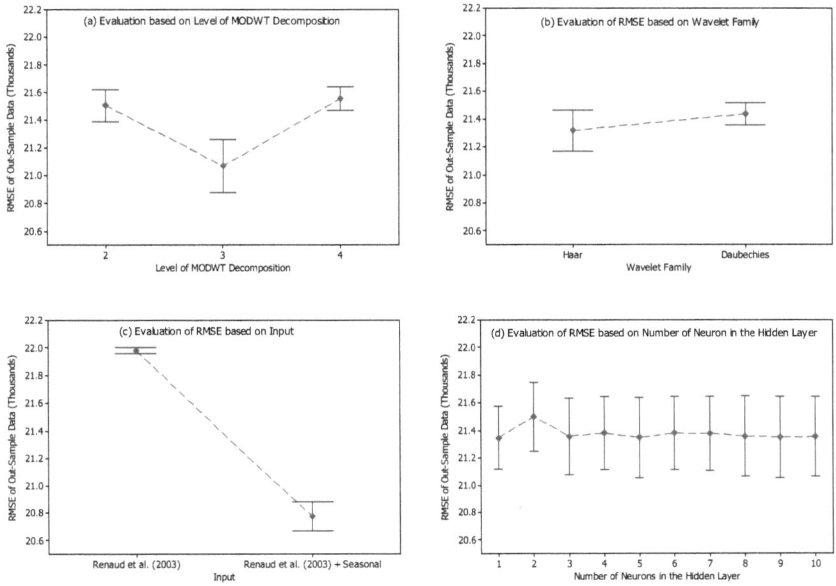

Fig. 5. Evaluation of RMSE at out-sample data based on (a) level of MODWT decomposition, (b) wavelet family, (c) input and (d) the number of neurons in the hidden layer for data in Ngurah Rai airport

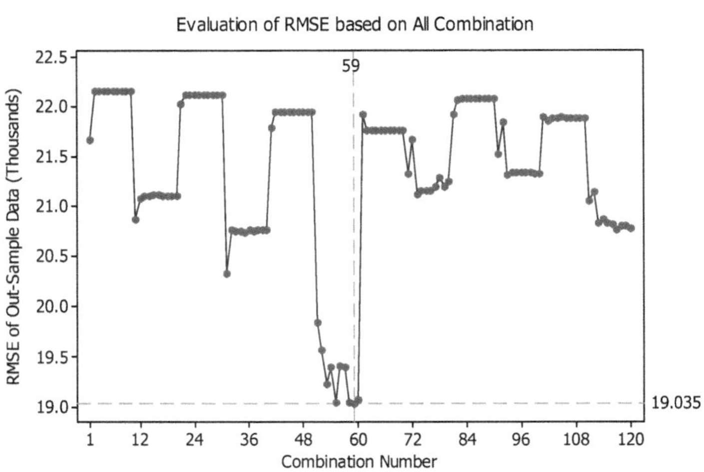

Fig. 6. Evaluation of RMSE of at-sample data based on combination of all factors for data in Ngurah Rai airport

The second dataset, the number of foreign tourist arrivals in Indonesia through Ngurah-Rai airport, is analyzed. The comparison of the factor effects is shown in

Fig. 5. This figure shows that the input is the most influence factor in the WNN for forecasting the tourist arrivals in Indonesia via Ngurah Rai airport because this factor brings larger variation among the levels. This is different from the first dataset. Based on the first factor, the level of MODWT decomposition, the use of level 3 in WNN yields the smallest RMSE of out-sample data. Based on the wavelet family, the use of Haar wavelet brings almost the same effect as of Daubechies wavelet, but WNN with Haar wavelet yields smaller RMSE of out-sample data. The use of input proposed by Renaud et al. [11] and the use of those inputs with the additional seasonal lags inputs yield a significant different effect. WNN with input proposed by Renaud et al. and the addition of seasonal lag input bring much less RMSE of out-sample data. The plot based on the number of neurons in the hidden layer shows that the use of 1 until 10 neurons in the hidden layer yield statistically same RMSE of out-sample data. Therefore, the best WNN based on the evaluation of each WNN factor for forecasting the number of foreign tourist arrivals in Indonesia through Ngurah Rai airport in Bali is by using MODWT decomposition level 3, Haar wavelet, and input proposed by Renaud et al. [11] with the addition of seasonal lag input.

Fig. 6 shows the average RMSE of out-sample data based on the experimental combination for the tourist arrival data in Ngurah Rai airport. Based on Fig. 6, the smallest RMSE of out-sample data is at combination number 59. From Table 1, combination number 59 is the combination of level 3 of MODWT decomposition, Haar wavelet, the input proposed by Renaud et al. [11] and the addition of seasonal lag input, and 9 neurons in the hidden layer. This result is the same as the result of the partial factor evaluation.

5 Conclusion

Design of experiments can be used as an alternative for conducting WNN design. The best WNN is selected by visual evaluation, by using the plot of the average response value (average RMSE of out-sample data). The number of tourist arrivals has different best architecture of WNN depends on the pattern.

For the number of tourist arrivals in Indonesia through Soekarno-Hatta airport, wavelet family, level of MODWT decomposition, and the number of neuron in the hidden layer, are influential on the performance of the WNN model. Based on the evaluation of each factor partially, the best WNN for this first dataset is WNN which is made of MODWT decomposition level 4, Daubechies wavelet, and 1 neuron in the hidden layer. Moreover, based on the best combination of all factors, the best WNN is WNN with level 4 of MODWT decomposition, Haar wavelet, input proposed by Renaud et al. [11] and seasonal lag input, and 1 neuron in the hidden layer.

Whereas, for the number of tourist arrivals in Indonesia through Ngurah Rai airport, level of MODWT decomposition and the input are influential on the goodness of the WNN. The partial evaluation of each factor shows that the best WNN for this dataset is WNN with MODWT decomposition level 3 and input Renaud et al. [11] and the additional seasonal lags. Based on the overall factor combination, the best WNN is also WNN with MODWT decomposition level 3, input Renaud et al. [11] and the additional seasonal lags, and 9 neurons in the hidden layer.

References

1. Abramovich, F., Bailey, T.C., Sapatinas, T.: Wavelet Analysis and Its Statistical Applications. The Statistician 49, 1–29 (2000)
2. Benaouda, D., Murtagh, F., Starck, J.L., Renaud, O.: Wavelet-Based Nonlinear Multiscale Decomposition Model for Electricity Load Forecasting. Neurocomputing 70, 139–154 (2006)
3. Chen, Y., Yang, B., Dong, J.: Time-Series Prediction Using A Local Linear Wavelet Neural Network. Neurocomputing 69, 449–465 (2006)
4. Daubechies, I.: Ten Lectures on Wavelets. Society for Industrial and Applied Mathematics. SIAM (1992)
5. Ismail, Z., Suhartono, Yahaya, A., Efendi, R.: Intervention Model for Analyzing the Impact of Terrorism to Tourism Industry. Journal of Mathematics and Statistics 5, 322–329 (2009)
6. Lasheras, F.S., Vilán, J.A.V., Nieto, P.J.G., Díaz, J.J.d.-C.: The Use of Design of Experiments to Improve A Neural Network Model in order to Predict The Thickness of The Chromium Layer in A Hard Chromium Plating Process. Mathematical and Computer Modelling 52(7-8), 1169–1176 (2010)
7. Lee, M.H., Suhartono, Sanugi, B.: Multi Input Intervention Model for Evaluating the Impact of the Asian Crisis and Terrorist Attacks on Tourist Arrivals. Matematika 26(1), 83–106 (2010)
8. Mitra, S., Mitra, A.: Modeling Exchange Rates Using Wavelet Decomposed Genetic Neural Networks. Statistical Methodology 3, 103–124 (2006)
9. Nason, G.P., Sachs, R.V.: Wavelets in Time Series Analysis. Phil. Trans. R. Soc. Lond. A 357(1760), 2511–2526 (1999)
10. Percival, D.B., Walden, A.T.: Wavelet Methods for Time Series Analysis. Cambridge University Press (2000)
11. Renaud, O., Stark, J.L., Murtagh, F.: Prediction Based on A Multiscale Decomposition. Int. Journal of Wavelets, Multiresolution and Information Processing 1, 217–232 (2003)
12. Suhartono, Ulama, B.S.S., Endharta, A.J.: Seasonal Time Series Data Forecasting by Using Neural Networks Multiscale Autoregressive Model. American Journal of Applied Sciences 7(10), 1372–1378 (2010)
13. Suhartono, Subanar.: Development of Model Building Procedures in Wavelet Neural Networks for Forecasting Non-Stationary Time Series. European Journal of Scientific Research 34(3), 416–427 (2009)
14. Sukhtomya, W., Tannock, J.: The Optimization of Neural Network Parameters Using Taguchi's Design of Experiments Approach: An Application in Manufacturing Process Modeling. Neural Comput. & Applic. 14, 337–344 (2005)
15. Tortum, A., Yayla, N., Celik, C., Gokdag, M.: The Investigation of Model Selection Criteria in Artificial Neural Networks by the Taguchi Method. Physica A 386, 446–468 (2007)
16. Ulagammai, M., Venkatesh, P., Kannan, P.S., Padhy, N.P.: Application of Bacterial Foraging Technique Trained Artificial and Wavelet Neural Networks in Load Forecasting. Neurocomputing 70, 2659–2667 (2007)
17. Zhang, B.L., Coggins, R., Jabri, M.A., Dersch, D., Flower, B.: Multiresolution Forecasting for Futures Trading Using Wavelet Decompositions. IEEE Transactions on Neural Networks 12(4), 765–775 (2001)
18. Zhang, B.L., Dong, Z.Y.: An Adaptive Neural-Wavelet Model for Short Term Load Forecasting. Electric Power Systems Research 59, 121–129 (2001)

A Review of Classification Approaches Using Support Vector Machine in Intrusion Detection

Noreen Kausar[1], Brahim Belhaouari Samir[2], Azween Abdullah[1], Iftikhar Ahmad[3], and Mohammad Hussain[4]

[1] Department of Computer and Information Sciences, Universiti Teknologi PETRONAS, Bandar Seri Iskandar, 31750 Tronoh, Perak, Malaysia
[2] Department of Fundamental and Applied Sciences, Universiti Teknologi PETRONAS, Bandar Seri Iskandar, 31750 Tronoh, Perak, Malaysia
[3] Department of Software Engineering, College of Computer and Information Sciences, P.O. Box 51178, Riyadh 11543, King Saud University, Riyadh, KSA
[4] Department of Computer Science, King Saud University, Riyadh, KSA
noreenkausar88@yahoo.com, brahim_belhaouari@petronas.com.my, azweenabdullah@petronas.com, wattoohu@gmail.com, mhussain@ksu.edu.sa

Abstract. Presently, Network security is the most concerned subject matter because with the rapid use of internet technology and further dependence on network for keeping our data secure, it's becoming impossible to protect from vulnerable attacks. Intrusion detection systems (IDS) are the key solution for detecting these attacks so that the network remains reliable. There are different classification approaches used to implement IDS in order to increase their efficiency in terms of detection rate. Support vector machine (SVM) is used for classification in IDS due to its good generalization ability and non linear classification using different kernel functions and performs well as compared to other classifiers. Different Kernels of SVM are used for different problems to enhance performance rate. In this paper, we provide a review of the SVM and its kernel approaches in IDS for future research and implementation towards the development of optimal approach in intrusion detection system with maximum detection rate and minimized false alarms.

Keywords: Intrusion Detection System (IDS), SVM, Kernel, RBF, Knowledge Discovery and Data Mining (KDD), Defense Advanced Research Projects Agency (DARPA).

1 Introduction

With the continuous advancement in the computer technology and specially the internet, the exposure of malicious attacks and illegal accesses to computer systems is also increasing at a high rate [1-3]. In order to protect network security, intrusion detection systems are the key to detect intrusions so that the network remains stable and functioning. Performance of the intrusion detection system depends on the technologies and the techniques used [4]. Intrusion detection system has become the research focus for security implementers in order to enhance the detection rate and

A. Abd Manaf et al. (Eds.): ICIEIS 2011, Part III, CCIS 253, pp. 24–34, 2011.

reduce false alarms by applying different approaches of feature selection and classifiers. The subject matter also includes decreasing training time and increasing the accuracy rate of detecting normal and intrusive activities. To overcome these issues SVM is the better choice to be used as classifier in intrusion detection systems [5]. Different approaches applied on intrusion detection using SVM is the focus of this paper.

In this paper, Section 2 gives an overview of intrusion detection system. Section 3 describes support vector machines. Section 4 discusses the approaches applied to intrusion detection using SVM with detail of their proposed model, experimental dataset used, IDS structure and result obtained. Section 5 provides discussion on the SVM approaches applied in IDS and finally Section 6 concludes with ideas for future research in the field of IDS.

2 Intrusion Detection System

An unauthorized access to a network for certain purpose is known as intrusion and the user who accesses the network illegally is known as intruder. Anderson introduced the theory of intrusion detection in 1980 [6]. The purpose of the intrusion detection system is to detect such attacks and respond in a suitable way [7]. The model for intrusion detection was proposed by Dr. Dorothy Denning in 1987. Her proposed model is the basic core of the methodologies of intrusion detection in use today [5]. The intrusion detection is either anomaly detection or misuse detection. Anomaly detection is the identification of the normal activities and misuse detection is the detection of attacks on the basis of attack signatures through pattern matching approach. There are many flaws in an intrusion detection system like false positive and false negative. In such cases the IDS needs more training data to be trained and more time to gain better performance rate [8]. Classifiers are used to separate normal and intrusive data accurately and to attain maximum detection rate and minimum false alarms.

3 Support Vector Machines

Support vector machine (SVM) is a machine learning method proposed by Vapnik which is based on statistical learning theory [9]. SVM solve problems related to classification, learning and prediction [10]. As compared to other classifiers, SVM adopts the principle of structural risk minimization, it avoids local minimum and solves the issues like over learning and provides good generalization ability [11]. It performs the classification of the data vectors by a hyperplane or set of hyperplanes in a high dimensional space [12]. For classification there can be several hyperplanes for separation but the best hyerplane produces maximum margin between the data points of two classes. In many cases the data points are not linearly separable in the input space so they need nonlinear transformation into a high dimensional space and then the linear maximum margin classifier can be applied [13].Kernel functions are used for this purpose [14]. They are used at the training time of the classifiers to select the support vectors along the surface of the function. Then SVM classify the data by using these support vectors which outline the hyperplane in the feature space [15].

Selection of an appropriate kernel for a certain classification problem influence the performance of the SVM because different kernel function constructs different SVMs and affects the generalization ability and learning ability of SVM [16]. There is no theoretical method for selecting kernel function and its parameters. Presently Gaussian kernel is the kernel function which is mostly used because of its good features [17,18]. But there are many other kernel functions which are not yet applied in intrusion detection. For intrusion detection, SVM provide high classification accuracy even there is less prior knowledge available and the IDS will have better performance in terms of detection [19].

4 SVM Approaches to Intrusion Detection

There are different approaches applied for intrusion detection using SVM kernels for classification and regression. Several techniques in IDS are used for features transformation and selection along with SVM kernel functions for classification are implemented and then evaluated for determination of detection accuracy in terms of true positives and true negatives. Improving existing techniques for reducing errors in intrusion detection like false positives and false negatives are also in focus for researchers in order to contribute their applied technique towards the designing of robust IDS with maximum detection rate and minimized false alarms. A review of applying SVM approach for intrusion detection systems is as below:

4.1 SVM Approach-1

One of the SVM based approach for IDS was performed by Xiao et al. [10] in which they suggested a technique for intrusion detection based on Ad hoc technology and Support vector machine. IDS performance was improved in two ways: feature subset selection and optimization of SVM parameters. They provided ad hoc based feature subset selection and then 10-fold cross validation was used for optimizing SVM parameters. The extracted features were classified with the help of Gaussian Kernel of SVM. For this experiment, they used DARPA 1998 containing all the 41 features with four different attack classes such as DOS, R2L, U2R and probe. The experiment showed that it was not only better than other data mining techniques but also intelligent paradigms as well. A review of their results is given in Table 1.

Table 1. SVM Approach-1

Author	Year	Data Source	Structure	Results
Xiao et al.	2007	DARPA 1998 randomly generated 11,982 records having 41 features.	Ad hoc based feature selection, SVM with Gaussian Kernel	Improving IDS performance (feature subset selection, optimization of SVM parameters).

4.2 SVM Approach-2

Another approach of SVMs was applied by Yendrapalli et al. [20] in 2007. They used SVM, BSVM (Biased support vector machine), Looms (leave–one-out model selection) based on BSVM on the DARPA dataset containing four attacks and the normal data. The experiment concluded that SVM performs well for Normal and U2R, BSVM for DOS and Looms (BSVM) for Probe and R2L. SVM achieved above 95% detection accuracy for all five classes of DARPA dataset. They also demonstrated that the ability of SVMs to classify intrusions highly depends on both kernel type and the parameter settings. The results of their approach are shown in Table 2.

Table 2. SVM Approach-2

Author	Year	Data Source	Structure	Results
Yendrapalli et al.	2007	DARPA	SVM with RBF kernel, BSVM, Looms based on BSVM	Classification accuracies: SVM for Normal: 98.42 SVM for U2R: 99.87 BSVM for DOS: 99.33 Looms for Probe: 99.65 Looms for R2L: 100.00

4.3 SVM Approach-3

Yuancheng et al. [21] proposed an IDS approach based on feature extraction using KICA (Kernel Independent Component Analysis) and then using KICA extracted features as input data to SVM for classification. The SVM kernel used in this approach is Radial basis function (RBF). They used KDDCUP99 for experiment with some rules like test data set and training data set from different probability distribution and test data set also included other attacks which do not exist in training data set. Due to the good generalization ability of SVM, the experimental results showed that it can also detect new attacks apart from existed attacks. The accuracy of this IDS was also increased remarkably by doing feature extraction. Even thought the detection rate decreased to some extent but the results were acceptable as false alarm rate also decreased considerably and these reduced false alarms had positive impact on the performance of the system. They also stated that different kernel functions for this method gives different performance results so still more work to be done to find optimal kernel for maximum accuracy. The results of their IDS are given in Table 3.

Table 3. SVM Approach-3

Author	Year	Data Source	Structure	Results
Yuancheng et al.	2008	KDDCUP 99	KCIA,SVM with RBF kernel	Accuracy : 98.9% Detection rate: 97.4%. False alarm: 1.1%

4.4 SVM Approach-4

Another work was done by Yuan et al. [22] in which they proposed machine learning method for accurate internet traffic classification. Their method classified internet traffic according to the network flow parameters taken from the packet headers. They represented a method based on SVM technique for a set of traffic data collected on Gbps Ethernet link. The application signatures were used for identification for collected traffic data via precise signatures matching. They adopted cross validation to evaluate the experiment accuracies. This SVM based classification was more computationally efficient as compared to previous methods having similar accuracies. It also lends well for real time traffic identification as all the features parameters were computable without storing of multiple packets. This internet traffic classification technique is also applicable to encrypted network traffic as it does not rely on application payload. The identification of the traffic was too late as it was done after collecting the network flow, so it is necessary to be done in the early stage of the traffic flow. The results for the biased and unbiased training and testing samples are shown below in Table 4.

Table 4. SVM Approach-4

Author	Year	Data Source	Structure	Results
Yuan et al.	2008	Traffic data collected from Gbps Ethernet link	SVM, RBF Kernel	Accuracy: Biased: 99.42% Unbiased: 97.17%

4.5 SVM Approach-5

Another attempt in the field of intrusion detection with SVM was done by Zaman et al. [23] in which they proposed a new method for selecting features using Enhanced Support Vector Decision Function (ESVDF) SVM technique. The features were selected on two factors, the features rank which was calculated using Support Vector Decision Function (SVDF) and the second was the correlation between the features based on Forward Selection Ranking (FSR) or Backward Elimination Ranking (BER). They used KDD cup that consist of 4 types of attacks (DOS, R2L, U2R and Probing). The experiment was done in two steps. In first the features were selected and secondly the results were validated using SVM and Neural Network (NN) classifier. The experiment showed high accuracy for both SVM and NN with decreasing the training and testing time. This proposed model performed very well by selecting best features regardless of the classifier's type and with minimum overhead and maximum performance. A review of their results is given in the Table 5.

Table 5. SVM Approach-5

Author	Year	Data Source	Structure	Results
Zaman et al.	2009	Subset of KDD cup 1999	SVM with FSR and BER	Improvement in false positive rate, training time and testing time.

4.6 SVM Approach-6

Gao et al. [11] presented a method based on classify SVM and used genetic algorithm (GA) to optimize SVM parameters in order to increase the detection rate. This new method detected intrusion behaviours quickly and efficiently with strong learning and generalization ability of SVM. They also used radial basis function neural network (RBFNN) to detect the anomaly intrusion behaviour to compare with the performance of SVM. They found that the classify SVM is stronger than RBFNN in generalization ability. SVM is less dependent of sample data and has smaller fluctuation range of generalize error than RBFNN. So this new approach is more stable and has high detection rate. Review of their work is mentioned below in Table 6.

Table 6. SVM Approach-6

Author	Year	Data Source	Structure	Results
Gao et al.	2009	Training and testing data based on MIT 1999	SVM, GA, RBFNN	SVM having higher stability and obtain higher recognition and detection accuracy.

4.7 SVM Approach-7

In 2009, Rung-Ching et al. [24] used rough set theory (RST) and SVM for the detection of the intrusion in network. The purpose of using RST was to do pre-processing of the data by reducing dimensions. Then the selected features were sent to SVM for training and testing respectively. The dataset used for experiment was KDD cup 99 having 41 features and containing four different types of attacks. The features were reduced to 29 by using RST. The performance evaluation of the system was done on three formulas [25]; attack detection rate (ADR), false positive rate (FPR) and system accuracy. The performance of this approach was compared with 41 features and with entropy. This system had higher accuracy with reduced features as compared to full features and entropy but its attack detection rate and false positive were worse than entropy. The results of this IDS is given below in Table 7.

Table 7. SVM Approach-7

Author	Year	Data Source	Structure	Results
Rung-Ching et al.	2009	KDD cup 99	Rough set, SVM with RBF Kernel	ADR: 86.72% FPR: 13.27% Accuracy: 89.13%

4.8 SVM Approach-8

Another work for intrusion detection was done by Yuan et al. [19]. They applied hypothesis test theory to SVM classifier (HTSVM) in order to get increased accuracy and decreased the impact of penalty factor. They selected RBF kernel of SVM in comparison with sigmoid and polynomial kernels. Experiment data was taken from KDD cup 99. In comparison with CSVM, the false positive rate (FPR) and false negative rate (FNR) of HTSVM were lower but the training and testing time was slightly increased. The results showed that HTSVM classifier had better generalization and learning ability and the performance of the IDS can be improved. The result of their work is given in Table 8.

Table 8. SVM Approach-8

Author	Year	Data Source	Structure	Results
Yuan et al.	2010	Experiment data KDD 99	SVM, HTSVM, CSVM, Gaussian Kernel	HTSVM: Detection Precision (%) : 93.97 FPR (%) : 0.11 FNR (%) : 0.68 Training time : 26.53 Testing Time : 18.98

4.9 SVM Approach-9

Another contribution in the field of intrusion detection using SVM and Agent was done by Guan et al. [26] in 2010. The experimental data selected for this IDS model was KDD CUP 99 containing four attacks including Probe, DOS, R2L and U2R to test their proposed SVM model. They explained IDS in which Agent was used for the detection of abnormal intrusion and four SVM classifiers were used to recognize the intrusion types. The results proved to have better detection accuracy than artificial neural network. The review of this work is given below in Table 9.

Table 9. SVM Approach-9

Author	Year	Data Source	Structure	Results
Guan et al.	2010	KDD CUP 99	Agent, SVM	Detection precision: SVM: 0.9457 BP neural network (BPNN): 0.8771

4.10 SVM Approach-10

Xiaomei et al. [27] combined adaptive genetic algorithm (AGA) and SVM for audit analysis by using KDD CUP 99 for experiment. SVM could work successfully as a classifier for security audit system but the problem was learning two parameters penalty factor and kernel function which were key factors that could affect the performance of SVM. So, in this approach AGA optimized the penalty factor and also kernel function parameters of SVM. The results showed that this technique is more efficient and has higher accuracy than SVM. The best security audit should obtained higher accuracy rate in shorter training time but AGA-SVM had longer training time than that of SVM as it used heuristic method which took a lot of time for the exhaustive search. The systematic review of this approach is given below in Table 10.

Table 10. SVM Approach-10

Author	Year	Data Source	Structure	Results
Xiaomei et al.	2010	KDD CUP 99	AGA, SVM	For Pure data: Average attack detection rate of AGA-SVM is 2.44% higher than SVM. For Noise data: Average attack detection rate of AGA-SVM is 8.04% higher than SVM.

4.11 SVM Approach-11

Another attempt was done by Ahmad et al. [28] in IDS by applying SVM and back propagation neural network were used to be applied on distributed denial of service (DDOS). The experiment data used was cooperative association for internet data analysis (CAIDA) which is a standard for evaluating security detection mechanisms. The proposed model performed well in experiments and was better than other approaches used in IDS like K-NN, PCA and LOF in terms of detection rate and false alarms. A review of their work approach is given below in Table 11.

Table 11. SVM Approach-11

Author	Year	Data Source	Structure	Results
Ahmad et al.	2010	CAIDA	SVM	SVM neural network True Positive (%) : 100 True Negative (%) : 90.32 False Positive (%) : 0 False Negative (%) : 9.67

5 Discussion

The above review about the approaches applied for intrusion detection using support vector machines provides a lot of details regarding the techniques combined together with SVM to enhance the performance of the IDS and to focus different issues that need to be solved or improved. The data for the training and testing is a very critical issue. They can be obtained from any of the three ways; real traffic, sanitized traffic or simulated traffic. The real traffic is very costly and sanitized is risky. Even creating simulated traffic is also a hard job [28].

In the beginning, DARPA was used as dataset for training and testing which has different attacks classes but then afterwards mostly approaches used KDD CUP and CIADA which are the standard datasets for evaluation of security mechanisms. The reason for choosing KDD CUP standard dataset is that it is easy to compare the result with other approaches to find optimal technique in IDS and also it is very hard to get any other dataset which contains rich types of attacks for training and testing purpose of IDS.

The performances of the approaches were observed on the basis of their detection rate, accuracy, false alarms, training time and testing time. In many cases mentioned above, some focused on the minimization of the false alarms which results either in decreasing the detection rate or increasing the training and testing time. Choosing different feature selection techniques apart from the classifier and its parameters selection also contributed in minimizing overhead and maximizing the performance. Good generalization ability and the less dependency on the dataset make SVM better in classification as compared to other classifiers. Also in case of CIADA dataset, experiment showed that SVM performed better than other approaches like K-NN, PCA and LOF in detection rate and false alarms [28].

The ability of the SVM classification depends mainly on the kernel type and the setting of the parameters. There are many kernel functions of SVM but the one which had mainly used in existing approaches is RBF. Other kernels should also be used in comparison to find optimal results for applying SVM based approach depending upon the nature of classification problem. The selection of different techniques for feature preprocessing and selection also affects directly to the result of the SVM classifier.

6 Conclusion and Future Suggestion

In this paper we presented a review of current researches of intrusion detection by using support vector machines as classifier. We discussed most recent approaches with a systematic review of their applied techniques, datasets used and results obtained from their proposed IDS model. Research in intrusion detection using SVM approach is still an ongoing area due to good performance and many hybrid techniques are also applied in order to maximize the performance rate and minimize the false alarms. Different kernel functions of SVM apart from RBF should also be applied for IDS classification purpose which may provide better accuracy and detection rate depending on different nonlinear separations. Different feature selection techniques can also be applied to dataset in combination with SVM classifier and its kernel functions so that the training time can be minimized instead of processing redundant data and to get enhanced accuracy rate from extracted features of dataset rather than processing large number of features which does not even affect the accuracy factor.

References

1. Ahmad, I., Abdullah, A.B., Alghamdi, A.S.: Artificial neural network approaches to intrusion detection: a review. In: Proceedings of the 8th Wseas International Conference on Telecommunications and Informatics, Istanbul, Turkey (2009)
2. Kabiri, P., Ghorbani, A.A.: Research on intrusion detection and response: A survey. International Journal of Network Security 1(2), 84–102 (2005)
3. Mitrokotsa, A., Douligeris, C.: Detecting denial of service attacks using emergent self-organizing maps. In: Proceedings of the Fifth IEEE International Symposium on Signal Processing and Information Technology 2005, pp. 375–380 (2005)
4. Yuxin, W., Muqing, W.: Intrusion detection technology based on CEGA-SVM. In: Third International Conference on Security and Privacy in Communications Networks and the Workshops, SecureComm 2007, pp. 244–249 (2007)
5. Denning, D.E.: An Intrusion-Detection Model. IEEE Trans. Softw. Eng. 13(2), 222–232 (1987)
6. Anderson, J.P.: Computer security threat monitoring and surveillance. Technical Report. pp. 1–56. Ford Washington PA (1980)
7. Ahmad, I., Abdullah, A.B., Alghamdi, A.S.: Application of artificial neural network in detection of DOS attacks. In: Proceedings of the 2nd International Conference on Security of Information and Networks, Famagusta, North Cyprus (2009)
8. Zhu, G., Liao, J.: Research of Intrusion Detection Based on Support Vector Machine. In: International Conference on Advanced Computer Theory and Engineering, pp. 434–438 (2008)
9. Vladimir, V.N.: The Nature of Statistical Learning Theory. Springer, Heidelberg (1995)
10. Xiao, H., Peng, F., Wang, L., Li, H.: Ad hoc-based feature selection and support vector machine classifier for intrusion detection. In: IEEE International Conference on Grey Systems and Intelligent Services (GSIS 2007), pp. 1117–1121 (2007)
11. Gao, M., Tian, J., Xia, M.: Intrusion Detection Method Based on Classify Support Vector Machine. In: Proceedings of the 2009 Second International Conference on Intelligent Computation Technology and Automation, pp. 391–394 (2009)
12. Ahmad, I., Abdulah, A., Alghamdi, A.: Towards the Designing of a Robust Intrusion Detection System through an Optimized Advancement of Neural Networks. In: Kim, T.-h., Adeli, H. (eds.) AST/UCMA/ISA/ACN 2010. LNCS, vol. 6059, pp. 597–602. Springer, Heidelberg (2010)
13. Yang, M.-h., Wang, R.-c.: DDoS detection based on wavelet kernel support vector machine. The Journal of China Universities of Posts and Telecommunications 15(3), 59–63, 94 (2008)
14. Kumar, G., Kumar, K., Sachdeva, M.: The use of artificial intelligence based techniques for intrusion detection: a review. Artificial Intelligence Review 34(4), 369–387 (2010)
15. Mulay, S.A., Devale, P.R., Garje, G.V.: Intrusion Detection System Using Support Vector Machine and Decision Tree. International Journal of Computer Applications 3(3), 40–43 (2010)
16. Li, C.-C., Guo, A.-l., Li, D.: Combined Kernel SVM and Its Application on Network Security Risk Evaluation. In: International Symposium on Intelligent Information Technology Application Workshops (IITAW 2008), pp. 36–39 (2008)
17. Jiancheng, S.: Fast tuning of SVM kernel parameter using distance between two classes. In: 3rd International Conference on Intelligent System and Knowledge Engineering (ISKE 2008), pp. 108–113 (2008)

18. Broomhead, D.S., Lowe, D.: Multivariable Functional Interpolation and Adaptive Networks. Complex Systems 2, 321–355 (1988)
19. Yuan, J., Li, H., Ding, S., Cao, L.: Intrusion Detection Model Based on Improved Support Vector Machine. In: Proceedings of the 2010 Third International Symposium on Intelligent Information Technology and Security Informatics, pp. 465–469 (2010)
20. Yendrapalli, K., Mukkamala, S., Sung, A.H., Ribeiro, B.: Biased Support Vector Machines and Kernel Methods for Intrusion Detection. In: Proceedings of the World Congress on Engineering (WCE 2007), London, U.K (2007)
21. Yuancheng, L., Zhongqiang, W., Yinglong, M.: An intrusion detection method based on KICA and SVM. In: 7th World Congress on Intelligent Control and Automation (WCICA 2008), pp. 2141–2144 (2008)
22. Yuan, R., Li, Z., Guan, X., Xu, L.: An SVM-based machine learning method for accurate internet traffic classification. Information Systems Frontiers 12(2), 149–156 (2010)
23. Zaman, S., Karray, F.: Features Selection for Intrusion Detection Systems Based on Support Vector Machines. In: 6th IEEE Consumer Communications and Networking Conference (CCNC 2009), pp. 1–8 (2009)
24. Rung-Ching, C., Kai-Fan, C., Ying-Hao, C., Chia-Fen, H.: Using Rough Set and Support Vector Machine for Network Intrusion Detection System. In: First Asian Conference on Intelligent Information and Database Systems (ACIIDS 2009), pp. 465–470 (2009)
25. Chen, R.C., Chen, S.P.: Intrusion Detection Using a Hybrid Support Vector Machine Based on Entropy and TF-IDF. International Journal of Innovative Computing, Information and Control (IJICIC) 4(2), 413–424 (2008)
26. Guan, X., Guo, H., Chen, L.: Network intrusion detection method based on Agent and SVM. In: The 2nd IEEE International Conference on Information Management and Engineering (ICIME), pp. 399–402 (2010)
27. Xiaomei, Y., Peng, W.: Security audit system using Adaptive Genetic Algorithm and Support Vector Machine. In: 3rd International Conference on Advanced Computer Theory and Engineering (ICACTE), pp. 265–268 (2010)
28. Ahmad, I., Abdullah, A.B., Alghamdi, A.S., Hussain, M.: Distributed Denial of Service attack detection using Support Vector Machine. Journal of Formation-Tokyo, 127–134 (2010)

Hybrid ARIMA and Neural Network Model for Measurement Estimation in Energy-Efficient Wireless Sensor Networks

Reza Askari Moghadam[1] and Mehrnaz Keshmirpour[2]

[1] Engineering Department, Payam Noor University, Tehran, Iran
askari@pnu.ac.ir
[2] Engineering Department, Payam Noor University, Tehran, Iran
keshmirpour@gmail.com

Abstract. Wireless Sensor Networks (WSNs) are composed of many sensor nodes using limited power resources. Therefore efficient power consumption is the most important issue in such networks. One way to reduce power consumption of sensor nodes is reducing the number of wireless communication between nodes by dual prediction. In this approach, the sink node instead of direct communication, exploits a time series model to predict local readings of sensor nodes with certain accuracy. There are different linear and non-linear models for time series forecasting. In this paper we will introduce a hybrid prediction model that is created from combination of ARIMA model as linear prediction model and neural network that is a non-linear model. Then, we will present a comparison between effectiveness of our approach and previous hybrid models. Experimental results show that the proposed method can be an effective way to reduce data transmission compared with existing hybrid models and also either of the components models used individually.

Keywords: Wireless Sensor Networks, Energy Conservation, Dual Prediction, ARIMA, Artificial Neural Networks, Hybrid Model.

1 Introduction

Wireless sensor networks have attracted great interests from many researchers because their wide range of applications in the military, industrial, commercial, health, environmental monitoring and control, and many other domains. Such networks are made up of many small sensor nodes that are randomly deployed in the area to be monitored [1,2]. These tiny sensor nodes include four basic components: a sensing unit for data acquisition, a processing unit for local data processing and storage, a communication unit for data transmission, and a power unit that often consists of a battery [3,4]. These devices must be small, light and inexpensive, so that they can be produced and deployed in large numbers, thus their resources in terms of energy, memory, computational speed and bandwidth are severely constrained [2].

A. Abd Manaf et al. (Eds.): ICIEIS 2011, Part III, CCIS 253, pp. 35–48, 2011.

In most applications recharging or replacing battery of sensor nodes is impossible because sensor nodes may be deployed in disastrous or inaccessible environment. Due to these limitations, energy conservation in WSNs is the most critical issue [4]. Energy saving in a wireless sensor network can be achieved by dual prediction methods. As energy consumption of communication unit is much higher than the other units, reducing the communication between nodes through dual prediction, leads to energy efficiency and prolonging the lifetime of the network.

In dual prediction, for each sensor node a prediction model that was trained from a history of sensor measurements is located at both sensor and the sink. Then sink node uses this model to forecast sensor samples with certain accuracy rather than transmit readings from the sensors. Therefore, the number of communications between nodes and sink is reduced and energy-expensive periodic radio transmission can be omitted [5,6].

To ensure that the difference between the predicted value by the sink and the actual value that measured by sensor is not more than predefined threshold, both sink and sensor node make identical prediction about the future measurement of sensor. In sensor node this predicted value is compared with the actual measurement, and if the difference between them didn't increase beyond the precision constraint, sensor doesn't transmit sampled data to the sink, thus avoiding unnecessary communication. In the absence of notification from the sensor node, the sink assumes that the value obtained from the prediction model is within the required error bound. Only when the difference between the actual and the predicted value exceeds user defined threshold, the prediction model needs to be updated. At this time sensor re-compute the parameters of the prediction model and send them to the sink. Predictions would then begin again, and continue, until the error tolerance condition is violated [5,6,8].

A common approach to predict the future sampled data is time series forecasting, where a set of historical values obtained by periodic samplings are used to predict the next value [4]. There are different algorithms to time series forecasting containing linear and nonlinear models. In this paper we will focus on the two most popular of them: ARIMA model for linear prediction and Neural Network based prediction model for nonlinear forecasting, and then we will propose a hybrid model to improve the forecasting results by combining these two models. We will evaluate our approach via simulation and compare its performance to ARIMA and neural network models used separately and other hybrid models.

2 Related Works

Typical methods for modeling stationary time series are autoregressive (AR), moving average (MA), or combination of these two models that make autoregressive-moving average (ARMA) model. But for nonstationary time series, the autoregressive integrated moving average (ARIMA) model also known as Box-Jenkins model can be applied, for example in Li et al. where seasonal ARIMA-based time series model has employed to forecast sensed data with the aim of reducing communication overhead [9].

Due to low complexity of AR model compared with ARIMA, this subclass of ARIMA model is more suitable for wireless sensor networks as it's used in many studies to forecast sensor measurements [10,11,12,13,14]. But the major limitation of ARIMA model and its subclasses is that ARIMA is a linear model and no nonlinear patterns can be captured by the ARIMA model. [15]

During last decade neural networks have been used successfully in modeling and forecasting nonlinear time series. The major advantage of neural networks is their flexible capability in nonlinear modeling. Numerous articles have been presented on time series forecasting by neural networks i.e. Zhang et al. [16], Mishra and Desai [17], Lee Giles et al. [18], Frank et al. [19], Bodyanskiy et al. [20], Yuehui Chen et al. [21], Giordano et al. [22], Zhang et al. [23], Hussain et al. [24], Han et al. [25], Zhang Yu [26], also in wireless sensor networks area, for example Park et al. proposed a non-linear neural network based approach for prediction of sensor measurements [6], Mandal et al. proposed a flood forecasting technique based on multilayer perceptron [27] and so on.

In some articles, the combination of ARIMA and Neural Network models is proposed to capture both linearity and nonlinearity parts of time series. Zhang proposed a hybrid system that linear ARIMA model and nonlinear Neural Network model are used jointly to improve forecasting performance. In this study it's assumed that time series to be composed of a linear autocorrelation structure and a nonlinear component. First, ARIMA model is used to forecast the linear component, and then residuals from the linear model that contain the nonlinear relationship are modeled using ANNs. Since the ARIMA model cannot capture the nonlinear structure of the data, the residuals of linear model will contain information about the nonlinearity. The results from the neural network can be used as predictions of the error terms for the ARIMA model [15]. Similar methods also proposed by Areekul et al. [28] and Faruk [29].

Sterba and Hilovska proposed a hybrid ARIMA-Neural Network prediction model for aggregate water consumption prediction. In the first step of their hybrid system, a seasonal ARIMA model is used to model the linear part of the time series, and to create the ARIMA forecast. In the next step, the ARIMA forecasts and time series data are used as inputs for artificial neural network, and trained using the known input and output training data to model the non-linearity part of the time series. Finally, the neural network is used to predict the future values of time series and output of artificial neural network is used as estimate of time series value for the next forecast [30].

Zeng et al. also proposed a hybrid predicting model that combines Autoregressive Integrated Moving Average (ARIMA) and Multilayer Artificial Neural Network (MLANN). The proposed methodology of the hybrid system consists of two steps. In the first step, a MLANN model is used to analyze the nonlinear part of traffic flow time series. In the second step, an ARIMA model is developed to model the residuals from the ANN model. Since the BPNN model cannot capture the linear structure of the data, the residuals of nonlinear model will contain information about the linearity. The results from the neural network can be used as predictions of the error terms for the ARIMA model [31].

3 Time Series Forecasting Models

The ARIMA and the neural network models are summarized in the following as foundation to describe the hybrid model.

3.1 Autoregressive Integrated Moving Average Model

The autoregressive-moving average model is a stochastic model for time series forecasting where the next value in time series is calculated from linear aggregation of previous values and error terms. The autoregressive-moving average model is denoted as ARMA(p, q) and is defined by:

$$y_t = \sum_{i=1}^{p} \emptyset_i y_{t-i} + \sum_{j=0}^{q} \theta_j \varepsilon_{t-j} \quad (\theta_0 = 1) \tag{1}$$

Where y_t is the time series value at time period t, $\emptyset_i$ and θ_j are the parameters of autoregressive and moving average model respectively, and ε_t is white noise that has mean zero and variance σ^2.

The prerequisite for using ARMA model is the stationarity of the time series, while many time series in industry or business exhibit nonstationary behavior. We can sometimes reduce the nonstationary time series to stationary by differencing. Doing so produces an autoregressive integrated moving average model where is a powerful model for describing time series and is defined by:

$$w_t = \nabla^d y_t = y_t - y_{t-d} \tag{2}$$

$$w_t = \sum_{i=1}^{p} \emptyset_i w_{t-i} + \sum_{j=0}^{q} \theta_j \varepsilon_{t-j} \tag{3}$$

The autoregressive integrated moving average model is denoted as ARIMA(p, d, q) that contains the autoregressive model of order p and the moving average model of order q and d is the order of differencing [32].

3.2 Structure of Neural Network Model

One of the most common neural network architectures called the feedforward multilayer perceptron (MLP). MLP network is composed of one input layer, one or more hidden layers and one output layer as shown in Fig. 1. For time series forecasting, input vector to the network consists of past samples of the time series and the output is the predicted value. There is a non-linear mapping relationship between the inputs and output as follow:

$$y_t = f(y_{t-1}, y_{t-2}, \dots, y_{t-p}) \tag{4}$$

Where y_t is the observation at time t, p is the dimension of the input vector or prediction order, and f is the transfer function that must be a nonlinear function.

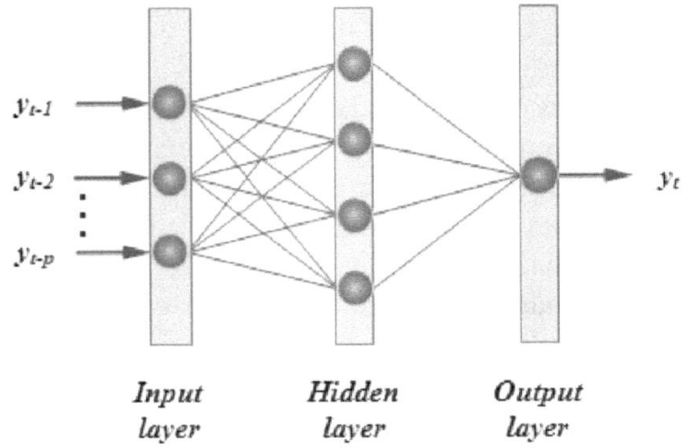

Fig. 1. Multilayer feedforward neural network architecture

According to Eq. (4) the feedforward network works as a general nonlinear autoregressive model [16,33].

4 Proposed Method

In ARIMA model, the next value in time series is calculated from linear combination of previous values plus white noise. Therefore, ARIMA model is appropriate for prediction of linear time series. On the other hand, using neural network is better in prediction of nonlinear time series because its nonlinear transfer function between input and output layers.

Both ARIMA and neural network models have achieved successes in their own linear or nonlinear domains. However, none of them is a universal model that is suitable for all circumstances. Using ARIMA models to approximation of nonlinear problems as well as neural networks to model linear problems may not yield good results.

Most real-world time series contain both linear and nonlinear parts. So, for an efficient prediction, individual linear and nonlinear models must be combined to create a single model. We will introduce a new method for hybridizing ARIMA as a linear model and Neural Network as a nonlinear model for prediction of sensor measurements in WSNs.

The main idea of our proposed method is using ARIMA model to forecast linear changes of data and neural network to recognize the trend of data changes.

By attention the acquired data from a sensor node (for example temperature data) we find that in some successive time periods, data changes are linear and monotonically increase or decrease. In these periods of time we use ARIMA model to estimate the next sampled data. But when non-linear changes occurred, the ARIMA model often fails. In this situation, neural network is engaged for detecting non-linearity relationships in data and tracks the trend of data changes. Thus, until the neural network is able to detect nonlinear relationships in data, the ARIMA model is prevented from updating.

By decreasing the number of model updates, total communications between sensor nodes and sink for resending new parameters of model are reduced. Since communication in wireless networks is not end to end, and for transmitting an update, data packets must pass through several nodes that are specified in routing mechanism, and as regards wireless communication is the main source of energy consumption in sensor nodes, reducing the number of update packets leads to saving energy in sensor nodes and prolonging the lifetime of the entire network.

In our proposed hybrid model, in the training phase ARIMA model and neural network are trained by actual data that acquired from the sensor separately, then ARIMA coefficients and neural network weights are computed and transmitted to the sink.

In the prediction phase, ARIMA model and neural network predict the next sampled data in parallel in both sensor node and the sink. Each of models uses its previous predicted values as input to forecast the next value recurrently. The output of ARIMA model is considered as estimation of sensor measurements in the sink.

In sensor node, this predicted value is compared with the actual sampled data. Until data changes are linear and the difference between the sensed and the predicted value doesn't exceed the predefined threshold, the predicted value obtained from the ARIMA model is assumed as sampled data with certain accuracy in sink node. When the difference or error become more than the threshold, instead of updating the ARIMA model coefficients, neural network is used for covering non-linearity of data changes. In this stage, the outputs of neural network that contain the trend of data changes are used as inputs for ARIMA model and eliminating the need for updating model.

To inform the sink that ARIMA model should use the output of neural network for prediction, sensor node sends a beacon signal to the sink. Beacon signal is a small message to signal the sink that output of neural network should be used for ARIMA model prediction. In calculating the total number of transmitted packets to the sink, the number of beacon signals also should be considered. Data packets for transmitting model update should be contain input values and the model parameters, while the size of beacon packets is very small. To take into account the size of packets, we calculate the total number of transmitted packets as follow:

$$p_t = p_u + cp_b \tag{5}$$

Where p_t is the total number of transmitted packets to the sink, p_u is the number of model update packets, p_b is the number of beacon packets and c is the ratio of the size of beacon packet to the size of model update packet.

Only when both models together fail to forecast measurements, the ARIMA model is re-trained for adapting new sampled data and the parameters of model is transmitted to the sink. Fig. 2 shows the block diagram of hybrid model. The procedures at the sensor and the sink are shown in Algorithm 1.

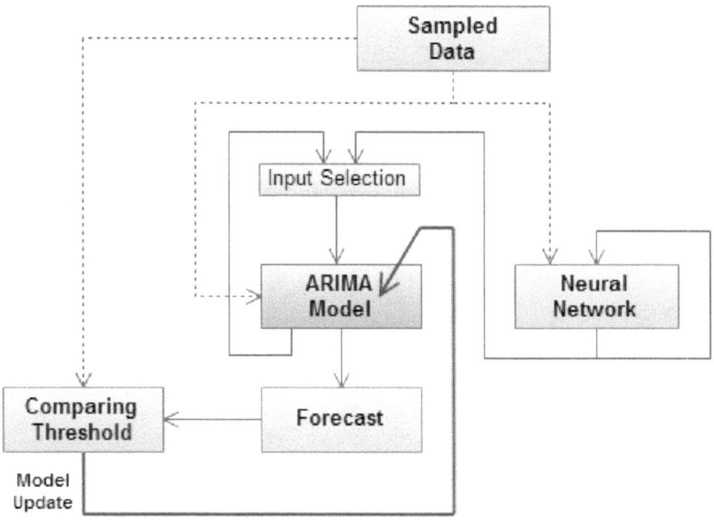

Fig. 2. Proposed hybrid model block diagram

Table 1. Three different data sets

Date	No. of Sensors	No. of Samples	Data set	Threshold	Min value	Max value
2004-02-29	53	31800	Temperature	0.3	14.9904	27.8284
			Humidity	0.3	32.2293	55.8884
			Voltage	0.03	2.3568	2.7496
2004-03-04	52	31200	Temperature	0.3	16.8034	122.1530
			Humidity	0.3	-4	43.9844
			Voltage	0.03	2.1597	2.6049
2004-03-07	52	31200	Temperature	0.3	17.2640	122.1530
			Humidity	0.3	-4	50.0966
			Voltage	0.03	2.0622	2.6164

Algorithm 1. Proposed Hybrid Model

Running at Sensor

```
initialize data and model parameters;
while true
{
  actual_value ← sampling data;
  arima_predict←predict_using_ARIMA(data);
  nn_predict←[nn_predict,predict_using_NN(nn_predict)];
  predicted_value ← arima_predict;
  if ( | actual_value – predicted_value | > threshold)
  {
    predicted_value ← predict_using_ARIMA(nn_predict);
    if ( | actual_value – predicted_value | > threshold)
    {
      send data to sink;
      update ARIMA model and send parameters to sink;
      data ← [data, actual_value];
    }
    else
    {
      send beacon singnal to sink;
    }
  }
  else
  {
    data ← [data, predicted_value]
  }
}
```

Running at Sink

```
receive data and model parameters from sensor;
while true
{
  actual _value ← data from sensor;
  beacon ← beacon signal from sensor;
  if (actual _value == null)
  {
    if (beacon == null)
    {
      actual_value ← predict_using_ARIMA(data);
    }
    else
    {
      actual_value ← predict_using_ARIMA(nn_predict);
    }
   nn_predict←[nn_predict,predict_using_NN(nn_predict)]
  }
  else
  {
    parameters ← ARIMA model parameters from sensor;
    update ARIMA model by received parameters;
  }
  data ← [data, actual_value];
}
```

5 Simulation Results

This section presents the simulation results in order to evaluate performance of the proposed hybrid model.

This simulation model was developed in Matlab and executed on a desktop PC with Intel Core2 Dou 2 GHz processor and 3GB of RAM. Three real-world datasets from the Intel Berkeley Research lab have been used for this experience [7]. We consider some epochs of data collected from all sensors during three days including temperature, humidity and voltage that are listed in Table 1. In this experience the one-step-ahead forecasting is considered.

The neural network used is a MLP network with $2\times1\times1$ network model and tan-sigmoid transfer function in the hidden layer and linear transfer function in the output layer. The input of the network are the past, lagged observations and the output is the predicted value. The network trained using Levenberg-Marquardt back propagation algorithm and network performance is measured by MSE (Mean squared error) function.

We modeled time series by ARIMA models, and select the best model based on minimum RMSE as autoregressive model of order 1 for these datasets. Parameters estimation of model is performed by Least Squares Method.

The objective of dual prediction is reducing data transmission between nodes and the sink. In Table 2 we show a comparison between transmitted packets in the proposed method and traditional ARIMA and neural network model used separately. Table 3 shows the results for Comparison of existing hybrid ARIMA-neural network models and proposed method by the number of model updates.

In this comparison we consider 3 hybrid models that we reviewed in the related works section.

In "Hybrid model 1" it's considered that time series to be composed of a linear and a nonlinear component. ARIMA model is used to forecast the linear component and the nonlinear relationship is modeled using ANN. The sum of linear and nonlinear parts makes the predicted value [15,28,29]. The procedures are shown in Algorithm 2.

Algorithm 2. Hybrid Model 1

Running at Sensor	Running at Sink

initialize data and model parameters;
while true
{
actual_value ← sampling data;
arima_predict←predict_using_ARIMA(data);
nn_predict ← predict_using_NN(data);
predicted_value ← arima_predict + nn_predict;
if (|actual_value – predicted_value| > threshold)
{
send data to sink;
update models and send parameters to sink;
data ← [data, actual_value];
}
else
{
data ← [data, predicted_value];
}
}
	receive data and model parameters from sensor;
	while true
	{
	actual _value ← data from sensor;
	if (actual _value == null)
	{
	arima_predict ← predict_using_ARIMA(data);
	nn_predict ← predict_using_NN(data);
	actual _value ← arima_predict + nn_predict;
	}
	else
	{
	parameters← model parameters from sensor;
	update ARIMA and NN model by received parameters;
	}
	data ← [data, actual_value];
	}

In "Hybrid model 2" first, an ARIMA model is used to model the linear part of the time series. Then the output of ARIMA model is used as input of neural network to model the non-linearity part of the time series. Finally, the output of artificial neural network is used as estimate of time series value as shown in Fig. 3 [30]. The procedures are shown in Algorithm 3.

Algorithm 3. Hybrid Model 2

Running at Sensor	Running at Sink

initialize data and model parameters;
while true
{
actual_value ← sampling data;
arima_predict←[arima_predict,
predict_using_ARIMA(data)];
predicted_value ← predict_using_NN(arima_predict);
if (| actual_value – predicted_value | > threshold)
{
send data to sink;
update models and send parameters to sink;
data ← [data, actual_value];
}
else
{
data ← [data, predicted_value];
}
}
	receive data and model parameters from sensor;
	while true
	{
	actual _value ← data from sensor;
	if (actual _value == null)
	{
	arima_predict←[arima_predict,
	predict_using_ARIMA(data)];
	actual_value ← predict_using_NN(arima_predict);
	}
	else
	{
	parameters ← model parameters from sensor;
	update ARIMA and NN model by received parameters;
	}
	data ← [data, actual_value];
	}

In "Hybrid model 3" first, ANN is used to analyze the nonlinear part of time series. Then ARIMA model is developed to model the residuals from the ANN model. The output of ARIMA model is used as predicted value as shown in Fig. 4 [31]. The procedures are shown in Algorithm 4.

The results shown in Table 2 and Table 3 indicate that the number of transmitted packets is reduced in proposed model compared with existing hybrid models and also either of the components models used individually. Since wireless communication is the main source of energy consumption in sensor nodes, reducing the number of transmitted packets eliminates wasted energy on nodes. Therefore, this method can be an energy-saving strategy for sensor nodes and leads to prolonging the lifetime of the sensor network.

Algorithm 4. Hybrid Model 3

Running at Sensor	**Running at Sink**

initialize data and model parameters;
while true
{
actual_value ← sampling data;
nn_predict ← [nn_predict , predict_using_NN(data)];
predicted_value←predict_using_ARIMA(nn_predict);
if (| actual_value – predicted_value | > threshold)
{
send data to sink;
update models and send parameters to sink;
data ← [data, actual_value];
}
else
{
data ← [data, predicted_value];
}
}
	receive data and model parameters from sensor;
	while true
	{
	actual _value ← data from sensor;
	if (actual _value == null)
	{
	nn_predict ← [nn_predict , predict_using_NN(data)];
	actual_value ← predict_using_ARIMA(nn_predict);
	}
	else
	{
	parameters ← model parameters from sensor;
	update ARIMA and NN model by received parameters;
	}
	data ← [data, actual_value];
	}

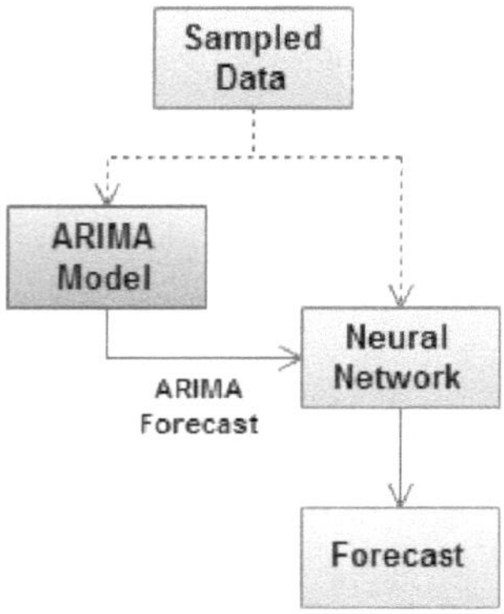

Fig. 3. Hybrid model 2 block diagram

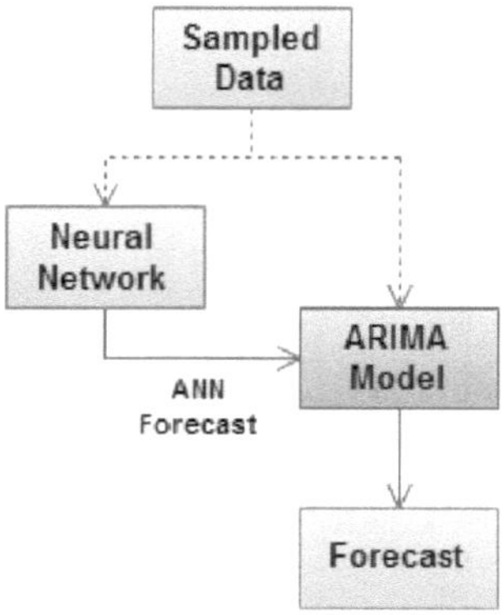

Fig. 4. Hybrid model 3 block diagram

Table 2. Comparison of prediction models by the number of transmitted packets

Date	Data set	Number of transmitted packets			
		Without Prediction	ARIMA model	Neural Network model	Proposed Hybrid Model + Beacon Signals
2004-02-29	Temperature	31800	502	574	438
	Humidity	31800	1837	2060	1286
	Voltage	31800	265	304	201
2004-03-04	Temperature	31200	1026	1092	868
	Humidity	31200	2023	2169	1687
	Voltage	31200	431	520	348
2004-03-07	Temperature	31200	350	410	346
	Humidity	31200	1324	1417	838
	Voltage	31200	224	286	185

Table 3. Comparison of prediction models by the number of model updates

Date	Data set	Number of model updates				
		Without Prediction	Hybrid Model 1 [15,28,29]	Hybrid Model 2 [30]	Hybrid Model 3 [31]	Proposed Hybrid Model
2004-02-29	Temperature	31800	545	669	588	432
	Humidity	31800	2066	1982	1737	1249
	Voltage	31800	258	419	277	177
2004-03-04	Temperature	31200	1141	1299	1109	852
	Humidity	31200	2194	2282	2052	1654
	Voltage	31200	466	556	418	322
2004-03-07	Temperature	31200	372	565	515	344
	Humidity	31200	1330	1374	1224	805
	Voltage	31200	227	361	238	164

The comparison between predicted values and the number of model updates using different models for humidity data set of sensor no.1 is shown in Fig. 5.

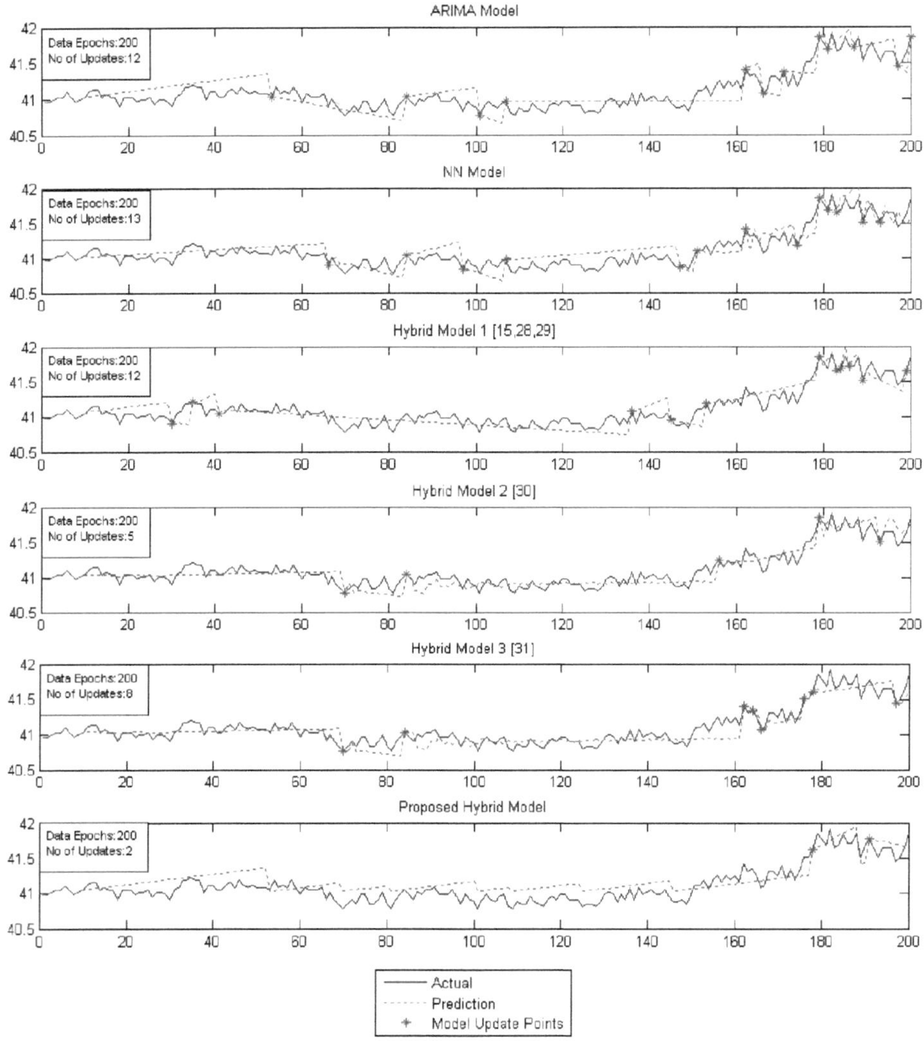

Fig. 5. Comparison of predicted values using different models for Humidity data set of sensor no.1

6 Conclusion

In this paper we proposed a hybrid prediction model that is created from combination of ARIMA model as linear prediction model and neural network as a non-linear model to forecast sensor measurements in order to reduce the number of communication between nodes and sink. Our goal is reducing energy consumption of nodes to prolong the lifetime of sensor networks while maintaining data accuracy. We evaluated our approach via simulation and compared its performance to ARIMA and neural network models used separately and other hybrid models. Experimental results show that the proposed hybrid method is able to outperform existing hybrid models and can be an effective way to reduce data transmission compared with traditional ARIMA and neural network models used separately.

An extension to this work would be to integrate dual prediction with adaptive sampling that conserves energy in both sensing and communication units.

References

1. Ning Xu, A.: Survey of Sensor Network Applications. IEEE Communications Magazine 40 (2002)
2. Culler, D., Estrin, D., Srivastava, M.: Overview of Sensor Networks. Computer 37(8), 41–49 (2004)
3. Akyildiz, I.F., Su, W., Sankarasubramaniam, Y., Cayirci, E.: A Survey on Sensor Networks. IEEE Communications Magazine, 102–114 (2002)
4. Anastasi, G., Conti, M., Di Francesco, M., Passarella, A.: Energy conservation in wireless sensor networks: A survey. Ad Hoc Networks 7, 537–568 (2009)
5. Tharini, C., Vanaja Ranjan, P.: An Energy Efficient Spatial Correlation Based Data Gathering Algorithm for Wireless Sensor Networks. International Journal of Distributed and Parallel Systems 2(3), 16–24 (2011)
6. Park, I., Mirikitani, D.T.: Energy Reduction in Wireless Sensor Networks through Measurement Estimation with Second Order Recurrent Neural Networks. In: Third International Conference on Networking and Services (ICNS 2007), pp. 103–103 (2007)
7. Intel Lab Data, `http://db.csail.mit.edu/labdata/labdata.html`
8. Le Borgne, Y.-A., Santini, S., Bontempi, G.: Adaptive model selection for time series prediction in wireless sensor networks. Signal Processing 87(12) (2007)
9. Li, M., Ganesan, D., Shenoy, P.: PRESTO: Feedback-driven Data Management in Sensor Networks. IEEE/ACM Transactions on Networking 17(4), 1256–1269 (2009)
10. Kim, W.-j., Ji, K., Srivastava, A.: Network-Based Control with Real-Time Prediction of Delayed/Lost Sensor Data. IEEE Transactions on Control Systems Technology 14(1), 182–185 (2006)
11. Mukhopadhyay, S., Schurgers, C., Panigrahi, D., Dey, S.: Model-Based Techniques for Data Reliability in Wireless Sensor Networks. IEEE Transactions on Mobile Computing 8(4), 528–543 (2009)
12. Arici, T., Akgun, T., Altunbasak, Y.: A Prediction Error-Based Hypothesis Testing Method for Sensor Data Acquisition. ACM Transactions on Sensor Networks (TOSN) 2(4) (2006)
13. Ling, Q., Tian, Z., Yin, Y., Li, Y.: Localized Structural Health Monitoring Using Energy-Efficient Wireless Sensor Networks. IEEE Sensors Journal 9(11), 1596–1604 (2009)
14. Jiang, H., Jin, S., Wang, C.: Prediction or Not? An Energy-Efficient Framework for Clustering-Based Data Collection in Wireless Sensor Networks. IEEE Transactions on Parallel and Distributed Systems 22(6), 1064–1071 (2011)
15. Peter Zhang, G.: Time series forecasting using a hybrid ARIMA and neural network model. Neurocomputing 50, 159–175 (2003)
16. Peter Zhang, G., Eddy Patuwo, B., Hu, M.Y.: A simulation study of artificial neural networks for nonlinear time-series forecasting. Computers and Operations Research 28(4), 381–396 (2001)

17. Mishra, A.K., Desai, V.R.: Drought forecasting using feed-forward recursive neural network. Ecological Modelling 198, 127–138 (2006)
18. Lee Giles, C., Lawrence, S., Chung Tsoi, A.: Noisy Time Series Prediction using a Recurrent Neural Network and Grammatical Inference. Machine Learning, 161–183 (2001)
19. Frank, R.J., Davey, N., Hunt, S.P.: Time Series Prediction and Neural Networks. Journal of Intelligent and Robotic Systems 31, 91–103 (2001)
20. Bodyanskiy, Y., Popov, S.: Neural network approach to forecasting of quasiperiodic financial time series. European Journal of Operational Research 175(3), 1357–1366 (2006)
21. Chen, Y., Yang, B., Dong, J.: Time-series prediction using a local linear wavelet neural network. Neurocomputing 69(4-6), 449–465 (2006)
22. Giordano, F., La Rocca, M., Perna, C.: Forecasting nonlinear time series with neural network sieve bootstrap. Computational Statistics & Data Analysis 51(8), 3871–3884 (2007)
23. Peter Zhang, G., Kline, D.M.: Quarterly Time-Series Forecasting With Neural Networks. IEEE Transactions on Neural Networks 18(6) (2007)
24. Hussain, A.J., Knowles, A., Lisboa, P.J.G., El-Deredy, W.: Financial time series prediction using polynomial pipelined neural networks. Expert Systems with Applications 35(3), 1186–1199 (2008)
25. Han, M., Wang, Y.: Analysis and modeling of multivariate chaotic time series based on neural network. Expert Systems with Applications 36(2), Part 1,1280–1290 (2009)
26. Yu, Z.: Research Of Time Series Finding Algorithm Based On Artificial Neural Network. In: 2009 World Congress on Computer Science and Information Engineering, Los Angeles, CA, vol. 4, pp. 400–403 (2009)
27. Mandal, S., Saha, D., Banerjee, T.: A neural network based prediction model for flood in a disaster management system with sensor networks. In: 2005 International Conference on Intelligent Sensing and Information Processing, pp. 78–82 (2005)
28. Areekul, P., Senjyu, T., Toyama, H., Yona, A.: A Hybrid ARIMA and Neural Network Model for Short-Term Price Forecasting in Deregulated Market. IEEE Transactions on Power Systems 25(1), 524–530 (2010)
29. Faruk, D.O.: A hybrid neural network and ARIMA model for water quality time series prediction. Engineering Applications of Artificial Intelligence 23(4), 586–594 (2010)
30. Sterba, J., Hilovska, K.: The Implementation Of Hybrid Arima-Neural Network Prediction Model For Agregate Water Consumtion Prediction. Journal of Applied Mathematics 3 (2010)
31. Zeng, D., Xu, J., Gu, J., Liu, L., Xu, G.: Short Term Traffic Flow Prediction Using Hybrid ARIMA and ANN Models. In: 2008 Workshop on Power Electronics and Intelligent Transportation System (2008)
32. Box, G.E.P., Jenkins, G.M., Reinsel, G.C.: Time Series Analyses Forecasting and Control, 3rd edn. Prentice Hall (1994)
33. Koskela, T., Lehtokangas, M., Saarinen, J., Kaski, K.: Time Series Prediction with Multilayer Perceptron, FIR and Elman Neural Networks. In: Proceedings of the World Congress on Neural Networks, pp. 491–496 (1996)

Recycling Resource of Furnitures for Reproductive Design with Support of Internet Community: A Case Study of Resource and Knowledge Discovery Using Social Networks

Masatoshi Imai[1] and Yoshiro Imai[2]

[1] Graduate School of Design, Tokyo Zokei University
1556 Utunuki-machi Hachioji-shi, Tokyo, 192-0992 Japan
320motoring.gmail.com
[2] Graduate School of Engineering, Kagawa University
2217-20 Hayashi-cho, Takamatsu-shi, Kagawa, 631-0396 Japan
imai@eng.kagawa-u.ac.jp

Abstract. Nowadays, Ecology and/or Recycling are one of very important keywords to improve our daily lives efficiently and comfortably. Some products have been not-used by owners but they have still now been available. In such a case, Resource and Knowledge Recovery are very much useful at the viewpoint of Ecology and Recycling. We have tried to demonstrate how to recover some resource of furniture in order to achieve recycling and reproducing. We have utilized social networks based on Internet to perform information sharing and exchanging. This time, our resources are currently not-used furnitures kindly provided from some company which has stored several mounts of them. By means of social network based on Internet, target resources can be found and selected into the next recycle process. And then discussion how to utilize such resources are carried out for redesign and reproduction with help of professional viewpoint. Someone, who is interesting in such resources, do redesign and reproduce new products for the sake of recycling and/or resource recovery. This paper describes a case study of recycling resource of furnitures into reproductive design as a sample of Resource and Knowledge Discovery Using Social Networks based on Internet.

Keywords: Recycling and Reproduction of Furnitures, Decision Making by means of Internet Community, Resource Discovery Using Social Networks.

1 Introduction

Recycle of resources becomes very much important in several domains from industrial fields to human lives. Diversification of values among the people had generated several problems to be adjusted and resolved in our history. Currently,

A. Abd Manaf et al. (Eds.): ICIEIS 2011, Part III, CCIS 253, pp. 49–61, 2011.

however, it is convenient for us to balance values in order to achieve recycling of resources. For example, someone may want to dispose of an object, at the same time, another may want to pick up the object. At the thought of more global area, values of people will be not similar and identical. In such cases, it is more probabilistic that something which is unnecessary for one is necessary for another at the same time. By the way, there must be suitable media and/or mechanism which can connect and transfer one's thought or decision making to another as fast as possible in order to recycle such resources.

Social networks based on Internet has been attractive and useful for us to perform information exchanging and sharing among the registered people who are living in the distance[1][4]. If one describes some resource is unnecessary in Social networks, others may rely those resources must be necessary in the same Social networks. And if one asks some questions which need knowledge to be resolved, others may reply the relevant answers which include suitable knowledge for resolution. Social networks are ones of the efficient and effective environments which can transfer information to the relevant position/people.

In order to perform resource recycling and recovering, it is very good to utilize Social networks and carry out information exchanging and sharing on the networks[2][3]. In our case, recycling resources of furnitures has been focused and illustrated in order to reproduce some useful products of furnitures with recycled resources. We will explain sample of utilization of Social networks, decision making on the networks (i.e. resource finding, knowledge obtaining to redesign, presenting by miniature, discussing, etc.), reproduction of real model, and evaluation.

This paper describes a case study of recycling resource of furnitures into reproductive design as a sample of Resource and Knowledge Discovery Using Social Networks based on Internet. The next section introduces our schematic procedure to utilize Social networks for reproduction of furnitures. The third section demonstrates practical reproduction processes of recycling furnitures. The fourth section explains some evaluation and application for reproduction of furnitures as recycling resources. And finally, the last section concludes our summaries and future problems.

2 Schematic Procedure for Utilization of Social Networks

This section introduces our schematic procedure to utilize Social networks for reproduction of furnitures. Before introduction of Social networks utilization, we show an example of real production process for furnitures in the first half of this section. And then we describe schematic procedure for reproduction of furniture using Social networks based on Internet secondarily.

2.1 Example of Real Production Process for Furnitures

A real production process of furniture includes the following steps;

1. Design of the target furniture: normally, some prototyping is necessary in the design process. Making miniature is a part of prototyping. It is convenient for overviewing such a target furniture.
2. Discussion of the target furniture: Designer(s) and sale manager(s) discuss the profile about the target furniture by means of miniature as a prototype. Some sale plan is to be prepared by means of prototyping, namely using miniature.
3. Production of the target furniture: After prototyping and discussing, producing process begins in accord with previous processes. Display and trial usage will be available with finished product(s).

Figure 1 shows prototyping a miniature of reference furniture on the work desk. In this case, prototyping includes coloring of miniature. Suitable coloring may be good for the sake of giving reality to miniature. Scaling of miniature will be from 1/10 to 1/8 possibly.

Figure 2 presents the according miniature of furniture with the same kind of miniature of seat sofas which have been made up of "foam polystyrene" because of easy forming. Such a prototype, however, may give someone a quality feeling so

Fig. 1. Prototyping and coloring of miniature for target furniture

Fig. 2. Display and evaluation with miniature of furniture

that some people say there is no special need to utilize Virtual reality rendering with expensive effect by computer.

Figure 3 displays a real model of furniture which is produced based on miniature after prototyping. A real model must be good and useful if previous prototyping is well-discussed and suitable enough to produce real furniture.

Fig. 3. Production of furniture based on miniature

As comparison with Figure 2 and Figure 3, not only designer(s) but also sale manager(s) can feel that real production is identical with prototyped miniature. As a consequence, potential buyers who may stand at the same position of sale manager can recognize and decide to pay their costs to buy the relevant furniture only through reference of prototype. As you know, not a few people sometimes buy products only with reference of catalogs or online browsing, instead of touching and checking real model.

2.2 Schematic Procedure for Reproduction Using Social Networks

Generally speaking, reproduction of furniture may be included with the following procedures, namely,

- Designer reforms his/her original model into a new one, which has both of a part of the same resources of the original model and other new parts.
- The designer must decide to keep what part of original resources and to design others newly.
- In order to decide to keep what part of original resources, it is necessary to retrieve past results. On the other hand, in order to decide to create new part, it may need to search future trends, namely, prediction of trend.
- The former must utilize retrieval of past track records just like as one of Database applications, while the latter had better employ market research, trend watching, questionary investigation for users and so on.

Of course, it is very difficult for only one or a few designers to manage the above procedures efficiently. Several staffs and/or support team must be necessary for such designer(s).

An idea of this time is "using Social networks" in order to support a series of procedures described above for reproduction of furniture. Namely, it is very much effective and efficient to utilize resources and knowledge of Social networks for the sake of retrieval of past track records in the target domain as well as prediction of trend. In this viewpoint, our research is one of applications to achieve "Resource and Knowledge Discovery Using Social Networks" based on Internet.

We describe schematic procedure for reproduction of furniture using Social networks based on Internet secondarily.

- In order to accomplish retrieval of past track records, we have utilized Social networks as well as Internet. Social network and Internet can play important roles to provide huge and excellent Database for retrieving.
- We have also utilized not only Social networks but also Internet to perform market research, trend watching, questionary investigation, and user's demands. Probabilistically speaking, small size of Social networks may have not large demands but steady ones even for furnitures.
- We have employed Social networks as suitable media to perform information sharing and exchanging. Namely, some members of Social networks may be able to provide and/or point out both of resources and know-how for reproduction of furnitures.
- As described before, values of people may be not similar and identical. If so, it must have possibilities that something which is unnecessary for someones is necessary for other ones from the global viewpoints.
- Especially, recycling will be more and more popular in many fields and may domain. Furnitures have relatively long lifetime such as 10 years or more, so resources of furnitures may be useful and available for multiple generation users. The problems are how to adjust changes and variation of their tasty, favorites and trends.

In the next section, we will introduce detail of recycling furniture using Social networks as a practical example.

3 Practical Example of Recycling Furniture

This section demonstrates practical reproduction processes of recycling furnitures. The section includes workflow of reproduction of furniture, explanation of detailed stages for real reproduction and modeling as resource recovery using Social networks.

3.1 Workflow of Practical Reproduction

First of all, workflow of reproduction of furnitures can be summarized as follows. Such workflow utilizes resources and know-how using Social networks based on Internet. All the operations and functions are especially geared towards Social networks and also intended for users of such network communities.

1. Furniture Designing stage:
   - Analyzing needs/demands
   - Choosing kinds of furnitures
   - Determining kinds of materials
2. Resource Finding stage:
   - Requesting information about furnitures to be constructed
   - Requesting information about materials of the furnitures
   - Searching resources for materials/furnitures
   - Obtaining information about resources
   - Obtaining information about resources
3. Knowledge Collecting stage:
   - Requesting information how to fabricate, manufacture and/or process such resources
   - Searching knowledge for fabrication, manufacturing and/or processing
   - Obtaining knowledge about the above techniques
   - Accumulating knowledge like Database
4. Furniture Constructing stage:
   - Selecting staffs and/or work places
   - Pouring resources and know-how(i.e. knowledge) into the above factory(i.e. workplace with staffs)
   - Reproducing(Constructing) the relevant furniture(s)

The above workflow can be separated into 4 major stages, which includes some more detailed steps.

3.2 Explanation of Real Reproduction

This part explains detailed stages for real reproduction of furniture as an example of Resource Recycling.

At first, some discussion has carried out during "Furniture Designing stage", where sometimes prototyped miniature can provide more constructive imagination shown in Figure 4. If such discussion is carried out in the environment of Social networks, it will be convenient and efficient so that participants at discussion can do in ways that can help save both costs and time.

Finding resources is one of the most time-consuming jobs so that "Resource Finding stage" must be considered to save time and perform efficiently. We had investigated whether there were any unused resources or not in building factories of furnitures. In such factories, there may be some resources which will be available for recycling, but almost always we cannot find such resources. So we want to utilize Social networks as one of attractive pools which store several kinds of resources. In this case, we have found some useful resource in kind furniture factory shown in Figure 5.

"Knowledge Collecting stage" needs several kinds of supports so that discussion may be required and retrieval of Database is also necessary. Through utilization of Social networks, we can obtain suitable know-how and idea in relatively short period. Even beginners, for example students, can reproduce a

Fig. 4. Discussion of reproduction of furniture with miniature

Fig. 5. Finding resources as elements for resigning of furniture

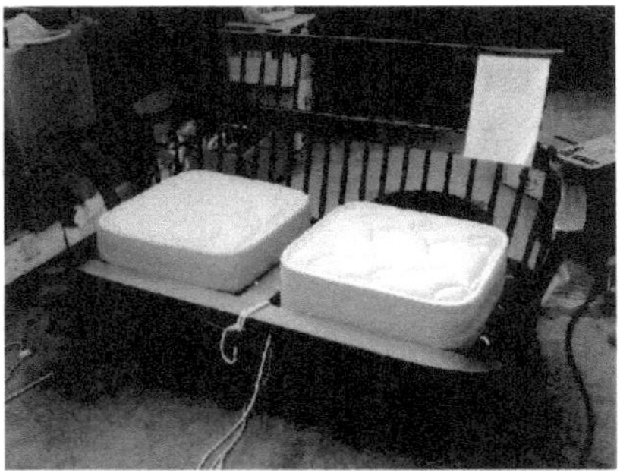

Fig. 6. Reproducing furniture with elements found as resources

new furniture by means of resources as recycled materials and with kindly suitable helps from Community supports. Figure 11 shows beginner's reproducing furniture in his/her car garage.

It is one of our specific problems to realize schematic procedure of recycling resource with community support just like the above example for utilization of Social networks into Resource and Knowledge Recovery. Especially, it is important how to apply the concept and practice of Resource and Knowledge Recovery using Social networks into Resource Recycling and Reproduction effectively and efficiently.

3.3 Modeling for Furniture Reproduction as Resource and Knowledge Recovery Using SNS

We have utilized Social networks based on Internet in order to obtain "Requests", "Resources", "Knowledge" and "Announcement" for reproduction of furnitures.

First of all, we have established Human relation for Demand analysis, Trend retrieval, Decision making, and so on. Social networks are powerful and reliable for us to achieve our aim relatively in a short period. They are very useful and suitable to perform information sharing and exchanging in convenient ways. Figure 7 shows such human relation realized in Social networks such as Facebook[6], Mixi[7] and so on. In such cases, however, it is not necessary to

Fig. 7. Establishment of Human Relation using Social Networks

restrict Social networks to so-called SNS(i.e. social network system like Facebook). Twitter[8] community and other similar ones may be sufficient enough to perform Human relation if it satisfies almost all conditions described in subsection 3.1.

In reproduction of furnitures, it is very much necessary to find useful resources efficiently. With utilization of Social networks, finding resources can be carried out more easily than others shown in Figure 8. If a user asks his colleagues in Social networks whether convenient resources exist close to your or not, some colleague replies his/her information about according resource. Of course, it is possible that others do not reply in a short period nor reply only they know nothing about such resources. Probably suitable resources will be found potentially in a short period through human relation established with Social networks.

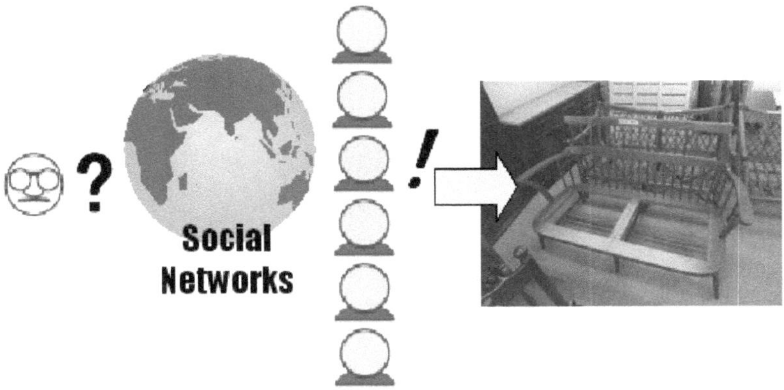

Fig. 8. Finding Resource of Furniture using Social Networks

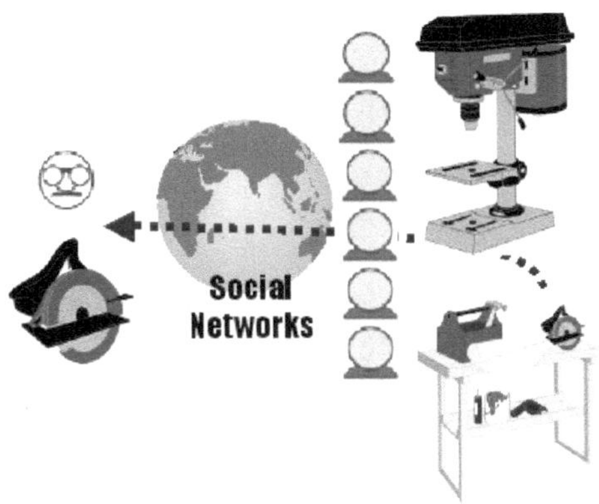

Fig. 9. Obtaining Tools for Reproduction of Furniture using Social Networks

In the same manners, if a user wants to obtain some tools and know-how to reproduce furnitures efficiently, he asks his colleagues, "Does anyone know where suitable tools are ?" or "Does anyone have adequate information how to reproduce such kind of furniture ?" Figure 9 shows that a user has obtained a necessary tool from Social networks and he can use the relevant tool to reproduce his furniture shown in Figure 11.

If a user is a beginner for furniture production, he may want to know how to (re)produce good furniture with his resources. So he needs several kinds of knowledge to use resources and to handle tools effectively and efficiently. With Social networks, a user may obtain suitable know-how to reproduce furnitures shown in Figure 10.

Even a beginner does reproduce furnitures with powerful supports from Social networks. With help of good tools and knowledge how to manipulate, the relevant beginner can reproduce some kinds of furnitures. Figure 11 shows that even a

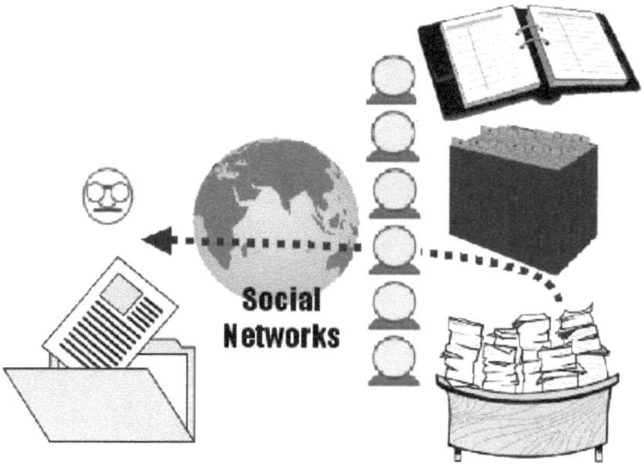

Fig. 10. Obtaining Knowledge for Reproduction of Furniture using Social Networks

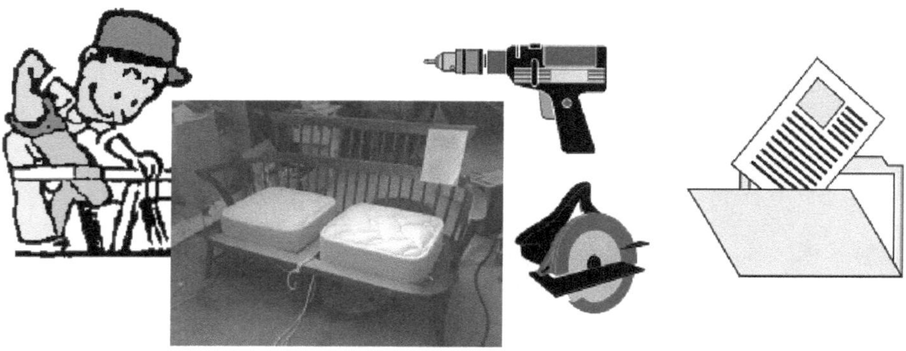

Fig. 11. Reproducing Furniture by means of Tools and Knowledge using Obtained from Social Networks

beginner can reproduce furniture by means of by means of tools and knowledge using obtained from Social networks. And he/she can accumulate not only all necessary techniques for tool manipulation but also knowledge about furniture reproduction.

On the other hand, Social networks can provide facility to offer information about reproduced furnitures towards not only colleagues but also others shown in Figure 12. With announcement about reproduction of furnitures, it is possible to stimulate potential demands from general users related to Social networks. If needs are not very few, the next demands about furniture reproduction may occur potentially. Such demands are steady and continuous so that it may be necessary to prepare some market research and securement of materials which are not only unused resources but also newly created ones.

Fig. 12. Announcing New Reproduced Furniture through Social Networks

4 Evaluation and Application for Reproduction of Furnitures Using Social Networks

The fourth section explains some evaluation and application for reproduction of furnitures as recycling resources.

4.1 Evaluation for Reproduction of Furniture as Recycling Resources

As evaluation of reproduction of furnitures described above, we explain the following three items, namely cost-performance, feasibility study@and human-relation based activity.

- cost-performance:
  Recycling of resources is positive and transferring of tools/resources/products is negative. The former is a good effect for ecology, cost-saving, and environmental protection. Resources for furnitures are almost woods so their recycling can reduce some impacts from deforestation. Recycling also brings cost-saving normally. The latter is a bad effect for emissions of carbon dioxide through traffic increasing and all-too-easy way of borrowing tools and know-how. Emission of carbon dioxide must increase by means of transferring resources and tools. If an imprudent person wants to participate in such Social networks, he/she frequently raises troubles based on borrowing tools and know-how in easy ways.
- feasibility study:
  Our viewpoint for reproduction of furnitures stands for the very best case to be performed. If some conditions are not satisfied, such reproduction cannot continue any more. for example, resources are necessary to be supplied in a low cost (although paying transferring fee) and Social networks kindly provide know-how about relevant requests from users. In order to keep and

satisfy the above conditions, we need to maintain and expand(= grown up) suitable human relation on Social networks. This may be one of most difficult problems!
- human-relation based activity:
Utilization of Social networks itself must be a good idea and it can be expected to make our life styles more fruitful. Although one person does not carry out works, many persons can perform such works probabilistically. Namely, activities based on human relation will be identical to times of single person's activity. It may be expected to have synergistic effect based on human relation through our practical experiences. Anyway, it is necessary to lay out a well-suited@goal to contribute to the maintenance of human relation on Social networks.

4.2 Trial Application of Reproducing Furnitures

As a utilization of reproduction of furnitures using social networks based on Internet, we will try to apply this mechanism into voluntary supply of recycled furnitures for people who had been attached by catastrophic@disasters. In some east districts of Japan, especially since the 11th of March, people living in such districts have been suffering from serious lack of several kinds of furnitures as well as living spaces.

Nowadays, "Disaster Recovery" is one of the most important and valuable words in Japan. Social networks also work together under the common concept to support people who had damages from such disasters. In order to help such people, we want to perform a trial application of reproducing furnitures. Not only because there are requests to need various kinds of furnitures as well as other living facilities, but also because people living there are still now suffering from lacks of several living facilities and supporting funds at the same time.

It is very much necessary to equip some good schema and mechanisms to consolidate several kinds of requests from such people and local governments, achieve arbitrations under many conditions and provide more suitable supports and supplies correctly according to the real requests. As one of such schema, we will discuss our procedure to recycle resources of furnitures with help from Social networks near future.

5 Conclusion

The paper has described the detail of recycling resource of furnitures for reproductive design with support from Social networks. This research can be summarized as a case study of resource and knowledge discovery using Social networks based on Internet.

First of all, we have illustrated an example of real production process for furnitures and schematic procedure for reproduction of furniture using Social networks based on Internet. And then we have explained workflow of reproduction of furniture, detailed stages for real reproduction and modeling as resource recovery using Social networks. Especially, it has been shown how to apply the concept and practice of Resource and Knowledge Recovery using Social networks into Resource Recycling and Reproduction effectively and efficiently. As a consequence, utilization of resources and know-how, such as recycling materials of furnitures with support from professionals, results in such significant values to the relevant community.

As evaluation and application of this research, we have introduced effect of reproduction of furniture with recycled resources and application of recycling furnitures to support daily lives of people who had received huge damages by disasters.

With the above discussion, it can be summarized in this paper as follows:

- Reproduction with furniture's elements has the effect of recycling, ecology and cost saving.
- Reproduction of furnitures, itself, can play a certain role of utilization of Resource and Knowledge from communities.
- Reproduction and recycling with support from Social networks seems to be some case study of Resource and Knowledge Recovery using Social networks.

Acknowledgments. The authors would like to express sincere thanks to Professor Hiroaki JINUSHI of Tokyo Zokei University for his supervised instruction about Recycled Resource Reproduction. They are also thankful to Mr. Motoharu YANA of Murauchi Furniture Access (`http://www.murauchi.net/`) for his kind and constructive support of Prof. JINUSHI's lecture in Graduate School of Design in Tokyo Zokei University.

References

1. Chakrabarti, S., Van Den Berg, M., Dom, B.: Focused crawling: A new approach to topic-specific Web resource discovery. Computer Networks 31(11), 1623–1640 (1999)
2. Colella, T.J.F., King, K.M.: Peer support. An under-recognized resource in cardiac recovery. European Journal of Cardiovascular Nursing 3(3), 211–217 (2004)
3. Davis, M.I., Jason, L.A.: Sex Differences in Social Support and Self-Efficacy Within a Recovery Community. American Journal of Community Psychology 36(3-4), 259–274 (2005)
4. White, C., Plotnick, L., Kushma, J., Hiltz, S.R., Turoff, M.: An online social network for emergency management. International Journal of Emergency Management 6(3-4), 369–382 (2009)
5. `http://en.wikipedia.org/wiki/Social_networking_service` (access on August 02, 2011)
6. `http://www.facebook.com/` (access on August 02, 2011)
7. `http://mixi.jp/` (access on August 02, 2011)
8. `http://twitter.com/` (access on August 02, 2011)

Towards an Understanding of Software Development Process Knowledge in Very Small Companies

Shuib Basri[1,2] and Rory V. O'Connor[1,3]

[1] Lero, the Irish Software Engineering Research Centre, Ireland
[2] Universiti Teknologi PETRONAS, Bandar Sri Iskandar, 31750 Tronoh, Perak, Malaysia
shuib_basri@petronas.com.my
[3] School of Computing, Dublin City University, Ireland
roconnor@computing.dcu.ie

Abstract. The influence of software team dynamics on well-organized software development knowledge process could prevent software development organizations from suffering from the knowledge atrophy problem. To explore this, we have studied several team dynamics factors that influence the Knowledge Management Processes (KMP) in Very Small Entities (VSEs) [1]. A survey was conducted in a variety of VSEs and through statistical and qualitative content analysis for the research data, results indicate that small teams, informal team process and structure have an important influence on the level of team dynamics in the software development process.

Keywords: SPI, VSEs, Team Dynamics, Grounded Theory (GT).

1 Introduction

Software development is a complex activity and depends strongly on human commitment for its implementation [3]. Furthermore since software development projects involve knowledge intensive exchanges and collaborations, the influence of team dynamics on the organization of software development knowledge could assist software companies to become more innovative and efficient. Hence KMP is more effective in an organization if the development teams have a good team culture with ability to share knowledge, collaborative relationship and personal responsible in creating and sharing knowledge [4]. In addition KMP is also reshaped by the attitudes and behaviour of team in order to ensure that both personal and organizational knowledge are always available [5]. The issues of limited resources; especially in cost and people almost always become an issue and can have an impact on the KMP in VSEs [6]. Therefore it is our belief that better understanding the influence of team dynamics in software projects could assist small companies to mitigate VSEs KMP against the knowledge atrophy problem.

2 Background

2.1 Very Small Entities (VSEs)

The definition of "*Small*" and "*Very Small*" companies is challengingly ambiguous, as there is no commonly accepted definition of the terms. In Europe, for instance, 85%

A. Abd Manaf et al. (Eds.): ICIEIS 2011, Part III, CCIS 253, pp. 62–71, 2011.

of the Information Technology (IT) sector's companies have 1-10 employees. In the context of indigenous Irish software firms 1.9% (10 companies), out of a total of 630 employed more than 100 people whilst 61% of the total employed 10 or fewer, with the average size of indigenous Irish software firms being about 16 employees [8]. The term "*Very Small Entity*" (VSE) had been defined by the ISO/IEC JTC1/SC7 Working Group 24 "*an entity (enterprise, organization, department or project) having up to 25 people*" [11]. Furthermore the issues of limited resources in VSEs always become a constraint in producing a competitive product in today's dynamic software business. [6] states that micro enterprise including VSEs whose have limited resources, particularly in financial and human resources, are practicing unique processes in managing their business. These unique characteristics have influenced VSEs in their business style and companies' process infrastructures compare to large companies' [11]. In addition due to the small number of peoples involved company's activities, most of the management processes are performed through an informal way and less documented.

2.2 Teams and Knowledge Management

According to [12] software development is a combination of two basic processes; social process and technological process. [13] argues that software production is more effected by social process rather than technological process. People are not only claimed as the greatest asset in a software organization [14] but also critical to software development success [12]. Software is always developed in a group rather on the individual basis [12] and the basis of every software project is a team [15]. [16] argue that the dynamic performance software project which involved many processes is always depends on team especially in quality of communication within team and between teams. They added that the communication can be applied in many ways not only in verbal but also in term of documentation form such as version control, guidelines, reports and many more. Moreover the communication also has a related impact with the team proximity [11]. They add that the increase distance from one team to another could effected the team dynamics in which it will interrupt team communication, coordination, mutual support, effort and cohesion [18]. Therefore in order to be success in KMP, organization must have a solid support from the software development and management team. The development and management team must be able to work together, share the knowledge and able to communication one another effectively. This is because the essence of software development is good relationship, effective communication and high esteem of teamwork among software development and management team.

2.3 Teams Dynamics

Team dynamics effect how team reacts, behaves or performs and the effects of team dynamics are often very complex [20]. There are various forces could influence team dynamics including nature of the task, the organizational context and team composition. [19] in her dissertation on dynamics of successful software team identified four characteristics of team dynamics; positive, negative, internal and external team dynamics. Positive team dynamics is the positive forces that can lead a team be a high performing successful team. [22] states the present of social relationship in a team could increase team productivity and could enhance social and interpersonal skill [23]. [25] argues that social interaction skill dimension can divide a team member to extrovert or introvert. Extroverts' team member is a people oriented, sociable person, who enjoys interaction with others. Meanwhile introvert person is a type of person who like to work alone and with less social interaction. Meanwhile, [26] believes that the positive mode of leadership (such as well focus directive, well plan and others) in software organization could enhance the positive team dynamics. Negative team dynamics is a negative force that could lead the decrease of team performance and preventing people from contributes with their full potential [19].

According to [14], from management point of view, in software development organization people are required three types of needs that have to be fulfilled and satisfied; social, self-esteem and self-realization needs. Social needs are related to social interaction and communication. The lack or ignorance of these needs will give a negative impact on the organization because people may feel unsecured, have low job satisfaction and decrease their motivation [27]. These will stop them from giving full commitment and cooperate in their work as a team member. Internal team dynamics are referring to the forces that exist within the team itself [19]. Team member also will not cooperate if they do not feel that that are a part of the team [28]. While internal social interaction between people could build team cohesion that will enhance team performance. [29]. External team dynamics are referring to the present of external forces that beyond the team control and could impact the team performance [19]. According to [30] the intrinsic and extrinsic factors in projects may motivate team. Intrinsic factors are the internal factors that consist in the task and team activity itself. Extrinsic factors are external factors that influence team from the outside such as reward and recognition, feedback from the organization and customer, team member pressure and the working environments. Moreover a better working environment also could enhance job satisfaction among team member [31].

3 Research Study

For this study we have developed and distributed a survey questionnaire to software VSEs (involved in software product development) in Dublin, Ireland. The survey questionnaires (which follow a GQM approach [24]) were consisted of quantitative and qualitative questions. In order to get a quick replied, we regularly contacted the respondents via email and phone. Each received and completed questionnaire were complied and analysis. The close-ended questionnaire were grouped according the issue and analyze using a statistical analysis. Meanwhile, on the open ended data, we analyze and categories the data according to the category that this study intends to understand. In summary we adopted the qualitative contents analysis approach in analyzing the open-ended answer [30]. At the end, we have merged the both analysis result in order to gain more understanding and validate the results. We have received a total of 70 filled questionnaires and have conducted 15 interviews for this study, In order to produce details analysis results, we have divided the survey respondents into 2 main group namely the Micro VSE (M) (1-9 employees) and Larger VSE (L) (10-25 employees) [1].

4 Study Findings and Discussion

4.1 A Team Dynamics and Structure

In this section, we explore the respondents' opinions on the companies' software development team status and study people working relationship and team environment in the companies.

Table 1. Team Dynamics

Grp		Clear Roles	Appropriate Size	Diverse Skill Range
M	Mean	3.60	3.20	3.60
L	Mean	3.60	3.40	4.00
Avg	Mean	3.60	3.30	3.80

Table 2. Team Structure

Grp		Good Working Relationship	Regular Share Opinion	Good Social Relationship	Good Interpersonal Skill	Closely Located
M	Mean	4.80	4.40	4.80	4.40	4.40
L	Mean	4.40	4.40	4.00	4.20	5.00
Avg	Mean	4.60	4.40	4.40	4.30	4.70

Table 1 indicates that the respondents' strongly agree that the development teams in their companies have a high level of team dynamics. The results shows that the team have a great working and social relationships, willing to share opinion and idea, having a good interpersonal skill and working closely each other. Results in table 2 have details regarding team environment in VSEs. The results show that even though VSEs having a small team and a flat structure but staff are clear about their roles, they have enough manpower and skill to do all the development tasks. Meanwhile from the qualitative analysis, indicated that all respondents claimed that their development teams are efficient and effective. They claimed that their development team are having all important criteria such as high skills, motivated, dynamic, socialize and good teamwork, open communication, able to meet project deadline and budget, active in sharing and involved in strategic planning. These points are illustrated in the extracts from interviews which are shown below:

"They get on well as a social group and communicate regularly and openly. Also the projects we manage are normally 1 to 2 man projects and hence easily manage in an ad-hoc manner by two people that get on and communicate well."

"We practice clear communication and we are active in informal knowledge sharing. Beside that our environment is a family culture and, following specific strategic planning... We also actively use communication tools."

Beside that the result on employee turnover rate question has strengthen the above finding regarding team environment in the VSEs. The result in this question shows that the companies do not have any serious problem with the staff turnover. They claimed that the company environment, management and working styles and team relationships that satisfied the employees have motivated people to stay longer in company. Below are the interview quotations which best explain the details of this situation.

"We handle many varying projects of different sizes and complexities and have a very loose/informal and friendly atmosphere. This means the work is challenging and rarely gets boring while it also being enjoyable here."
"We have 14 employees. Last one who resigned in was 3 years ago. The reason people stay is we operate in relaxed and informal environment."

In overall team environment issue give an indicator that all the above parts or processes are much related and depended to the organization team environment, process and culture in the organization

4.2 Communication

The results from the analysis as shown in table 3 indicate that the companies are practicing regular informal meetings (e.g stand-up meeting, online meeting) and practicing informal formal communication in their business operations. However the results also show that organization have clear communication process and channel. Moreover the results also indicated that that employee size has influence the formal communication process level in their VSEs daily business operations. This has been shown in comparison results between the L-VSEs and M –VSEs for this issue.

Table 3. Communication Process

Grp	Staff Knowledge	Project Exp. and Lesson Learned	Experience Doc	Works Progress and Procedure
M	2.20	2.20	2.20	2.20
L	2.80	3.20	2.80	2.60
Avg	2.50	2.70	2.50	2.40

In relation to the communication process in VSEs, the analysis on the open-ended question indicated that 90% of respondents are agreed that in development projects they regularly receive feedback from the project stakeholders. However the result showed that this process been done either in face to face, informal discussion, online communication, informal internal feedback or 'on the job training' process. The interview extracts below illustrate how the process has happened:

"Online communication, informal feedback, internal discussion, informal communication"
"We sit in one office so I talk to them all the time"

4.3 Learning and Sharing

In table 4, it is clear that all respondents' are agreed that their development team sharing and learning activities are active in the organization. This was shown from the research result which obtained more than 3.00 point in mean. This represents an indicator that in VSEs companies, they always utilize the knowledge and experience within the organization in performing their tasks. This analysis also found out that there are no big differences in term of company size in utilizing existing knowledge and experience in company.

Table 4. Learning and Sharing Process

Grp	Exploit Exist Org Knowledge	Learn Past Experience	Collect Past Experience
M	4.00	4.20	4.00
L	4.40	3.80	3.40
Avg	4.20	4.00	3.70

In the following extracts are illustrative of this point.

"We haven't done any formal training but we do give our employee an opportunity to attend various courses and seminars."

"It wasn't a formal training... what I mean once you get started you could find out, who to do certain things, someone have experience can show you the way of the main resources or he can read article with your interest you want to carried out certain task. It wasn't a formal training period, I just call training because I actually learn and still learning but now is not as before"

4.2 Documentation

Table 5 indicates that the documentation process has been done in informal process. In details it showed that people's knowledge, experience and activities are not documented properly or have been done personally. This was showed on the total mean score which presents that all respondents do not practice a formal documentation process in their documentation activities. Table 5 also indicates that number of employees working in the companies give an influence to the documentation formality process in VSEs.

Table 5. Documentation Process

Grp	Clear Com.	Reg. Feedback	Comm. Channel	Reg. Informal Comm.
M	4.80	4.40	4.80	5.00
L	4.40	4.40	4.40	4.60
Avg	4.60	4.40	4.60	4.80

In relation, the qualitative answers have highlighted that only business procedure and technical issues are being documented properly and organized. This could be identified in question on documentation process where 50% of the respondents claimed they felt that they are regularly update their document regularly especially on a specific works and procedures. Moreover the analysis results also showed that small team size issue is an obstacle to VSEs from performs seriously documenting their activities as shown by below interview extracts.

1)"We documented it electronically, and having an equal decision on it" 2)

"We are too small to do proper documentation process"

The result in this part of analysis demonstrates a pattern and indication that in VSEs documentations process are done in two ways; (1) the specific documentation process which is related to business and technical process and (2) informal documentation process which are inclined toward informal, personal and online documentation.

4.5 KM Process and Commitment

The questions on this part emphasize particularly on KM process and commitment in the software development projects as shown in table 6 and 7. The results from the analysis as shown indicate that the respondents were agreed that the level of KM process and commitment in VSEs are very significant. This could be identified with the average mean score for each question is relatively high. Table 6 indicates that in principle respondents are agreed they are having a clear KM strategy and a good leadership in their organization is important in organization software development knowledge as reflected in the mean score results for these two questions. However the results in table 6 indicate that activities related to KM within VSEs have not been performed properly. It is indicated in average total mean row that gained less than satisfied agreement level. Meanwhile, in table 7 showed that the management is very supportive in the KMP and peoples in the organization are always communicate, share and having good relationship among them. This issue could be identified in open-ended answer related to which indicates KMP were done informally through sharing activities and informal documentation such as personal or impromptu process as the interview extracts below show:

1)"We are doing more on self learning and sharing among us" 2)"Regular sharing process, internal sharing and team work"

Table 6. KM process and commitment

Grp	Mgmt C'ment	Working Relationship	Share /Thought Opinion	Share Experience
M	4.40	4.80	4.40	4.20
L	3.40	4.40	4.40	4.00
Avg	3.90	4.60	4.40	4.10

Table 7. KM commitment

Grp	KM Strategy	Good Leadership	Post mortem	Formal Training
M	3.40	4.60	2.40	1.40
L	4.00	4.40	2.00	2.40
Avg	3.70	4.50	2.20	1.90

In addition to the above analysis, the analysis of the knowledge loss issue have indicate that the informal process environment in VSEs helps the companies to mitigate knowledge loss problems from happened. The analysis in this part showed 90% of the respondents claimed that they do not face knowledge loss problem in their company due to the informal process. The interview extracts below illustrate this situation.

1)"Ensuring that no single member of staff has any exclusive knowledge by using a mentoring/buddy system." 2) "Not a problem since we using same technology and process in all our project.... We occasionally sharing and transferring knowledge among brothers"

5 Conclusions

The analysis has indicated that VSEs have a clear KMP in their organization. The results also show the knowledge atrophy problem is not a serious problem in VSEs. From the analysis we found that due to small team size which creates a flat work structure, direct and active communication, close relationship and open environment have created positive team dynamics environments in respondents' organization. These situations also have encouraged software development teams to share and create knowledge in organization. In addition the analysis in the first stage (qualitative) have indicated that management style in VSEs which is more informal and macro, and working style which more autonomous have helps to create team dynamics environments. This situation help VSEs enhance their KMP and mitigate several factors which lead to knowledge atrophy problems. This is shown from the analyses which have indicated that in VSEs knowledge sharing level is high; staff turnover rate is low, high levels of knowledge exploration, continuous guidance from the senior staff and active communication in exchanging idea or knowledge among staff. Meanwhile in second stage data analysis process indicates that 90% from our research respondents believed that informal process environment in their organization has helped the development team to become more dynamic and this situation has assisted them in KMP beside mitigated knowledge atrophy problem from happened. In addition, the second stage data analysis result also shows that 80% of respondents claimed that their software development activities are not affected by the knowledge atrophy problem. They claimed that by, having frequent guidance and mentoring activities, being active in knowledge sharing and proactive coaching could mitigate this problem from occurring.

Acknowledgments. This work were supported, between Science Foundation Ireland grant 03/CE2/I303_1 to Lero - the Irish Software Engineering Research Centre (www.lero.ie) and Universiti Teknologi PETRONAS, Malaysia (www.utp.edu.my).

References

1. Laporte, C.Y., Alxender, S., Renault, A.: Developing International Standards for Very Small Enterprises. Journal of Computer 41(3), 98 (2008)
2. Laporte, C.Y., Alexandre, S., O'Connor, R.: A Software Engineering Lifecycle Standard for Very Small Enterprises. In: O'Connor, R.V., et al. (eds.) Proceedings of EuroSPI. CCIS, vol. 16. Springer, Heidelberg (2008)
3. Bin Basri, S., O' Connor, R.: Organizational commitment towards software process improvement an irish software VSEs case study. In: 2010 International Symposium on Information Technology (ITSim), Kuala Lumpur, June15-17 (2010)
4. Plessis, M.: Knowledge management: what makes complex implementations successful? Journal of Knowledge Management 11(2), 91–101 (2007)
5. Basri, S., O' Connor, R.V.: Evaluation of Knowledge Management Process in Very Small Software Companies: A Survey. In: Proceeding of Knowledge Management" 5th International (KMICe 2010) Conference, Kuala Terengganu, Terengganu, May 25-27 (2010)

6. Sapovadia, V., Rajlal, K.: Micro Finance: The Pillars of a Tool to Socio-Economic Development. Development Gateway (2006) Available at SSRN, http://ssrn.com/abstract=955062
7. Coleman, G., O'Connor, R.V.: The influence of managerial experience and style on software development process. International Journal of Technology, Policy and Management 8(1) (2008)
8. ISO/IEC DTR 29110-1, Software Engineering - Lifecycle Profiles for Very Small Entities (VSE) – Part 1: VSE profiles Overview. Geneva: International Organization for Standardization (ISO) 2011
9. Basri, S., O' Connor, R.V.: Understanding the Perception of Very Small Software Companies towards the Adoption of Process Standards. In: Systems, Software and Services Process Improvement. CCIS, vol. 99, pp. 153–164 (2010)
10. Rosen, C.C.H.: The Influence of Intra Team relationships on the systems Development Process: A theoretical Framework of Intra-Group Dynamics. In: 17th Workshop of the Psychology off Programming Interest Group. Sussex University (2005)
11. Sawyer, S., Guinan, P.J.: Software development: processes and performance. IBM Systems Journal 37(4) (1998)
12. Sommerville, I.: Software Engineering, 9th edn. Pearson, NY (2011)
13. Cohen, S.G., Bailey, D.E.: What Makes Teams Work: Group effective Research from The Shop Floor to the Executive Suite. Journal of Management 23(3), 234–256 (1997)
14. Hall, T., Beecham, S., Verner, J., Wilson, D.: The Impact of Staff turnover on Software Project: The Importance of Understanding What makes Software Practitioners Tick. In: Proceedings of ACM SIGMIS CPR, pp. 30–39. ACM, New York (2008)
15. Basri, S.: Software Process Improvement in Very Small Entities, PhD Thesis, Dublin City University, Ireland (2010)
16. McCarty, B.: Dynamics of a successful Team. What are the enablers and barriers to High Performing Successful Teams? MSc Dissertation, Dublin City University (2005)
17. Scarnati, J.T.: On becoming a team player. Team Performance Management 7(1/2), 5–10 (2001)
18. Triplett, N.: The Dynamogenic Factors in Pace making and Competition. American Journal of Psychology 9(4), 507 (1998)
19. Katzenbach, J.R., Smith, D.K.: The Wisdom of Team. Creating the High Performance Organization. Harvard Business Scholl Press, Boston (1993)
20. Basili, V.R., Caldiera, G., Rombach, D.: The Goal Question Metric Approach. In: Encyclopedia of Software Engineering (1994)
21. Gorla, N., Lam, Y.W.: Who Should Work With Whom? Building Effective Software Project Teams. Communications of the ACM 47(6), 123 (2004)
22. Singh, S.K.: Role of leadership in knowledge management: A study. Journal of Knowledge Management 12(4), 3–15 (2008)
23. Sarma, A., Van der Hoek, A.: A Need Hierarchy for Teams (2004), http://www.ics.uci.edu/asarma/maslow.pdf
24. Furumo, K., Pearson, J.M.: An Empirical Investigation of how Trust, Cohesion and Performance Vary in Virtual and Face to Face Teams. In: Proceedings of the 39th Annual Hawaii International Conference System Sciences, vol. 1, pp. 26c (2006)
25. Levi, D.: Group Dynamics for Teams. Sage Publications (2001)

26. Kirkman, B.L., Rosen, B., Tesluk, P.E., Gibson, C.B.: The impact of team empowerment on virtual team performance: The moderating role of face-to-face Interaction. Academy of Management Journal 47(2), 175–192 (2004)
27. Javed, T., Maqsood, M., Durrani, Q.: A Survey to Examine the effect of Team Communication on Job satisfaction in Software Industry. ACM SIGSOFT Software Engineering Notes 29(2), 6

A New Model for Resource Discovery in Grid Environment

Mahdi MollaMotalebi, Abdul Samad Bin Haji Ismail,
and Aboamama Atahar Ahmed

Faculty of Computer Science and Information Systems, Universiti Teknologi Malaysia
81310, Universiti Teknologi Malaysia, Skudai, Malaysia
Motalebi@gmail.com, {Abdsamad,Aboamama}@utm.my

Abstract. Resource discovery is the most important challenge of Grid systems. Lately many researchers tried to improve indexing and searching methods. To this aim, there are several factors affecting improvement such as time and message complexities, scalability, dynamicity, reliability, support of different types of queries, and so on.

This paper proposes a new model for resource indexing and discovery, which reduces the time and message complexities significantly. It is based on indexing the nodes and resources in a tree schema. Peers on the leaves of the tree will be in a virtual super-peer schema. Nodes are categorized hierarchically relative to their resources, so that the domain of search narrows rapidly and queries can be replied quickly and without wasted messages.

Keywords: Grid, Resource discovery, Tree.

1 Introduction

Grid networks are increasing attention from all scientific and economic communities because of their capabilities to run burdensome jobs or applications that are impossible or very difficult to run by a single machine. There are several types of Grids with different structures, but all of them have some common features such as numerousness and heterogeneity of nodes, dynamicity of nodes and their resources.

To run a massive job, it is needed to co-operate some hardware and/or software resources. These resources often are owned by different nodes of a Grid. Thus, an important task in any Grid system is to find and gather required resources to run a user's job. It is critical and also difficult to do. Its criticality is due to sensitiveness of jobs to be completed as soon as possible. If a job waits for some resources for a while more than a threshold time, it is most likely to be crashed. The difficulty of finding the suitable resources is due to heterogeneity, dynamicity and excessiveness of nodes. Each node owns some resources with different characteristics. These nodes, resources and characteristics are unstable since at any time a node can join to the network, leave the network, or fail. Also node's resources may be used by some other nodes which affects on the accessibility, values, and other and other characteristics of resources.

With regard to above, in recent years, many researchers focused on Resource Discovery (RD) in Grid environments. There are some metrics to evaluate a RD

A. Abd Manaf et al. (Eds.): ICIEIS 2011, Part III, CCIS 253, pp. 72–81, 2011.

method: the number of messages transferring among the network during a RD process (message complexity), the amount of time or steps needed to complete a RD process (time complexity), reliability/stability and scalability of RD method, the number of nodes involved to find the resources, the average number of results, the rate of user satisfaction, and so on [1]. Considering the tradeoff between some of these metrics, it is likely impossible a RD method can cover and improve these metrics all together. Thus methods often focus on improving some particular features or metrics according to the network specifications. Different methods are suitable for various structures and scales. For example, although centralized methods act so quick and efficient in small-scale and low-dynamic Grids, they may fail in a large-scale Grid with a high degree of dynamicity.

Our contribution is to come up with a hierarchical tree model and protocol for resource discovery in Grid environment which decreases the message and time complexities significantly.

The remaining of this paper is organized as follows: section 2 contains the related work. In section 3, we represent our proposed model and its related algorithms for Grid RD. We analyze the proposed model in Section 4 and conclude the paper in Section 5.

2 Related Work

So far, a great deal of work on Grids has focused on RD since it is a key issue affecting the performance of a Grid system. RD methods can be considered in three main categories as follows:

The first category is centralized/hierarchical methods which are based on gathering resource information from all Grid nodes and maintain this information in one or more central index servers. Primitive methods were based on central databases due to the structure of client/server networks which all network information was maintained in central databases such as LDAP [1]. In this structure, any event such as joining/leaving a node and changing the node's resource information should be sent to the central servers. The main encumbrances of this structure are single point of failure and bottleneck. the former occurs since if central servers fail, disconnect or leave from the network, a lot of critical information of whole network (e.g. resource information) will be lost. The reason of the latter problem is that all messages of gathering, updating and querying resource information are exchanged through the central servers, so they suffer from heavy bandwidth and processing load. These problems raise more significantly if the size of network increases [1],[2],[3]. Thus, centralized methods are not reliable and efficient in large scale Grids. But they inherently are able to reply received queries quickly and accurately. Therefore, centralized methods are suitable for small-scale Grids with a medium amount of traffic.

The second category is distributed method (decentralized method) which uses the peer-to-peer (P2P) structure and concepts in Grid networks. P2P networks are used to share files/documents (e.g. music files) among anonymous users in a potentially wide area network (e.g. Internet). Each node shares its files with each other simply and rapidly, only by using a sharing application (e.g. KazzaA). In these networks, users send their query to the network and they expect to receive relevant responses within a reasonable time. P2P is similar to Grid from network structure's point of view, namely each node can communicate with each other without limitations. Also they are different in some aspects. (a) Finding the results in P2P is not as important as in Grid, since if a search does not reflect a suitable result in the Grid, then user job/application probably fails while in a P2P network, nodes can try again and the user is more patient to get arbitrary results. (b) In a P2P, resources are files/documents, while in a Grid, resources include heterogeneous hardware/software resources (e.g. CPU, memory, operating system, files). (c) Nodes and resources in a P2P are less dynamic than a Grid. Thus even though it is possible to use P2P methods in a Grid, but certain features of the Grid should also be considered. Most of RD methods in Grid environment are P2P-based. They may be Unstructured without organization on connections and they typically use flooding algorithms for RD (e.g. Gnutella[4], random-walks[5], and [6],[7],[8],[9],[10]). Most of these methods suffer from false-positive-errors, high message complexity, high time complexity, and low reliability. However load-balancing, lack of single point of failure, scalability, and dynamicity are their robustness [11]. Other case is Structured P2Ps which are organized by the specific criteria, algorithms, topologies and properties. They typically use distributed hash tables to index resource information (e.g. CAN[12], Chord[13], and [14],[15]). Although structured P2Ps find the resources quicker and with lower message exchange compared to the unstructured case, but they have some weaknesses such as requiring complicated maintenance considerations and poor support of dynamicity [16],[17],[18].

According to features of categories described above, the third category, Super-peer, prefers exploiting advantages and capabilities of both centralized and decentralized methods to do a more efficient RD. It strikes a balance between correctness and quickness of centralized search, and the autonomy, load balancing, scalability and reliability of decentralized search.

In a Super-peer network, each node can have the role of regular-peer or super-peer. Each super-peer is connected to a set of regular peers and forms a local cluster. Peers inside a cluster acts as a centralized system which the super-peer node is their central server. The super-peer nodes communicate with each other in a decentralized (e.g. P2P) manner. Regular peers send resource requests to their related local super-peer node, which does RD on behalf of the regular peers subsequently [19],[20],[17],[2], [21],[22].

Our method uses a tree structure that extends the Super-peer architecture so that it uses a hierarchical and multi-level structure of peers and index servers. There exist several index servers to store resource information. The resource information is aggregated from leaf nodes to their ancestors hierarchically. When searching, queries will not be flooded among the peers. Only a few passes, are necessary for traversing the tree to find the desired resource(s).

3 Description of Proposed Model

Considering the importance of finding the desired resources as quick as possible in Grid networks, we proposed a new model to gather, index and search the Grid resource information. It is based on a multi-level tree schema to index resource categories and also a super-peer schema for regular peers.

As illustrated in Fig. 1, regular peers are located on the leaves of tree, and they are a member of target clusters in the hierarchy (lowest level of tree). All other peers in the tree are Index Service Peers (ISP). Each ISP is the head of a cluster in the hierarchy and maintains resource categories of its descendants. It has some resources itself and may share them, but regular peers have higher priority to present resources due to indexing and routing responsibilities of ISPs. The location of each peer is the proper target cluster that is determined during the join process. Peers are chosen as an ISP in the virtual tree based on their robustness. Some metrics to be an ISP are having a high bandwidth, stability, and processing/storage capacities.

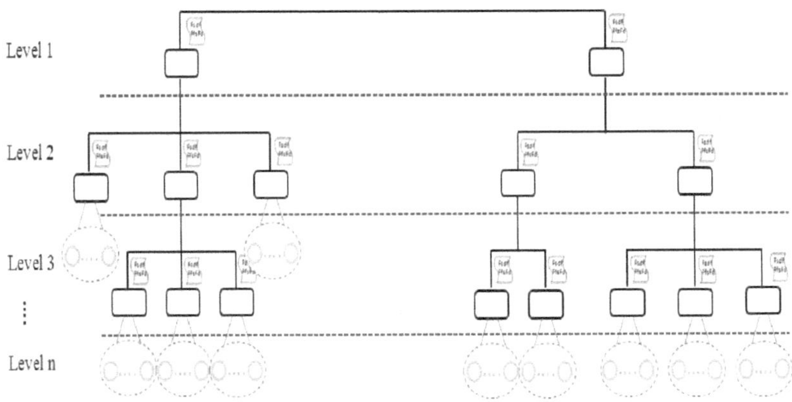

Fig. 1. Resource indexing tree schema. Rectangles are ISP peers. Leaves peers (circles) are regular peers in P2P structure.

As mentioned above, target clusters of tree include regular peers. These peers are in virtual Super-peer (VSP) schema in their cluster, see Fig. 2. Peers are not physically connected as a Super-peer network. They may be located at any place within the network, but they are supposed and indexed as connected together virtually.

The address of super-peer nodes inside each target cluster will be indexed in the related ISP (head of cluster). Some of regular peers within each cluster (e.g. ten percent) are chosen as super-peer nodes and other peers are member of them as a balanced division. Each super-peer node maintains the addresses of its peers. Each peer asks the address of its virtual neighbors from super-peer node whenever it is needed.

The description of main functions/algorithms in our model is represented below:

Peer Joining: In Grid systems, contrary to P2P systems which peers join anonymously, when a node decides to join the Grid, typically a join process (and probably some authentication/authorization steps) will be invoked. In our model, while joining, the applicant sends the request to one of the Grid's peers, and recipient

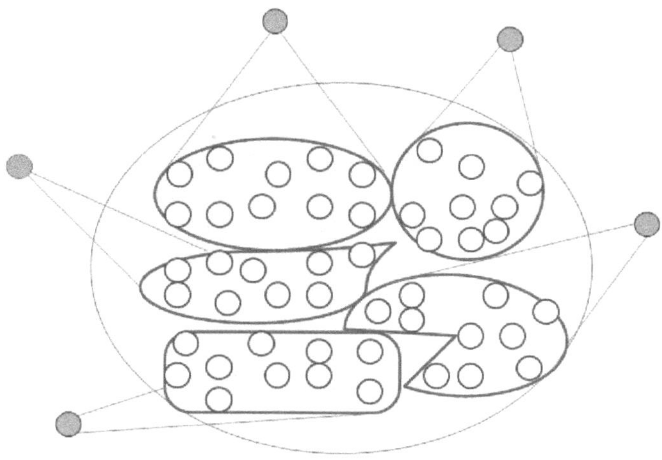

Fig. 2. Virtual Super-peers inside target clusters. Solid circles are super-peer nodes and hollow circles are regular peers.

forwards the request to its local ISP immediately, then it sends the ISP address to applicant peer. After that, new peer sends its resource information to ISP, in the form of a XML file or through a web interface. Each new node should send its resource information in a particular format which implies the hierarchical categorization of its resources. Certainly submitting through the web interface is more comfortable. Once the ISP receives the information, it invokes a resource discovery process for each resource independently. When the address of target ISP is returned by the resource discovery process, new node sends the resource information to target ISP. Intermediate ISPs which hierarchically are higher than target ISPs do not need to index the peer information. Only if the peer implies a new subcategory, intermediate ISPs will be updated.

To this stage, target cluster of new peer is found. Now new peers should be assigned to one of the existing VSPs in the cluster. A simple round robin method is used to assign peers to VSPs in the cluster to keep them balanced.

Peer Movement: Considering the dynamicity of Grid resources and nodes, whenever a peer moves in the network, nothing required to be done in the indexing since the indexing tree is independent of the physical location of peers in the real Grid. But if the address of an ISP (e.g. IP-Address) is changed, Grid DNS (GDNS) servers must be updated by replication between ISPs. As described formerly, in the old position, backup of ISP will be replaced and continues its role. Also any changes of super-peer nodes in VSPs will be updated in relevant ISPs.

Peer Leave/fail: If a regular peer fails or leaves the network nothing needed to be done in the indexes, because the detailed information of peers is not indexed in ISPs, but VSPs should update their address list of member peers.

To achieve more reliability, each cluster has an ISP backup. A powerful peer of the cluster, in terms of hardware and software capabilities, will be selected as a backup.

Every ISP and its backup check each other periodically for existence (e.g. by sending simple ping message). Once an ISP leaves/fails, its backup will be replaced and acts instead of old ISP additional to doing its own tasks, and then it chooses one peer of leaves to be new ISP backup. When the replication of information to new ISP backup completed, the new ISP does only its own tasks. Also addresses of new ISP and new ISP backup will be updated in GDNSs.

In target clusters, ISP maintains a backup of latest VSP's members address, so after leave/fail of each super-peer node, relevant ISP chooses another super-peer from regular peers and replicates the addresses.

Resource Modification: When resources of a peer altered, indexes of ISPs do not need to be modified; rather the cluster membership of the peer should be modified. Since our model categorized peers mostly based on the static value resources, in most of states it is not needed any modification on ISP indexes. However if it is needed, new target cluster will be defined by a resource discovery for new resource value, exactly like a normal resource request. It is carried out by sending the new information of resources from peer to local ISP. Local ISP tries to find an appropriate cluster in the network for new information, by doing the resource discovery process. Once the matched cluster is found, the peer joins to the new ISP. It is noteworthy that a peer may be located in several clusters relative to its different resources.

Most of modifications occur on dynamic values/attributes of resources but, forwarding the query to a target cluster will not change. In the target cluster, super-peers search the required resources inspecting the latest status of resources.

Resource Addressing: We considered a standard form of resource address, which is composed of two parts: a Grid Unified Resource Information (GURI) and a specific attribute/value. Considering that each resource is a member of a target subcategory in a category hierarchy, a GURI indicates the address of target subcategory (latest cluster's ISP). For example, a resource "*Intel* CPU 100MHz" is in the general category of "*hardware resources*", then a member of "*computing devices*", after that a member of "*CPUs*", and finally a member of "*Intel CPUs*". So, its GURI may be "*hw.computing.cpu.intel*". Using GURI makes the model independent of ISPs leave/move and IP address changing. We refer to the GURI as a stable addressing instead of relying to IP address or any other variable addresses. In the virtual tree of resource index, categories narrow down from top level to lower levels and make different GURIs. Every subcategory is independent from each other, so the tree is not a balanced tree necessarily.

Resource Discovery: Most of resources in our model are located in the leaves of virtual tree, also just a limited number are in ISPs. As for importance of ISPs performance, our algorithm tries to not using ISPs resources, thus using of regular nodes has a higher priority.

As shown in Fig. 3, User sends his/her resource request to its connecting peer by a XML document or a web interface. Then peer passes the query to local ISP. Local ISP firstly checks the received file contents in terms of an adapted request format. If the request format is in an accepted form, local ISP looks its cache for results which may be cached before, relative to similar queries. If a suitable resource owner exists, the query will be forwarded directly to the relevant owner, otherwise the query will be forwarded to the Query-Analyzer. If the query is a multi-attribute query, namely contains multiple resources requested, Query-Analyzer splits it to multiple independent sub-queries. Then it transforms the query(s) to standard form of GURI(s) and forwards it to GDNS.

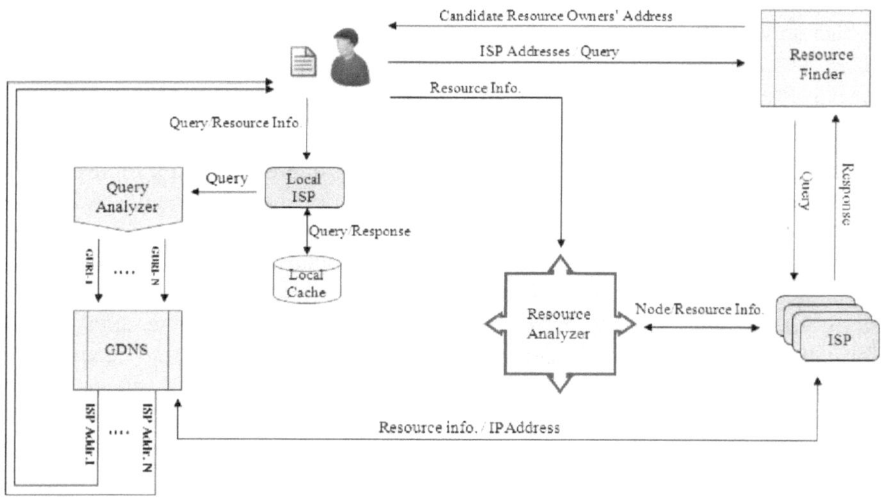

Fig. 3. Proposed resource discovery model

GDNS like an Internet DNS, maps each GURI address to corresponding address (e.g. IP Address) of appropriate target ISP and sends it back to requesting peer. This target ISP is the most matched target cluster's head which can lead the query to proper resource owner(s). It means that the resource owner certainly is located in descendants of target ISP. Then user sends his/her query to target ISP and it forwards the query to VSPs of its cluster subsequently. Apparently finding the suitable resource owner between this narrowed and limited domain of peers will be done much faster than a search in the whole Grid network.

When the candidate owners of desired resources are found, their address will be passed directly to the requesting peer. It records these addresses in its cache and then sends the resource request to owners directly. If still the resource exists (is not assigned to other requests), it will be reserved for peer for a limited while and an acknowledge message will be sent to peer. Finally Peer sends a confirm message to definite the assignment. If confirmation message is not received in a defined time, the resource will be released and available for other requests.

4 Performance Analysis

The proposed model categorizes resources based on their type and indexes them in a hierarchical tree. Each peer may include multiple resources, thus it can repeat in multiple positions of the tree. Peers in the hierarchy do not store the resource information of other peers, but they only maintain the categorization information so that they are able to forward a request to right path in the tree for a highest degree of matched resources. Also the model is independent of peers position or topology, namely resources are categorized and searched hierarchically. Because of heterogeneity and dynamicity nature of the Grid, the tree is not balanced necessarily. But, considering becoming more limited the scope in each step of request forwarding in the tree, the scope of investigating peers would be narrowed quickly. Assuming that each peer includes R_t type of resources to share, and the number of peers in the network is N, thus the total number of nodes in the virtual tree is $R_t \times N$. Also, considering hierarchical resource categorization, if we assume that in each level of the virtual tree, in average resources are divided to C_i subcategories and the number of levels is K, thus the total number of final subcategories in the virtual tree (total number of target clusters in the leaves of virtual tree) is $C_1 \times C_2 \times C_3 \times \ldots . \times C_k$. Therefore the number of nodes in each target cluster of virtual tree is:

$$\frac{N \times Rt}{C1 \times C2 \times C3 \times \ldots \times Ck}$$

For example, if we assume that resources in each level are divided to a same $C_i=3$ subcategories and total number of levels is k=4, thus each target cluster of virtual tree includes only 1/81 (1.2 percent) of all virtual tree nodes. Also inside the target clusters, nodes are divided more by super-peers. Assuming that inside a cluster, one percent nodes are super-peers, so the number of nodes managed by each super-peer in our example is 0.00012 out of total number of nodes in the virtual tree, means that if 100,000 peers exist in the Grid and each peer includes 5 types of resources in average, each super-peer searches resources among only 500,000 × 0.00012 = 60 nodes of virtual tree.

According to the above, this model improves the time and message complexity of resource discovery by its hierarchical virtual tree structure that narrows down the scope of the search quickly. This way, target super-peers do not need a huge storage to store resource information of a lot of nodes and also they would have fewer processing loads. Another advantage of this model is that each multi-attribute query can be divided to separated single-attribute queries and each of them can be handled independently and in parallel.

5 Conclusion

The most important function of Grid system is providing required resources for users and applications, but some particular features of Grid environments makes this function a challenging task. Grid participants are typically numerous and distributed widely, also their resources are heterogeneous and highly dynamic. An efficient resource providing in a Grid environment depends on resource information gathering, indexing, and discovery. Also, keeping the number of exchanged messages as minimal and finding desired resources in shortest time are critical.

We proposed a new model for resource information gathering, indexing and discovery based on a virtual hierarchical tree. Nodes in the leaves of tree are in a clustered P2P schema and use a particular case of logical super-peer structure. Other nodes of tree maintain the information of resource hierarchy and forward the received queries to a suitable path in the hierarchical tree. Considering the use of hierarchical search in this model, it reduces the number of messages and time significantly.

References

1. Cokuslu, D., Abdelkader, H., Erciyes, K.: Grid Resource Discovery Based on Centralized and Hierarchical Architectures. International Journal for Infonomics (IJI) 3(2), 283–292 (2010)
2. Ranjan, R., Harwood, A., Buyya, R.: Peer-to-peer-based resource discovery in global grids: a tutorial. IEEE Communications Surveys & Tutorials 10(2), 6–33 (2008)
3. Yin, Y., Cui, H., Chen, X.: The Grid resource discovery method based on hierarchical model. Information Technology Journal 6(7), 1090–1094 (2007)
4. The Gnutella protocol specification, `http://rfc-gnutella.sourceforge.net`
5. Lv, Q., et al.: Search and replication in unstructured peer-to-peer networks. In: SIGMETRICS, pp. 258–259 (2002)
6. Tsoumakos, D., Roussopoulos, N.: Adaptive probabilistic search for peer-to-peer networks. In: The Third International Conference on Peer-to-Peer Computing, pp. 102–109. IEEE Computer Society, Washington, DC, USA (2003)
7. Kalogeraki, V., Gunopulos, D., Zeinalipour-Yazti, D.: A local search mechanism for peer-to-peer networks. In: The Eleventh International Conference on Information and Knowledge Management, pp. 300–307. ACM, New York (2002)
8. Yang, B., Garcia-Molina, H.: Improving search in peer-to-peer networks. In: The 22nd International Conference on Distributed Computing Systems (ICDCS 2002), p. 5. IEEE Computer Society, Washington, DC, USA (2002)
9. Crespo, A., Garcia-Molina, H.: Routing indices for peer-to-peer systems. In: The 22nd International Conference on Distributed Computing Systems (ICDCS 2002), pp. 23–32. IEEE Computer Society (2002)
10. Menasce, D.A., Kanchanapalli, L.: Probabilistic scalable P2P resource location services. SIGMETRICS Perform. Eval. Rev. 30(2), 48–58 (2002)
11. Tsoumakos, D., Roussopoulos, N.: A Comparison of Peer-to-Peer Search Methods. In: WebDB 2003, pp. 61–66 (2003)
12. Ratnasamy, S., et al.: A scalable content-addressable network. SIGCOMM Comput. Commun. Rev. 31(4), 161–172 (2001)
13. Stoica, I., et al.: Chord: A scalable peer-to-peer lookup service for internet applications. SIGCOMM Comput. Commun. Rev. 31(4), 149–160 (2001)
14. Rowstron, A., Druschel, P.: Pastry: Scalable, Decentralized Object Location, and Routing for Large-Scale Peer-to-Peer Systems. In: The IFIP/ACM International Conference on Distributed Systems Platforms, Heidelberg, pp. 329–350 (2001)
15. Zhao, B. Y., John, K., Joseph, A. D.:Tapestry: An Infrastructure for Fault-tolerant Wide-area Location and Routing, EECS Department, University of California, Berkeley (2001)
16. Trunfio, P., et al.: Peer-to-Peer Models for Resource Discovery on Grids, Tech. Rep. TR-0028, Institute on System Architecture, CoreGRID - Network of Excellence (2006)
17. Hameurlain, A., Cokuslu, D., Erciyes, K.: Resource discovery in grid systems: a survey, Int. J. Metadata Semant. Ontologies 5(3), 251–263 (2010)
18. Trunfio, P., et al.: Peer-to-Peer resource discovery in Grids: Models and systems. Journal of Future Generation Computer Systems 23(7), 864–878 (2007)

19. Mastroianni, C., Talia, D., Verta, O.: A super-peer model for resource discovery services in large-scale Grids. Journal of Future Generation Computer Systems 21(8), 1235–1248 (2005)
20. Yang, B., Garcia-Molina, H.: Designing a super-peer network. In: 19th International Conference on Data Engineering (ICDE 2003), p. 49 (2003)
21. Marzolla, M., Mordacchini, M., Orlando, S.: Resource Discovery in a Dynamic Grid Environment. In: Sixteenth International Workshop on Database and Expert Systems Applications, pp. 356–360 (2005)
22. Zhao, C., Kan, L., Yushu, L.: A Multi-Level Super Peer Based P2P Architecture. In: International Conference on Information Networking (ICOIN 2008), Busan, pp. 1–5 (2008)

Staggered Grid Computation of Fluid Flow with an Improved Discretisation of Finite Differencing

Nursalasawati Rusli[1,2], Ahmad Beng Hong Kueh[2], and Erwan Hafizi Kasiman[2]

[1] Institute of Engineering Mathematics, Universiti Malaysia Perlis, 02000 Kuala Perlis, Perlis, Malaysia
[2] Steel Technology Centre, Faculty of Civil Engineering, Universiti Teknologi Malaysia, 81310 Skudai, Johor, Malaysia
nursalasawati@unimap.edu.my, {kbhahmad,erwanhafizi}@utm.my

Abstract. The present paper models the fundamental problems of fluid flow using a discretely improved finite difference method on a staggered computational grid. The developed finite difference formulation is applied to well-established benchmark problems, namely, the lid-driven cavity flow, the developing laminar flow in a straight rectangular duct and the backward-facing step flow. Excellent agreements have been found for all cases. Also, this approach has successfully handled the pressure of the flow that has been long considered as one of the main problems in using the finite difference method.

Keywords: finite difference method, Navier-Stokes equations, incompressible flow, staggered grid.

1 Introduction

Over the past few decades, numerical modelling of fluid flow has been a major topic of research in modern science and engineering [1]. Computational fluid dynamics (CFD) occupies one of the key physical disciplines that involve the description of fluid flow in terms of mathematical models which comprise convective and diffusive transports of matters. Basically, it constitutes the groundwork covering the fields of mechanical engineering, marine engineering, aeronautics and astronautics, civil engineering and bioengineering, to name a few. Inherent in the core of fluid flow study are the mathematical models that consist of a set of governing equations in the form of ordinary or partial differential equations. Although a great account of analytical solutions for CFD is available, in practical applications, it is customary to resolve the solutions in numerical form. One of the chief techniques frequently used in the investigation of CFD is the finite difference method (FDM).

In obtaining solutions for CFD problems, one of the main concerns of the FDM is the handling of the pressure of the flow. In general, physical specification of pressure is absent, as it is implicitly correlated to the problem description. Even though there are three equations for the three unknowns u, v, p, there is no explicit equation which can be used for pressure. In most finite difference solution schemes for incompressible steady flows, the pressure field is obtained from a Poisson equation which is derived

A. Abd Manaf et al. (Eds.): ICIEIS 2011, Part III, CCIS 253, pp. 82–94, 2011.

from the momentum equations and the continuity equation [2]. The difficulty inherited from this approach is the need to decide on additional boundary conditions on the pressure [3]. This problem has been discussed in details in [4].

To overcome this issue, [5] recently presented a point based compact finite difference method on a staggered grid, using a fully explicit second-order accurate time marching scheme, where the pressure Poisson equation is solved by a pseudo-time marching procedure. Elsewhere, a new scheme that is implemented with the SIMPLE-type algorithm for the pressure field calculation similar to that of finite volume methods was proposed by [6] to solve this problem. The discretised equations are developed as a purely finite difference formulation. The convective terms in the momentum equations are approximated using the first or second order finite difference formulae. [6] used unequally spaced grid points for handling u- and v-momentum equations at a wall boundary, whereas an equally spaced grid points are chosen in this study for the same nodes.

The present work concerns with the formulation of the scheme and the validation of the benchmark problems based on the improved model. First, the governing equations are presented in Section 2. Then, section 3 discusses the new scheme in details. Finally, section 4 presents the validation of this method and its analysis.

2 Governing Equations

In the current study, we shall be interested in the standard Navier-Stokes governing equations and continuity of incompressible fluid flow given as follows

continuity equation

$$\frac{\partial u^*}{\partial x^*}+\frac{\partial v^*}{\partial y^*}=0 \tag{1}$$

x-momentum equation

$$u^*\frac{\partial u^*}{\partial x^*}+v^*\frac{\partial u^*}{\partial y^*}=-\frac{1}{\rho}\frac{\partial p^*}{\partial x^*}+\nu\left(\frac{\partial^2 u^*}{\partial x^{*2}}+\frac{\partial^2 u^*}{\partial y^{*2}}\right) \tag{2}$$

y-momentum equation

$$u^*\frac{\partial v^*}{\partial x^*}+v^*\frac{\partial v^*}{\partial y^*}=-\frac{1}{\rho}\frac{\partial p^*}{\partial y^*}+\nu\left(\frac{\partial^2 v^*}{\partial x^{*2}}+\frac{\partial^2 v^*}{\partial y^{*2}}\right) \tag{3}$$

where u and v are the velocity components in the x and y directions respectively, p is the pressure, ρ is the constant density, and ν is the viscosity.

Using the dimensionless definitions as given by [7], the governing equations (1) to (3) become

$$\frac{\partial u}{\partial x}+\frac{\partial v}{\partial y}=0 \tag{4}$$

$$u\frac{\partial u}{\partial x}+v\frac{\partial u}{\partial y}=-\frac{\partial p}{\partial x}+\frac{1}{\mathrm{Re}}\left(\frac{\partial^2 u}{\partial x^2}+\frac{\partial^2 u}{\partial y^2}\right) \tag{5}$$

$$u\frac{\partial v}{\partial x}+v\frac{\partial v}{\partial y}=-\frac{\partial p}{\partial y}+\frac{1}{\mathrm{Re}}\left(\frac{\partial^2 v}{\partial x^2}+\frac{\partial^2 v}{\partial y^2}\right) \tag{6}$$

where $\mathrm{Re}=\dfrac{Uh}{\nu}$ is the Reynolds number.

3 Numerical Method

The governing equations presented in the previous section are solved using a new numerical algorithm proposed by [6]. The methodology is finite difference based, but essentially takes advantage of the best features of two well-established numerical formulations, the finite difference and the finite volume methods. Some weaknesses of the finite difference approach are removed by exploiting the strengths of the finite volume method.

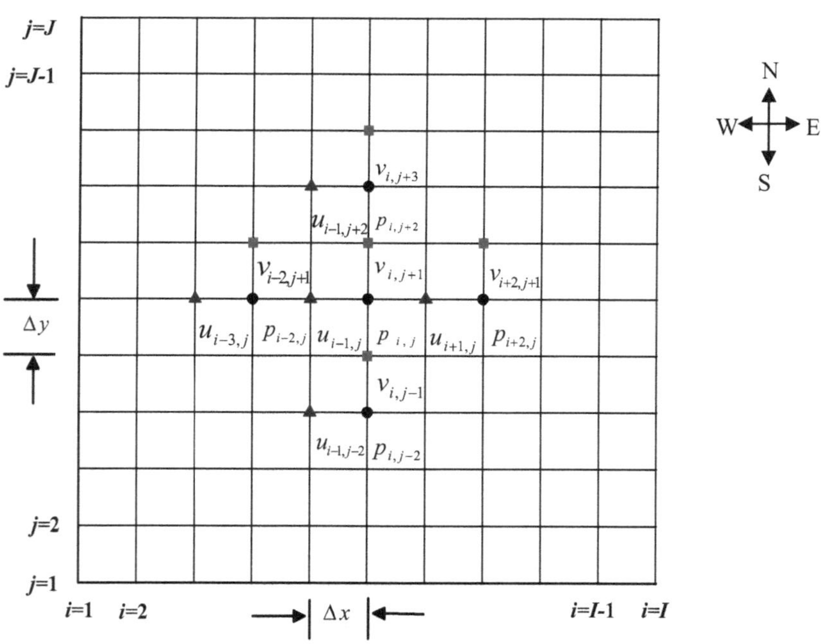

● p velocity component ▲ u velocity component ■ v velocity component

Fig. 1. Staggered grid arrangement

3.1 Finite Differencing on a Staggered Grid

We shall proceed next by considering a two-dimensional rectangular cavity flow domain which is subdivided using a regular Cartesian mesh as demonstrated in Figure 1. The mesh is evenly distributed in x and y directions. Here, a staggered grid is used to store the velocity components u and v and the pressure p.

We can see in Figure 1 that the values of u and v are stored at the i-$1,j$ and $i,j+1$ locations respectively and p is stored at i,j. A direct indication of such an arrangement is that the u-momentum (equation 5) is discretised at i-$1,j$, the v-momentum (equation 6) at $i,j+1$, and the continuity (equation 1) at i,j. Here, a first-order upwind differencing scheme has been employed to approximate the convective terms in the momentum equations, while a second-order central differencing is adopted for the diffusion terms. The pressure gradients are approximated by a second order central difference scheme.

3.2 Discretisation of the Momentum Equations

Unequally spaced grid points have been subscripted for the handling of u- and v-momentum equations at the wall boundary in [6]. As a result, the convective term is approximated using a second order accurate expression while the diffusion term takes the first order accurate expression, both of which lead to the formation of different formulae at different node location. For convenience, equally spaced grid points are chosen in this study. The advantage here is that the discretisation of the u- and v-momentum equations at interior nodes can be used at the wall boundary. To demonstrate the scheme, the discretisation of the momentum equations is summarized as below.

3.2.1 u-Momentum Equation

The discrete u-momentum equations at interior nodes are given by

$$a_P^{\text{int}} u_{i-1,j} + a_N^{\text{int}} u_{i-1,j+2} + a_S^{\text{int}} u_{i-1,j-2} + a_W^{\text{int}} u_{i-3,j} + a_E^{\text{int}} u_{i+1,j} = \frac{\hat{p}_{i-2,j} - \hat{p}_{i,j}}{2\rho\Delta x}$$

where

$$a_P^{\text{int}} = \frac{\hat{u}_{i-1,j}}{2\Delta x} + \nu\left(\frac{1}{2\Delta x^2} + \frac{1}{2\Delta y^2}\right)$$

$$a_N^{\text{int}} = \frac{\hat{v}_{i-1,j}}{4\Delta y} - \frac{\nu}{4\Delta y^2}$$

$$a_S^{\text{int}} = -\frac{\hat{v}_{i-1,j}}{4\Delta y} - \frac{\nu}{4\Delta y^2}$$

$$a_W^{\text{int}} = -\frac{\hat{u}_{i-1,j}}{2\Delta x} - \frac{\nu}{4\Delta x^2}$$

$$a_E^{\text{int}} = -\frac{\nu}{4\Delta x^2}$$

It shall be pointed out that the variables with the carets above them are the quantities to be calculated at the previous iteration. Because of the use of a staggered grid, the values of v in the u-momentum equation and u in the v-momentum equation, appearing as the coefficients of the convective derivatives, are not available at the desired points.

Consequently, these velocities are computed to a second order accuracy using the velocities of four surrounding grid points described as the followings,

$$u\big|_{i,j+1} = \frac{u_{i+1,j} + u_{i+1,j+2} + u_{i-1,j} + u_{i-1,j+2}}{4}$$

$$v\big|_{i-1,j} = \frac{v_{i,j-1} + v_{i,j+1} + v_{i-2,j-1} + v_{i-2,j+1}}{4}$$

Additional modifications have been made for the discrete u-momentum equations of interior nodes which are otherwise identical to those of boundary nodes. For example, the discrete u-momentum equations at the inlet nodes is the same as interior node except that the value of $u_{1,j}$ is known.

The u-momentum equation along the bottom of the wall $(j=2)$ takes the form

$$a_P^S u_{i-1,2} + a_N^S u_{i-1,4} + a_W^S u_{i-3,2} + a_E^S u_{i+1,2} = \frac{\hat{p}_{i-2,2} - \hat{p}_{i,2}}{2\rho\Delta x} + \left(\frac{2v}{3\Delta y^2} + \frac{2v_{i-1,2}}{3\Delta y}\right) u_{i-1,1}$$

where

$$a_P^S = \frac{\hat{u}_{i-1,2}}{2\Delta x} + \frac{\hat{v}_{i-1,2}}{2\Delta y} + v\left(\frac{1}{2\Delta x^2} + \frac{1}{2\Delta y^2}\right)$$

$$a_N^S = \frac{\hat{v}_{i-1,2}}{6\Delta y} - \frac{v}{3\Delta y^2}$$

$$a_W^S = -\frac{\hat{u}_{i-1,2}}{2\Delta x} - \frac{v}{4\Delta x^2}$$

$$a_E^S = -\frac{v}{4\Delta x^2}.$$

In a refined form, the current method presents the u-momentum equation along the bottom of the wall as

$$a_P^{\text{int}} u_{i-1,2} + a_N^{\text{int}} u_{i-1,4} + a_W^{\text{int}} u_{i-3,2} + a_E^{\text{int}} u_{i+1,2} = \frac{\hat{p}_{i-2,2} - \hat{p}_{i,2}}{2\rho\Delta x} - a_S^{\text{int}} u_{i-1,1}$$

Here, all other coefficients are the same as defined at the interior nodes.

3.2.2 v-Momentum Equation

Similar to the discrete u-momentum equations, the discrete v-momentum equations at the interior nodes take the following form

$$b_P^{\text{int}} v_{i,j+1} + b_N^{\text{int}} v_{i,j+3} + b_S^{\text{int}} v_{i,j-1} + b_W^{\text{int}} v_{i-2,j+1} + b_E^{\text{int}} v_{i+2,j+1} = \frac{\hat{p}_{i,j} - \hat{p}_{i,j+2}}{2\rho\Delta y}$$

where

$$b_P^{\text{int}} = \frac{\hat{u}_{i,j+1}}{2\Delta x} + \nu\left(\frac{1}{2\Delta x^2} + \frac{1}{2\Delta y^2}\right)$$

$$b_N^{\text{int}} = \frac{\hat{v}_{i,j+1}}{4\Delta y} - \frac{\nu}{4\Delta y^2}$$

$$b_S^{\text{int}} = -\frac{\hat{v}_{i,j+1}}{4\Delta y} - \frac{\nu}{4\Delta y^2}$$

$$b_W^{\text{int}} = -\frac{\hat{u}_{i,j+1}}{2\Delta x} - \frac{\nu}{4\Delta x^2}$$

$$b_E^{\text{int}} = -\frac{\nu}{4\Delta x^2}.$$

3.3 Discretisation of the Continuity Equation

For present model, the pressure correction equations that are identical to those given in [6] are employed for all boundary nodes. The pressure correction equations for the interior nodes are

$$c_P^{\text{int}} p'_{i,j} + c_E^{\text{int}} p'_{i+2,j} + c_W^{\text{int}} p'_{i-2,j} + c_N^{\text{int}} p'_{i,j+2} + c_S^{\text{int}} p'_{i,j-2} = \frac{u^{*'}_{i-1,j} - u^{*}_{i+1,j}}{2\Delta x} - \frac{v^{*'}_{i,j+1} - v^{*}_{i,j-1}}{2\Delta y}$$

where

$$c_P^{\text{int}} = \frac{1}{4\rho\Delta x^2 a_{i+1,j}} + \frac{1}{4\rho\Delta x^2 a_{i-1,j}} + \frac{1}{4\rho\Delta y^2 b_{i,j+1}} + \frac{1}{4\rho\Delta y^2 b_{i,j-1}}$$

$$c_E^{\text{int}} = -\frac{1}{4\rho\Delta x^2 a_{i+1,j}}$$

$$c_W^{\text{int}} = -\frac{1}{4\rho\Delta x^2 a_{i-1,j}}$$

$$c_N^{\text{int}} = -\frac{1}{4\rho\Delta y^2 b_{i,j+1}}$$

$$c_S^{\text{int}} = -\frac{1}{4\rho\Delta y^2 b_{i,j-1}}$$

3.4 Solution Algorithm

For convenience, we customarily use the SIMPLE scheme for the pressure-velocity coupling in the overall solution. The numerical algorithm for one complete cycle is given in the flow chart below.

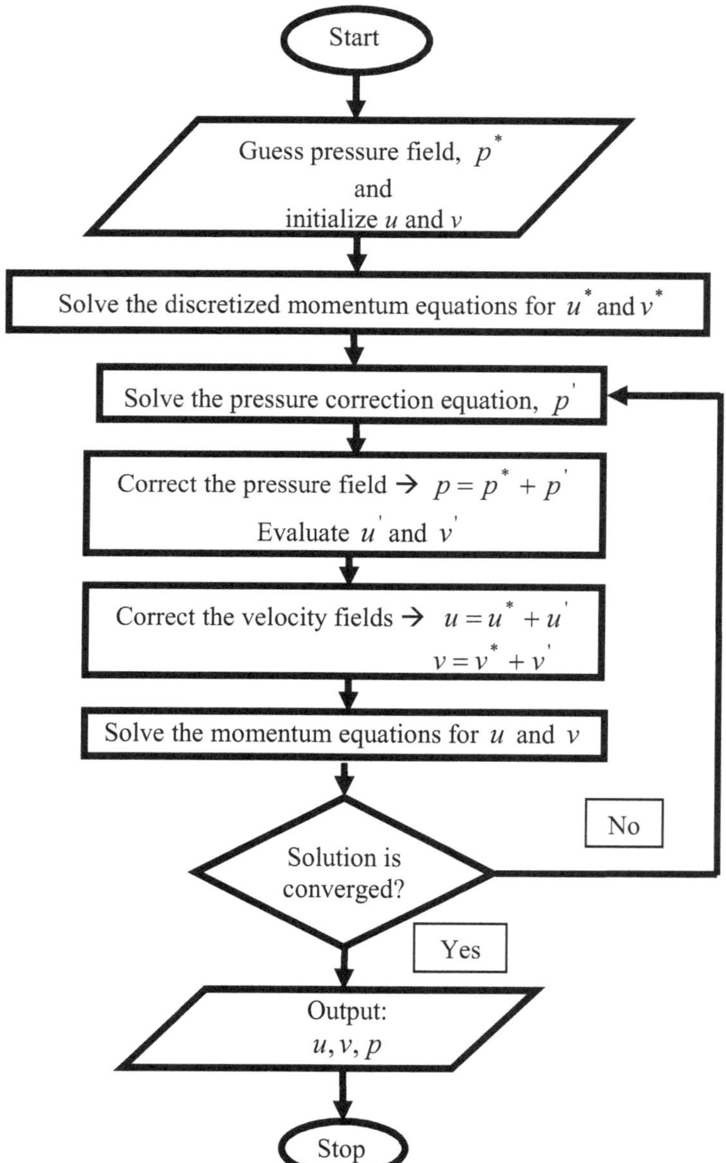

Fig. 2. Flow chart for the SIMPLE-type algorithm

It shall be stressed that the pressure-correction equation is prone to diverge from desired solution path unless an under-relaxation is implemented. For such a purpose, the following is used.

$$p = p^{*} + \alpha_P p^{'}$$

where α_P is the pressure under-relaxation parameter. Due to expensive computational time in achieving convergence, the Tri-Diagonal Matrix Algorithm (TDMA) used by [6] to solve the system of discretised equations is avoided. In the present algorithm, a modification is provided in the form of a direct method to remedy such a problem. It has been shown that a rapid convergence can be obtained through this method [8].

4 Test Problem

To measure the validity of current model, the developed finite difference formulation is used to simulate the well-established benchmark problems. In the following sections, we shall be interested in the comparison of currently modeled solution to those of classical problems, namely, the lid-driven cavity flow, the developing laminar flow in a straight rectangular duct and the backward-facing step flow. Note the comparisons are restricted to those of low Re numbers. Turbulent flow is not considered in the current study.

4.1 Lid-Driven Cavity Flow

The lid-driven cavity problem has long been considered as the test or validation case for new codes or new solution methods. Among the reasons for such popularity are the problem geometry is simple and two-dimensional. Furthermore, the boundary conditions are considerably simple. The standard case is fluid contained in a square domain with the Dirichlet boundary conditions on all sides, with three stationary sides and one moving side (with a prescribed velocity tangent to the side). The boundary conditions for the present problem are illustrated in Figure 3.

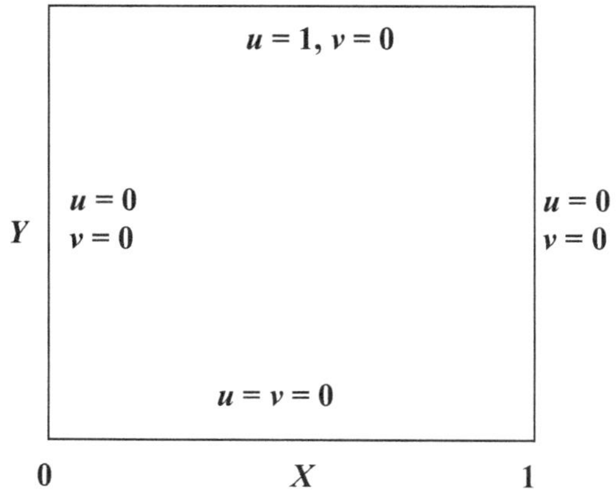

Fig. 3. Boundary conditions for the lid-driven cavity

Since this problem case has been solved and used frequently for verification, there exists a great deal of data to compare with. A good set of data for comparison is the data given in [1]. It includes tabulated results for various Reynolds numbers.

In the comparison, we shall consider the flow for aforementioned problem for $Re = 100$. Figure 4(a) illustrates the velocity component u along the vertical line through the geometric centre of cavity. Figure 4(b) shows the velocity component v along the horizontal line through the geometric centre of cavity. Obviously, one can see in the figures that very good agreements are demonstrated from the comparison of the present model with those obtained by [1] and [6].

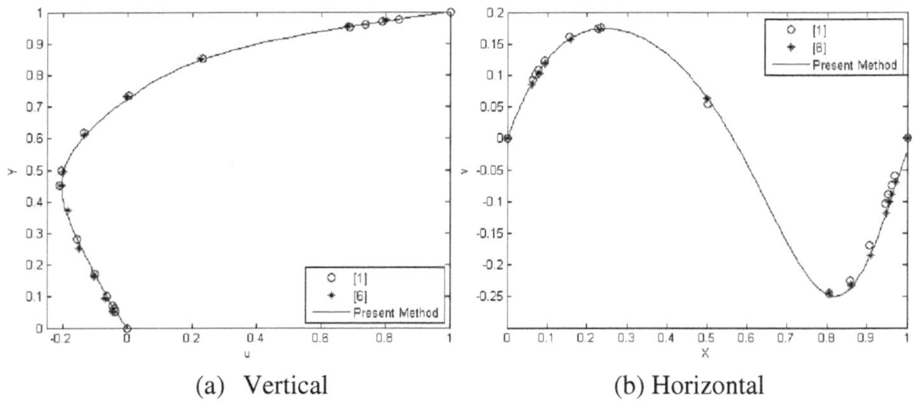

Fig. 4. Velocity along the vertical and horizontal lines through the geometric centre of cavity for $Re = 100$

The velocity vector plot and contour for $Re = 100$ are shown in Figure 5. One can see that the features of the cavity flow are excellently captured.

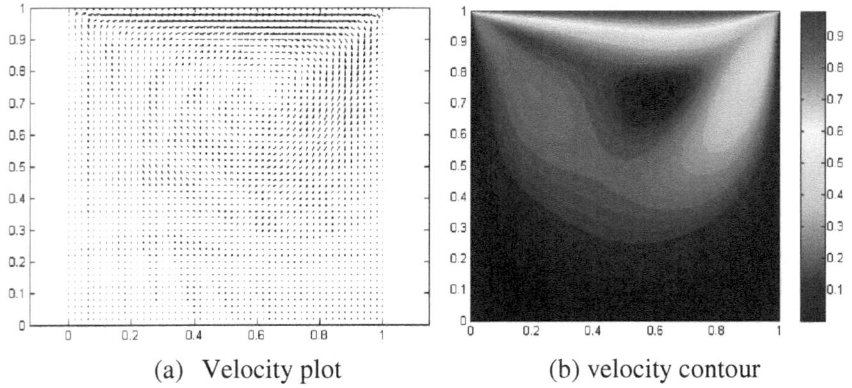

Fig. 5. Velocity plot and contour of the cavity flow for $Re = 100$

4.2 Developing Flow in a Rectangular Duct

Next, consider a developing flow in a straight two-dimensional channel as shown in Figure 6. The length *L* of the channel is taken to be ten times the width *D*, and we take $D = 1$.

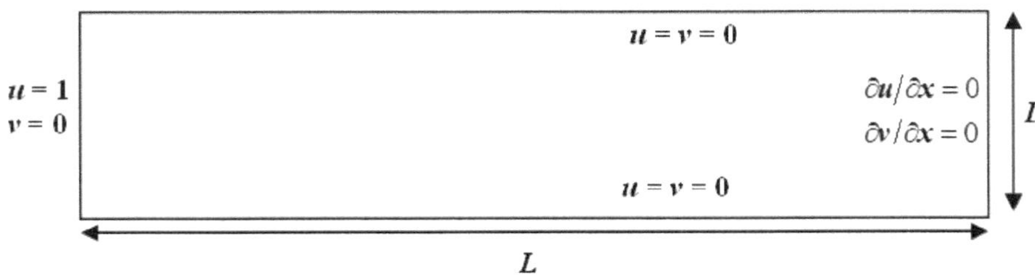

Fig. 6. Geometry of the channel with the prescribed boundary conditions

At the entrance of the channel, a uniform flow $(u = 1)$ is specified as the inlet velocity profile. The transverse velocity is set equal to zero at the inlet. A parallel flow condition is specified at the outlet, i.e. $\partial u/\partial x = 0$ and $\partial v/\partial x = 0$. The no-slip condition is applied at the lower and upper walls. As the fluid enters the channel, the wall boundary conditions distort the uniform flow due to the growth of boundary layers on the walls. The flow develops along the channel for some distance, until it becomes fully developed. At this point, the flow field is that described by the Poiseuille flow.

The numerical model is verified against the exact solution and Zogheib model for a fully developed flow formed at the outlet. Also, the predicted fully developed streamwise velocity profile for $\mathrm{Re} = 50$ is compared and the agreement is excellent, as given in Figure 7. In Figure 8, the result obtained for the present method closely matches the result from [6] and the agreement is better than that obtained from [9] where the parabolic profile of [9] starts further downstream, around $x = 4$. Velocity contour of the channel flow can be seen in Figure 9. Again, one can notice that it is considerably consistent with the behavior of the benchmark case (the latter is not shown here).

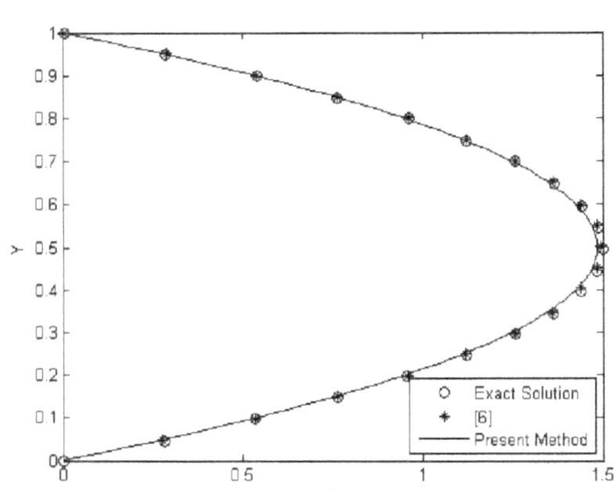

Fig. 7. Fully developed velocity profile

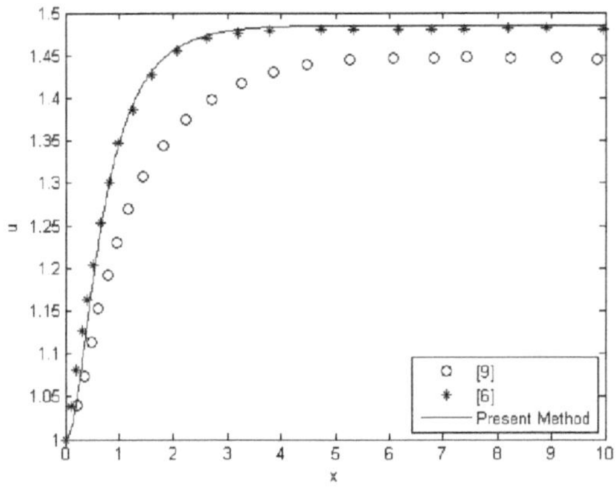

Fig. 8. Centreline velocity for $\mathrm{Re} = 50$

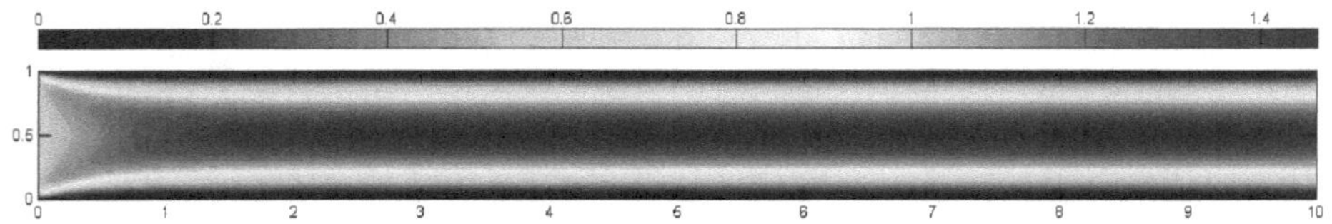

Fig. 9. Velocity contour of the flow

4.3 Backward-Facing Step Flow

The backward-facing step is one of the most fundamental geometries causing flow separation and is an important validation test for any numerical model.

Sketch of the geometry and boundary conditions for backward-facing step flow model is illustrated in Figure 10. The channel was defined to have height $2h$, with a step height and upstream inlet equal to h. In this work, we have taken $2h = 1$. The length L from the step to the end of the channel domain depends on Re. This length must be chosen to ensure the reattachment length is independent of the length of the calculation domain. Figure 11 shows the development of flow velocity vector in the channel.

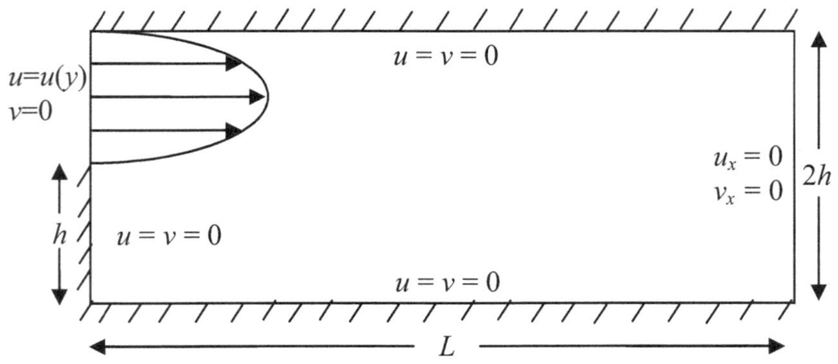

Fig. 10. Sketch of geometry for backward-facing step flow

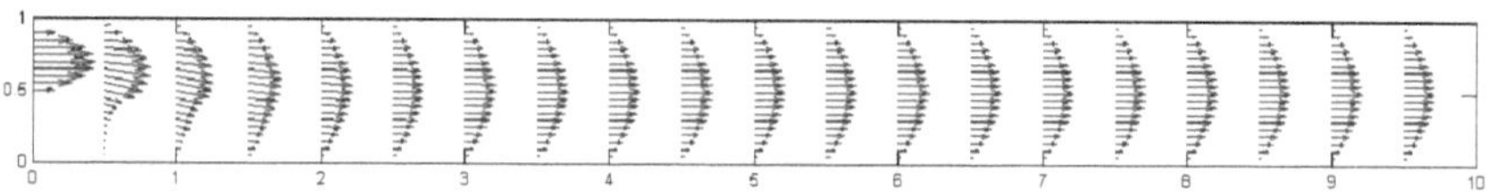

Fig. 11. Velocity plot of the flow

Table 12 gives a comparison of the reattachment length predicted by the present method with experimental and numerical results of [10] and [11]. It is clear that the computed results agree very well with those found in the literature.

Re	[10] (Experimental)	[11] (Numerical)	Present method (Numerical)
50	0.90	1.00	1.00
100	1.40	1.50	1.50
200	2.50	2.60	2.00

Fig. 12. Reattachment length as a function of Re

For demonstration purpose, we show next the contour and streamline plots for the channel for Re = 50 and Re = 100, respectively in Figures 13 and 14. It is obvious that an increase in Re boosts the velocity of flow especially near the entrance of channel. Nevertheless, the streamline plots display practically identical pattern for both flows.

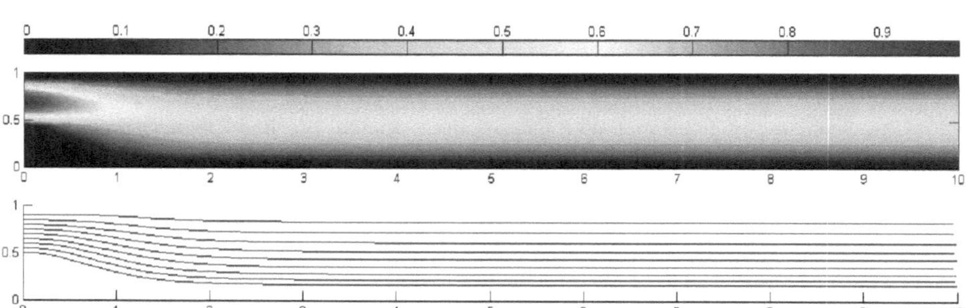

Fig. 13. u velocity contour and streamlines for Re=50

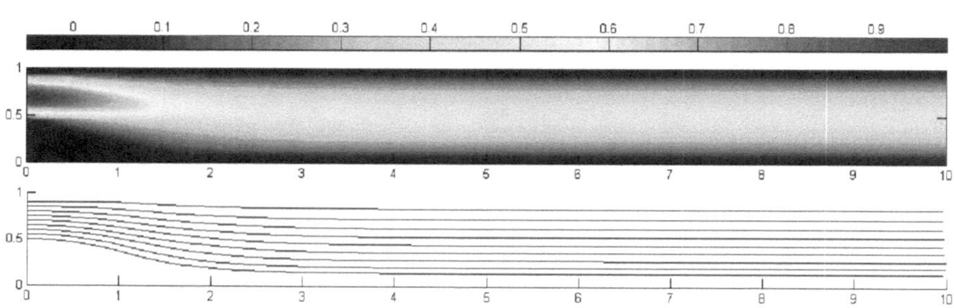

Fig. 14. u velocity contour and streamlines for Re=100

5 Conclusions

An improved finite difference discretisation method for solving the two-dimensional, steady, incompressible, laminar, viscous flow equations on a staggered grid is presented. The validation is done for the fundamental fluid flow problems, namely, the lid-driven cavity flow, the developing laminar flow in a straight rectangular duct and the backward-facing step flow. Good agreements are demonstrated by the current model with respect to these benchmark tests.

References

1. Ghia, U., Ghia, K.N., Shin, C.T.: High-Re Solutions for Incompressible Flow Using the Navier-Stokes Equations and a Multigrid Method. Journal of Computational Physics 48, 387–411 (1982)
2. Johnston, H., Liu, J.G.: Finite Difference Schemes for Incompressible Flow Based on Local Pressure Boundary Condition. Journal of Computational Physics 180, 120–154 (2002)
3. Strikwerda, J.C.: High Order-accurate Schemes for Incompressible Viscous Flow. International Journal for Numerical Methods in Fluids 24, 715–734 (1997)
4. Petersson, N.A.: Stability of Pressure Boundary Conditions for Stokes and Navier-Stokes Equations. Journal of Computational Physics 172, 40–70 (2001)
5. Zhang, K.K.Q., Shotorban, B., Minkowycz, W.J., Mashayek, F.A.: Compact Finite Difference Method on Staggered Grid for Navier–Stokes Flows. International Journal for Numerical Methods in Fluids 52, 867–881 (2006)
6. Zogheib, B.: Velocity-Pressure Coupling in Finite Difference Formulations for the Navier-Stokes Equations, Windsor, Ontario, Canada (2006)
7. Midya, C., Layek, G.C., Gupta, A.S., Mahapatra, T.R.: Magnetohydrodynamic Viscous Flow Separated in a Channel With Constrictions. Journal of Fluid Engineering 125, 952–962 (2003)
8. Ferziger, J.H., Peric, M.: Computational Methods for Fluid Dynamics, 3rd edn. Springer, USA (2002)
9. Reggio, M., Camarero, R.: Numerical Solution Procedure for Viscous Incompressible Flows. Numerical Heat Transfer 10, 131–146 (1986)
10. Armaly, B.F., Durst, F., Pereira, J.C.F., Schonung, B.: Experimental and Theoretical Investigation of Backward-facing Step Flow. Journal of Fluid Mechanics 127, 473–496 (1983)
11. Barber, R.W., Fonty, A.: Comparison of Vortex-element and Finite-volume Simulations of Low Reynolds Number Flow over a Confined Backward Facing Step. In: Proceedings of 11th Annual Conference of the CFD Society of Canada, CFD 2003, vol. 2, pp. 780–787 (2003)

Leveraging Wireless Sensors and Smart Phones to Study Gait Variability

E. Martin and R. Bajcsy

EECS Dept., University of California, Berkeley
emartin@eecs.berkeley.edu

Abstract. Recent research shows that cognitive load has an effect on gait, especially noticeable in people with neurodegenerative disorders. Most researchers in this field employ sophisticated and expensive systems to measure the variability of gait parameters under different cognitive loads. In this paper we propose the use of smart phones and off-the-shelf wireless accelerometers to implement a light-weight and low-cost system to study the influence of cognitive load on gait. Making use of this new approach, we study the effect on gait variability derived from imposing a speed while walking in a treadmill. We also compare "phone-texting" with other common "working memory" and "motor" tasks used by researchers to study the influence of cognitive load on gait. Our approach avoids the space constraints imposed by current systems during the tests, and delivers an accuracy comparable to that of the most sophisticated systems available in the market.

Keywords: Wireless communications; sensors; gait analysis; signal processing.

1 Introduction

There is a growing interest in clarifying the relationship between cognition and gait. In the past, walking was considered a motor activity independent of any cognitive processes and performed automatically by healthy adults. However, recent research shows that cognitive load has an effect on gait [1-4], clearly noticeable in neurodegenerative disorders such as Alzheimer's disease [5], vascular dementia, mixed dementia [6] or Parkinson's disease [7]. Psycho affective conditions such as anxiety and depression are also linked to specific gait disorders [8]. More specifically, a decrease in the frontal cerebral blood flow has been associated with modifications in gait [9]. As shown in [10, 11] and references therein, cerebral vascular abnormalities are associated with modifications of the gait pattern, namely an increased variability of spatio-temporal gait parameters. These observations are consistent with studies claiming that gait requires cognitive processes such as attention, memory and planning [12, 13], demanding frontal and parietal activity in the brain [14, 15]. In fact, changes in the frontal regions including the bilateral medial areas of the frontal cortex have been identified as a risk factor for dementia [16-18], and reductions in the motor strength associated with aging increase the attentional demands needed for walking.

The most popular method to analyze the effect of cognitive load on gait is the dual task test [3, 4, 10, 12, 19, 20, 21-29], in which the subject under study performs a cognitive task while simultaneously walking. Most researchers choose to avoid prioritizing any of the tasks. Since the dual task conditions impose a higher attentional

A. Abd Manaf et al. (Eds.): ICIEIS 2011, Part III, CCIS 253, pp. 95–111, 2011.

demand, the performance in one or both tasks can be impaired if the attentional reserve capacity available is challenged [22, 30, 31]. This is known as "dual task interference". The effect of the dual task test on gait can be quantified through the variability in the spatio-temporal parameters of gait, which will depend on the complexity of the task and the general condition of the subject [32-36]. For example, the effect of the cognitive task on gait can depend on factors such as age, gender, executive function, memory and verbal IQ [2, 32, 33, 37-42].

Researchers have also applied the dual task test to show the link between attentional demands and postural control [32, 43-49]. Recent studies claim that postural stability requires both cognitive and sensorimotor processes [50], and researchers are analyzing the impact of different details (e.g. speech complexity [51]) on postural control. In the same sense, the dual task test can be utilized to study the capacity of older adults to avoid obstacles [52]. In fact, gait stability can be a better predictor of falling than static measures of balance [40]. and recent studies have shown a relationship between dual task interference and fall risk [53, 54]. For instance, a simple measurement of the counting performance while walking in comparison with while seated has proved to be a good indicator of fall risk in the elderly [53]. In particular, there is a growing interest in studying the link between the variability of spatial-temporal parameters in gait under dual task conditions and the risk of falling in seniors [20, 37, 38, 55, 56-59].

In this paper we propose the use of smart phones and off-the-shelf wireless accelerometers to implement a light-weight and low-cost system to analyze dual task tests and study the effect of cognitive load on gait, avoiding the space constraints imposed by current systems. The rest of this paper is organized as follows. In Section 2, we review the state of the art in the analysis of the effect of cognitive load on gait, showing the different spatio-temporal parameters, systems, and dual task tests employed by researchers in this field. In Section 3, we present our proposed methodology, while in Section 4 we describe practical tests and results obtained making use of our approach. We draw conclusions in Section 5.

2 Related Work

In this Section we will review the state of the art in the analysis of the effect of cognitive load on gait, focusing on the types of dual task tests used, the most common systems employed, and the spatio-temporal parameters chosen by researchers in this field.

2.1 Dual Task Tests

Most of the existing research in this field involves the analysis of the effect of a second task on gait or postural control. Some researchers claim that dual task interference is only possible if the neural networks involved in the two processes overlap [2]. For instance, reference [33] suggests that only visual/spatial dual tasks would interfere with postural control, since postural control demands visual/spatial processing. However, there is no consensus on the optimum dual tasks with which to evaluate gait or postural control.

Some of the dual tasks employed by researchers are borrowed from neuropsychological tests, while others are created specifically for each experiment. And even if there is a lack of a standardized evaluation technique to compare the cognitive loads demanded by each task, most researchers follow practical guidelines to carry out the tests: the task should be difficult enough to load the attentional system, but it should not cause undue stress or anxiety. Also, the test should take into consideration the subject's skills (e.g. mathematical, verbal fluency), since the cognitive loads brought by a same task can vary depending on the subject's skills [2]. Tables 1 to 6 gather the most common tasks employed by researchers.

Table 1. Verbal Fluency tasks for dual task tests

Verbal fluency tasks	**Example reference articles**
Enumerating animals out loud	[22]
Modified Stroop test	[72]
Naming items that start with a certain letter or have a certain common characteristic (e.g., farm animals)	[73, 74, 76, 77]
Conducting a conversation	[54, 78]
Remembering similar sentences	[33]

Table 2. Auditory tasks for dual task tests

Auditory tasks	**Example reference articles**
Listening to a spoken word recording of a book excerpt, or simple white noise	[71]
Auditory Stroop test	[52]

Table 3. Working memory tasks for dual task tests

Working memory tasks	**Example reference articles**
Attention and articulation: counting backwards loud	[44]
Attention without demands for articulation: silent counting backwards	[44, 60]
Articulation alone: number repetition	[44]
Arithmetic task (backward counting, serial 3 or 7 subtractions)	[12, 21, 60-66]
Other arithmetic calculations	[67]
Counting backwards from 50 by steps of 2 out loud	[20]
Random digit generation	[60]
Backward digit recall	[60]
Digit span recall	[33]
Generating a monologue	[51]
Audibly reciting as many male names as possible	[68-70]
Backward spelling	[37]
Naming of months from December to January	[13]
Reciting the days of the week backwards	[51]
Counting backwards silently by 7's	[71]
Performing a rote repetition task	[51]

Table 4. Motor tasks for dual task tests

Motor tasks	Example reference articles
Fine motor task (opening and closing a coat button)	[33]
Finger tapping at 5 Hz or faster	[33]
Combination of memory-retention and fine motor tasks (digit recall and buttoning task)	[33]
Carrying a tray	[68-70]
Carrying a tray with four plastic glasses on it	[68-70]
Carrying a tray with filled glasses of water	[12, 79, 80-82]
Sequential finger movement	[67]
Transfer of coins between pockets	[65]
Other simple manual motor tasks	[83]

Table 5. Visual tasks for dual task tests

Visual tasks	Example reference articles
Brooks spatial memory task	[33, 60]
Tests under different visual conditions, no vision, static visual image, and a moving visual image	[44]
Color judgment	[84]
Other visual-spatial cognitive tasks	[85]

Table 6. Classical tests of executive function for dual task tests

Classical tests of executive function	Example reference articles
Wisconsin Card Sorting	[2]
Stroop test	[2]
Verbal fluency tests	[2]
The Executive Interview (EXIT25) test	[2]
CLOX (an executive clock drawing task)	[2]

2.2 Systems Employed to Analyze the Influence of Cognitive Load on Gait and Postural Control

Chronophotography is among the most basic approaches to analyze human kinematics [86]. More sophisticated motion tracking methods utilize mechanical, acoustic (including ultrasounds), radio-frequency, optical, magnetic, and inertial sensors. Descriptions and examples of all these systems can be found in [87]. The suitability of each system depends on the particular conditions and goals of each test, and the combination of different methods in a multi-modal approach allows an enhancement in accuracy and robustness in terms of security.

One of the most common and sophisticated commercial systems employed in research labs is the GAITRite walkway [88, 89], with a length of nearly 5 meters and with embedded force sensors to detect footfalls, allowing the estimation of gait parameters such as speed, length and width of the step, and symmetry of the gait pattern. This system enjoys high reliability and high concurrent validity when compared with video-based motion analysis systems for the estimation of spatiotemporal gait parameters such as gait speed, cadence, and stride length.

For the analysis of postural control, the most common methods use sensors or force plates installed on the floor [90-92]. Commercial examples of such systems employed in existing research are described in [20] and [51]. Other researchers utilize custom made plates attached to the subject to overcome the movement restriction due to the small size of force plates. Examples of these approaches include the employment of force transducers beneath the shoe, or pressure insoles and miniature triaxial piezoelectric transducers inside the shoe [87]. Table 7 gathers a summary of systems employed by researchers for the measurement of kinematic parameters in gait.

Additional methodologies utilized to diagnose clinical conditions that can influence gait are based on the analysis of electroencephalogram (EEG) signals and magnetic resonance imaging (MRI) [1]. Other techniques that can also be used to examine the link between clinical conditions and gait and to discover possible reasons for falling include Holter electrocardiography (ECG), 24-hour blood pressure monitoring, electromyography (EMG), and Doppler and duplex sonography of the extra- and intracranial vessels [20]. Methods such as single photon emission tomography, functional near infrared spectroscopy or functional magnetic resonance imaging (fMRI) and positron emission tomography, have also been employed to identify brain areas related to attentional resources during walking [21].

2.3 Spatio-Temporal Parameters Employed to Analyze the Effect of Cognitive Load on Gait

Gait velocity can be used as an indicator of the quality of life in the elderly [98]. In this sense, increased variability of spatio-temporal gait parameters has been linked to cognitive abnormalities [1, 11]. And although numerous gait parameters can be measured in sophisticated gait labs, many studies focus basically on mean gait speed and stride-to-stride variability in gait speed [37]. In fact, gait velocity and stride-to-stride variability in gait velocity have been identified as the best predictors of falls for the elderly [38, 99]. Stride-to-stride variability (V) in gait speed is commonly quantified as the percentage of the standard deviation (SD) to the mean [37]:

$$V(\%) = \frac{SD}{mean} * 100 \tag{1}$$

Other researchers also focus on stride time and swing time variabilities [100, 101]. Table 8 gathers representative gait parameters used by researchers to analyze the effect of cognitive load on gait, together with example reference literature.

Table 9 gathers a summary of the typical modifications measured for the spatio-temporal parameters of gait under dual task conditions.

Table 7. Common systems employed to analyze the spatio-temporal parameters of gait

Systems	Example reference articles
Absorbent paper to record wet footprint placements	[93]
Talcum powder dusted on the plantar surface of the foot to record footprint placements	[94]
Ink pads on the sole of the shoes with the person walking along a large piece of paper	[38, 95]
Shoe-integrated wireless sensor systems (e.g. Stride Analyzer; B&L Engineering, CA., USA)	[20]
Accelerometers (e.g. DynaPort MiniMod; McRoberts Moving Technology, The Netherlands)	[20]
Angular velocity transducer systems (e.g. Sway- Star; Balance Intern. Innov. GmbH, Switzerland)	[20]
Electronic walkways with integrated pressure sensors (e.g. GAITRite; CIR Systems, PA., USA)	[20, 32, 37, 12]
Video-based motion analysis systems (e.g. Vicon Motion Systems, CA., USA)	[20, 13, 88, 89]
On-body sensors based systems (e.g. STEP 32 gait analysis system by DEM, Italy)	[66]
Inner soles with 4 pressure-sensitive footswitches	[65]
Muscle activity measured with electromyography (EMG)	[21, 32, 96, 97]

Table 8. Common spatio-temporal gait parameters analyzed by researchers to study the influence of cognitive load on gait

Gait Parameters	Example Reference articles
Gait speed	[38, 37, 65, 12, 13]
Stride-to-stride variability in gait speed	[38, 37]
Stride time	[32, 12]
Double support time	[32]
Stride length	[65, 12]
Cadence	[65, 12]
Percentage of the gait cycle in double-limb stance	[65]
Range of motion and peak velocity of the center of mass	[52]
Duration of single and double support	[12]
Step time	[13]
Swing time	[13]
Stance time	[13]

Table 9. Summary of modifications in spatio-temporal gait parameters under dual task conditions

Gait Parameters	Example reference articles
Decreased gait velocity (natural compensation mechanism when stability is challenged). It is interesting to note that this parameter is associated with errors in the cognitive dual-task (e.g. poorer arithmetic ability [12] or verbal reaction time [52])	[12, 20, 35, 37, 38, 52, 65, 101-107]
Decreased stride length	[12, 65, 102]
Increased double support time	[102]
Increased gait cycle time variability	[19, 20, 38, 104–109]
Increased variability in stride length	[103, 104, 106, 109-112]
Increased variability in gait speed	[37]
Decreased cadence	[12]
Increased lateral gait instability (with arithmetic dual task, but not with verbal fluency task)	[35]
Increased postural sway, which is impacted by articulation and visual conditions, but not by attentional load (e.g. silent counting)	[44]

3 Proposed Methodology

We propose the use of wireless off-the-shelf accelerometers attached to the human body and communicating with a smart phone carried by the person being monitored, thus implementing a light-weight and low-cost system to enable the study of the effect of cognitive load on gait with an accuracy comparable to that of the most sophisticated and expensive systems available in the market. We will store all the acceleration signals in the smart phone for subsequent processing in the way that will be explained later in this Section. In particular, we use two wireless accelerometers (Shimmers by Intel) placed on the waist and the ankle. We sample the acceleration signals with a frequency of 30 Hz, since we will focus on the most representative frequencies of gait, which are commonly found between 0.5 Hz and 4 Hz. We choose the waist because it represents a good approximation of the center of mass of the human body (technically should be the L3 vertebra, but placing a sensor on the waist is usually easier and more comfortable to wear). The sensor on the ankle will allow us to extract the step frequency, leveraging the smoothed arctangent of the quotient between the vertical and anteroposterior components of the acceleration (see Fig. 2). The sensor on the waist will be leveraged to estimate the velocity of the person, through the application of the wavelet transform to the Signal Vector Magnitude (SVM) of the acceleration, as will be explained later in this Section. Both waist and ankle accelerometers will communicate with a smart phone via Bluetooth, making use of an application we have developed for the Android Operating System. Our application stores the acceleration signals on the phone, allowing total freedom of movement to the individual being monitored, since he/she can walk anywhere and anytime for as long as the battery lives of the sensors and the smart phone last (typically several hours). This represents a major contribution in this filed, since current systems constrain the space (typically a few meters within the lab) over which the person being monitored can walk during the tests.

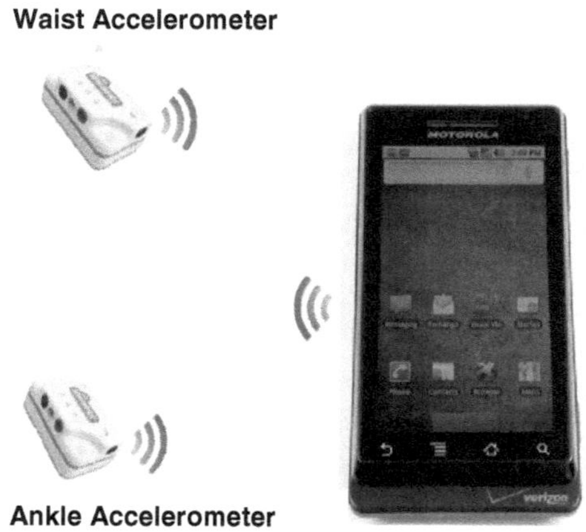

Fig. 1. Basic representation of our data acquisition system

To analyze the SVM of the waist acceleration, we can use a laptop or desktop PC equipped with wavelet processing software, even if we plan to implement the entire signal processing within the smart phone, making use of filters. Next we briefly summarize the wavelet transform based signal processing methodology we use.

The wavelet transform can decompose a signal *x(t)* into approximation $a_j(k)$ and detail $d_j(k)$ coefficients:

$$a_j(k) = \int x(t)\varphi_{j,k}(t)dt \tag{2}$$

$$d_j(k) = \int x(t)\psi_{j,k}^{*}(t)dt \tag{3}$$

Where $\varphi_{j,k}(t)$ represents the scaling function and $\psi_{j,k}(t)$ the wavelet function. We can see that to obtain these coefficients, we are integrating the signal *x(t)*, weighted by the $\varphi_{j,k}(t)$ and $\psi_{j,k}(t)$ functions. Since our signal *x(t)* represents accelerations, the application of the wavelet transform delivers the integration of weighted accelerations, and thus we are obtaining weighted velocities. Further analyzing the relationship between the wavelet transform coefficients and the kinetic energy of different walking patterns, we can actually infer the speed of the movement with the following expression:

$$Speed = \frac{1}{2}\sqrt{WE_{d_1} + \frac{WE_{d_2}}{2} + \frac{WE_{d_3}}{3} + \frac{WE_{d_4}}{4} + \frac{WE_{d_5}}{5}} \tag{4}$$

In which we include a new metric that we call "Weighted Energy":

$$WE_{d_i} = \begin{cases} \dfrac{\sum d_i^2}{n_0\sqrt{2}(J-i)} & i = 1..J-1 \\ \dfrac{\sum d_i^2}{n_0\sqrt{2}} & i = J \end{cases} \tag{5}$$

Where J represents the number of levels of decomposition we are using in the wavelet transform, i accounts for the specific level we are considering, d_i symbolizes the detail coefficients at level i, and n_0 represents the number of coefficients considered. We have previously tested this approach with a total of 14 individuals (males and females with ages ranging from 21 to 77), obtaining excellent accuracies in the velocities, with average errors around 5%. In fact, the accuracy of our approach is comparable to that obtained with more complex and expensive systems, and our results are achieved with significantly lower hardware requirements. Once we obtain the velocity of the movement, the step length can be calculated dividing the velocity by the step frequency, which we can obtain either from an accelerometer on the ankle or through the study of the wavelet transform of the waist acceleration (coefficients line offers precise information to extract the step frequency as the inverse of the time elapsed between two consecutive negative-to-positive transitions, as shown in Fig. 3).

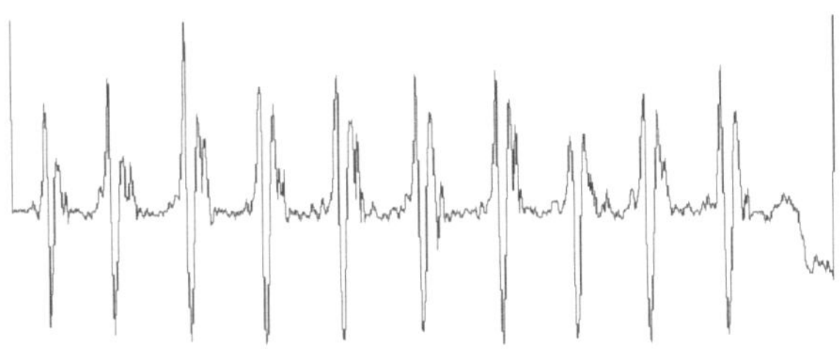

Fig. 2. Smoothed arctangent of the quotient between the vertical and anteroposterior components of the acceleration on the ankle, showing clear peaks which mark every step

4 Tests and Results

Making use of this new approach, we carried out tests to study the influence of cognitive load on gait. First, we analyzed the effect of imposing a velocity (the person should walk on a treadmill at a selected speed). For these tests, 20 individuals (ages ranging from 11 to 59) walked in a treadmill at the suggested speeds of 1 mph, 2 mph, 3 mph, 5 mph and 2 mph with inclination. The results regarding the variabilities in velocities (obtained as the percentage of the standard deviation to the mean) are summarized in Fig. 4. In this figure we have also included the values obtained from free walking conditions outside the treadmill averaged for the 20 individuals (3.94 mph corresponding to 11.21% variability).

We observe that the velocity variabilities obtained when the imposed velocities in the treadmill are very low (e.g. 1 mph with average variability of 19.14%), show noticeably higher values than the variabilities obtained without the cognitive load of

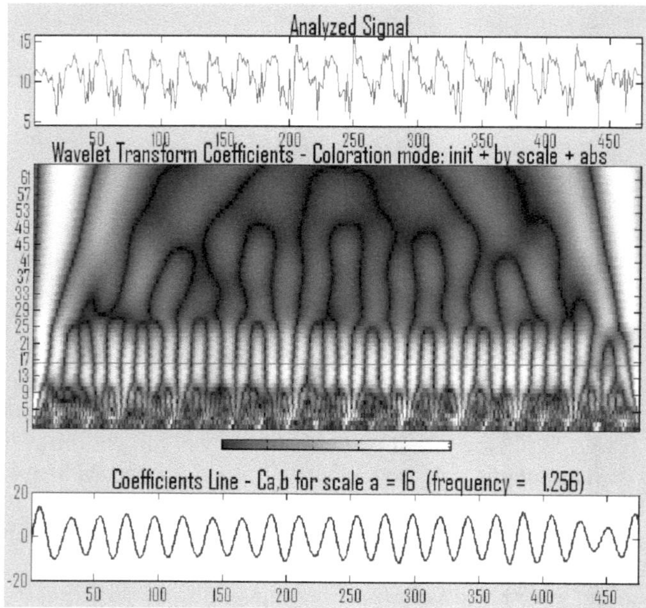

Fig. 3. Continuous wavelet transform of the waist acceleration for a typical walking pattern showing consecutive negative-to-positive transitions in the coefficients line from which the step frequency can be obtained

having to keep a fixed speed (free walk with average velocity of 3.94 mph and variability of 11.21%). On the other hand, the variabilities in the velocities decrease when the imposed speed in the treadmill is close to the average velocity followed under free walking conditions, and the minimum variabilities are obtained for imposed fixed velocities slightly lower than the average from free walk (e.g. 3 mph with variability of 10.39%).

As another original contribution in this field, we have also carried out mobile-phone related dual task tests in order to study the influence of activities such as "phone-texting" on gait. In particular, we have measured the variability of velocities and stride lengths (computed as the percentage of the standard deviation to the mean) for walking while "texting" long messages on a phone. To compare these results, we have also measured the variability of velocities and stride lengths under classical dual task tests such as walking while holding a tray with a glass full of water, or walking while performing arithmetic calculations out loud (serial 7 and 13 subtractions). Comparing all these variabilities with those obtained under free walking conditions (results gathered in Table 10), we can notice decreases in the mean velocities and stride lengths of the individuals while performing the dual tasks, including the phone-related ones. In fact, the measured reduction in speed for "phone-texting" is larger than those associated with serial subtractions. Regarding the percentage variabilities of velocity and stride length, these terms increase in all the dual task tests, with the effects of "phone-texting" being similar to serial subtractions. Finally, the mean stride lengths under dual task conditions experience a noticeable decrease, even if the reductions associated to "texting" are the lowest ones.

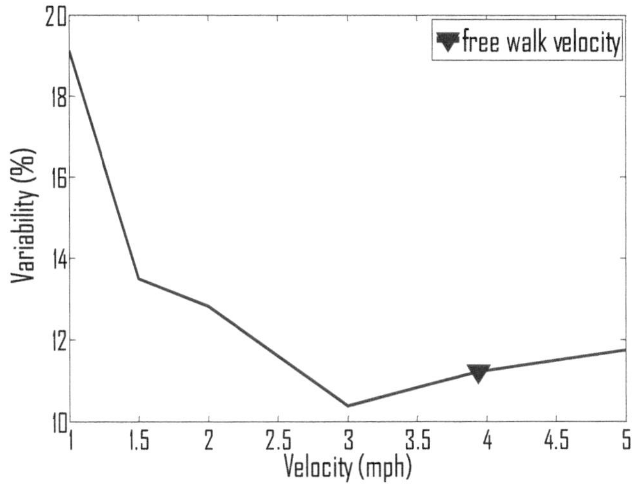

Fig. 4. Velocity variabilities (%) averaging for 20 individuals walking at different fixed speeds in a treadmill, and comparison with free walking conditions

Table 10. Measured effects of different dual tasks (including "phone-texting") on gait

	Mean Velocity (mph)	Velocity Variability (%)	Mean Stride Length (meters)	Stride Length Variability (%)
Free Walk	3.05	23.2	1.25	32.04
Walk while phone-texting	2.1	28.36	0.98	37.93
Carrying tray	1.82	24.93	0.65	61.9
Walk while calculating	2.6	25.17	0.85	35.29

5 Conclusions

In this paper we have shown the state of the art in the analysis of the effect of cognitive load on gait. In particular, we have reviewed the most common spatio-temporal parameters, dual tasks and systems employed by researchers in this field. We have also proposed a new methodology to study the effect of cognitive load on gait leveraging smart phones and off-the-shelf wireless accelerometers, avoiding the movement constraints imposed by common systems.

Making use of our new methodology, we have examined the influence on gait derived from the imposition of a fixed speed while walking on a treadmill, showing that the velocity variabilities obtained when the imposed velocities in the treadmill are very low (e.g. 1 mph), are particularly higher than those obtained without the cognitive load of having to keep an imposed speed. We have also examined the effect of "phone-texting" on gait, demonstrating that its influence is comparable to that of common "working memory" or "motor" tasks employed in dual task tests for the analysis of cognitive load on gait, and all these effects can be successfully measured leveraging current state-of-the-art smart phones and off-the-shelf wireless accelerometers, without the need of sophisticated and expensive equipment.

References

1. Gilles, A., Meulen, M., Assal, F.: Gait and cognition: the impact of executive function. Schweizer Archiv fur Neurologie und Psychiatrie 161(6), 195–199 (2010)
2. Galit, Y., Hausdorff, J., Giladi, N.: The role of executive function and attention in gait. Movement Disorders 23(3), 329–342 (2008)
3. Woollacott, M., Shumway-Cook, A.: Attention and the control of posture and gait: a review of an emerging area of research. Gait Posture 16(1), 1–14 (2002)
4. Beauchet, O., Kressig, R.W., Najafi, B., Aminian, K., Dubost, V., Mourey, F.: Age-related decline of gait control under a dual-task condition. J. Am. Geriatr. Soc. 51(8), 1187–1188 (2003)
5. Sheridan, P.: Influence of executive function on locomotor function. J. Am. Geriatr. Soc. 51(11), 1633–1637 (2003)
6. Allali, G., et al.: Impact of impaired executive function on gait stability. Dement Geriatr. Cogn. Disord. 26(4), 364–369 (2008)
7. Yogev, G.: Gait asymmetry in patients with Parkinson's disease and elderly fallers. Exp. Brain Res. 177(3), 336–346 (2007)
8. Hausdorff, J.M., Peng, C.K., Goldberger, A.L., Stoll, A.L.: Gait unsteadiness and fall risk in two affective disorders: a preliminary study. BMC Psychiatry, 4–39 (2004)
9. Nakamura, T.: Postural and gait disturbance correlated with decreased frontal cerebral blood flow in Alzheimer disease. Alzhe. Dis. Assoc. Disord. 11(3), 132–139 (1997)
10. Gilles, A., Meulen, M., Assal, F.: Gait and cognition: the impact of executive function. Schweizer Archiv fur Neurologie und Psychiatrie 161(6), 195–199 (2010)
11. Rosano, C.: Gait variability is associated with subclinical brain vascular abnormalities in high-functioning older adults. Neuroepidemiology 29(3-4), 193–200 (2007)
12. Paul, L.: The effect of a cognitive or motor task on gait parameters of diabetic patients, with and without neuropathy. Diabetic Medicine 26(3), 234–239 (2009)
13. Deepak, J., Sneh, A.: Cyclogram and cross correlation: A comparative study to quantify gait coordination in mental state. Journal of Biomedical Science and Engineering, 322–326 (2010)
14. Malouin, F., Richards, C.L., Jackson, P.L., Dumas, F., Doyon, J.: Brain activations during motor imagery of locomotor-related tasks: a PET study. Hum. Brain Mapp. 19, 47–62 (2003)
15. Sheridan, P.L., Hausdorff, J.M.: The role of higher-level cognitive function in gait: executive dysfunction contributes to fall risk in Alzheimer's disease. Dement Geriatr. Cogn. Disord. 24, 125–137 (2007)
16. Tombu, M., Jolicoeur, P.: A central capacity sharing model of dual-task performance. J. Exp. Psychol. Hum. Percept. Perform. 29, 3–18 (2003)
17. Mayer, Y.S., Barron, D.W.: Apraxia of gait: clinico-physiological study. Brain 83, 261–284 (1960)
18. Verghese, J.: Abnormality of gait as a predictor of non-Alzheimer's dementia. N. Engl. J. Med. 347(22), 1761–1768 (2002)

19. Allali, G., Kressig, R., Assal, F., Herrmann, F., Dubost, V.: Changes in gait while backward counting in demented older adults with frontal lobe dysfunction. Gait Posture 26(4), 572–576 (2007)
20. Bridenbaugh, S.A., Kressig, R.W.: Laboratory review: the role of gait analysis in seniors' mobility and fall prevention. Gerontology, 1–9 (October 2010)
21. Abbud, G.A.C., Li, K.Z.H., DeMont, R.G.: Attentional requirements of walking according to the gait phase and onset of auditory stimuli. Gait & Posture 30, 227–232 (2009)
22. Huang, H.J., Mercer, V.S.: Dual-task methodology: applications in studies of cognitive and motor performance in adults and children. Pediatr. Phys. Ther. 13, 133–140 (2001)
23. Yogev-Seligmann, G., Hausdorff, J.M., Giladi, N.: The role of executive function and attention in gait. Mov. Disord. 23, 329–342 (2008)
24. Pashler, H.: Dual-task interference in simple tasks: data and theory. Psychol. Bull. 116, 220–244 (1994)
25. Sheridan, P.L., Solomont, J., Kowall, N., Hausdorff, J.M.: Influence of executive function on locomotor function: divided attention increases gait variability in Alzheimer's disease. J. Am. Geriatr. Soc. 51, 1633–1637 (2003)
26. Sheridan, P.L., Solomont, J., Kowall, N.: Influence of executive function on locomotor function: divided attention increases gait variability in Alzheimer's disease. J. Am. Geriatr. Soc. 51, 1633–1637 (2003)
27. Allali, G., Kressig, R., Assal, F., Herrmann, F., Dubost, V.: Changes in gait while backward counting in demented older adults with frontal lobe dysfunction. Gait & Posture 26(4), 572–576 (2007)
28. Allali, G., Kressig, R., Assal, F., Herrmann, F., Dubost, V.: Changes in gait while backward counting in demented older adults with frontal lobe dysfunction. Gait Posture 26(4), 572–576 (2007)
29. Dubost, V.: Relationships between dual-task-related changes in stride velocity and stride time variability in healthy older adults. Hum. Mov. Sci. 25, 372–382 (2006)
30. Woollacott, M., Shumway-Cook, A.: Attention and the control of posture and gait: a review of an emerging area of research. Gait Posture 16, 1–14 (2002)
31. Abernethy, B.: Dual-task methodology and motor skills research: some applications and methodological constraints. J. Hum. Mov. Stud. 14, 101–132 (1988)
32. Ebersbach, G., Dimitrijevic, M.R., Poewe, W.: Influence of concurrent tasks on gait: a dual-task approach. Percept. Mot. Skills 81, 107–113 (1995)
33. Kerr, B., Condon, S.M., McDonald, L.: Cognitive spatial processing and the regulation of posture. J. Exp. Psychol. 11, 617–622 (1985)
34. Yogev-Seligmann, G., Hausdorff, J.M., Giladi, N.: The role of executive function and attention in gait. Movement Disorders 23(3), 329–342 (2008)
35. Beauchet, O.: Dual-task-related gait changes in transitionally frail older adults: the type of the walking-associated cognitive task matters. Gerontology 51, 48–52 (2005)
36. Bloem, B.R., Steijns, J.A.G., Smits, B.: An update on falls. Curr. Opin. Neurol. 16, 15–26 (2003)
37. Hollman, J.H., Youdas, J.W., Lanzino, D.J.: Gender differences in dual task gait performance in older adults. American Journal of Men's Health 5(1), 11–17 (2011)
38. Hollman, J.H., Kovash, F.M., Kubik, J.J., Linbo, R.A.: Age-related differences in spatiotemporal markers of gait stability during dual task walking 26(1), 113–119 (2007)
39. Hausdorff, J.M., Edelberg, H.K., Mitchell, S.L., Goldberger, A.L., Wei, J.Y.: Increased gait unsteadiness in community-dwelling elderly fallers. Arch. Phys. Med. Rehabil 78(3), 278–283 (1997)

40. Maki, B.E.: Gait changes in older adults: predictors of falls or indicators of fear. J. Am. Geriatr. Soc. 45(3), 313–320 (1997)
41. Krebs, D.E., Jette, A.M., Assmann, S.F.: Moderate exercise improves gait stability in disabled elders. Arch. Phys. Med. Rehabil. 79(12), 1489–1495 (1998)
42. Menz, H.B., Lord, S.R., Fitzpatrick, R.C.: Age-related differences in walking stability. Age Ageing 32(2), 137–142 (2003)
43. Woollacott, M., Shumway-Cook, A.: Attention and the control of posture and gait: a review of an emerging area of research. Gait Posture 16(1), 1–14 (2002)
44. Yardley, L., Yardley, L., Gardner, M., Leadbetter, A., Lavie, N.: Effect of articulatory and mental tasks on postural control. NeuroReport 10(2), 215–219 (1999)
45. Teasdale, N.: On the cognitive penetrability of postural control. Exp. Aging. Res. 19, 1–13 (1993)
46. Shumway-Cook, A., Woollacott, M.: Motor control: theory and practical applications, 2nd edn. Lippincott, Williams and Wilkens, Baltimore, MD (2000)
47. Shumway-Cook, A., Woollacott, M.: Attentional demands and postural control: the effect of sensory context. J. Gerontol. 55, M10–M16 (2000)
48. Maylor, E.A., Wing, A.M.: Age differences in postural stability are increased by additional cognitive demands. J. Gerontol. 51B, 143–154 (1996)
49. Shumway-Cook, A., Woollacott, M., Baldwin, M., Kerns, K.: The effects of cognitive demands on postural sway in elderly fallers and non-fallers. J. Gerontol. 52, M232–M240 (1997)
50. Woollacott, M., Shumway-Cook, A.: Attention and the control of posture and gait: a review of an emerging area of research. Gait Posture 16(1), 1–14 (2002)
51. Holmes, J.: Dual-Task Interference: The effects of verbal cognitive tasks on upright postural stability in Parkinson's disease. Parkinson's Disease, 1–5 (2010)
52. Siu, K.C.: Dual-task interference during obstacle clearance in healthy and balance-impaired older adults. Aging Clin. Exp. Res. 20(4), 349–354 (2008)
53. Beauchet, O., Dubost, V., Allali, G., Gonthier, R., Hermann, F.R., Kressig, R.W.: Faster counting while walking' as a predictor of falls in older adults. Age Ageing 36, 418–423 (2007)
54. Lundin-Olsson, L.: Stops walking when talking as a predictor of falls in elderly people. Lancet 349, 617 (1997)
55. Lundin Olsson, L.: Stops walking when talking as a predictor of falls in elderly people. Lancet, 617, 9052 (1997)
56. Verghese, J.: Validity of divided attention tasks in predicting falls in older individuals: a preliminary study. J. Am. Geriatr. Soc. 50, 1572–1576 (2002)
57. Kressig, R.W.: Longterm practice of Jaques-Dalcroze eurhythmics prevents age-related increase of gait variability under a dual task. J. Am. Geriatr. Soc. 53, 728–729 (2005)
58. Verghese, J.: Cognitive and mobility profile of older social dancers. J. Am. Geriatr. Soc. 54, 1241–1244 (2006)
59. Hayden, R.: The effect of rhythmic auditory stimulation (RAS) on physical therapy outcomes for patients in gait training following stroke: a feasibility study. Int. J. Neurosci. 119, 2183–2195 (2009)
60. Lajoie, Y.: Upright standing and gait: are there changes in attentional requirements related to normal aging? Exp. Aging. Res. 22, 185–198 (1996)
61. Springer, S.: Dual-tasking effects on gait variability: the role of aging, falls, and executive function. Mov. Disord. 21, 950–957 (2006)
62. Yogev, G.: Dual tasking, gait rhythmicity, and Parkinson's disease: which aspects of gait are attention demanding? Eur. J. Neurosci. 22, 1248–1256 (2005)

63. Beauchet, O.: Stride-tostride variability while backward counting among healthy young adults. J. Neuroengineering Rehabil. 2, 26 (2005)
64. Sheridan, P.L.: Influence of executive function on locomotor function: divided attention increases gait variability in Alzheimer's disease. J. Am. Geriatr. Soc. 51, 1633–1637 (2003)
65. O'Shea, S.: Dual task interference during gait in people with Parkinson disease: effects of motor versus cognitive secondary tasks. Phys. Ther. 82(9), 888–897 (2002)
66. Alberto, N.: Dual task interference during gait in patients with unilateral vestibular disorders. Journal of Neuro Engineering and Rehabilitation 7, 47–52 (2010)
67. Marchese, R.: Effect of cognitive and motor tasks on postural stability in Parkinson's disease: a posturographic study. Movement Disorders 18(6), 652–658 (2003)
68. Camicioli, R.: Verbal fluency task affects gait in Parkinson's disease with motor freezing. J. Geriatr. Psychiatry Neurol. 11, 181–185 (1998)
69. Brown, R.G., Marsden, D.C.: Dual task performance and processing resources in normal subjects and patients with Parkinson's disease. Brain 114, 215–231 (1991)
70. Bond, J.M., Morris, M.: Goal-directed secondary motor tasks: their effects on gait in subjects with Parkinson disease. Arch. Phys. Med. Rehabil. 81, 110–116 (2000)
71. Maki, B.E., McIlroy, W.E.: Influence of arousal and attention on the control of postural sway. J. Vestib. Res. 6(1), 53–59 (1996)
72. Guertz, A.C.H.: Dual task assessment of reorganization in persons with lower limb amputation. Arch. Phys. Med. Rehabil. 72, 1059–1064 (1991)
73. Bootsma-van der Wiel, A.: Walking and talking as predictors of falls in the general population: the Leiden 85-plus study. J. Am. Geriatr. Soc. 51, 1466–1471 (2003)
74. Dubost, V.: Relationships between dual-task related changes in stride velocity and stride time variability in healthy older adults. Hum. Mov. Sci. 25, 372–382 (2006)
75. Van Iersel, M.B.: The effect of cognitive dual tasks on balance during walking in physically fit elderly people. Arch. Phys. Med. Rehabil 88, 187–191 (2007)
76. Beauchet, O.: Dual-task-related gait changes in the elderly: does the type of cognitive task matter? J. Mot. Behav. 37, 259–264 (2005)
77. Camicioli, R.: Verbal fluency task affects gait in Parkinson's disease with motor freezing. J. Geriatr Psychiatry Neurol. 11, 181–185 (1998)
78. Camicioli, R.: Verbal fluency task affects gait in Parkinson's disease with motor freezing. J. Geriatr. Psychiatry Neurol. 11, 181–185 (1998)
79. Bond, J.M., Morris, M.: Goal-directed secondary motor tasks: their effects on gait in subjects with Parkinson disease. Arch. Phys. Med. Rehabil. 81, 110–116 (2000)
80. Canning, C.G.: The effect of directing attention during walking under dual-task conditions in Parkinson's disease. Parkinsonism Relat. Disord. 11, 95–99 (2005)
81. Rochester, L.: The effect of external rhythmic cues (auditory and visual) on walking during a functional task in homes of people with Parkinson's disease. Arch. Phys. Med. Rehabil. 86, 999–1006 (2005)
82. Yang, Y.R., Chen, Y.C., Lee, C.S., Cheng, S.J., Wang, R.Y.: Dual-task related gait changes in individuals with stroke. Gait Posture 25, 185–190 (2007)
83. Stelmach, G.E., Zelaznik, H.N., Lowe, D.: The influence of aging and attentional demands on recovery from postural instability. Aging 2, 155–161 (1990)
84. Ashburn, A.: A community-dwelling sample of people with Parkinson's disesase: characteristics of fallers and non-fallers. Age and Ageing 30(1), 47–52 (2001)
85. Schmit, J.: Deterministic center of pressure patterns characterize postural instability in Parkinson's disease. Experimental Brain Research 168(3), 357–367 (2006)

86. Burkow-Heikkinen, L.: Non-invasive physiological monitoring of exercise and fitness. Neurological Research 33(1), 3–17 (2011)
87. Schepers, H.M.: Ambulatory assessment of human body kinematics and kinetics, PhD Thesis, Universiteit Twente (June 2009)
88. Bilney, B.: Concurrent related validity of the GAITRite walkway system for quantification of the spatial and temporal parameters of gait. Gait & Posture 17, 68–74 (2003)
89. McDonough, A.L.: The validity and reliability of the GAITRite system's measurements: A preliminary evaluation. Archives of Physical Medicine and Rehabilitation 82, 419–425 (2001)
90. Orr, R.J., Abowd, G.D.: The smart floor: A mechanism for natural user identification and tracking. In: Proceedings of the Conference on Human Factors in Computing Systems (2000)
91. Suutala, J., Rning, J.: Towards the adaptive identification of walkers: Automated feature selection of footsteps using distinction sensitive LVQ. In: Int. Workshop on Processing Sensory Information for Proactive Systems, June 14-15 (2004)
92. Lee, M.: A floor sensor system for gait recognition. In: Fourth IEEE Workshop on Automatic Identification Advanced Technologies, pp. 171–176 (2005)
93. Clarkson, B.H.: Absorbent paper method for recording foot placement during gait: suggestion from the field. Phys. Ther. 63, 345–346 (1983)
94. Wilkinson, M.J., Menz, H.B.: Measurement of gait parameters from footprints: a reliability study. Foot 7, 19–23 (1997)
95. Maki, B.E.: Gait changes in older adults: predictors of falls or indicators of fear. J. Am. Geriatr. Soc. 45, 313–320 (1997)
96. McIlroy, W.E., Norrie, R.G., Brooke, J.D., Bishop, D.C., Nelson, A.J., Maki, B.E.: Temporal properties of attention sharing consequent to disturbed balance. NeuroReport 10, 2895–2899 (1999)
97. Rankin, J.K.: A neuromuscular analysis of the influence of a cognitive task on postural stability in young and older adults. J. Gerontol A Biol. Sci. Med. Sci. 55(3), M112–M119 (2000)
98. Ferrucci, L.: Disease severity and health-related quality of life across different chronic conditions. Journal of the American Geriatrics Society 48, 1490–1495 (2000)
99. Maki, B.E.: Gait changes in older adults: predictors of falls or indicators of fear. Journal of the American Geriatrics Society 45, 313–320 (1997)
100. Yogev, G.: Dual tasking, gait rhythmicity, and Parkinson's disease: which aspects of gait are attention demanding? Eur. J. Neurosci. 22(5), 1248–1256 (2005)
101. Springer, S.: Dual-tasking effects on gait variability: the role of aging, falls, and executive function. Mov. Disord. 21(7), 950–957 (2006)
102. Winter, D.A., Patla, A.E., Frank, J.S., Walt, S.E.: Biomechanical walking pattern changes in the fit and healthy elderly. Phys. Ther. 70, 340–347 (1990)
103. Hollman, J.H.: Age-related differences in stride-to-stride variability during dual task walking: a pilot study. J. Geriatr. Phys. Ther. 27(3), 83–87 (2004)
104. Hausdorff, J.M.: Effects of cognitive challenge on gait variability in patients with Parkinson's disease. J. Geriatr. Psychiatry Neurol. 16(1), 53–58 (2003)
105. Hausdorff, J.M.: Impaired regulation of stride variability in Parkinson's disease subjects with freezing of gait. Exp. Brain Res. 149(2), 187–194 (2003)
106. Sheridan, P.L.: Influence of executive function on locomotor function: divided attention increases gait variability in Alzheimer's disease. J. Am. Geriatr. Soc. 51(11), 1633–1637 (2003)

107. Beauchet, O.: Dualtask- related gait changes in the elderly: does the type of cognitive task matter? J. Mot. Behav. 37(4), 259–264 (2005)
108. Menz, H.B., Lord, S.R., Fitzpatrick, R.C.: Age-related differences in walking stability. Age and Ageing 32, 137–142 (2003)
109. Beauchet, O.: Age-related decline of gait control under a dual-task condition. J. Am. Geriatr. Soc. 51(8), 1187–1188 (2003)
110. Beauchet, O.: Age-related decline of gait control under a dual-task condition. Journal Am. Geriatr. Soc. 51(8), 1187–1188 (2003)
111. Grabiner, P.C., Biswas, S.T., Grabiner, M.D.: Age-related changes in spatial and temporal gait variables. Arch. Phys. Med. Rehabil. 82(1), 31–35 (2001)
112. Nakamura, T., Meguro, K., Sasaki, H.: Relationship between falls and stride length variability in senile dementia of the Alzheimer type. Gerontology 42(2), 108–113 (1996)

Recognizing Individual Sib in the Case of Siblings with Gait Biometric

W. Noorshahida Mohd-Isa, Junaidi Abdullah, Jahangir Alam, and Chikkanan Eswaran

Faculty of Information Technology, Multimedia University, 63100 Cyberjaya, Selangor, Malaysia
{noorsha,junaidi,md.jahangir.alam,eswaran}@mmu.edu.my

Abstract. Gait is another potential human biometrics to look into whenever face recognition fails in video-based systems as is the case with siblings that have similar faces. We perform analyses on 10 pairs of siblings where their faces are assumed to have similarities. Our gait features are the angular displacement trajectories of walking individuals. We apply smoothing with the Bezier polynomial in our root-finding algorithm for accurate gait cycle extraction. Then, we apply classification using two different classifiers; the linear discriminant analysis (LDA) and the *k*-nearest neighbour (*k*NN). The best average correct classification rate (CCR) is 100% with a city-block distance *k*NN classifier. Hence, it is suggested that in the case where face recognition fails, gait may be the better alternative for biometric identification.

Keywords: gait as a biometric, siblings/twins biometric, face similarity, Bezier smoothing, root-finding algorithm.

1 Motivation

Siblings are defined to be a number of individuals who share at least a parent by blood. They are genetically defined to have features from the parent/parents of whom they share. However each human is a unique individual, hence some features do uniquely belong to the individual sib in addition to some shared features. As for biometrics identification, fingerprints have been shown to be the unique identifier of each individual as is true in the case of siblings and twins. However, the faces of siblings are most of the times said to be almost similar; sometimes very similar in the cases of twins. Gait is a new biometric based on the way human walks. It has many advantages for use in video-based recognition systems, where face recognition may fail as in the case of siblings with almost similar faces and twins.

A gait recognition system may overcome the drawbacks arisen from other biometric recognition systems. In video-based recognition systems, the face seems to be seen as the biometric feature suitable for use as has been shown in much research [1] [2] [3] [4] [5]. However, when an individual face is covered or almost similar, as in the case of siblings or twins, a face recognition system may fail. On top of that, illumination changes (as in daylight, shadows) may affect the ability of the camera to

A. Abd Manaf et al. (Eds.): ICIEIS 2011, Part III, CCIS 253, pp. 112–122, 2011.

capture the features of an individual face in detail, which is highly required for recognizing a face. As opposed to face, gait is extracted by looking at its motion; hence it can be captured at low resolution when common closed-circuit cameras (CCTVs) are used. Also, a person's gait is difficult to conceal; it comes naturally to a person. In fact an individual who walks awkwardly may be oblivious to his/her surroundings where suspicions may be likely. Gait is non-invasive and cooperation of individuals is not a requisite making its system suitable for surveillance purpose.

Gait is believed to be unique to every person [6] and every person is said to have their own idiosyncratic ways of walking. Research in this domain has begun for more than 15 years ago and most research on gait focuses on looking into the features that make gait uniquely identifiable [7], [8], [9], [10] [11]. Also, there is numerous research on multimodal biometrics of face and gait that may suggest gait to be the complement of a face recognition system [12], [13], [14], [15]. In such settings, gait may either be used for recognition in parallel to face recognition system or as the alternative to face after a face recognition system fails. However, as in the usage of latter, there has never been a study on gait of twins where their faces may most definitely lead to the failure of the face recognition system, let alone a study on siblings with almost similar faces. With fraud cases on the rise as an example is the case of the Canseco brothers [16], where the twin brother was sent to box on behalf of the other, a research such as this may be useful. Especially when knowing cooperation is highly unlikely from these guys, meaning getting their fingerprints may be impossible. Gait may have been a useful identifier between these pair when they walk into the ring.

Thus far we have not found any research on siblings or twins study on gait. A study on multi biometrics recognition of twins has been performed in [17] aiming at identifying impostors through twins, and the usage of soft biometrics to enhanced face recognition [18]. Their works have shown results on irises, faces and fingerprints recognition of twins; nothing on gait. These data are gathered during an Annual Twin Fair in China. Several samples of twins are collected and analyses performed for recognition. The results show that fingerprints of twins are unique, as has been expected. Irises results show differentiability in twins. However, as anticipated, faces of twins have so much similarity, where a face recognition system may likely to fail.

Actually we faced difficulty in getting twins to participate in our study; hence the investigation is changed to a study of non twins (siblings) with the assumption that they may share similar face features. This is consistent with genealogy study on establishing family links, building family trees, and maintaining family heritage research as described here [19]. A project, known as 'myheritage' uses face similarity scores to establish blood-ties, where a score of 80% or more indicates a higher chance that the two persons are related. We put this assumption that due to sharing the similar face feature, it may lead a face recognition system to failure, where gait may be the biometrics to capture in such case.

This paper is laid out as follows: part 2 explains the data that we use; the data requirements and how they are collected including the description of the extracted features. Part 3 describes the methodology used to analyze the data. Here we will be describing the cycle extraction algorithm via root-finding using local Bezier polynomial smoothing. Also the classifiers used are mentioned here. In Part 4, we present the results with discussions. We conclude the work in Part 5 and lay out potential future works that may be attempted by us and others.

2 The Data

Our data are raw videos of 10 pairs of siblings, where they are young adults, aged between 18-28 years of age. This ensures an invariant analysis against age, since gait changes with age as has been shown by research within the rehabilitation and psychological domain [20]. Also, to ensure invariability against body weight; the subjects are having weights within the range of 'healthy' BMI (Body Mass Index). This carefully establishes a better height-to-weight ratio rather than just relying on weight measure alone. Additionally if we have male-female pair of siblings, the male ones tends to be taller than their female sibs.

The experimental setup requires an indoor setting, a homogeneous colour background with a defined straight path walkway. The video camera is fixed at a horizontal view to the walkway to enable all subjects to be captured sideways at their full heights. The walkway distance within the camera view is set to record at least two gait cycles. The subjects then walk at normal pace, with flat shoes and are not allowed to carry any objects while their gaits are recorded. To establish invariant walking on each leg, they have to be recorded walking from left side of the walkway to the right side of the walkway and vice versa. The previously described procedures follow the setup of other gait recognition databases [21].

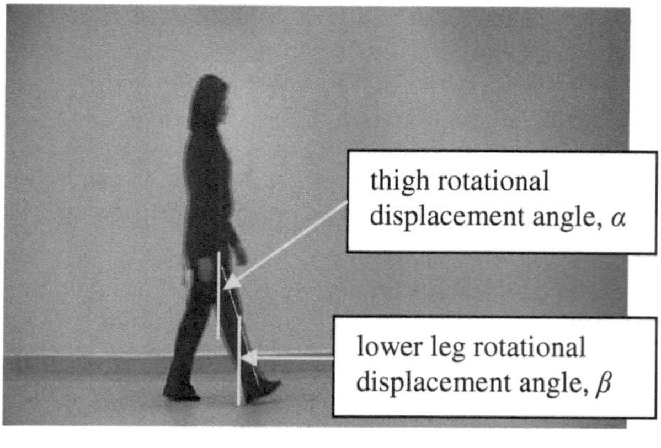

Fig. 1. Extracted features of interest; α (*thigh rotational displacement angle*) and β (*lower leg rotational displacement angle*)

Data that we gather are the angular displacements of the limbs while moving. This follows the successful recognition of gait on individuals by previous research [22] [23] [24]. By tracking the person's leg frame by frame, the features of interest are extracted and the angular measurements are calculated. They are the thigh angular displacement angles and lower leg displacement angles. The former measures the rotational angle for the thigh from side to side and the latter measures the rotational angle for the lower leg from side to side as shown in Fig. 1. The two measurements make up two separate signals' samples, α and β, to represent each individual as below:

Given a video of an individual, i we let L_i be the lengths of α and β with respect to time instance $t_{[n]}$, as

$$\boldsymbol{\alpha}_i = \alpha(t_{[n]}) \qquad \alpha \in \left[-\pi/2, \pi/2\right]^{L_i} \tag{1}$$

$$\boldsymbol{\beta}_i = \beta(t_{[n]}) \qquad \beta \in \left[-\pi/2, \pi/2\right]^{L_i} \tag{2}$$

The forward movement of the leg is assigned positive values and vice versa. The midpoints of α and β, at 0° is when the foot of the tracked leg falls flat on the ground, we call this position as "at vertical".

3 Methodology

3.1 Cycle Extraction

Due to differences in walking speeds for each individual, the lengths of L_i vary for each individual. To establish invariance to the walking speed, a cycle extraction procedure is performed to ensure a robust analysis. A complete gait cycle as defined by Murray [6] starts from a heel-strike of one leg and ends at the heel-strike of the same leg as shown in Fig. 2. The definition states that there are two steps in a gait cycle. Research in previous literature has been following this definition in their analyses. Due to the ambiguity in determining the time of heel-strike, we extract gait cycles beginning from the vertical of the individual to the successive vertical position (within two steps) as illustrated in Fig. 3.

Fig. 2. A *complete gait cycle* as defined by Murray with two *heel-strikes of the right leg* [4]

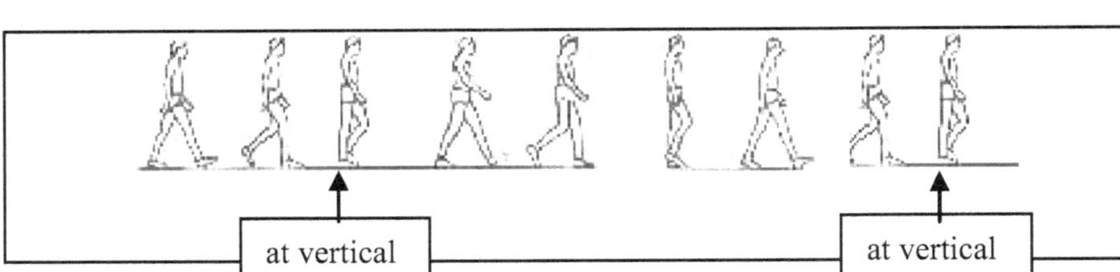

Fig. 3. Our proposed gait cycle extraction that starts from the individual to be *at vertical* and the successive *at vertical* position

The vertical positions can be found by locating the roots of the α and β signals. In this paper, we propose a root finding algorithm based on solving Bezier polynomials with $O(n)$ efficiency. Bezier polynomials are smoothing splines that have been used widely in the area of computer graphics [25]. The algorithm is described below:

```
Algorithm Bezier_Roots_Finding
 Input: α and β
 Output: root, τ

 Initialization of flag:
   if α[n] < 0, then
     flag = 0;
   else
     flag = 1;

 Loop:
   for each value n of α[n >= 2], do
       set diff = (α[n] - α[n-2]);

     if diff < 0 and flag = 1, then
       change flag = 0;
       solve Bezier;
     else if diff > 0 and flag = 0, then
       change flag = 1;
       solve Bezier;

     end if
   end for

return root.
```

The `solve Bezier` program finds the root, t by solving the Bezier polynomials. In this algorithm, the Bezier polynomials fit a smooth line between two endpoints whilst ensuring that the line to be fitted falls between and directionally follows two other control points. The four points required are the angle and time values of α and β at time instances $[n-2]$, $[n-1]$, $[n]$, and $[n+1]$. The $[n-2]$ and $[n-1]$ are values from one phase and the $[n]$ and $[n+1]$ are values representing the other phase. The two phases can either be between two peaks or two troughs of the signals characterized by the opening and closing of the legs while walking. The endpoints are the values at $[n-2]$ and $[n+1]$ and the other two are the control points. The mathematical formulation for α is shown next; the same formulation applies to β signals.

Given four time instances with their corresponding angle values$\left(\alpha_{[n-2]}, t_{[n-2]}\right)$, $\left(\alpha_{[n-1]}, t_{[n-1]}\right)$, $\left(\alpha_{[n]}, t_{[n]}\right)$, and $\left(\alpha_{[n+1]}, t_{[n+1]}\right)$, the Bezier polynomials are defined for $0 \leq \tau \leq 1$ as,

$$t(\tau) = t_{[n-2]} + b_t\tau + c_t\tau^2 + d_t\tau^3 \quad (3)$$

$$\alpha(\tau) = \alpha_{[n-2]} + b_\alpha\tau + c_\alpha\tau^2 + d_\alpha\tau^3 \quad (4)$$

where,

$$b_t = 3(t_{[n]} - t_{[n-2]})$$
$$c_t = 3(t_{[n]} - t_{[n-1]}) - b_t$$
$$d_t = t_{[n+1]} - t_{[n]} - b_t - c_t$$
$$b_\alpha = 3(\alpha_{[n]} - \alpha_{[n-2]})$$
$$c_\alpha = 3(\alpha_{[n]} - \alpha_{[n-1]}) - b_\alpha$$
$$d_\alpha = \alpha_{[n+1]} - \alpha_{[n]} - b_\alpha - c_\alpha$$

Solving for Eq. 3, three τ values can be found. However only real τ values within $0 \le \tau \le 1$ are considered and substituted into Eq. 4 to get τ. By setting $\alpha(\tau) = 0$, the actual root, t for each signal can be found.

Then a gait cycle is extracted between successive roots and resampled to $m = 25$ number of points as in Fig.4 and Fig.5. The α and β signals are concatenated to become a long feature vector and further analyzed using the linear discriminant analysis (LDA) and *k*-nearest neighbor (*k*NN) classifiers. These classifiers are standard classifiers and have been performing well for small sample problem in gait recognition research [22] [23] [24].

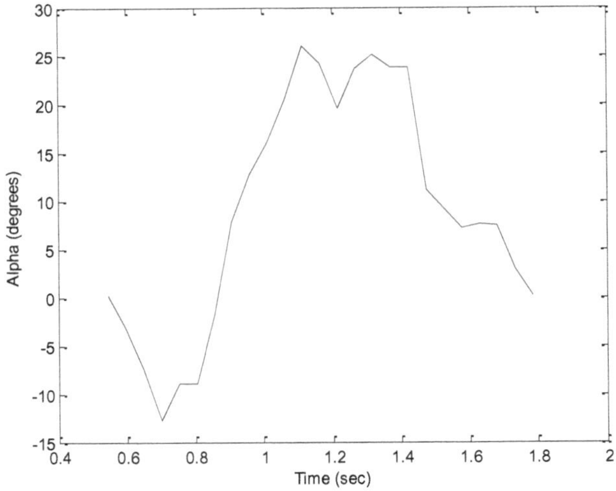

Fig. 4. A *complete gait cycle* extraction for an α signal

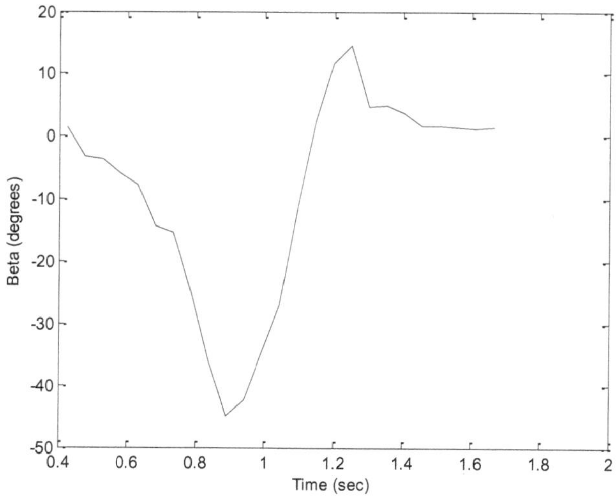

Fig. 5. A *complete gait cycle* extraction for a β signal

3.2 Linear Discriminant Analysis Classifier

LDA is a statistical transformational technique that aims to discriminate each class by deriving linear functions of the class' attributes. The linear functions are linear combinations of the independent features; in this paper, these are the α and β. Fisher, the innovator of LDA introduces a ratio that simultaneously maximizes the between class variance, $\mathbf{S_b}$ and minimizes the within class variance, $\mathbf{S_w}$ via solving an eigen equation, as below:

$$\mathbf{S_w}^{-1}\mathbf{S_b}\mathbf{v}_i = \lambda_i \mathbf{v}_i \tag{5}$$

where λ_i are the eigenvalues of the ratio, $\mathbf{S_w}^{-1}\mathbf{S_b}$ and $\mathbf{v}_i$ are the orthogonal eigenvectors that spans a $(C_T - 1)$-dimensional space with C_T as the total number of classes and $\mathbf{v}_i$ form the transformed matrix $\mathbf{V}$. Hence the decision function for the transformed input signals $f(i) = \mathbf{V}^T i$ is when $f(i) = 0$, where $i = [\alpha_i\,;\beta_i]$.

3.3 *k*-Nearest Neighbour Classifier

In a *k*NN classifier, a test sample point is classified into a class, C_j based on its nearest distances to the *k* training sample points. The *k* distances create a pool of *k* class decisions that then form a class majority. The class majority determines the class, C_j, which the test sample point should belong to. Generally, the *k* value is odd and ranging from one to five in order to eliminate cases of ties. The distance measures used may make a difference in classification results. In this paper, we use the standard measures; the Euclidean (Eq. 6) and the City-Block Distance (Eq. 7).

$$d(test, train) = \sum_{\substack{train\\data}} |test - train| \tag{6}$$

$$d(test, train) = \sqrt{\sum_{\substack{train\\data}} (test - train)^2} \tag{7}$$

4 Results and Discussions

There are in total 80 samples of 20 subjects (10 pairs) with four samples each; two samples walking from left to right and right to left, respectively. We perform three analyses with 20-fold (Experiment 1), 10-fold (Experiment 2) and 19-fold (Experiment 3) cross validations to calculate the average CCR.

4.1 Experiment 1

This analysis tests the ability of the classifiers to identify the individual sib as a unique individual in a population of 20 classes. Table 1 summarizes the average CCR where it shows the average CCR when the test sample is tested for its individuality. With the *k*NN classifier, $k = 1$ and via City-Block distance, an individual gait may be recognized as unique with an average CCR of 95% as can be seen from Table 1. The next highest result is through classification via *k*NN classifier with Euclidean distance at 87.5%, and the LDA classifier gives out 75% average CCR. This result is consistent with previous psychological gait literatures [26] that shows an individual can be recognized by his/her friends, where, in this case the friend is the classifier that has been trained using the individual past samples.

Table 1. Average CCR in Identification of a Sib as an Individual

Classifiers	Average CCR (%)
LDA	75.00
5-NN via Euclidean	55.00
3-NN via Euclidean	65.00
1-NN via Euclidean	87.50
5-NN via City-Block	70.00
3-NN via City-Block	76.25
1-NN via City-Block	**95.00**

4.2 Experiment 2

Experiment 2 tests the ability of the classifiers to identify the individual sib as a part of a larger class (its own family members). Table 2 tabulates the result where it shows the best average CCR is 100% and it is the result of using the City-block distance measure from the *k*NN classifier. In this test, the test sample is tested across a population of 10 classes, which means each class has larger learned samples than in Experiment 1. The second highest result is the *k*NN with Euclidean distance at 98.75% followed by the LDA classifier with 97.5%.

Table 2. Average CCR in Identification of an Individual as a Sibling to another Sib

Classifiers	Average CCR (%)
LDA	97.50
5-NN via Euclidean	63.75
3-NN via Euclidean	68.75
1-NN via Euclidean	98.75
5-NN via City-Block	77.50
3-NN via City-Block	78.75
1-NN via City-Block	**100.00**

Additionally, it is apparent that the results of Table 2 are higher than those in Table 1. This is because the analysis of Table 2 works on larger samples for each class than the analysis in Table 1. That is, Table 2 considers samples of both siblings as one class as compared to analysis of Table 1 where there are only four samples per class.

Further, we investigate the results of both Experiment 1 and Experiment 2 by looking at its data distribution. As suspected, in both experiments, the one neighbour that the test sample successfully recognizes is its own other samples. This explains the high average CCR for a k = 1 neighbour with both Euclidean and City-Block measures as compared to the LDA classifier results. The LDA results for both analyses are 75% and 97.5%, respectively. This is because LDA calculates the CCR by considering the statistics of the training data population as opposed to the kNN classifier where it looks at the location of the data in space.

Also between k = 3 and k = 5, the CCR for the former is better than the latter in both analyses. At the same time, the CCR for both k(s) in Table 2 is higher than those in Table 1. These may be the consequence of the number of samples per class in these analyses. Hence, we may expect that the performance of the classifiers to drop as the number classes increase (the increase of sample population).

4.3 Experiment 3

We proceed with another run of classification experiment. In this analysis, we let the test sample to run only with its siblings' samples as the training samples of its class. That is, we remove all other samples of the test samples. Then, the dataset goes through the classifiers. The rational for doing this is to check if the test sample can be classified into its sibling's class. This analysis is a classification of a test sample into 19 classes. Table 3 shows the result.

Table 3. Average CCR in Identification of an Individual as a Sibling to another Sib with Its Own Sample Removed

Classifiers	Average CCR (%)
LDA	0.02
5-NN via Euclidean	**6.25**
3-NN via Euclidean	**6.25**
1-NN via Euclidean	**6.25**
5-NN via City-Block	**6.25**
3-NN via City-Block	3.75
1-NN via City-Block	5.00

In contrasts with the previous two experiments, the best average CCR is only 6.25% from a *k*NN classifier. Via Euclidean distance, all *k*(s) neighbours produce the same average CCR of 6.25%. As for the *k*NN with City-Block distance, the best is when $k = 5$, where it seems that the test sample distances are coming from the same neighbours as with the Euclidean *k*NN.

The LDA classifier gives the worst of 0.02% average CCR. When the data is checked, the covariance matrix is said to be non-positive definite. In statistics, it is said that the data is close to being singular, which means probably having no unique solution. In pattern recognition, it means that the test sample has not been able to be classified into any of the 19 classes.

The resultant low average CCR from this experiment is consistent with previous literatures that states gait to be unique for each individual [6].

5 Conclusions and Future Work

All of the experiments above have been performed to analyze the ability to use gait as a mean of biometric identification with the assumption that a learning machine may have its siblings (or twins) data learned beforehand. This analysis is especially useful when dealing with twins data, where a face recognition system may fail. In this paper, we have used data from 10 pairs of siblings, where we put the assumption that these siblings have shared face features that may lead to the failure of a face recognition system. We have shown that the gait of a sib cannot be classified into his/her sib's class since gait is unique. However, we have not managed to explicitly show if gait is unique between twins because of lack of data. Hence, we are currently gathering twins' data for further analysis.

References

1. Martinez, A.M., Kak, A.C.: PCA versus LDA. IEEE Trans. on Pattern Analysis and Machine Intelligence 23(2), 228–233 (2001)
2. Jain, A., Nandakumar, K., Rozz, A.: Score normalization in multimodal biometric systems. Pattern Recognition 38, 2270–2285 (2005)
3. Chang, K.I., Bowyer, K.W., Flynn, P.J.: An evaluation of multimodal 2D+3D face biometrics. IEEE Trans. on Pattern Analysis and Machine Intelligence 27(4), 619–624 (2005)
4. Yang, C.T., Lai, S., Chang, L.: Hybrid image matching combining Hausdorff distance with normalized gradient matching. Pattern Recognition 40, 1173–1181 (2007)
5. Aurora The Face of Biometric, `http://www.facerec.com/`
6. Murray, M.P.: Gait as a total pattern of movement. American Journal of Physical Medicine 46(1), 290–332 (1967)
7. Bhanu, B., Han, J.: Human Recognition on Combining Kinematic and Stationary Features. In: Kittler, J., Nixon, M.S. (eds.) AVBPA 2003. LNCS, vol. 2688, pp. 600–608. Springer, Heidelberg (2003)
8. Nixon, M.S., Carter, J.N.: Automatic recognition by gait. Proceedings of the IEEE 94(11), 2013–2024 (2006)

9. Boyd, J.E., Little, J.J.: Biometric Gait Recognition. In: Tistarelli, M., Bigun, J., Grosso, E. (eds.) Advanced Studies in Biometrics. LNCS, vol. 3161, pp. 19–42. Springer, Heidelberg (2005)
10. Boulgouris, N.V., Hatzinakos, D., Plataniotis, K.N.: Gait recognition: A challenging signal processing technology for biometric identification. IEEE Signal Processing Magazine 22(6), 78–90 (2005)
11. Huang, K., Tan, T.: Vs-star: A visual interpretation system for visual surveillance. Pattern Recognition Letters 31(14), 2265–2285 (2010)
12. Pala, K.I., Bowyer, K.W., Flynn, P.J.: An evaluation of multimodal 2D+3D face biometrics. IEEE Trans. on Pattern Analysis and Machine Intelligence 27(4), 619–624 (2005)
13. Burton, A.M., Wilson, S., Cowan, M., et al.: Face recognition in poor quality videos: Evidence from security surveillance. Psychological Science 10(3), 243–248 (1999)
14. Hu, W.M., Tan, T.N., Wang, L., et al.: A survey on visual surveillance of object motion and behaviors. IEEE Trans. on Systems Man and Cybernetics Part C-Applications and Reviews 34(3), 334–352 (2004)
15. Zhang, T., Li, X., Tao, D., et al.: Multimodal biometrics using geometry preserving projections. Pattern Recognition 41(3), 805–813 (2008)
16. Jose Canseco gets punchy, sends twin brother to fight in his place, `http://sports.yahoo.com/mlb/blog/big_league_stew/post/Jose-Canseco-gets-punchy-sends-twin-brother-to-?urn=mlb-wp1507`
17. Sun, Z., Paulino, A.A., Feng, J., et al.: A study on multibiometric traits of identical twins. In: Proc. Conference on Biometric Technology for Human Identification VII, vol. 7667 (2010)
18. Park, U., Jain, A.K.: Face matching and retrieval using soft biometrics. IEEE Trans. on Information Forensics and Security 5(3), 406–415 (2010)
19. My Heritage, `http://www.myheritage.com/genealogy`
20. Grieve, D.W., Gear, R.J.: The relationship between length of stride and step frequency, time of swing and speed of walking in children and adults. Ergonomics 14(5), 379–399 (1966)
21. Automatic Gait Recognition for Human ID at a Distance, `http://www.gait.ecs.soton.ac.uk/`
22. Yam, C.Y., Nixon, M.S., Carter, J.N.: Automated person recognition by walking and running via model-based approaches. Pattern Recognition 37(5), 1057–1072 (2004)
23. Huang, P.S.: Automatic gait recognition via statistical approaches for extended template features. IEEE Trans. on Systems Man and Cybernetics Part B-Cybernetics 31(5), 818–824 (2001)
24. Bouchrika, I., Nixon, M.S.: Gait recognition by dynamic cues. In: Proc 19th International Conference on Pattern Recognition (ICPR), pp. 189–192 (2008)
25. Yamaguchi, F.: Curves and Surfaces in Computer-aided Geometric Design. Springer, New York (1998)
26. Cutting, J.E., Kozlowski, L.T.: Recognizing friends by their walk: Gait perception without familiarity clues. Bulletin of Psychonomic Society 9(5), 353–356 (1977)

Communications in Computer and Information Science: Diagnosis of Diabetes Using Intensified Fuzzy Verdict Mechanism

A.V. Senthil Kumar[1] and M. Kalpana[2]

[1] Department of MCA,
Hindusthan College of Arts & Science, Behind Nava India,
Coimbatore 641028, Tamil Nadu, India
[2] Department of Physical Science and Information Technology,
Agricultural Engineering College and Research Institute,
Tamil Nadu Agricultural University, Coimbatore 641 003, Tamil Nadu, India
{avsenthilkumar,kalpusiva}@gmail.com

Abstract. The use of Fuzzy Expert System has highly increased in the field of medicine, to diagnosis the illness of patient pursuit. By applying the intensified fuzzy verdict mechanism the diagnosis of diabetes becomes simple for medical practitioners. The intensified fuzzy verdict mechanism consists of fuzzy inference, implication and aggregation. For the diagnosis of diabetes, knowledge are represented in the form of fuzzification to convert crisp values into fuzzy values. This mechanism, contains set of rules with fuzzy operators. Defuzzification method is adopted to convert the fuzzy values into crisp values. In this paper, intensified fuzzy verdict mechanism is proposed to complete the knowledge representation and the inference model for diabetes data. The result of the proposed methods is compared with earlier method using accuracy as metrics. This mechanism is focused on increasing the accuracy and quality of knowledge for diabetes application.

Keywords: Fuzzy Expert System, Intensified Fuzzy Verdict Mechanism, Fuzzification, Diabetes application.

1 Introduction

Campos-Delgado et al. [1] developed fuzzy logic controller to regulate the blood glucose level that incorporates expert knowledge by using mamdani-type fuzzy logic.

Magni and Bellazzi [2] devised a methodology useful in variety of clinical contexts. The proposed model uses stochastic model to extract time course variability from a self-monitoring blood sugar level time series. Polat and Gunes [3] designed an expert system to diagnose the diabetes disease based on principal component analysis which improves the diagnostic accuracy of diabetes disease. Polat et al. [4] to diagnose the diabetes a cascade learning system based on generalized discriminant analysis and least square support vector machine is developed. Chang and Lilly [5] developed an evolutionary approach to derive a compact fuzzy classification system directly from data without any prior knowledge or assumptions on the distribution of

A. Abd Manaf et al. (Eds.): ICIEIS 2011, Part III, CCIS 253, pp. 123–135, 2011.

the data. Goncalves et al. [6] introduced an inverted hierarchical neuro-fuzzy BSP system for pattern classification and rule extraction in databases. Kahramanli and Allahverdi [7] designed a classification of the diabetes database for hybrid neural network system to increase the reliability of the result. Chang-Shing Lee [8] designed as fuzzy expert system for diabetes decision support application based on fuzzy decision making mechanism which simulates the semantic description of medical staff for diabetes. Ismail saritas et al.[9] developed a fuzzy expert system to determine drug dose in treatment of chronic interstine inflamation using the concept of fuzzification, fuzzy inference mechanism and defuzzification. The fuzzy expert system designed can be applied in complex and uncertain fields such as the treatment of illness, to determine the exact dose of medicine and evaluate clinic and laboratory data. Mehdi Fasanghari et al.[10] developed a fuzzy expert system for Tehran stock exchange using the concept of fuzzification. The American Diabetes Association [11] categorizes diabetes into type-1 diabetes, which is normally diagnosed in children and young adults, and type-2 diabetes, i.e., the most common form of diabetes that originates from a progressive insulin secretory defect so that the body does not produce adequate insulin or the insulin does not affect the cells. M. Kalpana and A. V Senthikumar [12] developed fuzzy expert system using fuzzy verdict mechanism for diabetes application using the concept of fuzzification using triangular membership function. Diabetes treatment focuses on controlling blood sugar levels to prevent various symptoms and complications through medicine, diet and exercise.

The Fuzzy Expert system developed helps to solve many challenging task in the field of medicine. The intensified fuzzy verdict mechanism gives the description for diabetes and support for the justification of the medical practitioners. The structure of the rest of this paper is as follows: Section 2 deals with the architecture of fuzzy expert system. The experimental results, implemented in MATLAB are presented in Section 3 and experimental results indicate that the proposed fuzzy expert system can work more effectively than other methods can [3], [5], [7],[8],[12] in section 4.

2 Fuzzy Expert System for Diabetes Application

This section describes a fuzzy expert system, including a Fuzzification, Intensified Fuzzy verdict mechanism for diabetes application and Defuzzification.

2.1 Pima Indians Diabetes Database

The National Institute of Diabetes and Digestive and Kidney Diseases (NIDDK) [14] has examined the Pima Indians Diabetes Database. This Database has one of the highest known rates of diabetes worldwide. The experimental PIDD is retrieved from the Internet (http://archive.ics.uci.edu/ml/) and it contains the collected personal data of the Pima Indian population. Table 1 lists the attributes of PIDD.

2.2 Architecture of the Fuzzy Expert System for Diabetes Application

Fuzzy expert system is the representation of the process in terms of fuzzy variables and fuzzy rules construction. Fuzzy concept is to transfer the information of the PIDD into the required knowledge. For the PIDD, each case has nine attributes, listed in Table 1, and each attribute can be constructed as a fuzzy variable with some fuzzy numbers. The relationship in the PIDD with respect to age is given in Table 2. The Architecture of the Fuzzy Expert System for diabetes application is given in Figure 1.

Table 1. Atttributes of PIDD

Abbreviation	Fullname	Units
Pregnant	Number of times pregnant	-
Glucose	Plasma glucose concentration in 2-hours OGTT	mg/dl
DBP	Diastolic blood pressure	mmHg
TSFT	Triceps skin fold thickness	mm
INS	2-hour serum insulin	mu U/ml
BMI	Body mass index	Kg/m^2
DPF	Diabetes pedigree function	-
Age	Age	-
DM	Diabetes Mellitus where '1' is interpreted as "tested positive for diabetes"	-

Table 2. Description of Fuzzy Relation

Fuzzy Relation	Description
RE≥FU(Age0_25)	Very Very Young
RE≥FU(Age25_30)	Very Young
RE≥FU(Age30_35)	More or Less Young
RE≥FU(Age35_40)	Slightly Young
RE≥FU(Age40_45)	Slightly Old
RE≥FU(Age45_50)	More or Less Old
RE≥FU(Age50_55)	Very Old
RE≥FU(Age55_60)	Very Very Old

2.3 Data Preparation

The data are taken from PIDD, the input variable are Plasma glucose concentration in 2-hours OGTT(Glucose), 2-hour serum insulin(INS), Body mass index(BMI), Diabetes pedigree function(DPF), Age(Age) and the output variable are Diabetes Mellitus(DM). The data with the age group from 25-30 are taken to test the Intensified Fuzzy Verdict Mechanism.

2.4 Fuzzification

Fuzzification simply refers to the process of taking a crisp input value and transforming it into the degree required by the terms[10]. If the form of uncertainty happens to arise because of imprecision, ambiguity, or vagueness, the variable is probably fuzzy and can be represented by a membership function.

Based on the constructed fuzzy concepts, the fuzzy numbers are built by the fuzzy relationship. Additionally, an interface is offered to tune and validate the parameters of the built fuzzy numbers. In this paper a triangular function as shown in (1) is adopted as the membership function of the fuzzy number and can be expressed as the parameter set[a,b,c]. The parameter is fixed with Minimum value, Mean, Standard Deviation, Maximum value for each variable. Then the membership function μ (x) of the triangular fuzzy number[13] is given by

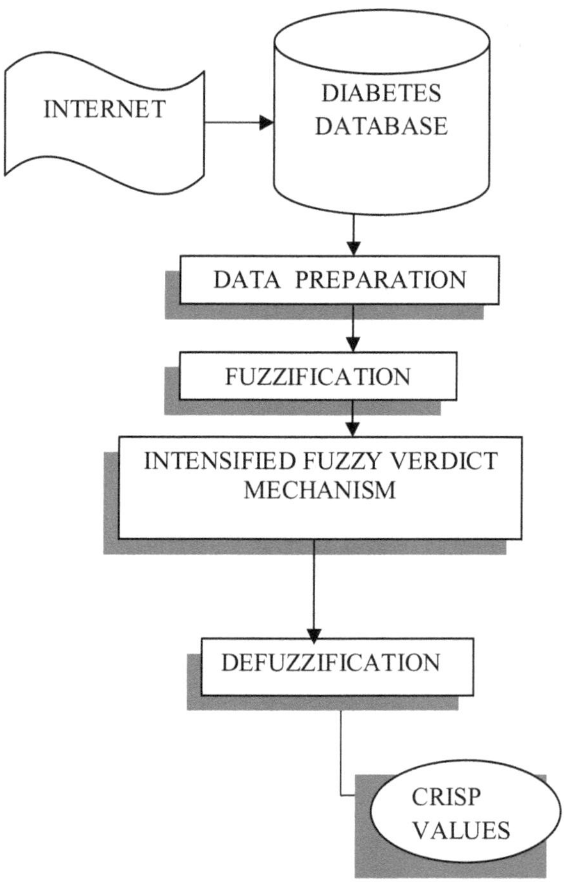

Fig. 1. Architecture of the Fuzzy Expert System for diabetes application

$$\mu(x)=\begin{cases}0, x \leq a \\ (x-a)/(b-a), a < x \leq b \\ (c-x)/(c-b), b < x < c \\ 0, x > c\end{cases} \tag{1}$$

The PIDD is first retrieved from the Internet to become the experimental database. By fuzzification the crisp input values, its membership values and degrees are obtained. These obtained fuzzy values are processed in intensified fuzzy verdict mechanism. Here, the output values which are also obtained by using rule-base are send to defuzzification unit and from this unit the final crisp values are obtained as output[9]. The fuzzy values are given in Figure 2 and Figure 3.

The input fuzzy value Glucose (let x), that varies from 71 to 196, the fuzzy expression will be

$$\mu_{low}(x)=\begin{cases}\frac{71-x}{71}; 71 \leq x \leq 121.27 \\ 0; otherwise\end{cases}$$

$$\mu_{medium}(x)=\begin{cases}\frac{121.27}{x}; 71 \leq x \leq 121.27 \\ \frac{196-x}{121.27}; 117 \leq x \leq 196 \\ 0; otherwise\end{cases} \tag{2}$$

$$\mu_{high}(x)=\begin{cases}0; x < 121.27 \\ \frac{x-121.27}{121.27}; 121.27 \leq x \leq 196 \\ 1; otherwise\end{cases}$$

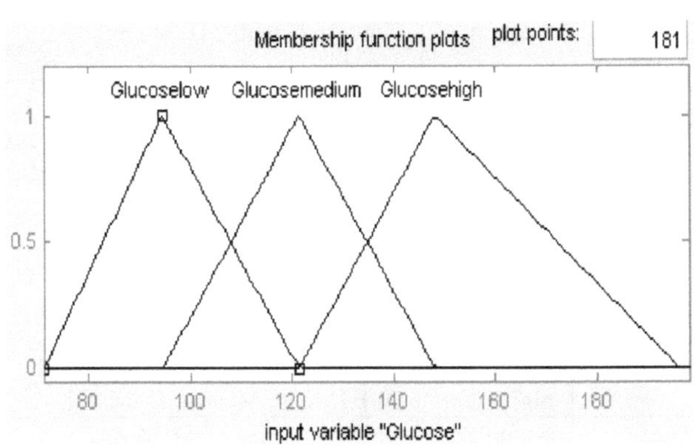

Fig. 2. Membership graphics for the fuzzy three values Glucose

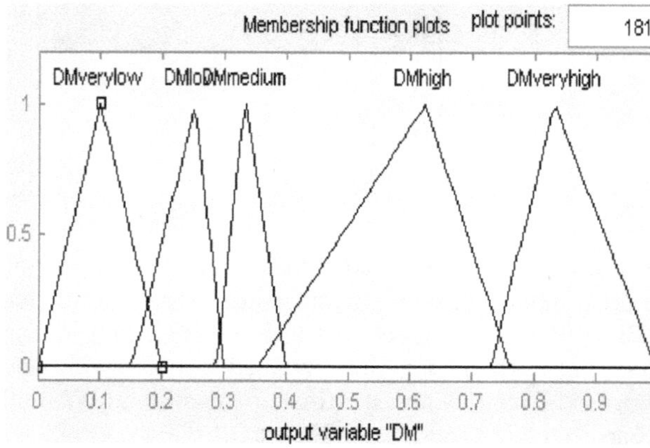

Fig. 3. Membership graphics for the fuzzy values DM

2.5 Intensified Fuzzy Verdict Mechanism

The Intensified Fuzzy Verdict Mechanism separately infers the possibility of individual developing diabetes for each instance in fuzzification and transfers the possibility into the form of statement. According to the American Diabetes Association [11], diabetes is associated with obesity, family history and age. Additionally, the American Diabetes Association also indicates that the 2-hour OGTT with measurement of plasma glucose and serum insulin concentrations are used as the criteria for diagnosing diabetes. Consequently, five attributes, i.e., Glucose, INS, BMI, DPF, and Age, are selected as the input fuzzy variables for the adopted intensified fuzzy verdict mechanism; in addition, the related information about fuzzy numbers is stored in the fuzzification. The parameters of the fuzzy numbers are listed in Table 3 and Table 4.

Table 3. Default constructed Fuzzy Numbers

Fuzzy Numbers	Fuzzy Numbers	Fuzzy triangular numbers
Glucose	low	Glucose[Min, Mean-SD, Mean]
	medium	Glucose [Mean-SD, Mean, Mean+SD]
	high	Glucose [Mean, Mean+SD, Max]
INS	low	INS [Min, Mean-SD, Mean]
	medium	INS [Mean-SD, Mean, Mean+SD]
	high	INS [Mean, Mean+SD, Max]
BMI	low	BMI [Min, Mean-SD, Mean]
	medium	BMI [Mean-SD, Mean, Mean+SD]
	high	BMI [Mean, Mean+SD, Max]
DPF	low	DPF [Min, Mean-SD, Mean]
	medium	DPF [Mean-SD, Mean, Mean+SD]
	high	DPF [Mean, Mean+SD, Max]
Age	young	Age [Min, Mean-SD, Mean]
	medium	Age [Mean-SD, Mean, Mean+SD]
	old	Age [Mean, Mean+SD, Max]

Table 4. Parameters of Triangular Membership Functions

Fuzzy Numbers	Fuzzy Numbers	Fuzzy triangular numbers
Glucose	low	[71 94.41 121.27]
	medium	[94.41 121.27 148.12]
	high	[121.27 148.12 196]
INS	low	[0 15.16 89.82]
	medium	[15.16 89.82 194.81]
	high	[89.82 194.81 579]
BMI	low	[0 24.46 33.24]
	medium	[24.46 33.24 42.03]
	high	[33.24 42.03 67.1]
DPF	low	[0.13 0.21 0.44]
	medium	[0.21 0.44 0.67]
	high	[0.44 0.67 0.96]
Age	young	[26 26 27]
	medium	[26 27 29]
	old	[27 29 30]
DM	verylow	[0 0.1 0.2]
	low	[0.1524 0.2524 0.3]
	medium	[0.287 0.333 0.3997]
	high	[0.355 0.623 0.762]
	veryhigh	[0.731 0.831 1]

The fuzzy variable Glucose has three fuzzy numbers, i.e., *Glucoselow*, *Glucosemedium*, and *Glucosehigh*. For the fuzzy variable INS, fuzzy concepts and knowledge of the 2-hour serum insulin are expressed in human communication by using the fuzzy numbers *INSlow*, *INSmedium*, and *INShigh*. The membership functions of BMI also have three fuzzy numbers, i.e., *BMIlow*, *BMImedium*, and *BMIhigh*. The fuzzy numbers *DPFlow*, *DPFmedium*, and *DPFhigh* are defined for the fuzzy variable DPF. The membership functions of the fuzzy variable *Age* are *Ageyoung*, *Agemedium*, and *Ageold*. The five fuzzy numbers, i.e., *DMverylow*, *DMlow*, *DMmedium*, *DMhigh*, and *DMveryhigh*, are adopted to represent the possibility of this instance with diabetes for output fuzzy variable DM. The proposed Intensified Fuzzy Verdict Mechanism consists of three steps, i.e., Fuzzy Inference, Implication and Aggregation.

Fuzzy Inference

Fuzzy Inference step is to take the fuzzified inputs and apply them to the antecedents of the fuzzy rules. After the inputs are fuzzified, the antecedent is satisfied for each rule. If the antecedent of a given rule has more than one part, the fuzzy operator is applied to obtain one number that represents the result of the antecedent for that rule. This number is then applied to the output function. The input to the fuzzy operator is two or more membership values from fuzzified input variables. The output is a single truth value. The OR operator max at work, evaluating the antecedent of the rule. The fifteen different pieces of the antecedent (Glucoselow, Glucosemedium, Glucosehigh, INSlow, INSmedium, INShigh, BMIlow, BMImedium, BMIhigh, DPFlow, DPFmedium,

DPFhigh, Ageyoung, Agemedium, Ageold) gives the fuzzy membership values respectively. The fuzzy OR operator simply selects the maximum values. The developed fuzzy rule has multiple antecedents, the fuzzy operator 'OR' is used to evaluate the rule antecedents.

Implication

Fuzzy Inference is invoked by using Mamdani's approach. Implication is the process of mapping result of the fuzzification from antecedent part into the consequence [18]. MIN operation is conducted by the system. The input for the implication process is a single number given by the antecedent and the output is a fuzzy set. Implication is implemented for each rule. The implication process is conducted when the appropriate fuzzy rules are fired. More than one fuzzy rule fired at same time. Implication results through the aggregation process.

Aggregation

Decisions are based on the all of the rules, combined in some manner in order to make a decision statement. Aggregation is the process by which the fuzzy sets that represent the outputs of each rule are combined into a single fuzzy set. The input of aggregation process is the list of developed clipped consequent membership function and the output is one fuzzy set of each output variables[19]. SUM operation is used by the system.

The membership degrees for all instances of the fuzzification are calculated. Intensified Fuzzy Verdict Mechanism analyzes the personal physical data, converts the inferred results into knowledge, and then presents the decision results through descriptions [15], [16]. The patterns of the statement of the output descriptions, including a statement analysis and a decision statement. Algorithm for the Intensified Fuzzy Verdict Mechanism is given below.

Algorithm for Intensified Fuzzy Verdict Mechanism

INPUT

Input the fuzzy set for Glucose, INS, BMI, DPF and Age

OUTPUT

Output the fuzzy set for DM

METHOD

Begin

Step1:Input the crisp values for Glucose ,INS, BMI, DPF and Age.

Step 2: Calculate Glucose[Min, Mean-SD, Mean+SD, Max], INS[Min, Mean-SD, Mean+-SD, Max], BMI[Min, Mean-SD, Mean+-SD, Max], DPF[Min, Mean-SD, Mean+-SD, Max] and

Age[Min, Mean-SD, Mean+-SD, Max].

Step 3: Set the triangular membership function for the fuzzy number with equation (1).

Step 4: Built the fuzzy numbers for Glucose, INS, BMI, DPF and Age for input set

Step 4.1: Built the fuzzy number for DM for the output set.

Step5: Fuzzy inference are executed by Mamdani 's method.

Step 5.1: Input the rule as {Rule 1,2.....n}

Step 5.2: The OR operator max, evaluate the antecedent of the rule. The antecedent of rule are calculated for fuzzy input set (Glucoselow, Glucosemedium,

Glucosehigh, INSlow, INSmedium, INShigh, BMIlow, BMImedium, BMIhigh, DPFlow, DPFmedium, DPFhigh, Ageyoung, Agemedium, Ageold) using MAX operation.

Step 5.3: Conduct Implication by MIN operation.

Step 5.4:Calculate the aggregation of the fired rules with SUM operation for fuzzy output set DM (DMverylow, DMlow, DMmedium, DMhigh, DMveryhigh).

Step6: Defuzzify into the crisp values by

$$DM_i \leftarrow \frac{\sum_{i=1}^{n} Z_i \mu(Z_i)}{\sum_{i=1}^{i=n} \mu(Z_i)}$$

Where Z_i means the weight for μ (Z_i) and μ (Z_i) means the number of fuzzy numbers of the output fuzzy variable DM.

Step6: Present the knowledge in the form of human nature language

End.

2.6 Defuzzification

The input for the defuzzification process is a fuzzy set (the aggregate output fuzzy set) and the output is a single number. As much as fuzziness helps the rule evaluation during the intermediate steps, the final desired output for each variable is generally a single number. Defuzzification process is conducted to convert aggregation result into crisp value for DM output. In this process the single number which represent the outcome of the fuzzy set evaluation. The final combined fuzzy conclusion is converted into a crisp value by using the centroid method[9].

Statement Pattern of Output Descriptions

Statement Analysis(SA)

The data exhibit that person is at [FN_{Age}:young,medium,old]age, meanwhile the plasma glucose concentration in 2-hour OGIT is [$FN_{Glucose}$:low,medium,high], 2-hour serum insulin is [FNI_{INS}:low,medium,high], body mass index is [FN_{BMI}:low,medium,high], and diabetes pedigree function is [FN_{DPF}:low,medium,high].

Decision Statement(DS)

The Decision statement justifies the possibility of suffering from diabetes for this person as [FN_{DM}:verylow,low,medium,high,veryhigh] (Possibility:[0,1]).

3 Experimental Results

The proposed fuzzy expert system for diabetes application was implemented with the MATLAB. The experimental environment was constructed to evaluate the performance of the proposed approach; in addition, PIDD was chosen as the evaluated data set. The proposed approach can analyze the data of the PIDD and generate corresponding human knowledge based on the Fuzzification for the parameter very young [8]. The first experiment shows sets of results in Table 5, indicating that the proposed approach automatically supports the analysis of the data. The acquired information is then transferred into knowledge, and finally the proposed method presents them in the form of the descriptions of humans.

Rule for Fuzzy Expert System 1. If(Glucose is Glucoselow) or(INS is INSlow) or (BMI is BMIlow) or (DPF is DPFlow) or(Age is Ageyoung)is DMverylow

2. If(Glucose is Glucoselow) or(INS is INSlow) or (BMI is BMIhigh) or (DPF is DPFlow) or(Age is Ageyoung) then (DM is DMlow)

3. If(Glucose is Glucosemedium) or(INS is INShigh) or (BMI is BMIhigh) or (DPF is DPFmedium) or(Age is Ageyoung) then (DM is DMmedium)

4. If(Glucose is Glucosehigh) or(INS is INSmedium) or (BMI is BMIhigh) or (DPF is DPFhigh) or(Age is Ageyoung) then (DM is DMhigh)

5. If(Glucose is Glucoselow) or(INS is INSlow) or (BMI is BMImedium) or (DPF is DPFlow) or(Age is Ageyoung) then (DM is DMverylow)

4 Evaluation of System Performance

The second experiment evaluates the performance of the Decision statement and the medical practitioner. Accuracy is the measuring scale for performance of this experiment. The True Positive (TP) and the True Negative (TN) denote the correct classification. False Positive (FP) is the outcome when the predicted class is yes

$$Accuracy = \frac{TN + TP}{TN + FP + FN + TP} X100\% \quad (3)$$

Table 5. Result obtained from MATLAB

Data	Glucose (mg/dl)	INS (mu U/ml)	BMI (Kg/m^2)	DPF	Age
	172	579	42.4	0.702	28
SA	If(Glucose is Glucosehigh) or(INS is INSmedium) or (BMI is BMIhigh) or (DPF is DPFhigh) or(Age is Ageyoung) then (DM is DMhigh)				
DS	The Decision statement justifies that the possibility of suffering from diabetes for this person is medium(possibility:**0.463**)				
Justification by Medical Practitioner	Medical practitioner justification is the person is diabetes				

(or positive) and actual class is no (or negative). Still, a False Negative (FN) is the outcome when the predicted class is no (or negative) and actual class is yes (or positive). Table 6 lists the various outcomes of a two-class prediction [17].Accuracy is the proportion of the total number of predictions that were correct. The precision is the proportion of the predicted positive cases that were correct. The eqn. (3) show the formula for accuracy.

Table 6. Different outcomes of a two-class predicton

Actual class	Predicted class	
	Yes	No
Yes	True positive (*TP*)	False Negative (*FN*)
No	False positive (*FP*)	True Negative (*TN*)

Table 7. Comparison of Proposed method Accuracy with earlier methods

Method	**Accuracy (%)**	**Author**
Our study for Very Young	88.35	Dr. A.V.Senthil Kumar and M.Kalpana
FES for diabetes using Fuzzy verdict Mechanism	85.03	M.Kalpana and Dr. A.V.Senthil Kumar
A FES for Diabetes Decision very young[8]	81.7	Lee and Wang
$HNFB^{-1}$[6]	78.26	Goncalves et al.
Logdisc	77.7	Statlog
IncNet	77.6	Norbert Jankowski
DIPOL 92	77.6	Statlog
Linear discr. Anal	77.5-77.2	Statlog, ster and Dobnikar
A FES for Diabetes Decision very very young[8]	77.3	Lee and Wang
VISIT[5]	77	Chang and Lilly
SMART	76.8	statlog
GTO DT(5 X CV)	76.8	Bennet and Blue
ASI	76.6	Ster and Dobnikar
Fisher discr. Analysis	76.5	Ster and Dobnika
MLP+BP	76.4	Ster and Dobnika
LVQ(20)	75.8	Ster and Dobnika
LFC	75.8	Ster and Dobnika

The final experiment compares the accuracy of the proposed method with results of studies involving the PIDD [5], [6], [8][12]. Comparing these methods, as listed in Table 7, reveals that the proposed method achieves the first highest accuracy values for "very young" based on the proposed fuzzy expert system. The accuracy values of the proposed method are compared with the earlier methods and represented graphically figure 4, which shows better accuracy.

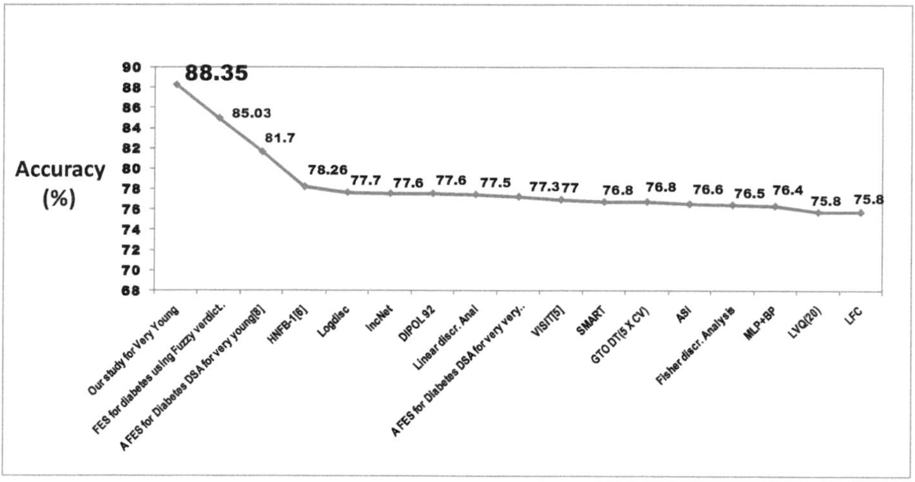

Fig. 4. Graphical represent of accuracy

5 Conclusions and Future Research

This paper presents fuzzy logic application to diagnosis the diabetes. The experimental data set, PIDD, is initially processed and the crisp values are converted into fuzzy values in the stage of fuzzification. The intensified fuzzy verdict mechanism undergoes three steps to execute rules with fuzzy operator, to make a decision on the possibility of individuals suffering from diabetes and to present the knowledge with descriptions. Defuzzification process is conducted to convert the result into crisp value for Diabetes Mellitus output. The results further demonstrate that the proposed method works more effectively for diabetes application than previously developed ones. Future works should test the fuzzification approach used herein for other similar tasks or other related data sets to evaluate its capability to produce a similar accuracy. Future works should undertake the composition and add more rules to improve the accuracy of Intensified Fuzzy Verdict Mechanism.

References

1. Campos-Delgado, D.U., Hernandez- Ordonez, M., Femat, R., Gordillo-Moscoso, A.: Fuzzy-based controller for glucose regulation in type-1 diabetic patients by subcutaneous route. IEEE Trans. Biomed. Eng. 53(11), 2201–2210 (2006)
2. Magni, P., Bellazzi, R.: A stochastic model to assess the variability of blood glucose time series in diabetic patients self-monitoring. IEEE Trans. Biomed. Eng. 53(6), 977–985 (2006)

3. Polat, K., Gunes, S.: An expert system approach based on principal component analysis and adaptive neuro-fuzzy inference system to diagnosis of diabetes disease. Dig. Signal Process. 17(4), 702–710 (2007)
4. Polat, K., Gunes, S., Arslan, A.: A cascade learning system for classification of diabetes disease: Generalized discriminant analysis and least square support vector machine. Expert Syst. Appl. 34(1), 482–487 (2008)
5. Chang, X., Lilly, J.H.: Evolutionary design of a fuzzy classifier from data. IEEE Trans. Syst. Man, Cybern. B, Cybern. 34(4), 1894–1906 (2004)
6. Goncalves, L.B., Vellasco, M.M.B.R., Pacheco, M.A.C., de Souza, F.J.: Inverted hierarchical neuro-fuzzy BSP system: A novel neuro-fuzzy model for pattern classification and rule extraction in databases. IEEE Trans. Syst. Man, Cybern. C, Appl. Rev. 36(2), 236–248 (2006)
7. Kahramanli, H., Allahverdi, N.: Design of a hybrid system for the diabetes and heart diseases. Expert Syst. Appl. 35(1/2), 82–89 (2008)
8. Lee, C.-S.: A Fuzzy Expert System for Diabetes Decision Support Application. IEEE Transactions on Systems, Man, and Cybernetics—Part B: Cybernetics 41(1) (February 2011)
9. Saritas, I., Ozkan, I.A., Allahverdi, N., Argindogan, M.: Determination of the drug dose by fuzzy expert system in treatment of chronic intestine inflammation. Springer Science+Business Media J. Intell. Manuf. 20, 169–176 (2009)
10. Fasanghari, M., Montazer, G.A.: Design and implementation of fuzzy expert system for Tehran Stock Exchange portfolio recommendation. Expert Systems with Applications 37, 6138–6147 (2010)
11. American Diabetes Association, Standards of medical care in diabetes—2007. Diabetes Care 30(1), S4–S41 (2007)
12. Kalpana, M., Senthilkumar, A.V.: Fuzzy Expert System for Diabetes using Fuzzy Verdict Mechanism. International Journal of Advanced Networking and Applications (onprint)
13. Siler, W., Buckley, J.: Fuzzy Expert System and Fuzzy Reasoning, pp. 49–50. Wiley & Sons, Inc. (2005)
14. Demouy, J., Chamberlain, J., Harris, M., Marchand, L.H.: The Pima Indians: Pathfinders of Health. Nat. Inst. Diabetes Digestive Kidney Diseases, Bethesda (1995)
15. Zadeh, L.A.: Toward human level machine intelligence—Is it achievable? The need for a paradigm shift. IEEE Comput. Intell. Mag. 3(3), 11–22 (2008)
16. Margaliot, M.: Biomimicry and fuzzy modeling: A match made in heaven. IEEE Comput. Intell. Mag. 3(3), 38–48 (2008)
17. Lee, C.S., Wang, M.H.: Ontology-based intelligent healthcare agent and its application to respiratory waveform recognition. Expert Syst. Appl. 33(3), 606–619 (2007)
18. Idrus, A., Nurulddin, M.F., Rohman, M.A.: Development of project cost contingency estimation model using risk analysis and fuzzy expert system. Expert System with Applications 38, 1501–1508 (2011)
19. Ho, T., Karri, V.: Fuzzy Expert System to Estimate Ignition timing for Hydrogen car. In: Sun, F., Zhang, J., Tan, Y., Cao, J., Yu, W. (eds.) ISNN 2008,, Part II. LNCS, vol. 5264, pp. 570–579. Springer, Heidelberg (2008)

An Implementation Scheme for Multidimensional Extendable Array Operations and Its Evaluation

Sk. Md. Masudul Ahsan and K.M. Azharul Hasan

Department of Computer Science and Engineering
Khulna University of Engineering & Technology
Khulna 9203, Bangladesh
smmasudulahsan@yahoo.com, azhasan@gmail.com

Abstract. In recent times, multidimensional arrays are extensively used to handle large amount of data in scientific research, engineering, and MOLAP applications. Most of the existing data structures are static in nature and cannot grow or shrink dynamically. The Traditional Multidimensional Array (TMA) is an efficient structure in terms of accessing the element of the array by straight computation of the addressing function, but TMA is not extendible during run time. There are some extendible data structures but they have the problem of address space overflow for large number of dimensions or length of dimension. In this paper we propose a new data structure, Extendible Karnaugh Array (EKA), to represent the multidimensional data. The main idea of this scheme is to represent *n* dimensional array by a set of two dimensional extendible arrays. The scheme can be extended in any direction during run time. We evaluate our proposed scheme by comparing for different operations with the Traditional Multidimensional Array (TMA). Our experimental result shows that the EKA scheme outperforms TMA.

Keywords: Multidimensional Array, Extendible Array, Karnaugh Map, Range Query, Dynamic Extension, MOLAP.

1 Introduction

There are few classes of data structures which are as well understood or as extensively used as arrays. It is quite often for scientific, statistical and engineering applications to have computation on large multidimensional arrays for modeling and analyzing scientific phenomena [1],[2]. The strong need to handle large scale data efficiently has been promoting comprehensive research themes on organization or implementation schemes for multidimensional arrays.

The fast random accessing capability of multidimensional arrays is a fascinating characteristic that enables various statistical computations including aggregation to be performed efficiently [3],[4]. But this capability depends on the fact that the size of each dimension should be fixed so that a simple addressing function can be used to access an arbitrary element of the array. However, such kind of multidimensional arrays go through following two important problems:

A. Abd Manaf et al. (Eds.): ICIEIS 2011, Part III, CCIS 253, pp. 136–150, 2011.

(i) The size of the multidimensional array is not dynamically extendible [5],[6]; when a new data value is added, size extension along the corresponding dimension is necessary and this implies reorganization of the entire array elements.

(ii) One more problem with the multidimensional array is address space requirement. To allocate memory, consecutive memory location is required for multidimensional array. But when the length of dimension and number of dimension of a multidimensional array is large then the address space overflows soon.

The introduction of extendible array [5],[6],[17] solves the problem (i) above. An extendible array can be extended in any dimension without any repositioning of previously stored data [5],[17]. Such advantage makes it possible for an extendible array to be applied into wide application area where required array size cannot be predicted before and / or can vary dynamically during operating time of the system. In this paper, we are going to propose a basic extendible data structure that will solve the problem (i) above. To solve the second problem we have segmented the subarrays in such a way that the subarrays are always 2 dimensional that solves the overflow situation in our model.

An extendible array, however, does not store an individual array; rather, it stores an array and all its potential extensions. In this paper, we propose a new scheme called Extendible Karnaugh Array (EKA). The main idea of our proposed EKA is to represent multidimensional array by a set of two dimensional extendible arrays. To evaluate our proposed scheme we have implemented and compared the results with TMA. The experimental result shows that EKA outperforms the TMA in various cases. The scheme is fully general to be applied in different applications such as implementation of multidimensional database systems [5],[8], or data warehouse systems [3],[9]. It can also be applied to design extendible and flexible database [10],[11] and parallel database design[12],[13].

2 Related Works

There are some existing multidimensional array systems to represent multidimensional data such as Traditional Multidimensional Array (TMA) [1],[2], Extended Karnaugh Map Representation (EKMR) [14],[15],[16], Extendible multidimensional Array [7],[17]. TMA is a good storage for storing multidimensional data set. The TMA represent *n* dimensional data by an array cell in an *n* dimensional array. The key to the structure of arrays resides in the familiar coordinate system, which pictures an n-dimensional array as being imbedded in the positive orthant of *n*-dimensional space, with array positions lay on the lattice points. To insert a new column value in the TMA entire reorganization of the array is necessary which causes massive cost [9]. Extended Karnaugh Map Representation (EKMR) represent *n* dimensional data by a set of two dimensional arrays [3]. But EKMR is not dynamically extendible.

The Extendible Array [7],[17] has the property of extendibility and the indices of the respective dimensions can be arbitrarily extended without reorganizing previously allocated elements. If the extendible array is *n* dimensional then the subarray is *n*-1 dimensional. Hence it will overflow soon for address space because the subarrays are n-1 dimensional although it can be extended dynamically. The extendible array is employed in [17] to extend the array and it only treats an organization scheme of the history tables. The subarrays are n dimensional hence it will be difficult to apply in actual implementation when address space overflow is concerned.

An extendible array model [18],[19] where there is record for each dimension called axis vector. Each element of the vector stores necessary information like the auxiliary tables in our EKA scheme to retrieve an element correctly. In this approach the sequence of the two consecutive extensions along the same dimension, although occurring at two different instances, is considered as an uninterrupted extension of that dimension and handled by only one expansion record entry in the axial-vector. Therefore number of element in an axial vector is always less than or equal to the number of indices of the corresponding dimension. If round robin expansion occurs, then it is similar to extendible array [17]. [4],[20] presents the chunking of multidimensional arrays. In this scheme the large multidimensional arrays are broken into chunks for storage and processing. All the chunks are n dimensional with smaller length than the original array. But the dynamic extension is not possible. In [21] there is an array system based on extendible array [7] presented that can insert a row in the middle of the dimension. All the array models mentioned in this Section do not handle the address space overflow which is handled in our EKA scheme.

3 The Extendible Karnaugh Representation of Array

The idea of EKA is based on Karnaugh Map (K-map) [22]. The K-map technique is used for minimizing Boolean expressions usually aided by mapping values for all possible combinations. Fig. 1 (a) shows a 4 variable K-map to represent possible 2^4 combinations of a Boolean function. The variables (w, x) represent the row and the variables (y, z) represent the column to indicate the possible combinations in a two dimensional array.

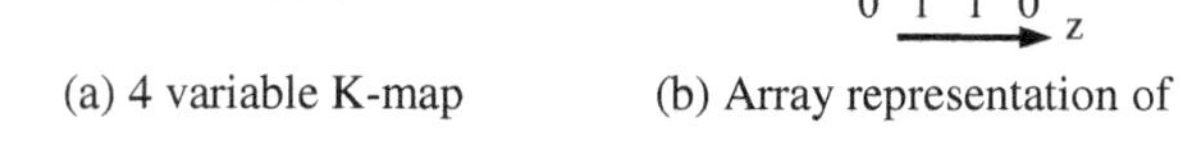

(a) 4 variable K-map (b) Array representation of K-map

Fig. 1. Realization of Boolean function using K-map

The array representation of K-map for 4 variable Boolean function is shown in Fig. 1(b). The length of each of the dimensions is 2 for both Fig. 1(a) and (b). This is because the Boolean variables are binary that causes the length to be 2.

Definition 1 (Adjacent Dimension): The dimensions (or index variables) that are placed together in the Boolean function representation of K-map are termed as adjacent dimensions (written as *adj*(i) = j). The dimensions (w, x) are the adjacent dimensions in Fig. 1, i.e. *adj*(w) = x or vice versa.

3.1 The Extension Realization of the EKA Scheme

EKA is the combination of subarrays. It has three types of auxiliary tables namely *history table*, *coefficient table*, and *address table*. For each of the four dimensions these tables exist. These tables help the elements of the EKA to be accessed very fast.

The extension subarrays are further sub divided into number of segments. The number of segments determines the number of entries in the address table and is calculated from the length of adjacent dimension. Since extension subarrays are three dimensional, the segmented subarrays are always two dimensional for an EKA(n). Throughout the paper, we write EKA(n) to mean an n dimensional EKA.

Consider the array in Fig. 2(a), the dimensions are d_1, d_2, d_3 and d_4 and the size of the array is $[l_1, l_2, l_3, l_4]$ where l_i indicates the length of dimension d_i and subscripts varies from 0 to l_i-1. In the current example $l_i = 2$. The dimension (d_1, d_3) and (d_2, d_4) are adjacent dimensions respectively. The logical extension in d_1 is shown in Fig. 2(b). The size of the extended subarray which is allocated dynamically is determined by $l_2 \times l_3 \times l_4$ (i.e. 3 other dimensions). The number of segments is the length of the adjacent dimension, $adj(d_1) = d_3$; In this case it is $l_3 = 2$. The size of each segmented subarray extended along dimension d_1 is determined by $l_2 \times l_4$. After extending along dimension d_1, the length of that dimension is incremented by 1. For each extension the corresponding auxiliary tables are maintained accordingly. Fig. 2(c), 2(d) and 2(e) shows the extension realization along dimension d_2, d_3 and d_4 respectively.

There is a history counter that counts the construction history of the subarrays. History table contains the construction history of the subarrays. For each history, the address table contains the first address of the extended subarrays for the

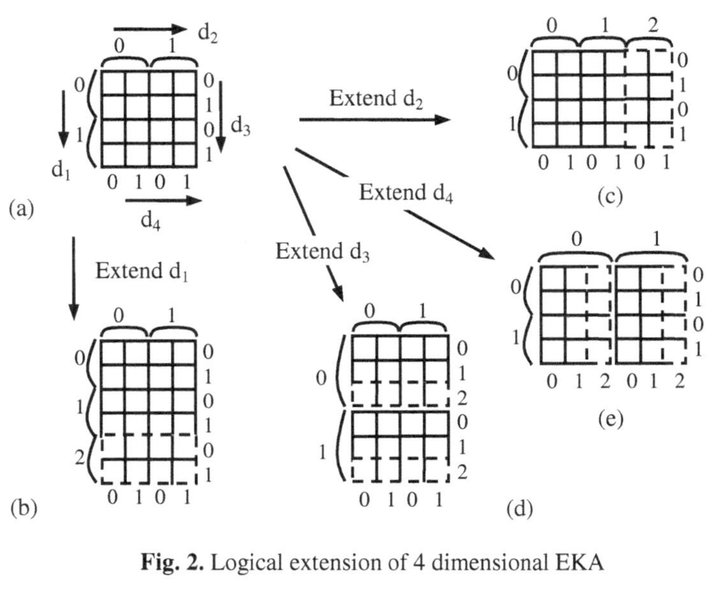

Fig. 2. Logical extension of 4 dimensional EKA

corresponding dimension. For each extension the subarrays are broken into segments (see Fig. 2). In fact, the address table stores the first addresses of each segments of the subarray. Hence for a single subarray (i.e. history value) the address table entry can be more than one. Coefficient table contains the coefficient of subarrays.

In an n dimensional conventional fixed size array of size $[l_n, l_{n-1}, ..., l_1]$ is allocated on memory using an addressing function like this:

$$f(x_n, x_{n-1}, x_{n-2}, ..., x_2, x_1) = l_1 l_2 ... l_{n-1} x_n + l_1 l_2 ... l_{n-2} x_{n-1} + ... + l_1 x_2 + x_1$$

Here, $l_1 l_2 ... l_{n-1}, l_1 l_2 ... l_{n-2}, ..., l_1 l_2, l_1$ is called as *coefficient vector*. As each segment of the subarray is 2 dimensional hence in our model the coefficient vector becomes $\langle l_1 \rangle$ only. The EKA can be extended along any dimension dynamically during runtime only by the cost of these three auxiliary tables.

An Illustrative Example. In this example we have taken an EKA(4) as an example that shown in Fig. 3. We are going to extend it in different dimensions in the following.

Fig. 3(a) illustrates the initial setup of the scheme. The history counter is zero and the history tables contain one entry namely 0. The address tables contain first address. Each of the coefficient table entry is 1 since length of each dimension is 1. During the extension of d_1 and d_3 dimension size of the segment is $l_2 \times l_4$ which is a two dimensional array, and so coefficient vector is one dimensional. Hence, for our example we use l_2 as coefficient vector for d_1 and d_3 dimensions. Similarly, l_3 is used as coefficient vector for d_2 and d_4 dimension and coefficient table is maintained. When an extension along d_2 direction is done as shown in Fig. 3(b), the history counter is increased by 1. The value of history counter is stored in the history table H_{d2}. The subarray size $[l_1, l_3, l_4]$ is calculated and dynamically allocated; the values of first address are stored in address table A_{d2}; since l_3 is 1 C_{d2} stores this value. Fig. 3(c) shows an extension along d_3 direction. Here the history counter incremented by 1 and this is stored in history table H_{d3}. The size of the subarray $[l_1, l_2, l_4]$ is calculated and the first address for this subarray is stored in the address table A_{d3}. In Fig. 3(d) an extension along direction d_4 is done. As a result of the extension history counter becomes 3, segmented subarray size becomes $l_1 \times l_3 = 1 \times 2 = 2$, and number of segments are $l_2 = 2$. Therefore, H_{d4} memorizes the history value 3, and A_{d4} has two entries. Similarly, the extension along direction d_1 is shown Fig. 3(e) and finally Fig. 3(f) shows one more extension along direction d_3.

3.2 Generalization to Higher Dimensions

The EKA scheme is generalized to n dimensions using a set of EKA(4)s. Fig. 4(a) shows the logical structure and Fig. 4(b) shows the physical implementation of a EKA(5) where the length of dimension d_5 is 2. Fig. 5 shows an EKA(6) represented by a set of EKA(4) in two level. If the current length of dimension d_5, and d_6 is 3 and 2 respectively, then the EKA(6) is represented by the two level structure as shown in Fig. 5. Each higher dimensions (d_5 and d_6) are represented as one dimensional array of pointers that points to the next lower dimension and each cell of d_5 points to each of the EKA(4). So each EKA(4) can be accessed simply by using the subscripts of higher dimensions. For the case of EKA(n), similar hierarchical structure will be

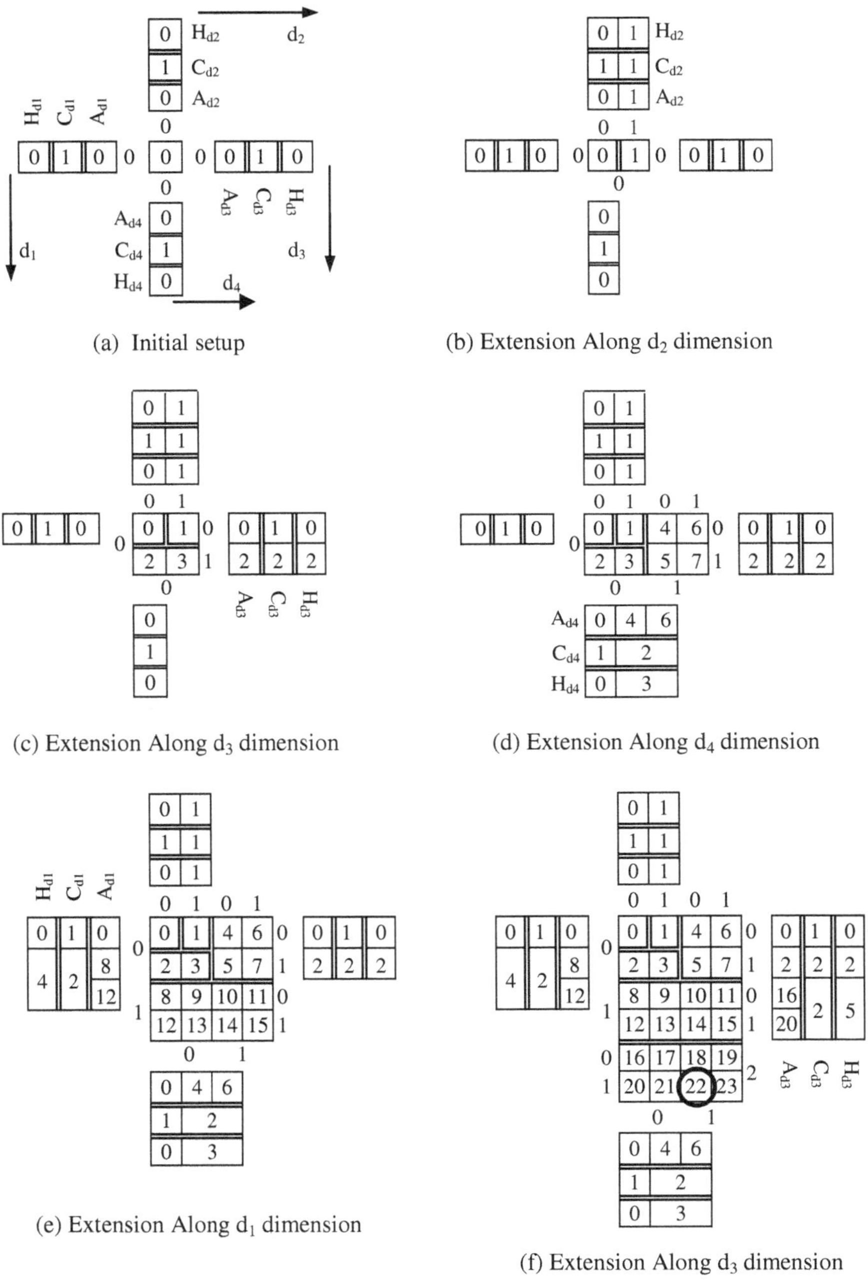

Fig. 3. Extension realization of EKA(4)

needed. The set of EKA(4)s stores the actual data values and the hierarchical arrays are indexes to EKA(4)s and used to locate the appropriate EKA(4). Hence the

EKA(n) is a set of EKA(4)s and a set of pointer is used for indexing purpose only. At this stage (Fig. 5), if dimension d_1 (or d_2, d_3, d_4) is extended dynamically, all the EKA(4)s will be extended along that dimension and the auxiliary tables are maintained.
At the end of this section we summarize the problems described in section 1.

(i) Since the EKA can be dynamically extended during runtime, the problem (i) is solved.
(ii) The subarrays are always 3-dimensional and are broken into segments which are 2-dimensional. When number of dimension is large (greater than 4), then one dimensional pointer arrays incorporated. Therefore overflow situation will be delayed even for vary large values of number of dimensions or length of dimension. Hence problem (ii) is resolved.

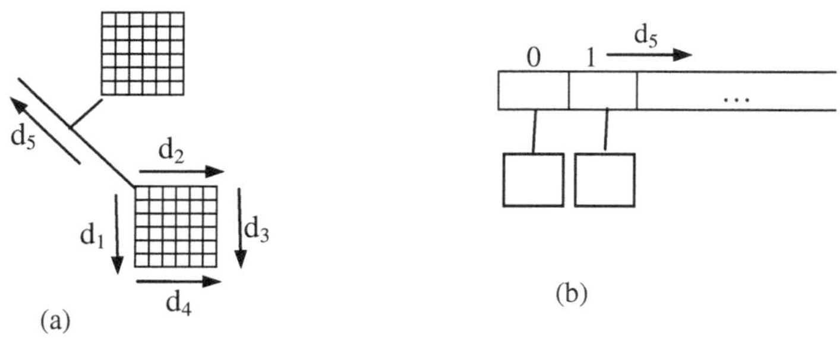

Fig. 4. Realization of 5 dimensional EKA

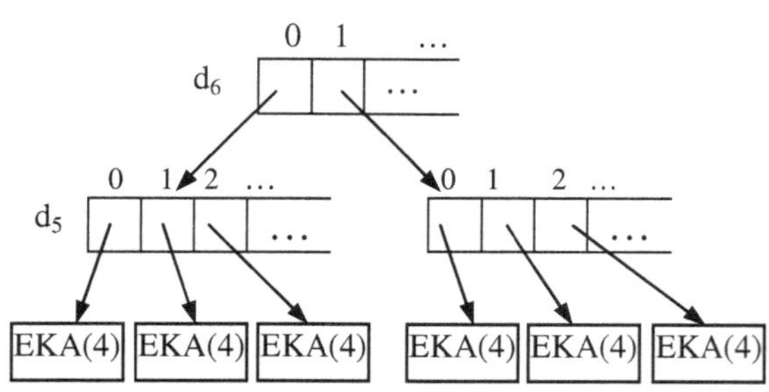

Fig. 5. Realization of 6 dimensional EKA

4 Operations on EKA

4.1 Retrieval

Retrieval in EKA(4)
Let the value to be retrieved is indicated by the subscript (x_1, x_2, x_3, x_4). The maximum history value among the subscripts $h_{max}= \max(H_{d1}[x_1], H_{d2}[x_2], H_{d3}[x_3], H_{d4}[x_4])$ and the dimension (say d_1) that corresponds to history value h_{max} is determined. h_{max} is the subarray that contains our desired element. This is because; the subarray that has the maximum history value was constructed at last (the history values are linear

numbers). Hence the desired element remains in the subarray having history value h_{max}. Now the first address and offset from the first address is to be found out. The adjacent dimension *adj*(d_1) (say d_3) and its subscript x_3 is found. Now the first address is found from $H_{d1}[x_1].A_{d1}[x_3]$. The *offset* from the first address is computed using the addressing function (described in Section 3.1); the coefficient vectors are stored in C_{d1}. Then adding the *offset* with the first address, the desired array cell (x_1, x_2, x_3, x_4) is found.

Example 1: Let four subscripts (1, 0, 2, 1) for dimension d_1, d_2, d_3, and d_4 is given (see Fig. 3(f)). Here h_{max} = max($H_{d1}[1] = 4$, $H_{d2}[0] = 0$, $H_{d3}[2] = 5$, $H_{d4}[1] = 3$) =5, and dimension corresponding to h_{max} is d_3 whose subscript is 2 and *adj*(d_3) = d_1 and x_1 = 1. So the first address is in $H_{d3}[2]A_{d3}[1] = 20$, and offset is calculated using the coefficient vector stored in coefficient table C_{d3} which is 2. Here, *offset* = $C_{d3}[2] * x_4 + x_2 = 2*1 + 0 = 2$. Finally adding the first address with the offset the desired location 20 + 2 = 22 is found (encircled in Fig. 3(f)).

Retrieval in higher dimensional EKA(n), n>4
Let the value to be retrieved is indicated by the subscript (x_n, x_{n-1}, …, x_2, x_1). Each of the higher dimensions (n > 4) is the set of one dimensional pointer arrays that points to next lower dimensions. Hence using subscripts x_k ($d_k > 4$) the pointer arrays are searched to locate the lower dimensions (see Fig. 5). If n ≤ 4, then using the above computation technique the location in EKA(4) can be found.

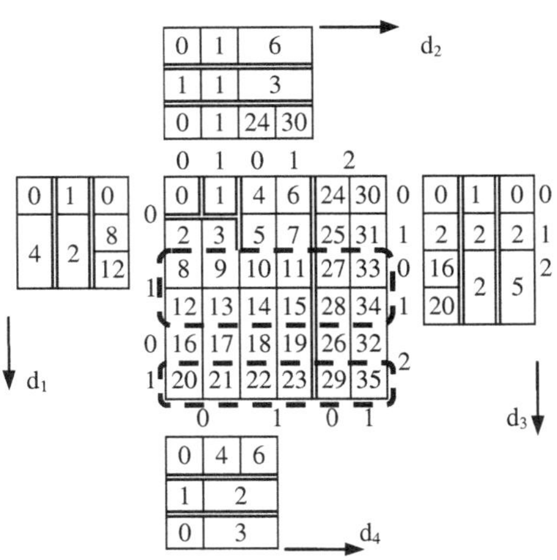

Fig. 6. Extension Along d2 dimension

4.2 Range Key Retrieval

A range key query [23] has a single predicate of the form (*column subscript < value*) or (*column subscript > value*) or (*column subscript between value₁ and value₂*). Fig. 6 (which is obtained by extending the Fig. 3(f) in d_2 dimension) shows the candidate range (bold dotted line) of a range key query for a EKA(4). Assume that the candidate range of the subscripts of the corresponding dimension d_1 has *NRQ* subscripts.

Let the specified range involve in the known column has subscripts x_{k1}, x_{k2}, …, x_{kNRQ} of dimension d_k. Let h_1, h_2, … h_{NRQ} be the history values that correspond to the subscripts and the minimum history value be $h_{min} = \min(h_1, h_2, \ldots h_{NRQ})$.

Definition 2 (Major and Minor subarray). All the elements of the subarrays corresponding to the history values h_1, h_2, … h_{NRQ} are candidate for retrieval (see Fig.6) and are called *Major subarray*. The subarrays that have history values greater than h_{min} and belong to the adjacent dimension $adj(d_k)$ are called *Minor subarray*. One segment of the minor subarrays is candidate for a range query. The candidate subarrays are those which are sufficient to be searched and these subarrays have history values greater than $h_{min.}$ The major and minor subarrays are candidate subarrays and rest of the candidate subarrays do not belong to the known dimension d_k and have history values greater than h_{min}.

Example 2: In Fig. 6, the subarray having history value 4 is the major subarray and the subarray having history values 5 is the minor subarray. Hence all the elements of subarray 4 are candidate for retrieval and one segment of subarray 5 are candidate for retrieval. The remaining candidate subarrays have history value greater than 4 (definition 2) and the elements inside those subarray are found by calculating the offsets and adding the first address as described in section 4.1

5 Performance Results

In this section, we simulate the retrieval operation for range key query for both TMA and EKA. The parameters are described in Table 1. All lengths or sizes of storage areas are in bytes. Some parameters are provided as input while others are derived from input parameters.

Table 1. Parameters for cost function for TMA and EKA

Parameter	Description
n	Number of dimension both for TMA and EKA
EKA(n)	An n dimensional Extendible Karnaugh Array
TMA(n)	An n dimensional Traditional Multidimensional Array
d_i	Dimension i, $1 \leq i \leq n$
l_i	Length of dimension d_i
V	Initial volume of both TMA and EKA, $V = \prod_{i=1}^{n} l_i$
s	Number of segments in a subarray for EKA
λ	Length of extension

We have constructed the TMA and EKA systems having the parameter values shown in Table 2 placing the TMA and EKA in secondary storage. The auxiliary tables of EKA are placed in main memory since the sizes of the auxiliary tables are negligible comparing to the main array. The test results for retrieval and extension operations are analyzed in this Section. All the tests are run on a machine (Dell Optiplex 380) of 2.93 GHz processor and 2 GB of memory having disk page size P = 4KB. We will show that the overall retrieval time has advantages for EKA than TMA. We also show that without any retrieval penalty we can extend the length of dimension of a multidimensional array effectively if implemented using EKA.

5.1 Retrieval Cost

In TMA, the array is linearized in a single data stream using the addressing function; (Section 4) therefore all the offset values of the array elements are consecutive. Hence the range of candidate offset values for a query can be determined uniquely. But for EKA; the same data stream is distributed over different subarrays (see Fig. 6).

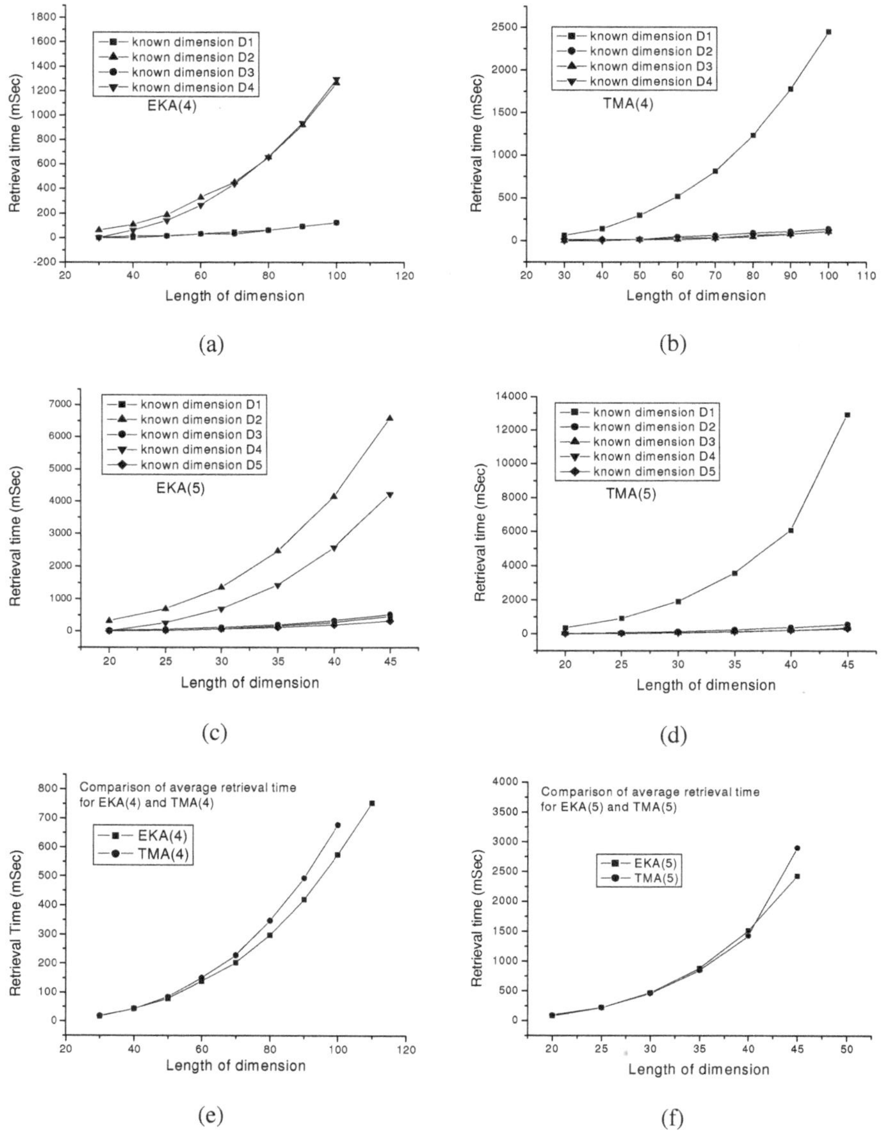

Fig. 7. Retrieval cost analysis for EKA and TMA

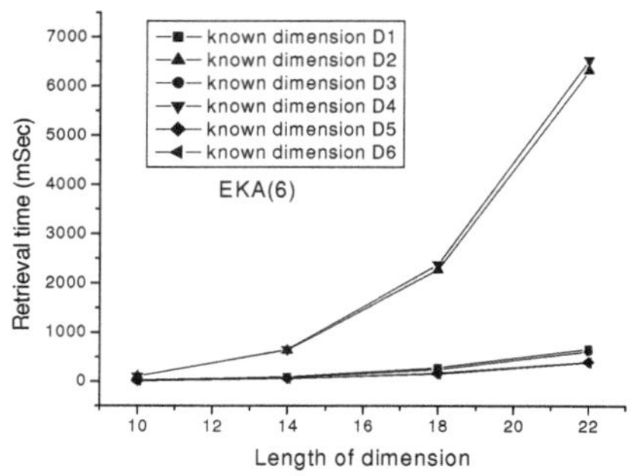

(g)

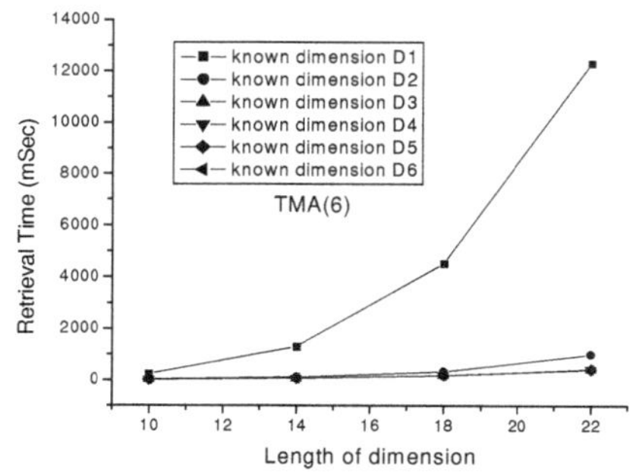

(h)

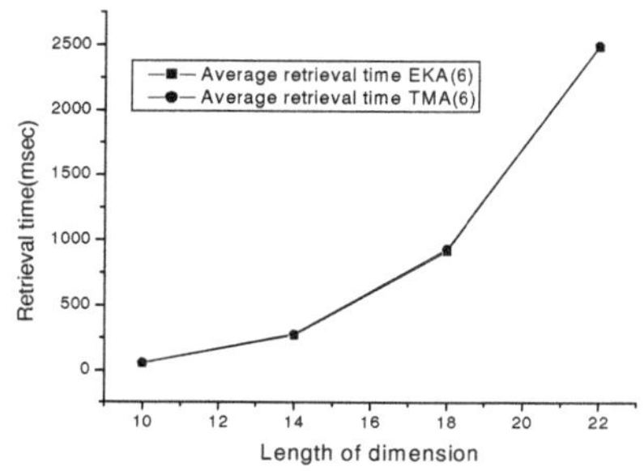

(i)

Fig. 7. *(Continued)*

Table 2. Assumed parameters for constructed prototypes

N	λ	max(l_i)	Initial V = l^n
4	10	100	$(30)^4$
5	5	45	$(20)^5$
6	2	22	$(10)^6$

The retrieval performance depends on the known dimension (i.e. the specified dimension) of query dimension. We use the term *known* dimension (or known subscript) to indicate the specified dimension of the query operation. For example if dimension 2 is the known or specified then we write subscript x_2 is *known*.

Fig. 7 shows the retrieval performance for range key query of TMA and EKA for the parameter values shown in Table 2. In Fig 7(a) the retrieval performance for EKA(4) for different known dimension is shown. It shows that, the retrieval time is higher when x_2 and x_4 are known. The retrieval time is lower when the x_1 and x_3 is known. This is because the segments of the subarrays of EKA(4) are two dimensional hence the element inside the subarrays can be organized as row major order or column major order. If the elements are organized in one order (say row major) then it is searched in column order; the target elements for the query are not consecutively organized. Therefore that known subscript takes longer time. Hence two known subscripts will take higher time than other two known subscripts. Please be noted a two dimension array is used as four dimensional (see Fig. 1) array. When number of dimension n increases for EKA then it (see Fig. 7(c) and 7(g)) shows that retrieval from EKA takes higher time for the known subscripts of only two values. Fig. 7(b) shows the retrieval time for TMA for $n = 4$. It shows that for the known dimension of x_1 takes higher time than other known dimensions. This is because when known dimension is x_1 then the entire array needs to be scanned as explained bellow:

The addressing function of a 4D array is $f(x_4, x_3, x_2, x_1) = l_1l_2l_3x_4 + l_1l_2x_3 + l_1x_2 + x_1$. Let $l_i = l$ for i=1... 4. Then the function becomes $f(x_4, x_3, x_2, x_1) = l^3x_4 + l^2x_3 + lx_2 + x_1$.

If $l = 6$ and x_4 is known (say, $x_4 = 0$, and $x_j = 0,\ldots,l\text{-}1$ for $j = 1,\ldots,3$) then the candidate offset values in the query are consecutive in the range 0 to 215 (total 216 offsets) out of 1296 offsets which is l^3 (i.e. 6^3). If x_1 is known (say, $x_1 = 0$) then the candidate offset values in the query are in the range 0 to 1290 (total 1291 offsets) out of 1296 offsets. From the above discussion, we can conclude that the retrieval in TMA is largely depends on the known dimension k and when $k = n$ then the retrieval time will be minimum and when $k = 1$ then the retrieval time will be maximum.

When $n = 5$, 6 for TMA, the same situation i.e for one known subscript TMA takes higher time than others as shown in fig. 7(d) and 7(h). Fig. 7(e) and 7(f) shows the average retrieval cost for EKA and TMA for $n = 4$ and 5. It shows that EKA has better performance than TMA and the average retrieval cost is almost same for both EKA and TMA when $n = 6$ (Fig. 7(i)). It can be concluded that, on average, the retrieval performance for EKA is better and there is no retrieval penalty for EKA over TMA.

5.2 Extension Cost

Fig. 8 shows the extension cost for TMA and EKA .The TMA reorganizes the array whenever there is an extension to it. That is, the whole array will be relinearized on disk to accommodate the new data due to the extension of length of dimension. The TMA scheme needs to face the existing elements then reorganize for the extension. On the other hand, the EKA extends the initial array with segment of subarrays containing the new data as described in Section 3. Hence the EKA strategy can reduce the cost of array extensions significantly. Extension gain is the difference between the extension time of TMA and EKA which is shown in Fig. 8(d).

The extension cost as well as extension gain depends on the initial volume of the array i.e. the values of n and l before the array is extended. Hence, if n and l increase, then the gain increases. We can conclude that if the initial volume is large then the extension cost for TMA is higher. It will be expensive to extend a large array even for small values of λ.

It can be shown that for TMA(n) with $l_i = l$, and an extension length λ in all dimensions, extension cost is $O(l^n)$ i.e O(initial volume). On the other hand extension cost for EKA(n) is $O(l^{n-1})$. We ignore the detail mathematical proof in this paper.

In Fig. 8(a), 8(b), and 8(c) the extension times are shown with $n = 4$, 5, 6 and maximum length l =120, 48, 24 for TMA and l = 170, 64, 32 for EKA respectively. The reason is as follows:

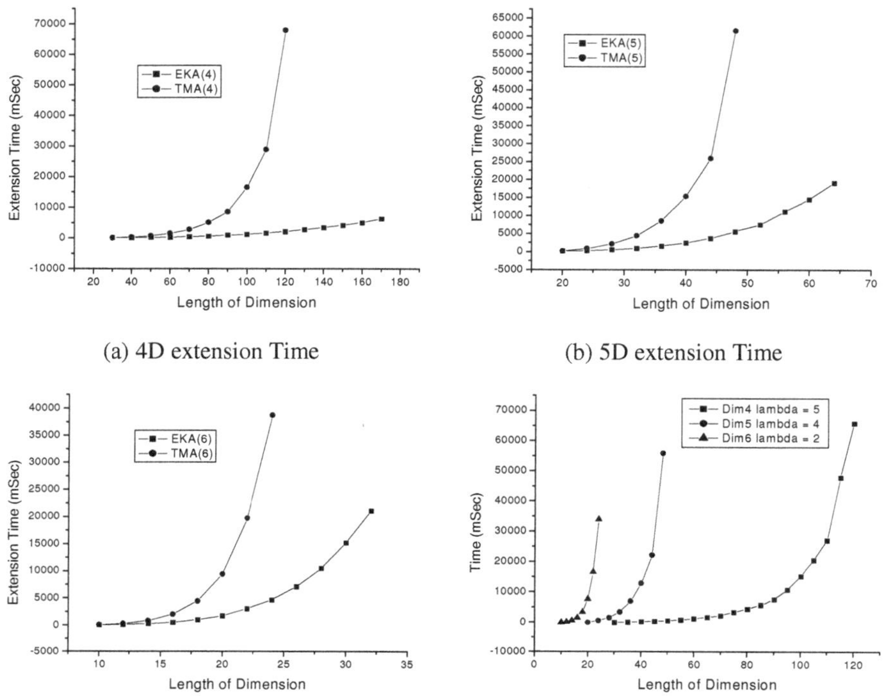

(a) 4D extension Time

(b) 5D extension Time

(c) 6D extension Time

(d) Extension gain

Fig. 8. Extension cost realization for EKA and TMA

In multidimensional array, we need to calculate the location of an element using the addressing function described in section 2. For an n dimensional array with each dimension length = l, maximum value of the coefficient vector can be l^n. This value quickly reaches the machine limit for TMA (eg. for 32 bit machine maximum value can be 2^{32}) and thus overflows. But in EKA since each of the segments are two dimensional, maximum value of the coefficient vector will be l^2, which greatly delays the overflow. One more reason is that TMA requires consecutive memory locations up to l^n and hence it overflows soon when l and n increases. On the other hand, in EKA the segments of the subarrays are always two dimensional and distributed. Hence consecutive memory location requirement is less in EKA than TMA. Therefore EKA delays the overflow situation even for large values of l.

6 Conclusion

In this paper, we proposed and evaluated a new scheme namely Extendible Karnaugh Array (EKA) for multidimensional array representation. We found better results for the proposed model than that of the traditional array representation. The main idea of the proposed model is to represent multidimensional array by a set of two dimensional extendible arrays. To extend the TMA re-linearization is necessary but this is very costly when if the array is large. Therefore we need an array system to extend in all dimensions without costly shuffling of the existing data. Our proposed EKA model serves this purpose efficiently. More over our model shows better performance for retrieval operations also. This scheme can be successfully applied to database applications especially for multidimensional database or multidimensional data warehousing system. One important future direction of the work is that, the scheme can be easily implemented in parallel platform. Because most of the operations described here is independent to each other. Hence it will be very efficient to apply this scheme in parallel and multiprocessor environment.

References

1. Seamons, K.E., Winslett, M.: Physical Schemas for Large Multidimensional Arrays in Scientific Computing Applications. In: 7th International Conference on Scientific and Statistical Database Management (SSDBM), pp. 218–227. IEEE CS, Washington, DC, USA (1994)
2. Sarawagi, S., Stonebraker, M.: Efficient Organization of Large multidimensional Arrays. In: 10th International Conference on Data Engineering, Houston, TX, USA, pp. 328–336 (1994)
3. Li, J., Srivastava, J.: Efficient Aggregation Algorithms for Compressed Data Warehouses. IEEE Transaction on Knowledge and Data Engineering 14(3), 515–529 (2002)
4. Zhao, Y., Deshpande, P.M., Naughton, J.F.: An Array Based Algorithm for Simultaneous Multidimensional Aggregates. ACM SIGMOD, 159–170 (1997)
5. Hasan, K.M.A., Kuroda, M., Azuma, N., Tsuji, T., Higuchi, K.: An Extendible Array Based Implementation of Relational Tables for Multi Dimensional Databases. In: Tjoa, A.M., Trujillo, J. (eds.) DaWaK 2005. LNCS, vol. 3589, pp. 233–242. Springer, Heidelberg (2005)
6. Hasan, K.M.A., Islam, K., Islam, M., Tsuji, T.: An Extendible Data Structure for Handling Large Multidimensional Data Sets. In: 12th International Conference on Computer and Information Technology, Dhaka, Bangladesh, pp. 669–674 (2009)
7. Rotem, D., Zhao, J.L.: Extendible Arrays for Statistical Databases and OLAP Applications. In: 8th International Conference on SSDBM, Stockholm, Sweden, pp. 108–117 (1996)
8. Pedersen, T.B., Jensen, C.S.: Multidimensional Database Technology. IEEE Computer 34(12), 40–46 (2001)
9. Hasan, K.M.A., Tsuji, T., Higuchi, K.: An Efficient Implementation for MOLAP Basic Data Structure and Its Evaluation. In: Kotagiri, R., Radha Krishna, P., Mohania, M., Nantajeewarawat, E. (eds.) DASFAA 2007. LNCS, vol. 4443, pp. 288–299. Springer, Heidelberg (2007)
10. Markus, B., Carsten, S., Gabriele, H.: On Schema Evolution in Multidimensional Databases. In: 1st International Conference on DaWaK, pp. 153–164. Springer, London (2005)
11. Acker, R., Pieringer, R., Bayer, R.: Towards Truly Extensible Database Systems. In: Andersen, K.V., Debenham, J., Wagner, R. (eds.) DEXA 2005. LNCS, vol. 3588, pp. 596–605. Springer, Heidelberg (2005)

12. Chen, Y., Dehne, F., Eavis, T., Chaplin, A.R.: Improved Data Partitioning for Building Large ROLAP Data Cubes in Parallel. Journal of Data Warehousing and Mining 2(1), 1–26 (2006)
13. Hasan, K.M.A., Tsuji, T., Higuchi, K.: A Parallel Implementation Scheme of Relational Tables Based on Multidimensional Extendible Array. Journal of Data Warehousing and Mining 2(4), 66–85 (2006)
14. Chun, Y.L., Yeh, C.C., Jen, S.L.: Efficient Representation Scheme for Multidimensional Array Operations. IEEE Transactions on Computers 51(3), 327–345 (2002)
15. Chun, Y.L., Yeh, C.C., Jen, S.L.: Efficient Data Parallel Algorithms for Multidimensional Array Operations Based on the EKMR Scheme for Distributed Memory Multicomputer. IEEE Transactions on Parallel and Distributed Systems 14(7), 625–639 (2003)
16. Chun, Y.L., Yeh, C.C., Jen, S.L.: Efficient Data Compression Method for Multidimensional Sparse Array Operations Based on EKMR Scheme. IEEE Transactions on Computers 52(12), 1640–1648 (2003)
17. Otoo, E.J., Merrett, T.H.: A Storage Scheme for Extendible Arrays. Computing 31, 1–9 (1983)
18. Otoo, E.J., Rotem, D.: A Storage Scheme for Multi-dimensional Databases Using Extendible Array Files. In: 3rd Workshop on STDBM, Seoul, Korea, pp. 67–76 (2006)
19. Otoo, E.J., Rotem, D.: Efficient Storage Allocation of Large-Scale Extendible Multi-dimensional Scientific Datasets. In: 18th International Conference on SSDBM, Vienna, Austria, pp. 179–183 (2006)
20. Rotem, D., Otoo, E. J., Seshadri, S.: Optimal Chunking of Large Multidimensional Arrays for Data Warehousing. Lawrence Berkeley National Laboratory, University of California, LBNL-63230 (2007)
21. Kumakiri, M., Bei, L., Tsuji, T., Higuchi, K.: Flexibly Resizable Multidimensional Arrays. In: 22nd International Conference on Data Engineering Workshops, Atlanta, GA, USA, pp. 83–88 (2006)
22. Mano, M.M.: Digital Logic and Computer Design. Prentice-Hall (2005)
23. Bertino, E., Kim, W.: Indexing Techniques for Queries on Nested Objects. IEEE Transactions on Knowledge and Data Engineering 1(2), 196–214 (1989)

Evaluation of Network Performance with Packet Measuring: A Trial Approach of Performance Evaluation for University Campus Network

Yoshiro Imai

Graduate School of Engineering, Kagawa University,
2217-20 Hayashi-cho, Takamatsu, Kagawa-pref. 761-0396 Japan
imai@eng.kagawa-u.ac.jp

Abstract. It is important for almost all users to know how their network environment can work correctly or suitably. Especially, it is considered to be significant whether really-provided (i.e. measured) performance is similar to theoretical one based on formulation or not. Sometimes the former performance may be rather different from the latter one from a viewpoint of our experience. We have utilized a kind of video transmission system which can be used as a network conference system. Not only because such a system becomes more and more useful in the distributed campus network environment, but also because the system must transmit certain amount of packet flows between and/or among its elements while it works. Such a video transmission system may be adequate and applicable to realize effective measurement of packet flow amount in the distributed campus network as a relatively wide experimental environment. This paper describes how to configure network conference scheme in order to formulate network performance and how to measure packet flow amount at specific points in the relevant network. A trial evaluation of network performance has been also carried out through comparison of packet flow amount for formulated (i.e theoretical) network performance and really measured one.

Keywords: Formulation of packet flow amount, Measurement of packet flow amount, Comparison of theoretical packet flow amount and really measured one, Performance evaluation based on comparison.

1 Introduction

Network is one of the very important environments to communicate and transfer information among users. Even in universities of the world, campus networks have been playing useful and essential roles to provide highly convenient communication between users, such as students, staffs and so on. In other words, network seems to be one of the most significant, necessary conditions that institutes and universities of the world can perform their duties and services to their users.

A. Abd Manaf et al. (Eds.): ICIEIS 2011, Part III, CCIS 253, pp. 151–160, 2011.

People say, "Networks are always considered to be working correctly. If is does not work, its users will complain allowing that they may make some mistakes." So network administrators must take care of their network and watch them to work correctly. And such administrators should check and investigate whether their network works correctly or not at regular intervals.

In order to check network facility and evaluate performance of network, we have formulated performance of our campus network based on theoretical prediction, measured packet flow amount[1][2] at the relevant points (namely with the network device which can report its packet flow amount), compared formulated packet flow amount with really measured one, and then try to evaluate network performance[4][3] by means of comparison and experimental situation.

This paper describes and reports our trial evaluation of network performance through comparison with formulated packet flow amount and really measured one in the network environment of our university. Our campus network environment is introduced in the next section. A kind of video transmission system is our target system, with which we formulated and measured packet flow amount. It is also explained in the same section. We formulated packet flow amount with model of network application with the above target system. Such a formulation is illustrated in the third and fourth sections.

We also measure packet flow amount with practical video transmission system which is implemented in our distributed campus network environment. The fifth and sixth sections demonstrate the result of measuring packet flow amount and its comparison with formulated one in the two typical cases. We have some discussion and consideration of performance evaluation of our networks with the above comparison and experience of using the above experimental video transmission system as a network conference system respectively. And finally we conclude our summary in the last (seventh) section.

2 Video Transmission System for Campus Network Environment

This section describes a brief introduction of our campus network environment and video transmission system as a target of our network performance evaluation.

First of all, we describe our campus network topology. It includes 4 major campuses, so that steering committee must move to one of them in order to participate in important meetings and university-level conferences. In such situations, some kinds of network conference scheme seem to be very much convenient and useful to reduce total movement of participants in the meetings and/or conferences.

This time, we tried to construct an element for such network conference scheme and apply it into one of real network conference systems. The element is organized with some clients, encoder and data exchanging /transferring server. A client is called digital video transmission system's client, which is abbreviated to "DVTS-client". A encoder is called digital video transmission system's encoder, which is abbreviated to "DVTS-encoder". And a data exchanging/transferring

Fig. 1. Elements of Video Transmission System

server is called an "IP-Tunneling Server" which is a server for digital video transmission system. Figure 1 shows elements of video transmission system for experimental network conference.

This IP-Tunneling Server is a special information server to catch the target information and/or signal generated by DVTS-encoder in each segment, encapsulate it into a special IP packet and throw the result to the another IP-Tunneling Server directly. When one IP-Tunneling Server receives encapsulated information/signal from another IP-Tunneling Server in another segment, the former IP-Tunneling Server decapsulates such information/ signal, in other words, it converts them to be viewed on DVTS-clients in its segment. It is why such a server called "IP-Tunneling Server", which is simply abbreviated to "IPTS" in the later explanation of this paper.

3 Estimation for Packet Flow Amount

This section presents an estimation of packet flow amount[5][7] of IPTS described in the previous section. It is assumed that there are n times of IPTS's in our scheme and the i-th IPTS in the focused segment has only one DVTS-encoder and mi times of DVTS-clients with focusing attention on the i-th IPTS.

Figure 2 shows an inter-multipoint video transmission scheme for network conference system, which consists of n times of IPTS's with one DVTS-encoder and mi times of DVTS-clients respectively. As focusing attention on the i-th IPTS, packet flow amount about it can be assumed as follows. We are separating input-bound packet flow amount and output-bound one for the i-th IPTS (focused IPTS). At first, in-bound packet flow amount includes $(n-1)$ times packet flow amount from other IPTS and e_i times of packet flow amount from its DVTS-encoders. Secondly, out-bound packet flow amount includes $(n-1)$

times packet flow amount to other IPTS and m_i times packet flow amount to its DVTS-clients. Generally speaking, with focusing attention to i-th IPTS, it is assumed that there are e_i times of DVTS-encoders, m_i times of DVTS-clients and $(n-1)$ times of other IPTS's. So the corresponding IPTS has $e_i + (n-1)$ times of packet flow amount for in-bound and $(n-1) + m_i$ times of packet flow amount for out-bound. Totally, the i-th IPTS has $e_i + 2(n-1) + m_i$ times of packet flow amount.

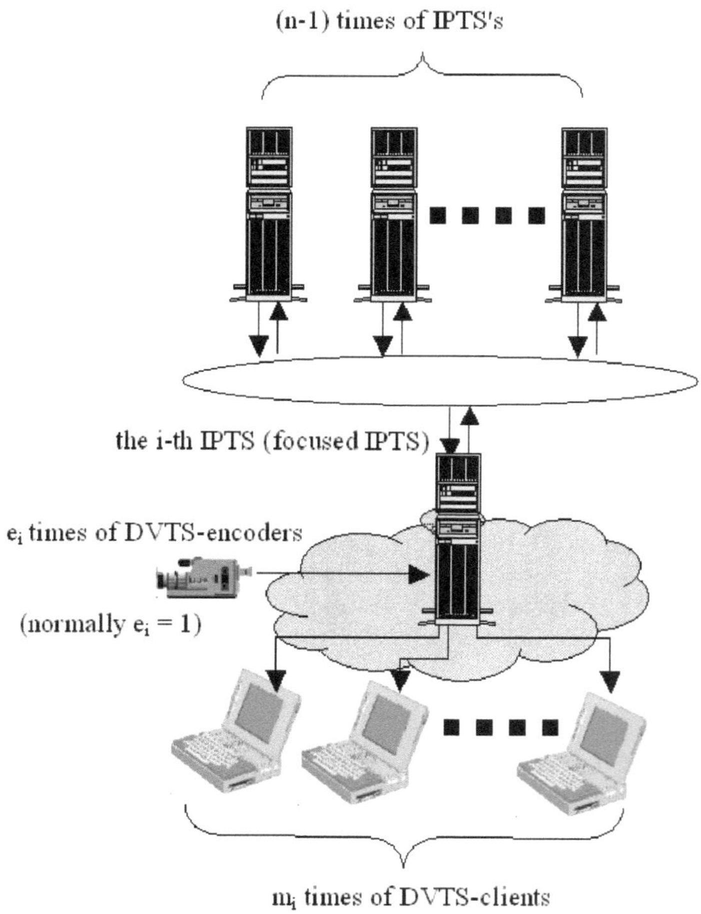

Fig. 2. Modeling of Video Transmission System for Network Conference

In order to evaluate system performance of the above inter-multipoint video transmission scheme, we assume the following three applicable conditions in using our prototype as network conference system:

- Each IPTS receives the same size of packet flow amount from every DVTS-encoder.

- Each DVTS-client can receive the same size of packet flow amount generated from the objective DVTS-encoder. Namely, it can be assumed to be almost loss less.
- The speed rate of packet is the same as other one. Namely, it is normally that speed rate is unique and the same as others in the whole system.

In this point, it is assumed that the size of packet flow amount from each DVTS-encoder is same and its value is N (bit per second: Bps). It is normal and never loses generality. So the i-th IPTS (i.e. each IPTS in the later section) has $Ne_i + 2(n-1) + m_i$ (bps). Frankly speaking, when our inter-multipoint video transmission scheme is applied to network conference system, organization of IPTS, DVTS-encoder and DVTS-client is simple and very much similar to one another. Almost always, the whole system may employ similar figure. For example, every IPTS has the same number of DVTS-encoder and the same ones of DVTS-clients naturally.

In order to realize a network conference system with our inter-multipoint video transmission scheme, we must define constant of general parameters as specific value. At first, it is supposed that there can be one video camera and one microphone in each conference room normally. So $e_i = 1$. Normally each conference room needs to communicate with the other conference ones. If such a conference room is corresponding to the i-th IPTS, numbers of the other conference ones are $(n-1)$ and it needs $m_i = (n-1)$ times of DVTS-clients for the other conference rooms. Sometimes, there are the only n times of DVTS-clients necessary because the last DVTS-client is corresponding to the i-th conference room itself. So $m_i = (n-1)$, sometimes $m_i = n$. There are at most 5 points of conference rooms simultaneously in usual network conference system of our University. So $n = 2, 3, 4, or 5$. N is the size of packet flow amount of DVTS-encoder, and we have employed such a DVTS-encoder that its output can be controlled by means of 10Mbps, 15Mbps, 20Mbps or 30Mbps. In other words, we can select N in the following mode: $N = 10M(bps), 15M(bps), 20M(bps) or 30M(bps)$. Secondly, it is described that specification of IPTS should transmit and/or receive $Ne_i + 2(n-1) + m_i$ of packet flow amount. In the case of $m_i = (n-1)$, the size of packet flow amount of IPTS is calculated in the following, $Ne_i + 2(n-1) + m_i = N1 + 2(n-1) + (n-1) = N(3n-2)$. In the case of $m_i = n$, it is also calculated as follows, $Ne_i + 2(n-1) + m_i = N1 + 2(n-1) + n = N(3n-1)$. On the other hand, it is assumed that there is only one IPTS in the according segment. It is one of normal conditions to use IPTS practically. Each IPTS can get packet flow amount from its DVTS-encoder and send it to the other IPTS's. So total amount of packet which each IPTS receives and transmit are $N2(n-1) = 2N(n-1)$ (bps). With the above parameters, we can express a formulation of packet flow amount of IPTS and inter-segment.

4 Formulation of Packet Flow Amount

On the condition of $N = 10Mbps, 15Mbps, 20Mbps, 30Mbps$ and $n = 2, 3, 4, or 5$, we can formulate the two-mode of packet flow amount size of IPTS and total amount of packet between each segment. Each value can be denoted as $N(3n-1)$, $N(3n-2)$ and $2N(n-1)$, respectively. For example, there are 3 inter-multipoint video transmission scheme employed for a real network conference system. We can control the volume of output from DVTS-encoder into 20Mbps. Such a case needs that $n = 3$, $N = 20$Mbps. Formulation about three values of $N(3n-1)$, $N(3n-2)$ and $2N(n-1)$ are simply specified as 160Mbps, 140Mbps and 80Mbps, respectively. We can define the formulation about the size of packet flow amount between IPTS's in the according segments theoretically which is shown in the Table 1.

Table 1. Packet Flow Amount Between IPTS'S in the According Segments (Theoretical Value, Unit: MBPS)

Output of DVTS-encoder	Packet Flow Amount			
	n=2	n=3	n=4	n=5
N= 10 (Mbps)	N(3n-1)= 50 N(3n-2)= 40 2N(n-1)= 20	N(3n-1)= 80 N(3n-2)= 70 2N(n-1)= 40	N(3n-1)= 110 N(3n-2)= 100 2N(n-1)= 60	N(3n-1)= 140 N(3n-2)= 130 2N(n-1)= 80
N= 15 (Mbps)	N(3n-1)= 75 N(3n-2)= 60 2N(n-1)= 30	N(3n-1)= 120 N(3n-2)= 105 2N(n-1)= 60	N(3n-1)= 165 N(3n-2)= 150 2N(n-1)= 90	N(3n-1)= 210 N(3n-2)= 195 2N(n-1)= 120
N= 20 (Mbps)	N(3n-1)= 100 N(3n-2)= 80 2N(n-1)= 40	N(3n-1)= 160 N(3n-2)= 140 2N(n-1)= 80	N(3n-1)= 220 N(3n-2)= 200 2N(n-1)= 120	N(3n-1)= 280 N(3n-2)= 260 2N(n-1)= 160
N= 30 (Mbps)	N(3n-1)= 150 N(3n-2)= 120 2N(n-1)= 60	N(3n-1)= 240 N(3n-2)= 210 2N(n-1)= 120	N(3n-1)= 330 N(3n-2)= 300 2N(n-1)= 180	N(3n-1)= 420 N(3n-2)= 390 2N(n-1)= 240

The upper limit of communication rate is at most 100Mbps. On the above case, $2N(n-1)$ becomes 80Mbps. It is similarly 100Mbps. Because other users communicate one another, so there may be over 100Mbps between specific segments. In such a case, packet flow can be regulated and some accidents may occur. By means of using boldface numbers, Table 1 indicates such cases with warning message. Such a formulation can be introduced theoretically and easily up to a case with $n = 10$ or more.

5 One-to-One Communication Using Video Transmission System

In the case of one-to-one communication using video transmission system, we have enjoyed a good environment as network conference system. Namely, when we need two or three times of packet throughput (i.e. packet speed) for more comfortable response, we can increase packet flow amount smoothly. As packet throughput comes higher, transferring video signals between two elements of video transmission system becomes faster and video information has been improved approximately in a linear function.

Figure 3 shows a graph for comparison of formulated packet flow amount and measured one at the One-to-one communication using video transmission system. As output level of DVTS-encoder becomes higher as step by step, measured result of packet flow amount, which IPTS can treat with at the same time, also increases linearly.

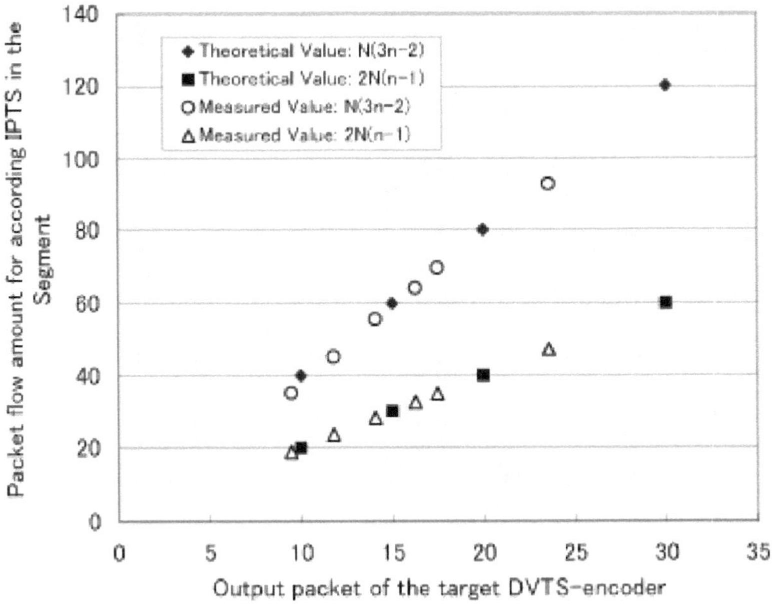

Fig. 3. Comparison of formulated packet flow amount and measured one at the One-to-one communication using video transmission system

Figure 3 also gives another good information about network performance, namely, it will be available in one to one communication for even other style applications to need linear growth of packet speed. For example, file transfer and data saving can be realized in the distributed network environment as far as communicating in one-to-one style.

In this case, we can perform evaluation of our network with formulated packet flow amount[6][8], because really-measured packet flow mount is simular with formulated one. And our network can provide very convenient performance to users who want to communicate with only one user in the network environment.

6 Inter-3 Point Areas Communication Using Video Transmission System

In the case of inter-3 point areas communication using video transmission system, we must have another result from experimental use as network conference system. Namely, we have some experience of saturation for packet flow amount in IPTS, and sometimes lose some packets from other video transmission system during communication among inter-3 point areas. Especially, when packet flow amount increases in high level, packet loss frequently occurs so that video signals receive a kind of block noises. In such a case, sound of video transferred from other system becomes not good enough to listen and motion of video also becomes "frozen" suddenly.

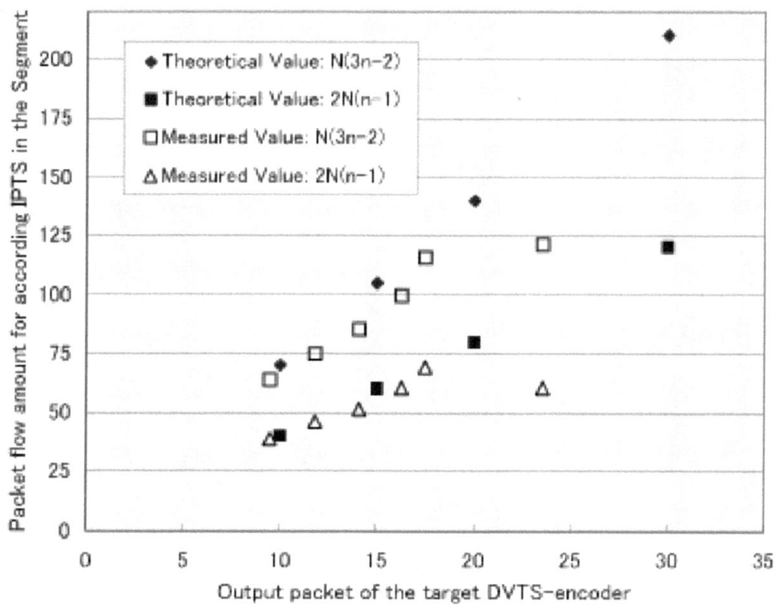

Fig. 4. Comparison of formulated packet flow amount and measured one at the Inter-3 point areas communication using video transmission system

Figure 4 shows a graph for comparison of formulated packet flow amount and measured one at the Inter-3 point areas communication using video transmission system. Although output level of DVTS-encoder becomes higher as step by step, measured result of packet flow amount, which IPTS can treat with at the same time, suddenly terminates linear growth and remain saturated with respect to more packet flow from DVTS-encoder .

Figure 4 also gives another information about network performance, namely, simultaneous communication among 3-point or more areas will probabilistically cause packet flow saturation which leads to communication stop or troubles among users. Of course, this situation may be attributable to not only network performance but also total performance of IT-Tunneling Server with DVTS-encoder and DVTS-client. We must investigate reasons of packet flow saturation as one of our future works.

7 Conclusion

This paper describes a trial performance evaluation of network with comparison of theoretical packet flow amount and really measured one. This experiment has been carried out by means of using a kind of video transmission system which plays a role of network conference system in distributed campus network environment.

We have employed DVTS-encoder, one of element for Video Transmission System, which can generate step-wise packet flow amount in the linear manner. So it is easy to apply step-wise input of packet flow amount into network servers and devices, which can measure real packet amount through its inner network channel. We can gain an understanding of packet flow amount and compare it with theoretical value of the relevant network device(or server).

After practical experiment of the two cases, we have obtained the following results. One case is a good result of performance so that it is convenient for users of campus network environment to utilize such network, while another is not so good because the result specifies that performance significantly depends on amount of packet. So it is summarized as follows:

- In the case of one-to-one communication, network performance is considered to be good enough to perform file transfer, data saving and so on. Because it is confirmed to be linear growth of packet speed, network can provide good performances during one-to-one communication.
- In the case of inter-3 point areas communication, network performance is considered to be unstable so that it is not suitable to achieve multiple connected communication. Especially, our university has 4 major campuses so there must be problems to be resolved if proposed video transmission system in inter-3 point or more areas communication is employed as network conference system

Acknowledgments. The Author would like to express his sincere thanks to Mr. Kazuyoshi Kawauchi, Mr. Kazutoshi Sone, Ms. Mayumi Kondo, Ms. Nobue Kawada, Ms. Shinobu Tada, Ms. Miho Yokoyama of Kagawa University and Mr. Hidetaka Noma, Mr. Toshiaki Yamashita of Net One Systems Inc. for their contributions to Experiments of Packet Measuring in Kagawa University Campus Network.

References

1. Lai, K., Baker, M.: Measuring link bandwidths using a deterministic model of packet delay. In: SIGCOMM 2000 Proceedings of the conference on Applications, Technologies, Architectures, and Protocols for Computer Communication, pp. 283–294. ACM, New York (2000)
2. Jain, M., Dovrolis, C.: End-to-end available bandwidth: measurement methodology, dynamics, and relation with TCP throughput. In: SIGCOMM 2002 Proceedings of the 2002 Conference on Applications, Technologies, Architectures, and Protocols for Computer Communications, pp. 295–308. ACM, New York (2002)
3. Wei, W., Wang, B., Towsley, D.: Continuous-time hidden Markov models for network performance evaluation. Performance Evaluation 49, 129–146 (2002)
4. Petrini, F., Frachtenberg, E., Hoisie, A., Coll, S.: Performance Evaluation of the Quadrics Interconnection Network. Cluster Computing 6, 125–142 (2003)
5. Pustisek, M., Savic, D., Humar, I., Bester, J.: Transport protocol dependent communications in different packet switch architectures. In: MELECON 2006 Proceedings of the IEEE Mediterranean Electrotechnical Conference, pp. 704–708 (2006)
6. Shi, L., Xia, G., Liu, B.: Performance Guarantees for Flow-Mapping Parallel Packet Switch. In: IPCCC 2007 Proceedings of the IEEE Conference on Performance, Computing, and Communications, pp. 109–116 (2007)
7. Celikoglu, H.B., Gedizlioglu, E., Dell'Orco, M.: A Node-Based Modeling Approach for the Continuous Dynamic Network Loading Problem. IEEE Transactions on Intelligent Transportation Systems 10(1), 165–174 (2009)
8. Prabhavat, S., Nishiyama, H., Ansari, N., Kato, N.: On the performance analysis of traffic splitting on load imbalancing and packet reordering of bursty traffic. In: IC-NIDC 2009 Proceedings of the IEEE Conference on Network Infrastructure and Digital Content, pp. 236–240 (2009)

Visualisation Support for the Protégé Ontology Competency Question Based Conceptual-Relationship Tracer

Muthukkaruppan Annamalai and Hamid Reza Mohseni

Faculty of Computer and Mathematical Sciences
Universiti Teknologi MARA
40450 Shah Alam, Selangor, Malaysia
mk@tmsk.uitm.edu.my, hrmohseni@gmail.com

Abstract. The competency evaluation of an ontology is a semantic analysis typically performed by an ontology engineer using a premeditated set of competency questions with the aid of evaluation tool such as the Competency Question based Conceptual-Relationship Tracer (CQ-CRT). A main limitation of the CQ-CRT that has been developed as a front-end application for the Protégé editor is that its result is represented in textual form, which is sometimes long winded and bogged with unwanted redundancies. It makes the result hard to trace and difficult to understand. We intend to assist the production of a visual representation of the textual result generated by the CQ-CRT in order to better promote the transparency and traceability of the analytic information. Jambalaya has been identified as a suitable visualiser plugin that can be adapted for providing the visualisation support. Consequently, this paper discusses the approach we have taken to adapt and integrate Jambalaya into CQ-CRT. A systematic testing and analysis was conducted to evaluate and improve the effective functioning of the integrated CQ-CRT visualisation tool. The analysis shows that the tool is able to afford the level of interactivity and visual expressiveness that meets the desired query requirements.

Keywords: Ontology, Competency evaluation, Information visualization, Software tool.

1 Introduction

Ontology is explicit specification of shared conceptualisation [1] that formally represents the entities that exist or may exist in a given domain. It serves as a semantic backbone of knowledge and information systems.

In this work, we considered the development of light-weight ontologies such as web-ontologies, which are simple models of knowledge. The concepts in these ontologies are defined as Frames, whose attributes are captured as properties and binary relations, which are defined as slots and constrained using facets. The hierarchical and domain-specific cross relations express the logical relationships between concepts. Instances are extensions of the defined concepts used in the description of knowledge base content.

A. Abd Manaf et al. (Eds.): ICIEIS 2011, Part III, CCIS 253, pp. 161–173, 2011.

Ontologies are often developed with the aid of special editing tools. Protégé [2], WebODE [3] and OntoWeb [4] are examples of editors that have been specifically developed to help users create and edit light-weight ontologies. The focus of our work is *Protégé ontologies*, i.e., ontologies developed using the Protégé ontology editor.

Protégé is selected because it is a popular, free and an open-source ontology editing platform. It provides a growing user community with a suite of tools to construct ontologies and knowledge-based applications. At its core, Protégé supports the creation and manipulation of ontologies which can be exported into a variety of web language formats such as OWL, RDF and XML schema.

Ontology evaluation is an important step in an ontology development life-cycle. Because ontologies are developed to serve as a semantic backbone of knowledge and information systems, the competency of an ontology is crucial for sake of the ontology's successful use [5]; and, some researchers contend that the competency evaluation ought to be part of the formative evaluation process, i.e., it should be performed while the ontology is being developed [6]. One way to evaluate the competency of an ontology is to check whether the ontology defines the necessary concepts, relations and properties to clearly express a set of predefined competency questions or their corresponding answers [7].

Competency questions were originally considered as a means to summatively assess the competency of knowledge-based systems [8, 9]. For example, a competency question to check the content of a knowledge base instantiated using concepts in a Family ontology (illustrated in Figure 1) is "*Who are the female members related to Adam [man]?*" Subsequently, the query answerer is expected to list all the female members in *Adam*'s family who are directly and indirectly related to him.

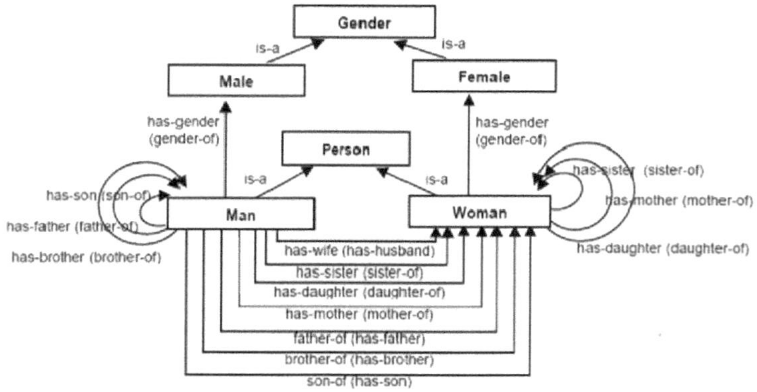

Fig. 1. A graphically reproduced segment of an example Family ontology. The concepts are shown in rectangles and the directed arrows represent the relations between a predecessor and its successor concepts.

In our case, the competency evaluation is performed over the terms defined in an ontology, and not over the instances in a knowledge base. The idea is to validate the functional adequacy of the conceptual definitions with respect to the competency questions.

Referring to the competency question for the family ontology mentioned earlier, the ontology engineer first needs to check whether the two key concepts in the question, i.e., *Man* and *Female*, are defined in the ontology, and are related in such way to appropriately respond to this question. It requires the tracing of the relationships involving these concepts in the ontology. For this purpose, a Competency Question based Conceptual-Relationship Tracer (CQ-CRT) for Protégé ontologies has been developed in a previous work to assist an ontology engineer to perform the competency evaluation [10]. The tool enables an engineer to make informative decisions about the modifications and extensions that are necessary to make the ontology amenable for future use.

A main limitation of the CQ-CRT is that its result is represented in textual form, which is sometimes long winded and bogged with unwanted redundancies. It makes the result hard to trace and at times difficult to understand as exemplified in the CQ-CRT's result describing the relationships between the concepts *Man* and *Female* defined in the Family ontology in Figure 2.

A graphical representation of the CQ-CRT's result could express the relevant background information about the ontology more simply and clearly, and free from redundancies. After all, visualisation is designed to enhance browsing, exploring and interaction with information spaces [11, 12] in order to promote a more intuitive and easy understanding of the investigated information. To an extent, this is evident in the visualisation in Figure 3, which provides a distinct graphical representation of the CQ-CRT's textual result shown in Figure 2.

There are currently three open source visualiser plugins for Protégé that support the visualisation of Frame based ontologies, namely TGViz [13], OntoViz [14] and Jambalaya [15]. Since we propose to find a visualisation support for the CQ-CRT that has been developed as a front-end application for Protégé, it would seem reasonable to adapt one of the above Protégé visualisers to support the visualisation of the CQ-CRT's result. Therefore, we have analysed the three visualiser plug-ins against a set of visualisation criteria to compare their utility and usability potentials, and identified Jambalaya as the closest visualisation fit for the CQ-CRT [16]. In this paper, we describe the approach we have taken to adapt and integrate Jambalaya into CQ-CRT.

Consequently, the paper is organised as follows. In section 2, we discuss the related works. In section 3, we detail the visualisation tool design and integration highlighting the modifications and enhancements to the CQ-CRT's and Jambalaya's classes. The evaluation of the integrated tool is described in section 4. Finally, in the concluding section, we summarise the contribution of this paper and point to the direction of future work.

2 Related Work

In this section, we provide a brief description about the purpose, design and the overall functions of each of the main constituents of the CQ-CRT visualisation tool, i.e., the CQ-CRT and the Jambalaya's QueryView applications.

2.1 Competency Question Based Conceptual-Relationship Tracer (CQ-CRT)

CQ-CRT is a Java based tool and has undergone several improvements since it was first developed by Annamalai and Teo [10]. It is designed to help an ontology engineer to interactively query and analyse the competency of a Protégé ontology under development. The CQ-CRT describes the background information about the concepts, relations and properties defined in an ontology using one of the following six pre-identified query options. We regard the expressiveness of these queries as the basic requirements to ascertain if the ontological commitments are adequate to support the ontology's use and need.

I. a particular concept (lists all relations that originate from the named concept or directed to it),
II. a particular property (lists all the concepts that are defined using the named property),
III. a particular relation (lists all the concept pairs that are directly related through the named relation),
IV. a particular relation directed from a certain source concept (lists all the concepts immediately succeeding the named source concept through the named relation),
V. a particular relation directed to a certain target concept (lists all the concepts immediately preceding the named target concept through the named relation), or
VI. a pair of source and target concepts (lists all the direct as well as the indirect relationships between the named source and target concepts).

Figure 2 shows the original interface of the CQ-CRT (that does not support query option II). The query panel at the top of the window contains three text boxes for user to enter the name(s) of a source concept, a relation and/ or a target concept. The user fills one or two of these input boxes, and then presses the Find button to generate the result, which comprises several conceptual-relationship statements of the form: "*predecessor concept – normal relation (inverse relation) – successor concept*".

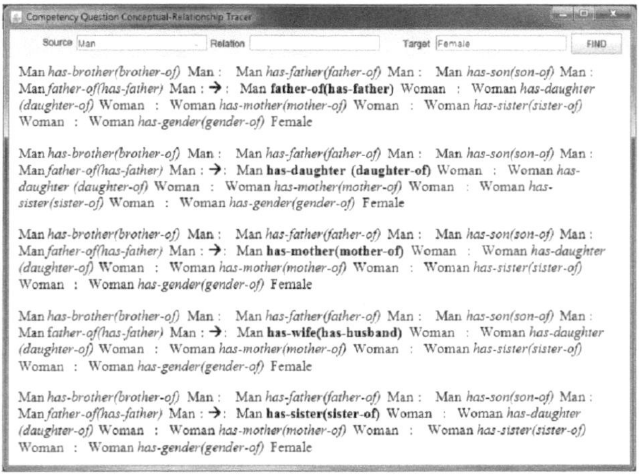

Fig. 2. CQ-CRT's result describing the relationships between *Man* and *Female* in the Family ontology

For example, the result in Figure 2 indicates that the concepts *Man* and *Female* are related through an intermediary concept *Woman* in five different ways, i.e., through each of the five parallel relations defined between *Man* and *Woman* (printed in bold), namely *father-of, has-daughter, has-mother, has-wife* and *has-sister*, and their respective inverse relations (in brackets). However, there are redundancies in the result that makes the information appear long winded. Note the self-referencing relations between *Man* (e.g. *brother-of*), the self-referencing relations between *Woman* (e.g. *has-daughter*) and the direct relation between *Woman* and *Female* (e.g. *has-gender*) are repeated in all the five text blocks.

Figure 3 graphically delineates the CQ-CRT's result tracing the relationships between *Man* and *Female* in the Family ontology. The concepts are represented as labelled nodes while the arcs denote the direct relationships between a pair of concepts. The relation names (arc labels) are not shown on this graph for the sake of visibility of the relationships.

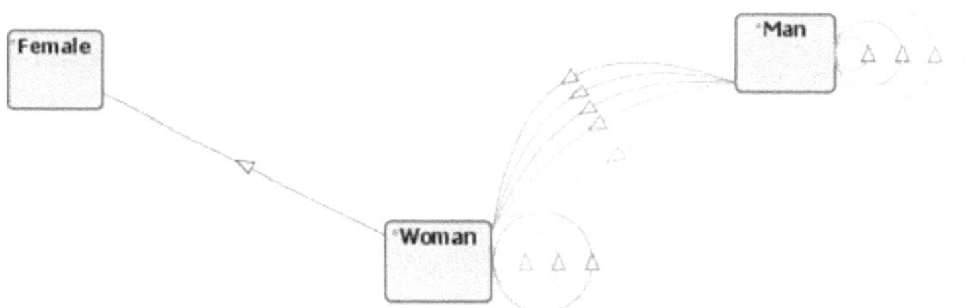

Fig. 3. Distinct visualisation of the CQ-CRT's result shown in Figure 2

Figure 4 (a) outlines the key functional components of the CQ-CRT. First the concept and relation terms defined in an ontology are extracted from the Protégé ontology file, and stored in three distinct vectors. Second, a Conceptual Adjacency Matrix (CAM) is constructed using the information about the normal relationships between concepts. The representation of the conceptual-relationships in the ontology in an adjacency matrix facilitates easy access and manipulation. Third, the inverse relationships are updated to the CAM. Next, the transitive closures of the relations are computed, and the indirect relationships are updated.

As a result, the processing and retrieval of the relevant information for query options I, III, IV and V can be implemented quite straightforwardly by performing systematic searches over the structured data in the term vectors and in the CAM.

On the other hand, the implementation of query option VI is rather challenging because of the need to find not only the direct relationships between two concepts, but also all the indirect relationships that exist between them. For this, the algorithm of Warshall [17] has been adapted to compute the transitive closure of the binary relationships in the ontology. The original Warshall algorithm simply manipulates Boolean values, and so can only indicate the presence or the absence of path connecting any two nodes in a graph. Therefore, the algorithm has been modified to allow the manipulation of textual information in the CAM. In addition, a marking scheme has been employed to represent the tracking information created during the computation of the transitive closure. The tracking information is updated to the CAM and is later utilised to generate the result by traversing the graph representation using a Coloured Depth-First Search algorithm.

2.2 Jambalaya Visualiser Plugin

Jambalaya has QuickView and QueryView application interfaces to visualise concepts and their corresponding instances defined in Protégé. They are designed using the SHriMP visualisation technique [18], which was originally created for software visualisation. It supports interactive environment, tree and nested layouts, zooming, multiple colours and other features.

QuickView helps users to browse the information space using custom views created by selecting the concepts or instances, and their relations that the users wish to include in a view. On the other hand, the QueryView runs a text matching query based on specified parameters that consists of a single concept and selected relations. The idea is to show the concept of interest and its surrounding neighbourhood. Because CQ-CRT is also a text matching query interface, it would seem logical to extend Jambalaya's QueryView interface to provide visualisation support for CQ-CRT.

The QueryView interface is shown in Figure 5 (a). It contains a Search panel layout *(A)*, a Node and Arc Types filter panel *(F)*, a Toolbar *(G)* and a Display window *(H)*. The Search panel contains the search components that comprises a text box *(B)* to select a concept in the ontology, a list box *(C)* to chose the regular expression type of search (*starts with, ends with, contains or exactly match*), another list box *(D)* to select the level of the search (*neighbourhood, parent, children or hierarchy*), and a submit query button *(E)*. The Node and Arc Types filter panel contains check boxes that can be used to select the type of nodes (concepts and instances) and arcs (relations) to show or hide. The Toolbar holds the display layout icons that help to centre, resize and reorder the visualisation linearly, hierarchically or in a star shape.

Jambalaya is an open source tool extended from Java Bean architecture [19], but without supporting technical documentation. Since there is only little knowledge in the literature about its development, we carried out reverse engineering to study its components, what they are used for, how they are structured and how they function. Based on this analysis, we delineate the core functional components of the QueryView application interface as shown in Figure 4 (b).

The QueryPanelComponent class handles the GUIs of the QueryView application. It manages the components of the Search panel layout, the Node and Arc Types filter panel and the Toolbar.

The QueryHelper class helps to manage the query parameters in QueryPanel Component and processes the input data to determine the concepts and relations that should be displayed. Next, the information is sent to the DataDisplayBridge, an adapter class that bridges the DataBean with the DisplayBean.

The DataBean is an internal database of the data objects (ontology terms) obtained from the Protégé project file. The DisplayBean is responsible for putting the graph on view in the display window. It holds information about the display objects such as their labels, their colours, the graph scale, its position and so on. The DataDisplayBridge contains mappings from the data objects, i.e., artefacts (concepts and instances) and relations (in the DataBean) to their corresponding display objects, i.e., nodes and arcs (in the DisplayBean).

3 CQ-CRT Visualisation Tool Design and Integration

The CQ-CRT visualisation tool is developed by integrating Jambalaya's QueryView into CQ-CRT. Figure 4 depicts the main components and the functioning of the integrated tool, and the dataflow among the components. The integration requires reworks on both ends involving five classes. We discuss the related issues and highlight the modifications and enhancements to these classes below.

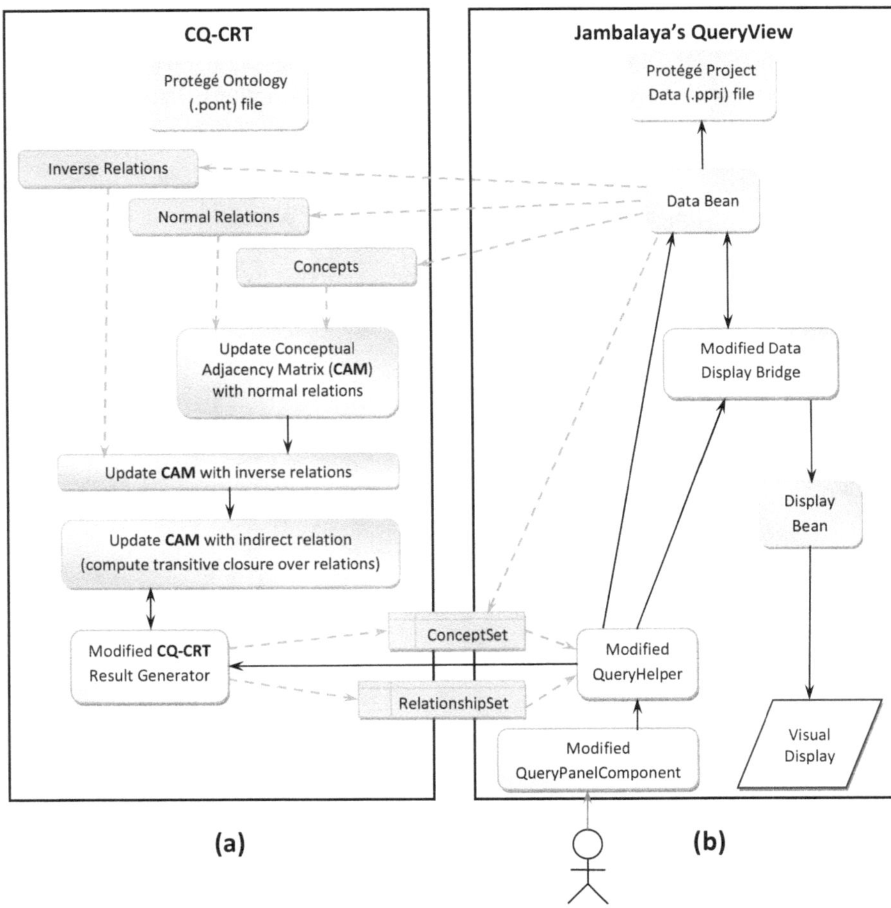

Fig. 4. The main components and functioning of the integrated CQ-CRT visualisation tool, and the dataflow among the components. The solid arrows represent transfer of process control, while the outlined arrows shows the flow of data between the different components and data stores.

3.1 Modifications to CQ-CRT Main

The CQ-CRT parses the Protégé ontology (*.pont*) file represented in Clips format to extract the concept and relationship terms defined in an ontology to populate the conceptual adjacency matrix, whereas Jambalaya obtains the same information from the Protégé project (*.pprj*) file. For sake of consistency, we amended the main class of CQ-CRT to obtain the information from a single source, i.e., from the DataBean in QueryView, which in turn obtains it from the Protege's KnowledgeBase class through an API.

3.2 Modifications to QueryPanelComponent

As mentioned in the previous section, we want the CQ-CRT visualisation tool to provide for the six text matching query options involving a pair of concepts, a relation and a property. On the other hand, the Jambalaya's QueryView just permits query based on a single concept and/ or relations. As a result, Jambalaya currently only supports query options I and V. It does not support query options II and VI. It is also unable to express all and only the relevant facts for query options III and IV. More details can be found in [16].

Moreover, there are unwanted features in the QueryView interface such as the Node and Arc Types filter panel and few irrelevant display layout icons in the Toolbar that can be removed.

Since QueryPanelComponent contains the components used in QueryView, changes are made to this class to accommodate the requirements of CQ-CRT. The re-designed QueryView interface is shown in Figure 5 (b).

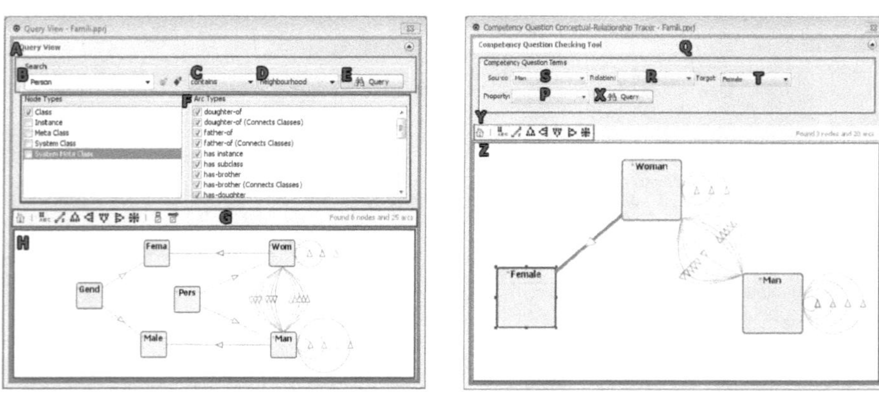

(a) Original QueryView interface **(b)** Re-designed QueryView interface

Fig. 5. Jambalaya's QueryView interface – before and after re-design screenshots

The Search panel layout *(Q)* now comprises four list boxes for users to enter the name(s) of Source concept *(S)*, Relation *(R)*, Target concept *(T)*, and/ or Property *(P)*, depending on the selected query option. The Toolbar *(Y)* only retains the Home and the display layout icons. The Node and Arc Types filter panel along with the icons that help to expand and collapse this panel are discarded. The Query button *(X)* to submit the query and the Display window *(Z)* are retained.

Consequently, we need to make modifications to some of the classes in CQ-CRT and Jambalaya to support the re-designed QueryView interface. This is discussed in the ensuing subsections.

3.3 Modifications to CQ-CRT Result Generator

The CQ-CRT Result Generator produces the result by searching, retrieving and processing the data in the term vectors and in the conceptual adjacency matrix. There is a query method for each of the query options (except for option II). First, we enabled the invocation of the query methods from an external class. Next, we collected the concept and relation terms that feature in the CQ-CRT's result and send the collection to the invocator. For this purpose, two Java collection variables: *ConceptSet* and *RelationshipSet* were created. A relation is identified uniquely by its source and target concepts, and is represented as a triple: *relation(source concept, target concept).*

3.4 Modifications to QueryHelper

The QueryHelper class originally mediates between the DataDisplayBridge and the QueryPanelComponent to handle the execution of a query. Now, we coerce this class to interact with the CQ-CRT and the DataBean, which is necessary to process the CQ-CRT's query options. The modified QueryHelper process is as follows:

a. Get user input from the QueryPanelComponent.
b. For query option II, send request to DataBean to obtain a collection of concepts that are defined by a given property.
c. For all other query options, identify the query parameters and send messages to evoke the corresponding methods in the CQ-CRT Result Generator.
d. In response to the information requests in steps (c) and (d) above, the concept and/or relation terms that ought to feature in the query result are obtained. These data objects are conveyed to the DataDisplayBridge.

3.5 Modifications to DataDisplayBridge

The DataDisplayBridge creates the display objects from the given data objects. To visualise the selected concepts, we add the corresponding artefacts using the *addObject* method of the DisplayBean. This will create and add the visual representation of the nodes associated with each artefact, as well as all the arcs (corresponding to relations) between them to the display. An arc is identified with a source and a target node.

Unfortunately, it is not possible to display only the nodes (e.g. Query option II) or only the arcs associated with a particular relations (e.g. Query options III, IV and V) using the *addObject* method. On the contrary, the DisplayBean's *removeObject* method allows us to remove selected arcs, leaving their related nodes in the display. Therefore, to overcome this problem, we compiled two sets of relations: the first one is the set of relations that we want to display (R_W), and the second one is the relations that we do not want to display (R_D), i.e., all relations defined in the ontology minus the relations in the first set ($R_D = R_{all} \setminus R_W$). Subsequently, we removed the represented arcs corresponding to the relations in the second set (R_D) from the display with the aid of the *removeObject* method. In this way, we were able to display all and only the nodes and arcs corresponding to the concepts and relations that ought to feature in the result.

4 Evaluation of the CQ-CRT Visualisation Tool

A systematic testing and analysis was conducted to validate the features of the integrated CQ-CRT visualisation tool, as well as to verify the effective functioning of this tool. The function verification test is part of the iterative development process to ensure that the visual information reflects the CQ-CRT's textual result. The test is organised to check the performance of the tool in response to the allowed user queries.

The general test cases for each of the six query options are outlined in Figure 6. The concept, relation and property terms are represented using rectangle, arrow and diamond shapes, respectively. The solid shapes indicate the terms in focus, while the outlined shapes denote the terms associated with the term(s) in focus.

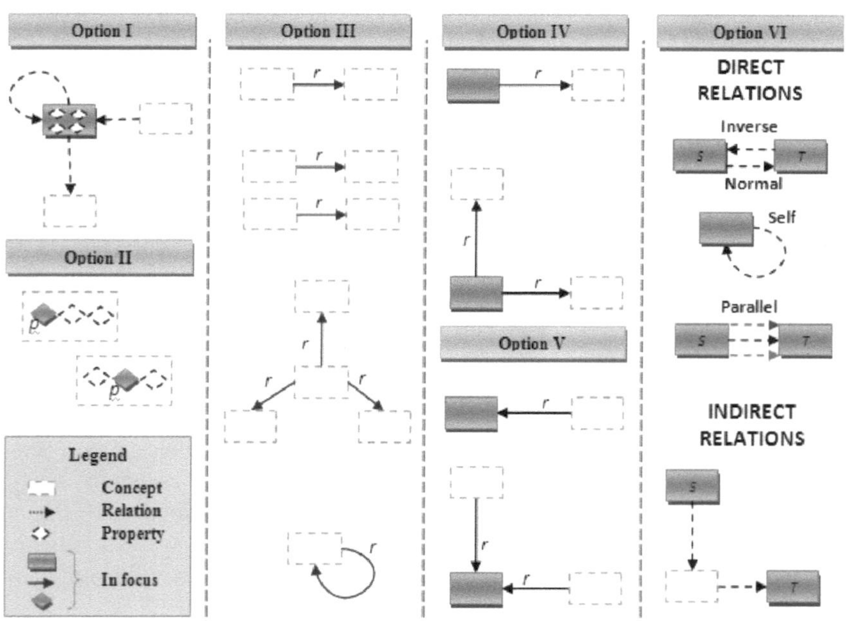

Fig. 6. The general test cases for each of the six query options

For option I, we checked the tool's ability to display a named concept with all relations that originate from or directed to it. In particular, we checked for six (6)

cases when the named concept has no relation, has only one or more incoming relations, has only one or more outgoing relations, has both incoming and outgoing relations. We also checked for the case when the named concept is not represented in the ontology.

For option II, we checked the tool's ability to show all the concepts that are defined using a named property *p*. We checked for two (2) cases when the property is defined in a single and in multiple concepts.

For option III, we checked the tool's ability to present all concept pairs that are directly related through the named relation *r*. We checked for two (2) cases when there is single or multiple relations *r* defined in the ontology. When there are multiple relations, we also checked for two (2) additional special cases when the relations *r* originate from or directed to a common concept.

For option IV, we checked the tool's ability to display all the concepts immediately succeeding the named predecessor concept through the named relation *r*. While for option V, we checked for its ability to put on view all the concepts immediately preceding the named successor concept through the named relation *r*. Options IV and V are actually subsets of option I, but centred on specific relation and its orientation. We also checked for cases when either the named concept or the named relation is not represented in the ontology. Accordingly, we checked for six (6) cases, i.e., three cases for each query option IV and V.

Finally, for option VI, we checked the tool's ability to visualise all the direct as well as the indirect (inferred) relationships between the named source concept *S* and the target concept *T*. In the case of indirect association between these concepts, there can be multiple ways and one or more intermediate relations to consider depending on the distance between the concepts in the ontology. We checked for fifty-four (54) cases involving only subsumption relations (*S* is above *T* in a hierarchy), only supersumption relations (*S* is below *T* in a hierarchy), only cross relations, both subsumption and cross relations, both supersumption and cross relation, and all types of (subsumption, supersumption and cross) relations.

We also checked for two (2) cases involving parallel relations (i.e., two or more distinct relations connecting a same pair of concepts).

While hierarchical relations are free of cycles, there can be admissible cycles involving indirect domain-specific cross relations. So, we checked for twenty-three (23) cases involving circularity at distance zero (self-referencing relation), one (with normal and inverse relation), two or more.

In total, the test suite consists of ninety-seven (97) cases involving three ontologies of varying sizes, namely the Family (6 concepts), Newspaper (26 concepts) and the Wine (109 concepts) ontologies. The Newspaper and Wine ontologies are obtained from the Protégé ontology library. In all cases, the CQ-CRT visualisation tool has demonstrated its ability to respond effectively to the six query options by producing the expected result as output.

From our observation, there is an apparent gain in the transparency and traceability of the interactive visualisation of the analytic information generated by the CQ-CRT; and, as a consequence, it would make the competency evaluation easier, less subjective, more complete and faster.

5 Conclusion and Future Work

We considered the development of a visualisation support for the CQ-CRT. CQ-CRT is an ontology evaluation supporting tool used by an ontology engineer to interactively query and analyse the competency of Protégé ontology under development. Jambalaya, a Protégé visualiser plugin, has been identified as a suitable visualisation fit for CQ-CRT in a previous work.

Consequently, this paper describes the integration of Jambalaya's QueryView application interface into CQ-CRT by addressing Jambalaya's expressiveness deficiencies before linking it up with CQ-CRT. It involves modifications and enhancements to five classes, which includes the re-design of the query interface.

A systematic testing and analysis was conducted to verify the effective functioning of the integrated tool, and we are convinced of the tool's present ability to afford the level of interactivity and visual expressiveness that meets the desired query requirements.

Currently, the integrated tool is dependent on Jambalaya, i.e., it is required to run on Jambalaya's environment. Therefore, our future work will be devoted to casting the CQ-CRT visualisation to work independent of Jambalaya, but as a tab plugin for Protégé. We also plan to equip the tool with a front-end natural language interface that would enable a competency question itself be used as a query parameter. This would help to dispense of the human effort to identify the terms in the ontology that could be linked to the keywords in a given competency question.

References

1. Gruber, T.R.: A Translation Approach to Portable Ontology Specification. Knowledge Acquisition 5(2), 199–220 (1993)
2. Noy, N.F., Sintek, M., Decker, S., Crubezy, M., Fergerson, R.W., Musen, M.: Creating Semantic Web Contents with Protégé-2000. IEEE Intelligent Systems 16, 60–71 (2001)
3. Arpírez, J.C., Corcho, O., Fernández-López, M., Gómez-Pérez, A.: WebODE: A Scalable Workbench for Ontological Engineering. In: Conference on Knowledge Capture, Victoria, British Columbia (2001)
4. Spyns, P., Oberle, D., Volz, R., Zheng, J., Jarrar, M., Sure, Y., Studer, R., Chung, S.: Ontoweb:A Semantic Web Community Portal. In: Karagiannis, D., Reimer, U. (eds.) PAKM 2002. LNCS (LNAI), vol. 2569, pp. 189–200. Springer, Heidelberg (2002)
5. Gangemi, A., Catenacci, C., Ciaramita, M., Lehmann, J.: A Theoretical Framework for Ontology Evaluation and Validation. In: Italian Semantic Web Workshop on Semantic Web Applications and Perspectives, Trento (2005)
6. Annamalai, M.: Formative Evaluations of Ontologies for Information Agents. In: Conference on Computer Science, Technology and Networking, Shah Alam (2005)
7. Annamalai, M., Sterling, L.: Guidelines for Constructing Reusable Domain Ontologies. In: Autonomous Agents and Multi-Agent Systems Conference Workshop on Ontologies in Agent Systems. CEUR Series, Melbourne, vol. 73 (2003)
8. Gruninger, M., Fox, M.: Methodology for the Design and Evaluation of Ontologies. In: Artificial Intelligence Conference Workshop on Basic Ontological Issues in Knowledge Sharing, Montreal (1995)

9. Noy, N., McGuinness, D.: Ontology Development 101: A Guide to Creating Your First Ontology. Technical Report, Stanford Knowledge Systems Laboratory (2001)
10. Annamalai, M., Teo, N.: Tool Support for Competency Evaluation of Web-Ontologies. In: Conference on Informatics, Petaling Jaya (2007)
11. Card, S.K., Mackinlay, J.D., Shneiderman, B.: Readings in Information Visualization: Using Vision to Think. Morgan Kaufmann (1999)
12. Freedman, E.G., Shah, P.: Toward a Model of Knowledge-Based Graph Comprehension. In: Conference on Diagrammatic Representation and Inference, Callaway Garden, Georgia (2002)
13. Alani, H.: TGVizTab: An Ontology Visualisation Extension for Protégé. In: Knowledge Capture Workshop on Visualization Information in Knowledge Engineering, Sanibel Island, Florida (2003)
14. Sintek, M.: OntoViz. Protégé Wikki (2001), `http://protegewiki.stanford.edu/wiki/OntoViz`
15. Storey, M., Noy, N., Musen, M., Best, C., Fergerson, R., Ernst, N.: Jambalaya: An Interactive Environment for Exploring Ontologies. In: Conference on Intelligent User Interfaces, San Francisco, California (2002)
16. Annamalai, M., Mohseni, H.R.: Jambalaya: The Closest Visualisation Fit for the Protégé Ontology Conceptual-Relationship Tracer. In: Conference on Science and Social Research, Kuala Lumpur (2010)
17. Warshall, S.: A Theorem on Boolean Matrices. Journal of the ACM 9(1), 11–12 (1962)
18. Storey, M., Wong, K., Fracchia, F., Mueller, H.: On Integrating Visualization Techniques for Effective Software Exploration. In: IEEE Symposium on Information Visualization, Phoenix, Arizona (1997)
19. Best, C.: Designing a Component-Based Framework for a Domain Independent Visualization Tool. Computer Science Department, University of Victoria (2002)

Empirical Study on Quality Requirements of Migration Metadata

Feng Luan, Mads Nygård, Guttorm Sindre, Trond Aalberg, and Shengtong Zhong

Department of Computer and Information Science,
Norwegian University of Science and Technology,
Trondheim, Norway
{luan,mads,guttors,trondaal,shket}@idi.ntnu.no

Abstract. Migration requires metadata about old hardware/software configurations or old computer technologies. However, current metadata schemas used in preservation systems are different and it is difficult to judge the actual quality requirement of metadata migration. This paper presents a set of quality requirements for migration metadata and the necessity and sufficiency of these requirements are evaluated with a questionnaire that was distributed internationally and followed up by several telephone interviews. The survey results indicate that our requirements are complete and can be classified into three levels, namely essentiality, necessity, and conditionality. The proposed quality requirements can be used by custodians as a checklist to examine their metadata schemas in terms of how well they can support migration.

Keywords: Information Management, Migration, Metadata Requirements, Long-term Preservation.

1 Introduction

Migration is "a set of organized tasks designed to achieve the periodic transfer of digital objects from one hardware/software configuration to another, or from one generation of computer technology to a subsequence generation" [1] (p. iii). Its objective is to ensure digital objects can be accessed, retrieved, manipulated, and preserved over time. However, for a migration procedure, one of the key factors is to have necessary and complete metadata. For example: the format migration workflow in [2] needs metadata about organization policies, file characteristics, migration process characteristics, cost requirements, old formats, new formats, a mechanism capturing migrated objects, assessment approaches, and evaluation approaches for the migration solution. The second example is the migration of hyperlinks of HTML files in [3]. Beside the current and previous file management system structures, the type and syntax of the hyperlinks are needed. The last example is to replace storage media. Even though there is no change to digital objects, custodians still need hardware metadata to find compatible replacements and need fixity metadata to prove the bit integrity.

A. Abd Manaf et al. (Eds.): ICIEIS 2011, Part III, CCIS 253, pp. 174–188, 2011.

Many national libraries, national archives, and governmental departments have designed their preservation metadata schemas for a long-term preservation purpose. Several examples are given in Section 2.1. Surprisingly, few studies formally examine how well those preservation metadata schemas perform in an actual migration. Even in some practical implementations of migration, e.g., [4-6], they used a set of particular metadata for their projects. We also did not find any discussion on quality requirements of migration metadata. Thus, we try to design a set of quality requirements. We believe that such requirements are more necessary than a particular metadata schema. It is because metadata schemas may be different in projects, whereas the high level requirements are more often similar. Moreover, the requirements can be reused as a checklist for helping people not to forget any important aspect.

This paper is a continuation of previous work [7] where we derived 24 quality requirements from recent works about preservation metadata and migration. Those 24 requirements cover metadata on storage, hardware, applications, specifications, characteristics, provenance, modification rights, and retention policies. In this paper, we use an on-line questionnaire and several telephone interviews to answer two research questions:

- ***RQ1:*** Are the proposed requirements necessary?
- ***RQ2:*** Are the proposed requirements complete?

This paper is organized as follows: Section 2 introduces recent work on preservation metadata schemas and quality criteria for building trustworthy preservation systems. Section 3 presents the design of two abstract migration procedures. Section 4 describes the quality requirements about migration metadata. Then, Sections 5 - 6 introduce and analyze the empirical study. Finally, Section 7 discusses the validity of the findings, and concludes the paper.

2 Related Work

2.1 Preservation Metadata

Preservation systems not only store digital objects, but also store a lot of metadata. These metadata are called preservation metadata, defined as "descriptive, structural, and administrative metadata that supports the long-term preservation of digital objects" in [8] (p. 5).

From 2000, a number of preservation metadata schemas were designed by libraries and archives. In 2002, the OCLC/RLG aggregated some metadata schemas and proposed a data model in [9], which complies with the Reference Model for an Open Archival Information System (OAIS) [10]. The OCLC/RLG also designed PREMIS-v1.0 and PREMIS-v2.0 in 2005 and 2008, respectively. Many national libraries, national archives and university libraries are now using PREMIS. Besides the OCLC/RLG, other organizations designed their own metadata schemas e.g., the National Library of New Zealand's preservation metadata [11] and the National Archive of Norway's Noark 5 [12]. In general, these preservation metadata elements cover and focus on:

- *Collection information*: As digital information is a group of digital objects, collection information should contain the description of this digital information and package structures between the digital objects.
- *Object information:* Object information provides metadata about the content of a digital object and the technique infrastructure for viewing the digital object.
- *Provenance information*: Provenance information describes previous events and corresponding outcomes for a digital object.
- *Rights information:* Rights information provides restrictions on how to store and use a given digital object.

2.2 Quality Criteria to Trustworthy Preservation Systems

Besides the above preservation metadata schemas, two quality criteria specify how to create a trustworthy preservation system. One is the Trustworthy Repositories Audit & Certification: Criteria and Checklist (TRAC) [13] and the other one is Nestor [14]. Both of the criteria cover three aspects:

- *Organization:* The preservation system should define its mandate, objectives, responsibility, organizational policy and structure, the staffing, and the financial issues.
- *Object management:* The preservation system should guarantee the integrity, authenticity, availability, and confidentiality of digital information in different management phases.
- *Technical infrastructure and security:* The preservation system should describe its general system infrastructure, appropriate technologies facilitating data management, and security technologies protecting the digital objects.

3 Abstract Migration Procedures

In terms of recent work on migration [5, 6, 10, 15], we propose two abstract migration procedures: *Replication* that focuses on copying and moving digital objects between storage media, and *Transformation* that focuses on converting digital objects and metadata to a new technique.

3.1 Replication

In *replication*, digital objects are copied and moved from Storage A to Storage B, so that the digital objects can be preserved in a healthy medium. Fig. 1 shows a generic design for this procedure: custodians are able to copy Bits-A to Bits-B only when they have the access rights. When the copy finishes, the custodians should use a software application to check bit integrity by comparing Bits-A and Bits-B in Step 4. If Bits-A = Bits-B, the new locations of the digital objects should be updated in a database or other location management systems in Step 6. Thus, the preservation system can know where the duplicated objects are. Moreover, provenance metadata about this event should be generated in Step 7. Finally, the new replica Bits-B with the provenance metadata will be stored to one or more storage media. If not equal, the process should attempt to duplicate Bits-A up to a certain threshold for the number of attempts.

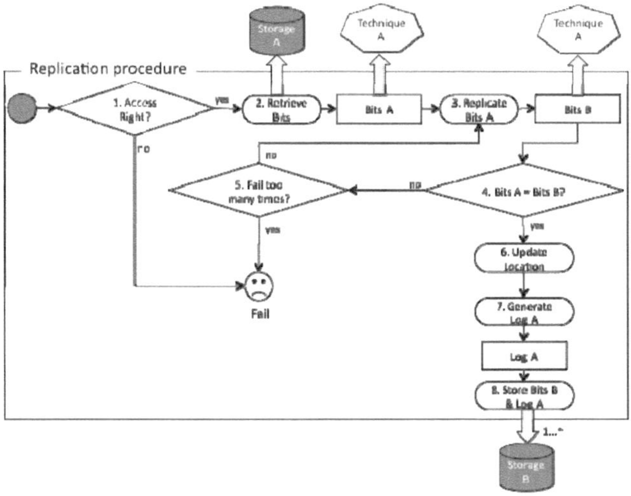

Fig. 1. Abstract Procedure for Replication

3.2 Transformation

In *transformation*, digital objects and metadata are transformed from Technique A to Technique B, so that the digital objects can be presented or processed with a new technique. This procedure is illustrated in Fig. 2: custodians can transform Bits-A only when they have legal modification rights and access rights. After the transformation, a manual validation procedure or an automatic validation procedure

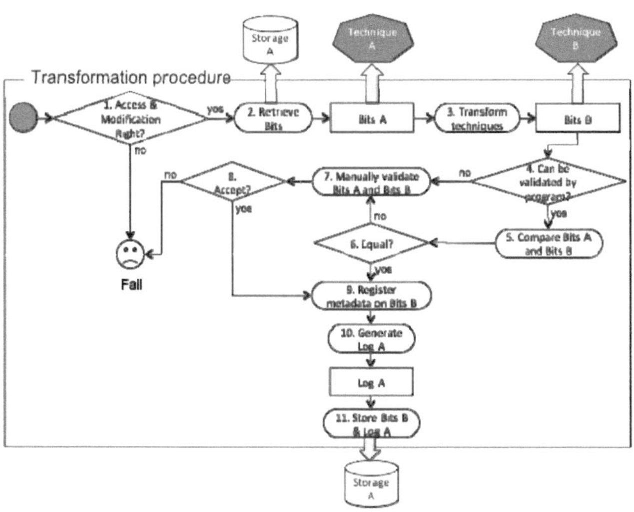

Fig. 2. Abstract Procedure for Transformation

should be performed. In the manual validation procedure, the custodians should compare each digital object before and after migration. Then, they decide whether they can accept the transformed digital object or not. On the other hand, in the automatic procedure, the program should determine the difference between Bits-A and Bits-B based on characteristics of a digital object. If the difference is within an acceptable level, this transformation should be deemed successful. If not, it requires the custodians to assess Bits-A and Bits-B manually. After the comparison, a set of new migration metadata and provenance metadata should be created. Finally, the Bits-B with its metadata is written to the storage.

4 Quality Requirements on Migration Metadata

24 migration data requirements were designed in [7]. Table 1 lists the descriptions of the quality requirements on migration metadata. In this paper, we just show how *replication* and *transformation* use them.

- *Storage*: Both *replication* and *transformation* should be able to read and write the bits from Storage A. This means that custodians need to know the storage medium type and the related storage medium driver.
- *Hardware*: Custodians may need to rebuild the old hardware system. Under the old system, *replication* and *transformation* can read and write the old storage medium. In addition, the custodians can examine the transformed objects by manually viewing them in the old system. To rebuild the hardware system, the custodians should know microprocessor, memory, motherboard and the related peripherals of the old system.
- *Application*: *Replication* and *transformation* need storage applications to read digital objects from Storage A. They also need interpretation applications to translate digital objects and/or validate their bits integrity. Moreover, in the manual comparison procedure of *transformation*, an interpretation application is required to view the original digital objects.
- *Specification*: In terms of the technical specification, new applications can be developed, or a compatible solution can be found. In *replication*, the specifications about a given encryption algorithm and fixity technique specifications may be needed when custodians access the digital object and check the bits integrity. In *transformation*, the encryption specification is needed. In addition, technical specifications including format, identifier, hyperlink, encryption and fixity may be required for developing interpretation or transformation applications.
- *Characteristics*: Characteristics are the important features of a digital object. They can be used for the validation task within a transformation procedure. As the number of digital objects will be huge, any manual comparison in a transformation procedure is impossible. Therefore, characteristics should be pre-defined and recorded, to support the consistency checks in Step 5 of *transformation*. Four kinds of features can be considered: content, appearance, behaviors, and references.

Table 1. Description of the Quality Requirements

Category	Req.	Description
Storage	R1	Metadata on a given storage medium should be preserved.
	R2	Metadata on a given storage medium driver should be preserved.
Hardware	R3	Metadata on a given microprocessor type should be preserved.
	R4	Metadata on a given memory type should be preserved.
	R5	Metadata on a given motherboard type should be preserved.
	R6	Metadata on a given related peripheral type should be preserved.
Application	R7	Metadata on a given storage transfer application should be preserved.
	R8	Metadata on a given technique interpretation application should be preserved.
Specification	R9	Metadata on a given format technique should be preserved.
	R10	Metadata on a given digital object identifier technique should be preserved.
	R11	Metadata on a given hyperlink technique should be preserved.
	R12	Metadata on a given encryption technique should be preserved.
	R13	Metadata on a given fixity technique should be preserved.
Characteristics	R14	Metadata on the content characteristics of any given digital object should be preserved.
	R15	Metadata on the appearance characteristics of any given digital object should be preserved.
	R16	Metadata on the behaviors characteristics of any given digital object should be preserved.
	R17	Metadata on the reference characteristics of any given digital object should be preserved.
Provenance	R18	Metadata on any migration activity event should be preserved.
	R19	Metadata on any changed parts of a digital object should be preserved.
Modification rights	R20	Metadata on any given intellectual property rights should be preserved.
	R21	Metadata on any restriction law should be preserved.
Retention policy	R22	Metadata on the preservation level of a given digital object should be preserved.
	R23	Metadata on the characteristics' important factors should be preserved.
	R24	Metadata on any given migration assessment method should be preserved.

– *Provenance*: Provenance metadata provide the history of the digital objects, so that future users can trust the preserved digital objects. For *replication* and *transformation*, the description of an event should be logged. If the digital object is modified in *transformation*, the changed parts should be recorded also.
– *Modification rights*: The violation of modification rights should terminate a transformation procedure. In order to make any transformation procedure legal, restrictions about intellectual property rights and laws should be recorded.
– *Retention policy*: A retention policy may affect a decision-making when choosing solutions of migration. In addition, for Step 5 of *transformation*, the type of digital objects could affect the score of the importance factors on the characteristics, and different assessment methods may have various rank lists for the transformation solutions. In general, it is advisable to pre-define the retention policy, so that the preservation consistency can be ensured.

5 Description of the Questionnaire

Since we did not find published quality requirements for migration metadata, we cannot compare our requirements against other requirements. Also, holding workshops to discuss the requirements is inconvenient and will typically only involve a small number of experts. Therefore, we decided to do an online survey. The online survey has some advantages: (a) it is cheap to get the respondent opinions; (b) we can easily analyze the survey results; and (c) we can contact many people whom we do not know at all. In addition, we performed follow-up interviews with a subset of the respondents to find explanation to some intriguing survey answers. In this section, we will provide an overview of the survey design. The survey results are discussed in the next section.

The questionnaire (see Appendix at the end of this paper) contains 30 questions in three parts. The first three questions are to discover the respondent's background. The next 24 questions are to investigate the necessity of each of the 24 requirements. The last three questions are to get comments and proposals for any missed requirements. We published the questionnaire in a web page and sent our invitation to several discussion groups on preservation systems, such as DCC[1], Dspace[2], iRODS[3], METS[4], PREMIS[5], PADI[6], SIG-DL[7], SHAMAN[8], and LongRec[9].

After three rounds of the call-for-participant, a total of 459 people had visited the questionnaire, but just 41 people completed and submitted their answers. Those respondents came from Europe (22), North America (15), Oceania (3), and Africa (1). They worked for research institutions (12), libraries (10), archives (9), government departments and commercial companies (5), repository providers (3), and preservation solution providers (2). The respondents' work experience within the fields of information management field or preservation systems was recorded as 6+ years (23), 2-6 years (14), and 0-2 years (4).

6 Analyzing the Survey Results

To find the answers of RQ1 – RQ2, we analyzed the survey results by the SPSS statistics program. The analysis includes the following two themes.

6.1 Necessary Requirements?

All the respondents of the questionnaire were requested to give an agreement score to each proposed requirements. 1 means the strongest disagreement and 7 means the strongest agreement. Table 2 summarizes the median and the frequency dispersion for each requirement. The median shows the middle value of the respondents' scores. When a requirement has a high median value, it means that the respondents strongly supported its necessity. The frequency dispersion shows the distributions of the agreement scores.

---

[1] The Digital Custodian Centre (DCC), `http://www.dcc.ac.uk/`
[2] `http://www.dspace.org/`
[3] The Integrated Rule-Oriented Data System (iRODS), `https://www.irods.org/index.php/Fedora`
[4] The Metadata Encoding and Transmission Standard (METS), `http://www.loc.gov/standards/mets/`
[5] The PREservation Metadata: Implementation Strategies (PREMIS), `http://www.loc.gov/standards/premis/`
[6] The Preservation Access to Digital Information (PADI), `http://www.nla.gov.au/padi/`
[7] The Special Interest Group in Digital Libraries (SIG-DL), `http://www.asis.org/SIG/sigdl/`
[8] `http://shaman-ip.eu/shaman/`
[9] The Long Term Records Management project (LongRec), `http://www.longrec.com`

In terms of the results of Table 2, we classify the requirements into three levels:

- *Essentiality*: It is essential for custodians to store metadata on format specification (R9), identifier specification (R10), encryption specification (R12), fixity specification (R13), migration event (R18), changed parts (R19), IPRs (R20) and law (R21). The median values of these requirements are 7. Moreover, the total percentage of the disagreement score with 1 – 3 is very small (< 10%), or the frequency of the strongest agreement is high (> 50%).
- *Necessity*: It is necessary for custodians to store metadata on interpretation application (R8), hyperlink specification (R11), content characteristics (R14) and preservation level (R22). Their median values are 5 or 6, and the total percentage of the agreement score with 5 – 7 is more than 70%. We have to mention that: even though some requirements' medians are 5, we still remove them from this set because the supporters are not so many (i.e., the total percentage of the agreement score with 5 – 7 < 70%). These requirements include storage medium (R1), storage medium application (R3), behaviors characteristics (R16), and assessment algorithm (R24).
- *Conditionality*: It is conditional for custodians to store metadata on storage medium (R1), storage medium player (R2), storage medium application (R3), microprocessor (R4), memory (R5), motherboard (R6), peripherals (R7), appearance characteristics (R15), behaviors characteristics (R16), reference characteristics (R17), important factors (R23), and assessment algorithm (R24). For these requirements, the percentage of the agreement and the percentage of the disagreement are not high enough.

By interviewing some respondents, we tried to uncover reasons why some requirements are at the conditional level. The possible answers are summarized in the following sub-sections.

When should Custodians Store Metadata on Storage Systems? Some digitized information may often be accessed and be stored in an online system, whilst some is rarely accessed and is stored in an offline system. Thus, it is needed to distinguish online and offline system. For online systems, the custodians may not need to preserve any metadata on the storage systems. However, for offline systems, they should document this storage system, because people may forget what this storage is after several years or decades.

When should Custodians Store Metadata on Computer Systems? It is suggested to make storage and software independent in preservation systems, and it is encouraging to find in this survey that many preservation systems comply with this rule. Hence, many deem these requirements are unnecessary. However, some people mentioned that some special video and audio digital objects still depend on a particular system. Hence, storing metadata about computer systems depends on the independency of the storage system and the related software applications.

When should Custodians Store Metadata on Characteristics? A respondent from the National Library of Britain (BL) told us that they do not preserve any characteristics for digital materials. However, they indeed need characteristics to evaluate the migrated digital objects. Every time when they plan to do migration, they

Table 2. Score of Agreement on the Quality Requirements

	Described Item	Frequency of the Agreement Score [a]							Median
		1	2	3	4	5	6	7	
R1	Storage medium	0.0%	22.0 %	7.3 %	9.8 %	22.0 %	2.4 %	36.6 %	5
R2	Storage medium player	14.6 %	14.6 %	12.2 %	9.8 %	24.4 %	4.9 %	19.5 %	4
R3	Storage medium application	7.3 %	12.2 %	9.8 %	14.6 %	17.1 %	7.3 %	31.7 %	5
R4	Microprocessor	22.0 %	12.2 %	7.3 %	9.8 %	14.6 %	9.8 %	24.4 %	4
R5	Memory stick	22.0 %	14.6 %	9.8 %	17.1 %	14.6 %	2.4 %	19.5 %	4
R6	Motherboard	22.0 %	19.5 %	4.9 %	17.1 %	22.0 %	7.3 %	7.3 %	4
R7	Peripherals	14.6 %	17.1 %	22.0 %	14.6 %	14.6 %	4.9 %	12.2 %	3
R8	Interpretation application	2.4 %	4.9 %	2.4 %	19.5 %	4.9 %	24.4 %	41.5 %	6
R9	Format specification	2.4 %	0.0%	0.0%	4.9 %	12.2 %	12.2 %	68.3 %	7
R10	Identifier specification	4.9 %	0.0%	4.9 %	7.3 %	12.2 %	9.8 %	61.0 %	7
R11	Hyperlink specification	4,9 %	0.0%	2.4 %	14.6 %	24.4 %	4.9 %	48.8 %	6
R12	Encryption specification	7.3 %	0.0%	0.0%	4.9 %	2.4 %	12.2 %	73.2 %	7
R13	Fixity specification	2.4 %	0.0%	2.4 %	4.9 %	9.8 %	17.1 %	63.4 %	7
R14	Content characteristics	9.8 %	7.3 %	2.4 %	7.3 %	24.4 %	2.4 %	46.3 %	5
R15	Appearance characteristics	12.2 %	4.9 %	22.0 %	12.2 %	14.6 %	7.3 %	26.8 %	4
R16	Behaviors characteristics	9.8 %	12.2 %	7.3 %	17.1 %	19.5 %	4,9 %	29.3 %	5
R17	Reference characteristics	9.8 %	7.3 %	12.2 %	24.4 %	12.2 %	7.3 %	26.8 %	4
R18	Migration event	2.4 %	4.9 %	0.0%	14.6 %	14.6 %	12.2 %	51.2 %	7
R19	Changed parts	2.4 %	4.9 %	4.9 %	7.3 %	12.2 %	14.6 %	53.7 %	7
R20	Intellectual property rights	4.9 %	4.9 %	2.4 %	12.2 %	9.8 %	4.9 %	61.0 %	7
R21	Law	4.9 %	7.3 %	7.3 %	14.6 %	9.8 %	4.9 %	51.2 %	7
R22	Preservation level	4.9 %	2.4 %	4.9 %	7.3 %	22.0 %	22.0 %	36.6 %	6
R23	Important factors to characteristics	2.4 %	2.4 %	12.2 %	39.0 %	14.6 %	9.8 %	19.5 %	4
R24	Assessment algorithm	7.3 %	7.3 %	12.2 %	22.0 %	19.5 %	9.8 %	22.0 %	5

a. "1" = the strongest disagreement, and "7" = the strongest agreement.

would determine a set of characteristics for a migration testing. After the testing completes, these characteristics would be discarded because currently no software can extract complete characteristics from every digital object. If they do this extraction task manually, the task would become too time-consuming and too expensive. On the other hand, several respondents also mentioned in the comments that metadata are now underused, as no sophisticated tools can completely utilize current metadata stored in the preservation system. Therefore, even though characteristics can help the assessment task of migration, the respondents still gave lower scores as few applications can extract and reuse those metadata in a migration procedure.

When should Custodians Store Metadata on Retention Policy? As the assessing task is the most essential task in a migration procedure, we deem that the requirements on the retention policy should be necessary also. When we tried to elicit the reason, the interviewees did not say much about it. They either did not know the methodology used in the PLANETS project, or they are learning this methodology. The possible reason why these requirements have lower agreement score is that the theory for retention policies is immature. When this theory become mature, the retention policy would be more important than now for an automatic rules-based migration procedure.

6.2 Complete Requirements?

Question 30 asked for additional comments, where the respondent could give any opinion or suggest any missing requirements in a free-text box. Unfortunately, only 24 respondents provided comments. Moreover, just two of them suggested a new requirement, namely that justification for performing a migration should be captured. However, R18 should include this new requirement, because the event should store information about a migration procedure, such as who, why, and how.

Besides the above requirement, the respondents did not mention any new requirement. This has two possible interpretations:

- Time pressure, laziness or other factors may have caused them to answer only what is required to answer. It might be the reason why 17 respondents do not give any comments.
- The respondents may feel that the suggested requirements are sufficient. In terms of the comments, a few of respondents mentioned that the migration data requirements ask for too many metadata. There are two reasons: (a) Base on current experience, metadata are often underused because effective tools do not yet exist. (b) A migration procedure may not need so many migration metadata, because the migration procedure is dependent upon a context, such as types of digital objects, preservation levels, and organization policies.

7 Discussion of the Validity of the Survey

7.1 Why a Low Response Rate?

We got 41 responses in our survey. However, in total, 459 people visited the questionnaire. The response rate is just 8.92%. The three most likely reasons for our low response rate are:

- Lack of strong network to potential respondents. Some potential respondents would not like to participate because they are too busy. Even though we sent the participation call three times in two months, we got only 10 more responses each time.
- Few experts on migration. In order to get more responses, we tried to contact some of the respondents who only viewed the questionnaire and left their email addresses in the questionnaire. Just two persons would like to finish the

questionnaire later. For the others, some did not respond us at all, and some declined because they had little experience and knowledge about migration.
- The third and last reason is that people might visit the web site several times, but only complete the questionnaire once. In addition, since we contacted some persons who did not finish this survey, they probably visited the questionnaire several times.

7.2 Threats to the Validity of the Survey

Survey outcomes may be biased by several threats relating to the design of questions, selection of the survey population, and collection of answers. Dillman summarizes four types of errors in mail and internet surveys [16] (p. 9). We will use this error classification to discuss what potential threats exist to our findings and what we did to mitigate them.

- Sampling error: The sample size relates to how well answers truly reflect the population opinion. In this survey, just 41 people filled out the questionnaire (despite our effort to invite and encourage experts to participate). Obviously, 41 for this survey is not a large number, compared to the number of experts on preservation around the world. Therefore, the sample size would be a substantial threat to the survey outcomes.
- Coverage error: Coverage error means selection bias, i.e., whether some parts of the population are not reached at all. In our survey method, two possible threats should be mentioned here. (a) The questionnaire was written in English. Non-English speaking experts might not give their answers. And (b) the invitation was sent by email to different discussion groups. The experts who did not join those discussion groups would not be aware of the survey. However, those two threats are not so serious for this study, because the questions on the quality requirements should not be affected by languages or discussion groups. The most possible threat factor might be the profession background. Based on the survey results, the answers come from libraries, archives, research institutions, government departments and commercial companies, repository providers, and preservation solution providers.
- Measurement error: This error is related to the questions themselves. We formulated all the questions as neutrally as possible. We also asked our project partners to review the questions before starting the survey to make the questions as clear and understandable as possible. Only one respondent mentioned that "it is not clear what is being asked" in the comment box. However, we did not disorder or rephrase the questions to do the survey again. This is because it would be hard to find other potential respondents and it is infeasible to invite the same people do the survey again. Therefore, we do not know whether the survey outcomes would be changed if we rearrange or rephrase those quality requirements.
- Non-response error: Non-response error concerns the problem that the invitees who did not give answers might hold rather different opinions than people who finished the questionnaire. This error may not be serious in our case, for two reasons: (a) some invitees who did not finish the survey because they had little experience in migration. However, they were interested in this research. They

wanted to browse this questionnaire. If they had completed the survey and submitted a response, their answers might have been much less reliable than those that we ended up receiving. And (b) the experienced experts gave us answers. 56.1% respondents had more than 6 years' work experience. Thus, we believe that the experienced experts joined in this survey.

8 Conclusion

Custodians of preservation systems lack a defined and published set of quality requirements on migration metadata, which can form a checklist to frame the design work of migration metadata elements or the examination work of current metadata elements. Hence, in this paper, we first showed the 24 requirements from an abstract migration procedure and second evaluated the necessity and the sufficiency of these requirements with two survey methods, i.e., questionnaire and telephone interview. Based on the survey results, these 24 requirements can be classified into three agreement levels. As for the sufficiency aspect, only two people mentioned an additional requirement that they felt missing, but we deem even this requirement to fit in as a sub-requirement of one of those that we have already defined.

Acknowledgements. This research is carried out under the LongRec project, which is sponsored by the Norwegian Research Council. We also thank all respondents who attended our survey and accepted the interview.

References

1. Waters, D., Garrett, J.: Preserving Digital Information. Report of the Task Force on Archiving of Digital Information (1996)
2. Strodl, S., Becker, C., Neumayer, R., Rauber, A.: How to choose a digital preservation strategy: evaluating a preservation planning procedure. In: Proceedings of the 7th ACM/IEEE-CS Joint Conference on Digital Libraries. ACM, Vancouver (2007)
3. Triebsees, T., Borghoff, U.M.: Towards automatic document migration: semantic preservation of embedded queries. In: Proceedings of the 2007 ACM Symposium on Document Engineering, pp. 209–218. ACM, Winnipeg (2007)
4. Hunter, J., Choudhury, S.: PANIC: an integrated approach to the preservation of composite digital objects using Semantic Web services. International Journal on Digital Libraries 6(2), 174–183 (2006)
5. Ferreira, M., Baptista, A., Ramalho, J.: An intelligent decision support system for digital preservation. International Journal on Digital Libraries 6(4), 295–304 (2007)
6. Becker, C., Kulovits, H., Guttenbrunner, M., Strodl, S., Rauber, A., Hofman, H.: Systematic planning for digital preservation: evaluating potential strategies and building preservation plans. International Journal on Digital Libraries 10(4), 157 (2009)
7. Luan, F., Mestl, T., Nygård, M.: Quality Requirements of Migration Metadata in Long-term Digital Preservation Systems. In: Sánchez-Alonso, S., Athanasiadis, I.N. (eds.) MTSR 2010. CCIS, vol. 108, pp. 172–182. Springer, Heidelberg (2010)

8. Lavoie, B., Gartner, R.: Technology Watch Report - Preservation Metadata. DPC Technology Watch Series Report 05-01 (2005)
9. The OCLC/RLG Working Group on Preservation Metadata: Preservation Metadata and the OAIS Information Model. A Metadata Framework to Support the Preservation of Digital Objects (2002), http://www.oclc.org/research/pmwg/pm_framework.pdf
10. The Consultative committee for Space Data Systems: The Reference Model for an Open Archival Information System (OAIS) (2002), http://public.ccsds.org/publications/archive/650x0b1.PDF
11. The National Library of New Zealand: Metadata Standards Framework - Preservation Metadata (2003), http://www.natlib.govt.nz/catalogues/library-documents/preservation-metadata-revised
12. The National Archive of Norway: Noark 5 - Standard for Records Management (2009)
13. Dale, R.L., Ambacher, B.: Trustworthy Repositories Audit & Certification: Criteria and Checklist, TRAC (2007)
14. Dobratz, S., Schoger, A., Strathmann, S.: The nestor Catalogue of Criteria for Trusted Digital Repository Evaluation and Certification. Journal of Digital Information 8(2) (2007)
15. Wheatley, P.: Migration–a CAMiLEON discussion paper. Ariadne 29(2) (2001)
16. Dillman, D.A.: Mail and Internet Surveys: The Tailored Design Method (2007)

Appendix: The Questionnaire Used in This Online Survey

Part I. Respondent Background

1. Your email address: (not mandatory, but we may contact you by this email address for further interviewing)

2. How many years have you worked in the information management system or the preservation system?

3. What item can best describe your organization type? If you choose "other type", please state your organization type.

Part II. Questions on the Quality Requirements

4. If a storage medium is used in the preservation system, the migration should have metadata that document this storage medium.

5. If a storage medium is used in the preservation system, the migration should have metadata that document this storage medium's driver.

6. If having software that depends on a hardware platform, the migration should have metadata that document the microprocessor used in this hardware platform.

7. If having software that depends on a hardware platform, the migration should have metadata that document the memory used in this hardware platform.

8. If having software that depends on a hardware platform, the migration should have metadata that document the motherboard used in this hardware platform.

9. If having software that depends on a hardware platform, the migration should have metadata that document the peripherals used in this hardware platform.

10. If having two storage media, the migration should have metadata that document a transfer application, which is able to read, transfer and write data between these two storage media.

11. If having a technique used for the digital objects, the migration should have metadata that document an interpretation application, which is able to interpret this technique. (PS: The technique may be a format, an encryption algorithm, a reference, or a communication protocol.)

12. If the preservation system has a format for its digital objects, the migration should have metadata that document this format.

13. If the preservation system has an identifier technique for its digital objects, the migration should have metadata that document this identifier technique. (PS: The identifier technique is a mechanism that assigns a unique name to a digital object.)

14. If the preservation system has a link technique for its preserved digital objects, the migration should have metadata that document this link technique.

15. If the preservation system has an encryption technique for its digital objects, the migration should have metadata that document this encryption technique. (PS: The encryption technique is used to limit access and operations to a digital object.)

16. If the preservation system has a fixity technique for its digital object, the migration should have metadata that document this fixity technique. (PS: The fixity technique is used to prove the integrity of the digital objects.)

17. The migration should have metadata that document the characteristics of the digital object's content. (E.g., the number of pages, the number of words, the dimension of an image, and the length of a video or audio)

18. The migration should have metadata that document characteristics of the digital object's appearance. (E.g., fort size, word style, columns per page, and positions of images)

19. The migration should have metadata that document the characteristics of the digital object's behaviors. (E.g., dynamically display the search results and automatically change the background color or image)

20. The migration should have metadata that document the characteristics of the digital object's references. (E.g., the number of the internal references that provide the internal structure of an archive package, and the number of the external references that provide the context of the archive package)

21. The migration should create metadata that document this migration activity for every migrated digital object.

22. The migration should create metadata that document the changed places of the migrated object.

23. The migration should have metadata that document intellectual property rights to a digital object.

24. The migration should have metadata that document a law that restricts a digital object.

25. The migration should have metadata that document a preservation level for a digital object. (PS: The example of the preservation level is "keep the bit integrity", "keep the content integrity", "keep the appearance integrity", and "keep the behavior integrity".)

26. The migration should have metadata that document the important factors, which specify the important degree of the above characteristics defined in Q17-Q20.

27. The migration should have metadata that document the assessment method, which is able to assess different migration solutions.

Part III. General Opinion

28. As a whole, I feel that the migration should have all the metadata in Q4-Q27.

29. As a whole, I feel that all the metadata in Q4-Q27 can ensure future migration executions

30. Comments to the migration metadata?

Workflow Engine Performance Evaluation by a Black-Box Approach

Florian Daniel[1], Giuseppe Pozzi[2], and Ye Zhang[2]

[1] Università degli Studi di Trento, via Sommarive 14 I-38100 Povo, Trento, Italy
[2] Politecnico di Milano, P.za L. da Vinci 32 I-20133 Milano, Italy
daniel@disi.unitn.it, giuseppe.pozzi@polimi.it
http://disi.unitn.it/users/florian.daniel,
http://home.dei.polimi.it/people/pozzi

Abstract. Workflow Management Systems (WfMSs) are complex software systems that require proper support in terms of WfMS performance. We propose here an approach to obtain some performance measurements for WfMSs (in order to compare them) by adopting a *black box* approach – an aspect that is not yet adequately studied in literature – and report some preliminary results: this allows us to evaluate at run-time the overall performance of a WfMS, comprising all of its constituent elements.

We set up two reference processes and four different experiments, to simulate real circumstances of load, ranging from one process instance to several process instances, entering the system either gradually or simultaneously. We identify some key performance indicators (CPU, main memory and disk workloads, and completion time) for the tests. We choose five WfMSs (some publicly available, some commercially available), and install them in their respective default configuration on five different and separate virtual machines (VMware). For every WfMS and for every experiment, we perform measurements and specifically focus on the completion time. Results enable us to measure how efficient the WfMSs are in general and how well they react to an increase of workload.

Keywords: Performance evaluation, Workflow management system, black-box approach, virtual machine.

1 Introduction

A *workflow* is the automation of a business process where atomic work units (*task*) are assigned to participants (*agent*) according to a *workflow schema* (*process model*). A workflow management system (WfMS) manages several process instances (*cases*), and relies on a database management system (DBMS).

We propose an approach to evaluate the performances of a WfMS treating it as a *black box* and a monolithic system purely observed from outside. To avoid the variability caused by using different computer systems, we use one unique computer system running several separate virtual machines, each machine featuring one WfMS. The tests we perform particularly aim at measuring the performance of the core of a WfMS, i.e., its engine.

A. Abd Manaf et al. (Eds.): ICIEIS 2011, Part III, CCIS 253, pp. 189–203, 2011.

The paper is structured as follows: Section 2 describes the state of the art and compares it with the proposed approach; Section 3 addresses the requirements of our approach; Section 4 recalls some basic concepts on performance evaluation; Sections 5 and 6 introduce our approach and the experiments; Section 7 draws some conclusions and sketches out some future research directions.

2 Related Work

The three main performance-related research areas in the domain focus on:
Impact of WfMSs addresses the changes from the use of a WfMS in managing business processes. Reijers and Van der Aalst [1] focus on analyzing business process performances on the basis of criteria including lead time, waiting time, service time, and usage of resource.

Workflow Process Modeling mostly relates to evaluating the capability of a workflow to meet the requirements of the business process, the workflow patterns [2], adopting as key performance indicators (KPI) maximal parallelism, throughput, service levels, and sensitivity [3]. Several studies focus on the performance issues of process modeling in distributed WfMSs (e.g., Reijers et al. [4] where actors are geographically distributed).

Architectural Issues discuss the inner architecture of WfMSs to improve their performances from the inside. Furthermore, WfMSs must cope with issues such as internet-based large-scale enterprize applications [5], dynamic change of the processes [6]. Kim and Ellis [5] describe three performance analytic models corresponding to the workflow architectural categories of passive, class-active and instance-active WfMS, especially on the aspect of scalability. Considering the configuration of a distributed enterprize-wide WfMS, Kim and Ahn [7] propose the workcase-oriented workflow enactment architecture.

Our Approach. Despite the many previous studies adopt a white box approach and focus on the business layer, on the service layer, or on the internal structure of a WfMS, very few studies address an effective performance evaluation method to assess the WfMS itself as a *black box* on a computer system level, especially on an IT infrastructure layer which is a fundamental component for every system. The *black box* concept here is derived from the *black box* method of software testing, where the inner architecture of programs is not examined. By this paper, we make an effort to design an approach that implements a *black box* performance analysis, to test some WfMSs on an IT infrastructure, thus trying to fill this gap on WfMS performance study.

Our approach builds on the work of Browne [8], evaluating the effective computer performance on the following three factors: 1) theories and models representing computer systems and computer processes; 2) evaluation techniques which generate accurate assessments of the system or of the program behavior from models and theories; 3) the technology for data gathering on executing systems or processes and technology for data analysis. As our performance evaluation is within the context of computer system performance evaluation, we develop three customized factors for WfMS in our approach in the light of [8].

3 Requirements

The paper aims at evaluating the *performance* of WfMSs as it is perceived from the outside, i.e., by system users. The *key idea* to do so is to test each system *as a whole*, instead of singling out individual elements, e.g., the resource scheduler (which decides whether to assign a given task to a human actor or to an automated resource, and to which instance thereof) or the DBMS underlying the WfMS, and testing them individually. Also, in order to test the systems under conditions that are as close to real production environments as possible, we do not want to simulate the functioning of the systems or to emulate individual functionalities. A thorough evaluation requires therefore *setting up full installations* of each WfMS, including the recommended operating system, the DBMS, and any other software required for a standard installation of the systems.

In order to guarantee similar hardware and software conditions for every WfMS, to eliminate the influence ad cross-interactions of already installed software (if the WfMSs are installed on the same machine) or of different hardware configurations (if the WfMSs are installed on different machines), we use a *dedicated virtual machine* for each installation, which can then easily be run and tested also on a single machine. Virtual machines also help the repeatability of the experiments and their portability on other computer systems. We call this requirement *independence from the host system.*

In our research in general, we aim at devising a set of generic performance metrics to assess WfMSs, whereas in this paper – as a first step – we specifically focus on the *workflow engine*, which is at the core of each WfMS and is in charge of advancing process instances according to their *control flows* and managing the necessary *process data* (the process variables). It is therefore necessary to devise a set of *reference processes* we use to study the performance of the engines and minimize the influence of the other components, e.g., the DBMS underlying the WfMS or the resource scheduler. We shall therefore define processes that do not make an intensive use of business data, and formulate tasks that are executed directly by the workflow engine under study. Note, however, that if a WfMS uses a DBMS internally to store its process data, such will be part of the evaluation.

More precisely, it is necessary to define tasks as automatic and self-contained software applications: we call this *autonomy of execution*. In this way, idle times and response times from agents are completely avoided, providing a pure measurement for the WfMS. Every WfMS comes with its own strategies to complete tasks by invoking external software applications: different strategies generate performance variability on both completion time and resource usage, e.g.,to startup suitable applications or persistent variable storage methods.

In order to be able to identify which system performs well in which execution contexts, it is further important to execute the reference processes under *varying workload conditions*. We expect each system will react differently to a growing number of running process instances, concurrently running in the system.

In this work, we are specifically interested in comparing a set of *commercial* and *non-commercial* WfMSs, in order to study if there are differences in how the products of these two families manage their coordination task. Although, at the first glance, the black box approach and the focus on the workflow engine appears to have a certain extent of limitation, we shall see, in the following sections, that this approach already allows us to draw some interesting conclusions on the performance of some state-of-art WfMSs.

4 Background

This section introduces some concepts related to the tests we perform and to key performance indicators (KPIs) for IT infrastructures.

4.1 Performance Testing

Performance testing is one of the computer system performance evaluation methods - also know as Application Performance Management (APM). APM measures the performance and the availability of an application while it is running: the main APM goals are monitoring, alerting, and providing data for incident and capacity management.

Purpose of Performance Testing. Performance testing aims at generating a simulated load to predict the behavior of the system under a real load. During performance testing, we verify what happens if the number of users or of the servers increases (load testing); we also evaluate the capacity of system (stress testing), and find the bottlenecks.

Types of Performance Testing. Two main types of performance testing are typically performed. *Load testing*, also called service level verification, aims at evaluating the behavior of the system under a simulated typical load, in order to verify if the performance goal is fulfilled. During load testing, users enter gradually the system, generating a progressively growing load.

Stress testing is considered a tuning test, as it aims at evaluating the performance of the system under a heavy load to find the maximum load sustainable by every component, helping to detect bottlenecks and providing us with inputs on performance tuning. During stress testing, all the users enter the system simultaneously.

Structure of Performance Testing for an Application. The performance testing structure includes three main components: load generator; controller; monitor. The *load generator* consists of one or more workstations or programs that generate the load on the application. The *controller* is a workstation that controls the load generators to manage the test: it triggers and drives the load generation, by controlling the ramp. The *monitor* is a workstation that measures the system load, performing both generic measurements (e.g., CPU usage) and specific measurements for any component (e.g., application server, DBMS).

4.2 KPI for Performance Testing of an IT Infrastructure

KPIs characterize the performance of the measured system and considers several layers of one service. Typically, the most relevant KPIs at the IT infrastructure level consider CPU, CPU idle time for I/O, CPU load (length of the process), main memory usage, disk throughput, and network bandwidth. In Section 5.2 we describe the KPI we shall consider for our goals.

5 Evaluating WfMS Performance

The approach we describe here aims at evaluating the performances of a WfMS. While the literature deeply considers the performances of the single components that set up a WfMS, we propose here a *black box* approach. Our interest mainly focuses on the overall evaluation of the IT infrastructure of a WfMS, as a monolithic system: we do not want to test a WfMS in an isolated fashion, instead we are interested in understanding its performances under real production conditions, that is, also taking into account the minimal system requirements.

While several types of business process can be identified, we introduce two reference processes used throughout the paper. Since we want to test the *pure* performance of a WfMS, any possible human intervention (agent's idle time) and any difference in the computing system must be avoided: all the activities are automatically performed with no human intervention; the same computing configuration and operating condition are used for any WfMS.

The main part of our approach is based on the effective computer performance evaluation framework by Browne [8]. We customize three main factors as follows: *workflow processes*, which are composed by automatic activities; *experimental evaluation procedures*, which generate an assessment of the load for the WfMS under different operational conditions; *performance indicators and data gathering methods*, which include performance measurement factors, tools for performance data gathering and tables for data analysis.

5.1 Workflow Process Design

We introduce two reference processes to evaluate the core behavior of the WfMS: both processes feature a limited set of workflow variables to avoid an intensive use of the underlying DBMS. Consequently, the following processes differ from business processes of the real world.

Although we look at two process models only, we are able to cover a wider set of real-world processes. The first process has a simple structure and a light load; the second one has a more complex structure and an heavier load.

Sample Process #1. The first reference process (SP1) is a very simple, typical, light and effective-running one: tasks are supposed simple, not requiring to execute big software codes. The process includes basic elements and patterns [2], decision nodes, automatic activities, one process variable (i), no temporary variable and no database operation. As the workflow variable can be set up to 1000, the process can cause continuous proper-weight load.

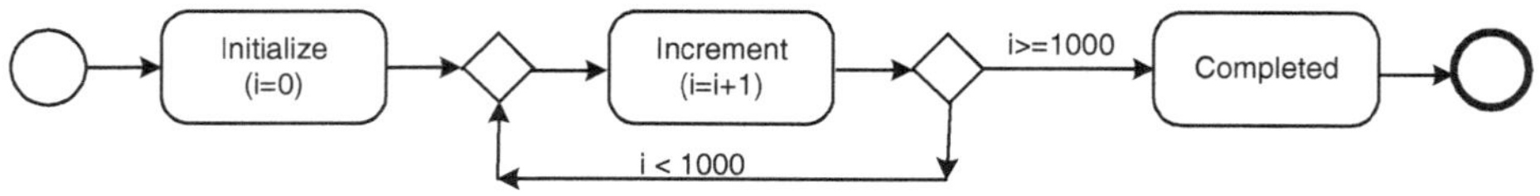

Fig. 1. A simple reference process - SP1

Sample Process #2. The second reference process (SP2) features two parallel execution branches and generates a relatively heavy load. The process contains every kind of routing tasks and patterns [2] (*and-split*, *or-split*, *and-join*, *or-join*), loops, and wait tasks. The task `Initialize` sets to 0 all the workflow variables i, j, k, m, and n. The task `RandomGenerate` randomly assigns values to a ($a > 0$) and b ($b < 100$): as a and b are randomly generated, every case goes through different execution paths and sets of branches. However, the overall length of the process flow is independent from the values randomly generated for a and b.

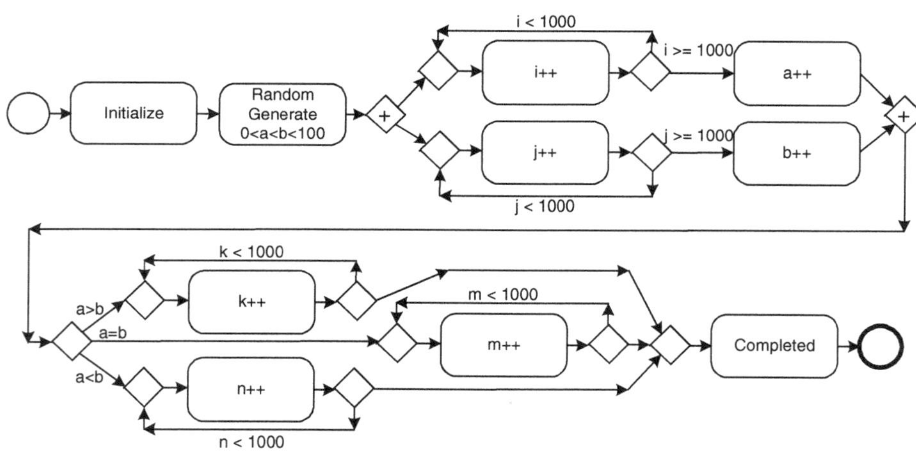

Fig. 2. A more complex reference process - SP2

5.2 Key Performance Indicators

The suitable KPIs are CPU workload, main memory usage and disk usage. The response time is also an important factor: we consider here the *process completion time*, i.e. the time required to complete the execution of the case.

CPU Workload. Several CPU performance metrics are defined, including CPU usage, system time, user time, idle time and waiting time. As measuring the workload that a certain process generates on the CPU is one of the main goals of our approach, we consider the $ProcessTime/ProcessorTime \times 100$ counter to measure the CPU workload.

Main Memory Workload. Main memory usage is a very critical issue when assessing the performance of a WfMS. Low memory conditions and frequent page faults slow down the execution of a process. Several performance indicators on main memory workload can be applied: free memory, swap usage and active/inactive memory. We choose *Available MBytes* as a measure of the main memory workload generated by a WfMS during its execution, i.e. the physical memory available, computed as the sum of the zeroed, free, and stand-by memory lists.

Disk Workload. Disk workload monitoring detects how efficiently the application reads/writes data from/to the disk, also exploiting the file-system cache. Considered factors include level of usage, throughput, amount of disk space available. Other activities arise from disk operations, such as interrupts generated by the disk system and paging activity, influencing other resources such as processor or main memory. We consider here the *disk transfer/sec*, as the rate of read and write operations on the disk: it depicts how many I/O operations per second are performed by the guest OS.

Completion Time. This indicator is the average amount of time required to complete a case, measured as the interval between the start time and the completion time of process execution. This is a very direct measurement on how efficiently the WfMS treats the process activity. When running several cases of the same process in parallel, the average process completion time is the interval between the earliest start time and the latest end time of all the cases divided by the number of cases. Consequently, the ability of a WfMS to execute many parallel processes simultaneously will be demonstrated and clarified by the average process completion time.

Observation. Installing several WfMSs on *one* unique system, to have *one* unique physical configuration for the experiments, is a very challenging issue. We use several, separate virtual machines on VMware, each of them running one WfMS, only. Consequently, the measurement of the CPU usage is performed on the *host* OS; main memory and disk workloads, as well as any other parameter, are measured on the *guest* OS. In fact, when we use a virtual machine, we are required to specify disk and memory usage for it. However, we theoretically permit the OS of the virtual machine to use as much CPU as possible. That is to say, we can get quite "comparable" results ("comparable" to the future measurements) by using either host CPU or CPU of the virtual machine. Thus, we use the performance monitoring tool in the host CPU instead of the virtual machine, in order not to put the load of the performance monitoring tool itself into the virtual machine to influence the WfMS.

5.3 Experiment Design

A minimum of *five* runs (Table 1) are executed per experiment and per WfMS. Every run is executed individually, with no overlap, and with no additional program running on the host computer. We set up the following four different types of experiments.

Experiment #1. It measures the performance of a WfMS while one single instance of SP1 is running. This experiment checks the efficiency of the WfMS performing a simple and typical process.

Experiment #2. It measures the performance of a WfMS while one single instance of SP2 is running. This experiment collects data on a WfMS when executing a relatively heavy, all-inclusive process with parallel sub-branches.

Experiment #3. It performs a load testing on the WfMS by SP2, where every *ten* seconds one new instance enters gradually the system till the number of simultaneously running instances is *five*. Theoretically, the maximum number of parallel instances that we should run in this experiment depends on when the workload generated by the current WfMS saturates. The experiment evaluates how the system behaves under the simulated typical operating load of SP2.

Experiment #4. It performs a stress test on the WfMS by SP2, where multiple instances start simultaneously. Experiment #4 can be divided in several parts, according to the number of total running cases: the total number of simultaneously running cases increases progressively, starting from 5 and rising up to 10, 25, 50, 100 or even higher.

Observation. Experiments #3 and #4 differ as instances enter the system gradually (Experiment #3) or simultaneously (Experiment #4). Experiment #4 evaluates the performances under an increasingly heavy load, to find the maximum load of every component and, possibly, the bottleneck.

Physical Configuration. For a fair comparison of the WfMSs, we use *the same* physical configuration for every experiment. We have two physical configurations: the *hardware configuration* includes type of computer/server, CPU, main memory, and hard disk; the *software configuration* includes operating system and the data gathering software, excluding any other user process. However, some WfMSs hold distinct OS compatibility requirements: one of the considered WfMS requires Windows 2003 Server, while the others run on Windows 2000. Windows 2003 Server will produce an additional load on the computer system, somehow affecting the performance evaluation: in order to reduce the impact of the OS, we increase the main memory allocated to balance this additional load.

Sampling Time. The sampling time describes the rate (how often) the monitoring system gathers data from the computer systems. A too high sampling rate introduces an additional and not negligible work load to the computer system itself. In our approach, we choose to acquire samples every 15 seconds, where any observation does not last for more than four hours.

5.4 Data Collection

The performance testing of our approach will produce a large amount of data. We set up some summary tables to collect and analyze results per experiment (Table 1) or per WfMS (Table 2).

For one experiment of one WfMS, the first row of Table 1 describes the considered process (Process template), and the number of cases simultaneously running (# or running instances). Table 1 also depicts all the parameters we collect during every run: the *completion time*, the *CPU workload (%)*, the *available main memory*, the *disk transfer/sec*. To obtain reliable results, we run the same experiment several times (one row of Table 1 for every run, identified by Run Number), computing then the average values for that experiment on that WfMS.

The three resource measurement columns (*CPU workload (%)*, *available main memory*, *disk transfer/sec*) have three sub-columns: *maximum*, *minimum* and *average*. For resource measurements, *maximum* and *minimum* statistics should be taken into consideration because *average* does not suffice to analyze the performances if data change dramatically. *Average* is computed as the mean of all the sampled data. As an example, Table 1 shows that the second run of Experiment #1 on process SP1 for WfMS#1 has a Completion Time of 72,818 msec, the Max value for CPU workload (%) is 10.938, its Min value is 0, its Avg value is 3.125 and so on.

We complete all the runs of Experiment #1 on every WfMS, obtaining 5 instances of Table 1, i.e., one instance per WfMS. We consider the average values (bottommost row) of any table, and put these average values in Table 2, which summarizes the average measurements per WfMS.

Table 1. Measurements for Experiment #1 on WfMS#1. Times are given in msec.

	Process template - SP1				# of running instances - 1					
Run	Single Process	CPU workload (%)			Main mem. (MB)			Disk transfer (MB/sec)		
Number	Completion Time	Max	Min	Avg	Max	Min	Avg	Max	Min	Avg
1	60,656	8.281	0.0	3.182	327	294	308.14	241.195	0.0	37.124
2	72,818	10.938	0.0	3.125	326	293	307.82	209.402	0.0	36.681
3	70,177	9.375	0.0	0.969	327	298	310.71	267.149	0.0	39.836
4	60,103	4.688	0.0	1.133	330	297	312.23	254.382	0.0	38.215
5	64,114	11.208	0.0	2.912	329	299	311.10	173.205	0.0	12.595
average	65,574	8.898	0.0	2.264	327.8	296.2	310.12	229.031	0.0	32.890

Table 2. Average measurements for Experiment #1 on every WfMS. Times are given in msec.

	Process template - SP1				# of running instances - 1					
WfMS	Single Process	CPU workload (%)			Main mem. (MB)			Disk transfer (MB/sec)		
Number	Completion Time	Max	Min	Avg	Max	Min	Avg	Max	Min	Avg
1	65,574	8.898	0.0	2.264	327.8	296.2	310.12	229.031	0.0	32.890
2	75,457	3.345	0.0	0.661	209.6	182.4	192.596	16.431	0.0	3.043
3	118,928	3.859	0.0	0.358	180.8	175.8	177.857	88.244	0.0	64.231
4	55,755	6.663	0.0	0.812	258.7	256.2	258.236	9.367	0.0	2.478
5	66,650	15.512	0.0	7.643	189.2	109.8	143.972	16.920	0.0	4.098

If the experiment (e.g., Experiment #3 and Experiment #4) requires several instances running simultaneously, the Total completion time for N simultaneously-started or gradually-entered cases is the interval between the earliest start time and the latest end time of all the processes, while Averaged Process completion time is computed as Total completion time divided by N. Table 3 summarizes the average measurements of Experiment #4 (25 process instances running simultaneously) per WfMS.

Table 3. Average measurements for Experiment #4 on every WfMS, with 25 process instances simultaneously running. Times are given in minutes - the smaller the better.

	Process template - SP2				# of running instances - 25					
WfMS	Averaged	CPU workload (%)			Main mem. (MB)			Disk transfer (MB/sec)		
Number	Completion Time	Max	Min	Avg	Max	Min	Avg	Max	Min	Avg
1	28.09	7.187	0.0	1.872	20.0	1.0	2.930	391.191	0.0	251.293
2	36.12	4.192	0.0	0.718	102.0	1.0	31.982	372.124	0.0	41.029
3	22.91	3.981	0.0	0.419	128.0	119.3	120.984	101.923	0.0	57.192
4	32.39	12.981	0.0	2.311	170.6	160.1	168.123	78.837	0.0	8.712
5	23.81	18.939	0.0	7.938	162.0	107.2	114.090	18.571	0.0	6.751

6 Experiments and Results

To validate our approach, we apply it to five WfMSs; for every WfMS, we perform the experiments of Section 5.3 and, next, evaluate the obtained results.

6.1 Tool Selection

The WfMSs. In order to obtain a wider scenario of WfMSs, we choose some of the leading, X-PDL-compliant, and open source WfMSs (we name them WfMS#1, WfMS#2, WfMS#4) and some of the top seller commercial WfMSs (we name them WfMS#3, WfMS#5). To avoid any conflict among the installed WfMSs, we install them on five *separate* virtual machines, run them on one unique PC to obtain comparable and hardware independent measurements. The virtual machines run Windows 2000 or Windows 2003 Server, while the host operating system is Windows XP.

The Virtual Machine. As virtual machine, we choose VMware Server rather than VMware ESX server, considering the possible migration of the virtual machine and the potential future extension of our approach.

ESX provides more accurate performance data, as ESX skips the OS level and takes full control of the hardware, directly. On the other hand, VMware Server is somehow influenced by the host OS, like Windows or Linux. However, by taking the direct control of the hardware, ESX has its own file system (VMFS) which provides faster I/O operations but makes it difficult to migrate the virtual machine to other system. Additionally, virtual machine files for VMware Server can be easily stored and transferred to other systems.

Moreover, ESX requires hardware-specific drivers, directly provided by VMware for that selected hardware. Instead, VMware Server clings to the host OS, which provides sufficient drivers to use the virtual machine. This feature makes VMware Server easy to run in a wide range of systems.

Accordingly, we choose VMware Server as our virtual machine environment. We assign to VMware Server an amount of 512 MBytes of main memory and of 8 GBytes of storage: the host machine has 2 GBytes of main memory, 320 GBytes of storage and the Windows XP operating system.

The Performance Monitoring Tool. We adopt the perfmon monitoring tool supported by Windows, collecting data every 15 seconds.

6.2 Experiment Implementation

Given the requirements of Section 3, we implement the autonomy of execution according to every WfMS's own strategy: e.g., in WfMS#1 automatic activities are defined by Java API of J2SE and the GUI structure of the WfMS itself, in WfMS#2 autonomy is achieved by JPDL and Java API.

As for the guest OS, we use Windows 2000 for WfMS#1, WfMS#2, WfMS#3, WfMS#4. We have to use Windows 2003 Server for WfMS#5, due to its strict software requirements (Visual Studio). This requirement influences the overall measurements, due to the different load on the host OS by the guest OS: to partially cope with it, we increase the total amount of main memory assigned to the guest OS to 768 MBytes.

Experiments #3 and #4 require a parallel execution of SP2. The simultaneous activation of several process instances generally differs from WfMS to WfMS: for example, for one WfMS, one process instance can be instantiated via the Web application, but the Web application does not support multiple instantiations. In order to instantiate multiple process simultaneously we program a suitable JUnit code.

We implement the reference processes (SP1 and SP2) on the five WfMSs. We have *five* runs (Table 1) per experiment and per WfMS for experiments #1, #2, and #3; for Experiment #4 we have *five* runs featuring 10 simultaneous instances, and *five* runs featuring 25 simultaneous instances, respectively. The final discussion will consider the average measurements of every set of five runs.

6.3 Analysis of the Results

A huge amount of experimental data support the final discussion and some conclusions on the performances from the five WfMSs. We mainly focus on the process completion time, considered as an overall performance indicator for the *black box* approach we adopt. We do not dig into the internal architecture of the five WfMSs: we rather focus on finding reasons, by combining the external performance data analysis and the general features of WfMSs.

Experiment #1. Experiment #1 features *one* single running instance of SP1. From Figure 3.a, WfMS#4 is the best performer since it requires the minimum amount of time to complete the test. As SP1 is a very simple process, one considerable amount of time is spent during process execution in accessing and updating data in the persistent layer and in loading the program from the logic layer: to our opinion, the great advantage for WfMS#1 comes from using its built-in small DBMS, while other WfMSs use a larger-scale, fully fledged DBMS.

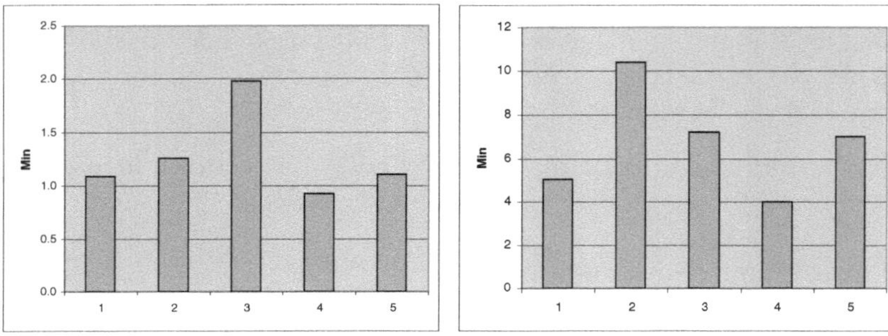

Fig. 3. a: Experiment #1 (left), b: Experiment #2 (right) - average execution time for the five WfMSs (x-axis). Times (y-axis) are given in minutes - the smaller the better.

On the other hand, WfMS#3 is the least efficient one for this experiment. To our opinion, this derives from its automatic execution of activities; WfMS#3 requires additional loading time for the activity-relevant executable files deployed in its server. On the contrary, the execution scripts fulfilling the same functionality in WfMS#1 and WfMS#4 do not require to be loaded because they are located in the process definition file using their self-defined API or script languages.

Experiment #2. As for Experiment #1, Experiment #2 features *one* single running instance of the process, which is now SP2. Comparing Figure 3.a and Figure 3.b, we observe that the efficiency rankings of WfMS#1, WfMS#4, and WfMS#5 remain unaltered. WfMS#2 and WfMS#3 switch their rankings to make WfMS#2 the slowest in executing SP2. Since in SP2 features many routing tasks and parallel task instances, to our opinion the mechanism of WfMS#2 to execute multiple simultaneous task instances is not robust.

Experiment #3. Experiment #3 comes with five instances of SP2 entering the system gradually. The leftmost bars for every WfMS of Figure 4 show that WfMS#1 is apparently the best performer. We identify the following reasons: a relatively small engine with respect to WfMS#3 and WfMS#5, so that WfMS#1 runs the automatic program more quickly without invoking several software layers; the hibernate layer of WfMS#1, which offers an optimized persistent layer solution to facilitate concurrent accesses to the database. This advantage of WfMS#1 is not obvious *a priori*, but shows up when the number of running instances increases within a small range. On the other hand, the process completion times of all the other WfMSs are almost identical within a small variability. This comes from the fact that some WfMSs, which perform fairly well under relatively light load, loose their advantages, while more robust WfMSs gradually catch up on simultaneous execution. Through our experiment results, we identify three of the main factors that have a certain impact on this kind of performance as: the mechanism to execute a small amount of simultaneous process instances; the strategy of space-time trade-off; and the persistent layer robustness.

By comparing Figures 3.a, 3.b, and the leftmost bars of Figure 4, we observe that WfMS#1 is the second fastest WfMS in experiments #1 and #2, and it takes the first place in Experiment #3. Thus, WfMS#1 efficiently executes those process models, both including and not including parallel work items, under a relatively light load (from 1 to 5 instances gradually entering the WfMS).

WfMS#4 is the best performer in experiments #1 and #2, but it is the worst performer in Experiment #3. This could mean that WfMS#4 performs well with *one* single running instance, but its performances fall down rapidly as more instances are executed simultaneously. One reason is that WfMS#4 comes with a persistent layer which interprets and encapsulates data between the logic layer and the persistent layer: consequently, additional time is required to access the database tables when handling simultaneous instances of the same process.

Experiment #4. Experiment #4 comes in two parts, both on SP2: one runs *10* simultaneous instances, the other runs *25*. The middle and rightmost bars of Figure 4 show some reverse trends compared to Figures 3.a, 3.b, and to left bars of Figure 4. WfMS#3 and WfMS#5 execute comparatively slow in experiments #1, #2, and #3 (especially WfMS#3), while WfMS#3 and WfMS#5 are the best performers in Experiment #4, with both 10 and 25 simultaneous instances.

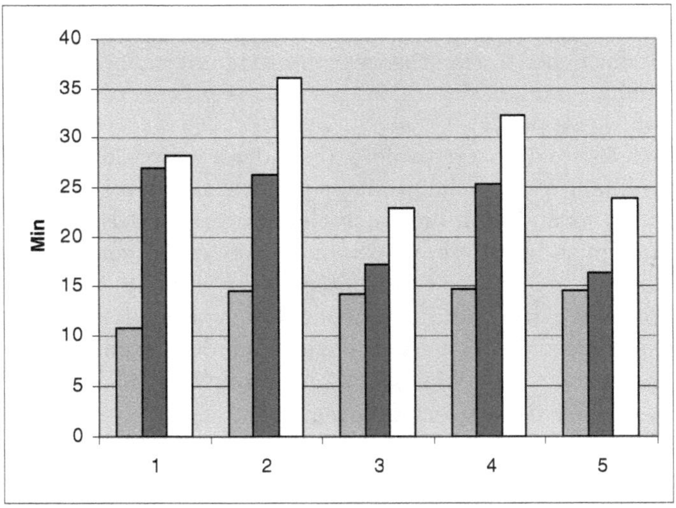

Fig. 4. Average execution time for the five WfMSs (x-axis) for: a: Experiment #3 (leftmost bars for every WfMS) - *five* instances of SP2 gradually enter the WfMS; b: Experiment #4 (middle bars) - *ten* instances of SP2 simultaneously enter the WfMS; c: Experiment #5 (rightmost bars) - *twentyfive* instances of SP2 simultaneously enter the WfMS. Times (y-axis) are given in minutes - the smaller the better.

These behaviors reveal that the two WfMSs show some advantages and robustness when dealing with several simultaneous process instances. For example, WfMS#3 might have a complex persistent layer, which is not so efficient in the simple situation, but is robust and stable as the workload increases. Moreover, some of the good performers under light load circumstances achieve an high execution speed by sacrificing their hardware resources; however, as the workload increases above a (small) threshold, the usage of the resources saturates, and no additional resource can be allocated to further enhance the speed. Therefore, those WfMSs which do not sacrifice their main memory and disk load to obtain a good execution speed, stand out when the number of simultaneous executions increases, despite they are relatively slow under light load circumstances.

7 Conclusions and Future Work

This paper describes a performance evaluation of five state-of-the-art Workflow Management Systems (WfMSs) and the approach we followed in order to compare their performances. We propose a *black box* approach for the performance analysis, as this allows us to study the systems as they are perceived by the actual users of the system, the perspective we are particularly interested in this work. We focus on the workflow engine, i.e., the core of each WfMS, and identify a set of requirements, such as autonomy of execution and independence from the host system, to guarantee a *fair* performance evaluation. The actual evaluation of the systems consists then in three main factors: selection of expressive reference processes; performance data collection; and experiment evaluation. The reference processes feature different levels of complexity; the experiments are defined on the basis of performance testing theory; collected performance indicators include CPU, main memory and disk workload, as well as *process completion time* (our main criterion in this paper).

The conclusions we draw are twofold: (i) under low workload conditions, both commercial and non-commercial products perform similarly; and (ii) under high workload conditions and with more complex process models, commercial products perform slightly better than their non-commercial competitors. Interestingly, this finding is in line with the intuitive decision the typical system designer would take: for less critical and less demanding workloads open-source or free products can suffice, while for mission-critical and demanding workloads a good choice is to invest some money in commercial products – not only to have better product support, but also better performance.

7.1 Future Research Direction

WfMSs are very complex systems and their analysis considers several issues; our approach requires further improvement to become more robust. Firstly, some more typical processes and WfMSs must be considered: next, optimization and fine tuning can significantly modify the behavior of a WfMS – especially for commercial systems, while insofar we just considered the *default* configuration. Further issues concern exception handling, scalability and distributed WfMSs.

Exception Handling. Expected exceptions describe a not negligible semantics of a business process [9]. Whenever a WfMS does not come with an exception handling unit, expected exceptions are mapped within the activity graph of the WfMS [10]. However, such a mapping severely affects the overall performances of the WfMS: our approach can measure the real incremental workload due to the pure exception management unit.

Scalability. WfMSs are growing up to accommodate an increasing number of users, work items, information items, and complex workflow applications. The architecture of a *robust* WfMS should be scalable up to thousands and millions of instances, with no serious degradation of the performances. Therefore, the total number of simultaneous instances of Experiment #4 is expected to be much larger, while at the same time, WfMSs should be implemented to smoothly operate under heavy load, too.

Distributed WfMS. Throughout the paper we assume that every process instance in a WfMS is executing on one single server. Large enterprizes demand the reliable execution of a wide variety of processes, demanding for a distributed WfMS [11]. Typically, in a distributed WfMS, the process instance is partitioned into several sub-processes, which are executed in a distributed environment on different engines connected via an intranet or even the Internet. Our approach can be enriched to analyze the performances on distributed WfMSs.

References

1. Reijers, H.A., van der Aalst, W.M.P.: The effectiveness of workflow management systems - predictions and lessons learned. Journal of Information Management, 457–471 (2005)
2. van der Aalst, W.M.P., ter Hofstede, A.H.M., Kiepuszewski, B., Barros, A.P.: Workflow patterns. Distributed and Parallel Databases 14, 5–51 (2003)
3. Li, J., Fan, Y., Zhou, M.: Performance modeling and analysis of workflow. IEEE Transactions on Systems, Man, and Cybernetics, Part A 34, 229–242 (2004)
4. Reijers, H.A., Song, M.S., Jeong, B.: On the Performance of Workflow Processes with Distributed Actors: Does Place Matter? In: Alonso, G., Dadam, P., Rosemann, M. (eds.) BPM 2007. LNCS, vol. 4714, pp. 32–47. Springer, Heidelberg (2007)
5. Kim, K.-H., Ellis, C.A.: Performance analytic models and analyses for workflow architectures. Information Systems Frontiers 3, 339–355 (2001)
6. Casati, F., Ceri, S., Pernici, B., Pozzi, G.: Workflow Evolution. Data Knowl. Eng. 24, 211–238 (1998)
7. Kim, K.-H., Ahn, H.-J.: An EJB-Based Very Large Scale Workflow System and its Performance Measurement. In: Fan, W., Wu, Z., Yang, J. (eds.) WAIM 2005. LNCS, vol. 3739, pp. 526–537. Springer, Heidelberg (2005)
8. Browne, J.C.: A critical overview of computer performance evaluation. In: ICSE, pp. 138–145 (1976)
9. Casati, F., Ceri, S., Paraboschi, S., Pozzi, G.: Specification and Implementation of Exceptions in Workflow Management Systems. ACM Trans. Database Syst. 24, 405–451 (1999)
10. Casati, F., Pozzi, G.: Modeling Exceptional Behaviors in Commercial Workflow Management Systems. In: CoopIS, pp. 127–138. IEEE Computer Society (1999)
11. Gillmann, M., Weißenfels, J., Weikum, G., Kraiss, A.: Performance assessment and configuration of enterprise-wide workflow management systems. In: Dadam, P., Reichert, M. (eds.) Enterprise-wide and Cross-enterprise Workflow Management. CEUR Workshop Proceedings, vol. 24, pp. 18–24. CEUR-WS.org (1999)

Third Order Accelerated Runge-Kutta Nyström Method for Solving Second-Order Ordinary Differential Equations

Faranak Rabiei[1], Fudziah Ismail[2], Norihan Arifin[3], and Saeid Emadi[4]

[1,2,3] Mathematics Department, universiti Putra Malaysia
43400 UPM Serdang, Selangor, Malaysia
[4] University of Derby, UK
{rabiei,fudziah,norihan}@math.upm.edu.my, s.emadi60@gmail.com

Abstract. In this paper, the explicit Accelerated Runge-Kutta Nyström (ARKN) method of order three with two stages for the numerical integration of second-order ordinary differential equations are developed. The method is two step in nature. Algebraic order conditions of the method are obtained and third order ARKN method is derived. Numerical examples are carried out to illustrate the efficiency of the proposed method compared to the existing Runge-Kutta Nyström (RKN) method.

Keywords: Accelerated Runge-Kutta Nyström method, Two step method, Second-order ordinary differential equations, Order conditions.

1 Introduction

Consider the special second-order ordinary differential equations of the form

$$y'' = f(x, y),\ y(x_0) = y_0,\ y'(x_0) = y'_0. \tag{1}$$

Such problem often arise in science and engineering fields such celestial mechanics, molecular dynamics , semi-discretization of wave equations, electronics and so on. The second-order equations can be directly solved by using Runge-Kutta Nyström (RKN) methods or multistep methods. Phohomsiri and Udwadia [1] constructed the third order Accelerated Runge-Kutta (ARK3) method for solving autonomous first-order ordinary differential equations with the form of $y' = f(y)$. In this paper, we developed the Accelerated Runge-Kutta Nyström method of order three (ARKN3) for solving autonomous second-order equation (1) with the form of $y'' = f(y)$. The method we presented here used only two stages while the existing RKN3 method used three stages.

In section 2, we presented the ARKN3 method and the order conditions of the method are obtained in section 3. In section 4, ARKN3 are derived and numerical examples to illustrate the efficiency of the method compared with the existing RKN3 are presented in the last section.

A. Abd Manaf et al. (Eds.): ICIEIS 2011, Part III, CCIS 253, pp. 204–209, 2011.

2 Construction of ARKN3 Method with Two Stages

Consider the ARK3 method from [1] as follows

$$\begin{aligned} y_{n+1} &= y_n + h(b_1 k_1 - b_{-1} k_{-1} + b_2(k_2 - k_{-2})), \\ k_1 &= f(y_n), \qquad k_{-1} = f(y_{n-1}), \\ k_2 &= f(y_n + ha_1 k_1), \qquad k_{-2} = f(y_{n-1} + ha_1 k_{-1}). \end{aligned} \tag{2}$$

where h is the fixed step size. Here based on the ARK3 method we developed the ARKN3 method for solving the autonomous second-order equation directly following the same approach as Dormand [2]. We define:

$$y_{n+1} = y_n + h(b_1 f_1 - b_{-1} f_{-1} + b_2(f_2 - f_{-2})), \tag{3}$$

$$y'_{n+1} = y'_n + h(b_1 g_1 - b_{-1} g_{-1} + b_2(g_2 - g_{-2})), \tag{4}$$

$$\begin{aligned} g_1 &= g(y_n), \qquad g_{-1} = g(y_{n-1}), \\ f_1 &= y'_n, \qquad f_{-1} = y'_{n-1}, \\ g_2 &= g(y_n + ha_1 f_1), \qquad g_{-2} = g(y_{n-1} + ha_1 f_{-1}) \\ f_2 &= y'_n + ha_1 g_1, \qquad f_{-2} = y'_{n-1} + ha_1 g_{-1}. \end{aligned}$$

by substituting the f_{-1}, f_1, f_{-2}, and f_2 into g_{-2} and g_2 we have

$$\begin{aligned} g_2 &= g(y_n + ha_1(y'_n + ha_1 g_1)) = g(y_n + ha_1 y'_n + h^2 a_1^2 g_1), \\ g_{-2} &= g(y_{n-1} + ha_1(y'_{n-1} + ha_1 g_{-1})) = g(y_{n-1} + ha_1 y'_{n-1} + h^2 a_1^2 g_{-1}), \end{aligned}$$

now substitute the f_{-1}, f_1, f_{-2}, f_2, g_{-1}, g_1, g_{-2}, g_2. into (3) obtain

$$\begin{aligned} y_{n+1} &= y_n + h(b_1 y'_n - b_{-1} y'_{n-1} + b_2 \left((y'_n + ha_1 g_1) - (y'_{n-1} + ha_1 g_{-1}) \right)), \\ &= y_n + h(b_1 + b_2) y'_n - h(b_{-1} + b_2) y'_{n-1} + h^2 a_1 b_2 (g_1 - g_{-1}). \end{aligned} \tag{5}$$

consider the following order conditions of ARK3 (see [1])

$$b_1 - b_{-1} = 1,$$

$$b_1 + b_2 = \frac{1}{2}.$$

simplifying the equation (5) we have

$$y_{n+1} = y_n + \frac{3h}{2} y'_n + \frac{h}{2} y'_{n-1} + h^2 \bar{b} \, (g_1 - g_{-1}).$$

where $\bar{b} = a_1 b_2$.

By writing Eqs. (3) and (4) in standard form in terms of k_i and function f, we define the ARKN3 method as follows :

$$
\begin{aligned}
y_{n+1} &= y_n + \frac{3h}{2}\, y_n' + \frac{h}{2}\, y_{n-1}' + h^2\bar{b}\,(k_1 - k_{-1}),\\
y_{n+1}' &= y_n' + h(b_1 k_1 - b_{-1}k_{-1} + b_2(k_2 - k_{-2})),
\end{aligned}
$$

$$
\begin{aligned}
k_1 &= f(y_n), & k_{-1} &= f(y_{n-1}),\\
k_2 &= f(y_n + ha_1k_1), & k_{-2} &= f(y_{n-1} + ha_1k_{-1}).
\end{aligned}
\tag{6}
$$

3 Order Conditions

To find the order conditions for ARKN3 method we applied the Taylor's series expansion to equations (6). Here, after using the Taylor's series expansion we obtained the order conditions for y_n and y_n' up to order three as follows:

order condition for y_n:

$$
\begin{aligned}
&\textit{first order} & b_1 - b_{-1} &= 1,\\
&\textit{second order} & b_1 + b_2 &= \frac{1}{2},\\
&\textit{third order} & b_2a_1 &= \frac{5}{12}.
\end{aligned}
$$

order condition for y_n':

$$
\textit{third order} \qquad \bar{b}_2 = \frac{5}{12}.
$$

4 Analysis of the Method

To find the coefficients of ARKN3 method in equations (6), all the above order conditions for y_n and y_n' must be satisfied. We choose the value of $b_{-1} \in [-1\ 1]$ as a free parameter, here we set $b_{-1} = -\frac{1}{3}$ and obtained the remaining parameters as follows:

$$
a_1 = \frac{1}{2}, \quad b_1 = \frac{2}{3}, \quad b_2 = \frac{5}{6}, \quad \bar{b}_2 = \frac{5}{12}.
$$

We compared the results of the new method with the existing RKN method of order three with dispersive order six and dissipative order five with three stages(see [3]). The RKN3 is computed by using the following formulas:

$$
\begin{aligned}
y_{n+1} &= y_n + hy_n' + h^2(b_1k_1 + b_2k_2 + b_3k_3),\\
y_{n+1}' &= y_n' + h(b_1'k_1 + b_2'k_2 + b_3'k_3),\\
k_1 &= f(y_n),
\end{aligned}
$$

$$k_2 = f(y_n + c_2 h y'_n + h^2 a_{21} k_1),$$
$$k_3 = f(y_n + c_3 h y'_n + h^2(a_{31} k_1 + a_{32} k_2)),$$

It is convenient to present the coefficients of RKN3 in in Table 1.
The coefficients of existing NRK3 are shown in Table 2.

Table 1. Table of coefficients for NRK3 method

0			
c_2	a_{21}		
c_3	a_{31}	a_{32}	
	b_1	b_2	b_3
	b'_1	b'_2	b'_3

Table 2. Table of coefficients for existing NRK3 method

0			
$\frac{1}{2}$	$\frac{4}{9}$		
1	$\frac{7}{20}$	$\frac{3}{20}$	
	$\frac{1}{3}$	0	$\frac{1}{6}$
	$\frac{1}{4}$	$\frac{3}{4}$	0

5 Numerical Examples

In this section, we tested a standard set of second-order initial value problems to show the efficiency and accuracy of the proposed method. The exact solution $y(x)$ and $y'(x)$ are used to estimate the global error as well as to approximate the starting values of y_1 and y'_1 at the first step $[x_0\ x_1]$. Consider the $y(x_i)$ is exact solution and $y^*(x_i)$ is approximated solution on ith iteration which computed using formulas (6), the global error of ith iteration will calculate as follow:

$$error_i = |y(x_i) - y^*(x_i)|.$$

The following problems are solved for $x \in [0\ 10]$.

Problem 1 (see [2])

$$y'' = -y, \quad y(0) = 0, \; y'(0) = 1,$$

exact solution: $y(x) = sin(x)$.

Problem 2 (see [4])

$$y_1'' = -\frac{y_1}{(\sqrt{y_1^2 + y_2^2})^3}, \quad y_1(0) = 1, \; y_1'(0) = 0,$$

$$y_2'' = -\frac{y_2}{(\sqrt{y_1^2 + y_2^2})^3}, \quad y_2(0) = 0, \; y_2'(0) = 1,$$

exact solutions: $y_1(x) = cos(x), \; y_2(x) = sin(x)$.
Here, the number of function evaluations are computed as follow :

Number of function evaluations= Number of stages $\times$ Number of steps.

where number of stages = 2, and

Number of steps $= \frac{10-0}{h}$, for $h = 0.5, \; 0.1, \; 0.05, \; 0.01, \; 0.005$.

The log(maximum global error) versus the number of function evaluations for the tested problems are shown in Figures 1 and 2.

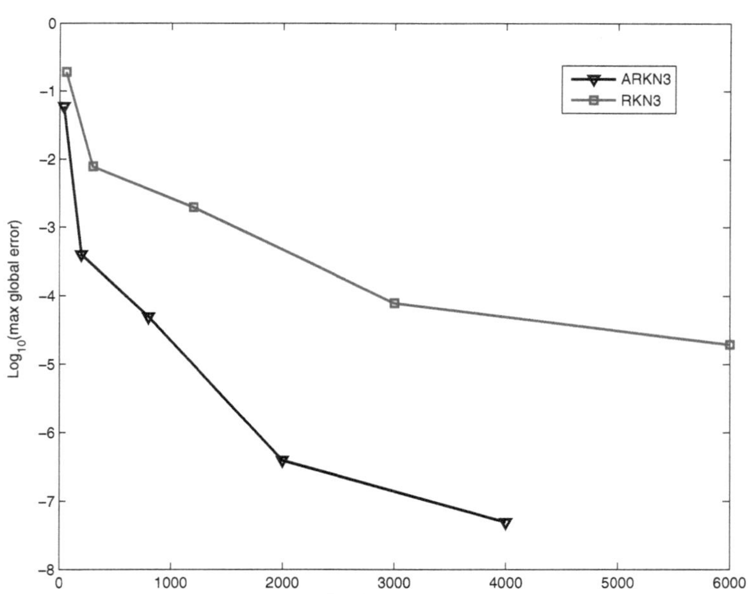

Fig. 1. Maximum global error versus number of function evaluations for problem 1

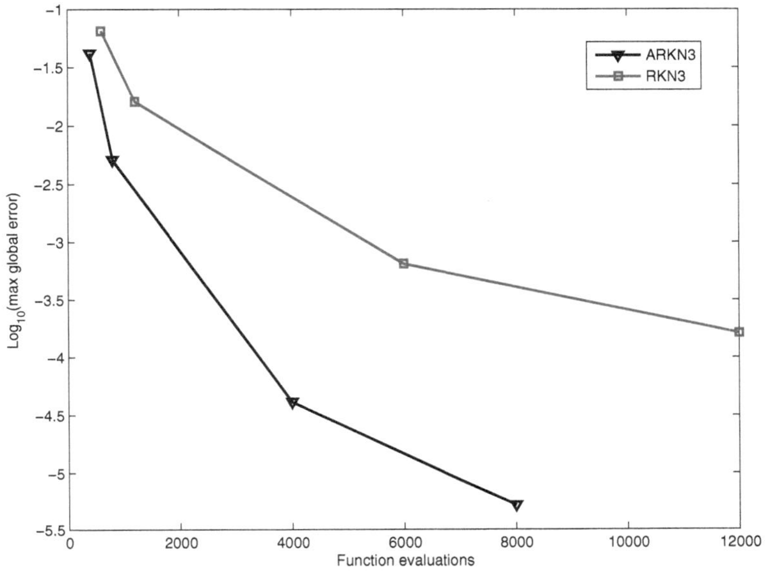

Fig. 2. Maximum global error versus number of function evaluations for problem 2

6 Discussion and Conclusion

From Figs. 1 and 2 we observe that for both problems the new method is more accurate and has lower number of function evaluations compared to the existing method.

As a conclusion, the third order ARKN method has been developed for numerical integration of second-order ordinary differential equations with reduced number of function evaluations required per step. The order conditions of the new method are derived up to order three and by satisfying the appropriate order conditions we obtained the method of order three. The ARKN3 method is almost two-step in nature and is computationally more efficient compared.

References

1. Phohomsiri, P., Udwadia, F.E.: Acceleration of Runge-Kutta Integeration Schemes. Discrit. Dynamic. Nature. Soci. 2, 307–314 (2004)
2. Dormand, J.R.: Numerical Method for Differential Equations. A Computational Approach. CRC Press Inc. (1996)
3. Norazak. B. S.,: Runge-Kutta Nyström Methods for Solving Osillatory Problems, Ph.D Thesis, Universiti Putra Malaysia (2010)
4. Franco, J.M.: A Class of Explicit Two Step Hybrid Methods for Second Order IVP's. J. Comput. Appl. Math. 187, 41–57 (2006)

New Model for Shariah-Compliant Portfolio Optimization under Fuzzy Environment

Younes Elahi* and Mohd Ismail Abd Aziz

Department of Mathematics, University Technology Malaysia
81310 Johor Bahru, Malaysia
elahi.math@gmail.com

Abstract. In this paper, a new fuzzy model is presented to improve methods for Shariah-compliant portfolio optimization, and provides an overview of faith-compliant portfolio optimization. The spread of fuzzy variable is adopted as criteria in practical risk management in Islamic finance. First, the effect of shariah-compliant strategy to portfolio optimization is covered in the literature review. After analyzing the literature, it was identified that the previous models lack the fuzzy environment so that they were unable to deal with uncertainty. Consequently, a new model is proposed to apply the fuzzy environment to Shariah-compliance portfolio optimization. In this research activity, an E-S model by the linear combination of the risk and reward for fuzzy shariah-compliant is proposed. Finally, some future works are presented along with a conclusion.

Keywords: Shariah guidelines, Portfolio model, Fuzzy Expectation-Spread (E-S) model.

1 Introduction and Outline

The growing capital value of the Muslim countries and they require of these investors to invest their capital in financial products that do not divergence with the Shariah triggered the development of Shariah-compliant investment products such as Islamic equity funds. Since Shariah prohibits the participation in interest-based assets [1], specific guidelines need to be introduced as more constraints into models for constructing Shariah-compliant portfolios [2].

The main problem of the classical problem (in theoretical and computational finance) is optimizing a portfolio of finitely numerous assets. As the determining work of Markowitz (1952, 1959, 1987) it is commonly agreed that portfolio performance must be measured in two distinct dimensions: the expected return rate with mean, and the risk for measured the uncertainty of the return rate. Another theoretic approach is stochastic dominance [3], [4].

The sense of stochastic dominance is referring to models of risk-averse predominance. It came from the theory of Majorization for the discrete case, was

* Corresponding author.

A. Abd Manaf et al. (Eds.): ICIEIS 2011, Part III, CCIS 253, pp. 210–217, 2011.

afterward extensive to common distributions, and was now generally used in economics and investment [5-10].

Current portfolio study is in progress from original research work by Markowitz [11]. Markowitz was presented mean–variance model, which is the first portfolio selection model. Founded on this model, absolute deviation portfolio optimization [12] and semi-absolute deviation models were propounded [13].

It is discussed that in actuality, many proceedings with fuzziness are characterized by probabilistic approaches, though they are not random events See [14]. Lately, some authors began to work on fuzzy portfolio selection problems[15]. Shariah-compliant Portfolio selection using fuzzy mathematical programming has been the focus of this paper.

The outline of this paper is as follows. In Sect. 2, we remember some fundamental concepts related to Islam and portfolio optimization. In Sect. 3, first we study on shariah-compliant portfolio optimization, and the second moment is referred to as some useful formulas for cases of strategies in Islamic finance; then we derive a model of portfolio compliance strategies. In Sect. 4, we formulate Fuzzy Portfolio Optimization. Then, according to the Fuzzy Expectation-Spread (E-S) model, we introduce the Shariah-compliant Fuzzy Portfolio Optimization model. Section 5 concludes the paper.

2 Fundamental Concepts

In this section, we present some basic primary senses for entrance the discussion:

2.1 Shariah-Compliant

Islamic finance is controlled by the Shariah, which prohibits speculation, but covenant that income must be derivative as profits from shared business risk rather than interest or guaranteed return[16]. Quran, Hadith and Ijtihad are the main Shariah sources for these rules. The Quran is the principal source of Islam, including the terminology of God as delivered to the prophet Mohammed while the Hadith consists of story minutes of the events and sayings of the prophet himself. Ijtihad is the third Shariah source, that the origin and formulation of Shariah laws by practiced scholars.

While there is no higher institution liable for religious faiths to be followed by all Muslims, Shariah scholars [17] take these sources and specify so called Shariah-compliance strategies to be followed within asset selection[18-20]. Despite these religious limitations and legal uncertainty encompassing the ability of investor interest under Islamic fiqh, Islamic finance can make balanced to equity, mortgages, and derivatives known in conservative finance[16].

2.2 Portfolio Optimization

The portfolio selection problem refers to form a good portfolio. It is complicated to choose which assets should be selected because of the doubt on their returns. The central purpose in a portfolio selection Problem is to find optimal proportions of the stock for creating a portfolio which complements the investor's preferences presumptuous that the investors' wish to strike a balance between maximizing the return and minimizing the risk of their investment [21].

Portfolio problem: Let $R_1, R_2, \ldots, R_n$ be stochastic return rates of assets $1,2,\ldots,n$. We suppose that $\mathbb{E}[|R_i| < \infty]$ for all $i = 1,\ldots,n$. Our plan is to invest our capital in these assets in order to get some attractive characteristics of the total return rate on the investment. Denoting by $x_1, x_2, \ldots, x_n$ the fractions of the original capital invested in assets $1,2,\ldots,n$ we can quickly gain the formula for the whole return rate:

$$R(x) = R_1 x_1 + R_2 x_2 + \cdots + R_n x_n \tag{1}$$

Obviously, the set of feasible asset allocations can be determined as follows:

$$X = \{\, x \in \mathbb{R}^n : x_1 + x_2 + \ldots + x_n = 1,\ x_i \geq 0,\ i = 1,\ldots,n\} \tag{2}$$

Usually, stochastic calculus instruments starting by the standard Black-Schole's theory for option pricing and portfolio optimization [22, 23].

3 Shariah-Compliant Portfolio Optimization

Common rules for Islamically allowable forms of financial activity can funded in The *Quran*, Islam's Holy Book, and the *hadıth* [24]. The main characteristic of Islamic economic behavior is Increase risk sharing between the procurer of funds (investor) and both the financial agent and the user of fund [25].

In this part, we review how Shariah-compliance can be modeled within the framework of portfolio optimization. We let the standard condition, i.e. an asset space, $I = \{1,\ldots,n\}$ from which a portfolio can be produced, and we imagine that the total wealth has to be invested and short-sellings is not permissible, which is practical since short-sellings is usually not allowed under Shariah. Then every portfolio can be exposed by a share vector

$x = (x_1, \ldots, x_n)$ where $x_i \in [0,1]$ represents the weight or fractional capital invested in each asset, $i \in I$ and

$\sum_{i=1}^{n} x_i = 1$ it hold [2].

For the following we as well suppose an objective function $f(x)$ by which the efficiency of a portfolio is measured and a set C of constraints stemming from investment guidelines other than Shariah guidelines. The objective function is cogitative the investment strategy. Moreover, the return/risk transaction and could stem, for example, from the mean-variance model [11], [26] or index tracking senses [27]. Furthermore, we supposed to have the following conventional portfolio optimization model that before or lacking about Shariah-compliance:

Min $f(x)$ Subject to x comply with constraints in C

$$\begin{aligned} &\textstyle\sum_{i=1}^{n} x_i = 1 \\ &x_i \geq 0 \quad \forall i \in I \end{aligned} \tag{3}$$

Sector rules have to be satisfied on the single assets or the total portfolio, whereas compliance is measured as an element of them.

We suppose an economic guideline $g \in G$ we have to compute a financial ratio $r_i(g)$ for each asset, $i \in I$ which measures the level of participation in a non-compliant financial activity, and to evaluate the value with a maximum permissible value $T(g)$, the so called threshold value. Thus, we have to organize a set of limitation of the following type:

$$r_i(g) \leq T(g) \tag{4}$$

Clearly, these guideline's consequences in an additional decrease of the asset universe and thus their achievement can be safe in a preprocessing phase analogously to the sector rules. Therefore, Shariah-fulfillment of a portfolio can be operationally generated by a preprocessing stage in which the asset universe for a conventional portfolio optimization model is specified. However, the useless way to model compliance with relate to a guideline is to formalize conditions (4) as set of mathematical inequalities, which are introduced as constraints into the portfolio model. Conceptually, a financial principle can be modeled by a set of logical limitations of the following type:

$$x_i = 0 \quad \text{If} \quad r_i(g) > T(g) \quad \forall i \in I \tag{5}$$

Unequal of (5) can be turned into a set of mathematical inequality like follows: We describe a binary variable z_i for each asset, $i \in I$ has been following form:

$$z_i = \begin{cases} 1 & \text{if} \quad i \text{ is complaint} \\ 0 & \text{otherwise} \end{cases} \tag{6}$$

and we use the constraints:

$$x_i \leq z_i \quad \forall i \in I \tag{7}$$

$$r_i(g).z_i \leq T(g) \quad \forall i \in I \tag{8}$$

Constraints (7) ensure that for every asset $i \in I$

$$x_i > 0 \text{ only if } z_i = 1 \tag{9}$$

According to constraints (8) guarantee, that z_i is 0 if the guideline (6) is not fulfilled.

3.1 Modeling Portfolio Compliance Strategies

A portfolio x complies with a specific rule g if the sum of the ratio values over all assets, $i \in I$ weighted by their share values x_i is less than the threshold, i.e.

$$\sum_{i \in I} r_i(g).x_i \leq T(g) \tag{10}$$

A portfolio x is acquiescent with related to a strategy $s \in S$ if x fulfils all guidelines $g \in G_s$. So, for a central strategy s and the set of rules G_s we find the following portfolio optimization model:

Min $f(x)$
Subject to (2)-(4) and

$$\sum_{i\in I} r_i(g).x_i \leq T(g) \quad \forall g \in G_s \tag{11}$$

The portfolio-based fulfillment strategies can now be modeled as follows:

Strategy 1: Best of Shariah strategy. In this strategy, we must solve the model for each $s \in S$ alone. In addition, the optimal portfolio related to this strategy is the one produced by the model yielding the best portfolio presentation.

Strategy 2: Consensus/Ijmaa Shariah strategy. To introduce Shariah-compliance under the Ijmaa strategy, we have got to substitute (11) by:

$$\sum_{i\in I} r_i(g).x_i \leq T(g) \quad \forall s \in S, \forall g \in G_s \tag{12}$$

Strategy 3: Liberal strategy. We define the binary variables for model of the liberal compliance strategy as the following:

$$zp(s) = \begin{cases} 1 & \text{if the portfolio } x \text{ is complaint for } s \in S \\ 0 & \text{otherwise} \end{cases}$$

There are nonlinear compulsions, and with attention to solvability of the optimization model must be present as follows:

$$\sum_{i\in I} r_i(g).x_i \leq (1 - zp(s)).M + T(g) \quad \forall s \in S, \forall g \in G_s, \tag{13}$$

That M is a being as much as needed great number. Now caused by (12) at least for one $s \in S$; s^0 , we attain

$$zp(s^0) = 1 \text{ and we have at least one } s \in S.$$

Strategy 4: Majority/Kasra strategy. We change in the model for the liberal strategy for the majority strategy via

$$\sum_{s\in S} zp_s \geq \left\lceil \frac{|S|}{2} \right\rceil , \tag{14}$$

Which certifies that at least the majority of main strategies $s \in S$ regards as the portfolio as being compliant [2].

4 Shariah-Compliant Fuzzy Portfolio Optimization

In this section, first, we present formula of the Fuzzy Portfolio Optimization. Then we showed the effect of shariah-compliant on this formula.

4.1 Fuzzy Portfolio Optimization

Definition: If ξ is a fuzzy variable with a possibility distribution function $\mu_\xi : \mapsto [0, 1]$, and its spread is defined by the following L-S integral

$$Sp[\xi] = \int_{(-\infty,+\infty)}(r - E[\xi])^2 \mathrm{d}\Phi(r), \tag{15}$$

Where $E[\xi]$ is the expected value of fuzzy variable ξ [28] and $\Phi(r)$ is the credibility distribution of the fuzzy variable [29]. Every financier has to decide on an appropriate combine of assets to comprise in his investment portfolio. Specified a set of potential investments indexed from 1 to n, allow ξ_i indicate the fuzzy return in the next time period on investment i, $i = 1,\ldots,n$. A portfolio is shown by specify what fraction of one's assets to situate into each investment. That is, a portfolio is a set of nonnegative numbers x_i, $(i = 1,\ldots,n)$ that summation to one. The return the investor would related achieve by using a given portfolio is introduced as $\sum_{i=1}^{n} x_i\xi_i$, which is also a fuzzy variable, then the reward with such a portfolio is shown as the expected return $E[\sum_{i=1}^{n} x_i\xi_i]$.

Now, we will describe the risk coupled with an investment to be the spread of the fuzzy return $\sum_{i=1}^{n} x_i\xi_i$, that is the quadratic deviation from the expected value. In our portfolio selection problem, we would like to minimize the risk and not incur too small reward. So, we formally build the following E-S model by a linear arrangement of the risk and the reward:

$$\begin{cases} \min & Sp[\sum_{i=1}^{n} x_i\xi_i] - \mu E[\sum_{i=1}^{n} x_i\xi_i] \\ & s.t. \quad \sum_{i=1}^{n} x_i = 1 \\ & x_i \geq 0, i = 1,2,\ldots,n \end{cases}, \tag{16}$$

The positive parameter μ denotes the important relation between risk and reward [30].

4.2 Shariah-Compliant Fuzzy Portfolio Optimization Model

We recall the criterion of shariah-compliant in portfolio optimization by [2] Ulrich Derigs, Shehab Marzban(2011). They used z_i as the same formula presented in equation (6):

$$z_i = \begin{cases} 1 & \text{if} \quad i \text{ is complaint} \\ 0 & \qquad\qquad \text{otherwise} \end{cases}$$

In a new model, with the above condition, we present the following E-S model by a linear combination of the risk and the reward for fuzzy shariah-compliant:

$$\begin{cases} \min & Sp[\sum_{i=1}^{n} z_i x_i\xi_i] - \mu E[\sum_{i=1}^{n} z_i x_i\xi_i] \\ & s.t. \quad \sum_{i=1}^{n} x_i = 1 \\ & x_i \geq 0, i = 1,2,\ldots,n \end{cases}, \tag{17}$$

where μ is a positive parameter. In the fuzzy environment, the positive parameter μ denotes the relation between risk and reward.

5 Conclusion

Within this paper, we have attention to the problem of Shariah-compliant portfolio construction. The analysis revealed that, fuzzy methodology allows us to add uncertainty into data bases and also to combine personal characteristics into the models. A financial asset comprises multi norm decision-making with the fuzzy deterministic formulation [21]. Monetary novelty will help to more growth and improve of Shariah-compliant derivative contracts. For example, extend of faith derivatives fine for the Islamic insurance *(taka ful)* industry, limitation the possible of risk diversification from a larger group of available assets [16].

In addition, the essential condition of such faith rules by the Shariah scholars the accessibility of modeling tools for setting up the Shariah-compliant portfolio optimization model is a main requirement, Although, not obligatory for trend the new paradigm in practice[2].

As a consequence, This model decreases complexity of computation and could be a fine replacement for Shariah-compliant portfolio optimization model, that present by Ulrich, D., Marzban, S . With sustaining this system, this model will develop in the future. Such as, Shariah-compliant Fuzzy risk and return optimization model and Shariah-compliant Fuzzy pricing optimization model.

Acknowledgment. This publication is supported by Ministry of Higher Education and Research University Grant (RUG), Universiti Teknologi Malaysia (No: Q.J130000.7108.01H56).

References

1. Wilson, R., Jaffer, S. (eds.): Screening criteria for islamic equity funds. In: Islamic Asset Management: Forming the Future for Shariah-Compliant Investment Strategies, pp. 35–45. Euromoney Books, London (2004)
2. Ulrich, D., Marzban, S.: A New strategies and a new paradigm for Shariah-compliant portfolio optimization. Journal of Banking & Finance 33, 1166–1176 (2009)
3. Mosler, K., Scarsini, M. (eds.): Stochastic Orders and Decision Under Risk. Institute of Mathematical Statistics, Hayward (1991)
4. Whitmore, G., Findlay, M. (eds.): Stochastic Dominance: An Approach to Decision-Making Under Risk. D.C.Heath, Lexington (1978)
5. Fishburn, P.: Decision and Value Theory. John Wiley & Sons, New York (1964)
6. Hardy, G., Littlewood, J.E., Pólya, G.: Inequalities. Cambridge University Press, Cambridge (1934)
7. Marshall, A., Olkin, I.: Inequalities: Theory of Majorization and Its Applications. Academic Press, San Diego (1979)
8. Quirk, J., Saposnik, R.: Admissibility and measurable utility functions. Review of Economic Studies 29, 140–146 (1962)
9. Hadar, J., Russell, W.: Rules for ordering uncertain prospects. American Economic Review 59, 25–34 (1969)
10. Rothschild, M., Stiglitz, J.E.: Increasing risk: I. A definition. Journal of Economic Theory 2, 225–243 (1969)
11. Markowitz, H.: Portfolio selection. Journal of Finance 7, 77–91 (1952)
12. Konno, H., Yamazaki, H.: Mean–absolute deviation portfolio optimization model and its applications to the Tokyo Stock Market. Management Science 37, 519–531 (1991)
13. Mansini, R., Speranza, M.: Heuristic algorithms for the portfolio selection problem with minimum transaction lots. European Journal of Operational Research 114, 219–233 (1999)

14. Wu, H.: The Karush–Kuhn–Tucker optimality conditions for the optimization problem with fuzzy-valued objective function. Mathematical Method of Operation Research 66, 203–224 (2007)
15. Zhang, X., Wei-Guo, Z., Wei-Jun, X.: An optimization model of the portfolio adjusting problem with fuzzy return and a SMO algorithm. Expert Systems with Applications 38, 3069–3074 (2011)
16. Jobst, A.: Derivatives in Islamic Finance. In: International Conference on Islamic Capital Markets, Jakarta, Indonesia during, August 27-29 (2007)
17. Delorenzo, Y.: Shariah Supervision of Islamic Mutual Funds. In: Proceedings of the Fourth Harvard University Forum on Islamic Finance. Harvard University, Cambridge (2000)
18. Derigs, U., Marzban, S.: Review and analysis of current Shariah-compliant equity screening practices. International Journal of Islamic and Middle Eastern Finance and Management 1(4), 285–303 (2008)
19. Renneboog, L., Ter Horst, J., Zhang, C.: Socially responsible investments: Institutional aspects, performance, and investor behavior. Journal of Banking and Finance 32, 1723–1742 (2008)
20. Galema, R., Plantinga, A., Scholtens, B.: The stocks at stake: Return and risk in socially responsible investment. Journal of Banking and Finance 32, 2646–2654 (2008)
21. Pankaj, G., Mukesh, K., Anand, S.: Asset portfolio optimization using fuzzy mathematical programming. Journal of Information Sciences 178, 1734–1755 (2008)
22. Darinka, D., Andrzej, R.: Portfolio optimization with stochastic dominance constraints. Journal of Banking & Finance 30, 433–451 (2006)
23. Ha-Young, K., Frederi, G.: Viens Portfolio optimization in discrete time with proportional transaction costs under stochastic volatility. onlin springer (2010)
24. Feisal, K.: How 'Islamic' is Islamic Banking? Journal of Economic Behavior & Organization 76, 805–820 (2010)
25. Iqbal, M., Ahmad, A., Khan.: Challenges facing Islamic banking. Islamic Development Bank. Islamic Research and Training Institute Occasional Paper (1998)
26. Dentcheva, D., Ruszczynski, A.: Portfolio optimization with stochastic dominance control. Journal of Banking and Finance 30, 433–451 (2006)
27. Corielli, F., Marcellino, M.: Factor based index tracking. Journal of Banking and Finance 30, 2215–2233 (2008)
28. Liu, B., Liu, Y.: Expected Value of Fuzzy Variable and Fuzzy Expected Value Models. IEEE Transactions on Fuzzy Systems 10, 445–450 (2002)
29. Liu, B.: Uncertainty Theory. Springer, Berlin (2004)
30. Liu, Y., Wu, X.: A Class of Fuzzy Portfolio Optimization Problems: E-S models. In: Tan, Y., Shi, Y., Tan, K.C. (eds.) ICSI 2010. LNCS, vol. 6146, pp. 43–50. Springer, Heidelberg (2010)
31. José, V., Enriqueta, V., Bermúdeza, J.D.: Fuzzy portfolio optimization under downside risk measures. Centro de Investigaci6n Operativa, Universidad Miguel Hernández de Elche (2005)

The Four Point-EDGMSOR Iterative Method for Solution of 2D Helmholtz Equations

Mohd Kamalrulzaman Md Akhir[1], Mohamed Othman[2], Jumat Sulaiman[3], Zanariah Abdul Majid[4], and Mohamed Suleiman[5]

[1] Institute for Mathematical Research, Universiti Putra Malaysia, 43400 UPM Serdang Selangor D.E, Malaysia
[2] Department of Communications Technology and Network, Faculty of Computer Science and Info Technology, Universiti Putra Malaysia, 43400 UPM Serdang Selangor D.E, Malaysia
[3] School of Science and Technology, Universiti Malaysia Sabah, 88400 Kota Kinabalu Sabah, Malaysia
[4,5] Department of Mathematics, Faculty of Science, Universiti Putra Malaysia, 43400 UPM Serdang Selangor D.E, Malaysia
mkamalrulzaman@gmail.com

Abstract. This paper examines the use of the Four Point-Explicit Decoupled Group (EDG) iterative method together with MSOR iterative method, namely 4 Point-*EDGMSOR*. The efficiency of this method will be investigated to solve two-dimensional Helmholtz equation by using half-sweep finite difference approximation. In fact, the formulation of and implementation of the proposed method are also presented. Some numerical examples are presented to point out efficiency of the proposed method.

Keywords: Helmholtz equation, Explicit Decoupled Group (EDG), Finite Difference, Modified Successive Over-Relaxation (MSOR).

1 Introduction

The applications and theory of partial differential equations (PDEs) have been one of the main principal tools in various area of science and engineering such as elastic waves in solids, time harmonic acoustic, electromagnetic fields and optical waveguide (Akhir *et al.*[4,5]). Recently, the half-sweep iterative method was initiated by Abdullah [1] through Explicit Decoupled Group (EDG) method to solve two-dimensional Poisson equations. The basic idea of half-sweep iterative method is to reduce computational complexity during iteration process, since the implementation of the half-sweep iterative method will only consider nearly half of all node points in a solution domain respectively. Following to that, there have been further discussion and works on the EDG method with half-sweep iterative method; see (Abdullah [1], Akhir *et al.* [5], Aruchunan and Sulaiman [6], Ibrahim and Abdullah [10], Muthuvalu and Sulaiman [12], Othman and Abdullah [13], Sulaiman *et al.* [16,17,18] and Yousif and Evans [20]).

A. Abd Manaf et al. (Eds.): ICIEIS 2011, Part III, CCIS 253, pp. 218–227, 2011.

In this paper, by using second order finite difference approximation equation, the effectiveness of the 4 Point-EDG*MSOR* iterative method will be investigated for solving two-dimensional Helmholtz equations. The 4 Point-EDG*MSOR* method will be compared to the existing 4 Point-EDG iterative methods. To certify the efficiency of the 4 Point-*EDGMSOR*, let us consider 2D Helmholtz equation as our model problem, which can be represented mathematically as

$$\frac{\partial^2 U}{\partial x^2} + \frac{\partial^2 U}{\partial y^2} - \alpha U = f(x,y), \quad (x,y) \in \Omega \tag{1}$$

subject to the Dirichlet boundary condition $U(x,y) = G(x,y), (x,y) \in \partial\Omega$, where α is a non-negative constant and $f(x,y)$ is given function with sufficient smoothness. For simplicity, we assume the domain Ω to be square unit $[0 \le x, y \le 1]$. To solve Eq. (1) numerically, we uniformly discretize the domain in both x and y directions with a grid size $h = 1/n$, where n is arbitrary positive integer. When Eq. (1) is discretized by finite difference scheme, the most commonly used approximation is the standard five points formula as

$$U_{i-1,j} + U_{i+1,j} + U_{i,j-1} + U_{i,j+1} - \left(4 + \alpha h^2\right) U_{i,j} = h^2 f_{i,j}, \tag{2}$$

Apart from Eq. (2), the rotated finite difference approximation can be formed by clockwise rotation of the x-y axis by $45°$. Thus rotated finite difference approximation for problem (1) becomes

$$U_{i+1,j+1} + U_{i-1,j-1} + U_{i+1,j-1} + U_{i-1,j+1} - \left(4 + 2\alpha h^2\right) U_{i,j} = 2ph^2 f_{i,j}, \tag{3}$$

Now it can be clearly seen that the application of either Eq. (2) or (3) to each internal mesh point will result in a large and sparse linear algebraic system

$$Au = f\ , \tag{4}$$

where A and f are a square nonsingular matrix and a column matrix, respectively. While u is a column matrix. The solution of Eq. (4) can be obtained by direct or iterative method. Since Eq. (4) is large and sparse, the iterative method is suitable to solve this type of problem and it can be solved either by point or block iterative methods. On the other hand, it was pointed out that iterative method that solves for a block for a several points at once will converge faster than the point method, see (Abdullah [1]).

The outline of this paper is organized in the following way. In section two, the formulation of the MSOR method will be elaborated. The latter section of this paper will discuss the formulation and implementation of the MSOR method together with 4 Point-EDG iterative method and some numerical results will be shown in fourth section to assert the performance of the proposed iterative method. Finally, section 5 contains some conclusion and directions of the future works.

2 The MSOR Iterative Method

The idea of MSOR method is without doubt one of the most efficient method in solving system of linear algebraic equation. The concept of the MSOR method was first considered by DeVogelaere [19], but it was mainly Young [21] who have been extensively studies for demonstrating the capability of MSOR methods for solving system linear algebraic equations. According to Kincaid *et al.* [11], MSOR method is best applied in solving the system of linear algebraic equations when the two matrices are two- cyclic consistently ordered of equation (excluding red and black equations). Thus the general scheme for MSOR iterative methods can be written as follows

$$\begin{aligned} u^{(k+1)} &= (D-\theta_r L)^{-1} + \left[\left(\theta_r U - (1-\theta_r)D\right) u^{(k)} + \theta_r f\right], \\ u^{(k+1)} &= (D-\theta_b L)^{-1} + \left[\left(\theta_b U - (1-\theta_b)D\right) u^{(k)} + \theta_b f\right], \end{aligned} \tag{5}$$

where $A=D-L-U$ in which D, L and U are the diagonal, negative lower triangulation and negative upper triangulation matrices, respectively. Here the relaxation parameter θ_r is for "red" equations and θ_b is for the "black" equations. The performance of the MSOR methods can be improved drastically with a proper choice of the relaxation parameter. Relaxation parameter can be calculated practically by consecutively choosing a value with some precision until the optimal value obtained. For the choice $\theta_r = \theta_b = 1$, MSOR method will reduce classical Gauss-Seidel (GS). Note that when $\theta_r = \theta_b$ will result in the MSOR method coincides with the original Successive Over-Relaxation (SOR) method with red black ordering. Further discussion on the MSOR method can be found in Akhir *et al.* [2,3,4,5].

3 Formulation and Implementation of Four Point-EDGMSOR Iterative Method

As explained in the previous section, a discretization scheme based on second order finite difference scheme was used to construct an approximation equation of 2D Helmholtz equation. To facilitate in formulating the approximation equations for 2D Helmholtz equation, further discussion will be restricted onto 4 Point-EDG*MSOR* iterative method.

In general the implementation of this method will be imposed onto solid node points of type • in Fig.1 until the convergence test criterion is reach. Then other approximate solutions at remaining points (points of the different type,) are obtained by using direct method, see (Abdullah [1], Hasan et.al [9], Ibrahim and

Abdullah [10], Yousif and Evans [20], Othman & Abdullah [13,14] and Sulaiman et.al [16,17,18]).

From Fig.1, let consider the solution at any group of four points on the solution domain can be solved using Eq. (3) and this will leads to the (4×4) linear system given as

$$\begin{bmatrix} 4+2h^2\alpha & -1 & 0 & 0 \\ -1 & 4+2h^2\alpha & 0 & 0 \\ 0 & 0 & 4+2h^2\alpha & -1 \\ 0 & 0 & -1 & 4+2h^2\alpha \end{bmatrix} \begin{bmatrix} u_{i,j} \\ u_{i+1,j} \\ u_{i,j+1} \\ u_{i+1,j+1} \end{bmatrix} = \begin{bmatrix} S_1 \\ S_2 \\ S_3 \\ S_4 \end{bmatrix}, \tag{6}$$

where

$$S_1 = U_{i-1,j-1} + U_{i+1,j-1} + U_{i-1,j+1} - 2h^2 f_{i,j},$$
$$S_2 = U_{i,j+2} + U_{i+2,j} + U_{i+2,j+2} - 2h^2 f_{i+1,j+1},$$
$$S_3 = U_{i,j-1} + U_{i+2,j-1} + U_{i+2,j+1} - 2h^2 f_{i+1,j},$$
$$S_4 = U_{i-1,j} + U_{i-1,j+2} + U_{i+1,j+2} - 2h^2 f_{i,j+1}.$$

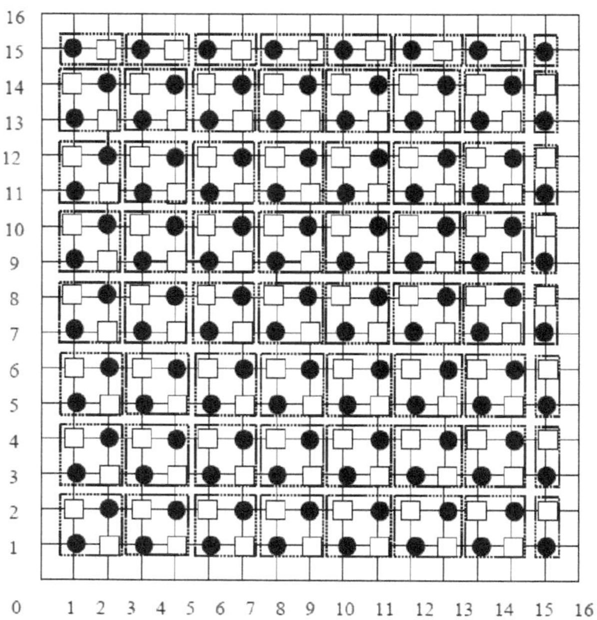

Fig. 1. The distribution of uniform nodal points for 4 Point-EDG*MSOR* at the solution domain for m=15

By splitting Eq. (6) this linear system can be written to a decoupled group of (2×2) linear systems, which are independently for each other. The 4 Point-EDG*MSOR* iterative method can be easily shown as

$$\begin{bmatrix} u_{i,j} \\ u_{i+1,j+1} \end{bmatrix}^{(k+1)} = \frac{1}{\beta}\begin{bmatrix} 4+2h^2\alpha & 1 \\ 1 & 4+2h^2\alpha \end{bmatrix}\begin{bmatrix} S_1 \\ S_2 \end{bmatrix}, \tag{7}$$

$$\begin{bmatrix} u_{i+1,j} \\ u_{i,j+1} \end{bmatrix}^{(k+1)} = \frac{1}{\beta}\begin{bmatrix} 4+2h^2\alpha & 1 \\ 1 & 4+2h^2\alpha \end{bmatrix}\begin{bmatrix} S_3 \\ S_4 \end{bmatrix}, \tag{8}$$

where

$$\beta = 1\Big/\left(2+h^2\alpha\right)\left(4+h^2 r\right)^2\left(6+h^2\alpha\right).$$

by adding the two accelerated parameters, θ_r and θ_b to Eqs. (8) and (9) the implementations of the 4 Point-EDG*MSOR* iterative method can be shown as

$$\begin{bmatrix} u_{i,j} \\ u_{i+1,j+1} \end{bmatrix}^{(k+1)} = \left(1-\theta_r\right)\begin{bmatrix} u_{i,j} \\ u_{i+1,j+1} \end{bmatrix}^{(k)} + \frac{\theta_r}{\beta}\begin{bmatrix} 4+2h^2\alpha & 1 \\ 1 & 4+2h^2\alpha \end{bmatrix}\begin{bmatrix} S_1 \\ S_2 \end{bmatrix}, \tag{9}$$

$$\begin{bmatrix} u_{i,j} \\ u_{i+1,j+1} \end{bmatrix}^{(k+1)} = \left(1-\theta_b\right)\begin{bmatrix} u_{i,j} \\ u_{i+1,j+1} \end{bmatrix}^{(k)} + \frac{\theta_b}{\beta}\begin{bmatrix} 4+2h^2\alpha & 1 \\ 1 & 4+2h^2\alpha \end{bmatrix}\begin{bmatrix} S_1 \\ S_2 \end{bmatrix}, \tag{10}$$

$$\begin{bmatrix} u_{i+1,j} \\ u_{i,j+1} \end{bmatrix}^{(k+1)} = \left(1-\theta_r\right)\begin{bmatrix} u_{i+1,j} \\ u_{i,j+1} \end{bmatrix}^{(k)} + \frac{\theta_r}{\beta}\begin{bmatrix} 4+2h^2\alpha & 1 \\ 1 & 4+2h^2\alpha \end{bmatrix}\begin{bmatrix} S_3 \\ S_4 \end{bmatrix}, \tag{11}$$

$$\begin{bmatrix} u_{i+1,j} \\ u_{i,j+1} \end{bmatrix}^{(k+1)} = \left(1-\theta_b\right)\begin{bmatrix} u_{i+1,j} \\ u_{i,j+1} \end{bmatrix}^{(k)} + \frac{\theta_b}{\beta}\begin{bmatrix} 4+2h^2\alpha & 1 \\ 1 & 4+2h^2\alpha \end{bmatrix}\begin{bmatrix} S_3 \\ S_4 \end{bmatrix}, \tag{12}$$

4 Numerical Experiments

In order to confirm 4 point-EDGMSOR is superior than other three methods, the following experiments are carried out on CPU Intel Core i7 Processor@2.80Ghz with memory is 4.00G. There are three parameters considered in the numerical comparison such as the number of iterations, the execution time and the maximum absolute error. In comparison, the Full-Sweep point Gauss-Seidel (FSGS) acts as the control of comparison of numerical simulations. Throughout the experiments, the convergence test is considered as the tolerance error in $\varepsilon = 10^{-10}$. The experiments were carried out based on several different mesh sizes such as 32, 64, 128 and 256. For comparisons purpose, this paper will also consider other two four point block iterative methods such as 4 Point-EDG*GS* and 4 Point-EDG*SOR* iterative methods. Results of numerical simulations, which were obtained from the implementations for all iterative methods for Example 1 and 2, have been recorded in Tables 1 and 2 respectively.

Example 1 (Evans, 1985)

$$\frac{\partial^2 U}{\partial x^2} + \frac{\partial^2 U}{\partial y^2} - 10U = 6 - 10\left(2x^2 + y^2\right), \quad (x, y) \in D = [0,1]\times[0,1]$$

Exact solution

$$U(x, y) = 2x^2 + y^2 .$$

Example 2 (Evans, 2003)

$$\frac{\partial^2 U}{\partial x^2} + \frac{\partial^2 U}{\partial y^2} - 2U = \left(12x^2 + 3x^4\right)\sin y, \quad (x, y) \in D = [0,1]\times[0,1]$$

Exact solution

$$U(x, y) = x^4 \sin y .$$

Table 1. Comparison of the number of iterations, execution time (seconds) and maximum absolute error for all methods (Example 1)

Mesh size	Methods	Number of iterations	Execution time (Seconds)	Maximum absolute error
32	FSGS	1326	0.29	6.8176E-10
	4-EDGGS	354 ($\theta_r = \theta_b = 1$)	0.14	1.6057E-9
	4-EDGSOR	221 ($\theta_r = \theta_b = 1.90$)	0.12	4.0473E-9
	4-EDGMSOR	93 ($\theta_r = 1.73, \theta_b = 1.74$)	0.07	4.0511E-9
64	FSGS	4910	1.38	2.7407E-10
	4-EDGGS	1321 ($\theta_r = \theta_b = 1$)	0.43	6.8224E-9
	4-EDGSOR	289 ($\theta_r = \theta_b = 1.91$)	0.19	4.5589E-9
	4-EDGMSOR	186 ($\theta_r = 1.86, \ \theta_b = 1.87$)	0.17	4.5585E-9
128	FSGS	18085	15.43	1.1004E-11
	4-EDGGS	4902 ($\theta_r = \theta_b = 1$)	3.72	2.7410E-10
	4-EDGSOR	770 ($\theta_r = \theta_b = 1.82$)	0.65	3.7483E-10
	4-EDGMSOR	480 ($\theta_r = 1.94, \ \theta_b = 1.95$)	0.49	3.3481E-10
256	FSGS	66177	210.11	4.4067E-11
	4-EDGGS	18071 ($\theta_r = \theta_b = 1$)	51.46	1.1004E-10
	4-EDGSOR	963 ($\theta_r = \theta_b = 1.97$)	3.29	2.6841E-10
	4-EDGMSOR	628 ($\theta_r = 1.95, \ \theta_b = 1.96$)	1.58	2.8463E-10

Table 2. Comparison of the number of iterations, execution time (seconds) and maximum absolute error for all methods (Example 2)

Mesh size	Methods	Number of iterations	Execution time (Seconds)	Maximum absolute Error
32	FSGS	1694	0.34	9.7880E-3
	4-EDGGS	458 ($\theta_r = \theta_b = 1$)	0.23	9.7819E-2
	4-EDGSOR	182 ($\theta_r = \theta_b = 1.89$)	0.12	9.7624E-2
	4-EDGMSOR	97 ($\theta_r = 1.79, \theta_b = 1.80$)	0.06	9.7621E-2
64	FSGS	6175	1.56	9.7889E-3
	4-EDGGS	1686 ($\theta_r = \theta_b = 1$)	0.55	9.7888E-2
	4-EDGSOR	302 ($\theta_r = \theta_b = 1.79$)	0.22	9.7819E-2
	4-EDGMSOR	230 ($\theta_r = 1.90,\ \theta_b = 1.91$)	0.17	9.7819E-E2
128	FSGS	22340	16.8	9.7906E-3
	4-EDGGS	6159 ($\theta_r = \theta_b = 1$)	4.24	9.7888E-2
	4-EDGSOR	637 ($\theta_r = \theta_b = 1.96$)	0.52	9.7888E-2
	4-EDGMSOR	421 ($\theta_r = 1.94,\ \theta_b = 1.95$)	0.35	9.7889E-2
256	FSGS	80028	225.82	9.7923E-3
	4-EDGGS	23307 ($\theta_r = \theta_b = 1$)	56.7	9.7921E-2
	4-EDGSOR	1184 ($\theta_r = \theta_b = 1.94$)	3.06	9.7922E-2
	4-EDGMSOR	893 ($\theta_r = 1.97,\ \theta_b = 1.98$)	2.64	9.7922E-2

Table 3. Decrement percentages of the number of iterations and execution time for all methods compared to the FSGS

Example	Methods	Numbers of iterations (%)	Execution time (%)
	4-EDGGS	72.67-73.30	51.72-71.51
1	4-EDGSOR	83.33-94.11	58.21-98.43
	4-EDGMSOR	92.99-99.05	75.86-99.25
	4-EDGGS	70.87-72.96	32.35-74.91
2	4-EDGSOR	89.26-95.11	64.71-96.90
	4-EDGMSOR	94.27-98.88	82.35-98.83

5 Conclusions and Future Research

In the previous section, we have presented formulation of full-sweep and half-sweep approximation equations based on second order finite difference scheme that can be easily generated system of linear algebraic equations as shown in Eqs. (6) till (12). Through numerical results recorded in Tables 1 and 2, it is clearly shown that by applying the MSOR method, the number of iterations can be reduced as compared to the FSGS method. Table 3 shows the decrement percentages number of iterations for 4 Point-EDG*GS*, 4 Point-EDG*SOR* and 4 Point-EDGM*SOR* iterative methods. Through the surveillance in Tables 2 and 3, we found that the application of the half-sweep iterations concepts have reduced the execution time of the proposed iterative method. Meanwhile, decrement percentages of the execution time for 4 Point-EDG*GS*, 4 Point-EDG*SOR* and 4 Point-EDG*MSOR* as compared to FSGS method have been summarized in Table 3. In addition, the accuracy approximate solutions for all methods are in good agreement compared to the FSGS. As a conclusion, the numerical results have proved that 4 Point-EDG*MSOR* iterative method is a better method compared to the 4 Point-EDG*GS*, 4 and Point-EDG*SOR* methods in a sense of complexity and execution time. For future works, this study will be extended to investigate on the use of 4 Point-EDG*MSOR* as a smoother for the half-sweep multigrid (Othman & Abdullah [13,14]) and the implementation of the Modified Explicit Group (MEG) (Othman & Abdullah [15]) by using finite difference approximations equations.

References

1. Abdullah, A.R.: The Four Point Explicit Decoupled Group (EDG) Method: A Fast Poisson Solver. Intern. Journal of Computer Mathematics 38, 61–70 (1991)
2. Akhir, M.K., Othman, M., Sulaiman, J.: Solving Two-Dimensional Steady Navier-Stokes Equations by Modified SOR Iterative Method. In: 4th International Conference on Research And Educations in Mathematics (ICREM4), pp. 744–749 (2009)

3. Akhir, M.K., Othman, M., Sulaiman, J.: Modified SOR Iterative Method to Solving Two-Dimensional Steady Burger Equations. In: 17th National Symposiums Science (SKSM17), pp. 148–153 (2009)
4. Akhir, M.K., Othman, M., Sulaiman, J., Majid, Z.A.: A New Half-Sweep Modified SOR Iterative Method for Solving Two-Dimensional Helmholtz Equations. In: Fundamental Science (FSC), pp. 88–89 (2010)
5. Akhir, M.K., Othman, M., Sulaiman, J., Majid, Z.A.: A New Half-Sweep Modified SOR for Solving Two-Dimensional Helmholtz Equations. In: International Conference on Intelligent Network and Computing (ICNIC), pp. 416–419. IEEE Press (2010)
6. Aruchunan, E., Sulaiman, J.: Half-sweep Conjugate Gradient Method for Solving First Order Linear Fredholm Integro-differential Equations Australian. Journal of Basic and Applied Sciences 5(3), 38–43 (2011)
7. Evans, D.J.: Group Explicit Iterative Methods for Solving Large Linear Systems. Intern. Journal of Computer Mathematics 17, 81–108 (1985)
8. Evans, D.J., Ergut, M., Bulut, H.: The Numerical Solution of Multidimensional Partial Differential Equations by Decomposition Method. Intern. Journal of Computer Mathematics 80, 1189–1198 (2003)
9. Hasan, M.K., Othman, M., Abbas, Z., Sulaiman, J., Ahmad, F.: Parallel Solution of High Speed Low Order FDTD on 2D Free Space Wave Propagation. In: Gervasi, O., Gavrilova, M.L. (eds.) ICCSA 2007, Part II. LNCS, vol. 4706, pp. 13–24. Springer, Heidelberg (2007)
10. Ibrahim, A., Abdullah, A.R.: Solving the Two-Dimensional Diffusion Equation by the Four Point Explicit Decoupled Group (EDG) Iterative Method. Intern. Journal of Computer Mathematics 58, 253–256 (1995)
11. Kincaid, D.R., Young, D.M.: The Modified Successive Over relaxation Method with Fixed Parameters. Journal Mathematics of Computation 26, 705–717 (1972)
12. Muthuvalu, M.S., Sulaiman, J.: Half-Sweep Arithmetic Mean method with composite trapezoidal scheme for solving linear Fredholm integral equations. Applied Mathematics and Computation 217(12), 5442–5448 (2011)
13. Othman, M., Abdullah, A.R.: The Half Sweeps Multigrid Method as a Fast Poisson Solver. Intern. Journal of Computer Mathematics 69, 219–229 (1998)
14. Othman, M., Abdullah, A.R.: An Efficient Multigrid Poisson Solver. Intern. Journal of Computer Mathematics 7, 541–553 (1999)
15. Othman, M., Abdullah, A.R.: An Efficient Four Points Modified Explicit Group Poisson Solver. Intern. Journal of Computer Mathematics 76, 203–217 (2000)
16. Sulaiman, J., Hasan, M. K., Othman, M.: The Half-Sweep Iterative Alternating Decomposition Explicit (HSIADE) Method for Diffusion Equation. In: Zhang, J., He, J.-H., Fu, Y. (eds.) CIS 2004. LNCS, vol. 3314, pp. 57–63. Springer, Heidelberg (2004)
17. Sulaiman, J., Othman, M., Hasan, M.K.: Red-Black EDG*SOR* Iterative Method Using Triangle Element Approximation for 2D Poisson Equations. In: Gervasi, O., Gavrilova, M.L. (eds.) ICCSA 2007, Part III. LNCS, vol. 4707, pp. 298–308. Springer, Heidelberg (2007)
18. Sulaiman, J., Othman, M., Hasan, M.K.: Red-black Half-sweep Iterative Method using Triangle Finite Element Approximation for 2D Poisson Equations. In: Shi, Y., van Albada, G.D., Dongarra, J., Sloot, P.M.A. (eds.) ICCS 2007. LNCS, vol. 4487, pp. 326–333. Springer, Heidelberg (2007)
19. Vogelaere, D.: Over-relaxations. Abstract #539-5. Notices Amer. Math. Soc. 147 (1958)
20. Yousif, W.S., Evans, D.J.: Explicit De-coupled Group Iterative Methods and Their Implementations. Parallel Algorithms and Applications 7, 53–71 (1995)
21. Young, D.M.: Iterative Solution of Large Linear Systems. Academic Press, London (1971)

Introducing Knowledge-Enrichment Techniques for Complex Event Processing

Sebastian Binnewies and Bela Stantic

School of Information and Communication Technology,
Griffith University, Brisbane, Australia
sebastian.binnewies@griffithuni.edu.au,
b.stantic@griffith.edu.au

Abstract. Complex event processing received an increasing interest during the last years with the adoption of event-driven architectures in various application domains. Despite a number of solutions that can process events in near real-time, their effectiveness for decision support relies heavily upon human domain knowledge. This poses a problem in areas that require vast amounts of specialized knowledge and background information, such as medical environments. We propose four techniques to enrich complex event processing with domain knowledge from ontologies to overcome this limitation. These techniques focus on preserving the strengths of state-of-the-art systems and enhancing them with existing ontologies to increase accuracy and effectiveness. The viability of our approach is demonstrated in a multifaceted experiment.

Keywords: Complex Event Processing, Ontologies, Rule Management, Semantic Complex Event Processing.

1 Introduction

Everyday life is surrounded by events – which can be any type of occurrence in an environment – and human actions are influenced by these events. Many organizations have adopted this perspective for their IT-supported processes and have incorporated an event-driven architecture [6]. A core component of these architectures is *complex event processing*. Complex event processing systems receive events in the form of data, process them to generate meaningful complex events, and trigger responses upon creation of complex events. Events can take a multitude of forms, e.g., clickstream data or sensor data from radio frequency identification (RFID) networks, and generally occur in high-volume streams.

Within the last ten years, complex event processing has replaced database-centric systems with real-time decision support in areas such as algorithmic trading, foreign exchange pricing, network security and energy smart metering. However, despite a wide range of potential application areas, complex event processing is not a silver bullet solution in itself. Processing is performed on the basis of rules, which have to reflect the requirements of each specific application domain. Therefore, rule specification and, consequently, the effectiveness of complex event processing for decision support are highly dependent on the amount

A. Abd Manaf et al. (Eds.): ICIEIS 2011, Part III, CCIS 253, pp. 228–242, 2011.

and quality of knowledge about that domain. This becomes an issue particularly when complex event processing is to be used in environments that are rich in domain knowledge, for instance, in hospital settings. The persons responsible for rule specification may possess enough knowledge to be considered medical domain experts, but a vast amount of specialized knowledge and background information is disregarded.

We propose to enrich complex event processing with *domain knowledge from ontologies* to address this issue. Ontologies model knowledge about a domain and enable automated reasoning over this knowledge. We present four techniques to increase the accuracy of rule specification and evaluation by accessing and reasoning over ontologies. The four techniques allow a relaxation of rule conditions and integration of background information into complex event processing. In contrast to existing work, our lightweight approach focuses on utilizing existing ontologies and preserving the strengths of recent advances in complex event processing. The viability of our approach is supported by the results of a multifaceted experiment.

2 Background

Our research incorporates the two disciplines complex event processing and knowledge representation in ontologies. The following two sections briefly introduce the recent advances in each area.

2.1 Complex Event Processing

In short, the term complex event processing stands for the processing of simple events to generate complex events. The notion of an *event* refers to any occurrence in an environment that can be expressed in the form of data, for example, the time, location and object identifier of an RFID reading. Events are sent from an event source to the complex event processing engine for processing. The engine filters incoming events, creates complex events upon detection of specific event patterns, and routes these complex events to an event sink or back to the engine for further processing. An essential component of complex event processing are event pattern rules. They specify a certain combination of events, their attributes and values – an event pattern – and an action to be executed if the event pattern is satisfied.

Despite several effective systems that address the inherent challenges of complex event processing, a single best solution does not exist. These challenges include, for instance, high volumes of input data, unordered event streams, uncertainty of event occurrences, temporal relationships, and processing performance, which are addressed by current commercial and academic systems (e.g., SASE [18], TESLA [4], ETALIS [2], TMS-RFID [11]). Yet, different systems have different strengths, suggesting that there is no single, silver bullet solution in complex event processing. In fact, a one-fits-all solution may not be feasible at all, due to the wide range of situations in which complex event processing is applied. Therefore, we emphasize that a system with its specific strengths should be chosen according to the area of application and its requirements.

2.2 Ontologies

Ontologies are used to model knowledge about a domain and to reason about this knowledge. Generally, an ontology represents the concepts of a domain as classes, individuals (instances of classes) and properties (relationships between classes and individuals). In addition, if an ontology captures the *formal semantics* of concepts, i.e., if it formally defines the meaning of these concepts through logical axioms, the semantics can be accessed and processed by an automated reasoner.

A growing number of ontologies are being developed by various communities and many of them are freely accessible on the World Wide Web. The Semantic Web community has produced several standards related to ontologies, such as RDF, OWL, RIF and SPARQL.[1] The life sciences have also adopted the technology of ontology modeling and its benefits, especially in the fields of biology and medicine, as evident in the prominent ontologies SNOMED CT[2], the Gene Ontology[3] and further ontologies from the OBO Foundry[4]. Our focus lies on utilizing existing ontologies to enrich the functionality of complex event processing. We are specifically interested in biomedical environments that are rich in domain knowledge, where ontologies can provide highly specialized information and background knowledge to increase processing accuracy.

3 Related Work

While research has been conducted in the individual fields of ontologies and event processing for years, finding possible synergies has only recently been undertaken. Combining ontologies and complex event processing is closely related to the broader research area of *semantic complex event processing*. The latter is a relatively new term and refers to complex event processing that is enhanced with reasoning capabilities. Reasoning over domain knowledge captured in an ontology is a sub-area of semantic complex event processing and still an emerging research field, where few publications exist to date.

A first complete solution was recently presented [1], introducing EP-SPARQL, an extension to SPARQL. EP-SPARQL combines event processing and SPARQL to retrieve the semantics of events captured in RDF serialized knowledge bases. While this may be a solution for event input in the form of RDF triples, data in other formats would have to be converted into RDF triples or graphs. Further investigation is required how this conversion affects event processing performance.

---
1 `http://www.w3.org/2001/sw/wiki`
2 `http://www.ihtsdo.org/snomed-ct/`
3 `http://www.geneontology.org/`
4 `http://www.obofoundry.org/`

In addition, EP-SPARQL queries would require the serialization of OWL concepts into less expressive RDF.

Only few other solutions have been proposed, which are limited in one way or another and differ greatly from our approach. Three different approaches ([5], [12], [14]) each implement a working combination of ontologies and complex event processing. However, each of them is restricted to one specific application domain. The remaining publications ([15], [16], [17]) primarily discuss the idea of a solution approach and lack the presentation of a working implementation. Two features are common to all these approaches. Firstly, they create a new ontology for the purpose of event processing. Secondly, they propose a tight integration of ontology and complex event processing by using a combined rule language and by executing event processing completely through reasoning over ontology concepts. Our approach, on the other hand, aims to utilize existing ontologies and does not restrict itself to a specific domain. It is a lightweight approach that focuses on preserving the strengths of existing complex event processing systems and ontologies, which stands in contrast to a tight integration.

Semantic complex event processing is surrounded by several related disciplines. *Event stream processing* shares similarities with complex event processing as it also evaluates a stream of events to detect specific events. However, it focuses on maximizing throughput and minimizing latency [13], rather than on the expressiveness of event pattern rules. On the other hand, *business rule management systems* strongly focus on rules. These rules can be quite similar to event pattern rules in complex event processing. Yet, business rules are checked when explicitly called from an application, not when an event arrives [6]. Furthermore, business rule processing is done through inferencing, in contrast to the three-step event processing procedure outlined above. *Stream reasoning* is also concerned with inferencing, albeit through reasoning over dynamically changing sets of knowledge. Existing work in this field has focused mainly on data in RDF format, e.g., [3], and stream reasoning has yet to address in detail such challenges mentioned in Section 2.1 as complex event processing has.

4 Enrichment Techniques and Their Benefits

As the previous section demonstrated, the concept of integrating complex event processing and ontologies is still an emerging research area, and only a few research projects have been conducted. However, none of these projects has clearly identified the general opportunities and benefits for complex event processing. We thoroughly analyzed the common characteristics of complex event processing, on the one hand, and of ontologies and Semantic Web technologies, on the other hand, to derive the potential of an integrated approach. The following sections introduce four techniques to enrich complex event processing with domain knowledge from ontologies, which we define as *ontology-enhanced complex event processing* (OECEP). Section 4.5 then emphasizes how these techniques can benefit complex event processing in general, since they can be used to increase its functionality irrespective of a specific implementation. To illustrate the four techniques and their benefits, we introduce a possible real-world scenario first:

At an airport, a large number of containers with food products arrive daily. Information about the containers and their content is often retrieved through scanning a barcode or reading an RFID tag at the airport's loading dock. The containers are then forwarded to the next destination based upon an evaluation of this information. Some of the containers may come from a different country and contain food products that have to be inspected by customs and quarantine. In this case, such critical containers have to be separated from non-critical containers and routed to quarantine. A complex event processing engine can be employed to evaluate container information on the basis of event pattern rules and trigger a response in the form of a routing decision. Nevertheless, due to the variety of food products and their ingredients, an impracticably large number of rules would be needed.

Assuming that information about the food domain is represented in an ontology, a complex event processing engine could use this ontology to significantly reduce the number of rules needed. Furthermore, rules may be stated in such a way that they use background knowledge encoded in the ontology. This can be achieved through the following four techniques.

4.1 Rule Rewriting

In 'standard' complex event processing, each condition of a rule has to be explicitly specified to create a complex event, e.g., all event types that will satisfy this rule. OECEP allows a relaxation of conditions while still creating the same complex event. This is realized through a rule rewriting process that includes reasoning over the ontology. The rule rewriting process is initiated with the engine passing a relaxed condition to the ontology reasoner. The reasoner then draws all inferences relating to this condition from the ontology. These inferences, called *inferred conditions*, are passed back to the engine. The engine then substitutes the relaxed condition with the inferred conditions.

In the airport example, one condition to deem a container as critical could be that the content is some kind of seafood. If a container with seafood in it arrives, the information gathered from the barcode or RFID tag (and possibly from a central database) would include the type of seafood, e.g., 'Tuna'. Normally, each type of seafood, i.e., 'Tuna', 'Swordfish', 'Flounder' etc., would have to be formulated in one or more rules so that the engine can correctly detect all seafood containers. With OECEP, it is only necessary to declare one rule, which has 'Seafood' as a condition. This condition is passed to the reasoner, which retrieves all instances of 'Seafood' and its subclasses from a food ontology. These instances are passed back to the engine. The engine then rewrites the rule and evaluates container information against the inferred conditions. Figures 1 and 2 depict the reasoning step and the process for this rule rewriting example, respectively.

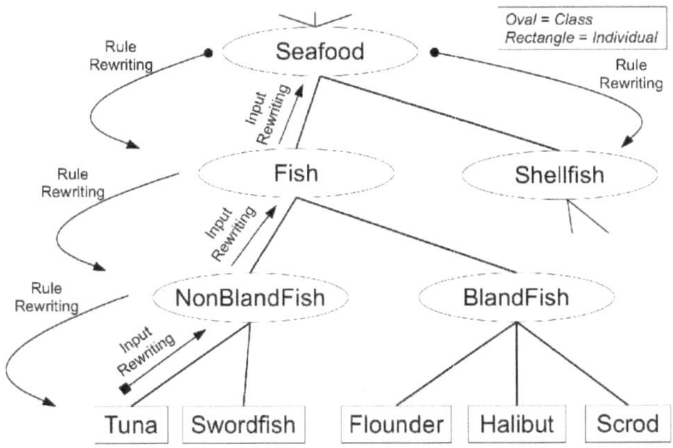

Fig. 1. Graph-based representation of ontology concepts including rule rewriting and input rewriting paths (based on the Food Ontology)

4.2 Input Rewriting

OECEP also makes it possible to rewrite input events. In input rewriting, information from an incoming event is passed to the ontology reasoner as a preprocessing step. The reasoner computes all relevant inferences and passes them back to the engine. The engine rewrites the input event with this inferred knowledge, creating *inferred event(s)*. These inferred events are then processed by the engine as usual.

Referring back to the airport example, the information that a recently arrived container holds a specific type of seafood, e.g., 'Tuna', is sent to the reasoner. The reasoner infers from the ontology that 'Tuna' is an instance of 'NonBlandFish' and of the superclasses 'Fish' and 'Seafood', and returns this information to the engine. The engine then substitutes the value 'Tuna' with the inferred information for the contents attribute of the event. This is done either by creating a new instance of this event for each inferred value, or by inserting multiple values in the contents attribute of this event if this is supported by the engine. The input rewriting path and process are displayed in Figures 1 and 2, respectively.

4.3 Output Rewriting

Output rewriting is a similar process to input rewriting, with the difference that a complex event is rewritten. When a complex event has just been created, its information is passed to the reasoner to infer further knowledge. This information is returned to the engine to rewrite the complex event into one or more *inferred complex event(s)*. Finally, the engine forwards these inferred complex events to the event sink or takes them as input for further processing.

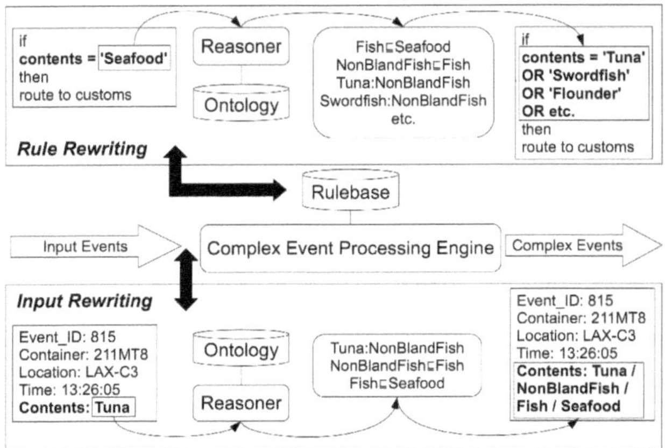

Fig. 2. Example processes of rule rewriting and input rewriting

In the airport example, a complex event is created when a container with fish is detected. This output could be rewritten into a complex event with the information that a container is detected whose contents need to be kept frozen.

4.4 Incorporating Domain Knowledge

In addition to the rewriting capabilities, OECEP also allows to include specific background knowledge in complex event processing. The extent to which this is possible depends the knowledge that is actually captured in the ontology and on the purpose of complex event processing in this domain. Incorporating such domain knowledge into complex event processing can happen in many forms. For instance, a rule may specify as a condition that an event has to be of type A, and A has to participate in at least one relationship α (to an event of type B). Although the engine can check the type of incoming events, the evaluation of the relationship α can only be executed by an ontology reasoner. As another example, a rule may state that the maximum path length between A and B can only be 5 (if the ontology is modeled as a graph).

A customs and quarantine rule could include a condition that checks if a food product has seeds. It is assumed that the ontology models a relationship 'hasSeed' between certain foods and their seeds – e.g., stone, single seed, multiple seeds. When the engine evaluates such a rule, it passes event information to the reasoner. The reasoner checks if there exists at least one relationship 'hasSeed' for this event and passes a boolean value back to the engine.

Conceptually, rule rewriting, input rewriting and output rewriting are a form of incorporating domain knowledge. Here, we define the concept of incorporating domain knowledge to refer to all enhancements, which do not belong to a rewriting technique. Obviously, it is possible to use any combination of rule rewriting, input rewriting and output rewriting, as well as incorporating domain knowledge, for rule specification and evaluation in complex event processing.

4.5 Benefits

From the descriptions above, it becomes evident that utilizing domain knowledge from ontologies enables *more intelligent* complex event processing. Firstly, rule rewriting, input rewriting and output rewriting can greatly reduce the number of rules that need to be formulated. This decreases the workload of human domain experts. Secondly, the engine can refer to background information. This allows specification of more expressive rules and increases the accuracy of processing. Thirdly, these general techniques have specifically been designed to be independent. They can be used independent of a specific ontology, complex event processing system or application domain. Nevertheless, a few challenges appear when looking more closely at the inherent features of complex event processing and ontologies, such as a formalization of complex event processing language to match the formal semantics in ontologies, a suitable interaction mechanism, expressiveness and conflicting characteristics of event and ontology languages, and processing performance.

4.6 Relevance

We see a high relevance of our approach specifically to the area of e-Health. In health care environments, we find an array of devices and sensors that monitor patients during an operation, recovery in hospital or at their home. Complex event processing can process this stream of data, detect complex events and trigger a response. However, most responses require a thorough understanding of medical background information related to an event, e.g., the type of illness [10]. Currently, complex event processing cannot effectively incorporate this kind of information, because it is stored in a variety of formats, such as electronic patient records, clinical databases and free text reports [7]. In order to access and interlink data from these diverse sources, a common definition of terms is needed. SNOMED CT has recently been chosen by the Australian National e-Health Transition Authority for standardizing clinical terminology [8] and already supports medical software in many other countries [9]. With the help of SNOMED CT, a complex event processing engine could access and utilize medical background information to generate more accurate responses, which would support better decision-making in e-Health environments.

5 Experimental Evaluation

To demonstrate the viability of our enrichment techniques, we conducted an extensive experiment. The experiment design variables are presented in the following section. Based on the experiment design, we formulated three hypotheses, which are given in Section 5.2. Section 5.3 discusses the experiment results.

5.1 Experiment Design

As shown in Table 1, we assessed two ontologies, two rewriting techniques and two interaction mechanisms in two possible real-world scenarios, which are explained in detail below. All tests were executed on a PC with Microsoft Windows XP Professional Version 2002 SP 3, Intel Core 2 CPU 1.80GHz and 2GB of RAM. Programming code was written in Java using Java 1.6.0.

Table 1. Experiment Design Variables

	Scenario 1	Scenario 2
Ontologies	Food Ontology (OWL DL $\mathcal{SHOIN}$)	Vaccine Ontology (OWL DL $\mathcal{SHOIN}$)
Techniques	Rule Rewriting / Input Rewriting	Rule Rewriting / Input Rewriting
Interaction Mechanism	OWL API 3.2.2 with HermiT 1.3.3 / SPARQL through Jena API 2.6.4	OWL API 3.2.2 with HermiT 1.3.3
Avg. Num. of Input Events	3050	83

Scenario 1. Scenario 1 resumes the airport example introduced in Section 4 and extracts domain knowledge from the Food Ontology[5]. To recapitulate, cases with food arrive by airplane, are checked for critical contents and are routed to quarantine if critical. An additional requirement in this scenario is that special food products should be processed quickly by quarantine. This is specified in the following two rules.

Rule 1:
If a case arrives at the loading dock that contains a critical food item,
then notify the pusher to route this case to quarantine.

Rule 2:
If a case waits to be assessed by quarantine for a certain period of time
and the case contains some seafood,
then produce a notification.

Each case is assumed to be equipped with an RFID tag and both the loading dock and the quarantine hall with RFID readers. It is further assumed that the data from a case reading can be mapped to information about the type of food that is in the case. Each reading represents a simple event and consists of data about the read time, the read place and the contents of the case that is read.

The Food Ontology models knowledge about food in 138 named classes, 206 individuals, 17 properties and 356 axioms. We utilize this ontology for two rewriting techniques – rule rewriting and input rewriting. In rule rewriting, all individuals of the classes which represent critical food items (for Rule 1) or fish items (for Rule 2) are computed and substituted for the original conditions. For instance, if Rule 2 specifies the class 'Seafood', it is rewritten to 'Tuna', 'Oysters',

[5] `http://www.w3.org/TR/2004/REC-owl-guide-20040210/food.rdf`

'Crab', ... Thus, if a case content matches any one of these individuals, the rule is satisfied. In input rewriting, all superclasses of the individual representing the case content are computed. Each input event is then rewritten by substituting the original case content with its superclasses. For example, if a case contains 'Tuna', the event would be rewritten to have as contents 'NonBlandFish', 'Fish', 'Seafood', ...

In the experiment, rule rewriting and input rewriting are evaluated separately. Evaluation is performed through an implementation of the Rete algorithm. For both rewriting techniques, we tested two different mechanisms to access the ontology, SPARQL and the OWL API. For each of these variations, we performed ten runs having an average number of 3050 events with randomly created timestamps. The results are given in Figure 3 and analyzed below.

Scenario 2. Scenario 2 describes a situation in which vaccines are transported between supply chain partners. Vaccines that do not contain a preservative have to be kept at a certain temperature. If such vaccines are transported and a refrigeration device fails, an alarm should be triggered. This is expressed in the following rule.

> If the temperature rises above 6 °C
> and the vaccine does not contain a preservative,
> then produce a notification.

Similar to Scenario 1, event data would arrive from RFID sensors, with tags attached to the vaccine containers and read at each station during transport, supplemented with data from temperature sensors.

We created this scenario to utilize the Vaccine Ontology[6], a much more comprehensive ontology than the Food Ontology, for rule rewriting and input rewriting. The Vaccine Ontology is an effort to standardize vaccine data such as vaccine components and vaccine categorization. At present, the Vaccine Ontology contains 3530 named classes, 120 individuals, 80 properties and 21,548 axioms. In rule rewriting, all subclasses of the class 'vaccine preservative' are computed and substituted for that class in the rule. In input rewriting, each input event representing a vaccine and its specific contents is rewritten with the superclasses of these contents. For example, if a vaccine contains the preservative 'phenoxyethanol', the input event would be rewritten with the information 'vaccine preservative', 'vaccine additive', ...

Again, we evaluated rule rewriting and input rewriting separately. The OWL API was used to access the ontology and compute the inferences. We executed ten runs with an average number of 83 events. The results are presented in Figure 4 and discussed below.

5.2 Hypotheses

Hypothesis 1. Rule rewriting is faster than input rewriting.

[6] `http://www.violinet.org/vaccineontology`

Rule rewriting is generally performed only once, i.e., when the rule is entered into the rulebase of the engine, and rule rewriting time is independent of the number of input events. Input rewriting, on the other hand, is performed for each input event that is represented in the ontology. Therefore, we expect its total time for all events to be larger than total rule rewriting time.

Hypothesis 2. The OWL API offers greater rewriting functionality but inferior scalability compared to SPARQL (through the Jena API) as a mechanism to interact with an ontology.

The OWL API offers direct access to OWL ontologies, whereas SPARQL requires the serialization of OWL into less expressive RDF. We thus expect a larger range of rewriting functionality from the OWL API. We also expect that greater functionality comes at the expense of scalability and anticipate that processing time with the OWL API is higher than with SPARQL.

Hypothesis 3. The complexity of an ontology is the key influence on rewriting time.

The complexity of an ontology can be measured along several metrics [19]. We chose the number of concepts as the crucial metric and expect a larger number of concepts to have a positive effect on rewriting time, i.e., the higher the complexity, the longer the processing time.

5.3 Results and Analysis

Figure 3 shows the average processing time per event in microseconds for each variation of Scenario 1, calculated and averaged over 10 runs each. When the OWL API was used, the processing time consisted of loading and pre-computing the ontology and reasoning over the ontology. As can be seen from the chart, the results are mixed across the variations, ranging from 460 μs (Rule Rewriting with SPARQL) to 7332 μs (Rule Rewriting with the OWL API). We can draw three conclusions from the results. Firstly, rule rewriting is not necessarily faster than input rewriting. While rule rewriting with SPARQL is approximately one fifth of the time for input rewriting with SPARQL, rule rewriting with the OWL API scales much worse than input rewriting with the OWL API. Secondly, SPARQL does not always perform better than the OWL API. Although SPARQL has a significantly lower processing time than the OWL API in rule rewriting, the OWL API outperforms SPARQL in input rewriting. Thirdly, when using the OWL API, it can be either the loading time or the reasoning time that is the major influence on total processing time. While loading the ontology makes up only 15% of the total time in rule rewriting, it accounts for 90% in input rewriting.

Figure 4 depicts the total processing time in milliseconds for rule rewriting and input rewriting with the OWL API in Scenarios 1 and 2, calculated and averaged over 10 runs each. We can again derive three conclusions from the chart. Firstly, the complexity of an ontology influences rewriting time. Utilizing the complex Vaccine Ontology for rewriting takes considerably longer than using the less comprehensive Food Ontology. Secondly, as already seen in Figure 3, rule rewriting

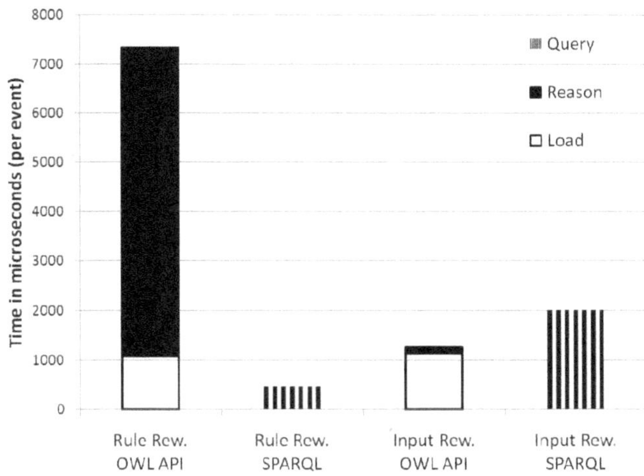

Fig. 3. Comparison of rewriting techniques and interaction mechanisms for Scenario 1 (Food Ontology)

is not necessarily faster than input rewriting. When using the Food Ontology, input rewriting performs better than rule rewriting. When using the Vaccine Ontology, both rewriting techniques perform similarly. Thirdly, SPARQL offers less rewriting functionalities than the OWL API. SPARQL (through the Jena API) could not be used for rule rewriting or input rewriting in Scenario 2 since it cannot handle relative URIs requiring specification of multiple base URIs. Therefore, only the OWL API was used in Scenario 2.

Hypothesis 1 could not be proven. Figure 3 showed that the superiority of rule rewriting over input rewriting (and vice versa) depends on the interaction mechanism. Additionally, input rewriting scaled significantly better than rule rewriting in Scenario 1, but only marginally better in Scenario 2. This can be explained by the type of reasoning that has to be executed. In Scenario 1, the reasoner has to compute relationships between classes and individuals, in Scenario 2 only between classes.

Hypothesis 2 was only partly supported by the results. Scenario 2 could not be evaluated with SPARQL because it lacks a functionality that the OWL API offers. In Scenario 1, the OWL API and SPARQL outperform each other depending on the rewriting technique. Thus, our hypothesis could be proven in regards to the superior functionality of the OWL API, but neither proven nor disproven in regards to scalability.

Hypothesis 3 was supported by the results. For both rule rewriting and input rewriting, reasoning over the more complex Vaccine Ontology took noticeably longer than reasoning over the Food Ontology, even though the reasoning task was more complex in the latter case.

In summary, although the scope of our experiment is limited, we obtained very interesting results. Both rule rewriting and input rewriting were realized, which suggests that the remaining two techniques – output rewriting and incorporating

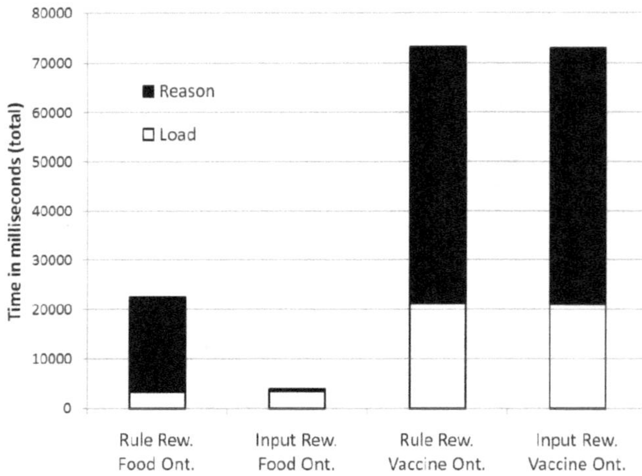

Fig. 4. Comparison of rewriting techniques in Scenarios 1 and 2 (Food Ontology and Vaccine Ontology)

domain knowledge – are also feasible. Yet, even the fastest variation yields no more than approximately 2200 rewrites per second. This certainly leaves room for optimization. Moreover, the performance is highly dependent on the complexity of the ontology and on the type of knowledge to be extracted. Further investigation into the influence of these factors is required to determine the best strategy for integrating domain knowledge into complex event processing.

6 Conclusion

Our study identified a shortcoming in the current procedure of rule specification and evaluation in complex event processing and analyzed how domain knowledge from ontologies could be utilized to overcome this limitation. We proposed four techniques that enable the use of domain knowledge to increase the accuracy of complex event processing and to reduce the workload of rule specification. Our approach emphasized the techniques' independence of a specific system or ontology, making them suitable for a wide range of application domains. Experimental results showed the feasibility of these techniques and indicated the direction for further research.

Future work will focus on the challenges mentioned throughout this paper and integrate our techniques into state-of-the-art complex event processing systems. We further aim to access modules of SNOMED CT with the help of the classifier Snorocket[7] to support complex event processing in e-Health environments.

Acknowledgments. The authors would like to thank Kewen Wang for his contribution to the initial idea of this project.

[7] `http://research.ict.csiro.au/software/snorocket`

References

1. Anicic, D., Fodor, P., Rudolph, S., Stojanovic, N.: EP-SPARQL: A unified language for event processing and stream reasoning. In: Proceedings of the 20th International Conference on World Wide Web, WWW 2011, pp. 635–644. ACM (2011)
2. Anicic, D., Fodor, P., Rudolph, S., Stühmer, R., Stojanovic, N., Studer, R.: A Rule-Based Language for Complex Event Processing and Reasoning. In: Hitzler, P., Lukasiewicz, T. (eds.) RR 2010. LNCS, vol. 6333, pp. 42–57. Springer, Heidelberg (2010)
3. Barbieri, D.F., Braga, D., Ceri, S., Della Valle, E., Grossniklaus, M.: Incremental Reasoning on Streams and Rich Background Knowledge. In: Aroyo, L., Antoniou, G., Hyvönen, E., ten Teije, A., Stuckenschmidt, H., Cabral, L., Tudorache, T. (eds.) ESWC 2010. LNCS, vol. 6088, pp. 1–15. Springer, Heidelberg (2010)
4. Cugola, G., Margara, A.: TESLA: A formally defined event specification language. In: Proceedings of the Fourth ACM International Conference on Distributed Event-Based Systems, DEBS 2010, pp. 50–61. ACM (2010)
5. Dunkel, J.: On complex event processing for sensor networks. In: 2009 International Symposium on Autonomous Decentralized Systems, pp. 1–6. IEEE (2009)
6. Etzion, O., Niblett, P.: Event Processing in Action. Manning, Greenwich (2011)
7. Hansen, D., Karunanithi, M., Lawley, M., Maeder, A., McBride, S., Morgan, G., Pang, C., Salvado, O., Sarela, A.: Improving the Use, Analysis and Integration of Patient Health Data. In: Ishikawa, Y., He, J., Xu, G., Shi, Y., Huang, G., Pang, C., Zhang, Q., Wang, G. (eds.) APWeb 2008 Workshops. LNCS, vol. 4977, pp. 74–84. Springer, Heidelberg (2008)
8. Hansen, D., Kemp, M., Mills, S., Mercer, M., Frosdick, P., Lawley, M.: Developing a national emergency department data reference set based on SNOMED CT. The Medical Journal of Australia 194(4), S8–S10 (2011)
9. International Health Terminology Standards Development Organisation: Results of Survey to Gather the Use, Benefits and Tools of SNOMED CT (2011), `http://www.ihtsdo.org/index.php?id=826` Date: 20110119, Version: 1.0
10. Lawley, M.: Exploiting fast classification of SNOMED CT for query and integration of health data. In: Proceedings of the 3rd International Conference on Knowledge Representation in Medicine (KR-MED 2008): Representing and Sharing Knowledge Using SNOMED, pp. 8–14 (2008)
11. Li, X., Liu, J., Sheng, Q., Zeadally, S., Zhong, W.: TMS-RFID: Temporal management of large-scale RFID applications. Information Systems Frontiers, 1–20 (2009)
12. Liu, D., Pedrinaci, C., Domingue, J.: A framework for feeding Linked Data to complex event processing engines. In: The 1st International Workshop on Consuming Linked Data (COLD 2010) at The 9th International Semantic Web Conference, ISWC 2010 (2010)
13. Paschke, A., Kozlenkov, A.: Rule-Based Event Processing and Reaction Rules. In: Governatori, G., Hall, J., Paschke, A. (eds.) RuleML 2009. LNCS, vol. 5858, pp. 53–66. Springer, Heidelberg (2009)
14. Paulheim, H.: Efficient Semantic Event Processing: Lessons Learned in User Interface Integration. In: Aroyo, L., Antoniou, G., Hyvönen, E., ten Teije, A., Stuckenschmidt, H., Cabral, L., Tudorache, T. (eds.) ESWC 2010. LNCS, vol. 6089, pp. 60–74. Springer, Heidelberg (2010)

15. Schmidt, K., Anicic, D., Stühmer, R.: Event-driven reactivity: A survey and requirements analysis. In: 3rd International Workshop on Semantic Business Process Management, pp. 72–86 (2008)
16. Teymourian, K.: Enabling knowledge-based complex event processing. In: Proceedings of the 2010 EDBT Workshops, pp. 1–7. ACM (2010)
17. Wienhofen, L.W.M., Toussaint, P.J.: Enriching events to support hospital care. In: Proceedings of the 7th Middleware Doctoral Symposium, MDS 2010, pp. 26–30. ACM (2010)
18. Zhang, H., Diao, Y., Immerman, N.: Recognizing patterns in streams with imprecise timestamps. Proceedings of the VLDB Endowment 3(1), 244–255 (2010)
19. Zhang, H., Li, Y., Tan, H.: Measuring design complexity of semantic web ontologies. Journal of Systems and Software 83(5), 803–814 (2010)

An Algorithm to Improve Cell Loss and Cell Delay Rate in ATM Networks by Adopting Dynamic Spacer

Changjin Kim* and Wu Woan Kim**

Division of Computer Science & Engineering, Kyungnam University
Kcjin00@nate.com, wukim@kyungnam.ac.kr

Abstract. In this paper, an improved User Parameter Control (UPC) algorithm is proposed to control traffic in ATM networks. The algorithm consists of delay elements such as Cell Buffer, Red Token Pool, Green Token Pool, and Dynamic Spacer. The token here is used to control traffics rather than to arbitrate the contention of buses. A token is generated during a random time period, and the accumulated tokens are consumed one each time a cell arrives. At this time, if the delay element, named Dynamic Spacer, is empty, the cell comes into the network. On the other hand, if the Spacer is not empty, the cell cannot come into the network. In addition, in the case that tokens do not exist in Token Pool, the corresponding cell is thrown away. This research proposes new UPC Algorithm to improve the cell delay rate and cell loss rate by adopting Dynamic Spacer. The proposed algorithm dynamically controls traffic in ATM networks with respect to the various traffic status.

Keywords: UPC algorithm, Traffic control, Dynamic spacer, ATM networks.

1 Introduction

In ATM networks, the service channel capacity is measured by the number of ATM cells. Therefore, the transferred data capacity is told by the number of ATM cells. The allocated transmitting capacity is determined when a call is established by the consuming capacity and the allocation capacity with negotiating a communication network[1][2]. So, in ATM, it is possible to connect networks flexibly and to allocate various bandwidths. In addition, ATM can communicate through various physical media and carrier networks because ATM is defined independently to means of carry in the physical layer. ATM has become the economical way to transfer information by transmitting traffics with various bit ratios with the statistical multiplexing. Also, one of the main purposes in ATM is to use network resources efficiently supporting the traffic having various statistical characteristics and QoS (Quality of Services)[3]. However, it happens frequently that the network resources cannot be activated

* Master Student, Dept. of Computer Engineering, Kyungnam Univ., S. Korea.
** Corresponding Author, Professor of Dept. of Computer Engineering, Kyungnam Univ.

A. Abd Manaf et al. (Eds.): ICIEIS 2011, Part III, CCIS 253, pp. 243–252, 2011.

efficiently due to the bursty property of the traffic. In order to prevent this problem, the application of techniques to controlling traffic becomes mandatory such as BMP, CAC (Connection Admission Control), UPC (User Parameter Control), priority control, congestion control, etc..

In this paper, the relationship of the UPC and BMP, is considered, and an improved UPC algorithm to control the traffic is proposed. The simulation result of the proposed algorithm shows that this algorithm decreases cell loss rate and cell delay.

2 ATM and Current Methods of Traffic Control

2.1 ATM

ATM, one of the communication methods to implement BISDN, has been suggested to support Teleconference, fast data transmission, VOD (Video on Demand) etc.. ATM is based on the packet transfer method using ATDM (Asynchronous Time Division Multiplexing).

ATM removes the inflexibility and ineffectiveness of STM. In BISDN, data transmission is performed by continuous data flow of the packet, named ATM cell. The cell is considered as a data frame of the fixed size in ATM. Service information is mapped to ATM with a constant size. Then, the internal transfer signal is established. In ATM, which is connection oriented method, service data is transferred with the established virtual channel. Every time a virtual channel is set up the identified number is given to the channel, and when the connection is released the identified number is also reset. The size of ATM cell is the fixed 53-byte including 5-byte cell header and 48-byte payload data. The 5-byte cell header consists of GFC, VPI, VCI, PT, CLP, and HEC. ATM performs a few of functions by using the cell header[1][3][4].

2.2 Current Methods of Traffic Control

In ATM networks, most traffic sources are exceeded. If such exceeded traffic sources make the traffic of PBR (Peak Bit Rate) simultaneously, the network loaded by sources falls in temporal congestion state. There are two ways to control traffic; the traffic control and the congestion control. The traffic control is the control action by network to prevent for the network falling in congestion state. On the other hand, the congestion control is that the control system, under the circumstance of network congestion already, checks the degree of congestion, decreases its lasting time and minimizes the affection of congestion state to other networks. Network resource management, fast reservation, CAC, UPC and priority control have been introduced as technologies of traffic control, so far.

3 The Current UPC Methods

UPC is the next step of CAC (Connection Admission Control), which always checks whether cell stream complies with the parameter value of VCC (Virtual Channel

Connection) and VPC (Virtual Path Connection), which are reported by users. If cell stream violates the parameter value, UPC discards the corresponding cell, or after UPC marks the violation tag, it transfers the cell. And, if the network is in congestion state, the algorithm abandons the cell. Popularly, the following surveillance algorithm have been known; LBA (Leaky Bucket Algorithm, VSA (Virtual Scheduling Algorithm), JW (Jumping Window), SW (Sliding Window) and PC (Peak Counter)[1][4][5][6].

4 The Proposed UPC Algorithm

4.1 Definition of UPC

In order to express the flexible and various characteristics of Bursty data, 2-state MMPP (Markov Modulated Poisson Process) model is used. 2-state MMPP is 2-state Poisson process in which the cell generating rate is determined by the state of Markov Chain. 2-state MMPP model has two states as [Fig. 1] shows.

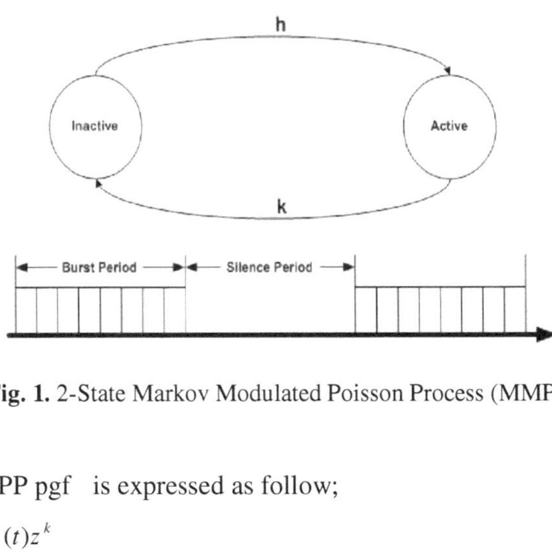

Fig. 1. 2-State Markov Modulated Poisson Process (MMPP)

2-state MMPP pgf is expressed as follow;

$$g(z,t) = \sum_{k=0}^{\infty} P_k(t) z^k$$

where,

k = the number of arrivals in an interval $(0, t]$

$g(z,t) = pgf$ of the number of arrival cells during in $(0, t]$

$Pk(t) = P$ [k arrivals in $(0, t]$]

$Pk_1(t) = P$ [k arrivals in $(0, t]$, current state $= 1$]

$Pk_2(t) = P$ [k arrivals in $(0, t]$, current state $= 2$]

The average lasting time of each state follows the Exponential Distribution. As it is in [Fig. 1], a cell is created in Burst period which has the property of the exponential function of h, and has the Idle period, too[5][7]. In ATM networks, there exist traffics with various characteristics such as CBR (Constant Bit Ratio) service and VBR (Variable Bit Rate) service. Therefore the user variable should be determined for these traffics to be applied in all cases. The user variable is expressed with the following several variables; PBR (Peak (Burst) Bit Rate), h (Mean Burst Duration), k (Mean Idle (Silence) Duration), (Mean Source Burstness), ABR (Average (Source) Bit Rate), T (Mean Cycle Duration), and t (Mean Burst Length in Bits). The result values of T, β, and ABR are as follow:

$$T = h + k \tag{1}$$

$$\beta = (h + k) / h = T / h \tag{2}$$

$$ABR = (PBR * h) / (h + k) = (PBR * h) / T \tag{3}$$

4.2 The Proposed Algorithm Adopting Dynamic Spacer

The improved UPC algorithm, proposed in this research, controls the user parameters at the user side in order to control congestion state. The algorithm consists of those of the basic model of LBA, such as Buffer, Bucket, and Spacer. Buffer is a FIFO queue. So, the arrived cell has to wait in the buffer until the previous cell goes out through Spacer. The buffer size is β, and the value is determined by CAC. Bucket consists of Green Token Pool and Red Token Pool. Green Token Pool generates legal cells while Red Token Pool generates illegal cells. The token generation rates of Green Token Pool and Red Token Pool are γ_g and γ_r, respectively. Being different from old ones, tokens here are for controlling traffic, not for arbitrating networks[5][7][8]The token generation rate of Green Token Pool is

$$\gamma_g = \frac{1}{ABR / CL}$$

The established γ_g controls ABR (Average Bit Ratio). The generation rate of Red Token Pool is determined by the characteristics of the traffic at the time of controlling connection admission. The Spacer is a delay element providing the function to smooth the load in a network. Spacer consists of token pool and decision part. The decision part estimates whether the token pool is empty or not, then if the token pool is empty, the decision part sends the corresponding cell to Bucket. Generally, there are two ways to establish the value of β. First, β is the value which is less than PBR and greater than $MAX[\gamma_g, \gamma_r]$. Second, β is established as the least cell transmission rate among middle nodes. The middle nodes are located in the networks. One of the purposes of middle nodes is for transferring cells, which come from the previous node through the network under UPC, to the next node. This structure of the middle node consists of Buffer and Token Pool. If the number of cells is greater than T , the control performs with two ways by the value of CLP as [Fig. 2].

Because BISDN supports various data services, the interval of cell arriving period is not constant every single traffic, and diverse by Burst characteristics of the traffic. Especially, in the case of Bursty traffic, when it passes the network without proper processing, cell delay becomes too long, and as its result it might bring out network congestion. In order to prevent the congestion, the interval of the arriving cell in the network should be mediated constantly by adopting the Spacer which passes cells at regular interval. Although LBA having a Spacer also reduces the cell loss, and burst characteristics, it does not have flexibility to cope with the various traffics. Therefore, the performance of a network is not actually increased except a special application field. The Spacer used in LBA is called Static Spacer[4][10][11].

In this paper, the Dynamic Spacer, which performs efficient and dynamic control considering with the state of traffic, is introduced. The proposed algorithm adopting the Dynamic Spacer improves problems such as increasing the cell loss due to managing networks inefficiently, and outbreak of cell delay due to paying no regards for the state and condition of the network. The improved UPC algorithm proposed in this research reduces both of the cell loss rate and cell delay rate. The algorithm consists of four main elements as follow; Buffer, Green Token Pool, Red Token Pool, and Dynamic Spacer. The elements build the model of the proposed UPC algorithm as seen in [Fig. 3].

[Fig. 4] shows the algorithm adopting Dynamic Spacer. It starts from the time at a cell's arriving on the input line of FIFO Queue (Buffer).

5 Simulation and Analysis

The simulation results for the cell loss and the cell delay rate of the proposed algorithm are compared with the existing algorithm. The results of the proposed algorithm show that it improves cell loss and cell delay rate of different Bursty traffics in ATM networks. However, although the main features of ATM technology are efficient and flexible for various services at the same time, there still exist a lot of problems which should be solved in the field of traffic control and resource management. In addition, the cell delay is dependent on the execution time and the buffer size of UPC algorithm. It means that there are so many factors to consider. In this paper, the cell loss rate and the delay rate are examined only when ABR control violation and Bursty violation happen.

```
START: begin
          if Arriving CLP of a Cell = 1
            go to DSCD_1;
           else /* Arriving CLP of a Cell = 0*/
             begin
              if CLP in the Buffer = 1
              if CLP = 1
                go to DSCD_2;
               else
                 go to DSCD_3;
              end;
           end.
DSCD _1: begin
            clear the Buffer;
            go to START;
            end;
DSCD _2: begin
            discard the corresponding cell;
            store arriving cell into Buffer;
            go to START;
            end;
DSCD _3: begin
            discard arriving cell;
            go to START;
            end;
```

Fig. 2. Control Ways by the Value of CLP

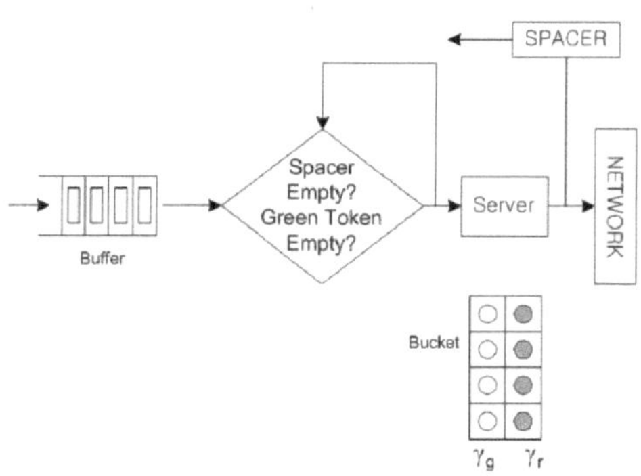

Fig. 3. Model for the Proposed UPC Algorithm

```
Begin
 get arrived cell into Buffer;
 DIFF: begin
         if N > T, then go to DISC;
         else
           begin
             if Green Token non-empty, then go to NET;
             else
               begin
                 if Dynamic Spacer non-empty, then go to DIFF;
                 else
                   begin
                     if Red Token empty, then go to NET;
                     else go to DIFF;
                   end;
               end;
           end;
       end;
end.

 DISC: begin
         discard the cell in Buffer;
       end;

 NET:  begin
         pass the cell to the Network;
       end;
```

Fig. 4. The Proposed UPC Algorithm with Dynamic Space

The simulation is performed with SMPL (Simulation Program Language) revised by M.H. McDougall. The required multimedia source loss rate in ATM is within the limit of 10^{-9} to 10^{-11} loss rate. Actually, finding the loss rate beyond 10^{-9} takes too long time to evaluate. So, the experiment is done until the loss rate becomes 10^{-5} order known as possible evaluating range. Each parameter value of services (Voice and Picture) is in [Table. 1][4][6]. The evaluating objects are existing algorithms LB and VLB. For the practical evaluation and comparison, the model and the variables defined in Section 4 are used.

Table 1. Service Characteristics

Parameter	Voice	Picture
PBR	32 Kb/s	2 Mb/s
h	352 ms	500 ms
k	650 ms	11,000 ms
m	11.2 b/s	87 Kb/s
β	2.85	23

The performance evaluation is expedited by the cell loss rate of ABR violation control and Bursty violation control. Here, the cell loss rate means the ratio of the number of total generated cells to the number of discarded cells. ABR violation occurs when Burst interval becomes abnormally long in the MMPP model. As soon as the abnormal traffic is produced, UPC algorithm has to discard the illegal cell or put CLP in the illegal cell and pass it into the network.

If UPC algorithm does not control fast and properly, the abnormal cell is transferred into the network and brings about congestion. It is the reason why UPC algorithm has to control efficienlyt and fast. On the other hand, Burst period violation occurs when Burst time interval grows longer and Idle time interval also proportionately grows longer at the same time. If Burst interval is too long, temporal crowd state happens. Therefore, UPC algorithm has to control accurately and propely to prevent congestion in the network.

In [Fig. 5], it is supposed that the Idle time interval is constant and the Burst time interval is longer. The cell loss rate under these consumptions is graphed. The graph expresses that if the cell arrival rate is between 1.0 and 1.4, the cell loss rate is less than that of the LBA. If it is greater than 1.1 the rate becomes nearly equal.

[Fig. 6] shows the simulation result for Burst interval violation. Here, with increasing Burst interval and Idle interval simultaneously, the cell loss rate, which is represented as the proportion of the number of total incoming cells and the number of lost cells among them, is graphed. Although we see there may be no big improvement for the slow data in [Fig. 6], both of the cell loss rate and the cell delay rate are reduced in case of the fast and massive data which is sensitive to the cell loss. The transmission of the massive and fast data is focused on in this research, so the cell loss and cell delay rate of the data must be improved practically.

Especially, LB reduced Burstness with minimizing CDV (Cell Delay Variation), so the increased network performance while the flexibility for Burst traffic became poor. The proposed algorithm makes it flexible for Burst traffic by adjusting Burst time interval with Dynamic Spacer, and guarantees QoS for users.

$$Cell\ Loss\ Rate = Number\ of\ Lost\ Cells\ /\ Number\ of\ Total\ Arrival\ Cells$$

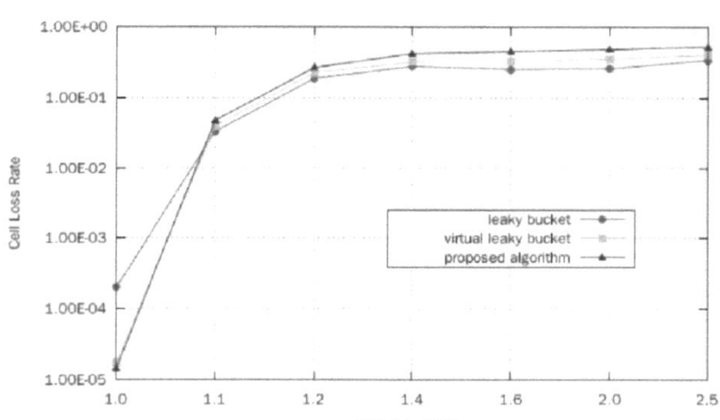

Fig. 5. ABR Violation

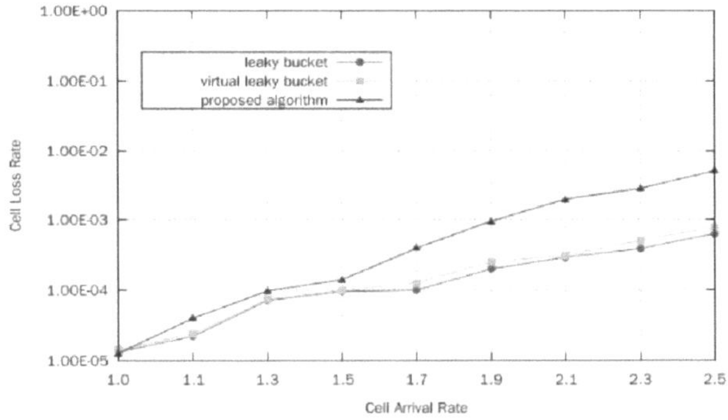

Fig. 6. Burst Interval Violation

6 Conclusions

In order to maximize usage of resources, and use them efficiently, the proper control is mandatory in ATM networks. Because the existing UPC algorithm performs only the preventive functions, they have the constant delay time due to the Buffer without regarding the network status. It is a serious defect. In this research, the four elements, Green Token Pool, Red Token Pool, Buffer, and Dynamic Spacer, perform the control actions dynamically with regarding to the network state and condition.

As the result, the cell loss rate and the cell delay rate are reduced and the traffic in the network is controlled properly. This paper suggests 2-State MMPP model for simulating, and the voice data is used for the traffic. The simulation results show that the cell loss rate is decreased in the part of the low cell arrival, and for the fast and massive data the cell loss rate and the cell delay rate should be decreased, too.

Currently in this paper, the various experiments for the different data transfer are not conducted because the simulation is done for only one channel. The research and simulation, for the various channels and networks with different states and variables, will be performed in near future.

References

1. Tanenbaum, A.S.: Computer Networks, 4th edn. Prentice Hall PTR, Upper Saddle River (2003)
2. Bae, J.J., Suda, T.: Survey of traffic control schemes and protocols in ATM networks. Proceedings of IEEE 79(2), 219–238 (1991)
3. Shimokoshi, K.: Evaluation of policing mechanisms for ATM network. IEEE JSAC E76-B(10) (November 1993)
4. Subramani, A., Krishnan, A.: Doubly Finite Queues (DFQ) supporting for ABR traffic load in ATM networks using MSVDR algorithm. In: 2009 IEEE International Advance Computing Conference (IACC 2009), pp. 13–19 (2009)
5. Mark, B.L., Ramamurthy, G.: Real-time estimation and dynamic renegotiation of UPC parameters for arbitrary traffic sources in ATM networks. IEEE/ACM Transactions on Networking 6(6), 811–827 (1998)

6. Wang, Q.: ATM Cell Scheduling and Learning by Function-level evolvable hardware. In: Pacific-Asia Workshop on Computational Intelligence and Industrial Application, PACIIA 2008, vol. 2, pp. 727–729 (2008)
7. Stiliadis, D., Varma, A.: Latency-rate servers: A general model for analysis of traffic scheduling algorithm. IEEE/ACM Transactions on Networking 6(5), 611–624 (1998)
8. Chan, M.C., Lee, T.T.: Statistical performance guarantees in large-scale cross-path packet switch. IEEE/ACM Transactions on Networking 11(2), 325–337 (2003)
9. Wang, Q.: ATM cell scheduling and learning by function-level evolvable hardware. In: Pacific-Asia Workshop on Computational Intelligence and Industrial Application, PACIIA 2008, vol. 2, pp. 727–729 (2008)
10. Jing, Y., Ren, T., Zhou, Y., Zheng, X.: ABR traffic control over ATM networks with time-varying multiple time-delays using fuzzy-immune controller. In: 46th IEEE Conference on Decision and Control, pp. 5851–5856 (2007)
11. Wang, L.-z., Fang, Y.-q.: An estimation suited for VBR service parameters in the ATM network. In: WASE International Conference on Information Engineering (ICIE 2009), vol. 1, pp. 278–281 (2009)

An Approximation Algorithm for the Achromatic Number of Hex Derived Networks

Bharati Rajan[1], Indra Rajasingh[1], Sharmila Mary Arul[2], and Varalakshmi[3]

[1] Department of Mathematics, Loyola College, Chennai – 600 034
[2] Department of Mathematics, Jeppiaar Engineering College, Chennai – 600 119
[3] Department of Mathematics, Ethiraj College, Chennai
sharmila_arul@rediffmail.com

Abstract. The achromatic number for a graph $G = (V, E)$ is the largest integer m such that there is a partition of V into disjoint independent sets $(V_1, \dots, V_m)$ such that for each pair of distinct sets $V_i, V_j, V_i \cup V_j$ is not an independent set in G. In this paper we present an $O(1)$-approximation algorithm to determine the achromatic number of Hex derived networks.

Keywords: achromatic number, approximation algorithms, NP-completeness, Graph algorithms.

1 Introduction

A *proper* coloring of a graph $G = (V, E)$ is an assignment of colors to the vertices of G such that adjacent vertices are assigned different colors. A proper coloring of a graph G is said to be *complete* if for every pair of colors i and j there are adjacent vertices u and v colored i and j, respectively. The *achromatic number* of the graph G is the largest number m such that G has a complete coloring with m colors. Equivalently there is a partition of V into disjoint independent sets $(V_1, \dots, V_m)$ such that for each pair of distinct sets $V_i, V_j, V_i \cup V_j$ is not an independent set in G. Yannakakis and Gavril [26] proved that determining this value for general graphs is NP-complete.

Scheduling problems with inter-processor communication delays are recent problems arising with the development of new message-passing architectures whose number of processors is increasing more and more. The scheduling problem with communication delays is NP-complete. Small Communication Time task systems show that the achromatic number of the co-comparability graph is an upper bound on the minimum number of processors [22].

The *chromatic number* problem is to minimize the number of colors over all proper colourings of a given graph. It is shown that the *achromatic number* is a maximinimal counterpart of *chromatic number*, by defining a partition-related partial order on the set of all proper colourings of G [20]. The *pseudoachromatic number* of a graph is the largest number of colours in a (not necessarily proper) vertex colouring of the graph

A. Abd Manaf et al. (Eds.): ICIEIS 2011, Part III, CCIS 253, pp. 253–261, 2011.

such that every pair of distinct colours appears on the endpoints of some edge. Yegnanarayanan [27] determined pseudoachromatic number for graphs such as cycles, paths, wheels, certain complete multipartite graphs, and for other classes of graphs. Hedetniemi [12] conjectured that the two parameters *achromatic number* and *pseudoachromatic number* are equal for all trees which was disproved later [6].

2 Overview of the Paper

The *achromatic number* was introduced by Harary, Hedetniemi and Prins [11, 12]. The survey articles by Hughes and MacGillivray [13] and Edwards [5] contain huge collection of references of research papers related to achromatic problem.

Computing achromatic number of a general graph was proved to be *NP*-complete by Yannakakis and Gavril [28]. A simple proof of this fact appears in [10]. Farber et al. [7] show that the problem is *NP*- hard on bipartite graphs. It was further proved that the achromatic number problem remains *NP*- complete even for connected graphs which are both interval graphs and cographs simultaneously [1]. Cairnie and Edwards [2], Manlove and McDiarmid [20] show that the problem is *NP*- hard even on trees. Further it is polynomially solvable for paths, cycles [5], complete bipartite graphs [19] and union of paths [21].

Since achromatic optimization problem is *NP*-hard, most of the research studies related to achromatic problem focus on approximation algorithms. An *approximation algorithm* for a problem, loosely speaking, is an algorithm that runs in polynomial time and produces an "approximate solution" to the problem. We say that an algorithm is α-approximation algorithm for a maximization problem if it always delivers a solution whose value is at least a factor $1/\alpha$ of the optimum. The parameter α is called the *approximation ratio* [8, 25].

Let n denote the number of vertices in the input graph G and let $\psi(G)$ be the achromatic number of G. It is conjectured in [3] that the achromatic number on general graphs admits an $O(\sqrt{n})$ approximation. Chaudhary and Vishwanathan [4] realize an algorithm for trees with a constant approximation ratio 7. For general graphs an algorithm that approximates the achromatic number within ratio of $O(n\,.\log\log n/\log n)$ is given in [18].

It is stated in [5] that "for achromatic numbers, there appear to be only a few results on special graphs apart from those for paths and cycles". Geller and Kronk [9] proved that there is almost optimal coloring for families of paths and cycles [5, 13]. This result was extended to bounded trees [2]. Also they generalized this result to all families of bounded degree graphs. Roichman, gives the achromatic number of Hypercubes [24].

In this paper we present an $O(1)$-approximation algorithm to determine the achromatic number of Hex derived networks.

3 Main Result

Our aim is to get an $O(1)$-approximation algorithm for the achromatic number of Hex derived networks. To achieve this goal, we begin with the following definitions.

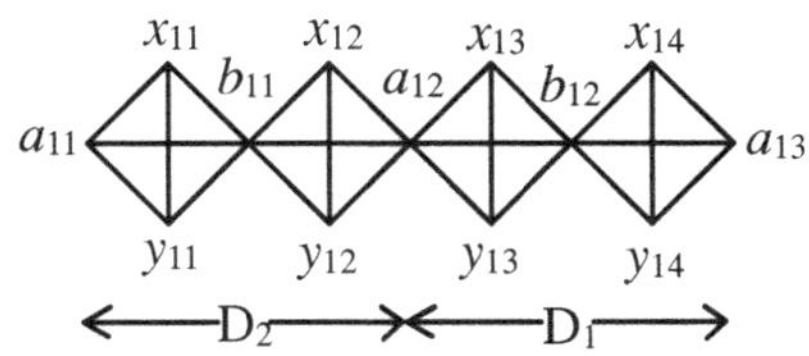

Fig. 1. $4K_4$ - chain

Definition 1: A $tK_4 - chain$ is a graph defined as the union of t number of complete graphs with a common vertex between two consecutive complete graphs. See Figure 1.

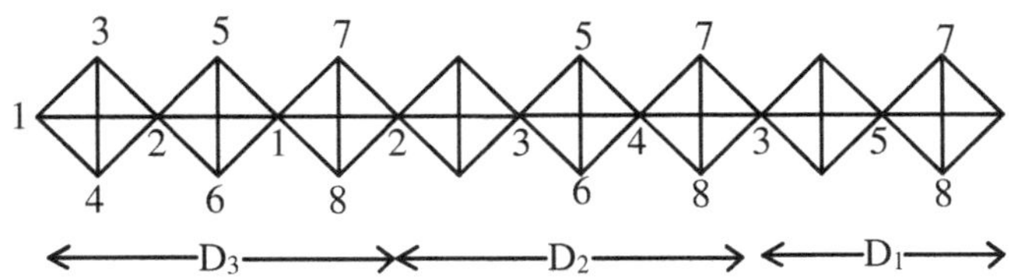

Fig. 2. Achromatic labeling of $8K_4$

3.1 Algorithm Achromatic $tK_4 - chain$

(i) Find maximum s such that $s \leq \left\lceil 3+\frac{\sqrt{8t+17}}{2} \right\rceil$

(ii) Partition D^k, $k=\frac{s-2i}{2}, i=1,2,\ldots,\frac{s-2}{2}$ into $D^k \cup D^{k-1} \cup \ldots \cup D^1$ where D^k and D^{k-1} consist of k-layer $tK_4 -$ sub chain, D^{k-2}, D^{k-3},... D^1 consist of $(k+1)$-layer $tK_4 -$ sub chain,

Group the first $(k+1)$-layer $tK_4 -$ sub chain as $D_{\frac{s-2}{2}}$, next as $D_{\frac{s-4}{2}}, \ldots$, last as $D_{\frac{s-2\left(\frac{s-2}{2}\right)}{2}}$. Call the edge (a_i, b_i) as a horizontal edge and the vertices a_i and b_i are called middle vertices.

For $0 \leq j \leq k-1$ label D^{k-j} as follows:

Label the middle vertices of D^{k-j} as $2j+1$ and $2j+2$ beginning from the first D in D^{k-j}. The remaining $2(k-j)$ vertices in D^{k-j} are labeled $2j+3, 2j+4, \ldots, 2j+[2(k-j)+2]$ from top to bottom. Here $2j+[2(k-j)+2] = 2k+2$. See Figure 2.

Since vertices labeled $2j+1$ and $2j+2$ are adjacent in D^{k-j}, they in turn are adjacent to vertices labeled $2j+3\ldots, 2k+2$. Since none of the adjacent vertices in D^{k-j} receive the same label, the labeling is proper. Therefore, the labeling of the vertices induces an achromatic labeling yielding the achromatic number for D^t to be at least $2k+2$.

Theorem 1: Let $k = \frac{s-2}{2}$ be the maximum integer such that $s \le \left\lceil 3 + \frac{\sqrt{8t+17}}{2} \right\rceil$

Then $\psi(tK_4 - chain) \ge 2k+2$.

We extend the achromatic labeling for $tK_4 - chain$ to union of $tK_4 - chains$.

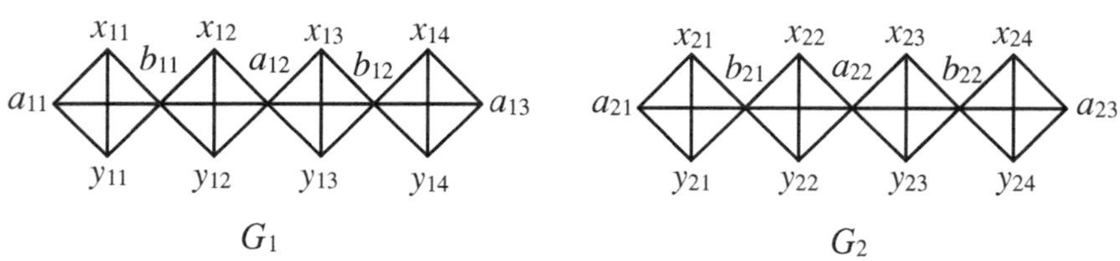

Fig. 3. $G = G_1 \cup G_2$

Definition 2: Let G_1, G_2 be two tK_4-chains with $3n_1+1$ and $3n_2+1$ vertices respectively. Then $G_1 \cup G_2$ is the disjoint union of G_1 and G_2 with $3n_1+3n_2+2$ vertices. See Figure 3.

Theorem 2: Let $G = \bigcup_{i=1}^{s} G_i$ be the disjoint union of tK_4-chains $G_1, G_2, \ldots, G_s$. Let $n = 3(n_1+n_2+\ldots+n_s)+s$. Then

$$\left\lceil \frac{1}{3}\left(\frac{1 \pm \sqrt{1+288(n-1)^2}}{2} \right) \right\rceil \le \psi(G) \le \frac{1 \pm \sqrt{1+288(n-1)^2}}{2}.$$

Proof: Let G be the union of tK_4-chains $G_1, G_2, \ldots, G_s$. See Figure 5.

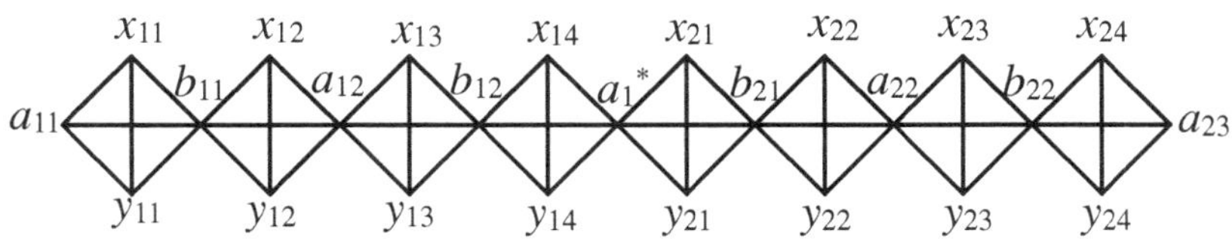

Fig. 4. G^* on 25 vertices

To get an achromatic coloring for G, we proceed as follows

Step 1: Identify the vertex (a_{i,n_i}) of G_i with $(a_{i+1,1})$ of $G_{i+1}, 1 \le i \le s-1$.

Call the new vertex as a_i^* and get a tK_4-chain G^* on $n = 3(n_1 + n_2 + ... + n_s) + s - 1$ vertices. See Figure 4.

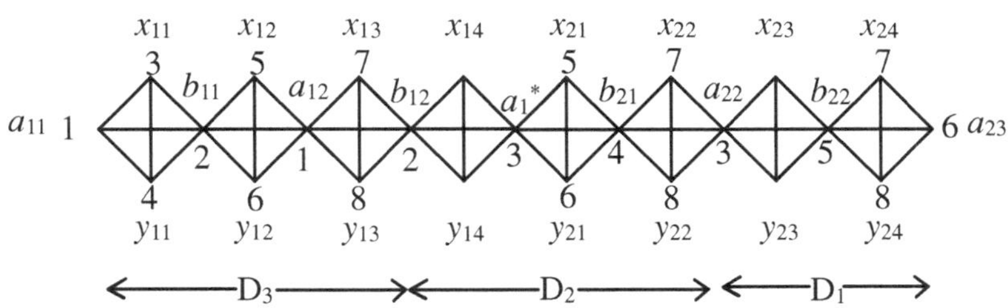

Fig. 5. Achromatic labeling of G^*

Step 2: Apply the **algorithm Achromatic** $tK_4 - chain$ to G^*. See Figure 5.

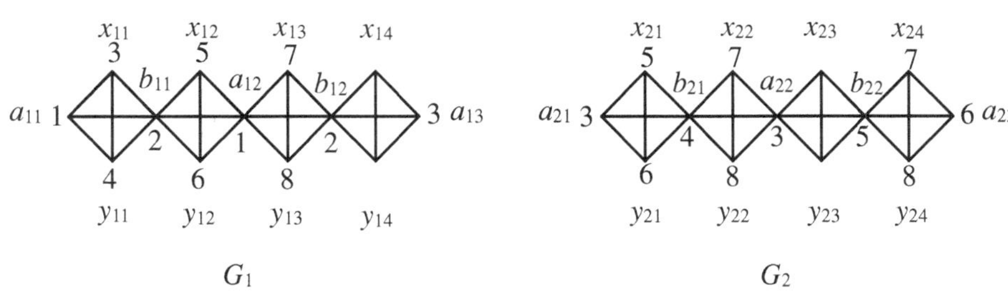

Fig. 6. Achromatic labeling of $G = G_1 \cup G_2$

Step 3: Replace G^* by G with the condition that (a_{i,n_i}) of G_i with $(a_{i+1,1})$ of $G_{i+1}, 1 \le i \le s-1$ receive same colors that are assigned to (a_i^*, a_{i+2}^*) in G^*, $1 \le i \le s-1$. See Figure 6. It is an easy consequence that this gives an achromatic labeling of union of tK_4 – chains.

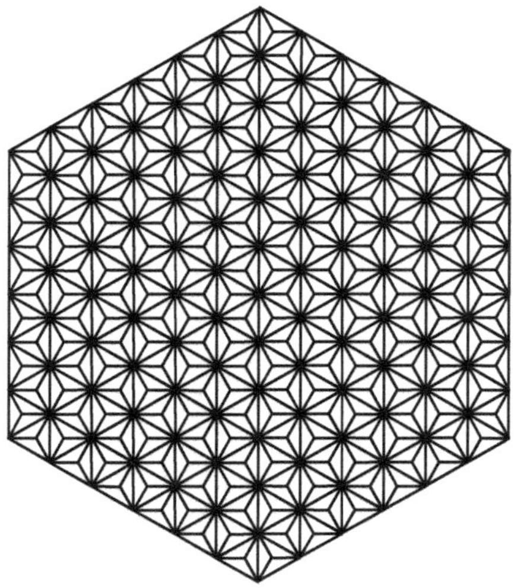

Fig. 7. Planar *HD*(7)

4 Achromatic Number of Hex Derived Networks

Definition 3: "We introduce two new architectures using the Hexagonal and Honeycomb networks. It is obtained from the union of $HX(n)$ and its bounded dual $HC(n-1)$ by joining each honeycomb vertex with the three vertices of the corresponding face of $HX(n)$. The resulting graph is non planar and it is called $HD(n)$. This graph has $9n^2 - 15n + 7$ vertices and $36n^2 - 72n + 36$ edges. The diameter is $2n - 2$". See Figure 7.

Using the fact that $tK_4 - chain$ is an induced subgraph in $HD(n)$, the following results are obtained. See Figure 8.

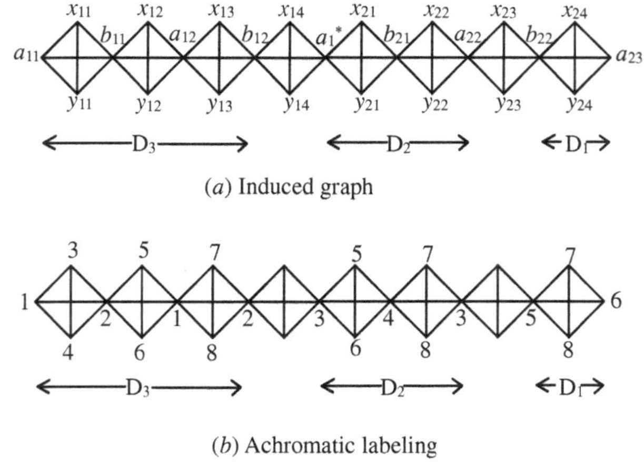

Fig. 8. Achromatic labeling of $tK_4 - chain$ in $HD(n)$

Lemma 1: Let $HD(r)$ be a Hex derived network of dimension r. Then $HD(r)$ contains a disjoint union of the induced $tK_4 - chain$ of the following type.

(i) When r is odd, the number of independent r-layer $K_4 - chain$ and $(r + 2)$-layer $K_4 - chain$ is two.

(ii) When r is even, in addition to (i) we get an extra $(r + 4)$ −layer $K_4 - chain$.

The following theorem is straightforward as the number of edges ε in a Hex derived network $HD(n)$ is $36n^2 - 72n + 36$ and $\varepsilon \geq \frac{\psi(\psi - 1)}{2}$.

Theorem 3: Let $HD(n)$ be a Hex derived network of dimension n. Then

$$\psi(HD(n)) \leq \frac{1 \pm \sqrt{1 + 288(n-1)^2}}{2}.$$

Theorem 4: There is an $O(1)$- approximation algorithm to determine the achromatic number of Hex derived network of dimension n.

Proof: The expected achromatic number for Hex derived network of dimension n is $\frac{1 \pm \sqrt{1 + 288(n-1)^2}}{2}$ and the lower bound realized is

$$\psi(HD(n)) \geq \left\lceil \frac{1}{3}\left(\frac{1 \pm \sqrt{1 + 288(n-1)^2}}{2}\right)\right\rceil.$$ This proves the theorem.

5 Conclusion

In this paper we present an $O(1)$ −approximation algorithm to determine the achromatic number of Hex derived networks. We have already obtained the same for Benes networks and butterfly networks [23], Mesh of trees [17], Petersen graphs, ladders and combs [14], Enhanced Hyper Petersen network [15] and Mesh [16]. Finding efficient approximation algorithms to determine achromatic number for other interconnection networks is quite challenging.

References

[1] Bodlaender, H.L.: Achromatic number is NP-complete for co-graphs and interval graphs. Inform. Proces. Lett. 31, 135–138 (1989)

[2] Cairnie, N., Edwards, K.J.: Some results on the achromatic number. Journal of Graph Theory 26, 129–136 (1997)

[3] Chaudhary, A., Vishwanathan.: Approximation algorithms for the achromatic number, pp. 558–563. ACM, New York (1997)

[4] Chaudhary, A., Vishwanathan: Approximation Algorithms for the Achromatic Number. Journal of Algorithms 41, 404–416 (2001)
[5] Edwards, K.J.: The harmonious chromatic number and the achromatic number. Surveys in Combinatorics, 13–47 (1997)
[6] Edwards, K.J.: Achromatic number versus pseudoachromatic number: a counterexample to a conjecture of Hedetniemi. Discrete Mathematics 219, 271–274 (2000)
[7] Farber, M., Hahn, G., Hell, P., Miller, D.J.: Concerning the achromatic number of graphs. J.Combin. Theory 40, 21–39 (1986)
[8] Garey, M.R., Johnson, D.S.: Computers and Intractability. Freeman, San Francisco (1979)
[9] Geller, D.P., Kronk, H.V.: Further results on the achromatic number. Fundamenta Mathematicae 85, 285–290 (1974)
[10] Goyal, N., Vishwanathan: A simple proof of NP- completeness of undirected grundy numbering and related problems. Personal Communication (2000)
[11] Harary, F., Hedetniemi, S.: The achromatic number of a graph. J. Combin. Theory 8, 154–161 (1970)
[12] Harary, F., Hedetniemi, S., Prins, G.: An interpolation theorem for graphical homomorphisms. Portugal. Math. 26, 453–462 (1967)
[13] Hughes, F., MacGillivray, G.: The achromatic number of graphs: a survey and some new results. Bull. Inst. Combin. Appl. 19, 27–56 (1997)
[14] Indra, R., Bharati, R., Sharmila, M.A.: Approximation Algorithms for the Achromatic Number of Combs, Ladders and Petersen Graphs. In: Conference Proceedings of National Conference on Computational Intelligence (2005)
[15] Indra, R., Bharati, R., Sharmila, M.A., Paul, M.: An Approximation Algorithm for the Achromatic Number of Enhanced Hyper-Petersen Network. In: Conference Proceedings of the 4th International Multiconference on Computer Science and Information Technology (CSIT), Amman, Jordan, vol. 1, pp. 89–94 (2006)
[16] Indra, R., Bharati, R., Sharmila, M.A.: An Approximation Algorithm for the Achromatic Number of Mesh Like Topologies. The International Journal of Mathematics and Computer Science 2, 155–162 (2007)
[17] Indra, R., Bharati, R., Sharmila, M.A., Paul, M.: An Approximation Algorithm for the Achromatic Number of Mesh of Trees. In: Conference Proceedings of the Fourteenth International Conference of the Forum for Interdisciplinary Mathematics (2007)
[18] Kortsarz, G., Krauthgamer, R.: On approximating the achromatic number. SIAM Journal on Discrete Mathematics 14, 408–422 (2001)
[19] Kortsarz, G., Shende, S.: An improved approximation of the achromatic number on bipartite graphs (2004)
[20] Manlove, D., McDiarmid, C.: The complexity of harmonious coloring for trees. Discrete Applied Mathematics 57, 133–144 (1995)
[21] MacGillivray, G., Rodriguez, A.: The achromatic number of the union of paths. Discrete Mathematics 231, 331–335 (2001)
[22] Moukrim, A.: On the minimum number of processors for scheduling problems with communication delays. Annals of Operations Research 86, 455–472 (1999)
[23] Paul, M., Indra, R., Bharati, R., Sharmila, M.A.: An Approximation Algorithm For the Achromatic Number of Butterfly and Benes Networks. In: Conference proceedings of the International Conference on Computer and Communication Engineering (ICCCE), Kuala Lumpur, Malaysia, pp. 304–308 (2006)
[24] Roichman, Y.: On the achromatic number of hypercubes. Journal of Combinatorial Theory 79, 177–182 (2000)

[25] Shmoys, D.B.: Computing near- optimal solutions to combinatorial optimization problems in Advances in Combinatorial Optimization, pp. 355–397. Math. Soc., Providence (1995)
[26] Yannakakis, M., Gavril, F.: Edge dominating sets in graphs. SIAM J. Appl. Math. 38, 364–372 (1980)
[27] Yegnanarayanan, V.: The Pseudoachromatic number of a graph. Southeast Asian Bulletin of Mathematics 24, 129–136 (2000)

Hybrid Local Polynomial Wavelet Shrinkage for Stationary Correlated Data

Alsaidi M. Altaher and Mohd Tahir Ismail

School of Mathematical Sciences,
Universiti Sains Malaysia, 11800, Penang, Malaysia
assaedi76@yahoo.com, mtahir@cs.usm.my

Abstract. Local Polynomial Wavelet Shrinkage estimator (LPWS) is an attractive technique used to cope with the boundary problem present in wavelet shrinkage. However, this combined estimator seems to be quite sensitive to the presence of correlated noise. In this paper, the practical consequences of this sensitivity are explained; including the breakdown of several popular thresholding selection methods. The term-by term level dependent thresholding has been investigated as an effective solution for recovering a signal contaminated with correlated noise. A simulation study is conducted to evaluate both EbayesThresh and level dependent cross validation under a variety of test function, noise structure, signal to noise ratio and sample size. Results showed that thresholding by level dependent cross validation is preferable.

Keywords: correlated noise, level dependent thresholding, boundary correction.

1 Introduction

Consider a noisy data set $y_1, y_2, \ldots, y_n$ from fixed design model:

$$y_i = f(x_i) + \varepsilon_i \quad ; i = 1,2,\ldots,n = 2^j;\ j = 1,2,\ldots \tag{1}$$

Where $x_i = i/n$. The aim is to estimate the unknown function, f for $x \in [0,1]$ using the noisy data $y_1, y_2, \ldots, y_n$.

The sequences $\{\varepsilon_i\}_{i=1}^{n}$ are usually assumed to be independent and identical, following Gaussian distribution with zero mean and constant variance, σ^2.

In this regard, there are several nonparametric techniques in literature for estimating the unknown function, f which allow flexible modeling of the data. See for example books by Eubank [1], Wahba [2], and Takezawa[3].

The past two decades have witnessed a great development of wavelet methods for estimating an unknown function observed in the presence of noise, see Donoho and Johnstone[4,5], where the concept of wavelet shrinkage has been introduced to the statistical literature.

A. Abd Manaf et al. (Eds.): ICIEIS 2011, Part III, CCIS 253, pp. 262–273, 2011.

Wavelet shrinkage can be viewed as orthonormal basis functions that are localized in both time and frequency domains, with time-widths adapted to their frequency. It has the advantages of ideal minimax property, spatial inhomogeneous adaptivity, and can be extended to high dimensions with fast algorithm.

Due to these key advantages, wavelet shrinkage has been proven to be highly effective at estimating the unknown function f as long as there are no boundary problems with f .Within boundaries; one side data information are available due to the bounded support of the underline function. As a result, the application of the wavelet transformation to a finite signal provides large biases at the edges, increasing the bias and creating artificial wiggles. This problem has been recognized as quite serious because final estimate results can easily get boosted and distorting substantially.

The usual way to account for the boundary effects upon using classical wavelet shrinkage is to impose on f some boundary assumptions such as symmetry or periodicity. Unfortunately, such assumptions are not always realistic and the problem still exists for some cases.

More recently, the Hybrid local polynomial wavelet regression fitting (LPWS, [6]) is proposed as an improvement boundary adjustment in wavelet shrinkage. Practical implementations have proved that LPWS performs much better than classical wavelet shrinkage with classical periodic assumption or the automatic boundary correction by a global polynomial model [6].

However, in realistic situations the noise structure is often correlated and sometimes highly correlated. Hence, the classical LPWS fails to construct a signal with correlated noise simply because wavelet transformations of a signal contaminated say, with stationary correlated noise lead to a sequence of wavelet coefficients which will generally be correlated as well. The variances of wavelet coefficients will depend on the level in the wavelet decomposition but will be constant at each level. As a result, the global thresholding methods (usually considered in LPWS) break down with lacking of providing a global threshold value to threshold wavelet coefficients at all desirable levels.

Researchers have begun looking at the situation where the noise is no longer independent, but instead contains a certain amount of structure in the form of correlation. See for example Chipman et al.[7]), Johnstone and Silverman [8], Opsomer et al. [9], Abramovich et al. [10] and Wang and Wood [11].

In all previous work, they either do not touch the boundary problem or using the classical way of boundary correction such periodicity and symmetric assumptions. Their approaches and techniques perform well when the boundary assumptions are satisfied. However, the practical achievement can be improved by using LPWS boundary correction when the boundary assumption is not satisfied.

The focus of this article is to look at the problem of estimating the unknown function using LPWS in the presence of stationary correlated noises. We then, investigate the so -called term by term -level dependent thresholding methodology. We show how EbayesThresh of Johnstone and Silverman [12] and level dependent cross validation of Oh et al. [13] deal with correlated noise problem. A simulation experiment is conducted to assess the practical performance of these two methods.

The rest of this paper is organized as follows: In section 2, we give a brief background to the Hybrid local polynomial wavelet shrinkage estimator. Section 3 shows some consequences of presences of correlated noise, following by level dependent thresholding in section 4. A simulation experiment is presented in section 5. Conclusion is drawn in section 6.

2 Hybrid Local Polynomial Wavelet Shrinkage

This section describes the Hybrid local polynomial shrinkage (Regression) proposed by Oh and Kim [6].

Let ϕ and ψ be father (scaling) and mother (dilation) wavelet functions respectively, the function f can be written in terms of wavelets as:

$$\hat{f}_W(x) = \sum_{k=1}^{\infty} \hat{c}_{0,k}\phi_k(x) + \sum_{j=0}^{j-1}\sum_{k=0}^{2^j-1} \hat{d}^s_{j,k}\psi_{j,k}(x)$$

Where: $\phi_k(x) = 2^{1/2}\phi(2x-k)$, $\psi_{j,k}(x) = 2^{1/2}\psi(2x-k)$, $\hat{c}_{0,k} = \sum y_i\phi_k(x_i)$ and $\hat{d}^s_{j,k}$ denotes the soft threshold coefficient.

Given a wavelet coefficient $d_{j,k}$ and threshold value λ, the soft threshold rule, $\hat{d}^s_{j,k}$ of the coefficient can be defined as:

$$\hat{d}^S_{j,k} = \text{sgn}(\hat{d}_{j,k})\ (\ |\hat{d}_{j,k}| - \lambda)\ I_{(\ |\hat{d}_{j,k}|>\lambda)}$$

Here I refers to the usual indicator function.

The Hybrid Local Polynomial wavelet Shrinkage method was introduced by Oh and Kim [6] as an improvement boundary adjustment in wavelet regression. Instead of using the global polynomial fit as in [14], it was proposed using a local polynomial fit, $\hat{f}_{Lp}$. Therefore, the Hybrid Local Polynomial wavelet Shrinkage estimator, $\hat{f}_H(x)$ can be written as:

$$\hat{f}_H(x) = \hat{f}_{Lp}(x) + \hat{f}_W(x)$$

As shown in [6] $\hat{f}_H(x)$ is computed through an iterative algorithm inspired by the back-fitting algorithm of Hastie and Tibshirani [15]. The following steps summarize the key points to find the final Hybrid Local polynomial wavelet regression fitting $\hat{f}_H$.

Select an initial estimate $\hat{f}_0$ for f and let $\hat{f}_H = \hat{f}_0$

1. For $j = 1, 2, \ldots$ iterate the following steps:
   a. Apply wavelet regression to the residuals $y_i - \hat{f}_H$ and obtain $\hat{f}_W^j$.
   b. Estimate $\hat{f}_{LP}^j$ by fitting local polynomial regression to $y_i - \hat{f}_W^j$.
2. Stop if $\hat{f}_H = \hat{f}_{LP}^j + \hat{f}_W^j$ converges.

The initial estimate, $\hat{f}_0$ can be found by using Friedman's (known as *supsmu*, available in R), while smoothing parameter is selected by cross validation or direct Plug-in criterion (available at *KernSmooth* package in R).

3 Problems with Correlation

Theoretically, much is known of how correlated noise can affect the theoretical performance in wavelet regression; see Opsomer et al. [9] for a general review of how wavelets and some other nonparametric approaches are affected by correlated noise. On the other hand, it is not clear enough to what extent the known theoretical results reflect and capture what happens in practical situations with correlated noise.

In this section, the target is showing some consequences of having data with stationary correlated noise. To do so, let's start by looking at the behavior of wavelet coefficients and their variances for different kinds of noise structure. We mainly focus on the cases in which the noise follows an autoregressive process (AR) of order p, or autoregressive moving process (ARMA) of order p, q. These processes can be defined respectively as:

$$AR(P): \quad \varepsilon_i = \alpha_1 \varepsilon_{i-1} + \alpha_2 \varepsilon_{i-2} + \ldots + \alpha_p \varepsilon_{i-p} + \eta_i$$

$$ARMA(p,q): \quad \varepsilon_i = \sum_{k=1}^{p} \alpha_k \varepsilon_{i-k} + \eta_i + \sum_{k=1}^{q} \alpha_k \varepsilon_{i-k}; \quad \eta \sim N(0, \sigma^2)$$

Based on these standard processes, we simulate data from AR(1) with parameter (0.5), and ARMA(1,1) with parameters (0.99,1). Autocorrelation functions, autocorrelations of finest-level discrete wavelet transform and the variances of the whole level of wavelet coefficients for each level are depicted in Figure 1 and Figure 2.

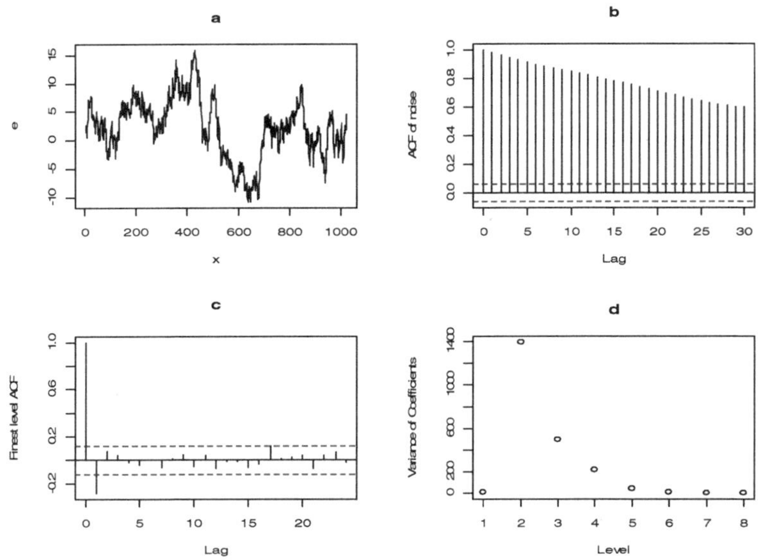

Fig. 1. (a) Realization of AR (1) process with parameter (0.5); (b) auto correlation function of (a); (c) autocorrelations of finest-level discrete wavelet transform; (d) the variances of the whole level of wavelet coefficients for each level

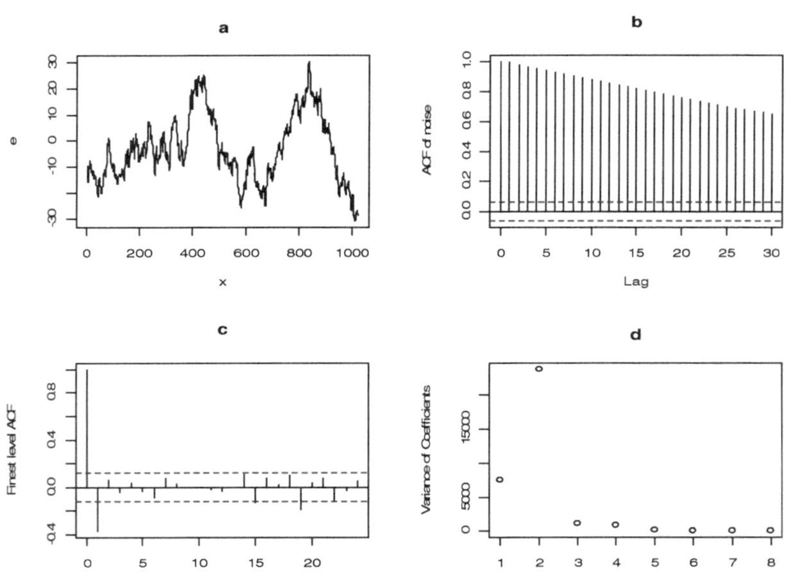

Fig. 2. (a) Realization of ARMA (1,1) process with parameters (0.99, 1); (b) auto correlation function of (a); (c) autocorrelations of finest-level discrete wavelet transform; (d) the variances of the whole level of wavelet coefficients for each level

As it can be seen in Figure1, 2, the auto correlation functions (panel b) show significant correlations even at quite high lags. However, auto correlations of wavelet coefficients at the finest level demonstrate much reduced correlations. It is also remarkable to notice that the variances of the entire level of coefficients show different variances.

Now let us carry on and see what would happen at wavelet reconstruction process in presence of such circumstances of correlations, and how the global thresholding criteria break down in smoothing a signal contaminated with correlated noise. We have used three well-known test functions: Blocks, HeavSin and Dopper; see Donoho and Johnstone [4,5]. Figure 3 displays three reconstructed signals contaminated with Gaussian noise (panel a,c,e); and with correlated noise from AR(1) with parameter (0.5) (panel b,d,f). Here, the global soft- Universal thresholding was used.

Obviously one can deduce that the global thresholding methodology work quite well to recover a signal with Gaussian noise(panel a,c,e) while having difficulty to recover a signal with correlated noise (panel *b,d,f*).

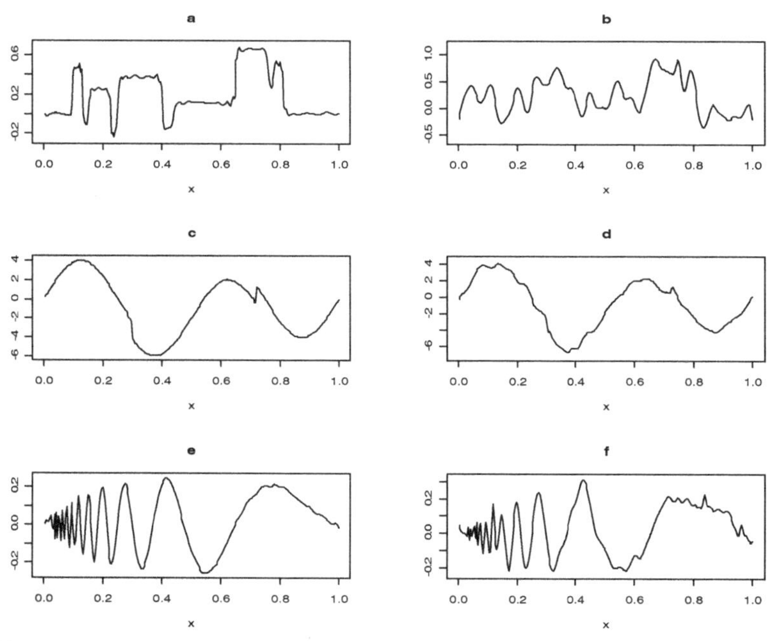

Fig. 3. First colum shows three reconstructed signals contaminated with Gaussian noise; second colum shows three reconstructed signals contaminated with correlated noise

4 Level Dependent Thresholding for LPWR

This method sometimes called term by term thresholding. It was introduced first by Johnstone and Silverman [8] to deal with correlation effects. As pointed in [8], if the noise structure is correlated and stationary, then wavelet coefficients will depend on the resolution level in wavelet decomposition process. Therefore it is recommended to use level dependent thresholding strategy. Different thresholding methods have been considered such Univeral of Donoho and Johnstone[4], SURE of Donoho and Johnstone[5] and translation–invariant denoising algorithm Coifman and Donoho [16]. Details can be found in [8].

We pick up this idea and apply it to more advance thresholding methods such Ebayesthresh of Johnstone and Silverman [12], and level dependent cross validation of Oh et al., [13].

Here we present some examples to show how effective the term by term thresholding reconstruct a signal with correlated noise. Three different test functions were used fg1, HeavSin and Bamps. See Donoho and Johnstone [4,5].

From Figure 4, it is clear that the term by term thresholding is able to a certain extent to overcome the correlation's effects.

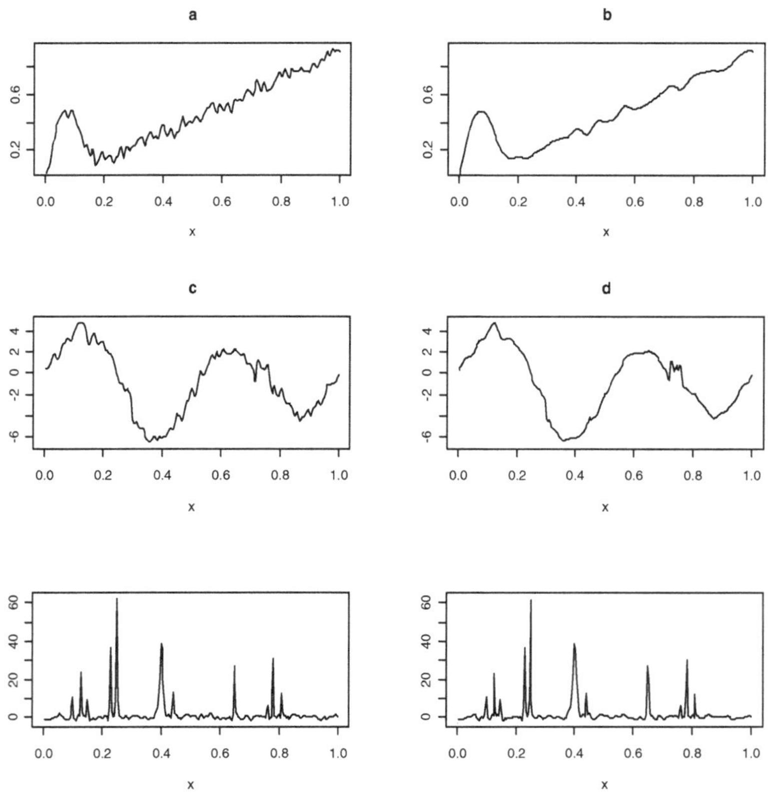

Fig. 4. First colum shows three reconstructed signals contaminated with correlation noise ARMA(2,1) using global Ebayesthresh; second colum shows three reconstructed signals contaminated correlation noise ARMA(2,1) using term by term thresholding via Ebayesthresh

5 Simulation Evaluation

5.1 Setup

In this section, we have used the codes of the R statistical package to contact a simulation study to compare the numerical performance of the Hybrid local polynomial wavelet shrinkage in presence of correlation using two thresholding methods:

- LPWS with EbayesThresh of Johnstone and Silverman [12].
- LPWS with level dependent cross validation of Oh et al. [13].

The purpose of this simulation is to examine these two methods using the global thresholding and term by term thresholding.

Throughout the whole simulation Mother wavelet $N = 10$ was used in every wavelet transform with soft thresholding rule. The median absolute deviation of the wavelet coefficients at the finest level was used to find variances for EbayesThresh. Laplace density and the median of posterior were used for EbayesThresh. For level dependent cross validation, we used 4-fold cross validation with block size 8.

Altogether four test functions were used. They are listed in Table 1 and are depicted in Figure 5. Each function has some abrupt changing features such as discontinuities or sharp bumps. It is reasonable to assume that functions 1 and 2 are periodic while the remaining as non-periodic case.

Three different kinds of correlated noise were used:

- Correlated noises from AR(1): first order autoregressive model with parameter (0.5)
- Correlated noises from AR(2): second order autoregressive model with parameter (0.7,-0.2).
- Correlated noises from ARMA(1,1): autoregressive moving average with parameters (0.5,0.8).

Two levels of signal to noise ratio (snr) were used: $snr = 5 \; and \; 10$.We consider two different sample sizes: $n = 256 \; and \; 512$. For every combination of test function, noise structure, signal to noise ratio and sample size, 100 samples were generated. For each generated data set, we applied the above two methods to obtain an estimate $(\hat{f})$ for each test function (f) and then the mean squared error was computed as a numerical measure for assessing the quality of $\hat{f}$.

$$MSE(\hat{f}) = \frac{1}{n}\sum_{i=1}^{n}[f(i/n) - \hat{f}(i/n)]^2$$

Since the boundary problem usually appears locally, it would be more precious to consider the mean squared error of the observations which lie only at the boundary region. Say; $[0, 0.05] \cup [0.95, 1]$ as considered by Lee and Oh [17]. In this case the mean squared error can be defined as:

$$MSE\,(\hat{f})=\frac{1}{n}\sum_{i\in N(\tau)}[f(x_i)-\hat{f}(x_i)]^2;\ \tau=1,2,\ldots,\ n/2\ ;\ x_i=i/n$$

Where $N(\tau)=\{1,\ldots\tau,n-\tau+1,\ldots,n\}$. Here τ refers to the observations number at the boundary region for each side. In our case since $n=256$, we have about 13 observations at each boundary side $(\tau=13)$.

Table 1. Mathematical description of four test functions used in simulation

Test Function	Formula	
1	Blocks of Donoho and Johnstone (1994)	
2	HeavSin of Donoho and Johnstone (1994)	
3	$4x(1-\sin x)$	$x\in[0,0.88]\cup[0.93,1]$
	1.10	$x\in[0.88,0.93]$
4	Piecewise polynomial functions of Nason and Silverman [18].	

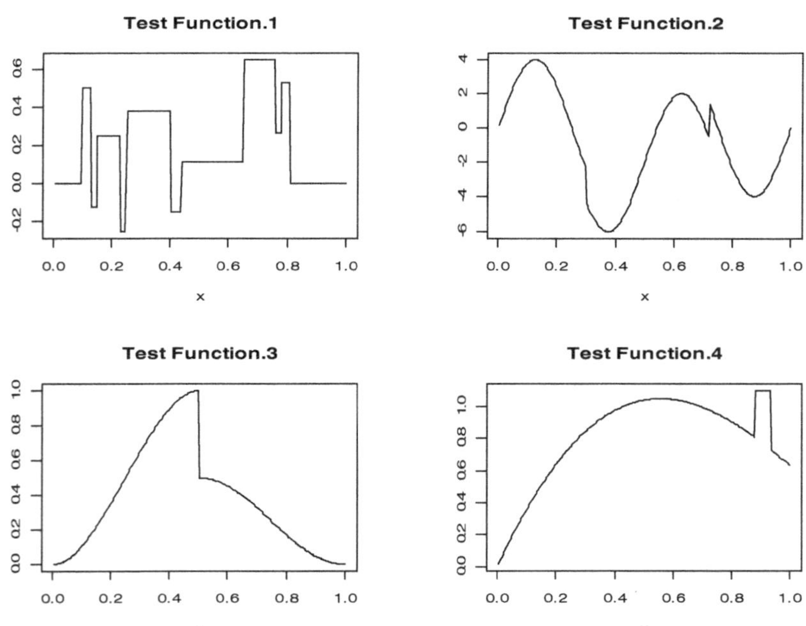

Fig. 5. Four test functions used in simulation

5.2 Results and Discussion

In this section we summarize and discus the numerical results from simulation study described above. Table 2 and Table 3 display the global and local mean squared error respectively for *snr*=5, *n*=256. Other results for (*snr*=10, *n*=256) and (*snr*=5,10, *n*=512) provide similar conclusions and hence, omitted.

Table 2. Simulation Results of global mean squared error at the boundary region for the two wavelet regression methods with snr=5, n=256

Global Level Dependent Cross Validation	Term by term Level Dependent Cross Validation	Global EbaysThresh	Term by term EbaysThresh
	AR(1)		
0.054796206	0.047438223	0.072036290	0.044085756
0.124410360	0.115407739	0.170893717	0.113858398
0.001404398	0.001294364	0.001876395	0.001213962
0.001451546	0.001408488	0.001897852	0.001381026
	AR(2)		
0.065953436	0.047703247	0.091156405	0.041580556
0.147085588	0.121369578	0.219611583	0.105703561
0.001516662	0.001302891	0.002332578	0.001173457
0.001568936	0.001404028	0.002372153	0.001315218
	ARMA(1,1)		
0.094435576	0.068405662	0.115590379	0.055519966
0.228863028	0.164344776	0.281538301	0.144385334
0.002196014	0.001715131	0.002931588	0.001540543
0.002372616	0.001841100	0.002947035	0.001668376

Having examined the results; In terms of the global and local mean squared error criteria, the following empirical remarks were observed:

1. By Using both EbayesThreh (Johnstone and Silverman, [12]) and Level dependent cross validation (Oh et al.,[13]) we found that term by term level dependent thresholding performs much better than the classical global thresholding when the noise structure is correlated.
2. The global Thresholding based on level dependent cross validation outperforms its corresponding based on EbayesThresh, regardless of noise structure.
3. The term by term level dependent thresholding based on level dependent cross validation works better than EbayesThresh for almost all used test functions except Test function 4.

Table 3. Simulation Results of mean squared error at the boundary region for the two wavelet regression methods with snr=5, n=256

Global Level Dependent Cross Validation	Term by term Level Dependent Cross Validation	Global EbaysThresh	Term by term EbaysThresh
	AR(1)		
0.262651938	0.225106937	0.356456058	0.202453781
0.623582561	0.568780282	0.844980538	0.557115632
0.007840417	0.007481517	0.009604456	0.006951197
0.009365276	0.009305340	0.010294287	0.009327620
	AR(2)		
0.314654899	0.219353842	0.44082171	0.184012661
0.737931716	0.604788740	1.10538984	0.512637739
0.008368686	0.007606753	0.01178819	0.006894004
0.009361630	0.009009119	0.01213235	0.009053392
	ARMA(1,1)		
0.46260240	0.323296837	0.57631055	0.24840768
1.10089455	0.773453535	1.36772750	0.67455351
0.01135314	0.009277444	0.01463827	0.00848832
0.01267567	0.010611046	0.01487706	0.01057069

6 Conclusion

In this paper the problem of correlated noise is considered for the Hybrid local polynomial wavelet shrinkage. The consequences of such correlations are illustrated through different noise structures such as first order autoregressive, second order autoregressive and autoregressive moving average process. A simulation experiment has been conducted to investigate the level dependent thresholding using two thresholding methods: EbayesThresh and level dependent cross validation. Results revealed that level dependent thresholding based on level dependent cross validation seems to be better than EbayesThresh.

Acknowledgement. The authors would like to thank Universiti Sains Malaysia for financial support.

References

1. Eubank, R.L.: Spline smoothing and nonparametric regression (1988)
2. Wahba, G.: Spline models for observational data. Society for Industrial Mathematics (1990)
3. Takezawa, K.: Introduction to nonparametric regression. Wiley Online Library (2006)

4. Donoho, D.L., Johnstone, J.M.: Ideal spatial adaptation by wavelet shrinkage. Biometrika 81(3), 425–455 (1994)
5. Donoho, D., Johnstone, I.: Adapting to Unknown Smoothness Via Wavelet Shrinkage. Journal of the American Statistical Association 90(432), 1200–1224 (1995)
6. Oh, H.S., Lee, T.C.M.: Hybrid local polynomial wavelet shrinkage: wavelet regression with automatic boundary adjustment. Computational Statistics and Data Analysis 48(4), 809–820 (2005)
7. Chipman, H.A., Kolaczyk, E.D., McCulloch, R.E.: Adaptive Bayesian wavelet shrinkage. Journal of the American Statistical Association, 1413–1421 (1997)
8. Johnstone, I.M., Silverman, B.W.: Wavelet threshold estimators for data with correlated noise. Journal of the Royal Statistical Society. Series B (Methodological), 319–351 (1997)
9. Opsomer, J., Wang, Y., Yang, Y.: Nonparametric Regressin with Correlated Errors Statistical Science 16(2), 134–153 (2001)
10. Abramovich, F., Bailey, T.C., Sapatinas, T.: Wavelet analysis and its statistical applications. Journal of the Royal Statistical Society: Series D (The Statistician) 49(1), 1–29 (2000)
11. Wang, X., Wood, A.T.A.: Wavelet Estimation of an Unknown Function Observed with Correlated Noise. Communications in Statistics - Simulation and Computation 39(2), 287–304 (2010)
12. Johnstone, I.M., Silverman, B.W.: Empirical Bayes selection of wavelet thresholds. Annals of Statistics 33(4), 1700–1752 (2005)
13. Oh, H.-S., Kim, D., Lee, Y.: Cross-validated wavelet shrinkage. Computational Statistics 24(3), 497–512 (2009)
14. Oh, H.S., Naveau, P., Lee, G.: Polynomial boundary treatment for wavelet regression. Biometrika 88, 291–298 (2001)
15. Hastie, T.J., Tibshirani, R.J.: Generalized Additive Models. Chapman & Hall/CRC (1990)
16. Coifman, R.R., Donoho, D.L.: Translation-invariant de-noising. Lecture Notes In Statistics, pp. 125–125. Springer, New York (1995)
17. Lee, T., Oh, H.S.: Automatic polynomial wavelet regression. Statistics and Computing 14, 337–341 (2004)
18. Nason, G.P., Silverman, B.W.: The discrete wavelet transform in S. Journal of Computational and Graphical Statistics 3, 163–191 (1994)

Low Complexity PSO-Based Multi-objective Algorithm for Delay-Constraint Applications

Yakubu S. Baguda, Norsheila Fisal, Rozeha A. Rashid, Sharifah K. Yusof, Sharifah H. Syed, and Dahiru S. Shuaibu

UTM-MIMOS Centre of Excellence,
Faculty of Electrical Engineering,
Universiti Teknologi Malaysia,
81310 UTM Skudai, Johor, Malaysia
{baguda_pg,sheila,rozeha,kamila,hafiza}@fke.utm.my

Abstract. There has been an alarming increase in demand for highly efficient and reliable scheme to ultimately support delay sensitive application and provide the necessary quality of service (QoS) needed. Multimedia applications are very susceptible to delay and its high bandwidth requirement. Consequently, it requires more sophisticated and low complexity algorithm to mitigate the aforementioned problems. In order to strategically select best optimal solution, there is dramatic need for efficient and effective optimization scheme to satisfy different QoS requirements in order to enhance the network performance. Multi-objective particle swarm optimization can be extremely useful and important in delay and mission-critical application. This is primarily due to its simplicity, high convergence and searching capability. In this paper, an optimal parameter selection strategy for time stringent application using particle swarm optimization has been proposed. The experimental result through well-known test functions clearly shows that multi-objective particle swarm optimization algorithm has extremely low computational time and it can be potentially applicable for delay sensitive applications.

Keywords: Optimal solution, particle swarm optimization (PSO), multi-objective optimization, Quality of service, computational complexity.

1 Introduction

Most of the engineering applications require multi-criteria decision making due to their nature in which more than one objective need to be satisfied in order to achieve optimal solution. The geometric increase in size and complexity of problems as a result of technological advancement has necessitated the need for more effective and efficient approach to solve optimization problem. For instance, Quality of service (QoS) in time-varying channel is challenging due to different application and service requirements. The complexity should be as low as possible in order to achieve optimal performance. More complex problems require highly efficient optimization techniques which are precise and efficient as well. Complexity has been a key issue to consider

A. Abd Manaf et al. (Eds.): ICIEIS 2011, Part III, CCIS 253, pp. 274–283, 2011.

while analyzing the algorithm performance as most applications are sensitive to delay. By substantially reducing the complexity will lead to decrease in energy and cost which is extremely important in today's competitive market.

Multi-objective optimization is becoming very popular nowadays and the nature of the problem can be efficiently tackle using evolutionary search algorithms. In [1], it has been used in minimizing the number of objectives for the optimization problem. Some research works focus mainly on producing more accurate solution close to the pareto front [2,3,4,5]. An optimization problem using genetic algorithm which based on strength pareto evolutionary algorithm has shown more prominence results. Also, [6] has demonstrated improvement when compared with other pareto based evolutionary algorithm. With integration of elitism in [7] has lead unified model with describes multi-objective evolutionary algorithm. This has been achieved by storing the non-dominated solutions and using genetic algorithm as well. [8,9,10] demonstrated the impact of restricting the number of solution on pareto front.

The fact that the swarm intelligent optimization deals with particles in form of groups will be suitable and applicable for multi-objective optimization in order to determine the pareto optimal solution to problem. Different evolutionary algorithms have been developed but mostly used genetic algorithm. In this paper, we proposed PSO-based multi-objective optimization algorithm which is relatively simple and low complex when compared to other techniques.

The remainder of this paper is organized as follows. Section 2 mainly focuses on the general overview of PSO. Section 3 formulates the multi-criteria decision using particle swarm optimization. Simulations results are presented in Section 4. Finally, conclusions are enumerated in Section 5.

2 Overview of Particle Swarm Optimization

Biologically-inspired algorithms have been used quite extensively in solving optimization problems due to their unique features. PSO has been one of the major optimization algorithms which mimic the movement of school of fish or flock of birds [11,12]. It has been extremely important tool and can potentially tackle complex optimization problems. Many different swarm optimization techniques exist today, but PSO has been very promising due to its fast convergence and simplicity [19, 20]. This can be applicable in supporting delay sensitive applications which require high efficiency and low computation complexity algorithm. It is very obvious that in order to enhance the performance of delay sensitive applications, many parameters and factors should be considered. Hence, multi-objective optimization PSO can eventually solve variety of multi-objective problems to achieve optimal performance. More importantly, multi-objective PSO can effectively search and determine the set of optimal solutions simultaneously [13,14]. The wireless channel characteristic can be represented by highly non-linear objective and constraint in order to potentially support time stringent applications.

It is very important to note that PSO is primarily governed by two fundamental equations representing the velocity and position of the particle at any particular time. After each iteration, the particle position and velocity is updated until the termination condition has been reached. The termination condition can be based on the number of iteration and achievable output required. Once the required number of iterations or predetermined output has been achieved, the searching process is terminated automatically. For a particle with n dimension can be represented by vector $\boldsymbol{X} = (x_1, x_2 \dots\dots\dots x_n)$. The position of the particcles at time t can be mathematically expressed as P= $(p_1, p_2 \dots\dots\dots p_n)$ while the corresponding velocity of the particles is represented as $\boldsymbol{V} = (v_1, v_2 \dots\dots\dots v_n)$. In general, the velocity and position of the particles at t+1 can be mathematically represented using equation (1) and (2) respectively

$$v(t+1) = \omega v(t) + c_1\big(P_l + x(t)\big) + c_2\left(P_g + x(t)\right) \quad (1)$$

$$x(t+1) = x(t) + v(t+1) \quad (2)$$

The velocity equation basically describes the velocity of the particles at time t+1. v(t) keeps track of the particle flight direction and it prevents the particle from sudden change in direction. $c_1(P_l-x(t))$ normally measures the performance of the particle i relative to the past performance. In a nutshell, it draws the particles to their best known position. $c_2(P_g-x(t))$ measures the performance of particle i relative to the neighbours. Generally, it serves as standard in which individuals want to reach. The global best (P_g) determines the best possible solution for the entire neighbourhood for each particle in the entire swarm. The position is then computed using the x(t+1) when the velocity is computed. It is very important to note that this will determine best possible position and velocity discovered by any particle at time (t+1).

3 Multi-objective Decision Criteria Using PSO

Generally, optimization problems which have more than one objective function termed as multi-objective optimization. It is absolutely possible that the objective functions conflict with one another while optimizing such a problem [15, 16]. Multi-objective optimization has different possible solution to particular problem. In this particular case, the multi-objective optimization primarily consists of objective function, constraint and optimal solution. The main optimization task is achieved through multi-objective optimization which is primarily based on the concept of particle swarm optimization. The equation (1) and (2) describes the velocity and position of the particle at any particular time. More importantly, the PSO capability depends greatly on the aforementioned functions. At any particular time, the values for these functions are computed and best possible value is selected. Also, it is very much necessary to include the constraint in order to set boundary for the search space.

In fact, wireless environment require multi-objective optimization due to multiple objective functions describing various parameters of the network. The minimization problem can be represented mathematically as

$$\text{Minimize} \quad f(x) = [f(x_1), f(x_2), \dots f(x_n)\,] \quad (3)$$
$$\text{Subject to} \quad x \in X$$

$$Objective\ function = \arg\min f(x) \tag{4}$$

$$Subject\ to: \ 0 \leq D_{max} \leq 250$$

As can be seen from equation (5) that we assumed f(x) is the function representing the multi-objective system with n objective functions and this can be expressed mathematically in matrix form by

$$f(x) = \begin{bmatrix} f(x_1) \\ . \\ f(x_n) \end{bmatrix} \tag{5}$$

Also, the constraints K for each of the above function can be represented in matrix form as shown in equation (6)

$$K(x) = \begin{bmatrix} K(x_1) \\ . \\ K(x_n) \end{bmatrix} \tag{6}$$

The matrix $K(x)$ describes the constraints which must be satisfied before achieving optimal solution without loss of generality. n is the number of constraints related to the above functions in equation (5).

For instance, the gradient of the continuous differential equation $f(x_i)$ representing the problem can be determine by finding the second derivative at x_i and hessian matrix can be represented mathematically as shown in equation (7)

$$\nabla \text{f}(x_i) = \left[\frac{\partial f(x_i)}{\partial x_1}, \frac{\partial f(x_i)}{\partial x_2}, \ldots \frac{\partial f(x_i)}{\partial x_n}\right]^T \tag{7}$$

By taking the partial derivative of hessian matrix in equation (7) will eventually yields equation (8).

$$\nabla^2 \text{f}(x_i) = \begin{bmatrix} \frac{\partial^2 f(x_i)}{\partial {x_1}^2} & \cdots & \frac{\partial^2 f(x_i)}{\partial x_1 x_n} \\ \frac{\partial^2 f(x_i)}{\partial x_2 x_n} & \ddots & \frac{\partial^2 f(x_i)}{\partial x_2 x_n} \\ \vdots & & \vdots \\ \frac{\partial^2 f(x_i)}{\partial x_n x_1} & \cdots & \frac{\partial^2 f(x_i)}{\partial {x_n}^2} \end{bmatrix} \tag{8}$$

The need for such multi-objective optimization scheme is very crucial especially with increasing demand for multimedia applications and services. The next generation communication system requires such scheme to significantly improve system performance and adapts with dynamically changing environment.

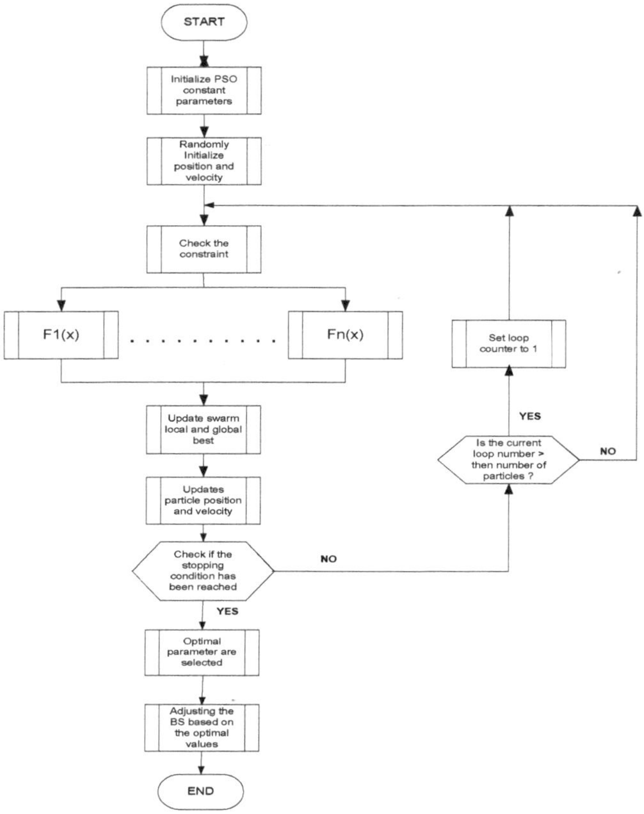

Fig. 1. Flowchart for multi-objective PSO algorithm

As shown in figure 1, the PSO constant parameters were set, and both the position and velocity are randomly initialized. The delay constraint is checked before evaluating the fitting for each objective function. Local and global best are determined and subsequently the position and velocity of the particles are updated. If the condition for termination has been reach, the current best optimal parameter configurations are selected. When the termination condition has not been reached, the loop counter is compared with the number of particles. The process is repeated until the termination condition has been reached.

The optimization parameters have been set based on the particle swarm to suit the QoS requirement for delay sensitive application. The maximum number of iterations and inertia weight were set to 30 and 0.5 respectively within which the optimal solution should determine or terminated. The cognitive c_1 and social c_2 constants have been set to 1. More details about the parameter settings used have been explained in table 1.

Table 1. Parameter settings

Parameters	Value
Number of particles	30
Number of iteration	30
Learning factors C1 & C2	1
Inertia weight ω	0.5

4 Simulation and Experimental Results

It has been a primary concern to determine the best possible solution in a system with multiple objective functions, in order to ultimately enhance the overall system performance. The parameters and settings used for the experimentation are as shown in Table 1. Having developed the optimization scheme, it is very important to determine the performance of the multi-objective optimizer to verify whether if it can efficiently optimize different parameters obtained from different layers of the protocol stalk. It has been assumed that the parameters are represented in terms of objective functions. Different test functions have been used to test the optimization scheme.

Firstly, the impact of having more objective functions on the optimizer performance have been investigated in order to verify the performance of the scheme as the number of functions increases. From table 2, it can be seen that the computational time increases with increase in number of particles and iterations as well. Selecting PSO configuration parameters to achieve the required results is important considering the application time constraint. Therefore, it is absolutely possible to use it in supporting delay applications such as video. It is very importantly to note that the minimum time delay for interactive applications such as video conferencing and surveillance is 250 milliseconds while streaming application normally requires a minimum delay of 5 to 10 seconds [17]. Hence, the multi-objective optimizer can be used for both applications.

Furthermore, the capability of the system to meet up with the time delay for multimedia application as the number of particles increase has been tested and investigated. It is primarily aimed at determining the number of particles to conveniently to conform to minimum time delay. Based on the experimentation, it has been observed that 30 particles can effectively yield better computational time for the multi-objective optimizer to converge. In order to achieve that, the number particles have been varied from 0 to 80 at interval of 20 particles and corresponding computation time has been noted for each case.

The tests functions of different parameters have been used primarily to test the heterogeneous nature of the network with different output obtained from each. The standard test functions used to investigate the performance of the multi-objective optimizer includes *Rastrigin*, and *Grienwack*. The *Rastrigin* function basically has large search space, local minima and maxima. The function is fairly difficult due to the aforementioned features. *Grienwack* function is very similar to *Rastrigin* function, but it has many local minima which are regularly distributed. The product term included in function makes more complex. The capability of multi-objective PSO to converge rapidly has clearly indicated its potential application in optimizing the performance of unpredictable environment. The experiments have been used to determine the minimum computational time, number of iteration, and number of particles to meet up with the delay constraint.

Test Case 1

Initially we consider grienwack test function in order to evaluate the performance of the algorithm. The parameter settings in table 1 are used in experimentation to verify the algorithm efficiency. As shown in fig 2, the fitness decreases with increase in number of iteration. The fact that rastrigin function is fairly complex due to the product and has many minima, it converges before 20th iteration. This indicated that the number of iteration should be relatively low such that the computational complexity is low as well.

$$f(x) = \sum_{i=1}^{n} \frac{x_i^2}{4000} - \prod_{i=1}^{n} \cos\left(\frac{x_i}{\sqrt{i}}\right) + 1 \tag{9}$$

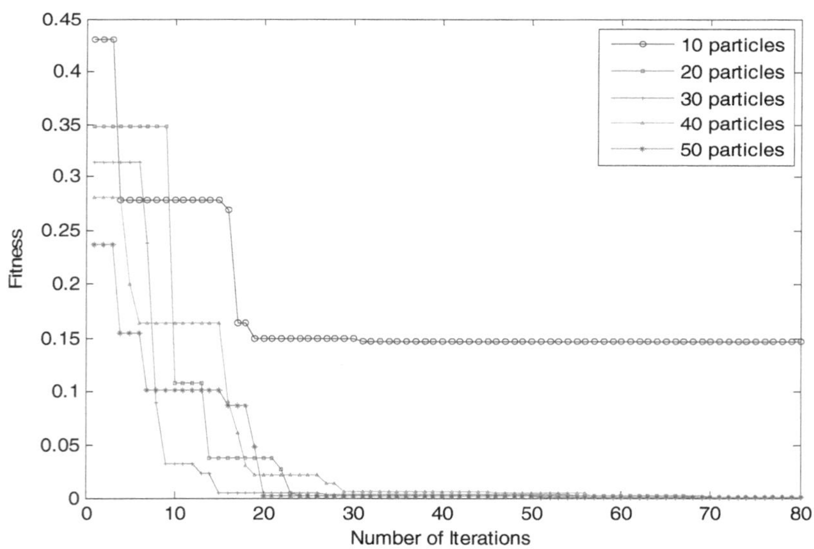

Fig. 2. Convergence of test function (grienwack) with number of iterations

Test Case 2

When considering the rastrigin test function, it contains cosine function which makes it multimodal and more complex in selecting the optima at a particular time. The fitness decreases with increase in number of iterations. As can be noticed from fig. 3

that it large search space but the algorithm can be able to achieve optimal performance within the first 8 iterations. The high convergence nature of the PSO algorithm will be useful in delay sensitive application. Based on the experimentation, less computational time and high efficiency can be achieve using the multi-objective PSO when each swarm is considered as objective function.

$$f(x) = 10.n + \sum_{i=1}^{n} (x_i^2 - 10.\cos(2.\pi.x_i)) \tag{10}$$

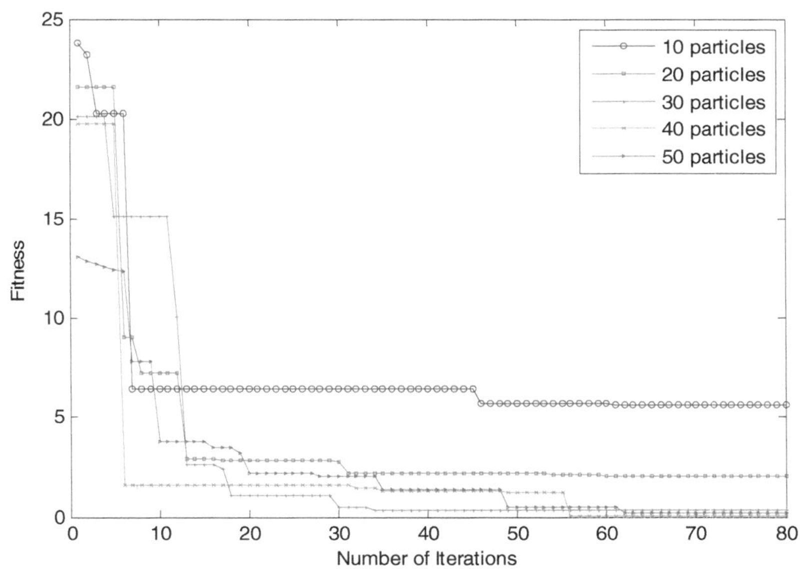

Fig. 3. Convergence of test function (rastrigin) with number of iterations

Table 2. Computational Complexity

S/No.	**No. of Iterations**		**No. of individuals**	
	Iteration	*Complexity (ms)*	*No. of particles*	*Complexity (ms)*
1.	20	16	20	16
2.	40	47	40	31
3.	60	48	60	47
4.	80	64	80	64

In order to determine the minimum number of iteration required to achieve convergence and at the same considering the time constraint for the delay sensitive application as well. It has been observed that multi-objective PSO can eventually determine the pareto optimal sets within a very short period of time. The performance of the multi-objective optimizer has been tested under different number of iterations to achieve optimal result. The computational time has been relatively low when compared to other optimization algorithms which require long period of time before it converges.

The ability to find and select the best optimal solution within the time limit is very important for delay sensitive application. In order to determine the efficiency of the developed scheme, the computational time is used as a metric to measure the scheme performance based on time. The computational time will tell about the amount of power used by the processor to execute the test algorithm. In a nutshell, the complexity of the optimization algorithm can be computed using the equation (11). As can be notice that the complexity is a function of the number of objection function and number of particles [18]. The performance of the low complexity multi-objective PSO-based algorithm outperforms single objective PSO-based algorithm described in [21].

Therefore, the complexity increases with increase in M and N. The complexity of the developed algorithm is tested using computational time required to execute the algorithm.

$$O(MN) \tag{11}$$

Where M is the number of objective function and N represents the number of parameters.

5 Conclusions

In this paper, we proposed an efficient strategy to select best possible optimal solution for multi criteria decision problem in order to ultimately support delay sensitive application. This is extremely important and challenging to conveniently optimize the network performance within the application time deadline especially in multimedia network. More importantly, the multi-objective optimization algorithm has shown more promising result for achieving high convergence with low complexity. The main primary objective is to fully explore the capability and potential of evolutionary computing for time and mission-critical applications. The proposed approach is effective, simple, flexible and high searching capability which can potentially meet with stringent time requirement. Our future work will adapts this technique in developing multi-objective cross layer optimization for wireless video streaming application.

Acknowledgement. The authors would like to thank all those who contributed toward making this research successful. Also, we would like to thanks to all the reviewers for their insightful comment. This work was sponsored by the research management unit (RMC), Universiti Teknologi Malaysia.

References

1. Beale, G.O., Cook, G.: Optimal digital simulation of aircraft via random search techniques. AIAA J. Guid. Control 1(4), 237–241 (1978)
2. Fonseca, C.M., Fleming, P.J.: Genetic algorithms for multiobjective optimization: Formulation, discussion and generalization. In: Proceedings of the Fifth International Conference on GeneticAlgorithms, San Mateo, CA, USA (1993)

3. Coello, C.A.C.: A comprehensive survey of evolutionary-based multiobjective optimization techniques. Knowl. Inf. Syst. An. Int. J. 1(3) (1999)
4. Horn, J., Nafpliotis, N., Goldberg, D.E.: A niched Pareto genetic algorithm for multiobjective optimization. In: Proceedings of the First IEEE Conference on Evolutionary Computation, IEEE World Congresson Computational Intelligence. IEEE Press, Piscataway (1994)
5. Srinivas, N., Deb, K.: Multiobjective optimization using nondominated sorting in genetic algorithms. Evolutionary Computation 2(3) (1995)
6. Knowles, J., Corne, D.: The Pareto archived evolution strategy: A new baseline algorithm for Pareto multiobjective optimisation. In: Proceedings of the 1999 Congress on Evolutionary Computation. IEEE Press, Piscataway (1999)
7. Laumanns, M., Zitzler, E., Thiele, L.: A unified model for multiobjective evolutionary algorithms with Elitism. In: Proceedings of the 2000 Congress on Evolutionary Computation. IEEE Press, Piscataway (2000)
8. Hanne, T.: On the convergence of multiobjective evolutionary algorithms. European Journal of Operational Research 117 (1999)
9. Laumanns, M., Thiele, L., Deb, K., Zitzler, E.: "On the convergence and diversity preservation properties of multi-objective evolutionary algorithms. ETH, Lausanne, Switzerland (June 2001)
10. Everson, R.M., Fieldsend, J.E., Singh, S.: Full elite sets for multiobjective optimisation. In: Parmee, I.C. (ed.) Adaptive Computing in Design and Manufacture V. Springer, New York (2002)
11. Kennedy, J., Eberhart, R.C.: Particle swarm optimization. In: Proc. IEEE International Conference on Neural Networks, Australia (1995)
12. Kennedy, J., Eberhart, R.C.: Swarm Intelligence. Morgan Kauffman Publishers, California (2001)
13. Coello, C.A., Pulido, G.T., Lechuga, M.S.: Handling Multiple Objectives with Particle Swarm Optimization. IEEE, Evolutionary Computing (2004)
14. Huang, V.L., Suganthan, P.N., Liang, J.J.: Comprehensive Learning Particle Swarm Optimizer for Solving Multi-objective Optimization Problems. International Journal of Intelligent System (2006)
15. Zitzler, E., Laumanns, M., Bleuler, S.: A tutorial on evolutionary multi-objective optimization (2004)
16. Coello, C.A.C., Lamont, G.B.: Application of Multi-objective Evolutionary Algorithms. World Scientific Publishing (2004)
17. Van der Schaar, M., Chou, P.A.: Multimedia over IP and Wireless network: Compression, networking and systems. Academic Press (2007)
18. Baguda, Y.S., Fisal, N., Shuaibu, D.S.: Multi-objective Particle Swarm Optimization for Wireless video Support. International Journal of Recent Trends in Engineering (2009)
19. Hu, X., Eberhart, R.C.: Multiobjective optimization using dynamic neighborhood particle swarm optimization. In: Proceedings of the Evolutionary Computation (2002)
20. Parsopoulos, K., Vrahatis, M.: Particle swarm optimization method in multiobjective problems. ACM (2002)
21. El-Saleh, A.A., Ismail, M., Viknesh, R., Mark, C.C., Chan, M.L.: Particle Swarm Optimization for Mobile Network Design. IEICE Electronic Express 6 (September 2009)

Irregular Total Labeling of Butterfly and Benes Networks

Indra Rajasingh[1], Bharati Rajan[1], and S. Teresa Arockiamary[2]

[1] Department of Mathematics, Loyola College, Chennai 600 034, India
[2] Department of Mathematics, Stella Maris College, Chennai 600 086, India
teresa_aroc@yahoo.co.in

Abstract. Given a graph G (V, E), a labeling $\partial: V \cup E \rightarrow \{1, 2\ldots k\}$ is called an *edge irregular total k-labeling* if for every pair of distinct edges uv and xy, $\partial(u) + \partial(uv) + \partial(v) \neq \partial(x) + \partial(y) + \partial(xy)$. The minimum k for which G has an edge irregular total k-labeling is called the *total edge irregularity strength* of G. In this paper we examine the total edge irregularity strength of the butterfly and the benes network.

Keywords: Irregular total labeling, interconnection network, butterfly network, benes network, graph labeling.

1 Introduction

Labeled graphs are becoming an increasingly useful family of Mathematical Models for a wide range of applications. While the qualitative labelings of graph elements have inspired research in diverse fields of human enquiry such as conflict resolution in social psychology, electrical circuit theory and energy crisis, these labelings have led to quite intricate fields of application such as coding theory problems, including the design of good radar location codes, synch-set codes; missile guidance codes and convolution codes with optimal autocorrelation properties. Labeled graphs have also been applied in determining ambiguities in X-Ray crystallographic analysis, to design communication network addressing systems, in determining optimal circuit layouts, radio-Astronomy., etc.

For a graph G (V, E), Baca et al.[1] define a labeling $\partial: V \cup E \rightarrow \{1, 2\ldots k\}$ to be an *edge irregular k-labeling* of the graph G if $\partial(u) + \partial(uv) + \partial(v) \neq \partial(x) + \partial(xy) + \partial(y)$ for every pair of distinct edges uv and xy. The minimum k for which the graph G has an edge irregular total k-labeling is called the *total edge irregularity strength* of the graph G, and is denoted by $tes(G)$. For a graph $G(V, E)$, with E not empty, it has been proved that $\left\lceil\frac{|E|+2}{3}\right\rceil \leq tes(G) \leq |E|$; $tes(G) \geq \frac{\Delta(G)+1}{2}$ and $tes(G) \leq |E| - \Delta(G)$ [1]. Brandt et al [2] conjecture that for any graph G other than K_5, $tes(G) = max\left\{\left\lceil\frac{\Delta(G)+1}{2}\right\rceil, \left\lceil\frac{|E|+2}{3}\right\rceil\right\}$. The conjecture has been proved to be true for all trees [5], and for large graphs whose maximum degree is not too large relative to its order and size [2]. Jendrol, Miskul, and Sotak [4] proved that $tes(K_5) = 5$ for $n \geq 6$,

A. Abd Manaf et al. (Eds.): ICIEIS 2011, Part III, CCIS 253, pp. 284–293, 2011.

$tes(K_n) = \left\lceil \frac{n^2-n+4}{6} \right\rceil$; and that $tes(K_{m,n}) = \left\lceil \frac{mn+2}{3} \right\rceil$. More complete results on irregular total labelings can be seen in the survey paper by Gallian [4]. In this paper we prove that $tes(BF(r)) = \left\lceil \frac{r2^{r+1}+2}{3} \right\rceil$ and $tes(B(r)) = \left\lceil \frac{r2^{r+2}+2}{3} \right\rceil$ where $BF(r)$ denotes the butterfly network of dimension r and $B(r)$ denotes the benes network of dimension r proving *Brandt's conjecture* [2] for these networks.

2 The Butterfly Network

Interconnection network is a scheme that connects the units of a multiprocessing system. It plays a central role in determining the overall performance of a multicomputer system. An interconnection network is modeled as a graph in which vertices represent the processing elements and edges represent the communication channel between them.

Interconnection networks play an important role for the architecture of parallel computers and PC-Clusters or Networks of Workstations. Much of the early work on interconnection networks was motivated by the needs of the communications industry, particularly in the context of telephone switching. With the growth of the computer industry, applications for interconnection networks within computing machines began to become apparent. Amongst the first of these was the sorting of sequences of numbers, but as interest in parallel processing grew, a large number of networks were proposed for processor to memory and processor to processor interconnection.

Butterfly network is an important and well known topological structure of interconnection networks. It is a bounded-degree derivative of the hypercube which aims at overcoming some drawbacks of hypercube. It is used to perform a method to illustrate *FFT*(Fast Fourier Transform), which is intensively used in the field of *signal processing*.

Definition. The set of nodes V of an r-dimensional Butterfly $BF(r)$ corresponds to the set of pairs $[w,i]$, where i is the dimension or level of a node ($0 \le i \le r$) and w is an r-bit binary number that denotes the row of the node. Two nodes $[w, i]$ and $[w', i']$ are linked by an edge if and only if $i' = i+1$ and either

i) w and w' are identical, or
ii) w and w' differ in precisely the ith bit.

The r- dimensional butterfly $BF(r)$ has $(r + 1) 2^r$ nodes and $r2^{r+1}$ edges.

Efficient representation for Butterfly and Benes networks have been obtained by Manuel et al.[10]. The Butterfly in Figure 1(a) is drawn in *normal representation*; an alternative representation, called the *diamond representation*, is given in Figure 1(b). By a diamond we mean a cycle of length 4. Two nodes $[w, i]$ and $[w', i]$ are said to be mirror images of each other if w and w' differ precisely in the first bit. The removal of level 0 vertices $v_1, v_2, \ldots, v_{2^r}$ of $BF(r)$ gives two subgraphs H_1 and H_2 of $BF(r)$, each isomorphic to $BF(r - 1)$. Since $\{v_1, v_2, \ldots, v_{2^r}\}$ is a vertex cut of $BF(r)$, the vertices are called *binding vertices* of $BF(r)$.

A 4-cycle xv_1yv_2x in $BF(r)$ where $x \in V(H_1)$, $y \in V(H_2)$ and v_1, v_2 are binding vertices of $BF(r)$ is called a *binding diamond*. The edges of the binding diamond are called *binding edges*. For convenience, we call the edges (x, v_i) as *upper binding edges* and edges (y, v_i) as *lower binding edges*. There are exactly two binding vertices of $BF(r)$ adjacent to a binding vertex of $BF(r - 1)$. One is called the *left binding vertex* and the other is called the *right binding vertex*. See Figure 2.

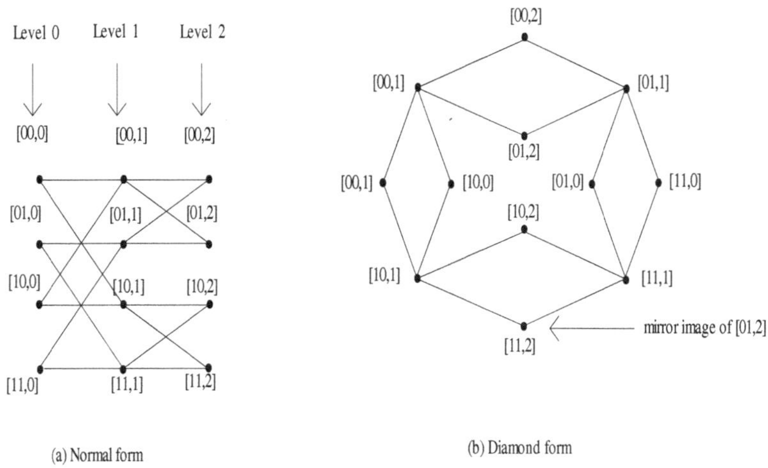

Fig. 1. Binary labeling of a 2-dimensional butterfly

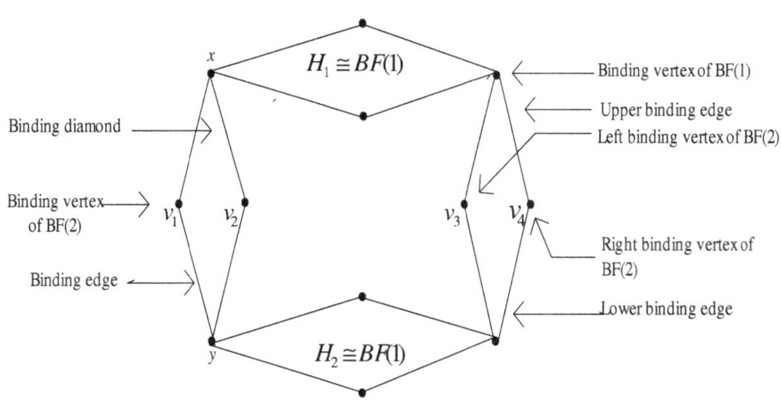

Fig. 2. Binding vertices and binding edges of $BF(2)$

2.1 Main Results

We begin with a few known results on $tes(G)$.

Theorem 1. [2] Every multigraph $G = (V, E)$ without loops, of order n, size m, and maximum degree $0 < \Delta < \frac{10^{-3}m}{\sqrt{8n}}$ satisfies $tes(G) = \left\lceil \frac{|E|+2}{3} \right\rceil$.

Theorem 2. [2] Every graph $G = (V, E)$ of order n, minimum degree $\delta > 0$, and maximum degree Δ such that $\frac{\Delta}{\delta} < \frac{10^{-3}\sqrt{n}}{4\sqrt{2}}$ satisfies $es(G) = \left\lceil \frac{m+2}{3} \right\rceil$.

Theorem 3. [2] For every integer $\Delta \geq 1$, there is some $n(\Delta)$ such that every graph $G = (V, E)$ without isolated vertices with order $n \geq n(\Delta)$, size m, and maximum degree at most Δ satisfies $tes(G) = \left\lceil \frac{m+2}{3} \right\rceil$.

It is easy to verify that the conditions in Theorem 1 are not satisfied for $BF(r)$, $r \leq 15$. Again condition in Theorem 2 is not satisfied for $BF(r)$, for any r. Hence it is interesting to study $tes(BF(r))$. The following algorithm determines tes of an r-dimensional butterfly network, $BF(r)$, $r \geq 3$.

2.2 Algorithm *tes*(*BF*(*r*))

Input : r- dimensional butterfly $BF(r)$, $r \geq 3$.

Algorithm

1. Label the vertices and edges of $BF(3)$ as shown in Figure 3.
2. Label the vertices and edges of $BF(r)$, $r \geq 4$, inductively as follows:

   Having labeled the vertices and edges of $H_1 \cong BF(r-1)$

   (i) Label the vertices and edges of $H_2 \cong BF(r-1)$ by adding $t = \left\lceil \frac{r2^{r+1}+2}{3} \right\rceil - \left\lceil \frac{(r-1)2^r+2}{3} \right\rceil$ to the vertex labels and $s = t - 1$ to the edge labels of H_1.

   (ii) Label the binding vertices of $BF(r)$ from left to right as 't'.

   (iii) Label the upper binding edges from left to right as $x, x+1, x+2, \ldots, x+(2^r-1)$ where $x = 3\left\lceil \frac{(r-1)2^r+2}{3} \right\rceil + \left\lceil \frac{(r-2)2^{r-1}+2}{3} \right\rceil - \left\lceil \frac{r2^{r+1}+2}{3} \right\rceil$.

   (iv) Label the lower binding edges from left to right as $y, y+1, y+2, \ldots, y+(2^r-1)$ where $y = 2^r - 2\left\lceil \frac{r2^{r+1}+2}{3} \right\rceil + 4\left\lceil \frac{(r-1)2^r+2}{3} \right\rceil + \left\lceil \frac{(r-2)2^{r+1}+2}{3} \right\rceil$.

Output: $tes(BF(r)) = \left\lceil \frac{r2^{r+1}+2}{3} \right\rceil$. Labeling of $BF(4)$ is shown in Figure 4.

Proof of Correctness

We prove the result by induction on r. By actual verification, it is easy to check that the labels given in Figure 3 yield $tes(BF(3)) = 17$. This proves the result when $r = 3$. Assume the result for $BF(r - 1)$. Consider $BF(r)$. Since the labeling of $H_1 \cong BF(r-1)$ is an edge irregular k- labeling, it is clear that the labeling of H_2 obtained by adding a constant to each label of H_1 using 2(i) is also an edge irregular k- labeling.

Let e_r denote the bottom rightmost edge of $BF(r\text{-}1)$ and e_l denote the leftmost top binding edge of $BF(r)$ respectively. If $e_r = (u, v)$ *and* $e_l = (p, q)$ and let $max_{(u,v)\in E(H_1)} \partial(u) + \partial(uv) + \partial(v) = a$ (say). Then label on e_l is

$$\begin{aligned}\partial(p)+\partial(q)+\partial(pq) &= [tes(BF(r\text{-}1))\text{-}tes(BF(r\text{-}2))] + [tes(BF(r))\text{-}tes(BF(r\text{-}1))] + x\\ &= [tes(BF(r\text{-}1))\text{-}tes(BF(r\text{-}2))] + [tes(BF(r))\text{-}tes(BF(r\text{-}1))] +\\ &\quad [3tes(BF(r\text{-}1)) + tes(BF(r\text{-}2))\text{-}tes(BF(r))].\\ &= [3tes(BF(r\text{-}1)) - 1] + 1\\ &= a + 1.\end{aligned}$$

Similarly we can prove that the label on the rightmost bottom binding edge of $BF(r)$ and the leftmost top edge of $BF(r)$ are consecutive. Thus the labels of all upper and lower binding edges are consecutive integers which are distinct.

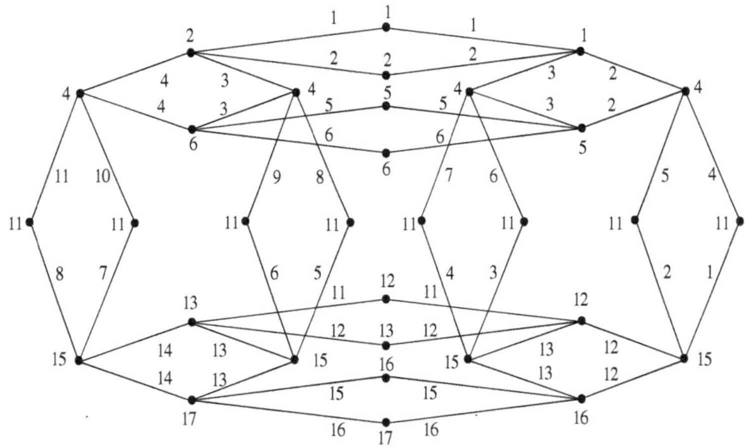

Fig. 3. Edge irregular k-labeling of $BF(3)$ when $k = 17$

3 The Benes Network

The Benes network is similar to the butterfly network, in terms of both its computational power and its network structure. As Butterfly is known for FFT, Benes is known for Permutation Routing. The Butterfly and Benes networks are important multistage interconnection networks, which possess attractive topological properties for communication networks [9]. They have been used in parallel computing systems such as IBM SP1/SP2, MIT transit project, and used as well in the internal structures of optical couplers, e.g., star couplers [7, 9]. The Benes network consists of back-to-back butterflies.

An r- dimensional Benes network has $2r + 1$ levels, each level with 2^r nodes. The level zero to level r vertices in the network form an r- dimensional butterfly. The middle level of the Benes network is shared by these butterflies. An r- dimensional Benes is denoted by B(r). The r- dimensional Benes has $(2r + 1)2^r$ nodes and $r2^{r+2}$ edges. See Figure 5.

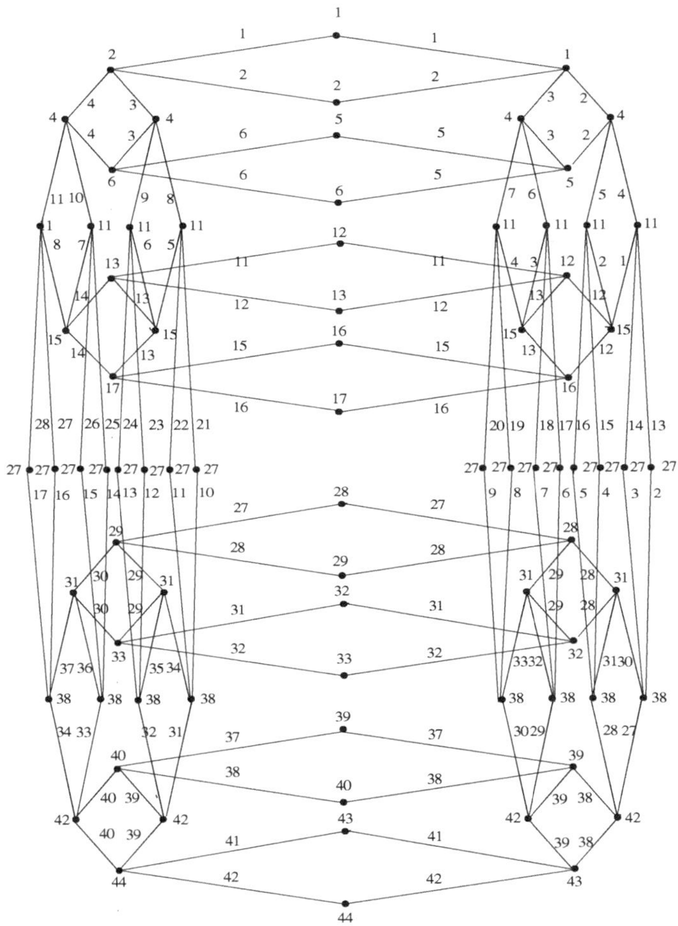

Fig. 4. Edge irregular *k*-labeling of $BF(4)$ when $k = 44$

The removal of level 0 vertices $v_1, v_2, \ldots, v_{2^r}$ and level $2r$ vertices $\{v_{2^r+1}, v_{2^r+2}, \ldots, v_{2^{r+1}}\}$ of $B(r)$ gives two subgraphs H_1 and H_2 of $B(r)$, each isomorphic to $B(r - 1)$. As in Butterfly Networks, we may define binding vertices, binding edges and binding diamonds for a Benes Network. See Figure 6.

As in the case of $BF(r)$, we proceed to prove that $tes(B(r)) = \left\lceil \frac{r2^{r+2}+2}{3} \right\rceil$.

Algorithm $\boldsymbol{tes(B(r))}$

Input **:** r- dimensional Benes $B(r)$, $r \geq 2$.

Algorithm

1. Label the vertices and edges of $B(2)$ as shown in Figure 7.
2. Label the vertices and edges of $B(r)$, $r \geq 3$ inductively as follows:

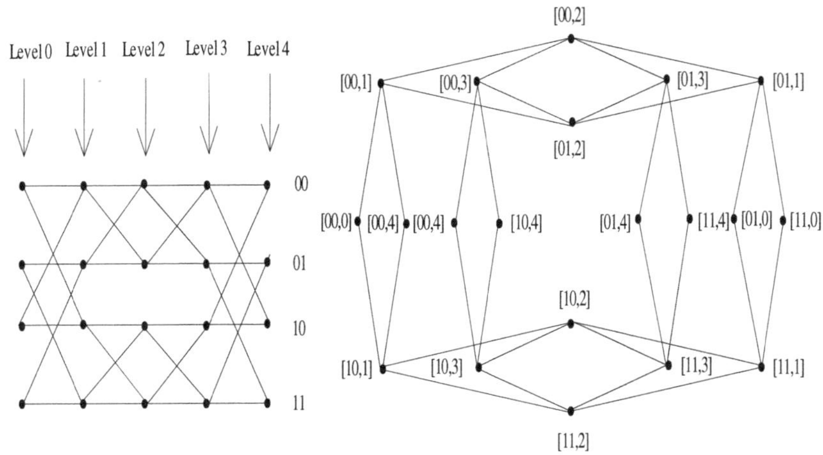

(a) Normal form (b) Diamond form

Fig. 5. Binary labeling of a 2-dimensional Benes network

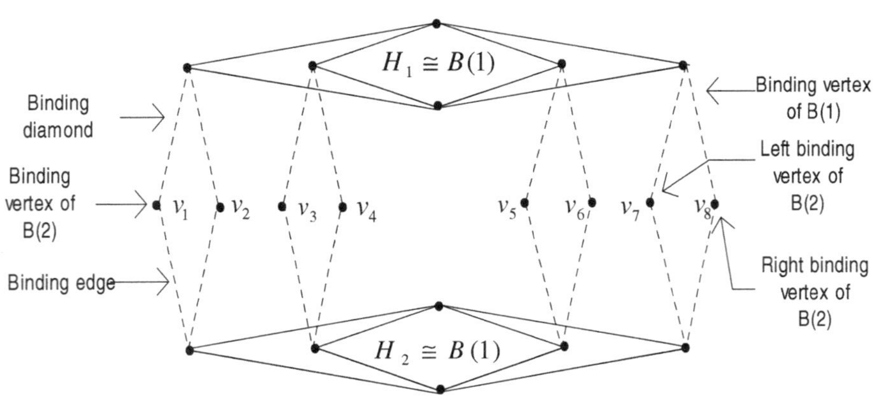

Fig. 6. Binding vertices and binding edges of $B(2)$

Having labeled the vertices and edges of $H_1 \cong B(r-1)$

(i) Label the vertices and edges of $H_2 \cong B(r-1)$by adding $c = \left\lceil \frac{r2^{r+2}+2}{3} \right\rceil - \left\lceil \frac{(r-1)2^{r+1}+2}{3} \right\rceil$ to the vertex labels and $d = c + 1$ to the edge labels of H_1.

(ii) Label the binding vertices of $B(r)$ from left to right as 'c '.
(iii) Label the upper binding edges from left to right as $x, x+1, \ldots, x+(2^{r+1}-1)$ where $x = 3\left\lceil\frac{(r-1)2^{r+1}+2}{3}\right\rceil + \left\lceil\frac{(r-2)2^{r}+2}{3}\right\rceil - \left\lceil\frac{r2^{r+2}+2}{3}\right\rceil$.
(iv) Label the lower binding edges from left to right as $y, y+1, \ldots, y+(2^{r+1}-1)$

$$\text{where} = 2^{r+1} - 2\left\lceil\frac{r2^{r+2}+2}{3}\right\rceil + 4\left\lceil\frac{(r-1)2^{r+1}+2}{3}\right\rceil + \left\lceil\frac{(r-2)2^{r}+2}{3}\right\rceil.$$

Output: $tes(B(r)) = \left\lceil\frac{r2^{r+2}+2}{3}\right\rceil$. Labeling of $B(3)$ is shown in Figure 8.

Proof of Correctness

We prove the result by induction on r. By actual verification, it is easy to check that the labels given in Figure 7 yield $tes(B(2)) = 12$. This proves the result when $r = 2$. Assume the result for $B(r-1)$. Consider $B(r)$. Since the labeling of $H_1 \cong B(r-1)$ is an edge irregular k- labeling, it is clear that the labeling of H_2 obtained by adding a constant to each label of H_1 using 2(i) is also an edge irregular k- labeling. Let e_r denote the bottom rightmost edge of $B(r$-1) and e_l denote the leftmost top binding

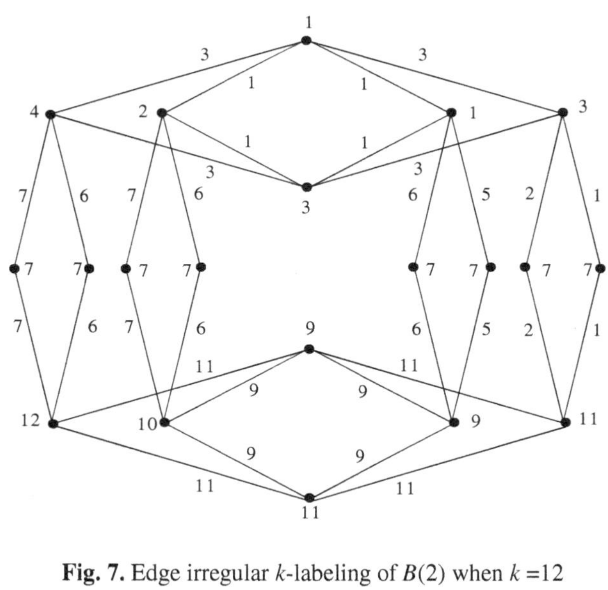

Fig. 7. Edge irregular k-labeling of $B(2)$ when k =12

edge of $B(r)$ respectively. If $e_r = (u, v)$ and $e_l = (p, q)$ then let $max_{(u,v)\in E(H_1)} \partial(u) + \partial(uv) + \partial(v) = b$ (say). The label on e_l is

$$\begin{aligned}\partial(p)+\partial(q)+\partial(pq) &= [tes(B(r-1)) - tes(B(r-2)) - 1] + [tes(B(r)) - tes(B(r-1))] + x.\\ &= [tes(B(r))-tes(B(r-2)) - 1] + 3tes(B(r-1)) + tes(B(r-2))-tes(B(r))\\ &= 3tes(B(r-1)) - 1\\ &= 3tes(B(r-1)) - 2 + 1.\\ &= b + 1.\end{aligned}$$

Similarly let e_m denote the bottom rightmost binding edge of $B(r)$ and e_n denote the leftmost edge of $B(r)$ respectively. If $e_m = (u, v)$ and $e_n = (p, q)$, then label on e_m is

$$\begin{aligned}\partial(u)+\partial(v)+\partial(uv) &= [tes(B(r)) - tes(B(r\text{-}1))] + [tes(B(r)) - tes(B(r\text{-}1)) + tes(B(r\text{-}1)) \\ &\quad - tes(B(r\text{-}2)) - 1] + [tes(B(r)) - tes(B(r\text{-}1)) - 4]. \\ &= 3\, tes(B(r)) - 2tes(B(r\text{-}1)) - tes(B(r\text{-}2)) - 5 \\ &= a \text{ (say).}\end{aligned}$$

Label on e_n is

$$\begin{aligned}\partial(p)+\partial(q)+\partial(pq) &= [tes(B(r)) - tes(B(r\text{-}1)) + 1] + [tes(B(r)) - tes(B(r\text{-}2)) - 6] + \\ &\quad [tes(B(r)) - tes(B(r\text{-}1)) + 1] \\ &= [3tes(B(r)) - tes(B(r\text{-}2)) - 2tes(B(r\text{-}1)) - 4] \\ &= 3tes(B(r)) - tes(B(r\text{-}2)) - 2tes(B(r\text{-}1)) - 5 + 1 \\ &= a + 1.\end{aligned}$$

Thus the labels of all upper and lower binding edges are consecutive integers which are distinct.

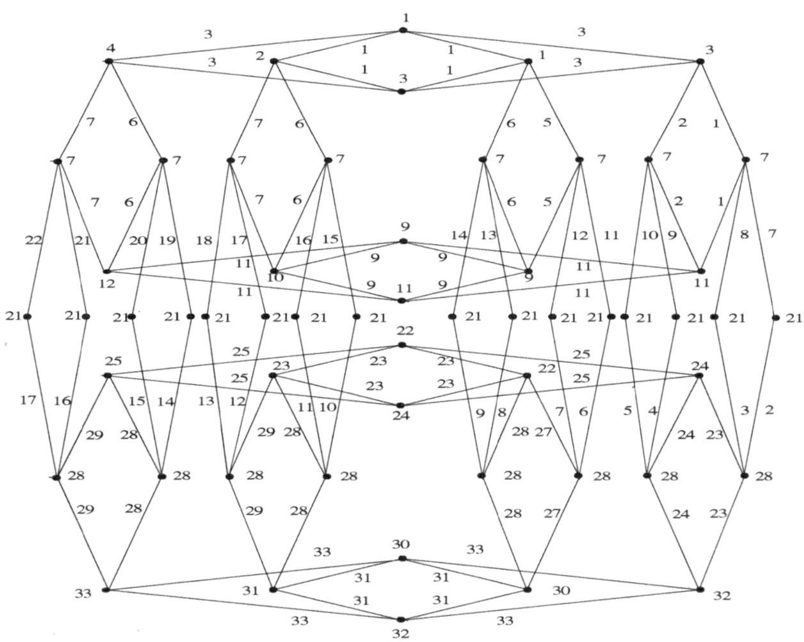

Fig. 8. Edge irregular k-labeling of $B(3)$ when $k = 33$

4 Conclusion

In this paper, we have obtained the total edge irregularity strength of butterfly networks and benes networks. This problem is under investigation for mesh and honeycomb networks.

References

1. Baca, M., Jendrol, S., Miller, M., Ryan, J.: On irregular total labeling. Discrete Math. 307, 1378–1388 (2007)
2. Brandt, S., Miskuf, J., Rautenbach, D.: On a conjecture about edge irregular total labeling. J. Graph Theory 57, 333–343 (2008)
3. Dimitz, J.H., Garnick, D.K., Gyarfas, A.: On total edge irregularity strength of the m x n grid. J. Graph Theory 16, 355–374 (1992)
4. Gallian, J.A.: A dynamic survey of graph labeling. Electronic Journal of Combinatorics, #DS6 (2010)
5. Jendrol, S., Missuf, J., Sotak, R.: Total edge irregularity strength of complete graphs and complete bipartite graphs. Elec. Notes Discr. Math. 28, 281–285 (2007)
6. Xu, J.: Topological Structure and Analysis of Interconnection Networks, China (2001)
7. Konstantinidou, S.: The selective Extras Butterfly. IEEE Transactions on Very Large Scale Integration Systems, I (1993)
8. Miskuf, J., Jendrol, S.: On total edge irregularity strength of the grids. Tatra Mt. Math. Publ. 36, 147–151 (2007)
9. Liu, X., Gu, Q.P.: Multicasts on WDM All-Optical Butterfly Networks. Journal of Information Science and Engineering 18, 1049–1058 (2002)
10. Manuel, P., Abd-El-Barr, M.I., Rajasingh, I., Rajan, B.: An Efficient Representation of Benes Networks its applications. In: Proc. of the Sixteenth Australasian Workshop on Combinatorial Algorithms, Ballarat, Australia, pp. 217–230 (2005)

A Process Model of KMS Adoption and Diffusion in Organization: An Exploratory Study

Sureena Matayong and Ahmad Kamil Bin Mahmood

Department of Computer and Information Sciences,
Universiti Teknologi Petronas, Malaysia
smatayong@gmail.com, kamilmh@petronas.com.my

Abstract. Today, many organizations have implemented knowledge management system (KMS) to facilitate activities in achieving their business objective and goal. Despite of the benefits that have been given by the system, its adoption and frequent use remain challenges. As acknowledged that KMS adoption is a complicated and context dependent, it is merit to investigate in understanding the phenomenon in a real setting. The purpose of this paper is to understand the nature of KMS adoption and diffusion in organization with the aim to provide recommendations which helping to increase adoption and utilization. The generated grounded results offer not only the identified factors and processes that could possibly lead to adoption but also those that make its diffusion and finally become part of daily practice.

Keywords: KMS, adoption and diffusion, an exploratory study.

1 Introduction

Now, many organizations are in the cross road of overcoming their "knowledge deficit" due to redeployment and retirement of employees [1]. This couple with the challenges from implementing KMS will certainly make the situation even more critical. Though managing knowledge through IT applications is considered as a new phenomenon and challenge [2], many organizations started their KMS by making significant investments in IT [3]. Despite, the large amount of money spent, the solely focus on technology does not promise its success [4]. As a result, the organizational efforts as well as their resources have been wasted [5]. It is estimated that the budget range for KMS implementation is from $25,000 to $50,000,000[6] but due to its failure, the Fortune 500 companies report that they lost at least $31.5 billion annually [7]. Taking into consideration of KMS adoption is one of the most critical factors to KMS success [8], currently it is the major concern for both practitioners and researchers to investigate and understand the phenomenon [9].

The main issue of this study concerns about KMS adoption and diffusion process in organization. Though there are several studies related to this topic, but those studies seem to concentrate more only on factors or variables to its adoption and diffusion [10][11][12][13][14]. However, they paid less attention on how those factors and variables affect its process. On the other hand, the adoption of KMS in organization is

A. Abd Manaf et al. (Eds.): ICIEIS 2011, Part III, CCIS 253, pp. 294–305, 2011.

considered as multifaceted and context dependent which related to such as users' experiences [15][16]. The experiences of users are the sets of eccentric to one's behavioral environment therefore it is suggested to develop autonomously [9]. While the literature on KMS adoption is scarcity at the same time the focus on its comprehensive study is very few [6][17]. Besides, those studies did not provide a theoretical understanding of its adoption process in regard to social context [18][6]. Subsequently, the study area has not been matured. For that reason, it is worthy to explore some concepts especially conducting the case at different context and process background.

In this study, a qualitative approach is taken within an interpretive case study and the context of action and the experience of individuals in a single, real-life setting are considered [19][20]. This will provide a complementary perspective to the existing studies within the oil and gas company in Malaysia. The exploratory case study with GT process of analysis is selected as the alternative methods to understand the process and context of KMS adoption and diffusion of this particular setting. In addition, the study will identify and explore its various influences and provides further insights into those influences [21].

2 Background on the Research Area

2.1 Knowledge Management System

KMS is an IT-based system developed to support and enhance KM processes of storage, sharing, retrieval, creation and application of knowledge [9][22]. The database management systems provide query languages as a tool to enhance knowledge storage and retrieval. Besides, the web applications allow online communities to share their common interest. Moreover, expert systems offer knowledge discovery and data mining to elicit knowledge from repositories [23]. Finally, workflow automation systems and rule-based expert systems are among the systems support the knowledge application, which embedded knowledge into organization routines and enforcing well-specified organization procedures [24].

Nevertheless, the main concern of KM is to make the right knowledge to the right person at the right time [25]. The organizations have to make sure of acquiring knowledge from experts and make it available throughout organizations when there is needed [26]. This is not an easy task and it is even more difficult when the majority of necessary knowledge is generated from many sources and it takes place beyond the formal structures with connections from other people [27]. Yet, these obstacles has turned down when ICT provided the solutions to facilitate almost all knowledge processes across organizations [4]. Throughout the decades, there are various technologies have been deployed for KM purpose and among those technologies are intranet, DBMS, groupware, search engines etc [6] These applications provided several applications, which embed in different business processes. Many researchers coincided that KMS implementation does not only facilitate the activities but also offers several benefits such as relevant, accurate, and timely manners [26]. In addition, it has brought organizations to move forward in quality improvement and business excellence, which eventually contributing to company competitive advantage.

At the earlier stage, organizations focused strongly on IT for KMS implementation. It started with simple access to the knowledge resource from building knowledge based repositories. Later there was exchange between users through collaborative interaction and learning by doing, which known as social software [28]. As a result, it could help organizations to learn and create not only creative solutions, but also radical innovations in the form of new tools, techniques, approaches, templates, and methodologies [29]. Through this accomplishment, KMS has been implemented in any industries and almost all organizations to achieve their goals. This led to the growth of its implementation in organization is at a rapid pace worldwide. Apparently, one system is not for all therefore it is no single approach that fits all industry. Recently, there are many studies conducted to understand the development of system in different disciplines and industrial types. In supporting and carrying out KM, the typology of system is identified broadly to architecture, size, knowledge type and functionality. The architecture is categorized to centralized or decentralized while size refers to platforms or application system. Knowledge type is classified to integrative/explicit or interactive/tacit. And functionality means of knowledge process; discovery, capture, sharing and application. As a summary, the development of KMS at this stage is related to design for suitable and appropriate tools to businesses need of various industries and organizations.

Broadly, there are 2 types of KMS approaches, hard and soft approaches. The hard part is about developing tools from IT while soft part focus on people essentially means of social mechanism [30]. These are described to technical and social perspective known as socio-technical aspects which is the combination of technology, organization, culture, knowledge and people. The recent findings have revealed that the successful implementation of KMS involves technical and social aspects [4].

However, the role of IT should not be over emphasized, and at the same time it should not be ignored, and beyond that there should be the intervention of the human component. Some empirical study reveals that IT plays only a part for users to share knowledge by using the system while social factors play the main role [9]. Overall, design patterns from the social sciences are very useful for providing systematic and approaches in system development. In addition, the system development to motivate some activities in working environment has also taken benefits from social science findings [31]. As supported by Kuo and Lee, a good KMS system is not only about the design but also the outputs and its balance with user that system could provide [25]. According to He et al., KMS is viewed as a social system based on IT support. As technology is not the main component of KMS to success, yet leveraging knowledge through ICT is not easy [9]. This has led to the difficulties for KM practitioners to carry out the task. Recently, the researchers and practitioners mainly concern and paid attention to understand the social aspect as the way to move forward for KMS development and success.

2.2 IT Adoption Theories

The KMS is an innovation in the field of IT and its adoption and diffusion rests within the literature of IT adoption. Though there is numerous literature reviews related to this area but their definitions, theories and models are different. The literatures of KMS adoption research have sought to understand the required conditions and motivations, indentified the inhibitors and barriers to KMS as an IT innovation in organization. This kind of knowledge is important to understand and improve technology evaluation and spread at an individual and organizational level. The following are the description of some theories related to IT adoption.

First, innovation diffusion theory of Rogers, he defined innovation as, "An idea, practice, or object that is perceived as new by an individual or other unit of adoption." He described diffusion as, "The process by which an innovation is communicated through certain channels over time among the members of a social system." [32]. Second, the theory of Perceived Characteristics of Innovations (PCI) by Moore and Benbasat [33]. They extended the work of Rogers [34] and Tornatzky and Klein [35] to form (PCI). Third, the theory of social cognitive suggested that the action is influenced by self efficacy, which the adoption and diffusion of innovation in organization will be based on self-efficacy [36]. Forth, The Theory of Reasoned Action (TRA) states that attitudes, beliefs and subjective norms lead to intentions and thereby behaviours. So, they used to study attitudes, beliefs and subjective norms to understand individual intention to adopt the innovation [37]. Fifth, the Theory of Planned Behaviour (TPB) improved TRA by adding behavioural control that involves internal and external factors of individual [38]. Sixth, The Technology Acceptance Model (TAM) also based on TRA to improve the theory [39]. It is very useful to apply for the study of user acceptance level of innovation adoption [40].

3 Methodology

As suggested by Yin, the case study research using the principle of Grounded Theory (GT) method can be designed to counterpart the conditions of the good case study practice. Therefore, this study uses qualitative approach of a single case study and the principles of GT for data collection and data analysis to investigate the phenomena [41]. The main design of qualitative research is generating understanding rather than testing assumptions with the aim to achieve the holistic view of the phenomenon in the case study. In line to this, the process perspective seeks to understand whole components instead of some parts, which focuses entire processes [42]. This viewpoint along with the case study method will facilitate researcher to have possibility to seize the complexity and dynamic of the phenomenon under study in its real life setting as well as to cover the relevant conditions in the context which are related to the phenomenon [43][44].

3.1 Participants

As the purpose of this study is to achieve a theory or model about the process of innovation adoption and diffusion of a KMS, the researchers interpret the perspectives, experiences and voices of people recruited in the sample according to theoretical relevance and purpose [44]. The selection of participants according to research questions is the criterion based sampling while collecting data based on concepts or categories emerged is considered as theoretical sampling [45][46]. The knowledgeable and experienced participants in the area of study are chosen instead of population size [47]. These participants are referred as key informants which they will direct the researchers to identify theoretically the next data to be collected for theory development [48]. The company selected in this study implemented technology for online knowledge sharing via virtual CoPs embedded in an overall knowledge management system. Therefore, the researcher identified different levels of administrators for the research sample. The diversity and variety of respondents represent a trustworthy population for theoretical saturation. This means that the categories eventually developed for the model would be dense along with the variations and processes.

3.2 The Study Design

The design for this study began with a broad literature review. Then the researcher identified a substantive area of interest. A more focused literature review followed wherein the researcher evaluated the most suitable research methodology and selected GT. The researcher came up with the problem statement and research objectives and began the field study with unstructured (open-ended) questions, which later became semi-structured questions as the interviews proceeded. The researcher conducted theoretical sampling, and interviewees were selected progressively. The researcher then collected the data until saturation and data analysis followed. Last, the researcher created diagrams and models grounded in the data. See Figure 1 for the process and design in this study.

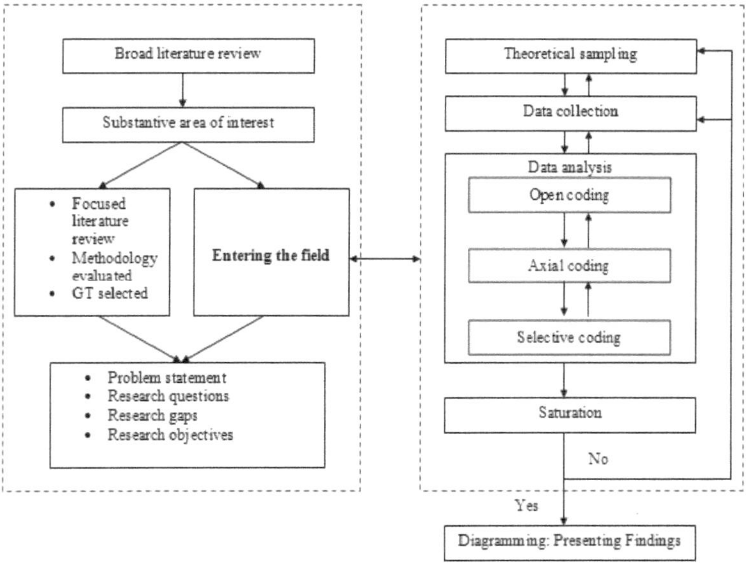

Fig. 1. The Study Process and Design

3.3 Data Collection

At the very beginning, the researchers interviewed 3 participants who were asked open-ended questions in an attempt to understand how KMS adoption and diffusion process occurred and the influences that affect the process and what are those processes. The researchers started with managers in different operating units and departments to get their views and experiences. After this initial stage, the concepts emerged and the next participants were selected based on categorical development and the emerging theory. These managers helped introduce the researcher to the persons to contact for the next interviews. At this time the researcher used theoretical sampling and the questions asked are semi-structured. When the data is saturated, the researchers stop collecting the data because there is nothing new added to the categories that had discovered [46][49]. All the interviews are tape recorded and later transcript into text for data analysis.

The first data collection started in August 2009, and the participants were invited through electronic mail. The interviews were conducted at the participants' offices located at different states in Malaysia. The following Table 1 includes the procedures for collecting data.

Table 1. Data Collection Procedures

• Theoretical sampling
• Unstructured & semi-structured interviews
• Open-ended & semi-structured questions
• Note taking during interviews
• Tape recordings
• Transcriptions
• Memos

3.4 Data Preparation

The researcher prepared the data by transcribing the interviews recorded in an mp3. Case by case the researcher typed and input the interviews into a computerized qualitative analytical tool known as ATLAS.TI. The researcher and a native speaker cleaned the data by English editing and appropriate paragraph formation. ATLAS.TI version 6 is a tool for qualitative analysis of large bodies of textual data. It performs knowledge management for researchers by transforming transcription data into useful knowledge. Furthermore, ATLAS.TI helps researchers to explore the complex phenomena hidden in the data. This is because the fundamental design of ATLAS.TI is to develop a tool that effectively supports human interpretation, especially in handling relatively large amounts of research materials, notes and associated theories.

ATLAS.TI offers support to the researcher without taking control of the intellectual process.

ATLAS.TI is designed specifically to use with GT [50]. It allows researchers to link, search and sort data. This tool is also capable of managing interview transcripts, creating codes, and storing quotations and memos. It can produce a network diagram from the categories and help researchers to understand more about the current research issue. This tool helps researchers to upload the interview scripts, identify the codes, create categories and link the categories in order to represent the overall picture of the current research issue as explained in an axial and selective coding process [47].

3.5 Data Analysis

This research employed the technique of constant comparison which is the heart or key process in GT. It allows for the emergence of theory. Constant comparison is the procedure for identifying codes/concepts, categories and themes, as well as, their properties and dimensions [46][49]. The researcher employed the process of constant comparison at each step of the data analysis as noted in Figure 2.

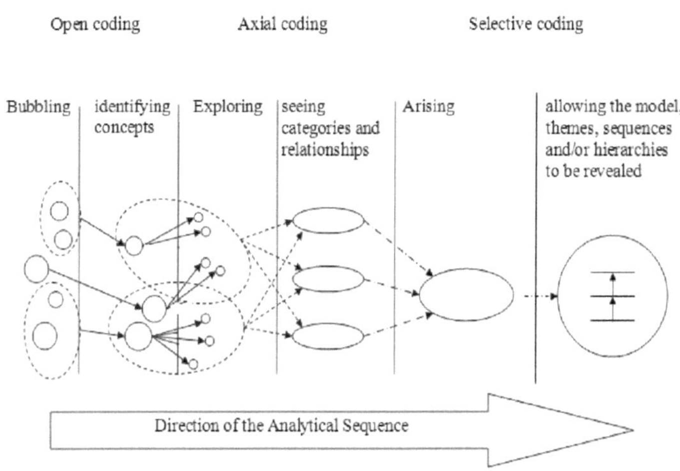

Fig. 2. The GT Analytical Process in the Data Analysis (adapted from Warburton, 2005)

There are 3 level of constant comparative data analysis; open coding, axial coding and selective coding [53]. At the open coding phase is to identify and label the data in the manuscript text. The codification was done with the ATLAS.TI software (see Figure 3). The codes are called in vivo codes because the codifications are from participants' words [51]. However, sometimes the codes were constructed based on concepts gained from the data [52]. Subsequently, a list of codes was compiled and compared against the original transcripts to make sure that the code was used constantly throughout all the transcripts.

These codes also refer to concepts as "words that stand for ideas contained in the data, are the interpretations, the products of analysis" [46]. The similar events, activities, functions, relationships, contexts, influences, outcomes are grouped together and coded to capture similarity. On the other hand, these codes or concepts are developed and identified in terms of their properties and dimensions. Properties are the characteristics that define and describe concepts while dimensions are variations within properties that give specificity and range to concepts [46]. The next step in this level was to compare the codes or concepts against each other for similarities and differences and the categories were created. At the same time, notes were taken of emerging concepts and categories, the ideas-at-hand and the relationships between the codes and categories [53]. Throughout the research process, the researcher also wrote memos to clarify and document the research process. Figure 3 offers a glimpse of the researcher's open-coding process along with the ATLAS.TI program capabilities.

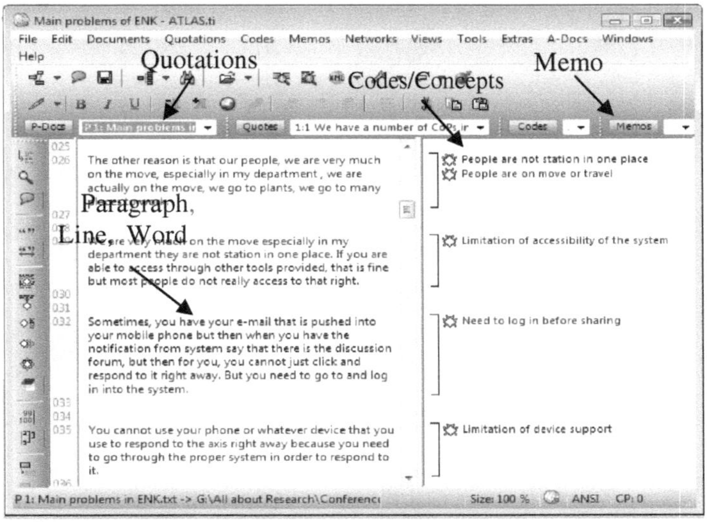

Fig. 3. ATLAS.TI Features

At the phase of axial coding, the researcher connected the relationships of categories and some categories had sub-categories. Indeed, the process of open coding and axial coding was not discrete or sequential rather both processes proceeded together. As the researcher saw the categories, their properties, and dimensions, at same time, the relationships of these categories were sorted out. Some analytical tools applied at this stage included: causal relationships, action/reaction strategies and consequences to link sub-categories to categories. Asking the questions of: where, why, how, and with what result, helped the researcher to unite the loose array of concepts and categories into patterns [46]. The concepts and categories needed to be put back into a pattern because they were unraveled and sorted in the open-coding process.

Finally, the themes were arising and the model was constructed at the selective coding phase. The categories that related to core categories will be selected to build the theory or model. [52].The sequences and hierarchies arose naturally and eventually theory building revealed a basic social process, along with model.

4 Results and Discussions

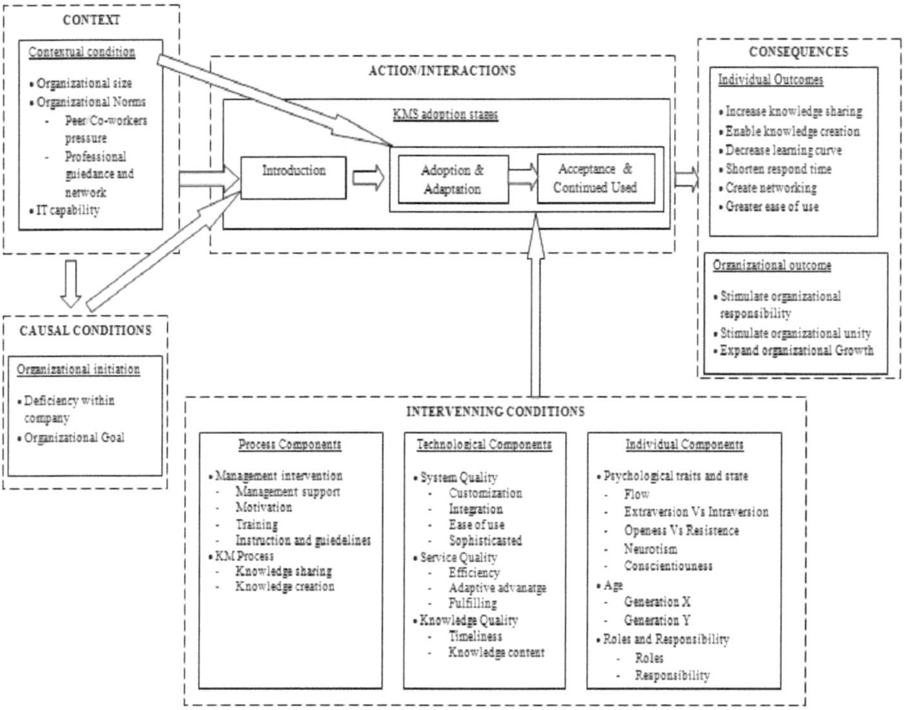

Fig. 4. The Process Model of KMS Adoption and Diffusion

The result on KMS adoption and diffusion reveal that this phenomenon is complex and multi-faceted as shown in figure 4. To illustrate its process model, the researchers apply the empirical examples from qualitative and interpretive case study. Based on pragmatic thinking, the categories are organized into a paradigm model as suggested by Strauss and Corbin when analyzing data [46]. The paradigm model consists of causal conditions, context, intervening conditions, actions/interactions, and consequences.

The causal conditions include the factors that influence KMS adoption. For contingent or authority adoption, the factor that triggers the adoption of KMS is organizational initiation. This is because there is the need for the system to handle deficiency within company as well as to achieve organizational goal. However, there are also some contextual factors that influence the adoption at this stage. There are organizational size, organizational norms such as peer pressure and professional guidance and network, and IT capability in organization. As depict in the model that the causal conditions and contextual conditions will primarily react at the early stages of adoption. An Intervening conditions consist of three components which arose easily and clearly from transcripts of the respondents. There are process, technology and people. The process involves with management intervention and KM process while technology is related to quality of the system which take account of system quality, service quality and knowledge quality. The individual components contain psychological traits/states, age and role and responsibility. The intervention conditions describe the attributes of each component to increase and expedite the adoption at individual level. For example when the person in the state of flow with the system, he/she will adopt the KMS. This section will respond to the later stage of adoption because it is related to user acceptance and adoption for daily use to support activities in organization. Also, the process model supported the finding in the outcome aspect as shown in the consequences box.

In addition, this study extends a new frontier by exploring the stage of adoption and diffusion of a KMS. The study identify 3 levels of its adoption and diffusion stages, there are introduction, adoption and adaptation and acceptance and continued used. Also, the factors that discovered will affect the adoption differently at different level adoption and diffusion stages.

5 Conclusion

As highlighted, the organizations are facing the adoption and diffusion gap related KMS which they are calling upon management team to support and increase the rate of system adoption and utilization. The following factors in this model have the potential to stimulate employees to adopt system, as well as, to enhance knowledge in the field of IT adoption for future scholars to explore. The generated model can also prove useful to understand the process of KMS adoption and diffusion in organization which provide a meaningful idea for organizations to deal with the situation in order to reach their KMS goals.

References

1. Danshy, A.: Consequences of People Shortage, Talent and Technology. SPE International 1(2) (2007)
2. Xu, J., Quaddus, M.: A Reality-Based Guide to KMS Diffusion Actively Involved in Its Adoption; Possess the Necessary Computing Skills. Journal of Management 24(4), 374–389 (2005)
3. Poston, R.S., Speier, C.: Effective use of knowledge management systems: a process model of content ratings and credibility indicators. MIS Quarterly 29(2), 221–244 (2005)
4. Dave, B., Koskela, L.: Collaborative Knowledge Management – A Construction Case Study. Automation in Construction 18(7), 894–902 (2009)
5. Hong, S.J., Thong, J.Y.L., Tam, K.Y.: Understanding continued information technology usage behavior: a comparison of three models in the context of mobile internet. Decision Support Systems 42(3), 1819–1834 (2006)
6. Xu, J., Quaddus, M.: A Six-Stage Model for the Effective Diffusion of Knowledge Management Systems. Journal of Management (1999) (2004)
7. Babcock, P.: Shedding Light on Knowledge Management. HR Magazine 49(5), 46–50 (2004)
8. Maier, R.: Knowledge Management Systems: Information and Communication Technologies for Knowledge Management, 3rd edn. Springer, Heidelberg (2007)

9. He, W., Qiao, Q., Wei, K.K.: Social Relationships and its Role in Knowledge Management Systems Usage. Information & Management 46(3), 175–180 (2009)
10. Lin, C., Hu, P.J.H., Chen, H.: Technology Implementation Management in law Enforcement; COPLINK system Usability and User Acceptance Evaluations. Social Science Computer Review 22(1), 24–36 (2004)
11. Money, W., Turner, A.: Application of the Technology Acceptance Model to a Knowledge Management System. In: Proceedings of the 37th Hawaii International Conference on System Sciences (2004)
12. Bals, C., Smolnik, S., Riempp, G.: Assessing User Acceptance of a Knowledge Management System in a Global Bank: Process Analysis and Concept Development. In: Proceedings of the 40th Hawaii International Conference on System Sciences (2007)
13. Chou, A.Y., Chou, D.C.: Knowledge Management Tools Adoption and Knowledge Workers' Performance. Int. J. Management and Decision Making 8(1), 52–63 (2007)
14. Wu, W.Y., Li, C.Y.: A Contingency Approach to Incorporate Human, Emotional and Social Influence into a TAM for KM Programs. Journal of Information Science 33(3), 275–297 (2007)
15. Davis, F.D., Bagozzi, R.P., Warshaw, P.R.: User Acceptance of Computer Technology: A Comparison of Two Theoretical Models. Management Science 35, 982–1003 (1989)
16. Denis, M.: Mcquail's Mass Communication Theory, 5th edn. SAGE Publications, London (2005)
17. Huang, L.-s., Quaddus, M.: Knowledge Management System Adoption and Practice in Taiwan Life Insurance Industry: Analysis via Partial Least Squares. Knowledge Management (2007)
18. Hayes, N., Walsham, G.: Knowledge sharing and ICTs: A Relational Perspective. In: Huysman, M., Wulf, V. (eds.) Social Capital and Information Technology. MITPress, London (2004)
19. Darke, P., Shanks, G., Broadbent, M.: Sucessful Completing Case Study Research: Combining Rigour, Relevant and Pragmatisim. Information System Journal 8(4), 273–289 (1998)
20. Carroll, J.M., Swatman, P.A.: Structured-case: A Methodological Framework for Building Theory in Information Systems Research. In: Proc. 8th European Conference on Information Systems, Vienna, July 3-5, pp. 116–123 (2000)
21. Denscombe, M.: The Good Research Guide: For Small-Scale Research Projects, 2nd edn. Open University Press, Buckingham (2003)
22. Heisig, P.: Harmonisation of Knowledge Management – Comparing 160 KM Frameworks Around the Globe. Journal of Knowledge Management 13(4), 4–31 (2009)
23. Liebowitz, J.: Knowledge Management and Its link to Artificial Intelligent. Expert Systems with Application 17, 99–103 (2001)
24. Alavi, M., Leidner, D.E.: Review: Knowledge Management and Knowledge Management Systems: Conceptual Foundations and Research Issues. MIS Quarterly 25(1), 107–136 (2001)
25. Kuo, R.-Z., Lee, G.-G.: KMS Adoption: The Effects of Information Quality. Management Decision 47(10), 1633–1651 (2009)
26. Tseng, S.-m.: Knowledge Management System Performance Measure Index. Expert Systems with Applications 34, 734–745 (2008)
27. Jung, J., Choi, I., Song, M.: An Architecture for Knowledge Management Systems and Business Process Management Systems. Computers in Industry 58, 21–34 (2007)
28. Bechina, A.A.A., Ndlela, M.N.: Success Factors in Implementing Knowledge Based Systems. Journal of Knowledge Management 7(2), 211–218 (2007)

29. Chikh, A., Berkani, L.: Communities of Practice of e-learning, an Innovative learning Space for e-learning Actors- Communities. Procedia Social and Behavioral Sciences 2, 5022–5027 (2010)
30. Shin, M.: A Framework for Evaluating Economics of Knowledgem Management Systems. Information and Management 42(1), 179–196 (2004)
31. Schümmer, T., Lukosch, S.: Patterns for Computer-Mediated Interaction. John Wiley & Sons, West Sussex (2007)
32. Rogers, E.M.: Diffusion of Innovations, 3rd edn. Free Press, New York (1983)
33. Moore, G., Benbasat, I.: Development of an Instrument to Measure perceptions of Adopting an Information Technology Innovation. Information Systems Research 2(3), 192–222 (1991)
34. Rogers, E.M.: Diffusion of innovations, 5th edn. Free Press, New York, NY (2003)
35. Tornatzky, L.G., Klein, K.J.: Innovation Characteristics and Innovation Adoption-Implementation: a Meta-analysis of Findings. IEEE Transactions on Engineering Management 29(1), 28–45 (1982)
36. Snyder, C.R., Shane, L.: Positive Psychology: The Scientific and Practical Explorations of Human Strengths. Sage, California (2007)
37. Fishbein, M., Ajzen, I.: Belief, Attitude, Intention, and Behavior. Addison-Wesley, Reading (1975)
38. Taylor, S., Todd, P.: Understanding Information Technology Usage: A test of competing models. Information Systems Research 6(2), 144–176 (1995)
39. Davis, F.D., Bagozzi, R.P., Warshaw, P.R.: User Acceptance of Computer Technology: A Comparison of Two Theoretical Models. Management Science 35, 982–1003 (1989)
40. Venkatesh, V., Davis, F.D.: A Theoretical Extension of the Technology Acceptance Model: Four longitudinal field studies. Management Science 46(2), 186–204 (2000)
41. Yin, R.K.: Case study research: Design and methods, 3rd edn. Sage, Thousand Oaks (2003)
42. Stake, R.E.: The art of case study research. Sage, Thousand Oaks (1995)
43. Eisenhardt, K.M.: Building Theories from Case Study Research. Academy of Management Review 14(4), 532–550 (1998)
44. Lin, F., Lin, S., Huang, T.: Knowledge Sharing and Creation in a Teachers' Professional Virtual Community. Computers & Education, 742–756 (2008)
45. Ader, H., Mellenbergh, G.: Research Methodology in the Life, Behavioral and Social Sciences. Sage, London (1999)
46. Strauss, A.L., Corbin, J.: Basics of Qualitative Research: Techniques and Procedures for Developing Grounded Theory, 3rd edn. Sage, Los Angeles (2008)
47. Green, J., Thorogood, N.: Qualitative Methods for Health Research. Sage, London (2005)
48. Goulding, C.: Grounded Theory, Ethnography and Phenomenology: A Comparative Analysis of Three Qualitative Strategies for Marketing Research. European Journal of Marketing 39(3/4), 294–309 (2005)
49. Glaser, B.: Basic Social Processes. Grounded Theory Review 4, 1–27 (2005)
50. Coleman, G.: Investigating Software Process in Practice: A Grounded Theory Perspective, PhD Thesis DCU, DCU (2006)
51. Stern, P.: Grounded Theory Methodology: Its Uses and Processes. Image (IN) 12, 20–23 (1980)
52. Mullen, P.D., Reynolds, R.: The Potential of Grounded Theory for Health Education Research: Linking Theory and Practice. Health Educ. Monographs 6, 280–294 (1978)
53. Razavi, M., Iverson, L.: A Grounded Theory of Information Sharing Behavior in a Personal Learning Space. In: ACM, CSCW, Banff, Alberta, Canada, November 4-6 (2006)

FMRI Brain Artifact Due to Normalization: A Study

J. SatheeshKumar[1,⋆], R. Rajesh[1,⋆], S. Arumugaperumal[2,⋆⋆], C. Kesavdass[3,⋆⋆⋆], and R. Rajeswari[1,⋆]

[1] Bharathiar University, Coimbatore, India
[2] ST Hindu College, Nagerkoil, India
[3] Sree Chitra Tirunal Institute for Medical Science and Technology, Trivandrum, India
{jsathee,kollamrajeshr}@ieee.org,
{arumugam.visvenk,chandrakesav,rrajeswari}@gmail.com

Abstract. Medical Imaging is an application of image processing in which normalization is one of the important process involved in most of the medical image analysis. Normalization is the process of mapping source image with same stereotaxic space. This can be done by registering each image to the same template, where template can be constructed by considering average of large number of high resolution MRImages. Normalizing source image with common existing template will help in analyzing inter subject relationships based on various factors, such as, age, sex etc. But for analyzing single patient data, normalization step can be skipped by registering source image with subject's/patient's anatomical data. Since there may be a variation between template and subject data, normalization step may either stretch or shrink the source image, where there are high chances of shift in motor activation area. This paper proves with experimental results of a trivial example of a subject, where normalization step have to be ignored for single subject analysis.

Keywords: Normalization, Realignment, MRI, Registration.

1 Introduction

Image processing has broad spectrum of applications in which Medical imaging is an interesting area for scientists and medical researcher. Medical imaging is a process of acquiring, analyzing and inferring known and unknown information from an image of a human or living organism. Latest developments and innovations in medical history show the role and importance of medical imaging applications and its significant influence on increasing average human life

⋆ Dr. J. Satheesh Kumar, Dr. R. Rajesh and Ms. R. Rajeswari are with Department of Computer Applications, School of Computer Science and Engineering.

⋆⋆ Dr.S. Arumugaperumal is with Department of Computer Science.

⋆⋆⋆ Dr. C. Kesavadas is with Department of Imaging Sciences and Interventional Radiology.

A. Abd Manaf et al. (Eds.): ICIEIS 2011, Part III, CCIS 253, pp. 306–319, 2011.

span time[4],[5],[6], [26], [42], [49]. Significant applications of medical imaging are Detection of cancerous region from the skin[16], Identifying tumor from human brain[18], [19],[29], [38], [39], Understanding the functionality and behavior of human brain structure[44], [46], [47], Identifying cancer from mammogram images[25], [32], [37], [48], analyzing the functionality of adrenal gland images[10],[17], [31], [51], etc.

Brain is an important part of human body which is having complex structure of neurons. Understanding structure and functionality of brain is still a challenging task for medical researchers due to significant increase in brain related diseases in the past decades. Significant studies which have been carried out on brain are Positron emission tomography study on emotional responses[22], Emotional analysis on human brain [2], [3], Neuroanatomical correlates of pleasant and unpleasant conditions on brain[27], Analysis on corpus callosum[14], Quantitative analysis on connectivity of brain[33], Behavioral responses of brain[20], [24], [30], [34], [43], etc.

Generally different modalities [PET, MRI, fMRI, MEG, SPECT] are available, which brings various information on brain activity based on some characteristics. The fMRI is one of the effective modality of acquiring brain images for analyzing motor activation area. Image Normalization is one of the important preprocessing step, where, the difference between source object and reference image are reduced by using different normalization methods. This paper discusses about the influence of image normalization during image pre processing among inter subject comparison and role of normalization in intra subject analysis. This paper proves that normalization step can be ignored for single subject analysis. Section 2 elucidates various image preprocessing steps needed for medical image analysis of brain and section 3 deals with the importance of normalization as well as the place where the normalization process seems to be difficult during image analysis. Section 4 deals with results and discussions and section 5 concludes the paper.

2 Image Preprocessing Steps for Brain Image Analysis

2.1 Image Acquisition

The first step involves reading T1 weighted MR images of patients by using single scanner with high resolution, in which, each image refers to sequence of tissue with some specific thickness [of 1.6mm]. Even slight variation in resolution between two different scanner may have higher influence during analysis phase. Two types of data can be resulted by most of the scanners namely structured and functional data, where structured data have more resolution compare with functional data. Functional images of patient's data can be overlaid with structural data of the same subject for identifying specific motor activation area [1], [8], [9], [11], [15], [28],[35],[36], [50].

2.2 Spatial Normalization and Transformation

Spatial normalization is the process of mapping source image with some reference image shown in Figure 1 for reducing residual errors between source and target images. An advantage using spatially normalized images shown in Figure 2 is that the motor activation area for different functionalities can be analyzed accurately based on set of meaningful coordinates with in standard space [7]. The first step of normalization is spatial transformation shown in Figure 3, which can be broadly classified as label-based techniques and non-label based techniques [7], [12]. Similar features (labels) in the image and template can be identified by label-based approach, where as, spatial transformation that minimizes some index of the difference between an object and a template image can be analyzed by non-label based approaches.

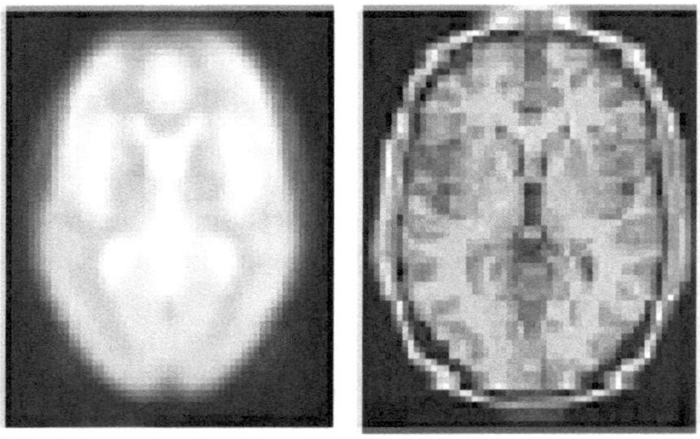

Fig. 1. Reference Images used to map with source image: MNI Template image (left), Single subject T1 mean image (right)

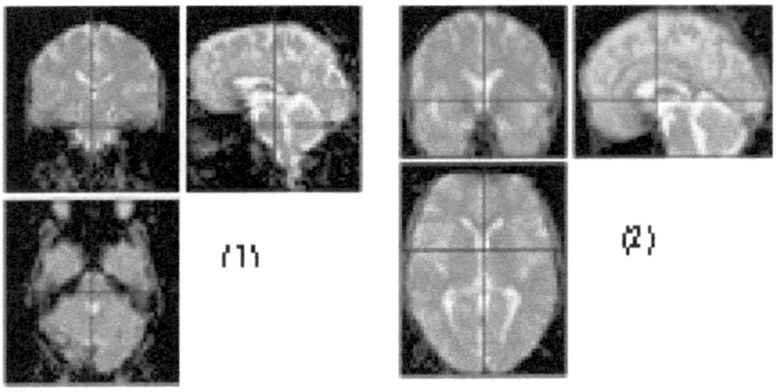

Fig. 2. (1).Results before normalization in a study, where, multiple subjects were analyzed by playing auditory words. (2). Result after normalization.

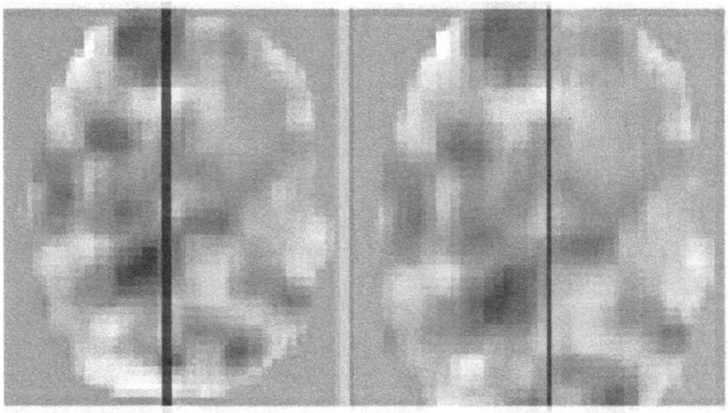

Fig. 3. Reorientation of images: Source Image(left), translation of source image through zooms and shears(right)

2.3 Segmentation and Extraction

By using segmentation techniques, the images after normalization can be decomposed into various factor like gray matter [GM], white matter[WM] and cerebrospinal fluid [CSF] based on intensities of voxels or pixels. Image extraction is also one of the process of removing noise. Some non-brain voxels may have the similar intensities of tissue like gray matter that can be removed by taking some effective brain extraction step[37].

2.4 Smoothing

The process of smoothing takes place after effective image extraction technique. Smoothing is a kind of enhancing an image for accurately analyzing target. Generally Isotropic Gaussian kernel are used for smoothing. The images to analyze the differences between groups and local volume of various tissues (such as, gray matter and white matter) can be calculated from the smoothed images based on intensity value of pixel or voxel value of an image. Finally, results can be compared by applying various statistical approaches[45].

2.5 Statistical Analysis

Many techniques have been proposed for statistically analyzing fMRI data like, multi variate analysis of co-variance (MANCOV), canonical correlation analysis (CCA) can be used to analyze the difference between groups of images, and a variety of these are in general use. The aim of such analysis is to produce an image identifying the regions, which show significant signal change in response to the task. Each pixel is assigned a value dependent on the likelihood of the null hypothesis, that the observed signal changes can be explained purely by random variation in the data consistent with its variance, being false. Such an image is called a statistical parametric map [13], [21], [23].

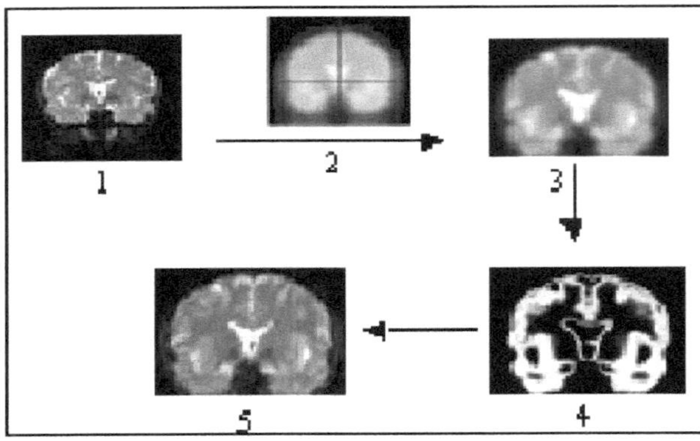

Fig. 4. Steps involved in medical image processing: (1). Source image (2).High resolution mean MR image(template, used to map with source image) (3). Image after normalization (4) Images after reducing noise by taking effective segmentation techniques (5) result after smoothing segmented images.

3 Normalization - As a Dragon Creating Disadvantages

As mentioned earlier, normalization is the process of adjusting images by superimposing source image with the reference image or template. The template is a mean image, which can be constructed by considering average of large number of high resolution MR images. When a study like, identifying relational differences with same modality, the concept of normalization is needed so as to reduce errors or differences (like sum of squared differences) between source image and template image shown in Figure 2. After successful image acquisition and co registration of multiple subjects with similar modality based on several factors (like, age, sex, diseases etc.,), there are higher chances of variations in every patient's brain shapes[45], [40], [41]. In order to get correct and best-known result, all the images can be mapped with same stereotaxic space, where by noise and unnecessary portions can be removed so that relationship between subjects can be accurately identified. Figure 4 clearly shows sequence of image pre processing steps during image analysis. Source images are generally mapped with predefined templates (MNI) or it can be mapped with user defined reference image that can be constructed by using structural data of the patient or subject.

Due to the realignment by motion correction parameters during inter subject analysis of normalization phase, some subjects might have changed to make best fit with reference image as well as to reduce the residual error between object and template image. In a study about single subjects brain, the mapping process of subject image with pre defined template (MNI created based on considering 13 subjects high resolution MR images) is not suggestible during image analysis. When the mean image is used for mapping, there may be higher possibilities of variation between object and reference image. Because of stretching and shrinking based on template, there may be higher chances of losing data Figure 5 or significant shift in motor activation area.

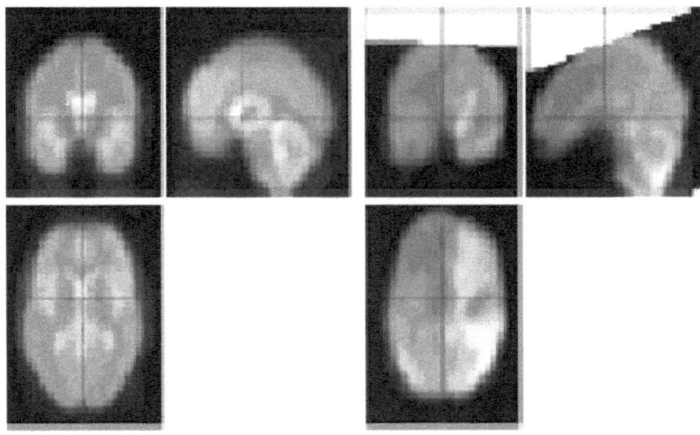

Fig. 5. Complexities in images after normalization, where, single subject data is superimposed with predefined template. Higher chances of data lose (top right figures) because of variation between source image and template image.

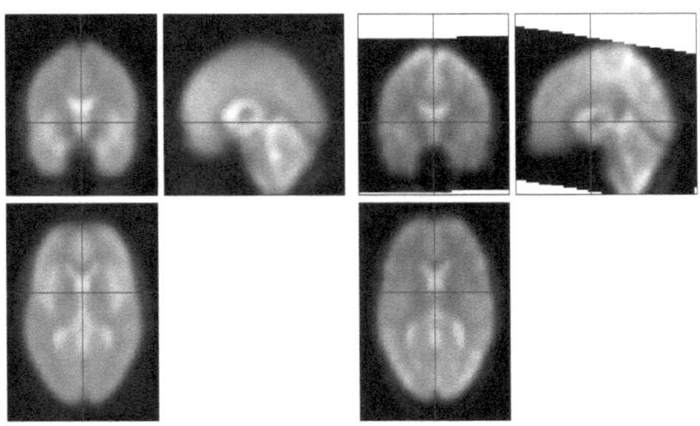

Fig. 6. Normalized images of a subject during the study of different music

4 Results and Discussions

Functional magnetic resonance images used in this study was obtained from Sree Chitra Tirunal Institute for Medical Science and Technology, Tiruvananthapuram, using 1.5 T MRI system (Siemens Avanto). A structural image of the subject's brain with 176 slices of 1 mm thickness was imaged for overlaying final results. The subject was asked to hear different types of music like karnatic, instrumental and white noise during the experiment. Functional images of 336 volumes were obtained, where each volume consist of 36 slices of 3 mm thickness at the scanning rate of 3.58 seconds per volume. The boxcar paradigm used in this experimental analysis is shown in the Figure 7. The total experiment took around 20 minutes to complete the scan.

Experiment have carried out with a trivial example of subject, where the normalization seems to be difficult. The shape of the patient left and right brain

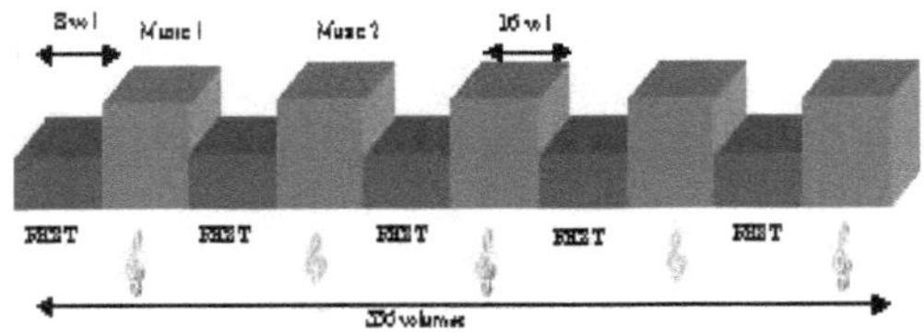

Fig. 7. Boxcar design paradigm for the experiment

vary significantly. Hence the normalization with template seems to be difficult and the results obtained after normalization are shown in the Figure 6. It is clear from the figure that data loses due to normalization. Fields significantly activated by music 1 and music 2 for normalized and unnormalized images are shown in the tables 1, 2, 3, 4.

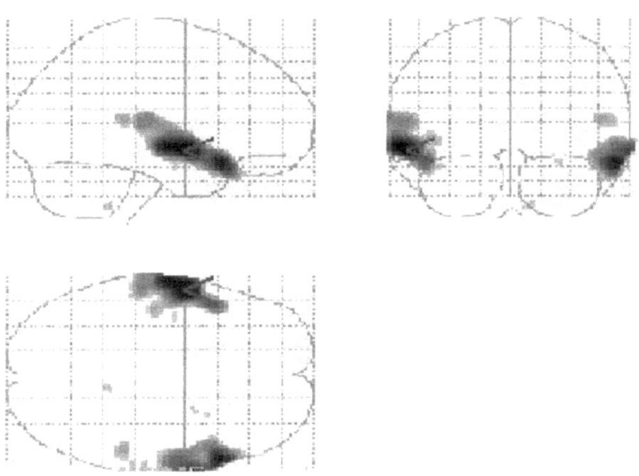

Fig. 8. Maximum Intensity projection of normalized images activated by music1

The results shows maximum intensity projection(MIP) for music 1 and music 2 on so called glass brain. Figure 9 shows MIP for music 1 at position [-58 -10 -29] and Figure 11 shows MIP for music 2 at position [8 55 -40] with out performing normalization during preprocessing of images. The MIP for normalized images are shown in the Figure 8 and Figure 10 at position [-58 0 -10] for music 1 and at position [18 -90 -38] for music 2. The results clearly shows that the MIP position for music has changed from actual location to some other position due to normalization. MNI coordinate position for these MIP can be identified by using a meta analysis matlab tool box(AMAT). Table 5 shows brain region for MIP coordinates on MNI space. These micro level changes will lead the radiologists and medical researchers for miss-understanding about hidden information in

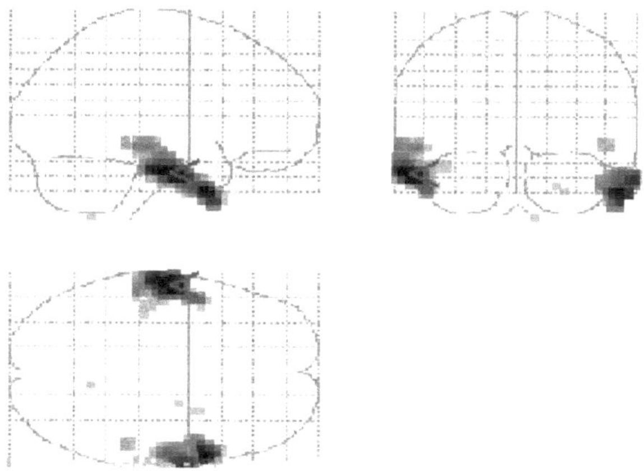

Fig. 9. Maximum Intensity projection for music1 without performing normalization

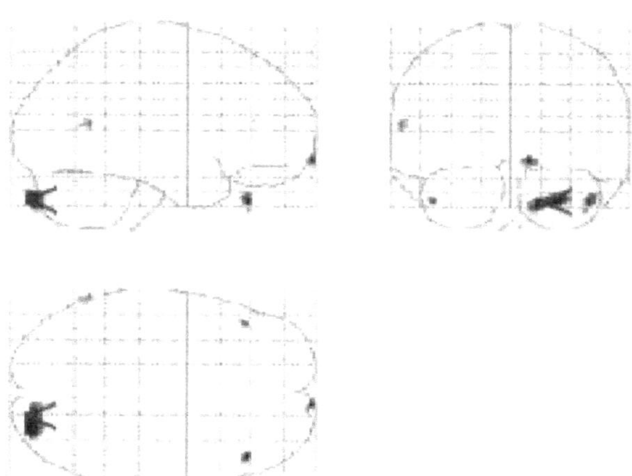

Fig. 10. Maximum Intensity projection of normalized images activated by music2

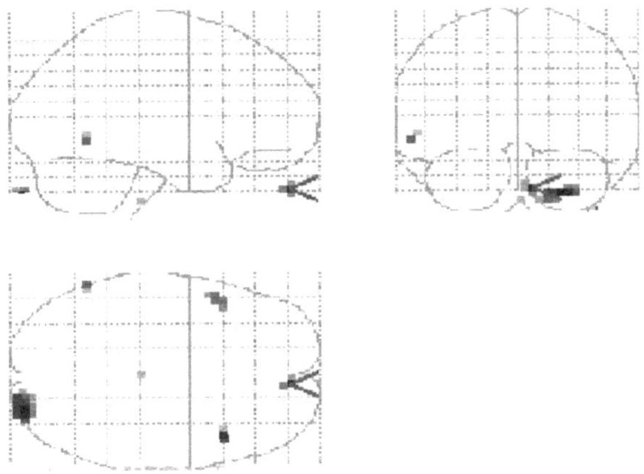

Fig. 11. Maximum Intensity projection for music2 without performing normalization

Table 1. Fields significantly activated, patients image without performing normalization, by music 1 obtained after t-test (p-values are adjusted for search volume)

Cluster-level			voxel-level					x, y, z {mm}		
p_{corr}	k_E	p_{uncorr}	$p_{FWE-corr}$	$p_{FDR-corr}$	T	Z_E	p_{uncorr}			
0.000	203	0.000	0.000	0.000	6.01	5.84	0.000	-59	-10	-29
			0.044	0.001	4.72	4.63	0.000	-51	-2	-37
			0.249	0.004	4.22	4.16	0.000	-66	-22	-11
0.000	141	0.000	0.000	0.000	5.72	5.58	0.000	58	8	-41
			0.003	0.000	5.31	5.20	0.000	66	-4	-33
0.794	6	0.207	0.915	0.026	3.55	3.51	0.000	52	-36	-11
0.972	2	0.469	0.999	0.070	3.17	3.15	0.001	27	6	-41
0.991	1	0.621	0.999	0.073	3.14	3.12	0.001	10	-54	-59
0.991	1	0.621	0.999	0.077	3.13	3.10	0.001	23	-6	-37

Table 2. Fields significantly activated, patients image without performing normalization, by music 2 obtained after t-test (p-values are adjusted for search volume)

Cluster-level			voxel-level					x, y, z {mm}		
p_{corr}	k_E	p_{uncorr}	$p_{FWE-corr}$	$p_{FDR-corr}$	T	Z_E	p_{uncorr}			
0.850	5	0.248	0.813	0.530	3.68	3.64	0.000	8	56	-41
0.183	21	0.027	0.882	0.530	3.60	3.56	0.000	24	-92	-44
			0.936	0.530	3.51	3.47	0.000	16	-96	-44
0.794	6	0.207	0.910	0.530	3.56	3.52	0.000	42	18	-59
0.972	2	0.469	0.974	0.530	3.41	3.37	0.000	-60	-57	-7
0.566	10	0.109	0.980	0.530	3.38	3.35	0.000	-48	14	-59
0.991	1	0.621	0.998	0.557	3.18	3.16	0.001	1	-27	-48

Table 3. Fields significantly activated normalized images by music 1 obtained after t-test (p-values are adjusted for search volume)

Cluster-level			voxel-level					x, y, z {mm}		
p_{corr}	k_E	p_{uncorr}	$p_{FWE-corr}$	$p_{FDR-corr}$	T	Z_E	p_{uncorr}			
0.000	1683	0.000	0.000	0.000	6.17	5.99	0.000	-58	0	-10
			0.000	0.000	5.86	5.70	0.000	-64	-10	-8
			0.032	0.001	4.83	4.74	0.000	-48	14	-20
0.000	1072	0.000	0.001	0.000	5.74	5.60	0.000	58	20	-18
			0.003	0.000	5.41	5.29	0.000	66	4	-10
			0.417	0.006	4.08	4.02	0.000	52	8	-12
0.714	61	0.144	0.836	0.017	3.70	3.66	0.000	52	-36	12
0.994	9	0.582	0.979	0.035	3.43	3.40	0.000	10	-42	-50
1.000	1	0.882	0.999	0.068	3.18	3.15	0.001	24	4 -	14
0.999	3	0.771	1.000	0.070	3.17	3.14	0.001	-42	-6	-20
1.000	1	0.882	1.000	0.073	3.15	3.12	0.001	26	6	-18
0.999	2	0.820	1.000	0.076	3.14	3.11	0.001	28	12	-18

Table 4. Fields significantly activated normalized images by music 2 obtained after t-test (p-values are adjusted for search volume)

Cluster-level			voxel-level					x, y, z {mm}		
p_{corr}	k_E	p_{uncorr}	$p_{FWE-corr}$	$p_{FDR-corr}$	T	Z_E	p_{uncorr}			
0.280	134	0.038	0.823	1.000	3.71	3.67	0.000	18	-90	-38
			0.838	1.000	3.70	3.65	0.000	28	-88	-36
0.991	11	0.539	0.919	1.000	3.59	3.55	0.000	10	70	-10
0.983	15	0.467	0.920	1.000	3.59	3.55	0.000	44	34	-38
0.999	3	0.771	0.988	1.000	3.39	3.35	0.000	-44	32	-38
0.995	8	0.606	0.993	1.000	3.34	3.31	0.000	-62	-56	14
1.000	1	0.882	0.998	1.000	3.24	3.21	0.001	42	34	-44

Table 5. Maximum Intensity Projection on MNI space

Experiment	*with/without normalization*	*MIPValues*	*Brainregionbased onMNItemplate*
Music 1	Un Normalized images	-59 -10 -29	inferior temporal cortex
	Normalized Images	-58 00 -10	anterior middle temporal gyrus
Music 2	Un Normalized images	08 56 -41	medial orbitofrontal cortex
	Normalized Images	18 -90 -38	Right cerebellum

complex human brain structure and hence normalization phase can be avoided for single subject data.

5 Conclusion

This paper explains various image processing steps and the role of normalization in medical image analysis. This paper proves by contradiction that due to higher chances of variation between source and predefined template, normalization can be ignored for single patient data to get best-known result so that data lost can be avoided.

Acknowledgement. The first two authors are thankful to the Department of Imaging Sciences and Interventional Radiology, Sree Chitra Tirunal Institute for Medical Sciences and Technology for supporting them to do their research training in the institution. They are also thankful to all staff of the Department of Computer Applications, School of Computer Science and Engineering, Bharathiar University, India for their support. The first, second and fifth authors are thankful for the partial funding support received from University Grants Commission(UGC), India.

References

1. Klautau, A.: Multiplicative Homomorphic Processing and its Application to Image Enhancement (2000)
2. Ahren, G.L., Schwartz, G.E.: Differential lateralization for positive and negative emotion in the human brain: EEG spectral analysis. Neuropsychologia 23, 745–755 (1985)
3. Angrilli, A., Palomba, D., Cantagallo, A., Maietti, A., Stegagno, L.: Emotional impairment after right orbitofrontal lesion in a patient without cognitive deficits. NeuroReport 10, 1741–1746 (1999)
4. Sherbondy, A., Akers, D., Mackenzie, R., Dougherty, R., Wandell, B.: Exploring Connectivity of the Brains White Matter with Dynamic Queries. IEEE Transactions on Visualization and Computer Graphics 11(4), 419–430 (2005)
5. May, A., Gaser, C.: Magnetic resonance-based morphometry: A window into structural plasticity of the brain. Current Opinion in Neurology 19, 407–411 (2006)
6. Ashburner, Friston, K.: Morphometry, PhD Thesis, Chapter 6 (2000)
7. Ashburner, J.: Friston K, Nonlinear Spatial Normalization using Basis Functions, Welcome department of cognitive neurology. Human Brain Mapping 7(4), 254–266 (1999)
8. Ashburner, J., Friston, K.J.: Voxel-based morphometry-The Methods. Neuro. Image 11, 805–821 (2000)
9. Bogorodzki, P., Rogowska, J., Yurgelun-Todd, D.A.: Structural group classification technique based on regional fMRI BOLD responses. IEEE Transactions Medical Imaging 24(3), 389–398 (2005)
10. Chang, A., Glazer, H.S., Lee, J.K.T., Ling, D., Heiken, J.: Adrenal gland: MR imaging. Radiology 163, 123–128 (1987)
11. Daniel, N.R., Dennis Jr., M.H.: Modern Signal Processing, vol. 46. MSRI Publications
12. Davatzikos, C.: Computational neuroanatomy using shape transformations - Handbook of medical imaging, vol. 16, pp. 249–260. Academic Press (2000)
13. Cahn, D.A., Sullivan, E.V., Shear, P.K., Marsh, L., Fama, R., Lim, K.O., Yesavage, J.A., Tinklenberg, J.R.: Adolf Pfefferbaum: Structural MRI correlates of recognition memory in Alzheimer's disease. Journal of the International Neuropsychological Society 4, 106–114 (1998)
14. Lee, D.J., Chen, Y., Schlaug, G.: Corpus Callosum: Musician and Gender Ejects 14(2), 205–209 (2003)
15. Selle, D., Spindler, W., Preim, B., Peitgen, H.-O.: Mathematical Methods in Medical Imaging: Analysis of Vascular Structures for Liver Surgery Planning (2000)
16. Ercal, F., Moganti, M., Stoecker, W.V., Moss, R.H.: Detection Of Skin Tumor Boundaries In Color Images. IEEE Transactions on Medical Imaging 12(3) (1993)
17. Krestin, G.P., Steinbrich, W., Friedmann, G.: Adrenal masses: Evaluation with fast dynamic gradient echo MR imaging and Gd-DTPA-enhanced dynamic studies. Radiology 171, 675–680 (1989)
18. Gibbs, P., Buckley, D., Blackb, S., Horsman, A.: Tumour volume determination from MR images by morphological segmentation. Physics in Medicine and Biology 41, 2437–2446 (1996)
19. Görlitz, L., Menze, B.H., Weber, M.-A., Kelm, B.M., Hamprecht, F.A.: Semi-supervised Tumor Detection in Magnetic Resonance Spectroscopic Images using Discriminative Random Fields. In: Hamprecht, F.A., Schnörr, C., Jähne, B. (eds.) DAGM 2007. LNCS, vol. 4713, pp. 224–233. Springer, Heidelberg (2007)

20. Guimaraes, A.R., Melcher, J.R., Talavage, T.M., Baker, J.R., Ledden, P., Rosen, B.R., Kiang, N.K.S., Fullerton, B.C., Weisskoff, R.M.: Imaging Subcortical Auditory Activity in Humans. Human Brain Mapping 6, 33–41 (1998)
21. Friedl, H., Kauermann, G.: Standard Errors for EM Estimates in Generalized Linear Models with Random Effects. Biometrics 56(3), 761–767
22. Royet, J.P., Zald, D., Versace, R., Costes, N., Lavenne, F., Koenig, O., Gervais, R.: Emotional Responses to Pleasant and Unpleasant factory, Visual, and Auditory Stimuli: a Positron Emission Tomography Study. The Journal of Neuroscience 20(20), 7752–7759 (2000)
23. Keller, S.S., Wieshmann, U.C., Mackay, C.E., Denby, C.E., Webb, J., Roberts, N.: Voxel based morphometry of grey matter abnormalities in patients with medically intractable temporal lobe epilepsy: effects of side of seizure onset and epilepsy duration. Journal of Neurology Neurosurgery and Psychiatry 73, 648–655 (2002)
24. Kling, A., Steklis, H.D.: A neural basis for affiliative behavior in non-human primates. Brain, Behavior, and Evolution 13, 216–238 (1976)
25. Kobatake, H., Yoshinaga, Y., Murakami, M.: Automated detection of malignant tumors on mammogram. In: Proceedings of the IEEE International Conference on Image Processing, vol. 1, pp. 407–410 (1994)
26. Kubota, J., et al.: Neurol Neurosurg Psychiatry, Alcohol consumption and frontal lobe shrinkage: study of 1432 non-alcoholic subjects. JNNP 71, 104–106 (2001)
27. Lane, R.D., Reiman, E., Bradley, M.M., Lang, P.J., Ahern, G.L., Davidson, R.J.: Neuroanatomical correlates of pleasant and unpleasant emotion. Neuropsychologia 35, 1437–1444 (1997)
28. Lawrence, A.A., Ritter, G.X.: Cellular topology and its applications in image processing. International Journal of Parallel Programming 12 (1983)
29. Lefohn, A.E., Cates, J.E., Whitaker, R.T.: Interactive, GPU-Based Level Sets for 3D Brain Tumor Segmentation. In: Ellis, R.E., Peters, T.M. (eds.) MICCAI 2003. LNCS, vol. 2878, pp. 564–572. Springer, Heidelberg (2003)
30. McEwen, B.S.: Physiology and neurobiology of stress and adaptation: Central role of the brain. Physiological Reviews 87, 873–904 (2007)
31. Mitchell, D.G., Crovello, M., Matteucci, T., Petersen, R.O.: Miettinen MM Benign adrenocortical masses: diagnosis with chemical shift MR imaging. Radiology 185, 345–351 (1992)
32. Wirth, M., Lyan, J., Nikitenko, D., Stapinski, A.: Removing radiopaque artifacts from mammograms using area morphology. In: Proceedings of SPIE Medical Imaging: Image processing, vol. 5370, pp. 1054–1065 (2004)
33. Murre, J., Sturdy, D.: The connectivity of the brain: multi-level quantitative analysis. Biological cybernetics, Neuroreport 73(6), 529–545 (1995)
34. Noriuchi, M., Kikuchi, Y., Senoo, A.: The functional neuroanatomy of maternal love: Mothers response to infants attachment behaviors. Biological Psychiatry 63, 415–423 (2008)
35. Ohser, J.,Schladitz, K., Koch, K., Nothe, M.: Diffraction by image processing and its application in materials science. ITWM, Nr.67 (2004)
36. Patel, J., Lee, K.F., Goldberg, B.: The role of ultra sonography in the diagnosis of certain neurologic disorders. Neuroradiology, 1432–1920 (Online)
37. Petrick, N., Chan, H.P., Sahiner, B., Helvie, M.A.: Combined adaptive enhancement and region-growing segmentation of breast masses on digitized mammograms. Medical Physics 26(8), 1642–1654 (1999)
38. Prastawa, M., Bullitt, E., Ho, S., Gerig, G.: A brain tumor segmentation framework based on outlier detection. Medical Image Analysis 8(3), 275–283 (2004)

39. Prastawa, M., Bullitt, E., Moon, N., Leemput, K.V., Gerig, G.: Automatic brain tumor segmentation by subject specific modification of atlas priors. Acad. Radiol. 10, 1341–1348 (2003)
40. Rajesh, R., SatheeshKumar, J., Arumugaperumal, S., Kesavdas, C.: Have a look at the 3 dimensional view of t-statistics? - Isn't it cute ginger. The Neuroradiology 21, 31–34 (2008)
41. Rajesh, R., SatheeshKumar, J., Arumugaperumal, S., Kesavdas, C.: On identifying micro level error in realignment phase of statistical parametric mapping. The Neuroradiology Journal 20, 491–493 (2007)
42. Rowland, Clinical, legal, and research issues in dementia. Am. J. Alzheimers Disorders Other Demen 21, NP (2006)
43. Rusch, N., van Elst, L.T., Ludaescher, P., Wilke, M., Huppertz, H.J., Thiel, T., Ebert, D.: A voxel-based morphometric MRI study in female patients with borderline personality disorder. NeuroImage 20, 385–392 (2003)
44. SatheeshKumar, J., Arumugaperumal, S., Rajesh, R., Kesavdas, C.: A Note on Visualization of Information from Three Dimensional Time Series of Brain. International Journal of Recent Trends in Engineering 1(2), 173–175 (2009)
45. SatheeshKumar, J., Rajesh, R., Arumugaperumal, S., Kesavdas, C.: A Novel Algorithm for an Efficient Realigning of fMRI Data Series of Brain. ICGST International Journal on Graphics, Vision and Image Processing 9(I), 35–40 (2009)
46. SatheeshKumar, J., Arumugaperumal, S., Rajesh, R., Kesavdas, C.: On experimenting with functional magnetic resonance imaging on lip movement. The Neuroradiology Journal 21, 23–30 (2008)
47. SatheeshKumar, J., Arumugaperumal, S., Kesavdas, C., Rajesh, R.: Does Brain react on Indian music? - An functional Magnetic Resonance Imaging study. In: IEEE International Joint Conference on Neural Networks (IJCNN 2008), pp. 2696–2703 (2008)
48. Sahiner, B., Chan, H.P., Wei, D., Petrick, N., Hlvie, M.A., Adler, D.D., Goodsit, M.M.: Image feature selection by a genetic algorithm: Application to classifications of mass and normal breast tissue. Medical Physics 23, 1671–1684 (1996)
49. Dehaene, S., Le Clec'H, G., Cohen, L., Poline, J.-B., van de Moortele, P.-F., Le Bihan, D.: Inferring behavior from functional brain images. Nature Neuroscience 1, 549 (1998)
50. Perry, S.W.: Applications of Image processing to mine warfare sonar, DSTO-GD-0237
51. Tsushima, Y., Ishizaka, H., Matsumoto, M.: Adrenal masses: differentiation with chemical shift, fast low-angle shot MR imaging. Radiology 186, 705–709 (1993)

A Parallel Abstract Machine for the RPC Calculus

Kensuke Narita* and Shin-ya Nishizaki

Department of Computer Science,
Tokyo Institute of Technology,
2-12-1-W8-69, O-okayama, Meguro-ku, Tokyo, 152-8552, Japan
nisizaki@cs.titech.ac.jp

Abstract. Cooper and Wadler introduced the RPC calculus, which is obtained by incorporating a mechanism for remote procedure calls (RPC) into the lambda calculus. The location where a caller's code is executed is designated in a lambda abstraction in the RPC calculus. Nishizaki et al. proposed a simplified abstract machine for the lambda calculus, known as a Simple Abstract Machine (SAM). The configuration of an SECD machine is a quadruple of data sequences: Stack, Environment, Code, and Dump. In contrast, the SAM configuration is a double of data sequences: Stack and Code. In this paper, we introduce a SAM-based abstract machine for the RPC calculus, called a Location-aware Simple Abstract Machine (LSAM). This machine makes it possible to model parallelism more clearly. We provide a translation of the RPC calculus into LSAM, and prove a correctness theorem for the translation. We then show that the translation can be extended to allow parallel execution in LSAM.

1 Introduction

1.1 The RPC Calculus

A *remote procedure call*, or *RPC*, is an inter-process communication that allows a program to cause a procedure to be executed on another computer, in exactly the same manner as the usual procedure call. RPC has been widely used since SUN Microsystems implemented it as the basis for the Network File System. RPC lightens the programmer's burden by making the transport layer of the network transparent[2].

The RPC calculus [3] $\lambda_{\mathbf{RPC}}$, proposed by Cooper et al., is an extension of the lambda calculus that incorporates the concepts of location and remote procedure call. The terms of the calculus are defined by the grammar:

* The first author, Kensuke Narita, completed this research when he was a student at Tokyo Institute of Technology. He is now with Hitachi, Ltd.

A. Abd Manaf et al. (Eds.): ICIEIS 2011, Part III, CCIS 253, pp. 320–332, 2011.

$$
\begin{array}{rll}
a, b ::= & & \text{locations} \\
& \mathbf{c} & \text{client} \\
| & \mathbf{s} & \text{server} \\
M ::= & & \text{terms} \\
| & c & \text{constants} \\
| & x & \text{variables} \\
| & (MN) & \text{function application} \\
| & \lambda^a x.\, M & \text{lambda abstraction}
\end{array}
$$

The operational semantics $\Downarrow_a$ is defined by the following rules:

$$V \Downarrow_a V$$

$$\frac{L \Downarrow_a \lambda^b x.\, N \quad M \Downarrow_a W \quad N[x := W] \Downarrow_b V}{(LM) \Downarrow_a V}$$

The expression $M \Downarrow_a V$ is a big-step reduction relation, and is read "the term M, evaluated at location a, results in value V." Each evaluation is connected with a location where it is processed. The term $\lambda^b x.\, N$ is called *b-annotated abstraction* and its body N is evaluated at location b. This is obtained by formalizing the remote procedure call. Cooper and Wadler proposed the client-server calculus λ_{CS} [3], which defines a state-transition machine for the operational semantics of the RPC calculus. A state in the state-transition machine denotes a client and server configuration. The calculus only formalizes *sequential* computations with remote procedure calls.

1.2 The SAM Abstract Machine

Several kinds of abstract machines have been proposed for functional languages, including the SECD machine[6], the Categorical Abstract Machine[4], and the Krivine machine[1]. The SECD machine is an abstract machine for the call-by-value lambda calculus. Narita et al. proposed the Simple Abstract Machine (SAM), which is obtained by simplifying the SECD machine [7].

The instruction set of SAM consists of primitive functions $f, f', \ldots$, numerals $0, 1, 2, \ldots, -1, -2, \ldots$, variables $x, y, z, \ldots$, lambda abstractions $\mathbf{lam}(x, C)$, and application **app**. To simplify the instruction set, we postulate that the primitive functions are unary. We use $I, I', I_1, I_2, \ldots$ for instructions and $C, C', C_1, C_2, \ldots$ for instruction sequences, which are called *codes*.

$$
\begin{aligned}
I &::= f \mid n \mid x \mid \mathbf{lam}(x, C) \mid \mathbf{app} \\
C &::= I_1 : I_2 : \cdots I_n
\end{aligned}
$$

A set of *Values* is a subset of the set of instructions, defined by the following grammar:

$$V ::= n \mid f \mid f(V) \mid \mathbf{lam}(x, C).$$

The internal configuration of SAM is represented as a pair consisting of a stack S and a code C. A SAM stack is sequence of values. A SAM computation is formulated as a transition between the configurations defined by the following rules:

$$\begin{array}{ll}
\textsf{num} & (S,\ n : C) \to (n : S,\ C) \\
\textsf{prim} & (S, f : C) \to (f : S,\ C) \\
\textsf{lam} & (S,\ \mathbf{lam}(x, C') : C) \to (\mathbf{lam}(x, C') : S,\ C) \\
\textsf{app-lam} & (V : \mathbf{lam}(x, C') : S, \mathbf{app} : C) \\
& \to (S, C'[x{:=}V] : C) \\
\textsf{app-prim} & (V : f : S,\ \mathbf{app} : C) \to (f(V) : S,\ C)
\end{array}$$

The variable reference mechanism is abstracted as substitutions in SAM, and consequently (unlike the SECD machine configuration) an environment sequence becomes unnecessary (which was the crucial point of simplification introduced in SAM).

2 The LSAM Abstract Machine

2.1 Syntax of LSAM

In this section, we introduce the *Location-aware Simple Abstract Machine*, or *LSAM*, into which we incorporate the concept of location. We first present a set of instructions and configurations for LSAM.

We assume in advance that countable sets of variables and locations are given, denoted by $x, y, z, \ldots$ and $l, l', l'', \ldots$, respectively.

Definition 1 (Instructions and Configurations). *The LSAM* Instructions *are defined by*

$$\begin{array}{rll}
I ::= & V & \textsf{value} \\
\mid & \mathbf{app} & \textsf{application} \\
\mid & \mathbf{wait}(l) & \textsf{waiting} \\
\mid & \mathbf{ret}(l) & \textsf{return}
\end{array}$$

where the values *and* code sequences *are defined by*

$$\begin{array}{rll}
V ::= & x & \textsf{variable} \\
\mid & \mathbf{lam}(l, x, C) & \textsf{abstraction,}
\end{array}$$

$$C ::= [\,] \mid I : C,$$

respectively. The Stack sequences *are defined by*

$$S ::= [\,] \mid V : S.$$

An LSAM configuration, *or* machine, *is a pair of stack and code sequences annotated by a label:*

$$M ::= (S, C)_l.$$

2.2 Operational Semantics of LSAM

We first introduce the idea of being *well-located.* A set of machines is well-located if no two distinct machines occupy the same location.

Definition 2 (Well-located set of machines). *A set of machines W is* well-located *if $l_1 \neq l_2$ for any pair of distinct machines $(S_1, C_1)_{l_1}$, $(S_2, C_2)_{l_2}$.*

We next define a transition relation between two machines at the same location.

Definition 3 (Intra-location Transition). *An* intra-location transition $\rightarrow$ *between machines at the same location is defined by the following rules:*

$$\begin{array}{lrrr} \mathsf{var} & (& S, & x : C)_l \\ & \rightarrow(& x : S, & C)_l \\ \\ \mathsf{lam} & (& S, & \mathbf{lam}(l, x, C') : C)_l \\ & \rightarrow(& \mathbf{lam}(l, x, C') : S, & C)_l \\ \\ \mathsf{beta} & (V : & \mathbf{lam}(l, x, C') : S, & \mathbf{app} : C)_l \\ & \rightarrow(& S, & C'[x{:=}V] : C)_l \end{array}$$

We then define a transition relation between two well-located sets of machines. This transition is denoted by the same symbol as the intra-location transition.

Definition 4 (Transition between sets of machines). *A transition $A \rightarrow A'$ between well-located sets A, A' of machines is defined by the following rules:*

$$\begin{array}{ll} \mathsf{indiv} & \textit{if } (S, C)_l \rightarrow (S', C')_l \textit{ then } \{(S, C)_l\} \cup A \rightarrow \{(S', C')_l\} \cup A \\ \mathsf{app\text{-}lam\text{-}rpc} & \{(V : \mathbf{lam}(m, x, C') : S_1,\ \mathbf{app} : C_1)_l, (S_2, C_2)_m\} \cup A \\ & \rightarrow \{(S_1,\ \ \mathbf{wait}(m) : C_1)_l, (S_2,\ \ C'[x{:=}V] : \mathbf{ret}(l) : C_2)_m\} \cup A \\ \mathsf{ret\text{-}rpc} & \{(S_1,\ \ \mathbf{wait}(m) : C_1)_l, (V : S_2,\ \ \mathbf{ret}(l) : C_2)_m\} \cup A \\ & \rightarrow \{(S_1,\ \ V : C_1)_l, (S_2,\ \ C_2)_m\} \cup A \end{array}$$

The rule indiv specifies that a machine in a well-located set is run by an intra-location transition. The rule app-lam-rpc specifies the initiation of an RPC from location l to location m. The rule ret-rpc specifies the return of an RPC from l to m. The instruction $\mathbf{wait}(m)$ means await the return of a result from m. The instruction $\mathbf{ret}(l)$ means return a result to l.

We define an n-times transition $\twoheadrightarrow_n$ between well-located sets of machines and the reflexive-transitive closure $\twoheadrightarrow$ of the transition $\rightarrow$.

Definition 5. *We define $A \twoheadrightarrow_n A'$ as $A \underbrace{\rightarrow \cdots \rightarrow}_{n} A'$. We define $A \twoheadrightarrow A'$ as $A \twoheadrightarrow_n A'$ for some integer $n \geq 0$.*

We next present an example of a transition sequence. Three locations l, m, n are utilized in this example. A code is first placed at location l. An RPC passes the code from l to m, and then another RPC passes it from m to n. Subsequently, the code returns from n to m, and then returns from m to l. A value a is passed unaltered from l to m, and then from m to n.

The transitions of the example are illustrated in Fig. 1.

Example 1 (Mobile Code)

$$
\begin{aligned}
& \{(,\mathbf{lam}(m, x, \mathbf{lam}(n, y, y) : x : \mathbf{app}) : a : \mathbf{app})_l,\ ([\,],[\,])_m,\ ([\,],[\,])_n\} && (1)\\
\twoheadrightarrow_2\ & \{(a : \mathbf{lam}(m, x, \mathbf{lam}(n, y, y) : x : \mathbf{app}), \mathbf{app})_l,\ ([\,],[\,])_m,\ ([\,],[\,])_n\} && (2)\\
\twoheadrightarrow\ & \{([\,],\ \mathbf{wait}(m))_l, ([\,],\ \mathbf{lam}(n, y, y) : a : \mathbf{app} : \mathbf{ret}(l))_m,\ ([\,],[\,])_n\} && (3)\\
\twoheadrightarrow_2\ & \{([\,],\ \mathbf{wait}(m))_l, (a : \mathbf{lam}(n, y, y), \mathbf{app} : \mathbf{ret}(l))_m,\ ([\,],[\,])_n\} && (4)\\
\rightarrow\ & \{([\,],\ \mathbf{wait}(m))_l, (\mathbf{wait}(n), \mathbf{ret}(l))_m,\ ([\,], a : \mathbf{ret}(m))_n\} && (5)\\
\rightarrow\ & \{([\,],\ \mathbf{wait}(m))_l, (\mathbf{wait}(n), \mathbf{ret}(l))_m,\ (a, \mathbf{ret}(m))_n\} && (6)\\
\rightarrow\ & \{([\,],\ \mathbf{wait}(m))_l, (\mathbf{wait}(n), a : \mathbf{ret}(l))_m,\ ([\,],[\,])_n\} && (7)\\
\rightarrow\ & \{([\,],\ \mathbf{wait}(m))_l, (a, \mathbf{ret}(l))_m,\ ([\,],[\,])_n\} && (8)\\
\rightarrow\ & \{([\,], a)_l, ([\,],[\,])_m,\ ([\,],[\,])_n\} && (9)\\
\rightarrow\ & \{(a, [\,])_l, ([\,],[\,])_m,\ ([\,],[\,])_n\} && (10)
\end{aligned}
$$

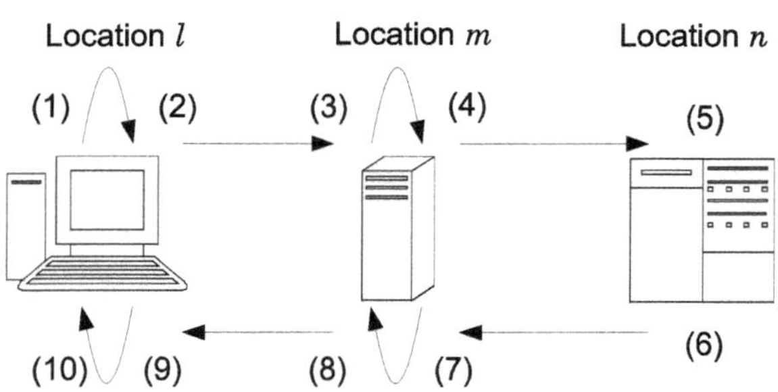

Fig. 1. Transition sequence of Example 1

The following example shows that if a client machine (location m) sends a value a to a server machine (location m), then the server returns the value a to the client.

Example 2 (Server-client Model)

$$
\begin{aligned}
& \{(\mathbf{lam}(l, x, x), [\,])_l, (a : \mathbf{lam}(l, x, x : \mathbf{app}), \mathbf{app})_m\} && (11)\\
\rightarrow\ & \{(\mathbf{lam}(l, x, x), a : \mathbf{app} : \mathbf{ret}(m))_l, ([\,], \mathbf{wait}(l))_m\} && (12)\\
\rightarrow\ & \{(a : \mathbf{lam}(l, x, x), \mathbf{app} : \mathbf{ret}(m))_l, ([\,], \mathbf{wait}(l))_m\} && (13)\\
\rightarrow\ & \{([\,], a : \mathbf{ret}(m))_l, ([\,], \mathbf{wait}(l))_m\} && (14)\\
\rightarrow\ & \{(a, \mathbf{ret}(m))_l, ([\,], \mathbf{wait}(l))_m\} && (15)\\
\rightarrow\ & \{([\,],[\,])_l, ([\,], a)_m\} && (16)\\
\rightarrow\ & \{([\,],[\,])_l, (a, [\,])_m\} && (17)
\end{aligned}
$$

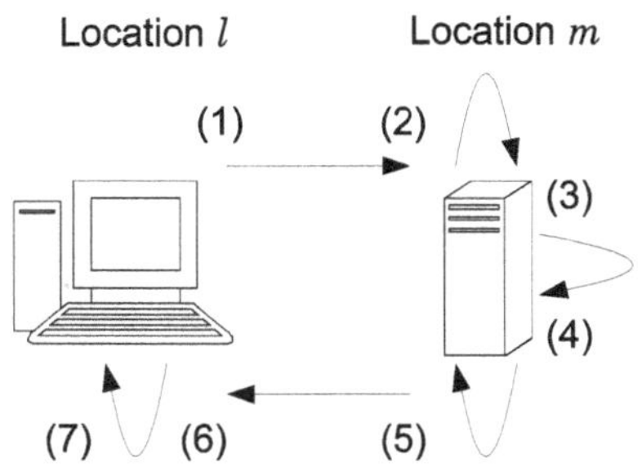

Fig. 2. Transition sequence of Example 2

3 Translation of the RPC Calculus into LSAM

In this section, we present a translation of RPC calculus terms into LSAM codes, and assess its correctness. First, we define a translation function $\mathcal{T}[\![M]\!]$.

Definition 6 (Translation function $\mathcal{T}[\![M]\!]$). *A function $\mathcal{T}[\![-]\!]$ that maps an RPC calculus term to an LSAM code is defined by induction on the structure of the term:*

$$\begin{aligned} \mathcal{T}[\![x]\!] &= x, \\ \mathcal{T}[\![\lambda^l x.\, M]\!] &= \mathbf{lam}(l, x, \mathcal{T}[\![M]\!]), \\ \mathcal{T}[\![(MN)]\!] &= \mathcal{T}[\![M]\!] : \mathcal{T}[\![N]\!] : \mathbf{app}. \end{aligned}$$

A substitution lemma holds for the translation $\mathcal{T}[\![-]\!]$.

Lemma 1 (Substitution Lemma for $\mathcal{T}[\![-]\!]$). *For any RPC calculus term M and variable x,*

$$\mathcal{T}[\![M]\!][x := \mathcal{T}[\![N]\!]] = \mathcal{T}[\![M[x := N]]\!]$$

This lemma is proved by straightforward induction on the structure of the term M.

We next define a function that maps an RPC calculus term to a finite set of locations $\mathsf{LS}(M)$. The locations in $\mathsf{LS}(M)$ appear in the term M.

Definition 7 (Location Set of an RPC Term). *For an RPC calculus term M, a set $\mathsf{LS}(M)$ of locations that appear in M is defined inductively by the following equations:*

$$\begin{aligned} \mathsf{LS}(x) &= \emptyset, \\ \mathsf{LS}(M_1\ M_2) &= \mathsf{LS}(M_1) \cup \mathsf{LS}(M_2), \\ \mathsf{LS}(\lambda^l x.\, M) &= \{l\} \cup \mathsf{LS}(M). \end{aligned}$$

$\mathsf{IS}(M, l)$ denotes the set of machines that may be traversed in executing a code $\mathcal{T}[\![M]\!]$ at location l. It is formally defined as follows:

Definition 8 (Initial Set IS). *For an RPC calculus term M and a location l, a finite set $\mathsf{IS}(M, l)$ of locations, called an* initial set, *is defined by*

$$\mathsf{IS}(M, l) = \{([\,], [\,])_m \mid m \in \mathsf{LS}(M) - \{l\}\}.$$

In order to prove the correctness theorem for the translation, the following lemma is required:

Lemma 2. *Let M and N be RPC calculus terms, V a value, l a location, and n a nonnegative integer.*

The following two conditions are equivalent.

1. $\{([\,], \mathcal{T}[\![LM]\!])_l\} \cup \mathsf{IS}(LM, l) \twoheadrightarrow_n \{(\mathcal{T}[\![V]\!], [\,])_l\} \cup \mathsf{IS}(LM, l)$
2. There exist a term N, a value W, a location m, a variable x, and nonnegative integers n_1, n_2, n_3 less than n such that

$$\{([\,], \mathcal{T}[\![L]\!])_l\} \cup \mathsf{IS}(L, l) \twoheadrightarrow_{n_1} \{(\mathcal{T}[\![\lambda^m x.\, N]\!], [\,])_l\} \cup \mathsf{IS}(L, l)$$

and

$$\{([\,], \mathcal{T}[\![M]\!])_l\} \cup \mathsf{IS}(M, l) \twoheadrightarrow_{n_2} \{(\mathcal{T}[\![W]\!], [\,])_l\} \cup \mathsf{IS}(M, l)$$

and

$$\begin{array}{l}\{([\,], \mathcal{T}[\![N[x := W]]\!])_m\} \cup \mathsf{IS}(N[x := W], m) \\ \twoheadrightarrow_{n_3} \{(\mathcal{T}[\![V]\!], [\,])_m\} \cup \mathsf{IS}(N[x := W], m).\end{array}$$

This lemma is proved by showing that the reduction sequence can be divided into three subsequences that are essentially similar to the ones in the condition 2.

Theorem 1 (Correctness of the Translation). *Let M be a term, V a value, and l a location. The following two conditions are equivalent:*

1. $M \Downarrow_l V$.
2. $\{([\,],\ \mathcal{T}[\![M]\!])_l\} \cup \mathsf{IS}(M, l) \twoheadrightarrow \{(\mathcal{T}[\![V]\!], [\,])_l\} \cup \mathsf{IS}(M, l)$.

Proof. $1 \Longrightarrow 2$: We prove this part of the theorem by induction on the structure of the derivation tree of $M \Downarrow_l V$.

The base case of value: Suppose that $M = V$ and $V \Downarrow_l V$ is derived by the rule value. Then by rule var or lam, we obtain

$$\{([\,],\ \mathcal{T}[\![V]\!])_l\} \cup \mathsf{IS}(M, l) \twoheadrightarrow \{(\mathcal{T}[\![V]\!], [\,])_l\} \cup \mathsf{IS}(M, l).$$

The step case of beta: We assume that the last rule applied in the derivation tree is

$$\dfrac{\begin{array}{ccc}\vdots & \vdots & \vdots \\ L \Downarrow_l \lambda^m x.\, N & K \Downarrow_l W & N[x := W] \Downarrow_m V\end{array}}{LK \Downarrow_l V}\ \mathsf{beta}$$

By the induction hypothesis,

- $\{([\,], \mathcal{T}[\![L]\!])_l\} \cup \mathsf{IS}(L,l) \twoheadrightarrow \{(\mathcal{T}[\![\lambda^m x.\,N]\!], [\,])_l\} \cup \mathsf{IS}(L,l)$,
- $\{([\,], \mathcal{T}[\![K]\!])_l\} \cup \mathsf{IS}(K,l) \twoheadrightarrow \{(\mathcal{T}[\![W]\!], [\,])_l\} \cup \mathsf{IS}(K,l)$, and
- $\{([\,], \mathcal{T}[\![N[x := W]]\!])_m\} \cup \mathsf{IS}(N[x := W],m) \twoheadrightarrow \{(\mathcal{T}[\![V]\!], [\,])_m\} \cup \mathsf{IS}(N[x := W],m)$.

We consider the two cases $l = m$ and $l \neq m$.

Case 1. We assume that $l = m$. We then have

- $\{([\,], \mathcal{T}[\![L]\!] : \mathcal{T}[\![K]\!] : \mathbf{app})_l\} \cup \mathsf{IS}(LK,l) \twoheadrightarrow \{(\mathcal{T}[\![\lambda^l x.\,N]\!], \mathcal{T}[\![K]\!] : \mathbf{app})_l\} \cup \mathsf{IS}(LK,l)$,
- $\{(\mathcal{T}[\![\lambda^l x.\,N]\!], \mathcal{T}[\![K]\!] : \mathbf{app})_l\} \cup \mathsf{IS}(LK,l) \twoheadrightarrow \{(\mathcal{T}[\![W]\!] : \mathcal{T}[\![\lambda^l x.\,N]\!], \mathbf{app})_l\} \cup \mathsf{IS}(LK,l)$, and
- $\{([\,], \mathcal{T}[\![N[x := W]]\!])_l\} \cup \mathsf{IS}(LK,l) \twoheadrightarrow \{(\mathcal{T}[\![V]\!], [\,])_l\} \cup \mathsf{IS}(LK,l)$.

From Lemma 1, we have

$$\{(\mathcal{T}[\![W]\!] : \mathcal{T}[\![\lambda^l x.\,N]\!], \mathbf{app})_l\} \cup \mathsf{IS}(LK,l) \to \{([\,], \mathcal{T}[\![N[x := W]]\!])_l\} \cup \mathsf{IS}(LK,l).$$

Therefore,

$$\{([\,], \mathcal{T}[\![L]\!] : \mathcal{T}[\![K]\!] : \mathbf{app})_l\} \cup \mathsf{IS}(LK,l) \twoheadrightarrow \{(\mathcal{T}[\![V]\!], [\,])_l\} \cup \mathsf{IS}(LK,l),$$

and hence $\{([\,], \mathcal{T}[\![LK]\!])_l\} \cup \mathsf{IS}(LK,l) \twoheadrightarrow \{(\mathcal{T}[\![V]\!], [\,])_l\} \cup \mathsf{IS}(LK,l)$.

Case 2. We assume that $l \neq m$.

- $\{([\,], \mathcal{T}[\![L]\!] : \mathcal{T}[\![K]\!] : \mathbf{app})_l\} \cup \mathsf{IS}(LK,l) \twoheadrightarrow \{(\mathcal{T}[\![\lambda^m x.\,N]\!], \mathcal{T}[\![K]\!] : \mathbf{app})_l\} \cup \mathsf{IS}(LK,l)$,
- $\{(\mathcal{T}[\![\lambda^m x.\,N]\!], \mathcal{T}[\![K]\!] : \mathbf{app})_l\} \cup \mathsf{IS}(LK,l) \twoheadrightarrow \{(\mathcal{T}[\![W]\!] : \mathcal{T}[\![\lambda^m x.\,N]\!], \mathbf{app})_l\} \cup \mathsf{IS}(LK,l)$, and
- $\{([\,], \mathbf{wait}(m))_l, ([\,], \mathcal{T}[\![N[x := W]]\!] : \mathbf{ret}(l))_m\} \cup \mathsf{IS}(LK,l) - \{([\,],[\,])_m\}$
  $\twoheadrightarrow \{([\,], \mathbf{wait}(m))_l, (\mathcal{T}[\![V]\!], \mathbf{ret}(l))_m\} \cup \mathsf{IS}(LK,l) - \{([\,],[\,])_m\}$.

Furthermore,

$$\begin{aligned} &\{([\,], \mathbf{wait}(m))_l, (\mathcal{T}[\![V]\!], \mathbf{ret}(l))_m\} \cup \mathsf{IS}(LK,l) - \{([\,],[\,])_m\} \\ \to\ &\{([\,], \mathcal{T}[\![V]\!])_l\} \cup \mathsf{IS}(LK,l) \\ \to\ &\{(\mathcal{T}[\![V]\!], [\,])_l\} \cup \mathsf{IS}(LK,l). \end{aligned}$$

By Lemma 1, we have

$$\begin{aligned} &\{(\mathcal{T}[\![W]\!] : \mathcal{T}[\![\lambda^m x.\,N]\!], \mathbf{app})_l\} \cup \mathsf{IS}(LK,l) \\ \to\ &\{([\,], \mathbf{wait}(m))_l, ([\,], \mathcal{T}[\![N[x := W]]\!] : \mathbf{ret}(l))_m\} \cup \mathsf{IS}(LK,l) - \{([\,],[\,])_m\}. \end{aligned}$$

Thus $\{([\,], \mathcal{T}[\![LK]\!])_l\} \cup \mathsf{IS}(LK,l) \twoheadrightarrow \{(\mathcal{T}[\![V]\!], [\,])_l\} \cup \mathsf{IS}(LK,l)$.

$2 \Longrightarrow 1$: We prove this part of the theorem by mathematical induction on the length of the reduction sequence $\{([\,],\ \mathcal{T}[\![M]\!])_l\} \cup \mathsf{IS}(M,l) \twoheadrightarrow \{(\mathcal{T}[\![V]\!], [\,])_l\} \cup \mathsf{IS}(M,l)$.

The base case: We assume that $n = 1$. The reduction

$$\{([\,],\ \mathcal{T}[\![M]\!])_l\} \cup \mathsf{IS}(M,l) \to \{(\mathcal{T}[\![V]\!], [\,])_l\} \cup \mathsf{IS}(M,l)$$

can be derived only by rule var or lam. In both cases, $\mathcal{T}[\![M]\!]$ must be a value and $M = V$. By applying rule value, we have $V \Downarrow_l V$.

The step case: We assume that $n > 1$. Because M must not be a value, we can assume that $M = LK$ for some terms L and K. By Lemma 2, there exist a term N, a value W, a location m, and a variable x such that

$$\{([\,], \mathcal{T}[\![L]\!])\} \cup \mathsf{IS}(L, l) \twoheadrightarrow \{(\mathcal{T}[\![\lambda^m x.\, N]\!], [\,])_l\} \cup \mathsf{IS}(L, l),$$

$$\{([\,], \mathcal{T}[\![K]\!])_l\} \cup \mathsf{IS}(K, l) \twoheadrightarrow \{([\,], \mathcal{T}[\![W]\!])_l\} \cup \mathsf{IS}(K, l), \text{ and}$$

$$\begin{aligned}&\{([\,], \mathcal{T}[\![N[x := W]]\!])_m\} \cup \mathsf{IS}(N[x := W], m)\\ &\twoheadrightarrow \{(\mathcal{T}[\![V]\!], [\,])_m\} \cup \mathsf{IS}(N[x := W], m).\end{aligned}$$

Because the lengths of the three reduction sequences are shorter than n, we can apply the induction hypothesis to them and obtain $L \Downarrow_l \lambda^m n.\, N$, $K \Downarrow_l W$, and $N[x := W] \Downarrow_m V$. By beta, we have $LK \Downarrow_l V$. **Q.E.D.**

4 Parallel Execution

In the previous section, we discussed the translation of the RPC calculus into LSAM, and proved the correctness of the translation. We assumed sequential execution of the RPC calculus and the translated LSAM code. In this section, we extend the results to parallel execution of sequential codes.

Definition 9 (Extended Initial Set ISX). *For a set T of terms and a set L of locations, $\mathsf{ISX}(T, L)$ is defined by*

$$\mathsf{ISX}(T, L) = \left\{ ([\,], [\,])_m \;\middle|\; m \in \bigcup_{M \in T} \mathsf{LS}(M) - L \right\}.$$

If T and L are singleton sets (i.e. $T = \{M\}$ and $L = \{l\}$),then $\mathsf{ISX}(T, L) = \mathsf{IS}(M, l)$, which means that IS is a special case of ISX.

The correctness of the translation is extended via the following theorem.

Theorem 2 (Correctness of the Translation in Parallel Execution). *Let $M_1, \ldots, M_n$ be RPC calculus terms, $V_1, \ldots, V_n$ values, and $l_1, \ldots, l_n$ distinct locations. The following two conditions are equivalent:*

1. $M_1 \Downarrow_{l_1} V_1, \ldots,$ *and* $M_n \Downarrow_{l_n} V_n$
2. $\{([\,], \mathcal{T}[\![M_1]\!])_{l_1}, \ldots, ([\,], \mathcal{T}[\![M_n]\!])_{l_n}\} \cup \mathsf{ISX}(\{M_1, \ldots, M_n\}, \{l_1, \ldots, l_n\})$ $\twoheadrightarrow \{(\mathcal{T}[\![V_1]\!], [\,])_{l_1}, \ldots (\mathcal{T}[\![V_n]\!], [\,])_{l_n}, \} \cup \mathsf{ISX}(\{M_1, \ldots, M_n\}, \{l_1, \ldots, l_n\})$.

In order to prove this theorem, we can apply a modified LSAM that includes process names. Process names enable us to distinguish between processes that are executed in parallel. Each computation $M_i \Downarrow_{l_i} V_i$ $(i = 1, .., n)$ in the RPC calculus corresponds to a process labelled by a process name p_i $(i = 1, .., n)$. The modified LSAM is called *LSAM with process names*, or $\mathrm{LSAM_{PN}}$.

A countable set of process names is specified in advance. The symbols $p, q, r, \ldots$ denote metavariables over process names.

Definition 10 (Syntax of LSAM$_{\mathrm{PN}}$). *An LSAM$_{\mathrm{PN}}$ instruction H and value U are defined by*

$$H ::= \langle I \rangle^p \text{ and } U ::= \langle V \rangle^p,$$

respectively, where I denotes an LSAM instruction, and V an LSAM value.

An LSAM$_{\mathrm{PN}}$ code sequence B and stack sequence R are defined by

$$B ::= [\,] \mid H : B \text{ and } R ::= [\,] \mid U : R,$$

respectively.

An LSAM$_{\mathrm{PN}}$ configuration, *or* machine, *consists of a pair of stack and code sequences annotated by a label:*

$$L ::= (R, B)_l.$$

The notation $\langle I \rangle^p$ is extended to a function on code sequences as follows:

Definition 11. *For each LSAM code sequence C, $\langle C \rangle^p$ is defined by the equations*

$$\langle [\,] \rangle^p = [\,] \text{ and } \langle I : C \rangle^p = \langle I \rangle^p : \langle C \rangle^p.$$

The transition relation of LSAM is extended to LSAM$_{\mathrm{PN}}$. The relation is annotated with a process name.

Definition 12 (Intra-location Transition for LSAM$_{\mathrm{PN}}$). *The* intra-location transition $\rightarrow_p$ *is a ternary relation on two machines and a process name, defined by the following rules:*

$$
\begin{array}{llrr}
\mathsf{var} & (& R, & \langle x \rangle^p : B)_l \\
 & \rightarrow^p (& \langle x \rangle^p : R, & B)_l \\[1em]
\mathsf{lam} & (& R, & \langle \mathbf{lam}(l, x, C') \rangle^p : B)_l \\
 & \rightarrow^p (& \langle \mathbf{lam}(l, x, C') \rangle^p : R, & B)_l \\[1em]
\mathsf{beta} & (& \langle V \rangle^p : \langle \mathbf{lam}(l, x, C') \rangle^p : R, & \langle \mathbf{app} \rangle^p : B)_l \\
 & \rightarrow^p (& R, & \langle C'[x{:=}V] \rangle^p : B)_l
\end{array}
$$

Definition 13 (Transition between sets of machines). *The transition $A \rightarrow^p A'$ between well-located sets A, A' of machines with a process name p is defined by the following rules:*

$$
\begin{array}{ll}
\mathsf{indiv} & \textit{if } (R, B)_l \rightarrow^p (R', B')_l \textit{ then } \{(R, B)_l\} \cup A \rightarrow^p \{(R', B')_l\} \cup A \\[1em]
\mathsf{app\text{-}lam\text{-}rpc} & \{(\langle V \rangle^p : \langle \mathbf{lam}(m, x, C') \rangle^p : R_1,\ \langle \mathbf{app} \rangle^p : B_1)_l, (R_2, B_2)_m\} \cup A \\
 & \rightarrow^p \{(R_1,\ \langle \mathbf{wait}(m) \rangle^p : B_1)_l, (R_2,\ \langle C'[x{:=}V] \rangle^p : \langle \mathbf{ret}(l) \rangle^p : B_2)_m\} \cup A \\[1em]
\mathsf{ret\text{-}rpc} & \{(R_1,\ \langle \mathbf{wait}(m) \rangle^p : B_1)_l, (\langle V \rangle^p : R_2,\ \langle \mathbf{ret}(l) \rangle^p : B_2)_m\} \cup A \\
 & \rightarrow^p \{(R_1,\ \langle V \rangle^p : B_1)_l, (R_2,\ B_2)_m\} \cup A
\end{array}
$$

We sometimes write $W \rightarrow^p W'$ simply as $W \rightarrow W'$. The relations $\twoheadrightarrow_n$ and $\twoheadrightarrow$ are defined in a manner similar to those of LSAM.

Definition 14 (Extraction of instructions). *For a code B and a set P of process names, a code $\mathsf{PF}(B, P)$ of LSAM is defined inductively by the following equations:*

$$\begin{aligned}\mathsf{PF}([\,], P) &= [\,],\\ \mathsf{PF}(\langle I\rangle^p : B, P) &= I : \mathsf{PF}(B, P) \text{ if } p \in P,\\ \mathsf{PF}(\langle I\rangle^p : B, P) &= \mathsf{PF}(B, P) \text{ if } p \notin P.\end{aligned}$$

The following lemma implies that a reduction sequence in parallel execution corresponds to a reduction sequence with process names.

Lemma 3. *For terms $M_1, \ldots, M_n$, values $V_1, \ldots, V_n$, and process names $p_1, \ldots, p_n$, if*

$$\begin{aligned}&\{([\,], \mathcal{T}[\![M_1]\!])_{l_1}, \ldots, ([\,], \mathcal{T}[\![M_n]\!])_{l_n}\} \cup \mathsf{ISX}(\{M_1, \ldots, M_n\}, \{l_1, \ldots, l_n\})\\ \twoheadrightarrow\ &\{(\mathcal{T}[\![V_1]\!], [\,])_{l_1}, \ldots, (\mathcal{T}[\![V_n]\!], [\,])_{l_n}, \} \cup \mathsf{ISX}(\{M_1, \ldots, M_n\}, \{l_1, \ldots, l_n\}),\end{aligned}$$

then

$$\begin{aligned}&\{([\,], \langle\mathcal{T}[\![M_1]\!]\rangle^{p_1})_{l_1}, \ldots, ([\,], \langle\mathcal{T}[\![M_n]\!]\rangle^{p_n})_{l_n}\} \cup \mathsf{ISX}(\{M_1, \ldots, M_n\}, \{l_1, \ldots, l_n\})\\ \twoheadrightarrow\ &\{(\langle\mathcal{T}[\![V_1]\!]\rangle^{p_1}, [\,])_{l_1}, \ldots, (\langle\mathcal{T}[\![V_n]\!]\rangle^{p_n}, [\,])_{l_n}, \} \cup \mathsf{ISX}(\{M_1, \ldots, M_n\}, \{l_1, \ldots, l_n\}).\end{aligned}$$

The following result is the inverse of the previous lemma.

Lemma 4. *For a set P of process names, if*

$$\{(R_1, B_1)_{l_1}, \ldots (R_n, B_n)_{l_n}\} \twoheadrightarrow \{(R'_1, B'_1)_{l_1}, \ldots (R'_n, B'_n)_{l_n}\}$$

then

$$\begin{aligned}&\{(\mathsf{PF}(R_1, P), \mathsf{PF}(B_1, P))_{l_1}, \ldots (\mathsf{PF}(R_n, P), \mathsf{PF}(B_n, P))_{l_n}, \}\\ \twoheadrightarrow\ &\{(\mathsf{PF}(R'_1, P), \mathsf{PF}(B'_1, P))_{l_1}, \ldots (\mathsf{PF}(R'_n, P), \mathsf{PF}(B'_n, P))_{l_n}, \}.\end{aligned}$$

We conclude this section with a proof of Theorem 2.

Proof. $1 \Longrightarrow 2$. We prove the theorem by mathematical induction on n.

The base case: We assume that $n = 1$. This case is directly derived from Theorem 1.

The step case: We assume that $n = k + 1$. By Theorem 1,

$$\{([\,], \mathcal{T}[\![M_n]\!])_{l_n}\} \cup \mathsf{IS}(M_n, l_n) \twoheadrightarrow \{(\mathcal{T}[\![V_n]\!], [\,])_{l_n}\} \cup \mathsf{IS}(M_n, l_n).$$

Hence we have

$$\begin{aligned}&\{\ldots, ([\,], \mathcal{T}[\![M_k]\!])_{l_k}, ([\,], \mathcal{T}[\![M_n]\!])_{l_n}\} \cup \mathsf{ISX}(\{M_1, \ldots, M_n\}, \{l_1, \ldots, l_n\})\\ \twoheadrightarrow\ &\{\ldots, ([\,], \mathcal{T}[\![M_k]\!])_{l_k}, (\mathcal{T}[\![V_n]\!], [\,])_{l_n}\} \cup \mathsf{ISX}(\{M_1, \ldots, M_n\}, \{l_1, \ldots, l_n\})\end{aligned}$$

In contrast, from the induction hypothesis, we obtain

$$\begin{aligned}&\{([\,], \mathcal{T}[\![M_1]\!])_{l_1}, \ldots, ([\,], \mathcal{T}[\![M_k]\!])_{l_k}\} \cup \mathsf{ISX}(\{M_1, \ldots, M_k\}, \{l_1, \ldots, l_k\})\\ \twoheadrightarrow\ &\{(\mathcal{T}[\![V_1]\!], [\,])_{l_1} \ldots, (\mathcal{T}[\![V_k]\!], [\,])_{l_k}\} \cup \mathsf{ISX}(\{M_1, \ldots, M_k\}, \{l_1, \ldots, l_k\}).\end{aligned}$$

These two reduction sequences imply that

$$\begin{aligned}&\{([\,], \mathcal{T}[\![M_1]\!])_{l_1}, \ldots, ([\,], \mathcal{T}[\![M_n]\!])_{l_n}\} \cup \mathsf{ISX}(\{M_1, \ldots, M_n\}, \{l_1, \ldots, l_n\}) \\ \twoheadrightarrow\ &\{(\mathcal{T}[\![V_1]\!], [\,])_{l_1} \ldots, (\mathcal{T}[\![V_n]\!], [\,])_{l_n}\} \cup \mathsf{ISX}(\{M_1, \ldots, M_n\}, \{l_1, \ldots, l_n\}).\end{aligned}$$

$2 \implies 1$. Suppose that $p_1, \ldots, p_n$ are distinct process names. By Lemma 3, we have

$$\begin{aligned}&\{([\,], \langle\mathcal{T}[\![M_1]\!]\rangle^{p_1})_{l_1}, \ldots, ([\,], \langle\mathcal{T}[\![M_n]\!]\rangle^{p_n})_{l_n}\} \cup \mathsf{ISX}(\{M_1, \ldots, M_n\}, \{l_1, \ldots, l_n\}) \\ \twoheadrightarrow\ &\{(\langle\mathcal{T}[\![V_1]\!]\rangle^{p_1}, [\,])_{l_1} \ldots, (\langle\mathcal{T}[\![V_n]\!]\rangle^{p_n}, [\,])_{l_n}\} \cup \mathsf{ISX}(\{M_1, \ldots, M_n\}, \{l_1, \ldots, l_n\}).\end{aligned}$$

Applying Lemma 4, it follows that for $i = 1, \ldots, n$,

$$\begin{aligned}&\{([\,], \langle\mathcal{T}[\![M_i]\!]\rangle^{p_i})_{l_i}\} \cup \{([\,], [\,])_{l_j} \mid j = 1, \ldots, n,\ j \neq i\} \\ &\cup \mathsf{ISX}(\{M_1, \ldots, M_n\}, \{l_1, \ldots, l_n\}) \\ \twoheadrightarrow\ &\{(\langle\mathcal{T}[\![V_i]\!]\rangle^{p_i}, [\,])_{l_i}\} \cup \{([\,], [\,])_{l_j} \mid j = 1, \ldots, n,\ j \neq i\} \\ &\cup \mathsf{ISX}(\{M_1, \ldots, M_n\}, \{l_1, \ldots, l_n\}),\end{aligned}$$

and consequently,

$$\{([\,], \langle\mathcal{T}[\![M_i]\!]\rangle^{p_i})_{l_i}\}\} \cup \mathsf{IS}(M_i, l_i) \twoheadrightarrow \{(\langle\mathcal{T}[\![V_i]\!]\rangle^{p_i}, [\,])_{l_i}\}\} \cup \mathsf{IS}(M_i, l_i).$$

By Theorem 1, $M_i \Downarrow_{l_i} V_i$. **Q.E.D.**

5 Conclusions

In this paper, we proposed a Location-aware Simple Abstract Machine, or LSAM, which was extended to incorporate the concept of locations into LSAM[7]. The operational semantics of LSAM is given as a transition relation between finite sets of LSAM configurations. Each lambda abstraction instruction has an attached location where its body is to be evaluated.

We next established a translation of Cooper and Wadler's RPC calculus into LSAM, and proved the correctness of the translation. Moreover, we studied parallel execution of codes in LSAM, and developed a translation of parallel execution of the RPC calculus into LSAM. In order to prove the correctness of the translation, we introduced the concept of process names into LSAM, enabling us to distinguish between processes in LSAM and clarify the correspondence between the RPC calculus and LSAM.

6 Future Work

Stateless Behaviour on a Server

In the RPC calculus[3], only two locations are permitted: client **c** and server **s**. The RPC calculus is translated into the client-server calculus λ_{CS}. Just after a remote procedure call from a server to a client, the server's configuration becomes empty. In the translated codes of the client-server calculus λ_{CS}, the server is used in the *stateless* style. The translation is implemented via CPS transformation in the trampolined style[5]. In contrast, our translation of the RPC calculus into LSAM generates a code that functions on a server in the *stateful* style. Future research should focus on a translation of the RPC calculus into LSAM in the stateless style.

Concurrency in LSAM

Although parallel execution is allowed in LSAM, synchronization is only allowed between remote procedure calls. Synchronization between processes executing in parallel is not provided. It would be interesting to find a way to introduce other concurrent constructs into LSAM.

First-Class Continuations and Environments

One of the authors, Nishizaki, previously studied first-class continuations [9] and environments [8] in the framework of the lambda calculus. It would be interesting to incorporate such computational mechanisms into the RPC calculus and LSAM. The combination of remote procedure calls and extensions of this type would make the calculus synergistically powerful.

References

1. Amadio, R.M., Curien, P.L.: Domains and Lambda-Calculi. Cambridge University Press (1998)
2. Birrell, A.D., Nelson, B.J.: Implementing remote procedure calls. ACM Transactions on Computer Systems 2(1), 39–59 (1984)
3. Cooper, E., Wadler, P.: The RPC calculus. In: Proceedings of the 11th ACM SIGPLAN Conference on Principles and Practice of Declarative Programming, PPDP 2009, pp. 231–242 (2009)
4. Cousineau, G., Curien, P.L., Mauny, M.: The categorical abstract machine. Science of Computer Programming 8(2), 173–202 (1987)
5. Ganz, S.E., Friedman, D.P., Wand, M.: Trampolined style. In: Proceedings of the 4th ACM SIGPLAN International Conference on Functional Programming, ICFP 1999, pp. 18–27 (1999)
6. Landin, P.J.: The mechanical evaluation of expressions. The Computer Journal 6(4), 308–320 (1964)
7. Narita, K., Nishizaki, S., Mizuno, T.: A Simple Abstract Machine for Functional First-class Continuations. In: Proceedings of International Symposium on Communications and Information Technologies 2010, pp. 111–114. IEEE (2010)
8. Nishizaki, S.: Polymorphic Environment Calculus and Its Type Inference Algorithm. Higher-Order and Symbolic Computation 13(3) (2000)
9. Nishizaki, S.: Programs with Continuations and Linear Logic. Science of Computer Programming 21(2), 165–190 (1993)

Optimization of Task Processing Schedules in Distributed Information Systems

Janusz R. Getta

School of Computer Science and Software Engineering,
University of Wollongong, Wollongong, Australia
jrg@uow.edu.au

Abstract. The performance of data processing in distributed information systems strongly depends on the efficient scheduling of the applications that access data at the remote sites. This work assumes a typical model of distributed information system where a central site is connected to a number of remote and highly autonomous remote sites. An application started by a user at a central site is decomposed into several data processing tasks to be independently processed at the remote sites. The objective of this work is to find a method for optimization of task processing schedules at a central site. We define an abstract model of data and a system of operations that implements the data processing tasks. Our abstract data model is general enough to represent many specific data models. We show how an entirely parallel schedule can be transformed into a more optimal hybrid schedule where certain tasks are processed simultaneously while the other tasks are processed sequentially. The transformations proposed in this work are guided by the cost-based optimization model whose objective is to reduce the total data transmission time between the remote sites and a central site. We show how the properties of data integration expressions can be used to find more efficient schedules of data processing tasks in distributed information systems.

Keywords: Distributed information system, data processing, scheduling, data integration, optimization.

1 Introduction

The rapid growth in the number of distributed applications and the users of these applications creates an ever increasing pressure on the performance of data processing in distributed information systems. To satisfy the increasing performance requirements we investigate more sophisticated and more efficient algorithms for distributed data processing. A factor, that has a significant impact on the performance of distributed data processing is scheduling of the individual data processing tasks over the remote sites. In a typical approach a central site decomposes a task submitted by a user into a number of individual tasks, to be processed at one of the remote sites. A partial order in which the individual tasks

A. Abd Manaf et al. (Eds.): ICIEIS 2011, Part III, CCIS 253, pp. 333–345, 2011.

are submitted to the remote sites and a way how their results are assembled into the final result is called as a *task processing schedule.*

Two generic task processing schedules are either *entirely sequential* or *entirely parallel* schedules. In an *entirely sequential* schedule the tasks $t_1, \ldots, t_n$ are processed one by one in a way where a task t_i can be processed only when all results of the tasks $t_1, \ldots, t_{i-1}$ are available at a central site. Accordingly to an *entirely parallel* schedule all tasks $t_1, \ldots, t_n$ are simultaneously submitted for processing at the remote sites. When looking at the performance, our intuition always favor an entirely parallel schedule over a sequential one because processing of several tasks is done in the same time at many remote sites. An entirely parallel schedule attempts to save time on processing of all tasks. However, if we consider time spent on transmission of the results from the remote sites then in some cases a sequential schedule is more appropriate than a parallel one because the intermediate results received so far can be used to reduce the size of the other results. For example, if an individual task t_i returns a lot of data then processing of t_i and transmission of its results to a central site may take more time than parallel processing of the tasks $t_1, \ldots, t_{i-1}$, modification of task t_i with the results $r_1, \ldots, r_{i-1}$, processing of updated t_i, and transmission of its results. In such a case simultaneous processing of the tasks $t_1, \ldots, t_{i-1}$ followed by simultaneous processing of the tasks $t_{i-1}1, \ldots, t_n$ may provide better performance than entirely parallel schedule.

An *entirely sequential* schedule attempts to minimize data transmission time of the results while an entirely parallel schedule minimizes the total processing time of the individual tasks. As the efficiency of both methods depend on a number of factors like for instance the computational complexity of the individual tasks, computational power of local systems, data transmission speed, etc, then usually a *hybrid schedule* where some of the individual tasks are processed sequentially while the others simultaneously, provides the best results.

The objectives of this work are the following. We consider a model of distributed information system where a user application running at a central site submits a data processing task T against a global view of the system. An abstract model of data containers represents a data component of a distributed system and a system of operations on data containers is used to implement the data processing tasks. The task is decomposed into a number of individual tasks $t_1, \ldots, t_n$ to be processed at the local sites of the distributed system. A *data integration expression* $e(t_1, \ldots, t_n)$ determines how the results $r_1, \ldots, r_n$ of the individual tasks suppose to be assembled into the final result of a task T. A starting point for the optimization is an entirely parallel schedule where the individual tasks are in the same moment submitted for the simultaneous processing at the remote sites. We show how an entirely parallel task processing schedule can be transformed into a hybrid schedule that minimizes the total amount of time spent on transmission of data from the local sites. To minimize total transmission time we estimate the amounts of time needed for transmission of the results $r_1, \ldots, r_n$ and we find if it is possible to reduce the amounts of transmission if some of the tasks are processed before the others. Then, we find how the results of the tasks processed earlier can be used to transform the tasks processed later.

The paper is organized in the following way. An overview of the works related to an area of optimization of data processing in distributed systems is included in the next section. A section 3 introduces an abstract data model used in this work. A method used for the estimation of the costs of alternative data processing schedules is presented in a section 4. Transformation and optimization of data processing schedules is described in the sections 5 and 6. Finally, section 7 concludes the paper.

2 Previous Works

The previous works concentrated on three aspects of distributed data processing: optimization of query processing in distributed systems, estimation of processing time at the remote site and transmission time, and optimization of data integration.

Optimization of data processing in distributed systems has its roots in optimization of query processing in multidatabase and federated database systems [17,15]. Due to the syntactical and semantic heterogeneities of the remote systems [16] optimization of distributed query processing is conceptually different from optimization of query processing in homogeneous and centralized systems [14]. One of the recent solutions to speed up distributed query processing in distributed systems considers the contents of cache in the remote systems and prediction of cache contents [10]. Wireless networks and mobile devices triggered research in mobile data services and in particular in location-dependent queries that amalgamate the features of both distributed and mobile systems. The existing literature related to location-dependent query processing is reviewed in [7]. A framework for distributed query scheduling has been proposed in [13]. The framework allows for the dynamic information gathering across distributed systems without relying on a unified global data model of the remote systems. [20] introduces an adaptive distributed query processing architecture where fluctuations in selectivities of operations, transmission speeds, and workloads of remote systems, can change the operation order distributed query processing.

Optimization of data processing schedules in distributed systems strongly depends on the precise estimation of data processing time at the remotes sites and on the amounts of data transmitted from the remote sites. Due to the strong autonomy of the remote sites a central site has no impact on processing of subqueries there and because of that the estimation of the local performance indicators is pretty hard [21]. A solution proposed in [5] categorizes the local databases into three groups and uses such classification to estimate the cost functions for data processing at the remote sites. In [21] the query sampling methods is used to estimated the query processing costs at the local systems. [11] proposes a clustering algorithm to classify the queries and to derive the cost functions. Query scheduling strategy in a grid-enabled distributed database proposed in [4] takes under the consideration so called "site reputation" for ranking response time of the remote systems. A new approach to estimation of workload completion time based on sampling the query interactions has been proposed in [1] and in [2]. Query monitoring can be used to collect information about expected database load, resource allocation, and expected size of the results [9].

Efficient integration of the partial results obtained from the remote sites is one of subproblems in optimization data processing schedules in distributed systems. Data integration combines data stored at the remote sites and provides a single unified view of the contents of remote sites. The reviews of research on data integration are included in [8],[22]. The implementations of experimental data integration systems systems based on application of ontologies and data sharing are described in [19],[18], [12]. A distributed and open query processor that integrates Internet data sources was proposed in [3].

3 Basic Concepts

To remain at a high level of generality we define an abstract data model where a data component of an information system is a set $\mathcal{D}$ of *data containers*. A data container $d \in \mathcal{D}$ includes *data objects*. A data object is either a *simple data object* or a *composite data object*. A *simple data object* includes the pairs of data items $(name, value)$ where *name* is a name of data item and *value* is a value of data item. An *internal data structure* can be used to "assemble" the data items into a simple data object. At an abstract level we do note refer to any particular internal data structure. In a *concrete data model* an internal data structure could be a sequence of tuples of data items, a hierarchical structure of data items, a graph of data items, a vector of data items etc.

A *composite data object* is a pair (o_i, o_j) where o_i and o_j are either simple data objects or composite data objects.

An operation of *composition* on data containers r_i and r_j is defined as

$$r_i +_f r_j = \{(o_i, o_j) : o_i \in r_i \text{ and } o_j \in r_j \text{ and } f(o_i, o_j)\} \tag{1}$$

where f is an *evaluation function* $f : r_i \times r_j \rightarrow \{true, false\}$.

An operation of *semicomposition* on data containers r_i and r_j is defined as

$$r_i \dashv_f r_j = \{(o_i : o_i \in r_i \text{ and } \exists o_j \in r_j f(o_i, o_j)\} \tag{2}$$

where f is an *evaluation function* $f : r_i \times r_j \rightarrow \{true, false\}$.

An operation of *elimination* on data containers r_i and r_j is defined as

$$r_i -_f r_j = \{o_i : o_i \in r_i \text{ and not } \exists o_j \in r_j f(o_i, o_j)\} \tag{3}$$

where f is an *evaluation function* $f : r_i \times r_j \rightarrow \{true, false\}$.

An operation of *union* on data containers r_i and r_j is defined as

$$r_i \cup_f r_j = \{o_i : (o_i \in r_i \text{ or } o_i \in r_j) \text{ and } f(o_i)\} \tag{4}$$

were f is an *evaluation function* $f : r_i \rightarrow \{true, false\}$.

An operation of *elimination* on a data container r_i is defined as

$$\sigma_f(r_i) = \{o_i : o_i \in r_i \; and \; f(o_i)\} \tag{5}$$

where f is an *evaluation function* $f : r_i \rightarrow \{true, false\}$.

Like for an internal structure of data objects, a precise syntax of an evaluation function is not determined in the abstract data model. Selection of the particular internal structures for the simple and composite data objects and a syntax for an elimination function defines a concrete data model. For example, a choice of n-tuples as a unified internal structure of all data objects and a syntax of formulas of prepositional logic for an elimination function defines a relational data model with the operations of join, semijoin, antijoin, union, and selection.

A *query* is an expression whose arguments are simple and composite data objects and all its operations belong to a set $\{+_f, \dashv_f, -_f, \cup_f, \sigma_f\}$.

Let $f(x, y)$ be an evaluation function $f : r_i \times r_j \rightarrow \{true, false\}$. A *signature* of f is a pair (r_i, r_j).

A *Projection of function* $f(x, y)$ on an object $o_j \in r_j$ is denoted as $f(x|o_j)$ and it is defined as $f(x|o_j) : r_i \rightarrow \{true, false\}$. A projection of a function $f(x, y)$ on an object $o_j \in r_j$ is obtained through a systematic replacement of an argument y with a constant object o_j. For example if an evaluation function $f(x, y)$ is implemented as `return((x.a+y.b)>5)` then projection of the function on an object o_j such that $o_j.b = 3$ is a function $f(x|o_j)$ implemented as `return((x.a+3)>5)`.

Let T denotes a task submitted at a central site of a distributed information system and let $t_1, \ldots, t_n$ be its decomposition into the individual tasks to be processed at the remote sites of the system. Let $S = \{\top, \bot, t_1, \ldots, t_n\}$ be a set where $\top$ is a *start of processing* symbol, $\bot$ is an *end of processing* symbol. Then, a partial order $P \subseteq S \times S$ such that $< S, P >$ is a lattice where $sup(S) = \top$ and $inf(S) = \bot$ and any pair $(t_i, t_j) \in P$ is called as a *task processing schedule.* For instance, a lattice given in a Figure 1 represents a task processing schedule where the system starts from the simultaneous submission of the tasks t_1, t_2, t_3. When the results of t_2 are available, the system submits t_4. When both results of t_2 and t_3 are available the system submits t_5.

Let $r_1, \ldots, r_n$ denote the results of the tasks $t_1, \ldots, t_n$. An expression that determines how to combine $r_1, \ldots, r_n$ into the final answer is called as a *data integration expression* and it is denoted as $e(r_1, \ldots, r_n)$.

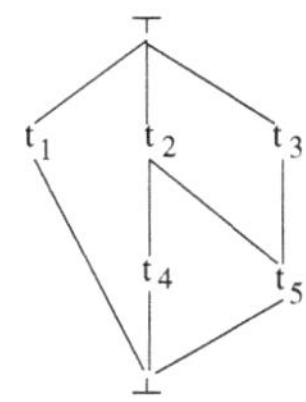

Fig. 1. A sample task processing schedule

4 Evaluation of Integration Strategies

Consider a task processing schedule $S \subseteq T \times T$ where $T = \{\top, \bot, t_1, \ldots, t_n\}$ The cost of a schedule S is measured as the total amount of time required to transmit the results $r_1, \ldots, r_n$ to a central site. The total transmission time depends on the amounts of transmitted data and transmission speed of a network. With an entirely parallel processing schedule the total transmission time is equal to

$$max(|r_1|/\tau_1, \ldots, |r_n|/\tau_n) \tag{6}$$

where τ_i is a transmission speed from a remote system i and $|r_i|$ is the total amount of data transmitted from a remote system i. When one of $|r_i|/\tau_i$ is significantly bigger then the others then it is beneficial to delay the processing of t_i until the results of $r_1, \ldots, r_{i-1}, r_{i+1}, \ldots, r_n$ are available at a central site and to use these results to modify t_i to t'_i such that its result r'_i is smaller than r_i. Then, the total transmission time is equal to

$$max(|r_1|/\tau_1, \ldots, |r_{i-1}|/\tau_{i-1}, |r_{i+1}|/\tau_{i+1}, \ldots, |r_n|/\tau_n) + |r'_i|/\tau_i, \tag{7}$$

When a value of (7) is smaller than a value of (6) then a hybrid task processing schedule, that delays processing of a task t_i and transforms it to reduce transmission time is better than entirely parallel schedule.

An important problem in the evaluation of alternative task processing schedules is estimation of the sizes $|r_i|$ and $|r'_i|$. In the database systems where the query processors use cost based optimization techniques it is possible to get information about an estimated total amount of data returned by a query. For example the cost based query optimizers in relational database systems use histograms on columns of relational tables to estimate the total number of rows returned by a query and SQL statement `EXPLAIN PLAN` can be used find a query execution plan and estimated amounts of data processed accordingly to the plan. Then, it is possible to estimate the values $|r_1|, \ldots, |r_n|$ before the queries are processed. These results can also be used to estimate the reductions of data transmission time when a task t_i is transformed into $t'_i = \sigma_{f(x|r_j)}(t_i)$ where $f(x|r_j)$ is a projection of elimination function on the results r_j. The transformations of t_i are explained in the next section. If an elimination operation removes from r_i data objects that do not satisfy a condition $f(x|r_j)$ then smaller r_j reduces r_i to a larger extent. On the other hand, if elimination removes from r_i data objects that do not have matching data items in the data objects in r_j then larger r_j reduces r_i more than smaller r_j. When it is possible to get information about the total number of data objects included in r_i and r_j then together with a known projection of elimination function $f(x|r_j)$ and known the distributions of data items in objects in r_i and r_j it is possible to estimate the size of $\sigma_{f(x|r_j)}(t_i)$ and find whether processing of t_j before t_i is beneficial.

5 Transformations of Task Processing Schedules

In this section we consider the tasks t_i and t_j to be processed at the remote systems and we show when and how a task t_i can be transformed by the results

r_j. We start from an example that explains an idea of transformations of task processing schedules.

Consider a task T submitted at a central site and decomposed into the tasks t_1, t_2, t_3, and t_4 to be processed at the remote sites. Let r_1, r_2, r_3, r_4 denote data containers with the results of the individual tasks and let a data integration expression $(r_1 +_{f_1} r_2) +_{f_3} (r_3 -_{f_2} r_4)$ determines how the results of individual tasks must be "assembled" into the final result. Assume, that an evaluation function f_3 has a signature (r_1, r_3). It means that implementation of f_3 uses only the data items from the data containers r_1 and r_3. Then it is possible to transform the data integration expression into an equivalent form $((r_1 \dashv_{f_3} r_3) +_{f_1} r_2) +_{f_3} (r_3 -_{f_2} r_4)$. The result of the transformed expression is the same as the result of the original expression because a subexpression $r_1 \dashv_{f_3} r_3$ removes from r_1 data objects which would not contribute to the result of operation $+_{f_3}$ in the transformed expression. It means that a task t_1 can be transformed into an expression $t_1 \dashv_{f_3} r_3$. Unfortunately, due to a high level of autonomy of a remote system the expression cannot be computed in its present form. A remote system does not accept any tasks that include the input data containers like for example r_3. Therefore the expression must be transformed into a form that can be processed by a remote system. We consider an evaluation function $f_3(x, y) : r_1 \times r_3 \rightarrow \{true, false\}$ and its projections $f_3(x|o_1), \ldots, f_3(x|o_n)$ on the objects $o_1, \ldots o_n \in r_3$. Next, we replace an expression $t_1 \dashv_{f_3} r_3$ with $\sigma_{f_3(x|o_1) \text{ or } \ldots \text{ or } f_3(x|o_n)}(t_1)$. It means that we construct a new task that filters the results of t_1 with a condition built over the values of data items in the objects $o_1, \ldots o_n \in r_3$. As a consequence, an entirely parallel task processing schedule of can be changed into a schedule where processing of t_3 precedes processing of t_1 while t_2 and t_4 are still processed simultaneously.

A problem how to transform an entirely parallel schedule can be expressed in the following way. Let T be a task submitted at a central site and decomposed into the tasks $t_1, \ldots, t_n$ to be processed at the remote systems. Let $e(r_1, \ldots, r_n)$ be a data integration expression build over the operations $\{+_f, -_f, \cup_f\}$ and the partial results $r_1, \ldots, r_n$ obtained from the processing of $t_1, \ldots, t_n$ at the remote systems. A question is when and how a task t_i can be transformed into a task t'_i using the results r_j of a task t_j such that a result of data integration expression $e(r_1, \ldots, r_i, \ldots, r_n)$ is the same as a result of expression $e(r_1, \ldots, r'_i, \ldots, r_n)$ where r'_i is the result of transformed task t'_i.

We consider a syntax tree T_e of data integration expression $e(r_1, \ldots, r_n)$ and the smallest subtree T_{ij} of T_e that contain both arguments r_i and r_j. A syntax tree T_e is constructed such that the arguments $r_1, \ldots, r_n$ are located at the leaf nodes and the operations of data integration expression are located at non-leaf nodes. Let $\alpha_f \in \{+_f, -_f, \cup_f\}$ be an operation located at the root node of a subtree T_{ij}. If a signature of an elimination function f is equal to (r_i, r_j) then a task t_i can be transformed using a result r_j or a task t_j can be transformed using a result r_i of a task t_i.

In the example above t_1 can be reduced with the results of t_3 and the opposite because a signature of an operation $+_{f_3}$ in the root of the smallest syntax tree that contains r_1 and r_3 is equal to (r_1, r_3).

In the specific cases the condition determined above may not be satisfied and still it is possible to transform a data integration expression. For example if in expression $(r_1 +_{f_1} r_2) +_{f_3} (r_3 -_{f_2} r_4)$ a signature of f_3 is equal to (r_2, r_3) and signature of f_2 is equal to (r_3, r_4) and $f_2(x_3, x_4)$ is implemented as $\texttt{return}(x_3 = x_4)$ then it is still possible to transform a task t_2 to a form $\sigma_{not\ f_3(x|o_1)\ or\ \ldots\ or\ not\ f_3(x|o_n)}(t_2)$ where $o_1, \ldots, o_n \in r_4$. This is because an equality condition $x_3 = x_4$ in implementation of a function f_2 makes r_3 in in a signature of f_3 equal to r_4 and the second argument of an operation $+_{f_3}$ does not contain objects included in r_4. In the specific cases it is possible to transform the queries despite that signature does not satisfy a condition above.

Table 1. The labeling rules for syntax trees of data integration expressions

	$+_f$	$(left)-_f$	$-_f(right)$	$\cup_f$
d	$d-$	$d-$	$-d$	$d*$
$d-$	$d-$	$d-$	$d*$	$d*$
$-d$	$-d$	$-d$	$d*$	$d*$
$d*$	$d*$	$d*$	$d*$	$d*$

The next problem is to find a transformation that in a general case can be applied to a given task t_i to reduce transmission time of its results r_i. To discover a transformation we label a syntax tree T_e in the following way.

(i) An edge between a leaf node that represent an argument d is labeled with d.
(ii) If a node n in T_e represents an operation α that produces a result r and "child" edge of a node n is labeled with one of the symbols d, $d-$, $-d$, $d*$ then a "parent" edge of n can be labeled with a symbol located in a row indicated by a label of "child" edge and a column indicated by an operation α in Table 1.

The interpretations of the labels are the following. A label d attached to a "child" edge of composition operation at root node of the tree indicate that all d data objects are processed by the operation. A label $d-$ attached to a "child" edge of the same operation indicates that only a subset of data objects of an argument d are processed by the operation. A label $-d$ attached to the same edge indicates that none of data objects d are processed by the operation. A label $d*$ indicates that some of data objects in d and some other data objects are processed by the operation.

As an example, consider an integration expression $(r_1 -_{f_1} r_2) +_{f_2} r_3$. The "parent" edges of the nodes r_1, r_2, and r_3 obtain the labels r_1, r_2, and r_3. A left "child" edge of the root node obtained a label r_1- indicated by a location in the first row and the second column in Table 1. Moreover, the same edge obtains a label $-r_2$ indicated by a location in the first row and the third column in Table 1. A complete labeling is given in a Figure 2.

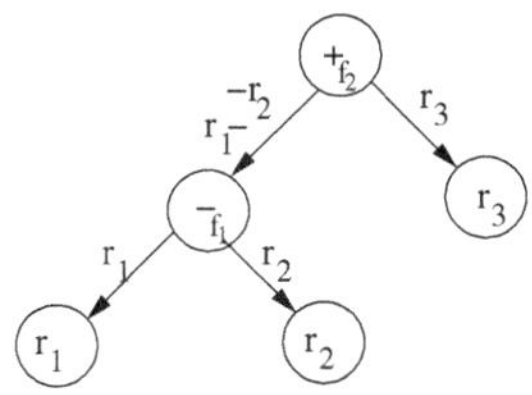

Fig. 2. A labeled syntax tree of data integration plan $(r_1 -_{f_1} r_2)) +_{f_2} r_3$

Table 2. The transformations of arguments in task processing schedules (1)

$+_f$	r_j	r_j-	$-r_j$	r_j*
r_i	$\sigma_{f(x\|r_j)}(t_i)$ $\sigma_{f(r_i\|y)}(t_j)$	$\sigma_{f(x\|r_j)}(t_i)$ $\sigma_{f(r_i\|y)}(t_j)$	$\sigma_{not\ f(x\|r_j)}(t_i)$ $\sigma_{f(r_i\|y)}(t_j)$	$\sigma_{f(r_i\|y)}(t_j)$
r_i-	$\sigma_{f(x\|r_j)}(t_i)$ $\sigma_{f(r_i\|y)}(t_j)$	$\sigma_{f(x\|r_j)}(t_i)$ $\sigma_{f(r_i\|y)}(t_j)$	$\sigma_{not\ f(x\|r_j)}(t_i)$ $\sigma_{not\ f(r_i\|y)}(t_j)$	$\sigma_{f(r_i\|y)}(t_j)$
$-r_i$	$\sigma_{not\ f(r_i\|y)}(t_j)$ $\sigma_{f(x\|r_j)}(t_i)$	$\sigma_{not\ f(x\|r_j)}(t_i)$ $\sigma_{not\ f(r_i\|y)}(t_j)$	$\sigma_{not\ f(r_i\|y)}(t_j)$ $\sigma_{not\ f(x\|r_j)}(t_i)$	$\sigma_{not\ f(r_i\|y)}(t_j)$
r_i*	$\sigma_{f(x\|r_j)}(t_i)$	$\sigma_{f(x\|r_j)}(t_i)$	$\sigma_{not\ f(x\|r_j)}(t_i)$	*none*

Table 3. The transformations of arguments in task processing schedules (2)

$-_f$	r_j	r_j-	$-r_j$	r_j*
r_i	$\sigma_{f(r_i\|y)}(t_j)$ $\sigma_{not\ f(x\|r_j)}(t_i)$	$\sigma_{f(r_i\|y)}(t_j)$	$\sigma_{f(r_i\|y)}(t_j)$	$\sigma_{f(r_i\|y)}(t_j)$
r_i-	$\sigma_{f(r_i\|y)}(t_j)$	$\sigma_{f(r_i\|y)}(t_j)$	$\sigma_{f(r_i\|y)}(t_j)$	$\sigma_{f(r_i\|y)}(t_j)$
$-r_i$	$\sigma_{not\ f(r_i\|y)}(t_j)$ $\sigma_{not\ f(x\|r_j)}(t_i)$	$\sigma_{not\ f(r_i\|y)}(t_j)$	$\sigma_{not\ f(r_i\|y)}(t_j)$ $\sigma_{not\ f(x\|r_j)}(t_i)$	$\sigma_{not\ f(r_i\|y)}(t_j)$
r_i*	$\sigma_{not\ f(x\|r_j)}(t_i)$	$\sigma_{not\ f(x\|r_j)}(t_i)$	*none*	*none*

The interpretation of the transformations included in the Tables 2 and 3 is the following. Consider the arguments r_i and r_j included in the smallest subtree of a syntax tree of data integration expression If an operation in the root of the subtree is $+_f$ then the possible transformations r_i and r_j are included in a Table 2. If an operation in the root of the subtree is $-_f$ then the possible transformations r_i and r_j are included in a Table 3. The replacements of the arguments r_i and r_j can be found after the labeling of both paths from the leaf nodes representing the both arguments towards the root node of the subtree. The transformations of the arguments r_i and r_j are located at the intersection of a row labeled with a label of left "child" edge and a column labeled with a label of "right" child edge of the root node. For instance, consider a subtree of the arguments r_i and r_j such that an operation $+_f$ is in the root node of the subtree. If a left "child" edge of the root node is labeled with $-r_i$, and a right "child" edge of the root node is labeled with r_j* then a Table 2 indicates that it is possible to replace the contents of an argument t_j with an expression $\sigma_{not\ f(r_i|y)}(t_j)$.

As an example consider a data integration expression $(r_1 -_{f_1} r_2)) +_{f_2} r_3$ and its labeling is given in a Figure 2. The following transformations of the arguments are possible. A query t_1 can be replaced with $\sigma_{not\ f_1(x|r_2)}(t_1)$ or with $\sigma_{f_2(x|r_3)}(t_1)$. A query t_2 can be replaced with $\sigma_{f_1(r_1|y)}(t_2)$ or with $\sigma_{f_2(x|r_3)}(t_2)$. A query t_3 can be replaced with $\sigma_{not\ f_2(r_2|y)}(t_3)$ or with $\sigma_{f_2(r_1|y)}(t_3)$. It is possible to apply both transformations. For example, if we plan to process both t_1 and t_2 before t_3 then t_3 can replaced with $\sigma_{not\ f_2(r_2|y)}(\sigma_{f_2(r_1|y)}(t_3))$.

6 Optimization of Task Processing Schedules

At an early stage of data processing at a central site a task T is decomposed into the tasks $t_1, \ldots, t_n$ to be submitted for processing at the remote sites and a data integration expression $e(r_1, \ldots, r_n)$ determines how to combine the results $r_1, \ldots, r_n$ into the final answer. Optimization of a task processing schedule finds an order in which the individual tasks $t_1, \ldots, t_n$ are submitted for processing to minimize the total data transmission time from the remote systems to a central site. The initial task processing schedule is an entirely parallel schedule where all tasks $t_1, \ldots, t_n$ are submitted for processing in one moment in time and processed simultaneously at the remote systems. Optimization of an entirely parallel task processing schedule consists of the following steps.
For all pairs of results (r_i, r_j) perform the following actions:

(1) Find in a syntax tree T_e of a data integration expression $e(r_1, \ldots, r_n)$ the smallest subtree that contain both arguments r_i and r_j. Find an operation α_f in the root node of the subtree. If a signature of an elimination function f is (r_i, r_j) then progress to the next step, otherwise consider the next pair of arguments (r_i, r_j).
(2) Use a Table 1 to label the paths from the leaf nodes r_i and r_j to the root node α_f of the subtree.
(3) Use the Tables 2 and 3 to find the transformations of t_i by a result r_j and t_j by a result r_i.
(4) Compare the costs of the following data integrations plans: (i) t_i processed simultaneously with t_j, (ii) t_i processed before a transformed t_j, (iii) t_j processed before a transformed t_i' and record the best processing order, i.e. a pair (t_i, t_j) or a pair (t_i, t_j) or nothing if simultaneous processing of t_i and t_j provides the smallest costs.

Next, we use the pairs of queries obtained from a procedure above to construct a scheduling lattice. The queries $t_1, \ldots, t_n$ are the labels of the nodes in the lattice and each pair (t_i, t_j) contributes to an edge from node t_i to a node t_j where t_i is located "above" t_j in the lattice. Finally the nodes labeled with $\top$ and $\bot$ are added to the scheduling lattice.

As an example consider a data integration expression $(r_1 -_{f_1} r_2)) +_{f_2} r_3$ and its labeling is given in a Figure 2. The following transformations of the arguments are possible. A query t_1 can be replaced with $\sigma_{not\ f_1(x|r_2)}(t_1)$ or with $\sigma_{f_2(x|r_3)}(t_1)$. A query t_2 can be replaced with $\sigma_{f_1(r_1|y)}(t_2)$ or with $\sigma_{f_2(x|r_3)}(t_2)$. A query t_3 can be replaced with $\sigma_{not\ f_2(r_2|y)}(t_3)$ or with $\sigma_{f_2(r_1|y)}(t_3)$. It is possible to apply both transformations. For example, if we plan to process both t_1 and t_2 before t_3 then t_3 can replaced with $\sigma_{not\ f_2(r_2|y)}(\sigma_{f_2(r_1|y)}(t_3))$. If estimation of the processing times indicated that the results r_2 and r_2 used to transformation of task t_3 into $t'_3 = \sigma_{not\ f_2(r_2|y)}(\sigma_{f_2(r_1|y)}(t_3))$ reduce the transmission of the results d'_3 such that $max(|r_1|/\tau_1, |r_2|/\tau_2)+|d'_3|/\tau_3| < max(|r_1|/\tau_1, |r_2|/\tau_2, |r_3|/\tau_3|)$ then simultaneous processing of the tasks t_1 and t_2 followed processing of t_3 is more efficient than entirely parallel processing of t_1, t_2, and t_3.

7 Summary and Open Problems

In this work we consider optimization of task processing schedules in distributed information system. A task submitted for processing at a central site of the system is decomposed into a number of individual tasks to be processed at the remote sites. A parallel processing schedule of the individual tasks does not always minimize data transmission time and its transformation into a sequential or hybrid schedule may provide shorter response time. This work shows how to transforms entirely parallel task processing schedules into more optimal hybrid schedules where certain tasks are processed simultaneously while the other tasks are processed sequentially. The transformations are guided by the cost-based optimizations whose objective is to reduce the total data transmission time. We show that the properties of data integration expressions can be used to find more efficient schedules. We propose a technique of labeling of syntax trees of data integration expressions to find the coincidences between the arguments. Different types of coincidences between the arguments determine possible transformations of data processing tasks. We show how to use the results of the tasks processed earlier to transform the tasks still waiting for processing in a way that reduce transmission time of their results.

The avenues for further research in this area include the analysis of previous results to estimate the amounts of time needed to transfer the results of individual tasks, and binding optimization of data processing schedules with optimization of processing of data integration expressions. An important factor in optimization of task processing schedules is the ability to precisely predict the amounts of data transmitted from the remote sites by the individual tasks. Recording the characteristics of data processing tasks and the respective amount of data would provide statistical information that later on can be used to more precisely estimate the future transmission size. At the moment processing of data integration expression is resumed only whenever the complete partial results of task processing are available at a central site. An interesting idea would be to process a data integration expression in an online mode where an increment of the partial results would trigger the computations of data integration expression. Such technique would better utilize the available computing resources and it will more evenly spread processing load in time. The other interesting problems include an extension of cost based optimization on both task processing time at a remote site and data transmission time and investigation of an impact of different types of elimination function on transformations of data processing tasks.

References

1. Ahmad, M., Aboulnaga, A., Babu, S.: Query interactions in database workloads. In: Proceedings of the Second International Workshop on Testing Database Systems, pp. 1–6 (2009)
2. Ahmad, M., Duan, S., Aboulnaga, A., Babu, S.: Predicting completion times of batch query workloads using interaction-aware models and simulation. In: Proceedings of the 14th International Conference on Extending Database Technology, pp. 449–460 (2011)
3. Braumandl, R., Keidl, M., Kemper, A., Kossmann, D., Kreutz, A., Seltzsam, S., Stocker, K.: ObjectGlobe: Ubiquitous query processing on the Internet. The VLDB Journal 10(1), 48–71 (2001)
4. Costa, R.L.-C., Furtado, P.: Runtime Estimations, Reputation and Elections for Top Performing Distributed Query Scheduling. In: Proceedings of the 2009 9th IEEE/ACM International Symposium on Cluster Computing and the Grid, pp. 28–35 (2009)
5. Du, W., Krishnamurthy, R., Shan, M.-C.: Query Optimization in Heterogeneous DBMS. In: Proceedings of the 18th VLDB Conference, pp. 277–299 (1992)
6. Friedman, M., Levy, A., Millstein, T.: Navigational plans For Data Integration. In: Proceedings of the National Conference on Artificial Intelligence, pp. 67–73 (1999)
7. Ilarri, S., Mena, E., Illarramendi, A.: Location-dependent query processing: Where we are and where we are heading. ACM Computing Surveys 42(3), 1–73 (2010)
8. Lenzerini, M.: Data Integration: A Theoretical Perspective (2002)
9. Mishra, C., Koudas, N.: The design of a query monitoring system. ACM Transactions on Database Systems 34(1), 1–51 (2009)
10. Nam, B., Shin, M., Andrade, H., Sussman, A.: Multiple query scheduling for distributed semantic caches. Journal of Parallel and Distributed Computing 70(5), 598–611 (2010)
11. Harangsri, B., Shepherd, J., Ngu, A.: Query Classification in Multidatabase Systems. In: Proceedings of the 7th Australasian Database Conference, pp. 147–156 (1996)
12. Ives, Z.G., Green, T.J., Karvounarakis, G., Taylor, N.E., Tannen, V., Talukdar, P.P., Jacob, M., Pereira, F.: The ORCHESTRA Collaborative Data Sharing System. SIGMOD Record (2008)
13. Liu, L., Pu, C.: A Dynamic Query Scheduling Framework for Distributed and Evolving Information Systems. In: Proceedings of the 17th International Conference on Distributed Computing Systems (1997)
14. Lu, H., Ooi, B.-C., Goh, C.-H.: Multidatabase Query Optimization: Issues and Solutions. In: Proceedings RIDE-IMS 1993, Research Issues in Data Engineering: Interoperability in Multidatabase Systems, pp. 137–143 (April 1993)
15. Ozcan, F., Nural, S., Koksal, P., Evrendilek, C., Dogac, A.: Dynamic Query Optimization in Multidatabases. Bulletin of the Technical Committee on Data Engineering 20(3), 38–45 (1997)
16. Sheth, A.P., Larson, J.A.: Federated Database Systems for Managing Distributed, Heterogeneous, and Autonomous Databases. ACM Computing Surveys 22(3), 183–236 (1990)

17. Srinivasan, V., Carey, M.J.: Compensation-Based On-Line Query Processing. In: Proceedings of the 1992 ACM SIGMOD International Conference on Management of Data, pp. 331–340 (1992)
18. Thain, D., Tannenbaum, T., Livny, M.: Distributed computing in practice: the Condor experience: Research Articles. Concurrency Computing: Practice and Experience 17(2-4), 323–356 (2005)
19. Wache, H., Vogele, T., Visser, U., Stuckenschmidt, H., Schuster, G., Neuman, H., Hubner, S.: Ontology-Based Integration of information - A Survey of Existing Approaches (2001)
20. Zhou, Y., Ooi, B.C., Tan, K.-L., Tok, W.H.: An adaptable distributed query processing architecture. Data and Knowledge Engineering 53(3), 283–309 (2005)
21. Zhu, Q., Larson, P.A.: Solving Local Cost Estimation Problem for Global Query Optimization in Multidatabase Systems. Distributed and Parallel Databases 6(4), 373–420 (1998)
22. Ziegler, P.: Three Decades of Data Integration - All problems Solved? In: 18th IFIP World Computer Congress, vol. 12 (2004)

On Rewriting of Planar 3-Regular Graphs

Kohji Tomita[1], Yasuwo Ikeda[2], and Chiharu Hosono[3]

[1] National Institute of Advanced Industrial Science and Technology (AIST), Tsukuba, Japan
k.tomita@aist.go.jp
[2] Department of Media Presentation, Faculty of Studies on Contemporary Society, Mejiro University, Tokyo, Japan
yikeda@krd.biglobe.ne.jp
[3] Department of Computer Science, University of Tsukuba, Tsukuba, Japan
hosono@ailab.is.tsukuba.ac.jp

Abstract. In this paper, we consider a class of connected planar 3-regular graphs (rotation systems) and show that, for any two such graphs with the same number of vertices, one kind of local rewriting rule is capable of rewriting one graph to the other. On the basis of such graph development systems, emergent systems including self-organizing systems will be considered in a uniform manner.

Keywords: graph rewriting, graph automata, local rewriting rule, emergence.

1 Introduction

Graphs are useful concept which provides various levels of abstraction for describing, analyzing, or designing systems. They have been studied in diverse contexts [2]. Usually, each vertex corresponds to an element or a component of a system, and an edge between vertices represent some relation among them.

When the systems have some dynamic nature, rewriting of graphs is necessary, in accordance with their physical or logical change. We have many such systems, e.g., biological development systems with emergent behavior. Due to diverse nature of graphs and their possible rewritings, there are variety of ways to rewrite graphs. They include node replacement, hyper edge replacement and so on [6].

Instead of considering general cases, in this paper, we focus on rewriting of 3-regular graphs (also called cubic graphs or trivalent graphs) to simplify the discussion owing to the regularity. In 3-regular graphs, each vertex has three incident edges. In spite of apparent simplicity of 3-regular graphs, they are important and interesting as surveyed in [3]. In addition to the regularity, we assume a cyclic order of the edges around each vertex. Such a graph is called a (graph) rotation system. Rotation systems correspond to embeddings on surfaces.

Rewriting of 3-regular graphs has been studied in several aspects [10,1,7]. In [8], two types of local rewriting rules were shown to be enough for rewriting one connected planar 3-regular graph to the other. In this paper, we extend

A. Abd Manaf et al. (Eds.): ICIEIS 2011, Part III, CCIS 253, pp. 346–352, 2011.

the result by considering the case such that one type of local rewriting rule is employed and show that, when two connected planar 3-regular graphs have the same number of vertices, there is a rewriting sequence from one to the other by the rule.

This study is motivated by studies of self-organizing systems including adaptive networks [4]. By assigning states to the vertices and giving a rule set, this study extends to graph development systems for self-organizing systems. In such systems, structures and states are coupled closely in the sense that the global structure constrains the behavior of each element and the behaviors of the elements affect on the structure. On this basis we will be able to provide a simple framework for understanding emerging behavior such as self-organization.

2 Formulation

In this section, we review the framework that we consider in this paper. We assume that the base graph structure is a 3-regular graph rotation system; for every vertex the number of edges which are incident into the vertex is three. Different from ordinary graphs, cyclic order of the edges is assigned at each vertex. More formally, it is defined as follows.

Let I be an index set $\{0, 1, 2\}$ for the cyclic order. The set of all two element subsets of a set A is denoted by $\mathcal{P}_2(A)$, i.e., $\mathcal{P}_2(A) = \{\{x, y\} | x, y \in A \text{ and } x \neq y\}$.

Definition 1. A base graph G is a pair $\langle V, E\rangle$, where V is a (possibly empty) finite set of vertices and E is a set of edges defined in the following. Each edge specifies two incident vertices with indices; more formally, E is a subset of $\mathcal{P}_2(V \times I)$ such that for every $\langle u, i\rangle \in V \times I$ there exists just one $\langle v, j\rangle \in V \times I$ such that $\{\langle u, i\rangle, \langle v, j\rangle\} \in E$.

This definition permits multiple edges and self-edges (loops). For a graph G, V_G and E_G denote the vertices and edges of G, respectively.

We use $\oplus$ to indicate the addition modulo three. A function $\psi : I \to I$ is said to preserve cyclic ordering if there exits $d \in I$ such that $\psi(i) = i \oplus d$ holds for every $i \in I$.

Definition 2. Two base graphs $G = \langle V, E\rangle$ and $G' = \langle V', E'\rangle$ are isomorphic, denoted as $G \simeq G'$, if there exist bijections $\varphi : V \to V'$ and $\psi_u : I \to I$, for each $u \in V$, such that ψ_u preserves cyclic ordering and $\{\langle u, i\rangle, \langle v, j\rangle\} \in E$ iff $\{\langle \varphi(u), \psi_u(i)\rangle, \langle \varphi(v), \psi_v(j)\rangle\} \in E'$ for $u, v \in V$ and $i, j \in I$.

Hereafter, base graphs are called just graphs for simplicity if there is no confusion. In this paper, isomorphic graphs are identified. A base graph is called planar if it can be drawn on a plane, i.e., embedded without crossing the edges, so that the cyclic order agrees on all the vertices; three edges are drawn in the same cyclic order (clockwise, in the figures hereafter) around every vertex.

For notational convenience, we introduce replacement of vertices and indices in a set E of edges;

$$E[\langle v'_0, x'_0\rangle/\langle v_0, x_0\rangle, \ \ldots, \ \langle v'_n, x'_n\rangle/\langle v_n, x_n\rangle]$$

is the result of replacing each $\langle v_i, x_i\rangle$ in the edges in E by $\langle v_i', x_i'\rangle$ for $0 \le i \le n$ simultaneously.

We introduce one kind of rewriting, called commutation, in the following.

Definition 3. A rewriting of $G = \langle V, E\rangle$ for $e \in E$, denoted as com_e, is a function in the following. If e is a loop, $com_e(G) = G$. Otherwise, let $e = \{\langle u, i\rangle, \langle v, j\rangle\}$ for $u \ne v$. Then, $com_e(G) = \langle V, E'\rangle$, where

$$E' = E[\langle u, i\oplus 1\rangle/\langle u, i\oplus 2\rangle, \langle u, i\oplus 2\rangle/\langle v, j\oplus 1\rangle, \langle v, j\oplus 1\rangle/\langle v, j\oplus 2\rangle, \langle v, j\oplus 2\rangle/\langle u, i\oplus 1\rangle].$$

Figure 1 illustrates structural change of this rewriting. Note that any two neighbor vertices of u or v, denoted as u_i and v_i with dotted line in the figure, may coincide (possibly with u or v). This rewriting preserves planarity of the graphs.

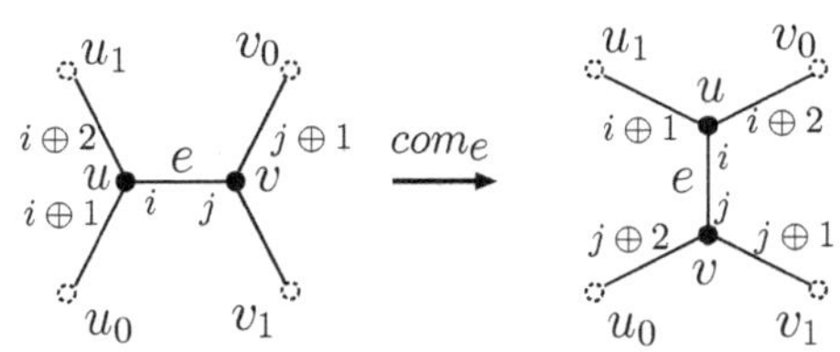

Fig. 1. Structural change by commutation. i and j indicate cyclic order of the edges. Vertices with dotted line may coincide (possibly with u or v).

Definition 4. Let G_0 be a graph, and $e \in E_{G_0}$. If $G_1 \simeq com_e(G_0)$, we write $G_0 \xrightarrow{e} G_1$ or simply $G_0 \to G_1$. If $G_i \to G_{i+1}$ for $0 \le i \le n-1$, we write $G_0 \to^* G_n$, and say G_0 is rewritten into G_n.

Lemma 1. *Rewriting relation '$\to$' is symmetric, i.e., if $G \to H$, then $H \to G$.*

Proof. For any $e \in E_G$, e is an edge of $com_e(G)$ and $com_e(com_e(G)) \simeq G$. □

3 Reachability

In this section, we show that, for any connected planar graphs G and H with n vertices, $G \to^* H$ holds. For this purpose, we introduce canonical graphs N_n with n vertices, and show $G \to^* N_n$.

Definition 5. Graphs N_{2n} with $2n$ vertices in the following are called canonical: $N_{2n} = \langle V, E\rangle$, where

$$\begin{aligned} V &= \{v_0, \ldots, v_{2n-1}\}, \\ E &= \{\{\langle v_i, 0\rangle, \langle v_{(i+1) \bmod n}, 2\rangle\} | 0 \le i \le n-2\} \\ &\cup \{\{\langle v_i, 0\rangle, \langle v_{(i+1) \bmod 2n}, 2\rangle\} | n \le i \le 2n-2\} \\ &\cup \{\{\langle v_i, 1\rangle, \langle v_{n+i}, 1\rangle\} | n \le 0 \le n-1\}. \end{aligned}$$

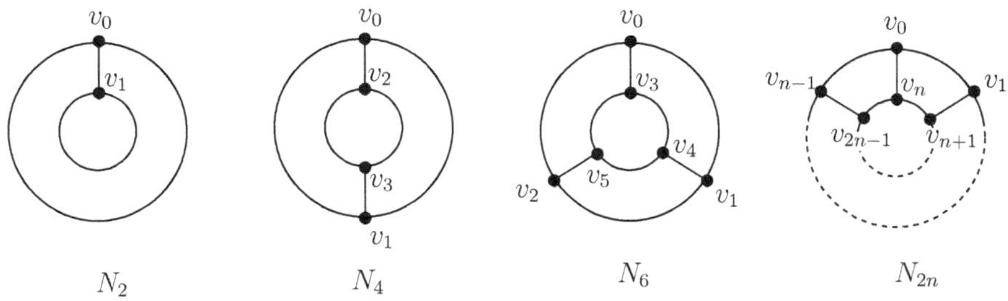

Fig. 2. Examples of canonical graphs

Examples of canonical graphs are shown in Fig. 2. Each vertex in N_{2n} is equivalent in the sense that, for any vertices v and v' in N_{2n}, there exists an isomorphism from N_{2n} to N_{2n} that maps v into v' .

Figure 3 illustrates all the planar connected 3-regular graphs with four vertices, and some rewriting among them. Bold and two types of dashed lines indicate the vertices to which corresponding rewriting, denoted by arrows, are applied.

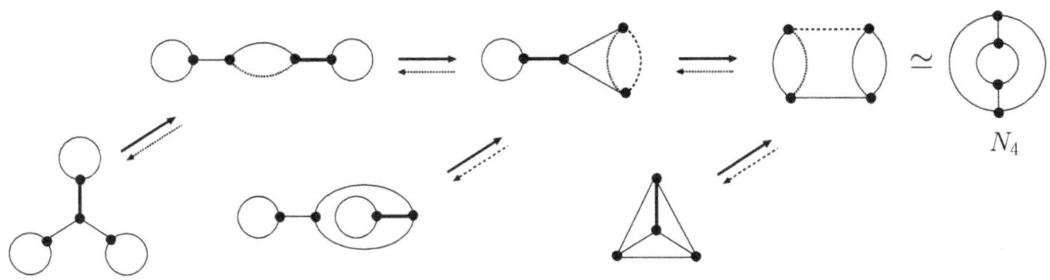

Fig. 3. Examples of rewriting sequence for all possible planar 3-regular graphs with four vertices. Bold and two types of dashed lines indicate the vertices to which corresponding rewriting, denoted by arrows, are applied.

In order that induction on the number of vertices runs, we introduce a method to regard a subgraph of three vertices as one vertex.

Definition 6. A cycle of the form

$$v_0, \{\langle v_0, d_0\rangle, \langle v_1, d_1 \oplus 1\rangle\}, v_1, \{\langle v_1, d_1\rangle, \langle v_k, d_2 \oplus 1\rangle\}, v_2, \ldots,$$
$$v_n, \{\langle v_n, d_n\rangle, \langle v_0, d_0 \oplus 1\rangle\}, v_0,$$

is called uniform. A uniform cycle of length three is called a triangle.

Triangles may be specified by three vertices. When H is obtained from G by replacing a vertex v with a triangle (v_0, v_1, v_2) as shown in Fig. 4, we denote this by $H = G[(v_0, v_1, v_2)/v]$. This replacement keeps the constraint of 3-regular graphs. This vertex v is called a meta vertex. This is formally defined as follows.

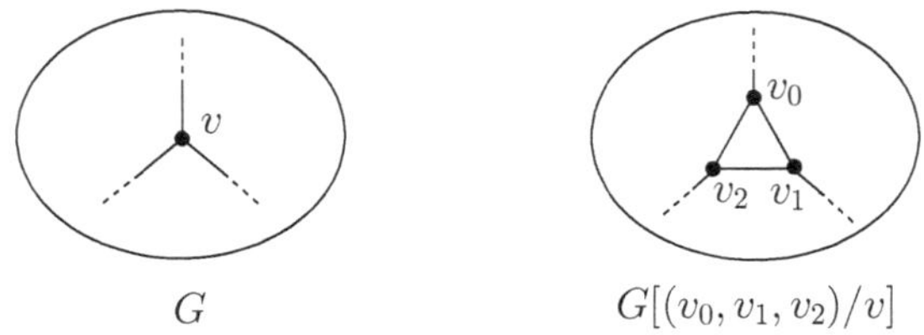

Fig. 4. Meta vertex

Definition 7. For a graph $G = \langle V, E\rangle$, where $v \in V$ and $\{v_0, v_1, v_2\} \cap V = \phi$, $G[(v_0, v_1, v_2)/v] = \langle V', E'\rangle$, where

$$\begin{aligned} V' &= (V\backslash\{v\}) \cup \{v_0, v_1, v_2\},\\ E' &= E[\langle v_0, 0\rangle/\langle v, 0\rangle, \langle v_1, 1\rangle/\langle v, 1\rangle, \langle v_2, 2\rangle/\langle v, 2\rangle]\\ &\quad \cup\{\{\langle v_0, 1\rangle, \langle v_1, 0\rangle\}, \{\langle v_1, 2\rangle, \langle v_2, 1\rangle\}, \{\langle v_2, 0\rangle, \langle v_0, 2\rangle\}\}. \end{aligned}$$

Lemma 2. *Let $G = \langle V, E\rangle$ and $H = \langle V, E'\rangle$ be connected planar 3-regular graphs. If $G \rightarrow^* H$, then, for every $v \in V$, $G[(v_0, v_1, v_2)/v] \rightarrow^* H[(v_0, v_1, v_2)/v]$, where $\{v_0, v_1, v_2\} \cap V = \phi$.*

Proof. By the induction on the length of rewriting $G = G_0 \rightarrow \cdots \rightarrow G_n = H$.

If $n = 0$, it is evident. If $n = 1$, we have $G \overset{e}{\rightarrow} H$ for some $e \in E_G$. If e is not incident to v, $G[(v_0, v_1, v_2)/v] \overset{e}{\rightarrow} H[(v_0, v_1, v_2)/v]$. Otherwise, by extending the meta vertex into three vertices, we obtain a rewriting sequence from $G[(v_0, v_1, v_2)/v]$ into $H[(v_0, v_1, v_2)/v]$ by two steps as shown in Fig. 5. Large dotted circles in the first and last graphs represent meta vertices. Bold lines indicate edges to which commutation is applied in this and the following figures.

The cases for $n > 1$ are shown from the induction hypothesis and transitivity of rewriting. □

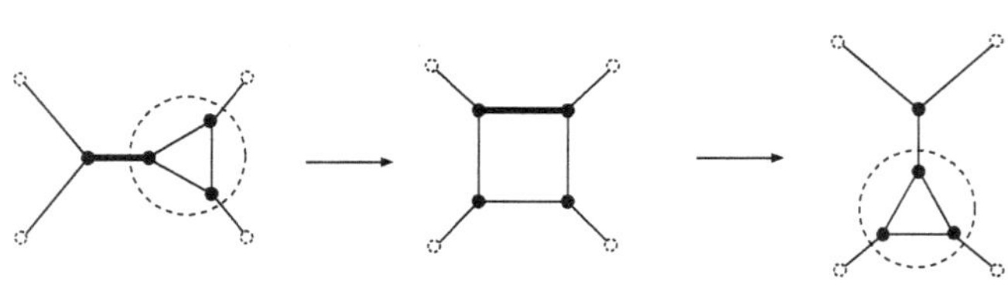

Fig. 5. Commutation of a meta vertex by two steps. Dashed circles with three vertices in the left and right graphs represent meta vertices. Bold lines indicate edges to which rewriting is applied.

Lemma 3. *Any connected planar 3-regular graph $G = \langle V, E\rangle$, where $|V| \geq 4$, can be rewritten into a graph $G' = \langle V, E'\rangle$ with a triangle.*

Proof. If there is a uniform cycle of length n (≥ 3), it is inductively shown as follows. If $n = 3$, we have $G' = G$. Otherwise, let the cycle be $v_0, e_0, ..., v_{n-1}, e_{n-1}, v_0$.

Then, for any e_j in this cycle, application of com_{e_j} generates a uniform cycle of length $n-1$. Thus, the induction step follows from the induction hypothesis and transitivity.

If G includes a loop, a triangle can be generated as follows. Depending on the connective relation of its neighbor vertices, local connection around the vertex is one of two cases: Fig. 6(a) or Fig. 6(b). In each case, rewritings indicated in Fig. 6 generate a triangle.

In the following, we show that if there is not a uniform cycle of length at least three, G has a loop. If G has no cycle of length greater than two, by removing loops and merging multiple edges, the graph becomes a tree in ordinary sense, and a leaf corresponds to a vertex with a loop in G. Otherwise, G has a non-uniform cycle of length at least three. We assume a fixed drawing of G on a plane. Then, there is an edge to its inner face of the cycle. Without loss of generality, we can assume this cycle is an innermost one. Then, similarly to the above reasoning, there exists a vertex with a loop in this face. □

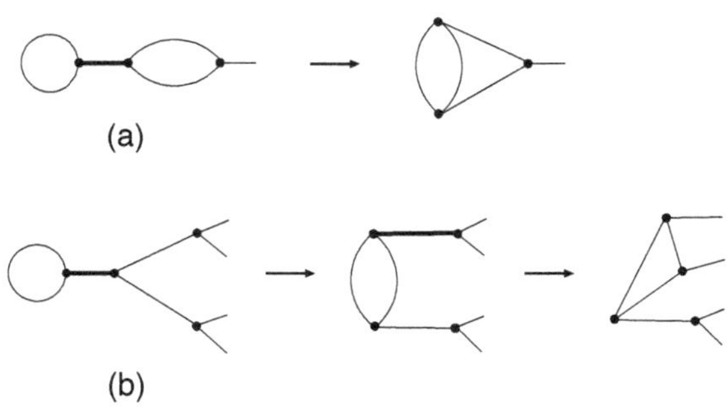

Fig. 6. Two cases of rewriting steps for loops. Bold lines indicate edges to which rewriting is applied.

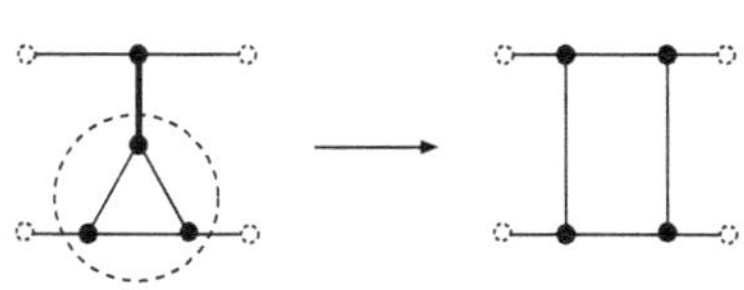

Fig. 7. Rearranging three nodes in a meta vertex into a canonical graph. Bold lines indicate edges to which rewriting is applied.

Lemma 4. *For any connected planar 3-regular graph G with n vertices, $G \to^* N_n$.*

Proof. We show this by the induction on the number of vertices. If $n = 2$, then $G \simeq N_2$, or G has triple edges. In the latter case, for any edge e in G, $G \xrightarrow{e} N_2$.

If $n \geq 4$, G can be written into N_{2n} as follows. (1) G can be rewritten into G' with a triangle from Lemma 3, i.e., $G \to^* G'$. (2) By regarding a triangle

(v_0, v_1, v_2) in G' as a meta-vertex, G' is isomorphic to a graph $G''[(v_0, v_1, v_2)/v]$ for some graph G'' with $n - 2$ vertices, i.e., $G' \simeq G''[(v_0, v_1, v_2)/v]$. Then, from the induction hypothesis, $G'' \rightarrow^* N_{n-2}$. Thus, from Lemma 2, we have $G''[(v_0, v_1, v_2)/v] \rightarrow^* N_{n-2}[(v_0, v_1, v_2)/v]$. (3) Since each vertex in N_n is equivalent, $N_{n-2}[(v_0, v_1, v_2)/v]$ can be rewritten into N_n as in Fig. 7, independent of the location of the meta vertex. That is, $N_{n-2}[(v_0, v_1, v_2)/v] \rightarrow^* N_n$. Therefore, from transitivity, we have $G \rightarrow^* N_n$. □

Theorem 1. *Let G and H be connected planar 3-regular graphs with the same number of vertices. Then, $G \rightarrow^* H$.*

Proof. Clear from Lemmas 1 and 4. □

4 Conclusion

In this paper, we considered a class of connected planar 3-regular graphs (rotation systems) and showed that, for any two such graphs with the same number of vertices, one kind of local rewriting rule is capable of rewriting one graph to the other. It is also possible to perform the obtained rewriting in the system in [8], by assigning appropriate states to the vertices, and giving a rewriting rule set. On the basis of such graph development, emerging behavior including self-organization can be considered in a uniform manner.

Acknowledgment. This work was supported by JSPS KAKENHI (21500231).

References

1. Bolognesi, T.: Planar Trivalent Network Computation. In: Durand-Lose, J., Margenstern, M. (eds.) MCU 2007. LNCS, vol. 4664, pp. 146–157. Springer, Heidelberg (2007)
2. Diestel, R.: Graph Theory, 4th edn. Springer, Heidelberg (2010)
3. Greenlaw, R., Petreschi, R.: Cubic graphs. ACM Computing Surveys 27(4), 471–495 (1995)
4. Gross, T., Sayama, H. (eds.): Adaptive Networks: Theory. Models and Applications. Springer, Heidelberg (2009)
5. Milner, R.: The Space and Motion of Communicating Agents. Cambridge University Press (2009)
6. Rozenberg, R. (ed.): Handbook of Graph Grammars and Computing by Graph Transformation. Foundations, vol. 1. World Scientific (1997)
7. Tomita, K., Kurokawa, H., Murata, S.: Graph automata: natural expression of self-reproduction. Physica D 171(4), 197–210 (2002)
8. Tomita, K., Kurokawa, H.: On the reachability of a version of graph-rewriting system. Information Processing Letters 109(14), 777–782 (2009)
9. von Neumann, J.: Theory of Self-Reproducing Automata. Univ. of Illinois Press (1966)
10. Wolfram, S.: A New Kind of Science. Wolfram Media (2002)

An Intelligent Query Routing Mechanism for Distributed Service Discovery with IP-Layer Awareness

Mohamed Saleem H[1,*], Mohd Fadzil Hassan[2], and Vijanth Sagayan Asirvadam[3]

[1] Computer and Information Sciences, Universiti Teknologi PETRONAS, Perak, Malaysia
Dual affiliation with Faculty of Information and Communication Technology, Universiti Tunku Abdul Rahman, Perak, Malaysia
saleem@utar.edu.my
[2] Computer and Information Sciences
[3] Fundamental and Applied Science, Universiti Teknologi PETRONAS, Perak, Malaysia
{mfadzil_hassan,vijanth_sagayan}@petronas.com.my

Abstract. Traditional query routing mechanisms for service and resource discovery in distributed systems function purely at the overlay layer by isolating itself from the underlying IP-layer. This leads to large amount of inter-ISP traffic and unbalanced utilization of underlying links which affect the performance of the network. In this paper we address this problem by proposing a novel distributed service discovery algorithm, which enables IP-layer awareness so that query routing is performed without the involvement of the overlay peers. In our algorithm, message level intelligence is exploited using Application Oriented Networking (AON) and thus query forwarding is performed in the IP layer. We also classify services in the registry based on industries so that queries could be forwarded selectively. We present the conceptual design of our framework and analyze its effectiveness through simulation. Our simulation results prove the performance gain obtained by moving down the overlay query routing mechanism to the IP-layer.

Keywords: Web services, service discovery, AON, P2P, multicasting, clustering, SOA.

1 Introduction

As more and more services are made available both from within and outside organizations, the centralized service discovery based on client/server architecture turns out to be unsuccessful in terms of scalability and single point of failure [1], which paved way for decentralized approach. Many contributions have been made earlier regarding distributed service discovery (DSD) (as well as resources), which has its roots from Peer-to-Peer (P2P) file sharing systems. Amongst various P2P approaches, only a few are suitable to be implemented in the service discovery domain, as they were designed for file sharing applications, where file download efficiency is one of the major concerns.

* Corresponding author.

A. Abd Manaf et al. (Eds.): ICIEIS 2011, Part III, CCIS 253, pp. 353–363, 2011.

However, as of service and resource discovery are concerned other constraints such as range queries, their cost and multiple matches are taken into account.

The current DSD systems could be classified into unstructured, structured and hybrid. The main shortcoming of the decentralized unstructured architecture is their scalability, whereas the structured architectures are prone to complex administration, tight coupling and poor performances in dynamic environment [2]. On the other hand hybrid systems are focused towards key mapping mechanisms that are inclined towards tightly controlled structured approach. In this paper our focus is towards unstructured systems which are widely deployed due to their flexibility with dynamic entry and exit options for the peers.

Currently, most of the query routing mechanisms are implemented in the overlay layer which results in IP-layer-ignorant query forwarding. Due to this neighbors that appear closer in the overlay layer could be far apart in the physical underlying network. This leads to three major problems. First, it heavily increases the inter-ISP network traffic [3] which is expensive for the service providers. Second, the network links are stressed in unbalanced manner resulting in poor performance and thirdly it introduces interlayer communication overhead. To alleviate these problems several contributions have been made in making the peers IP-layer aware while choosing their neighbors. However, these solutions just provide the knowledge of network proximity to the peers in the overlay and let the peers decide on their own [4]. Letting the peers aware of network related parameters may lead to privacy and security issues both for the peers and the ISPs.

In order to improve the efficiency and performance of the query routing, we propose a novel approach by moving the query routing mechanism to the IP-layer that enhances awareness of underlying network topology in terms of the proximity of the neighbors and class based selective query forwarding with message level intelligence. Our proposal is also more secure as the routing information is not revealed to the peers in the overlay layer. We prove that the performance can be significantly improved through our approach.

In addition to performance gain, our architecture also provides enhancements like,

1. Non-involvement of peers in the locality aware query forwarding that results in improved efficiency.
2. Increased peer privacy.
3. Increased response time with the elimination of interlayer communication overhead.

The rest of the paper is organized as follows. Section 2 discusses the related work, Section 3 demonstrates our design, Section 4 analyzes the performance analytically, Section 5 proves the analysis with simulation results and Section 6 concludes the paper with future work.

2 Related Work

In our previous work [5], we had demonstrated the modeling of AON based routing with message level intelligence and discussed its benefits in intelligent query routing.

This prototype simulation analyzed the registry (and not query) processing at the IP-layer over application layer and proved that processing at the IP-layer provides better time efficiency. In this paper we have extended our prototype to implement typical service discovery with AON based routing and analyzes its performance which is detailed further in section 5. Various other approaches have been proposed and investigated towards improving the network layer awareness in query routing mechanisms.

TOPLUS [6] organizes peers into group of IP addresses and uses longest prefix match to determine the target node to forward the query. Here the peers use an API in the application layer to identify the neighbor. Moving the query routing functionality to the IP layer is out of their scope.

PIPPON [7] is closer to our effort in trying to match the overlay with the underlying network. The clustering mechanism in the overlay layer of PIPPON is based on network membership and proximity (latency). However, the similarity of the services provided is not taken into consideration in cluster formation. Moreover, it ends up in a highly structured system with high administrative overhead.

The contribution made in [8] is a technique called *biased neighbor selection*. This technique works by selecting a certain number of neighboring peers within the same ISP and the remaining from different ISPs. This helps in reducing the inter-ISP traffic. This approach is well suited for file sharing systems like BitTorrent. However, the neighbors still function at the overlay layer.

In [3] authors have discussed the problem space for the Application Layer Traffic Optimization (ALTO) working group, which is initiated by IETF. This approach allows the peer to choose the best target peer for file downloading by querying the ALTO service which has acquired static topological information from the ISP. Here the ALTO service is provided as a complementary service to an existing DHT or a tracker service. The problem space here is the final downloading of the file and not the query search mechanism itself.

A framework that is used for conveying network layer information to the P2P applications has been proposed by P4P [4]. Peers make use of *iTrackers* and *appTrackers* to obtain the network information. The network information is used for the overlay query routing mechanism. However, the scope of the work is not in moving the query routing to the network layer which is the focus of our contribution.

Plethora [9] proposes a locality enhanced overlay network for semi-static peer to peer system. It is designed to have a two-level overlay that comprises a global overlay spanning all nodes in the network, and a local overlay that is specific to the autonomous system (AS). In dynamic environments, entry and exit of peers are common and thus this architecture is not appropriate due to its high structured nature.

There has been substantial contribution made in clustering as well. One such recent contribution is [10]. Our contribution contrasts with this and all others in making network provider based clustering, which aids in reduction of number of super registries that needs to be handled by Application Oriented Networking (AON) multicasting.

Deploying message level intelligence in network layer multicasting and dealing with QoS requirements in the service discovery domain are discussed in [11-13]. In [14], authors have initiated the discussion of employing AON in the service discovery but have not given a concrete implementation model, which is where our contribution fits in. The increasing trends in deployment of AON in other areas of SOA are provided in [15].

3 Framework for IP-Layer Query Routing

3.1 Layered Approach

The layered framework of our design is as shown in figure 1. Our contribution is at layer 2, where AON is employed for carrying query messages to the target peers with the help of message level intelligence. As redundant query forwarding in the underlying IP-layer is minimized by AON with message level multicasting, the performance gain is very close to the IP level multicasting [16]. In order to further exploit the feature of AON, the design at layer 3 should be adapted in such a way that only multicasting is required for DSD. This leads to the design of AS based clustering and service classifications at layer 3, which leverages the message level multicasting by AON. Our work assumes that there exists a suitable service class encoding method and its details are out of the scope of our research. At layer 2 our framework can also support the interoperability with routers that does not support message level routing. This is an added advantage which is explained in section 3.3.

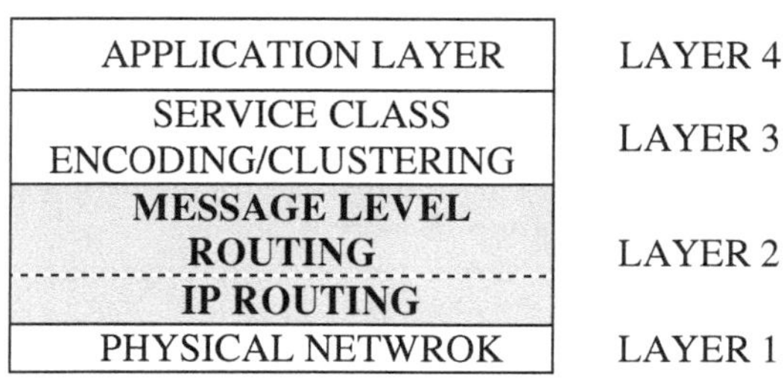

Fig. 1. Layers of P2P service discovery

3.2 Registry Clustering

Our clustering approach at layer 3 is with respect to the AS so as to reduce the inter-ISP traffic. A registry which has the highest hardware configuration is elected as super registry (SR) that is responsible for accepting queries for the whole AS. The services published in the registries are classified in accordance with Global Industry Classification Standard (GICS) [17]. Our architecture uses these coding for the implementation of AON routing at the underlying layer. A sample of GICS industry classification is shown in Table 1.

Table 1. Sample Industry Types and Their Codes

Industries	Class codes
Air Freight & Logistics	20301010
Airlines	20302010
Hotels, Resorts & Cruise	25301020
Leisure Facilities	25301030

This AS based SR approach leverages the following characteristics of our system.

1. Enables the AON router in layer 2 to learn the query forwarding interface(s) that are specific to particular class of services.
2. Improves the scalability and dynamism of the system as new registries can enter and exit the cluster with minimal overhead.

We also propose to use crawling technique to update the entries in the super registries so that queries forwarded within the AS could be minimized.

3.3 Intelligent Query Routing Mechanism

AON routers are capable of taking routing decisions based on application level messages [14]. We find this feature fits quite nicely into the distributed service discovery. Any query generated from an AS needs to be forwarded to the super registry in the AS which has an interface for classifying the query into one or more of its service classes. Then the message is constructed by encapsulating the query and its class and forwarded to the neighbors in the overlay routing table. Our packet structure in the IP layer is designed to record the interface(s) of the intermediate routers through which a particular router has received its query and reply, along with the intended source and destination IP addresses. This feature can be easily incorporated with the help of extension headers in case if IPv6 or within the payload in case of IPv4. The AON router uses this feature to inspect and update these fields and its AON specific routing table which is used for selective query forwarding to multiple SRs. This approach which is a multicast does not maintain any group memberships and forwarding is purely based on AON specific routing table. Possible scenarios that could be encountered during query forwarding are depicted in table 2.

Table 2. Scenarios encountered in query forwarding

Router	Packet	Remark
AON	AON	Routing based on extension headers (message level intelligence)
AON	Non-AON	Classical routing based on IP header
Non-AON	AON	Classical routing based on IP header
Non-AON	Non-AON	Classical routing based on IP header

Figure 2a depicts an illustrative scenario of four ASs each with its own super registries connected via AON routers. A query forwarded from an AS is received by the border routers of ASs, in this case router R1. The routing algorithm employed by AON routers is shown below. Figure 2a demonstrates a sample query forwarding from SR1 to SR2, SR3 and SR4 during the learning state. In such situation the query is forwarded through all interfaces of the router except the incoming interface. The looping of the query is prevented by providing a unique id for each query so that the router does not forward the query if it has already done so. During this state the AON routing table is updated along the path of the reply as shown in condition 1 where r is the existing routes of routing table RT and r_{new} is new routes learned through the query reply Q_{reply}.

$$RT \cup Q_{reply} \mid r \in RT, r_{new} \in Q_{reply} \quad (1)$$

Figure 2b demonstrates a typical scenario of steady state in query forwarding. SR1 forwards the query to its border router R1. AON-router R1 inspects the query and finds that this query should be forwarded to R2 as per its AON routing table and this process continues until the query reaches its destination. The same process is used if a query could be answered by multiple SRs in which case queries are forwarded to more than one SR.

Routing algorithm

```
IF AON_RT = empty AND query not forwarded already
   Forward packet to all outgoing interface except
incoming interface
ELSE
 Forward as per the AON_RT
```

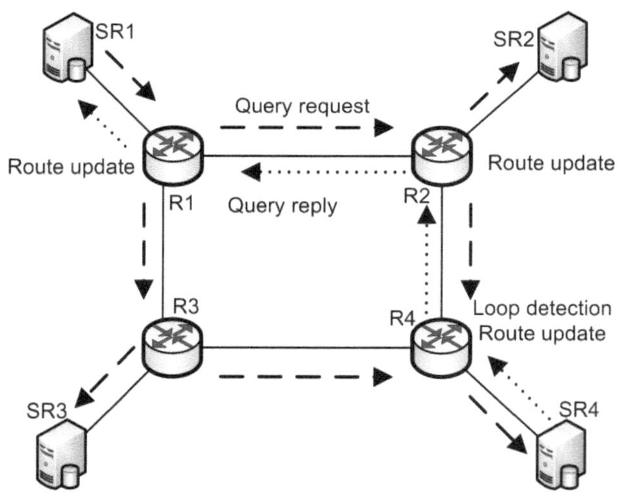

Fig. 2a. Query routing in learning state

4 Analysis

The following features are enhanced in our implementation.

1. **Enhanced Security:** Network aware query routing is delegated to the underlying IP-layer and is kept transparent to the overlay layer so that network related information is not revealed to the peer in the overlay.
2. **Reduced Inter-ISP Traffic:** The peers in the system are not used as an intermediary for query routing between the source and the targeted peer. This enormously reduces the inter-ISP traffic as our SRs are based on AS.

3. **Reduced Stress Level:** The network layer is relieved from the stress due to reduction in the amount of redundant traffic generated in the IP-layer.
4. **Interoperability:** Our design integrates seamlessly with non-AON routers, if encountered, along the path of query forwarding.

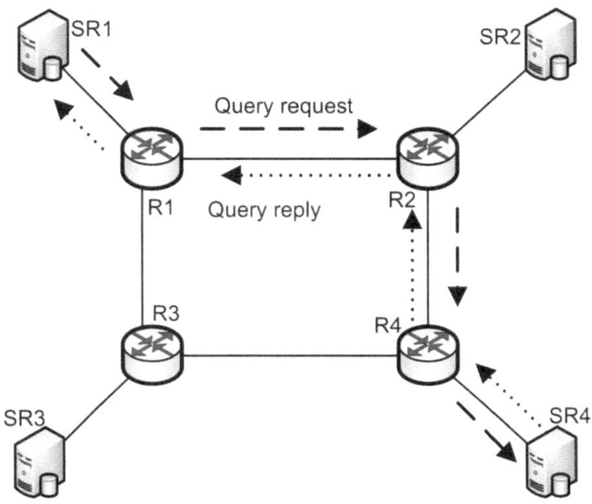

Fig. 2b. Query routing in steady state

Table 3. Performance Analysis for the Given Scenario

Query propagation method	No. of peers involved	No. of links involved
Flooding (select all 3 neighbors)	4 (SR1,SR2, SR3,SR4)	13 (SR1→R1 * 3 , R1→R2 * 2, R1→R3 * 2, R2→R4, R3→SR3, R4→SR4 * 2 R3→R4, R2→SR2)
Random/Probabilistic (selects 2/3 neighbors)	3 (SR1, SR2, SR4)	7 (SR1→R1, R1→R2 * 2, R2→SR *2, R2→R4, R4→SR4)
AON based	2 (SR1, SR4)	4 (SR1→R1, R1→R2, R2→R4, R4→SR4)

In a pure overlay based routing, for instance, Gnutella like systems, considering the worst case scenario (Flooding), query from SR1 to SR2, SR3 and SR4 would generate traffic along the paths SR1→SR2, SR1→SR3, SR1→SR4. Particularly the link R1→R2, and R1→R3 would carry the same request twice as the routing is performed in the overlay. However, if AON routing is employed the traffic generated is just along the path SR1→SR4. Even during the learning stage the redundant queries are eliminated. This clearly illustrates that ineffective query propagation could effectively be overcome by AON to improve the efficiency of search mechanism. The same can be visualized in terms of inter-ISP traffic as well. In our illustration the only inter-ISP traffic is from the source to the AS in which the target SR resides, as the intermediary peers are not involved in query forwarding. Whereas in the overlay routing all the four peers belonging to different ISPs are involved in query processing. Performance can also be improved in case of other query forwarding heuristics like random or probabilistic selection of neighbors which is summarized in table 3.

Current Issues

1. **Security Issues:** Chances are there that a compromised router could generate malformed query replies that could corrupt the AON based routing entries. As per our design the system functions even if some routers along the path are non-AON-routers. In the event of an attack the ISP could detect it and switch the respective router(s) to classical routing until the attack is neutralized.
2. **Router Performance:** There could be overhead in the router which processes the AON packets and in maintaining the second routing table. However, we argue that with tremendous increase in processing power and memory capacity of current routers, this issue can be resolved.
3. **Involvement of ISPs:** It needs to be studied that how ISPs could be encouraged to provide AON service. The reduction of cost due to reduced inter-ISP traffic could be the incentive.
4. **File Sharing and Downloading:** Our focus in this paper has been in resource discovery process. Its applicability in file sharing and downloading, such as BitTorrent like systems needs to be studied.

5 Simulation and Evaluation

In order to test our proposed mechanism we have modeled and implemented message level routing in Java based discrete event simulation tool J-Sim. J-Sim is object oriented and aids rapid development by providing extensible components. In our case in order to develop an AON router model, an existing router model has been inherited and AON functionality has been programmed into it.

We have constructed a topology with 10 SRs and 12 AON routers with network parameters shown in table 4. Three different scenarios namely, AON based, overlay flooding and selective overlay forwarding were implemented.

The performance comparison of the RTT of the query messages is shown in figure 3. AON has the least RTT compared to the other scenarios which proves our claim in section 4. It is also interesting to note that Overlay Flooding perfoms better compared to Overlay Profiling. This is due to the fact that Overlay Flooding forwards reply messages straight to the query originator whereas the reply is forwarded along the same path of request in case of Overlay Profiling so that the peers could be profiled. However the profiled peer selection in the overlay has the advantage of reducing the network stress by minimizing the number of query messages compared to pure flooding. In AON based query forwarding the stress is further reduced by avoiding redundant traffic in the underlay links. The results obtained reiterate our analysis in section 4.

Table 4. Simulation metrics

Parameters	Values
Bandwidth	10Kbps
Router buffer size	10 packets
Packet size	30 bytes
Link propagation delay	300 ms

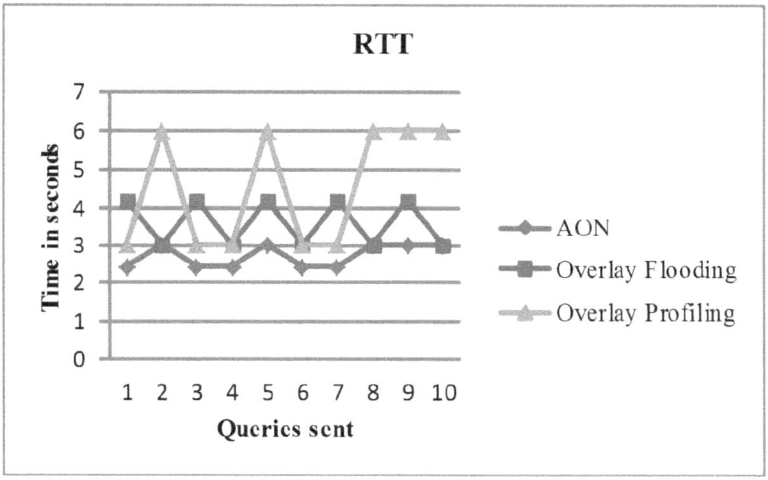

Fig. 3. Round Trip Time (RTT)

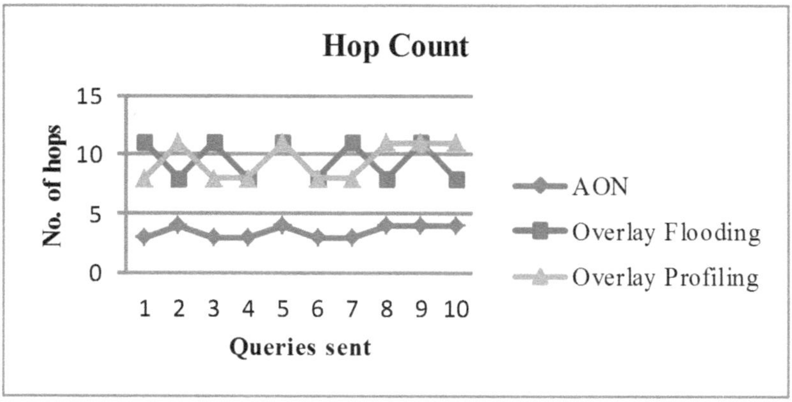

Fig. 4. Number of hops crossed

Figure 4 demonstrates the number of routers crossed by each queries sent in different scenarios. The results clearly shows that overlay routing are no match to

AON based intelligent routing in terms of reducing the network stress. The queries in the overlay routing take the same amount of hops for both the scenarios.

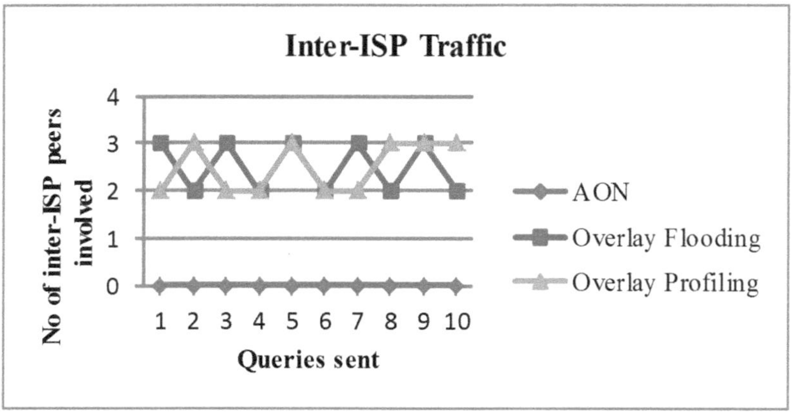

Fig. 5. Inter-ISP traffic generated

Figure 5 demonstrates the reduction in the inter-ISP traffic. Here the inter-ISP traffic is measured in terms of the number of peers involved in the overlay. The validity of this can be seen from our implementation of SR per AS. AON based intelligent routing eliminates the inter-ISP traffic completely.

6 Conclusion and Future Work

We have proposed an IP-layer aware query routing mechanism for distributed service discovery with message level intelligence. We have proved that our query routing is performed in synchronization with the underlying physical topology with the awareness of the target location. We have also demonstrated its effectiveness in terms of privacy and security of peers in the overlay, efficient query forwarding, and performance. We have proved through simulation results that AON based intelligent query routing mechanism performs better in all aspects mentioned above. In future we plan to study the effects of our system in conditions like bandwidth throttling, dynamic entry and exit of peers and its resilience to router related security threats.

References

1. Michael, P.T., Papazoglou, P., Dustdar, S., Leymann, F., Krämer, B.J.: Service-Oriented Computing Research Roadmap. In: Dagstuhl Seminar Proceedings 05462, Service Oriented Computing, SOC (2006), `http://drops.dagstuhl.de/opus/volltexte/2006/524`
2. Meshkova, E., Riihijärvi, J., Petrova, M., Mähönen, P.: A survey on resource discovery mechanisms, peer-to-peer and service discovery frameworks. Computer Networks 52, 2097–2128 (2008)

3. Seedorf, J., Kiesel, S., Stiemerling, M.: Traffic localization for P2P-applications: The ALTO approach. Presented at P2P 2009. IEEE Ninth International Conference on Peer-to-Peer Computing (2009)
4. Xie, H., Yang, Y.R., Krishnamurthy, A., Liu, Y.G., Silberschatz, A.: P4p: provider portal for applications. In: Proceedings of the ACM SIGCOMM 2008 Conference on Data Communication, pp. 351–362. ACM, Seattle (2008)
5. Mohamed Saleem, H., Hassan, M.F., Asirvadam, V.S.: Modelling and Simulation of Underlay aware Distributed Service Discovery. To be presented at The 17th Asia-Pacific Conference on Communications, Malaysia (accepted for publication, 2011)
6. Garcés-Erice, L., Ross, K.W., Biersack, E.W., Felber, P., Urvoy-Keller, G.: Topology-Centric Look-Up Service. In: Stiller, B., Carle, G., Karsten, M., Reichl, P. (eds.) NGC 2003 and ICQT 2003. LNCS, vol. 2816, pp. 58–69. Springer, Heidelberg (2003)
7. Hoang, D.B., Le, H., Simmonds, A.: PIPPON: A Physical Infrastructure-aware Peer-to-Peer Overlay Network. Presented at TENCON 2005 2005 IEEE Region, vol. 10 (2005)
8. Bindal, R., Pei, C., Chan, W., Medved, J., Suwala, G., Bates, T., Zhang, A.: Improving Traffic Locality in BitTorrent via Biased Neighbor Selection. Presented at 26th IEEE International Conference on Distributed Computing Systems, ICDCS (2006)
9. Ferreira, R.A., Grama, A., Jia, L.: Plethora: An Efficient Wide-Area Storage System. In: Bougé, L., Prasanna, V.K. (eds.) HiPC 2004. LNCS, vol. 3296, pp. 252–261. Springer, Heidelberg (2004)
10. Xin, S., Kan, L., Yushu, L., Yong, T.: SLUP: A Semantic-Based and Location-Aware Unstructured P2P Network. Presented at 10th IEEE International Conference on High Performance Computing and Communications, HPCC (2008)
11. Menasce, D.A., Kanchanapalli, L.: Probabilistic scalable P2P resource location services. SIGMETRICS Perform. Eval. Rev. 30, 48–58 (2002), http://doi.acm.org/10.1145/588160.588167
12. Tsoumakos, D., Roussopoulos, N.: Adaptive probabilistic search for peer-to-peer networks. Presented at 2003 Proceedings of Third International Conference on Peer-to-Peer Computing, P2P 2003 (2003)
13. Kalogeraki, V., Gunopulos, D., Zeinalipour-Yazti, D.: A local search mechanism for peer-to-peer networks. In: Proceedings of the Eleventh International Conference on Information and Knowledge Management McLean, pp. 300–307. ACM, Virginia (2002), http://doi.acm.org/10.1145/584792.584842
14. Yu Cheng, I.I.o.T., Alberto Leon-Garcia, U.o.T., Ian Foster, U.o.C.: Toward an Autonomic Service Management Framework:A Holistic Vision of SOA, AON, and Autonomic Computing. IEEE Communications Magazine (2008), http://soa.sys-con.com/node/155657
15. Tian, X., Cheng, Y., Ren, K., Liu, B.: Multicast with an Application-Oriented Networking (AON) Approach. Presented at 2008 IEEE International Conference on Communications, ICC 2008 (2008), http://www.mscibarra.com/products/indices/gics/

A Comparative Study on Quorum-Based Replica Control Protocols for Grid Environment

Zulaile Mabni and Rohaya Latip

Faculty of Computer Science and Information Technology, University Putra Malaysia
Serdang, 43400 Selangor, Malaysia
zulaile@tmsk.uitm.edu.my, rohaya@fsktm.upm.edu.my

Abstract. Grid Computing handles huge amount of data which is stored in geographically distributed sites. It is a great challenge to ensure that data is managed, distributed and accessed efficiently in the distributed systems such as the data grid. To address the challenge, various techniques have been proposed in the literature. One of the widely used techniques is data replication since it offers high data availability, fault-tolerance and improve the performance of the system. In replication-based systems, replica control protocols are implemented for managing and accessing the data. In this paper, we present a comparison of various quorum-based replica control protocols that have been proposed in the distributed environment. This paper attempts to compare these replica control protocols based on the strengths, weaknesses and performance of the protocols.

Keywords: Replica control protocol, Data replication, Data availability, Communication cost.

1 Introduction

Grid computing is a form of distributed computing that is designed to provide reliable access to data and computational resources over a wide area network and across organizational domains. Data grid is a grid computing system that provides a scalable infrastructure for managing and storing data files to support variety of scientific applications ranging from high-energy physics to computational genomics which require access to large amount of data in the size of terabyte or petabyte [1]. Thus, it is a great challenge to manage such huge and geographically distributed data in a data grid. To address the challenge, various techniques have been proposed in the literature. One of the widely used techniques is data replication. Data replication has been implemented for distributed database system to provide a high availability, fault tolerance, and increase the performance of the system [2]. In Data replication, exact copies of data are created and stored at distributed sites to increase data access and reliability. Replication-based systems implement replica control protocol for managing and accessing the data.

In this paper, we present a brief review of past and current research on data replication techniques. Our focus is on the quorum-based replica control protocols that have been proposed to be used in the data grid environment. We compare the

A. Abd Manaf et al. (Eds.): ICIEIS 2011, Part III, CCIS 253, pp. 364–377, 2011.

strengths, weaknesses and performance in terms of communication cost and data availability of the replica control protocols. In this paper, the terms node and site will be used interchangeably, without loss of generality. The paper is organized as follows. Sections 2 reviews some of the quorum-based replica control protocols with focus on the read and write operations for the communication cost and data availability. In Section 3, comparisons on the strengths, weaknesses and also the performance of the replica control protocols are presented. Section 4 concludes the paper.

2 Quorum-Based Replica Control Protocols

In a replicated database, copies of an object may be stored at several sites in the network. To interact with the database, users need to invoke a transaction program that is a partially ordered sequence of read and write operations that are executed atomically [3, 4]. Multiple copies of an object must appear as a single logical object to the transaction which is known as one-copy equivalence [4] and is enforced by the replica control protocol.

Quorum is grouping of nodes or databases into small cluster to manage the replica for read and write operations. A read or write operation quorum is defined a set of copies whose number is sufficient to execute the read or write operation. This protocol imposes an intersection requirement between read and write operations. The selection of a quorum must satisfy the quorum intersection property to ensure one-copy equivalence. The property stated that for any two operations $o[x]$ and $o'[x]$ on an object x, where at least one of them is a write, the quorums must have a nonempty intersection [5]. The write quorum needs to satisfy read-write and write-write intersections to ensure that a read operation will access the updated data [6]. However, a read quorum does not have to satisfy the intersection property since it does not change the value of the accessed data object.

Some of the quorum-based replica control protocols that have been proposed for used in data grid environment are as follows:

2.1 Read-One Write-All (ROWA)

Read-One Write-All (ROWA) protocol is a straightforward protocol, proposed by Bernstein and Goodman in [4]. In this approach, a read operation needs to access only one copy and a write operation needs to access a number of copies, n [7,8]. The ROWA communication cost for read operation $C_{ROWA,R}$ as given in [8] is represented in Eq. (1):

$$C_{ROWA,R} = 1 \ , \tag{1}$$

and write operation $C_{ROWA,W}$ is represented in Eq. (2):

$$C_{ROWA,W} = n \ . \tag{2}$$

On the other hand, the read and write availability of ROWA can be represented as one out of n and n out of n, respectively. Thus, in [8] the formulation for read availability $A_{ROWA,R}$ is as given in Eq. (3):

$$A_{ROWA,R} = \sum_{i=1}^{n} \binom{n}{i} p^i (1-p)^{n-i} = 1 - (1-p)^n \quad (3)$$

whereas, the write availability $A_{ROWA,W}$ is given in Eq. (4):

$$A_{ROWA,W} = \sum_{i=n}^{n} \binom{n}{i} p^i (1-p)^{n-i} = p^n \quad (4)$$

where p is the probability of data file accessing between 0.1 to 0.9 and i is the increment of n.

2.2 Voting Protocol

The voting protocol (VT) was first proposed by Thomas in [9]. It was later generalized by Gifford in [5] and called weighted voting protocol. In this protocol, each copy of replicated data object is assigned a certain number of votes. Every transaction has to collect a read quorum of r votes to read a data object, and a write quorum of w votes to write the data object. A quorum must satisfy the following conditions:

i) $r + w > v$
ii) $w > v/2$

The first condition where $r + w$ must be larger than the total number of votes v assigned to the copies of data object, ensures that there is non-empty intersection between every read quorum and every write quorum. Whereas, the second condition where the total of write quorum of w votes must be larger than half of the total number of votes v assigned to the copies of data object, ensures that the write operations cannot occur in two different partitions for the same copies of data objects.

Communication cost for voting is depending on a quorum. The bigger the size of the read or write quorum, the higher the communication cost. Thus, the VT communication cost for read $C_{VT,R}$ and write $C_{VT,W}$ operations, are given in Eq. (5):

$$C_{VT,R} = C_{VT,W} = \left\lceil \frac{n+1}{2} \right\rceil \quad (5)$$

where n is the total number of votes assigned to the copies [8].

Meanwhile, the VT read availability $A_{VT,R}$ is as given in Eq. (6):

$$A_{VT,R} = \sum_{i=k}^{n} \binom{n}{i} p^i (1-p)^{n-i}, k \geq 1 \tag{6}$$

and the VT write availability $A_{VT,W}$ is as given in Eq. (7):

$$A_{VT,W} = \sum_{i=n+1-k}^{n} \binom{n}{i} p^i (1-p)^{n-i}, k \geq 1 \tag{7}$$

where p is the probability of data file accessing between 0.1 to 0.9, i is the increment of n and k is the chosen read quorum such as $k = \lceil n/4 \rceil$ selected by [10].

2.3 Tree Quorum Protocol

Tree quorum (TQ) protocol proposed by Agrawal and El Abbadi [3], imposed a logical tree structure on the set of copies of the replicas. Fig. 1 illustrates the diagram of a tree quorum structure with thirteen copies. In this protocol, a read operation needs to access a majority of copies at any single level of the tree. For example, a read quorum can be formed by the root, or a majority copies from {2,3,4}, or a majority copies from {5,6,7,8,9,10,11,12,13} as illustrated in Fig. 1. On the other hand, a write operation must write a majority of copies at all levels of the tree. In Fig. 1, a write quorum can be formed by the root, and any two copies from {2,3,4}, and a majority copies from {5,6,7,8,9,10,11,12,13}. For example, a write operation could be executed by writing the following set of copies only: {1, 2, 3, 5, 6, 8, 9}.

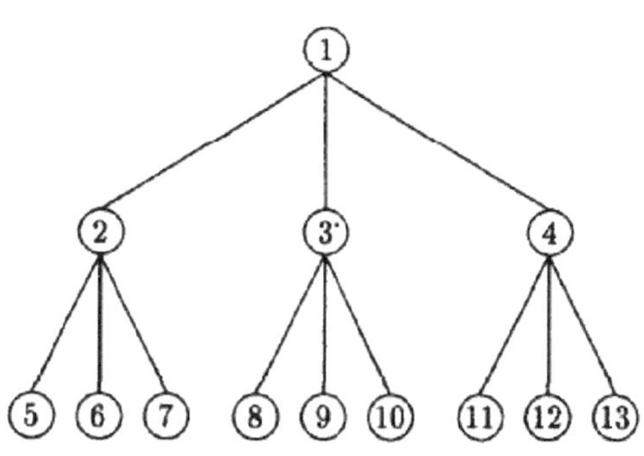

Fig. 1. A tree organization of 13 copies of data objects [3]

In estimating the TQ communication cost operation, h denotes the height of the tree, D is the degree of nodes in the tree, and M is the majority of D where:

$$M = \left\lceil \frac{D+1}{2} \right\rceil.$$

In TQ, when the root is available, a read quorum size is equal to 1. But if the root fails, the majority of its children will replace it and thus, will increase the quorum size. Therefore, for a tree of height h, the maximum quorum size is M^h [7] and the TQ communication cost for read operation $C_{TQ,R}$ is in the range of $1 \leq C_{TQ,R} \leq M^h$. Meanwhile, the TQ communication cost for write operation $C_{TQ,W}$ is given in Eq. (8):

$$C_{TQ,W} = \sum M^i, \text{ where } i = 0,\ldots,h . \tag{8}$$

The TQ availability for read and write operations can be estimated by using recurrence equations based on the tree height h [8]. Thus, the formulation for read availability A_{TQ,R_h} for height $h + 1$ is as given in Eq. (9):

$$A_{TQ,R_{h+1}} = p + (1 - p) \sum_{i=M}^{D} \binom{D}{i} A_{TQ,R_h}{}^{i} (1 - A_{TQ,R_h})^{D-i}. \tag{9}$$

Meanwhile, the availability of a write operation A_{TQ,W_h} for a tree of height h + 1 is as given in Eq. (10):

$$A_{TQ,W_{h+1}} = p \sum_{i=M}^{D} \binom{D}{i} A_{TQ,W_h}{}^{i} (1 - A_{TQ,W_h})^{D-i} \tag{10}$$

where, p is the probability that a copy is available, and R_0 and W_0 are equal to p.

2.4 The Grid Structure (GS) Protocol

Maekawa [11] proposed a technique by using the notion of finite projective planes that achieved mutual exclusion in a distributed system, where all quorums are of equal size. Maekawa's grid protocol was extended by Cheung et al. [12], to further increase data availability and fault-tolerance. In this protocol, n copies of data objects are logically organized in the form of $\sqrt{n}$ x $\sqrt{n}$ grid as illustrated in Fig. 2. Read

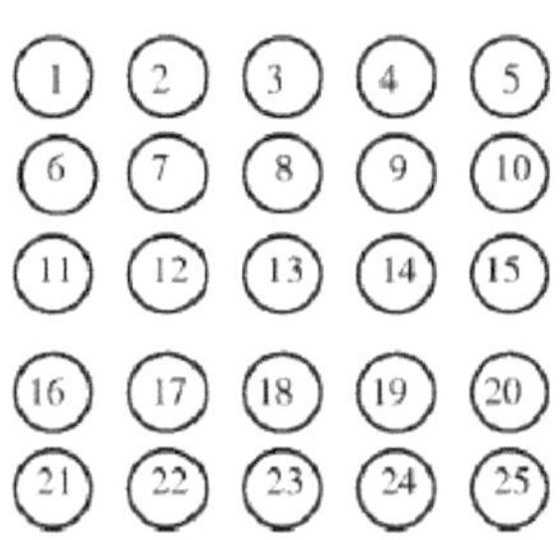

Fig. 2. A grid structure with 25 copies of data objects [7]

operations are executed by accessing a read quorum that consists of one copy in each column. On the other hand, write operations are executed by accessing a write quorum that consists of all copies in one column and a copy from each of the remaining column. As an example, in Fig. 2, copies {1,7,13,19,25} are sufficient to execute a read operation, whereas, copies {1,6,11,16,21,7,13,4,20} are required to execute a write operation.

The GS communication cost for read operation $C_{GS,R}$ as given in [7] is represented in Eq. (11):

$$C_{GS,R} = \sqrt{n} \tag{11}$$

and write operation $C_{GS,W}$ is as given in Eq. (12):

$$C_{GS,W} = \sqrt{n} + \left(\sqrt{n} - 1\right) = 2\sqrt{n} - 1\,. \tag{12}$$

On the other hand, for the read availability $A_{GS,R}$ in GS protocol, the formulation is as given in Eq. (13):

$$A_{GS,R} = \left[1 - (1-p)^{\sqrt{n}}\right]^{\sqrt{n}} \tag{13}$$

and write availability $A_{GS,W}$ is as given in Eq. (14):

$$A_{GS,W} = \left[1 - (1-p)^{\sqrt{n}}\right]^{\sqrt{n}} - \left[1 - p^{\sqrt{n}} - (1-p)^{\sqrt{n}}\right]^{\sqrt{n}}. \tag{14}$$

2.5 Three Dimension Grid Structure (TDGS) Protocol

In TDGS protocol [6], given N copies of a data object, the N copies are organized into a box-shaped structure with four planes as shown in Fig. 4. The read operations in TDGS are executed by acquiring a read quorum that consists of hypotenuse copies. For example, in Fig. 4, copies {A,H}, {B,G}, {C,F}, and {D,E} are hypotenuse copies, where any one of these pairs is sufficient to execute a read operation. On the other hand, write operations are executed by acquiring a write quorum from any plane that consists of hypotenuse copies and all vertices copies. For example, in Fig. 4, to execute a write operation, copies from {A, H} and copies from {H, A, B, C, D} must be accessible.

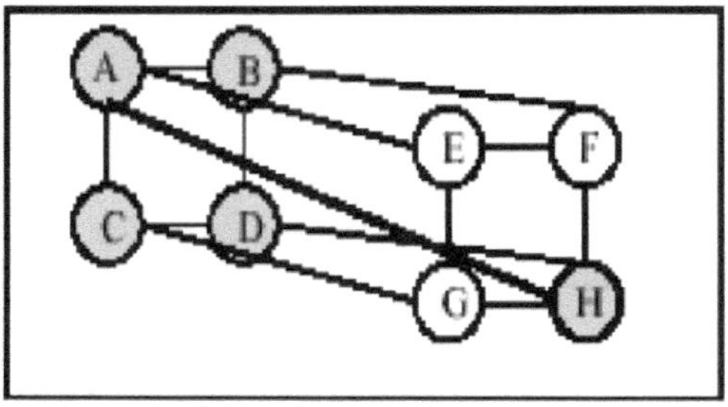

Fig. 4. A TDGS organization with eight copies of data objects [13]

The communication cost of TDGS protocol is represented by the quorum size [6]. The communication cost for read operation $C_{TDGS,R}$ is represented in Eq. (15):

$$C_{TDGS,R} = 2 \tag{15}$$

and write operation $C_{TDGS,W}$ is represented in Eq. (16):

$$C_{TDGS,W} = \text{Hypotenuse copies} + (\text{All copies of vertices in plane} - \text{Hypotenuse copy in the same plane}) = 2 + (4 - 1) = 5 \tag{16}$$

In [6], all copies in this protocol are assumed to have the same probability, p and since TDGS has 4 hypotenuse copies then the read availability $A_{TDGS,R}$ is presented in Eq. (17):

$$A_{TDGS,R} = 1 - (1 - p^2)^4\ , \tag{17}$$

whereas, formulation of write availability, $A_{TDGS,W}$ is as given in Eq. (18):

$$A_{TDGS,W} = 1 - (1 - \beta)^4$$

$$\text{where } \beta = p\varphi + p\phi - p^2\,(\varphi * \phi),\ \varphi = p^4(1 + p - p^2) \text{ and} \tag{18}$$

$$\phi = p^4(2 - p^2)\ .$$

2.6 Diagonal Replication on 2D Mesh Structure (DR2M)

Diagonal Replication on 2D Mesh Structure (DR2M) protocol proposed by [13,14], is a protocol where all nodes are logically organized into two-dimensional mesh structure. In this protocol, few assumptions are made where, the replica copies are in the form of text files and all replicas are operational meaning that the copies at all replicas are always available. This protocol uses quorum to arrange nodes in cluster. The data are replicated to only one node of the diagonal site which is the middle node of the diagonal site in each quorum. Fig. 5 illustrates how the quorums for network size of 81 nodes are grouped by nodes of 5 x 5 in each quorum. Nodes which are formed in a quorum intersect with other quorums. This is to ensure that each quorum can communicate or read other data from other nodes which is in another quorum. The number of nodes grouped in quorum, R must be odd so that only one middle node from the diagonal sites can be selected. For example, s(3,3) in Fig. 5 is selected to have the copy of data.

In DR2M, voting approach is used to assign a certain number of votes to every copy of the replicated data objects [14]. The selected node in the diagonal sites is assigned with vote one or zero. The communication cost for read and write operation is directly proportional to the size of the quorum. The DR2M communication cost for read operation $C_{DR2M,R}$ formulated from [10] is as given in Eq. (19):

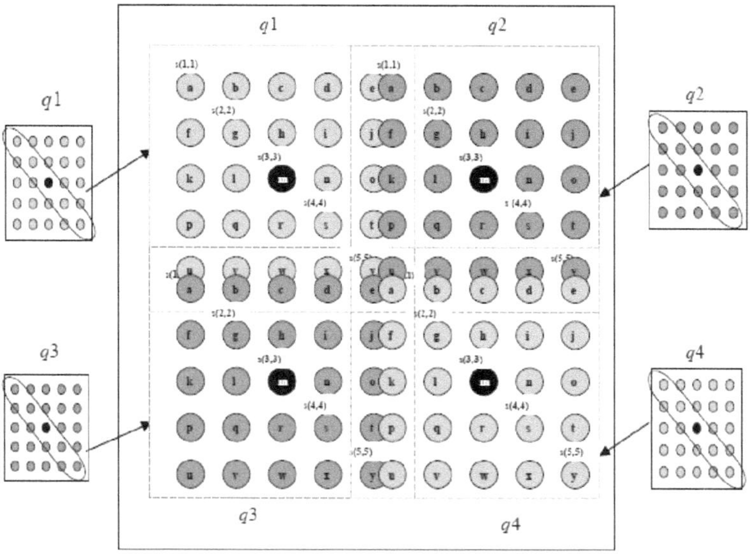

Fig. 5. A grid organization with 81 nodes, each of the nodeshas a data file a, b,…, and y respectively [14]

$$C_{DR2M,R} = \lfloor r/2 \rfloor \ , \tag{19}$$

whereas, the communication cost for write operation $C_{DR2M,W}$ is as given in Eq. (20):

$$C_{DR2M,W} = \lfloor (r+1)/2 \rfloor \tag{20}$$

where r is the number of replicas in the whole network for executing read or write operations.

On the other hand, the DR2M read availability $A_{DR2M,R}$ formulated from [10] is represented in Eq. (21):

$$A_{DR2M,R} = \sum_{i=q_r}^{n} \binom{n}{i} (p^i(1-p)^{n-i}) \tag{21}$$

and write availability $A_{DR2M,W}$ is represented in Eq. (22):

$$A_{DR2M,W} = \sum_{i=q_w}^{n} \binom{n}{i} (p^i(1-p)^{n-i}) \tag{22}$$

where n is the number of the column or row of the grid. For example, in Fig. 5, the value of n is 5. p is the probability that a copy is available with value between 0 to 1. The q_R and q_W are the number of quorums for read and write operations, respectively.

2.7 Arbitrary 2D Structured (A2DS) Protocol

Recently, an Arbitrary 2D Structured Replica Control Protocol (A2DS) has been proposed by Basmadjian et. al. in [15]. This protocol can be applied to any 2D structure to achieve near optimal performance in terms of communication cost, availability and system load of their read and write operations. Several basic 2D structures where replicas of the system are arranged logically based on its width *w* and height *h* into a *straight line*, a *triangle*, a *square*, a *trapezoid*, and a *rectangle* are presented as illustrated in Fig. 6. Other 2D structures where replicas are arranged logically into a hexagon and an octagon are also obtained by the composition of several basic 2D structures.

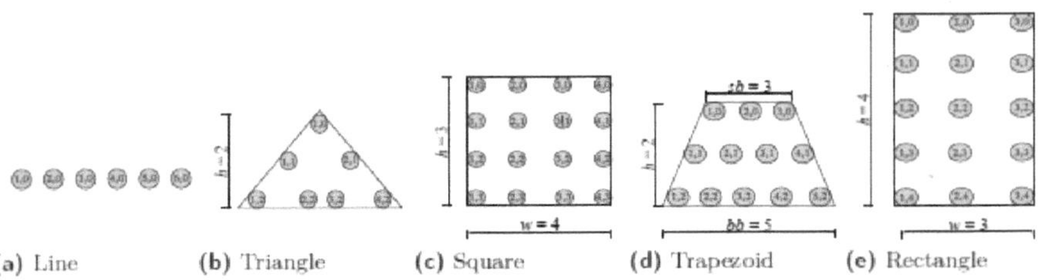

Fig. 6. An example of A2DS basic structures for $n = 6, 7, 16, 12$ and 15 replicas respectively [15]

In this protocol, a read operation is carried out on any single replica at every level of the 2D structure. A write operation, on the other hand, is performed on all replicas of any single level of the structure [15].

The communication cost for read operation $C_{A2DS,R}$ of this protocol is as given in Eq. (23):

$$C_{A2DS,R} = 1 + h \tag{23}$$

and write operation $C_{A2DS,W}$ is as given in Eq. (24):

$$C_{A2DS,W} = \frac{n}{1+h} \tag{24}$$

where *h* is the height of the 2D structure and *n* is the number of replicas [15]. As an example, for replicas that are arranged logically into a *square* of height $h > 0$, width $w = h + 1$, and $n = w \times (h + 1)$, its operations have a cost of $\sqrt{n}$.

On the other hand, the availability for read operation $A_{A2DS,R}$ for A2DS protocol formulated from [15] is as given in Eq. (25):

$$A_{A2DS,R}\,(p) = \prod_{k=0}^{h}(1 - (1 - p)^{m_k}) \tag{25}$$

and the availability for write operation $A_{A2DS,W}$ is as given in Eq. (26):

$$A_{A2DS,W}(p) = 1 - \prod_{k=0}^{h}(1-p)^{m_k} \quad (26)$$

where m_k denotes the total number of replicas at level k.

As an example, for replicas that are arranged logically into a *square* of height $h > 0$, width $w = h + 1$, and $n = w \times (h + 1)$, the read and write operations have an availability of $(1-(1-p)^{\sqrt{n}})^{\sqrt{n}}$ and $1-(1-p^{\sqrt{n}})^{\sqrt{n}}$ respectively [15].

3 Comparative Analysis

In this section, we compare the strengths and weaknesses of the quorum-based replica control protocols discussed in Section 2. Comparisons on the read and write communication cost of the quorum-based replica control protocols are also made.

3.1 Comparisons of Strengths and Weaknesses

The strength of ROWA protocol is that the read operation can be done from any replica, thus, produces a high degree of read availability at a very low communication cost. However, the write operation has a low write availability and high communication cost since write operation is done on all replicas [3,6]. This protocol is good for distributed environment where the data is mostly read-only. A significant weakness of ROWA is a write operation cannot be executed if one of the replicas is unavailable. Nevertheless, ROWA is still popular and has been used in mobile, peer to peer environment [16], database systems [17], and grid computing [18].

The voting protocol (VT) is another popular technique because they are flexible and easily implemented [8,19]. This protocol has been used to address the issue of increasing fault-tolerance of the ROWA protocol [3]. The strength of VT approach is, it does not require write operations to write all copies, thus increases their fault-tolerance. However, in this protocol, a read operation must read several copies which made the read operation more costly than the ROWA protocol. A weakness of this technique is that writing an object is fairly expensive since a write quorum of copies must be larger than the majority votes [8].

Another technique called tree quorum (TQ) protocol has comparable cost of executing the read operations, as compared to ROWA protocol. Whereas, the availability of TQ write operations is significantly better than ROWA protocol [3]. The strength of this protocol is that a read operation may access only one copy and a write operation must access number of copies which is usually less than the majority of the copies. However, this protocol has a weakness, where if more than a majority of the copies at any level of the tree become unavailable write operations cannot be performed. For example, if the root of the tree is unavailable, no write operations can be executed.

The strength of grid structure (GS) protocol is that it provides low communication cost for the operations compared to VT protocol, while providing a comparable degree of availability for both read and write operations [7]. However, there are several weaknesses of this protocol. One of the weaknesses is, if copies in an entire column are unavailable, read and write operations cannot be executed. Similarly, if copies in an entire row are unavailable, write operations cannot also be executed.

Another weakness is that it still has a larger number of copies for read and write quorums, thus, decrease the communication cost and increase data availability.

To address the limitation in the GS protocol, TDGS protocol is proposed to tolerate the failure of more than three quarter of the copies [6]. This is due to TDGS protocol can still construct a write quorum even if three out of four planes are unavailable as long as the hypotenuse copies are accessible. Thus, this protocol enhances the fault-tolerance in write operations as compared to GS protocol. The other strength of this protocol is that the read operation only needs two copies to be executed, whereas, the write operation requires only five copies to execute the operation, thus reduce the communication cost. However, there are several weaknesses of TDGS protocol. The first weakness is that for a read operation, if one of the copies of each pairs is not available, then the hypotenuse copies are not accessible, thus the read operation cannot be performed. Meanwhile, a write operation cannot be executed at that plane. Therefore, this has affected the consistency of the data. Another weakness is that, in TDGS, a perfect square box must be formed, and if new copies are added, more copies are needed at the other plane of the box to get a perfect square box. Therefore, this has increased the read and write quorum size and thus, affects the communication cost.

The strength of DR2M protocol is that it uses quorum to arrange nodes in cluster and the data are replicated to only one node of the diagonal site which is the middle node of the diagonal site in each quorum. Since the data file is replicated only to one node in each quorum, thus, this has reduced the number of database update operations because the number of quorum is minimized. In comparison to the TDGS technique, DR2M provides higher read or write availability while requiring a lower communication cost. Nevertheless, DR2M technique has few weaknesses, where this protocol requires the number of nodes in each quorum must be odd and the number of nodes for each quorum is limited to 2401 nodes.

A2DS protocol has been recently proposed to provide a single protocol that can be applied to any 2D structure. The strength of this protocol is that unlike the existing proposed protocols, it can be adapted to any 2D structure [15]. In this protocol, replicas of the system are arranged logically based on its width w and height h into any 2D structure such as a *straight line*, a *triangle*, a *square*, a *trapezoid*, and a *rectangle*. For the replicas that are arranged logically into a *straight line*, it has the same cost and availability of ROWA for both read and write operations. However, when the replicas are arranged logically into a *square* with number of copies, $n > 25$, its availability for the write operations becomes poor [15].

3.2 Comparisons of Communication Cost

The communication cost of an operation is directly proportional to the size of the quorum required to execute the operation [8]. Therefore, the communication cost is presented in terms of the quorum size. Fig. 7 and Fig. 8 illustrate the read and write communication costs of the seven algorithms (ROWA, VT, GS, TQ, TDGS, DR2M, A2DS), respectively, for different total number of copies, n = 25, 49, 81, and 121. In Fig. 7, for the TQ protocol, the maximum communication cost for read operation is plotted when D = 3 and for the VT protocol, the read and write quorum is selected as the majority of the total copies. As for the A2DS protocol, the *square* structure is selected for the comparison.

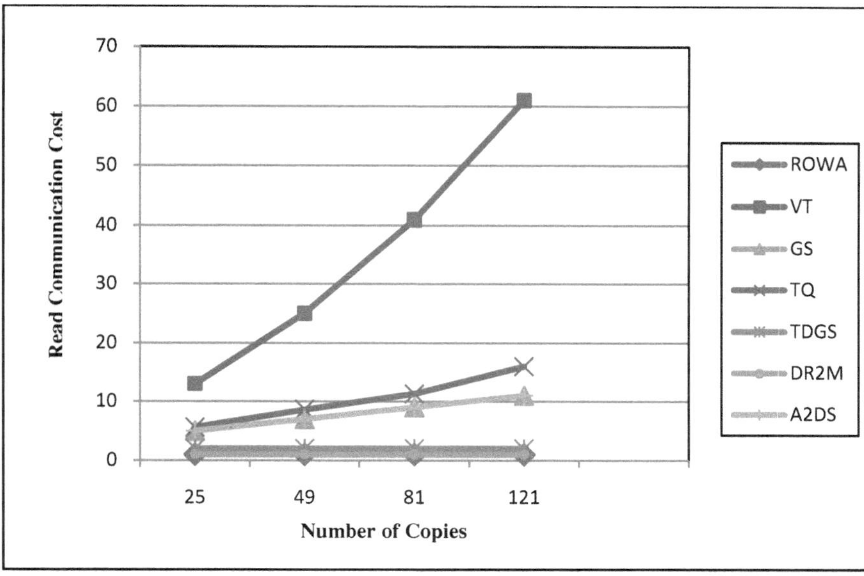

Fig. 7. Comparison of the Read Communication Cost

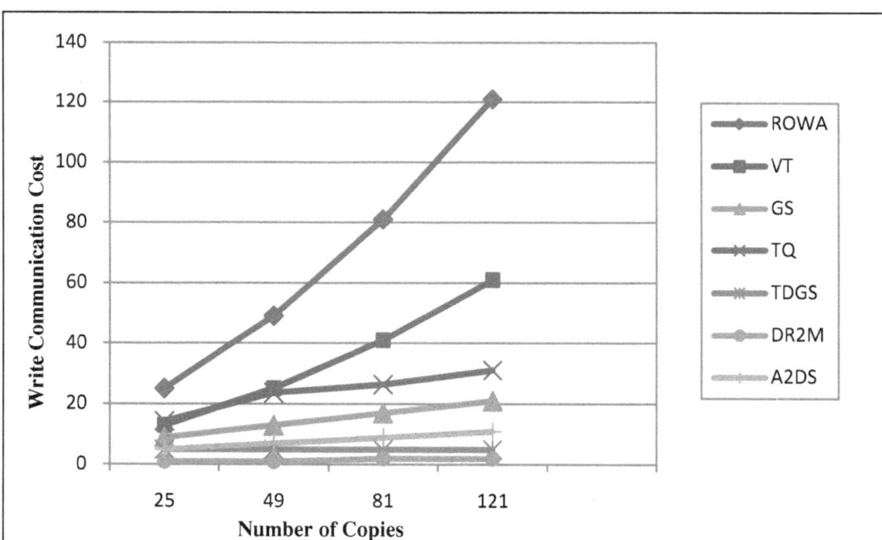

Fig. 8. Comparison of the Write Communication Cost

From Fig. 7, for the read operation, ROWA has the lowest communication cost since a read operation needs only one copy for all instances. DR2M also has a low communication cost which is comparable to ROWA for 25, 49, 81, and 121 copies. It is shown that TDGS needs only 2 copies for the read operation for all instances. The read costs for GS and A2DS protocols are the same because the read operation needs to access one copy in each column of GS protocol and one copy in every level of A2DS structure. On the other hand, VT protocols has higher read cost than the other protocols since its read and write quorum is selected as the majority of the total copies.

For the write operation as illustrated in Fig. 8, DR2M has the lowest communication cost because data file is replicated only to one node in each quorum, thus, this has reduced the number of database update operations. Meanwhile, TDGS needs only 5 copies for the write operation for all instances. The ROWA protocol has the highest communication cost since write operation is done on all replicas simultaneously.

4 Conclusion

In this paper, a comparison of various quorum-based replica control protocols namely: ROWA, VT, GS, TQ, TDGS, DR2M and A2DS that have been proposed in the distributed environment has been presented. Comparison has been done based on the strengths, weaknesses and performance in terms of the communication cost of the protocols. For a distributed environment where the data is mostly read-only, ROWA is the best protocol compared to other existing proposed protocols as it provides a read operation with the lowest communication cost. On the other hand, for an environment where write operations are critical, DR2M is the recommended protocol as it has the lowest communication cost compared to the other protocols. Moreover, DR2M and TDGS protocols can be considered for environment that requires low communication cost for both read and write operations.

References

1. Chervenak, A., Foster, I., Kesselman, C., Salisbury, C., Tuecke, S.: The Data Grid: Towards Architecture for the Distributed Management and Analysis of Large Scientific Datasets. Journal of Network and Computer Applications 23, 187–200 (2001)
2. Lamehamedi, H., Syzmanski, B., Shentu, Z., Deelman, E.: Data Replication in Grid Environment. In: Proceedings of the Fifth International Conference on Algorithms and Architectures for Parallel Processing (ICA3PP 2002), pp. 378–383. IEEE Press, Beijing (2002)
3. Agrawal, D., El Abbadi, A.: The Tree Quorum Protocol: An Efficient Approach for Managing Replicated Data. In: Proceeding 16th International Conference on Very Large Databases, pp. 243–254 (1990)
4. Bernstein, P.A., Goodman, N.: An Algorithm for Concurrency Control and Recovery in Replicated Distributed Database. ACM Transaction Database System 9(4), 596–615 (1984)
5. Gifford, D.K.: Weighted Voting for Replicated Data. In: Proceedings of the 7th Symposium on Operating System Principles, pp. 150–162. ACM, New York (1979)
6. Mat Deris, M., Abawajy, J.H., Suzuri, H.M.: An Efficient Replicated Data Access Approach for Large-Scale Distributed Systems. In: IEEE International Symposium on Cluster Computing and the Grid, pp. 588–594 (2004)

7. Agrawal, D., El Abbadi, A.: Using Configuration for Efficient Management of Replicated Data. IEEE Transactions on Knowledge and Data Engineering 8(5), 786–801 (1996)
8. Chung, S.M.: Enhanced Tree Quorum Algorithm for Replica Control in Distributed Database. Data and Knowledge Engineering, Elsevier 12, 63–81 (1994)
9. Thomas, R.H.: A Majority Consensus Approach to Concurrency Control. ACM Transaction Database System 4(2), 180–209 (1979)
10. Mat Deris, M., Bakar, N., Rabiei, M., Suzuri, H.M.: Diagonal Replication on Grid for Efficient Access of Data in Distributed Database Systems. In: Bubak, M., van Albada, G.D., Sloot, P.M.A., Dongarra, J. (eds.) ICCS 2004. LNCS, vol. 3038, pp. 379–387. Springer, Heidelberg (2004)
11. Maekawa, M.: A $\sqrt{n}$ Algorithm for Mutual Exclusion in Decentralized Systems. ACM Transactions Computer System 3(2), 145–159 (1992)
12. Cheung, S.Y., Ammar, M.H., Ahamad, M.: The Grid Protocol A High Performance Scheme for Maintaining Replicated Data. IEEE Transaction Knowledge and Data Engineering 4(6), 582–592 (1992)
13. Latip, R.: Data Replication with 2D Mesh Protocol for Data Grid. PhD Thesis, Universiti Putra Malaysia (2009)
14. Latip, R., Ibrahim, H., Othman, M., Abdullah, A., Sulaiman, M.N.: Quorum-based Data Replication in Grid Environment. International Journal of Computational Intelligence Systems (IJCIS) 2(4), 386–397 (2009)
15. Basmadjian, R., de Meer, H.: An Arbitrary 2D Structured Replica Control Protocol (A2DS). In: 17th GI/ITG Conference On Communication in Distributed System (KiVS 2011), pp. 157–168 (2011)
16. Budiarto, Nishio, S., Tsukamoto, M.: Data Management Issues in Mobile and Peer To Peer Environment. Data and Knowledge Engineering 41, 391–402 (2002)
17. Zhou, W., Goscinki, A.: Managing Replication Remote Procedure Call Transaction. The Computer Journal 42(7), 592–608 (1999)
18. Kunszt, P.Z., Laure, E., Stockinger, H., Stockinger, K.: File Based Replica Management. Future Generation Computer System 21(1), 115–123 (2005)
19. Mat Deris, M., Evans, D.J., Saman, M.Y., Ahmad, N.: Binary Vote Assignment on Grid For Efficient Access of Replicated Data. International Journal of Computer Mathematics 80(12), 1489–1498 (2003)

A Methodology for Distributed Virtual Memory Improvement

Sahel Alouneh[1], Sa'ed Abed[2], Ashraf Hasan Bqerat[2], and Bassam Jamil Mohd[2]

[1] Computer Engineering Department, German-Jordanian University, Jordan
sahel.alouneh@gju.edu.jo
[2] Computer Engineering Department, Hashemite University, Jordan
{sabed,bassam}@hu.edu.jo, aihetchbe@hotmail.com

Abstract. In this paper, we present a methodology for managing the Distributed Virtual Memory (DVM). The methodology includes distributed algorithms for DVM management to detect the memory status which will enhance previous DVM techniques. The DVM data structure tables are similar to those found in current Conventional Virtual Memory (CVM) with some modifications. Finally, we evaluate our methodology through experimental results to show the effectiveness of our approach.

Keywords: Distributed Virtual Memory (DVM), Conventional Virtual Memory (CVM), Page faults.

1 Introduction

Distributed Virtual Memory (DVM) is a technique which exploits all of the first storage devices (commonly RAMs), in such way that it maximizes the utilization of these devices as much as possible depending on the techniques used in Page out, Page replacement and Page fault. For example, if a page has to get out of the memory of a certain node, instead of sending it to its Hard Disk (HD), which will consume a massive time in storing and retrieving this page, this node may ask other nodes in the system to store its page in their memory in order to get it back when needed. Of course the enhancement here comes from the fact that memory to memory transfer time is much less than memory to HD transfer time. The aim of this work is to make load balancing through the distribution of some processes of a certain node to other nodes which may have some unused resources and thus leads to an increased throughput of the system.

DVM is used in multi-node systems which contains many nodes. The node is a single independent computer (which has its own CPU, Memory and input/output subsystems). So, our targeted system should contain the following:

- Nodes,
- Backbone network,
- A protocol which controls the communication process between these nodes.

A. Abd Manaf et al. (Eds.): ICIEIS 2011, Part III, CCIS 253, pp. 378–384, 2011.

Based on this, DVM technique adds another level of storage devices named as the memory of other nodes as shown in Figure 1.

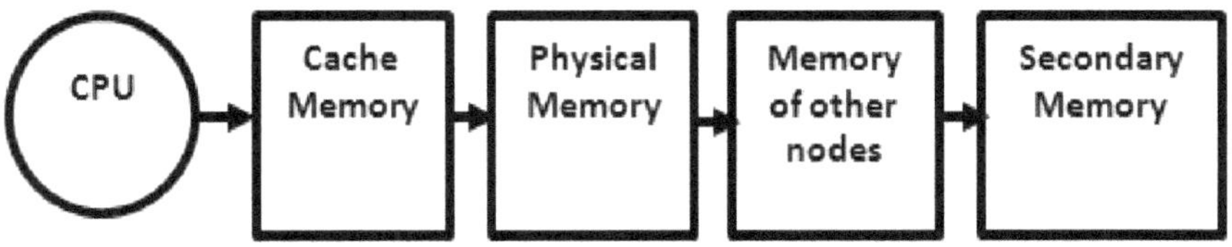

Fig. 1. Memory hierarchy of the DVM

DVM was introduced by many researchers at the level of processes and at level of pages. In this paper, we are interested in DVM at the level of pages. Memory sharing at the level of pages was firstly introduced by Li [1, 2], Clancey and Francioni [3], Abaza and Malkawi [4, 5], later on Abaza and Fellah [6] and also by others [7].

In [4], the author proposed a new way to manage virtual memory through the use of a node page table (NPT) instead of using process page table as in Conventional Virtual Memory (CVM). The node page table keeps information about the pages that are currently resides at the node and the pages departed the node to an immediate neighbor. Each entry of NPT contains the name of the owner process (PID), virtual page number (VPN), the physical address of the page if currently located in memory, and the destination of the page if transferred to another node.

Later on an optimization was carried out by Qanzu'a [8] to replace the NPT by two new structures which are: PPT (Process page table) and PrPT (Processor Page Table). He simulated his work and proved that it has improved the throughput of the whole system compared to [4].

Our work mainly states the problem of the second back storage devices which commonly are HDs (Hard desks) which use the magnetic nature to encode and store data in terms of north and south poles. Due to mechanical and physical limitations, these kinds of storage devices are much slower compared to CPU speed, caches speed and memory (most of times it is RAM) speed which is used as a first storage device commonly. Of course, we have a lot of options to go over this problem such as:

- Increasing cache size and memory size (need Hardware).
- Using some techniques for the pages and processes to decide which one should reside in memory and which should not, aiming to decrease the thrashing level as much as possible which leads to minimize the necessity of the HD (needs massive processing time) such as Least Recently Used (LRU) technique.
- Using DVM technique which we will spotlight on and introduce some methods that were done by many researchers and compare with them.

Our optimization will be modeled in terms of decreasing the traffic over the backbone network and decreasing the time needed to find a page that is reclaimed by its own original node.

We have deferent data structures that may implement DVM such using NPT as proposed in [4] and its optimization method in [8] which uses Process Page Table (PPT) and Processor Page Table (PrPT). Our work will have two steps: first, we will use the approach in reference in [8] and then divide the system into clusters. Second, we will add another memory level which is a cache for each cluster. A question may arise, what the benefits shall we have by adding a cache for each cluster? The points below summarize these benefits:

- Caches are used for the aim of:
- Reducing access time to find the node which may have a page related to another node.
- Reducing the traffic on local lines inside each cluster.
- The optimization comes from reducing the number of pages moving between different nodes which results in reducing the traffic.
- The amount of optimization will depend on caching techniques.

Thus, considering the above points will result in the following advantages:

1. Increase the scalability of the system by a massive factor.
2. Increase throughput through the time saved in caches' hits.

The structure of this paper is organized as follows: Section 2 describes the proposed methodology. Section 3 evaluates the proposed methodology through some experimental results. Finally, Section 4 concludes the paper with directions for future research.

2 Design Methodology

The DVM technique is used to increase the system throughput with some drawbacks such as: high traffic density and other problems that will be discussed later. Our methodology is based on adding another level of memory which is the cluster cache by dividing the system into clusters and each cluster has its own cache (memory). We will show the criteria step by step based on enhancements on previous techniques presented in reference [8].

Figure 2 illustrates our methodology and compares it with CVM and DVM techniques as well as shows different approaches that organize paged memory. For CVM, when a process, during execution, needs a page it directly asks for it in the cache memory (1). Then, if cache miss happens, it will ask the physical memory for such a page (2). If also page is not found, the process will go directly to the second storage device (5) to bring the page which will be so slow. Thus, pages in CVM are exchanges between memory and the second storage device. While in DVM, the process asks for the page in other nodes' memory (4) before going to the second storage device (5) in case the page is not found in other nodes. Thus, pages in DVM are exchanged firstly between memory and other nodes' memory, and secondly, between memory and second storage device. In our model, the process will ask for the page following 1,2,3,4,5 route.

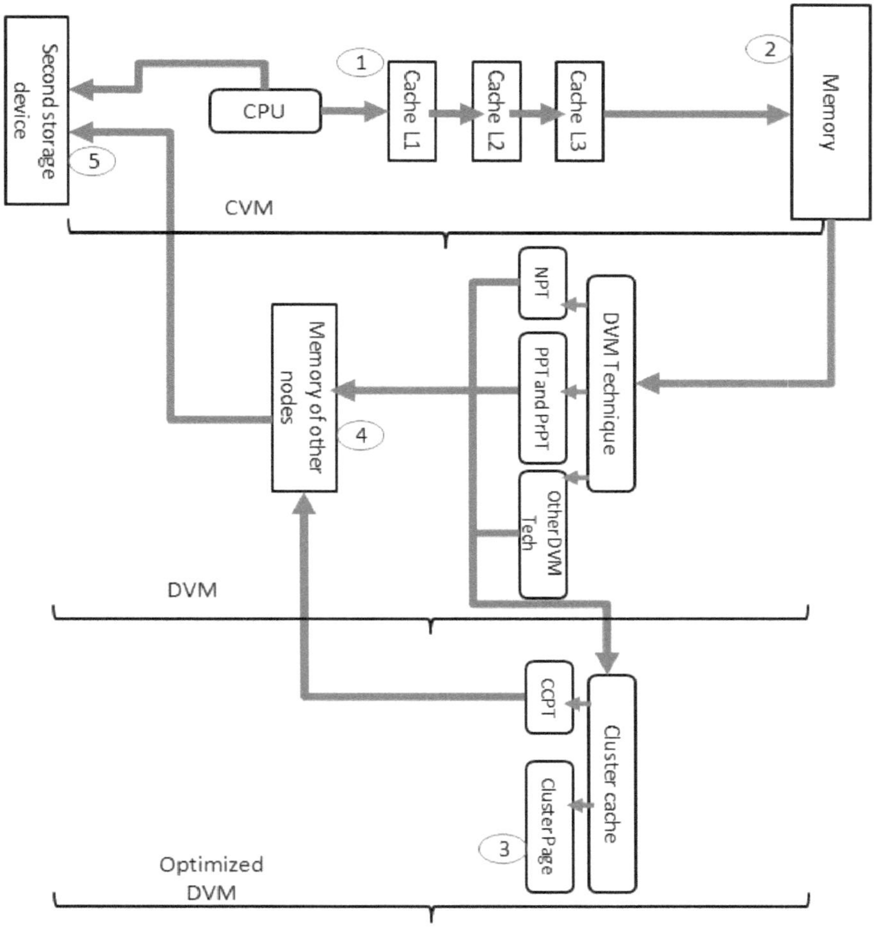

Fig. 2. CVM, DVM and optimized DVM Models

The methodology is based on dividing the whole system into different groups and making one of its node as a master node which has to be the most advanced and capable node. This master node has some additional functionality to be done. First, we will take off 10% of its memory and name it a cluster cache which seems reasonable especially with current computer capabilities which has RAM larger than 2GB. This cluster cache has to be accessible by all nodes of the local cluster. Also, it will contain the LLN table and it will have some pages of the pages of the local nodes.

Our methodology for page look up is illustrated in the following algorithm. When a process p is asking for page x which resides at node N, firstly, check page x at node n which is the local node of process p. If page x is in memory of node n, then page is found otherwise, check the node's cluster cache to see if page resides in it. If so, then the page is found and cache hit is made, otherwise check the LLN table to see if page is at one of other nodes either in its cluster or out of it. If so, then page is found otherwise, page is residing in node's n HD. Thus, in our methodology it is clear that the aim of placing a cluster cache is to increase the throughput by cache hits which are clearly a distinguished approach in DVM.

Algorithm: A process P is asking for page X which resides in node N.

1. *Process startCheck page X at node N*

   If (Page X is in memory of node N) then
   Page found go to START
   Else
2. *Check the nodes cluster cache to see if page resides in it*

   If (Page X is in cluster cache) then
   page is found go to START
   Else
3. *Check the nodes cluster cache (Cluster Page Table CCPT) to see if page is at one of its node*

   If (Page X is in memory of node M<> N) then
   page is found go to START
   Else
4. *Check the other clusters' caches by send messages to see if the page resides in it*

   If (Page X is in cluster cache) then
   page is found go to START
   Else
5. *Check the other clusters' caches by send messages to see if the page is in its*

   (Cluster Page Table CCPT) cache to see if page is at one of its node
   If (Page X is in memory of node k<> N& M) then
   Page is found goto START
   Else
   Goto HD of Node N to bring the page

END

3 Simulation Results

Simulation has been carried out for our methodology in terms of page fault rate and the results proved our enhancement over [8] and also over CVM.

In our simulation, we considered a system with 12 nodes; each 4 of them formulate a cluster. So, we have 3 clusters with 3 master nodes. They are connected in a star topology. Each node has 50 frames of memory. And has large HD. The cluster cache is at each master node with 5 frames size so the master node has 45 frames. Also, work load varies from 82 to 263 pages.

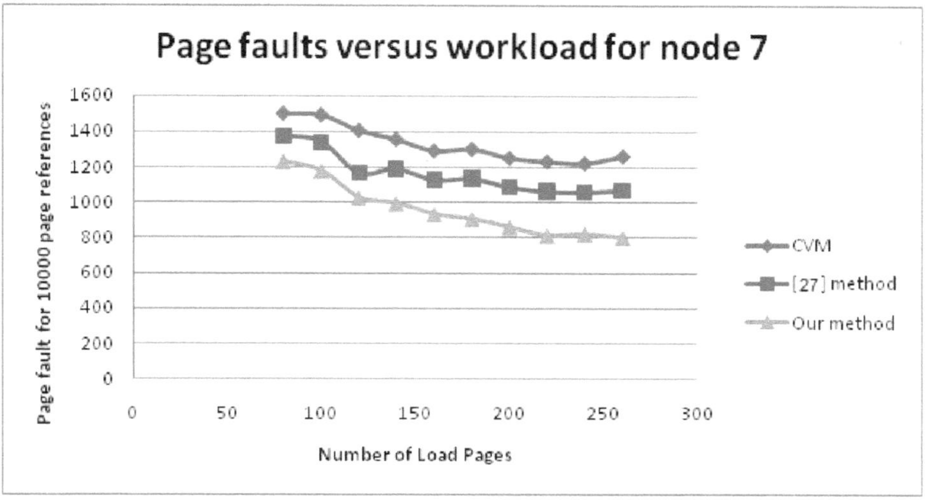

Fig. 3. Page Faults for Every Approximately 10000 Page References

Figure 3 shows the page fault rate compared to CVM for node 7. X-axis shows number of pages of the work load and Y-axis shows number of page faults for approximately 10000 page references. Notice that the enhancement that our methodology has over [8] method in terms of page faults. Also, as the work load increases, fault rate decreases compared to CVM and [8] method. So our methodology becomes more efficient as work load increases, until it shows some stability at the right most side. But on the other hand, as work load increases context switching will increase, so there is a trade off. From simulation we can notice that page faults rate decreased at average of 25% of CVM, and 15% of [8] method, which is considered as a good enhancement.

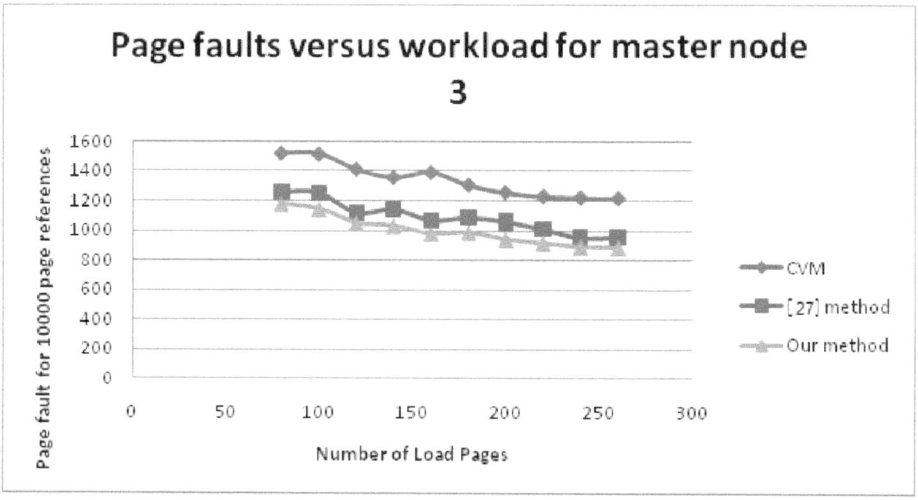

Fig. 4. Master Node Page Faults for Every Approximately 10000 Page References

Figure 4 shows the page fault rate to work load for node 3 which is a master node of cluster 1. Using our methodology, [8] methodology and CVM. Notice that the page fault rate compared to CVM has been decreased by average of 12.5 %. The enhancement over [8] is not obtained since the master node has smaller memory equals to 45 frames which have an effect over number of page faults.

4 Conclusion and Future Work

As was introduced, our work mainly depends on dividing the whole system into clusters and adding a cache for each one. As seen in the simulation, our methodology has optimized the DVM by increasing system throughput and decreasing the traffic in backbone network and as well the scalability of the system has been increased by a significant ratio. The experimental results based on benchmarks, have shown that the page fault rate has decreased by 25% compared to CVM and 15% compared to [27] methodology.

In the future, we might generalize our method by adding up the cache to the core switch commercially which will be built into it. So, the DVM technique accordingly will be applied and the throughput will be increased. Moreover, we intend to formalize the time complexity of the proposed algorithm and do more comparisons with our techniques.

References

1. Kai, L.: IVY: A Shared Virtual Memory System for Parallel Computing. In: International Conference on Parallel Processing, vol. 2, pp. 94–101 (1988)
2. Barrera III, J.S.: Odin: A Virtual Memory System for Massively Parallel Processors. Microsoft Research, Microsoft Corporation One Microsoft Way Redmond, WA 98052
3. Clancey, P.M., Francioni, J.M.: Distribution of Pages in a Distributed Virtual Memory. In: International Conference on Parallel Processing, pp. 258–265 (1990)
4. Abaza, M.: Distributed Virtual Memory Systems' Ph.D Thesis, The University of Wisconsin-Milwaukee (July 1992)
5. Malkawi, M., Knox, D., Abaza, M.: Dynamic Page Distribution in Distributed Virtual Memory Systems. In: Proceedings of the Forth ISSM International Conf. on Parallel and Distributed Computing and Systems, pp. 87–91 (1991)
6. Fellah, A., Abaza, M.: On page blocks in distributed virtual memory systems. In: IEEE Pacific Rim Conference on Communications, Computers and Signal Processing (PACRIM), pp. 605–607 (1999)
7. Geva, M., Wiseman, Y.: Distributed Shared Memory Integration. In: IEEE International Conference on Information Reuse and Integration (IRI), August 13-15, pp. 146–151 (2007)
8. Qanzu'a, G.E.L.: Practical Enhancements of Distributed Virtual Memory. M.S Thesis, Jordan University of Science and Technology (March 1996)
9. Abaza, M., Fellah, A.: Distributed virtual memory in the CSMA/CD environment. In: IEEE Pacific Rim Conference on Communications, Computers and Signal Processing (PACRIM), August 20-22, vol. 2, pp. 778–781 (1997)
10. Fellah, A.: On virtual page-based and object-based memory managements in distributed environments. In: IEEE Pacific Rim Conference on Communications, Computers and signal Processing (PACRIM), vol. 1, pp. 311–314 (2001)
11. Fellah, A., Abaza, M.: On page blocks in distributed virtual memory systems. In: IEEE Pacific Rim Conference on Communications, Computers and Signal Processing, pp. 605–607 (1999)

Radio Antipodal Number of Certain Graphs

Albert William and Charles Robert Kenneth

Department of Mathematics, Loyola College, Chennai, India
charlesrobert2@yahoo.co.in

Abstract. Let $G = (V, E)$ be a graph with vertex set V and edge set E. Let $diam(G)$ denote the diameter of G and $d(u, v)$ denote the distance between the vertices u and v in G. An antipodal labeling of G with diameter d is a function f that assigns to each vertex u, a positive integer $f(u)$, such that $d(u, v) + |f(u) - f(v)| \geq d$, for all $u, v \in V$. The span of an antipodal labeling f is $max\{|f(u) - f(v)|: u, v \in V(G)\}$. The antipodal number for G, denoted by $an(G)$, is the minimum span of all antipodal labelings of G. Determining the antipodal number of a graph G is an NP-complete problem. In this paper we determine the antipodal number of certain graphs .

Keywords: Labeling, radio antipodal numbering, diameter.

1 Introduction

Let G be a connected graph and let k be an integer, $k \geq 1$. A radio k- labeling f of G is an assignment of positive integers to the vertices of G such that $d(u, v) + |f(u) - f(v)| \geq k + 1$ for every two distinct vertices u and v of$G$, where $d(u, v)$is the distance between any two vertices u and v of G. The span of such a function$f$, denoted by sp $(f) = max\{|f(u) - f(v)|: u, v \in V(G)\}$. Radio $k -$ labeling was motivated by the frequency assignment problem [3]. The maximum distance among all pairs of vetices in G is the diameter of G. The radio labeling is a radio k- labeling when $k = diam(G)$. When $k = diam(G) - 1$, a radio k- labeling is called a radio antipodal labeling. In otherwords, an antipodal labeling for a graph G is a function, $f: V(G) \rightarrow \{0,1,2, \ldots\}$ such that $d(u, v) + |f(u) - f(v)| \geq diam(G)$. The radio antipodal number for G, denoted by $an(G)$, is the minimum span of an antipodal labeling admitted by G. A radio labeling is a one-to –one function, while in an antipodal labeling, two vertices of distance $diam(G)$ apart may receive the same label.

The antipodal labeling for graphs was first studied by Chartrand et al.[5], in which, among other results, general bounds of $an(G)$ were obtained. Khennoufa and Togni [7] determined the exact value of $an(P_n)$ for paths P_n. The antipodal labeling for cycles C_n was studied in [4], in which lower bounds for $an(C_n)$ are obtained. In addition, the bound for the case $n \equiv 2(mod\ 4)$ was proved to be the exact value of $an(C_n)$, and the bound for the case $n \equiv 1(mod\ 4)$ was conjectured to be the exact value as well [6]. Justie Su-tzu Juan and Daphne Der-Fen Liu confirmed the conjecture mentioned above. Moreover they determined the value of $an(C_n)$ for the case $n \equiv 3(mod\ 4)$ and also for the case $n \equiv 0(mod\ 4)$. They improve the known lower bound [4] and give an upper bound. They also conjecture that the upper bound is sharp.

A. Abd Manaf et al. (Eds.): ICIEIS 2011, Part III, CCIS 253, pp. 385–389, 2011.

In this paper we obtain an upper bound for the radio antipodal number of the Lobster and Extended mesh.

2 The Radio Antipodal Number of Lobster

A caterpillar is a tree in which the removal of pendant vertices leaves a path P called is its spine.

Let C(r, k) denote the caterpillar is which P is on k vertices and there are exactly r pendant edges incident at each vertex of P.

A lobster is a tree in which the removal of pendant vertices leaves a caterpillar.

Let $L(m, r, k)$ denote the lobster in which there are m pendant vertices incident at each of the pendant vertices of $C(r, k)$.

$L(m, r, k)$ of diameter d has $k = d$-3 vertices on P. Let $u_1, u_2, \dots, u_k$ be the vertices on P. Let v_{ij} denote the jth child from right to left of the vertex u_i $1 \leq i \leq k, 1 \leq j \leq r$. Again, let w_{ij}^s denote the sth child from right to left of the vertex v_{ij}, $1 \leq i \leq k, 1 \leq j \leq r$ and $1 \leq s \leq m$. In this paper we consider lobster $L(m, r, k)$ of diameter 7. This implies that P is on 4 vertices, namely u_1, u_2, u_3, u_4.

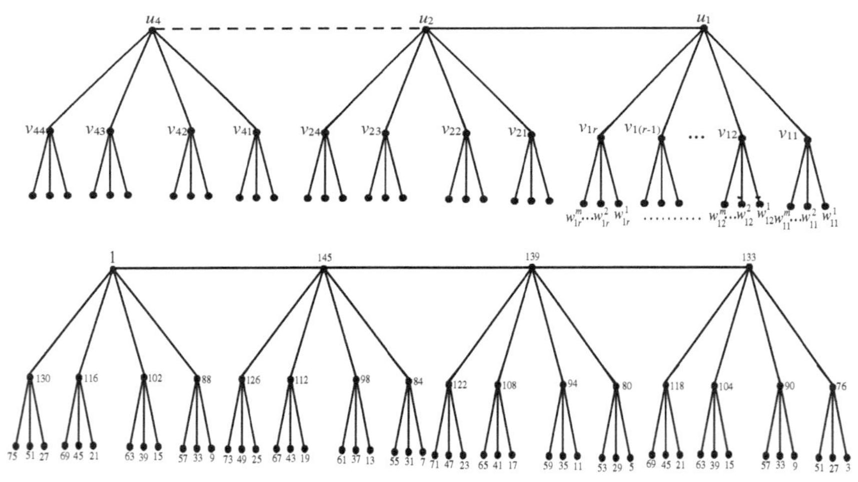

Fig. 1. Radio antipodal number of Lobster with diameter 7

Theorem 1. *The radio antipodal number of Lobster satisfies* $an\big(L(m,r,k)\big) \leq 24r + 20k - 7$.

Proof. Define a mapping $f\colon V\big(L(m,r,k)\big) \to N$

$$f\left(w_{ij}^{s}\right) = 3 + 4(j-1)6 + 6(i-1) + 2(u_k - 1), 1 \leq i \leq k, 1 \leq j \leq r, 1 \leq s \leq m, 1 \leq u_k \leq 4.$$

$$f(v_{ij}) = 3 + 4(j-1)6 + 6(i-1) + 2(u_k - 1) + \big(14v_{ij} - 13\big) + 4(u_k - 1), 1 \leq i \leq k, 1 \leq j \leq r,$$

$$1 \le u_k \le 4$$
$$f(u_i) = 3 + 4(j-1)6 + 6(i-1) + 2(u_k - 1) + \left(14v_{ij} - 13\right) + 4(u_k - 1) + (6u_l - 3), u_l = 1,2,3.$$

In other words label the vertices of the spine of $L(m,r,k)$ from right to left as $rm(2k-2) + (4k+1) + 12(k-1) + 8$, $rm(2k-2) + (4k+1) + 12(k-1) + 14$, $rm(2k-2) + (4k+1) + 12(k-1) + 20$ and 1.

Label the r pendent edges incident at vertex labeled $rm(2k-2) + (4k+1) + 12(k-1) + 8$ as $rm(2k-2) + 4$, $rm(2k-2) + 4k + 2$, $rm(2k-2) + 4(k-1) + 4k + 4$, $rm(2k-2) + 8(k-1) + 4k + 6$.

Label the r pendent edges incident at vertex labeled $rm(2k-2) + (4k+1) + 12(k-1) + 13$ as $rm(2k-2) + 8$, $rm(2k-2) + 4k + 6$, $rm(2k-2) + 4(k-1) + 4k + 8$, $rm(2k-2) + 8(k-1) + 4k + 10$.

Label the r pendent edges incident at vertex labeled $rm(2k-2) + (4k+1) + 12(k-1) + 20$ as $rm(2k-2) + 12$, $rm(2k-2) + 4k + 10$, $rm(2k-2) + 4(k-1) + 4k + 12$, $rm(2k-2) + 8(k-1) + 4k + 14$.

Label the r pendent edges incident at vertex labeled 1 as $rm(2k-2) + 16$, $rm(2k-2) + 4k + 14$, $rm(2k-2) + 4(k-1) + 4k + 16$, $rm(2k-2) + 8(k-1) + 4k + 18$.

Label the mth right most pendant vertex at level 3 incident at the ith right most vertex at level 2.

Consider vertex u and v in G.

Case 1: If $u = u_i$ and $v = u_j$ for $i \ne j$, then $d(u,v) + |f(u) - f(v)| = 1 + |(rm(2k-2) + (4k+1) + 12(k-1) + 8) - (rm(2k-2) + (4k+1) + 12(k-1) + 14)| \ge diam(G)$.

Case 2: If $u = u_i$ and $v = v_{ij}$ for $i \ne j$, then $d(u,v) + |f(u) - f(v)| = 1 + |(rm(2k-2) + (4k+1) + 12(k-1) + 8) - (rm(2k-2) + 4)| \ge diam(G)$.

3 The Radio Antipodal Number of Extended Mesh

Let P_n be a path on n vertices. Then an $m \times n$ mesh denoted $M(m,n)$ is defined to be the Cartesian product $P_m \times P_n$. The number of vertices in $M(m,n)$ is mn and the diameter is $m + n - 2$.

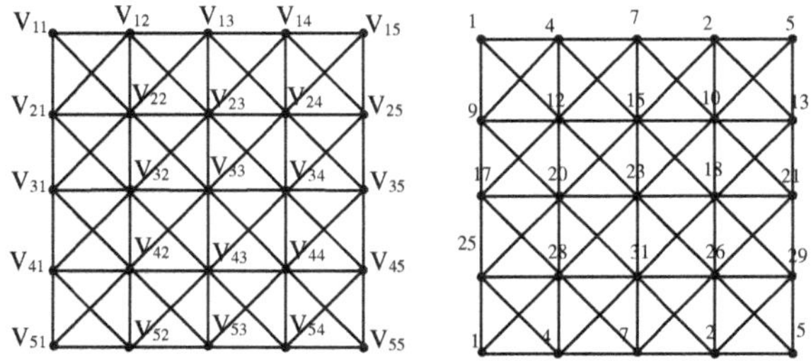

Fig. 2. Radio antipodal number of $EM(m,n)$ with diameter 5

The architecture obtained by making each 4-cycle in $M(m,n)$ into a complete graph is called an extended mesh. It is denoted by $EM(m,n)$. The number of vertices in $EM(m,n)$ is mn and diameter is $\min\{m,n\} - 1$.

Theorem 2. *If n is odd, then the radio antipodal number of the extended mesh $EM(m,n)$ satisfies* $an(EM(m,n)) \leq (n-2)\left(\left\lceil\frac{n}{2}\right\rceil - 1\right)(n-1) + \frac{(n-1)^2}{2} - \left\lfloor\frac{n-2}{2}\right\rfloor$.

Proof. Define a mapping $f\colon V(EM(m,n)) \to N$.

$$f(a_{ij}) = (i-1)(n-2)\left(\left\lceil\frac{n}{2}\right\rceil - 1\right) + \left(\frac{n-1}{2}\right)i - \left(\left\lfloor\frac{n-2}{2}\right\rfloor\right) + (n-2)(j-1),$$
$$i = 1,2,\ldots n-1, j = 1,2,\ldots \left\lceil\frac{n}{2}\right\rceil$$

$$f\left(a_{i,\left\lceil\frac{n}{2}\right\rceil+j}\right) = (i-1)(n-2)\left(\left\lfloor\frac{n}{2}\right\rfloor - 1\right) + (n-2)\left(j - \left\lceil\frac{n}{2}\right\rceil - 1\right) + \left\lfloor\frac{n}{2}\right\rfloor$$
$$+ (i-1)(n-1) - (i-1) - \left\lfloor\frac{n}{2}\right\rfloor(i-1), i = 1,2,\ldots n-1,$$

$j = 1,2,\ldots n$. It is easy to verify that $d(u,v) + |f(u) - f(v)| \geq (n-2)\left(\left\lceil\frac{n}{2}\right\rceil - 1\right)(n-1) + \frac{(n-1)^2}{2} - \left\lfloor\frac{n-2}{2}\right\rfloor$ for all $u, v \in V(EM(m,n))$.

4 Conclusion

The study of radio antipodal number of graphs has gained momentum in recent years. Very few graphs have been proved to have radio antipodal labeling that attains the radio antipodal number. In this paper we have determined the bounds of the radio antipodal number of the lobster and extended mesh. Further study is taken up for various other classes of graphs.

References

[1] Calamoneri, T., Petreschi, R.: L(2,1)-Labeling of Planar Graphs, pp. 28–33. ACM (2001)

[2] Chang, G.J., Lu, C.: Distance-Two Labeling of Graphs. European Journal of Combinatorics 24, 53–58 (2003)

[3] Chartrand, G., Erwin, D., Zhang, P.: Radio k-Colorings of Paths. Disscus Math. Graph Theory 24, 5–21 (2004)

[4] Chartrand, G., Erwin, D., Zhang, P.: Radio Antipodal Colorings of Cycles. Congressus Numerantium 144 (2000)

[5] Chartrand, G., Erwin, D., Zhang, P.: Radio Antipodal Colorings of Graphs. Math. Bohem. 127, 57–69 (2002)

[6] Chartrand, G., Erwin, D., Zhang, P.: Radio Labeling of Graphs. Bull. Inst. Combin. Appl. 33, 77–85 (2001)

[7] Khennoufa, R., Tongni, O.: A Note On Radio Antipodal Colouring of Paths. Math. Bohem. 130 (2005)

[8] Kchikech, M., Khennoufa, R., Tongi, O.: Linear And Cyclic Radio k-Labelings Of Trees. Discussiones Mathematicae Graph theory (2007)

[9] Ringel, G.: Theory Of Graphs And Its Applications. In: Proceedings of the Symposium Smolenice 1963, p. 162. Prague Publ. House of Czechoslovak Academy of Science (1964)

[10] Rosa, A.: Cyclic Steiner Triple Systems And Labeling Of Triangular Cacti. Scientia 1, 87–95 (1988)

[11] Rajan, B., Rajasingh, I., Kins, Y., Manuel, P.: Radio Number Of Graphs With Small Diameter. International Journal of Mathematics and Computer Science 2, 209–220 (2007)

[12] Rajan, B., Rajasingh, I., Cynthia, J.A.: Minimum Metric Dimension Of Mesh Derived Architectures. In: International Conference of Mathematics and Computer Science, vol. 1, pp. 153–156 (2009)

Induced Matching Partition of Sierpinski and Honeycomb Networks

Indra Rajasingh, Bharati Rajan, A.S. Shanthi, and Albert Muthumalai

Department of Mathematics, Loyola College, Chennai 600 034, India
shanthu.a.s@gmail.com

Abstract. Graph partitioning has several important applications in Computer Science, including VLSI circuit layout, image processing, solving sparse linear systems, computing fill-reducing orderings for sparse matrices, and distributing workloads for parallel computation. In this paper we have determined the induced matching partition number for certain classes of bipartite graphs, sierpinski graphs, sierpinski gaskets, honeycomb tori and honeycomb networks.

Keywords: Matching, Bipartite graphs, Honeycomb networks, Sierpinski graphs, Induced matching partition.

1 Introduction

A balanced distribution of the total workload in diverse fields such as modelling of solar radiation, climate, environmental and biochemical changes as well as VLSI designs has been shown to be the key element in achieving high speed-ups. The need for huge computational power arising in such applications to simulate complicated physical phenomenon accurately, on the other hand, demands the use of massively parallel computer architectures. The issue of distributing the overall workload evenly amongst a set of processors has been widely studied as a graph partitioning problem [4].

A matching in a graph $G = (V, E)$ is a subset M of edges, no two of which have a vertex in common. The vertices belonging to the edges of a matching are saturated by the matching. The others are unsaturated. A matching is called *induced* if the subgraph of G induced by the endpoints of edges in M is 1-regular. A matching M is said to *perfect* if every vertex in G is an endpoint of one of the edges in M. A *near-perfect* matching covers all but exactly one vertex. Let G be a graph with a perfect matching. An induced matching k-partition of a graph G which has a perfect matching is a k-partition $(V_1, V_2, \ldots, V_k)$ of $V(G)$ such that, for each i $(1 \leq i \leq k)$, $E(V_i)$ is an induced matching of G that covers V_i, or equivalently, the sub graph $G[V_i]$ of G induced by V_i is 1-regular. The induced matching partition number of a graph G, denoted by $imp(G)$, is the minimum integer k such that G has an induced matching k-partition. The induced matching partition problem is to determine $imp(G)$ of a graph G.

The induced matching k-partition problem was first studied as a combinatorial optimization problem [5]. The induced matching k-partition problem is NP-complete, and also NP-complete for $k = 2$ and for 3-regular planar graphs, respectively [5, 9]. Yuan and Wang [14] have characterized graphs G with $imp(G) = 2\Delta(G) - 1$.

A. Abd Manaf et al. (Eds.): ICIEIS 2011, Part III, CCIS 253, pp. 390–399, 2011.

The problem was studied for certain interconnection networks such as butterfly networks, hypercubes, cube-connected cycles and grids [8].

In this paper we have determined the induced matching partition number for certain classes of bipartite graphs, sierpinski graphs, sierpinski gaskets, honeycomb tori and honeycomb networks.

2 Main Results

It is easy to check that an acyclic graph with perfect matching has *imp* equal to 2.

Theorem 1. *If G is a tree with perfect matching then imp(G) = 2.*

Let $\hat{G}$ be a graph containing the graph H shown in Figure 1 as an induced subgraph where $deg_{\hat{G}}v_1 = 2$, $deg_{\hat{G}}v_2 = deg_{\hat{G}}v_3 = deg_{\hat{G}}v_5 = 4$, $deg_{\hat{G}}v_4 \geq 2$ and $deg_{\hat{G}}v_6 \geq 2$.

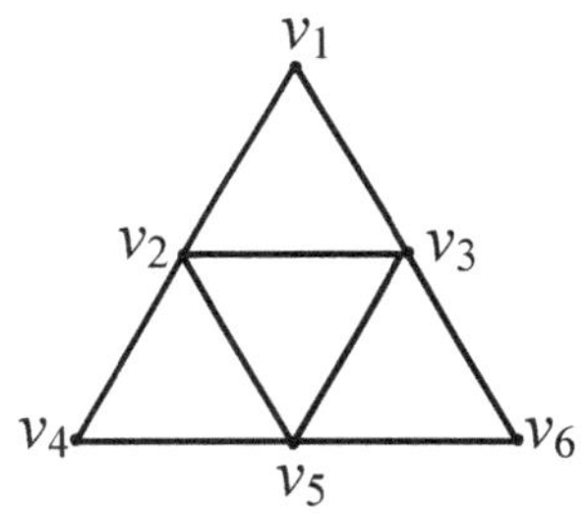

Fig. 1. Graph H

Theorem 2. *imp*($\hat{G}$) ≥ 3.

Proof. Let $V_1, V_2, \ldots, V_k$ be an induced matching k-partition of $\hat{G}$. We claim that $k \geq 3$. Suppose not, let V_1, V_2 be an induced matching 2-partition of $\hat{G}$. To saturate v_1, either $(v_1, v_2) \in E(V_1)$ or $(v_1, v_3) \in E(V_1)$. Without loss of generality let $(v_1, v_2) \in E(V_1)$. Now $(v_3, v_5) \in E(V_2)$ or $(v_3, v_6) \in E(V_2)$. Then $v_4 \notin V_1$ or V_2. Therefore $imp(\hat{G}) \geq 3$. □

In this section B_{XY} denotes a bipartite graph with $|X| = |Y| = n$ and $K_{n,n}$ is a complete bipartite graph on $2n$ vertices. For given m, let $\theta_G(m) = min_{A \subseteq V,\ |A| = m}|\theta_G(A)|$ where $\theta_G(A) = \{(u, v) \in E: u \in A, v \notin A\}$.

Theorem 3. *Let G be B_{XY} on 4k + 2 vertices, k ≥ 1 and admit a perfect matching. Then imp(G) ≥ 3.*

Proof. Suppose on the contrary that V_1 and V_2 form an induced matching 2-partition of G. Let $V = (X, Y)$ be a bipartition of G. Since G has a perfect matching, $|X| = |Y| = 2k + 1$ and $\theta(V_1) = \theta(V_2)$. Hence $|V_1| = |V_2| = 2k + 1$. Moreover $|X| = \frac{|V_1|}{2} + \frac{|V_2|}{2}$. Therefore X is partitioned into two sets of cardinality $\frac{2k+1}{2}$ each. But $\frac{2k+1}{2}$ is not an integer, a contradiction. □

Theorem 4. *Let G(V, E) be the bipartite graph B_{XY} and let d(v) = n – 1 for every v ∈ V. Then* $imp(G) = \begin{cases} \frac{n}{2} & if\ n\ is\ even \\ \left\lceil \frac{n}{2} \right\rceil + 1 & if\ n\ is\ odd \end{cases}$.

Proof. Let $V = V_1, V_2, \ldots, V_k$ be an induced matching partition of V and let $x \in X$. Since $deg\ x = n - 1$, there exists $y \in Y$ such that $xy \notin E$. Select $xv \in E$ and put x, v in V_1. Since $deg\ v = n - 1$, there exists $u \neq x$ in X such that $uv \notin E$ and $yu \in E$. We include the vertices y, u in V_1. Every edge in G with one end in X is incident with either y or v. Similarly every edge in G with one end in Y is incident with either x or u. Hence $|V_1| = 4$. We continue this procedure of selecting subsets of vertices of cardinality 4. If n is even, we proceed till all vertices are saturated. Thus $imp(G) = \frac{2n}{4} = \frac{n}{2}$. If n is odd, a pair of vertices $a \in X$ and $b \in Y$ will be left unsaturated such that $ab \notin E$. Consider $V_1 = \{x, y, u, v\}$. Delete V_1 and add $V_{\frac{n}{2}+1} = \{a, y\}$, $V_{\frac{n}{2}+2} = \{x, u\}$ and $V_{\frac{n}{2}+3} = \{v, b\}$. Hence $imp(G) = \left\lceil \frac{n}{2} \right\rceil + 1$. □

Theorem 5. *Let G be the complete bipartite graph $K_{n,n}$. Then imp(G) = n.*

Proof. Let (X, Y) be the bipartition of G with $|X| = |Y| = n$. The result is obvious since every vertex in X is adjacent to all vertices in Y. □

Remark 1. Let G be a bipartite graph B_{XY} with at most one vertex of degree $n - 2$ and all other vertices of degree $n - 1$. Then $imp(G) = n$.

Remark 2. Perfect matchings do not exist for a bipartite graph $G(V, E)$ with $V = X \cup Y$, $|X| = m$, $|Y| = n$ and $m \neq n$.

3 Honeycomb

A honeycomb network can be built in various ways. The honeycomb network $HC(1)$ is a hexagon; see Figure 2 (*a*). The honeycomb network $HC(2)$ is obtained by adding a layer of six hexagons to the boundary edges of $HC(1)$ as shown in Figure 2 (*b*). Inductively honeycomb network $HC(n)$ is obtained from $HC(n - 1)$ by adding a layer of hexagons around the boundary of $HC(n - 1)$. The number of vertices and edges of $HC(n)$ are $6n^2$ and $9n^2 - 3n$ respectively [10].

Honeycomb networks, thus built recursively using hexagonal tessellation, are widely used in computer graphics, cellular phone base station [11], image processing [2], and in chemistry as the representation of benzenoid hydrocarbons [10, 13]. Honeycomb networks bear resemblance to atomic or molecular lattice structures of chemical compounds. In the sequel let C_n and P_n denote a cycle and a path on n vertices respectively. The vertices of $HC(n)$ are labelled as shown in the Figure 2 (*b*). If C_o^n denotes the outer cycle of $HC(n)$, then the number of vertices in C_o^n is $12n - 6$. We introduce co-ordinate axes for the honeycomb networks as follows.

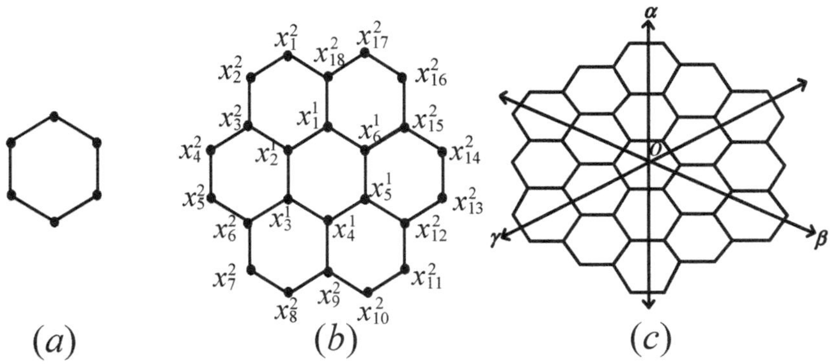

Fig. 2. (*a*) *HC*(1) (*b*)*HC*(2) (*c*) *HC*(3)

The edges of *HC*(1) are in 3 different directions. The point *O* at which the perpendicular bisectors of these edges meet is called the centre of the honeycomb network *HC*(1). *O* is also considered to be the centre of *HC*(*n*). Through *O* draw three lines perpendicular to the three edge directions and name them as α, β, γ axes. See Figure 2 (*c*). The α line through *O*, denoted by α_o, passes through $2n-1$ hexagons. Any line parallel to α_o and passing through $2n-1-i$ hexagons is denoted by α_i, $1 \le i \le n-1$ if the hexagons are taken in the clockwise sense about α_o and by α_{-i}, $1 \le i \le n-1$ if the hexagons are taken in the anti-clockwise sense about α_o. In the same way β_j, β_{-j}, $0 \le j \le n-1$, and γ_k, γ_{-k}, $0 \le k \le n-1$ are defined.

Theorem 6. *Let G(V, E) be HC(n). Then imp(G)* ≥ 3.

Proof. Suppose on the contrary that V_1, V_2 form an induced matching 2-partition of *G*. Label vertices in V_1 as 1 and V_2 as 2. Since *HC*(*n*) is a C_6 tessellation, the vertex set of every hexagon say *abcdefa* can be partitioned in any one of the three ways (*i*) $a, c, e \in V_1$ and $b, d, f \in V_2$, (*ii*) $a, c, d, f \in V_1$ and $b, e \in V_2$ and (*iii*) $a, d, f \in V_1$ and $b, c, e \in V_2$. See Figure 3.

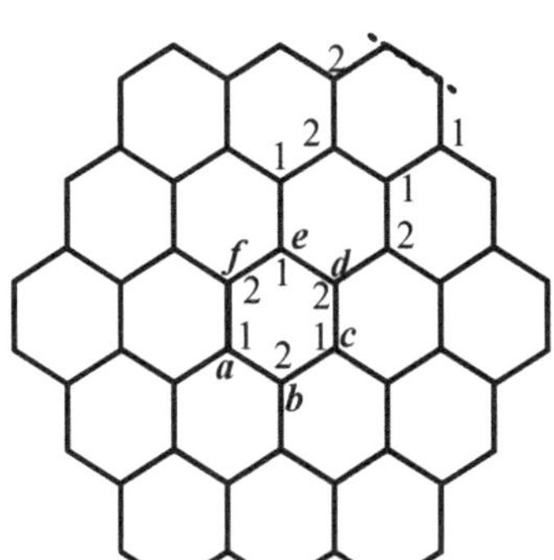

Fig. 3. *HC*(3)

If the partition is as in (*i*) or (*iii*) then the hexagons in the axis perpendicular to *ed* ∈ *E* are labelled with 1 or 2 except the outer hexagon and in the outer hexagon *ed* ∉ $E(V_1)$ and $E(V_2)$. Since all the outer hexagons in *HC*(*n*) cannot be in form (*ii*) there exists at least one hexagon in form (*i*) or (*iii*). Therefore $imp(G) \geq 3$. □

Procedure INDUCED MATCHING PARTITION *HC*(*n*)

Input: A honeycomb network *G* of dimension *n*.

Algorithm

While $k = 1$ to *n* Do

If *k* is odd, label the vertices x_i^k of C_o^k as 1 or 2 according as $i \equiv 1, 2 \; mod \; 4$ or $i \equiv 0, 3 \; mod \; 4$ respectively whenever $i \leq 12k - 8$ and label x^k_{12k-7} and x^k_{12k-6} as 3. If *k* is even, label the vertices x_i^k of C_o^k as 2 or 1 according as $i \equiv 1, 2 \bmod 4$ or $i \equiv 0, 3 \bmod 4$ respectively whenever $i \leq 12k - 10$ and label x^k_{12k-9}, x^k_{12k-8} as 3 and x^k_{12k-7} and x^k_{12k-6} as 1.

$k \leftarrow k + 1$

Repeat

End Induced Matching Partition *HC*(*n*)

Output: $imp(HC(n)) = 3$.

Theorem 7. *Let G(V, E) be HC(n). Then imp(G) = 3.*

Proof. Let V_i be the set of all vertices that receive label *i*, $i = 1, 2, 3$ by the Procedure INDUCED MATCHING PARTITION *HC*(*n*). For $u \in V_i$, $|N(u) \cap V_i| = 1$, $i = 1, 2, 3$. Thus $G[V_1]$, $G[V_2]$ and $G[V_3]$ are 1-regular. Therefore $imp(G) = 3$. □

4 Honeycomb Torus

Honeycomb torus network can be obtained by joining pairs of nodes of degree two of the honeycomb network. In order to achieve edge and vertex symmetry, the best

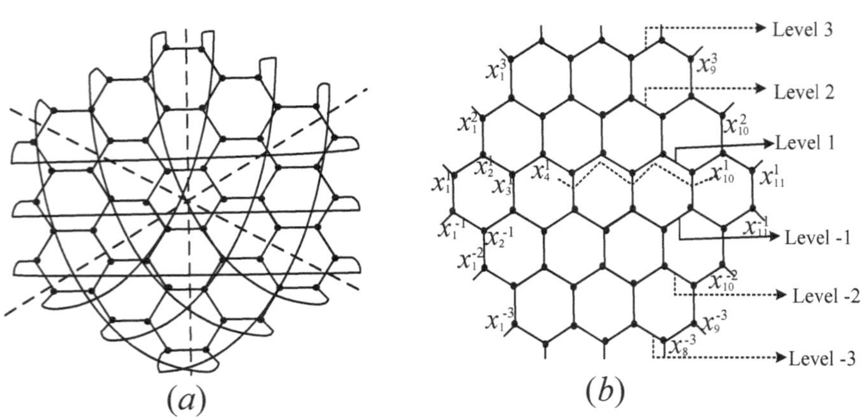

Fig. 4. Honeycomb Torus of size three

choice for wrapping around seems to be the pairs of nodes that are mirror symmetric with respect to three lines, passing through the centre of the hexagonal network, and normal to each of the three edge orientations. Figure 4 (*a*) shows how to wraparound honeycomb network of size three (*HC*(3)) to obtain *HT*(3), the honeycomb torus of dimension three. Let us label the vertices of honeycomb torus as shown in the Figure 4 (*b*). The vertices x_i^k are in level k where $-n \le k \le n$. Level k has $4n - 2k + 1$ vertices.

The following result is an easy consequence of Theorem 3.

Theorem 8. *Let G be HT(n), n odd. Then imp(G)* ≥ 3.

Procedure INDUCED MATCHING PARTITION *HT*(*n*)

Input: A honeycomb torus G of dimension n.

Algorithm: Let $-n \le k \le n$ and $1 \le i \le 4n - 2k + 1$.

Case 1 (*n* even): For i and k both even or both odd, label x_i^k as 1, and as 2 otherwise.

Case 2 (*n* odd): For $k \equiv 0 \bmod 3$, label x_i^k as 1, 2 or 3 according as $i \equiv 2 \bmod 3$, $i \equiv 0 \bmod 3$ or $i \equiv 1 \bmod 3$. For $k \equiv 1 \bmod 3$, label x_i^k as 1, 2 or 3 according as $i \equiv 1 \bmod 3$, $i \equiv 2 \bmod 3$ or $i \equiv 0 \bmod 3$. For $k \equiv 2 \bmod 3$, label x_i^k as 1, 2 or 3 according as $i \equiv 0 \bmod 3$, $i \equiv 1 \bmod 3$ or $i \equiv 2 \bmod 3$.

Output: $imp(HT(n)) = 2$ if n is even and $imp(HT(n)) = 3$ if n is odd.

Theorem 9. *Let G be HT(n). Then imp(G) = 3 if n is odd and imp(G) = 2 if n is even.*

Proof. Let V_i be the set of all vertices that receive label i, $i = 1, 2, 3$ by the procedure INDUCED MATCHING PARTITION *HT*(*n*). For any x_i^k in level k, two vertices of $N(x_i^k)$ are in level k itself and adjacent vertices in the same level do not receive the same label. Thus $G[V_1]$, $G[V_2]$ and $G[V_3]$ are 1-regular. Therefore $imp(G) = 2$ for n even and 3 for n odd. □

5 Sierpinski Graphs

The Sierpinski graphs $S(n, 3)$, $n \geq 1$, are defined in this following way [7]:

$V(S(n, 3)) = \{1, 2, 3\}^n$, two different vertices $u = (u_1, ..., u_n)$ and $v = (v_1, ..., v_n)$ being adjacent if and only if there exist an $h \in \{1, ..., n\}$ such that

(i) $u_t = v_t$, for $t = 1, ..., h - 1$;
(ii) $u_h \neq v_h$; and
(iii) $u_t = v_h$ and $v_t = u_h$ for $t = h + 1, ..., n$.

We will shortly write $< u_1u_2...u_n >$ for $(u_1, u_2, ..., u_n)$. The graph $S(3,3)$ is shown in Figure 5 (*a*). The vertices < 1...1 >, < 2...2 >, and < 3...3 > are called the extreme vertices of $S(n, 3)$.

The set of edges {< 122...2 >< 211...1 >, < 133...3 >< 311...1 >, < 233...3 >< 322...2 >} is an edge-cut whose removal yields 3 components namely A, B and C each isomorphic to $S(n - 1, 3)$. The extreme vertices of A are < 11...1 >, < 12...2 > and <

13...3 > of S_n, the extreme vertices of B are < 21...1 >, < 22...2 > and < 23...3 > of S_n and for C the extreme vertices are < 31...1 >, < 32...2 > and < 33...3 > of S_n.

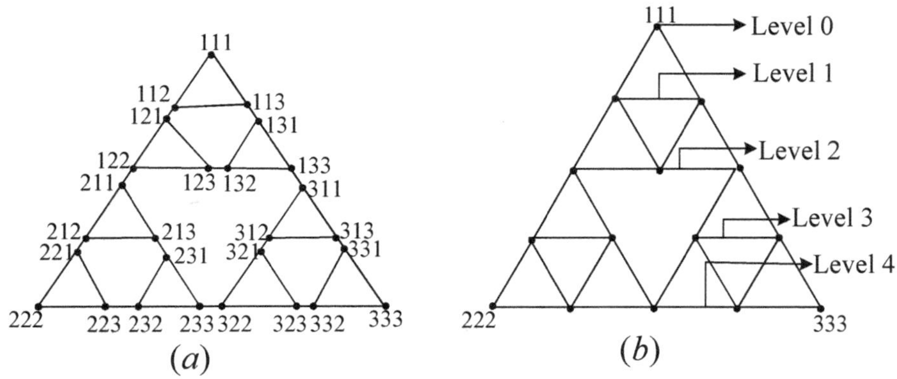

Fig. 5. *(a)* $S(3, 3)$ *(b)* S_3

Procedure INDUCED MATCHING PARTITION $S(n, 3)$

Input: A Sierpinski graph G of dimension n.

Algorithm: $S(2, 3)$ is labelled as shown in the Figure 6 *(a)*. The component A in $S(n, 3)$ is labelled as $S(n - 1, 3)$ with labels of extreme vertices < 11...1 >, < 12...2 > and < 13...3 > identified with labels of < 11...1 >, < 22...2 > and < 33...3 > respectively.

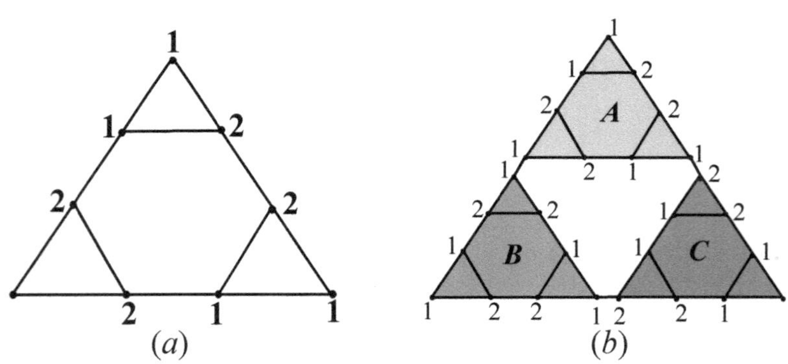

Fig. 6. *(a)* $S(2, 3)$ *(b)* $S(3, 3)$

If n is odd, the component B in $S(n, 3)$ is labelled as $S(n - 1, 3)$ with labels of extreme vertices < 21...1 >, < 22...2 > and < 23...3 > identified with labels of < 22...2 >, < 11...1 > and < 33...3 > respectively. The component C in $S(n, 3)$ is labelled as the complement of $S(n - 1, 3)$ with labels of extreme vertices < 31...1 >, < 32...2 > and < 33...3 > identified with labels of < 11...1 >, < 33...3 > and < 22...2 > respectively. Label the vertices < 12...2 > and < 21...1 > as 1. See Figure 6 *(b)*.

If n is even, the component C in $S(n, 3)$ is labelled as $S(n - 1, 3)$ with labels of extreme vertices < 31...1 >, < 32...2 > and < 33...3 > identified with labels of < 33...3 >, < 22...2 > and < 11...1 > respectively. The component B in $S(n, 3)$ is labelled as the complement of $S(n - 1, 3)$ with labels of extreme vertices < 21...1 >, < 22...2 > and < 23...3 > identified with labels of < 11...1 >, < 33...3 > and < 22...2 > respectively. Label the vertices < 13...3 > and < 31...1 > as 2.

Output: $imp(S_n) = 2$.

Proof of Correctness: Suppose the vertices that receive label i are in V_i, $i = 1, 2$. If n is odd, B is isomorphic to A with labelling as that of A. Resolving the edges of A into 1-factors also implies resolving B into 1-factors except < 12...2 > and < 21...1 >. Label the two vertices as 1. Again since A and C are isomorphic and the labels of C are complements of labels of A, both A and C can be resolved into 1-factors.

If n is even, C is isomorphic to A with labelling as that of A. Resolving the edges of A into 1-factors also implies resolving C into 1-factors except < 13...3 > and < 31...1 >. Label the two vertices as 2. Again since A and B are isomorphic and the labels of B are complements of labels of A, both A and B can be resolved into 1-factors. Therefore $imp(G) = 2$. □

6 Sierpinski Gasket Graphs

The sierpinski gasket graphs S_n, $n \geq 1$, are defined geometrically as the graphs whose vertices are the intersection points of the line segments of the finite sierpinski gasket σ_n and the line segments of the gasket as edges. The sierpinski gasket graph S_3 is shown in Figure 5 (*b*). S_n is the graph with three special vertices < 1...1 >, < 2...2 >, and < 3...3 > are called the extreme vertices of S_n, together with the three vertices of the form < $u_1...u_r$ > $\{i, j\}$, where $0 \leq r \leq n - 2$, and all the u_k's, i and j are form {1, 2, 3} [7].

There have been some studies on sierpinski gasket graphs in recent years. In [6, 12], the authors consider the vertex coloring, edge-coloring and total-coloring of sierpinski graphs, domination number and pebbling number of sierpinski gasket graphs.

The vertex <1...1> in S_n is called the root vertex and it is in level 0. The children of the root vertex are in level 1. The children of vertices in level 1 are in level 2. In general the vertices in 2^{n-1}th level are the children of vertices in level 2^{n-2}. See Figure 5 (*b*). For $v \in V$, let $N_1(v)$ denote the set of all vertices adjacent to v in G. Let $N_2(v)$ denote vertices adjacent to members of $N_1(v)$.

The vertices of sierpinski gasket graphs are traversed as follows. We start at the left most vertex u in the level $i = 2^{n-1}$. We next visit a vertex adjacent to u in level i which has not yet been visited. Move from left to right passing through all the vertices in the level i. On reaching the right most vertex x in the level i, the next vertex in the traversal belongs to $N(x)$ in the level $i - 1$ and move from right to left. Thus the traversal in alternate levels beginning from level 2^{n-1} is from left to right and all other traversals are from right to left till we reach level 0.

The following result is an easy consequence of Theorem 2.

Theorem 10. *Let G be S_n. Then imp(G) ≥ 3.*

Procedure INDUCED MATCHING PARTITION S_n

Input: A Sierpinski gasket graph G of dimension n.

Algorithm: Label the left most vertex v in the level 2^{n-1} as 1. The labelling follows the sierpinski gasket traversal. Let u be a vertex in level i. If $N_1(u)$ has a vertex w labelled k, $k = 1$ or 2 or 3 and if $N_1(w)$ does not contain label k then label u as k. Otherwise label u as 1, 2 or 3 according as $N_1(u)$ are labelled as 2 or 3, 1, 1 and 2 and the graph induced by $N_2(u)$ is K_2 are not labelled as 1, 2 or 3. If the graph induced by $N_2(u)$ is K_2 and are labelled as 1 or 2 and elements of $N_1(u)$ are labelled as 2 or 1 then label u as 3 where $N_2(u)$ is $N_1(w)$ and w is an unvisited vertex.

Output: $imp(S_n) = 3$.

Theorem 11. *Let G be S_n. Then imp(G) = 3.*

Proof. The vertices that receive label 1, 2 or 3 are in V_1, V_2 and V_3 respectively by the Procedure INDUCED MATCHING PARTITION S_n. For any $u \in V_i$, $i = 1, 2, 3$, exactly one vertex in $N(u) \in V_i$. Thus $G[V_1]$, $G[V_2]$ and $G[V_3]$ are 1-regular. Therefore $imp(G) = 3$. □

7 Conclusion

In this paper, the induced matching partition numbers of certain classes bipartite graphs have been determined. As the induced matching k-partition problem is *NP*-complete even for $k = 2$, it would be interesting to identify other interconnection networks for which $k = 2$. We have also identified classes of trees, even honeycomb torus and sierpinski graphs for which $k = 2$ and classes of honeycomb, odd honeycomb torus and sierpinski gasket graphs with $k = 3$. It is worth investigating interconnection networks for which $k > 2$.

Acknowledgement. This work is supported by the Department of Science and Technology, Government of India, Project No. SR/S4/MS: 595/09.

References

1. Arora, S., Karger, D.R., Karpinski, M.: Polynomial Time Approximation Schemes for Dense Instances of NP-Hard Problems. J. Comput. Syst. Sci. 58, 193–210 (1999)
2. Bell, S.B.M., Holroyd, F.C., Mason, D.C.: A Digital Geometry for Hexagonal Pixels. Image and Vision Computing 7, 194–204 (1989)
3. Czumaj, A., Sohler, C.: Testing Hypergraph Colorability. Theoretical Computer Science 331, 37–52 (2005)
4. Evrendilek, C.: Vertex Separators for Partitioning a Graph. Sensors 8, 635–657 (2008)

5. Garey, M.R., Johnson, D.S.: Computers and Intractability: A Guide to the Theory of NP-Completeness. W.H. Freeman, San Francisco (1979)
6. Jakovac, M., Klavazar, S.: Vertex-, Edge-, and Total-Colorings of Sierpinski-like Graphs. Discrete Mathematics 309(6), 1548–1556 (2009)
7. Klavzar, S.: Coloring Sierpinski Graphs and Sierpinski Gasket Graphs. Taiwanese J. Math. 12, 513–522 (2008)
8. Manuel, P., Rajasingh, I., Rajan, B., Muthumalai, A.: On Induced Matching Partitions of Certain Interconnection Networks. In: FCS, pp. 57–63 (2006)
9. Schaefer, T.J.: The Complexity of Satisfiability Problems. In: Proceedings of the 10th Annual ACM Symposium on Theory of Computing, Association for Computing Machinery, New York, pp. 216–226 (1976)
10. Stojmenovic, I.: Honeycomb Networks: Topological Properties and Communication Algorithms. IEEE Transactions on Parallel and Distributed Systems 8(10), 1036–1042 (1997)
11. Tajozzakerin, H.R., Sarbazi-Azad, H.: Enhanced-Star: A New Topology Based on the Star Graph. In: Cao, J., Yang, L.T., Guo, M., Lau, F. (eds.) ISPA 2004. LNCS, vol. 3358, pp. 1030–1038. Springer, Heidelberg (2004)
12. Teguia, A.M., Godbole, A.P.: Sierpinski Gasket Graphs and Some of their Properties. Australasian Journal of Combinatorics 35, 181 (2006)
13. Xu, J.: Topological Structure and Analysis of Interconnection Networks. Kluwer Academic Publishers (2001)
14. Yuan, J., Wang, Q.: Partition the Vertices of a Graph into Induced Matching. Discrete Mathematics 263, 323–329 (2003)

PI Index of Mesh Structured Chemicals

S. Little Joice[1], Jasintha Quadras[2], S. Sarah Surya[2], and A. Shanthakumari[1]

[1] Department of Mathematics, Loyola College, Chennai 600 034, India
[2] Department of Mathematics, Stella Maris College, Chennai 600 086, India
sara24solomon@gmail.com

Abstract. The *PI* index of a graph *G* is defined as $PI(G) = \Sigma[\eta_{eu}(e|G) + \eta_{ev}(e|G)]$, where for the edge $e = (u,v)$, $\eta_{eu}(e|G)$ is the number of edges of *G* lying closer to *u* than *v*; $\eta_{ev}(e|G)$ is the number of edges of *G* lying closer to *v* than *u* and summation goes over all edges of *G*. In this paper, we have introduced a new strategy to compute *PI* indices of graphs. Using this strategy, the *PI* index of mesh, torus and honeycomb mesh, *NaCl* molecule and benzenoid graph have been computed.

Keywords: *PI* index, mesh, torus, honeycomb mesh, *NaCl* molecule and benzenoid graph.

1 Introduction

Graph theory represents a very natural formalism for chemistry and has already been employed in a variety of implicit forms. Its applications began to multiply so fast that chemical graph theory bifurcated in manifold ways to evolve into an assortment of different specialisms. The current panorama of chemical graph theory has been erected on foundations that are essentially graph - theoretical in nature.

The chemical graphs are now being used for many different purposes in all the major branches of chemical engineering and this renders the origin of the earliest implicit application of graph theory of some considerable interest.

The mesh, honeycomb and diamond networks are not only important interconnection networks but also bear resemblance to atomic or molecular lattice structures of chemical compounds. These networks can be modeled by graphs with nodes corresponding to processors and edges corresponding to communication links between them. A survey of these networks is given in [13].

There are three possible tessellations of a plane with regular polygons of the same kind: square, triangular and hexagonal, corresponding to dividing a plane into regular squares, triangles and hexagons respectively. The mesh network is based on square tessellation whereas the honeycomb mesh is based on hexagonal tessellation.

Honeycomb and hexagonal networks have been studied in variety of contexts. They have been applied in chemistry to model benzenoid hydrocarbons [15], in image processing, in computer graphics [9], and in cellular networks [4]. The honeycomb architecture was proposed in [14], where a suitable addressing scheme together with routing and broadcasting algorithms were investigated. Some topological properties

A. Abd Manaf et al. (Eds.): ICIEIS 2011, Part III, CCIS 253, pp. 400–409, 2011.

and communication algorithms for the honeycomb network and tori have been also investigated in [3, 10, 11, 12].

In order to obtain the structure-activity relationships in which theoretical and computational methods are based, it is necessary to find appropriate representations of the molecular structure of chemical compounds. These representations are realized through the molecular descriptors. One such kind of molecular descriptors is the topological indices. A topological representation of a molecule can be carried out through the molecular graph.

Numbers reflecting certain structural features of organic molecules that are obtained from the molecular graph are usually called graph invariants or more commonly topological indices. Many topological indices have been defined and several of them have found applications as means to model chemical, pharmaceutical and other properties of molecules. Padmakar V. Khadikar introduced a new topological index called Padmakar – Ivan index [5, 6], which is abbreviated as *PI* index.

In a series of papers, Khadikar et. al. computed the *PI* index of some chemical graphs [6, 7, 8]. Ali Reza Ashrafi and Amir Loghman computed the *PI* index of a zig-zag polyhex nanotube [1] and they also computed *PI* index of some benzenoid graphs [2].In this paper, we compute the *PI* index of mesh, torus and honeycomb mesh. Further, we derive the *PI* index of *NaCl* molecule.

PI Index of Graphs

Definition 1. [5] *The PI index of a graph G is defined as* $PI(G) = \Sigma[\eta_{eu}(e|G) + \eta_{ev}(e|G)]$, *where for the edge e = (u,v),* $\eta_{eu}(e|G)$ *is the number of edges of G lying closer to u than v;* $\eta_{ev}(e|G)$ *is the number of edges of G lying closer to v than u and summation goes over all edges of G. When there is no ambiguity, we denote PI(G) by PI and define* $PI = \sum_{e\epsilon E}[\eta_{eu} + \eta_{ev}]$.

We prove the following lemma, which enables another way of counting the *PI* index of a graph *G*.

Lemma 1. *The PI index of a graph G(p,q) is given by* $PI = q^2 - \sum_{e\epsilon E}|\tau_e|$, *where q is the number of edges in G and for any edge e = (u, v),* τ_e *is the set of edges which are equidistant from both u and v.*

Proof. We know that for any graph *G*, $PI(G) = \Sigma[\eta_{eu}(e|G) + \eta_{ev}(e|G)]$, where for the edge *e* = (*u,v*), $\eta_{eu}(e|G)$ is the number of edges of *G* lying closer to *u* than *v*; $\eta_{ev}(e|G)$ is the number of edges of *G* lying closer to *v* than *u* and summation goes over all edges of *G*. We note that τ_e is not empty as edge *uv* is equidistant from both *u* and *v*. Now $\eta_{eu} + \eta_{ev} = q - |\tau_e|$. Hence taking summation over all the edges of *G*, we have $PI = \sum_{e\epsilon E}[\eta_{eu} + \eta_{ev}] = \sum_{e\epsilon E}[q - |\tau_e|] = q^2 - \sum_{e\epsilon E}|\tau_e|$.

The above lemma has been proved for any connected, planar, bipartite graph in the Euclidean plane [17]. We make use of the following lemma throughout this paper.

Lemma 2. *Let G = (V, E) be a graph and let $\{E_1, E_2,\ldots, E_k\}$ be a partition of E such that for,* $e, e' \epsilon E_i, 1 \leq i \leq k$, $\tau_e = \tau_{e'}$ *then* $PI(G) = q^2 - \sum_{i=1}^{k}|\tau_{e_i}|\, t_i$ *where* $t_i = |E_i|$ *and* $e_i \epsilon E_i$, $1 \leq i \leq k$.

Proof. $\sum_{e\epsilon E}|\tau_e| = \sum_{i=1}^{k}\sum_{e_i\epsilon E_i}|\tau_{e_i}| = \sum_{i=1}^{k}|\tau_{e_i}|\, t_i$ *where* $t_i = |E_i|$, $1 \leq i \leq k$ *and since* $\tau_e = \tau_{e'}$ *for any two edges* $e, e' \epsilon E_i, 1 \leq i \leq k$.

2 Meshes

Let P_n denote a path on n vertices. For m, $n \geq 2, P_m \times P_n$ is defined as a two dimensional (2-*D*) mesh with *m* rows and *n* columns. See Fig 1.

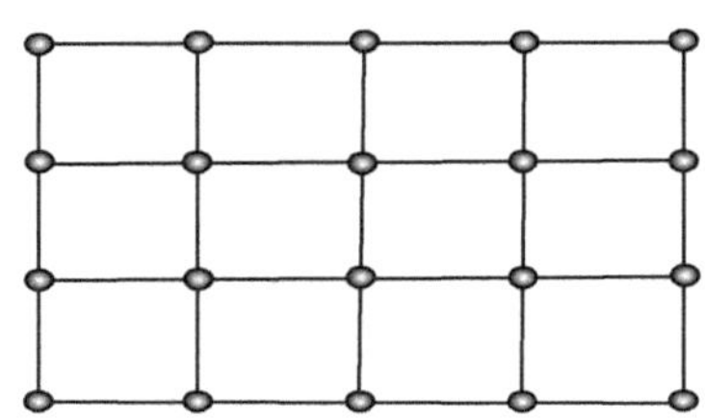

Fig. 1. *M* (4,5)

A three dimensional (3-*D*) mesh *M*(*r*, *s*,*t*) is nothing but $P_r \times P_s \times P_t$. In a 3-*D* mesh there are *str* number of vertices and (2*rs*-*r*-*s*)*t* + (*t*-1)*sr* number of edges. See Fig 2.

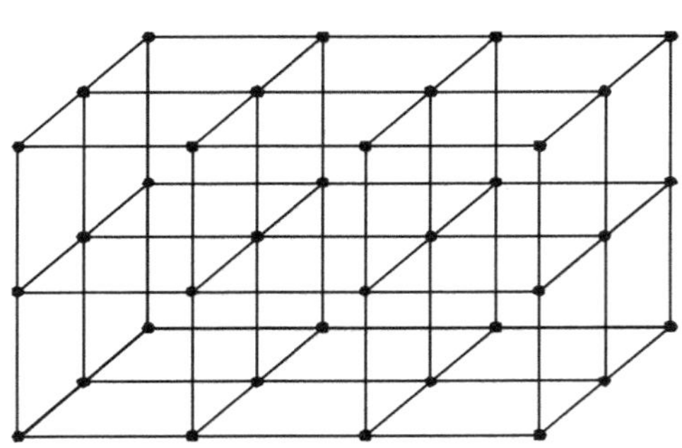

Fig. 2. *M* (4, 3, 3)

For convenience we shall make use of the cartesian coordinate system for the 3-D mesh. Let the mutually perpendicular lines through *O* be the *X*- axis, *Y*- axis and *Z*-axis respectively. See Fig 3.

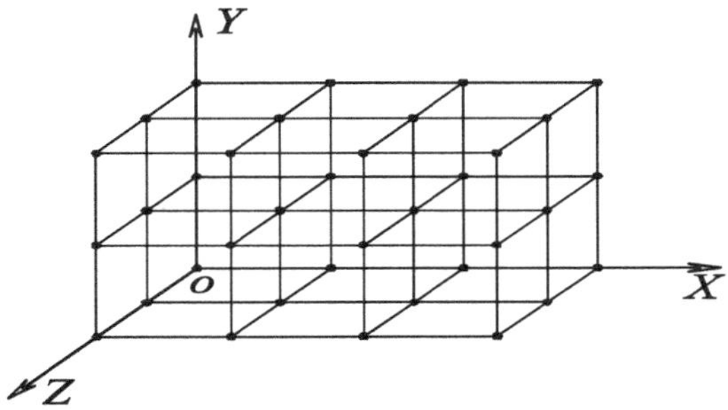

Fig. 3. Coordinate system in 3-*D* mesh *M* (4, 3, 3)

In *M*(*r*, *s*, *t*), let C_{x_i} denote planes (also called cuts) parallel to *YOZ* plane at distance $i - 1/2$ from the *YOZ* plane where *i* = 1, 2,…,*r*-1. See Fig 4. Similarly, let C_{y_j}, C_{z_k} denote the cuts parallel to *XOZ*, *XOY* planes at distances $j - 1/2, k - 1/2$, from these planes respectively, where *j* = 1, 2,...*s*-1 and *k* = 1, 2,…*t*-1. See Fig 5 & 6.

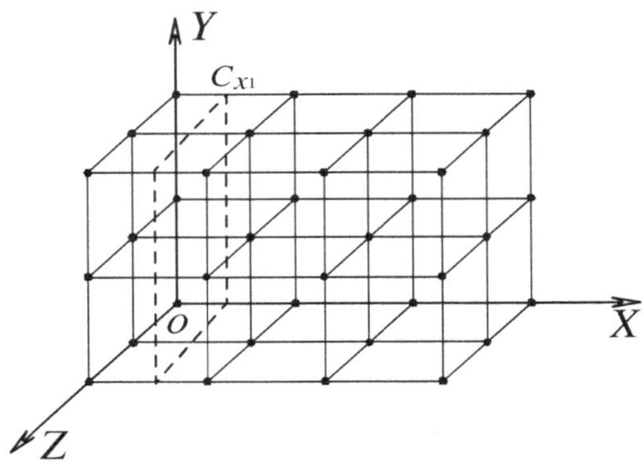

Fig. 4. Cut C_{x_1} parallel to *YOZ* plane

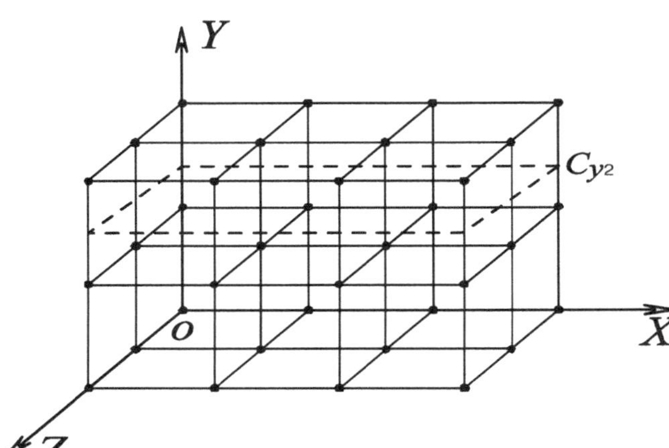

Fig. 5. Cut C_{y_2} parallel to *XOZ* plane

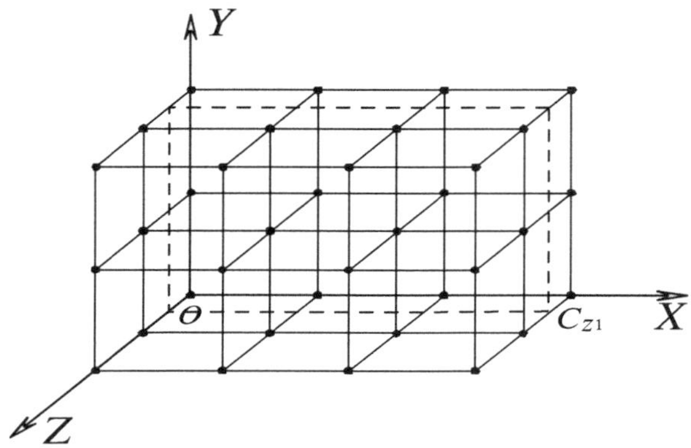

Fig. 6. Cut C_{z_1} parallel to *XOY* plane

The 2-*D* and 3-*D* meshes have applications in computer graphics and virtual reality, fluid mechanics, modeling of 3-*D* systems in earth sciences and astronomy etc. They are also natural topologies for linear algebra problems.

A mesh is a bipartite graph but not regular. If atleast one side has even length, the mesh has a hamiltonian cycle. Many optimal communication and parallel algorithms have been developed for meshes. The most important mesh based parallel computers are Intel's Paragon (2-*D* mesh) and MIT J-Machine (3-*D* mesh).

Theorem 1. *The PI index of the 3-dimensional mesh M(r, s, t) is given by* $PI(M(r,s,t)) = (3rst-(rs+st+tr))^2 - (r-1)s^2t^2 - (s-1)t^2r^2 - (t-1)r^2s^2$.

Proof. In $M(r,s,t)$, $C_{x_1}, C_{x_2}, \ldots, C_{x_{r-1}}$ are cuts parallel to *YOZ* plane. Each cut contains *st* number of edges. $C_{y_1}, C_{y_2}, \ldots, C_{y_{s-1}}$ are cuts with *rt* edges each and parallel to *XOZ* plane. Similarly $C_{z_1}, C_{z_2}, \ldots, C_{z_{t-1}}$ are cuts with *rs* edges each and parallel to *XOY* plane. Thus the edge set of $M(r,s,t)$ is partitioned into C_X, C_Y, C_Z and where $C_X = \{e/e \in C_{x_i}, 1 \le i \le r-1\}$, $C_Y = \{e/e \in C_{y_j}, 1 \le j \le s-1\}$ and $C_Z = \{e/e \in C_{z_k}, 1 \le k \le t-1\}$.

Let $e \in C_X$. Then $e \in C_{x_i}$, for some i, $1 \le i \le r-1$. Now every edge on the cut C_{x_i} is equidistant from *e*. All other edges in *M* are at unequal distance from *e*. Thus $|\tau_e| = st$. Similarly for any edge *e* on the cut C_{y_j}, $1 \le i \le s-1$, $|\tau_e| = rt$ and for *e* on C_{z_k}, $1 \le i \le t-1$, $|\tau_e| = rs$. By lemma 2,

$$\begin{aligned} PI(M(r,s,t)) &= q^2 - \left(\textstyle\sum_{e\epsilon C_X}|\tau_e| + \sum_{e\epsilon C_Y}|\tau_e| + \sum_{e\epsilon C_Z}|\tau_e|\right) \\ &= q^2 - \left(\textstyle\sum_{i=1}^{r-1}\sum_{e\epsilon C_{x_i}}|\tau_e| + \sum_{j=1}^{s-1}\sum_{e\epsilon C_{y_j}}|\tau_e| + \sum_{k=1}^{t-1}\sum_{e\epsilon C_{z_k}}|\tau_e|\right) \\ &= (3rst-(rs+st+tr))^2 - (r-1)s^2t^2 - (s-1)t^2r^2 - (t-1)r^2s^2 \end{aligned}$$

In our day-to-day life, the common salt *NaCl* is used as an important preservative because it retards the growth of micro - organisms. It also improves the flavour of food items. Chlorine products are used in metal cleaners, paper bleach, plastics and water treatment. They are also used in medicines. We find that the unit cell representation of

Sodium Chloride (*NaCl*) is the same as the 3-*D* mesh *M*(3, 3, 3). Infact in Fig 7, the hollow circles represent Na^+ and solid circles represent Cl^- ions.

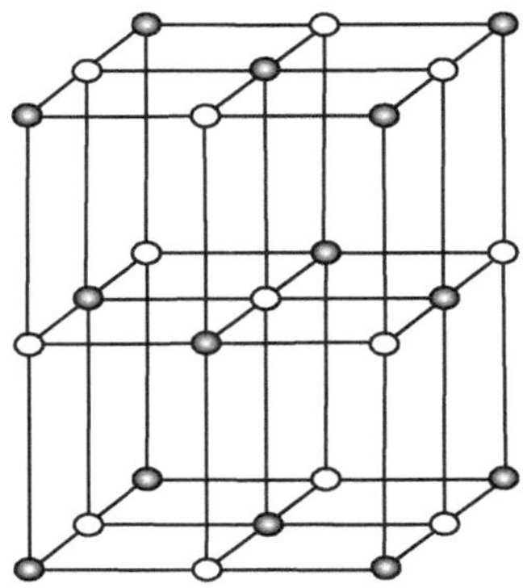

Fig. 7. Unit cell representation of *NaCl* structure

Theorem 2. The *PI* index of the sodium chloride *NaCl* is given by *PI*(*NaCl*) = 2430.

Proof. The unit cell representation of sodium chloride (*NaCl*) is *M*(3, 3, 3). Taking $r = s = t = 3$ and applying Theorem 1, we have *PI*(*NaCl*) = *PI*(*M*(3, 3, 3) = 2430 .

3 Torus

Consider the mesh *M*(*m*, *n*). If there are wraparound edges that connect the vertices of the first column to those of the last column and wraparound edges that connect the vertices of the first row to those of the last row, then the resulting architecture is called a torus denoted by *T*(*m*, *n*). See Fig 8.

Tori *T*(*m*, *n*) are bipartite if and only if *m* and *n* are even. Any torus has a hamiltonian cycle and they are regular and vertex symmetric. Each torus can be canonically decomposed into a cartesian product of cycles. The torus network has been recognized as a versatile interconnection network for massively parallel computing [16].

Theorem 3. *The PI index of the torus T(m, n) is given by*

$$PI(T(m,n)) = \begin{cases} 2mn(2mn - m - n); & \text{when } m, n \text{ are even} \\ mn(4mn - m - n); & \text{when } m, n \text{ are odd} \\ mn(4mn - m - 2n); & \text{when } m \text{ is even and } n \text{ is odd} \\ mn(4mn - 2m - n); & \text{when } m \text{ is odd and } n \text{ is even} \end{cases}$$

Proof. The torus *T*(*m*, *n*) contains *M*(*m*, *n*) as a subgraph together with the wraparound edges. Let $C_{x_1}, C_{x_2}, \dots, C_{x_{n-1}}$ be lines parallel to *Y*- axis at distance $i - {}^1\!/_2$ from the axis, i = 1, 2,..,n-1. Let C_{x_n} be the set consisting of the wraparound edges joining the vertices of the first column to those of the last column. Similarly let $C_{y_1}, C_{y_2}, \dots, C_{y_{m-1}}$

be lines parallel to X- axis at distance $j - {}^{1}/_{2}$ from the axis, j = 1, 2,…,m-1 and C_{y_m} be the set consisting of the wraparound edges joining the vertices of the first row to those of the last row. Now, the edges of $T(m, n)$ is partitioned into C_X and C_Y where $C_X = \{e/e \in C_{x_i}, 1 \leq i \leq n\}$, $C_Y = \{e/e \in C_{y_j}, 1 \leq j \leq m\}$.

When n is odd we see that for any $e \in C_{x_i}$, $1 \leq i \leq n$, τ_e consists of all edges in C_{x_i} and no other edges. On the other hand when n is even for any $e \in C_{x_i}$, $1 \leq i \leq n$, τ_e consists of all edges in C_{x_i} and all the edges in, $C_{x_{i+\frac{n}{2}(mod\, n)}}$, $1 \leq i \leq n$. A similar argument holds good for C_{y_j}, $1 \leq j \leq m$.

We now proceed to calculate the PI index of $T(m, n)$.

Case 1: m and n even. Let $e \in C_X$. Then $e \in C_{x_i}$, for some i, $1 \leq i \leq n$. Now, $|\tau_e| = |C_{x_i}| + \left|C_{x_{i+\frac{n}{2}(mod\, n)}}\right| = 2m$. Similarly, for any edge $e \in C_Y$, $|\tau_e| = 2n$. Thus $PI(T(m, n)) = 2mn(2mn - m - n)$.

Case 2: m and n odd. Let $e \in C_X$. Then $e \in C_{x_i}$, for some i, $1 \leq i \leq n$. Now, $|\tau_e| = |C_{x_i}| = m$. Similarly, for any edge $e \in C_Y$, $|\tau_e| = n$. Thus $PI(T(m, n)) = mn(4mn - m - n)$.

Case 3: m even and n odd. Let $e \in C_X$. Then $e \in C_{x_i}$, for some i, $1 \leq i \leq n$. Now, $|\tau_e| = |C_{x_i}| = m$ and for any edge $e \in C_Y$, $|\tau_e| = |C_{y_j}| + \left|C_{y_{j+\frac{m}{2}(mod\, m)}}\right| = 2n$. Thus, $PI(T(m, n)) = mn(4mn - m - 2n)$.

Case 4: m odd and n even. As in case 3, $PI(T(m, n)) = mn(4mn - 2m - n)$.

4 Topological Properties of Honeycomb Meshes

Honeycomb meshes can be built from hexagons in various ways. The simplest way to define them is to consider the portion of the hexagonal tessellation, which is inside a given convex polygon. To maximize the symmetry, honeycomb (hexagonal) meshes can be built as follows: One hexagon is a honeycomb mesh of size one, denoted by HM_1. See Fig 9 (a). The honeycomb mesh HM_2 of size two is obtained by adding six hexagons to the boundary edges of HM_1. See Fig 9 (b). Inductively, honeycomb mesh

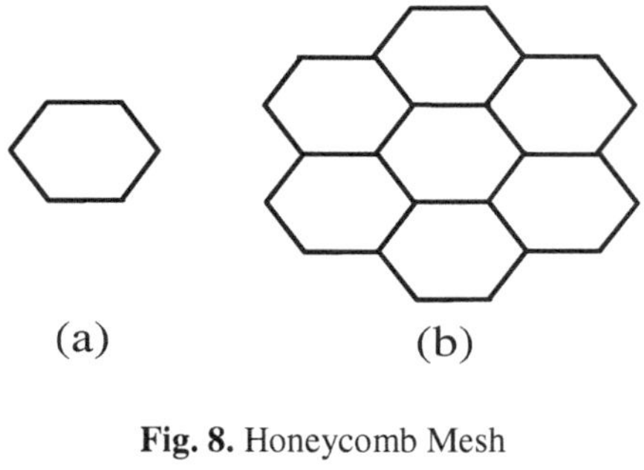

Fig. 8. Honeycomb Mesh

HM_d of size d is obtained from HM_{d-1} by adding a layer of hexagons around the boundary of HM_{d-1}. Alternatively, the size d of HM_d is determined as the number of hexagons between the center and boundary of HM_d (inclusive) and the number of vertices and edges of HM_d are $6d^2$ and $9d^2 - 3d$ respectively [14].

Theorem 4. *The PI index of the honeycomb mesh HM_d of dimension d, is given by* $PI(HM_d) = (9d^2 - 3d)^2 - 12d^2 - 6\sum_{i=1}^{d-1}(2d-i)^2$.

Proof. For convenience, we shall introduce a coordinate system for the honeycomb mesh. Through O, the centroid of HM_d draw 3 lines mutually inclined at 120° to each other. Name the lines as α, β and γ axes. See Fig 10. The α axis denoted by α_0 passes through $2d - 1$ hexagons. Any line parallel to α_0 and passing through $2d - 1 - i$ hexagons is denoted by α_i, if the hexagons are above α_0 and are denoted by α_{-i}, if the hexagons are below α_0, *where* $0 \le i \le d-1$. Similarly, β_j, β_{-j}, $0 \le j \le d-1$ and γ_k, γ_{-k} where $0 \le k \le d-1$ are defined.

Let H_{α_i} denote the set of all edges cut by α_i, $|i| \le d-1$. We note that $|H_{\alpha_i}| = 2d - |i|$. Similarly H_{β_j} and H_{γ_k}, $|j| \le d-1, |k| \le d-1$ are defined. The collection $\{H_{\alpha_i}, H_{\beta_i}, H_{\gamma_i}\}$, $|i| \le d-1$ is a partition of the edge set of HM_d. For any edge e in $H_{\alpha_i}, H_{\beta_i}$, or H_{γ_i}, $|\tau_e| = 2d - |i|$, for all $|i| \le d-1$.

$$PI(HM_d) = q^2 - \left(\sum_{i=-(d-1)}^{d-1}\sum_{e\epsilon H_{\alpha_i}}|\tau_e| + \sum_{j=-(d-1)}^{d-1}\sum_{e\epsilon H_{\beta_j}}|\tau_e| + \sum_{k=-(d-1)}^{d-1}\sum_{e\epsilon H_{\gamma_k}}|\tau_e|\right)$$

$$= q^2 - \{3\sum_{e\epsilon H_{\alpha_0}, H_{\beta_0}, H_{\gamma_0}}|\tau_e| + 6\sum_{i=1}^{d-1}\sum_{e\epsilon H_{\alpha_i}, H_{\beta_i}, H_{\gamma_i}}|\tau_e|\}$$

$$= (9d^2 - 3d)^2 - 12d^2 - 6\sum_{i=1}^{d-1}(2d-i)^2$$

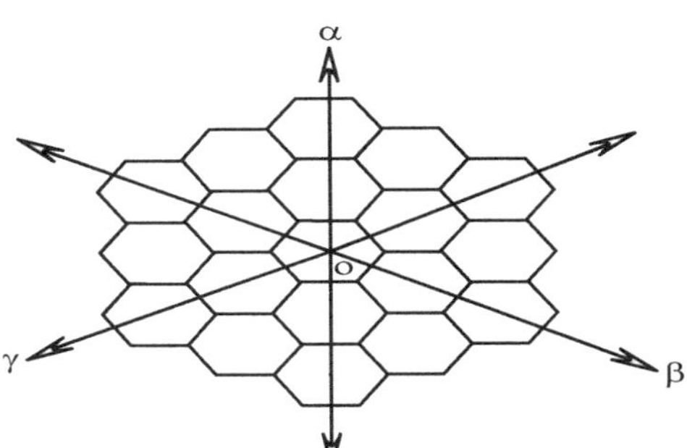

Fig. 9. Dimension Honey comb HM_3

Definition 2. [2] Let $G(m, n)$, $m \le n$ be a graph consisting of two rows of n and m hexagons respectively. In chemistry, it is called as the benzenoid graph. See Fig 11.

The following theorem has been proved in [2] but with an error in the calculation. The corrected version is given below.

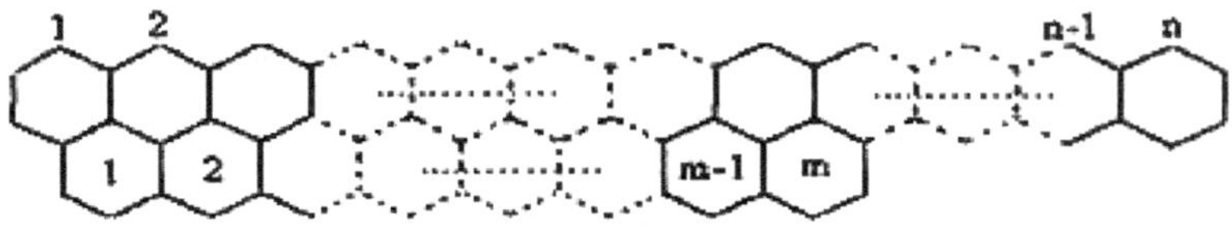

Fig. 10. A pericondensed benzenoid graphs consisting of two rows of n and m hexagons, respectively, $m \leq n$

Theorem 5. *The PI index of benzenoid graph G(m, n) is given by*

$$PI(G(m,n)) = \begin{cases} 8m^2 + 24n^2 + 30mn + 10n + 2 \,; n > m \\ 62n^2 + 26n + 8 \quad ; n = m \end{cases}$$

5 Conclusion

In this paper, we have introduced a new strategy to compute the *PI* indices of graphs. The same strategy is used to compute the *PI* index of mesh structured chemicals. Further work is going on with respect to star and pancake graphs.

References

1. Ashrafi, A.R., Loghman, A.: MATCH Commun. Math. Comput. Chem. 55, 447 (2006)
2. Ashrafi, A.R., Loghman, A.: PI index of some Benzenoid Graphs. Chil, J. Chem. Soc. 51(3), 968–970 (2006)
3. Carle, J., Myoupo, F., Seme, D.: All-to-all broadcasting algorithms on honeycomb networks and applications. Parallel Process. Lett. 9(4), 539–550 (1999)
4. Garcia, F., Stojmenovic, I., Zhang, J.: Addressing and routing in hexagonal networks with applications for location update and connection rerouting in cellular networks. IEEE Trans. Parallel Distrib. Systems 13(9), 963–971 (2002)
5. Khadikar, P.V.: On a novel Structural Descriptor PI. Nat. Acad. Sci. Letters 23, 113–118 (2000)
6. Khadikar, P.V., Karmarkar, S., Agarwal, V.K.: A Novel PI index and its Applications to QSPR/QSAR Studies. J. Chem. Inf. Comput. Sci. 41, 934–949 (2001)
7. Khadikar, P.V., Kale, P.P., Deshpande, N.V., Karmarkar, S., Agrawal, V.K.: Novel PI Indices of Hexagonal Chains. J. Math. Chem. 29, 143–150 (2001)
8. Khadikar, P.V., Karmakar, S., Varma, R.G.: On the Estimation of PI Index of Polyacenes. Acta Chim. Slov. 49, 755–771 (2002)
9. Laster, L.N., Sandor, J.: Computer graphics on hexagonal grid. Comput. Graph, 8401–409 (1984)
10. Megason, G.M., Liu, X.: Yang: Fault-tolerant ring embedding in a honeycomb torus with node failures. Parallel Process. Lett. 9(4), 551–562 (1999)
11. Megason, G.M., Liu, X.: Yang: Honeycomb tori are Hamiltonian. Inform. Process. Lett. 72, 99–103 (1999)
12. Parhami, G., Kwau, D.M.: A unified formulation of honeycomb and diamond networks. IEEE Trans. Parallel Distrib. Systems 12(1), 74–79 (2001)

13. Stojmenovic, P., Zomaya, A.Y.: Direct interconnection networks. In: Paralel and Distributed Computing Handbook, pp. 537–567. McGraw-Hill, Inc., Tokyo (1996)
14. Stojmenovic, I.: Honeycomb networks: topological properties and communication algorithms. IEEE Trans. Parallel Distrib. Systems 8(10), 1036–1042 (1997)
15. Tosic, Y., Masulovic, I., Stojmenovic, J., Brunvoll, B.N., Cyvin, S.J., Cyvin, S.J.: Enumeration of polyhex hydrocarbons upto h=17. J.Chem. Inform. Comput Sci. 35, 181–187 (1995)
16. Ishigami, Y.: The wide-diameter of the n-dimensional toroidal mesh. Networks 27, 257–266 (1996)
17. John, P.E., Khadikar, P.V., Singh, J.: A Method of Computing the PI index of Benzenoid hydrocarbons Using Orthogonal Cuts. Journal of Mathematical Chemistry 42(1), 37–45 (2006)

Enabling GPU Acceleration with Messaging Middleware

Randall E. Duran[1,2], Li Zhang[1,2], and Tom Hayhurst[2]

[1] Singapore Management University, 80 Stamford Road, Singapore 178902
[2] Catena Technologies Pte Ltd, #11-04, 30 Robinson Road, Singapore 048546
{randallduran,lizhang}@smu.edu.sg, tom@catena-technologies.com

Abstract. Graphics processing units (GPUs) offer great potential for accelerating processing for a wide range of scientific and business applications. However, complexities associated with using GPU technology have limited its use in applications. This paper reviews earlier approaches improving GPU accessibility, and explores how integration with middleware messaging technologies can further improve the accessibility and usability of GPU-enabled platforms. The results of a proof-of-concept integration between an open-source messaging middleware platform and a general-purpose GPU platform using the CUDA framework are presented. Additional applications of this technique are identified and discussed as potential areas for further research.

Keywords: GPU, GPGPU, middleware, messaging, CUDA, k-means, clustering, ZeroMQ, stream processing.

1 Introduction

General-purpose graphics processing units (GPGPUs) offer great potential for accelerating processing for a wide range of scientific and business applications. The rate of advancement of GPU technology has been exceeding that of mainstream CPUs, and they can be utilized by a wide range of computationally intensive applications. For instance, GPUs have been found to be superior in terms of both performance and power utilization for N-body particle simulations [1]. For these computations, GPU-based solutions were found to be the simplest to implement and required the least tuning, as compared with multi-core CPU and Cell processor implementations. For all their benefits though, significant time is required to design and tune algorithms that make optimal use of GPUs' memory architectures.

GPU processing can be used for a variety of scientific and business applications. GPUs have been used to accelerate DNA analysis and sequencing [19], biomedical image analysis [8], seismic data interpretation [10], and more recently in the derivatives pricing and risk analytics domain of the financial services industry [3]. As a case in point, many of the algorithms used for seismic data analysis – Fourier transforms, calculation of finite differences, and image convolutions – are especially well suited for parallel implementation on GPUs. GPUs have been shown to perform 20-100 times faster than CPUs for these types of computations.

A. Abd Manaf et al. (Eds.): ICIEIS 2011, Part III, CCIS 253, pp. 410–423, 2011.

Nevertheless, GPU platforms have seen only limited use in scientific applications. While GPUs are commonly found in desktop computer systems, only a small proportion of consumer-grade systems readily support GPGPU programming and have the memory bandwidth and number of processing cores needed to perform faster than typical CPUs. High-end GPU cards or dedicated GPGPU computing processors are often used with server-class hardware configurations. Hence, in many cases providing a GPGPU-enabled workstation on every desk is impractical.

Another factor that has limited the use of GPUs is the need for application designers to understand the intricacies of GPU architectures and programming models. To take advantage of GPU acceleration, developers must determine how the computational aspects of an application should be mapped to advantage of the parallelism of the GPU platform. They must also understand the GPU's limitations and work around them. In particular, device-specific memory access constraints must be considered and catered for.

While some middleware has emerged that helps simplify GPU programming and provide remote access to GPUs, ease of use still creates a significant barrier to their widespread adoption. Device-specific programming considerations, such as the number of cores, size of memory and performance for floating point precision calculations, are still critical factors. Likewise, little attention has been given to using GPUs to accelerate real-time applications.

Outside the field of GPU processing, message-oriented middleware, referred to henceforth as messaging for brevity, has proliferated over the past two decades and has become a mainstay for distributed computing applications. Request-reply and publish-subscribe communications are commonly used for remote invocation of services and data stream processing. Furthermore, most messaging platforms promote and facilitate the development of common, reusable services. Access is commonly provided to such services through abstract interfaces that seek to minimize application-specific functionality and hide details of the underlying implementation.

Given this context, this paper explores how the integration of messaging technologies can help improve the accessibility and usability of GPU platforms. Messaging can help to hide the complexities of the underlying GPU platform and programming environment and also facilitate remote access to GPU-enabled hardware platforms. The paper is organized as follows. First, a brief survey of background and related research is presented. Second, the design of a messaging-accessible, GPU-enabled platform is described. Third, practical applications of accessing GPU-enabled services over messaging are identified. Fourth, the results of a proof-of-concept integration between an open-source messaging platform and a general-purpose GPU platform built on the CUDA framework are provided. Finally, further areas of potential research are discussed.

2 Background and Related Work

Three different aspects of background and previous research are reviewed in this section. The types of calculations that are well suited to GPU acceleration are considered in relation to which functions might be best implemented in conjunction with messaging. Other middleware approaches that have been used to simplify local and remote access to GPUs are also examined. The use of messaging to support GPU acceleration is also reviewed.

A number of different types of calculations have been mapped to GPUs to achieve improved performance for both scientific and financial applications. Monte Carlo simulations – which are used in computational physics, engineering, and computational biology – are one type of calculation that has been shown to benefit from execution on GPUs [16]. Hidden Markov models and other Bayesian algorithms – which are used in bioinformatics and real-time image processing – can also benefit significantly from GPU acceleration [6][13]. Likewise, k-means clustering – used in computational biology, image analysis, and pattern recognition – has been a common target for GPU acceleration [12][20].

The ease by which these different types of calculations can be implemented as common, abstracted services that can be executed remotely using messaging varies. On one hand, Monte Carlo simulations are not well suited for remote invocation because they require application-specific algorithms to be loaded and run on the server that hosts the GPU. There is no simple device-independent means of bundling up application-specific logic for remote execution on remote servers. On the other hand, k-means clustering calculations can be easily separated from application logic, parameterized, and presented as remote services that can be accessed through request-reply messaging functions. Accordingly, the research described in this paper focuses on the k-means algorithm for the proof-of-concept implementation.

There have also been a number of industry and research efforts focused on developing middleware that helps simplify GPU programming, including CUDA, HiCUDA, and OpenCL. CUDA (Compute Unified Device Architecture) is a framework that provides C language programming extensions that can be used to access the GPU hardware through a general purpose hardware interface opposed to a graphics processing-oriented API [15]. HiCUDA [7] goes further, providing higher-level programming abstractions that hide the complexity of the underlying GPU architecture. Alternatively, OpenCL [14] provides a device-level API similar to CUDA that is portable across different types of processors and GPUs, whereas CUDA is only supported on GPUs made by NVIDA. While these middleware implementations have improved the usability of GPU devices, they only support access to GPUs cards installed locally on the server that are controlled by the local operating system.

vCUDA and rCUDA help improve GPU accessibility by enabling applications to access GPUs indirectly. vCUDA [17] provides guest operating systems that run inside virtual machines with CUDA-based access to the host server's GPU. CUDA API calls are intercepted by a proxy client library installed in the guest OS that routes the calls to a vCUDA server component running in the host OS. The vCUDA server component then passes the API request to the GPU and returns the response to the proxy, which in turn delivers it to the application running in the guest OS. rCUDA [5] takes a similar approach to provide remote access to GPUs over the network. A client proxy library intercepts applications' CUDA API calls and forwards them using TCP/IP sockets to an rCUDA server component running on the remote host where the GPU physically resides. These two approaches help address the problem of needing local access to the GPU, but they still require the application developer to be aware of and design around device-specific considerations of the remote systems' hardware configurations.

While a wealth of information on messaging middleware has been developed over the past two decades, little research to date has focused on how GPUs can be combined with messaging. To this effect, King et al [11] demonstrated how convertible bond pricing calculations could be accelerated by GPUs and accessed remotely via a request-reply style web service interface. They reported performance gains of 60x of the GPU-based hardware cluster over CPU-based hardware cluster configuration. Furthermore, the GPU-based cluster was substantially less expensive and consumed half the power of the CPU-based cluster. This example demonstrated the benefits of and potential for middleware-based GPU services; however, its use is limited. The calculation implemented on the GPU was domain specific and could not be easily leveraged for other purposes.

The design and prototype presented in this paper continues in the direction that King et al began, but seeks to provide a more generic and widely applicable model. As a proof of concept, a broadly applicable algorithm, k-means clustering, was implemented on the GPU and remotely accessed using an off-the-shelf messaging platform, ZeroMQ [9]. Access to the GPU was implemented in request-reply mode, as with King et al, and also in publish-subscribe mode, to help assess the practicality of using the GPU to accelerate network-based, real-time data stream processing applications. ZeroMQ was used as the messaging middleware because it is a readily available open source platform that provides a lightweight messaging implementation with low end-to-end latency. No unique features of ZeroMQ were used, though, and similar results would be expected were other messaging platforms to be used instead.

The aim of this effort was to answer several questions and help set the stage for further research. Specifically, the goal was to determine whether:

- From an architectural standpoint, it is possible to package certain types of computations so that they can be executed remotely on GPUs to achieve faster processing
- The CPU interacting simultaneously with the network interface and GPU would cause any conflicts or performance degradation
- It is practical to use GPUs to act as pipeline components processing real-time data streams using publish-subscribe messaging facilities

The main of the focus of this paper is on the request-reply oriented GPU-enabled services. Preliminary results are also briefly described regarding the feasibility and potential gains that might be achieved for publish-subscribe-oriented GPU applications.

3 Architecture

Traditional local-access GPGPU computing architectures are structured as shown in Fig. 1. Each client application runs on a separate GPU server that hosts the GPU processor. Each application has its own computation-intensive algorithms that have been designed to run on the GPU, and each application is implemented independently. Hence, two applications may use the same basic algorithm, but have different source code and have been tuned for different GPU processor configurations. Moreover, the GPU processor on each server may remain idle when the application is not run, and the GPU capabilities of on one server cannot be shared by an application running on another server.

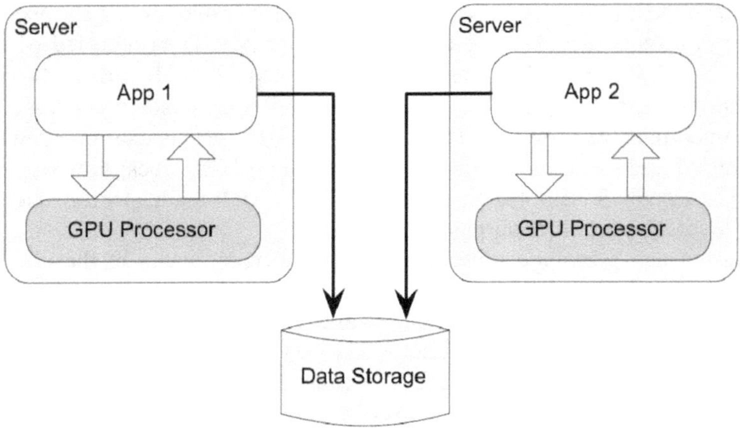

Fig. 1. A traditional local-access GPGPU architecture

Alternatively, by integrating middleware-messaging technologies with GPU platforms, it is possible to improve the accessibility, usability, and hardware utilization rates of GPU processors for general purpose computing. Fig. 2 shows a service-oriented architecture view of the middleware-accessible GPU-enabled platform. As compared to the traditional local-access model, client applications can run on remote workstations. Computation-intensive algorithms are invoked by passing data using request-reply messaging. These algorithms can run on servers that host high-performance GPU processors that serve multiple remote client applications. The algorithm implementation can be tuned specifically for each host platform's hardware configuration, without requiring each client application to address this concern. Likewise, the GPU-based algorithm implementation can be updated when the GPU hardware is upgraded without requiring changes to the client applications, assuming that the API remains constant.

In summary, the benefits of this architecture are to:

- Enable remote access to GPU processors
- Hide the complexity of underlying GPU platform and programming environment
- Provide abstract interfaces to common services
- Allow the GPU resources to be shared more efficiently across multiple applications
- Simplify maintenance of GPU-accelerated applications

The algorithm's input data may be passed directly across the messaging layer, or it may be more practical to include a reference to a remote data location – such as a

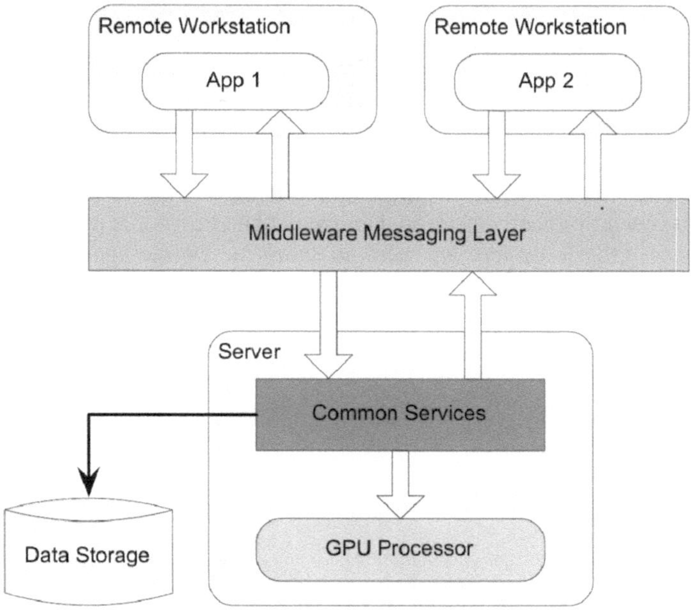

Fig. 2. The architecture of a middleware-accessible GPU-enabled platform

database stored procedure or URL – as part of the service request message. The service can then directly retrieve the data for processing.

4 Application

Messaging middleware could provide scientific applications with access to a range of computationally intensive algorithms that run on high performance GPU processors. To demonstrate the feasibility of this idea, two proof-of-concept applications were implemented and tested. The first application implemented a k-means clustering algorithm on the GPU and exposed it as a shared service that was made accessible to applications running on different servers through ZeroMQ's request-reply messaging interface. In a real-world scenario, remote computer vision, data mining, and computational biology applications could similarly make use of a GPU-accelerated clustering algorithm to partition and find common sets in collections of data.

The second application implemented filtering algorithms on the GPU and was made accessible via ZeroMQ's publish-subscribe interface. In this real-time scenario, raw streams of seismic data could be published using ZeroMQ, and then processed by GPU-accelerated filter algorithms, with the filtered results then being published back on the messaging middleware so that they can be accessed by downstream applications running on different servers.

4.1 GPU-Based K-Means Clustering Accessed Using Request-Reply Messaging

Cluster analysis has been used in the fields of computer vision, data mining, and machine learning, amongst others, to divide data objects into groups based on their features and patterns. K-means is a widely used partitional clustering algorithm. It randomly chooses a number of points to form the centers of each cluster, and then assigns each datum to the cluster whose centre is nearest it, in a process called labeling. The center of each cluster is then recalculated from the points assigned to it, and these new cluster centers are used to label the points again. This process is repeated until the recalculated cluster centers stop moving between successive iterations. Fig. 3 shows an example of clustering output using the k-means algorithm with 3 clusters.

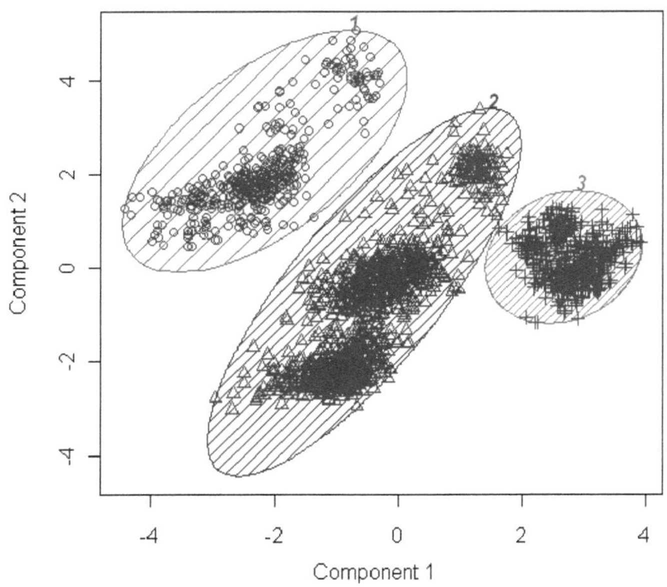

Fig. 3. Example of k-means clustering results with three clusters

The traditional k-means clustering algorithm has a known problem whereby non-optimal solutions may be found, depending on the initial random selection of cluster centers. To address this, the algorithm is normally repeated multiple times, to increase the chance of finding a near-optimal solution. Hence, k-means is a computationally intensive algorithm, especially for large data sets.

When executing the k-means algorithm, the time-consuming process of labeling can be transferred to the GPU for parallel execution to increase performance [2]. In the proof-of-concept implementation, the k-means algorithm was implemented using CUDA. Distance calculations were performed in parallel on the GPU while the CPU sequentially updated cluster centroids according to the results of the distance calculations [12]. Fig. 4 illustrates the processing flow of the GPU-based k-means algorithm. A CPU thread begins by reading the data points from the source location and randomly initializing K cluster centers. To save data transfer cost between CPU and GPU, the data points are copied to the GPU's global memory only once. The GPU processor then labels the data points and transfers the new labels back to the CPU. Again, transferring only the new labels helps to save on data transfer between the GPU and CPU. The CPU thread calculates new centroids based on the updated labels and determines whether to invoke the GPU again to label the data points. Once the algorithm terminates, the final data labels can be downloaded to the CPU and stored.

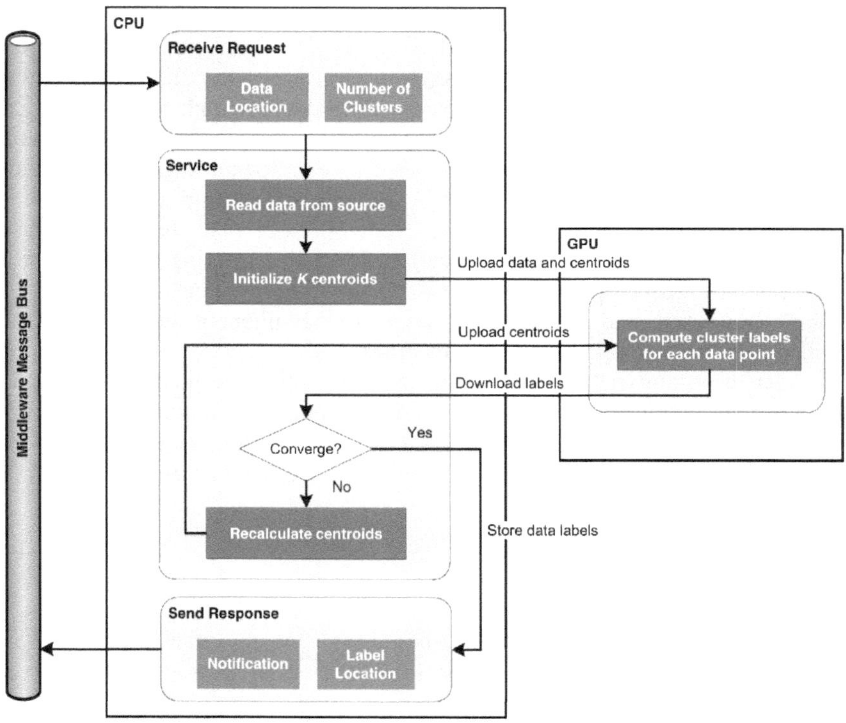

Fig. 4. Process flow of the GPU-based k-means clustering algorithm

The GPU-based k-means algorithm was then exposed as a shared service, accessed by remote client applications using a request-reply message interface as described in section 3. A client sends a request message specifying the location of the input data points (in a database table or file) and the number of clusters to be generated. After receiving the request, the service retrieves the input data and invokes the clustering algorithm. Once the algorithm has completed, the server will notify the client, which can then retrieve the clustered data set from the same location as the input data.

4.2 GPU-Based Filtering Using Publish-Subscribe Messaging

Sensor networks are commonly used to collect data for seismic data analysis generating large volumes of real-time data. Query-based filtering mechanisms, which compare sensor readings against a large number of predicates, help identify patterns that correspond to or may predict specific types of events [4]. The process of comparing the current reading with a set of predicates is a time-consuming process that can be parallelized. Therefore, performance benefits may be achieved, especially for large data streams, by migrating the comparison function to a GPU [18]. Messaging middleware can provide a convenient and efficient mechanism for collecting and distributing data from remote sensors for analysis. Sensors typically publish their measurements asynchronously, filters consume these data and republish information when patterns match, and interested downstream applications will subscribe to the relevant information from the filters.

A proof-of-concept GPU-based filtering service was implemented and made available via a publish-subscribe messaging interface. The filtering service uses a binary "greater than" operator to compare current data readings with a historical data set read from a data source stored either as a file on disk or in a database table. For example, this filtering service could be used to monitor an ongoing stream of real-time sensor readings. If the filter detected that a current reading was greater than 90% of previous movement readings, another event would be published on the messaging middleware. While quite simple in its current form, this filtering mechanism could be easily extended to compare data with more complex predicates. Likewise, a large number of different predicates could be compared simultaneously by the GPU, taking advantage of its massively parallel architecture.

To test the prototype, an application that simulates a remote sensor publishes a stream of measurement readings. The filtering component running on the GPU server subscribes to this data stream compares each data reading to the filtering criteria. When a match occurs, filtering service publishes a message on a new topic, creating a derivative event stream.

5 Experimental Results

To compare the performance of a CPU-based k-means algorithm and the GPU-based version that were invoked through messaging, a set of tests were performed on a quad-core Intel i5-760 2.80 GHz machine with 8 GB of RAM, and a NVIDIA GeForce 450GTS graphics card [15]. For comparison purpose, the GPU-based algorithm was run on both a GeForce 450GTS graphics card with 192 cores and a Tesla C1060 graphics card with 240 cores, respectively. Each test used a different number of 3-dimensional data points and ran the k-means algorithm repeatedly 10000 times with 10 iterations per run to cluster the data points into different number of clusters. For the GPU-based algorithm, the number of threads per block was fixed at 32 for the GeForce 450GTS card, and 1024 for the Tesla C1060 card, and the number of blocks was computed based on the number of data points and the number of threads. Table 1 shows the average total time taken to generate five clusters using the CPU-based algorithm and the GPU-based version, respectively. The GPU total time is the total service processing time as shown by the Service component in Fig. 4, which includes the data upload and download time. The results obtained from the Tesla C1060 card surpass those from the GeForce 450GTS card significantly. This also shows that fine-tuning the number of threads per block as appropriate to the data size has a large effect on the GPU performance.

Table 1. CPU-based and GPU-based k-means service processing times

Processing Time	No. of Data Points 100	1K	10K	100K	1M
Avg single CPU total time (ms)	0.06	0.85	8.99	81.8	817
Avg GPU total time (ms) GeForce 450GTS	0.38	0.84	2.83	24.3	232
Avg GPU total time (ms) Tesla C1060	0.20	0.37	0.47	1.2	6

Fig. 5 shows the average total time taken for running the k-means clustering service when invoked remotely over messaging both on a single CPU, an estimated quad-core CPU, a GeForce 450GTS GPU, and a Tesla C1060 GPU, respectively. For simplicity, the time for the quad-core CPU is estimated based on a 3.4 speedup factor from the single CPU results. The results show that the processing time of the single CPU-based algorithm is very low for a small number of points, but it increases exponentially when the number of points increases. In contrast, the processing time of the GPU-based algorithm for a small number of points is relatively high, but it increases less as the number of points increases. The GPU shows superior performance at around 1000 points.

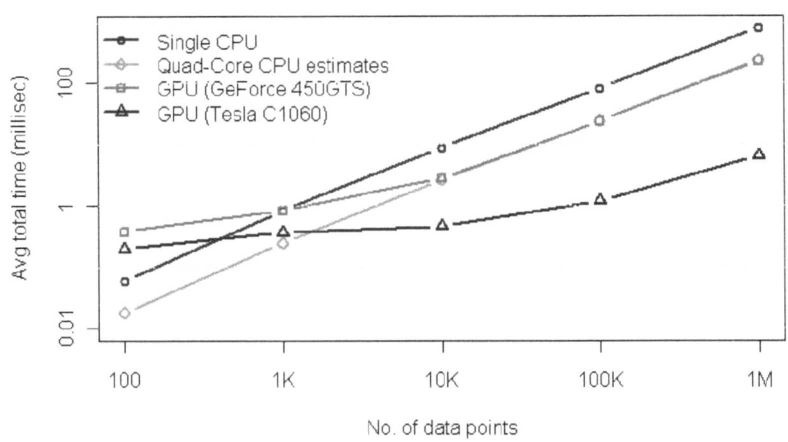

Fig. 5. Average total processing time for different number of data points using CPU-based and GPU-based k-means algorithm

Fig. 6 shows the average total time taken for invoking CPU and GPU versions of k-means algorithm using request-reply messaging to process one million points with different number of clusters. It demonstrates that the time taken for the single CPU-based algorithm as well as the quad-core estimate increases more rapidly than the GPU-based version. The GPU's performance benefits increase as the number of points and their dimension increase.

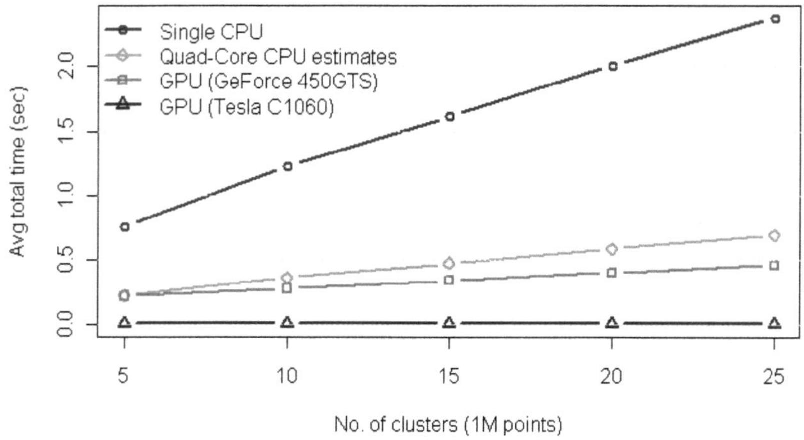

Fig. 6. Average total processing time for different number of clusters using CPU-based and GPU-based k-means algorithm

Preliminary experiments were also conducted on a publish-subscribe-based GPU service, as described in Section 4, to determine the latency involved when using messaging and GPUs to process real-time data streams. Fig. 7 shows the latencies that were measured. The input message latency measures the time taken for the input data message to reach the remote GPU service. The GPU processing time corresponds to the time taken by the GPU to process the input data received from the messaging layer. The output latency measures the time taken for a remote subscriber to receive event notifications once the GPU identified a criteria match.

As part of the tests, a client application published a stream of floating point data readings. After receiving each data reading, the server ran the GPU-based filtering algorithm to check whether the current data reading is greater than a set of historical readings read from the same data source. If the criteria matched, the corresponding cell of the bit map will be updated to 1, otherwise 0. The CPU thread on the server then determined, based on the bit map, whether current reading should be republished with an alert flag attached.

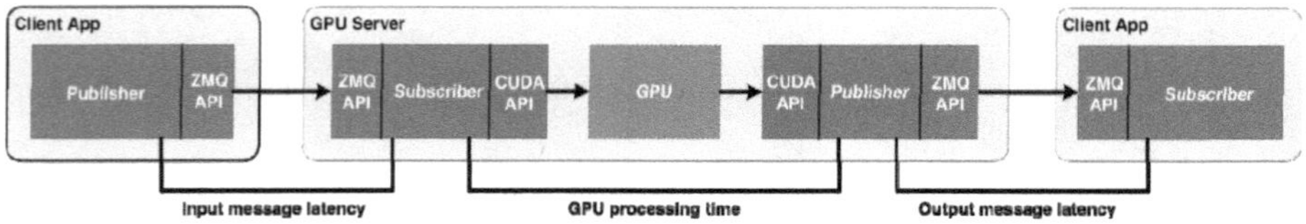

Fig. 7. Latency definitions for the publisher-subscriber model

The streaming data tests were carried out on the same hardware as for the k-means test described above. Table 2 shows the CPU and GPU processing time of the filtering algorithm and the two pub-sub latencies described above for 1,000 data readings each comparing with 10K, 100K, and 1 million historical readings. The results show that for this simple filtering algorithm, running on GPU did not provide performance benefits as compared to running it on a single CPU due to the higher memory allocation and data transfer cost. However, if more complex filtering algorithms, such as complex predicate comparisons or Fourier transforms, were applied, it is more likely that the GPU-based implementation would outperform the CPU-based version. The input message latency is measured with a message publishing rate of 5000 messages per second. It is observed that as the publishing rate decreases, the input message latency is reduced as well but to a certain extent. When the publishing rate becomes too low, the input message latency increases. The same pattern is observed for the output message latency. The output message latency shown in Table 2 is comparable with the input message latency because the publishing rate is about the same as well. These preliminary results demonstrate the feasibility of the proposed architecture. Further work is necessary to fine-tune the performance of GPU-based filtering algorithm for real-time data stream processing.

Table 2. CPU-based and GPU-based filtering service processing times and input/output message latency

Median Processing Time	No. of Comparisons		
	10K	100K	1M
CPU processing time (μs)	28	260	1,820
GPU processing time (μs) GeForce 450GTS	156	717	5,065
GPU processing time (μs) Tesla C1060	205	721	4,189
Input message latency (μs)	46	54	55
Output message latency (μs)	36	51	56

6 Conclusion and Future Work

The aim of this paper was to answer several questions and help set the stage for further research. First, it was determined that from architectural standpoint, it is possible to encapsulate k-means computations so that they can be executed remotely on GPUs to achieve faster processing than locally on CPUs. Second, no significant conflicts arose when integrating messaging with the GPU processing. It is beneficial, however, to multithread services so that receipt of inbound messages and invoking local processing on the GPU are managed independently. Third, while using GPU-based services to process real-time data streams, borne by messaging middleware, was shown to be feasible, further work is required to demonstrate this approach can outperform similar CPU-based configurations.

Moreover, an important and easily measured benefit of messaging-enabled GPU architectures is cost and environment savings from reduced power consumption. Making GPUs more easily accessible can offload traditional CPU server implementations and reduce the number of GPU cards that are required to support some types of computationally intensive algorithms and processing of high throughput real-time data flows. In this regard, Duato et al [5] estimated that halving the number of GPUs used in a high performance server cluster – which could be easily achieved through more efficient sharing of GPU resources – could reduce the cluster's overall power consumption by 12%.

Several areas of further research would be beneficial. One area is exploring how more advanced features of messaging middleware, such as one-of-N delivery semantics, could be used to support load balancing across different servers in GPU-enabled server clusters. Another area of interest is whether other computation types, such as hidden Markov models and Bayesian algorithms, are suitable for abstraction, parameterization, and remote invocation as a similar manner as was demonstrated for k-means clustering. Finally, further investigation of the potential for GPUs to support the analysis and filtering of high-throughput, real-time data flows would be beneficial.

References

1. Arora, N., Shringarpure, A., Vuduc, R.W.: Direct N-body Kernels for Multicore Platforms. In: 2009 International Conference on Parallel Processing, pp. 379–387 (2009)
2. Bai, H.T., He, L.L., Ouyang, D.T., Li, Z.T., Li, H.: K-Means on Commodity GPUs with CUDA. In: World Congress Computer Science and Information Engineering, pp. 651–655 (2009)
3. Clive, D.: Speed is the key - Balancing the benefits and costs of GPUs (2010), http://www.risk.net/risk-magazine/feature/1741590/balancing-benefits-costs-gpus
4. Daniel, J.A., Samuel, M., Wolfgang, L.: REED: Robust, Efficient Filtering and Event Detection in Sensor Networks. In: 31st VLDB Conference, pp. 769–780 (2005)
5. Duato, J., Peña, A.J., Silla, F., Mayo, R., Quintana-Orti, E.S.: rCUDA: Reducing the number of GPU-based accelerators in high performance clusters. In: 2010 International Conference on High Performance Computing and Simulation (HPCS), pp. 224–231 (2010)
6. Ferreira, J.F., Lobo, J., Dias, J.: Bayesian Real-Time Perception Algorithms on GPU - Real-Time Implementation of Bayesian Models for Multimodal Perception Using CUDA. Journal of Real-Time Image Processing (published online February 26, 2010)
7. Han, T.D., Abdelrahman, T.S.: hiCUDA: High-Level GPGPU Programming. IEEE Transactions on Parallel and Distributed Systems 22(1) (2011)
8. Hartley, T.D.R., Catalyurek, U., Ruiz, A., Igual, F., Mayo, R., Ujaldon, M.: Biomedical image analysis on a cooperative cluster of GPUs and multicores. In: 22nd Annual International Conference on Supercomputing ICS 2008, pp. 15–25 (2008)
9. Hintjens, P.: ØMQ - The Guide, http://zguide.zeromq.org/ (accessed April 2011)
10. Kadlec, B.J., Dorn, G.A.: Leveraging graphics processing units (GPUs) for real-time seismic interpretation. The Leading Edge (2010)
11. King, G.H., Cai, Z.Y., Lu, Y.Y., Wu, J.J., Shih, H.P., Chang, C.R.: A High-Performance Multi-user Service System for Financial Analytics Based on Web Service and GPU Computation. In: International Symposium on Parallel and Distributed Processing with Applications (ISPA 2010), pp. 327–333 (2010)
12. Li, Y., Zhao, K., Chu, X., Liu, J.: Speeding up K-Means Algorithm by GPUs. In: 2010 IEEE 10th International Conference on Computer and Information Technology (CIT), pp. 115–122 (2010)

13. Ling, C., Benkrid, K., Hamada, T.: A parameterisable and scalable Smith-Waterman algorithm implementation on CUDA-compatible GPUs. In: 2009 IEEE 7th Symposium on Application Specific Processors, pp. 94–100 (2009)
14. Munshi, A.: OpenCL Specification Version 1.0. In: The Khronos Group (2008), http://www.khronos.org/registry/cl
15. NVIDIA Corporation. NVIDIA® CUDATM Architecture. Version 1.1 (April 2009)
16. Preisa, T., Virnaua, P., Paula, W., Schneidera, J.J.: GPU accelerated Monte Carlo simulation of the 2D and 3D Ising modelstar, open. Journal of Computational Physics 228(12), 4468–4477 (2009)
17. Shi, L., Chen, H., Sun, J.: vCUDA: GPU Accelerated High Performance Computing in Virtual Machines. In: 2009 IEEE International Symposium on Parallel & Distributed Processing (2009)
18. Tsakalozos, K., Tsangaris, M., Delis, A.: Using the Graphics Processor Unit to realize data streaming operations. In: 6th Middleware Doctoral Symposium, pp. 274–291 (2009)
19. Tumeo, A., Villa, O.: Accelerating DNA analysis applications on GPU clusters. In: 2010 IEEE 8th Symposium on Application Specific Processors (SASP), pp. 71–76 (2010)
20. Zechner, M., Granitzer, M.: Accelerating K-Means on the Graphics Processor via CUDA. In: The First International Conference on Intensive Applications and Services, INTENSIVE 2009, pp. 7–15 (2009)

Wide Diameter of Generalized Fat Tree

Indra Rajasingh*, Bharati Rajan, and R. Sundara Rajan

Department of Mathematics, Loyola College,
Chennai 600 034, India
vprsundar@gmail.com

Abstract. The wide diameter of a graph is a natural generalization of diameter in a graph when we take account of the connectivity of the graph. The concept of wide diameter has been discussed and used in practical applications, especially in the distributed and parallel computer networks. In this paper, we find the wide diameter of generalized fat tree. Moreover we obtain the bisection width of generalized fat tree.

Keywords: wide diameter, bisection width, generalized fat tree.

1 Introduction

The reliability of computer, communication and storage devices has been recognized early as one of the key issues in computer systems. Since the 1950's, techniques that enhance the reliability of computer and communication systems were developed both in academia and industry. It has been also recognized that as complexity of computing and communication devices increases, fault-tolerance will gain more importance. Surprisingly, fault tolerance has never been the major design objective. While there are a number of reasons for this situation, the most important is that the reliability of individual components has been increasing at a much more rapid pace than it was expected. In addition, creative packaging and cooling schemes tremendously reduced the stress factor on computation and communication systems [1].

The only component of fault tolerance that has received a great deal of attention in industry is off-line testing. The modern testers are $10+ million systems that are contributing increasingly to the cost of modern microprocessors. The rapid growth of the Internet in the last 10 years was the first major facilitator of the renewed interest in fault tolerance and related techniques such as self-repair. Internet requires the constant mode of operation and therefore special effort has been placed to develop fault tolerant data canters [1]. Due to the widespread use of reliable, efficient, and fault-tolerant networks, these three parameters have been the subject of extensive study over the past decade [2]. In the sequal, $(x_1, x_2, ..., x_n)$ denotes a path from x_1 to x_n.

Leiserson [3,4] proposed fat trees as a hardware-efficient, general-purpose interconnection network. Several architectures including the Connection Machine

* This work is supported by DST Project No.SR/S4/MS: 494/07, New Delhi, India.

A. Abd Manaf et al. (Eds.): ICIEIS 2011, Part III, CCIS 253, pp. 424–430, 2011.

CM-5 of Thinking Machines, the memory hierarchy of the KSR-1 parallel machine of Kendall Square Research [5], and Meiko supercomputer CS-2 [6,7] are based on the fat trees. A different fat tree topology called "pruned butterfly" is proposed in [8], and other variants are informally described in [9], where the increase in channel bandwidth is modified compared to the original fat trees [3].

The generalized fat tree $GFT(h,m,w)$ [10] of height h consists of m^h processors in the leaf-level and routers or switching-nodes in the non-leaf levels. Each non-root has w parent nodes and each non-leaf has m children. Informally, $GFT(h+1,m,w)$ is recursively generated from m distinct copies of $GFT(h,m,w)$, denoted as $GFT^j(h,m,w) = (V_h^j, E_h^j)$, $0 \leq j \leq m-1$, and w^{h+1} additional nodes such that each top-level node $(h, k + j \cdot w^h)$ of each $GFT^j(h,m,w)$ for $0 \leq k \leq w^h - 1$, is adjacent to w consecutive new top-level nodes (*i.e.* level $h+1$ nodes), given by $(h+1, k \cdot w), ..., (h+1, (k+1) \cdot w - 1)$. The graph $GFT^j(h,m,w)$ is also called a sub-fat tree of $GFT(h+1,m,w)$. See Figure 1.

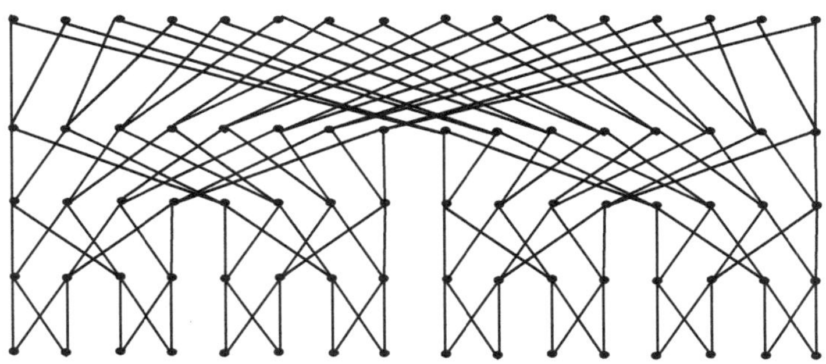

Fig. 1. Generalized fat tree $GFT(4,2,2)$

Definition 1. [11] *A container $C(x,y)$ between two distinct nodes x and y in a network G is a set of node-disjoint paths between x and y. The number of paths in $C(x,y)$ is called the width of $C(x,y)$. An $C(x,y)$ container with width w is denoted by $C_w(x,y)$. The length of $C_w(x,y)$, written as $l(C_w(x,y))$, is the length of a longest path in $C_w(x,y)$.*

Definition 2. [12] *For $w \leq k(G)$, the w-wide distance from x to y in a network G is defined to be*

$$d_w(x,y) = \min\{l(C_w(x,y))/C_w(x,y) \text{ is a container with width } w \text{ between } x \text{ and } y\}$$

The w-wide diameter of G is defined to be

$$d_w(G) = \max_{x,y \in V(G)} \{d_w(x,y)\}. \tag{1}$$

In other words, for $w \leq k(G)$, the w-wide diameter $d_w(G)$ of a network G is the minimum l such that for any two distinct vertices x and y there exist w vertex-disjoint paths of length at most l from x to y.

The notion of w-wide diameter was introduced by Hsu [2] to unify the concepts of diameter and connectivity. It is desirous that an ideal interconnection network G should be one with connectivity $k(G)$ as large as possible and diameter $d(G)$ as small as possible. The wide-diameter $d_w(G)$ combines connectivity $k(G)$ and diameter $d(G)$, where $1 \leq w \leq k(G)$. Hence $d_w(G)$ is a more suitable parameter than $d_w(G)$ to measure fault-tolerance and efficiency of parallel processing computer networks. Thus, determining the value of $d_w(G)$ is of significance for a given graph G and an integer w. Hsu [2] proved that this problem is NP-complete [13].

Remark 1. If there exist a container $C_w^*(x,y)$ such that each of the w paths in $C_w^*(x,y)$ is a shortest path between x and y in G, then

$$d_w(x,y) = l(C_w^*(x,y)) \tag{2}$$

Definition 3. [14] *For $w \leq k(G)$, the $(w-1)$-fault distance from x to y in a network G is*

$$D_w(x,y) = max\{d_{G-S}(x,y) : S \subseteq V \text{ with } |S| = w-1 \text{ and } x,y \text{ are not in } S\}$$

where $d_{G-S}(x,y)$ denoted the shortest distance between x and y in $G-S$.

The $(w-1)$-fault diameter of G is

$$D_w(G) = max\{D_w(x,y) : x \text{ and } y \text{ are in } G\} \tag{3}$$

The notion of $D_w(G)$ was defined by Hsu [2] and the special case in which $w = k(G)$ was studied by Krishnamoorthy et al. [15]. It is clear that when $w = 1$, $d_1(G) = D_1(G) = d(G)$ for any network G. Hsu and Luczak [16] showed that $d_k(G) = \frac{n}{2}$ for some k-regular graphs G on n vertices having connectivity k. For a graph (network) G with connectivity $k(G)$, the two parameters $d_w(G)$ and $D_w(G)$ for any $w \leq k(G)$ arise from the study of parallel routing, fault-tolerant systems, and randomized routing respectively [2,15,17,18].

Note: In [10] the processors are considered at the leaf-level of $GFT(h,m,w)$. In this paper, we consider all the nodes as processors.

In 1994, Chen et al. determined the wide diameter of the cycle prefix network [12]. In 1998, Liaw et al. found fault-tolerant routing in circulant directed graphs and cycle prefix networks [19]. The line connectivity and the fault diameters in pyramid networks were studied by Cao et al. in 1999 [11]. In the same year Liaw et al. determined the Rabin number and wide diameter of butterfly networks [14,17]. In 2005, Liaw et al. found the wide diameters and Rabin numbers of generalized folded hypercube networks [20]. In 2009, Jia and Zhang found the wide diameter of Cayley graphs of Z_m, the cyclic group of residue classes modulo m and they proved that the k-wide diameter of the Cayley graph Cay(Z_m, A)

generated by a k-element set A is $d+1$ for $k=2$ and is bounded above by $d+1$ for $k=3$, where d is the diameter of Cay(Z_m, A) [21]. In 2011, Rajasingh et al. found the wide diameter of circulant network [22].

In this paper, we compute the m-wide diameter $d_m(G)$ of generalized fat tree $GFT(h,m,m)$. Also, we compute the bisection width of generalized fat tree $GFT(h,m,m)$.

2 Main Results

2.1 Wide Diameter

The following are basic properties and relationships among $d_w(G)$ and $D_w(G)$.

Lemma 1. [14] *The following statements hold for any network G of connectivity k:*

1. $D_1(G) \leq D_2(G) \leq \cdots \leq D_k(G)$.
2. $d_1(G) \leq d_2(G) \leq \cdots \leq d_k(G)$.
3. $D_w(G) \leq d_w(G)$ *for* $1 \leq w \leq k$. □

Theorem 1. *Let G be a generalized fat tree $GFT(h,m,m)$ for all h. Then* $d_m(G) = 3h$.

Proof. We will prove this theorem by method of induction on the diameter of h. If $h=1$, by the definition of GFT the diameter of $GFT(1,m,m)=2$. Thus $d_m(GFT(1,m,m))=3$. Atleast one of these three disjoint paths has 3. Hence the result is true for $h=1$. Now, let us assume that the result is true for $h=k$. That is, $d_m(GFT(k,m,m))=3k$ for all k. Since $d(GFT(k-1,m,m))=2(k-1)$. Let us prove that the result is true for $h=k+1$.

Consider the graph $GFT(k+1,m,m)$. Let us assume that $u=(0,0)$ and $v=(k+1,0)$. Since the neighbourhood of $(k+1,0)$ namely $N\{(k+1,0)\}$ is the set $N\{(k+1,0)\}=\{(k,0),(k,3(k+1)+1),(k,6(k+1)+1)\}$, each path in the container $C_3(u,v)$ contains exactly one member from $N(v)$.

Consider a path P in $C_3(u,v)$ passing through $(k,6(k+1)+1)$. Then one of the route for P is

$$P = ((0,0),\cdots,(k+1,m^h-1),(k,m^h-1),\cdots,(k,2m^{h-1}),(k+1,0)) \quad (4)$$

Also $V(P) \cap (N(v) \backslash (k,6(k+1)+1)) = \phi$. In order to compute $d_m(G)$ we choose P to be a shortest path between u and v. Thus

$$P = ((0,0),\cdots,(k+1,m^h-1),(k,m^h-1),\cdots,(k,2m^{h-1}),(k+1,0)) \quad (5)$$

of length $3(k+1)$. By induction hypothesis the shortest diatance between (k,m^h-1) and $(k,2m^{h-1})$ is nothing but the diameter of $GFT(k,m,m)$ and is equal to $2k$. See Figure 2. Similarly the length of other paths are less than or equal to $3(k+1)$. Also it is easy to see that $d_m(u,v)=3(k+1) \geq d_m(i,j)$ for all vertices i,j in G. □

Corollary 1. *Let G be a generalized fat tree $GFT(h,m,w)$. Then* $D_2(G) = 2h$.

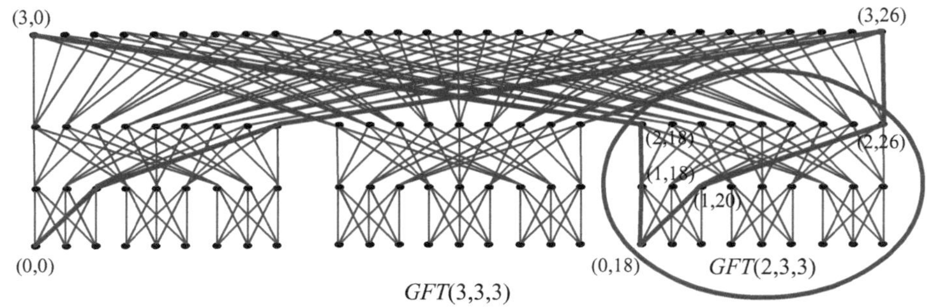

Fig. 2. 3-wide diameter of generalized fat tree $GFT(3,3,3)$ is 9

2.2 Bisection Width

The bisection width of a network is an important indicator of its power as a communications network. There are a large number of problems for which it is possible to prove some lower bound, I, on the number of messages that must cross a bisection of a parallel machine in order to solve the problem. In each case, $I/BW(G)$ is a lower bound on the time, T, to solve the problem. The bisection width of a network also gives a lower bound on the VLSI layout area, A, of a network G. In particular, Thompson proved that $A \geq (BW(G))^2$ [23]. Combining this inequality with the inequality $T^2 \geq (I = BW(G))^2$ for any particular problem yields the so-called "AT^2" bound $AT^2 \geq \Omega(I^2)$ [23]. The bisection width of an N-node network $G = (V, E)$ is defined as follows:

Definition 4. [24] *A cut $(S, \overline{S})$ of G is a partition of its nodes into two sets S and $\overline{S}$, where $\overline{S} = V - S$. The capacity of a cut $C(S, \overline{S})$, is the number of (undirected) edges with one endpoint in S and the other in $\overline{S}$. A bisection of a network is a cut $(S, \overline{S})$ such that $|S| \leq \lceil \frac{N}{2} \rceil$ and $|\overline{S}| \leq \lceil \frac{N}{2} \rceil$. The bisection width $BW(G)$ is the minimum, over all bisections $(S, \overline{S})$, of $C(S, \overline{S})$. In other words, the bisection width is the minimum number of edges that must be removed in order to partition the nodes into two sets of equal cardinality (to within one node).*

Theorem 2. *If m is even, then $BW(GFT(h, m, m)) \leq \frac{m^{h+1}}{2}$.*

Proof. By definition, $GFT(h, m, m)$ has $\sum_{i=0}^{h} m^h$ nodes, such that level i contains m^h nodes. Also the degree of each leaf is m and the degree of each intermediate node is $2m$. The degree of the roots, i.e., the nodes in level h, is m. For each non-root (l, i), the parent nodes are $(l+1, m\cdot i), ..., (l+1, m\cdot(i+1)-1)$. For each non-leaf (l, i) the child nodes are $(l-1, \lfloor \frac{i}{m} \rfloor + 0\cdot m^{l-1}), ..., (l-1, \lfloor \frac{i}{m} \rfloor + (m-1)\cdot m^{l-1})$. Since we know that $GFT(h, m, m)$ contains m copies of $(h-1)$ height generalized fat tree, say $GFT'(h-1, m, m)$, $GFT''(h-1, m, m)$,...,$GFT^{m'}(h-1, m, m)$.

Also by the definition of generalized fat tree, none of the vertex in $GFT^{i'}(h-1,m,m)$ is adjacent to any vertex in $GFT^{j'}(h-1,m,m)$ for all i and j. So, upto $\frac{m'}{2}$ copies, there is no edge can be removed for partitioned into two subgraph of equal size. Also, in the hth level, each vertex have degree 2. So, atleast we can remove $\frac{m^{h+1}}{2}$ edges for partitioned into two subgraph of equal cardinality. □

Conjucture: If m is even, then $BW(GFT(h,m,m)) = \frac{m^{h+1}}{2}$. □

Theorem 3. *If m is odd, then*

$$BW(GFT(h,m,m)) \text{ is } \left\lfloor \frac{m}{2} \right\rfloor m^h + BW(GFT(h-1,m,m)) + \left\lceil \frac{m}{2} \right\rceil, \tag{6}$$

where $GFT(1,m,m) \leq \left\lceil \frac{m^2}{2} \right\rceil$. □

Conjucture: If m is odd, then

$$BW(GFT(h,m,m)) \text{ is } \left\lfloor \frac{m}{2} \right\rfloor m^h + BW(GFT(h-1,m,m)) + \left\lceil \frac{m}{2} \right\rceil, \tag{7}$$

where $GFT(1,m,m) = \left\lceil \frac{m^2}{2} \right\rceil$. □

3 Conclusion

In this paper, we compute the wide diameter of generalized fat tree $GFT(h,m,m)$. Also, we have obtained the bisection width of generalized fat tree $GFT(h,m,m)$. It would be a good line of research to prove the conjuctures cited in this paper.

References

1. Koushanfar, F., Potkonjak, M., Vincentelli, A.S.: Fault Tolerance in Wireless Sensor Networks. IEEE Sensors 2, 1491–1496 (2002)
2. Hsu, D.F.: On Container Width and Length in Graphs, Groups and Networks. IEICE Trans. Fundamentals of Electronics, Comm. and Computer Sciences 77A, 668–680 (1994)
3. Leiserson, C.E.: Fat-trees: Universal Networks for Hardware Efficient Supercomputing. IEEE Transactions on Computers C-34, 892–901 (1985)
4. Leiserson, C.E., Abumadeh, Z.S., Douglas, D.C., Ekynman, C.H., Ganmukhi, M.N., Hill, J.V., Hillis, W.D., Kuszmaul, B.C., Pierre, M.A., Wells, D.S., Wong, M.C., Yang, S.W., Zak, R.: The Network Architecture of the Connectionmachine CM-5. In: Proceedings of the Symposium on Parallel Algorithms and Architectures, pp. 272–285 (1992)
5. Frank, S., Rothnie, J., Burkhardt, H.: The KSRl: Bridging the Gap between Shared Memory and MPPS. In: Proceedings Compcon 1993, San Francisco, CA, pp. 285–294 (1993)
6. Schauser, K.E., Scheiman, C.J.: Experiments with active messages on the Meiko CS-2. To appear in the Proceedings of the 9th International Parallel Processing Symposium, Santa Barbara, pp. 140–149 (1995)

7. Ramanathan, G., Oren, J.: Survey of Commercial Parallel Machines. ACM SIGARCH Compuler Architecture News 21(3), 13–33 (1993)
8. Bay, P., Bilardi, G.: Deterministic on-line Routing on Area Universal Networks. In: Proceedings of the Annual Symp. on Foundations of Computer Science, pp. 297–306 (1990)
9. Greenberg, R.I., Leiserson, C.E.: Randomized Routing on Fat Trees. In: Micali, S. (ed.) Advances in Computing Research, Book 5: Randomness and Computation, pp. 345–374. JAI Press, Greenwich (1989)
10. Öhring, S.R., Ibel, M., Das, S.K., Kumar, M.J.: On Generalized Fat Trees. In: IPPS, Proceedings of the 9th International Symposium on Parallel Processing, vol. 37. IEEE Computer Society, Washington, DC, USA (1995)
11. Cao, F., Du, D., Hsu, D.F., Teng, S.: Fault Tolerance Properties of Pyramid Networks. IEEE Transactions on Computers 48(1), 88–93 (1999)
12. Chen, W.Y.C., Faber, V., Knill, E.: Restricted Routing and Wide Diameter of the Cycle Prefix Network. DIMACS Series in Discrete Mathematics and Theoretial Computer Science 21, 31–46 (1994)
13. Zhang, J., Xu, X.R., Wang, J.: Wide Diameter of Generalized Petersen Graphs. Journal of Mathematical Research & Exposition 30(3), 562–566 (2010)
14. Liaw, S.C., Chang, G.J.: Rabin Number of Butterfly Networks. Discrete Math. 196, 219–227 (1999)
15. Krishnamoorthy, M.S., Krishnamurthy, B.: Fault Diameter of Interconnection Networks. Comput. Math. Appl. 13, 577–582 (1987)
16. Hsu, D.F., Luczak, T.: Note on the k-diameter of k -regular k-connected Graphs. Discrete Math. 133, 291–296 (1994)
17. Liaw, S.C., Chang, G.J.: Wide Diameters of Butterfly Networks. Taiwanese Journal of Mathematics 3(1), 83–88 (1999)
18. Rabin, M.O.: Efficient Dispersal of Information for Security, Load Balancing and Fault Tolerance. J. Assoc. Comput. Mach. 36, 335–348 (1989)
19. Liaw, S.C., Chang, G.J., Cao, F., Hsu, D.F.: Fault-tolerant Routing in Circulant Networks and Cycle Prefix Networks. Annals of Combinatorics 2(2), 165–172 (1998)
20. Liaw, S.C., Lan, P.S.: Wide Diameters and Rabin Numbers of Generalized Folded Hypercube Networks. PhD Thesis, Taiwan, Republic of China (2005)
21. Jia, K.E., Zhang, A.Q.: On Wide diameter of Cayley graphs. Journal of Interconnection Networks 10(3), 219–231 (2009)
22. Rajasingh, I., Rajan, B., Rajan, R.S.: Reliability Measures in Circulant Network. In: Proceedings of The World Congress on Engineering. Lecture Notes in Engineering and Computer Science, pp. 98–102 (2011)
23. Thompson, C.D.: A Complexity Theory for VLSI. PhD thesis, Department of Computer Science, Carnegie-Mellon University, Pittsburgh, PA (1980)
24. Bornstein, C., Litman, A., Maggs, B., Sitaraman, R., Yatzkar, T.: On the Bisection Width and Expansion of Butterfly Networks. In: Proceedings of the 12th International Parallel Processing Symposium, pp. 144–150 (1998)

Topological Properties of Sierpinski Gasket Pyramid Network

Albert William, Indra Rajasingh, Bharati Rajan, and A. Shanthakumari

Department of Mathematics, Loyola College, Chennai 600 034, India
shanthakumari9775@gmail.com

Abstract. In this paper a new pyramidal topology for multicomputer interconnection networks based on the sierpinski gasket network is proposed. The Sierpinski fractal or Sierpinski gasket is a familiar object studied by specialists in dynamical systems and probability. The new network is referred to as the sierpinski gasket pyramid. We study the topological properties such as connectivity, diameter, chromatic number, hamiltonicity, pancyclicity and K_4-decomposition of the new pyramid network.

Keywords: Sierpinski gasket pyramid, Sierpinski gasket graph, Chromatic number, Hamilton cycle, Pancyclic, Decomposition.

1 Introduction and Background

Designing parallel computers is a popular trend for cost-effectiveness. In these parallel computers, many processors interconnected by an interconnection network, cooperate to solve a large problem. Interconnection networks are currently being used for many different applications, ranging from internal buses and inter-IP connections in VLSI circuits to wide area computer networks. An interconnection network can be modeled by a graph in which a processor is represented by a node and a communication channel between two nodes is represented by an edge between corresponding nodes. Various topologies for interconnection networks have been proposed in the literature [6, 20]. The tree, mesh, hypercube, k-ary n-cube, star graph, chordal rings, OTIS-Network and WK-recursive mesh are examples of common interconnection network topologies. Desirable properties of interconnection networks include symmetry, small node degree, diameter, network cost, high connectivity, scalability, modularity and fault-tolerance. Most of the topologies introduced by researchers try to compromise between cost and performance resulting in a wide range of different interconnection topologies each with some advantages and disadvantages [17].

A famous network topology which has been used as the base of both hardware architectures and software structures is the Pyramid. By exploring the inherent hierarchy at each level, pyramid structures can be efficiently used to handle various problems in graph theory, digital geometry, machine vision and image processing [5, 15]. Fault-tolerant properties of the pyramid network [4] make it also a promising network for reliable computing. Pyramids have therefore gained much attention in past studies [16].

A. Abd Manaf et al. (Eds.): ICIEIS 2011, Part III, CCIS 253, pp. 431–439, 2011.

Motivated by the pyramidal topology which is based on the triangular mesh network introduced in [17], the present paper introduces a new pyramidal topology, which is based on the sierpinski gasket network. This network preserves almost all desirable properties of the traditional pyramid networks and displays even better topological properties in some cases.

Fractal antennas have been studied, built, commercialized for a considerable while. Properly synthesized fractal antennas feature multi-band properties. Some of the modern mobile radio communication systems are based on sierpinski fractals or sierpinski gasket like structures and have a log-periodic behaviour as far as radiation patterns are concerned. Fractal geometries also have electromagnetic applications [16]. In the sequel, we refer to Bondy and Murty [3] for the definitions in Graph Theory.

2 Sierpinski Graphs and Sierpinski Gasket Graphs

The *Generalised Sierpinski graph* $S(n, k)$, $n \geq 1$, $k \geq 1$ is defined in the following way:

$V(S(n, k)) = \{1, 2, ..., k\}^n$, two distinct vertices $u = (u_1, u_2, ..., u_n)$ and $v = (v_1, v_2, ..., v_n)$ being adjacent if and only if there exists an $h \in \{1, 2, ..., n\}$ such that

(i) $u_t = v_t$, for $t = 1, ..., h - 1$;
(ii) $u_h \neq v_h$; and
(iii) $u_t = v_h$ and $v_t = u_h$ for $t = h + 1, ..., n$.

We shortly write the vertex $(u_1, u_2, ..., u_n)$ as $(u_1u_2...u_n)$. The vertices (1...1), (2...2), ..., $(k...k)$ are called the *extreme vertices* of $S(n, k)$ [8]. In the literature, $S(n, 3)$, $n \geq 1$ is known as the *Sierpinski graph*. For $i = 1, 2, 3$, let $S(n + 1, 3)_i$ be the subgraph induced by the vertices that have i as the first entry. Clearly $S(n + 1, 3)_i$ is isomorphic to $S(n, 3)$ [10]. In the Figures, we denote the vertex $(u_1u_2...u_n)$ as $u_1u_2...u_n$.

The *Sierpinski gasket graph* S_n, $n \geq 1$, can be obtained by contracting all the edges of $S(n, 3)$ that lie in no triangle. If $(u_1...u_r, i, j, ..., j)$ and $(u_1...u_r, j, i, ..., i)$ are the end vertices of such an edge, then we will denote the corresponding vertex of S_n by $(u_1...u_r)\{i, j\}$, $r \leq n - 2$. Thus S_n is the graph with three special vertices (1...1), (2...2) and (3...3) called the *extreme vertices* of S_n, together with vertices of the form $(u_1...u_r)\{i, j\}$, $0 \leq r \leq n - 2$ where all u_k's, i and j are from $\{1, 2, 3\}$. This labeling is called *quotient labeling* of S_n [10] and $(u_1...u_r)$ is called the prefix of $(u_1...u_r)\{i, j\}$. S_{n+1} contains three isomorphic copies of S_n that can be described as follows: For $i = 1$, 2, 3 let $S_{n, i}$ be the subgraph of S_{n+1} induced by $(i...i)$, $\{i, j\}$, $\{i, k\}$ where $\{i, j, k\}=\{1, 2, 3\}$ and all the vertices whose prefix starts with i [10]. The graph $S(3, 3)$ and S_3 are shown in Figure 1.

Geometrically, S_n is a graph whose vertices are the intersection points of the line segments of the finite sierpinski gasket σ_n and line segment of the gasket as edges. The sierpinski gasket graph S_n is the finite structure obtained by n iterations of the process [19].

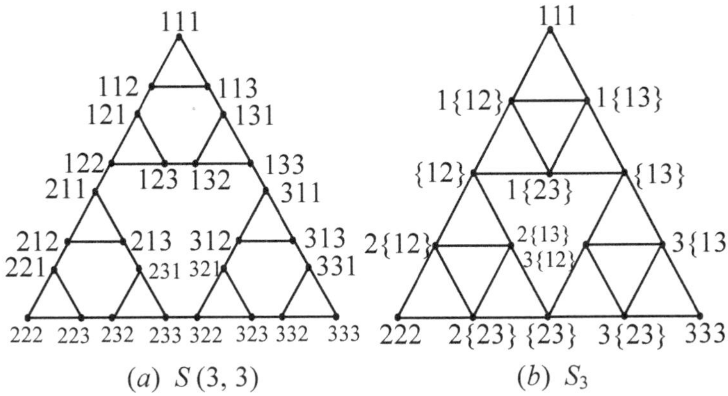

Fig. 1. Quotient Labeling

The definition of sierpinski graphs $S(n, k)$ originated from the topological studies of the Lipscomb's space [14]. The motivation for the introduction of these graphs is the fact that $S(n, 3)$, $n \geq 1$, is isomorphic to the graphs of the Tower of Hanoi with n disks [11]. The graphs $S(n, k)$ have many appealing properties and are studied from different points of view. They possess unique 1-perfect codes [7, 12]. Moreover, sierpinski graphs are the first nontrivial families of graphs of fractal type for which the crossing number is known [13] and several metric invariants of these graphs are determined. Hinz and Schief used the connection between the graphs $S(n, 3)$ with the sierpinski gasket to compute the average distance of the latter [9]. Teguia and Godbole [19] studied several properties of these graphs, in particular hamiltonicity, pancyclicity, cycle structure, domination number, chromatic number, pebbling number, cover pebbling number. Also, the vertex colouring, edge-colouring and total-colouring of sierpinki gaskets have been obtained.

The sierpinski graph S_n is hamiltonian for each n and pancyclic, that is, it has cycles of all possible sizes. It has $\frac{3}{2}(3^{n-1} + 1)$vertices, the number of edges in S_n may thus be easily determined using the fact that the sum of the vertex degrees equals twice the number of edges. S_n is properly three-colourable, that is, $\chi(S_n) = 3$ for each n. S_n has two hamiltonian paths both starting at the same vertex of degree two and ending at different vertices of degree two. Its diameter is 2^{n-1}.

3 Sierpinski Gasket Pyramid Network (SP_n)

The pyramid is a promising and powerful architecture in image processing, image understanding, in the area of computer vision and scalespace (or multiresolution) and coarse-to-fine operations [16]. In this paper we introduce a new architecture called the *Sierpinski gasket pyramid network* (SP_n) and study a few topological properties of the new pyramidal network. We begin with the concept of merging vertices. Let $G_1(V_1, E_1)$ and $G_2(V_2, E_2)$ be two graphs. Let the vertex u be from the boundary of the exterior face of G_1 and the vertex v from the exterior face of G_2. If we merge

u and v to form a new vertex x, creating a new graph G with x as cut vertex, then we call G is obtained by vertex merging of G_1 and G_2.

The *Sierpinski gasket pyramid graph* SP_n is defined recursively as follows:

1. SP_1 is the complete graph on 4 vertices. See Figure 2.
2. The $(n - 1)$-dimensional sierpinski gasket pyramid SP_n comprises of four copies of SP_{n-1} referred to as the *top*, *bottom left*, *bottom right* and *bottom middle* parts of SP_n and denoted as SP_n^T, SP_n^L, SP_n^R and SP_n^M respectively, each isomorphic to SP_{n-1} with the following pairs of vertices merged: $\{SP_n^{TL}, SP_n^{LT}\}$, $\{SP_n^{TR}, SP_n^{RT}\}$, $\{SP_n^{TM}, SP_n^{MT}\}$, $\{SP_n^{LR}, SP_n^{RL}\}$ $\{SP_n^{LM}, SP_n^{ML}\}$ and $\{SP_n^{RM}, SP_n^{MR}\}$ where SP_n^{XY} denotes Y node of the X sierpinski gasket pyramid of dimension $n - 1$ and $X, Y \in \{Top, Left, Right, Middle\}$.

The sierpinski gasket pyramid graphs SP_1, SP_2 are shown in Figure 2.

Theorem 1. *SP_n has $2^{2n-1} + 2$ vertices and $3 \times 2^{2n-1}$ edges.*

Proof. We have $|V(SP_n)| = 4|V(SP_{n-1})| - 6 = 4^{n-1}|V(SP_1)| - 6(4^0 + 4^1 + \ldots + 4^{n-2}) = 2^{2n-1} + 2$. The number of edges is given by $|E(SP_n)| = 4|E(SP_{n-1})| = 4^{n-1}|E(SP_1)| = 3 \times 2^{2n-1}$. □

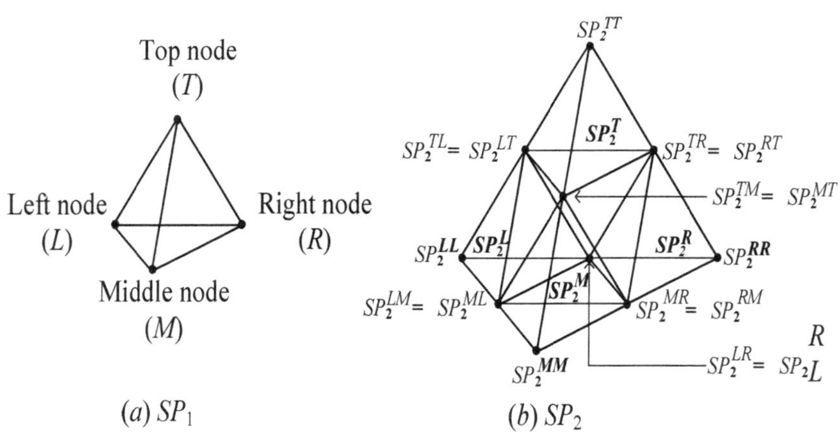

Fig. 2. Construction of SP_2 from SP_1

From the construction of the sierpinski gasket pyramid graph and Theorem 1, we observe the following:

1. SP_n is nothing but the tessellation of each triangular face of a tetrahedron into sierpinski gasket graph.
2. Any two copies of $(n - 1)$-dimensional sierpinski gasket pyramids share exactly one vertex.
3. SP_n^R is the mirror image of SP_n^T with the mirror placed along the line passing through SP_n^{TR} and SP_n^{ML}. SP_n^M is the mirror image of SP_n^R or SP_n^L with the mirror placed along the line passing through SP_n^{TL} and SP_n^{MR} according as the vertex being shared is SP_n^{RL} or SP_n^{LR}.

4. SP_n is a biregular graph with 4 vertices of degree 3 and the remaining vertices of degree 6.
5. The vertex connectivity is 3 and the edge connectivity is also 3.
6. SP_n is not Eulerian since it has odd degree vertices.

4 Diameter, Chromatic Number and K_4-Decomposition

The *diameter* of a graph G denoted by $d(G)$, is defined as the maximum distance between any two vertices of G. In other words, $d(G) = max\{d(G; x, y) : x, y \in V(G)\}$.

Theorem 2. *For $n \geq 1$, $diam(SP_n) = 2^{n-1}$.*

Proof. We prove the result by induction on n. It is obvious that $diam(SP_1) = 1$. Assume the result is true for SP_{n-1}. In other words $diam(SP_{n-1}) = 2^{n-2}$. Let u, $v \in SP_n$. A path from u to v has to pass through any of the six merged vertices only. Hence $diam(SP_n) = 2diam(SP_{n-1}) = 2^{n-1}$. □

A *k-vertex colouring* of G is an assignment of k colours to the vertices of G. The colouring is *proper* if no two distinct adjacent vertices have the same colour. G is *k-vertex colourable* if G has a proper k-vertex coloring abbreviated as *k-colourable*. The chromatic number, $\chi(G)$ of G is the minimum k for which G is k-colourable. If $\chi(G) = k$, then G is said to be *k-chromatic*.

Theorem 3. *The chromatic number of SP_n is 4, for all $n \geq 1$.*

Proof. K_4 is a subgraph of SP_n, so $\chi(SP_n) \geq 4$. Hence it is enough to prove that 4 colours are sufficient for SP_n. We prove the result by induction on n. Since SP_1 is isomorphic to K_4, $\chi(SP_1) = 4$. See Figure 3. Assume $\chi(SP_{n-1}) = 4$. Consider an arbitrary 4-colouring of SP_n^T in SP_n. By construction, each copy of SP_{n-1} in SP_n is a mirror image of SP_n^T and hence receives the same four colours. □

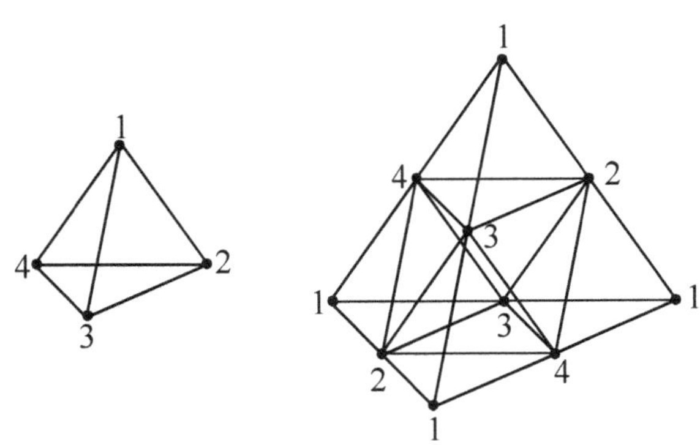

Fig. 3. Colouring of SP_1 and SP_2

A *decomposition* of G is a family of subgraphs $G_1, G_2, ..., G_k$ of G such that their edge sets form a partition of the edge set of G. An *H-decomposition* of G is a family of edge-disjoint subgraphs each isomorphic to the graph H of G whose union is G. In this case, we say G is *H-decomposable*. A graph G is said to be *randomly H-decomposable* if any edge-disjoint family of subgraphs of G each isomorphic to H can be extended to an H-decomposition of G [18].

The concept of random decomposition was introduced by Ruiz in [18]. Beineke, Hamburger and Goddard studied randomly K_n-decomposable graphs and characterised randomly tK_2-decomposable graphs with sufficiently many edges [2]. Arumugam et al. [1] characterised randomly H-decomposable graphs for H isomorphic to some disconnected graphs namely $K_n \cup K_{1,n-1}$ and $K_n \cup K_{1,n}$.

Theorem 4. *SP_n is randomly K_4-decomposable with 4^{n-1} copies of K_4.*

Proof. We prove the result by induction on n. Since SP_1 is isomorphic to K_4, the result is trivial. Assume the result is true for SP_{n-1}. In other words, it consists of 4^{n-2} edge-disjoint subgraphs each isomorphic to K_4 whose union is SP_{n-1}. Now, SP_n contains $4(4^{n-2}) = 4^{n-1}$ copies of K_4. □

5 Hamiltonian and Pancyclic Properties

A path that contains every vertex of G is called a *Hamilton path*. A cycle that contains every vertex of G is called a *Hamilton cycle*. G is said to be *hamiltonian* if it contains a Hamilton cycle. G is *hamiltonian-connected* if a hamiltonian path exists between every pair of vertices in G.

Theorem 5. *The Sierpinski gasket pyramid is hamiltonian, $n \geq 1$.*

Proof. We prove the result by induction on n. Since $SP_1 \simeq K_4$, it contains a Hamilton cycle. Assume that SP_{n-1} is hamiltonian. We prove that SP_n is hamiltonian. SP_n is a four-fold "repetition" of SP_{n-1}. By induction, there exists a hamiltonian path from SP_n^T to SP_n^R. Let it be P: $SP_n^{TL} \rightarrow SP_n^{TR} \rightarrow SP_n^{RM}$ where $x \rightarrow y$ denotes the subpath traced between two vertices x and y. If a mirror is placed along the line passing through SP_n^{TL} and SP_n^{RM}, then the hamiltonian path in the other two copies SP_n^M and SP_n^L is the mirror image of P with a critical modification of avoiding the two merged vertices namely SP_n^{TM} and SP_n^{RL} still maintaining the order of the sequence of the vertices. Since every merged vertex has two triangles sharing the same vertex, the edge not incident with the merged vertex is used in the traversal of the mirror image of P. □

Using quotient labeling, Theorem 5 may be formulated as an algorithm for determining a Hamilton cycle in SP_3. See Figure 4.

Procedure HAMILTONIAN SP_n

Input: A Sierpinski gasket pyramid of dimension 3.

Algorithm

(i) The hamiltonian path P with origin SP_3^{TL} and end point SP_3^{RM} is traced as follows: {{0, 1}, 0{0, 1}, 0{0, 2}, 000, 0{0, 3}, 0{1, 3}, 0{1, 2}, {0, 2}, 0{2, 3}, {0, 3}, 3{0, 1}, {1, 3}, 3{1, 2}, 3{0, 2}, 3{0, 3}, 333, 3{1, 3}, 3{2, 3}, {2, 3}}.

(ii) The mirror image of P from SP_3^{RM} to SP_3^{LT} is {{2, 3}, 2{2, 3}, 2{0, 2}, 222, 2{1, 2}, 2{1, 3}, 2{0, 3}, {0, 2}, 2{0, 1}, {1, 2}, 1{2, 3}, {1, 3}, 1{0, 3}, 1{0, 2}, 1{1, 2}, 111, 1{1, 3}, 1{0, 1}, {0, 1}}

(iii) Omit the merged vertices {0, 2} and {1, 3} in (ii) such that the order of the sequence of the vertices is retained.

Output: A Hamilton cycle.

Corollary 1. *The Sierpinski gasket pyramid SP_n is hamiltonian-connected, $n \geq 1$.*

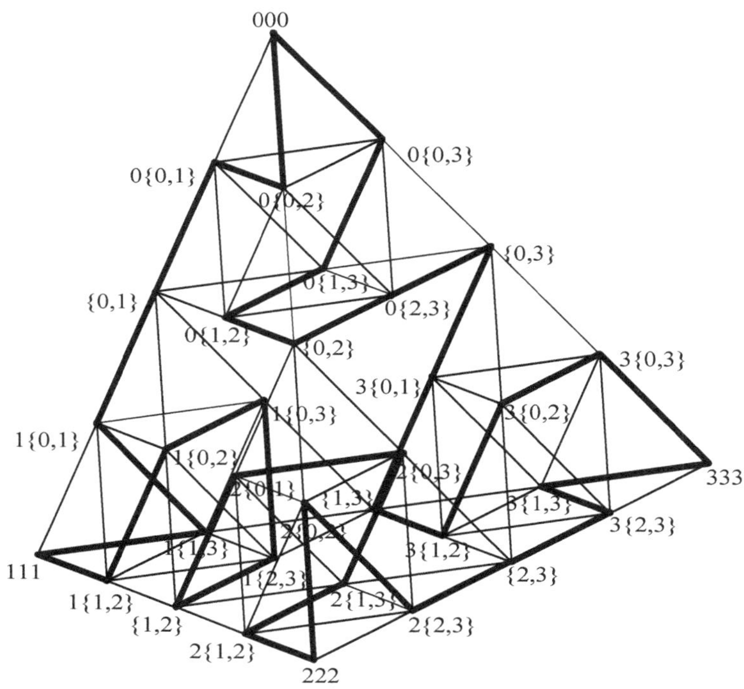

Fig. 4. A Hamilton cycle in SP_3

Theorem 6. *The Sierpinski gasket pyramid SP_n is pancyclic, $n \geq 1$.*

Proof. We prove the result by induction on n. The induction base is SP_1, for which the constructed cycles of length 3 and 4 are shown in Figure 5. Let H_{n-1} be a hamiltonian path of length $2^{2n-3} + 1$ in SP_{n-1}, $n \geq 2$. Let C_j be a cycle on j vertices and $3 \leq j \leq \frac{1}{2}((5 \times 3^{n-1}) - 1)$ passing through the vertices of the base $SP_n \cong S_n$. We observe that there exist 3, 4, 5 and 6-cycles passing through exactly a pair of vertices of base SP_n.

There are 3^{n-2} such pair of vertices in base SP_n. By induction hypothesis, SP_{n-1} is pancyclic, $n \geq 2$. We must prove that cycles of lengths 3, 4, ... and $2^{2n-1} + 2$ can be embedded in SP_n. We note that SP_n consists of copies of SP_{n-1}, SP_{n-2}., ..., SP_1 and C_j 's. Let x, y be a pair of vertices lying both in H_{n-1} and the base sierpinski gasket graph S_{n-1}. Since the diameter of SP_{n-1} is 2^{n-2}, for every pair of vertices x, y there exists a pair of vertices u, v in base SP_n such that there are paths of length 2^{n-2} from x to u and y to v. Since both SP_{n-1} and S_n are pancyclic, the lengths of H_i's, C_j 's where $2 \leq i \leq n-1$, $3 \leq j \leq \frac{1}{2}((5 \times 3^{n-1}) - 1)$ and the two paths from x to u and y to v can be modified to form cycles of lengths 3, 4, ... and $2^{2n-1} + 2$. See Figure 6. □

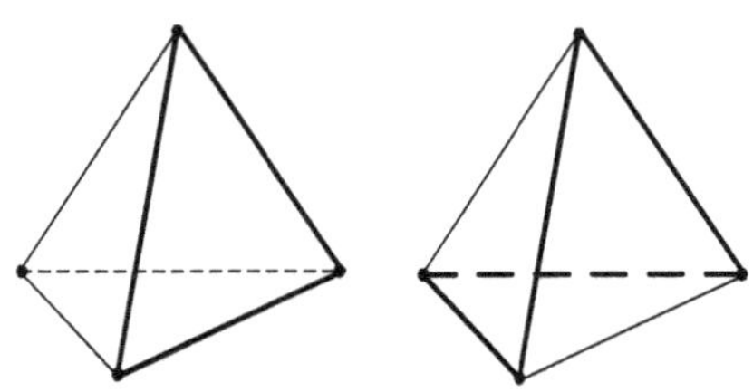

Fig. 5. Cycles C_3 and C_4 in SP_1

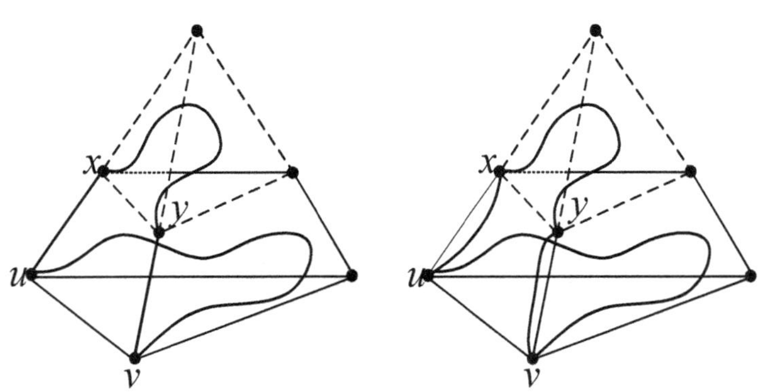

Fig. 6. Cycle construction in SP_n

6 Conclusion

Numerous network topologies have been proposed for multicomputer interconnection networks in the literature. In this paper, we have introduced a new pyramidal topology based on Sierpinski gasket network. Some important properties of the proposed pyramid network have been investigated. We conjecture that this is a good cost-effective network for interconnecting processing nodes in a multicomputer compared to the conventional pyramid topology. We also propose to study *message routing* and *broadcasting* in this network.

References

1. Arumugam, S., Meena, S.: Graphs that are Randomly Packable by some common Disconnected Graphs. Indian J. Pure Appl. Math. 29, 1129–1136 (1998)
2. Beineke, L., Hamburger, P., Goddard, W.: Random Packing of Graphs. Discrete Mathematics 125, 45–54 (1994)
3. Bondy, J.A., Murty, U.S.R.: Graph Theory with Applications. The Macmillan Press Ltd (1977)
4. Cao, F., Hsu, D.F.: Fault-Tolerance Properties of Pyramid Networks. IEEE Transactions on Computers 48, 88–93 (1999)
5. Dingle, A., Sudborough, I.H.: Simulation of Binary Trees and X-trees on Pyramid Networks. In: Proc. IEEE Symp. Parallel and Distributed Processing, pp. 220–229 (1992)
6. Farahabady, M.H., Azad, H.S.: The Recursive Transpose-Connected Cycles (RTCC) Interconnection Network for Multiprocessors. In: ACM SAC 2005 (2005)
7. Gravier, S., Klavzar, S., Mollard, M.: Codes and L(2, 1)-Labelings in Sierpinski Graphs. Taiwan. J. Math. 9, 671–681 (2005)
8. Hilfer, R., Blumen, A.: Renormalisation on Sierpinski-Type Fractals. J. Phys. A: Math. Gen. 17, 537–545 (1984)
9. Hinz, A.M., Schief, A.: The Average Distance on the Sierpinski Gasket. Probab. Theory Related Fields 87, 129–138 (1990)
10. Klavzar, S.: Coloring Sierpinski Graphs and Sierpinski Gasket Graphs. Taiwan. J. Math. 12, 513–522 (2008)
11. Klavzar, S., Milutinovic, U.: Graphs S(n,k) and a Variant of the Tower of Hanoi Problem. Czechoslovak Math. 47, 95–104 (1997)
12. Klavzar, S., Milutinovic, U., Petr, C.: 1-perfect codes in Sierpinski graphs. Bull. Austral. Math. Soc. 66, 369–384 (2002)
13. Klavzar, S., Mohar, B.: Crossing Numbers of Sierpinski-Like Graphs. J. Graph Theory 50, 186–198 (2005)
14. Lipscomb, S.L., Perry, J.C.: Lipscomb's L(A) Space Fractalized in Hilbert's l2(A) Space. Proc. Amer. Math. Soc. 115, 1157–1165 (1992)
15. Miller, R., Stout, Q.: Data Movement Techniques for the Pyramid Computer. SIAM Journal of Computing 16, 38–60 (1987)
16. Ng, C.K.Y.: Embedding Pyramids into 3D Meshes. Journal of Parallel and Distributed Computing 36, 173–184 (1996)
17. Razavi, S., Azad, H.S.: The Triangle-Pyramid: Routing and Topological Properties. Information Sciences 180, 2328–2339 (2010)
18. Ruiz, S.: Randomly Decomposable Graphs. Discrete Mathematics 57, 123–128 (1985)
19. Teguia, A.M., Godbole, A.P.: Sierpinski Gasket Graphs and Some of their Properties. Australas. J. Combin. 35, 181 (2006)
20. Xu, J.: Topological Structure and Analysis of Interconnection Networks. Kluwer Academic Publishers (2001)

On the Crossing Number of Generalized Fat Trees*

Bharati Rajan[1], Indra Rajasingh[1], and P. Vasanthi Beulah[2]

[1] Department of Mathematics, Loyola College, Chennai, India
[2] Department of Mathematics, Queen Mary's College, Chennai, India
vbeulah@yahoo.com

Abstract. The crossing number of a graph G is the minimum number of crossings of its edges among the drawings of G in the plane and is denoted by $cr(G)$. Bhatt and Leighton proved that the crossing number of a network is closely related to the minimum layout area required for the implementation of the VLSI circuit for that network. In this paper, we find an upper bound for the crossing number of a special case of the generalized fat tree based on the underlying graph model found in the literature. We also improve this bound for a new drawing of the same structure. The proofs are based on the drawing rules introduced in this paper.

Keywords: Drawing of a graph, planar graph, crossing number, generalized fat trees.

1 Introduction

Crossing number minimization is one of the fundamental optimization problems in the sense that it is related to various other widely used notions. Besides its mathematical interest, there are numerous applications, most notably those in VLSI design [1, 7, 8, 17] and in computational geometry [19]. Minimizing the number of wire crossings in a circuit greatly reduces the chance of cross-talk in long crossing wires carrying the same signal and also allows for faster operation and less power dissipation. When fabricating a VLSI layout for a network, crossing numbers can be used to obtain lower bounds on the chip area which contributes largely to the cost of making the chip. It is also an important measure of non-planarity of a graph.

A drawing D of a graph G is a representation of G in the Euclidean plane R^2 where vertices are represented as distinct points and edges by simple polygonal arcs joining points that correspond to their end vertices. A drawing D is *good* or *clean* if it has the following properties.

1. No edge crosses itself.
2. No pair of adjacent edges cross.
3. Two edges cross at most once.
4. No more than two edges cross at one point.

* This work is supported by The Minor Project - No.F.1-2/2010-2011 (RO/SERO/MRP) PNO. 345 of University Grants Commission, Hyderabad, India.

A. Abd Manaf et al. (Eds.): ICIEIS 2011, Part III, CCIS 253, pp. 440–448, 2011.

The number of crossings of D is denoted by $cr(D)$ and is called the crossing number of the drawing D. The crossing number $cr(G)$ of a graph G is the minimum $cr(D)$ taken over all good or clean drawings D of G. If a graph G admits a drawing D with $cr(D) = 0$ then G is said to be planar; otherwise non-planar. It is well known that K_5, the complete graph on 5 vertices and $K_{3,3}$, the complete bipartite graph with 3 vertices in its classes are non-planar. According to Kuratowski's famous theorem, a graph is planar if and only if contains no subdivision of K_5 or $K_{3,3}$.

The study of crossing numbers began during the Second World War with Paul Turán. For an arbitrary graph, computing $cr(G)$ is NP-hard [5]. Hence from a computational standpoint, it is infeasible to obtain exact solutions for graphs, in general, but more practical to explore bounds for the parameter values [3]. Richter and Thomassen [16] discussed the relation between crossing numbers of the complete graphs and the complete bipartite graphs. The bound for $cr(K_n)$ and $cr(K_{m,n})$ are obtained by Guy [6]. In particular, Pan et al. [13] have shown that $cr(K_{11}) = 100$ and $cr(K_{12}) = 153$. Nahas [11] has obtained an improved lower bound for $cr(K_{m,n})$. In [4, 15] the crossing number of some generalized Petersen graphs $P(2n + 1, 2)$ and $P(3k + h, 3)$ has been discussed.

Another family of graphs whose crossing numbers have received a good deal of attention is the interconnection networks proposed for parallel computer architecture. The vertices of the graph correspond to processors and the edges represent the communication links between the processors. For hypercubes and cube connected cycles, the crossing number problem is investigated by Sýkora et al. [18]. Cimikowski [3] has obtained the bound for the crossing number of mesh of trees.

For various other networks like torus, butterfly and Benes networks, Cimikowski [2] has given the upper bound for the crossing number based on the combinatorial analysis of the adjacency structure of the underlying graph theoretic model of the network. We have obtained improved bounds for the crossing number for two different drawings of the standard butterfly as well as Benes networks [10]. We have also obtained upper bounds for the crossing number for the honeycomb rectangular torus and the honeycomb rhombic torus [14]. To our knowledge, the crossing number of generalized fat trees has not been considered in the literature so far. In this paper we find an upper bound for the crossing number of a special case of the generalized fat tree based on the underlying graph model. We also improve this bound for a new drawing of the same structure.

2 Generalized Fat Trees

Several topologies have been proposed as interconnection networks for multicomputer systems [9]. However, hypercubes suffer from wirability and packing problems for VLSI implementation and a mesh topology has larger diameter and low edge bisection. To overcome these difficulties, Ohring et al. [12] introduced a new family of multiprocessor interconnection networks called *generalized fat trees* denoted by $GFT(h, m, w)$. This consists of m^h processors in the leaf level and routers or switches in the non-leaf levels. In a $GFT(h, m, w) = (V_h, E_h)$ of height h, level h nodes (top level nodes) are called the *root nodes* and level 0 nodes are called the *leaf nodes*. Each non-root has w parent nodes and each non-leaf has m children. Generalized fat trees include as special cases the fat trees used for the connection machine architecture *CM*-5, pruned butterflies and various other fat trees proposed in the literature. They also provide a formal unifying concept to design and analyze a fat tree based architecture. In this paper, we have obtained upper bounds for the crossing number for a special case of generalized fat trees.

Definition 1. [12] A generalized fat tree $GFT(h,m,w)$ is recursively generated from m distinct copies of $GFT(h-1,m,w)$, denoted as $GFT^j(h-1,m,w) = (V^j_{h-1}, E^j_{h-1})$, $0 \le j \le m-1$, and w^h additional nodes such that each top level node $(h-1, k + j\,w^{h-1})$ of each $GFT^j(h-1,m,w)$ for $0 \le k \le w^{h-1} - 1$ is adjacent to w consecutive new top level nodes (ie., level h nodes), given by (h, kw), $(h, kw+1)$, …, $(h, (k+1)w-1)$. The graph $GFT^j(h-1,m,w)$ is also called the sub-fat tree of $GFT(h,m,w)$. A $GFT(2,4,2)$ is shown in Figure 1.

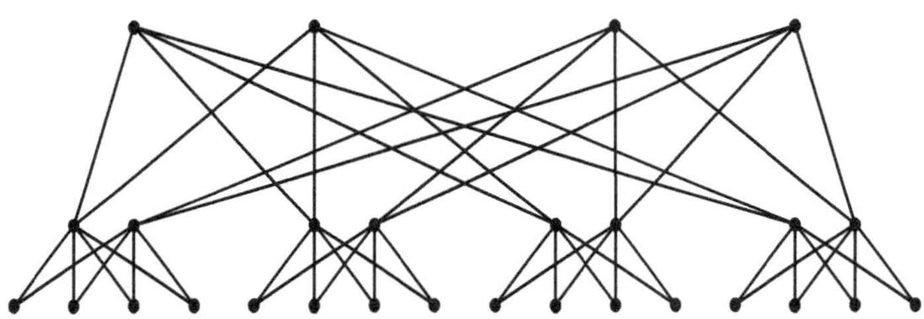

Fig. 1. The Generalized Fat Tree $GFT(2,4,2)$

The vertex set of $GFT(h,m,w)$ is given by $V_h = \{(l,i) : 0 \le l \le h,\ 0 \le i \le m^{h-l}w^l - 1\}$, where l is the level of the node and i denotes the position of this node in level l. The distance between two leaves $(0, i_1)$ and $(0, i_2)$ of $GFT(h,m,w)$ is two times the height of the smallest sub-fat tree of $GFT(h,m,w)$ which contains both of them. In this paper we consider the generalized fat tree $GFT(h,3,3)$. A formal definition is given below.

Definition 2. A generalized fat tree $GFT(h,3,3)$ of height h is recursively generated from 3 distinct copies of $GFT(h-1,3,3)$, denoted as $GFT^j(h-1,3,3) = (V^j_{h-1}, E^j_{h-1})$, $0 \le j \le 2$, and 3^h additional nodes such that each top level node $(h-1, k + j\,3^h)$ of each $GFT^j(h-1,3,3)$ for $0 \le k \le 3^{h-1} - 1$ is adjacent to 3 consecutive new top level nodes (ie., level h nodes), given by $(h, 3k)$, $(h, 3k+1)$ and $(h, 3k+2)$. The graph $GFT^j(h-1,3,3)$ is also called the sub-fat tree of $GFT(h,3,3)$. This construction is sketched in Figure 2 for $h = 2$.

The vertex set of $GFT(h,3,3)$ is given by $V_h = \{(l,i) : 0 \le l \le h,\ 0 \le i \le 3^h - 1\}$, where l is the level of the node and i denotes the position of this node in level l. Here the degree of each root node is 3 and that of each leaf node is also 3. Degree of each intermediate node is 6.

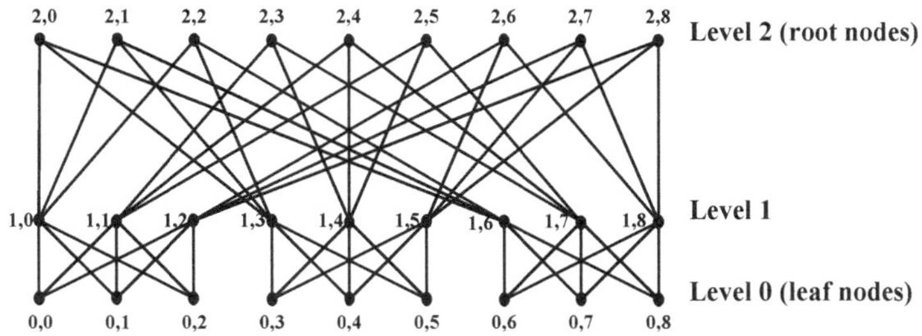

Fig. 2. *GFT*(2,3,3)

3 Crossing Number for *GFT*(*h*,3,3)

Theorem 1. Let *G* be *GFT*(*h*,3,3). Then $cr(G) \leq 3^{h+1}\left[\frac{3^{h+1}}{4}-\frac{h}{2}-\frac{3}{4}\right]$.

Proof. We prove the result by induction on the height *h*.
Base case *h* = 1.

Let *D* be the drawing of *GFT*(1,3,3). We describe the method of counting the number of crossings in the diagram *D* of *GFT*(1,3,3). The edges from the leaf node (0,0) to the top level nodes (1,0), (1,1) and (1,2) do not contribute to the crossing number as shown in Figure 3(a). The edges from the leaf node (0,1) to the top level nodes (1,0), (1,1) and (1,2) contribute (2 + 1 + 0) crossings as in Figure 3(b) and the edges from (0,2) to the root nodes contribute (4 + 2 + 0) crossings as in Figure 3(c). Thus the number of crossings in the diagram *D* of

$$GFT(1,3,3) = 3(2+1+0) = 9 = 3^2\left[\frac{3^2}{4}-\frac{1}{2}-\frac{3}{4}\right]. \qquad \square$$

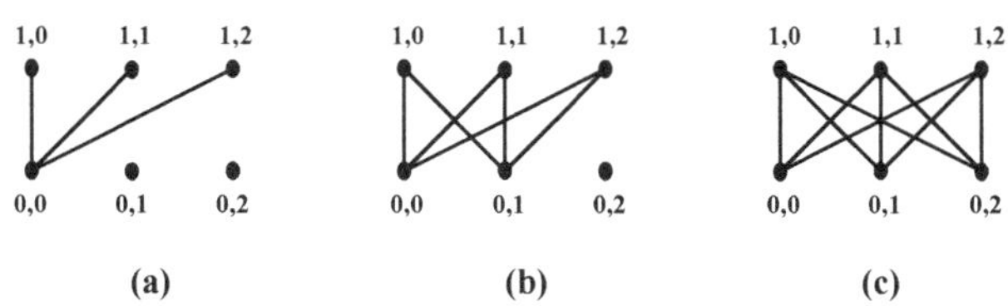

Fig. 3. Edges of *GFT*(1,3,3)

Assume that the theorem is true for *GFT*(*h* – 1,3,3). Let *G* be *GFT*(*h*,3,3) and let G_1, G_2 and G_3 be the three copies of *GFT*(*h* – 1,3,3) in the drawing of *D* of *G*. The crossing number of *D* is the number of crossings of G_1, G_2 and G_3 together with the number of crossings contributed by the additional edges from level $(h-1)$ to the level h nodes of G. We describe the method of including the additional edges in order to count the number of crossings. The additional nodes are drawn from left to right from the top level nodes of G_1, G_2, G_3 respectively. The edges from the top level nodes of G_1 to the root nodes of G do not contribute to the crossing number. The edges from the top level nodes of G_2 to the root nodes of G contribute $(3^h-1)+(3^h-2)+...+2+1+0$ crossings. Similarly the edges from the top level nodes of G_3 to the root nodes of G contribute $2[(3^h-1)+(3^h-2)+...+2+1+0]$ crossings. Hence,

$$
\begin{aligned}
cr(D) &= cr(G_1)+cr(G_2)+cr(G_3)+3[(3^h-1)+(3^h-2)+...+2+1+0] \\
&\le 3\times 3^h\left[\frac{3^h}{4}-\frac{h-1}{2}-\frac{3}{4}\right]+3\times(0+1+...+3^h-1) \\
&= 3^{h+1}\left[\frac{3^{h+1}}{4}-\frac{h}{2}-\frac{3}{4}\right].
\end{aligned}
$$

Figure 4 shows the inclusion of additional edges in *GFT*(2,3,3).

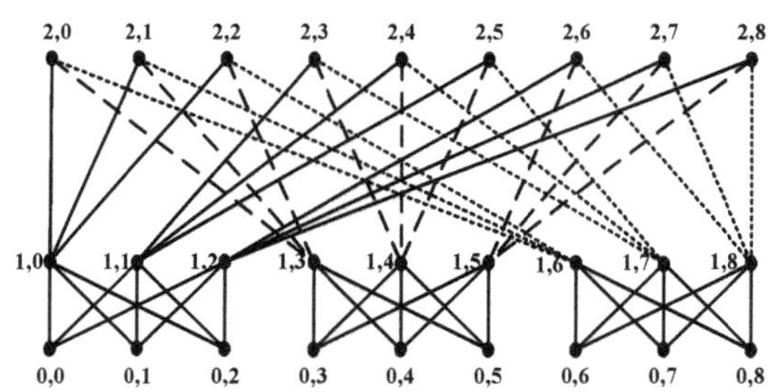

Fig. 4. Additional Edges in *GFT*(2,3,3)

4 Proposed Representation for *GFT*(*h*,3,3)

We propose a new representation of *GFT*(*h*,3,3) denoted by *NGFT*(*h*,3,3). The following observation in *GFT*(2,3,3) is useful in drawing the recursive structure of *NGFT*(*h*,3,3).

In *GFT*(2,3,3) each node in level 2 is the root of a complete ternary tree with leaf nodes at level 0. Let T denote all complete ternary trees having the middle one-third nodes in level 2 as roots (shown by broken lines in Figure 5(a)). Take the mirror image of T about the level 0 nodes. In this process, the middle one third nodes in the top level of *GFT*(2,3,3) and the middle one third nodes in the top levels of the 3 distinct copies of *GFT*(1,3,3) are brought down the level 0 nodes. Let us name the nodes which are brought down from the level 2 and level 1 nodes as level –2 and level –1 nodes respectively. The resultant graph is a *NGFT*(2,3,3).

In a similar way, a *NGFT*(h,3,3) can be drawn from a *GFT*(h,3,3) by taking the mirror image of all complete ternary trees having the middle one-third nodes at level h as root nodes, about the level 0 nodes.

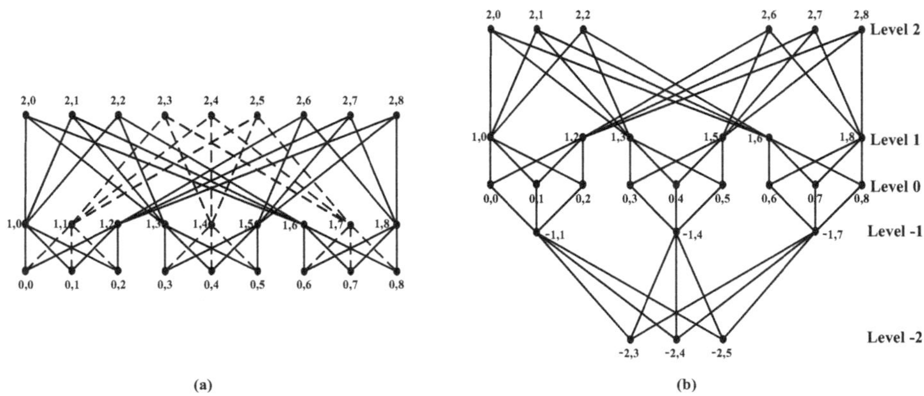

Fig. 5. *GFT*(2,3,3) and *NGFT*(2,3,3)

4.1 Crossing Number for *NGFT*(*h*,3,3)

In this section we obtain an improved bound for the crossing number of the new representation.

Theorem 2. Let G be *NGFT*(h,3,3). Then $cr(G) \le 3^h + \frac{1}{4}\left[5 \cdot 3^{2h} - (3+2h)3^{h+1}\right]$.

Proof. We prove the result by induction on the height h.
Base case $h = 1$.

Let D be the drawing of *NGFT*(1,3,3). The edges are added as shown in figures 6(a), 6(b) and 6(c). The edges from the node (1,0) to the nodes (0,0), (0,1) and (0,2)

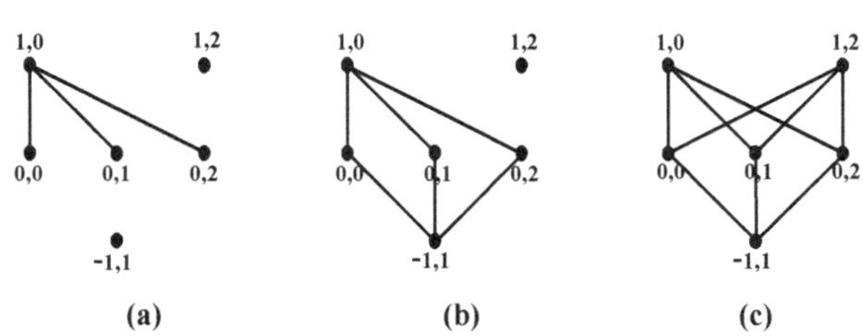

Fig. 6. Edges of *NGFT*(1,3,3)

do not contribute to the crossing number. The edges from the node (−1,1) to the nodes (0,0), (0,1) and (0,2) also do not contribute to the crossing number. But the edges from (1,2) to the nodes (0,0), (0,1) and (0,2) contribute (2 + 1 + 0) crossings. Thus the number of crossings in the diagram D of

$$NGFT(1,3,3) = (2+1+0) = 3 = 3^1 + \frac{1}{4}\left[5\cdot 3^2 - (3+2)3^2\right].$$

Assume that the result is true for $NGFT(h-1,3,3)$. Let G be $NGFT(h,3,3)$ and let G_1, G_2 and G_3 be the three copies of $NGFT(h-1,3,3)$ in the drawing of G. The crossing number of D is the number of crossings of G_1, G_2 and G_3 together with the number of crossings contributed by the additional edges from level $(h-1)$ to the level h nodes of G as well as from level $-(h-1)$ to the level $-h$ nodes of G. Let us first find the number of crossings contributed by the additional edges from level $(h-1)$ nodes to the level h nodes of G. While in the process of including the additional edges, the edges from the top level nodes of G_1 to the top level nodes of G do not contribute to the crossing number. The edges from the top level nodes of G_2 to the top level nodes of G contribute

$$[(3^{h-1}+3^{h-1}-1)+(3^{h-1}+3^{h-1}-2)+...+(3^{h-1}+1)+(3^{h-1}+0)]$$
$$+[(3^{h-1}-1)+(3^{h-1}-2)+...+2+1+0]$$

crossings. Similarly the edges from the top level nodes of G_3 to the top level nodes of G contribute

$$2[(3^{h-1}+3^{h-1}-1)+(3^{h-1}+3^{h-1}-2)+...+(3^{h-1}+1)+(3^{h-1}+0)]$$
$$+2[(3^{h-1}-1)+(3^{h-1}-2)+...+2+1+0]$$

crossings. Also the edges from level $-h$ nodes to level $-(h-1)$ nodes contribute $[(3^{h-1}-1)+(3^{h-1}-2)+...+1+0]+(3^{h-1}-1)\times 3^{h-1}$ crossings.

Hence,

$$cr(D) = cr(G_1)+cr(G_2)+cr(G_3)+7[(3^{h-1}-1)+(3^{h-1}-2)+...+2+1+0]+$$
$$3[3^{h-1}\times 3^{h-1}]+(3^{h-1}-1)3^{h-1}$$
$$\leq 3\times\left\{3^{h-1}+\frac{1}{4}\left[5\cdot 3^{2(h-1)}-(3+2(h-1))3^h\right]\right\}+3^{2h-1}+\frac{9}{2}(3^{h-1}-1)\times 3^{h-1}$$
$$=3^h+\frac{1}{4}\left[5\cdot 3^{2h}-(3+2h)3^{h+1}\right].$$

□

***Conjecture*:** Let G be a generalized fat tree denoted by $GFT(h,m,w)$. Then

$$cr(G) \le \begin{cases} \dfrac{w^h m(m-1)}{4}\left\{ w^{h+2}\dfrac{1-\left(\dfrac{m}{w^2}\right)^h}{w^2-m} - h \right\} & \text{if } m = w \\ \dfrac{w^h m(m-1)}{4}\left\{ w^h h - w\dfrac{1-\left(\dfrac{m}{w}\right)^h}{w-m} \right\} & \text{if } m = w^2 \\ \dfrac{w^{h+1} m(m-1)}{4}\left\{ w^{h+1}\dfrac{1-\left(\dfrac{m}{w^2}\right)^h}{w^2-m} - \dfrac{1-\left(\dfrac{m}{w}\right)^h}{w-m} \right\} & \text{otherwise} \end{cases}$$

where $G=K_{m,w}$ if $h=1$.

4.2 Comparison of Crossing Numbers

The following table gives the number of crossings of the generalized fat tree *GFT*(*h*,3,3) and the new representation *NGFT*(*h*,3,3).

***cr*(*D*)**	***h* = 1**	***h* = 2**	***h* = 3**	***h* = 4**	***h* = 5**
GFT(*h*,3,3)	9	135	1458	14094	130491
NGFT(*h*,3,3)	3	63	756	7614	73386

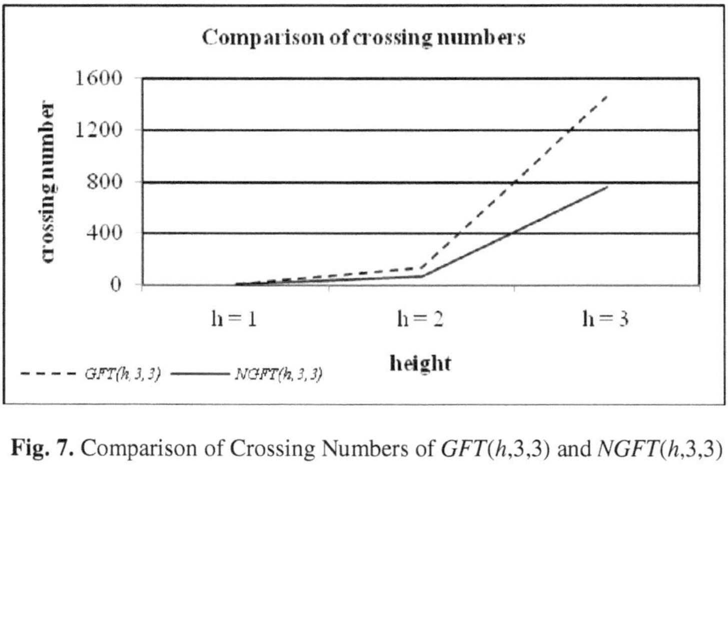

Fig. 7. Comparison of Crossing Numbers of *GFT*(*h*,3,3) and *NGFT*(*h*,3,3)

5 Conclusion

The ratio of the upper bound for the crossing number of the proposed drawing of *GFT*(h,3,3) to that of the original drawing of *GFT*(h,3,3) is 5/9. The proof of the conjecture on $cr(GFT(h,m,w))$ for different values of m and w is under investigation.

References

1. Bhatt, S.N., Leighton, F.T.: A Framework for Solving VLSI Graph Layout Problems. Journal of Computer and System Sciences 28, 300–343 (1984)
2. Cimikowski, R.: Topological Properties of some Interconnection Network Graphs. Congressus Numerantium 121, 19–32 (1996)
3. Cimikowski, R., Vrt'o, I.: Improved Bounds for the Crossing Number of the Mesh of Trees. Journal of Interconnection Networks 4, 17–36 (2003)
4. Exoo, G., Harary, F., Kabell, J.: The Crossing Number of some Generalized Petersen graph. Math. Scand. 48, 184–188 (1981)
5. Garey, M.R., Johnson, D.S.: Crossing Number is NP-complete. SIAM J. Algebraic and Discrete Methods 4, 312–316 (1983)
6. Guy, R.K.: Crossing Numbers of Graphs. Graph Theory and Applications. In: Proceedings of the Conference at Western Michigan University, pp. 111–124. Springer, New York (1972)
7. Leighton, F.T.: Complexity Issues in VLSI. MIT Press, Cambridge (1983)
8. Leighton, F.T.: New Lower Bound Techniques for VLSI. Mathematical Systems Theory 17, 47–70 (1984)
9. Leighton, F.T.: Introduction to Parallel Algorithms and Architectures: Arrays, Trees, Hypercubes. Morgan Kaufmann, San Mateo (1992)
10. Manuel, P., Rajan, B., Rajasingh, I., Beulah, P.V.: On the Bounds for the Crossing Number of Butterfly and Benes Networks (submitted for publication)
11. Nahas, N.H.: On the Crossing Number of $K_{m,n}$. The Electronic Journal of Combinatorics 10 (2003)
12. Ohring, S.R., Ibel, M., Das, S.K., Kumar, M.J.: On Generalized Fat Trees. In: Proceedings of 9th International Parallel Processing Symposium, Santa Barbara, CA, pp. 37–44 (1995)
13. Pan, S., Richter, R.B.: The Crossing Number of K_{11} is 100. Journal of Graph Theory 56, 128–134 (2007)
14. Rajan, B., Rajasingh, I., Beulah, P.V.: On the Crossing Number of Honeycomb Related Networks. Accepted for publication. Journal of Combinatorial Mathematics and Combinatorial Computing (2011)
15. Richter, R.B., Salazar, G.: The Crossing Number of P(N,3). Graphs and Combinatorics 18, 381–394 (2002)
16. Richter, R.B., Thomassen, C.: Relations between Crossing Numbers of Complete and Complete Bipartite Graphs. The American Mathematical Monthly 104, 131–137 (1997)
17. Shahrokhi, F., Sýkora, O., Székely, L.A., Vrt'o, I.: Crossing numbers: Bounds and Applications. J. Bolyai Math. Soc. 31, 179–206 (1997)
18. Sýkora, O., Vrt'o, I.: On Crossing Numbers of Hypercubes and Cube Connected Cycles. BIT Numerical Mathematics 33, 232–237 (1993)
19. Székely, L.A.: A Successful Concept for Measuring Nonplanarity of Graphs: The Crossing Number. Discrete Math. 276, 331–352 (2004)

Relay Node Deployment for a Reliable and Energy Efficient Wireless Sensor Network

Ali Tufail

Division of Information and Computer Engineering,
Ajou University, Suwon, South Korea
alitufail@ajou.ac.kr

Abstract. Wireless sensor networks (WSNs) have been increasingly deployed for ambient data reporting for varied settings. Certain applications like industrial monitoring, healthcare and military require a highly reliable source to the sink communication link. Due to limited energy WSNs pose additional challenge to the reliable source to the sink communication. Fast energy drainage can cause a link failure, hence affecting the overall reliability. In this paper, a novel three tiered multi-hop scheme has been introduced. At first level there are sensor nodes for sensing, at second level there are relay nodes for relaying and at the third level there are gateway nodes for managing the cluster and communicating to and from the cluster. By distributing the load among these three tiered nodes, overall node and network lifetime can be greatly increased. With the help of reduced energy consumption and less end-to-end hops this schemes guarantees a reliable source to the sink communication.

Keywords: WSNs, Relay Node, Reliability, Gateways.

1 Introduction

The technological revolution and the advancement in the field of communication technologies have paved the way for the large scale production of low-priced sensor nodes. These sensor nodes are not only simple and cost effective but also have the capability of sensing, computing and communicating. A typical WSN comprises of a large number of low powered, low cost, memory/computationally-constrained, intelligent sensor devices. These sensors are generally involved in detecting and measuring some target phenomena.

Due to its intrinsic energy, footprint and deployment limitations, a WSN is prone to errors and malfunctioning. These errors can be due to hardware/software failures or energy exhaustion. In antagonistic deployments, the errors may be caused by natural or human adversaries, e.g., natural disasters in calamity-struck regions or radio jamming in a battlefield [1]. Despite WSN's fault-prone characteristics, mission-critical natures of emerging WSN applications (e.g., military, healthcare, industrial monitoring, target tracking, smart homes, habitat monitoring etc [2], [3]) require that communication to/from sensors is dependable and reliable. The source to sink

A. Abd Manaf et al. (Eds.): ICIEIS 2011, Part III, CCIS 253, pp. 449–457, 2011.

communication in WSNs is generally dependent on the intermediate relaying sensor nodes. Therefore the reliability of a transmission is dependent on the topology, energy efficiency and routing techniques being deployed in the WSN.

In the end-to-end communication a sensor node deployed in the field typically senses the environment and sends the reading back to the sink node via a gateway or a relaying node. As these sensor nodes have limited energy supply, therefore all the operations should be low powered so that minimum amount of energy is consumed and the network lifetime is enhanced. Usually, all the multi-hop routing schemes have to be designed with a focus on energy efficiency. Energy efficiency and reliability are interdependent. If a WSN is designed to give high reliability then it must make sure that the energy consumption by nodes is kept to its low and the load on the nodes is balanced. In a multi-hop network even if a single link failure is found it can lead to a very low reliability. Link failure is likely to be caused by a dead node.

This paper, suggests a scheme that not only enhances the reliability but also the overall energy efficiency of the WSN. Minimum number of hops from source to the sink is guaranteed under the suggested scheme. A WSN typically contains multiple resourceful gateway nodes that provide load balancing, local cluster management and energy saving [4], [5]. Gateway nodes (GNs) are connected using a high speed link like hotlines [6]. However, just a high speed and a reliable link between GNs does not ensure the high reliability from the source to the sink. Moreover, usually the sensor nodes in a cluster can reach the cluster head i.e. the GN in multiple hops. All these added wireless hops add a likelihood of failure hence reduces the overall reliability. Therefore, the suggested scheme in this paper adds a special category of the WSN nodes called the relay nodes (RNs). RNs are usually more resourceful as compared to the normal sensor nodes and they are deployed just for the purpose of relaying and not of sensing. This paper suggests deploying RNs in a cluster under the GNs. These RNs will not only share the burden of the GNs but also would serve to provide a means of making the overall network energy efficient. The effect of this would automatically enhance the overall reliability of the network. Moreover, RNs help the normal sensor nodes (NSNs) do less work by taking the relaying part of those nodes away. Instead of relaying and sensing NSNs would just be involved in sensing. It will help to preserve the energy even further. The number of hops for the source to sink communication can be reduced greatly. The suggested scheme reduces the source to sink communication to a minimum of 3 hops.

The rest of the paper is organized as follows. Section 2 describes related work. Section 3 discuses our network model and assumptions. Section 4 introduces the proposed reliable and energy efficient scheme. Section 5 summarizes key conclusions of this work.

2 Related Work

In [7] authors suggest deploying relay nodes for WSNs. However, their deployment is just focused on tunnel applications. Moreover, they do not address reliability issue directly. Similarly, [8], [9] suggest using relay nodes in WSNs but a) they talk about it from an application point of view b) multi-tier communication structure has not been explored c) reliability has not been addressed directly.

[10] talks about a delay aware reliable transport (DART) protocol. Authors focus on timely event detection with a focus on congestion and energy efficiency. Quite recently an effort has been made to enhance the reliability of WSN using emergency routing paths [11]. Authors in [11] presents an AODV based routing protocol that uses multipath algorithm to increase the reliability in a sensor network. However, their routing protocol fails to provide reliable packet delivery for a network having high degree of failed or sleeping nodes. Authors in [12] try to improve the reliability and availability of WSNs by proposing a data forwarding algorithm. However, they just focus on low duty cycle WSNs and they have not presented any good comparison of their approach with other existing reliable routing approaches for WSNs.

In [13], authors formulate a WSN reliability measure that considers the aggregate flow of sensor data into a sink node. This measure is based on a given estimation of the data generation rate and the failure probability of each sensor. Common cause failures (CCF) have been discussed and identified as the cause of unreliability in WSN in [14], [15]. Authors in [14] consider the problem of modeling and evaluating the coverage-oriented reliability of WSN subject to CCF whereas in [15] the main emphasis is on addressing the problem of modeling and evaluating the infrastructure communication reliability of WSN. Authors in [16] present a reliable routing protocol that forms the reliable routing path by utilizing network topology and routing information of the network. However, their protocol and analysis is application specific. Moreover, they have not provided any comparison with existing reliability schemes.

3 Network Model

In this paper we consider a WSN with three-level heterogeneity. At the first level, we have resource-constrained sensor nodes (NSNs) which are deployed densely on a two-dimensional grid. NSNs have the same resources and are just deployed for sensing the required object. They do not perform any relaying. NSNs communicate directly to the second level nodes. At the second level we have relay nodes (RNs) which are bit more resourceful than the first level sensor nodes. RNs just do the relaying and are not involved in any kind of sensing.

Density of the RNs is much less than those of the NSNs. RNs communicate to the first level and the third level nodes. We assume that the RNs are deployed manually. At the third level, we have sensor gateway nodes (GN) that operate as cluster heads to regulate the flow of traffic and to manage sensor motes (including NSNs and RNs) deployed in the given geographical region. The GNs are not resource-constrained and their density is many orders of magnitude lesser than the density of the NSNs and the RNs. GNs are connected to each other in a bus topology via highly reliable links e.g., Ethernet cables or point-to-point wireless links. GNs report directly to the command or the sink node (SN) or the command node. The communication from source to destination is multi-hop and it usually involves GNs and RNs. We assume that the sink node passes its query, like sensing a particular object in a particular area, to the particular GN. GN in turn passes on the query to the concerned RN. The query is then finally passed on the NSNs in the particular area. The report or the reading then travels back to the SN in the reverse order. The source to sink communication is typically completed in three hops. We assume a fixed network topology where GNs, RNs and the NSNs are static. We further assume that all the nodes have to ability to switch on/off their transmitter and receivers.

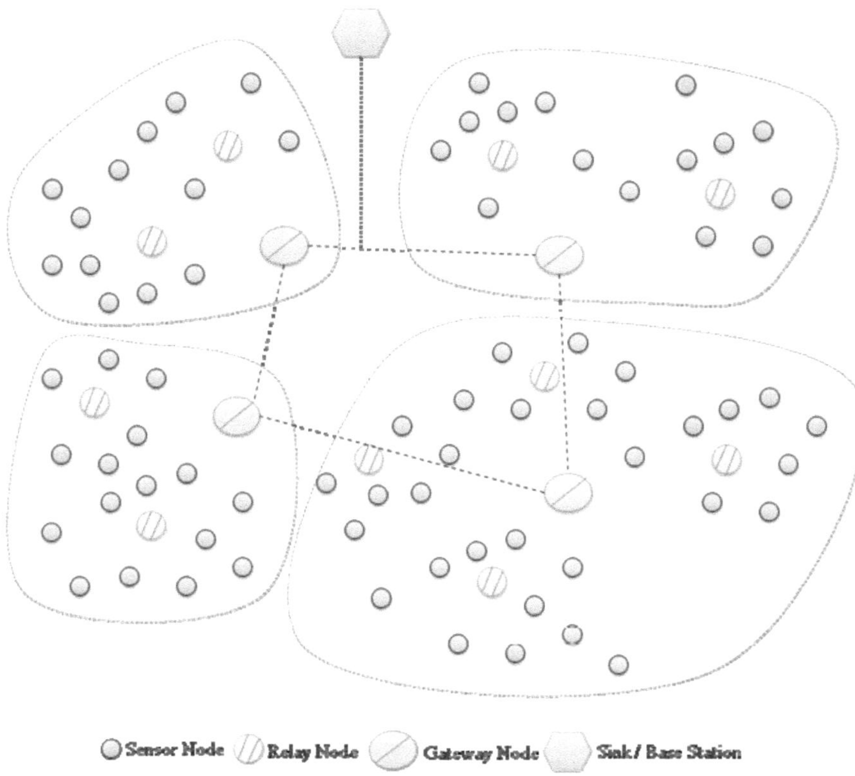

Fig. 1. Network Model

4 Overview of the Scheme

In this section, we introduce the basic concepts of the proposed scheme. Fig. 2 shows the GNs, RNs, and the NSNs along with their respective communication ranges. The communication range of the GNs is more than that of the RNs and the NSNs. Similarly, the communication range of RNs is more than that of the NSNs. NSNs are energy constrained and in order to enhance the lifetime of the network and decrease the overall energy consumption of the network, NSNs are configured in a way that the communication range is sufficient enough to reach the associated RN. Moreover, NSNs are just involved in the sensing and not relaying so it further helps to preserve energy. As shown in the Fig. 2 there can be a scenario where the RN is not in range of any of the GNs but it is in the range of any of the RNs. Then this out of range RN will get associated to that RN and will become part of the same cluster. Please note that in this case the NSNs would be three hops away from the GN instead of being two hops away as in other cases.

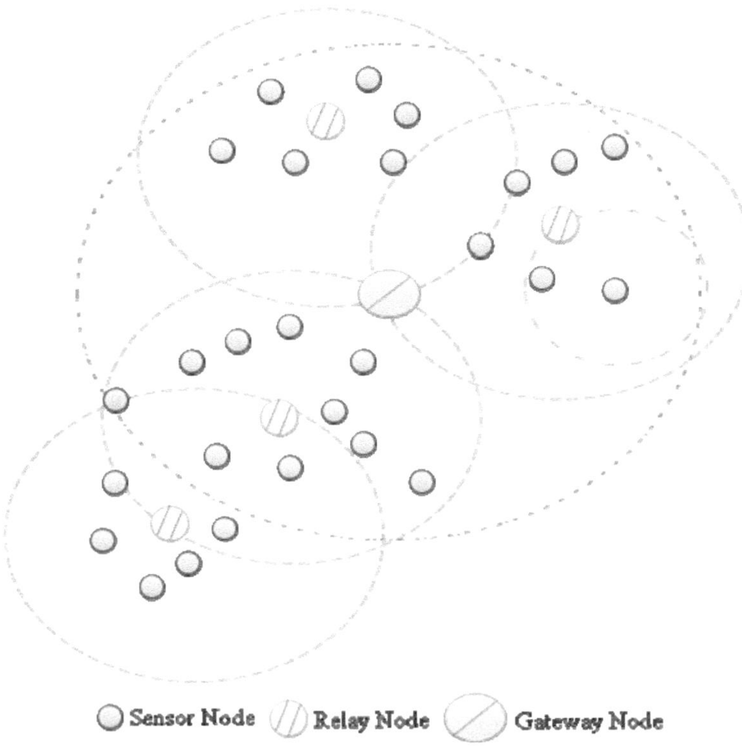

Fig. 2. Communication range of the gateway nodes (GNs), relay nodes (RNs) and the sensor nodes (NSNs)

4.1 Gateway Node Deployment and Association

Gateway nodes act as the cluster head and serve to manage the cluster. GNs are connected to each other and to the SN. The connection is very high speed and constitutes of a single hop [6]. In a single cluster there is only one GN but there can be multiple RNs and hundreds of the NSNs. GNs are deployed optimally so that they can balance the load of the network.

The overall association process and cluster formation process is defined in the Fig. 3. GN association is done with the help of the router advertisement message [6]. The first step in association involves all the RN association to the closest GN. Once the RN gets the router advertisement message, they check the hop count. RN joins only that GN which is just single hop away. If there are more than one GNs with a single hop then there can be other factors involved in decision making like minimum delay, strength of the communication signal etc. Once the RN chooses it's desired GN it will send a confirmation request to the GN to become part of that cluster. It will conclude this phase of the association.

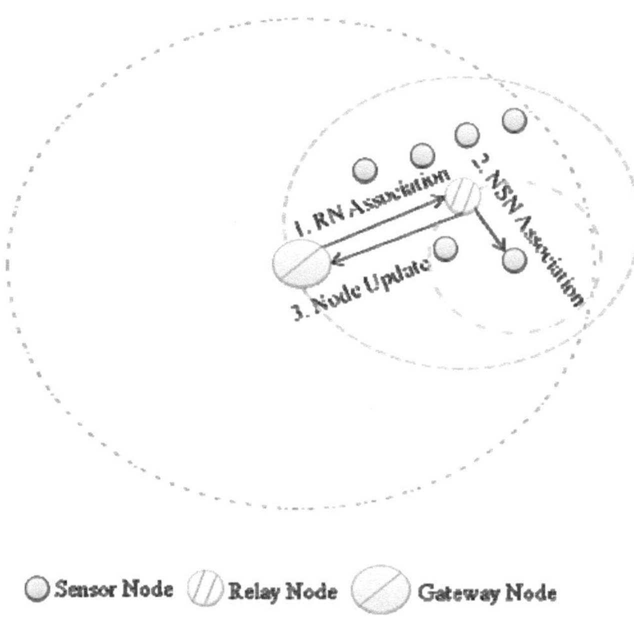

Fig. 3. The process of node association

4.2 Relay Node Deployment and Association

As mentioned before, RNs are deployed manually in order to make sure that they optimally cover the maximum area of the WSN. It means that the number and place of the RNs are pre-determined.

RNs are supposed to be a part of one of the clusters. They become part of the cluster by associating with any of the GNs. This process has been defined in the previous section. After becoming the part of a cluster, the next step is of making other sensor nodes part of the same cluster. RNs now send their own advertisement message to its neighboring NSNs. NSNs get the message and decide to join the closest RN in terms of hop count. This process is highlighted in the Fig. 3. Once the RN accepts the NSN it then reports the GN. The GN updates the list of the NSNs that are part of its cluster. This step concludes the overall association mechanism. The first part of the step was the RN association with the GN and the second part was the NSN association with the RN. Finally, the cluster list update process at the GN concludes this phase.

4.3 End-to-End Communication

A typical WSN works by sensing some reading or collecting some target information at a particular geographical area and then sending it back to the base station. This sensing is triggered by the query or the command from the base station, at first place. As mentioned before, there are several applications that require reliable end-to-end communication. Reliability can be enhanced by providing better or high speed links between several hops from source to destination [6]. However, as the sensor nodes are energy constrained and if energy of any of the node is depleted it will break the path and hence will reduce the reliability literally to zero. It means only high speed or better links cannot guarantee a high degree of reliability but there should a balanced consumption of energy throughout the network. Therefore, in order to enhance the reliability at the same time making the network energy efficient this paper introduce the use of RNs along with the GNs. RNs will not only share the burden of the GNs but also would serve to provide a means of making the overall network energy efficient. The effect of this would automatically enhance the overall reliability of the network.

The suggested scheme reduces the number of hops from source to the destination. SN requests a reading by sending the request to the GN, which is just one hop away from the SN, the request is then forwarded to the concerned RN, which is again just a hop away, the RN in turn forwards the request to the concerned NSN or couple of NSNs, which are just one hop away. The defined overall communication will reduce the source to sink hops and will help to make the communication more reliable.

Fig. 4 shows the overall communication phase. Please note that the Fig. highlights two different source nodes. The source node on the top right corner is just two hops away from the GN and the source node shown at the bottom left corner is three hops away from the GN. Although, this source node is part of the same cluster but because it's associated RN is not in the communication range of the GN so this RN is

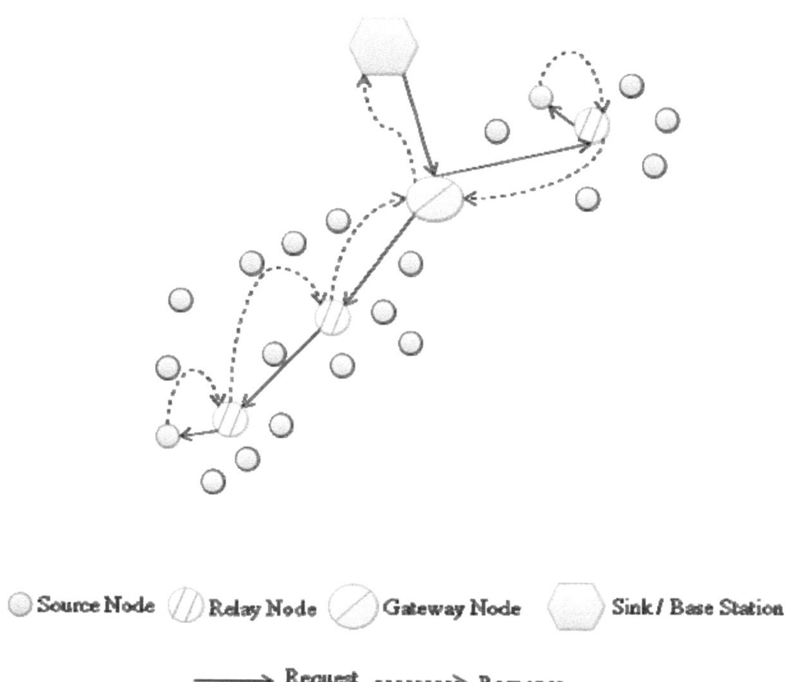

Fig. 4. Source to the sink communication

associated to the other RN instead of being associated to the GN directly. Therefore, one additional hop is added from source to the destination. Fig. 4 shows two types of messages, one is the request message initiated by the SN and other is the response message initiated by the source node or NSN as a response to the request.

5 Conclusion

This paper discuses the issue of reliability and energy efficiency pertaining to WSNs. It has been deliberated that gateway nodes can help to serve the reliability of WSNs. The paper shows that the addition of relay nodes and by their appropriate positioning in the WSN clusters not only reduces the load on the gateway nodes but also reduces the energy consumption of the sensing nodes manifolds. Furthermore, the suggested scheme reduces the number of end-to-end hops from the source to the destination. Therefore, it can be claimed that the source to the destination reliability has been increased by guaranteeing a stable and less prone to failure path. With the help of the novel three tiered multi-hop scheme the source to the sink hops have been reduced to a minimum of 3.

References

1. Abdelsalam, H.S., Rizvi, S.R.: Energy efficient workforce selection in special-purpose wireless sensor networks. In: IEEE INFOCOM Workshops, pp. 1–4 (2008)
2. Fiorenzo, F., Maurizio, G., Domenico, M., Luca, M.: A Review of Localization Algorithms for Distributed Wireless Sensor Networks in Manufacturing. International Journal of Computer Integrated Manufacturing 22, 698–716 (2009)
3. Wang, Y.C., Hsieh, Y.Y., Tseng, Y.C.: Multiresolution Spatial and Temporal Coding in a Wireless Sensor Network for Long-Term Monitoring Applications. IEEE Transaction on Computers 58, 827–838 (2009)
4. Youssef, W., Younis, M.: Intelligent Gateways Placement for Reduced Data Latency in Wireless Sensor Networks. In: IEEE International Conference on Communications (ICC), pp. 3805–3810 (2007)
5. Chor, P.L., Can, F., Jim, M., Yew, H.A.: Load-balanced clustering algorithms for wireless sensor networks. In: IEEE International Conference on Communications, ICC (2007)
6. Tufail, A., Khayam, S.A., Raza, M.T., Ali, A., Kim, K.H.: An Enhanced Backbone-Assisted Reliable Framework for Wireless Sensor Networks. Sensors 3, 1619–1651 (2010)
7. Ruoshui, L., Ian, J.W., Kenichi, S.: Relay Node Placement for Wireless Sensor Networks Deployed in Tunnels. In: IEEE International Conference on Wireless and Mobile Computing, Networking Communications (2010)
8. Feng, W., Dan, W., Jiangchuan, L.: Traffic-Aware Relay Node Deployment for Data Collection in Wireless Sensor Networks. In: SECON (2009)
9. Ergen, S.C., Varaiya, P.: Optimal Placement of Relay Nodes for Energy Efficiency in Sensor Networks. In: IEEE International Conference on Communication, ICC, pp. 3473–3479 (2006)
10. Vehbi, C.G., Akan, O.B.: Delay aware reliable transport in wireless sensor networks. Int. J. Commun. Syst. 20, 1155–1177 (2007)

11. Mainaud, B., Zekri, M., Afifi, H.: Improving routing reliability on wireless sensors network with emergency paths. In: Distributed Computing Systems Workshops, pp. 545–550 (2008)
12. Suhonen, J., Hämäläinen, T.D., Hännikäinen, M.: Availability and End-to-end Reliability in Low Duty Cycle MultihopWireless Sensor Networks. Sensors 9, 2088–2116 (2009)
13. AboElFotoh, H.M.F., ElMallah, E.S., Hassanein, H.S.: On the Reliability of Wireless Sensor Networks. In: IEEE International Conference on Communications, ICC (2006)
14. Shrestha, A., Liudong, X., Hong, L.: Modeling and Evaluating the Reliability of Wireless Sensor Networks. In: Reliability and Maintainability Symposium (2007)
15. Shrestha, A., Liudong, X., Hong, L.: Infrastructure Communication Reliability of Wireless Sensor Networks. In: IEEE International Symposium on Dependable, Autonomic and Secure Computing (2006)
16. Dong, J., Qianping, W., Yan, Z., Ke, W.: The Research and Design of High Reliability Routing Protocol of Wireless Sensor Network in Coal Mine. In: International Conference on Networks Security, Wireless Communications and Trusted Computing, NSWCTC 2009, vol. 1, pp. 568–571 (2009)

Precise Multimodal Localization with Smart Phones

E. Martin and R. Bajcsy

EECS Dept., University of California, Berkeley
emartin@eecs.berkeley.edu

Abstract. In this paper we propose the integration of computer vision with accelerometry and the magnetometer and radios available in current state-of-the-art smart phones, in order to provide a precise localization solution feasible for indoor environments. In terms of accelerometry, we apply the wavelet transform to the signal of a single off-the-shelf accelerometer on the waist to obtain the velocity and stride length of the user. This allows us to link accelerometry and computer vision through the kinetic energy of the user. Additionally, our system leverages the capabilities of current state-of-the-art smart phones to integrate both offline and online phases of radio fingerprinting with WiFi, achieving an accuracy of 1.5 meters. We have also studied the possibilities offered by the cellular communications radio, with the intention to build a multimodal solution for localization, delivering an accuracy of up to 0.5 meters when all the information is combined with a Kalman filter.

Keywords: Localization, wireless networks, multimode.

1 Introduction

Context awareness is a key factor for multiple applications, and location is a fundamental parameter to consider. The research community is focusing on multimodal systems for localization, since the combination of different technologies increases the robustness and accuracy of the solution. Most of the recently proposed applications requiring location information in smart phones make use of the embedded GPS radio and accelerometers [1]. However, GPS is only reliable in certain outdoor environments with direct visibility to the satellites, and the existing approaches to leverage off-the-shelf accelerometers (like those embedded in current state-of-the-art smart phones) fail to deliver precise information for localization. Consequently, there is a need to optimize the existing technologies already embedded in smart phones (e.g. accelerometer, magnetometer, camera, and different radios) or commonly available in buildings (e.g. WiFi access points, surveillance cameras) to develop a precise multimodal localization solution feasible for indoor environments. In this article, we propose the fusion of computer vision, accelerometry, magnetometry and the radios embedded within smart phones to obtain precise location information. In particular, we use a new approach to process acceleration signals and precisely obtain the velocity and stride length of the user, which allows us to link this technology with computer vision through the kinetic energy of the user. Using a Kalman filter to combine all these data with information from the radios embedded in smart phones, we can obtain a localization accuracy of up to 0.5 meters.

A. Abd Manaf et al. (Eds.): ICIEIS 2011, Part III, CCIS 253, pp. 458–472, 2011.

To the best of our knowledge, our application represents the first approach for indoor localization fusing precise kinematic information obtained from a single off-the-shelf accelerometer (like those in current state-of-the-art smart phones) with computer vision and radio fingerprinting, integrating both online and offline phases of fingerprinting within the same device. In Section 2 we summarize the related work in this area, while in Section 3, technical details about our solution are presented, gathering the conclusions in Section 4.

2 Related Work

In this Section we present the state of the art in the estimation of kinematic parameters by means of accelerometry, we summarize related work on the integration of computer vision with accelerometers for localization, and we review existing research on radio-localization through fingerprinting, focusing on its implementation on smart phones.

2.1 Related Work in the Estimation of Kinematic Parameters through Accelerometry

The knowledge of the kinematics of a person can be successfully applied for localization. Since acceleration, velocity and displacement are physical magnitudes linked through integration, the calculation of stride length (displacement) represents the biggest challenge in this field. Consequently, next we will review the state of the art in stride length estimation by means of accelerometry. Throughout the existing literature, we have found six main methods leveraging accelerometers for the estimation of stride length in straight line walking [2]-[4]:

1) *Double integration of acceleration data:* it can suffer from low accuracies due to the drift increasing over time, together with the fact that acceleration values obtained from commercial accelerometers are very noisy (especially for low accelerations). A solution to overcome the drift consists on restarting the integration for each step, taking into account that velocity is zero at each footfall [5]. Nevertheless, the main drawback of this method is the need for very precise and expensive hardware (accelerometers and gyroscopes), careful calibration and extensive computation.

2) The modeling of human gait through the *Weiberg algorithm* [4], assumes that the stride length is proportional to the vertical displacement of the hip at every step. These methods employ empirical expressions to estimate the stride length:

$$SL = K \times \sqrt[4]{a_{\max} - a_{\min}} \tag{1}$$

Where a_{max} and a_{min} represent the maximum and minimum values of the acceleration within each stride, and K is a constant that depends on the individual and needs to be calibrated experimentally [2], which represents a disadvantage.

Building on this algorithm, and through the consideration of human gait as an inverted pendulum model, the relationship between the vertical displacements of the center of mass of the human body at each step (*h*) and the stride length (*SL*) can be expressed by empirical expressions (again requiring individual calibration) [3]:

$$SL = 2K\sqrt{2hl - h^2} \tag{2}$$

Where *l* represents the length of the individual's leg, and *K* is a constant to be calibrated for each individual. The main drawback of this method is the need for a double integration of the vertical acceleration of the center of mass in order to obtain *h*, which is prone to drift errors, therefore requiring very expensive hardware to deliver accurate results.

3) As an *extension of the inverted pendulum model* explained before, the third model focuses on the elimination of drift through a very precise double integration of accelerations, assuming that at the time of foot-flat, the velocity is zero and the vertical coordinate of the center of mass equals that at the start of the step [3].

4) Building on the two previous approaches and assuming a more complex model, the fourth method considers the vertical displacement of the center of mass through double integration of the acceleration and ruled by two pendulums: first, an inverted pendulum with the leg's length during the swing phase, and a second pendulum, during the double-stance phase of the step. Again, the complexity of this methodology represents its main drawback.

5) The fifth method develops an empirical relationship between the first harmonic (low pass filter at 3 Hz) of the vertical acceleration of the center of mass of the human body, the stride length and the step count, but it requires individual calibration and can suffer from important errors.

6) The sixth method focuses on the development of an empirical linear relationship between the length and the frequency of the steps, claiming a good correlation (> 0.6) between both terms [7]. However, the accuracy of this approach can be seriously jeopardized by different gait patterns.

Comparing the methods described above, the double integration with zero-velocity-update approach delivers the best accuracy (errors close to 5%) [4]. However, its complexity and hardware requirements (several expensive accelerometers and gyroscopes are needed) represent important drawbacks. Consequently, in order to minimize hardware requirements, in Section 3 we propose a new approach to precisely estimate kinematic parameters (based on a single off-the-shelf accelerometer) feasible for lightweight systems.

2.2 Related Work in the Integration of Computer Vision with Accelerometry

In order to correct the drift inherent to Inertial Navigation Systems (INS), computer vision has been suggested as a potential complementary solution. Commonly, observation equations are developed to relate the computer vision measurements with the INS data by means of a Kalman filter [8]. It is important to note that there is a trade-off between localization and identification when employing computer vision, since localization usually needs to cover a wide area, which demands low resolution from the camera, while identification requires high resolution. Background subtraction and silhouette information are often used for localization in many computer vision applications [9, 10]. As a recent example, the research work on person localization using multiple cameras described in [11] employs background modeling and foreground subtraction to determine the person region in each image, and by means of the corresponding homography, a set of projected foreground pixels is obtained. The authors model the localization of the person as an optimization problem subject to geometric constraints. In particular, given the observations, the objective is to maximize the posterior probability distribution representing the location.

Identification of a tracked object is also a difficult task. The integration of computer vision and accelerometry data can assist in this challenge. In this sense, several researchers have used the correlation between accelerometry and visual tracking signals for identification [12, 13]. As a recent research work on identification, reference [14] employs the Normalized Cross-Correlation of the signal vector magnitude (to avoid dependency on the coordinate system) of the signals from the accelerometer and the camera. Likewise, reference [15] combines computer vision and accelerometers for identification and localization, modeling the measurements from both the accelerometer and the camera by means of kinematics. In particular, for the accelerometer data, the authors assume the velocity of the center of mass of the human body to be proportional to the standard deviation of the vertical acceleration, proposing a linear relationship between both terms with a set of parameters that require calibration; however, this approach suffers from errors due to inconsistent orientation of the measuring device with respect to gravity when the person moves. For the computer vision signal, the authors in [15] compute the velocity of the center of mass of the human body leveraging the displacement of the centroid of the silhouette detected by the camera:

$$V_{COM} = \frac{\sqrt{(x_k - x_{k-1})^2 + (y_k - y_{k-1})^2}}{\Delta t} \tag{3}$$

Where (x_k, y_k) represent the image coordinates of the silhouette centroid (considered a very good estimate of the person's center of mass) at the kth frame, and Δt represents the time between frames. The authors use the correlation coefficient of the two velocities to quantify their similarity. Within the same field, reference [16] describes a multimode approach for people identification combining computer vision and body-worn accelerometers due to the difficulty of obtaining step lengths leveraging only accelerometer data and the fact that the stepping period by itself is not sufficient to disambiguate people. Assuming that people walk with a movement transversal to the camera, and that cameras and accelerometers are synchronized to a few milliseconds, the authors use the Pearson coefficient $\rho(A,B)$ to determine signal similarity [16]:

$$\rho(A,B) = \frac{1}{N-1} \frac{\sum_{k=1}^{N} (a_k - \bar{a})(b_k - \bar{b})}{\sigma_a \sigma_b} \tag{4}$$

Where A= $(a_1,\ldots,a_N)$ and B= $(b_1,\ldots,b_N)$ represent the time series of uniformly sampled data from both sensors (cameras and accelerometers must be sampled at the same rate or interpolated). The authors conclude that the correlation between time series of accelerations can work as an effective indicator to determine whether both accelerations originated from the same subject. Nevertheless, this method assumes frequent changes in acceleration. Additionally, the Pearson coefficient requires a large number of samples to converge, which translates into processing delays. Moreover, increases in the standard deviation of the signal noise and decreases in the sampling rate increase the delay, which can render this approach unfeasible.

Other models for identification and localization integrating accelerometry and computer vision (e.g. working independently at separate time slots, or prioritizing computer vision and relying on INS when the cameras fail to deliver information) are described in [17] and references therein. In this sense, recent examples include navigation systems integrating cameras, gyroscopes and accelerometers, combining the data with an extended Kalman filter [18], an unscented Kalman filter [19], or the employment of Bayesian segmentation to detect a moving person (with "Mixtures of Gaussians" for background modeling), and a particle filter to track the person in the scene [20].

2.3 State of the Art in Radio Fingerprinting

Radio Signal Strength Indications (RSSI) can be translated into distances from beacon points by means of theoretical or empirical radio propagation models. The two main approaches for the estimation of location making use of RSSI values are: 1) "fingerprinting", where a pre-recorded radio map of the area of interest is leveraged to infer locations through best matching, and 2) "propagation based", in which RSSI values are used to calculate distances through the computation of the path loss. "Propagation based" techniques can face errors of up to 50% [21] due to multipath, non line-of-sight conditions, interferences and other shadowing effects, rendering this technique unreliable and inaccurate, especially for indoor environments, where multipath is very important. Several authors have tried to improve the efficiency of this technique for indoor environments, introducing new factors in the path loss model to account for wall attenuation, multipath or noise [22], but the hardware and software requirements due to the complexity of the method and the overall poor accuracy achieved makes this approach unfeasible for current state of the art smart phones. On the other hand, fingerprinting techniques have already proved to be able to deliver better accuracies [23]. In these techniques, the mobile terminal estimates its location through best matching between the measured radio signals and those corresponding to locations previously registered in the radio map. This process consists of two stages:

1) Training phase, also called offline phase, in which a radio map of the area in study is built.
2) Online phase, in which the mobile terminal infers its location through best matching between the radio signals being received and those previously recorded in the radio map.

Considering GSM as an example for cellular communications technology, although it makes use of power control both at the mobile terminal and base station, the data on the Broadcast Control Channel (BCCH) is transmitted at full and constant power, making this channel suitable for fingerprinting. Several authors have tried this approach for localization, but with the need of dedicated and complex hardware.

Regarding WiFi technology, several research groups have already tried to leverage RSSI fingerprinting for localization:

- Radar [24]: represents the first fingerprinting system achieving the localization of portable devices, with accuracies of 2 to 3 meters.
- Horus [25]: based on the Radar system, it manages a performance improvement making use of probabilistic analysis.
- Compass [26]: applies probabilistic methods and leverages object orientation to improve precision, claiming errors below 1.65 meters.
- Ekahau [27]: commercial solution using 802.11 b/g networks, achieving precisions from 1 to 3 meters in normal conditions.

Nevertheless, all the existing approaches use dedicated and complex hardware, making them unfeasible for direct implementation in current state of the art smart phones.

Besides cellular communications and WiFi technologies, the RSSI fingerprinting technique for localization can be utilized with other radiofrequency technologies including:

- Bluetooth, which despite the extra infrastructure requirements in comparison with WiFi, it can achieve accuracies in the range of 1.2 meters.
- Conventional radio, can also be used for localization. However, the requirement of dedicated hardware and the fact that devices can be located only down to a suburb, represent important drawbacks.
- Digital TV signals have also proved to be suitable for localization, but subject to dedicated hardware requirements and low resolutions.
- Zigbee technology can also be applied for localization through fingerprinting [28], achieving accuracies of approximately 2 meters. However, this technology also requires extra hardware for a correct implementation, constituting a major drawback.

3 Technical Details of Our Multimodal Approach

In this paper we propose the integration of computer vision with accelerometry and the magnetometer and radios available in current state-of-the-art smart phones for localization. In particular, we use a new approach to process acceleration signals and precisely obtain the velocity and stride length of the user, which allows us to link this technology with computer vision through the kinetic energy of the user. We have also studied the possibilities offered by the WiFi and cellular communications radios embedded in smart phones. Next we will summarize the technical details of each component in our system, summarizing the results from the integration of the different modalities with a Kalman filter at the end of this Section.

3.1 Proposed Approach to Estimate Kinematic Parameters from Accelerometry

In this Section we describe our approach to use a single accelerometer placed on the waist to obtain the velocity and stride length of the person wearing it. Our methodology is based on the application of the wavelet transform to the acceleration signal, and it is feasible for implementation in lightweight systems including current state-of-the-art smart phones (using filters).

To test our approach, we took measurements for 9 different types of walking, classified according to 3 different speeds (fast, medium and slow) and 3 different stride lengths (long, normal and short). A total of 14 individuals participated in the tests (males and females with ages ranging from 21 to 77). We employed a Shimmer accelerometer on the waist with a sampling frequency of 30 Hz, analyzing the signal with the wavelet transform.

Reviewing the wavelet transform decomposition of a signal *x(t)* into approximation $a_j(k)$ and detail $d_j(k)$ coefficients [29]:

$$a_j(k) = \int x(t)\varphi_{j,k}(t)dt \tag{5}$$

$$d_j(k) = \int x(t)\psi_{j,k}^{*}(t)dt \tag{6}$$

Where $\varphi_{j,k}(t)$ represents the scaling function and $\psi_{j,k}(t)$ the wavelet function, it can be seen that we are integrating the signal *x(t)*, which in our case represents the acceleration from the human body center of mass (near the waist), weighted by the $\varphi_{j,k}(t)$ and $\psi_{j,k}(t)$ functions. Consequently, we are integrating weighted accelerations, therefore obtaining weighted velocities. Further analyzing the relationship between the energies of the detail coefficients and the kinetic energy of the walking patterns, we can actually infer the speed of the person, with the following expressions:

$$Speed|_1 = \frac{1}{2}\sqrt{WE_{d_1} + \frac{WE_{d_2}}{2} + \frac{WE_{d_3}}{3} + \frac{WE_{d_4}}{4} + \frac{WE_{d_5}}{5}} \tag{7}$$

$$Speed|_2 = \frac{1}{2}\sqrt{\frac{WE_{d_2}}{2} + \frac{WE_{d_3}}{3} + \frac{WE_{d_4}}{4} + \frac{WE_{d_5}}{5}} \tag{8}$$

$$Speed|_3 = \frac{1}{2}\sqrt{WE_{d_1} + \frac{WE_{d_2}}{2} + \frac{WE_{d_3}}{3} + \frac{WE_{d_4}}{4} + \frac{WE_{d_5}}{5} + WE_{d_6}} \tag{9}$$

$$Speed|_4 = \frac{1}{2}\sqrt{\frac{WE_{d_2}}{2} + \frac{WE_{d_3}}{3} + \frac{WE_{d_4}}{4} + \frac{WE_{d_5}}{5} + WE_{d_6}} \tag{10}$$

In which we include a new metric that we call "Weighted Energy":

$$WE_{d_i} = \begin{cases} \dfrac{\sum d_i^2}{n_0\sqrt{2}(J-i)} & i = 1..J-1 \\[2ex] \dfrac{\sum d_i^2}{n_0\sqrt{2}} & i = J \end{cases} \tag{11}$$

Where *J* represents the number of levels of decomposition we are using in the wavelet transform, *i* accounts for the specific level we are considering, d_i symbolizes the detail coefficients at level i, and n_0 represent the number of coefficients considered. The differences between (8) to (11) are based on the consideration of the wavelet transform detail coefficients at levels 1 and 6, which account for the trade-off between accuracy and computational costs of the results.

Taking into account that the step frequency can be easily extracted as the inverse of the time elapsed between two consecutive negative-to-positive transitions in the waist acceleration signal filtered through the wavelet transform (example in Figure 1), the step length can be calculated leveraging its relationship with the strep frequency and the speed:

$$Speed = Step\_Length \cdot Step\_frequency \tag{12}$$

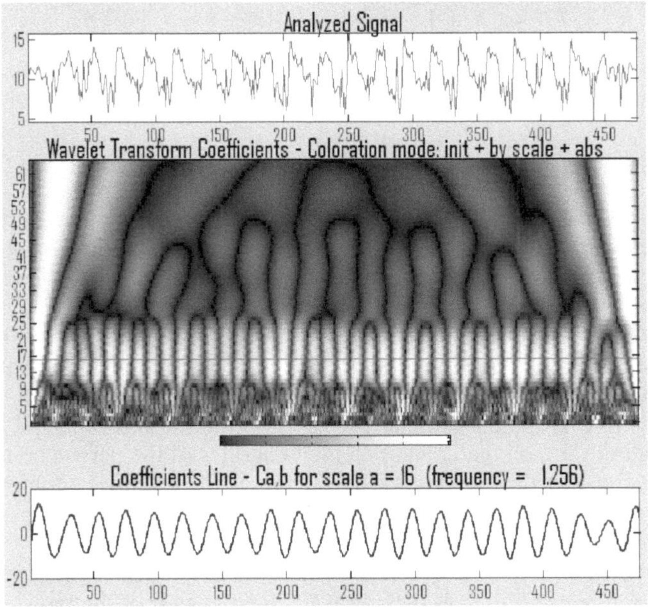

Fig. 1. Application of the wavelet transform to the waist acceleration signal (upper plot), delivering a smooth oscillation (lower plot) from which the step frequency can be easily obtained (from the number of negative-to-positive transitions)

A graphical comparison between actual velocities and the results obtained with our new methodology can be observed in Figure 2, showing that the performance of an adaptive optimum approach is excellent, with average errors below 5%.

This accuracy is comparable to that obtained with the most sophisticated and expensive methods, but our results are achieved with significantly lower hardware requirements, since a single accelerometer on the waist is enough to obtain the step frequency, step length and velocity.

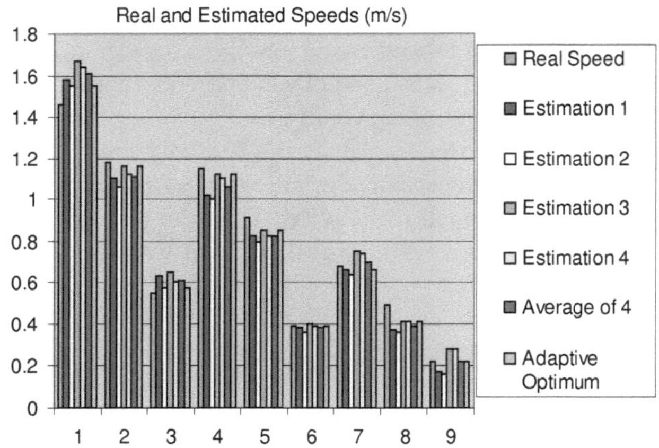

Fig. 2. Graphical comparison between actual speeds and the estimations obtained through our proposed equations, for 9 different walking patterns (from 1 to 9 over the horizontal axis)

3.2 Linking Computer Vision with Accelerometry through Kinetic Energy

Already deployed surveillance cameras or even the cameras from smart phones can be used for localization cooperating with different technologies in a multimodal approach. For our tests, we used video from different cameras (including from Motorola Droid and HTC G1 smart phones), with different formats, ranging from 5 to 49 frames per second and resolutions of 352x288, 640x240 and 720x480 pixels. With the camera data, we employ segmentation of local regions of motion in the motion history image, using the gradients within these regions to compute their motion. Additionally, we leverage the number of pixels within the movement silhouettes as a metric accounting for the kinetic and potential energies of the person being tracked. In particular, we consider the location of the camera as the origin of coordinates, and we use the distance between the tracked person and the camera as the parameter to account for his/her potential energy.

Figure 3 shows an example of the evolution of movement silhouettes, where we represent the number of points in their ROI by the diameter of the blue circle tracking the person.

The diameter of the blue tracking circle in Figure 3 is proportional to: 1) the velocity (kinetic energy) of the person in the video frames and 2) the volume of the silhouettes, which depends mainly on the distance (potential energy) between the person and the camera (assuming average size people).

Taking into account that the center of the blue tracking circle represents the center of mass of the movement silhouettes, and we use the distance from this point to the camera as the parameter to obtain the potential energy of the person, we can isolate this potential energy (in terms of distance to the camera) if we know the velocity of the person. And this parameter (velocity) is precisely obtained from the accelerometer on the waist through the application of the wavelet transform, as previously explained. Consequently we can successfully leverage these results for localization, and we will show detailed accuracy levels in the localization solution at the end of this Section.

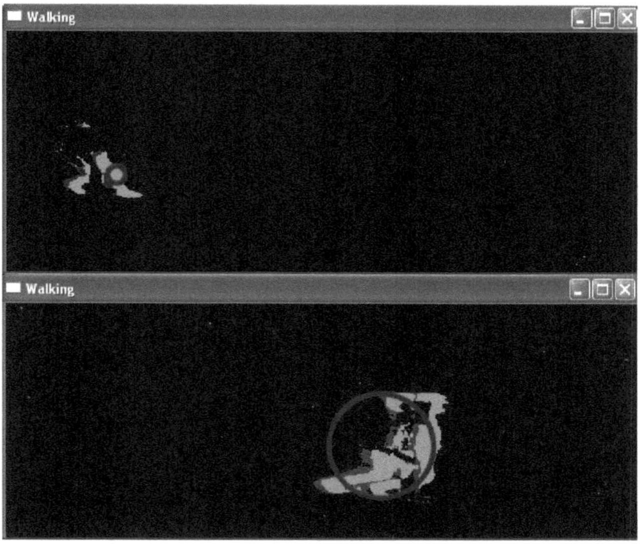

Fig. 3. Example of evolution in the number of points within the silhouette ROI (represented by the diameter of the blue circle tracking the person) at two different video frames

As a simple example illustrating the previous reasoning, Figure 4 shows the regularity in the evolution of the number of pixels within the silhouettes for a constant velocity movement.

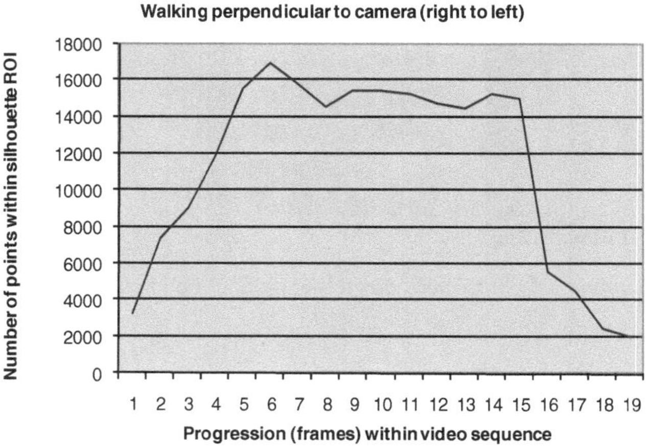

Fig. 4. Evolution in the number of points within the silhouette ROI in a video sequence for a constant velocity movement

3.3 Radio Fingerprinting Approach

RSSI information from WiFi access points deployed within buildings allows us to obtain a radio map of different locations (technique called fingerprinting), and we can estimate locations through the comparison of the current RSSI measurements with those stored in the radio map. Different attempts to obtain RSSI-based indoor localization without fingerprinting show an important loss of accuracy [30]. Also, many fingerprinting-based localization systems make use of dedicated hardware for the collection of data in the training phase, while in the measurement phase, the actual mobile device used for localization is different, resulting in an error called "signal reception bias" [31], due to the differences in antennas characteristics and measurement acquisitions schemes between different equipments. In fact, we have carried out tests showing a difference of approximately 10 dB in average between RSSI values measured with a Dell Latitude laptop and those measured with a Motorola Droid cell-phone. Consequently, we have integrated both the training and measurement phases in fingerprinting within the same mobile device. Moreover, the way the fingerprints are taken in the training phase should reproduce as accurately as possible the way the measurements will be carried out in the localization phase. In this sense, the orientation of the phone (obtainable from accelerometer and magnetometer data) helps enhance the localization accuracy. And in order to minimize errors due to human body effect [32], the cell-phone should be handled during the training phase as close as possible to the normal conditions in which it will be used in the measurement phase.

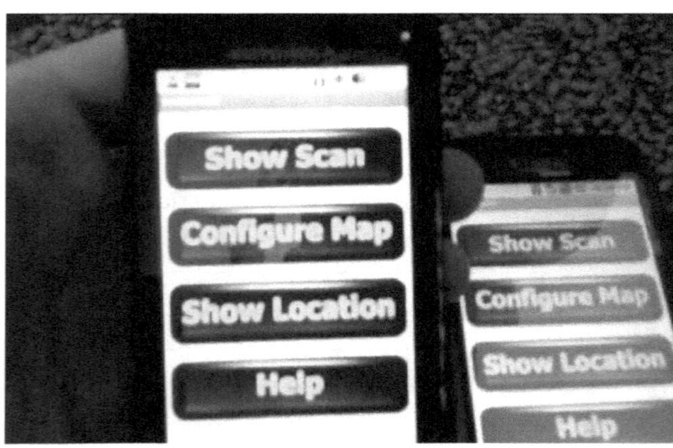

Fig. 5. Main interface of our Localization application in the Droid (left) and G1 (right) smart phones

Experimental Setup for Radio Fingerprinting: We have carried out tests to measure different radiofrequency signal strengths within the Cory building in the University of California, Berkeley campus. As will be explained further in this Section, WiFi technology offers the most reliable approach for indoor localization in our building, because of the important deployed infrastructure of WiFi Access Points. For the measurement of the signals and practical implementation of our localization application, we have used smart phones running on Android, in particular the G1 and the Droid. The sensitivity of these smart phones ranges from -45 dBm to -104 dBm. Subsequently, we have built an Android application for localization, and we have tested it in locations where 25 WiFi radios in average were listened (approximately

40% of them with RSSI above -80 dBm), obtaining accuracies in the order of 1.5 meters even within a same room, and with real-time dynamicity (refreshment of location information every second).

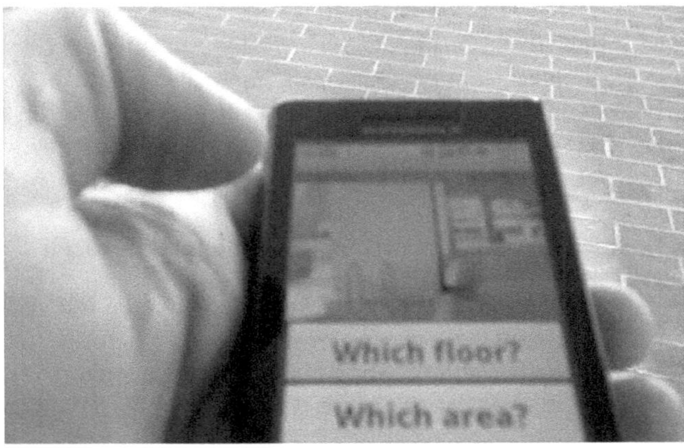

Fig. 6. Localization Application in the Droid showing location information as multimedia messages

In our experimental setup, each WiFi Access Point has 5 radios (each represented by a MAC address). For example, 00:23:04:89:db:20, 00:23:04:89:db:21, 00:23:04:89:db:22, 00:23:04:89:db:25 and 00:23:04:89:db:26 are 5 radios belonging to the same Access Point. RSSI values (in dBm) from the same Access Point can show important standard deviations in between consecutive scans (within the same radio) and also in between different radios within the same Access Point. Consequently, averaging of values both within the same Access Point and over time provides much more stable values that can successfully be used as a fingerprint component of each particular location. We call this approach "Nearest Neighbor in signal space and Access Point averages", and the results summarized in Table 1 show that our approach can outperform existing deterministic techniques (the resolution metric, in percentage, accounts for the number of true positives obtained during localization tests).

Table 1. Comparison of accuracies of different radio fingerprinting approaches in terms of success in location estimation

Technique	**Resolution (% of success)**		
	Room	**2 meters**	**1 meter**
Closest Point	85%	39%	18%
Nearest Neighbor in Signal Average	78%	39%	26%
Smallest Polygon	84%	45%	26%
Nearest Neighbor in Signal and Access Point averages	87%	48%	32%

RSSI information from cellular base stations could theoretically be used to disambiguate locations for which the WiFi radio map offers doubts. Nevertheless, we have found this approach unfeasible with current state of the art smart phones, because the refreshment rate of RSSI values is very slow (not dynamic enough for indoor walking) and the granularity in the RSSI values is poor and hardware dependent (e.g. G1 only distinguishes between 4 bars of coverage, and Droid only provides a few more intermediate values ranging from -56 dBm to -115 dBm). Moreover, we could only read RSSI information from neighboring base stations belonging to the same SIM card operator, constraining the practicality of this approach.

3.4 Summary of Accuracy Results for the Multimodal Approach

Combining the data from the different technologies (computer vision, accelerometry and WiFi radio-fingerprinting) by means of a Kalman filter, the accuracy levels obtained are summarized in Table 2, showing an important improvement over the WiFi-only approach.

Table 2. Comparison of accuracies for the multimodal solution with different radio fingerprinting approaches in terms of success in location estimation

Technique used in WiFi fingerpriting	**Resolution of multimodal approach (% of success)**		
	2 meters	**1 meter**	**0.5 meters**
Closest Point	98%	59%	40%
Nearest Neighbor in Signal Average	97%	58%	38%
Smallest Polygon	95%	62%	42%
Nearest Neighbor in Signal and Access Point averages	99%	67%	46%

4 Conclusions

We have proposed the fusion of computer vision with accelerometry and the magnetometer and radios available in current state-of-the-art smart phones, in order to provide a precise localization solution feasible for indoor environments. In terms of accelerometry, our approach makes use of a single off-the-shelf accelerometer on the waist, obtaining velocity and stride length with a precision comparable to the most sophisticated and expensive systems available in the market. Leveraging these results, we subsequently link accelerometry and computer vision through the kinetic energy of the user. Additionally, our system optimizes the capabilities of current state-of-the-art smart phones to integrate both offline and online phases of radio fingerprinting, with the implementation of a new approach for the statistical processing of radio signal strengths. We have also studied the possibilities offered by the cellular communications radio, in order to build a multimodal solution for localization, delivering an accuracy of up to 0.5 meters when all the information is combined with a Kalman filter. To the best of our knowledge, our application represents the first approach for indoor localization fusing precise kinematic information obtained from a single off-the-shelf accelerometer (like those in current state-of-the-art smart phones) with computer vision and radio fingerprinting, and integrating both online and offline phases of fingerprinting within the same device.

References

1. Ryder, J., Longstaff, B., Reddy, S., Estrin, D.: Ambulation: A tool for monitoring mobility patterns over time using mobile phones. In: Proceedings - 12th IEEE Int. Conf., vol. 4, pp. 927–931 (2009)
2. Li, Q., et al.: Walking speed and slope estimation using shank-mounted inertial measurement units. In: IEEE International Conference on Rehabilitation Robotics, pp. 839–844 (2009)
3. Alvarez, D., et al.: Comparison of step length estimators from weareable accelerometer devices. In: Interl. Conf. of the IEEE Engineering in Medicine and Biology Society, pp. 5964–5967 (2006)
4. Jiménez, A.R., et al.: A comparison of pedestrian dead-reckoning algorithms using a low-cost MEMS IMU. In: Proceedings, pp. 37–42 (2009)
5. Liu, R., Zhou, J., Liu, M., Hou, X.: A wearable acceleration sensor system for gait recognition. In: IEEE Conference on Industrial Electronics and Applications, pp. 2654–2659 (2007)
6. Kim, J.W., Jang, H.J., Hwang, D.H., Park, C.: A step, stride and heading determination for the pedestrian navigation system. J. Global Positioning Syst 3(1-2), 273–279 (2004)
7. Ladetto, Q.: On foot navigation: continuous step calibration using both complementary recursive prediction and adaptive Kalman filtering. Intern. Techn. Meeting of Sat., 1735–1740 (2000)
8. Hide, C., Moore, T., Andreotti, M.: Integrating computer vision and inertial navigation for pedestrian navigation. GPS World (January 2011)
9. Havasi, L., Szlávik, Z.: A statistical method for object localization in multi-camera tracking. In: Proceedings - International Conference on Image Processing, pp. 3925–3928 (2010)
10. Lee, T.-Y., et al.: People localization in a camera network combining background subtraction and scene-aware human detection. In: International Multimedia Modeling Conference, pp. 151–160 (2011)
11. Sun, L., Di, H., Tao, L., Xu, G.: A robust approach for person localization in multi-camera environment. In: International Conference on Pattern Recognition, pp. 4036–4039 (2010)
12. Kawai, J., et al.: Identification And Positioning Based on Motion Sensors And A Video Camera. In: IASTED International Conference on Web-Based Education, pp. 461–809 (2005)
13. Shigeta, O., Kagami, S., Hashimoto, K.: Identifying a Moving object with an Accelerometer in a Camera View. In: Proceedings of IEEE/RSJ International (2008)
14. Maki, Y., et al.: Accelerometer detection in a camera view based on feature point tracking. In: IEEE/SICE International Symposium on System Integration: SI International, pp. 448–453 (2010)
15. Jung, D., Teixeira, T., Savvides, A.: Towards cooperative localization of wearable sensors using accelerometers and cameras. In: Proceedings - IEEE INFOCOM (2010)

16. Teixeira, T., et al.: PEM-ID: Identifying people by gait-matching using cameras and wearable accelerometers. In: 3rd ACM/IEEE International Conference on Distributed Smart Cameras (2009)
17. Eyjolfsdottir, E., Turk, M.: Multisensory embedded pose estimation. In: IEEE Workshop on Applications of Computer Vision, pp. 23–30 (2011)
18. Barabanov, Andrey, E., et al.: Adaptive filtering of tracking camera data and onboard sensors for a small helicopter autopilot. In: IEEE International Conference on Control Applications, pp. 1696–1701 (2009)
19. Kelly, J., Sukhatme, Gaurav, S.: Visual-inertial simultaneous localization, mapping and sensor-to-sensor self-calibration. In: International Symposium on Computational Intelligence, pp. 360–368 (2009)
20. Grassi, M., et al.: An integrated system for people fall-detection with data fusion capabilities based on 3D ToF camera and wireless accelerometer. In: Proceedings of IEEE Sensors, pp. 1016–1019 (2010)
21. Poovendran, R., Wang, C., Sumit, R.: Secure Localization and Time Synchronization for Wireless Sensor and Ad Hoc Networks. Springer, Heidelberg (2006)
22. Singh, R., et al.: A novel positioning system for static location estimation employing WLAN in indoor environment. IEEE PIMRC 3, 1762–1766 (2004)
23. Brida, P., Cepel, P., Duha, J.: Geometric Algorithm for Received Signal Strength Based Mobile Positioning. In: Proc. Of Czech Slovak Technical Universities & URSI, vol. 5 (2005)
24. Bahl, P., Padmanabhan, V., Balachandran, A.: Enhancements to the RADAR user location and tracking system, Technical Report MSR-TR-00-12, Microsoft Research (February 2000)
25. Youssef, M.: HORUS: A WLAN-Based indoor location determination system, Ph.D. Dissertation, University of Maryland (2004)
26. King, T., Kopf, S., Haenselmann, T., Lubberger, C., Effelsberg, W.: COMPASS: A Probabilistic Indoor Positioning System Based on 802.11 and Digital Compasses. In: 1st WiNTECH, pp. 34–40 (September 2006)
27. Ekahau (August 2011), http://www.ekahau.com
28. Noh, A.S.-I., Lee, W.J., Ye, J.Y.: Comparison of the Mechanisms of the Zigbee's Indoor Localization Algorithm Software Engineering. In: 9th ACIS Int. Conf., pp. 13–18 (August 2008)
29. Mallat, S.: A wavelet tour of signal processing, 2nd edn. Academic Press (1999)
30. Li, X.: Ratio-based zero-profiling indoor localization. In: IEEE 6th Int. Conf. MASS, pp. 40–49 (2009)
31. Hsu, C., Yu, C.: An Accelerometer based approach for indoor localization. In: Symposia and Workshops on UIC'09 and ATC 2009 Conferences, pp. 223–227 (2009)
32. Pathanawongthum, N., Cherntanomwong, P.: Empirical evaluation of RFID-based indoor localization with human body effect. In: 15th Asia-Pacific Conf. on Communications, pp. 479–482 (2009)

Analysis of the Influence of Location Update and Paging Costs Reduction Factors on the Total Location Management Costs

E. Martin and M. Woodward

EECS Dept., University of California, Berkeley
emartin@eecs.berkeley.edu

Abstract. In this paper, we develop an analytical model of the signaling costs due to location update and paging for the radio interface in mobile communications networks. This model accounts for the effects that the savings brought by different algorithms have on the total Location Management (LM) costs. It also takes into account the trade-off between the location update and paging costs, showing that those strategies that achieve savings in the location update costs deliver a larger overall improvement in the total LM costs than those algorithms focusing on the minimization of the paging costs. Moreover, leveraging the factors studied to obtain this model, we also analyze the overall LM costs including the fixed network part.

Keywords: Location Management, mobility, signaling costs.

1 Introduction

Location Management (LM) has become a key research topic because of the rise in the number of users in mobile communications networks, bringing large signaling burdens that should be optimized. The aim of LM is to enable the roaming of the users through the coverage area, and for this purpose, the two basic procedures involved are location update and paging. Most of the existing research on LM tends to focus on the signaling costs involved in the radio interface, which is a critical point due to the scarcity of the radio resources. In this sense, several strategies have been proposed to minimize the components of the costs. However, not all the strategies have the same global influence on the LM costs. In this article, considering the different factors that our previous research (see [1-11] and references therein) has leveraged for the analysis of the signaling overhead, we develop a model to account for the costs in the radio interface. This model will be useful to examine the effect of the savings achieved by each particular algorithm on the optimum point that minimizes the LM costs.

Due to the fact that most of the LM concepts are not protocol dependent [12], the issues dealt with in this article are applicable to all Personal Communications Services (PCS) networks, and also to third generation wireless networks [13]. Moreover, the basic concepts of LM in Mobile IP are the same as in PCS, with three slight differences [14]: first, in Internet, a subnet cannot be abstracted with a geometric shape; second, distances in Internet are usually counted in terms of the

A. Abd Manaf et al. (Eds.): ICIEIS 2011, Part III, CCIS 253, pp. 473–483, 2011.

number of hops that the packets travel; and third, instead of paging cost, packet delivery cost should be used to calculate the total LM costs. Furthermore, although a change in backbone network can bring new considerations, many of the concepts used for PCS networks, and some for Mobile IP, will be applicable in some way to the Wireless Asynchronous Transfer Mode (WATM) and Satellite networks [12].

In the next Section, we introduce a first analytical model for the costs in the radio interface. Section 3 examines the different costs reduction coefficients that will be considered to develop a more complex model for the costs. Section 4 focuses on the global costs involved in LM and provides suggestions for further research. The paper is concluded in Section 5.

2 Analytical Model

Assuming a Poisson process for the arrival of calls, with rate λ_c (number of calls per user and per time unit). Calling C_{LU} the signaling cost for the radio interface due to a location update operation, C_{Pcell} the signaling cost for the radio interface involved in paging a single cell, and ρ and $E[v]$ the density and mean velocity respectively of the users in study. Considering a fluid flow mobility model and a deployment of square cells of side length L, we can obtain an expression to approximate the LM costs in the radio interface per amount of users in a cell and per time unit, using blanket paging [1]:

$$C_{Tc} \approx (\lambda_c \cdot \rho \cdot L^2) \cdot C_{Pcell} \cdot x + \frac{C_{LU} \cdot 4\rho \cdot E[v] \cdot L}{\pi} \cdot \frac{1}{\sqrt{x}}, \tag{1}$$

where x represents the number of cells per Location Area (LA).

Choosing $\lambda_c = 0.5$ call/hour per user, $\rho = 200$ users/km^2, $L = 1$ km, $E[v] = 4$ km/h, and the C_{LU}/C_{Pcell} ratio as 17 [1], we obtain the results in Fig. 1.

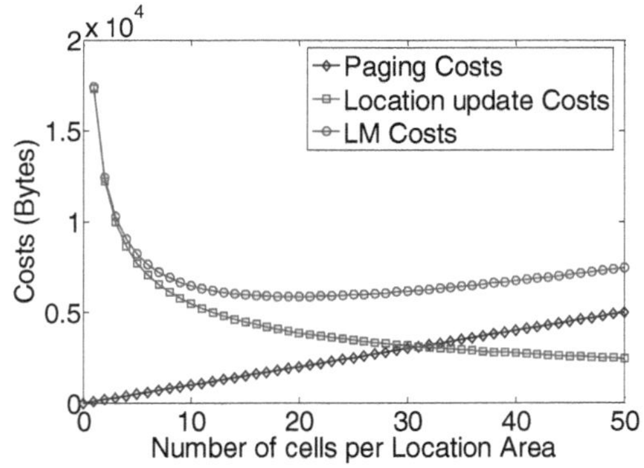

Fig. 1. Representation of location update, paging and LM costs. Square cells configuration.

If instead of square cells, we consider hexagonal cells of side length L, we can obtain a new expression for the C_{Tc}, following the steps indicated in [1]:

$$C_{Tc} \approx (\lambda_c \cdot \rho \cdot \frac{3\sqrt{3}}{2} L^2) \cdot C_{Pcell} \cdot \left(3d^2 - 3d + 1\right) + \frac{C_{LU} \cdot \rho \cdot E[v] \cdot (12d - 6) \cdot L}{\pi} \cdot \frac{1}{\left(3d^2 - 3d + 1\right)}, \quad (2)$$

where d is the number of rings of hexagonal cells that form the LAs. Taking values of $\lambda_c = 1$ call/hour/user, $\rho = 100$ users/km^2, $L = 1$ km, $E[v] = 8$ km/h, and C_{LU} / C_{Pcell} ratio as 17, we obtain the results shown in Fig. 2.

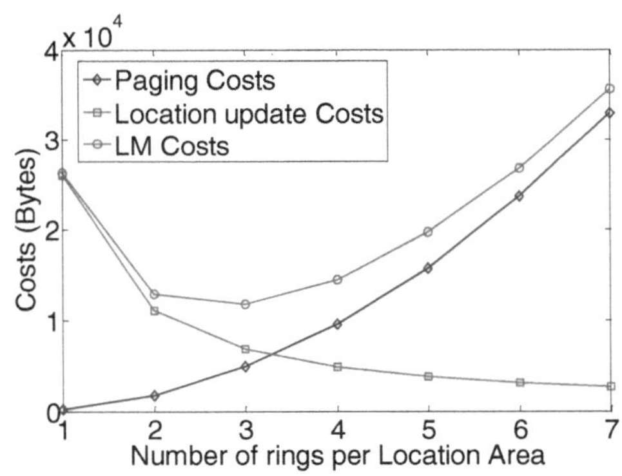

Fig. 2. Representation of location update, paging and LM costs. LAs formed by rings of hexagonal cells.

Both (1) and (2) take into account the two main procedures involved in LM: paging and location update. In the rest of this paper, the first term of these expressions will be referred as *PG*, while the second term accounting for the location update procedure, will be referred as *LU*.

An important proportion of the existing literature about LM proposes particular algorithms aimed at minimizing the signaling costs. Some of the proposed algorithms achieve savings in the location update costs [15-17], usually measured in percentage terms, and which we will name in this paper as S_{LU}. For each LM algorithm the values of S_{LU} will range between 0 (if no savings in the location update costs are achieved) and 1 (theoretical value which would correspond to the case in which the savings for *LU* were 100%). Other algorithms achieve savings in the paging costs [18-20], which we will refer by S_P, whose values range within [0,1) in analogy to S_{LU}. As conveyed in [21], the trade-off between *LU* and *PG* should be taken into account at the time of analyzing the performance of a particular LM algorithm, because for example, reductions in *LU* can bring rises in the uncertainty of the users' location, therefore increasing the *PG* term, a detail that not all researchers consider [21]. To study this trade-off, we will examine the general evolution of the LM costs leveraging the model we introduced in [1], and introducing a new term to account for the trade-off (*TO*), with the following expression:

$$TO = (1 - S_{LU})^{\frac{2}{3}} \cdot (1 - S_P)^{\frac{1}{3}}. \tag{3}$$

The *TO* term reflects the fact that those LM algorithms that achieve savings in the location update costs, deliver a bigger overall improvement in the total LM costs than those algorithms focusing on reductions in the paging costs. This detail is illustrated in Fig. 3, where it can be observed that the overall reductions in the trade-off term due to savings in the location update costs are always more important than those due to savings of the same value in the paging costs. Consequently, we can obtain a new expression to approximate the LM costs in the radio interface per amount of users in a cell and per time unit:

$$C_{Tc} \approx [PG + LU] \cdot TO. \tag{4}$$

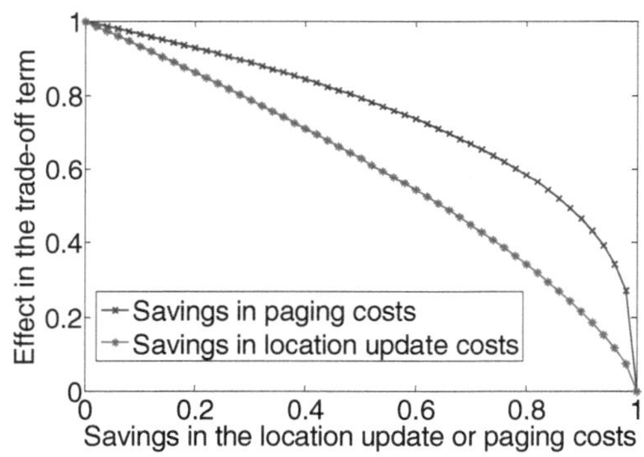

Fig. 3. Reductions in the trade-off term due to savings in the location update or paging costs

3 Coefficients to Account for the Factors Affecting the LM Costs

Studying the different factors that affect the LM costs in the radio interface (see [1-11] and references therein), we can introduce the following coefficients:

- *RCr*: reduction coefficient for the LM costs accounting for the sensitivity of the optimal total costs to the variance of the cell residence time. As shown in [22], the optimal total LM costs can experience noticeable reductions in absolute terms when the variance of the cell residence time rises. It must be noticed that the relevance of this factor is only important for low Call-to-Mobility Ratios (CMRs), a detail that could be considered through the introduction of a filtering factor, *F*, to account for the influence of the CMR. In this sense, assuming that the savings achievable due to the sensitivity to the variance of the cell residence time, *Sr*, are the product of a fixed quantity *S* and the factor *F*, the value of *RCr* can be expressed as follows:

$$RCr = 1 - Sr = 1 - S \cdot F \ , \tag{5}$$

where F can be approximated by the following expression:

$$F = \frac{\frac{\pi}{2} - \arctan(CMR - \pi)}{\pi} . \tag{6}$$

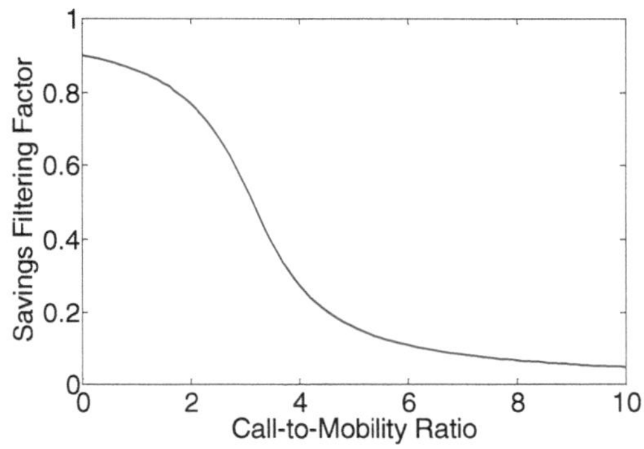

Fig. 4. Evolution of the Savings Filtering Factor, *F*, with the Call-to-Mobility Ratio

- *RCi*: reduction coefficient for the *LU* costs due to the optimum integration of cells with high inter-cell mobile traffic within a same LA, in order to minimize the number of crossings of LAs borders and therefore minimize the number of location updates. An optimum design of LAs would also assign cells with low inter-cell mobile traffic to the borders of different LAs. This effect has been studied in [15, 23-24], and signaling savings of 30% have been reported for deployments with hexagonal cells [15]. Therefore, we will consider typical values of this coefficient ranging between 0.6 (for savings of 40%) and 1 (for savings of 0%). It must be noticed that this improvement in the *LU* costs does not increase the uncertainty of the users' whereabouts and consequently, in a new analytical expression for the LM costs that takes into account the *RCi* coefficient, this coefficient would not be included within *TO*, but it would multiply directly to the *LU* term, as will be shown in (7).
- RC_{dLA}: reduction coefficient for the LM costs as a consequence of the use of dynamic designs of LAs instead of static ones. Studies such as [25] show the convenience of dynamic LA schemes adaptable to the time-varying call and mobility patterns of the user. As in general, the adaptations of the LAs are for both call and mobility models of the user, we will assume that the savings in the signaling costs affect in the same way to *LU* and *PG*, and therefore this term will not be included within *TO*, but will multiply directly to both *LU* and *PG*.
- *RCo*: reduction coefficient for *LU* costs due to the overlapping of LAs. Several studies, such as [25-26] show the savings that can be achieved in the number of location updates when some regions around the borders of LAs are overlapped, so that the user only updates its location when the borders of the overlapping region are crossed. This coefficient will be included within *TO*, as will be shown in (8).

- *RCs*: reduction coefficient for LU costs due to the optimum choice of the shape of LAs. Studies such as [16] show that the rate of updates can be minimized by means of optimal shapes of LAs, which turn out to be irregular. In the same sense, [25] shows that ring LA configurations around the city center outperform sector shaped LAs. Consequently, the choice of an optimal shape for the LA brings savings in the *LU* term without increasing the uncertainty of the user's location. Therefore this *RCs* factor will not be included within the *TO* term, but will directly multiply to the *LU* term.
- *RCd*: reduction coefficient for *PG* costs due to the consideration of more than one paging step. Research works such as [18-20] and [27] analyze the trade-off between the paging costs and the call delivery delay, showing that big savings can be achieved in the paging costs when two paging steps are considered, while further savings brought by three-step paging are not so important. Typical savings when 2 or 3 paging steps are considered range between 20% and 40%, and thus typical *RCd* values would be between 0.8 and 0.6 respectively, although it should be taken as 1 if blanket paging (single step) is performed. It must be noticed that these savings in the *PG* term do not modify the *LU* costs, and therefore *RCd* will not be included within the *TO* term, but will directly multiply the *PG* term.

Taking all these factors into account, the LM costs per amount of users in a cell and per time unit for the radio interface can be approximated by:

$$C_{Tc} \approx RCr \cdot RC_{dLA} \cdot \left[PG \cdot RCd + LU \cdot RCi \cdot RCs\right] \cdot TO, \tag{7}$$

and the new expression for the *TO* term is:

$$TO = \left(1 - S_{LU}\right)^{\frac{2}{3}} \cdot \left(RCo\right)^{\frac{2}{3}} \cdot \left(1 - S_P\right)^{\frac{1}{3}}. \tag{8}$$

Focusing on the scenario described in Fig. 1, next we will show the effect of the different reduction coefficients and savings brought by the application of particular LM strategies. Fig. 5 presents the modifications in the LM costs' curve due to reductions of 20% in each one of the factors separately. It must be noticed that according to (7) and (8), both *RCr* and RC_{dLA} have the same influence on C_{Tc}, and for simplicity, we have only included in Fig. 5 the curve resulting from the variation of one of them. The same applies to *RCi* and *RCs*, and to $\left(1 - S_{LU}\right)$ and *RCo*.

It can be observed that the reductions brought by *RCr* or RC_{dLA} translate into the largest overall savings for the LM costs, while the reductions due to S_P or *RCd* achieve the lowest decreases in the LM costs. It can also be noticed that the savings reflected by *RCr*, RC_{dLA} , *RCo*, S_{LU} and S_P do not involve a change in the optimum number of cells per LA; on the other hand, the savings from *RCd* enlarge the optimum number of cells per LA while the savings from *RCi* and *RCs* diminish that optimum number. The size of these variations in the optimum point increase with the value of the savings, and for the same value, it is more important for *RCd* than for *RCi* or *RCs*.

From a designer's point of view, it is interesting to notice that the freedom to choose between different numbers of cells per LA with a value of the LM costs similar to that of the optimum point, decreases when the minimum of the LM costs' curve becomes more distinguished (sharper shape of the curve). This happens with savings achieved through *RCi* or *RCs*. The opposite takes place with reductions from *RCd*.

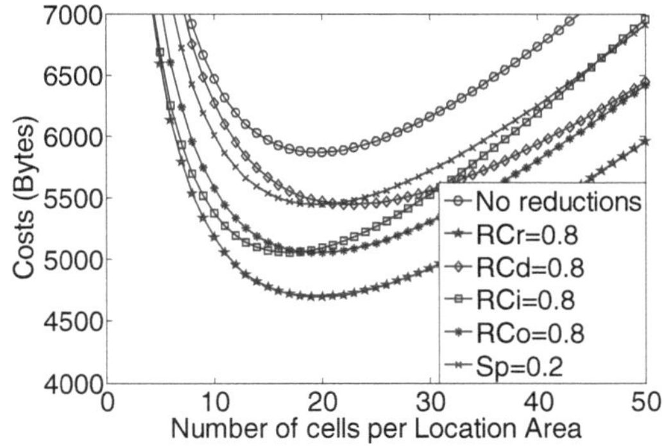

Fig. 5. Influence of the different costs reduction coefficients in the LM costs. 20% reductions.

In analogy to Fig. 5, the effects of 40% reductions are illustrated in Fig. 6.

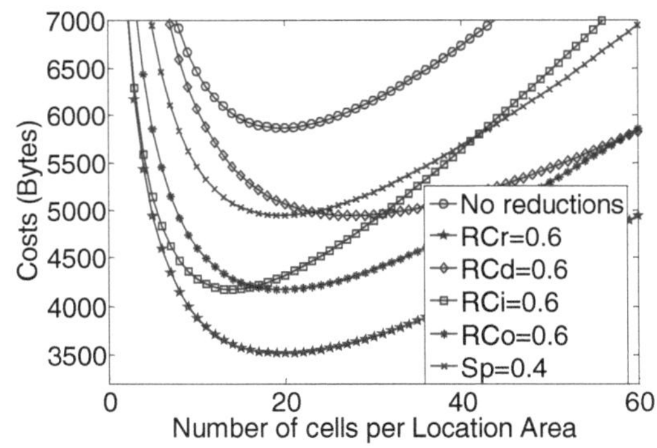

Fig. 6. Influence of the different costs reduction coefficients in the LM costs. 40% reductions.

4 Consideration of the Costs in Monetary Units

From a network operator's point of view, it would be interesting to translate the costs obtained in (7) into monetary units by means of a conversion factor, C_{RB} (cost of the radio bandwidth), whose value will reflect the price of the frequencies used. Referring to the costs for LM in the radio interface in terms of monetary units as MC_{RI} we have:

$$MC_{RI} = C_{Tc} \cdot C_{RB} \tag{9}$$

Apart from the costs involved in the radio interface, LM implies costs in the fixed network side and mobile terminal, which will mainly depend on the particular LM strategies chosen. These costs can be accounted for in a simplified way by two factors: storage and computing capabilities. To study these factors, we can define the following terms:

- ST_T : storage capabilities in the mobile terminal.
- ST_N : storage capabilities in the fixed network side.
- CP_T: computing capabilities in the mobile terminal.
- CP_N : computing capabilities in the fixed network side.
- C_{ST} : conversion factor into monetary units for the storage capabilities in the mobile terminal.
- C_{SN} : conversion factor into monetary units for the storage capabilities in the fixed network side.
- C_{CT} : conversion factor into monetary units for the computing capabilities in the mobile terminal.
- C_{CN} : conversion factor into monetary units for the computing capabilities in the fixed network side.

The values of these parameters would be determined by specifications from the network operators, the terminal manufacturers, the applications developers, and the services provided. In a simplified way, a first approximation for the monetary costs for LM in the mobile terminal and fixed network side, $MC_{T\&N}$, can be expressed as:

$$MC_{T\&N} \approx ST_T \cdot C_{ST} + CP_T \cdot C_{CT} + ST_N \cdot C_{SN} + CP_N \cdot C_{CN}. \quad (10)$$

Next, we will consider the influence of some of the costs reductions factors and particular LM strategies in each one of the terms in (10). The application of a LM algorithm usually implies an increase in the storage and computing capabilities both at the mobile terminal and fixed network side. Moreover, in general, the bigger the savings achieved, the larger the needed increase of those capabilities. For instance, the distance-based algorithm outperforms the movement-based method [28] in minimizing the number of location update messages, but demands a higher implementation complexity. Therefore, in order to reflect these requirements, we can define a term called "requirements due to the algorithm," R_A , which will be a function of $(1-S_{LU})$ and $(1-S_P)$:

$$R_A = f((1-S_{LU}),(1-S_P)), \quad (11)$$

and which will be included in $MC_{T\&N}$ in the following way:

$$MC_{T\&N} \approx R_A \cdot (ST_T \cdot C_{ST} + CP_T \cdot C_{CT} + ST_N \cdot C_{SN} + CP_N \cdot C_{CN}). \quad (12)$$

It must be noticed that the $(1-S_{LU})$ and $(1-S_P)$ terms will affect in an inversely proportional way to the storage and computing capabilities of the mobile terminal and fixed network. For simplicity, we have assumed equal increases in all the capabilities, although the exact influence of S_{LU} and S_P in the referred capabilities would depend on the specifications of each particular case in study.

In an analogous way, we can study the influence of some of the costs reduction factors in each one of the storage and computing capabilities. In this sense, the following general trends can be outlined:

Regarding RC_{dLA}, the main requirements brought by the application of dynamic LA designs adaptable to the time-varying call and mobility patterns of the user will be the storage of the users' profiles in the network side and the modifications of the LAs according to those profiles; i.e. increases in the storage and computing capabilities at the network side. In case the mobile terminal was required to keep a copy of its profile, it would mean a demand for larger storage in the mobile terminal. Regarding *RCo*, the most important demand of resources due to the overlapping of LAs borders will be on the mobile terminal in order to be able to deal with the new working conditions established for the overlapping regions. In relation to *RCd*, the introduction of paging steps to reduce the paging costs will require additional complexity in the network side. In particular, the optimum division of a LA in several paging zones would require to keep users' statistics in the network side in order to obtain the users' location probability distributions and perform the search in decreasing order of probabilities to minimize the costs [19]. This will involve higher demands for the storage and computing capabilities at the network side. Regarding *RCs*, the choice of the optimum shape for the LAs will involve additional computing resources at the network side, for instance if the design of LAs is dynamically adjusted to the call and mobility patterns of the users.

And taking into account these guidelines, the following terms can be defined in analogy to R_A:

- R_{FST}: Requirements due to factors affecting the storage capabilities in the mobile terminal.
- R_{FSN}: Requirements due to factors affecting the storage capabilities in the fixed network side.
- R_{FCT}: Requirements due to factors affecting the computing capabilities in the mobile terminal.
- R_{FCN}: Requirements due to factors affecting the computing capabilities in the fixed network side.

These four terms will be functions of the different costs reduction factors. And to reflect the influence of R_{FST}, R_{FSN}, R_{FCT} and R_{FCN} in the different capabilities, the new expression for $MC_{T\&N}$ is:

$$MC_{T\&N} \approx R_A \cdot (R_{FST} \cdot ST_T \cdot C_{ST} + R_{FCT} \cdot CP_T \cdot C_{CT} + \\ + R_{FSN} \cdot ST_N \cdot C_{SN} + R_{FCN} \cdot CP_N \cdot C_{CN}). \tag{13}$$

Apart from the costs for the radio interface and the costs involved in the storage and computing capabilities both at the mobile terminal and fixed network side, the effect of the different LM strategies in the quality of service provided should also be taken into account. For instance, the reductions in the paging costs achieved by the multiple step paging strategy bring an increase in the call delivery delay, which could translate into a lower acceptance of the service and therefore monetary losses. The type of service provided will play a major role in this case. A term called "monetary costs from the quality of service," MC_{QoS}, would account for this detail. And consequently, the general expression for the total monetary costs involved in LM is:

$$MC_{LM} = MC_{RI} + MC_{T\&N} + MC_{QoS}\,. \tag{14}$$

5 Conclusions

For the analysis of the LM costs in the radio interface, an analytical model has been developed that takes into account the effect of the savings achieved by different LM strategies in each one of the components of the costs. The *TO* term introduced shows that those algorithms that achieve savings in the location update costs, bring larger overall savings in the total costs than those strategies aiming at the minimization of the paging costs. From the study of the influence of the different costs reduction coefficients in the LM costs, it can be concluded that the best overall performance is accomplished when the savings are due to increases in the variance of the users' cell residence time or due to the use of dynamic designs of LAs. Moreover, the reductions that these factors bring to the LM costs do not involve modifications in the optimum number of cells per LA, and the minimum of the costs does not become more distinguished (sharper in shape). On the other hand, the worst overall improvement is managed by means of the savings achieved through multiple step paging.

References

1. Martin, E., Liu, L., Pesti, P., Weber, M., Woodward, M.: Unified analytical models for location management costs and optimum design of location areas. In: Proceedings of 2009 International Conference on Collaborative Computing, Washington D.C, November 1-10, pp. 12–14 (2009)
2. Martin, E., Bajcsy, R.: Variability of Location Management Costs with Different Mobilities and Timer Periods to Update Locations. International Journal of Computer Networks & Communications, 1–15 (July 2011)
3. Martin, E., Bajcsy, R.: Savings in Location Management Costs Leveraging User Statistics. International Journal of Ubiquitous Computing, 1–20 (July 2011)
4. Martin, E., Bajcsy, R.: Enhancements in Multimode Localization Accuracy Brought by a Smart Phone-Embedded Magnetometer. In: IEEE International Conference on Signal Processing Systems (2011)
5. Martin, E.: Multimode Radio Fingerprinting for Localization. In: IEEE Conference on Wireless Sensors and Sensor Networks (2011)
6. Martin, E.: Solving Training Issues in the Application of the Wavelet Transform to Precisely Analyze Human Body Acceleration Signals. In: IEEE International Conference on Bioinformatics and Biomedicine (2010)
7. Martin, E., Bajcsy, R.: Considerations on Time Window Length for the Application of the Wavelet Transform to Analyze Human Body Accelerations. In: IEEE International Conference on Signal Processing Systems (2011)
8. Martin, E.: Optimized Gait Analysis Leveraging Wavelet Transform Coefficients from Body Acceleration. In: International Conference on Bioinformatics and Biomedical Technology (2011)
9. Martin, E.: A graphical Study of the Timer Based Method for Location Management with the Blocking Probability. In: International Conference on Wireless Communications, Networking and Mobile Computing (2011)
10. Martin, E.: Characterization of the Costs Provided by the Timer-based Method in Location Management. In: International Conference on Wireless Communications, Networking and Mobile Computing (2011)

11. Martin, E.: New Algorithms to Obtain the Different Components of the Location Management Costs. In: International Conference on Wireless Communications, Networking and Mobile Computing (2011)
12. Akyildiz, I.F., McNair, J.: Mobility Management in next generation wireless systems. Proceedings of the IEEE 87, 1347–1384 (1999)
13. Fang, Y.: General modeling and performance analysis for location management in wireless mobile networks. IEEE Transactions on Computers 51(10), 1169–1181 (2002)
14. Xie, J., Akyildiz, I.: An optimal location management scheme for minimizing signaling cost in Mobile IP. In: Proceedings IEEE International Conference on Communications, vol. 5, pp. 3313–3317 (2002)
15. Cayirci, E., Erdal, I., Akyildiz, F.: Optimal location area design to minimize registration signaling traffic in wireless systems. IEEE Transactions on Mobile Computing 2(1), 76–85 (2003)
16. Abutaleb, A., Li, V.: Location update optimization in personal communication systems. Wireless Networks 3(3), 205–216 (1997)
17. Akyildiz, I., Ho, M., Lin, Y.: Movement-based location update and selective paging for PCS networks. IEEE/ACM Transactions on Networking 4(4), 629–638 (1996)
18. Akyildiz, I., Ho, J.: Mobile user location update and paging mechanism under delay constraints. Computer Communications Review 25(4), 244–255 (1995)
19. Rose, R., Yates, R.: Minimizing the average cost of paging under delay constraints. Wireless Networks 2(2), 109–116 (1996)
20. Krishnamachari, B., Gau, R., Wicker, S., Haas, S.: Optimal Sequential Paging in Cellular Wireless Networks. Wireless Networks 10(2), 121–131 (2004)
21. Chung, Y., Sung, D., Aghvami, A.: Effect of uncertainty of the position of mobile terminals on the paging cost of an improved movement-based registration scheme. IEICE Transactions on Communications E86-B(2), 859–861 (2003)
22. Giner, V.C., Oltra, J.M.: Global versus distance-based local mobility tracking strategies: A unified approach. IEEE Transactions on Vehicular Technology 51(3), 472–485 (2002)
23. Lo, W., et al.: Efficient location area planning for cellular networks with hierarchical location databases. Computer Networks 45(6), 715–730 (2004)
24. Demirkol, I., Ersoy, C., Caglayan, C., Delic, H.: Location area planning and cell-to-switch assignment in cellular networks. IEEE Transactions on Wireless Communications 3(3), 880–890 (2004)
25. Markoulidakis, J., Lyberopoulos, J., Tsirkas, D., Sykas, D.: Evaluation of location area planning scenarios in future mobile telecommunications systems. Wireless Networks 1, 17–29 (1995)
26. Bejerano, Y., Cidon, I.: Efficient location management based on moving location areas. In: Proceedings - IEEE INFOCOM, vol. 1, pp. 3–12 (2001)
27. Giner, V., Oltra, J.: On movement-based mobility tracking strategy - an enhanced version. Communications Letters 2(1), 45–47 (1998)
28. Bar-Noy, A., Kessler, I., Sidi, M.: Mobile users: to update or not to update? ACM-Baltzer Wireless Networks, 175–185 (1995)

Data Compression Algorithms for Visual Information

Jonathan Gana Kolo, Kah Phooi Seng, Li-Minn Ang, and S.R.S. Prabaharan

Department of Electrical and Electronics Engineering, The University of Nottingham Malaysia Campus, Jalan Broga 43500 Semenyih, Selangor Darul Ehsan, Malaysia
{keyx1jgk,jasmine.seng,kenneth.ang,
prabaharan.sahaya}@nottingham.edu.my

Abstract. Audio-visual information is one of the richest but also most bandwidth-consuming modes of communication. To meet the requirements of new applications, powerful data compression schemes are needed to reduce the global bit rate drastically. In this paper, we proposed a simple lossless visual image compression scheme that will be used to compress visual images. In this scheme, the two dimensional visual image data is converted to a one dimensional data using our proposed pixel scanning method. The difference between consecutive pixel values in the resulting one dimensional image data is taken and the residues are encoded losslessly using an entropy encoder. The working principles of this our approach is presented together with the image compression algorithm used. We developed a software algorithm and implemented it to compress some standard test images using Huffman style coding techniques in a MATLAB platform.

Keywords: Lossless Image Compression, Huffman coding, Audio-Visual information, Wireless Sensor Network.

1 Introduction

The recent availability of inexpensive hardware such as CMOS cameras and microphones that are able to ubiquitously capture multimedia content from the environment has encouraged the development of Multimedia Wireless Sensor Networks (MWSNs) which are networks of wirelessly interconnected sensor nodes that collect video and audio streams, still images, and scalar sensor data. With increasing technological advancements and miniaturization in hardware, a single sensor node can be equipped with audio and visual information collection modules. MWSNs will not only enhance existing sensor network applications such as tracking, home automation, and environmental monitoring, but they will also enable several new applications such as security and surveillance in which a network of nodes identify and track objects from their visual information. MWSNs will also greatly enhance the application area of environmental monitoring [1].

Generally, a wireless sensor network (WSN) is a network of many autonomous sensor nodes that are deployed inside the phenomenon or very close to it. The sensor nodes which communicate with each other over a wireless channel are deployed to sense or monitor physical or environmental conditions cooperatively. WSN are used in many applications such as habitat monitoring, structural health monitoring,

A. Abd Manaf et al. (Eds.): ICIEIS 2011, Part III, CCIS 253, pp. 484–497, 2011.

environmental monitoring, medical monitoring, industrial monitoring, target tracking, prediction and detection of natural calamities, video surveillance, satellite imaging, military applications and so on [2] – [6].

WSN has serious resource constraints. Each sensor node in WSN has short communication range, low bandwidth, limited amount of energy, and limited processing and storage [3]. Since sensor nodes operate on limited amount of battery power, power efficiency in WSN is therefore an important performance metric that influences the network lifetime directly [3][4]. Network lifetime is dependent on the number of active nodes and the connectivity of the network, so energy must be used efficiently at each node [3]. By minimizing energy consumption at each node, the network lifetime of the WSN will be maximized. Sensor nodes in WSN consume energy during sensing, processing and transmission. But the energy spent by a sensing node in the communication module for data transmission is more than the energy for processing [4][7] - [14]. One way to conserve energy and maximize network lifetime in WSN is through the use of efficient data compression schemes [3][4].

Data compression schemes reduce data size before transmitting in wireless medium which translate to reduce total power consumption. This savings due to compression directly translate into lifetime extension for the network nodes [15]. Both the local single node that compresses the data as well as the intermediate routing nodes benefits from handling less data [16].

Any data compression algorithm proposed for use on a sensor node should have low complexity since the node has limited computational resources. Also, the compression efficiency of the algorithm should be high since the node has limited bandwidth for communication, and there is a high energy cost for communication. These requirements are contradictory since a more complex encoder usually produce higher compression rate. Thus, the choice of the algorithm will depend on the application domain.

In this paper, we proposed a simple lossless visual image compression scheme. In this scheme, the two dimensional visual image data is converted to a one dimensional data using our proposed pixel scanning method which systematically exploits the natural correlation that exist between neighboring image pixels. In order to keep our proposed scheme simple, we adapt the Lossless Entropy Compression (LEC) algorithm proposed in [12] for use with our proposed scheme. We focus on lossless image compression in MWSN due to the fact that some applications such as digital medical image processing and transmission, visual recognition, security and surveillance monitoring just to mention a few cannot tolerate information loss.

The remainder of this paper is structured as follows: In section 2, we discuss related work. Section 3 discusses Huffman coding and also reviews the LEC algorithm that was proposed in [12] and [14]. In section 4, our proposed visual image compression algorithm is presented. Experiments and results are presented in section 5 follow by the conclusion in section 6.

2 Related Work

In visual sensor networks, cameras are used to capture visual information (digital image) which is then processed locally and independently of data from other visual sensor nodes in the network. This captured still image requires an enormous amount of storage and or bandwidth for transmission. For example, a 24-bit colour image with 512X512 pixels will require 768 Kbyte of storage space. The main aim of image compression is to reduce the cost of storage and transmission of the digital image by representing the digital image more compactly. The images to be compressed by our proposed algorithm are grayscale images with pixel values between 0-255.

Data compression algorithms can be categorized into two main groups: lossless and lossy compression algorithms. In lossless algorithms, there is no loss of information during compression and/or decompression and thus, the integrity of the image is guaranteed. That is, the image reconstructed from the compressed image is identical to the original image. On the other hand, information loss is incurred and a higher compression ratio is achieved during lossy data compression. That is, the image reconstructed from the compressed image is similar to the original image but not identical to it. Thus, the choice of the algorithm type to use is dependent on the specific area of application. In this work we are going to use a lossless compression algorithm by using Huffman coding technique.

Some numbers of image compression schemes have been proposed in the literature for WSN [17-23]. These image compression schemes are complex and some requires additional hardware for their implementation. To ensure that the complexity of our design is as simple as possible and to also avoid the use of additional hardware for the implementation of our proposed lossless image compression algorithm, we surveyed lossless data compression algorithms for WSN with the aim of adapting any suitable and efficient algorithm to image compression. To the best of our knowledge, the two best lossless data compression algorithms for WSN from our study are S-LZW [16] and LEC [12]. The S-LZW algorithm was tailored towards LZW [24] that have received significant research attention. The memory usage of LZW and its embedded versions exceeds the tens of kilobytes that is typical in a sensor node even though it uses less memory than it counterpart algorithms that are aimed at high - end machines. Also LZW fixed dictionary entries do not make it suitable for sensor nodes where data could vary significantly over the duration of the deployment. S-LZW which is a distinct variant of LZW is specifically tailored to the energy and memory constraints of sensor nodes. Because of limited RAM of the sensor nodes for this dictionary-based algorithm, S-LZW introduced the following limitations compared to LZW [25][26]: (1) S-LZW divides the uncompressed input bitstreams into fixed size blocks of 528 bytes (two flash pages) and compresses each block separately.(2) S-LZW uses 512 entries dictionary. At the start, the algorithm initializes the dictionary to all standard characters of the ASCII code extended to 255 that represent the first 256 entries of the dictionary. For every block used in the compression, the dictionary is re-initialized. A new entry is created in the dictionary for every new string in the input bitstream. That is why the data to be compressed are limited. (3) To solve the problem of full dictionary, the dictionary is freeze and use as it is to compress the remainder of the data in the block, or it is reset and started from the scratch. However, this problem does not arise when the data block is small, thus the dictionary is not full. (4) A mini-cache of 32 entries was added to S-LZW to take advantage of the repetitiousness of the sensor data. The mini-cache is a hash-indexed dictionary of size N, where N is a power of 2, which stores recently used and created dictionary entries.

The values of the four parameters discussed above have great impact on the compression ratios. Therefore, they have to be properly set before deploying S-LZW into sensor nodes. See section 3.2 for the detailed description of the LEC algorithm. The LEC algorithm is chosen for adaptation because of its simplicity and efficiency since it outperforms the S-LZW algorithm.

3 Entropy Coding

In entropy encoding, digital data are compressed by representing frequently occurring symbols with less bits and rarely occurring symbols with more bits. Huffman coding and Arithmetic coding are two well known entropy coding techniques with Arithmetic coding almost achieving the theoretical near-optimal performance if the alphabet is small and highly skewed. In our approach, the difference between consecutive pixel values in the 1-D representation of the image data is taken and the residues forms sequence of decimal symbols. The frequency distribution of the symbols for the different test images is highly skewed with maximum frequency around '0' as shown in Fig. 4. We choice Huffman coding as the preferable coding scheme over arithmetic coding since arithmetic coding will be difficult to implement on the resource constrained sensor node.

3.1 Huffman Coding

Huffman coding is a popular lossless compression method for any kind of digital data [25]. The main idea in Huffman coding is to compress data by representing frequently occurring symbols with less bits and rarely occurring symbols with more bits based on their relative frequency of occurrence. The more frequent a symbol is, the shorter its code. The codes are prefix-free of each other. Thus, decoding can easily be done by parsing the encoded bitstream from left to right bitwise. The distribution of difference plots in Fig. 4 clearly shows that the difference between consecutive pixels values are unevenly distributed, hence Huffman compression method could be used effectively. Huffman coding, however, cannot be applied on a wireless sensor in its basic form because it is a CPU demanding method. Also, a lot of bandwidth would be wasted for online calculation of codes for each symbol which would require sending the list of codes to the sink. To overcome these problems, we could pre-calculate the Huffman codes for each possible symbol. For this the relative frequency of occurrence of each symbol is needed. In order to avoid the cost of computing frequency on the sensor nodes, the amount of work already carried out on JPEG [26] algorithm and further modified in the LEC [12] algorithm was exploited. This way encoding is done by the sensor node by reading the appropriate code for each symbol from a lookup table. The varying length of the codes was taken into account. Decoding by the sink could be done by parsing the incoming bitstream bitwise, as in the original Huffman algorithm. Since Huffman coding is a lossless compression, the quality of the resulting image is not affected.

3.2 Simple Lossless Entropy Compression (LEC) Scheme [12]

LEC is a simple lossless compression algorithm that was designed specifically for resource constrained WSN node. LEC algorithm exploits the natural correlation that exists in the data that are collected by wireless sensor nodes and the principle of entropy compression. LEC compresses data on the fly by using a very short fixed dictionary, the size of which depends on the resolution of the analog-to-digital converter. Since the dictionary size is fixed *a priori*, LEC does not suffer from the growing dictionary problem that affected other algorithms proposed in the literature for WSNs. The statistical characteristic of the natural correlation that exists in the data that are collected by wireless sensor nodes is similar to those characterizing DC coefficients of a digital image. Thus, LEC algorithm follows a scheme similar to the one that was used by the baseline JPEG algorithm for compressing the DC coefficients of a digital image. In LEC algorithm, a codeword is a hybrid of unary and binary code: the unary code is a variable length code that specifies the group, while the binary code which is a fixed length code represents the index within the group. LEC also adopts a differential compression scheme. Despite the simplicity of LEC, it outperforms Sensor node LZW (S-LZW) Compression Scheme [16] and Lightweight Temporal Compression (LTC) [15]. Its performances are comparable to five well known compression algorithms namely, gzip, bzip2, rar, classical Huffman and classical arithmetic encodings all of which are computationally complex and requires large memory. These are the reasons that motivate us to adapt LEC for visual image compression.

In the LEC algorithm, each sensor node measure m_i is converted by an ADC to binary representation r_i using R bits, where R is the resolution of the ADC. For each new measure m_i, the compression algorithm computes the difference $d_i = r_i - r_{i-1}$, which is input to an entropy encoder. The encoder performs compression losslessly by encoding differences d_i more compactly based on their statistical characteristics. Each d_i is represented as a bit sequence bs_i composed of two parts s_i and a_i, where s_i gives the number of bits required to represent d_i and a_i is the representation of d_i. Code s_i is a variable length code generated by using Huffman coding. The basic idea of Huffman coding is that symbols that occur frequently have a smaller representation than those that occur rarely. The a_i part of the bit sequence bs_i is a variable length integer code generated as follows: If $d_i = 0$, s_i is coded as 00 and a_i is not represented. For any non-zero d_i, n_i is trivially computed as $\lfloor \log_2(|d_i|) \rfloor$. If $d_i>0$, a_i corresponds to the n_i lower-order bits of the direct representation of d_i. If $d_i<0$, a_i corresponds to the n_i lower-order bits of the two's complement representation of $(d_i -1)$. The procedure used to generate a_i guarantees that all the possible values have different codes. Once bs_i is generated, it is appended to the bit stream which forms the compressed version of the sequence of measures m_i. Since transmission of a bit needs energy comparable to the execution of thousand instructions, just saving only a bit by compressing original data corresponds to reduce power consumption. Table 1 is the dictionary used by the LEC algorithm. It was constructed based on the explanations above.

4 Proposed Compression Scheme

The dynamic range of source symbols is a key factor in achieving compression ratio. The block diagram of the new image compression technique proposed to reduce the original image size is given Fig. 1. From the block diagram, the original grayscale image is first applied to the pixel re-ordering block where the original image pixels are scanned according to the pixel scanning method given in Fig. 2 to take advantage of the high correlation that normally exist between neighboring pixels. The output of the pixel re-ordering block is a one dimensional image signal r_i. The difference between consecutive pixel values in the one dimensional image signal is taken to lower the dynamic range of the source symbols (pixels). Because of the high correlation that exists between neighboring pixels, the most frequent difference between consecutive re-ordered pixels is 0. And in order to avoid the cost of computing frequencies on the sensor node, we took advantage of the amount of work already carried out on LEC algorithm by adopting Table 2 which coincides with the first 9 rows of the dictionary used in both the JPEG and the LEC algorithms for compression. Each output d_i of the differential scheme unit is then encoded by the entropy encoder as a bit sequence c_i made up of two parts $h_i \mid l_i$ where h_i codifies the number b_i of bits needed to represent d_i and l_i is the representation of d_i. For each d_i, the algorithm determines the number b_i of bits needed to represent d_i. For $d_i = 0$, $b_i = 0$, else $b_i = \lfloor floor(\log_2(|d_i|)) + 1 \rfloor$. Next, using the value of b_i, the prefix code h_i is extracted from the lookup table, h_i being the higher-order bits of the compressed data. Next, the suffix code l_i which is the low-order bits of the compressed difference data is then computed using 2's complement representation of d_i in b_i bits.

Table 1. Compression Rule Used By LEC Algorithm

n_i	s_i	d_i
0	00	0
1	010	−1,+1
2	011	−3,−2,+2,+3
3	100	−7, . . . ,−4,+4, . . .,+7
4	101	−15, . . . ,−8,+8, . . .,+15
5	110	−31, . . . ,−16,+16, . . .,+31
6	1110	−63, . . . ,−32,+32, . . .,+63
7	11110	−127, . . . ,−64,+64, . . .,+127
8	111110	−255, . . . ,−128,+128, . . .,+255
9	1111110	−511, . . . ,−256,+256, . . .,+511
10	11111110	−1023, . . . ,−512,+512, . . .,+1023
11	111111110	−2047, . . . ,−1024,+1024, . . .,+2047
12	1111111110	−4095, . . . ,−2048,+2048, . . .,+4095
13	11111111110	−8191, . . . ,−4096,+4096, . . .,+8191
14	111111111110	−16383, . . . ,−8192,+8192, . . .,+16383

When $d_i = 0$, l_i is not represented. Whenever $d_i > 0$, l_i is the direct binary representation of d_i using b_i bits. Whenever $d_i < 0$, l_i is the b_i low-order bits of the 2's complement representation of $(d_i - 1)$. The way l_i is generated ensures that all possible values of d_i have different codes. Finally, the higher-order bits h_i and the low-order bits l_i are concatenated to generate a compressed data c_i. c_i is then appended to the bit stream that forms the compressed version of the pixel values sequence r_i.

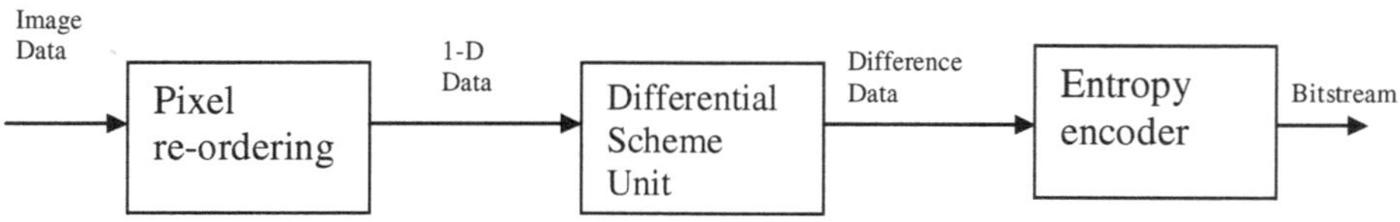

Fig. 1. Block diagram of our proposed image compression scheme

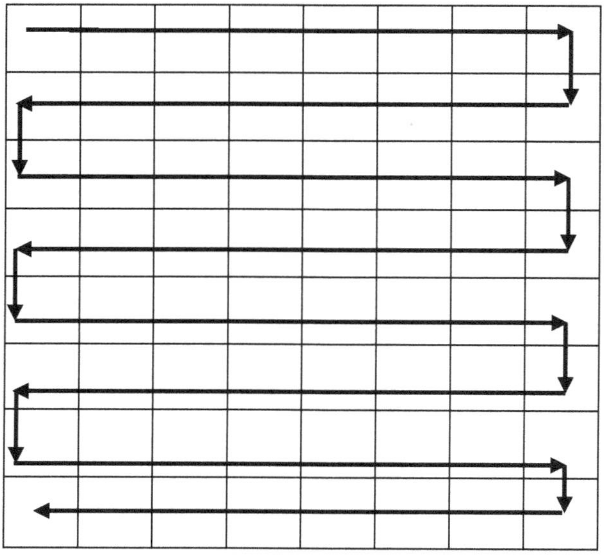

Fig. 2. Our proposed pixel scanning method to take advantage of the correlation between neighboring pixels

Our proposed lossless visual image compression algorithm is summarized below:

1. The grayscale image is read onto the MATLAB workspace.
2. Call a function that scans the image matrix according to our proposed scanning pattern and return a 1-D image vector array r_i.
3. Call a function that computes the difference between consecutive pixel values of the 1-D image vector array and returns the difference d_i.
4. Call a function that computes and returns the difference category b_i.
5. Call a function that extracts from the lookup table the variable length prefix-free code h_i that corresponds to b_i.
6. Call a function that computes the 2's complement of d_i using b_i bits and returns l_i.
7. Call a function that concatenates h_i and l_i and returns c_i.
8. Call a function that appends c_i to the bitstream.

5 Experiments and Results

To show the effectiveness of our image compression algorithm, we use it to compress 8 grayscale images out of which 6 are 256 X 256 standard grayscale test images available at [27-29]. All the test images used by us are 256 X 256 each with the exception of the horizon image which is 170 X 170. These grayscale images namely David, Lena, Bird, Camera, Horizon, Seagull, Tiffany and Circles are shown in Fig. 3. These test images are loaded into MATLAB workspace individually and scanned using our proposed scanning method in Fig. 2. The statistical analysis of all the resultant 1-D image data sets was performed and recorded in Table 3. Most importantly, we computed the mean $\bar{s}$ and the standard deviation $\sigma_{\bar{s}}$ of the pixels in the original 1-D image data sets. The mean $\bar{d}$ and the standard deviation $\sigma_{\bar{d}}$ of the differences between consecutive pixel values in the 1-D image data sets were also computed. We also computed the information entropy $H = -\sum_{i=1}^{N} p(r_i).\log_2 p(r_i)$ of the original 1-D image data sets, where N is the number of possible values of r_i (the output of the pixel re-ordering block) and $p(r_i)$ is the probability mass function of r_i. Finally, the information entropy $H_d = -\sum_{i=1}^{N} p(d_i).\log_2 p(d_i)$ of the difference between consecutive pixel values of the 1-D image data sets was also computed. These are all recorded in Table 3. In addition, we plotted the distribution of difference between consecutive pixel values of the 1-D image data set for each of the 8 test images used. The plots are shown in Fig. 4.

From Table 3 we observe that the image "circles" have the lowest entropy value followed by seagull, horizon, bird, Tiffany, camera, David and Lena in that order. That is, Lena image has the highest entropy value. Similarly, we also observe from Fig. 4 that the image 'circles' have the highest level of correlation between pixel values with frequency of 64733 for difference value of "0". The next in terms of high correlation is the seagull and the least is Lena. Thus, the differential scheme (differencing) applied to the 1-D 1mage data sets have increased the compressibility of the image data as the dynamic range of the pixel values is greatly reduced. From the foregoing, the performance of the entropy compression algorithm should be highest for the circles and least for Lena image.

The performance of our proposed image compression algorithm will be determined in terms of compression ratio (CR) which is defined as

$$CR = 100.\left(1 - \frac{CS}{OS}\right). \tag{1}$$

where CS is the compressed image size in bytes and OS is the original image size in bytes. Each uncompress grayscale image pixel is represented by 8-bits (1 byte) unsigned integers since grayscale image pixels take value in the range 0-255. For the computation of the first difference by the differential scheme (differencing) unit, the difference is taken between the first pixel value in the 1-D image data set and 128, 128 being the centre value among 256 discrete pixel values. Table 4 shows the results we obtained after the application of the proposed lossless entropy image compression algorithm to all the 8 test images. From Table 4, the compression ratio performance obtained by our proposed lossless entropy image compression algorithm agrees with the statistical characteristics in Table 3. The image "circles" that is characterized by the lowest mean of the difference between consecutive pixel values in the 1-D image data and also characterized by lowest entropies (1.78 and 0.13 for H and H_d respectively) achieves the highest compression ratio of 73.22%. This is due to the high correlation that exists between the image background (that is black all through) pixels and the high correlation that also exist between the object pixels. See Fig. 3 for a view of the circles image. Following next in terms of high compression ratio is the "seagull" image that records compression ratio of 59.67%. The "seagull" is also characterized by lowest mean of the difference data and low entropies (4.73 and 2.57 for H and H_d respectively). Note also that the background (white all through) pixels of the seagull image are highly correlated and the object "seagull" itself have region of high correlation on it in terms of neighboring pixel values. Following next in terms of high compression ratio is the "horizon" image that records a compression ratio of 47.06%. The "horizon" is characterized by low mean and low standard deviation of the difference data and low entropy (3.96 for H_d). It has highly correlated regions. Following next in terms of high compression ratio is the "bird" image that records compression ratio of 42.00%. The "bird" image is characterized by low mean and low standard deviation of the difference data and low entropy (4.19 for H_d). The "bird" image has highly correlated background and the object (bird) also has regions of high correlation. Following next in terms of high compression ratio is the "camera" image that records compression ratio of 33.96%. The "camera" image is characterized by low mean of the difference data and entropy of 5.03 for H_d that is slightly high. The "camera" image has medially correlated background and the object (camera man) also has regions of medial correlation. Next in line in terms of compression ratio is the "Tiffany" image which records compression ratio of 33.51%. Its 1-D difference image data set is characterized by low mean and entropy of 4.97 (slightly high). The image is medially correlated. Next is "David" image which is characterized by low mean of the difference between consecutive pixel values in the 1-D image data and high entropy values of 7.46 and 5.27 for H and H_d respectively. It records compression ratio of 30.30%. David image is characterized by medially correlated background and object. Lastly, "Lena" image is characterized by the highest entropy values (7.57 and 5.58 for H and H_d respectively) when compared to the remaining test images and there is no doubt it performed least in terms of compression ratio with a value of 26.21%. Lena image has the least correlation as evident from Fig. 3 and Fig. 4. The background and the object on the "Lena" image are poorly correlated and that led to the poor performance. From the foregoing, it can be seen that the level of correlation between the pixels of the image background together with the level of correlation of the object in the image greatly affect the compression performance.

Therefore, our proposed lossless image compression algorithm shows better compression ratio for images having higher redundancy when compared with the images of lower redundancy. Our proposed lossless image compression algorithm can find use in applications such as smart farming, visual recognition, security and surveillance monitoring, etc. To enhance the compression performance of our proposed algorithm, the camera mounted on the visual sensor node could be positioned such that the background of the captured image will be highly correlated. This way compression ratio of about 40% and above will be attainable as evident from bird, horizon, seagull and circles images.

The compressed images could then be sent over the wireless network to the sink in short amount of time thereby increasing the energy efficiency of the visual sensor node. The network lifetime is also improved.

Our proposed simple lossless compression scheme was compared with the schemes proposed in [17] and [21]. The scheme proposed in [17] is computationally more complex than our proposed scheme and needs additional hardware (field programmable gate array) for its implementation. It also needs more memory for processing and buffering. The scheme proposed in [21] called Image Subtraction with Quantization of Image (ISQ) was proposed for fixed standalone sensor nodes. It needs additional memory for storing the image of the environment it is installed in. The scheme is simple and can easily be implemented in WSNs since it only computes the small changes between the stored image and the new captured image. However, the changes are quantized before encoding which makes the scheme lossy.

Table 2. The Dictionary Used In Our Proposed Algorithm

b_i	h_i	d_i
0	00	0
1	010	−1,+1
2	011	−3,−2,+2,+3
3	100	−7, . . . ,−4,+4, . . .,+7
4	101	−15, . . . ,−8,+8, . . .,+15
5	110	−31, . . . ,−16,+16, . . .,+31
6	1110	−63, . . . ,−32,+32, . . .,+63
7	11110	−127, . . . ,−64,+64, . . .,+127
8	111110	−255, . . . ,−128,+128, . . .,+255

Table 3. Statistical characteristics of the 1-D dataset of test images

Image	$\bar{s} \pm \sigma_{\bar{s}}$	$\bar{d} \pm \sigma_{\bar{d}}$	H	H_d
David (256X256)	110.07 ± 48.03	-9.46E-04 ± 14.03	7.46	5.27
Lena (256X256)	98.68 ± 52.29	-0.0018 ± 18.07	7.57	5.58
Bird (256X256)	125.39 ± 46.01	-5.95E-04 ± 8.92	6.77	4.19
camera (256X256)	118.72 ± 62.34	-5.34E-04 ± 22.74	7.01	5.03
Horizon(170X170)	129.48 ± 66.40	0.0031 ± 8.76	7.70	3.96
Seagull(256X256)	178.85 ± 91.98	0 ± 10.46	4.73	2.57
Tiffany(256X256)	150.79 ± 35.30	-2.59E-04 ± 12.84	6.81	4.97
circles (256X256)	94.17 ± 87.17	0 ± 19.24	1.78	0.13

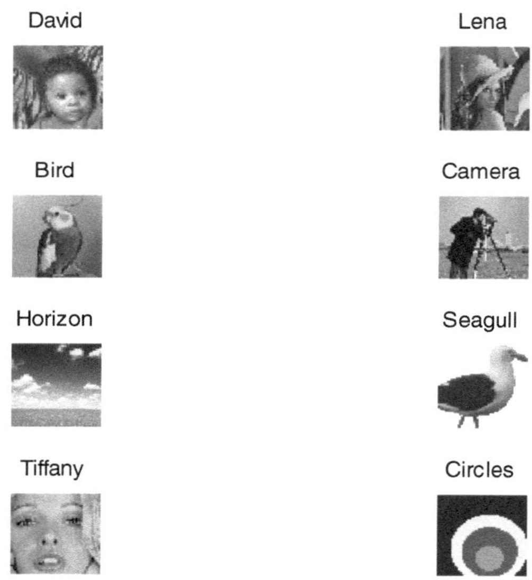

Fig. 3. Test images used to assess the performance of our algorithm

Table 4. Compression performance obtained by our algorithm on the test images (File size in Bytes)

Image	Original size	Compressed size	Compression Ratio
David (256X256)	65536	45679	30.30%
Lena (256X256)	65536	48359	26.21%
Bird (256X256)	65536	38009	42.00%
camera (256X256)	65536	43277	33.96%
Horizon(170X170)	28900	15301	47.06%
Seagull(256X256)	65536	26433	59.67%
Tiffany(256X256)	65536	43573	33.51%
circles (256X256)	65536	17549	73.22%

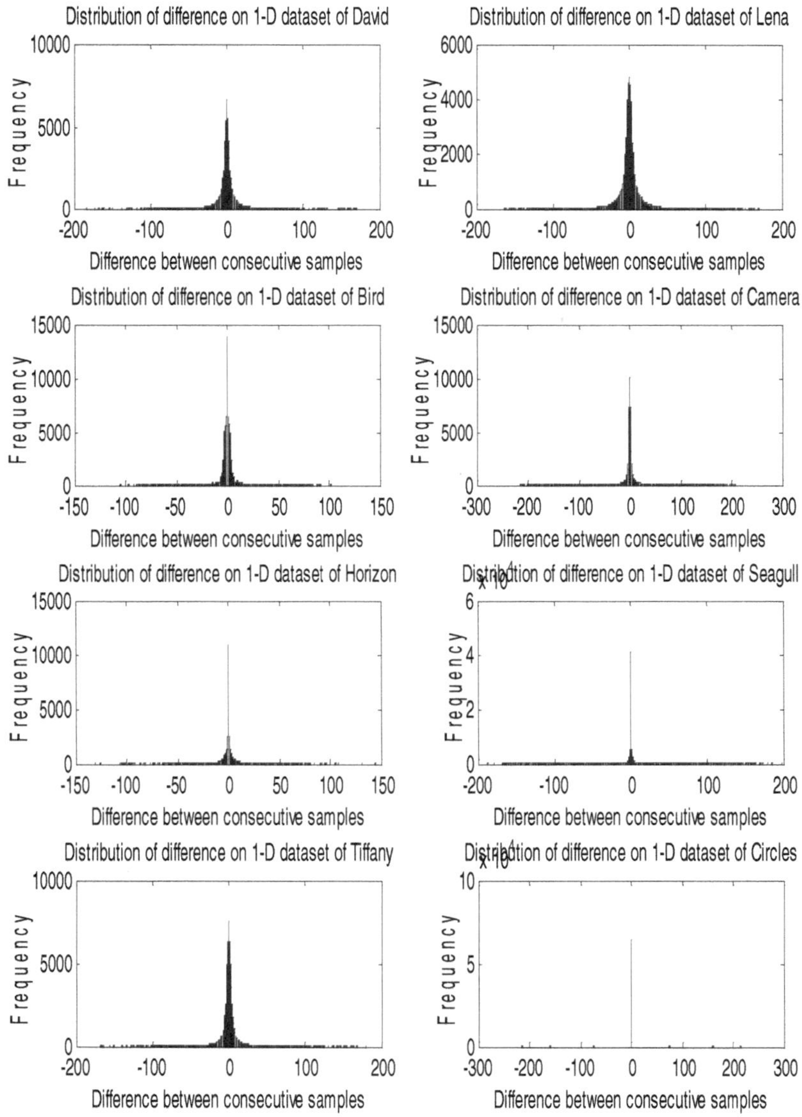

Fig. 4. The distribution of difference on the 1-D 1mage data sets of the 8 test images

6 Conclusion

In this paper, we proposed a simple lossless entropy image compression scheme for the compression of image data in visual sensor nodes. We applied differential scheme to the original image data to exploits the high correlation that exists between neighboring pixels. To ensure that our compression algorithm is simple since wireless sensors usually have extreme resource constraints like low processing power and storage, we modified a traditional WSN data compression scheme to make it suitable for image compression. From our experimental results, we obtained a compression ratio of up to 73.22% for a highly correlated image data without incurring information loss. Thus, the proposed scheme will be suitable for the compression of visual images.

References

1. Akyildiz, I.F., Melodia, T., Chowdhury, K.R.: A survey on wireless multimedia sensor networks. Computer Networks 51, 921–960 (2007)
2. Kulkarni, R.V., Forster, A., Venayagamoorthy, G.K.: Computational Intelligence in Wireless Sensor Networks: A Survey. IEEE Communications Surveys & Tutorials 13, 68–96 (2011)
3. Yick, J., Mukherjee, B., Ghosal, D.: Wireless sensor network survey. Computer Networks 52, 2292–2330 (2008)
4. Akyildiz, I.: Wireless sensor networks: a survey. Computer Networks 38, 393–422 (2002)
5. Chew, L.W., Ang, L., Seng, K.: Survey of image compression algorithms in wireless sensor networks. In: International Symposium on Information Technology, ITSim 2008, vol. 4, pp. 1–9 (2008)
6. Anastasi, G., Conti, M., Di Francesco, M., Passarella, A.: Energy conservation in wireless sensor networks: A survey. Ad Hoc Networks 7, 537–568 (2009)
7. Kimura, N., Latifi, S.: A survey on data compression in wireless sensor networks. In: International Conference on Information Technology: Coding and Computing (ITCC 2005), vol. II, pp. 8–13 (2005)
8. Tharini, C.: An Efficient Data Gathering Scheme for Wireless Sensor Networks. European Journal of Scientific Research 43, 148–155 (2010)
9. Dolfus, K., Braun, T.: An Evaluation of Compression Schemes for Wireless Networks. In: International Congress on Ultra Modern Telecommunications and Control Systems and Workshops (ICUMT), pp. 1183–1188 (2010)
10. van der Byl, A., Neilson, R., Wilkinson, R.H.: An evaluation of compression techniques for Wireless Sensor Networks. In: Africon 2009, pp. 1–6 (2009)
11. Tharini, C., Vanaja Ranjan, P.: Design of Modified Adaptive Huffman Data Compression Algorithm for Wireless Sensor Network. Journal of Computer Science 5, 466–470 (2009)
12. Marcelloni, F., Vecchio, M.: An Efficient Lossless Compression Algorithm for Tiny Nodes of Monitoring Wireless Sensor Networks. The Computer Journal 52, 969–987 (2009)
13. Barr, K.C., Asanović, K.: Energy-aware lossless data compression. ACM Transactions on Computer Systems 24, 250–291 (2006)
14. Marcelloni, F., Vecchio, M.: A Simple Algorithm for Data Compression in Wireless Sensor Networks. IEEE Communications Letters 12, 411–413 (2008)

15. Schoellhammer, T., Greenstein, B., Osterweil, E., Wimbrow, M., Estrin, D.: Lightweight temporal compression of microclimate datasets. In: 29th Annual IEEE International Conference on Local Computer Networks, pp. 516–524 (2004)
16. Sadler, C.M., Martonosi, M.: Data compression algorithms for energy-constrained devices in delay tolerant networks. In: Proceedings of the 4th International Conference on Embedded Networked Sensor Systems - SenSys 2006, p. 265 (2006)
17. Chew, L.W., Chia, W.C., Ang, L.-M., Seng, K.P.: Very Low-Memory Wavelet Compression Architecture Using Strip-Based Processing for Implementation in Wireless Sensor Networks. EURASIP Journal on Embedded Systems 2009, 1–16 (2009)
18. Huu, P.N., Tran-quang, V., Miyoshi, T.: Image Compression Algorithm Considering Energy Balance on Wireless Sensor Networks. Image, 1005–1010 (2010)
19. Enesi, I., Zanaj, E., Kamo, B., Kolici, V., Shurdi, O.: Image Compression for Wireless Outdoor Sensor Networks Related research. In: BALWOIS 2010 - Ohrid, Republic of Macedonia, May 29-25, pp. 1–11 (2010)
20. Razzak, M.I., Hussain, S.A., Minhas, A.A., Sher, M.: Collaborative Image Compression in Wireless Sensor Networks. International Journal of Computational Cognition 8(1), 24–29 (2010), http://Www.Ijcc.Us
21. Hussain, S.A., Razzak, M.I., Minhas, A.A., Sher, M., Tahir, G.R.: Energy Efficient Image Compression in Wireless Sensor Networks. International Journal of Recent Trends in Engineering 2(1), 2–5 (2009)
22. Wugnef, R., Nowak, R., Baruniuk, R.: Distributed Image Compression For Sensor Networks Using Correspondence Analysis and Super-Resolution. Analysis, 597–600 (2003)
23. Chow, K.-Y., Lui, K.-S., Lam, E.Y.: Efficient On-Demand Image Transmission in Visual Sensor Networks. EURASIP Journal on Advances in Signal Processing 2007, 1–12 (2007)
24. Welch, T.: A Technique for High-Performance Data Compression. Computer 17(6), 8–19 (1984)
25. Huffman, D.A.: A method for the construction of minimum-redundancy codes. Proceedings of the Institute of Radio Engineers 40(9), 1098–1101 (1952)
26. Pennebaker, W.B., Mitchell, J.L.: JPEG Still Image Data Compression Standard. Kluwer Academic Publishers, Norwell (1992)
27. 256X256 Grayscale Test Images, http://www2.isye.gatech.edu/~brani/datapro.html (accessed June 17, 2011)
28. Standard test images, http://pami.uwaterloo.ca/tizhoosh/images.htm (accessed June 17, 2011)
29. Seagull, http://photo-info.co.nz/articles/removing-image-backgrounds-gimp (accessed June 17, 2011)

Cluster - Head Selection by Remaining Energy Consideration in a Wireless Sensor Network

Norah Tuah, Mahamod Ismail, and Kasmiran Jumari

Department of electrical, electronic and system engineering,
Universiti Kebangsaan Malaysia, UKM Bangi, Selangor, 43600, Malaysia
{norah,mahamod,kbj}@eng.ukm.my

Abstract. Energy competence is a very important study in order to find ways to prolong the lifetime of a wireless sensor network. Therefore a good routing protocol and mechanism need to be design. Cluster based architecture is a well known method to optimize the energy competence in the network and have been applied in LEACH routing protocol. However the LEACH routing protocol that used a round concept have a problem because each node will suffer its rest energy in the current round and will die in the next round due to insufficient energy management in the network. Then, we make an alteration of LEACH's cluster-head selection algorithm by considering an outstanding energy available in each node in order to extend the lifetime of the network. It is known as the Residual Energy (ResEn) algorithm. Consequently, at the end of this paper a comparison analysis for LEACH and ResEn has been simulated using Matlab. As a result, it shows that ResEn algorithm can extended the lifetime of the network.

Keywords: Energy, Cluster-based routing protocols, Wireless Sensor Networks.

1 Introduction

Wireless Sensor Networks (WSNs) are made up of many sensor nodes which work together in data transmission throughout the network. Each of the sensor nodes can sense environmental phenomena such as temperature, sound, wind, and pollution at different locations. So it has been widely used in military, environment, health, home and commercial application. However, each node in the wireless sensor network consumes more energy during data transmission compared to for sensing and computation. Therefore, the node required transmission power grows exponentially with an increase in transmission distance [1]. In order to prolong the network lifetime the amount of traffic and transmission distance has to be considered.

Data transmission over a wireless networks can be use a single hop or multi hop scheme. For short distance a single hop scheme is more practical then multi-hop distance. However, a multi-hop scheme that transmit data by each intermediate hop is more practical for long-data transmission which less costly in terms of energy consumption. A multi-hop scheme may be organized into flat and hierarchical architecture. In a flat network, each node uses its peer nodes as a relays when

A. Abd Manaf et al. (Eds.): ICIEIS 2011, Part III, CCIS 253, pp. 498–507, 2011.

communicating with the sink as shown in Fig. 1. Some examples of flat routing protocol are Flooding, Gossiping, Sequential Assignment Routing (SAR), Directed Diffusion and Sensor Protocol for Information via negotiation (SPIN).

In a hierarchical network, sensor nodes are structured into clusters, each member node in the cluster will send their data to the cluster heads which serve as relays for transmitting the data to the sink. Low Energy Adaptive Clustering Hierarchy (LEACH), Power Efficient Gathering in Sensor Information System (PEGASIS), Threshold Sensitive Energy Efficient sensor Network protocol (TEEN) etc is an example of hierarchical routing protocol. Fig. 2 and Fig.3 shows an example of two types of hierarchical architecture according to the distance between the cluster members and their cluster head.

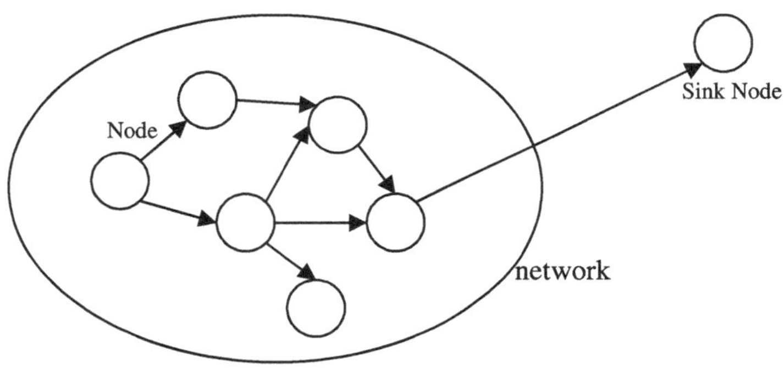

Fig. 1. Flat Network architecture

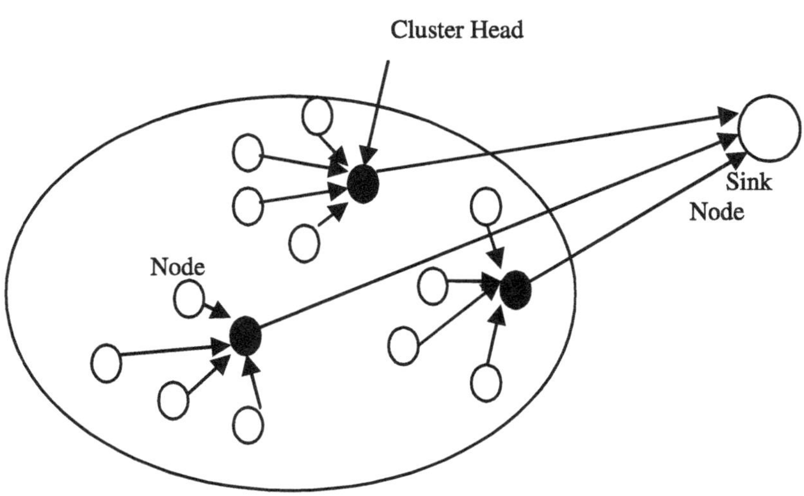

Fig. 2. Single-hop clustering architecture

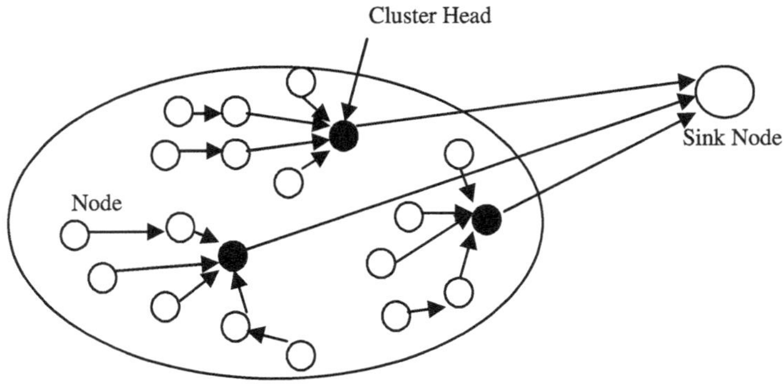

Fig. 3. Multi-hop clustering architecture

1.1 Related Works

A cluster-based wireless sensor network has been the subject of widespread studies by considering the energy competence as the main focus of many clustering protocols proposed so far. Heinzelman et al. [2] were among the first researchers who worked on the cluster- based networks. They proposed a routing protocol with self-organizing and adaptive clustering that used randomization to distribute the energy load among the sensors in the network which was called Low-Energy Adaptive Clustering Hierarchy (LEACH). It used a localized coordination to enable scalability and robustness for active networks. It applied a data fusion in the network to reduce the amount of information that must be sent to the base station.

M.J.Handy et al [3] modified this LEACH protocol by extending LEACH's stochastic cluster head selection algorithm using a deterministic component. With_this selection method, the nodes only need local information and no global information (communication with base station) is necessary to become the cluster-head. With this modification, the network lifetime has been increased to 30%.

M.S.Ali et al. [4] proposed selecting the highest energy node as the cluster head to ensure that all nodes die at approximately the same time. This can be achieved by introducing new threshold equation of cluster head selection called general probability and current state probability. As a result, the death rate of the nodes is reduced which in turn prolongs the lifetime of the network.

M.C.M.Thein et al. [5] customized the LEACH's stochastic cluster head selection algorithm according to the residual energy of a node in relation to the residual energy of a network. Their proposed model can stabilize the energy in the network, prolonging the network's lifespan.

X.L.Long et al. [6] made an improvement algorithm which was based on multi-hop LEACH cluster head (LEACH-M) algorithm by considering current node energy taking into account in the cluster head election. Selecting the nodes with huge energy as the cluster head can resolve the problem of nodes with less energy being selected as the cluster head. This improved algorithm effectively extended lifetime of the network.

2 The Developed ResEn Algorithm

In this section we describe ResEn algorithm, which improve the lifetime of the network. Generally ResEn algorithm is based on deterministic cluster-head selection [3] which inclusion of the remaining energy level available in each node. Consequently the network model, radio dissipation energy model and the working procedure have been explained in the following part.

2.1 Network Model

Some assumptions behind the implementation of this algorithm is:

1. The sensor node is homogeneous.
2. The BS located is fixed with far distance from the network area.
3. Immobility of sensor nodes.

2.2 Radio Energy Dissipation Model

A free-space energy model as defined in [7] was used, whereby the power expended conveying a *k*-bit message per distance *d* is calculated by equation 1, while power expended in receiving a *k*-bit message is calculated by equation 2. We assumed that the sensor nodes could make an adjustment to their transmission power based on the distance of the receiving node.

$$E_T(k,d) = k\,(E_{Tx\text{-}elec} + \varepsilon_{amp}.d^2) \qquad (1)$$

$$E_R(k) = k\,(E_{Rx\text{-}elec}) \qquad (2)$$

$E_{Tx\text{-}elec}$ and $E_{Rx\text{-}elec}$ means that the power dissipated to operate the transmitter or receiver circuitry and ε_{amp} is the power for transmitting the amplifier.

2.3 The Working Procedure

The algorithm operation can be split into three different phases which are cluster head selection, cluster creation and data transmission. All the phases are explained as follows:

a. Cluster head selection

Each *n* node has a chance to be selected as the cluster head in each round. It will choose a random number between 0 and 1. If the selected random number is less than the threshold *T(n)*, the node becomes a cluster-head for the present round. The threshold *T(n)* was calculated using the equation 3 below.

$$T(n) = \begin{cases} \frac{p}{1-p*(r \bmod \frac{1}{p})} \times \frac{E_{cur}}{E_{init}} & n \in G \\ 0 & otherwise \end{cases} \qquad (3)$$

Where *p* is the preferred percentage of cluster heads, *r* is the current round, E_{cur} is the nodes' current energy, E_{init} is the initial energy of the node and *G* is the set of nodes that have not become as cluster-heads in the last 1/p rounds. The algorithm for cluster head selection is shown in Fig. 4 below. The definition for terms used in the algorithm is *MaxInteral* = total round, *NodeNums* = Number of nodes in the network, *T(i)* = generate threshold value of node i, *Random (1,1)* = generate random number between 0 and 1 and *Broadcast_cluster(i)* = broadcast cluster announcement message for cluster head i

```
for round = 0 to MaxInteral
   for every node i ∈ NodeNums
      if node i was CH in round then
        T(i) = 0
      elseif Random (1,1) < T(i) then
        Broadcast_Cluster(i)
      end if
   end for
end for
```

Fig. 4. The cluster head selection algorithm

b. Cluster creation

After the cluster head node is determined, the cluster head will advertise itself as the new cluster head to the other common nodes (not cluster head). It will broadcast the message which contains the information qualifying itself as the cluster-head and its ID. The common nodes will decide which cluster to follow according to the strength of the advertisement signal by sending a *follow-req* message back to the corresponding cluster-head. After the cluster head has received the *follow-req* message from each node member in its cluster, the cluster head will create a TDMA schedule, informing each node when it can transmit data. The algorithm for cluster formation is shown in Fig. 5 below. The terms used in the algorithm are *NodeNums* = Number of nodes in the network, *CH* = cluster head, *Head_msg* = Cluster head message and *Follow_clstr_msg* = Following cluster message

```
for every node i ∈ NodeNums
    if node is CH
       Broadcast Head_msg
       Wait for follow cluster
    End if
end for
for every node i ∈ NodeNums
  if node is not CH
       Receive all Head_msg
       Compute the distance for each CH
       Choose the CH with min(distance) and broadcast follow_clstr_msg
  End if
End for
```

Fig. 5. The cluster creation algorithm

c. Data transmission

Data transmission starts after the cluster is formed and the TDMA schedule is fixed. In this work, a 10 TDMA frames each round have been set to reduce clustering cost. The cluster head will combine data from all common nodes in its cluster before sending it to the base station. It requires a high-energy consumption for transmission the data to the base station which is located far away.

3 Simulation and Results

Table 1 shows the parameters that have been used in the simulation using MATLAB.

Table 1. Lists of simulation parameters

Parameter	Value
The size of the network	$[0,150]^2$
Number of sensor nodes	100
Location of BS	[75,200]
Original Energy	2J
E_{elec}	50 nJ/bits
E_{amf}	100 pJ/bit/m^2
Data Size	2000 bits
Probability	0.05
Communication range	10m

We simulated the network for 1000 rounds and calculated the average lifetime, the energy consumption in each round and the average remaining energy for the cluster head. Communication between sensors and their_cluster head and between cluster heads to base Station was single-hop. The radio model was similar to that of [2], in which E_{elec} = 50 nJ/bits, E_{amf} = 100 pJ/bit/m^2 and data size was 2000 bits.

To analyze the performance of ResEn algorithm, we compared it with LEACH. LEACH is a routing protocol with self-organizing and adaptive clustering that uses randomization to distribute the energy load among the sensors in the network. Fig. 6 shows the energy dissemination for each node during the setup phase. The setup phase occurs throughout the cluster head selection and cluster formation. The node uses energy to receive and transmit data. From the graph, it shows that the ResEn , as an algorithm with remaining energy among cluster node members consideration, has a better energy consumption capacity compared to LEACH.

Fig. 7 shows the average remaining energy of the chosen cluster head nodes over time. The LEACH graph was decreased slightly until it reached the minimum average remaining energy of 0.2 J after 500 rounds. For ResEn, the graph was decreased until it reached the minimum average remaining energy between 1 J to 0.6J after 300 rounds. When LEACH is used, it is not considered the remaining energy in the network during selecting the nodes as the cluster head. Comparatively, ResEn, which considers the remaining energy in the network in selecting the cluster head nodes, has shown a better performance than LEACH.

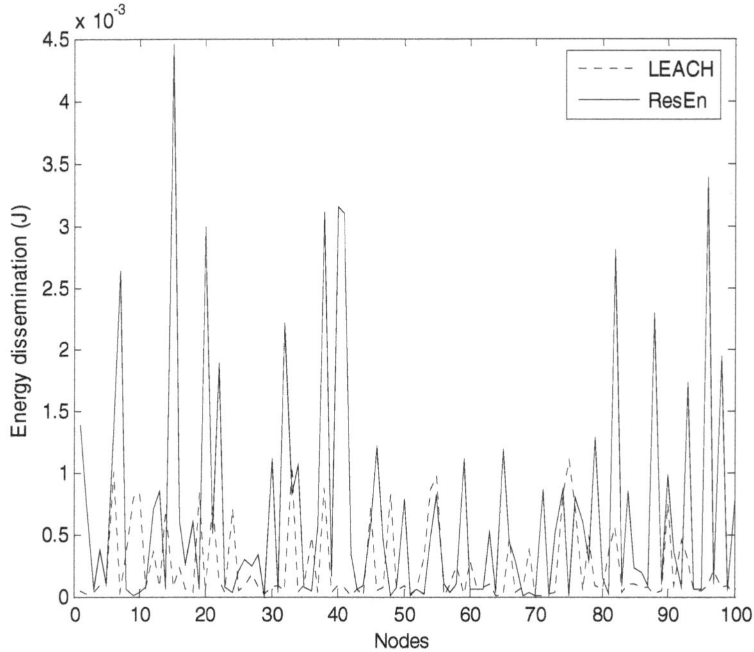

Fig. 6. Energy dissemination for each node during the setup phase

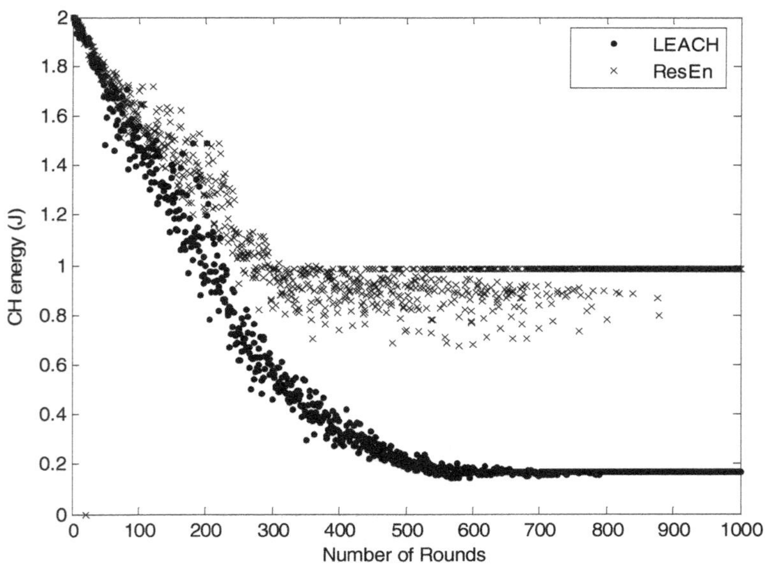

Fig. 7. Average remaining energy of the cluster head

Fig. 8 shows the comparison of the lifetime of the nodes of both routing protocols after 1000 rounds. According to this graph, ResEn may expand the lifetime of the network longer than LEACH. In LEACH, each time a node becomes a cluster head, it dissolves the same amount of energy. As a result, it leads to inefficient selection of heads which depletes the network faster.

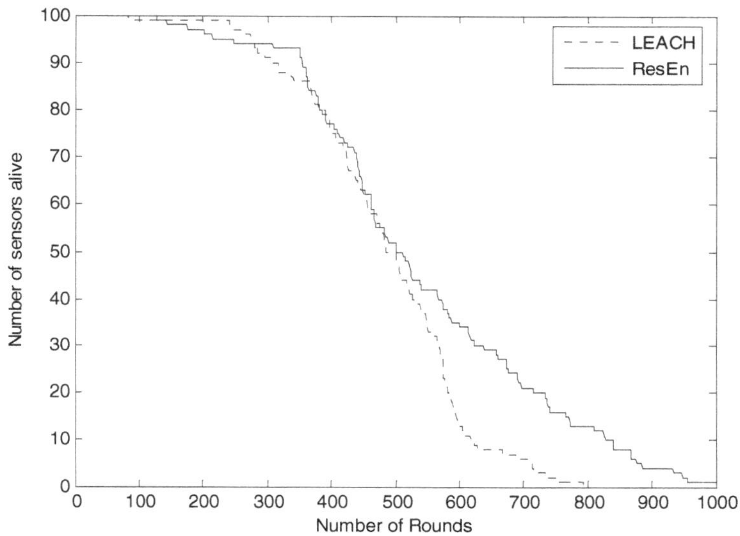

Fig. 8. Number of live sensors

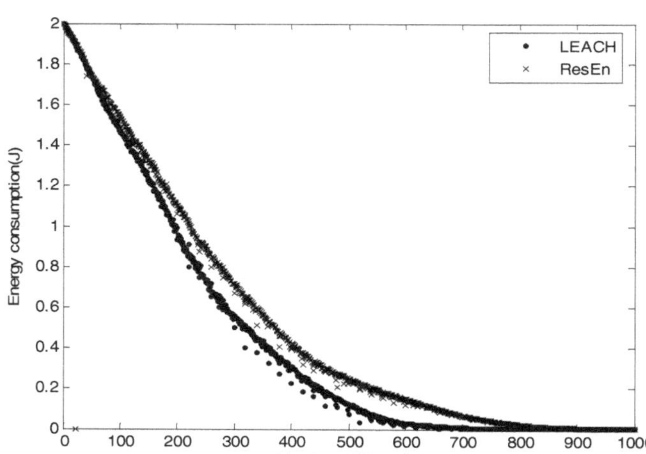

Fig. 9. Energy consumption throughout the rounds

Fig. 9 shows the comparison of energy consumption with respect to the number of rounds for both protocols. The energy consumption decreased with the reduction of the number of live nodes with each round (as shown in Fig.8), nodes that transmit data are reduced in number. This indicates that ResEN is more energy efficient compared to LEACH.

According to Fig. 10, if the number of TDMA frames is increased to 20, the network lifetime is reduced to almost half. It occurs because the cluster head has to send more messages to the sink during each round. So the cluster head has to use twice the amount of energy in each round. From the graph, it shows that the ResEn graph decreased earlier than LEACH before it went back to its normal ability to extend the network's lifetime after 450 rounds.

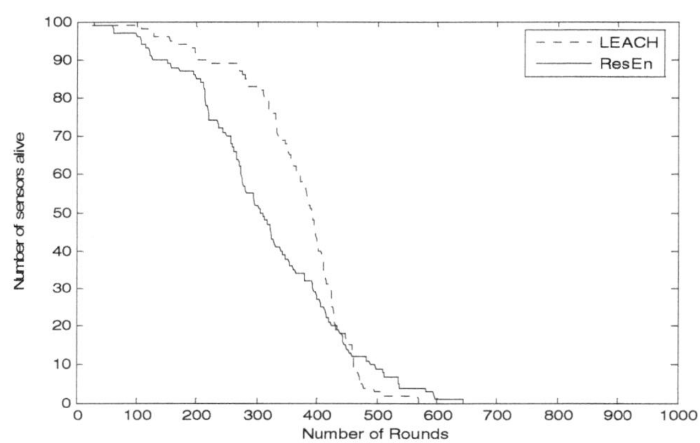

Fig. 10. Number of sensors alive for TDMA with 20 frames

4 Conclusion

The cluster head generation algorithm with the original LEACH clustering protocol may lead to the redundancy of cluster heads in a small region which causes a significant energy loss. To overcome this problem, residual energy has been consider during cluster head selection algorithm in this paper. As a result, it shows that ResEn algorithm can extended the lifetime of the network. For future work, we plan to do some consideration on the network as: 1. In order to increase the lifetime of the network, we will work in intra and inter- cluster communication (Hierarchical architecture) 2. The improvement of our proposed algorithm by combining different approaches introduced by other researchers such as distance, voting-based clustering, optimal cluster number selection and others. 3. Network coverage consideration in a cluster head determination for wireless sensor networks.

Acknowledgments. We would like to thank the reviewers for their comments. This research was supported by research grant UKM-OUP-ICT-36-185/2011 and Universiti Teknologi MARA Malaysia.

References

1. Zheng, J., Jamalipour, A.: Wireless sensor networks: A Networking Perspective. John Wiley & Sons, Inc. (2009)
2. Heinzelman, W., Chandrakasan, A., Balakrishnan, H.: Energy-efficient communication protocol for wireless sensor networks. In: Proceeding of the 33rd Hawaii International Conference on System Sciences (2000)
3. Handy, M.J., Haase, M., Timmermann, D.: Low energy adaptive clustering hierarchy with deterministic cluster-head selection. In: Proceeding of IEEE Mobile and Wireless Communication Network (2002)
4. Ali, M.S., Dey, T., Biswas, R.: ALEACH:Advanced LEACH routing protocol for wireless microsensor networks. In: Proceeding of IEEE 5th International Conference on Electrical and Computer Engineering (2008)
5. Thein, M.C.M., Thein, T.: An energy efficient cluster-head selection for wireless sensor networks. In: Proceeding of IEEE International Conference on Intelligent Systems, Modelling and Simulation (2010)
6. Long, X.L., Jun, Z.J.: Improved LEACH cluster head multi-hops algorithm in wireless sensor networks. In: Proceeding of IEEE 9th International Symposium on Distributed Computing and Applications to Business, Engineering and Sciences (2010)
7. Heinzelman, W.R., Sinha, A., Wang, A., Chandakasan, A.P.: Energy- scalable algorithms and protocols for wireless micro sensor networks. In: Proceeding of IEEE Acoustic, Speech and Signal Processing (2000)

Bluetooth Inter-piconet Congestion Avoidance Protocol through Network Restructuring

Sabeen Tahir and Abas Md Said

Department of Computer and Information Sciences, Universiti Teknologi PETRONAS, Bandar Seri Iskandar, 31750 Tronoh, Perak, Malaysia
Sabeen135@hotmail.com, abass@petronas.com.my

Abstract. Bluetooth is a low cost wireless technology for short range device. The Bluetooth system can be used for different kinds of data exchange; it carries both synchronous and asynchronous data traffic. Bluetooth basic network is called piconet; multiple connected piconets are called scatternet. The scatternet structure has a great impact on the network performance. Without considering the traffic flow, a scatternet may suffer from serious congestion problem. The objective of this research work is to propose a new Bluetooth Inter-piconet Congestion Avoidance (ICA) protocol by network restructuring. The main objectives of proposed protocol are to share the traffic load and find the shortest routing path for pairs of Bluetooth sources and destinations. Simulation results show that proposed protocol reduces control overhead, decreases delay and improves network throughput.

Keywords: Congestion, Restructuring, Fairness, Bluetooth scatternet.

1 Introduction

In 1998, a cluster of manufacturers proposed an open standard for short range 10m wireless connectivity that works in an ad hoc fashion entitled as Bluetooth (BT) technology. The essential system of Bluetooth consists of a radio frequency transceiver, baseband and protocol stack. Bluetooth is playing a key role in communications with electronic devices, and it is now an emerging standard for Wireless Personal Area Networks (WPANs) [1]. Initially Bluetooth was introduced as cable replacement technology; hence, its radio frequency range was only 10m. However, it used to connect different type of devices in ad hoc fashion, such as PDAs, mobile phone, computers, etc. The Bluetooth radios function in the unlicensed ISM band at 2.4 GHz, which is available worldwide. Bluetooth uses frequency hopping spread spectrum (FHSS) to combat interference. Hopping covers 79 channels in the band with 1 MHz spacing at a rate of 1600 hops per second, which means that each transmission exists in each carrier for $625\mu s$ [2].

Bluetooth defines two types of ad hoc networks: piconet and scatternet [2, 3]. A piconet is a small network within the range of 10m as shown in Fig. 1. A piconet consists of maximum eight active devices, one of the device plays master role and remaining devices act as slaves. In piconet, slave devices cannot directly communicate; they always communicate through a master node. Devices in a piconet always share the same frequency through time division duplex (TDD) technique.

A. Abd Manaf et al. (Eds.): ICIEIS 2011, Part III, CCIS 253, pp. 508–518, 2011.

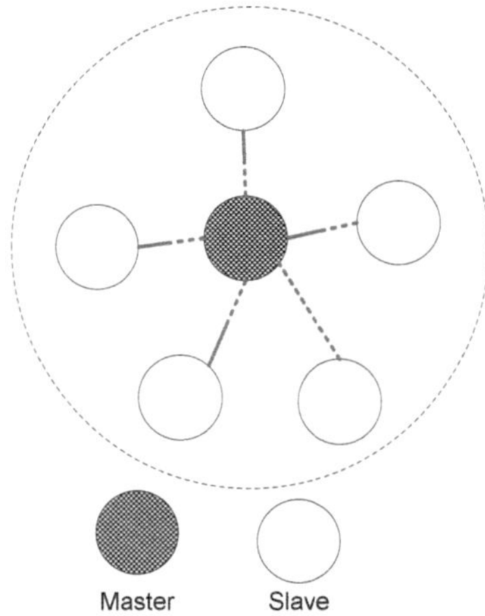

Fig. 1. A simple piconet

Multiple connected piconets are called a scatternet. Devices in different piconets can communicate through bridge node [4, 5], as shown in Fig. 2. A bridge device is responsible for the communication of different piconets, but it has some limitations, e.g., it can be a slave in more than one piconets but it cannot be master within more then one piconet. As a bridge performs scheduling between piconets, the performance of scatternet is highly dependent on the performance of the bridge device, number of bridges and their degree. Before communication, all Bluetooth devices are stay in standby mode. In the second step, a master device executes inquiry whereas the slave devices listen from the master in an inquiry scan procedure. In third step, the master enters into the page mode and slave devices enter into the page scan mode to receive page messages from the master device. Thus, Bluetooth devices make connections for communication.

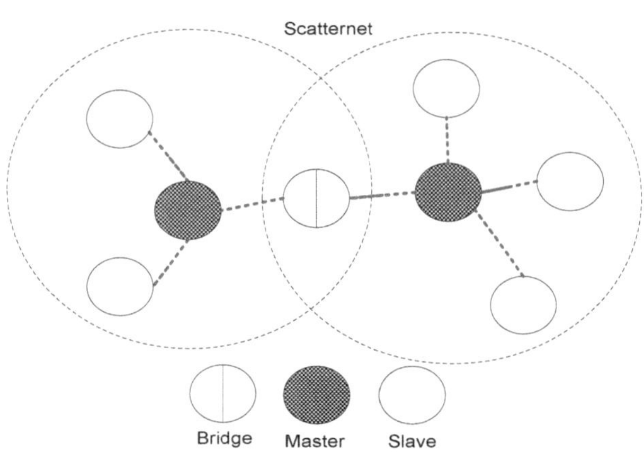

Fig. 2. Bluetooth Scatternet

There are many protocols for inter-piconet communication, but for this research only the most relevant protocol was selected, which is called congestion control of Bluetooth radio system by piconet restructuring (CCPR) [13]. The CCPR was proposed for congestion control, it shares the traffic load by changing some node role to auxiliary masters and bridges. This protocol has some serious drawbacks like loss of AM_Addrs and having the longest route selection for a pair of source and destination. To overcome these problems, we propose a new protocol called Bluetooth Inter-piconet Congestion Avoidance (ICA) by Network Restructuring. The proposed protocol performs network restructuring by a role switch action for congestion avoidance and ensures the shortest path between pair of source and destination.

The rest of the paper is structured as follow: in Section 2, we discuss basics of Bluetooth and some related works. The proposed protocol is described in Section 3. Section 4 discusses the results and comparison. Finally, the paper is summarized in Section 5.

2 Related Work

Scatternet formation protocols proposed until now are not much efficient to establish the network for many applications types. Although there are many studies done on Bluetooth inter-piconet communication [7, 8,9,10, 11], it is still an open research issue because it has not been defined in the Bluetooth specification [3]. Many techniques for Bluetooth scatternet have been proposed by different researchers. As a new technique Dynamic Congestion Control (DCC) [12], protocol has been proposed for congestion avoidance. This technique was implemented for intra-piconet congestion control through the formation of backup relay node. When a single relay node participates in multiple piconets, it may create a problem of bottleneck in the scatternet due to heavy data traffic that the relay handles. Since a master device is always involved for the communication of different slave devices, handling the incoming and outgoing data traffic, thus the master can easily regulate the traffic load. The master monitors the piconet's traffic pattern, and when it detects heavy traffic load on the existing relay, it creates and activates a backup relay to share the load. The DCC protocol can be explained by the Fig. 3. For example, suppose that B_1 is the only relay that is participating in the communication among four different piconets. When the load increases in P3, the master of P3 uses backup relay BR_2 to avoid the local congestion (intra-piconet). Although, DCC is useful to avoid congestion, a serious problem occurs when a single relay participates in multiple piconets and none of the piconets have heavy data traffic.

CCPR [13] tries to avoid congestion in a Bluetooth scatternet. According to CCPR technique, when a master node monitors the traffic load, it performs role switching and reconstructs the piconet. This technique has some serious drawbacks, which are explained by an example. As shown in Fig 4a, (A, M_1, B), (D, M_1, B_1, M_2, G), (B_1, H) and (E, M_2, F) communicate using this technique, to share the traffic load on masters. It reconstructs piconets by making auxiliary masters.

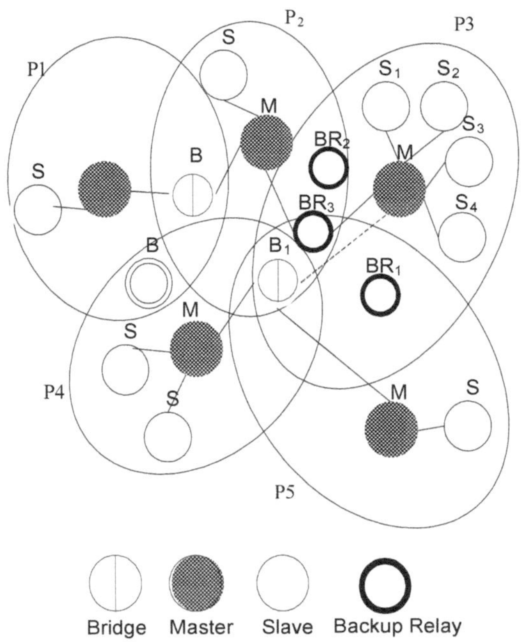

Fig. 3. Congestion control in DCC by using backup relay

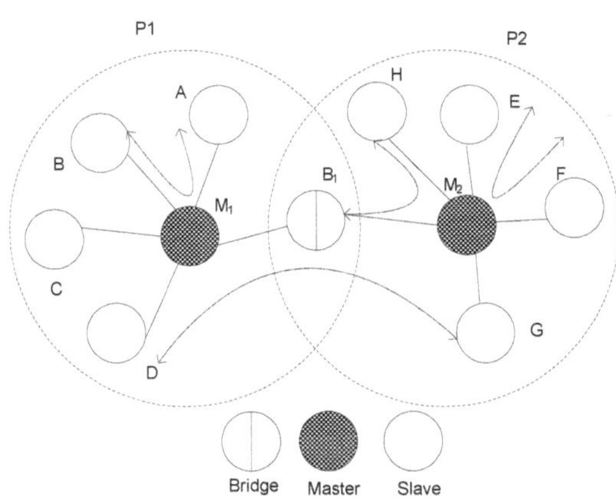

Fig. 4a. Analysis of communication pairs before restructuring of piconets

As shown in Fig. 4b, it reconstructs new piconets by making auxiliary masters (temporary master) B, D, B_1 and E. This technique breaks the links between (A, M_1, B), (D, M_1, B_1, M_2, G), (B_1, H) and (E, M_2, F) and make new links (B, A), (E, F), (B_1, H) and (D, G).

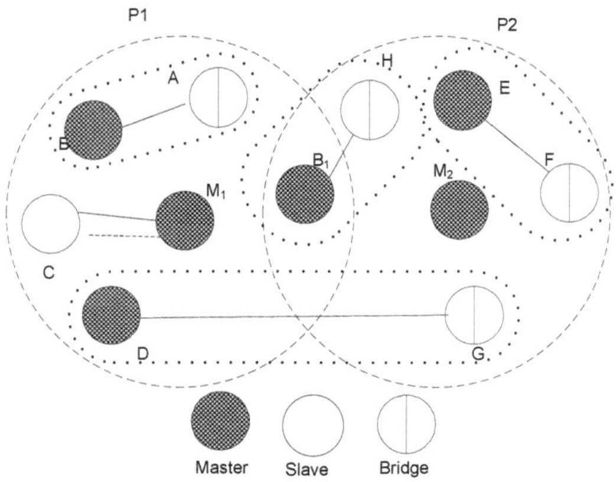

Fig. 4b. Analysis of communication pairs after restructuring of piconets

Suppose, at this point in time, node C wants to communicate with node F or M_2 in another piconet. It cannot send data through the shortest link because of link breakage. Therefore it will follow the longer path and we can see in Fig. 4b the bridge node B_1 has changed its status from a bridge to an auxiliary master, so there is no link between piconets. Another serious problem with this technique is that after t+1 time (any given time), nodes will come back in original states. In this case, due to link breakage, when a new node comes into the piconet, then the master allocates AM_Addr and reaches the limit of AM_Addr. Thus the old node cannot be given AM_Addr as master has no more AM_Addrs.

To solve the issues of inter-piconet formation and communication in a decentralized manner, where dynamic topology alterations are challenging tasks for Bluetooth scatternet, a model for scatternet formation is required. Thus, the inefficiency of DCC and CCPR provides an opportunity to propose a new inter-piconet congestion avoidance protocol for Bluetooth scatternet.

3 The Proposed Inter-piconet Congestion Avoidance (ICA) Protocol

The proposed protocol overcomes the problems in previous techniques. According to the proposed protocol, a network restructuring is performed due to the following situations:

1. Inter piconet congestion
2. When a new devices arrives within the domain of a piconet that already comprises eight devices
3. To find shortest path between a pair of source and destination

For inter-piconet congestion avoidance, a bridge data flow table is maintained on each bridge node, which contains the list of all connected masters. Thus, a bridge node can easily determine the traffic load within network, since a bridge is always involved for incoming and outgoing data traffic. If there is congestion on the bridge device, it checks its data flow table and transmits a request packet for the role switch action.

As shown in Fig 5, A, B, C, D BT devices in P_1 are communicating through $M_1$with each other and E, F, G, H in P_2 are communicating through M_2 with each other therefore congestion may occur on masters $M_1$and M_2. If devices in different piconets are communicating frequently through bridge B_1 then congestion may occur due to B_1.

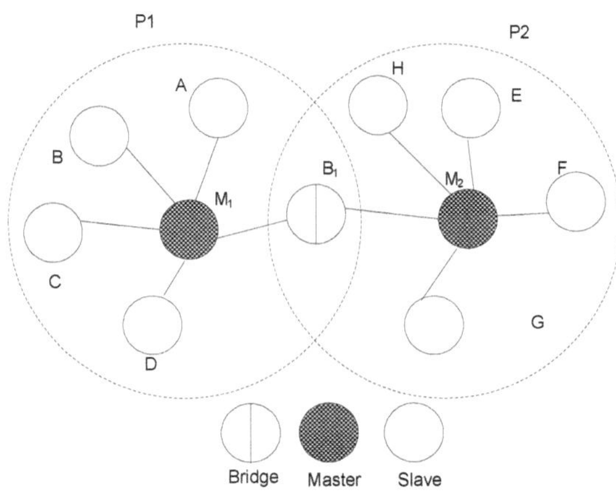

Fig. 5. Construction of scatternet before assigning role switch action

Therefore, the proposed protocol avoids Inter-piconet congestion. The steps of the proposed protocol are given below:

1. Master device has a record of all outgoing and incoming data traffic of slave devices.
2. Bridge device maintains a data flow table, which maintains information of data traffic across the piconets.
3. Performing the role switch action.
   3.1. If congestion occurs on a bridge device, it checks data flow table and transmit a request packet for role switch action to the corresponding masters.
   3.2. If there is a longest route between a pair of source and destination devices while nodes are in the proximity of each other.
4. Data is continually coming from slaves, then corresponding master transmit a request packet, and go to Park Mode (low power) and change status for network restructuring.
5. A slave device is selected as an auxiliary master that has less data traffic and has ability to construct direct connection between devices. If there are two nodes then one will become auxiliary master and other will become slave. In

case if there is an intermediate device then that can perform the function of bridge.

6. If the transmission is over, all devices involved in a scatternet restructuring return to their original states.

Through the fair Bluetooth network restructuring, the traffic load may be shared, and the shortest path for pair of source and destination may be selected. Fig. 6 shows the operation of network restructuring. For example, device D wants to communicate with device G but there is congestion on M_1, B_1, and M_2due to other communications. If D follows the path D-M_1-B_1-M_2-G, that is the longest path. So, for the purpose of sharing traffic load and for the shortest path, masters M_1 and M_2 perform network restructuring. Devices D and G enter into Park mode for a certain period of time and make direct link for communication. According to the proposed protocol, during network reformation, the old link would not be broken so nodes will not lose their AM-Addr. Hence, the resynchronization time of nodes can be saved, which reduces network delay.

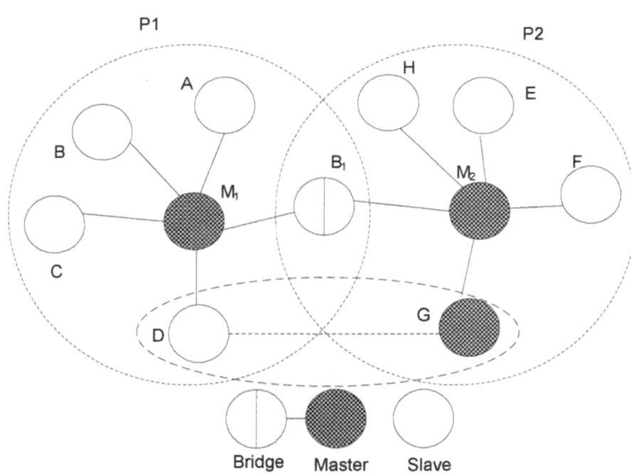

Fig. 6. Construction of scatternet after assigning role switch action

4 Performance Measurement

In this section we discuss the results and compare the proposed Inter-piconet Congestion Avoidance (ICA) protocol with existing CCPR. The results are compared in terms of delay, control overhead and throughput. It is observed that the proposed ICA protocol outperform the CCPR for same issues in inter-piconet communication. The proposed protocol is implemented on the University of Cincinnati's Bluetooth simulator [14], which is based on NS-2 [15]. The parameters [20] used in the simulation are listed in Table. 1. The space size is set to 70m x70m and the number of devices is varied from 15 to 75. Total simulation time is 300s, where the first 60s are used for network construction. The CBR (Constant Bit Rate) traffic is started at 55th s. and the intervals between packets transmissions are set to 0.015s.

Table 1. Simulation parameters

Parameter	Value
The number of nodes	15-75
Network size	70 x 70 m^2
Communication range	10 m
Traffic model	Constant Bit Rate (CBR)
Number of pairs	25 pairs source and destination
Bridge Algorithm	Maximum Distance Rendezvous Point [16]
Scheduling Algorithm	Round Robin
Packet type	DH3, DH5
Simulation time	300s

4.1 Control Packet Overhead

Bluetooth uses different types of control packets for connection activation and exchanging information. Furthermore, each packet requires some extra bytes to store format information in packet header. It is observed that proposed protocol perform better than CCRP in term of control packet. CCPR uses heavy control packets that create overhead for different mobile nodes as shown in Fig. 7. As a master breaks the existing links for constructing new links, therefore, rebuilding the connection may need unnecessary control packet to resynchronize. The proposed ICA protocol uses the park mode for slave nodes, which reduces the number of control packet overhead.

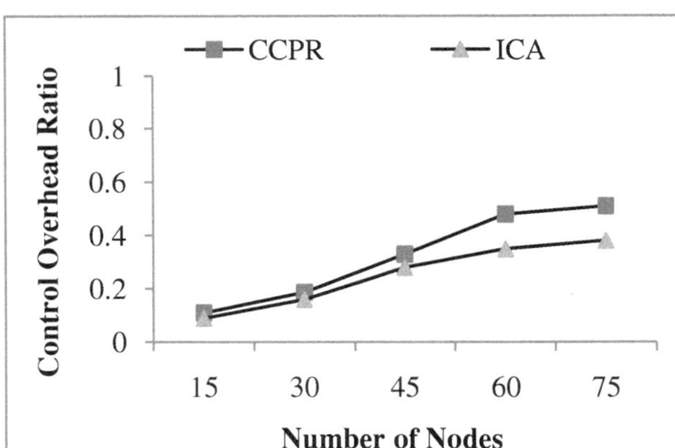

Fig. 7. Control overhead vs. Number of nodes

4.2 Network Delay

The time taken for a bit to travel from a source to a destination is called delay. The average delays of the two protocols are compared for different number of node. The proposed protocol monitors the traffic load on the relay node, and restructures the network to avoid congestion. When a relay switches between different piconets, it needs to adjust its frequency according to the piconet, and this has increased the delay time. As a result, communication is blocked due to unavailability of the relay node. The proposed ICA protocol does not break the slaves' links; therefore, it has less delay compared to CCPR as shown in Fig. 8. It is observed that due to traffic load of inter-piconet the proposed protocol fairly shares its traffic load in Bluetooth scatternet and performs better than CCPR.

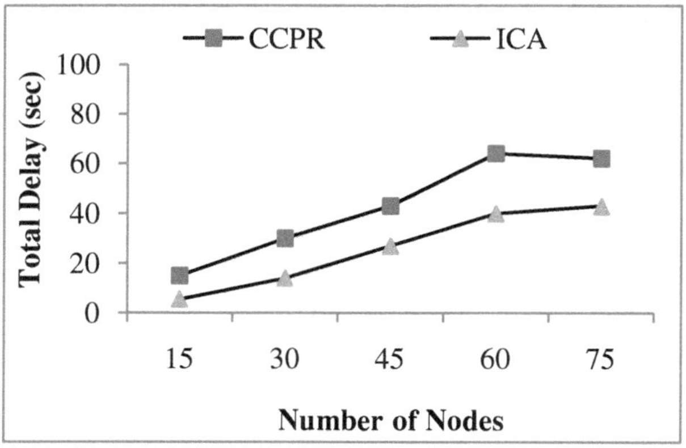

Fig. 8. Delay vs. Number of nodes

4.3 Network Throughput

The average rate of sucessful message transmissions in a netwok is known as throughput. To evaluate the system performance, throughputs of both the protocols are measured. It is observed that as number of nodes increase in the scatternet throughput also incrasing, as shown in the Fig. 9. It is observed that the shortest route ensures higher network throughput. As in proposed protocol keeps track of traffic load on the relay node, and due to congestion avoidance, it has increased network throughput.

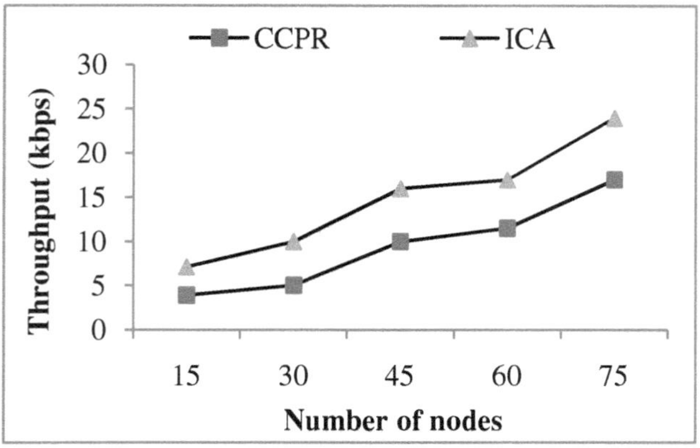

Fig. 9. Throughput vs. Number of nodes

5 Conclusion

The paper proposed a dynamic scatternet reformation protocol, which can regulate the structure of Bluetooth scatternet globally to share the traffic load of bridge device. The proposed protocols performs network restructuring for finding shortest path for any pair of source and destination. Simulation results show that the proposed protocol has the following benefits: it can find the shortest routing path so it reduces the number of hop counts, it decreases delay time and increases network throughput. The proposed ICA protocol will contribute to standardize the Bluetooth scatternet specification.

References

[1] Hassan, T., Kayssi, A., Chehab, A.: Ring of Masters (ROM): A new ring structure for Bluetooth scatternets with dynamic routing and adaptive scheduling schemes. Journal of Elsevier (2008)

[2] The Bluetooth Specification, http://www.bluetooth.org 1.0b and 1.1

[3] McDermott-Wells, P.: What is Bluetooth? IEEE Potentials (December 2004/January 2005)

[4] Sun, M., Chang, C.K., Lai, T.H.: A Self-Routing Topology for Bluetooth Scatternets. In: The International Symposium on Parallel Architectures, Philippines (May 2002)

[5] Kapoor, R., Gerla, M.: A zone routing protocol for Bluetooth scatternets. In: Proc. of IEEE Wireless Communications and Networking Conference, pp. 1459–1464 (2003)

[6] http://www.palowireless.com/bluearticles/baseband.asp

[7] Altundag, S., Gokturk, M.: A Practical approach to scatternet formation and routing on Bluetooth. In: Proceedings of the Seventh IEEE International Symposium on Computer Networks, ISCN 2006, pp. 1-4244-0491-6 (2006)

[8] Royer, E., Toh, C.-K.: A review of current routing protocols for ad hoc wireless networks. IEEE Personal Communications, 46–55 (April 1999)

[9] Broch, J., Maltz, D., Johnson, D., Hu, Y.-C., Jetcheva, J.: A performance comparison of multi-hop wireless ad hoc network routing protocols. In: Proc. of the 4th ACM/IEEE Int. Conf. on Mobile Computing and Networking (MOBICOM 1998), Dallas, TX, USA, pp. 85–97 (1998)

[10] Safa, H., Artail, H., Karam, M., Ollaic, H., Abdallah, R.: HAODV: a New Routing Protocol to Support Interoperability in Heterogeneous MANET, 1-4244-1031-2/07/2007 IEEE

[11] Yu, G.-J., Chang, C.-Y., Shih, K.-P., Lee, S.-C.: Relay Reduction and Route Construction for Scatternet over Bluetooth Radio Systems. Journal of Network and Computer Applications 30, 728–749 (2007)

[12] Tahir, S.-H., Hasbullah, H.: Dynamic Congestion Control through Backup Relay in Bluetooth Scatternet. Journal of Network and Computer Applications (2011)

[13] Yu, G.-J., Chang, C.-Y.: Congestion control of bluetooth radio system by piconet restructuring. Journal of Network and Computer Applications Elsevier (2008)

[14] University of Cinicinnati Bluetooth simulator (UCBT) (2010), http://www.ececs.uc.edu/_cdmc/ucbt/

[15] The Network Simulator ns-2,
http://www.isi.edu/nsnam/ns/ns-build.html
[16] Johansson, P., Kapoor, R., Kazantzidis, A., Gerla, M.: Rendezvous scheduling in Bluetooth scatternets. In: ICC IEEE International Conference, vol. 1, pp. 318–324 (2002)

Capacity Analysis of G.711 and G.729 Codec for VoIP over 802.11b WLANs

Haniyeh Kazemitabar and Abas Md. Said

Computer & Information Science Department, University of PETRONAS
Bandar Seri Iskandar, 31750, Malaysia
hanieh80@gmail.com, abass@petronas.com.my

Abstract. Voice over IP (VoIP) or IP telephony is a very popular way of communication not only for single users but also for big enterprises. Due to fast-growing wireless technology and ease of use of wireless networks, VoIP is now being deployed over Wireless LANs (VoWLANs). The main issues in communication of real time application on IP networks, however, are providing Quality of Service (QoS), security and capacity. Capacity planning is an essential factor to consider at the time of developing VoIP network. Wireless links provide different capacity due to multi-rate transmission that affects all active calls. This paper focuses on the capacity problem and attempts to determine the maximum number of calls the bandwidth can support in each transmission rate based on different speech codecs and packetization intervals.

Keywords: Capacity, Codec, IEEE 802.11, VoIP, WLAN.

1 Introduction

The Institute of IEEE is responsible for setting standards for LANs and 802.11 workgroup in IEEE is tasked to develop standards for wireless LANs. Characters such as “a”, “b”, “g” or “n” have been assigned beside 802.11 to categorize this standard to even more specific tasks [1].

Multi-rate transmission is one of the IEEE 802.11 features, which means the PHY layer has “multiple data transmission rates” to provide different bandwidth based on the link condition [2]. If the wireless signal becomes weak, link cannot provide high transmission, so this standard enables wireless stations to implement lower rate transmission to prevent transmission errors (such as signal to noise ratio). Hence, with the objective of improving performance of wireless link, stations perform rate switching dynamically [3].

In this work, IEEE 802.11b series was used to study the maximum number of calls possible. The possible data rates for 802.11b are 1, 2, 5.5 and 11 Mbps which means that this standard provides four different capacities for VoIP calls.

The principal components of a VoIP system are CODEC (Coder-Decoder), Packetizer and playout buffer [4]. Voice codecs are the algorithms which run on sender and receiver sides to enable digital lines to transmit analog voice. In addition they provide compression methods to save network bandwidth. Different codecs have

A. Abd Manaf et al. (Eds.): ICIEIS 2011, Part III, CCIS 253, pp. 519–529, 2011.

different bit-rate[1], packet length, speech quality, algorithmic delay, complexity and robustness to background noise. Bit rate is a very important parameter of codec which affects the quality and capacity of encoded speech.

The next component is the packetizer which divides encoded voice into packets. The playout buffer is the last main component at the receiver side which is used to rearrange packets according to the schedule of their playout time [4].

The most common voice codecs include G.711, G.723, G.726, G.728 and G.729. Due to popularity of G.711 and G.729 codec, they have been studied in this paper. G.711 codec doesn't have licensing fee so it can be used in VoIP applications freely. G.729 is a licensed codec but most of the well-known VoIP phone and gateway have implemented this codec in their chipset [5].

2 Motivation of Work

Multi rate WLANs make different transmission rate and hence, different bandwidths possible. If the number of calls exceed the capacity of link (available bandwidth), the quality of perceived voice can be affected by packet loss, jitter and delay [6]. Thus, the capacity of link and voice quality of calls is in a direct relation. In order to use the WLAN link capacity at the efficient level while the voice quality is kept at the acceptable level, it is necessary to know maximum number of calls for each rate.

As we mentioned earlier, choosing a proper codec for voice signals is an important factor because it can affect the voice quality and bandwidth consumption together [7].

Some of the codecs provide higher compression and as a result, lower utilization of bandwidth, so they can support more calls on the opposite side, some others provide lower compression and so less number of calls [8].

From another point of view, higher compression codecs has lower bit rate which means lower perceived quality as it is shown in Table 1 [9].

Table 1. Characteristics of two well known codecs

Codec	Bit Rate (Kbps)	MOS[2]	Quality	Compression type
G.711	64	4.1	Excellent	PCM
G.729	8	3.9	Good	CS-ACELP

Two main speech codecs namely G.711 with 64 kbps and G.729 with 8 kbps bit rate are widely used. G.729 utilizes one eighth of the bandwidth compared to G.711. This means that G.729 supports more calls but they have less quality.

Therefore to choose the optimal codec for VoWLAN at the network development time, it is important to consider which factor is more important; higher quality or minimum utilization of bandwidth.

[1] Bit-rate is the number of bits per unit of time required to get samples of analog speech to encode it to digital format.

[2] Mean Opinion Score (MOS) gives a numerical indication from 1 to 5 for perceived speech quality. The MOS score for G.729 (A) is 3.7.

Besides codec, different packet sizes also affect bandwidth usage in speech transmission. The amount of encoded voice which can be allocated in each IP packet depends on the frame size feature of each codec. For example some of the codecs like GSM uses a fixed 20 ms frame and consequently packets must be a multiple of 20 ms, while G.711 packet length is optional [10].

Oouch et al. [11] investigated the effects of different packet sizes on speech quality levels. They have shown that a VoIP system with large packet sizes has higher transmission efficiency but in the case of packet dropping, larger amount of voice will be lost. In addition, longer delay will occur due to the longer time which is taken by the packetizer. On the other hand small packet sizes tolerate packet loss and delay and present better quality but lower transmission efficiency.

At the time of developing a VoIP system over WLANs, we need to know the limitation of the capacity and the number of possible calls for each transmission rate to design the network properly. Our work attempts to show the effect of different transmission rate of 802.11b on the number of connections and to demonstrate the effects of changing codecs and packet sizes on the capacity.

3 Related Works

With respect to fast deployment of real time application, especially VoIP, a lot of studies have been done on WLAN networks in terms of quality and capacity.

Hole and Tobagi in [12] examine the capacity of VoIP over an IEEE 802.11b network. They have considered G.711 and G.729 speech coder and different packetization intervals with different wireless network delay budget to observe upper bound of capacity in different scenarios. They have shown codecs upper bound capacity in ideal channel also in different Bit Error Rate (BER), but they did not specify maximum number of calls based on transmission rate. Sfairopoulou et al. [13] study an IEEE 802.11b/e hotspot capacity based on estimation on previous work. Garg and Kappes also evaluate different codecs using a range of voice packet intervals [14].

Keegan and Davis in [15] performed an experimental study on 802.11b WLAN. They achieved to 16 calls using G.711and 240 bytes payload for packets.

The summary of all previous works about capacity is gathered by Cai et al. [16] within one table. Table 2 shows the maximum call for 802.11b WLAN which is obtained from [16].

Table 2. The maximum number of VoIP connections over 802.11 b, according to the previous works

Packet Interval (ms)	G.711 Connections	G. 729 Connections
10	6	6
20	11	13
30	15	19
40	19	25
50	22	31
60	25	37

The work in [17] is an experimental study on maximum number of VoIP connections using G.711 codec with 10 milliseconds of audio data per RTP packet which is six calls.

Trad et al. [18] have studied maximum number of calls IEEE 802.11e standard which is uses HCF[3] instead of DCF/PCF[4] in MAC layer.

Previous research on VoIP capacity on WLANs had studied the effect of different codec on the capacity at the highest transmission rate of each series without consideration of lower transmission rates. This study has even taken the lower transmission rates of 802.11b into account and has found maximum number of calls for all possible rates.

4 Simulation Methodology

The simulation approach taken to achieve the results is discussed in this section. A WLAN infrastructure has been designed with two wireless workstations which are connected through an Access Point (AP) as a sender/receiver. The attributes are given in table 3.

Table 3. The station attributes

Attribute	*Value*
Transmit Power (W)	0.005
Packet Reception-Power Threshold (dBm)	-95
Max Receive Lifetime (Millisecond.)	30
Buffer Size (Byte)	32000

In OPNET, modeling of any application such as VoIP needs some parameters like codec and size of packet to be set by "Application Configuration" node. Further, it is necessary to set "Profile Configuration" node for defining the network behavior such as application start time, repeatability and duration of simulation run.

In this study, the objective is to calculate network capacity (the maximum number of possible calls) while maintaining the quality at the good level. In order to calculate the capacity, a VoIP call is added to the network in every certain time period which should be set in the profile configuration. In our methodology instead of adding one station with one call, we used one station which generates *one* call *every minute* and we can examine network performance after each run to monitoring the network performance after each simulation's run. This method is easier to implement, but it has a small impact on the queuing delay which is negligible [19].

Based on the result of the simulation we can determine the maximum number of calls. When there is a mismatch between the traffic sent and received or other quality key parameter such as delay drops in the range of 80 to 150 ms, or packet loss exceed 2% or MOS decrease below 4 or at worse case below 3.6, it means the number of

[3] Hybrid Coordination Function.

[4] Distributed coordination function/ Point coordination function.

VoIP calls is more than the network capacity to provide satisfactory quality, Hence, we can estimate upper bound of each rate.

We repeated the same scenario for different rates and for each rate we evaluated codec G.711 and G.729 with different packet sizes from 1 to 5 frames per packet (frames are 10 milliseconds). We did not consider more than 5 frames per packet due to low quality produced (MOS lower than 3.6) [20].

5 Simulation Results

The simulation run time was 20 min for all runs according to our profile, VoIP traffic starts after 1 minute from start time of the simulation and then, every 1 minute 1 VoIP call is added to the simulation which means a total of 19 calls are generated but it does not mean the capacity of network is 19 calls. To find the proper capacity of network, as we mentioned in methodology section some indices like the difference between sent and received traffic, delay and MOS should be considered.

In the first scenario observed the capacity of 11 Mbps using codec G.711 with 5 frames per packet (fpp). Fig. 1 shows the mismatch of voice packets sent and received during the simulation. According to the results, after the 13th minute, the sent and received traffic do not trace eachother. Since in the profile, one VoIP call was added to the network every minute and the profile started transmission after the first minute, we can conclude that after the 12th, the call capacity of this network is full.

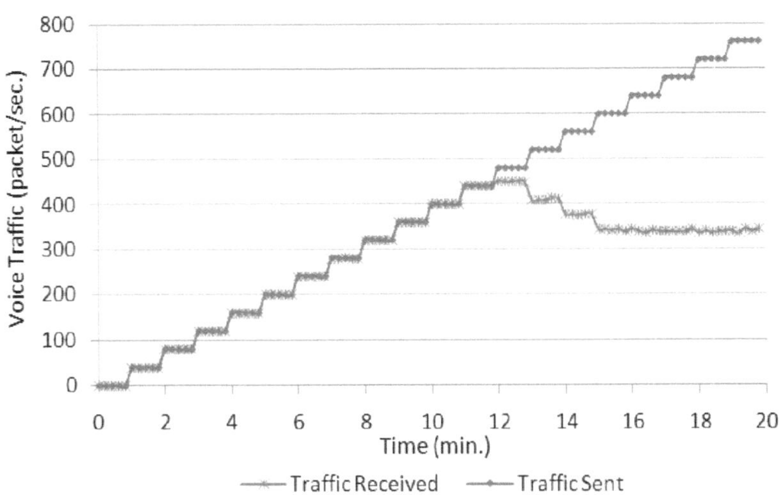

Fig. 1. Voice traffic sends & receives using codec G.711/5fpp/11Mbps

For further illustration, we also used MOS which is used to indicate the voice quality of calls. Fig. 2 also shows that after the 12th minute, the quality has degraded sharply.

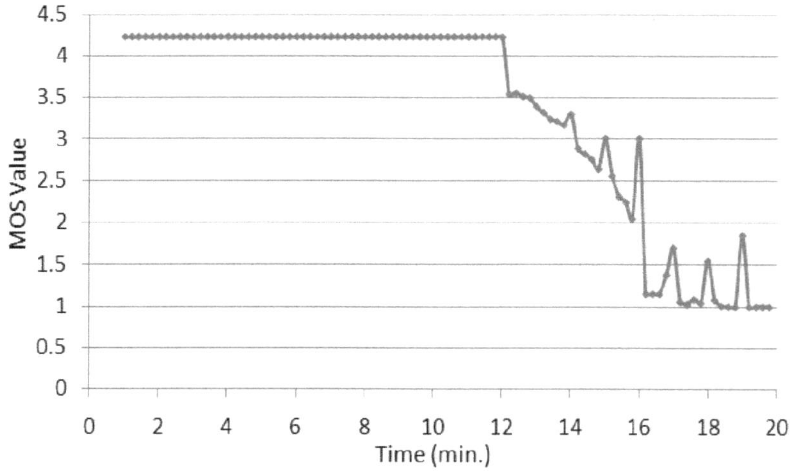

Fig. 2. MOS level during calls using codec G.711/5fpp/11Mbps

Fig. 3 shows when delay is within acceptable range (less than 150 ms) the number of calls is less than 12.

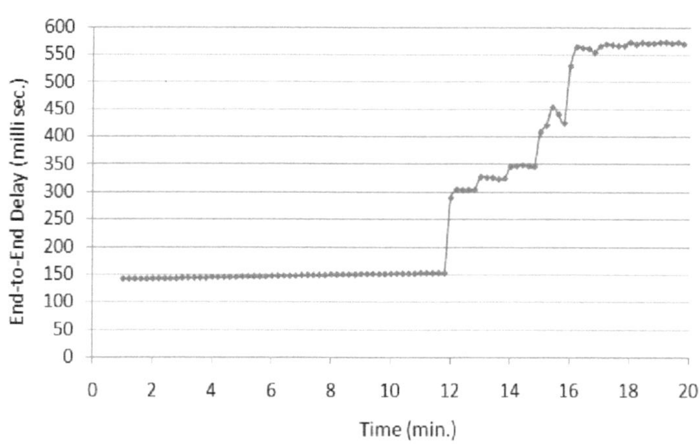

Fig. 3. End to end delay for voice and delay in WLAN using codec G.711/5fpp/11Mbps

The second scenario has been done using the same methodology as the first scenario (adding one call per minute and start calls after 1 minute).

Fig. 4 shows the relation of voice packets sent and received during the simulation run using codec G.729 with 1 fpp in 1Mbps transmission rate. The result shows that after the 2nd minute, mismatched traffic sent and received start increasing. Based on the profile, we can conclude that after one or at most two calls, the capacity of this network (1Mbps/G.729/1 fpp) is full. We will demonstrate the results later using MOS and delay graphs.

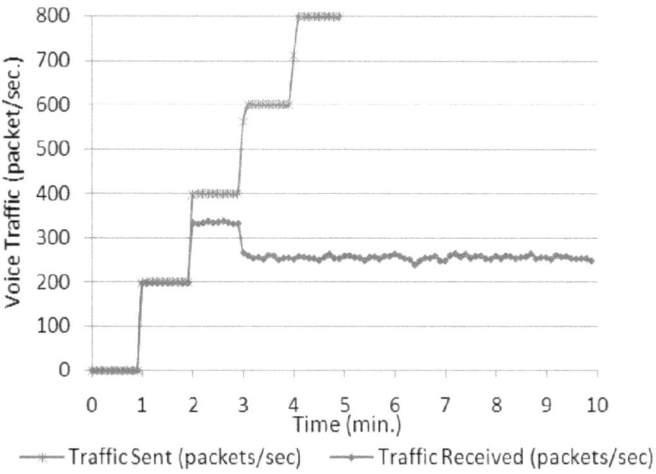

Fig. 4. Voice traffic sends and receives using codec G.729/1fpp/1Mbps

The MOS plot in Fig. 5 supports the results in the previous figure. It can be observed after 2 minutes, the quality has fallen down very sharply, giving the capacity of only one call.

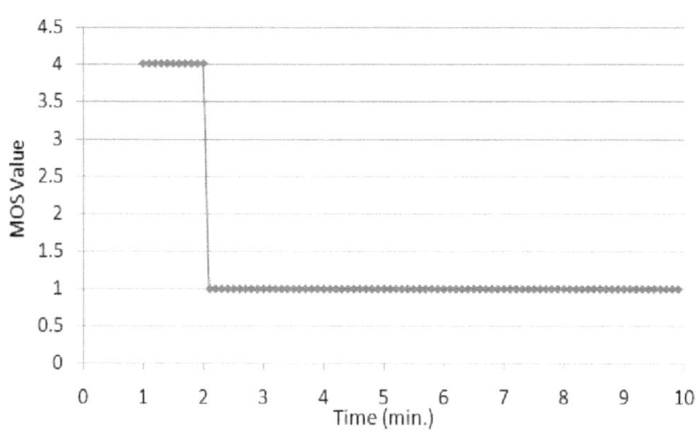

Fig. 5. MOS level during calls using codec G.729/1fpp/1Mbps

Fig. 6 also shows the delay exceed the acceptable range after 1 call.

We applied the same methodology for all IEEE 802.11b transmission rates (11, 5.5, 2 and 1 Mbps) using G.711 and G.729 codec and different frames per packet (fpp). The maximum number of calls where each rate could support were collected and tabulated in Tables 4 and 5.

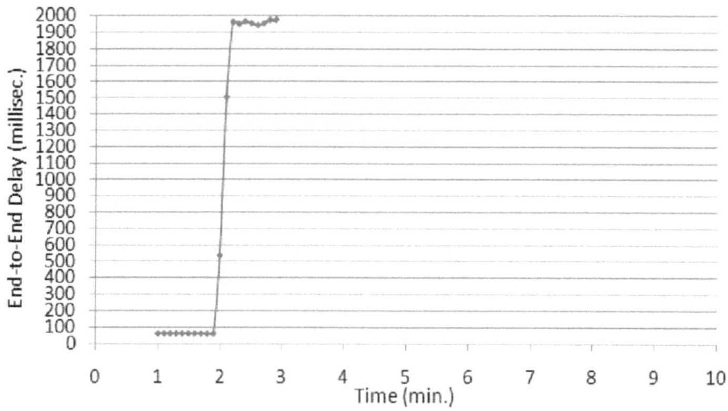

Fig. 6. End to end delay in voice and delay in WLAN using codec G.729/1fpp/1Mbps

Table 4. The maximum number of calls for G.729

Transmission Rate (Mbps) \ Packet size (frame per packet)	1	2	3	4	5
1	1	3	4	6	7
2	2	4	6	8	10
5.5	2	5	8	11	13
11	3	6	9	12	15

Table 5. The maximum number of calls for G.711

Transmission Rate (Mbps) \ Packet size (frame per packet)	1	2	3	4	5
1	1	1	2	2	2
2	1	2	3	4	4
5.5	2	4	6	7	8
11	2	5	7	9	12

Fig. 7 and Fig. 8, show the number of call for each transmission rate using different packet size to have maximum number of calls without compromising the quality using G.711 codec and G.729 codec.

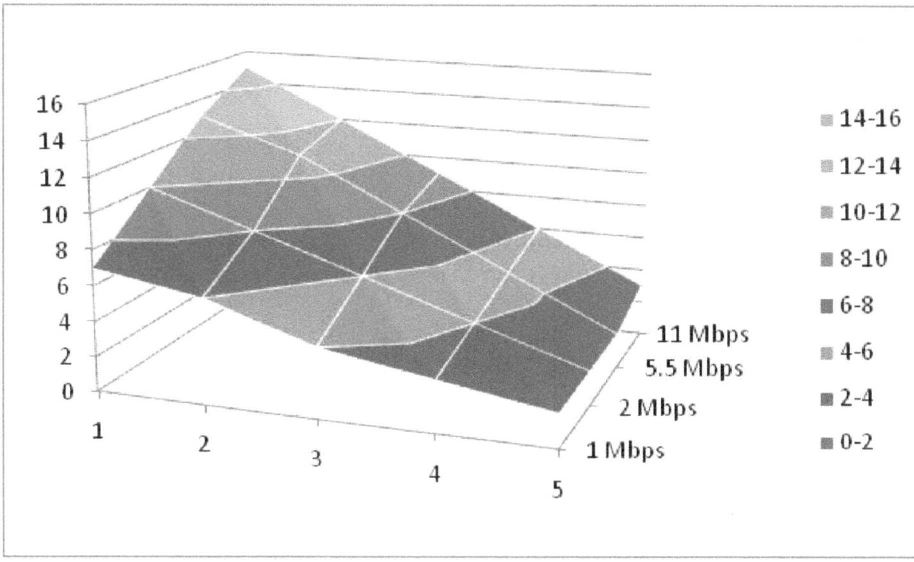

Fig. 7. Calls capacity in different transmission rate for G.729 codec with different number of frames per packet

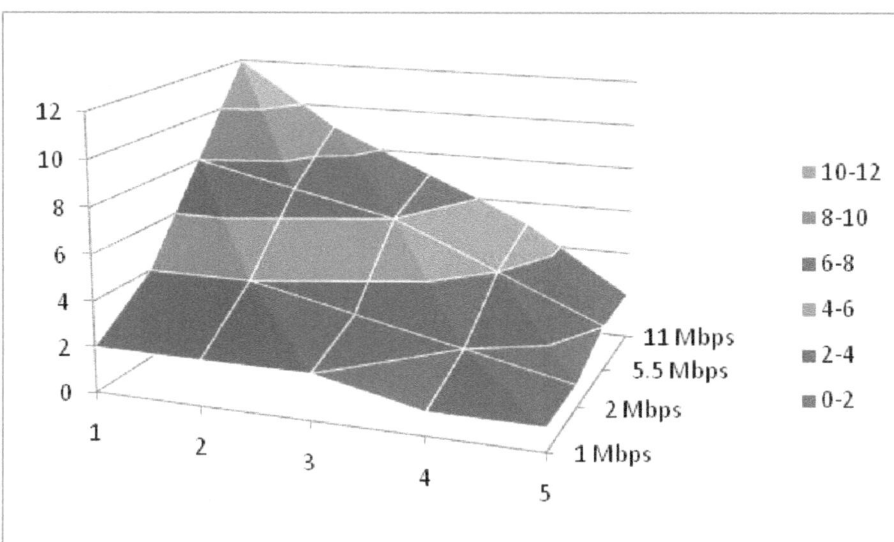

Fig. 8. Calls capacity in different transmission rate for G.711 codec with different number of frames per packet

6 Conclusion

In WLAN, the capacity changes according to the transmission rate which in turn is affected by distance from AP, the presence of walls or the atmospheric condition. At the time of developing a VoIP system over WLANs, we need to know the limitation of capacity and number of possible calls for each transmission rate to design our network properly.

According to the results of the simulation which is comprised the different transmission rate of WLAN stations shown in the table 4 and 5 also illustrated in Fig. 7 and Fig. 8, we analyzed the effect of different codec (G.711, G.729) and a range of payload size (10-50 millisecond) on the number of call. Further we have shown maximum number of calls without compromising the quality in each transmission rate of WLAN 802.11b.

In spite of previous work have studied only the upper bound of 802.11b standard, here, we tried to show network capacity (number of calls) for different transmission rate of 802.11b using two famous codecs with different packet size.

It should be mentioned here, that the difference between the results of previous work (Table 2) and results in this work (Table 4 and 5) could be due to dissimilar network design and/or special network attribute and/or use of different simulator. For example our network design is totally includes wireless stations, nevertheless having some of stations (call parties) in wired part of WLAN causes less delay, less packet loss and better quality and as result increases the capacity to make more number of calls.

References

[1] Lipiczky, B.: Voice over WLAN. In: Information Security Management Handbook, pp. 145–153. Auerbach Publications (2007)

[2] IEEE, Wireless LAN Medium Access Control (MAC) and Physical Layer (PHY) Specifications, in Telecommunications and information exchange between systems. Local and metropolitan area networks. IEEE (2007)

[3] Abu-Sharkh, O., Tewfik, A.H.: Multi-rate 802.11 WLANs. In: Global Telecommunications Conference, GLOBECOM 2005, p. 6, 3133. IEEE (2005)

[4] Kazemitabar, H., Ahmed, S., Nisar, K., Said, A.B., Hasbullah, H.B.: A Survey on Voice over IP over Wireless LANs. World Academy of Science, Engineering and Technology (2010)

[5] Cisco. Cisco Codec Support FAQ (2005), http://www.cisco.com/en/US/products/sw/voicesw/ps556/products_qanda_item09186a00801b34cc.shtml

[6] Karam, M.J., Tobagi, F.A.: Analysis of the delay and jitter of voice traffic over the Internet. In: Proceedings of INFOCOM 2001. Twentieth Annual Joint Conference of the IEEE Computer and Communications Societies, vol. 2, pp. 824–833. IEEE (2001)

[7] Cisco. Voice Over IP - Per Call Bandwidth Consumption, Document ID: 7934 (2006), http://www.cisco.com/application/pdf/paws/7934/bwidth_consume.pdf

[8] Light, J., Bhuvaneshwari, A.: Performance analysis of audio codecs over real-time transmission protocol (RTP) for voice services over Internet protocol. In: Proceedings. Second Annual Conference on Communication Networks and Services Research, pp. 351–356 (2004)
[9] Karapantazis, S., Pavlidou, F.-N.: VoIP: A comprehensive survey on a promising technology. Computer Networks 53, 2050–2090 (2009)
[10] Reynolds, R.J.B., Rix, A.W.: Quality VoIP - An Engineering Challenge. BT Technology Journal 19, 23–32 (2001)
[11] Oouch, H., Takenaga, T., Sugawara, H., Masugi, M.: Study on appropriate voice data length of IP packets for VoIP network adjustment. In: Global Telecommunications Conference, GLOBECOM 2002, vol. 2, pp. 1618–1622. IEEE (2002)
[12] Hole, D.P., Tobagi, F.A.: Capacity of an IEEE 802.11b wireless LAN supporting VoIP. In: 2004 IEEE International Conference on Communications, pp. 196–201 (2004)
[13] Sfairopoulou, A., Bellalta, B., Macian, C.: How to tune VoIP codec selection in WLANs. IEEE Communications Letters 12, 551–553 (2008)
[14] Garg, S., Kappes, M.: Can I add a VoIP call? In: IEEE International Conference on Communications, ICC 2003, vol. 2, pp. 779–783 (2003)
[15] Keegan, B., Davis, M.: An Experimental Analysis of the Call Capacity of IEEE 802.11b Wireless Local Area Networks for VoIP Telephony. In: Irish Signals and Systems Conference IET 2006, pp. 283–287 (2006)
[16] Cai, L., Xiao, Y., Shen, X., Mark, J.W.: VoIP over WLAN: voice capacity, admission control, QoS, and MAC: Research Articles. Int. J. Commun. Syst. 19, 491–508 (2006)
[17] Garg, S., Kappes, M.: An experimental study of throughput for UDP and VoIP traffic (2003)
[18] Trad, A., Munir, F., Afifi, H.: Capacity evaluation of VoIP in IEEE 802.11e WLAN environment. In: 3rd IEEE Consumer Communications and Networking Conference, CCNC 2006, pp. 828–832 (2006)
[19] Salah, K., Alkhoraidly, A.: An OPNET-based simulation approach for deploying VoIP. Int. J. Netw. Manag. 16, 159–183 (2006)
[20] Kazemitabar, H., Said, A.B.M.: Performance Analysis of VoIP over Multi-Rate WLANs. Presented at the 3rd International Conference on Machine Learning and Computing (ICMLC), Singapore (2011)

Design and Verification of a Self-organisation Algorithm for Sensor Networks

Nacéra Benaouda[1], Hervé Guyennet[2], Ahmed Hammad[2], and Mohamed Lehsaini[3]

[1] Department of Computer Science
Sétif Automatic Laboratory, Faculty of engineering Science, Sétif, Algeria
nacbenaouda@gmail.com
[2] UFC-LIFC
16, route de Gray, 25030 Besançon-cedex France
{ahmed.hammad,herve.guyennet}@univ-fcomte.fr
[3] Department of Computer Science,
STIC Laboratory
Faculty of Technology
Tlemcen Univeristy, Algeria
m_lehsaini@mail.univ-tlemcen.dz

Abstract. For ad hoc networks, clustering is the organization method that groups the nodes into clusters managed by nodes called cluster-heads. This hierarchical organization allows an effective way of improving performance, security, fault tolerance and scalability of the platform. In this paper, we introduce a new approach to self-organize an ad hoc network, and define communication protocols so that to optimize communication in the routing. We implement a hierarchy structure to the ad hoc network, that is: many clusters with one leader per group, and a coordinator for the whole network. In order to optimize the communication process, decent metrics are chosen in group formation and in leader election. To illustrate the performance of our algorithm, we verify it using model checking; we simulate it and compare its performance with a geographical-based algorithm.

Keywords: Sensor networks, Verification, Organisation, Clustering, Simulation.

1 Introduction

For the last few years, we can observe a boost development of ad-hoc networks and wireless network techniques. An ad-hoc network consists of independent wireless nodes that have the ability to dynamically form connections with each other to create a network. It does not require any central infrastructure and it can grow, shrink and fragment without having to make any requests or reports to a central authority. Each node participates in routing by forwarding data for other nodes, and so the determination of which nodes forward data is made dynamically based on the network connectivity. Organization and a strategy of process

A. Abd Manaf et al. (Eds.): ICIEIS 2011, Part III, CCIS 253, pp. 530–543, 2011.

partitioning on a distributed system depends on the nature of the distributed components, on communication support, on the flow of exchanged data, and the constraints imposed by the application needs. Applications on ad hoc networks are increasingly used in different sectors (industrial, medical, commercial, etc) because it is easy to install an ad hoc network anywhere, when appropriate equipment exist (ad hoc nodes). An ad hoc network is independent not only on wire line infrastructure, but also on access points such as wireless cellular network. An ad hoc network, being nothing else than a distributed system, the issue of partitioning must take place in any design of application on this type of network. Since mobile network, Zigbee and ad hoc network, today, research in wireless networks has been much focused on the wireless sensor networks. A sensor network is composed of a large number of sensor nodes that are densely deployed either inside the event or very close to it. These tiny sensor nodes consist of sensing, data processing, and communicating components. The position of sensor nodes need not be engineered or predetermined. This allows random deployment in inaccessible terrains or disaster relief operations. This means that sensor network protocols and algorithms must possess self-organizing capabilities. This paper presents a new approach for partitioning a set of nodes in multiple clusters in order to optimize communications on this particular distributed system. We first propose an algorithm based on k-density to partition the network into clusters of nodes with the election of a clusterhead. Then, we implement such architecture on a network of wireless sensors and we perform simulations to verify the scalability. Finally, we propose values of number of nodes per group to allow maximum efficiency. Safety and liveness properties are verified using Model Checking. The rest of this paper is organized as follows: In section 2, we present related works about clustering. Then in section 3, we give our clustering algorithm which is simulated to verify scalability property in section 4. In section 5, we implement this algorithm using wireless sensors network. In section 6, we verify safety and liveness properties using Model Checking. Finally, in section 7, we conclude and present several perspectives of our work.

2 Related Works

Organizing in clusters a system consists of putting together some objects, materials or machinery in clusters cooperating and communicating. The cluster concept allows to define a group of entities as a single virtual entity: it assigns the same name to each member of a particular group, and communicates with them using the same address. Generally, in a distributed system, communication between nodes, objects or processes transfer, and decisions are difficult problems that can not be resolved for all nodes.

To solve these problems, one can use the formation of subsets of entities called clusters, cells, domains, partitions or clusters. They are composed of members. In each cluster, one member plays a particular role, and is called leader, manager, interconnection point, clusterhead [6] or local coordinator. This one is responsible for communication between various members or levels, receiving information and referring to the other members, and overseeing the internal organization of the group. The notion of cluster can be extended by the definition of several level hierarchy structure. A two level hierarchy structure [1], [12] requires, in addition to clusters formation, and the choice of a coordinator for each group, the election of an overall coordinator that is called global coordinator or Superleader, playing the role of interconnection point of all clusters.

Many cluster formation algorithms have been conceived, widely studied and classified. Generally, the term clustering is used in a great number of publications [17] and thesis that speak about clustering on the basis of: mobility [11], [14], [16], signal power [11], node weight [11], density [14], distance between nodes [2], [3], lowest identifier. We propose a new cluster formation approach in following paragraph. The clustering improves the performance of dynamicity and scalability when network size is important with high mobility. All of the characteristics and constraints imposed by sensors make the design of an efficient scheme for the self-organisation of WSNs a real challenge. In response to this challenge, authors gives several solutions based on clustering for WSNs, which consists of grouping sensors into a set of disjoint clusters as opposed to a flat topology. Each cluster has a designated leader called cluster-head, which is the node with the greatest weight in its 2-hop neighbourhood not affiliated to other clusters.

In [10], the authors have proposed LEACH, which is a distributed, single hop clustering algorithm for homogeneous WSNs. In LEACH, the cluster-head role is periodically rotated among the sensor nodes to evenly distribute energy dissipation. To implement this protocol, the authors assume that all sensors support different MAC protocols, and perform long distance transmissions to the base station.

[11] has proposed an efficient cluster-based self-organisation algorithm (ECSA) for partitioning Wireless Sensor Networks (WSNs) into clusters, thus giving at the network a hierarchical organisation. Each sensor uses its weight based on its k-density and its residual energy to elect a cluster-head in its 2-hop neighbourhood.

[9] has given an energy aware clustered-based multipath routing, which forms several clusters, finds energy aware node-disjoint multiple routes from a source to destination and increases the network life time by using optimal routes. The Combined Higher Connectivity Lower ID (CONID) clustering algorithm is used to generate the clusters where each clusterhead finds its all neighbor clusterheads.

[8] has demonstrated a hierarchical routing protocol design (ECP) that can conserve significant energy in its setup phase as well as during its steady state data dissemination phase. ECP achieves clustering and routing in a distributed manner and thus provides good scalability. The protocol is divided into 3 phases: clustering, route management, and data dissemination. Phase one is to cluster sensor nodes together to achieve a maximum number of border nodes and minimum number of clusters.

[7] has proposed a stable and low-maintenance clustering scheme (NSLOC) that simultaneously aims to provide network. stability combined with a low cluster maintenance cost. In an algorithm [6] using location information, the sensor

field is partitioned by regions called cells, and the cell size affects the energy efficiency of the protocols. In his paper, Bani and all propose a modification of CBRP protocol called Vice Cluster Head Cluster Based Routing Protocol that elect one Vice Cluster Head in each cluster rather than one cluster head to increase the lifetime of the cluster in the network.

[4] has proposed structuring nodes in zones, meant to reduce the global view of the network to a local one. His paper presents a distributed and low-cost topology construction algorithm, addressing the following issues: large-scale, random network deployment, energy efficiency and small overhead.

[5] has presented a security policy for wireless sensor networks which provide to fine-tune access to sensor resources. They build on the notion of group-based key establishment to show how group membership can be utilized in deploying a dynamic and robust security policy.

Finally, we can find a short survey on clustering algorithms for wireless sensor networks in [17] where authors ask how to compute the optimal cluster size, and how to determine the optimal frequency for cluster head rotation in order to maximize the network lifetime.

3 Clustering Algorithm

In this section, we propose a weight-based clustering algorithm called *CSOS* that consists of grouping sensors into a set of disjoint clusters, hence giving at the network a hierarchical organisation. In [11], each cluster has a cluster-head that is elected among its 2-hop neighbourhood based on nodes weight. The weight of each sensor is a combination of the following parameters: 2-density and residual energy, as presented in equation 1. We used the 2-density as parameter instead of 2-degree to generate homogeneous clusters and to favour the node that has the most 2-neighbours related to become clusterhead. The coefficient of each parameter can be chosen depending on the application.

Therefore, we attribute adequate values to the different coefficients in the purpose to generate stable clusters and guarantee a long network lifetime.

$$Weight(u) = \alpha * P_{K-density} + \beta * P_{res-Energy} + \gamma * P_{mobility} \tag{1}$$

with

$$\alpha + \beta + \gamma = 1 \tag{2}$$

3.1 k-Density

The k-density of a node u represents the ratio between the number of links in its k-neighborhood (links between u and its neighbors and links between two k-neighbors of u) and k-degree of u. Formally, it is represented by the following equation:

$$k\text{-}density(u) = \frac{|(v,w) \in E : \; v,w \in N^k[u]|}{\delta_k(u)} \tag{3}$$

where

$$N^k[u] = \{v \in E \ : \ d(u,v) \leq k\} \quad (4)$$

$N^k[u]$ is the closed set of u's k-neighbors which contains all nodes being at a distance less than or equal to k hops.

$$\delta_k(u) = |N^k(u)| \quad (5)$$

$\delta_k(u)$ represents the k-degree of u However, in our contribution we are interested only to calculate the 2-density nodes not to weaken the proposed algorithm's performance. Hence, the equation presented below follows the general equation presented above.

$$\textit{2-density(u)} = \frac{|(v,w) \in E : \ v,w \in N^2[u]|}{\delta_2(u)} \quad (6)$$

3.2 Clusters Formation

Since cluster-head is responsible to coordinate among the cluster members and transmit their aggregate data to the remote sink, we proposed to set up periodically cluster- head election process not to exhaust its battery power. Moreover, for better management of clusters formed, cluster formation takes into account the following constraints: each cluster has a size ranging between two thresholds $Thresh_{Upper}$ and $Thresh_{Lower}$ except in certain case its value can be lower than $Thresh_{Lower}$, and in which cluster members are at most 2-hops from their respective cluster-head. If during set-up phase, there is formation of clusters whose size is lower than $Thresh_{Lower}$, then re- affiliation process will be triggered. Furthermore, a cluster-head could be able to manage its cluster members, to accept or refuse adhesion of new arrivals based on its capacity without perturbing the functionality of the other cluster members.

In the proposed strategy, each node u is identified by a state vector: ($Node_{Id}$, $Node_{CH}$, $Weight$, Hop, $Size$, $Thresh_{Lower}$,$Thresh_{Upper}$) where $Node_{Id}$ is the identifier of sensor, $Node_{CH}$ represents the identifier of its cluster-head. If this node is a cluster-head then its identifier will be assigned to NodeCH. Hop indicates the number of hops separating it from its respective cluster-head, and Size represents cluster size to which it belongs. Moreover, each node is responsible to maintain a table called "TableCluster", in which the information of the local members cluster is stored. The format of this table is defined as TableCluster($Node_{Id}$, $Node_{CH}$, $Weight$). Sensors could coordinate and collaborate between each other to construct and update the above stated table by using Hello message. Furthermore each cluster-head maintains another cluster-head information table so called "TableCH", in which the information about the other cluster-heads is stored. The format of these tables is represented as $Table_{CH}$($Node_{CH}$, $Weight$). These above tables contain the state vector of nodes, which should be periodically exchanged either between cluster-heads or between each cluster-head and its cluster members.

In our approach, we tried to organize sensors into clusters by affiliating each sensor to the nearest cluster-head from it. We used Hello messages for cluster formation in order to minimize broadcast overhead and not degrade algorithm of its performance. Hence, at the beginning each sensor calculates its weight and generates a Hello message, which includes two extra fields addition to other regular contents: *weight* and $Node_{CH}$, where $Node_{CH}$ is set to zero. Furthermore, clustering process is performed in two consecutive phases as well as clusters are formed the ones after the others.

First Phase. Cluster-head election process proceeds in the following way. Initially, a random node initiates clustering process while broadcasting a Hello message to its $N^2[u]$ neighbors. Then, node having greatest *weight* among its $N^2[u]$ neighbors will be elected as cluster-head (CH).

This latter updates its state vector by assigning to $Node_{CH}$ the value of its identifier $(Node_{Id})$, sets respectively Hop value and Size value with 0 and 1. After that, it broadcasts advertisement message ADV_CH including its state vector to its 2-hop neighborhood to request them to join it. Each node belonging to N1$(Node_{CH})$ whose NodeCH value is equal to zero i.e. does not belong to any cluster and its weight is lower than CHs weight, transmits REQ_JOIN message to CH to join it. Corresponding cluster-head checks if the size of its own cluster does not reach. $Thresh_{Upper}$ i.e. Size value is lower than $Thresh_{Upper}$, it will transmit $ACCEPT\_CH$ message to this node, otherwise it will simply drop the message of affiliation demand. Thereafter, CH increments its Size and the affiliated node sets Hop value with 1 and NodeCH with $Node_{CH}$ of its corresponding cluster-head, then it broadcasts received message again with the same transmission power to its neighbors. Similarly, each node belonging to N2$(Node_{CH})$, which is not affiliated to any cluster as its weight is lower than that of CH, transmits REQ_JOIN message to corresponding CH. In the same way, CH checks if its Size value is always less than ThreshUpper, so yes it updates its state vector; otherwise it drops message of affiliation demand. Finally, when no more Hello messages are broadcasted in the network, each node will know which cluster it belongs to and which node is its cluster-head. Clustering process will end after a fixed interval of time, which should be long enough to guarantee that every node can find its nearest cluster-head.

Second Phase. During the first phase, it may not be possible for all clusters to reach $Thresh_{Upper}$ threshold. On the other hand, since there is no constraint relating to the generation of clusters having a number of nodes lower than $Thresh_{Lower}$ during the execution of first phase; it is possible that there is creation of this type of clusters during this phase. For that, we tried to reduce the number of clusters formed

during this second phase. Hence, we proposed to re- affiliate the nodes belonging to clusters that have not attained cluster size $Thresh_{Lower}$ to clusters that did not reach cluster size $Thresh_{Upper}$. The execution of the second phase proceeds in the following way. Cluster-heads that belong to clusters whose size is strictly lower than $Thresh_{Upper}$, broadcast a new message called $RE-AFF_CH$

to re-affiliate nodes belonging to the small clusters to them. Then, each node that receives this message and belongs to a small cluster, should re-affiliate to the nearest cluster-head whose weight is greater than its and the size of its own cluster does not always reach$Thresh_{Upper}$. After the unfolding of our algorithm, we obtain balanced and stable clusters considering that we have involved k-density, residual energy and to structure network in clusters.

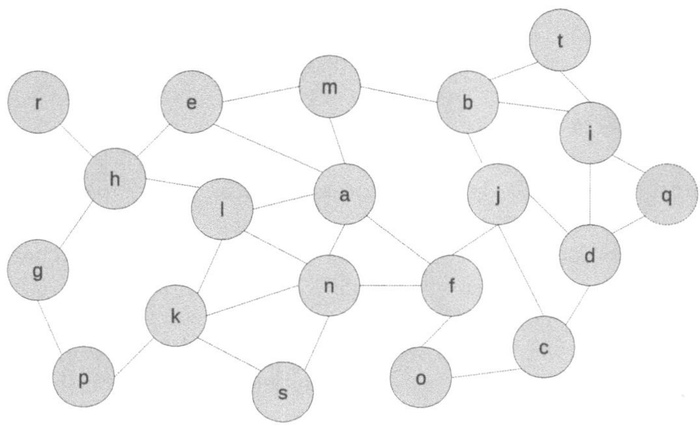

Fig. 1. Example of a wireless network modeled by an undirected graph

Example. After running *CSOS*, we obtain the following clusters (see figure 2):

4 Simulation

Before the use of experimental platforms, a deep simulation work was conducted with NS2. Our goal was to see the behavior of CSOS in the scaling of nodes number, and then, compare it to other approach. Indeed, WSN that are available in research laboratories allow to verify the feasibility of approaches with tests on a limited number of sensors, simulation is needful if we want to do tests on a larger number of sensors. In this paper, our simulation study consists of comparing CSOS to HSL-2-AN (A Two Level Hierarchy structuring for Ad hoc Networks)[12] on the basis of the running time. HSL-2-AN is a simple algorithm that takes into account the geographical criteria, after having study many aspects of both approaches, we simulated each of them for 20, 50, 100, 200 and 300 nodes. We calculated the running time, and observed the formed clusters in each approach, for each number of nodes. Comparative simulation studies have often led to new approaches which have, as much as possible benefits of the compared approaches.

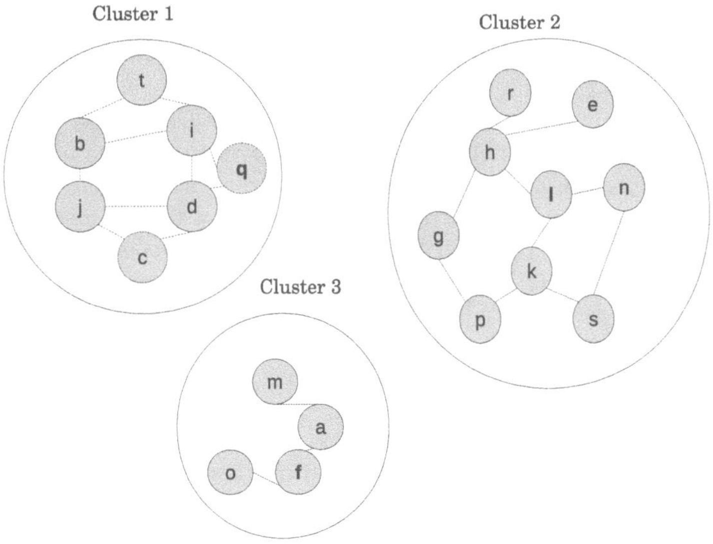

Fig. 2. Following clusters

4.1 HSL-2-AN Principle

HSL-2-AN [12] allows to organize the network into a two level tree structure: several clusters with a leader per cluster, and a superleader for the entire network. It takes place according to three stages: cluster formation, leader election and finally, the superleader election. Groups/clusters are formed on the basis of the simple geographical metric, expressed by the distance between two nodes and the node scope. In each group, a leader is elected. The group leader is the node with the average distance between it and other group nodes is minimal. This reflects the fact that the leader should be as close to the maximum of nodes in the group. The superleader is the network node that has the maximum of leaders in its scope. Between the same group members the communication passes through the leader. Between different group members the communication passes through the coordinator. HSL-2-AN includes three parameters baptized cohesion parameters to measure connectivity in the network. $Group\_cohesion_k$ is calculated for each group and represents the percentage of nodes in the leader scope in the group number k. $Network\_Cohesion$ is calculated for the entire network and represents the percentage of leaders in the superleader scope. $Taux\_Group\_Cohesion$ is also calculated for the entire network and represents the percentage of clusters in cohesion. The use of these parameters is based on threshold values defined for each application. Three situations were identified and considered significant for the network: Cohesion, strong cohesion and absolute Cohesion. The latter refers to the state in which communication is optimal.

4.2 Comparative Study of CSOS and HSL-2-AN

The approach of forming clusters in CSOS is based on a generic metric (weight) chosen for the leader election: the formula defining the weight (see equation 1) takes into account three parameters at once, the geographical criterion, the remaining energy and the node mobility. By varying the value of α, β or γ we can increase, decrease or cancel the importance of a criterion in the metric. For instance, assuming $\alpha = 0.5$, $\beta = 0.5$ and $\gamma = 0$, the metric takes into account only the geographical criterion and the rest of energy, but mobility is neglected. In this case, the metric can be used in applications where nodes are not very mobile. Such is the case in most applications of environmental monitoring using wireless sensors. In simulation, CSOS takes place according to two phases: the first stage or the preparatory phase concerns some calculations used to fill *density_table* on which is based the group formation; the second stage is the group formation itself. Our simulation study has shown that the time of the group formation itself is negligible compared to the time $T_{Preparatory}$ consumed in the preparatory phase. And we can affirm that in the simulation, the elapsed time in CSOS can be likened to $T_{Preparatory}$. Note that during the preparatory phase, the node remains inert and cannot communicate with any other node.

In $HSL-2-AN$ approach, the group formation stage, takes into account only the geographical criterion, and which poses no constraint on the number of nodes. Hence, the resulting clusters can be very different in number of nodes, and may even be composed of a single node. This imbalance in the number of nodes per group, leads to an unbalanced load in the network between clusters and between nodes. However, the cohesion parameters, provide information about the state of network connectivity. These parameters are defined according to the established structure (A two level hierarchy), and their meaning depends strongly on the

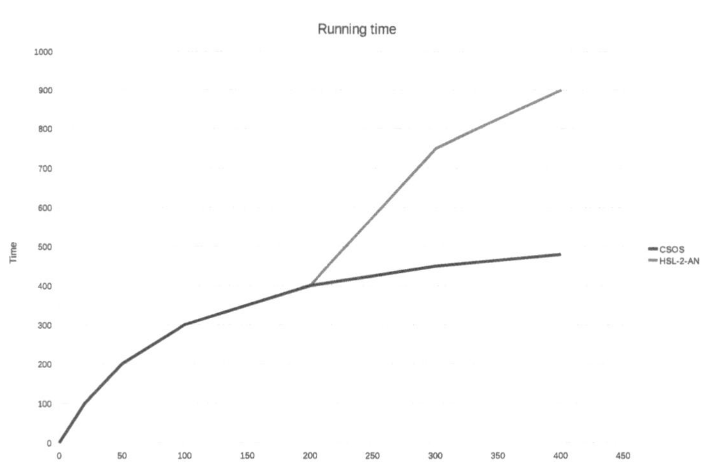

Fig. 3. Comparison of CSOS and HSL-2-AN running time curves

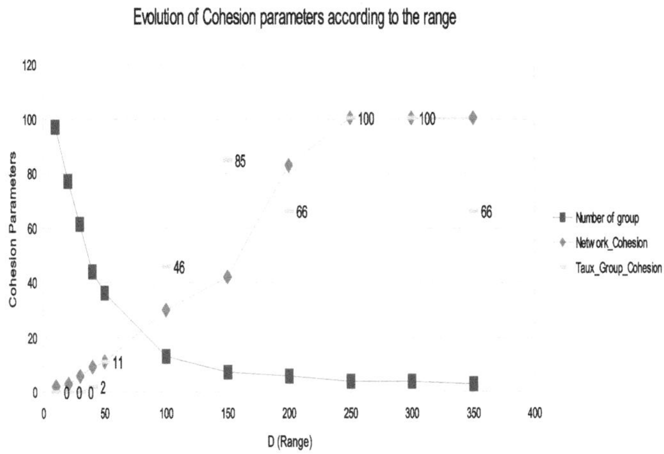

Fig. 4. Cohesion Parameters provided by HSL-2-AN

defined communication protocols. Figure 4 shows the evolution of the number of nodes, *Network_Cohesion* and *Taux_Group_Cohesion* according to the range. In this graph, we remark that the number of clusters, increases when the range decreases. However, *Network_cohesion* and *Taux_group_Cohesion* increase with the range. They reach they maximum value (100) when the range=250. The value 66 of *Taux_Group_Cohesion* when the range=350 is due to the fact that the number of clusters is reduced to 3, and one of these clusters is one member composed, it's the reason why, *Taux_Group_Cohesion* decreased. In running time, from 200 nodes, CSOS becomes a bit slower than HSL-2-AN. This is mainly due to the preparatory phase of CSOS. Figure 3 compares HSL-2-AN and GSOS running time curves.

5 Implementation on a Wireless Sensors Network Platform

Our wireless sensor network platform is composed of 20 Tmote Sky. This sensor type is ultra low power wireless module manufactured by Sentilla. It belongs to the family of Telos motes which are USB devices. The Tmote Sky is an IEEE 802.15.4 compliant device using the Chipcon CC2420 radio (250kbps), providing reliable wireless communication. It consists of TI MSP430 ultra low power microcontrollers, 10 kB RAM, 48 kB Flash memory, 1 MB storage and integrated Humidity, Temperature, and Light sensors. It runs the TinyOS operating system.

The sensors send data only when certain events occur. For example, a wireless sensor network is deployed in a forest to prevent fires. Sensors sense the temperature and send an alarm message to the cluster-head when there is increase in temperature. Cluster-heads in turn send alert messages to the sink. But many sensors collect the same information and send them to the sink. So they lose energy to send redundant data. Moreover, since there is many transmissions at the same time, the network contention becomes more seriously, which is likely to generate more collisions in the network. Several methods of medium access control specific to the event-driven application of wireless sensor networks have been developed [16]. They reduce the number of redundant messages as well as the network congestion. So the nodes reduce energy waste and the network lifetime is maximized.

6 Formal Verification

6.1 Introduction

Formal verification means creating a mathematical model system, using a language to specify the system properties in concise and unambiguous manner, and the use of verification methods to prove that model satisfies the specified properties. Thus, the verification shows that all the system behaviors satisfy the properties. A system mathematical model is described by the use of a formal language such as action systems. The system properties can be specified by a specification language as temporal logic. Two major approaches exist for formal verification: Proof and Model checking. We present below, the model checking approach.

6.2 LTL Model Checking

The term model checking [13] subsumes several algorithmic techniques for the verification of reactive and concurrent systems, in particular with respect to properties expressed as formulae of temporal logics. More specifically, the context of our work are LTL (linear temporal logic) model checking algorithms based on Büchi automata [15]. In this approach, the system to be verified is modelled as a finite transition system and the property is expressed as a formula ϕ of (LTL). The formula ϕ constrains executions, and the transition system is deemed correct (with respect to the property) if all its executions satisfy ϕ. After translating the formula into a Büchi automaton, the model checking problem can be rephrased in terms of language inclusion between the transition system (interpreted as a Buchi automaton) and the automaton representing ϕ or, technically more convenient, as an emptiness problem for the product of the transition system and the automaton representing ϕ.The following decision problem : Given finite transition system TS and LTL-formula ϕ : yields yes if $TS \models \phi$, and no (plus a counterexample) if no $TS \models \phi$.

6.3 Properties

In order to verify our system, we defined two properties that the system must verify: a safety property and a liveness property. The chosen properties concern a fundamental aspect of our system and if checked, they are enough to ensure that *CSOS* runs correctly. we define below the two properties.

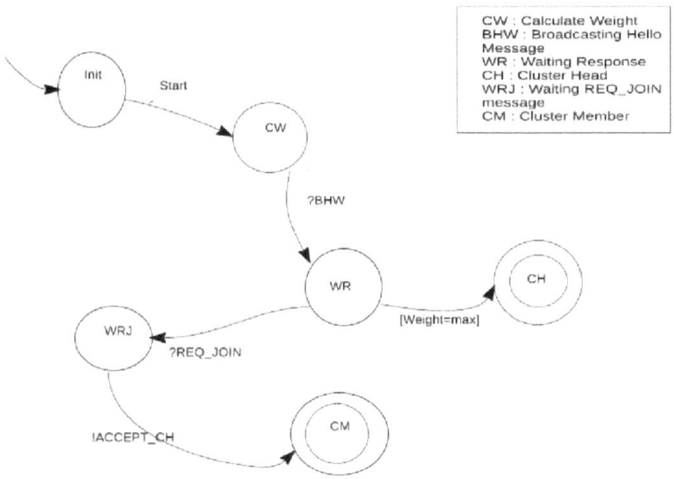

Fig. 5. Automaton of the CSOS algorithm

- Safety property definition
  "Being in the *init* state, a node doesn't remain indefinitely in this state". A LTL formula φ_1 is of the form :

$$\Box(p \Rightarrow \bigcirc q) \tag{7}$$

- Liveness property definition
  "Being in the *init* state, if the node will not be the cluster-head hence it will be a cluster member."
  This property expresses the fact that the node must incorporate a cluster at the end of *CSOS*. A LTL formula φ_2 is of the form :

$$\Box(p \Rightarrow \Diamond q) \tag{8}$$

Lets P, P_M, P_H atomic propositions :

- P="init state",
- P_M="to be a cluster member",
- P_H="to be a cluster head".

In LTL, we may write:

$$\varphi_1 \equiv P \Rightarrow \diamond(\neg P) \tag{9}$$

$$\varphi_2 \equiv P \Rightarrow (\diamond(\neg P_H) \Rightarrow \diamond P_M) \tag{10}$$

6.4 Interpretation and Verification Deduction

On the basis of this automaton, safety property is checked because the passage from the state "init" to the state "CM" (Cluster Member) is reliable, this transition is carried out at the first stage of *CSOS* execution, that concerns clusters formation on the basis of nodes coordinates.

Vivacity property is, also checked, because it's clear on the automaton, that the node has three issues from the initial state: either to be a member of a cluster or to re-affiliate node to an other cluster and stop there, or to be a cluster head as result to *CSOS* second stage and stop there, Therefore, we conclude that the two properties expressed by φ_1 and φ_2 are verified and the node does not remain, indefinitely in the state "init", and it will have a status that may be: a member of a cluster or a cluster head. This fact expresses that *CSOS* runs properly. Given that any node checks the defined safety and liveness properties, and given that the network nodes run *CSOS* independently of each other, the two properties are assumed in the whole network.

7 Conclusion

In this paper, we have presented an algorithm for wireless sensor networks called self-organization CSOS based on the concept of clustering. This algorithm consists of grouping sensors into a set of disjoint clusters, hence giving at the network a hierarchical organisation. Each cluster has a cluster-head that is elected among its 2-hop neighbourhood based on nodes weight. The weight of each sensor is a combination of the following parameters: 2-density and residual energy. We used the 2-density as parameter instead of 2-degree to generate homogeneous clusters and to favour the node that has the most 2-neighbours related to become clusterhead.

To test the performance of our contributions, we performed several simulations and compared the results with respect to the results of other protocols. We have it compared to a classical approach geographical-based and we have evaluated its performance in terms of clusters number formed and distribution balancing.

Using model checking technique, we have formally verified our proposition with the both properties of safety and liveness. Finally, we have deployed an example with classicals sensors and validate its implementation. A future work will be to develop a surveillance application on your architecture.

References

1. Wagenknecht, G., Anwander, M., Braun, T., Staub, T., Matheka, J., Morgenthaler, S.: MARWIS: A Management Architecture for Heterogeneous Wireless Sensor Networks. In: Harju, J., Heijenk, G., Langendörfer, P., Siris, V.A. (eds.) WWIC 2008. LNCS, vol. 5031, pp. 177–188. Springer, Heidelberg (2008)
2. Capo-Chichi, E.P., Guyennet, H., Friedt, J.-M.: IEEE 802.15.4 Performance on a Hierarchical Hybrid Sensor Network Platform. In: The Fifth International Conference on Networking and Services (ICNS), Valence, Spain (2009)
3. Capo-Chichi, E.P., Guyennet, H., Friedt, J.-M., Johnson, I., Duffy, C.: Design and implementation of a generic hybrid Wireless Sensor Network platform. In: The 8th IEEE International Workshop on Wireless Local Networks, LCN, Montreal Canada (2008)
4. Beydoun, K., Felea, V., Guyennet, H.: Wireless Sensor Network Infrastructure: Construction and Evaluation. In: ICWMC 2009, Int. Conf. on Wireless and Mobile Communications, Cannes, France (2009)

5. Claycomb, W., Lopez, R., Shin, D.: A Group-Based Security Policy for Wireless Sensor Networks. In: The 25th ACM Symposium on Applied Computing (SAC 2010), Sierre, Switzerland (2010)
6. Bani Yassein, M., Hijazi, N.: Improvement on Cluster Based Routing Protocol By using Vice Cluster Head. In: NGMAST 2010 Proceedings of the 2010 Fourth International Conference on Next Generation Mobile Applications, Services and Technologies. IEEE Computer Society Press, Washington, DC, USA (2010)
7. Conceicao, L., Palma, D., Curado, M.: A Novel Stable and Low-maintenance Clustering Scheme. In: The 25th ACM Symposium on Applied Computing (SAC 2010), Sierre, Switzerland (2010)
8. Loh, P.K., Pan, Y.: An Energy-Aware Clustering Approach for Wireless Sensor Networks. I. J. Communications, Network and System Sciences 2, 91–168 (2009)
9. Bheemalingaiah, M., Naidu, M.M., Rao, D.S.: Energy Aware Clustered Based Multipath Routing in Mobile Ad Hoc Networks. I. J. Communications, Network and System Sciences 2, 91–168 (2009)
10. Heinzelman, W.R., Chandrakasan, A., Balakrishnan, H.: Energy-efficient communication protocol for wireless micro sensor networks. In: IEEE Proceedings of 33rd Annual Hawaii International Conference on System Sciences (HICSS 2000), Maui, Hawaii, USA, vol. 2 (2000)
11. Lehsaini, M., Guyennet, H., Feham, M.: An efficient cluster-based self-organisation algorithm for wireless sensor networks. Int. J. Sensor Networks 7(1/2) (2010)
12. Benaouda, N., Guyennet, H., Hammad, A., Mostefai, M.: A New Two Level Hierarchy Structuring for node Partitionning in Ad Hoc Networks. In: SAC 2010, 25th ACM Symposium on Applied Computing, Zurich, Switzerland, pp. 719–726 (2010)
13. Clarke, E.M., Grumberg, O., Peled, D.A.: Model checking. MIT Press, Cambridge (2001)
14. Lehsaini, M., Guyennet, H., Feham, M.: CES: Cluster-based Energy-efficient Scheme for Mobile Wireless Sensor Networks. Wireless Sensor and Actor Networks II 264, 13–24 (2008)
15. Büchi, J.R.: On a Decision Method in Restricted Second-order Arithmetic. In: Proceedings of the 1960 Congress on Logic, Methdology and Philosophy of Science. Stanford Univeristy Press, Stanford (1962)
16. Le, C., Guyennet, H., Zerhouni, N.: Over-hearing for Energy Efficient in Event-Driven Wireless Sensor NetworkWorkshop on Intelligent Systems Techniques for Wireless Sensor Networks. In: The Third IEEE Internat. Conf. Mobile Ad-hoc and Sensor Systems, Vancouver, Canada (2006)
17. Boyinbode, O., Le, H., Mbogho, A., Takizawa, M., Poliah, R.: A survey on clustering algorithms for wireless sensor networks. In: The 13th Int. Conf. on Network-Based Information Systems, Takayama, Gifu, Japan (2010)

Wireless Controller Area Network Using Token Frame Scheme

Wei Lun Ng, Chee Kyun Ng, Borhanuddin Mohd. Ali, and Nor Kamariah Noordin

Department of Computer and Communication Systems Engineering,
Faculty of Engineering, University Putra Malaysia,
UPM Serdang, 43400 Selangor, Malaysia
william_2909@hotmail.com,
{mpnck,borhan,nknordin}@eng.upm.edu.my

Abstract. The controller area network (CAN) has been long regarded as the pioneer in standardizing vehicle bus standard. Its influence has even been reached out to various applications in industrial automation; which includes military, aviation, electronics and many others. With wireless technology becoming more pervasive, there is a need for CAN too to migrate and evolve to its wireless counterpart. In this paper, a new wireless protocol named wireless controller area network (WCAN) is introduced. WCAN is an adaptation of its wired cousin, controller area network (CAN) protocol which has not being properly defined. The proposed WCAN uses the concept introduced in wireless token ring protocol (WTRP); a MAC protocol for wireless networks and efficient in a sense to reduce the number of retransmission due to collisions. Additionally, it follows most of its wired cousin attributes on message-based communication. Message with higher priority has the first priority in transmitting their message into the medium. In WCAN, stations or nodes take turns in transmitting upon receiving the token frame that are circulating around the network for a specified amount of time. WCAN was tested in a simulation environment and is found that it outperform IEEE 802.11 in a ring network environment.

Keywords: MAC, controller area network, wireless controller area network, wireless token ring protocol, token.

1 Introduction

The Controller area network (CAN) was created by Robert Boush in mid-1980s as a new vehicle bus communication between control units in automobile industries. In the past, vehicle bus communication uses point to point wiring systems; which cause wiring to become more complex, bulky, heavy and expensive with increasing electronics and controllers deployed in a vehicle [1]. This problem can be seen in Fig 1(a), where the abundance of wiring required makes the whole circuit even more complicated.

CAN solves this abundance problem by utilizing twisted pair cable which all control units shares as shown in Fig 1(b). This allows the overall connection to be less

A. Abd Manaf et al. (Eds.): ICIEIS 2011, Part III, CCIS 253, pp. 544–556, 2011.

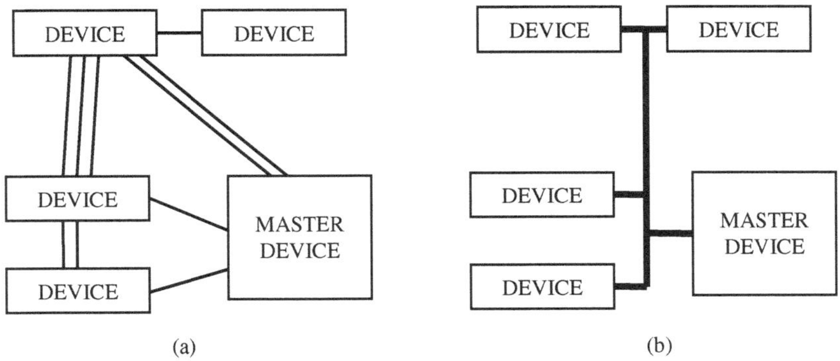

Fig. 1. The differences between (a) traditional wiring and (b) CAN methods

complex. Additionally, CAN protocol allow microcontrollers, devices and sensors to communicate within a vehicle without a host computer. Having the advantages of high immunity towards electrical interference and ability to self diagnose, CAN was seen deployed in various automation industry that requires high quality of service (QoS) [1] - [4]. Wireless network on the other hand, has become so pervasive that there are huge demands for higher data rate and better QoS to support services. Unfortunately, the features of wired CAN cannot be adopted in providing ubiquitous service.

This paper presents a new approach in utilizing the advantageous of CAN into a wireless network system called wireless controller area network (WCAN). The proposed protocol follows the concept of token as shown in [14] - [17]. It is proven that using token concept has its advantages; in terms of improving efficiency by reducing the number of retransmissions due to collisions; and more fair as all stations use the channel for the same amount of time.

The outline of the paper is as follows. Section 2 presents an overview of CAN protocol. An overview of different method in defining WCAN is shown in Section 3. The proposed wireless protocol of WCAN using token frame scheme is described in Section 4. The performance evaluations are discussed in Section 5 and finally this paper is concluded in the last section.

2 CAN Protocol

Controller area network (CAN) was first defined by Robert Boush in mid-1980s as a new robust serial communication between control units in automobile such as cars, trucks, and many others. CAN not only reduce the wiring complexity but also made it possible to interconnect several devices using only single pair of wires and allowing them to have simultaneous data exchange [5], [6]. CAN protocol is a message-based protocol, meaning that messages are not transmitted from one node to another based on addresses. Instead, all nodes in the network receive the transmitted messages in the bus and decide whether the message received is to be discarded or processed. Depending on the system, a message can be destined to either one node or many nodes [1] - [3]. This has several important consequences such as system flexibility, message routing and filtering, multicast, together with data consistency [4].

In CAN, collisions of messages are resolved through bit-wise arbitration based on priority of the message. This means that higher priority messages are remain intact even if collisions are detected. Uniquely in CAN, the lower identifier value has the highest priority. This is because the identifier bit value is located at the beginning of the packet and the electrical signal for zero is designed to overwrite the signal for one. Therefore, the logic bit ‘0’ is defined as the dominant bit whereas logic bit ‘1’ as the recessive bit [7]. Figure 2 shows an example of CAN bus arbitration process between 3 nodes with different identifier value.

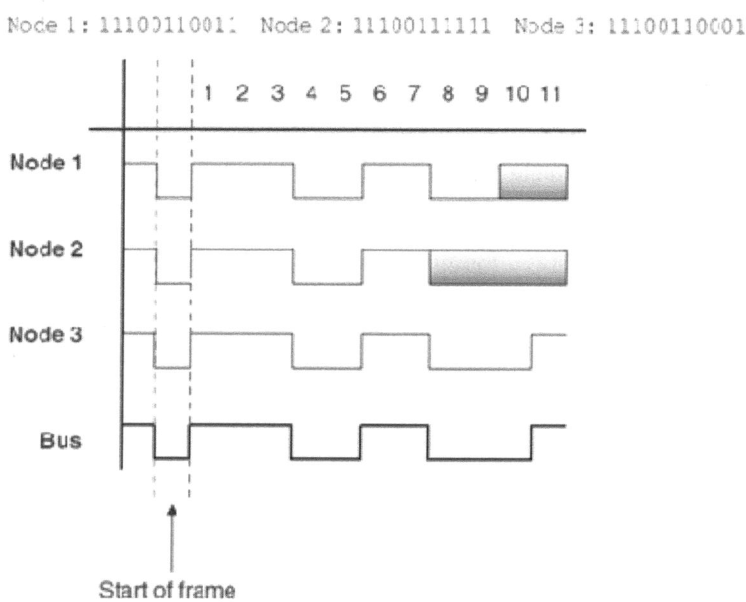

Fig. 2. CAN bus arbitration [8]

In Fig 2, all nodes start transmitting simultaneously by sending SOF bits first and followed by corresponding identifier bits. The 8th bit of Node 2 is in the recessive state or ‘1’, while the corresponding bits of Nodes 1 and 3 are in the dominant state or ‘0’. Therefore Node 2 stops transmitting and returns to receive mode. The receiving phase is indicated by the grey field. The 10th bit of Node 1 is in the recessive state, while the same bit of Node 3 is in dominant state. Thus Node 1 stops transmitting and returns to receive mode. The bus is now left for Node 3, which can send its control and data fields at will.

3 Wireless Controller Area Network

The wireless controller area network (WCAN) is a new approach of using CAN message-based protocol in wireless network. Various ideas have been proposed by researchers to allow an ease of transition from CAN into WCAN [9] - [13]. Most research centered on the MAC layer in providing protocol to WCAN.

3.1 WCAN Using RTS / CTS Scheme

Dridi et. al in [9] - [11] proposed to apply contention based WCAN protocol using RTS/CTS mechanism that are used in IEEE 802.11 protocol. The RTS/CTS mechanism is used to reduce frame collisions introduced by the hidden node problem. Dridi et. al uses RTS/CTS mechanism in managing priority considerations between nodes. Changes are done to the standard RTS/CTS frame that allows message identifier. The MAC-addresses in RTS and CTS frame are replaced by the 29-bit CAN message identifier to allow message-based protocol. Additionally, RTS/CTS mechanism is used to enable a station or node to reserve the medium for a specified amount of time by specifying the duration field that the station/node requires for a subsequent transmission. This reservation information is stored in all stations in a variable called Network Allocation Variable (NAV) and represents the Virtual Carrier Sense. Inter- Frame Space (IFS) are used to control the priority access of the station to the wireless medium and it represents the time interval between each transmission of frames with Short IFS (SIFS) as the smallest type of IFS.

3.2 WCAN with RFMAC and WMAC Access Method

The authors in [12], [13] propose RFMAC and WMAC protocols to be operated in both centralized and distributed WCAN networks. The RFMAC protocol operates in a centralized WCAN manner that consists of a master node and a number of slave nodes that are in the range of master node. The RFMAC method uses the Idle Signal Multiple Access (ISMA) as its reference method. This access method enables upstream (to central node) and downstream (to terminals) to be transmitted on a same shared channel. Instead of using the message identifier, the central or master node periodically broadcast out remote frames to all terminals in the network. If the master node wishes to have data from any node, it broadcast a remote frame to the channel. All nodes on the network receive the remote frame and decide whether the remote frame belongs to the node by using acceptance filtering. If the remote frame identifier does not match with the acceptance filter, the terminal node stays idle. Else, a data frame is sent out by the terminal node with the same frame identifier. Fig. 3 displays how the remote frame traffic works in RFMAC.

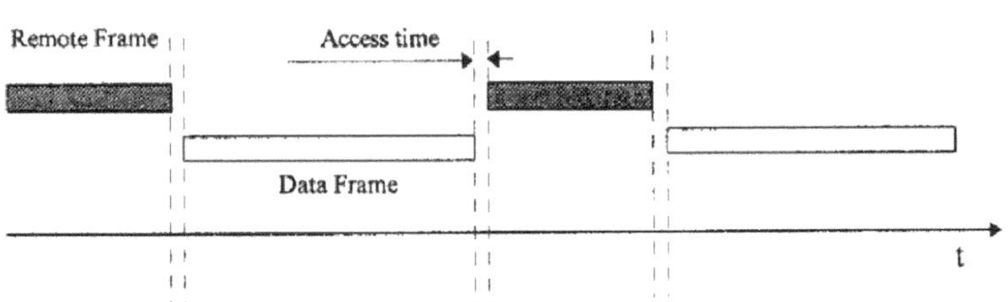

Fig. 3. Remote frame message traffic

The WMAC WCAN on the other hand, allows several nodes to communicate with each other without the assistance of a central node. Contention situation is solved by utilizing different Priority IFS (PIFS) for each message. Each node must wait messages for PIFS time before they are allowed to send their message. PIFS times provide message priority and are derived from the scheduling method which is performed by the user application. The shortest PIFS takes the highest priority as it requires the shortest delay to access the channel. Figure 4 shows how PIFS provides channel access to two nodes.

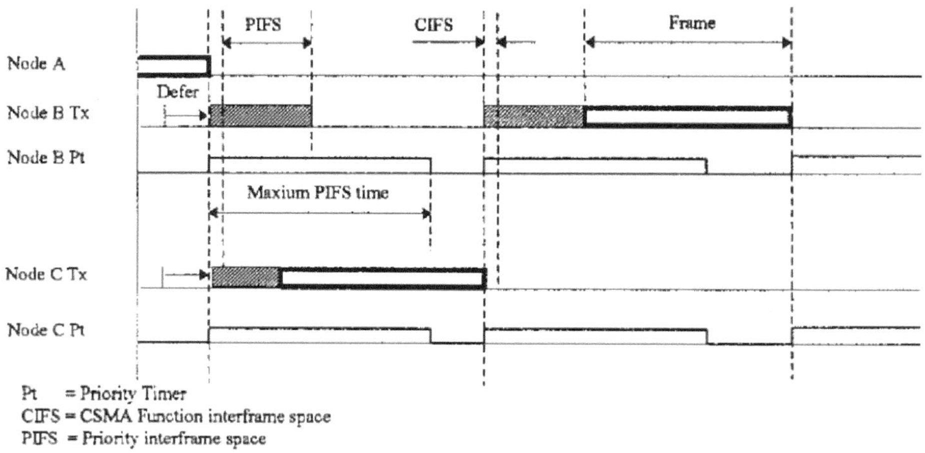

Fig. 4. WMAC timing diagram

In Fig 4, node B and node C tries to access the channel at the same time. As node C has the shortest PIFS, it sense the channel is idle and starts transmitting its message. After a short while, node B's PIFS expires and it sense that the channel is currently occupied by node C. Therefore, node B waits for node C to conclude its transmission before transmit out its message packet.

4 Wireless Controller Area Network Using Token Frame

Inspired by the token frame scheme introduced in [14] - [17], WCAN uses token frame in transmitting messages around the network. Also, the token defines the ring network by setting the successor and predecessor field present in each node. Following the scheme, the proposed WCAN is a wireless based distributed medium access control (MAC) protocol for ad-hoc network. Having a wireless based distributed MAC has its advantageous of being robust against single node failure as it can recover gracefully from it. Additionally, nodes are connected in a loose and partially connected manner.

4.1 WCAN Token Format

Transmission of messages proceeds in one direction along the ring network of WCAN. As such, each node requires a unique successor and predecessor present in the network. The token is the crucial part in WCAN network as it allows a smooth transmission of packet between nodes. Furthermore, it defines the current mode of operation running in the network. Fig 5 shows the proposed token format used in WCAN.

FC	RA	DA	SA	Seq	
4	6	6	6	4	bytes

Fig. 5. WCAN token frame

The Frame Control (FC) contains the frame type indicator and message identifier CAN format. The frame type indicator allows the receiving node identifies the type of token received; such as Token, Soliciting Successor, Data Token, Token Delete Token, Implicit Acknowledgement, Set Successor and Set Predecessor. Message identifier of the token follows the principal as used in CAN protocol, which is a message broadcast. In addition to FC, the token also includes the ring address (RA), destination address (DA), and the source address (SA) that defines the direction and the flow of the token frame. RA refers to the ring which the token frame belongs to. The sequence number is used to build an ordered list and determine the number of stations or nodes that present in the ring.

As previously stated, the WCAN token allows a smooth transmission of packet between nodes in the wireless medium. Therefore, in order for a node to gain access to the medium, the node must first capture the token that circulates around the network. The token is generated first by a ring master assigned in the network. Once a token is captured, a node wins the arbitration by comparing the message identifier located in FC. The arbitration access follows the same concept as in CAN which is lower message identifier value has the highest priority. Once a node wins the arbitration, it will place its message identifier into the FC field and start transmitting its data to the next node on its list.

The next node captures the token and examines the message identifier first. If the message identifier of the receiving node has lower priority than the token had, the node will relay the token to the next node on its ordered list. However, if the node wants to transmit a message or information which is in turn having higher priority, it will replace the message identifier in the token with its own and transmits it to the next node. A node will only know if its transmission is successful when the token it receives next contains the same message identifier it has. Otherwise, it will be in receiving mode until it receives the token back with a lower priority message identifier.

Fig 6 shows an example of how the token transmission works in the network. In Fig 6, station D monitors the successive token transmission from B to C before the token comes back to E. At time 0, D transmits the token with sequence number 0. At time 1, E transmits the token with the sequence number 1 and so on. D will not hear the transmission from F and A but when it hears transmission from B, it will notice that the sequence number has been increased by 3 instead of 1, This indicates that

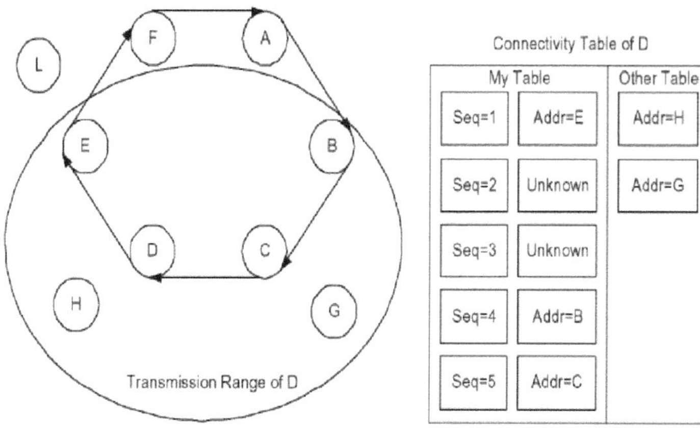

Fig. 6. The ordered list and system architecture of station D

there were two stations that it could not hear between A and F. With this information, station D could build an ordered list of nodes that are available in the ring as shown in the connectivity of D.

4.2 WCAN Operation

The WCAN operation can be divided into two main operations; namely the normal operation and the soliciting operation. The normal operation only involves data packet transmission within WCAN network with a set number of nodes. The soliciting operation however engages a lot of decision making as it involves soliciting operation with nodes that are outside of the network.

4.2.1 Normal Operation

In normal operation, nodes only made certain changes on its operating module. In this operation, there is no joining process, which means either the ring is full or there is no station outside of the ring. When a node gets the token in its idle state, it goes to have token and monitoring state. The station goes back to the idle state from the monitoring state when it receives the implicit ack.

4.2.2 Soliciting Operation

The soliciting operation involves many procedures in order for a node to join or leave the network. In order for the ring to be flexible in its network topology, partial connectivity has been introduced. Nodes are allowed to join the ring in a dynamic manner. Nodes can join if the rotation time (sum of token holding times per node) would not grow unacceptably with the addition of the new node. A different approach is done to enable a node to leave the network. For a node to leave the network, it must first inform its successor and predecessor that it is leaving the network.

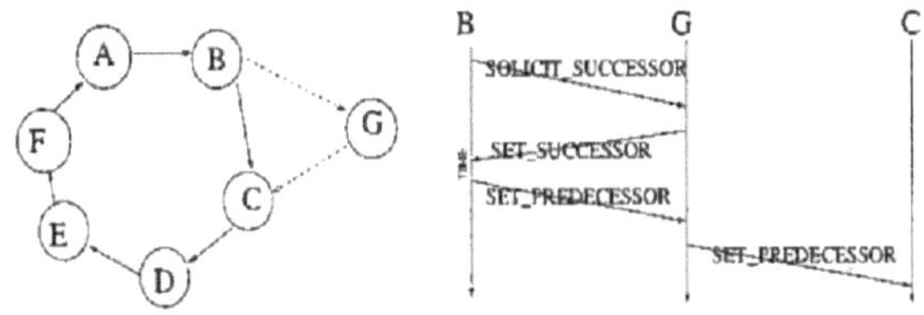

Fig. 7. Node G joining the network

Fig 7 illustrates an example of node G joining the network. Node B invites node G to join by sending out a SOLICIT_SUCCESSOR token. Node G accepts the token and responds by sending out a SET_SUCCESSOR token to node B. The node B will then transmit yet another token, SET_PREDECESSOR to node G indicating that node C will be node G predecessor node. Node G sends the SET_PREDECESSOR token to node C and brings the joining process to completion.

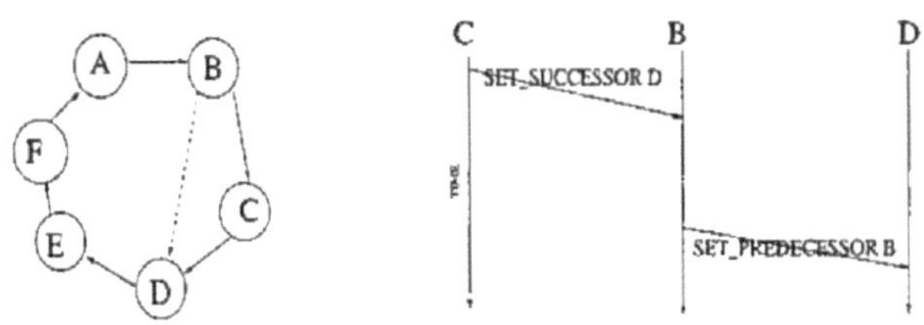

Fig. 8. Node C leaving the network

On the other hand, Fig 8 illustrates how node C leaves the ring network. Firstly, node C waits for the right to transmit. Upon reception of the right to transmit, node C sends the SET_SUCCESSOR token to its predecessor node B with the address of its new predecessor node D. If B can hear D, B tries to connect to node D by sending a SET_PREDECESSOR token. If B cannot be connected to node D, node B will find the following connected node and send the SET_PREDECESSOR token.

4.3 Timing

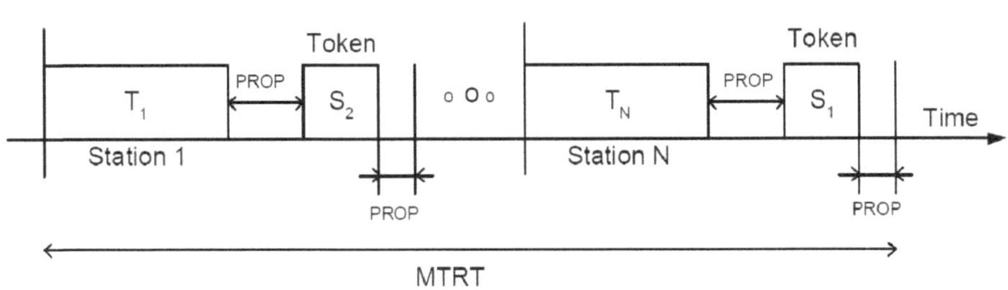

Fig. 9. Timing diagram of WCAN

As stated earlier, the transmission of messages in WCAN proceeds in one direction along the ring network. Fig 9 shows the timing diagram of WCAN token and message. Assume that there are N nodes on the said ring network. Also, T_n and T_t is defined as the time needed in transmitting messages and token respectively. Out of the total N nodes in the network, another assumption is that only n active nodes are actively operating while the other nodes are inactively operating. By assuming the propagation delay (PROP) as DCF interframe space (DIFS), the token rotation time (TRT) can be calculated as

$$TRT = n \times (T_n + DIFS) + N \times (T_t + DIFS) \quad (1)$$

In WCAN, the active nodes may send one packet and one token in a token rotation cycle, while the inactive nodes just forward the token. Thus, the aggregate throughput, S for a token ring network with n active nodes may derive as

$$S = \frac{n \times T_m}{n \times T_m + N \times (T_t + DIFS)} \times R \quad (2)$$

4.4 WCAN Implementation

The proposed WCAN protocol is simulated and deployed using QualNet simulator. The QualNet simulator is chosen for its many model libraries for well-known protocol and its performance evaluation technique. Additionally, the simulator allows programmer to build a new protocol over its existing libraries easily using C++ programming. Moreover, it reduces costs by providing support for visual and hierarchal model design. A snapshot of one of the scenario built using QualNet can be seen in Fig 10.

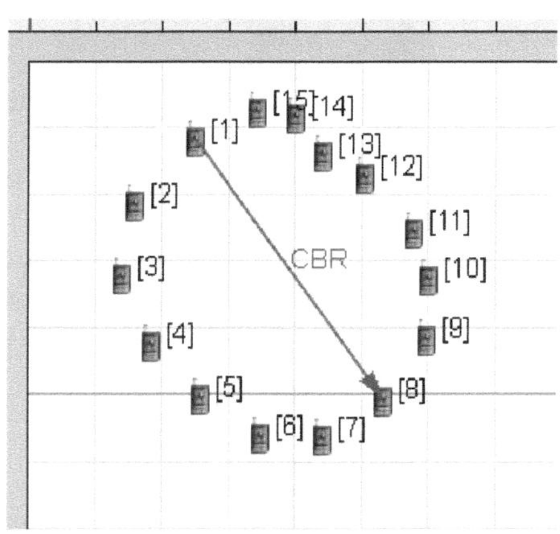

Fig. 10. The snapshot of implementation of WCAN in QualNet

The proposed WCAN protocol is compared with the standard IEEE 802.11 using QualNet simulator. Table 1 shows the simulation scenario parameter for both IEEE 802.11 and WCAN standards. In terms of network size, the simulation is done from 10 to 70 nodes which covers scenario from small to large networks. As for the node placement, the nodes are all placed in a ring manner. The IEEE 802.11b has been chosen as the physical layer for both the standards.

Table 1. Simulation parameter of WCAN and IEEE 802.11 in QualNet simulator

Parameter	Value
Traffic type	CBR
Nodes	10 to 70 nodes
Simulation Time	25 seconds
MAC layer protocol	WCAN and IEEE 802.11b
Physical layer radio type	IEEE 802.11b
Packet payload	512 bytes
Node Placement	Ring Network

5 Performance Evaluation of Simulated WCAN

The performances of WCAN are evaluated in terms of its throughput and the average end-to-end delay. The performances metric are simulated out using QualNet simulator as discussed previously. Throughput is defined as the average rate of data packets received at destination successfully. It is often in the measurement of bits per second (bit/s or bps), and occasionally in data packets per second. In other words, throughput is the total amount of data that a receiver receives from the sender divided by the time it takes for the receiver to get the last packet. Lower throughput is obtained with a high delay in the network. The other affecting factors which are out of the scope of this study include bandwidth, area, routing overhead and so on. Throughput provides the ratio of the channel capacity utilized for positive transmission and is one of the useful network dimensional parameters.

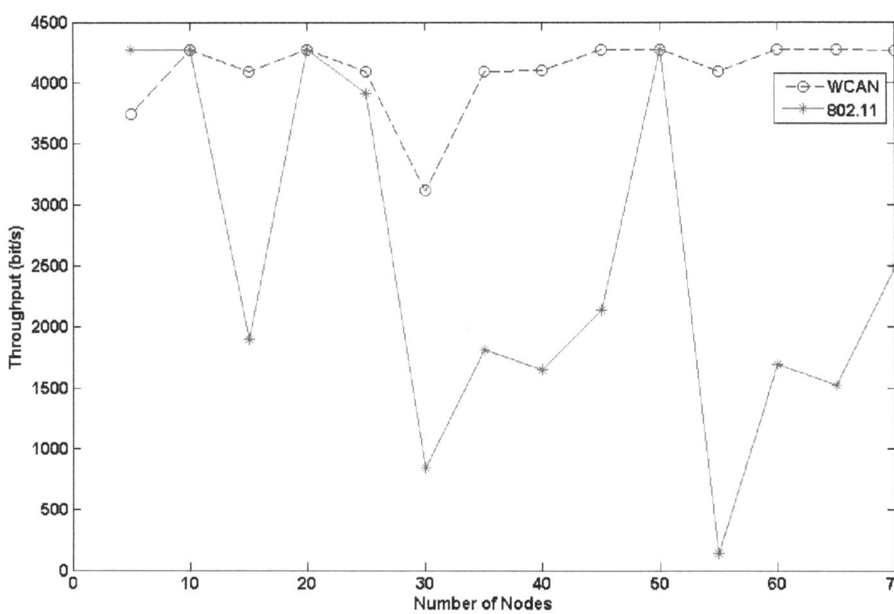

Fig. 11. The throughput performance between WCAN and IEEE 802.11

From Fig 11, it can be seen that WCAN protocol slightly maintains its throughput regardless of its number of nodes in a ring environment. However, the IEEE 802.11 protocol has an irregular throughput value in the same environment. Additionally, its overall throughput is lower than that of WCAN in a ring network environment. This may be due to the placement of nodes that causes the nodes to have contentions between its neighboring nodes [18]. Another possible situation is the unusual role of wireless node as router and hosts simultaneously that cause this abnormality [19].

On the other hand, the average end-to-end delay is defined as the time taken for a particular packet transmitting from the source to destination and the discrepancy is computed between send times and received time. The delay metric includes delays due to transfer time, queuing, route discovery, propagation and so on; meaning that it is regarded as how long it took for a packet to travel across a network from source node to destination node. Commonly, lower end-to-end delay shows that a said protocol to be good in its performance due to lack of network congestion.

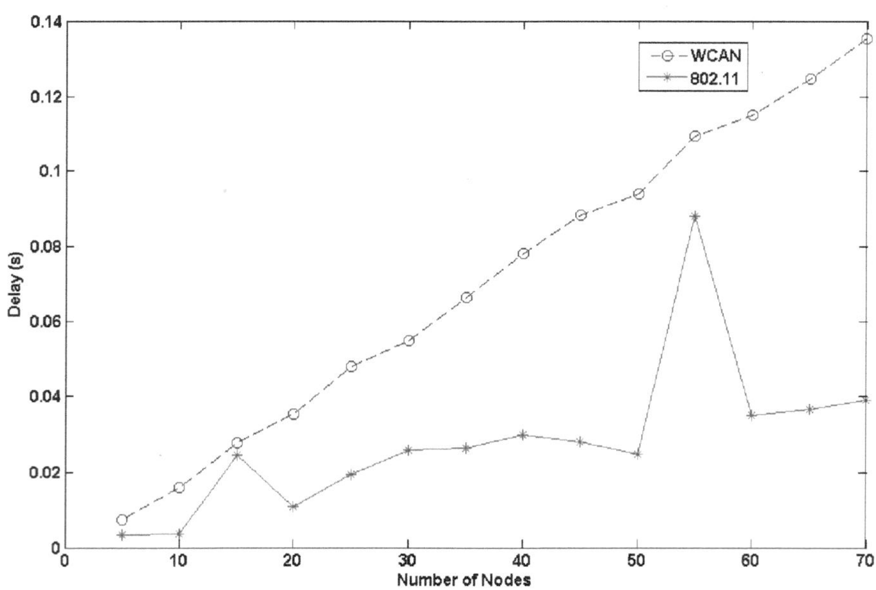

Fig. 12. The average end-to-end delay performance between WCAN and IEEE 802.11.

Looking at Fig 12, it can be seen that the average end-to-end delay of WCAN increases linearly with increasing number of nodes in a ring network. However, the IEEE 802.11 shows a much lower value for its average end-to-end delay. This is because the packet in WCAN environment is passed through each of the nodes present in the ring network in a circular motion. Comparing to IEEE 802.11, the packets are directly transmitted to the destination node using mesh network capability.

6 Conclusion

This paper presents a new wireless protocol namely wireless controller area network (WCAN). WCAN uses the token frame scheme as depicted in [26 - 29] with some modification on the token format and its operation. Furthermore, the flexibility of topologies allows nodes to join and leave the network dynamically. This characteristic gives rise to easier and more versatile design of a home automation system. The developed WCAN is built on the MAC layer as a wireless based distributed MAC protocol for ad-hoc network. WCAN was deployed using QualNet simulator and achieve mixed reaction results. Simulation results show that WCAN outperform IEEE 802.11 in terms of throughput in a ring network environment. However, in terms of average end-to-end delay, WCAN increases linearly with increasing number of nodes and is slightly higher than IEEE 802.11. This is due to the fact that every node takes turn in transmitting the token around the ring network causing the overall delay to increase. From the results, it's shown that WCAN provide 'fair' share for all nodes by scheduling the transmission with token reception. Additionally, WCAN is advantageous by reducing collision probability, by distributing the resource fairly among each node.

References

1. Pazul, K.: Controller Area Network (CAN) Basics. Microchip Technology Inc. (1999)
2. Chen, H., Tian, J.: Research on the Controller Area Network. In: International Conference on Networking and Digital Society, vol. 2, pp. 251–254 (2009)
3. Corrigan, S.: Introduction to the Controller Area Network (CAN). Texas Instrument, Application Report (2008)
4. Robert Bosch GmbH.: CAN Specification, Version 2.0 (1991)
5. Farsi, M., Ratcliff, K., Barbosa, M.: An overview of controller area network. Computing & Control Engineering Journal 10, 113–120 (1999)
6. Lee, K.C., Lee, H.H.: Network-based fire-detection system via controller area network for smart home automation. IEEE Transactions on Consumer Electronics 50, 1093–1100 (2004)
7. Pérez Acle, J., Sonza Reorda, M., Violante, M.: Early, Accurate Dependability Analysis of CAN-Based Networked Systems. IEEE Design and Test of Computers 23(1), 38–45 (2006)
8. Ng, W.L., Ng, C.K., Noordin, N.K., Rokhani, F.Z., Ali, B.M.: Home appliances controller using wireless controller area network (WCAN) system. In: 2010 International Conference on Computer and Communication Engineering (ICCCE), pp. 1–6 (2010)
9. Dridi, S., Gouissem, B., Hasnaoui, S.: Performance Analysis of Wireless Controller Area Network with Priority Scheme. In: The Sixth Annual Mediterranean Ad Hoc Networking Workshop, pp. 153–158 (2007)
10. Dridi, S., Kallel, O., Hasnoui, S.: Performance Analysis of Wireless Controller Area Network. International Journal of Computer Science and Network Security (2007)
11. BenGouissem, B., Dridi, S.: Data centric communication using the wireless Control Area Networks. In: IEEE International Conference on Industrial Technology, pp. 1654–1658 (2006)

12. Kutlu, A., Ekiz, H., Powner, E.T.: Performance analysis of MAC protocols for wireless control area network. In: Proceedings of Second International Symposium on Parallel Architectures, Algorithms, and Networks, pp. 494–499 (1996)
13. Kutlu, A., Ekiz, H., Powner, E.T.: Wireless control area network. In: IEE Colloquium on Networking Aspects of Radio Communication Systems, pp. 3/1 –3/4 (1996)
14. Ergen, M., Lee, D., Sengupta, R., Varaiya, P.: WTRP - wireless token ring protocol. IEEE Transactions on Vehicular Technology 53(6), 1863–1881 (2004)
15. Ergen, M., Lee, D., Sengupta, R., Varaiya, P.: Wireless token ring protocol-performance comparison with IEEE 802.11. In: Eighth IEEE International Symposium on Computers and Communication, pp. 710–715 (2003)
16. Lee, D., Puri, A., Varaiya, P., Sengupta, R., Attias, R., Tripakis, S.: A wireless token ring protocol for adhoc networks. In: IEEE Aerospace Conference Proceedings, vol. 3, pp. 3-1219 – 3-1228 (2002)
17. Lee, D., Attias, R., Puri, A., Sengupta, R., Tripakis, S., Varaiya, P.: A wireless token ring protocol for intelligent transportation systems. IEEE Intelligent Transportation Systems, 1152–1157 (2001)
18. Akyildiz, I.F., Wang, X.: A Survey on Wireless Mesh Networks. IEEE Commun. Mag. 43(9), S23–S30 (2005)
19. Sichitiu, M.L.: Wireless mesh networks: Opportunities and challenges. In: Proceedings of World Wireless Congress (2005)

Low-Dropout Regulator in an Active RFID System Using Zigbee Standard with Non-beacon Mode

M.A. Shahimi[1], K. Hasbullah[1], Z. Abdul Halim[1], and W. Ismail[2]

[1] CEDEC (Collaborative μElectronic Design Excellent Center)
[2] School of Electrical&Electronic Engineering
Universiti Sains Malaysia, Engineering Campus
14300 Nibong Tebal, Seberang Perai Selatan, Pulau Pinang, Malaysia
zaini@cedec.usm.my

Abstract. The use of the low-dropout (LDO) voltage regulator in reducing current consumption in the active tag RFID system using the ZigBee standard was studied. The tag was set with a cyclic mode configuration with non-beacon data transmission mode, and was programmed to sleep for 1.5 s and wake up for 5 s to check for signals coming from the reader. The LDO voltage regulator from the TPS7800 series with ultra-low quiescent current was used in the experiments. Two sets of experiments were conducted using tags with and without LDO voltage regulators, respectively. The current consumed by the active tag was measured, and the results showed that the current consumption was reduced to 32% if the LDO was used to regulate the input voltage from 3 V to 2.2 V. The current consumption remained stable although the voltage source dropped from 3 to 1.8 V. The transmission range also increased when the LDO was adopted in the system.

Keywords: Low-dropout regulator (LDO), Active RFID tag, ZigBee.

1 Introduction

ZigBee is designed for low power consumption, low cost, and various wireless networking applications [1]. In addition, it provides wireless personal area network (WPAN) in the form of digital radio connections between computers and related devices. It is applicable in home automation, smart energy telecommunication, and personal and home application. ZigBee builds on the IEEE 802.15.4 standard, which details the physical layer and MAC layer for low cost and low data rate for the personal area network. The physical layer supports three bands, namely, 2.45 GHz, 915 MHz, and 868 MHz. A total of 16 channels are available in the 2.45 GHz band, 10 channels in the 915 MHz band, and a single channel in the 868 MHz band. All the channels in the frequency range use the direct-sequence spread spectrum (DSSS) access mode. The physical layer supports on/off operation, functionalities for channel selection, link quality estimation, energy detection measurement, and clear channel assessment.

A. Abd Manaf et al. (Eds.): ICIEIS 2011, Part III, CCIS 253, pp. 557–567, 2011.

The MAC layer provides two types of nodes, namely, the reduced function devices (RFDs) and the full function devices (FFDs). Normally, the RFD is integrated with the sensors or actuators such as light switches, temperature sensors, and lamps. The FFD is used as a coordinator or a network end device, whereas the RFD is used only as an end device.

Star topology and peer-to-peer topology are the two types of networks supported by IEEE 802.15.4. The working concept of star topology is similar to a master-slave network concept. The FFD has the role of a PAN (Personal Area Network) coordinator. The other nodes can be RFD or FFD and can only communicate with the PAN coordinator. In peer-to-peer topology, the FFD communicates with the other FFDs through an intermediate FFD, thus allowing communication outside of its radio coverage area. The communication now forms a multi-hop network, and the PAN coordinator administers the network operation.

The PAN coordinator operates the network with a super-frame (beacon) or without a super-frame (non-beacon) [2]. In communication without super-frame (non-beacon), the PAN never sends beacons, and communication occurs based on the unslotted CSMA-CA. The end device periodically wakes up and polls coordinator for any pending message. The coordinator is always on and ready to receive data. Once it receives a signal from the end device, the coordinator sends the messages or signals that no message is available.

Radio frequency identification (RFID) is a telecommunication application, which uses ZigBee technology [3]. Specifically, it can be utilized in asset inventory, in which star topology with non-beacon mode can be applied. For instance, when the reader sends a command to all tags, the tags should respond immediately once they receive the signal. A missing response indicates that the tag or asset is unavailable. A movement sensor can be integrated with the tag as well. The movement of the tag or the asset can generate a stimulus triggering the tag to immediately send a signal to the reader. The reader then sounds an alarm to notify that the asset has moved to another place.

In asset inventory, low power consumption and longer battery lifetime are important factors that ensure battery life efficiency, thus delaying battery replacement. One of the methods to reduce power consumption is to put the tag in the sleep mode when there is no communication activity. In the sleep mode, the current consumption is only a few microamperes, but in idle mode, the current consumption can reach a few miliamperes. Another method to reduce power consumption is the use of a low dropout (LDO) voltage regulator, which minimizes the output saturation of the pass transistor and its drive requirements [4].

This paper discusses the use of the LDO TPS7800 series with ultra-low quiescent current in an active RFID system to reduce power consumption. In addition, the effect on the transmission range was investigated. The tag was programmed in the cyclic non-beacon mode, and two sets of experiments were performed to observe the significance of the LDO in the RFID system. The first experiment was conducted without the LDO, while the second experiment was with the LDO. The current was measured in both experiments, and analyses were based on the current consumption and transmission range in both experiments.

2 Hardware Development

The two main components of an active RFID system are the tag and the reader [5]. Basically, the reader contains a module consisting of a transmitter, a receiver, a control unit, and a coupling element of the antenna. Fig. 1 shows a block diagram of the reader, which consists of a ZigBee module (Xbee module), a single LED indicator, a reset button, and a voltage regulator. The Xbee module operates at 2.45 GHz with a data rate of 250 kbps. The working voltage of the module was between 1.6 V and 3.3 V. The Max3232 converts at the data level between the Zigbee module and the host (PC). A voltage regulator (LM1117) was used to regulate the input voltage from 9 to 3.3 V. The LED indicator demonstrated the status of the reader and a button was used to reset the reader.

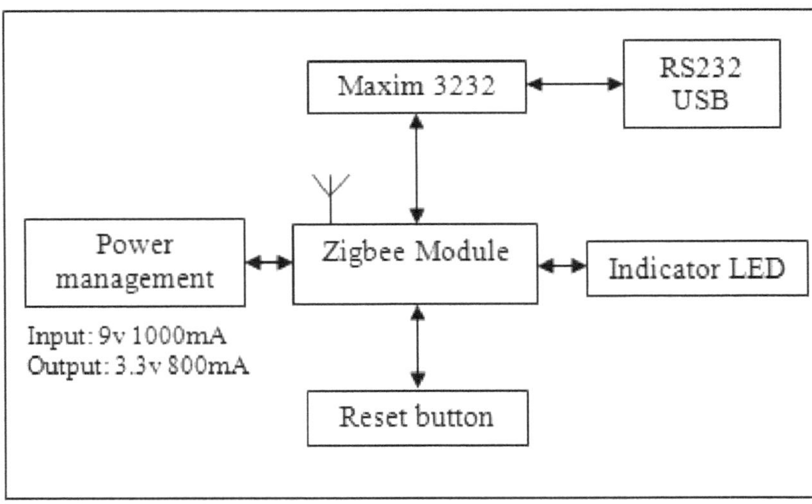

Fig. 1. Block diagram of the reader

The reader has its own channel to communicate with the tags. It searches for its channel continuously if the channel is in conflict with other readers [6]. In one system, the tag's address must be the same as that of the reader. The identity of the tag can be programmed until 20 characters, implying that every system can consist of up to 1,048,576 tags. The tags respond to the reader when they are in the coverage zone, depending on the output power levels of the reader.

Fig 2 shows the block diagram of an RFID tag using periodic data communication. The tag consisted of a power management circuit and a ZigBee module. The tag was programmed with a cyclic mode configuration, during which the tag slept for 1.5 s and woke up for 5 s to check whether or not there was a signal from the reader. The tag responded if there was a signal from the reader; it resumed its sleep mode if there was no signal from the reader after 5 s.

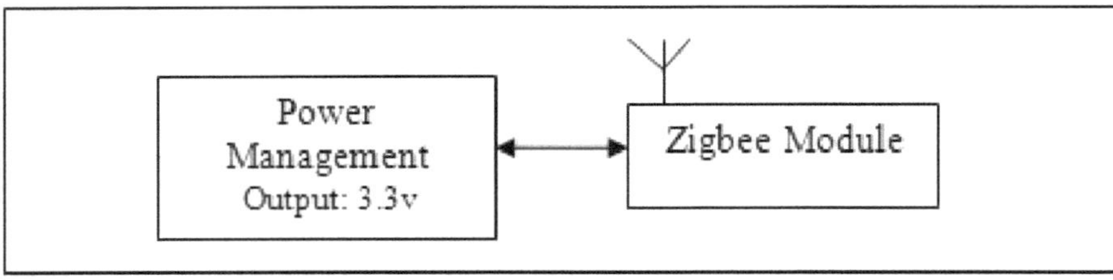

Fig. 2. Block diagram of the RFID tag using periodic data communication

Fig. 3 shows the block diagram of the tag with the LDO device. The tag was programmed under sleep mode configuration. The LDO, which was connected to a power source, was used to minimize current consumption. The output voltage of the LDO was used to supply power constantly to the ZigBee module.

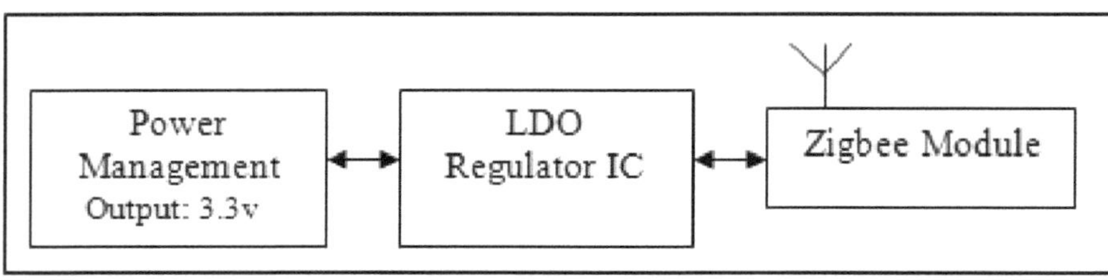

Fig. 3. Block diagram of combination of the LDO and the tag using periodic data communication

Fig. 4 shows the circuit, which controls the output voltage of the LDO. Input and output capacitors were used to stabilize the circuit and were connected to the ground. A feedback pin was used to adjust the output voltage of the LDO, with feedback voltage at 1.216 V. The output voltage varied from 1.2 V to 5.1 V. The output voltage of the LDO was calculated using Equation 1.

$$V_{out} = V_{fb}\left(\frac{R_1}{R_2} + 1\right). \tag{1}$$

The values of R1 and R2 should be chosen in order to get approximately 1.2 μA current divider. The recommended value of R2 is 1MΩ. Using Eq. 1, R1 can be calculated as follows:

$$R_1 = \left(\frac{V_{out}}{V_{fb}} - 1\right) \text{ x } R_2. \tag{2}$$

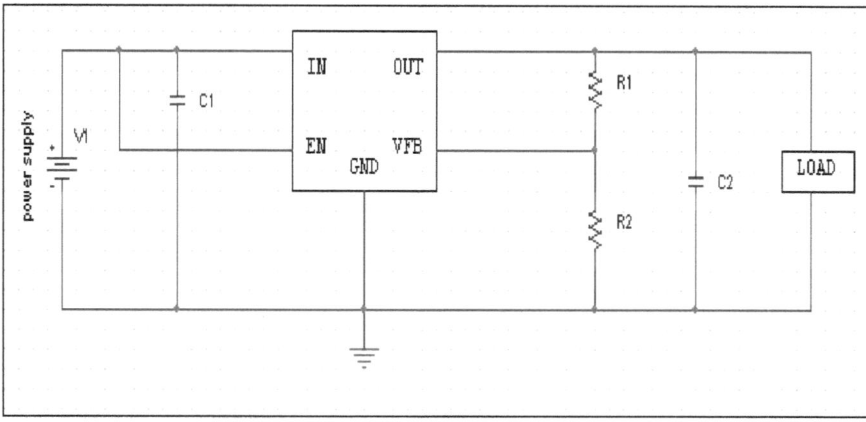

Fig. 4. Block diagram of the LDO circuit

3 Experimental Setup

The first experiment determined the current consumed by the tag at different voltage levels without LDO. The current was measured directly from the source, as shown in Fig. 5.

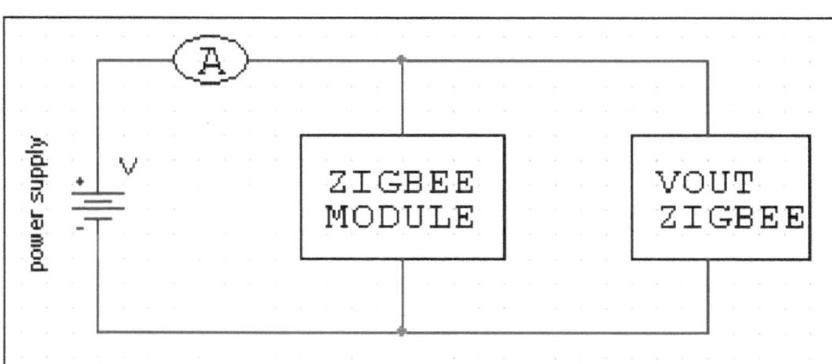

Fig. 5. Experimental setup for tag periodic data communication without LDO

The voltage varied from 1.8 V to 3.3 V. In the experiment, the reader sent a command to the tag; when the tag received the signal, it responded to the reader by sending message "Tag 1," and the message was displayed on the PC.

The second experiment was carried out with LDO. The output voltage of the LDO was set to different values ranging from 1.8 V to 3.3V. The currents consumed by the circuit at these different voltage values were measured. The tag used input voltage from the LDO. Similar to the first experiment, the reader sent a command to the tag; when the tag received the signal, it sent a message of "Tag 2" to the PC. The experiment is shown in Fig 6.

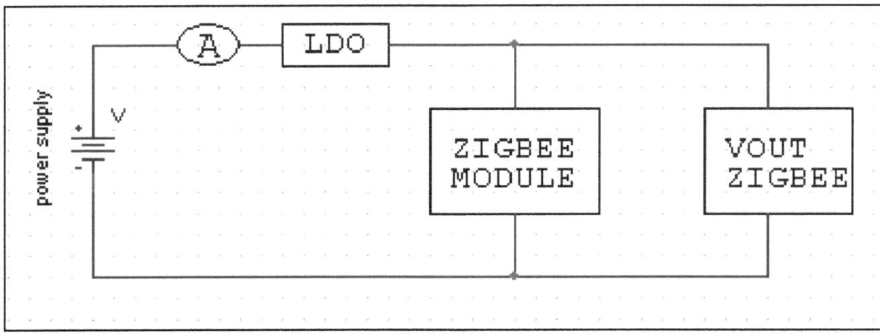

Fig. 6. Experimental setup for tag periodic data with LDO

4 Results and Discussion

In the experiment, an association pin checked whether or not the tag was ready for communication. After a wake up, the tag began to find a channel to communicate with the reader. After acquiring the channel, the tag was associated to the network and was considered ready to transmit or receive data. Fig. 7 shows the voltage signal at the associated indicator pin, where the tag is in sleep mode for 1.5s (logic '0') and wake up for 5s (logic '1'). During the wake up period, it is ready to communicate with the reader for 5 s. After 5s, it goes back to sleep mode.

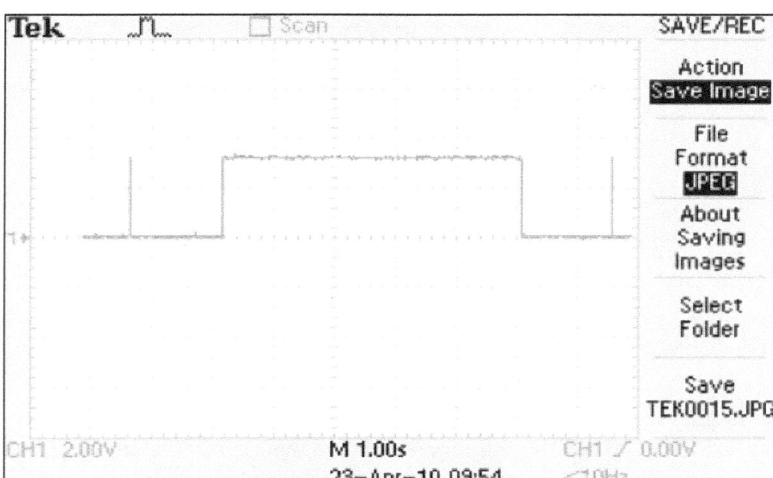

Fig. 7. Voltage signal at the associated indicator pin for the tag with periodic data communication

Table 1 shows the tabulated results for the experiment without LDO. The data show that when the input voltage increases, the current also increases. The lowest

Table 1. Current consumption versus output voltage

Voltage (V)	Current, I ($^{Tx}/_{Rx}$) (mA)
1.8	11.05055
2	11.6649
2.2	11.4328
2.4	13.11755
2.6	14.25075
2.8	15.20865
3	16.31115
3.2	16.87370
3.3	17.58765

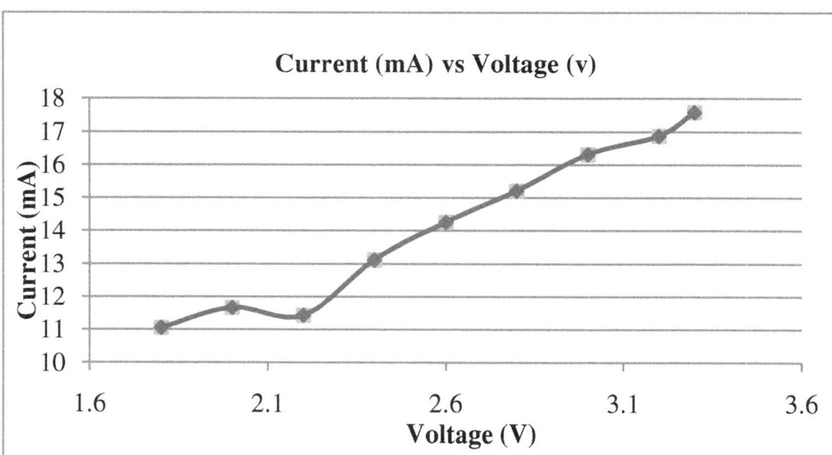

Fig. 8. Current consumption during transmit mode (without LDO)

input voltage to power up the circuit is 1.8 V. Fig. 8 shows the graph of the Current consumption during transmit mode (without LDO).

Table 2 shows the tabulated data for the experiment with LDO. Figure 9 shows the graph of the results.

Table 2. Current consumption versus output voltage

V	Input Voltage								
	1.8	**2.0**	**2.2**	**2.4**	**2.6**	**2.8**	**3.0**	**3.2**	**3.3**
(LDO) = 2.2v	11.5	11.8	12.0	11.5	11.8	12.1	12.4	12.0	12.2
(LDO) = 2.4v	11.0	11.1	12.6	12.5	12.9	13.0	12.2	12.8	12.4
(LDO) = 2.6v	11.3	11.4	12.4	13.1	13.5	13.8	13.8	13.9	13.9
(LDO) = 2.8v	11.5	11.6	12.4	12.9	13.8	14.3	14.7	14.6	15.4
(LDO) = 3.0v	11.2	11.4	12.4	12.8	14.4	15.2	15.9	16.3	15.6
(LDO) = 3.2v	11.0	11.9	12.0	12.1	14.2	15.5	16.4	17.2	16.7
(LDO) = 3.3v	11.7	11.4	12.2	12.7	14.4	15.7	15.9	17.0	17.7
Without LDO	11.1	11.7	11.4	13.1	14.3	15.2	16.3	16.9	17.6

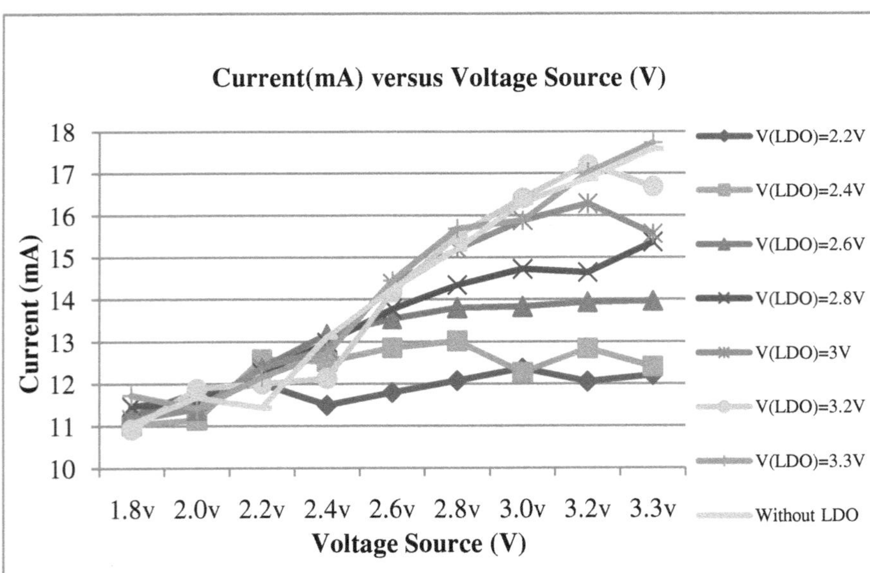

Fig. 9. Current consumption versus input voltage source at different values of output voltage from LDO

The graph shows that the current increases if the voltage source increases, especially at a higher output voltage from the LDO. However, the current is almost constant when the output voltage from LDO is set to 2.2 V. This is because 2.2 V is the optimum working voltage for this application. As shown in Fig. 10, the current of the tag with LDO is nine times more stable than the tag without LDO. Although the voltage source from the battery drops from 3.3 to 1.8 V, the current is still maintained at around 12 mA. The data also show that if the tag is using a 3 V battery, by using LDO, the current consumption can be reduced until 32%, which is quite significant in this application.

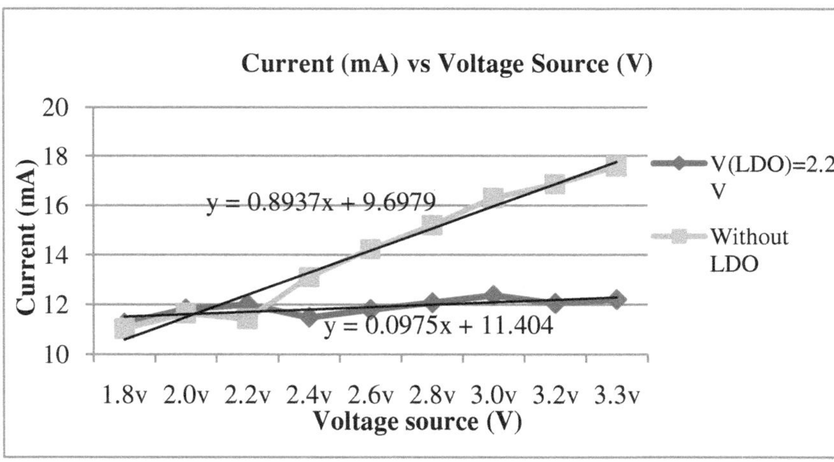

Fig. 10. The comparison between the currents of the tag with and without LDO

5 Transmission Range

Apart from measuring current, the experiments also measured the transmission range. This is done in order to see whether or not the LDO has influenced the transmission range. A different output voltage from the LDO was set, while the input voltage source was fixed at 3 V. The experiment was conducted in the lab, which established that the transmission range was in indoor range. The output power level of the tag was set to 3 dBm.

Fig. 11 shows that the maximum distance is 67.5 m, with an output voltage of 2.2 V from the LDO. The optimum working voltage for this application is 2.2 V, thus giving the longest distance for the transmission range.

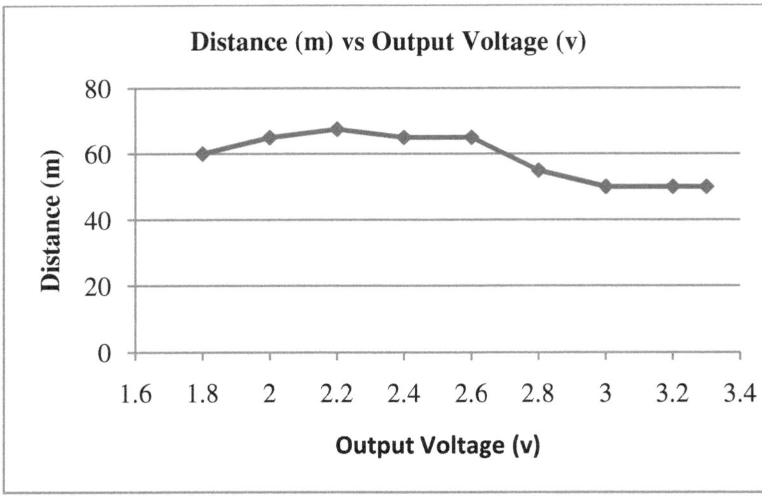

Fig. 11. Distance versus output voltage

In the experiment without LDO, the voltage source was supplied directly to the RFID tag. The input voltage was varied from 3.3 to 1.8 V. The experiment was conducted in a lab, and the output power level of the tag was set at 3dBm.

The results show that the maximum transmission range is 38.9 m, which is 42% shorter than the range of the tag with the LDO voltage regulator. The graph in Fig 12 shows that the transmission range is almost constant until the input voltage drops to 2.2 V, and the tag is unable to transmit any signal at the voltage level of 1.8 V.

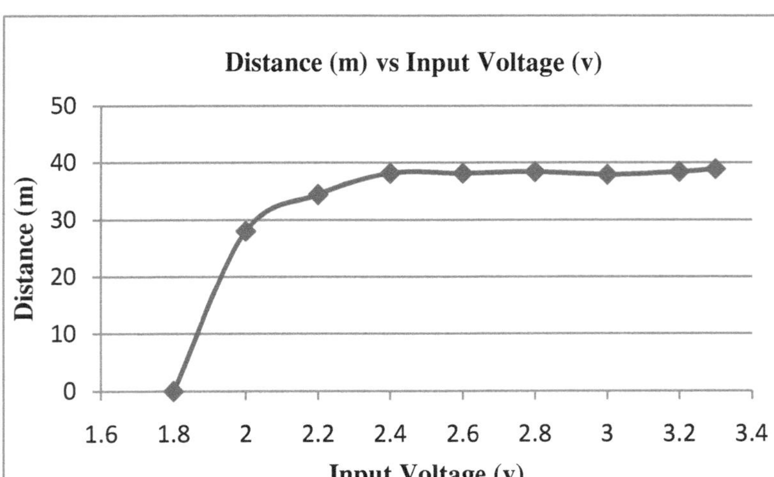

Fig. 12. Distance versus output voltage

6 Conclusion

This paper discusses the use of the LDO in an active RFID tag for the star topology network with non-beacon mode. The tag was configured under the cyclic mode, in which the tag slept for 1.5 s and woke up for 5 s. The LDO from the TPS7800 series with ultra low quiescent current was used in these experiments. Using the LDO, the current consumption remained constant even though the voltage level decreased. The minimum voltage level for the working tag was 1.8 V, and the optimum voltage level for the TPS7800 was 2.2 V. The LDO voltage regulator also reduced the current consumption in this application, where the data showed that current consumption was reduced until 32%, which proved to be significant for this application. Moreover, the indoor transmissions range of the active tag also increased by 42% when the LDO voltage regulator was adopted in the system.

References

1. Ahamed, S.S.R.: The role of zigbee technology in future data communication system. Journal of Theoretical and Applied Information Technology 5, 129 (2009)
2. Baronti, P., Pillai, P., Chook, V.W.C., Chessa, S., Gotta, A., Hu, Y.F.: Wireless sensor networks: A survey on the state of the art and the 802.15. 4 and ZigBee standards. Computer communications 30, 1655–1695 (2007)
3. Shahimi, M.A., Halim, Z.A., Ismail, W.: Development of active RFID system using zigbee standard with non beacon mode. In: Asia Pacific Conference on Circuits and Systems, IEEE, Kuala lumpur (2010)
4. Kugelstadt, T.: Fundamental theory of PMOS low-dropout voltage regulators. Application Report SLVA068. Texas Instruments Inc. (1999)
5. Kitsos, P., Zhang, Y., Hagl, A., Aslanidis, K.: RFID: Fundamentals and Applications RFID Security. Springer, US (2009)
6. Eady, F.: Go Wireless with the XBee. Circuit cellar: The magazine for computer applications, 48–56 (2006)
7. Wolbert, B.: Designing With Low-Dropout Voltage Regulators (1998)
8. Karmakar, N.C., Roy, S.M., Preradovic, S., Vo, T.D., Jenvey, S.: Development of Low-Cost Active RFID Tag at 2.4 GHz. In: 36th European Microwave Conference, pp. 1602–1605 (2006)

Distributed, Energy-Efficient, Fault Tolerant, Weighted Clustering

Javad Memariani, Zuriati Ahmad Zukarnain, Azizol Abdullah, and Zurina Mohd. Hanapi

Department of Communication Techology and Network, Universiti Putra Malaysia University Putra Malaysia, 43400 Serdong, Malaysia
javad.memariani@gmail.com,
{zuriati,azizol,zurina}@fsktm.upm.edu.my

Abstract. In distributed sensor networks, a large number of small sensors are deployed to create a network which cooperates together to set up a sensing network. The main duty of sensors is to prepare access to environmental information anytime, anywhere by collecting, processing, analyzing and transmitting data. Scalability, load balancing and increasing network lifetime are significant parameters for wireless sensor networks [1]. Clustering is a useful technique to address these issues. In this paper, we propose a distributed, energy-efficient, fault tolerant and weighted clustering algorithm that extends the network lifetime by using some parameters such as energy, centrality, density, in addition distances between nodes and the base station. We consider a backup node for each cluster, that will be replaced while the cluster head drain out of its energy, and also cluster head list [2] for every node. These mechanisms cause increasing the network lifetime and lead the network to become fault tolerant.

Keywords: Clustering, Fault Tolerant, Life Time, Wireless Sensor Network.

1 Introduction

The development of micro devices and wireless communication technology created the tiny sensor device called sensor node. Over the past few years, wireless sensor networks for various applications including target tracking, military surveillance, etc. have been used. Major benefits are pleaded for the sensor technology is that it has high capability for wireless communications, sensing and data processing despite its low price. However, these sensor nodes restricted with the small memory, limited energy power and constrained processing capability. Depending on the application, the nodes gather observed data from the environment and sending the processed data to the base station.

The design of energy-efficient and scalable clustering protocols is one of the significant challenges in WSNs, because of the non-rechargeable and non-exchangeable power energy characteristic of sensor nodes. To address these issues, vast research for the clustering has been done.

The basic concept of clustering scheme is to separate a network into several sections, which are called clusters and cluster heads are assigned to each cluster.

A. Abd Manaf et al. (Eds.): ICIEIS 2011, Part III, CCIS 253, pp. 568–577, 2011.

The cluster heads are nodes with higher energy, that are responsible for aggregating, processing and transmitting information to the base station, while the regular nodes with lower energy are used to sense the desired area and sending data to cluster heads. The key benefit of the clustering scheme is to reduce the distance of transferring data by communicating with cluster heads, which are obviously having shorter distance against transmission data to the base station directly. Furthermore, it reduces unnecessarily repetitive transmissions by minimizing the network traffic towards the base station that impacts on energy consumption.

In this paper, we propose a distributed, energy-efficient, fault tolerant and weighted clustering algorithm which takes into account battery power of nodes, density, centrality, in addition distance between nodes and the base station. Also, to address the fault tolerant of clustering in the network two mechanisms are used. The first one by assigning to each cluster a backup node and second, making a cluster head list [2] for each node that leads to prolong the network life time.

We compare our approach with two famous algorithms LEACH and HEED. Simulation results show that the proposed approach yields better results than LEACH and HEED in network life time.

The rest of the paper is organized as follows. In Section 2, we review several clustering algorithm proposed previously. Then we describe our clustering algorithm in Section 3. In section 4, the performance analysis of the proposed algorithm is described. At last, section 5 concludes the paper.

2 Related Work

Several kinds of clustering algorithms have been proposed in the literature. Each of them pondered different principle such as weights as a priority standard or probabilistic approach to elect cluster heads. In LEACH [3], authors propose a distributed algorithm which each node makes a decision independently without any centralized control. In LEACH, a formula proposed for calculating the probability distribution p in each round. At the beginning of each round, each node selects a random number between 0 and 1. If this number is less than the threshold $T(n)$, the node can be cluster head. Then, it disseminates this fact to other nodes. The proposed probability formula is:

$$T(n) = \begin{cases} \dfrac{p}{1 - p \times (r \, mod \, \frac{1}{p})} & if \; n \in G \\ 0 & if \; n \notin G \end{cases} \tag{1}$$

Where n is the number of the nodes in the network, r is the number of round, p is the optimal number of cluster head that is desired to be 0.05 of the total number of nodes and G is referred to the set of nodes that have not been elected as cluster head in the last $1/p$ rounds. LEACH, generates a high number of cluster in each round, which increases the overhead of inter-cluster communication but in overall this algorithm tries to provide a balancing of energy dissipation by random rotation of cluster heads.

HEAD [4] for intra-cluster communication and inter-cluster communication uses two different radio transmission level [5]. This algorithm does not opt cluster head randomly, thus provides more balanced cluster head in size. Each sensor becomes a cluster head according to its residual energy. The probability to be selected as cluster head can be calculated as follows:

$$CH_{prob} = C_{prob} \times \frac{E_{residual}}{E_{initial}} \tag{2}$$

If CH_{prob} is less than 1, a node introduces itself as a temporary cluster head. With probability equal or greater than 1, the node introduces itself as a final cluster head. After that, node broadcasts its decision.

The PEGASIS [6] protocol aims to reduce the overhead causes by the iteration of reclustering in LEACH by constructing chains of sensor nodes by using a greedy algorithm. By assuming that each node has a global knowledge of the network, each node selects nearest neighbors as next hops in the current chain. The disadvantage of this protocol is that the significant delays caused by passing the packet data sequentially in the chain and the chain leader has to wait to all the packets are received before sending them to the base station.

TEEN [7] is designed for event-based applications where information is generated only when an event occurs. This protocol provides hierarchical levels of nodes. Data are sent to cluster heads which have the duty of collect, aggregate and transmitting these data to a higher cluster head until it is received by the base station. TEEN constructs communication through two thresholds: hard threshold (HT) and soft threshold (ST). When a node has sensed-attribute changes such as temperature, it compares that value to HT, if it is exceeded HT the node sends the observed data to cluster head. The HT restricts the packet transmissions of those observed data that match the base station's interest. The ST will diminish the number of transmissions if there is little or no change in the value of sensed attribute.

The Adaptive Threshold Sensitive Energy Efficient sensor network protocol (APTEEN) [8] is an improvement of TEEN, which controls when and how data can be sent frequently using the hard and soft threshold. The complexity of forming clusters at hierarchical levels and also the overhead are the main disadvantages of TEEN and APTEEN.

The Weighted Clustering Algorithm (WCA) [9] proposed a weight-based distributed clustering algorithm, which takes into account the transmission power, battery power, ideal degree and mobility of nodes. In WCA, the number of nodes is limited in a cluster thus the performance of the MAC protocol is not decreased.

Uniformly Distributed Adaptive Clustering Hierarchy (UDACH) [10] is based on energy balancing to select cluster head but not randomly. This clustering algorithm performs in three steps: cluster construction which establishes a cluster head tree and in this step cluster head are selected and nodes around the cluster heads are able to identify the near cluster head. The tree in the step of building a cluster head is created based upon the weight of each cluster head. The cluster heads near to the base station becomes the root of the cluster head tree, and it communicates with the base station directly. In the last step, each member of a cluster head collects the sensed data and sends it to the base station by its cluster head.

In [11], Maximum Energy Cluster Head (MECH), the clusters are constructed in a certain area based on the number of the node members and radio transmission range.

A hierarchical tree is used to reduce the distance of cluster heads to the base station. High broadcasting of the control message is the weakness of this protocol.

EADC [12] selects a cluster head with higher energy by using cluster head competition range which is based upon the ratio between the residual energy of the node and the average remaining of neighbor nodes. Furthermore, the competition range causes to construct clusters of balanced size which uniforms the energy consumption through cluster members. A cluster-based routing algorithm is proposed to overcome the problem of imbalanced energy consumption caused by non-uniform node distribution by controlling the inter-cluster and the intra-cluster energy consumption of cluster heads.

Location-based Unequal Clustering Algorithm (LUCA) [13] proposed a clustering algorithm, which each cluster based upon its location information has a different cluster size. This information includes the distance between the base station and a cluster head. The clusters with larger size are farther away from the base station, where makes the cluster head the ability to collect more local data and decrease the energy consumption for inter-cluster communication. A cluster head near to the base station has smaller size to reduce the energy consumption for intra-cluster communication.

3 The Proposed Algorithm

3.1 Assumptions

We adopt some reasonable assumptions for our algorithm as follows:

1. All the sensor nodes are homogenous.
2. Each sensor node is aware of its own location.
3. Each node has a unique ID.
4. Position of the base station is at point (1, 1).
5. All sensor nodes always have a packet ready to transmit.
6. There is no mobility for nodes.

3.2 Description of Proposed Algorithm

There are five parameters in our algorithm which are as follows.

1. **Energy:** obviously, the cluster head consumes much more energy than regular sensors because the burden of routing, processing and communicating with much more nodes. To ensure that the cluster heads perform their task without interrupt, the nodes are more eligible than the other nodes in terms of residual energy that have the maximum remaining energy.
2. **Centrality:** sometimes density of a node is high, but most of the neighbors are in one side of that node. The nodes located in the center of regions usually get higher structural significance than those positioned in the border hence, whenever there exists data following, central nodes play a significant role to pass data to next hop. Therefore, cluster heads are preferred to locate at the center of their corresponding neighbors that this causes more load-balancing.

3. **Density:** the algorithm aims to select cluster head from the areas containing high density [14]. In a real network most nodes may focus in certain areas, and in other areas may exist quite sparse or even no node. In this paper, the density factor is calculated according to the number of nodes around a node [1].
4. **Distance Between Nodes:** in proposed approach, a cluster head is selected by other nodes when the node located close to other respective nodes. Far nodes in a region are given a negative score, thus they have a little chance to become a cluster head.
5. **Distance to the Base Station:** it is desirable to select cluster heads, which are close to base station. This causes less inter-cluster communication, because a packet to be received by base station has to pass in fewer hops [15].

3.3 Clustering Phase

In the proposed algorithm, all nodes are separated into some regions called cluster and at the end of the algorithm, there are a cluster head for each cluster and backup node. Other nodes are called cluster member. The algorithm ensures that the clustering is thoroughly distributed. It consists of a number of control messages, which executed by each node.

1. Initially, each node disseminates to all perspective nodes around itself a message called Preliminary Advertisement Message (PAM). We refer this stage as *initial phase*. This message contains the node' ID, and its geographical coordinate. Nodes can use location services such as [16, 17] to estimate their locations coordinate and no GPS receiver is required. Each node computes the distance between itself and neighbors by knowing the information about their coordinates. If the retrieved distance is less than a threshold *d* then the node can update its neighbor's table and compute the density parameter. This threshold considered for the size of clusters. Reducing the value of the *d* causes a smaller cluster head, thus the intra-communication will reduce and vice versa.
2. Afterwards, each node received a PAM from all its neighbors, computes the centrality factor according to the proposed algorithm in [1]. We call a node is a volunteer when neither is not positioned in the border nor density is greater than the threshold *s*. Increasing this threshold causes nodes with fewer neighbors have a small chance to become a volunteer and vice versa. To identifying the nodes located in the border, we referred to centrality factor. The value of the centrality should be higher than half of the density value.
3. A volunteer should be voted by its neighbors to be nominated as a cluster head. All nodes are aware about their residual energy. Therefore, each node gives itself a score according to each neighbor's distance and sends it for the neighbor. Clearly, each neighbor may receive a different score from the other neighbors because the distance between nodes defers from a node to other. The score can be computed using following linear formula.

$$Score(i) = E + \omega_1\, De - \omega_2 Ce - \omega_3\, Dis_n - \omega_4\, Dis_{bs} \qquad (3)$$

Where ω_1, ω_2, ω_3 and ω_4 are the weighting coefficients for the density, centrality, distance between nodes and distance between nodes and the base station respectively. This score will be sent as Volunteer Advertisement Message (VAM).

4. All the nodes are aware about the VAM of their neighbors. When a node receives a VAM, it computes a score for that particular volunteer and stores it in its volunteer list. The score can be calculated as follows.

$$Score(v) = \sum \varphi \times \gamma \tag{4}$$

As we can see, the number of voters is very significant for volunteers to become a cluster head. Each time a VAM receives, the volunteer list will be updated with a new score. For the remaining of this phase, each node selects a node with a high score from the volunteer list. If the highest score belongs to itself, thus the node is a cluster head then introduces itself to neighbors as cluster head and goes to the next phase; otherwise it looks forward receiving the join message from the near cluster head.

5. In this phase, each cluster head sends a join message to its neighbors. Then each neighbor stores the received join message to its cluster head list. Finally regular nodes decide to join to which cluster head. Here, it is preferable to join the closest cluster head. After deciding about choosing a cluster head, the node sends an acceptance message which also contains the residual energy of that node. Then the members go to *steady phase*, and periodically sense information from the environment and send the data to their cluster head.
6. The corresponding cluster head then chooses the nearest member with high residual energy as a backup node for that particular cluster. The cluster head informs its members about the cluster's backup node.
7. Whenever a cluster head dies after a while, the members of that cluster switch to the backup node. After the backup node dies, the members can use their cluster head list to find a closest cluster head and send their data to that certain cluster head.

3.4 Weighting Coefficients

Based upon the preceding discussion, for existing five parameters of formula (3), there is no exact mathematical way to calculate the weighting coefficient. We empirically compute them by using linear regression to estimate the best coefficient values. Because we assumed a homogenous network, all nodes commence their job with the same level of energy, thus the changes of energy level are very low before the steady state. Hence, the weighting value calculated by regression for energy is meaning-less. Therefore, we considered the energy factor for the homogenous network as a constant. The estimated coefficients are shown in Table (1).

Table 1. Coefficients table

Area	Node	ω_1	ω_2	ω_3	ω_4
100	100	-0.874	2.370	-0.117	0.054
200	200	-2.809	3.299	-0.094	-0.011
300	300	-4.316	5.332	-0.127	-0.016

4 Simulation

4.1 Radio Model

We use the same radio model described in [18]. The wireless channel model is composed of the free space model and the multipath fading model. Transmission and reception energy consumption for an l-bit message over distance d is calculated as follows.

$$E_{Tx}(l,d) = \begin{cases} l \times E_{elec} + l \times \epsilon_{fs} \times d^2, d < d_0 \\ l \times E_{elec} + l \times \epsilon_{mp} \times d^2, d \geq d_0 \end{cases} \tag{5}$$

$$E_r(l) = l \times E_{elec} \tag{6}$$

Where d is the transmission range, l is the size of the packet. E_{elec}, ϵ_{fs}, and ϵ_{mp} are parameters of the transmission/reception circuitry, respectively.

4.2 Performance Evaluation

In this section, we will verify the performance of proposed approach via computer simulation. We developed our own discrete event simulation program in C++. The data packets are generated twice in every one second by members. We ran simulations with 100, 200 and 300 sensor nodes, which are uniformly distributed into an area with dimensions 100, 200 and 300 respectively. The parameters of simulations are listed in Table 2.

Table 2. Parameters of simulations

Parameters	Value
Initial Energy	6 J
Data Packet Size	500 bytes
Transmission Range	30
Simulation Time	900 s
E_{elec}	50 nJ/bit
ϵ_{fs}	10 pJ/(bit·m^2)
ϵ_{mp}	0.0013 pJ/(bit·m^4)

We compared the performance of our approach to prominent protocols, LEACH and HEED. All the simulation parameters for above algorithms and our algorithm are exactly the same.

The simulation starts from the initial phase, which every node sends the PAM message to neighbors. Then each volunteer sends VAM to its neighbors. After identifying the cluster head for each cluster, the cluster heads send the join message to their neighbors, and steady phase will begin. In this phase, each regular node performs sensing from the environment and then sends the observed data to its corresponding cluster head. Obviously, the cluster head gathers and aggregates received data from their members and send them hop-to-hop to the base station.

After the network running for certain time in steady phase, the cluster heads drain out their energy and become unavailable. Progressively, backup cluster heads became active, and send the join message to neighbors around themselves and form a new different set of clusters in the network. Furthermore, after the backups lost their energy, the regular node still can continue their job by using their cluster head list, and find an available cluster head to send their data. This fault tolerance characteristic of the proposed algorithm insures the area to be covered even when the cluster heads are drained out of their energy, and also leads to increase the network life time. Here, the nodes die when their remaining energy is less than 1%.

The simulation result of the three models, LEACH, HEED and our model, depicted in Fig. 1, 2 and 3. As shown, our model increased the network life time around six times and about two times more than LEACH and HEED respectively. One of the significant shortcomings of LEACH and HEED is the iteration of selecting cluster heads in each round [19]. This causes considerable lost of energy due to redundant transmission [20]. However, in our algorithm, backup node replacement and cluster head list usage are a reason for the improvement. Also, the numbers of alive nodes almost remain constant and much more than two other algorithms. The load to broadcast data to base station is uniformly distributed among all sensor nodes in the proposed algorithm, thus nodes exhausted their energy almost at the same time.

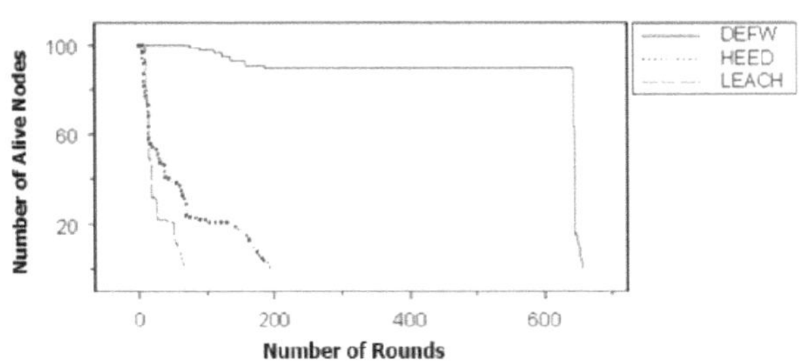

Fig. 1. Total number of alive node pre round for area 100 and 100 nodes

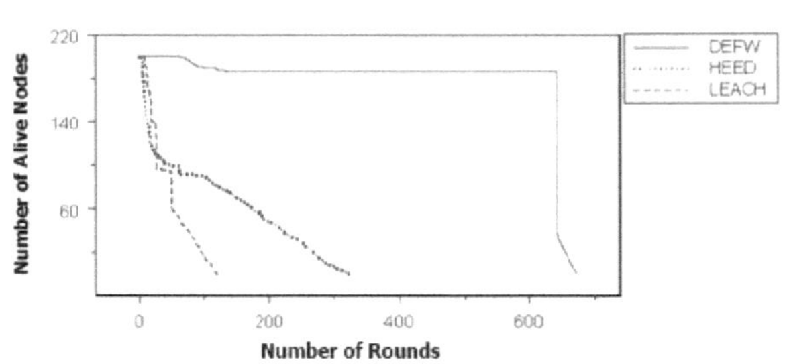

Fig. 2. Total number of alive node pre round for area 200 and 200 nodes

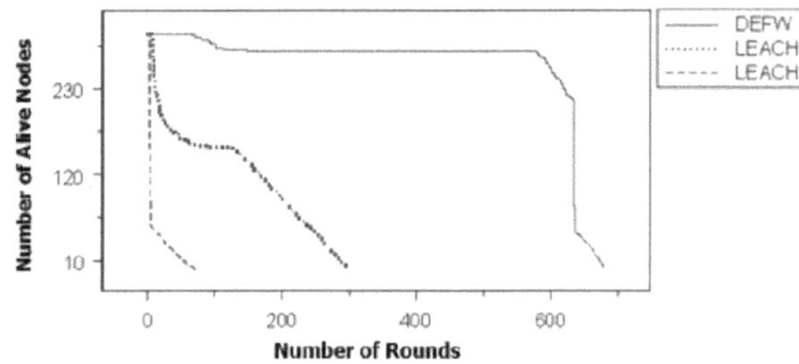

Fig. 3. Total number of alive node pre round for area 300 and 300 nodes

5 Conclusion

In this paper, we have presented an energy-efficient and distributed clustering algorithm for wireless sensor networks, which prolongs the network lifetime. Proposed algorithm can dynamically adjust itself with the ever network topology and selects a backup node for each cluster. This causes the whole network to be thoroughly covered, and the network will be faulting tolerant. As a future work, we expect to design and implement a fuzzy-logic approach to calculate the weighing coefficients for counting their average amount.

References

1. Mehrani, M., Shanbehzadeh, J., Sarrafzadeh, A., Mirabedini, S.J., Manford, C.: FEED: Fault tolerant, energy efficient, distributed Clustering for WSN. In: The 12th International Conference on Advanced Communication Technology (ICACT), pp. 580–585. IEEE (2010)
2. Du, X., Xiao, Y.: Energy efficient Chessboard Clustering and routing in heterogeneous sensor networks. International Journal of Wireless and Mobile Computing 1, 121–130 (2006)
3. Heinzelman, W.R., Chandrakasan, A., Balakrishnan, H.: Energy-efficient communication protocol for wireless microsensor networks. In: Proceedings of the 33rd Annual Hawaii Conference on System Sciences, p. 10 (2000)
4. Younis, O., Fahmy, S.: Distributed clustering in ad-hoc sensor networks: A hybrid, energy-efficient approach. In: Twenty-third Annual Joint Conference of the IEEE Computer and Communications Societies, p. 4. IEEE (2004)
5. Bajaber, F., Awan, I.: Energy efficient clustering protocol to enhance lifetime of wireless sensor network. Journal of Ambient Intelligence and Humanized Computing, 1–10 (2010)
6. Lindsey, S., Raghavendra, C.S.: PEGASIS: Power-efficient gathering in sensor information systems. In: Aerospace Conference Proceedings, pp. 1125–1130. IEEE (2002)
7. Manjeshwar, A., Agrawal, D.P.: TEEN: a routing protocol for enhanced efficiency in wireless sensor networks. In: 15th International Proceedings Parallel and Distributed Processing Symposium, pp. 2009–2015. IEEE (2001)
8. Manjeshwar, A., Agrawal, D.P.: APTEEN: A hybrid protocol for efficient routing and comprehensive information retrieval in wireless sensor networks, pp. 195–202. IEEE (2002)

9. Chatterjee, M., Das, S.K., Turgut, D.: WCA: A weighted clustering algorithm for mobile ad hoc networks. Cluster Computing 5, 193–204 (2002)
10. Chen, J., Yu, F.: A Uniformly Distributed Adaptive Clustering Hierarchy Routing Protocol. In: IEEE International Conference on Integration Technology, pp. 628–632. IEEE (2007)
11. Chang, R.S., Kuo, C.J.: An energy efficient routing mechanism for wireless sensor networks. In: 20th International Conference on Advanced Information Networking and Applications, p. 5. IEEE (2006)
12. Yu, J., Qi, Y., Wang, G., Gu, X.: A cluster-based routing protocol for wireless sensor networks with nonuniform node distribution. AEU-International Journal of Electronics and Communications (2011)
13. Lee, S., Choe, H., Park, B., Song, Y., Kim, C.: LUCA: An Energy-efficient Unequal Clustering Algorithm Using Location Information for Wireless Sensor Networks. Wireless Personal Communications, 1–17 (2011)
14. Yi, G., Guiling, S., Weixiang, L., Yong, P.: Recluster-LEACH: A recluster control algorithm based on density for wireless sensor network. In: 2nd International Conference on Power Electronics and Intelligent Transportation System, pp. 198–202. IEEE (2009)
15. Lee, G., Kong, J., Lee, M., Byeon, O.: A Cluster-Based Energy-Efficient Routing Protocol without Location Information for Sensor Networks. The Journal of Information Processing Systems 1, 49–54 (2005)
16. Doherty, L., pister, K.S.J., El Ghaoui, L.: Convex position estimation in wireless sensor networks. In: Twentieth Annual Joint Conference of the IEEE Computer and Communications Societies, pp. 1655–1663. IEEE (2001)
17. Savvides, A., Han, C.C., Strivastava, M.B.: Dynamic fine-grained localization in ad-hoc networks of sensors. In: Proceedings of the 7th Annual International Conference on Mobile Computing and Networking, pp. 166–179. ACM (2001)
18. Zhao, C., Zhou, T., Liu, X., Xiong, H.: Prediction-based Energy Efficient Clustering Approach for Wireless Sensor Networks. Journal of Convergence Information Technology 6 (2011)
19. Deng, J., Han, Y.S., Heinzelman, W.B., Varshney, P.K.: Scheduling sleeping nodes in high density cluster-based sensor networks. Mobile Networks and Applications 10, 825–835 (2005)
20. Chamam, A., Pierre, S.: A distributed energy-efficient clustering protocol for wireless sensor networks. Computers & Electrical Engineering 36, 303–312 (2010)

Location Estimation and Filtering of Wireless Nodes in an Open Environment

A. Muhammad[1,2,5], M.S. Mazliham[3], Patrice Boursier[1,4], and M. Shahrulniza[5]

[1] Laboratoire Informatique Image Interaction (L3i) Université de La Rochelle, France
[2] Institute of Research and Postgraguate Studies, UniKL (BMI), Kuala Lumpur, Malaysia
[3] Malaysia France Institute (UniKL MFI), Bandar Baru Bangi, Malaysia
[4] Faculty of Computer Science & IT Universiti Malaya, Kuala Lumpur, Malaysia
[5] Malaysian Institute of Information Technology (UniKL MIIT), Kuala Lumpur Malaysia
muhammad.ulr@gmail.com, {mazliham,shahrulniza}@unikl.edu.my,
patrice.boursier@univ-lr.fr, patrice@um.edu.my

Abstract. The research is on the location estimation and filtering of wireless nodes in an open environment. This research is based on our previous findings in which we categorized the geographical area into thirteen different terrains/clutters based on the signal to noise ratio. As signal to noise ratio differs from terrain to terrain therefore data points are calculated for each terrain. A C# program is used with the WiFi architecture to calculate the available signal strength and the receive signal strength. Estimation is done by using triangulation method with the construction of three triangles. As each experiment is repeated five times which estimated five different positions due to the effect of signal to noise ratio, therefore fifteen locations are estimated based on three triangles. Filtering is further done by using average and mean of means calculations. Results show that terrains/clutters based location estimation and filtering produce better results. Only terrains with high attenuation such as sea, dense forest, highway/motorway and high dense urban areas has high error rate after filtering. This research work helps to minimize location error in an open environment.

Keywords: Location estimation, location filtering, terrains/clutters, signal to noise ratio.

1 Introduction

Location estimation of wireless nodes is a very popular research area for the past few years. The research in location estimation is not limited to satellite communication [1], but also in WLAN [2], MANET [3], WSN [4] and Cellular communication [5]. Because of the growth and advancement in cellular communication architecture the usage of handheld devices has increasing rapidly, therefore mobile users originating calls are also increasing [6]. It is estimated that more than 50% emergency calls are originated by mobile phones [7]. Researchers have used different location estimation techniques such as satellite based, geometrical, statistical and mapping techniques [8,9]. In order to achieve accuracy sometime researchers have combined two or more techniques [10].

A. Abd Manaf et al. (Eds.): ICIEIS 2011, Part III, CCIS 253, pp. 578–593, 2011.

However the terrain based location estimation is an area which is not considered by researchers extensively. As radiowaves behave differently in different atmosphere, the calculation of few parameters is not sufficient to achieve accuracy especially when it is totally based on Receive Signal Strength (RSS) which carries impairments. Behavior of radiowaves can be categorize as [11,12]

- Reflection
- Refraction
- Diffraction
- Scattering
- Absorption

Radio waves are directly infected by terrains atmosphere [13]. When the transmit signal (Tx) passes from different terrains then the above mentioned behaviors apply on that Tx. Because of the noise addition the Rx value differs from the Tx value [13]. The difference between the Tx and the Rx values is known as loss. The receive signal strength is inversely proportional to loss, if the loss increases the receive signal strength decreases. For location estimation researchers use this receive signal as a primary value for parameters calculation. If we do not consider the terrain error rate then it will not give us accurate position of a wireless node. Every terrain has different error rate because of its specific environment. If we ignore the terrains/clutters impairments then the calculated location will not be précised. In our previous research work [14], we proposed thirteen different terrains based on the geographical areas. These terrains are divided into four environment groups which are [14, 15]:

A. Urban Terrains/Clutters
- Low Dense Urban (LDU)
- Medium Dense Urban (MDU)
- High Dense Urban (HDU)

B. Rural Terrains/Clutters
- Low Dense Rural (LDR)
- Medium Dense Rural (MDR)
- High Dense Rural (HDR)

C. Plantation
- Agriculture/Field (A/F)
- Low Forest/ Plantation (LF/P)
- Dense Forest (DF)

D. Highways & Water Bodies
- Highway/Motorway (H/M)
- River/Lake (R/L)
- Sea

(We propose desert as a 13th category in the terrain division but has not been considered in this research). All testing results presented in this research article are taken in WiFi environment.

This research paper is divided into seven sections. Section two is dedicated to the problem statement. Triangulation based location estimation is included in section three and location filtering is discussed in section four. Experimental results are presented in section five. Comparison of filtering results with actual locations is presented in section six. Finally conclusion and limitations of this research is added in section seven.

2 Problem Statement

Corrected location of wireless nodes is always the main issue faced by the researchers. Transmitted signals (The Tx) and received signals (The Rx) are the main parameters used for the calculation of location of wireless nodes. Because of the atmospheric attenuation in the free space the Available Signal Strength (ASS) or Tx and the Receive Signal Strength (RSS) or Rx values always comes with error. A procedure is required to calculate the accurate location by considering terrains impairments.

3 Triangulation Implementation with Three Antennas for Location Estimation

We use triangulation method to estimate position in different terrains (figure 1). The combination of RSS and Available Signal Strength (ASS) is used to avoid terrain attenuation and for better location. We repeat our experiment 5 times on each node and construct three triangles. As a result we calculate fifteen location of a wireless node.

Based on the data points the Angle of Arrival (AOA) is calculated and a triangle is constructed as shown in figure 2. For error correction three (3) antennas are used which provides overlapping coverage feature. Constructed triangles are ΔABM, ΔACM and ΔBCM as shown in the figure 3 [14-17].

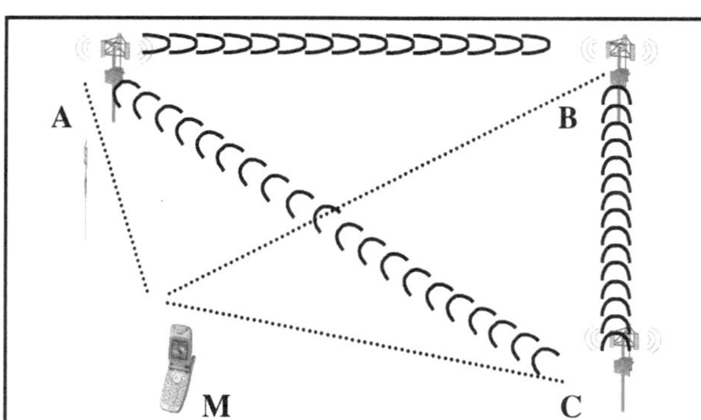

Fig. 1. Mobile node (M) is receiving signals from antennas

where A, B, C are antennas (transmitters)
M is a wireless node (receiver)

By using the ASS and the RSS, the distance between points AB, AM and AC is calculated.

where ASS is Actual Signal Strength at A and B at t_0
RSS is Receive Signal Strength from A, B and M at time t_0.

As the location and the distance between points A, B and C are known, by using the ASS and the RSS, the distance between points AB, AM and BM is calculated.

$$D_{(AB)t0} = (ASS_{(A)t0}+ASS_{(B)t0}) / 2 - (RSS_{(A)t0} + RSS_{(B)t0}) / 2 \quad (1)$$
$$D_{(AM)t0} = ASS_{(A)t0} - RSS_{(M)t0} \quad (2)$$
$$D_{(BM)t0} = ASS_{(B)t0} - RSS_{(M)t0} \quad (3)$$

where

$D_{(AB)}$ is distance between point A and B.
$D_{(AM)}$ is distance between point A and M
$D_{(BM)}$ is distance between point B and M

As the location of points A, B and C are known and now also the distance between A, B and M is calculated, so by using the simple trigonometry formula angles α, β and γ are calculated.

By using basic trigonometric *formula for angle calculation with three known sides,*

$$Cos\alpha = (b^2 + c^2 - a^2) / 2bc$$
$$Cos\beta = (a^2 + c^2 - b^2) / 2ac$$
$$Cos\gamma = (a^2 + b^2 - c^2) / 2bc$$

$$Cos\alpha = [\{D_{(AM)t0}\}^2 + \{D_{(AB)t0}\}^2 - \{D_{(BM)t0}\}^2] / 2 D_{(AM)t0} D_{(AB)t0} \quad (4)$$
$$Cos\beta = [\{D_{(BM)t0}\}^2 + \{D_{(AB)t0}\}^2 - \{D_{(AM)t0}\}^2] / 2 D_{(BM)t0} D_{(AB)t0} \quad (5)$$
$$Cos\gamma = [\{D_{(BM)t0}\}^2 + \{D_{(AM)t0}\}^2 - \{D_{(AB)t0}\}^2] / 2 D_{(BM)t0} D_{(AM)t0} \quad (6)$$

By using the distance between AB, AM and BM and the angles α and β a triangle is plotted to estimate the location of M (Loc M) at time t_0 by using ΔABM, as shown in figure 2 [14-17].

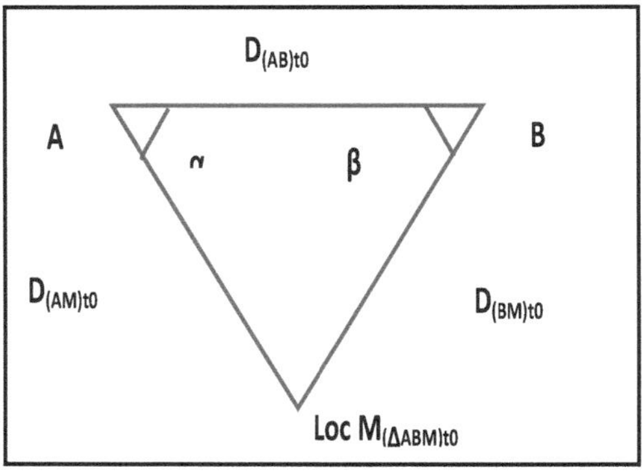

Fig. 2. Mapping of M by using distances AB, AM and BM and the angles α and β

Similarly by using triangles ΔACM and ΔBCM two other locations of M are calculated as shown in figure 3[14-17].

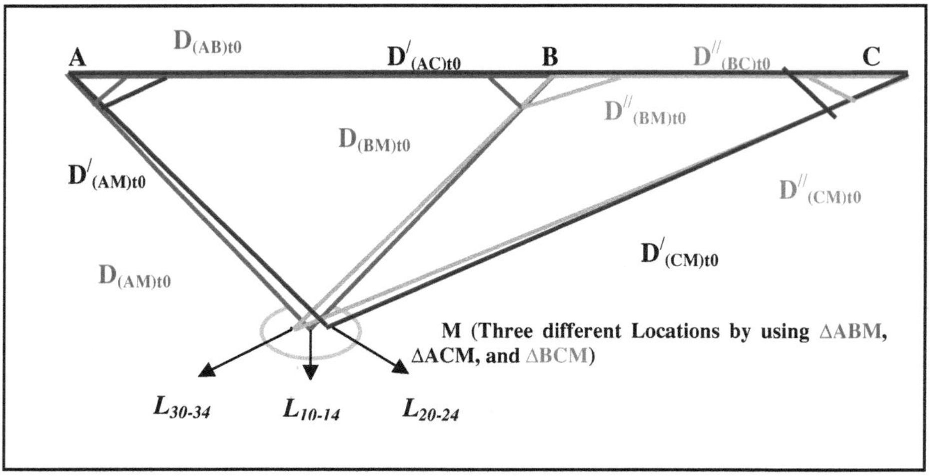

Fig. 3. Location estimation of Mobile by using three triangles, where D is the distance calculated by ΔABM, $D^{/}$ is calculated by ΔACM and $D^{//}$ is calculated ΔBCM

4 Location Filtering

As shown in figure 3, after estimation we come up with fifteen different locations. Filtering is done by using average and mean of means method to achieve precise location out of fifteen locations.

4.1 Average Based Filtering

The experiment is repeated 5 times for every triangle (as shown in figure 3), therefore 15 different locations are calculated which are from $L_{10\text{-}14}$, $L_{20\text{-}24}$ and $L_{30\text{-}34}$. As we have five (5) different locations from ΔABM at t_0 to t_4, averaging is applied on timestamp to filter one location of ΔABM and similarly on ΔACM and ΔBCM.

$$LocM_{\Delta ABM}=[LocM_{(\Delta ABM)t0}+LocM_{(\Delta ABM)t1}+LocM_{(\Delta ABM)t2}+LocM_{(\Delta ABM)t3}+LocM_{(\Delta ABM)t4}]/5 \quad (7)$$

$$LocM_{\Delta ACM}=[LocM_{(\Delta ACM)t0}+LocM_{(\Delta ACM)t1}+LocM_{(\Delta ACM)t2}+LocM_{(\Delta ACM)t3}+LocM_{(\Delta ACM)t4}]/5 \quad (8)$$

$$LocM_{\Delta BCM}=[LocM_{(\Delta BCM)t0}+LocM_{(\Delta BCM)t1}+LocM_{(\Delta BCM)t2}+LocM_{(\Delta BCM)t3}+LocM_{(\Delta BCM)t4}]/5 \quad (9)$$

Finally to calculate a single filtered location mean is calculated from averages calculated in equations 7, 8 and 9.

$$Loc\ M = [Loc\ M_{\Delta ABM} + Loc\ M_{\Delta ACM} + Loc\ M_{\Delta BCM}] / \quad 3 \tag{10}$$

We use simple and cost effective averaging method to calculate single location out of fifteen different locations.

5 Experimental Results of Estimation and Filtering

Tables 1 to 4 are representing the estimation and filtering results. Column 2 is representing estimation/triangulation results. Filtering results are displayed in column 3. Finally last column is representing error of average in each terrain. Selected case is based on the zones ranging from 40 to 60 meters.

5.1 Terrain/Clutter Type: Rural (Low, Medium and High Dense)

Table 1 is representing the estimation and filtering results by using Low Dense Rural terrain. Estimation errors after triangulation are mentioned in last column of table.

Table 1. Estimation and Filtering in Low Dense Rural terrain type

Terrain Type	**Triangulation Location (w.r.t α, β, γ) in meters**	**$\bar{Y}$ (Mean)**	**Error of each estimated location**
Actual location of wireless node in LDR with respect from antenna A is 58.70 m			
LDR (ΔABM, t_0)	57		1.7
LDR (ΔABM, t_1)	57.4		1.3
LDR (ΔABM, t_2)	58.1	57.38	0.6
LDR (ΔABM, t_3)	57.3		1.4
LDR (ΔABM, t_4)	57.1		1.6
LDR (ΔACM, t_0)	56.8		1.9
LDR (ΔACM, t_1)	57.1		1.6
LDR (ΔACM, t_2)	57.3	56.94	1.4
LDR (ΔACM, t_3)	57		1.7
LDR (ΔACM, t_4)	56.5		2.2
LDR (ΔBCM, t_0)	56.7		2
LDR (ΔBCM, t_1)	57.2		1.5
LDR (ΔBCM, t_2)	57.7	57.02	1
LDR (ΔBCM, t_3)	56.9		1.8
LDR (ΔBCM, t_4)	56.6		2.1
Location M (LDR)		**57.11**	

Distance of wireless node from antenna A is 58.70 meters whereas filtered location by using average and mean of means is 57.11 meters. The error in distance is 1.59 meters.

In selected case of MDR actual distance of wireless node from antenna A is 56.90 meters whereas filtered location by using average and mean of means is 54.88 meters. The error in distance is 2.02 meters.

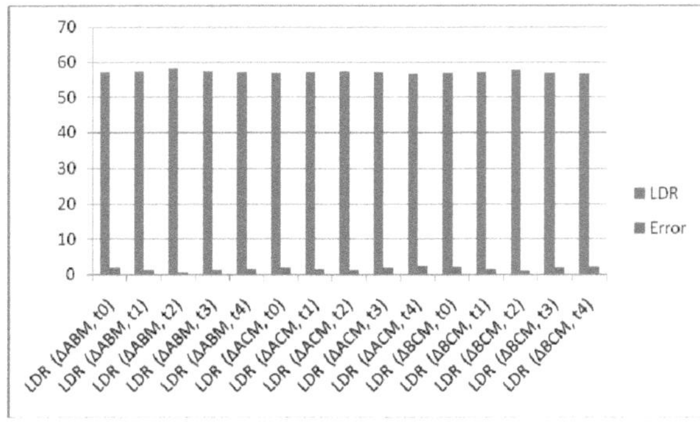

Fig. 4. Graphical representation of LDR terrain error by using triangle ABM, ACM & BCM (from $t_0 - t_4$)

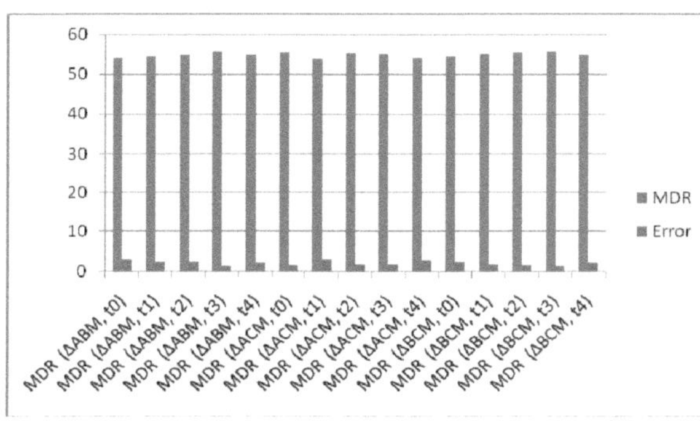

Fig. 5. MDR terrain error by using triangle ABM, ACM & BCM (from $t_0 - t_4$)

Similarly in selected case of HDR actual distance of wireless node from antenna A is 61.0 meters whereas filtered location by using average and mean of means is 58.11 meters. The error in distance is 2.89 meters.

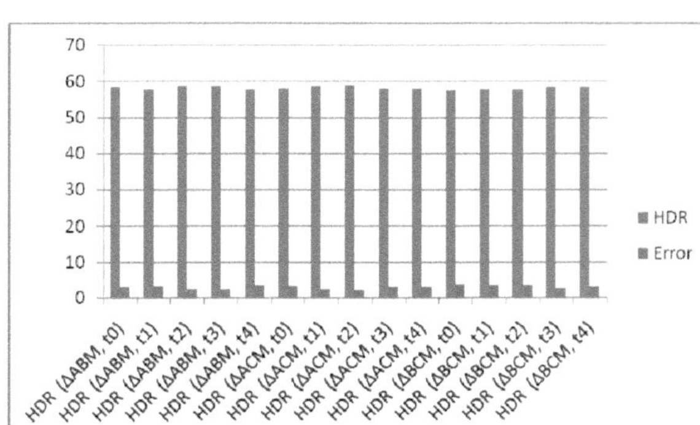

Fig. 6. HDR terrain error by using triangle ABM, ACM & BCM (from $t_0 - t_4$)

5.2 Terrain/Clutter Type: Urban (Low, Medium and High Dense)

Table 2 is representing the location estimation and filtering in Low Dense Urban terrain. Figures 7, 8 and 9 are representing the comparison error in LDU, MDU and HDU terrains.

Table 2. Estimation and Filtering in Low Dense Urban terrain type

Terrain Type	Triangulation Location (w.r.t α, β, γ) in meters	$\bar{Y}$ (Mean)	Error of each estimated location
Actual location of Mobile node in LDU with respect from antenna A is 56.90 m			
LDU (ΔABM, t_0)	55	55.08	1.9
LDU (ΔABM, t_1)	54.6		2.3
LDU (ΔABM, t_2)	55.7		1.2
LDU (ΔABM, t_3)	54.2		2.7
LDU (ΔABM, t_4)	55.9		1
LDU (ΔACM, t_0)	54.6	54.72	2.3
LDU (ΔACM, t_1)	53.8		3.1
LDU (ΔACM, t_2)	55.8		1.1
LDU (ΔACM, t_3)	55.3		1.6
LDU (ΔACM, t_4)	54.1		2.8
LDU (ΔBCM, t_0)	55.8	55.06	1.1
LDU (ΔBCM, t_1)	54.6		2.3
LDU (ΔBCM, t_2)	55.6		1.3
LDU (ΔBCM, t_3)	54.9		2
LDU (ΔBCM, t_4)	54.4		2.5
Location M (LDU)		**54.95**	

In selected case of LDU actual distance of wireless node from antenna A is 56.90 meters whereas filtered location by using average and mean of means is 54.95 meters. The error in distance is 1.95 meters.

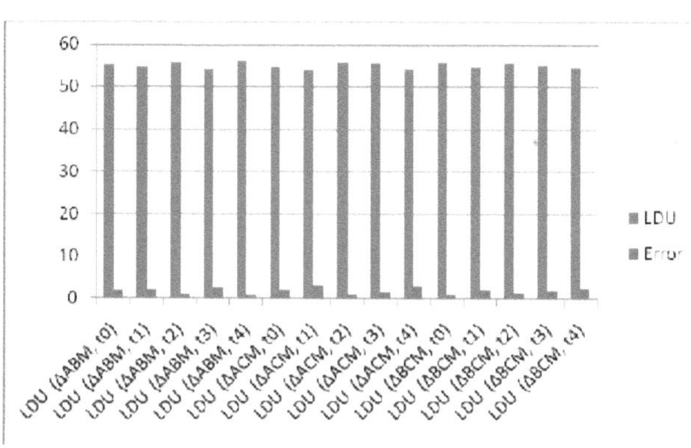

Fig. 7. LDU terrain error by using triangle ABM, ACM & BCM (from $t_0 - t_4$)

In selected case of MDU actual distance of wireless node from antenna A is 54.80 meters whereas filtered location by using average and mean of means is 52.63 meters. The error in distance is 2.17meters.

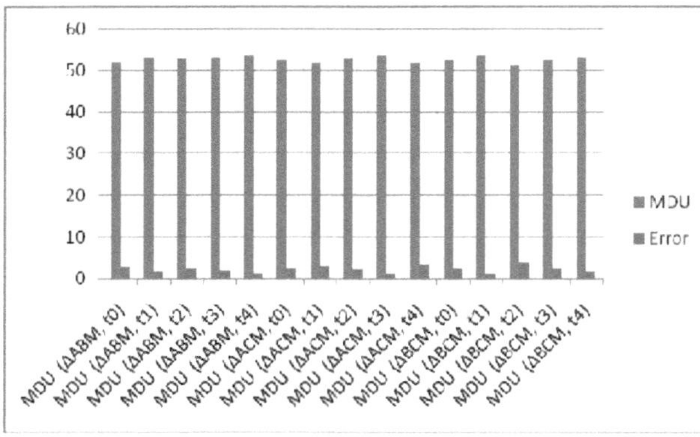

Fig. 8. MDU terrain error by using triangle ABM, ACM & BCM (from $t_0 - t_4$)

Similarly in selected case of HDU actual distance of wireless node from antenna A is 58.90 meters whereas filtered location by using average and mean of means is 55.60 meters. The error in distance is 3.30 meters.

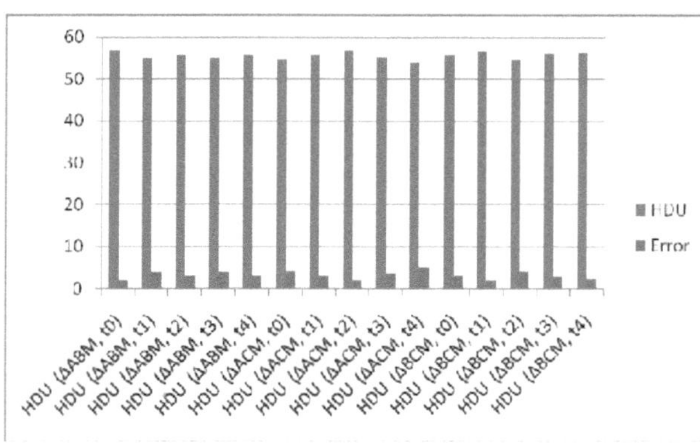

Fig. 9. HDU terrain error by using triangle ABM, ACM & BCM (from $t_0 - t_4$)

5.3 Terrain/Clutter Type: Plantation (Field, Low & Dense Forest)

In selected case of A/F actual distance of wireless node from antenna A is 59.60 meters whereas filtered location by using average and mean of means is 58.58 meters. The error in distance is 1.02 meters.

Table 3. Estimation and Filtering in Agriculture/Field terrain type

Terrain Type	Triangulation Location (w.r.t α, β, γ) in meters	$\bar{Y}$ (Mean)	Error of each estimated location
Actual location of wireless node in A/F with respect from antenna A is 59.60 m			
A/F (ΔABM, t_0)	57.4		2.2
A/F (ΔABM, t_1)	58.6		1
A/F (ΔABM, t_2)	59.8	58.28	-0.2
A/F (ΔABM, t_3)	57.7		1.9
A/F (ΔABM, t_4)	57.9		1.7
A/F (ΔACM, t_0)	58.6		1
A/F (ΔACM, t_1)	59.2		0.4
A/F (ΔACM, t_2)	58.4	58.56	1.2
A/F (ΔACM, t_3)	57.3		2.3
A/F (ΔACM, t_4)	59.3		0.3
A/F (ΔBCM, t_0)	58.8		0.8
A/F (ΔBCM, t_1)	59.4		0.2
A/F (ΔBCM, t_2)	57.8	58.9	1.8
A/F (ΔBCM, t_3)	58.9		0.7
A/F (ΔBCM, t_4)	59.6		0
Location M (A/F)		**58.58**	

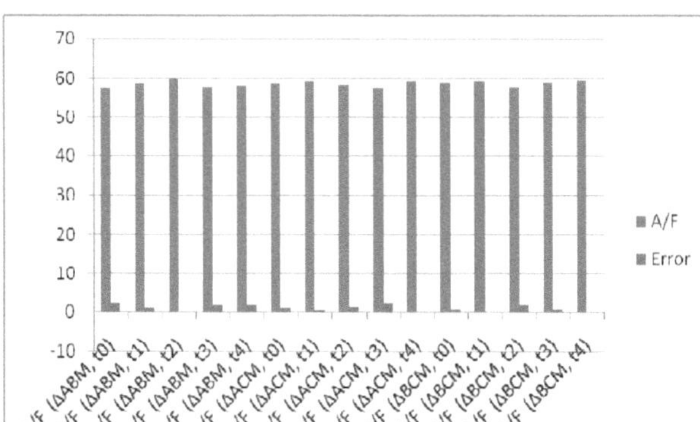

Fig. 10. A/F terrain error by using triangle ABM, ACM & BCM (from $t_0 - t_4$)

In selected case of LF/P (as shown in figure 11) actual distance of wireless node from antenna A is 56.80 meters whereas filtered location by using average and mean of means is 54.86 meters. The error in distance is 1.94 meters. Similarly in selected case of DF (figure 12) actual distance of wireless node from antenna A is 60.20 meters whereas filtered location by using average and mean of means is 56.61 meters. The error in distance is 3.59 meters.

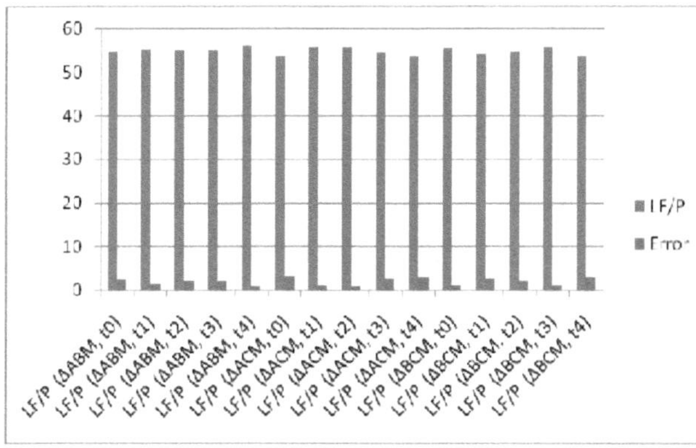

Fig. 11. LF/P terrain error by using triangle ABM, ACM & BCM (from $t_0 - t_4$)

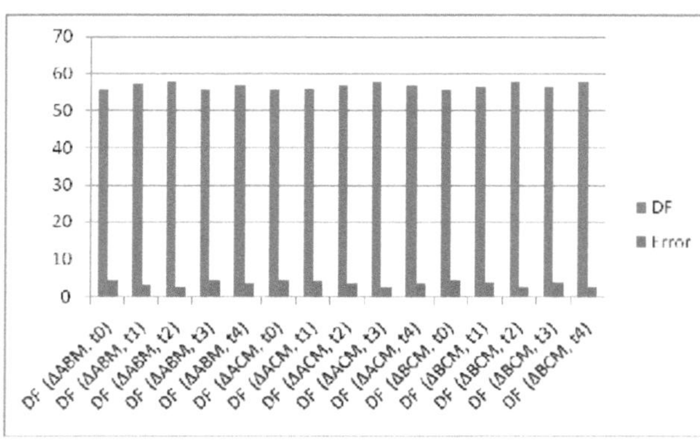

Fig. 12. DF terrain error by using triangle ABM, ACM & BCM (from $t_0 - t_4$)

5.4 Terrain/Clutter Type: Highway/Motorway and Water Bodies

In selected case of R/L actual distance of wireless node from antenna A is 55.10 meters whereas filtered location by using average and mean of means is 52.07 meters. The error in distance is 3.03 meters.

In selected case of Sea actual distance of wireless node from antenna A is 59.40 meters whereas filtered location by using average and mean of means is 55.39 meters. The error in distance is 4.01 meters.

In selected case of H/M actual distance of wireless node from antenna A is 61.20 meters whereas filtered location by using average and mean of means is 58.17 meters. The error in distance is 3.03 meters.

Table 4. Filtering and Estimation River/Lake in terrain type

Terrain Type	Triangulation Location (w.r.t α, β, γ) in meters	$\bar{Y}$ (Mean)	Error of each estimated location
Actual location of wireless node in R/L with respect from antenna A is 55.10 m			
R/L (ΔABM, t_0)	51.2		3.9
R/L (ΔABM, t_1)	50.3		4.8
R/L (ΔABM, t_2)	53.6	51.88	1.5
R/L (ΔABM, t_3)	51.8		3.3
R/L (ΔABM, t_4)	52.5		2.6
R/L (ΔACM, t_0)	53.5		1.6
R/L (ΔACM, t_1)	52.3		2.8
R/L (ΔACM, t_2)	53.4	52.18	1.7
R/L (ΔACM, t_3)	51.2		3.9
R/L (ΔACM, t_4)	50.5		4.6
R/L (ΔBCM, t_0)	52.6		2.5
R/L (ΔBCM, t_1)	52.9		2.2
R/L (ΔBCM, t_2)	53.8	52.16	1.3
R/L (ΔBCM, t_3)	51.1		4
R/L (ΔBCM, t_4)	50.4		4.7
Location M (R/L)		**52.07**	

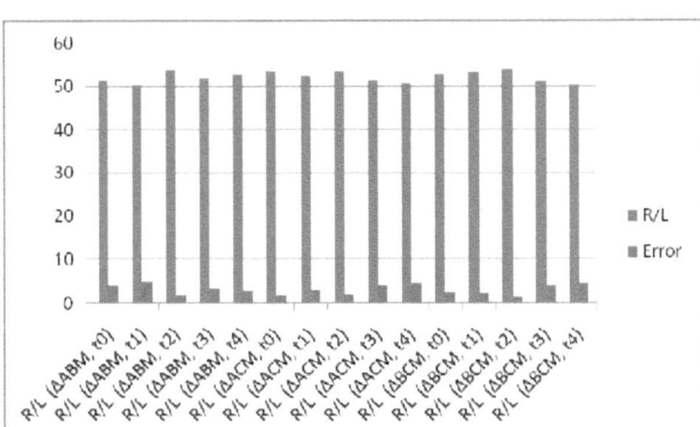

Fig. 13. R/L terrain error by using triangle ABM, ACM & BCM (from $t_0 - t_4$)

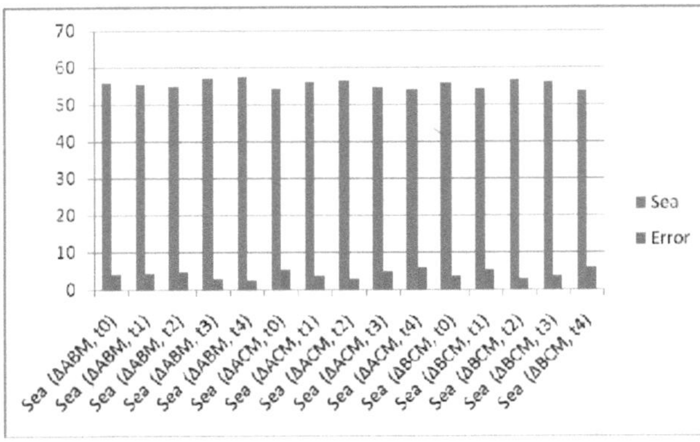

Fig. 14. Sea terrain error by using triangle ABM, ACM & BCM (from $t_0 - t_4$)

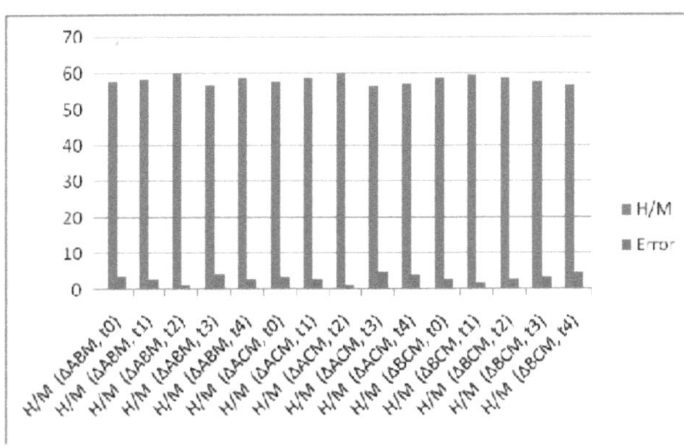

Fig. 15. H/M terrain error by using triangle ABM, ACM & BCM (from $t_0 - t_4$)

6 Filtered Location Comparison with Actual Location

Table 5 is the comparison between the selected cases filtered locations by using average technique with the actual location.

Table 5. Comparison of average based filtering and actual distance

Terrain Type	Actual Location (in meters)	Filtered Location (in meters)	Error (in meters)
LDR	58.7	57.11	1.59
MDR	56.9	54.88	2.02

Table 5. *(Continued)*

HDR	61	58.11	**2.89**
LDU	56.9	54.95	1.95
MDU	54.8	52.63	2.17
HDU	58.9	55.6	**3.3**
A/F	59.6	58.58	1.02
LF/P	56.8	54.86	1.94
DF	60.2	56.61	**3.59**
R/L	55.1	52.07	**3.03**
SEA	59.4	55.39	**4.01**
H/M	61.2	58.17	**3.03**

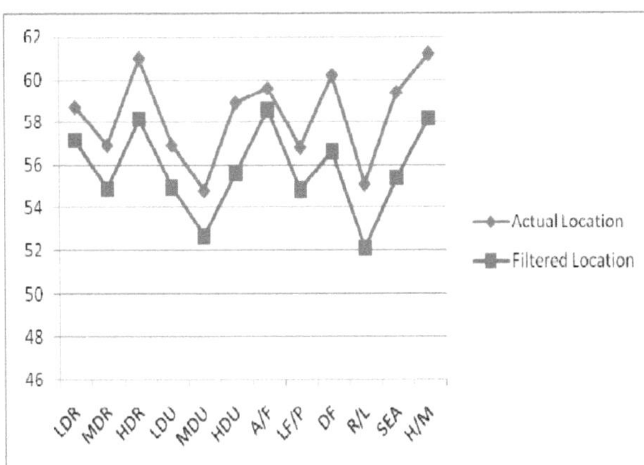

Fig. 16. Average based filtering Error

Table 5 and figure 16 are explaining the concept that the error in high attenuated terrain is still much higher as compared with low attenuated terrains.

7 Conclusion

This research is focusing on the terrain/clutter based location estimation and filtering. Signal to noise ratio plays a vital role in the signal distortion. If we use the same distorted signal without refering the attenuated factors then the calculated location will not be précised. We proposed thirteen terrains based on the atteunation/impairment. By considering the atteunated signals we estimate and filter the wireless node position. Results show that atteunation can change the predicted position of wireless node if terrain impairments are not considered. In this specific case by considering the terrain impairments results improvement are from 45% to 60% depend on the terrain/clutter we are dealing with.

Limitations: Although the terrain impairments are considered in this research but external effects such as bright sunlight, humidity factors, heavy rain and others are not considered. The presence of one or the combination may produce unpredictable results. Furthermore the combination of any two terrains may result in varying the estimated and filtered locations.

References

1. Wang, S., Min, J., Yi, B.K.: Location Based Services for Mobiles: Technologies and Standards. In: IEEE ICC 2008- Beijing, LG Electronics MobileComm, U.S.A. Inc. (2008)
2. Roos, T., Myllymäki, P., Tirri, H., Misikangas, P., Sievänen, J.: A Probabilistic Approach to WLAN User Location Estimation. International Journal of Wireless Information Networks 9(3), 155–164, doi:10.1023/A:1016003126882
3. Laurendeau, C., Barbeau, M.: Insider attack attribution using signal strength-based hyperbolic location estimation. Security and Communication Networks 1, 337–349 (2008), doi:10.1002/sec.35
4. Patwari, N., Hero III, A.O., Perkins, M., Correal, N.S., O'Dea, R.J.: Relative location estimation in wireless sensor networks. IEEE Transactions on Signal Processing 51(8), 2137–2148 (2003); ISSN: 1053-587X
5. Muhammad, A., Mazliham, M.S., Boursier, P., Shahrulniza, M., Yusuf, J.C.M.: Location Estimation and Power Management of Cellular Nodes for rescue operation. In: ICET Kuala Lumpur, Malaysia, December 08-10 (2009)
6. `http://www.guardian.co.uk/world/2008/feb/27/nokia.mobilephones`
7. EU Institutions Press Release, Commission Pushes for Rapid Deployment of Location Enhanced 112 Emergency Services, DN: IP/03/1122, Brussels (2003)
8. Khalaf-Allah, M.: A Novel GPS-free Method for Mobile Unit Global Positioning in Outdoor Wireless Environments. Wireless Personal Communications Journal 44(3) (February 2008)
9. Gezici, S.: A Survey on Wireless Position Estimation. Wireless Personal Communications: An International Journal 44(3) (February 2008); ISSN: 0929-6212
10. Muhammad, A., Mazliham, M.S., Boursier, P., Shahrulniza, M., Yusuf, J.C.M.: Predicted and Corrected Location Estimation of Mobile Nodes Based on the Combination of Kalman Filter and the Bayesian Decision Theory. In: Cai, Y., Magedanz, T., Li, M., Xia, J., Giannelli, C. (eds.) Mobilware 2010. Lecture Notes of the Institute for Computer Sciences, Social Informatics and Telecommunications Engineering, vol. 48, pp. 313–325. Springer, Heidelberg (2010)
11. Dalela, P.K., Prasad, M.V.S.N., Mohan, A.: A New Method of Realistic GSM Network planning for Rural Indian Terrains. IJCSNS International Journal of Computer Science and Network Security 8(8) (August 2008)
12. Lecture notes on RF fundamentals Universitas Bina Darma, `http://images.ilmanzuhriyadi`
13. Integrated Publishing, Electrical Engineering Training Series, `http://www.tpub.com/neets/book10/40c.htm`

14. Muhammad, A., Mazliham, M.S., Boursier, P., Shahrulniza, M., Mustapha, J.C.: Terrain/Clutter Based Error Calculation in Location Estimation of Wireless Nodes by using Receive Signal Strength. In: 2nd International Conference on Computer Technology and Development (ICCTD), Cairo, Egypt, November 2-4 (2010); ISBN: 978-1-4244-8844-5
15. Muhammad, A., Mazliham, M.S., Boursier, P., Shahrulniza, M., Mustapha, J.C.: Clutter based Enhance Error Rate Table (CERT) for Error Correction in Location Estimation of Mobile Nodes. In: International Conference on Information and Computer Networks, ICICN 2011, Guiyang, China, January 26-28 (2011); IEEE Catalog Number: CFP1145M-PRT ISBN: 978-1-4244-9514-6
16. Muhammad, A., Mazliham, M.S., Shahrulniza, M.: Power Management of Portable Devices by Using Clutter Based Information. IJCSNS, International Journal of Computer Science and Network Security 9(4), 237–244 (2009)
17. Muhammad, A., Mazliham, M.S., Shahrulniza, M., Amir, M.: Posterior Probabilities based Location Estimation (P^2LE) Algorithm for Locating a Mobile Node in a Disaster Area. In: MULTICONF 2009, July 13-16, American Mathematical Society, Orlando (2009)

Multichannel MAC Protocol with Discontiguous-OFDM for Cognitive Radio Networks*

Mingyu Lee and Tae-Jin Lee**

School of Information and Communication Engineering
Sungkyunkwan University
440-746, Suwon, South Korea
lmk0218@skku.edu,tjlee@ece.skku.ac.kr

Abstract. Medium access control (MAC) protocols in a cognitive radio network (CRN) are required to increase spectral efficiency and achieve high data rate for secondary users (SUs). Many MAC protocols use a single control channel with a bottleneck problem. In this paper, we propose a multichannel MAC protocol using dicontiguous orthogonal frequency division multiplexing (D-OFDM) in a CRN. Since D-OFDM technology enables SUs to receive multiple packets on discontiguous multiple channels, the proposed MAC protocol adopting D-OFDM has an effect of utilizing multiple control channels, which mitigates the control channel bottleneck problem. Simulations show that the throughput of the proposed protocol outperforms the split phase control channel (SPCC) approach.

Keywords: Cognitive Radio, Multichannel, D-OFDM, MAC.

1 Introduction

Discontiguous-orthogonal frequency division multiplexing (D-OFDM) [1], [2] has been proposed to utilize spectrum holes by dicontiguous frequency channels in cognitive radio networks (CRNs). By using the D-OFDM technology, spectral efficiency can be improved and high data rate can be achieved [3], [4]. In [3] and [4], the transceivers adopting the D-OFDM technology have been proposed. Discontiguous subcarriers and channels can be utilized by the transceivers. The transceiver of a secondary user (SU) in [3] runs D-OFDM by the fast fourier transform (FFT) pruning algorithm to combine the subcarriers as a channel

* This work was supported by Priority Research Centers Program through the National Research Foundation of Korea(NRF) funded by the Ministry of Education, Science and Technology(2011-0018397), and the MKE(The Ministry of Knowledge Economy), Korea, under the ITRC (Information Technology Research Center) support program supervised by the NIPA (National IT Industry Promotion Agency)(NIPA-2011-(C1090-1111-0005)).
** Corresponding author.

A. Abd Manaf et al. (Eds.): ICIEIS 2011, Part III, CCIS 253, pp. 594–603, 2011.

excluding the deactivated subcarriers to avoid interfering with primary users (PUs). And multiple data chunks can be transmitted and received simultaneously on multiple channels by using the D-OFDM transceiver. The authors in [4] present a method of relay selection and channel allocation for a medium access control (MAC) protocol in a CRN. It requires a centralized SU access point (SUAP), which decides efficient relays and allocates channel resources to SUs. The MAC protocol attempts to improve the throughput of a network, but it is hard to apply the centralized mechanism to an ad-hoc CRN. For an ad-hoc CRN, it is required to design a distributed MAC protocol.

To utilize multiple channels in an ad-hoc CRN, MAC protocols using the concept of opportunistic spectrum access (OSA) have been proposed. In [5], MAC protocols to control access to multiple channels by a control channel have been presented. In [5]-[7], two types of multi-channel MACs are introduced: *Single Rendezvous Control Channel* (SRCC), and *Multiple Rendezvous Control Channel* (MRCC). The SRCC approach can be classified into *Dedicated (Common) Control Channel* (DCC), *Hopping Control Channel* (HCC), and *Split Phase Control Channel* (SPCC). MRCC uses all available channels as control channels while SRCC uses a single control channel. MRCC has better control capability and capacity by evading from PUs activity in a flexible way than SRCC and overcomes the single channel bottleneck problem. The MRCC approach in [5]-[7], however, requires SUs to operate channel hopping and to share the hopping patterns of other SUs to transmit data. Moreover, SRCC and MRCC do not utilize the advantage of D-OFDM. So it is desirable to have an efficient MAC with D-OFDM and not requiring channel hopping.

In this paper, we propose a new distributed multichannel D-OFDM MAC protocol in an ad-hoc CRN. The objective of our proposal is to overcome the single channel bottleneck problem by utilizing the D-OFDM technology which enables sources/destinations to send and receive multiple data frames on multiple channels simultaneously while it does not need to hop channels. In the proposed D-OFDM MAC protocol, each SU randomly chooses one of the multiple available channels and slots in a distributed way and contend it to acquire the channel in a distributed way to transmit data.

The rest of this paper is organized as follows. Section 2 proposes a novel multichannel D-OFDM MAC protocol for an ad-hoc CRN. Section 3 presents simulation results to demonstrate the effectiveness of our protocol. Finally we conclude in Section 4.

2 Proposed MAC Protocol

We assume that SUs in a CRN are within the transmission range of other SUs. A device in a CRN is assumed to be equipped with a single D-OFDM transceiver with software defined radio (SDR) [8]. SUs can use up to N_{ch} PU channels for data transmission by sensing. All SUs are assumed to be synchronized to the cycle times. A cycle time consists of three parts: sensing, contention-overhearing, and transmission time. In the sensing time, SUs sense the channels and decide

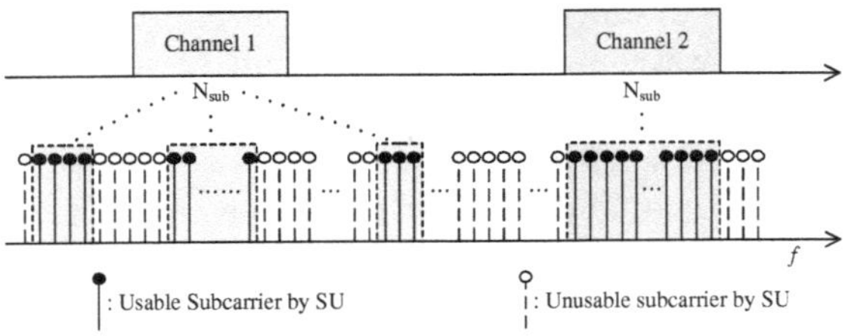

Fig. 1. An example of available channels

idle channels for the transmission of SUs. The contention-overhearing time consists of T slots, during which SUs compete with one another to reserve the sensed idle channels. After the contention-overhearing time, successful SUs can transmit data frames during the transmission time.

In the proposed MAC protocol, an SU is assumed to use a D-OFDM transceiver. The transceiver enables SUs to sense subcarriers and to receive multiple data on discontiguous multichannels at the same time. SUs sense and find the unoccupied subcarriers by PUs to avoid interference with PUs, and N_{sub} unoccupied subcarriers constitute a channel as in [3]. The subcarriers to form a channel dynamically change by the channel usage of PUs. In Fig. 1, we show an example of such channels sensed by SUs. SUs are assumed to achieve the common sensing information on the idle subcarriers by independent sensing to encode and decode their data after the sensing time.

After the sensing period, SUs are ready to compete with one another on the available idle channels for data transmission. At the beginning of a time slot in the contention-overhearing period, each SU randomly selects a channel among H available channels and a time slot among T slots. The interval of a time slot is decided to hold a Request To Send-Clear To Send (RTS-CTS) frame and two Short Interframe Space (SIFS). A source SU sends an RTS frame in its selected contention slot and channel and waits for a CTS frame from the destination SU. If the source SU receives the CTS correctly without collision, the source SU now reserves the available idle channel successfully. Otherwise, it recognizes a collision with other SUs. Since RTSs can be transmitted in more than one channel during a certain slot, there may be three kinds of collision: RTS-RTS (RR) collision, destination-destination (DD) collision, and absent destination (AD) collision.

1. RR collision: If the same contention time slot is selected by more than one SU, RR collision occurs. Then both RTSs can not be reached to their destinations.
2. DD collision: If the same destination SU is chosen by more than one source SU, DD collision occurs. Then the destination SU has to select one source SU and discard the other source SUs.
3. AD collision: While an SU sends RTS to its destination SU on a channel in a time slot, the destination SU tries to send RTS to another SU on a different channel in the same time slot. Then AD collision happens. Since a single radio do not support simultaneous receiving and transmitting of a

Channel (1 byte)	Address of Source (6byte)	Address of Destination (6byte)
Channel 1	MAC address of Source SU	MAC address of Destination SU
. . .	. . .	. . .
Channel H	MAC address of Source SU	MAC address of Destination SU

Fig. 2. The structure of Channels Information Table (CIT)

frame, the destination SU cannot send CTS to the source SU. As a result, the source SU can not succeed in sending RTS.

If an SU receives CTS from another SU on a channel successfully, the SU gives up sending RTS in the remaining slots. And if an SU is selected as a destination SU before transmitting RTS, the SU does the same. If an SU knows that a destination SU is already chosen by an other SU before transmitting RTS, the SU does the same.

Based on the D-OFDM transceiver sensing, all SUs keep the Channel Information Table (CIT) that includes the MAC addresses of source and destination SUs for each channel (see Fig. 2). The CIT is empty when an SU enters a network. By overhearing RTS/CTS frames, SUs update CIT. By D-OFDM, other SUs except for the source SUs which are transmitting RTS frames can decode RTSs simultaneously on different channels in a certain time slot. In the same way, CTSs can be decoded by SUs except for the destination SUs. The SUs receiving RTS/CTS can update CITs with the MAC addresses of the SUs in the MAC Protocol Data Unit (MPDU).

In the data transmission time, the successful source SUs with available channels transmit data in the beginning of the data transmission time. If the duration is enough for additional transmissions, source SUs can send data as much as possible. In the transmitter of an SU, for data transmission, only the subcarriers of a selected available channel are used. In the receiver of an SU, signals are decoded for the selected channel of the SU. Thus multiple data frames transmitted from different source SUs can be received at a destination SU.

Fig. 3 shows an example of the proposed D-OFDM MAC protocol. After the sensing interval T_s, all SUs are trying to occupy their selected random channels and slots during the contention-overhearing interval T_{co}. In the first slot, SU 1 and SU 2 send RTS to SU 2 and SU 3, respectively. Since SU 1 tries to send RTS to SU 2 while SU 2 tries to send RTS in the same time slot, SU 1 experiences an AD collision, and, SU 2 receives CTS from SU 3. In the second time slot, since SU 5 and SU 6 send in the same time slot, they experience an RR collision. And SU 4 and SU 7 try to send RTSs to SU 8. Since SU 8 chooses SU 4 as the source SU, SU 7 experiences a DD collision. In the Tth slot, SU 9 and SU 10 send RTSs to SU 11 and SU 12, respectively, and receive CTSs from their destinations after transmitting RTSs. As a result, SU 2, SU 4, SU 9, and SU 10 reserve channels CH 4, CH 1, CH 3, and CH 5, respectively for data transmission in the contention interval. In the data transmission duration T_{tr}, SU 2 and SU

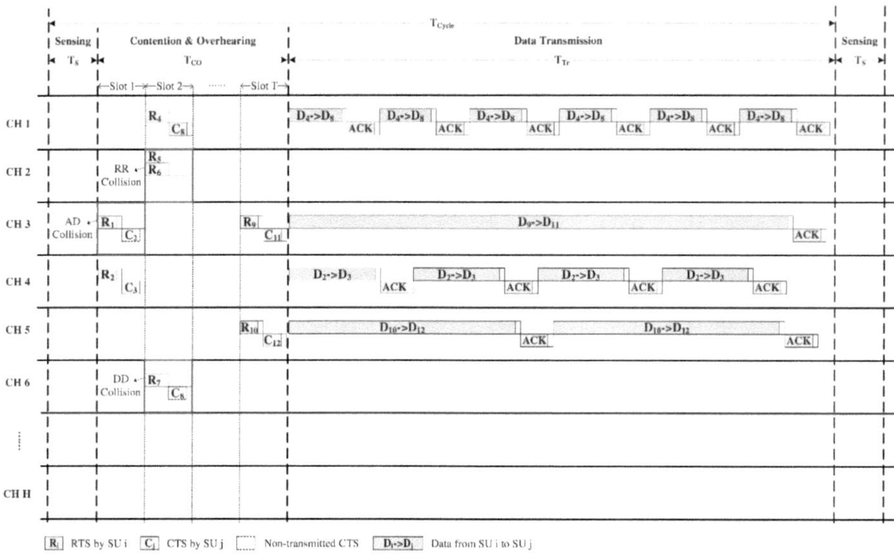

Fig. 3. An example of the proposed MAC protocol

4 send data to SU 3 and SU 8 on CH 4 and CH 1, respectively. SU 9 and SU 10 send data to SU 11, and SU 12 on CH 3 and CH 5, respectively. After the data transmission duration, a new cycle begins.

3 Simulation Results

In this section, we show various simulation results of the proposed MAC protocol. We consider a IEEE 802.11a-based D-OFDM system. Destination SUs are assumed to be positioned at the center of a circle area and they are called a destination group in a network. The number of destination SUs is the same as that of source SUs. Depending on the distance from the center (i.e., rate), SUs are grouped. The number of groups by data rates is 8 in IEEE 802.11a [9]-[11]. SUs are randomly distributed in a network and can be source SUs if they obtain available channels. Destination SUs are randomly selected by source SUs. The parameters in the simulation are summarized in Table 1, 2, and 3.

The proposed protocol is similar to the type of MAC protocol using the SPCC approach. In this paper, the MAC protocol using the SPCC approach in [7] is used for comparison. For comparative purpose, we have modified SPCC MAC to have the same cycle time. The sensing time which has the same duration as the proposed protocol is added to the MAC to find available channels. And only one pair of source-destination can transmit data in the data transmission phase since SUs are not allowed to reserve multiple channels if there are no free channels.

Fig. 4 and Fig. 5 show the performances of the proposed MAC and SPCC for the various numbers of SUs. In Fig. 4, the throughputs of the protocols increase

Table 1. Time Parameters

Parameter	Value
T_{slot}	9μs
T_{SIFS}	16μs
T_{DIFS}	34μs
$T_{Preamble}$	16μs
T_{SIGNAL}	4μs
T_{Symbol}	4μs
T_S	34μs
T_{RTS}	51μs
T_{CTS}	43μs

Table 2. Size of Frames and Headers

Parameter	Value
$S_{SERVICE}$	16 bits
$S_{MACheader}$	28×8 bits
S_{TAIL}	6 bits
S_{DATA}	2048×8 bits
S_{RTS}	20×8 bits
S_{CTS}	14×8 bits
S_{ACK}	14×8 bits

Table 3. Data Rates for Different Groups

Group	Data rates	bits/symbol
1	6Mbps	24
2	9Mbps	36
3	12Mbps	48
4	18Mbps	72
5	24Mbps	96
6	36Mbps	144
7	48Mbps	192
8	54Mbps	216

by increasing the number of available channels. Since the proposed MAC protocol is affected largely by the number of SUs and the number of channels and time slots, the throughput of the proposed MAC protocol is less than that of

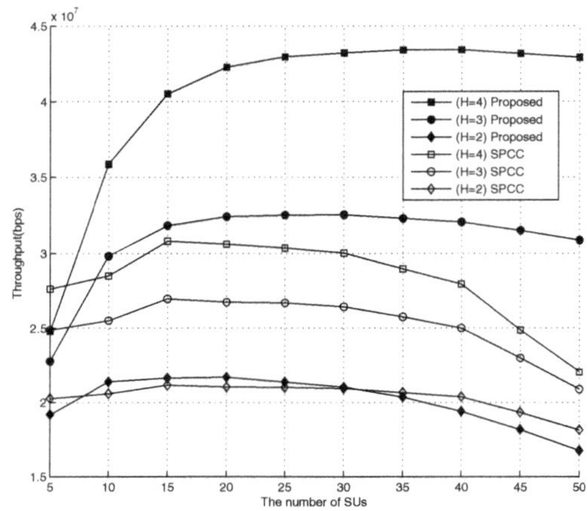

Fig. 4. Throughput for varying number of SUs and available channels ($T = 8$)

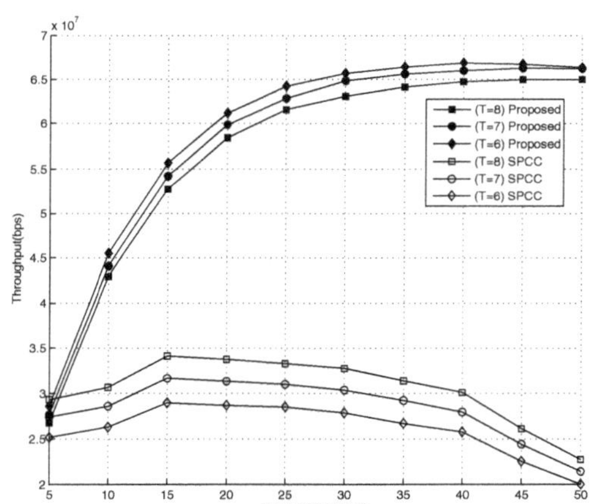

Fig. 5. Throughput for varying number of SUs and time slots ($H = 6$)

SPCC when the number of SUs exceeds 20 where the number of available channels is 2. However, this effect is mitigated by increasing the number of available channels. Since the available contention slots increase by increasing the available channels in the proposed MAC protocol, SUs have more chances to choose different contention slots than SPCC. Thus, the success probability to achieve channels improves and the throughput of the proposed MAC protocol improves accordingly.

In Fig. 5, we investigate the effect of time slots. Fig. 5 shows that the throughput of the proposed MAC protocol decreases since the number of contention slots is not sufficient for the required one for a large number of SUs. Once the

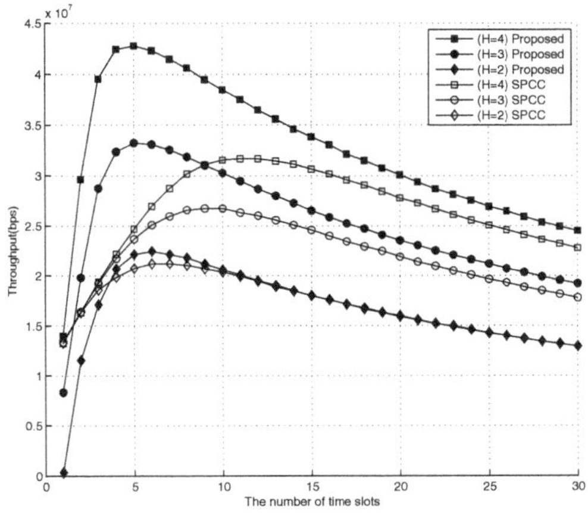

Fig. 6. Throughput for varying number of time slots and available channels ($N = 15$)

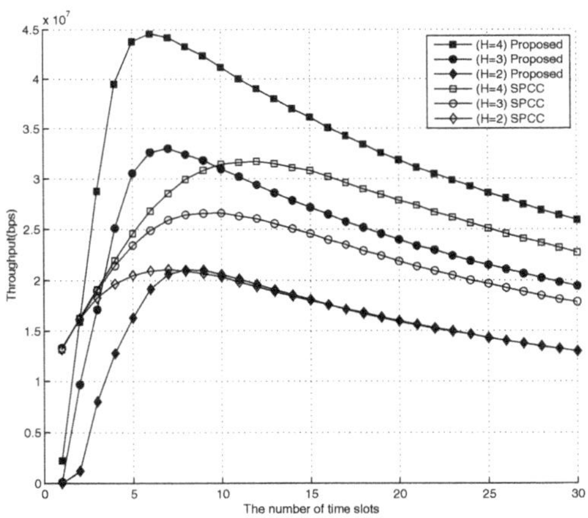

Fig. 7. Throughput for varying number of time slots and available channels ($N = 30$)

maximum throughput is achieved, the performance of the proposed MAC protocol decreases by increasing the number of time slots due to overprovisioned time slots. The throughput of SPCC is limited although increasing number of time slots improves the throughput of SPCC. The proposed MAC protocol is shown to be less sensitive to the number of SUs compared to SPCC. The throughput of the proposed MAC protocol also improves for increasing number of time slots as the number of SUs increases.

We can figure out that the optimum number of time slots which maximizes the throughput. Figs. 6 and 7 show the performances when the number of increasing time slots increases. It needs more time slots for increasing number of

SUs. However more than the required time slots for a given number of SUs may degrade performance. To obtain the maximum throughput, the proposed MAC needs fewer time slots than SPCC. The number of contention slots of the proposed MAC protocol increases by increasing the number of available channels. In SPCC, the more available channels, the more contention slots are needed to reserve channels since a single control channel is used. In Figs. 6 and 7, the throughput of the proposed MAC protocol increases rapidly by increasing the number of time slots it until achieves the maximum throughput. The optimal number of time slots for the proposed MAC protocol in Fig. 6 is 5 while that in Fig. 7 decreases from 8 to 6 when the number of available channels increases from 2 to 4. Since the number of SUs in Fig. 7 is more than that in Fig. 6, additional time slots are needed to obtain the maximum throughput. The required number of time slots for SPCC, however, increases to obtain the maximum throughput by increasing the number of channels in Figs. 6 and 7.

4 Conclusion

In this paper, we have proposed a new multichannel MAC protocol in a CRN. Our MAC protocol with D-OFDM enables SUs to send and receive multiple packets on multiple channels. Since the number of contention slots increases by the number of channels, the bottleneck problem effect of a single control channel for a large number of SUs is mitigated. So, the proposed MAC protocol improves throughput in a CRN. The proposed MAC protocol is shown to enhance the throughput compared to the MAC protocol using the SPCC approach. For the future work, we plan to analyze the performance and to consider cooperative communication among SUs.

References

1. Tang, H.: Some Physical Layer Issues of Wide-band Cognitive Radio Systems. In: 1st IEEE Symposium on New Frontiers in Dynamic Spectrum Access Networks, Baltimore MD, USA, pp. 151–159 (2005)
2. Poston, J., Horne, J.W.: Discontiguous OFDM Considerations for Dynamic Spectrum Access in Idle TV channels. In: 1st IEEE Symposium on New Frontiers in Dynamic Spectrum Access Networks, Baltimore MD, USA, pp. 607–610 (2005)
3. Rakesh, R., Wyglinski, A.M., Minden, G.J.: An Efficient Implementation of NC-OFDM Transceivers for Cognitive Radios. In: 1st International Conference on Cognitive Radio Oriented Wireless Networks and Communications, Mykonos Island, Greece, pp. 1–5 (2006)
4. Zhang, Q., Jia, J., Zhang, J.: Cooperative Relay to Improve Diversity in Cognitive Radio Network. IEEE Commun. Mag. 47(2), 111–117 (2009)
5. Pawelczak, P., Pollin, S., So, H.-S.W., Motamedi, A., Bahai, A., Prasad, R.V., Hekmat, R.: State of the Art in Opportunistic Spectrum Access Medium Access Control Design. In: 3rd International Conference on Cognitive Radio Oriented Wireless Networks and Communications, Singapore, pp. 1–6 (2008)

6. Pawelczak, P., Pollin, S., So, H.-S.W., Motamedi, A., Bahai, A., Prasad, R.V., Hekmat, R.: Comparison of Opportunistic Spectrum Multichannel Medium Access Control Protocols. In: IEEE Global Communications Conference, New Orleans, LA, USA, pp. 1–6 (2008)
7. Mo, J., So, H.-S.W., Walrand, J.: Comparison of Multichannel MAC Protocols. IEEE Trans. Mobile Comput. 7(1), 50–65 (2008)
8. Mitola, J.: Cognitive Radio Architecture Evolution. Proceedings of the IEEE 97(4), 626–641 (2009)
9. Broadcom, IEEE 802.11g: The New Mainstream Wireless LAN Standard.: 802.11g-WP104-R, white paper (July 2003)
10. IEEE 802.11, Wireless LAN Medium Access Control (MAC) and Physical Layer (PHY) Specifications (June 2007)
11. Qiao, D., Choi, S., Shin, K.: Goodput Analysis and Link Adaptation for IEEE 802.11a Wireless LANs. IEEE Trans. Wireless Commun. 8(5), 2410–2416 (2009)
12. Bianchi, G.: Performance Analysis of the IEEE 802.11 Distributed Coordination Function. IEEE J. Selected Areas Comm. 18(3), 535–547 (2000)

Adaptive Cell Management in a Femto-Cell System

Dong Ho Kim, Kwang-hyun Cho, and Ye Hoon Lee*

Seoul National University of Science and Technology, 172 Kongneung-dong
Nowon-gu, Seoul, Korea
{dongho.kim,khyun,y.lee}@snut.ac.kr

Abstract. Recently mobile communication systems such as 3GPP LTE, IEEE802.16e have been growing interest in the femto-cell systems for increase of data rates and enhanced call quality. Cell management method for handover in a femto-cell system is very important issue because it includes heavy control management information of macro-cell and a large number of femto-cells and can be a burden to a system. In this paper, we propose an adaptive construction of control management message (MOB_NBR-ADV) and cell management method in a femto-cell system. The proposed scheme provides fast scanning and efficient handover by means of preselecting the candidate target femto-cells. The simulation results show that the proposed schemes improve the MS's handover-related performance in terms of scanning power and scanning time compared with the conventional management scheme of femto-cell systems.

Keywords: Femto-cell, cell management, handover.

1 Introduction

Recently smart phone users have increased the data traffic in the mobile networks. Femto-cell system is a small base station providing wireless communications services to the terminal in the small office (or home) environment with very low price and a high data rate. Latest mobile communication systems such as 3GPP LTE, IEEE802.16e have been growing interest in the femto-cell systems for increase of data rates and enhanced call quality.

In the femto-cell system, various technical issues should be resolved such as interference problems and synchronization between the MBS (macro-cell BS) and the FBS (femto-cell BS). Also, the cell management method for the efficient handover is one of the most important issues in the femto-cell systems [1]. In this paper, we propose efficient cell management methods and a construction of control message for the handover in a femto-cell system. The proposed method can reduce the control messages for the cell management and also increase the exactness of handover.

This paper is organized as follows. In Section 2, we will consider the issues of cell management in an IEEE 802.16e femto-cell system. We propose a load-balanced cell management method and present the performance with computer simulation in Section 3 and Section 4, respectively. Finally, conclusions are made in Section 5.

---

* Corresponding author.

A. Abd Manaf et al. (Eds.): ICIEIS 2011, Part III, CCIS 253, pp. 604–613, 2011.

2 Cell Management in IEEE 802.16e Femto-Cell System

In this Section, we describe system model and cell management methods in the IEEE 802.16e femto-cell system.

2.1 Handover Process in IEEE 802.16e System

In the handover process, mobile station (MS) which moves from a serving base station (BS) to a target BS collects the information on the neighboring BSs and makes a decision of best BS for handover. The process of collecting the information of neighboring BS is called 'scanning'. To ease the scanning process, serving BS periodically broadcasts a control message of MOB_NBR-ADV (Mobile Neighboring-BS Advertisement message). MOB_NBR-ADV includes neighboring BS's information such as channel status, frequency, BS identifier (BSID), preamble index and downlink channel descriptor (DCD). MS can reduce the scanning time and power with the help of MOB_NBR-ADV message [2-4]. Also, fast handover to the target BS with best channel condition is possible because MS has the information on network topology and channel state information using MOB-NBR-ADV.

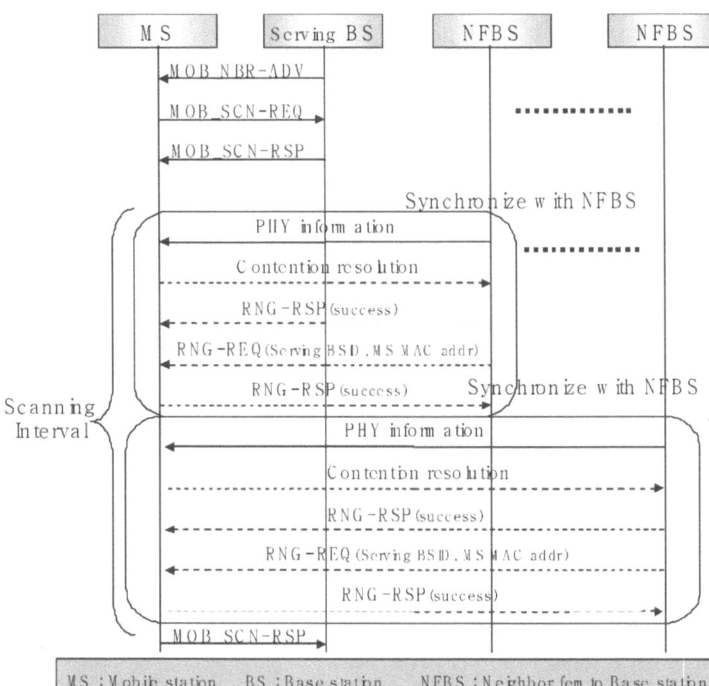

Fig. 1. Handover process in IEEE 802.16e system

In Figure 1, scanning process in the IEEE802.16e system is shown. When MS meets the target BS which is included in the MOB-NBR-ADV, it begins scanning process with sending MOB_SCN-REQ (Mobile Scanning Request) message to serving BS. The MOB_SCN-REQ message includes the target BS's ID and the scanning type, scanning time and scanning number, etc. BS responds to the scanning request using MOB_SCN-RSP (Mobile Scanning Response) which includes permission or modification to MOB_SCN-REQ. MS can collect channel conditions of neighboring BS without additional reception of neighboring BS's broadcast information. After the scanning process, MS keeps scanning results such as CINR, RSSI of neighboring BSs and in addition sends MOB-SCN-REP (Mobile Scanning Report) message to serving BS if necessary [2-4].

2.2 Cell Management in IEEE802.16e Femto-Cell System

In Figure 2, conventional construction of MOB_NBR-ADV message is shown when the femto-cell system is applied to the IEEE802.16e system. MOB_NBR-ADV includes every macro BS (MBS) and femto BSs (FBS) list. In case that a number of femto-cells are placed, MOB_NBR-ADV message gets bigger in proportional to the number of femto-cell number. Therefore the MBS may have the burden of broadcasting a heavy MOB_NBR-ADV message. Also MS which receives a heavy MOB_NBR-ADV message should scan a number of candidate neighboring BSs (both MBSs and FBSs) with much power and time consumption. There have been several researches on femto-cell management. In [2], MRU/MFU (most recently/frequently used) method was proposed in which the scanning time can be reduced using the user preferences and past handover history. In MRU/MFU, MS have the memory burden because of the past handover history. In [3], fast group scanning (FGS) was proposed in which related several MS make a group and exchange the scanning information.

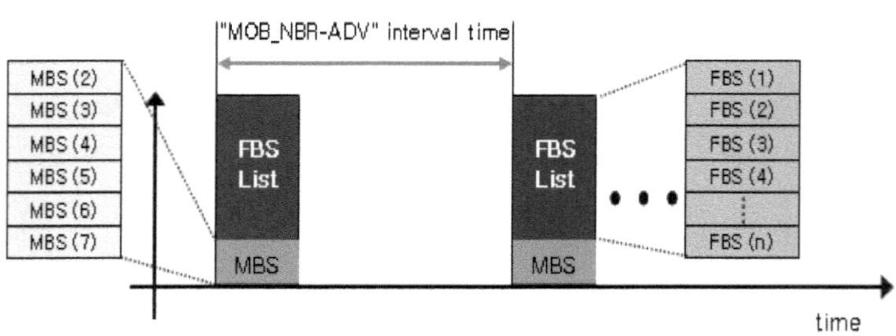

Fig. 2. Conventional MOB_NBR-ADV Message in IEEE 802.16e femto-cell system

In [1], modified construction of MOB_NBR-ADV and cell management method which distinguishes cell regions with sectors and tiers are proposed. Modified MOB_NBR-ADV is divided into the macro-cell message (MacMSG) and location-based message (PosMSG). MS should listen to the MacMSG for MBS regardless of its location and listen to PosMSG for FBS selectively according to its location. In Figure 3, femto-cell system with cell sector and cell tier is shown. When the cell is divided into cell sector and cell tier, the amount of MOB_NBR-ADV message can also be divided into smaller one which provides the selective FBS's information belonging to the specific MBS. In [1], MS is assumed to know its location with detecting preamble signal's attenuation of the serving MBS and the preamble signal strength of adjacent MBSs. After MS finds out its location, it selectively listens to the location-dependent PosMSG message of specific cell sector/tier as shown in Figure 4.

The modified construction of MOB_NBR-ADV proposed in [1] can reduce the amount of MOB_NBR-ADV and save the scanning time and scanning power compared to conventional method in IEEE 802.16e system. However, it may happen that MS cannot be handover to the best FBS just because the best FBS belongs to another sector/tier region. In other words, MS cannot listen to the MOB_NBR-ADV message of best FBS and don't have any information of best FBS. Such a case will happen in cell sector/tier edge.

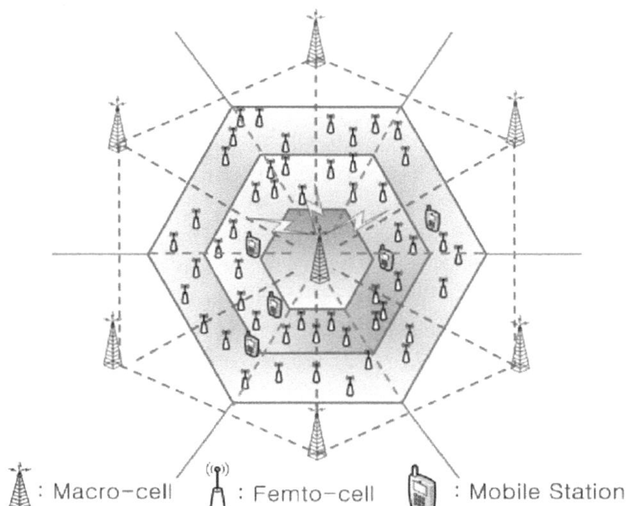

Fig. 3. Cell sectoring and cell tiering in IEEE 802.16e femto-cell system [1]

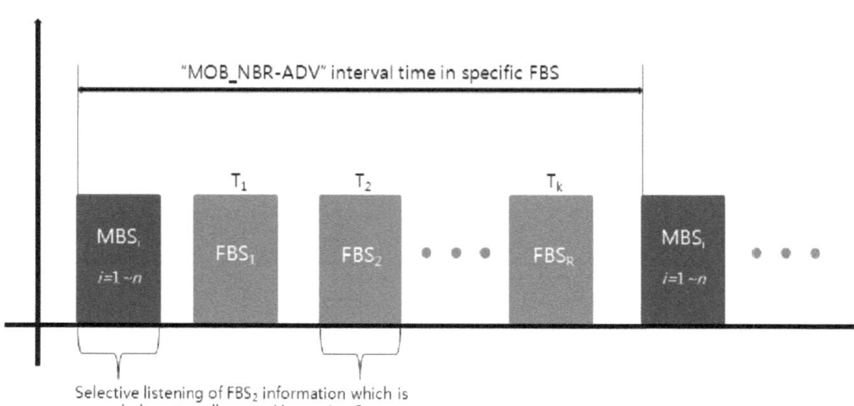

Fig. 4. MOB_NBR-ADV Messages in cell sectoring and cell tiering [1]

3 Proposed Load Balanced Cell Management Method

As described in Section 2, modified construction of MOB_NBR-ADV with cell sector/tier proposed in [1] has some drawback that the MS cannot be handover to the best FBS in cell sector or tier edge environment. In case MS is located in cell sector or cell tier edge region, the probability of handover hit gets lower than the conventional IEEE 802.16e femto-cell system. On the other hands, in a conventional IEEE802.16e femto-cell system the MS is handover to the appropriate FBS with hit probability of almost 1, however the MOB_NBR-ADV gets bigger.

In this section, we propose load balanced cell management in femto-cell system.

3.1 Proposed Cell Management in IEEE 802.16e Femto-Cell System

In the proposed method, we construct MOB_NBR-ADV as shown in Figure 5. We assume that serving MBS is MBS_0 and MacMSG for MBS_i (where i is 1~n) represents the adjacent MBS list. Also, PosMSG for FBS_k (where k is 1~R) represents FBS list in kth region. MBS_0 periodically broadcasts MacMSG for MBS_i and PosMSG for FBS_k. MS should listen to MacMSG mandatorily and FBS_k selectively when it is located in region k. When serving BS is femto-cell BS (FBS_k), MS also listen in the same way under the assumption that MS knows its location of region k and MBS_0. We noted the situation that MS is located in cell sector or tier edge region. In that case, because MS just listens to FBS_k it does not notice the presence of the better FBS which is located in another region k' as shown in Figure 6. In the proposed construction of MOB_NBR-ADV message for FBS_k, additional FBS information located in edge of region (k+1) and region (k-1) are included. Compared with construction method in [1], proposed method increases MOB_NBR-ADV slightly because additional FBS information is included twice. However, the hit probability of handover to the nearest cell P_{hit} improves dramatically.

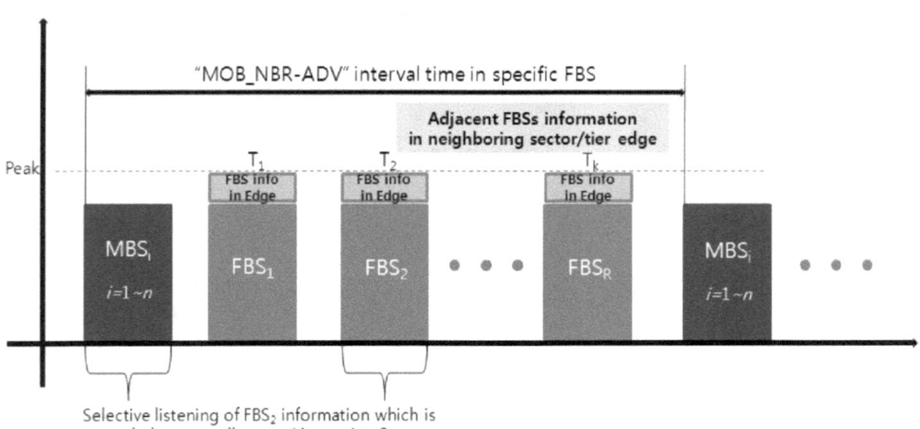

Fig. 5. Proposed MOB_NBR-ADV Messages in cell sectoring and cell tiering

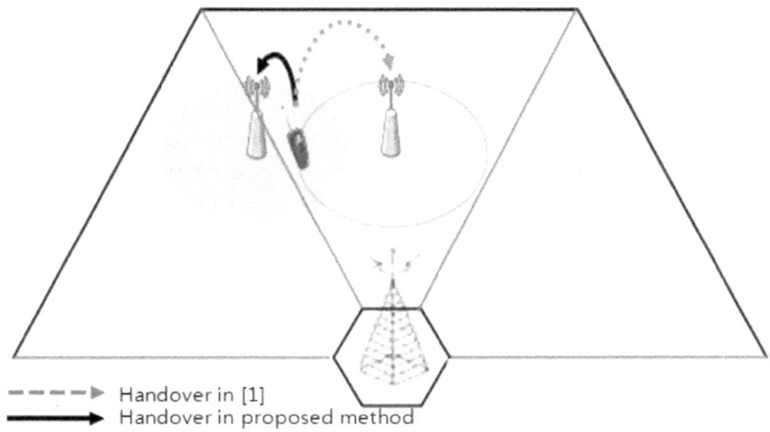

Fig. 6. Comparison of Handover between conventional method [1] and proposed method

In the proposed MOB_NBR-ADV construction, the peak value of additional message can be specified. Within the peak value, the amount of MOB_NBR-ADV message can be determined adaptively considering the number of MBS and the distribution of MS which connects to the FBS, service traffic, etc.

3.2 Procedure of Access in IEEE 802.16e Femto-Cell System

When MS intends to access the network, it first finds out serving MBS using preamble signal or the previous records of access to the specific MBS. After MS knows its serving MBS, it receives MOB_NBR-ADV message. In IEEE 802.16e system, next broadcast time for MOB_NBR-ADV is provided in downlink MAP in a type of timing offset [4]. Also, MOB_NBR-ADV interval is provided and we consider the information as MacMSG interval. In order for MS to get its PosMSG, MS needs to know its exact location. The location information can be obtained with the received signal strength of preamble from serving MBS and neighboring MBSs as given in [1] and [5]. When MS listens to MOB_NBR-ADV which is composed of MacMSG and PosMSG, it can make a full-scanning of MBS and FBS and the handover procedure is made.

In the proposed method, we also consider the construction of the MOB_NBR-ADV with prioritized FBSs. In other words, serving BS constructs MOB_NBR-ADV with prioritized FBSs considering the current channel allocation of candidate FBSs. For example, we assume that there are three candidate FBSs, FBS_A, FBS_B, FBS_C in a cell region and FBS_A has more vacant channel than other FBSs. In that case, serving BS lists up FBS_A in the MOB_NBR-ADV with highest priority and MS selects FBS_A as a target FBS in case other criterions for handover are meet. The proposed construction of MOB_NBR-ADV with prioritized FBSs can reduce the outage probability and improve the QoS.

4 Simulation Results

In this section, we present simulation results with proposed method. We assume a simulation environment with one MBS and a number of FBS. MBS and FBS are uniformly distributed with radius of 1km and 10~20m respectively. Also we consider Gaussian Markovian model for mobile movement. Also we assume that the scanning time and power for each FBS are same and normalized to 1 hour and 1W.

We consider the same model of cell sector/tier structure in [1] and compare the performance between the conventional system [1] and the proposed system. The simulation parameters are given in Table 1 where N_f denotes the number of FBSs which MS scans.

Table 1. Parameter for Simulation

Simulation Parameters	Range of Value	Value
N_f : Num. of FBS in MBS	24, 48, ..., 96	24
Service Coverage of FBS (m)	5, 10, ... 20	10
Average Velocity of MS (m/s)	0.5, 1.5, 2.5, ... 5.5	1 (Pedestrian)
Message Interval of MOB_NBR-ADV (sec)	5, 10, 15, ..., 30	15
Number of MBS	Sectoring: 1, 2, 4, 12	2

First we analyze the amount of broadcasting control message M_{MS} according to the number of FBSs in macro-cell as shown in Figure 7. As the number of FBSs in a macrocell gets larger, M_{MS} increases and MS scans more broadcasting message with much power and time consumption. In terms of M_{MS} the construction method given in [1] is best. But the difference of M_{MS} between the conventional and proposed method is negligible.

We also analyze P_{hit} which is defined as the hit probability of handover to the best (nearest) BS and the probability of handover failure when the MS is located in the femto-cell overlapping region. In Figure 8, the probability of handover to the best BS P_{hit} with conventional IEEE 802.16e scheme, the modified scheme in [1] and the proposed scheme are shown. When the number of sectors in a macrocell is 1, all the schemes are same. As the number of sectors in a macrocell gets larger, the proposed method improves P_{hit} dramatically compared with the method in [1]. P_{hit} can approach to probability of 1 if we applied more adjacent FBS information at the sector/tier edge. In Figure 9, the probability of handover failure with conventional IEEE 802.16e scheme and the proposed scheme are shown. When MS is located in overlapping region of femto-cell system, the ping-pong phenomenon is likely to happen. The proposed method decreases the probability of handover failure compared with conventional IEEE 802.16e system when the MS is located in overlapping region of femto-cell system. The performance improvement gets larger as the overlapping femto-cell number increases.

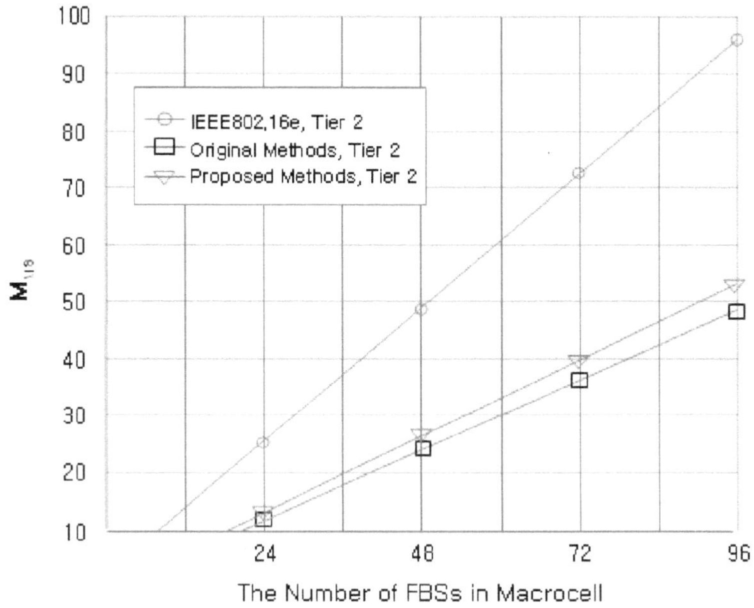

Fig. 7. Amount of Control Message (M_{MS}) vs. the number of FBSs in macro-cell

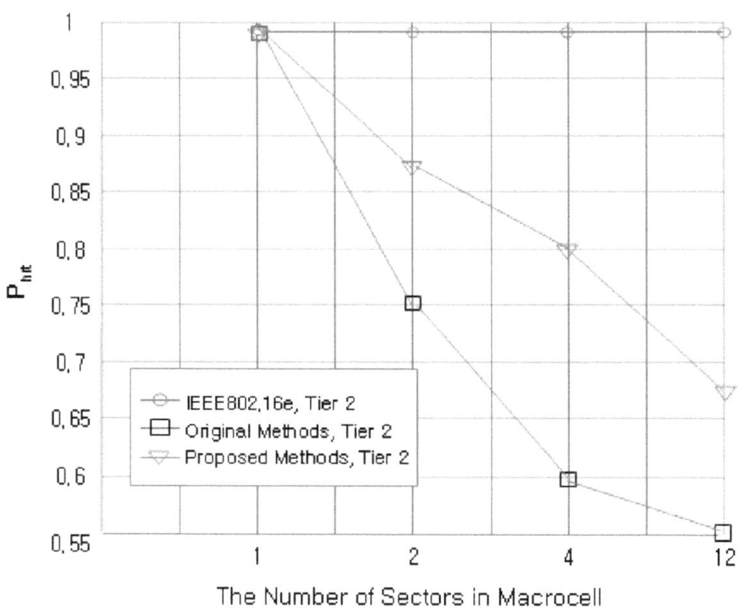

Fig. 8. The hit probability of handover P_{hit}

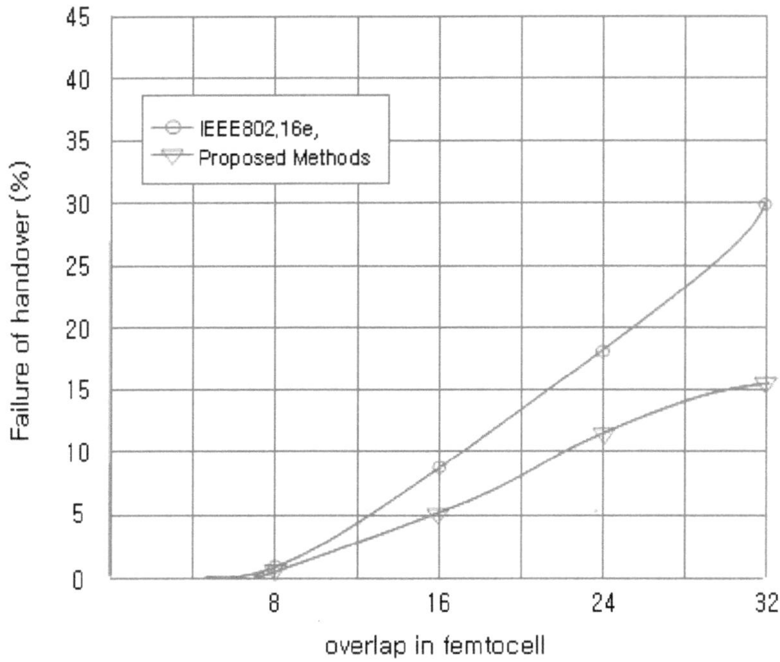

Fig. 9. The probability of handover failure when MS is located in overlapping femto-cell region

5 Conclusions

In this paper, we proposed an adaptive cell management and construction method of MOB_NBR-ADV message in an IEEE802.16e based femto-cell systems. The proposed method provides fast scanning and efficient handover by means of preselecting the candidate target femto-cells. The simulation results showed that the proposed schemes improve the MS's handover-related performance compared with the conventional management scheme of femto-cell systems.

Acknowledgments. This work was supported in part by the Basic Science Research Program through the National Research Foundation of Korea(NRF) funded by the Ministry of Education, Science and Technology (No. 2011-0005356) and in part by the Korea Research Foundation(KRF) grant funded by the Korea government(MEST) (No. 2010-0015495)

References

1. Nam, J., Shin, J., Yoon, C., Cho, H.: Management of neighboring BS lists for the fast scanning and efficient handover. Journal of Korean Institute of Communications Society 34(6), 445–457 (2009)
2. 3GPP TR 25.820 V8.2.0: 3GPP Home NodeB Study Item Technical Report (2008)

3. 3GPP TR R3.020: Home (e)NodeB; Network aspect (2008)
4. IEEE 802.16e 2005: IEEE Standard for Local and Metropolitan Area Networks - Part 16: Air Interface for Fixed and Mobile Broadband Wireless Access Systems–Amendment 2: Physical and medium access control layers for combined fixed and mobile operation in licensed band and corrigendum 1, IEEE 802.16e (2006)
5. IEEE C80216m-08_1157r1: Proposed Updates to IEEE 802.16m System Requirements to Reflect Operators Requirements on Femtocells, IEEE 802.16m (2008)

Feasibility of Electromagnetic Communication in Underwater Wireless Sensor Networks

Yasser K. Zahedi, Hamidreza Ghafghazi,
S.H.S. Ariffin, and Norazan M. Kassim

Faculty of Electrical Engineering
Universiti Teknologi Malaysia
Johor D. T, Malaysia
yasserzahedi@gmail.com

Abstract. Underwater Wireless Sensor networks (UWSNs) comprised of a number of sensor nodes that are deployed to perform collaborative monitoring tasks. Sensor nodes are connected to each other through wireless signals. Acoustic signal is the dominant wave used for UWSNs communications. Acoustic signals face a lot of challenges such as ambient noise, manmade noise, limited bandwidth, multipath and low propagation speed. These challenges become more severe in shallow water environment where a high level of ambient and manmade noise, turbidity and multipath is available. Therefore, Electromagnetic signals can be applied for using as a communication signal for UWSNs. In this work, the performance of electromagnetic communication in the water environment is investigated. The investigation is conducted for fresh and seawater environment. Results show that freshwater environment can permit short range communication while the communication is more difficult for seawater due to the high value of attenuation.

Keywords: Underwater wireless sensor networks, underwater electromagnetic communication, underwater acoustic communication.

1 Introduction

Shallow water environments can be regarded as the shallow water in rivers or the shallow coastal environments of seas. Shallow water is one of the most marine environments that can be affected directly due to the human activities comparing to other environments. Due to its ecological significance, shallow water requires critical management and monitoring tasks. Increased pollution, turbidity or temperature could affect the echo system in this particular region.

Underwater wireless sensor networks (UWSNs) can be used for monitoring the condition of the shallow water environment. Sensor nodes (also named as *motes*) can be deployed to sense the temperature, turbidity, or pollution of the water. The communication between the sensor motes is done using a wireless medium. The best wireless medium that can be used in this environment should be determined because shallow water with a good ecological condition can result in a good marine life.

Although the acoustic signals are the most used signals for underwater wireless sensor network, they are not preferred for shallow water. Acoustic signals are subject

A. Abd Manaf et al. (Eds.): ICIEIS 2011, Part III, CCIS 253, pp. 614–623, 2011.

to many problems including ambient noise, multipath and the affection on marine life. These disadvantages of acoustic signals are subject for increasing in the shallow water. Shallow water contains a higher percentage of turbidity, sink object, ambient noise, manmade noise due to the human activities, and a rich marine life that can be affected by these signals. In addition, acoustic signals have a limited bandwidth. Therefore, electromagnetic signals can be used in shallow water instead of acoustics.

Electromagnetic (EM) signals are more preferred for using in shallow water environments. EM signals do not experience most of the problems that the acoustics do. These waves are not affected by the interference that comes from other sound sources such as ambient noise and manmade noise. In addition, no interference would happen with the acoustic communication used by some marine livings. Moreover, one of the most important advantages is the less multipath encountered due to the short path of signals. In addition, these signals have much higher bandwidth and velocity than acoustics.

In the present digital era, the benefits of short range and high bandwidth communication systems have become a preferred issue [1]. Therefore, there is a requirement to analyze the performance of EM communication and its feasibility in underwater wireless sensor networks.

The organization of the paper is as follows. Section 2 illustrates the disadvantages of using Acoustic signals. In section 3, the advantages of EM signals underwater are explained. The related work of using EM signal for underwater propagation and underwater WSN is shown in section 4. Section 5 contains the explanation about the propagation of EM signals and the equations used in our analyses. Section 6 illustrates the results. Illustration about the suitable antennae sizes for sensor mote is explained in section 7 followed by the discussion section 8. Finally, section 9 concludes the paper and presents a future work.

2 Disadvantages of Acoustic Signals

Although acoustic signals are dominant for communication in underwater WSNs, many disadvantages appeared from these signals. These disadvantages can be listed as follows:

A. Multipath Propagation. Due to the long range communication in the acoustic signals, multi-path propagation is one of the main disadvantages. This multi-path propagation leads to a significant inter-symbol interference. Therefore, adaptive equalization should be used in the receiver to recover the bit stream from the received signal [2].

B. Ambient and Manmade Noise. The frequency of the acoustic signals is approximately the same as the other sound waves. Consequently, ambient noise can affect and interfere with the acoustic signals used in the underwater communication. The ambient noise comes from sources such as turbulence, breaking waves, rain, and distant shipping [3]. In addition, noise generated from the human activities (Manmade noise), such as turbines, engines and fans, can also interfere.

C. High Propagation Delay. Propagation speed of the acoustic signals is five orders of magnitude less than the radio signals. The bit rate of the system can be reduced significantly due to this large propagation delay (0.67 s/km) [4].

D. Synchronization between Nodes. High propagation delay causes more difficulties to achieve proper time synchronization between the nodes. This prevents from developing efficient protocols to create a precise synchronization.

E. Limited Bandwidth. Acoustic signals have a limited bandwidth due to their low frequencies. These values of Bandwidths are very small comparing to the EM signals.

3 Advantages of Underwater EM Communication

Electromagnetic technology can be used specifically in shallow water environment due to the high level of sediment and turbidity that exist in this environment. In addition, the ambient and manmade noise exist more in this water environment. The advantages of using EM communication in UWSNs can be listed as follows:

- EM signals can be used for coastal monitoring applications, where the sediment and aeration are at high level [5].
- Smooth transition through the air and water interfaces cannot be done by acoustic or optical signals. This transition is performed easily by EM signals.
- As opposed to the case in optical and acoustic signals, EM waves can tolerate the tidal waves, ambient noise, manmade noise and other human activities.
- EM signals can work in dirty water and other types of high turbid water.
- High bandwidth can be achieved through the use of EM radio signals. The typical bandwidth of the acoustics is 20Kbps while for radio signal is up to 100Mbps [5].
- Propagation speed of EM signals is similar to the speed of light. On the other hand, acoustics have a very low propagation speed (1500 m/s).
- Due to the faster propagation, radio signals can lead to more efficient communication protocols.
- Short ranges available for radio signals results in a lack of multi-path propagation. Therefore, less complicated equalization would be required in the receiver compared to the acoustic one [2].

4 Related Work

Due to the challenges arise in shallow water, EM communication is proposed to be an alternative to acoustic in this type of environment. Therefore, some research has been done in this issue.

Using EM communication for swarms of autonomous underwater vehicles (AUVs) is proposed in [2]. It has been found that the EM communication is feasible for this type of networks. In addition, it facilitates higher throughput compared to acoustic communication. In [5], EM communication for small scale underwater WSN was investigated through a simulation which showed the effectiveness and feasibility of using EM communication.

In the previous researches, low frequency EM signals were proposed due to the low attenuation that can be experienced there. In [1], a case study was presented for using electromagnetic technology in a small scale underwater wireless sensor network. The investigations revealed that the EM communication coupled with a digital technology and signal compression technique can be suitable for niche underwater applications. The analyses showed that EM communication in the shallow water environment is feasible.

The physical fundamentals and engineering implementations of acoustic, radio and light waves were elaborated in [6]. In terms of electromagnetic communication, the authors suggest that the used signal frequency for propagation should be larger than the transition frequency. For example, the used frequency in seawater should be larger than 888 MHz. Further studies were recommended for using EM communication underwater.

5 Underwater EM Communication

During EM signal propagation underwater, many factors can affect the signal. The most important factor is attenuation. EM signal attenuates due to propagating through water. Depending on the frequency and the water environment, the attenuation can increase or decrease. To understand the behavior of the signal while propagating underwater, the following factors should be understood.

5.1 Loss Tangent

Loss tangent is a parameter of a dielectric material that quantifies its inherent dissipation of electromagnetic energy. It is an important factor to recognize the type of the material whether it is a lossy dielectric, lossless dielectric or good conductor.

Loss tangent can be found from the following equation [7].

$$\tan\theta = \frac{\sigma}{\omega\varepsilon} \tag{1}$$

Where σ is the conductivity in S/m, ω is the angular frequency in radians/s, and ε is the permittivity of the material.

For underwater WSN water is considered as the material the signal propagate through. The water permittivity is $\varepsilon_r \varepsilon_\circ$. The relative permittivity of water is 81 while $\varepsilon_\circ$ is equal to $\frac{10^{-9}}{36\pi}$.

A medium is said to be a good (lossless or perfect) dielectric if the loss tangent is very small. This means $\sigma << \omega\varepsilon$. On the other hand, the material is considered as a good conductor if the loss tangent value is very large i.e. $\sigma >> \omega\varepsilon$ [7].

The characteristics of the medium is not just depending on the σ, ω and ε, but depends also on the frequency. Frequency value affects the magnitude of the loss tangent. In turn, the loss tangent value would determine the type of the material whether it is lossy, lossless dielectric or good conductor. Therefore, the same material that is regarded as dielectric for a particular frequency can be regarded as a good conductor for another selected frequency[7].

5.2 Attenuation

Generally, the electromagnetic signals attenuate when passing through a water medium. The attenuation values are different depending on the medium that the signals pass through. Moreover, water conductivity increases the attenuation proportionally. Therefore, signals suffer from higher attenuation in seawater than in freshwater due to the higher conductivity of the sea water.

Frequency is an important factor in increasing the attenuation. The attenuation increases with the increasing of frequency. Signals propagate with higher frequency is more likely to suffer from higher values of attenuation. On the other hand, lower frequency signals experience lower values of attenuation.

For getting accurate results, the equation of attenuation of EM signals in lossy dielectric material is used. The lossy dielectric equation is the general equation. Other equations such as equations for EM signal propagation through a good conductor and free space have been derived from the lossy dielectric equation. Equation (2) represents the attenuation of EM signal in a lossy dielectric material [7].

$$\alpha = \omega\sqrt{\frac{\mu\varepsilon}{2}\left[\sqrt{1+\left[\frac{\sigma}{\omega\varepsilon}\right]^2}-1\right]} \tag{2}$$

Where α is the attenuation factor in nepers per meter (Np/m).

5.3 Velocity of Underwater EM Communication

As it explained earlier, low propagation speed is an important drawback in using underwater acoustic communication for underwater WSNs. Low propagation speed affects proper communication protocols design. On the other hand, EM communication has high propagation speed underwater. The velocity of an EM signal propagating through a material is expressed mathematically in equation (3) [7].

$$u = \frac{\omega}{\beta} \tag{3}$$

Where ω is the angular frequency in (radians/s), and β is the wave number in (radians/m). β value is obtained from the following equation [7].

$$\beta = \omega \sqrt{\frac{\mu\varepsilon}{2}\left[\sqrt{1+\left[\frac{\sigma}{\omega\varepsilon}\right]^2}+1\right]} \tag{4}$$

6 Simulation Results

This section contains the results of attenuation, loss tangent and velocity for EM signals propagating through fresh and seawater. The analysis of these graphs and its contribution to underwater WSNs is explained. MATLAB was used to obtain the results. For freshwater, the conductivity is set to 0.01 S/m while it is set to 4 S/m for seawater. Results were obtained for different EM signal frequencies.

6.1 Loss Tangent of Underwater EM signals

The Loss Tangent is calculated as in equation (1)

As it is shown in fig. 1, the loss tangent for both sea and fresh water has a larger value in low frequencies and started to decrease as the frequency of the signal goes higher. A larger value of loss tangent means the signal is seems to be a conductor more than a dielectric. When the loss tangent elevated to be lower, the signal will tend to be more dielectric.

Material with higher dielectric behavior makes the propagation of electromagnetic signal to be more difficult. As a result, low frequency EM can propagate better in the water medium than for high frequency EM signal.

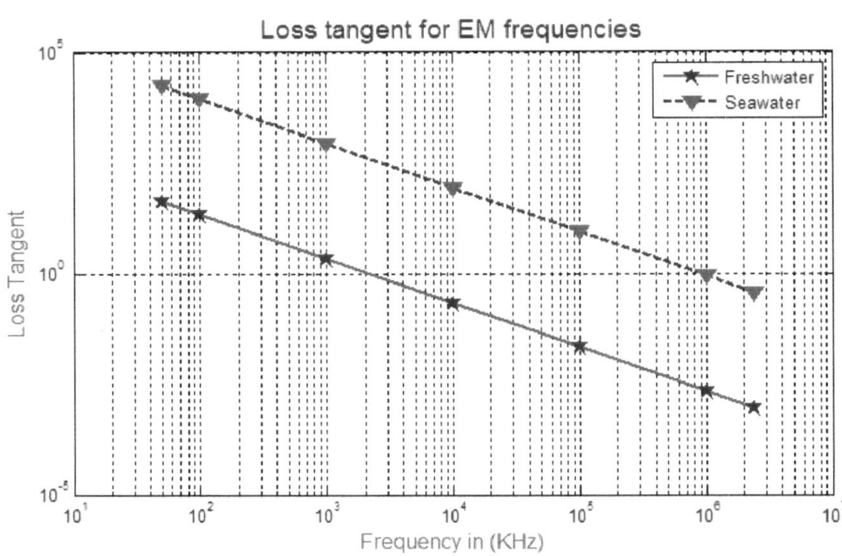

Fig. 1. Loss tangent for EM signals in fresh and seawater

6.2 Attenuation

Attenuation is simulated using equation (2). The results of underwater EM propagation in fresh and seawater is shown in fig 2.

As it is shown in fig. 2, EM signal suffers from higher attenuation in seawater than in freshwater. The conductivity of seawater is higher than the conductivity of freshwater. For example, the attenuation experienced by an EM signal at 2.4 GHz frequency for propagation through seawater is above 700 dB/m while it is slightly above 1 dB/m for fresh water. Similar situation is applicable to other frequencies as it is shown figure 2. Therefore, the very high attenuation that the signal will suffer in seawater makes the communication tend to be impossible for high frequencies.

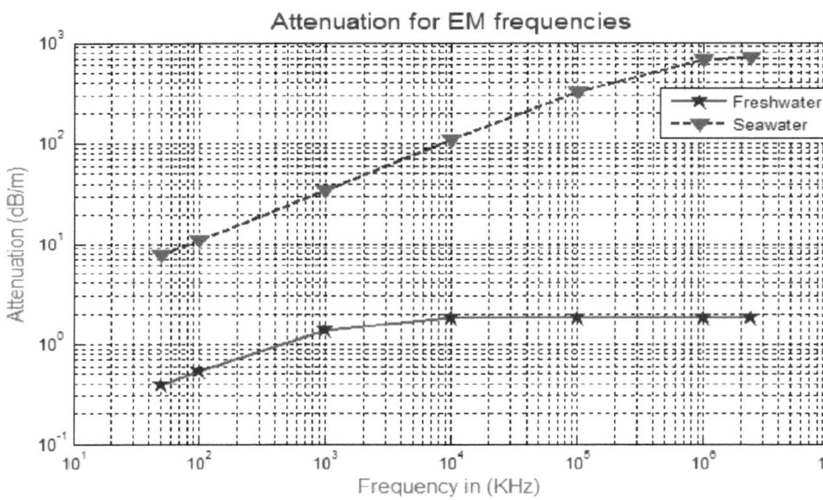

Fig. 2. Attenuation experienced by EM signals in fresh and seawater for different frequencies

6.3 Velocity

Velocity values for the EM signal propagating through sea and freshwater is shown in fig. 3. The values are calculated for different frequencies.

The velocity of the EM signals propagating through the water medium increases as the frequency increases. As the frequency of the transmitted signal is set to 1 GHz and higher, the velocity of the signal is settled (as shown in the figure). Velocity of the signal was investigated till 2.4 GHz frequency because this frequency is the one used for terrestrial communication in wireless sensor networks.

It can be noticed that the velocity of the EM signal is extremely higher than the acoustic one even for low frequencies. This can facilitate and improve the function of the communication protocols in underwater WSNs.

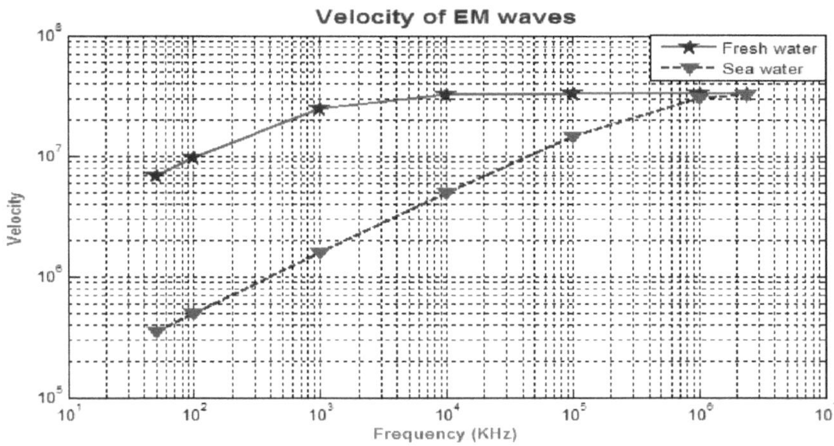

Fig. 3. Velocity of EM waves in fresh and seawater

7 Antenna Size in Underwater EM Communication

A small form factor is an important issue in designing sensor motes. Sensor motes should be small enough to be deployed easily in a particular sensing environment. The value of the transmitted EM signal frequency leads to a specific antenna size. As the frequency increases, the antenna size decreases. For example, in terms of MICAz sensor mote, the antenna used is a quarter-wave monopole antenna. Therefore, antenna size will be determined as:

$$D = \lambda / 4 \tag{5}$$

Where D is the physical dimension of the antenna, λ is the wavelength of the EM signal. λ is calculated by dividing the velocity of the underwater EM signal over its frequency.

$$\lambda = \frac{u}{f} \tag{6}$$

Depends on the velocity of the EM signal, the antenna size of the sensor mote is different for fresh and seawater. These sizes should be taken in regards in order to get the exact frequency of transmission. It can be seen that the antenna size is small for high frequency compared to the low frequencies. Therefore, for UWSNs using high frequency EM signals can be more practical to obtain a suitable form factor for sensor motes.

8 Discussion

In terms of terrestrial wireless sensor networks, the attenuation for free space communication approaches zero. For UWSNs, the attenuation is very high for seawater and available with lower value in freshwater. Therefore, attenuation value degrades signal strength considerably. To find the power strength of the signal received by the receiving sensor node, the attenuation value along with the path loss value must be subtracted from the value of the transmitted power. Path loss value of the signal should be obtained based on a path loss model specified for underwater environment.

Depending on the results obtained from the theoretical calculations, Freshwater environment permits a short range communication for high frequency EM signals due to the lower value of attenuation (comparing to attenuation in seawater) that equals to 1.8192 dB/m for 2.4 GHz. This can be useful for the applications that do not need a long range communication between the sensor motes. In terms of seawater results, it can be concluded that the communication is very difficult for high frequency EM signals. This is due to the high attenuation in seawater environment (715 dB/m for 2.4 GHz) because of the high value of conductivity. Therefore, lower frequencies should be used to get longer communication ranges in sea and even in freshwater environments. However, antenna size should be considered in order to preserve a suitable size for sensor motes.

9 Conclusion and Future Works

EM communication in UWSNs has been investigated. The performance advantage of underwater EM communication is the high bandwidth achieved and the elimination of the challenges of shallow water acoustic communication. However, EM communication permits lower ranges of communication compared to acoustic one. High frequency EM communication experienced higher attenuation. In addition, water behaves as more dielectric medium for high frequency signals resulting in difficulty of propagation. Low frequency EM signals permits longer range of communication. On the other hand, antenna size will be bigger which limits the achievement of small form factor of sensor motes. As a future work, practical experiments will be conducted to obtain the performance of underwater EM communication especially for high frequency signals.

Acknowledgement. This work was supported by Minister of Higher Education (MOHE) grant under FRGS J13000078234F046 and RMC UTM.

References

1. Che, X., et al.: Re-evaluation of RF electromagnetic communication in underwater sensor networks. IEEE Communications Magazine, 143–151 (2010)
2. Frater, M.R., Ryan, M.J., Dunbar, R.M.: Electromagnetic communications within swarms of autonomous underwater vehicles. In: 1st ACM International Workshop on Underwater Networks (2006)
3. Stojanovic, M. and J. Preisig:Underwater Acoustic Communication Channels: Propagation Models and Statistical Characterization. IEEE Communications Magazine, 84–89 (2009)
4. Akyildiz, I.F., Pompili, D., Melodia, T.: Underwater acoustic sensor networks: research challenges. Ad Hoc Networks, 257-279 (2005)

5. Che, X., et al.: A Static Multi-hop Underwater Wireless Sensor Network Using RF Electromagnetic Communications. In: 29th IEEE International Conference on Distributed Computing Systems Workshops (2009)
6. Lanbo, L., Shengli, Z., Jun Hong, C.: Prospects and problems of wireless communication for underwater sensor networks. Wireless Communications and Mobile Computing, 977–994 (2008)
7. Sadiku, M.N.O.: Elements of electromagnetics, 4th edn., Oxford city (2007)

Communications in Computer and Information Science: Techniques on Relaying for LTE-Advanced Network

Aimi Syamimi Ab Ghafar, Nurulashikin Satiman, Norsheila Fisal, Siti Marwangi Mohamad Maharum, Faiz Asraf Saparudin, Rozeha Abdul Rashid, Sharifah Kamilah Syed Yusof, and Norshida Katiran

UTM-MIMOS Center of Excellence in Telecommunication Technology, Faculty of Electrical Engineering, Universiti Teknologi Malaysia, Skudai, Johor, Malaysia

aimisyamimi@fkegraduate.utm.my, sheila@fke.utm.my

Abstract. Relay-assisted cellular network is a major concern in research studies around the world as it can aid the cell to achieve coverage extension and capacity enhancement. Long Term Evolution-Advanced (LTE-A), a candidate from Third Generation Partnership Project (3GPP) has include relaying as one of its key technologies to meet International Mobile Telecommunications (IMT) Advanced requirements. This article focuses on relay architectures from LTE-A and the types of relay defined in the standard. Pros and cons of developed relaying strategies, transmission schemes together with relay selection pairing scheme are also reviewed. This article also provides simulation results comparing performance between transmission with and without the usage of relay. In addition, recent studies extending the relaying concept such as cognitive and cooperative relaying as a hot research topic are also discussed.

Keywords: LTE-A, relay architectures, relay strategies, transmission schemes, pairing schemes, performance comparison, cognitive and cooperative relaying.

1 Introduction

Recently, relay technology is one of the main technologies broadly studied for standardization of LTE-Advanced in meeting IMT-Advanced requirements. The requirements are enhanced peak data rates to support advanced services and applications (100 Mbit/s for high and 1 Gbit/s for low mobility) where the mobility classes are defined as stationary: 0 km/h, pedestrian: > 0 km/h to 10 km/h, vehicular: 10 to 120 km/h, high speed vehicular: 120 to 350 km/h. After that, peak spectral efficiencies of downlink is 15 bit/s/Hz and for uplink is 6.75 bit/s/Hz. The minimum requirements on voice over IP (VoIP) capacities in high-mobility and low-mobility environments are 30 and 50 active users/sector/MHz. Finally, latency for control and user planes should be less than 100 ms and 10 ms, respectively.

A. Abd Manaf et al. (Eds.): ICIEIS 2011, Part III, CCIS 253, pp. 624–638, 2011.

The function of relay node (RN) can be described simply as a device which assists transmissions between local eNodeB (eNB)/base station (BS) and user equipment (UE) /mobile station (MS) [2]. Two main concerns in deploying relay technology are coverage extension and capacity improvement as mentioned in [3]. Coverage extension was further described by using a scenario as shown in Fig.1. User equipments in a moving vehicle at highway can still receive signal coverage from the eNodeB by using multi-hop relays. In the latter case, which is to enhance the network capacity, multi-hop links are used to lessen the distance between eNodeB and its corresponding UEs. As shown in Fig.2 [3], usage of relay helps to attain higher data rates comparing to single-hop links.

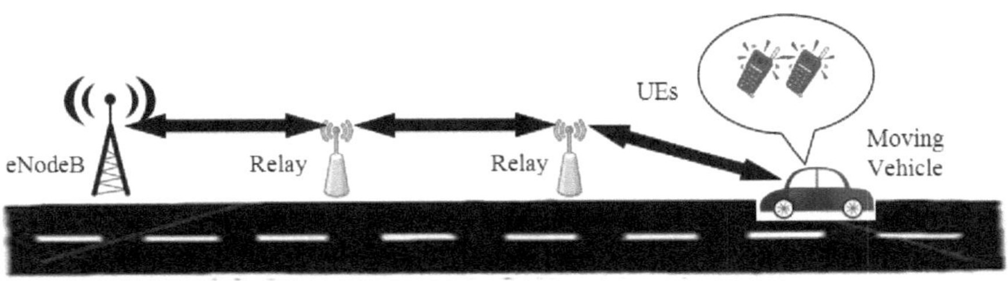

Fig. 1. Extension of coverage by using relay

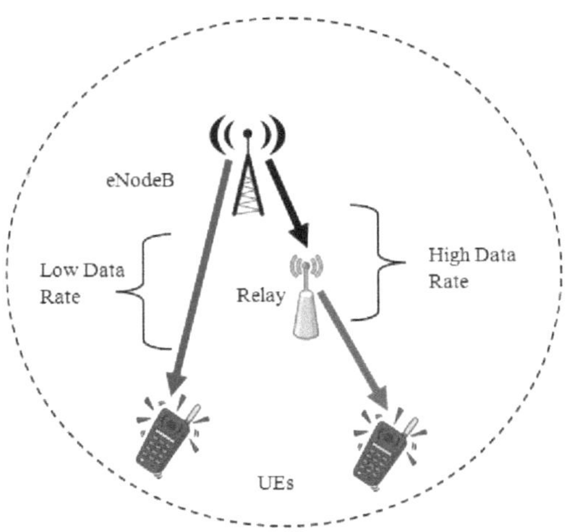

Fig. 2. Increased capacity

This article is organized as follows. Section 2 provides explanation two relay types in terms of its contribution to the network performance. Subsequently, in section 3, multi-hop relay architectures in LTE-A network are explained followed by relaying strategies in section 4. Several relay transmission schemes are described in section 5. Pairing schemes for relay selection and parameters involved in evaluating relay-equipped network are described next, in section 6 and section 7 respectively. We also explained simulation results comparing network with and without usage of relay in section 8, extension to relaying concept in section 9 and finally draw the conclusion in section 10.

2 Relay Types

There are two types of relay defined in 3GPP LTE-Advanced standards, specifically Type-I and Type-II relay or in WiMAX standards, also known as non-transparent and transparent relay [2]. Categorization of relay is made according to its ability to manage the resources, which means the relay can generate cell control message [4]. As shown in Fig.3 [2], type-I (or non-transparent) RN in specific is responsible to assist a remote UE to access the eNodeB. This remote UE is usually located far away from the eNodeB and out of the cell coverage. Thus, type-I relay is equipped with the ability to generate its own cell control messages and has distinct cell IDs.

One characteristic of type-I relay is that it controls cells, each of which appears to UE as a separate cell distinct from eNodeB [5]. The cells shall have their own physical cell IDs, and the relay node (RN) shall transmit its own synchronization channels, reference symbols, and etc. Type-I RN used to extend signal and service coverage. At the same time, in allowing communications for remote UEs, it improves overall system capacity.

Type-II RN (transparent) is accountable to help UE within the coverage of eNodeB. Although this local UE can communicate directly with the eNodeB, deployment of RN can help to improve its service quality and link capacity. This type of relay is a part of the donor cell and does not have a cell identity of its own. In other words, type-II relay will share cell IDs and cell control messages with its donor cell (served by corresponding eNodeB). By using this relay, the overall system improvement can be obtained by multipath diversity and transmission gains for local UEs.

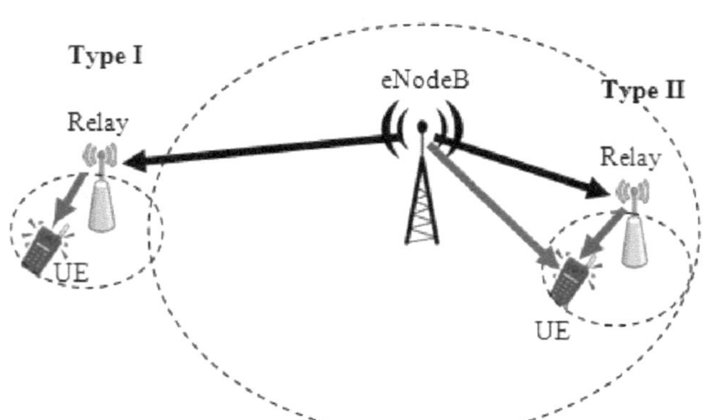

Fig. 3. Type-I and type-II relay

3 Multi-hop Relay Architectures

Before going into more details about relaying techniques, the architecture of LTE-Advanced networks will be discussed. Technically, a multi-hop LTE-A network consists of eNodeB, relays (can be one or more) and UEs. For *n* number of hops, the number of relays is *n-1*. Limitation has been set by 3GPP where the *n* is bounded to two. Thus, only one relay can be implemented producing two-hop network.

LTE-A network consists of UE, eNodeB, Mobility Management Entity (MME), Serving Gateway, Packet Data Network (PDN) Gateway and Policy and Charging Rules Function (PCRF). Protocols architecture of LTE-A network is shown in Fig.4 [3] (a) and (b), consisting of user plane and control plane. The relay protocol stacks are left blank because its protocol functions depend on types of relaying schemes used.

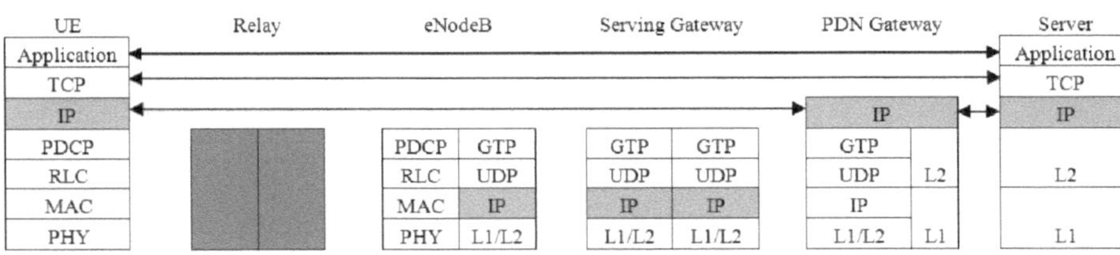

a) LTE-Advanced protocol architecture – User Plane

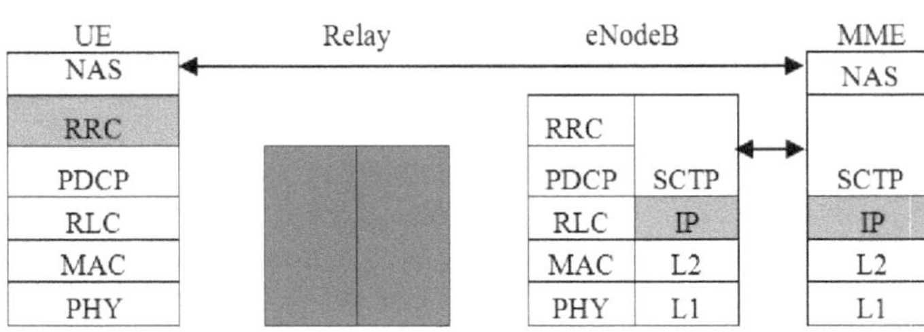

b) LTE-Advanced protocol architecture – Control Plane

Fig. 4. Protocols in LTE-A architecture

Table 1. Protocol and layer functions

User plane	Packet Data Convergence Protocol (PDCP)	Compressing & decompressing the headers of user-level IP packets
	IP (transport-level)	Carry signal between eNodeB and PDN gateway
	Radio link control (RLC)	Responsible for error recovery and flow control for data transportation between UE and eNodeB
	Medium Access Control (MAC)	Provides hybrid automatic repeat request (HARQ) -responsible for logical-to-transport channel mapping, scheduling operation & random access
	Physical (PHY)	Adaptive modulation & coding, and OFDM modulation
	GRPS Tunneling Protocol (GTP)	Transfer IP datagrams between eNodeB and PDN gateway
Control plane	Non Access Stratum (NAS)	Session management, security control, & aunthentication
	Stream Control Transmission Protocol (SCTP)	Carry NAS
	Radio Resource Control (RRC)	Setting up and maintenance of radio bearers, plus mobility management
	PDCP, RLC, MAC, PHY	Same as user plane

4 Relaying Strategies

There are three relaying strategies discussed by Peters et. al [6] which are one-way relaying, two-way relaying and shared relaying as illustrated in the following Fig.5 [6]. As shown in the figure, the eNodeB is equipped with one antenna per sector and one RN serving a single UE in its vicinity. On the other hand, the relay station nodes are shared between eNodeBs of three adjacent cells which use the same frequency.

The concept of one-way relaying is illustrated in the following Fig.6. The data transmission is divided into four frames as denoted by the number: In the downlink, 1) the eNodeB transmits to RN, followed by 2) RN forwards the signal to UE. Then, during uplink, 3) UE transmits to RN and finally 4) RN forwards UE's signal to eNodeB.

As an enhancement to one-way relaying, two-way relaying is more efficient where the data transmission is done in two phases as shown in Fig.7. During the first phase, both eNodeB and UE transmit their signals to the RN and then in second phase, after proper signal processing, the RN forwards the signals to both eNodeB and UE. Therefore, the transmission duration would be half of the time taken for one-way relaying.

Shared relaying is cost-saving as number of RNs to be deployed is reduced by allowing the RN to be shared by three cells. Also, as mentioned in [6], shared relay has advantage over one-way relaying compared to two-way relaying. This is due to the interference that might occur during the simultaneous transmissions of two-way relay, combining with the fact that the shared relay itself has to handle the multiple signals from eNodeBs of the three adjacent cells.

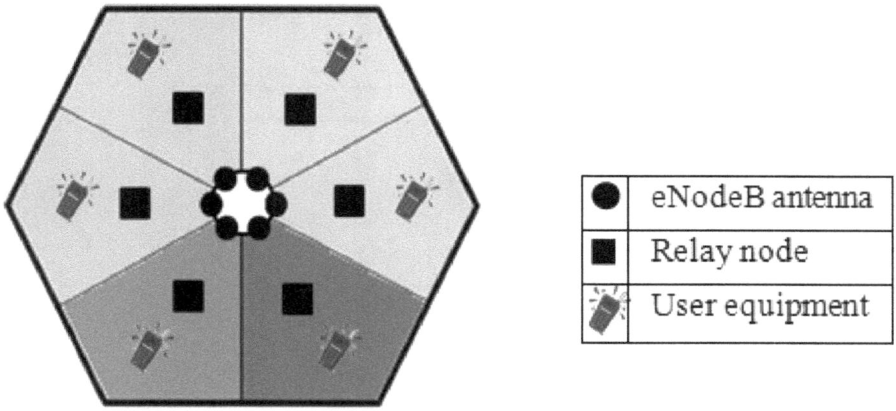

a) One-way and two-way relaying

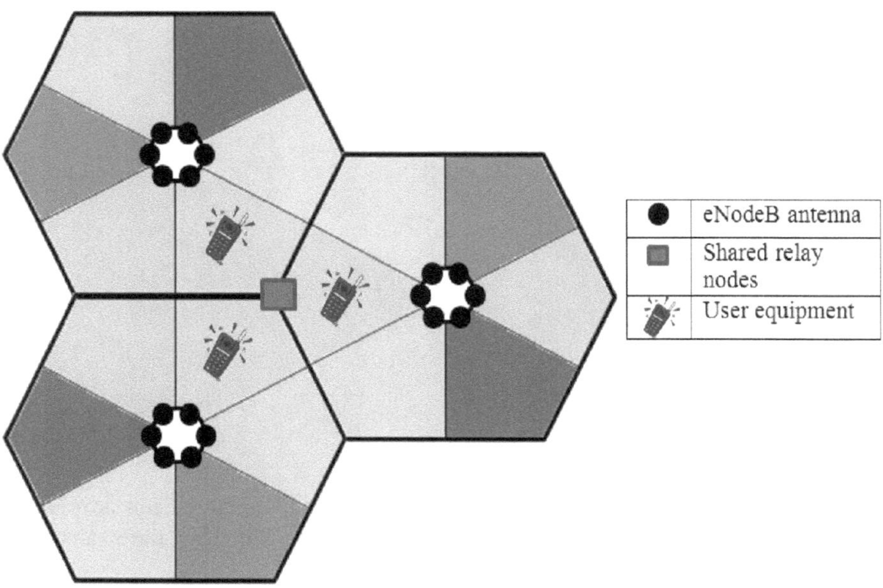

b) Shared relaying

Fig. 5. Relaying strategies with frequency reuse of factor 6 where each cell is divided into 6 sectors. a) Frequency reuse pattern for one-way and two-way relays deployed in one cell. b) Frequency reuse pattern for shared relay deployed in 3 adjacent cells.

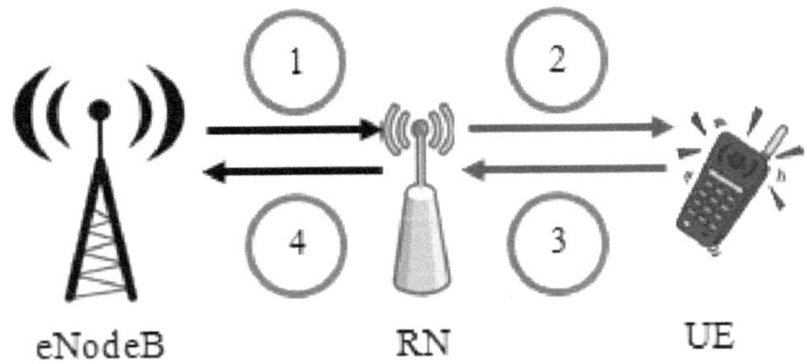

Fig. 6. One-way relaying

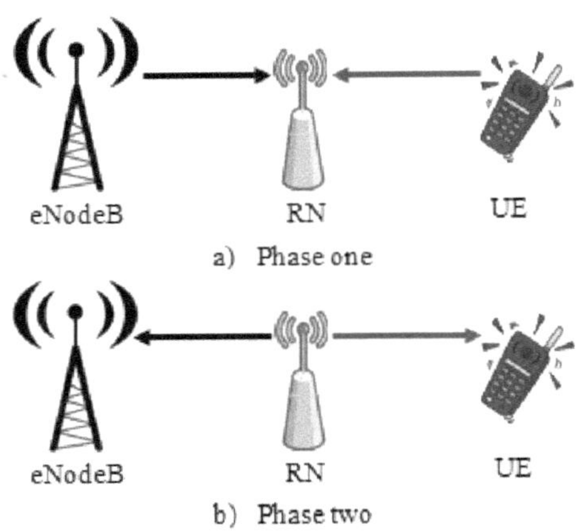

Fig. 7. Two-way relaying

5 Relay Transmission Schemes

Over the past decade, numerous relay transmission schemes have been developed to be implemented in our cellular network technology. In [6], the transmission techniques include:

i. Analog repeater which repeats transmit signal using combination of directional antennas and a power amplifier
ii. Amplify-and-forward which transforms the received signal directly
iii. Decode-and-forward which decodes the received signal and then re-encode it for transmission
iv. Compress-and-forward
v. Demodulate-and-forward.

In this article, only three relay transmission schemes will be discussed which are amplify-and-forward (AF), decode-and-forward (DCF) and demodulate-and-forward (DMF) [2]-[3].

AF relay, namely wireless repeater or Layer 1 (L1) relay involves only the PHY layer. The operation of RN can be divided into two phases. First, RN receives signals and next, amplifies and forwards it. Operation of L1 relay transceiver can be either on the same carrier frequency (inband) or on orthogonal carrier frequency (outband).

For inband operation, directional antennas are used to diminish the interference produced by concurrent transmissions of eNodeB-to-relay and relay-to-UE. Outband operation assures that the repeated signal would not interfere with any direct signal received at the destination. To assign frequency bands for transmissions of eNodeB-relay and relay-UE, this operation is assisted by radio resource management (RRM) function at eNodeB.

Benefits of using this relay include simplicity, low cost and having low delay. The main trade-off is that repeaters do not have the capability to distinguish real signals with noise and interference. Thus, those undesired signals are also amplified and retransmitted along with the original signals.

Another relaying strategy is decode-and-forward where the signals are decoded by the relay node, re-encoded and lastly forwarded to desired destination. In this relaying strategy, noise and interference are discarded from being transmitted together with the real signals but with the price of longer delay due to decoding and re-encoding process. The relay structures can be categorized into Layer 2 (L2) relay and Layer 3 (L3) relay, depending on its function. The transmissions involved can be both inband and outband as well, as in L1 relay.

L3 relay is proposed with the self-backhauling configuration as shown in Fig.8 [3]. This self-backhauling relay has the same function as base station but it transmits lower power and smaller cell size. Connection of self-backhauling relay to eNodeB is called backhaul link and must support LTE radio interface protocols in communicating with eNodeB. Self-backhauling and nonself-backhauling IP packets need to be differentiated. For self-backhauling IP packets, eNodeB bypasses GTP and UDP to be processed at self-backhauling relay. To make it cost-effective, the relay must also use the same radio interface technology as UE. The limitation of this approach is that the LTE radio protocol stack is meant for single-hop rather than multi-hop transmission.

L2 protocol includes three sub-layers which are Packet Data Convergence Protocol (PDCP), Radio Link Control (RLC) and Medium Access Control (MAC). There are two approaches of implementing L2 which are per hop and end-to-end basis as shown in Fig.9 and Fig.10 respectively [3]. For per hop basis, the concept is quite similar to self-backhauling approach. The difference is L2 forwards PDCP packets, not IP packets as in self-backhauling case. In the latter case, L2 protocols are employed at eNodeB and UE. This protocol can be innovatively designed for multi-hop relaying purpose. Currently, multi-hop automatic repeat request (ARQ) schemes are developed and optimized for multi-hop communications. It can be seen that UE and eNodeB has RLC protocol functioning as end-to-end recovery tool while at relay, the RLC is for local error recovery. As for per hop basis, it is only equipped with local error recovery.

Another important notation is that only L2 and L3 relays are equipped with RRM function in MAC layer, which hold the responsibility to handle radio resources efficiently. L1 relay does not come with this functionality as it is limited to PHY layer only [7].

Regarding the DMF relay, RN demodulates the received signal without decoding it. It was then re-modulated and forwarded to eNodeB/UE. This strategy is simple and having low processing delay but cannot avoid propagation error as the decision is made without decoding the received signal to discard noise.

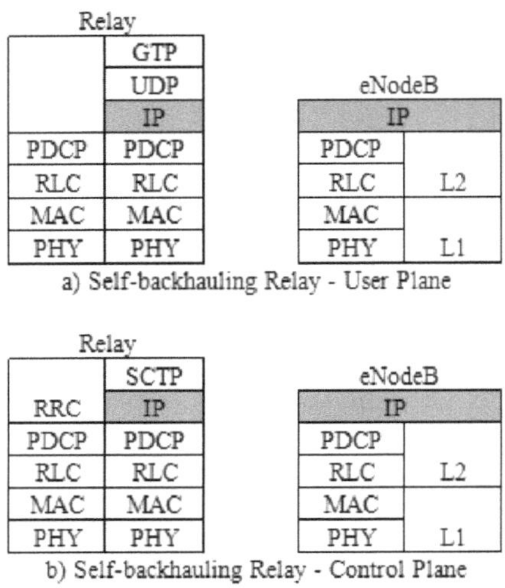

Fig. 8. L3: Self-backhauling relay architecture

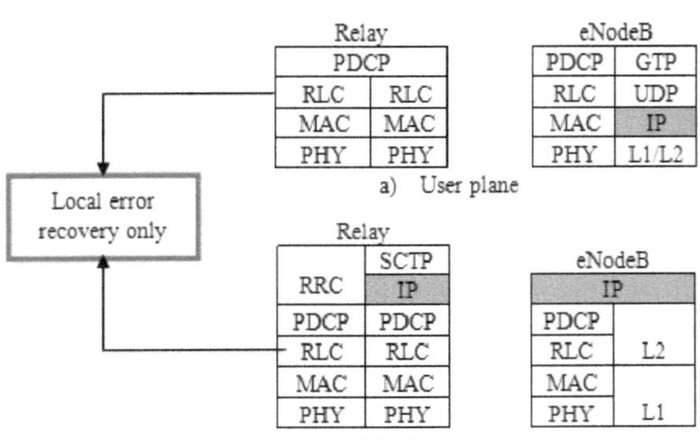

Fig. 9. L2: Per hop approach

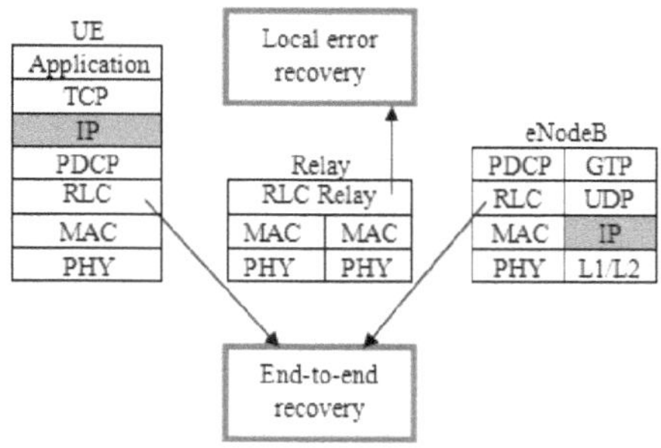

Fig. 10. L2: End-to-end approach

6 Relay Selection Pairing Schemes

In this section, four types of pairing schemes are discussed briefly in [2], [7] and [8] namely random, opportunistic, centralized and distributed.

In random pairing scheme, RS will randomly select any UEs in its service coverage without taking any consideration in decision-making such as UE location, the gains, achievable data rates or etc.

Opportunistic pairing scheme UE chooses RN according to signal strength, which means the closest RN which has strongest signal is chosen consecutively.

As for centralized scheduling, the resource allocation of all the links is done by eNodeB. Thus, RN has to periodically report the channel state information (CSI) for the links between RN-UE and RN-eNodeB. Upon achieving the links quality information, eNodeB will construct pairing result and broadcast it to all RNs and UEs under its coverage and can maximize number of served UEs. However, as RN feedback CSI of all the links to eNodeB, it causes huge overhead in the network which leads to latency problem.

In reducing periodic information exchange and signaling overhead from centralized scheduling, distributed pairing scheme is proposed. In this case, RN is responsible to make decisions on resource allocation RN-UE links transmission. The feedback overhead is reduced since the need for RN to report CSI of RN-UE link has been discarded. Nevertheless, optimization for resource allocation cannot be achieved due to nonexistence of central node to efficiently control and coordinate resource usage among all the links in the network.

Centralized and distributed scheduling can only be applied L2 and L3 relays only as these scheduling require RRM function.

7 Parameters in Concern for Relay-Enhanced Network

Typically, key parameters to assess the performance of a multi-hop cellular network consisting of relays are by monitoring its throughput and delay. Throughput or data rate which is measured in bit per second (bps) reflects the efficiency to successfully deliver the packets in the transmission between eNodeB and UE. Users of mobile phone usually encounter performance degradation (low data rate) due to several reasons such as constraint of distance and interference from other cells. As for delay, we take the example of UE which is located at cell edge. As this UE transmits its signal to corresponding eNodeB, the signal may suffer distortion from interference and causing packet loss. Thus, UE needs to retransmit the lost packets which consequently increase more latency on the data transmission. Relay technology is introduced to resolve these problems by providing multipath diversity while simultaneously reduce the cost as relay is a low power node.

8 Performance Evaluation

We have done performance evaluation of the network shown in Fig.2 in terms of throughput and delay. We compare two scenarios which are direct transmission of UE-eNodeB and transmission with relaying UE-RN-eNodeB. The parameters used for the simulation is shown in Table 2. Based on Fig.11 and Fig.12, both throughput and delay with relaying are better compared to direct transmission. Since UE is located at the cell edge, the performance for direct transmission is poor. The SNR is low that makes it easier to be fluctuated by noise while transmitting. Furthermore, due to its location at the cell edge, UE may suffer interference from other cells. Relay transmission overcome this problem because it enhances the SNR of the transmission. As mentioned earlier, there are many transmission schemes for relaying that can be used to further boost the performance of the system.

According to [2] and [3], DCF scheme can be considered the best among other (AF and DMF) relay schemes since it provides the function to distinguish noise and interference plus its complexity and processing delay are still acceptable. Thus, DCF scheme is now widely considered to be deployed in multi-hop cellular networks.

Also, from [2] and [7], centralized and distributed can help the network to optimize number of served UE units and higher cell throughput performance compared to other schemes. However, there are still much room for investigation and research to highly utilize the concept of relay selection pairing scheme in meeting IMT-Advanced requirements.

Apart from that, as discussed in [4], there are still many challenges to be studied for future releases such as mobility, power saving, multi-hop architecture, transparent relaying (since current researches are based only on nontransparent relaying), and multi-carrier transmission.

Table 2. Parameters used for simulation

Parameter	Value
Channel frequency	2.3 GHz
Transmission Power (eNodeB)	46 dbm
Transmission Power (RN)	30 dbm
Channel bandwidth	10 MHz
Frame Duration	5 ms
Payload size	512 byte

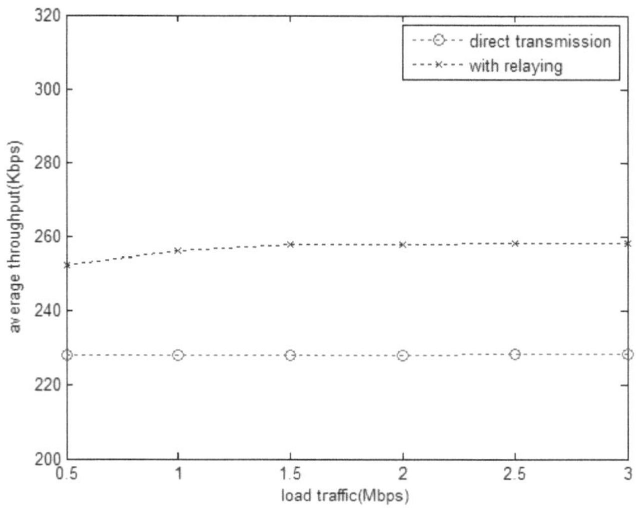

Fig. 11. Average throughput comparison

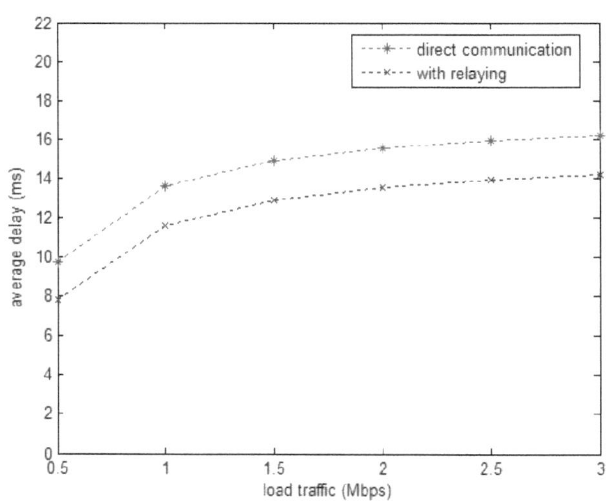

Fig. 12. Average delay comparison

9 Extension to Relay Network and Its Open Issues

Cognitive relaying [8]-[11] is also one attractive field to be embarked. In cognitive radio network, spectrum sharing between licensed (primary) user and unlicensed (secondary) user has been made possible with the advantage of mitigating spectrum scarcity and improving spectrum utilization effectively [12]. Cognitive relay has been introduced to make use of spectrum holes in a cellular network to forward information for either primary or secondary users in order to improve system throughput.

However, Zhang et. al [14]-[15] has brought up the concern of unbalanced spectrum usage in cognitive radio network due to different traffic demands of different users. Some users might have high traffic demand but run out of resources while the others are wasting their resources due to low traffic demand. The open research issue is the selection of RNs so that traffic demand is satisfied and spectrum is utilized efficiently.

The functionality of a RN is further enhanced in order to acquire better QoS. Cooperative relaying is an extension of basic connection of one eNB to one RN, where multiple RNs are allowed to be connected to single eNB. A lot of researches have been done and still going regarding the deployment of cooperative relaying concept for various wireless network platforms, as discussed in [12]-[16]. Spatial diversity is exploited through cooperation of a set of RNs to forward data to the UE. There are two categories of cooperative relaying as shown in the following Fig.13.

a) Cooperative transmission between secondary users – the secondary users in a wireless network, which have their own data to be sent, cooperate between each other to increase the network throughput by forwarding signals of other users. In this scenario, the users act as relays.
b) Cooperative transmission by RNs – the RNs do not have their own packets. They are deployed in a cell mainly to help in forwarding users data. In this project, this type of cooperation is considered.

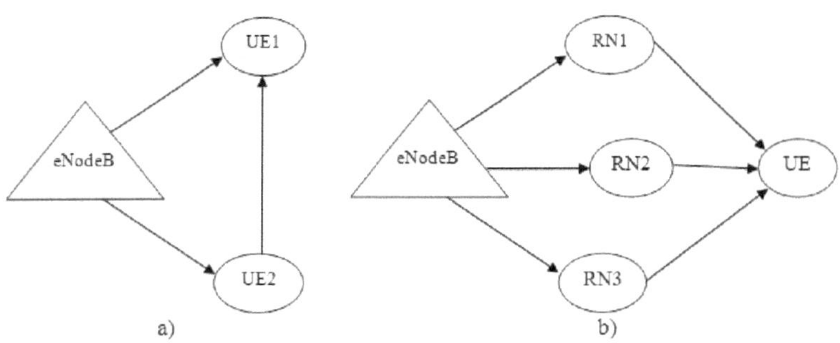

Fig. 13. Cooperative transmission categories

Cooperative transmission is also being considered heavily in LTE-A. In [16], relay is said to be one of the key component in applying virtual MIMO concept into practice to obtain higher spectral efficiency and data throughput. Recent studies showed that cooperative relay technology is also applied in cognitive radio networks to improve transmission diversity gain while making use of the spectrum holes [14]-[15]. Nevertheless, there are still open issues and combination of cooperative and cognitive network is a promising technology in obtaining a better network performance.

10 Conclusion

In this paper we have explained two main targets of relaying in LTE-Advanced studied by 3GPP working group, which is to extend cell coverage and improve its capacity. Then, type-I and type-II relays are defined and its contribution to the system is explained. Multi-hop relay architectures defined in the latest release of LTE-A standard are also discussed in terms of the functional elements and functionality of each layer/protocol of user-plane and control-plane. Three relaying strategies for implementation are also discussed. Review of three relay transmission schemes is given together with their advantages and disadvantages. Performance comparison between direct and relaying transmission are discussed based on simulation results. Finally, further study on the potential of cognitive as one of the research areas to be investigated in realizing cost-effective networks is discussed, together with the cooperative communications as a promising technology to achieve end-to-end throughput enhancement of a network while utilizing the spectrum efficiently.

Acknowledgement. The authors would like to thank to the UTM-MIMOS Center of Excellent and Research Management Center (RMC) of Universiti Teknologi Malaysia for their full support and advice in realizing this research project. Also, thanks to all anonymous reviewers for their invaluable comments and the guest editors for handling the review for this paper. The work is financed by Institutional Scholarship provided by Ministry of Higher Education and Ministry of Science, Technology and Innovation of Malaysia.

References

1. ITU-R Rep. M.2134. Requirements Related to Technical Performance for IMT-Advanced Radio Interface(s). Technical Report, 3GPP (2008)
2. Yang, Y., Hu, H., Xu, J., Mao, G.: Relay Technologies for WiMAX and LTE-Advanced Mobile Systems. IEEE Communications Magazine 47(10), 100–105 (2009)
3. Lo, A., Niemegeers, I.: Multi-hop Relay Architectures for 3GPP LTE-Advanced. In: Proceedings of the 9th IEEE Malaysia International Conference on Communications (MICC), Malaysia, pp. 123–127 (2009)
4. Loa, K., Wu, C., Sheu, S., Yuan, Y., Chion, M., Huo, D., Xu, L.: IMT-Advanced Relay Standards. IEEE Communications Magazine 48(8), 40–48 (2010)
5. 3GPP TR 36.814. Evolved Universal Terrestrial Radio Access (E-UTRA); Further Advancements for E-UTRA Physical Layer Aspects. Technical Report, 3GPP (2010)
6. Peters, S.W., Panah, A.Y., Truong, K.T., Heath Jr., R.W.: Relay Architectures for 3GPP LTE-Advanced. EURASIP Journal on Wireless Communications and Networking (2009)
7. Zheng, K., Fan, B., Ma, Z., Liu, G., Shen, X., Wang, W.: Multihop Cellular Networks Toward LTE-Advanced: Its Architecture and Performance. IEEE Vehicular Technology Magazine 4(3), 40–47 (2009)
8. Luo, H., Zhang, Z., Chen, Y., Wang, W., Li, S.: Opportunistic Cognitive Relaying: A Win-Win Spectrum Sharing Scheme. EURASIP Journal on Wireless Communications and Networking (2010)
9. Jovicic, A., Viswanath, P.: Cognitive Radio: An Information-Theoretic Perspective. IEEE Transactions on Information Theory 55(9), 3945–3958 (2009)
10. Xiaomao, M., Peiliang, Q.: Cognitive Relay. In: IEEE Conference on Future Generation Communication and Networking (FGCN), vol. 2, pp. 264–269 (2007)

11. Song, C., Shiba, H., Shimamoto, S.: A Cognitive Relay Approach for Multi-hop Wireless Ad Hoc Communication. In: Third International Conference on Communications and Networking, China, pp. 1230–1234 (2008)
12. Luo, H., Zhang, Z., Yu, G.: Cognitive Cooperative Relaying. In: 11th IEEE Singapore International Conference on Communication Systems, ICCS, pp. 1499–1503 (2008)
13. Laneman, J.N., Tse, D.N.C., Wornell, G.W.: Cooperative Diversity in Wireless Networks: Efficient Protocols and Outage Behavior. IEEE Transactions on Information Theory 50(12), 3062–3080 (2004)
14. Jia, J., Zhang, J., Zhang, Q.: Cooperative Relay for Cognitive Radio Networks, Rio de Janeiro (2009)
15. Zhang, Q., Jia, J., Zhang, J.: Cooperative Relay to Improve Diversity in Cognitive Radio Networks. IEEE Communications Magazine 47(2), 111–117 (2009)
16. Nam, Y.H., Liu, L., Wang, Y., Zhang, C., Cho, J., Han, J.: Cooperative Communication Technologies for LTE-Advanced. In: ICASSP, pp. 5610–5613 (2010)

Retracted: Communications in Computer and Information Science: A New Scalable Anonymous Authentication Protocol for RFID

Mohammad Shirafkan, Naser Modiri, Mohammad Mansour Riahi Kashani, and Koosha Sadeghi Oskooyee

Islamic Azad University, North Tehran branch,
Department of Computer Engineering, Tehran, Iran
{Mohammadshirafkan,Nasermodiri}@yahoo.com,
{M_Riahi_Kashani,K_Sadeghi_Oskooyee}@iau-tnb.ac.ir

Abstract. RFID tags are becoming more and more widespread, but their privacy issue has remained yet as a major concern. Due to resource limitations on these tags, providing the privacy is challenging while it is undoubtedly critical before their full deployment. A considerable number of protocols have been proposed, improved over the time and crypt analyzed to provide descent solutions to RFID privacy problem, each of which with strengths and weaknesses. This paper addresses privacy weaknesses of some of them and in the main part of this paper; we propose a scalable anonymous RFID authentication protocol and describe its design and implementation issues. Our protocol mainly substitutes the hash function used for identification with anonymous tickets, which uniquely identify tags and are reusable. As the result, it considerably strengthens untraceability feature and it needs just O(1) search time and query with small storage overhead on the back-end system.

Keywords: Authentication Protocol, RFID, Security, Hash function, Anonymous tickets.

1 Introduction

Radio Frequency Identification (RFID) is a radio wave technology to enable objects identification with no need for line-of-sight. The flexibility of this technology and its several important advantages, make it a promising replacement for barcodes to be deployed in novel applications, such as the use of RFID tags in market products, or to provide access control to physical locations/resources. RFID tags are embedded in many things, including credit cards, big bank notes, student cards etc, and have been embedding into every product realizing the internet of things [1].

In the paper, we introduce a privacy-friendly protocol which replaces the hash functions with anonymous tickets. Anonymous tickets uniquely identify a tag and are reused by tags if revoked by others. In this way, seeing the same ticket twice does not necessary mean that it belongs to the same tag and hence the untraceability is considerably strengthened comparing to the first group (related work). This protocol

A. Abd Manaf et al. (Eds.): ICIEIS 2011, Part III, CCIS 253, pp. 639–653, 2011.

is designed in a way that it requires a little storage and just a few queries in the back-end server/database, improving scalability, considerably in comparison to the second group (related work). Throughout the paper, we use the notations in Table 1 In addition, wherever a new symbol is required, we will also add and define in its place.

Table 1. Table of notation

Symbol	Explanation
||	Concatenation
Hash or *H( )*	One-way cryptographic hash function
XOR or ⊕	Exclusive OR operation
k or *sk*	Secret/shared key
ID	A tag's real identity
O( )	Algorithmic order, the so-called big-o notation
N	Total number of tags
δ	Level of anonymity

2 Related Work

A considerable number of protocols have been proposed to provide privacy for RFID systems and some of them been attacked [4]. In the following, we categorize related works in two general yet major groups, and point out to their weaknesses.

2.1 Group One

Protocols in this group normally use a *H(X)* in order to hide a real identity of a tag (*X* is different for every tag), and the value of *X* is the same as long as the entire (request-response) protocol is not executed. *X* for example can be an identity *ID* as depicted in Fig. 1(a), and having the table indexed with *H(ID)*, the system thus ends up with O(1) search complexity on the back-end server. For some of them including the work of Henrici and Muller [5], *X* is updated after successfully running of the whole protocol.

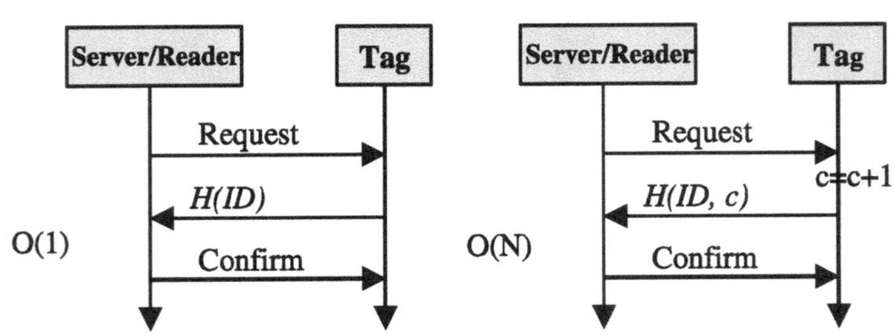

Fig. 1. Related works: (a) group one, (b) group two

At the moment we are not concerned with the value of X for the sake of generality as well as the burden on the back-end database. Here we show that all of these protocols suffer from a tracking problem.

Untraceability Attack. As depicted in Fig. 2, in such a protocol a tag responds with a $Y = H(X)$ in the first round to every request, no matter who is requesting as there is no server authentication in place. Therefore, if an attacker having a rogue reader just performs the first part of this protocol without going on to the next step, she will always receive the same value Y as long as X is not updated on the tag (or an attacker deliberately prevents it from updating).The main problem is that due to the collision resistance property of hash functions (as though it is infeasible to find two different tags with different Xs having the same Y), the attacker by seeing the same Y can infer that it is definitely the same tag, with high probability. The attacker does not know who is really this tag, but she at least knows a certain tag is appeared in which places before. So imagine an attacker has several readers scattered around in crowded locations and just requests present tags for the first response and nothing more. She can collect all the data in several places and then cross-check to see for example this tag was previously in this place and so on. If in an application updates rarely happen on RFID tags, the problem aggravates. Keeping in mind that for most applications people always tend to carry RFID enabled devices with themselves (e.g. a credit card), but occasionally they use their tags to get a service.

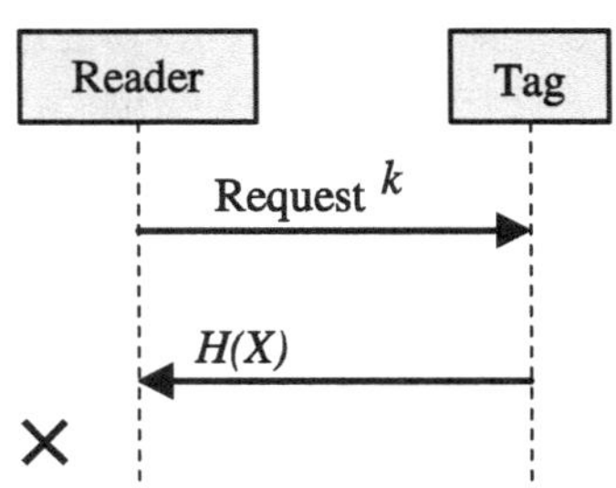

Fig. 2. Group one and its untraceability attack

2.2 Group Two

Papers in this group normally use a $H(X_n)$ in which X_n is changed whenever a reader (genuine or rogue) requests the tag, no matter the entire request-response protocol is run or not (e.g. [6]). X_n for example can be an identity ID alongside a counter c as depicted in Fig. 1(b), but since the back-end server has to exhaustively search for $H(ID,c)$ on its table, it typically ends up with O(N) search complexity.

A good and recent example of this group could be the work of Alomair et al. [7]. The authors claim that their work is the only protocol achieves high level of anonymity having constant time burden on the back-end database.

3 Requirements

Before we propose a new anonymous RFID authentication protocol, we should investigate on the necessary requirements for such an environment first. In what follows, we summarize the major requirements of such a protocol.

3.1 Privacy

Obviously a privacy-friendly RFID protocol should preserve the privacy as the name speaks for itself. Generally speaking, privacy is defined in terms of ability to infer ID relations from the messages exchanged in the protocol [2]. Remember that there is a database of *ID*s, and the goal is to hide them from an adversary. In other words, the definition can be divided into two subparts:

1. Anonymity: *ID* of tags cannot be inferred from the messages.
2. Untraceability: messages of two tags cannot be linked, implying that they represent the same tag.

In the following we bring different privacy-related properties required for RFID privacy-friendly protocols. Note the definition of forward and backward untraceability in particular, as different definitions (and even opposite) exist.

Tag Anonymity. An RFID system is said to be anonymous, if the real identity of a tag, *ID*, cannot be inferred from the exchanged messages in the protocol.

Tag Untraceability. Sometimes the identity *ID* of a tag may not be inferred from the exchange messages, but still two identities of the same tag in different protocol runs can be linked to each other. In this way the corresponding tag is tracked down and traced by an adversary.

Backward Untraceability. RFID tags are not tamper resistant and thus can be physically corrupted and the secret data (such as the secret key or identity) can be simply obtained. Therefore, another important requirement here is that even in this case, the privacy of past events made by the corrupted tag is still preserved.

Forward Untraceability. Forward untraceability requires that knowledge of a tag's current state should not help identify the tag's future/forward interactions.

3.2 Security Requirements

Alongside the mentioned privacy properties, an RFID protocol should undoubtedly preserve some other security features as well. These features include mutual authentication between every tag and the back-end server and resistance against some attacks.

Mutual Authentication. An RFID protocol is said to provide mutual authentication if and only if both of the tag authentication and server (or reader) authentication are successfully achieved.

Denial of Service. In denial of service attacks, an adversary typically tries to consume resources of the server, preventing legitimate tags from accessing them, or tries to corrupt messages sent by tags, making the server busy and the like.

Password Guessing Resilience. The term is also used for the secret guessing, where an adversary attempts to guess the shared secret key between a tag and the server, and verify her guesses by means of the exchange messages in an off-line manner.

3.3 Performance

The back-end server should handle tremendous amount of requests from RFID tags. Therefore, a designed protocol, in addition to the mentioned security and privacy guarantees, should also be efficient from a performance perspective. It is not just the matter of the back-end server; the tag side too should have a good performance, considering all its memory and computational limits.

Tag Side. On the tag side, we struggle with limited memory and computational power.

Scalability of the Back-end Server. As mentioned, at the back-end server the issue of performance and efficiency is even more critical. The term scalability is also applied here. Scalability in this context means that the system be able to cope with and handle the growing number of RFID tags in a graceful manner.

Communication. Communication cost between a tag and a reader consists of 1- the number of message exchanges, and 2- The total bit size of the transmitted messages, per each communication.

Unique Identification. Uniquely identifying a tag by a server is also an important issue that may encounter serious performance and security problems.

4 Our Protocol

In this section we describe our proposal for a constant time privacy-friendly RFID protocol.

4.1 Assumption

We have RFID tags, readers and a back-end server/database, and assume that there is a secret key shared between each tag and the server, and hence there is initially a table of tuples *(ID, k)* (*ID* is a tag's identity and k the shared key) at the database. At the tag side we keep *ID* and *k* too. Our main goal is to hide *ID* from an attacker in order to stipulate anonymity. Alongside the tuple *(ID,k)*, we add T_b as a randomly assigned ticket and n as a counter starting from 0. Similar changes should be made on the database side that it will come later.

We reserve two tickets for every tag for synchronization purposes, and the realization of these tickets could be simply numbers from 1 to $2N+\delta$, given N the number of all tags and δ the level of anonymity we demand (the bigger the value, the stronger the anonymity).

Adversary. Two types of adversaries are considered:

- Type1: this type is a typical Dolev-Yao intruder [10], which we assume that she can eavesdrop on the radio link between a tag and a reader, can modify messages, can add messages of her own and is able to block some messages from a tag to reader or vice versa.

- Type2: this type is a stronger adversary having all the capabilities mentioned for the first type, and additionally she is able to corrupt a tag and acquire its secret data.

We assume several readers in the system, which is more realistic, and the adversary has control on subset of them not all of them. Having a secure channel between readers and the server is also a common assumption; therefore an adversary cannot do anything on that link. Also we assume that the adversary does not know initially which tickets are assigned to which tags. Moreover similar to the related works, distinction by a physical layer behavior of RFID tags is out of the scope of this work and thus not discussed here.

4.2 Protocol Steps

This section is devoted to presenting the protocol steps. Here, we aim to hide the identity even from a reader which gives us a stronger privacy (i.e. end to end privacy between a tag and the back-end server). As discussed before, we shall also consider a tag impersonation/corruption attack as RFID tags are not tamper resistant. Respective to what depicted in Fig. 3, the protocol steps are:

1. The reader interrogates the tag with a random challenge r_1.
2. The tag first increments the internal counter n, and calculates $r_2=H(k||n)$ and $r_3=H(k||T_b||r_1||r_2)$. H is a public one-way hash function and k means concatenation. It eventually sends the anonymous ticket T_b (instead of *ID*) along with r_2 and r_3. The term r_2 mainly acts as a random number and r_3 mainly as a tag authenticator for the server.
3. The reader then forwards the message as well as the random challenge r_1 to the back-end server via a secure channel.
4. Using T_b the server is able to obtain the corresponding record of this tag, i.e. *ID*, and k. (The details of this database procedure will be explained soon.) Using k and the received r_1 and r_2, the server is able to verify $r_3=H(k||T_b||r_1||r_2)$ and so authenticate the tag. The server randomly chooses a new ticket from available/free ones, say T_c, and further generates a session key $H(k||T_b||r_3)$ for encryption.
5. For our encryption we use a simple XOR ($\oplus$) operation. The server encrypts the new anonymous ticket T_c with $H(k||T_b||r_3)$: i.e. $T_c \oplus H(k||T_b||r_3)$. It sends the encrypted ticket along with $H(k||r_3||T_c)$ (for integrity checking) to the reader. The server updates two records belonging to this tag, for the one next to T_c it stores incremented n and $H(k)$ instead of k. The reader subsequently forwards it to the corresponding tag.
6. The tag takes the r_3 and its k to compute $H(k||T_b||r_3)$, the so-called session key. Using this session key, it can de-cipher the received $T_c \oplus H(k||T_b||r_3)$ and hence obtain T_c.
7. After successfully acquiring the new ticket, the tag invokes hash operation on the key and substitutes it as the new key (i.e. $k \Leftarrow H(k)$) in order to empower the scheme with the backward untraceability property. (At the server side, the same changes would have happened.)

8. Finally it updates its tickets to T_c, besides having new values for k and n. Just to emphasize it more, next time this tag is going to reply with T_c in the above protocol.

Usage of n

The use of n in this protocol for both sides is three-fold:

1. to have different hash outputs every time on the tag side,
2. to impart for the server a notion of time so that it can detect this ticket is newer or older than the other ticket of this tag (by checking the value of n next to each anonymous ticket), and
3. To customize this protocol in a case that in an application, if executing the ticket assigning procedure every time be costly for the server side. We can set an upper bound η on n, and as long as $n \bmod \eta \neq 0$ the server does not invoke that procedure (so to say every η times it is executed in a triggered fashion).

Moreover, optionally using the stored n, the server can also validate $r_2 = H(k \,||\, n)$ to make sure that the tag was not probably under attack attempt by a rogue reader. If it is not validated, the server in free times can go and check it for values bigger than the current n until a correct one is found. This mechanism gives the server a rough number of attack attempts which from organizational point of view it is a useful knowledge.

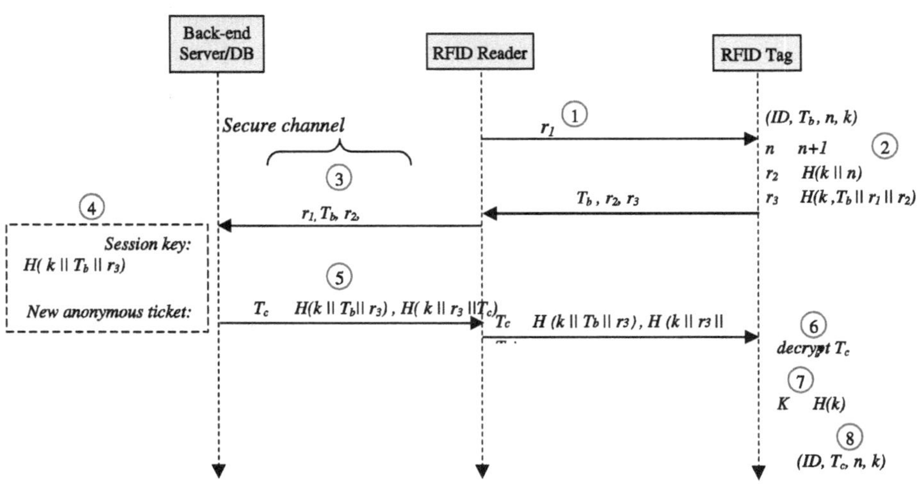

Fig. 3. Protocol steps

4.3 Database Operations

We concentrate here on the back-end database to show how we achieve constant time identification while preserving anonymity. In order to handle requests from tags in the database, we maintain a table and one pool.

Tickets Table. As we assumed, a table of identities already exists in RFID systems to find out the shared key k given an identity ID. We only adjust it and hence rename it for our purpose (see Fig. 4):

- Ticket is now the primary index of this table and can give us back at least *ID* and *k*. By each of a tag's tickets we can thus retrieve the real identity and the shared key in O(1), the fastest possible time in database context.
- The table has a column "ref." (Stands for reference), which corresponds a ticket of one tag to its previous ticket/record and vice versa. The ticket column is the primary key, so the table gives out *ID* if we provide one of the tickets T_a or T_b, in O(1) too.
- Num also represents how many tickets are assigned to a tag so far. (In other words, the value of tag's n from the server's point of view.)

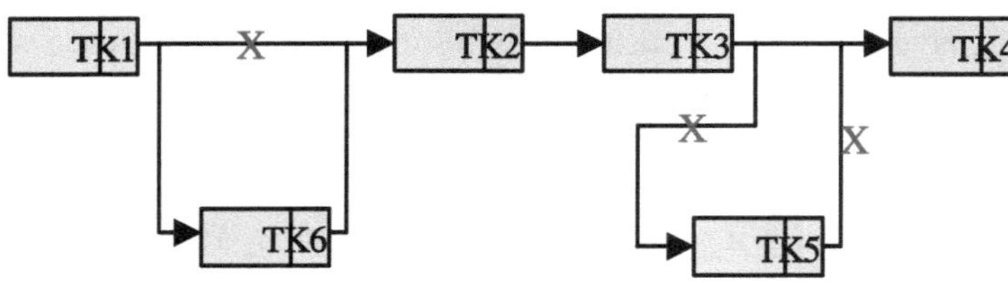

Fig. 4. Linked list for a free ticket pool: (a) inserting TK6, (b) removing TK5

Free Tickets Pool. Free tickets pool contains those tickets not assigned to any tag (in total of size δ). It can be implemented using a simple table of free tickets or a link list that is efficiently permutable (by easily adding or removing tickets, see Fig. 5), in order to randomize the assignment.

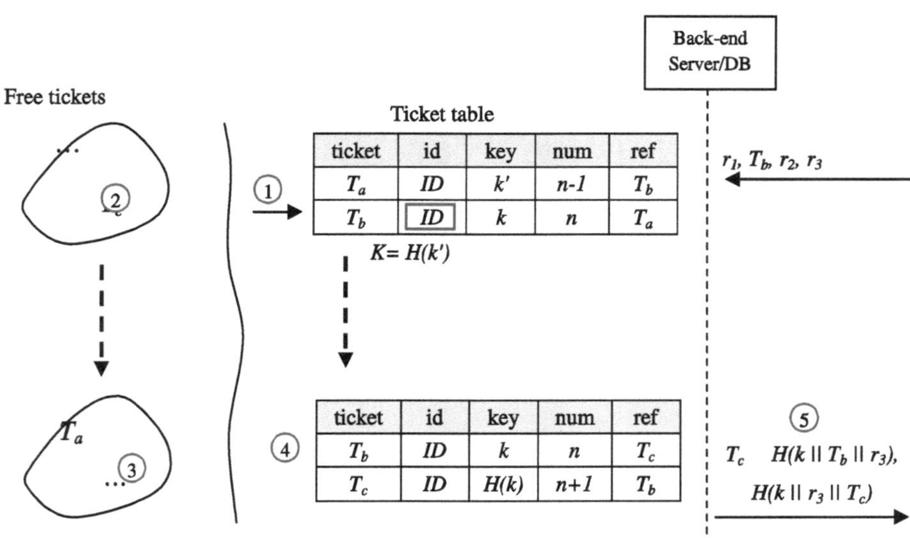

Fig. 5. Steps at the back-end database side

Procedure. In the initialization phase, the server fills the Ticket table with two randomly assigned tickets to every tag (e.g. T_a and T_b in Fig. 5) while setting the other fields correctly (e.g. num is 0 for the first ticket). Therefore, in the very first run a tag responds with T_a and the server could immediately send back T_b in the encrypted format (as explained before) with no further operation, as though we already have T_b reserved for this tag. For the other runs, steps are (in respect to steps illustrated in Fig. 5):

1. Using T_b on the *Ticket table*, the server is able to quickly obtain the corresponding *ID*, *k* and previous ticket T_a by a single lookup query. By Checking the row belongs to T_a (another query) the server can ensure that T_b is the recent ticket by comparing the value of num fields (the bigger the value, the newer the ticket). By *k* and T_b, the server validates correctness of the received values.
2. The server randomly chooses a new ticket from the free tickets, let say T_c. This random selecting operation is important as it removes any link between the current ticket T_b and the new ticket T_c. We assume that a strong random number generator is available at the server as this side is not limited.
3. T_a is released and returned back to the Free Tickets pool.
4. The server updates the Ticket table accordingly: T_a is updated to the new anonymous ticket T_c (as primary index), num field is incremented by one, and the ref: columns of T_b and T_c are pointed to each other. More importantly, the key *k* becomes $H(k)$ in the new row.
5. As mentioned before, the server finally generates a session key $H(k||T_b||r_3)$ and returns back T_c in encrypted format alongside a $H(k||r_3||T_c)$ for integrity checking.

Another important feature to notice is that every time a new/free ticket (from *free tickets* pool) is removed, another one is added to the free tickets (in the example above, T_c and T_a respectively). Therefore no ticket is assigned to two different tags and the unique identification is preserved.

4.4 De-synchronization Resilience

We keep two rows for every tag in the back-end database in the case that the server's response (i.e. carrying the new ticket T_c) does not reach the requested tag, due to noise, denial-of-service attacks, etc. In this situation, the server expects that next ticket from this tag will be T_c but the tag will start over by sending T_b. After receiving such a request with T_b, the server obtains the corresponding ticket T_c (using ref: field in the Ticket table) and by checking the value of num field could realize that in fact the tag has not received its new ticket previously. So, without going through the new ticket assigning procedure, just the same as before returns back T_c with no update on the Ticket table. So in this way, this protocol handles de-synchronization attempts, with no extra queries.

4.5 Unique Identification

In our scheme we guarantee the unique identification by putting one entity (i.e. the server) in charge of ticket assignment and sending an anonymous unique ticket for identification.

In the server side, we leverage a well-design database having at least two tables to guarantee this issue:

- Initially we have a series of unique tickets in the system.
- We keep the assigned tickets in Ticket table and non-assigned tickets in free tickets pool to easily manage both of them.
- Then whenever the server updates a tag's identity, it releases one assigned ticket to, and subsequently retrieves one from the free tickets pool.

Therefore in this way, we guarantee no ticket is assigned to two different tags at the same time, thus the unique identification is preserved (inductively).

4.6 Password Guessing Resilience

Password or key guessing attack is also an important issue in RFID systems, although it is overlooked by many of related works in the field. The main reason is due to the fact that we can enlarge the key space to considerably big values depending on the available memory on the tags. In practice, something around 128-bit key likely gives enough security in this respect [11], and reduces the possibility of launching a key guessing attack. If we assume that due to memory limitations and the like, the number of bits is not sufficient anyhow, a protocol should provide resistance against password guessing, as this attack may be easily plausible, especially because of using light weight operations. These light weight operations make an adversary's attack job way easier.

Altogether, the password guessing is not a major strong attack but still it is worthwhile considering it in a designed protocol. In the following, we give a solution to resist password guessing in our protocol. Beside this attack, in the next section we will argue that this simple solution will enhance the protocol yielding another nice property, the forward untraceability.

A Potential Weakness. On the tag side of our protocol, we keep a secret key k and feed it inside of hash function to encrypt or stipulate integrity. A possible drawback from the password guessing perspective is that, in the last server's response, the two messages $H(k||r_3||T_c)$ and $T_c \oplus H(k||T_b||r_3)$ can give the adversary a way to verify her guess on the value of k. In other words, the adversary having these values is able to launch a brute force attack (in an off-line manner) by:

1. picking different values for k as k',
2. feeding her guess k' into a hash and calculating $Y = H(k'||T_b||r_3)$ (note that the values T_b and r_3 are given from the first transmitted response),
3. XORing the Y with the $Tc \oplus H(k||T_b||r_3)$, obtaining a T'_c,
4. And finally verifying by comparing the value of $H(k'||r_3||T'_c)$ with the $H(k||r_3||T_c)$.

If the final values are equivalent, therefore $k = k'$ and the secret key is compromised. As the result, the adversary is able to act like a genuine tag in the rest of the protocol running due to knowing the secret key.

Solution. In order to withstand this drawback (apart from implausibility of such an attack due to a big enough key space), we can slightly modify our protocol this way:

- We divide the secret key k into two sub-keys or would be better to add another secret key to both sides, let say k'. Therefore in the tag as well as the server side, alongside the secret key k we also store k'.
- The rest of the protocol is just as explained before, except the last phase of updating the secret key for the purpose of backward untraceability.
- For updating, instead of updating k to $H(k)$, we update it to $H(k||k')$: i.e. $k \Leftarrow H(k||k')$.

This update is performed in both the tag and the server, just as before. As the result, we hide a part of the overall secret key as k' and do not use it in the exchanged messages. In this way, we incapacitate the adversary of verifying her guess for k, if she solely Works on the transmitted data (and not using her corruption capability).

4.7 Forward Untraceability

Surprisingly, the solution given for the password guessing resilience also yields another yet more important property of the forward untraceability. Again, the forward untraceability is defined as: knowledge of a tag's current state/secret should not help identify the tag's future/forward interactions. In the previous solution, we use two secret keys k and k': k is used in every hash operation, but k' is never used in the exchanged messages. In the update phase however k becomes $H(k||k')$. So assume that an adversary without corruption capability, somehow acquired the secret key k (probably by guessing), but she does not have the k'. Not having the second key, she does not know accordingly the new secret key, due to being updated to $H(k||k')$. Therefore she is not able to use her obtained key to compromise further in the future interactions.

5 Performance Analysis

This section is devoted to performance analysis of the proposed protocol on the tag side, and the back-end server side (as well as its database).

Selected Works. To compare, we select two recent candidate protocols: Henrici and Muller [5] (from the group one, it has a replay attack problem though [12]) and the recent work by Alomair et al. [7] assuming big value for the counter C (from the group two). One common thing with these two and ours is that all claim to provide privacy imposing just a constant time on the back-end database. Actually all of protocols from both discussed groups lie in the category of hash-based RFID protocols, for a performance (and security) analysis of such protocols.

5.1 Tag Side

Tag side of an RFID system should be fast enough to give the readers freedom of working with multiple tags in parallel. In the following we study computation, memory and communication costs of the selected protocols plus ours.

Computation. In our protocol, a tag performs (totally):

- five hash operations,
- one XOR operation, and
- One addition (incrementing n).

The other two schemes impose these burdens: Henrici and Muller [5] with 3 hash operations; Alomair et al. [7] with 6 hashes, 1 XOR, and 1 addition.

Memory. The amount of memory a tag should store is also another important issue in RFID systems, with strict memory limitations. In our protocol, a tag should keep 3 items (plus ID which is not necessary):

1. Secret key k
2. An anonymous ticket like T_b
3. An internal counter n

The other two related works also keep the same number of items on the tag side. The amount of bits for every item could be also similar. Apparently, this amount of memory is completely suitable even for inexpensive tags, as many protocols in the group use up roughly similar amount of memory.

5.2 Communication Overhead

The number of message exchanges between a tag and a reader (including the server) incurs an overhead on the whole system; the smaller this value is, the better the performance would be. Therefore, in a protocol design should be also considered, as it contributes some costs on the performance of the whole system. Using a 3-way protocol is actually a common approach in RFID systems: 1-it starts with an interrogation from a reader, 2-then with a reply from the tag, 3-and finally a confirmation from the reader (server) mostly for synchronization purposes.

Our protocol, as we have seen earlier, follows the same approach ending up with 3 exchanged messages. In Alomair et al. [7] also the authors use 3 communications, however in contrary to ours they put majority of the tasks including the hash calculations on the reader. On the other hand, Henrici and Muller's protocol [5] normally is performed in 2 communications, but in the case of a "triggered hash chain" [5], it also ends up with 3 exchanges as the others.

5.3 Back-end Server Side

The back-end server side plays a big role in performance, since it may receive a huge number of requests by RFID tags. In the following, generally speaking we deal with computation and memory of this side of the RFID system.

Computation. We can analyze this side separately: the reader and the back-end server. On the reader side, it should generate a random number and subsequently interrogate a tag with it. And on the back back-end server side, it should perform four hash operations, one XOR operation, one random selection, two update queries on tables all on primary keys per each request.

Altogether, we could say for some low cost operations such as random generations, hash or XOR operation are not that much cost for most of the ordinary servers. Henrici and Muller's protocol computes as much as the tag side in their protocol, and puts no load on the reader (actually they assume both the reader and the back-end server as one single entity). On the other hand, in Alomair et al., the authors put the reader in charge of most of the operations and the back-end server just on the database queries: the reader should perform one random number generation, 4 hash operations, and 1 XOR; the back-end server should perform 1 hash and some database queries.

Database Queries. The amount of database query for every request is considered here. In our protocol, all of the database operations are being run on primary keys of tables (so to speak, the fastest possible in database context). Moreover, for every tag request, the back-end server just needs to run two queries. On the other hand, the mentioned schemes have a constant query burden on the back-end database, however there is a considerable difference between the amount of database queries needed to be executed in Alomair et al.'s and the rest: It is constant in big-o notation but definitely a lot more costlier than the other two schemes in reality, as the big-o does not reflect well the practical issues.

Alomair et al.'s scheme performs roughly $2C$ update queries (if de-synchronization resilience is supported too), and assuming $C = 1000$ (as the authors' example), it means 2000 database queries per each request, while in our scheme we just need at most two update queries. Henrici and Muller's protocol also executes two queries per each request.

Storage. From the storage point of view, Alomair et al.'s scheme considerably differs from the other two schemes. That is however because, as the authors of this paper also state, they want to tradeoff database storage for the sake of stronger untraceability. They maintain three tables (M-I, M-II and M-III) each of which approximately needs $N \times C$ (N number of pseudonyms/tags and C the maximum counter). Considering the fact that we have to double this space for synchronization purposes, it eventually eats up in the magnitude of 40 terabytes (following the author's example with 10^9 tags in the system), although Avoine et al. [9] proposes a way to save up almost one-third of it. Requiring this huge amount of storage might seem feasible but not very practical [9]. But in our scheme, considering the fact that we already have a database of identity and keys (this one also assumed by Alomair et al.), we need just to add three columns to the Ticket table and double the number of rows. With the same example of 10^9 tags, our scheme adds roughly 4×10^9 bytes which is way less than one terabyte (i.e. 0:004 terabytes). Proposed protocol of Henrici and Muller [5] consumes almost the same amount of storage as ours.

Unique Identification. Additionally, as mentioned, uniquely identifying a tag by a back-end server is also an important performance issue. As discussed by the other two related papers [7, 13] unique identification is not guaranteed and may cause problems for them as they use the output of hash functions for identification. At least, one non-unique identification enforces the server to run extra checking to make sure that it is the right tag, and thus imposes performance inefficiency.

In our scheme however we guarantee the uniqueness by putting the server in charge of ticket/identity assignment and sending an anonymous unique ticket for identification. The server leverages a well-designed database system to deal with the issue: Briefly it has a ticket table to keep all of the assigned ones and a so-called pool to keep all of the free tickets.

Summary. Fig. 6 brings an intuitive comparison among the selected works, just to give an impression about two major requirements: untraceability and scalability.

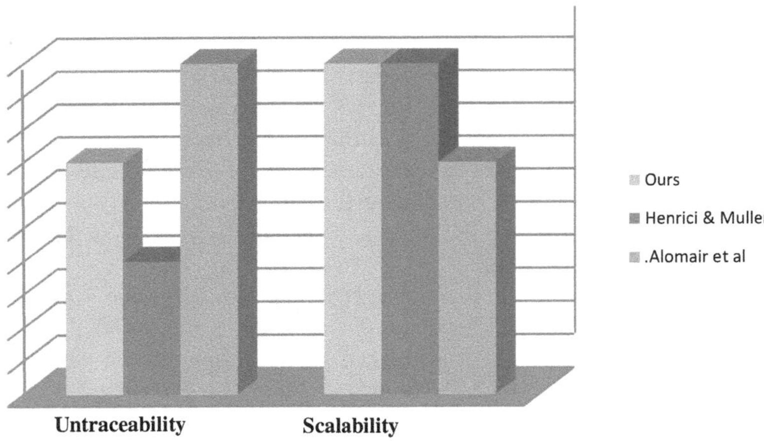

Fig. 6. An intuitive comparison of the selected works

6 Conclusion

We pointed out that some of the existing privacy-friendly RFID protocols suffer from a traceability problem, as a tag outputs the result of a collision resistance hash function as a means of anonymous identification. The distinct and constant value of hash output can differentiate this tag from others as long as update on input values does not occur.

In other words, the collision resistance property conveys that whenever or wherever the same value is observed, it definitely belongs to the same tag. Also we argued that if we accept a small collision in the hash outputs, they still suffer from a unique identification problem. All together, it may be better to revise the use of hash functions for the purpose of anonymous identifications: either they harm untraceability (if we assume perfect collision resistance) or they harm unique identification (if they are not that collision resistant).

In order to strengthen untraceability, we introduced anonymous tickets in place of using hash functions. We showed that these tickets can uniquely identify a tag and since the server reuses and assigns them randomly to other tags, an adversary cannot be sure it is the same tag by observing the same ticket.

For handling these tickets efficiently at the back-end database side, we employed one free tickets pool to store all free/non-allocated tickets, and we extended one existing ticket table by adding anonymous tickets columns to it. This solution imposes a little storage overhead and just a few queries on the primary index in the back-end server/database, which is fast and cheap.

Finally we analyzed the proposed protocol from a performance perspective, the burden on each tag and the back-end database. We showed that our protocol outperforms the group one of the related works in particular in untraceability, and outperforms the group two in efficiency and scalability issues.

References

1. MIT Auto-ID Center, `http://www.autoidcenter.org` (Online; accessed January 24, 2011)
2. Vaudenay, S.: On Privacy Models for RFID. In: Kurosawa, K. (ed.) ASIACRYPT 2007. LNCS, vol. 4833, pp. 68–87. Springer, Heidelberg (2007)
3. Lim, C., Kwon, T.: Strong and robust RFID authentication enabling perfect ownership transfer. Information and Communications Security, 1–20 (2006)
4. Van Deursen, T. and Radomirovic, S.: Attacks on RFID protocols, IACR eprint archive 2008,310 (2008)
5. Henrici, D., Muller, P.: Providing security and privacy in RFID systems using triggered hash chains. In: Sixth Annual IEEE International Conference on Pervasive Computing and Communications, pp. 50–59. IEEE (2008)
6. Weis, S., Sarma, S., Rivest, R., Engels, D.: Security and privacy aspects of low-cost radio frequency identification systems. In: Security in Pervasive Computing, pp. 50–59 (2004)
7. Alomair, B., Clark, A., Cuellar, J., Poovendran, R.: Scalable RFID systems: a privacy-preserving protocol with constant-time identification. In: 2010 IEEE/IFIP International Conference on Dependable Systems and Networks (DSN), pp. 1–10. IEEE (2010)
8. Zanetti, D., Danev, B.: Physical-layer identification of UHF RFID tags. In: Proceedings of the Sixteenth Annual International Conference on Mobile Computing and Networking, pp. 353–364. ACM (2010)
9. Avoine, G., Coisel, I., Martin, T.: Time Measurement Threatens Privacy-Friendly RFID Authentication Protocols. In: Workshop on RFID Security (2010)
10. Dolev, D., Yao, A.: On the security of public key protocols. IEEE Transactions on Information Theory 29(2), 198–208 (2002)
11. Tsudik, G.: Ya-trap: Yet another trivial RFID authentication protocol. In: PerCom Workshops, pp. 640–643 (2006)
12. Lim, T.-L., Li, T., Li, Y.: A Security and Performance Evaluation of Hash-Based RFID Protocols. In: Yung, M., Liu, P., Lin, D. (eds.) Inscrypt 2008. LNCS, vol. 5487, pp. 406–424. Springer, Heidelberg (2009)
13. Henrici, D.: RFID Security and Privacy. Lecture Notes in Electrical Engineering. Springer, Heidelberg (2008)

Inter-cell Interference Mitigation and Coordination in CoMP Systems

Norshidah Katiran, Norsheila Fisal, Sharifah Kamilah Syed Yusof, Siti Marwangi Mohamad Maharum, Aimi Syamimi Ab Ghafar, and Faiz Asraf Saparudin

UTM-MIMOS CoE Telecommunication Technology, Universiti Teknologi Malaysia, 81310 Skudai, Johor, Malaysia
norshida@uthm.edu.my, {sheila,kamilah}@fke.utm.my, smarwangi@yahoo.com, {aimisyamimi,faiz.asraf}@gmail.com

Abstract. Coordinated Multi-Point (CoMP) transmission and reception is seen as a promising technology to achieve higher spectral efficiency in LTE-Advanced systems. Base stations cooperation can be one of the most important enabling technologies beneficial in scenarios with high inter-cell interference (ICI). In this paper, interference mitigation and coordination schemes in CoMP are being discussed. Simulation study to show the significant effect of ICI to cell-edge performance is presented. In this work, we proposed an interference cancellation scheme with minimal backhaul requirements in addition to existing inter-cell interference coordination (ICIC) schemes.

Keywords: CoMP, ICI, eNB, coordination.

1 Introduction

The goal of LTE-Advanced (LTE-A) standard is to further enhance system data rates and spectral efficiency while supporting backward compatibility with LTE Release 8. As part of LTE-A standard development, several enhancements including support for up to 100 MHz bandwidth and higher- order MIMO are being investigated to meet the IMT-advanced requirements [1].

An important requirement for the LTE-A system is to improve cell-edge performance and throughput. Unlike the other cellular system (e.g., CDMA) which has robust interference capability, OFDM-based cellular system (e.g., WiMAX, LTE, LTE-A) suffers from ICI at the cell boundary, especially when all frequency channels are fully reused [2]. Therefore, some means of mitigating the ICI is required to support a full frequency-reuse operation. This problem has attracted much attention and some strategies have been proposed in order to improve cell edge performance.

Recently, cooperative communications (e.g., base stations, relays) have been studied extensively to exploit diversity in order to achieve better network performance [2-4]. As for LTE-A systems, Coordinated Multi-Point transmission and reception (CoMP) has been proposed as one of the key technology to enhance cell average and cell edge throughput. CoMP refers to a system where the transmission and/or

A. Abd Manaf et al. (Eds.): ICIEIS 2011, Part III, CCIS 253, pp. 654–665, 2011.

reception at multiple, geographically separated antenna sites is dynamically coordinated in order to improve system performance.

There are two types of coordination strategy in CoMP: Joint Processing (JP) and Coordinated Scheduling/ Beamforming (CS/CB). In the first strategy, data to a single user end (UE) is simultaneously transmitted from multiple transmission points [3]. This strategy puts higher requirements on the coordination links and the backhaul since user data need to be made available at multiple coordinated transmission points. The amount of data to be exchanged over the coordination links is also large. By contrast, in coordinated scheduling (CS) scheme, a resource block (RB) is transmitted only from the serving cell [3]. An RB is assigned to the UE by scheduling of the serving cell. Scheduling/ beamforming is coordinated among multiple coordinated cells where the transmit beamforming weights are generated to reduce unnecessary interference to other UE scheduled within the coordinated cells.

The rest of the paper is organized as follows: Section 2 discusses related work on ICI mitigation schemes in CoMP. Section 3 presents ICI problem formulation. Section 4 shows simulation result for ICI problem mentioned in Section 3. We proposed our ICIC strategy in Section 5. Finally, the conclusion and recommendations for future work are drawn in Section 6.

2 Related Work

The goal of the ICIC scheme is to apply certain restrictions (e.g., transmit power, RB) on the resources used in different cells in a coordinated way. Such restrictions in a cell provide the possibility for improvement in SNR, and cell-edge data rates on the corresponding time-frequency resources in a neighbor cell [4]. The ICI coordination requires certain inter-eNB communication in order to configure the scheduler restrictions. From literature, we identified some ICIC schemes recently used to mitigate ICI in CoMP systems [5-17] and here we classified these schemes into three main categories.

2.1 Interference Avoiding Schemes

Interference avoidance technique focuses on finding an optimal effective frequency reuse factor. It is often achieved through restrictions on frequency and power allocations to fulfill network performance goal. When frequency reuse factor, K=1 as in Fig. 1a), the entire bandwidth available for transmission is used in all sectors or cells [5]. In this case, the UEs near the cell-center will experience high signal-to-interference noise ratio (SINR) due to large path loss from adjacent cells. On the other hand, the UEs at the cell boundary will suffer from a small SINR (signal-to-interference plus noise ratio), which may increase an outage rate at the cell boundary. In order to improve the SINR throughout the cell coverage area while reducing the outage rate at the cell boundary, the whole bandwidth can be divided into three channels (Fig. 1b)). Each channel is allocated to adjacent cells in an orthogonal manner. It corresponds to K=3 and reduces the usable bandwidth for each cell. However, the UEs at the cell boundary will experience improved SINR, reducing ICI.

A fractional frequency reuse (FFR) scheme is based on the concept of reuse partitioning. In reuse partitioning, the UEs with the highest signal quality use a lower reuse factor while UEs with low SINR use a higher reuse factor. The FFR scheme, for example uses frequency reuse of one for cell-center UEs while a reuse of three is used for the cell-edge UEs as shown in Fig. 1d) [5]. In FFR schemes, the frequency resources for cell-edge UEs in the neighboring cells are left empty in a given cell. By contrast, all the frequency resources can be used in all the cells in soft frequency reuse (SFR) schemes (Fig. 1c)). The frequency resource used for cell-center UEs in a cell is used for cell-edge UEs in neighboring cells. Although static interference schemes such as FFR and SFR achieve improved throughput [5]-[8], they may suffer seriously in terms of sector or cell throughput. An optimal partitioning approach needs to consider the distribution of the UEs, traffic arrival and channel dynamism. Therefore, any static reuse partitioning scheme always results in suboptimal solution.

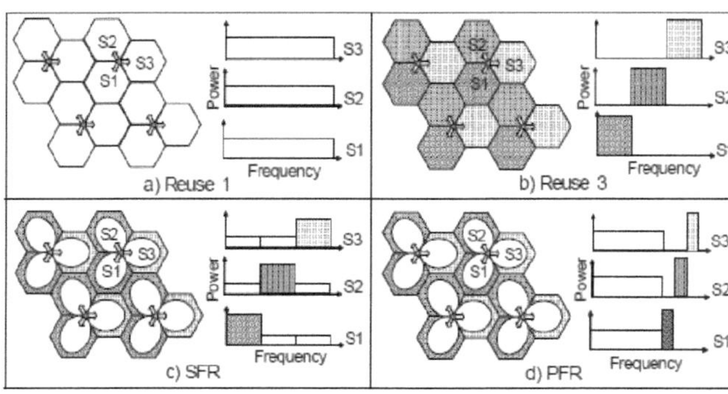

Fig. 1. Some static interference avoidance schemes [5]

For LTE downlink, an interference avoidance scheme that uses dynamic ICIC facilitated through X2 interfaces among neighboring eNBs has been evaluated for LTE downlink [9]. A UE restricts I inter-eNB most dominant interferers and then determines the achievable rates on physical resource block (PRB), n. A pair of sectors will have restrictions for the same PRB in some cases (e.g., when ICI received at particular sector/cell is unacceptable). In this case, the corresponding eNB communicates with the neighboring eNBs using X2 interfaces about restricting the PRB. Then, the corresponding eNB will decide either the restricted PRB are unused or used with lower power. [10] considered the objective of network-wide proportional fairness (PF) through load balancing where under-loaded cells avoid using the same RBs as used by cell-edge UEs in neighboring over-loaded cells. Thus, ICI imposed on them can be reduced and further increase the capacity of over-loaded cells.

In another approach, [11] presented a decentralized ICIC scheme in order to mitigate ICI and enhance the capacity of the users found near the cell-edge area of a wireless multi-cell OFDMA system. The scheme aims at maximizing the throughput of the cell-edge users which experience the most severe form of ICI with a minimal coordination between eNBs. The algorithm tries to find the subchannel that is less reused by neighboring eNBs and then finds the pair of cell-edge user and subchannel that yields the higher channel gain. Then, it allocates equal amount of power to all users of the cell-edge group. Each cell solves its own problem with a minimal coordination via information exchange through X2 interface.

2.2 Coordinated Scheduling/Beamforming (CS/CB)

In CB/CS coordination strategy, it is not necessary to share the UE's data across multiple eNBs. To achieve the coordination, the UE needs to feed back information about the CSIs of the serving cell and the other cells in the CoMP set. [12] presented coordinated scheduling method based on FFR and multi-cell precoding matrix index PMI coordination in CoMP system (Fig. 2). To support PMI coordination, the cell-edge UE is required to feedback information that includes the preferred PMI indices for each frequency sub-band to its serving cell. Also, it recommends or restricts precoding index for neighboring cells. Through multi-cell coordination, the neighboring cell is requested to either use the recommended precoder or not to use the restricted precoder. PMI recommendation is more effective than PMI restriction in suppressing the interference. In order to avoid excessive feedback overhead, the PMI information can be limited to one or two strongly interfering cells.

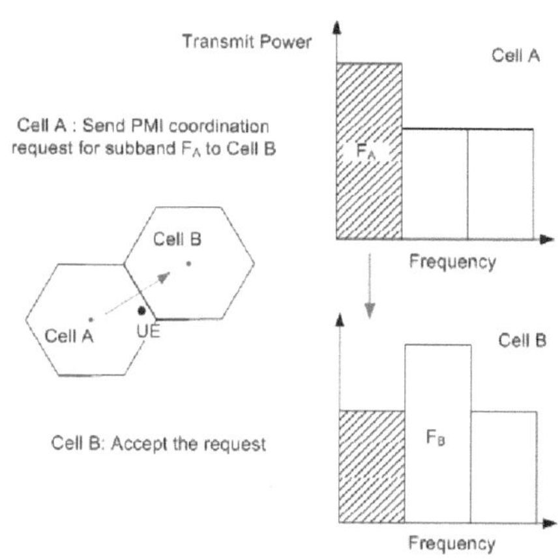

Fig. 2. Inter-eNB signaling for PMI coordination [12]

By comparison, [13] proposed a CB scheme with explicit feedback which denotes full CSI and designed the precoding vector through exploitation of the signal leakage information to other cells to reduce ICI. To mitigate ICI in CoMP based on CS/CB, [14] used a downlink transmit beamforming with nulling under partial channel state information (CSI) and no data sharing condition for cell-edge users with low mobility. By considering all possible interfering channel direction to UEs in adjacent cell, both inter-user interference (IUI) and ICI can be canceled perfectly. However, this strategy induces a trade-off between mitigating interference for cell-edge users and maximizing the total throughput.

2.3 High Interference Indicator (HII) and Overload Indicator (OI) Mechanisms

The LTE system defines a load indication procedure for uplink ICIC. This mechanism is used to send an interference overload indication when an eNB experiences too high interference on some resource blocks. The eNB experiencing excessive interference initiates the procedure by sending an uplink interference overload indication (OI) message to intra-frequency neighboring eNBs. The information exchanged consists of high interference, medium interference or low interference indication for each PRB. On the other hand, HII is in general a proactive operation, aiming at preventing the occurrence of ICI. The serving cell informs the neighboring cells of which resources will be used by its edge users. Then neighboring cells control the allocation of resources, such as lowering the power or resources re-allocation. While work in [15] and [16] employed OI and HII separately which will incur inevitable shortcomings, [17] used an OI and HII hybrid scheme that can enhance system performance and reduce backhaul signaling.

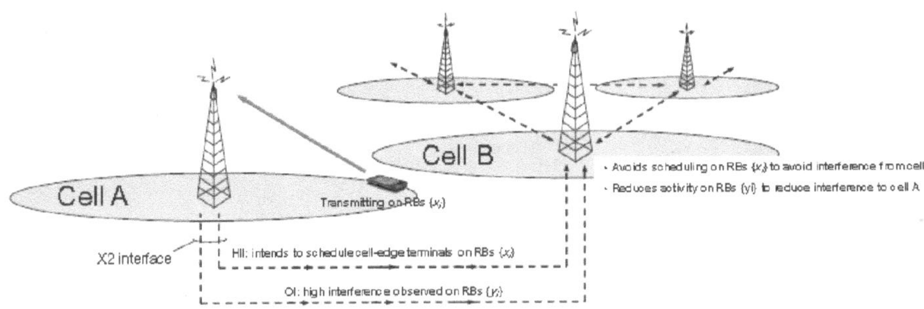

Fig. 3. ICIC based on HII and OI X2 signaling [18]

3 System Model

3.1 ICI Problem

As a UE moves away from the cell-center, SINR degrades due to two factors. Firstly, the received signal strength goes down as the path-loss increases with distance from the serving eNB. Secondly, the ICI goes up because when a UE moves away from one eNB, it is generally getting closer to another eNB as shown in Fig. 4. We assume that the UE is connected to eNB1 and moving away from eNB1 towards eNB2. Furthermore, we assume frequency reuse of one, which means that both eNB1 and eNB2 transmit on the same frequency resources. Therefore, the signal transmitted from eNB2 appears as interference to the UE.

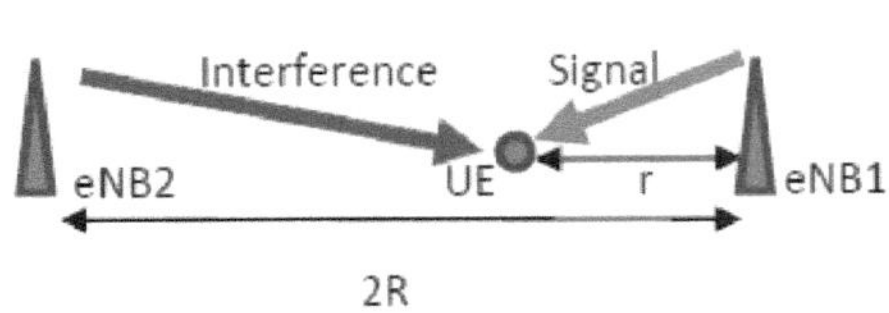

Fig. 4. Inter-cell Interference (ICI)

The SINR experienced by the UE at a distance r from eNB2 can be expressed as [4]:

$$\rho = \frac{P_1 r^{-\alpha}}{N_0 W + P_2 (2R - r)^{-\alpha}}. \tag{1}$$

where α is the path-loss exponent and P_k is the transmit power for the kth eNB. Also, R is the cell-radius with $2R$ the distance between eNB1 and eNB2. In general, all the eNBs in a system use the same transmit power and therefore we will assume $P_1 = P_2$. In a severely interference-limited scenario, the background noise, N_0 can be ignored and Equation (1) can be simplified as:

$$\rho = \left(\frac{2R}{r} - 1 \right)^{\alpha}. \tag{2}$$

Let us assume the path loss model for 2 GHz frequency:

$$PL_s = 128.1 + 37.8 \log_{10}(r) \text{ dB}. \tag{3}$$

where r is the distance between the UE and eNB in kilometers. In addition, we assume in-building penetration loss of 20 dB. The same path-loss model is assumed for the interferer eNB2.

$$PL_i = 128.1 + 37.8 \log_{10}(2R - r) \text{ dB}. \tag{4}$$

The SINR experienced by the UE can be written as:

$$\rho_{ICI} = \frac{P\left(10^{\frac{PL_s}{10}}\right)}{N_0 + P\left(10^{\frac{PLi}{10}}\right)}. \tag{5}$$

When the ICI is not present, the SINR experienced by the UE can be written as:

$$\rho_{No-ICI} = \frac{P\left(10^{\frac{PL_s}{10}}\right)}{N_0}. \tag{6}$$

Shannon showed that the system capacity C of a channel perturbed by additive white Gaussian noise (AWGN) is a function of the average received signal power S, the average noise power, N and the bandwidth, W [19]. The capacity relationship according to Shannon theorem can be stated as:

$$C = W \log_2 (1 + \frac{S}{N}). \tag{7}$$

3.2 Conventional Non-cooperative Scheme

The conventional system is characterized by single cell signal reception and suffers from ICI from its neighboring cell (shown as shaded hexagonal cell area).

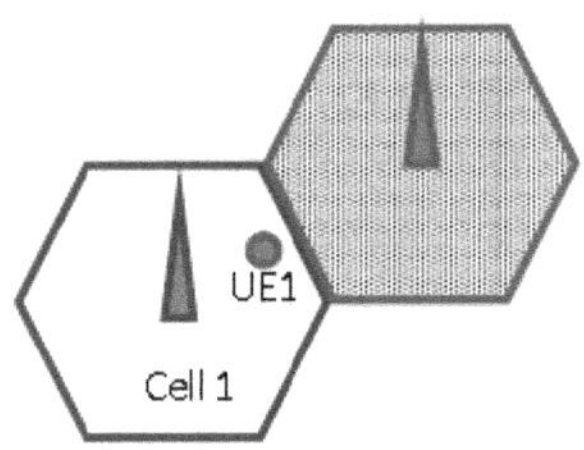

Fig. 5. Non-cooperative system

3.2 2-Cell CoMP (JP)

In the class of joint processing (JP), multiple eNBs jointly transmit signals to a single UE terminal improve the received signal quality [20]. In this case, data intended for a particular UE terminal is shared by the neighboring cell (Cell 2) and is jointly processed at this cell.

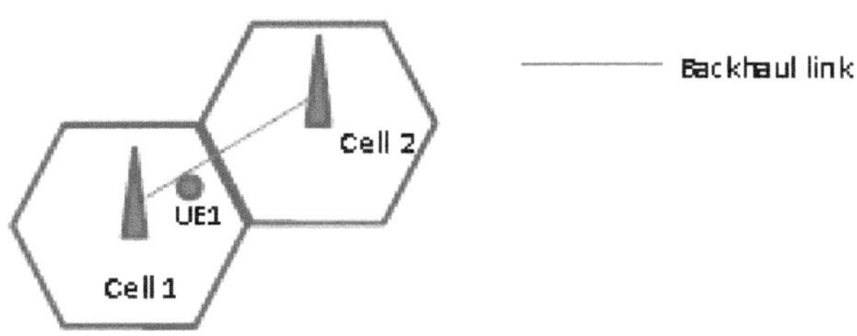

Fig. 6. CoMP system with 2 cells

We assume that UE1 is receiving signals from the two cells: Cell 1 and Cell 2 (denoted as C1 and C2). Assume $H_{i1}$is the channel gain from Ci to UE1, the received signal Y_1 at UE1 can be expressed as

$$Y_1 = H_{11}W_1X_1 + H_{21}W_2X_2 + Z_1. \tag{8}$$

where X_i is the signal transmitted at Ci, W_i is the precoding matrix at Ci, and Z_1 is the adaptive white Gaussian noise (AWGN) at the receiver.

4 Results and Discussion

4.1 ICI Analysis

In Fig. 7, we presented SINR with and without assuming ICI as a function of distance from the cell-center, r for a UE receiving transmission over a 20 MHz bandwidth.

The total background noise is *No* = -104 dBm. We also assume eNB transmit power of *P* = 43 dBm. We note that SINR degrades with increasing *r*, which is the case for cell-edge UEs. Also, for a given $r < R$, the SINR is higher for a larger path-loss exponent α. This is because the interference travels a longer distance for $r < R$ and is attenuated more for larger α.

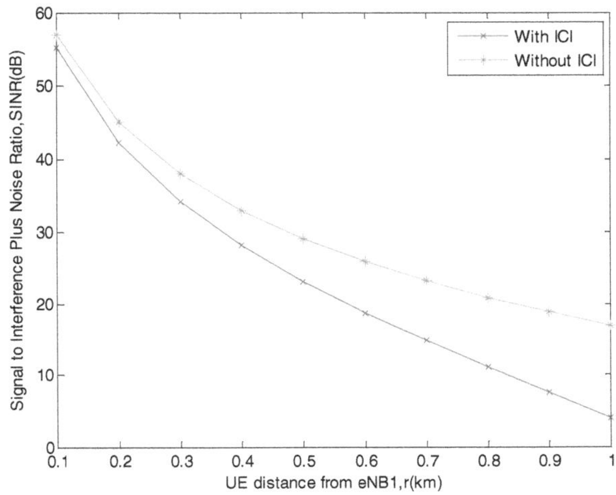

Fig. 7. SINR as a function of distance from the cell-center

Interference is the major limiting factor in the performance of cellular radio systems. The relative gains in throughput by eliminating ICI are expected to be even larger for low SINR UEs as the capacity scales almost linearly at lower SINR. For high SINR UEs, small gains in SINR by ICI elimination do not translate into any meaningful gains in throughput as shown in Fig. 8. From this discussion, we can

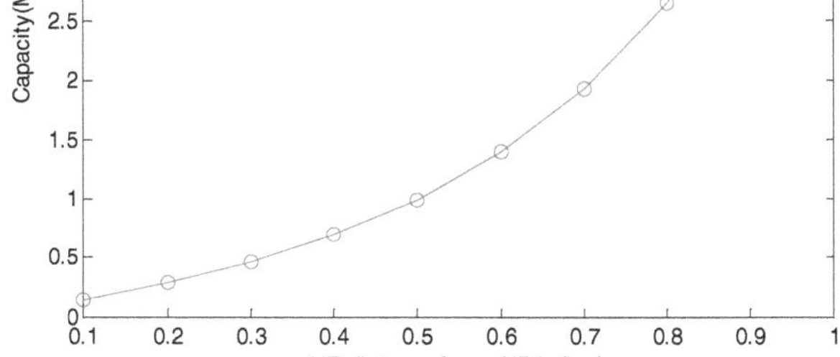

Fig. 8. Capacity gain result

conclude that ICI is more important for cell-edge UEs than for the cell-center UEs. Therefore, ICI mitigation schemes can be used to improve system cell-edge performance.

4.2 CoMP Performance

We further evaluated the performance of the CoMP (JP) scheme and compared to the conventional non-cooperative system. At this stage, we assumed that both systems are single-input single-output (SISO) based. In Fig. 9 we compare the error performance of the CoMP scheme and the conventional scheme over Rayleigh fading channel for downlink.

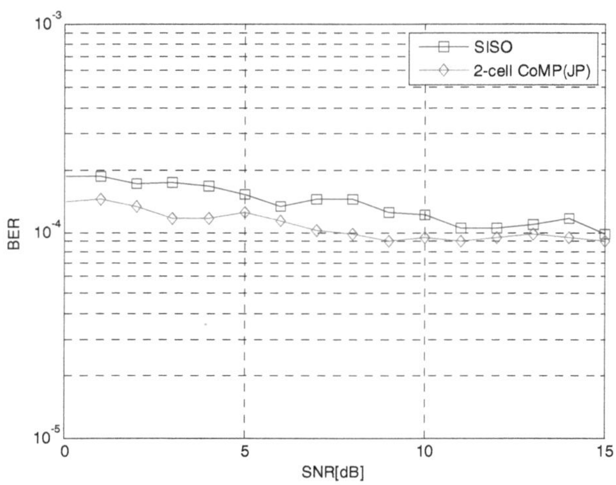

Fig. 9. Error performance comparison

The CoMP scheme gives better error performance over the conventional non-cooperative. Cooperation among eNBs can effectively turn harmful ICI into useful signals, allowing significant power gain to be exploited. Note that the above analysis is based on the fact only one UE is served by the CoMP cluster which is called CoMP single user (SU) MIMO mode.

It is expected that CoMP (JP) will bring more significant system improvement at a higher implementation cost [19]. In CoMP (JP), the data together with channel related information for different UEs need to be exchanged among the cells within the CoMP cluster. This data exchange can be done in wired backhaul. However, this will cause additional latency and impose stringent requirements for backhaul technologies.

5 Proposed ICIC Strategy

We consider a CoMP-JP system with N cooperative eNBs assigned with the same carrier frequency. Each eNB tries to detect the UEs transmitting in their own sector without any support from other eNBs. In case that the cell-edge UEs have been detected, the data transmitted by them is signaled to all cooperating eNBs. When all cooperating eNBs have accurate multi-cell CSI, they can accurately reconstruct the interference caused by these UEs and subtract it from their own received signals. As a result, the probability that the UE transmitting in the respective cells can be decoded can be improved. Note that this interference cancellation scheme is applied to cell-edge users only so that we do not burden the backhaul link with excessive data and information exchange. This is one of the main contributions of our proposed scheme.

As shown in Fig. 11, assume there are 3 cooperating eNBs in the system and signal transmitted by UEI to its own eNB interfers the signal transmitted by UE2 and UE3 to their respective eNBs as both of them are located at cell boundary region. All cells decode their own user's data and then transmit their cell-edge user's data to the neighboring cells. For example, Cell 1 decodes transmitting data by UE1 and signals it to Cell 2 and Cell 3 on the backhaul links. Then, Cell 2 and Cell 3 subtract the interfering signal (from UE1) before detecting their own received signal. In general, the proposed scheme can reduce the requirements on backhaul link since only data of users located at cell boundary region is shared by the cooperating eNBs. Besides, its capability to mitigate ICI is feasible and undoubted.

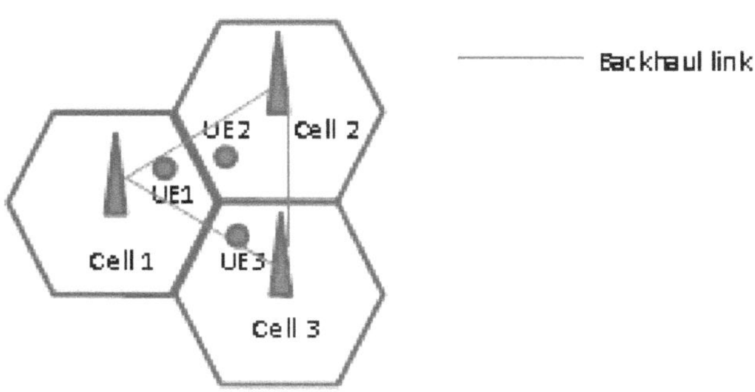

Fig. 11. System model of the proposed scheme

6 Conclusion

The LTE system targets better cell-edge performance in order to provide service consistency in terms of geographical coverage and throughput. In interference-limited scenarios, the cell-edge performance can be improved via ICIC. In this paper, inter-cell interference coordination (ICIC) schemes in CoMP system have been discussed. However, there are some limitation and drawback that we have addressed throughout our review on these schemes. In FFR and SFR schemes for example, interference is mitigated by sacrificing cell throughput and are suboptimal since the nature of channel dynamism in wireless environment has not been considered. As for CoMP (CS/CB) schemes, the challenge lies in the precoder design complexity that can optimally suppress interference. In addition, excessive feedback overhead (e.g. CSI, PMI) from UE to eNB should be avoided. Utilizing HII and OI mechanism to mitigate

ICI should be performed with minimum inter-eNB signaling to minimize signaling delay and overhead. In general there is tradeoff between cooperation and information exchange which needs be further explored. We have shown simulation results and discussed the significant effect of ICI to the received SNR and capacity. We also performed basic system performance of CoMP scheme over conventional non-cooperative scheme. Besides, we also proposed an interference cancellation scheme in CoMP system with minimal signaling as to reduce the X2 bandwidth requirements and processing delay. Currently, the proposed work is still in progress and in future we will be sharing the resulting outcomes.

Acknowledgement. The authors would like to thank to Ministry of Higher Education, Malaysia (MOHE), Research Management Centre (UTM-RMC), and Universiti Teknologi Malaysia (UTM) for their support. This work was funded by Vote No. Q.J130000.7123.01F.01H35 grant.

References

1. Sawahashi, M., Kishiyama, Y., Morimoto, A., Nishikawa, D., Tanno, M.: Coordinated Multipoint Transmission/Reception Techniques for LTE-Advanced. IEEE Wireless Communications, 26–34 (2011)
2. Nam, Y., Liu, L., Wang, Y., Zhang, C., Cho, J., Han, J.: Cooperative Communication Technologies for LTE-Advanced. In: 2010 IEEE International Conference on Acoustics speech and Signal Processing, pp. 5610–5613 (2010)
3. Anis Izzati, A.Z., Rozeha, A.R., Sharifah Kamilah, S.Y., Norsheila, F.: Performance Analysis for Cooperative Relay with Power Control Scheme over Fading Channel. In: First UK-India International Workshop on Cognitive Wireless Systems (2009)
4. Rashid, R.A., Aripin, N.M., Fisal, N., Yusof, S.K.S.: Inner Bound Capacity Analysis of Cooperative Relay in Cognitive Radio Using Information Theoretic Approach. In: IEEE Malaysia International Conference On Communications (MICC 2009), Kuala Lumpur, Malaysia (2009)
5. Immer, R., Droste, H., Marsh, P., Brueck, S., Mayer, H., Thiele, L., Jungnickel, V.: Coordinated Multipoint: Concepts, Performance and Field Trial Results. IEEE Communications Magazine, 102–111 (2011)
6. Khan, F.: LTE for 4G Mobile Broadband : Air-interface Technologies and Performance. Cambridge University Press (2009)
7. Porjazoski, M., Popovski, B.: Analysis of Inter-cell Interference Coordination by Fractional Frequency Reuse in LTE. In: International Conference on Software, Telecommunications and Computer Networks (2010)
8. Ghaffar, R., Knopp, R.: Fractional Frequency Reuse and Interference Suppression for OFDMA Networks. In: Proceedings of the 8th International Symposium on Modeling and Optimization in Mobile, Ad Hoc and Wireless Networks (2010)
9. Yu, Y., Dutkiewicz, E., Huang, X., Mueck, M., Fang, G.: Performance Analysis of Soft Frequency Reuse for Inter-cell Interference Coordination in LTE Networks. In: International Symposium on Communications and Information Technologies, pp. 504–509 (2010)
10. Al-Shalash, M., Khafizov, F., Chao, Z.: Uplink Inter-cell Interference Coordination Through Soft Frequency Reuse. In: IEEE Global Telecommunications Conference (2010)

11. Rahman, M., Yanikomeroglu, H., Wong, W.: Interference Avoidance with Dynamic Inter-cell Coordination for Downlink LTE System. IEEE Transactions on Wireless Communications 10(5), 1414–1425 (2011)
12. Zheng, S., Tian, H., Hu, Z., Chen, L., Zhu, J.: QoS-Guaranteed Radio Resource Allocation with Distributed Inter-Cell Interference Coordination for Multi-Cell OFDMA Systems. In: IEEE 71st Vehicular Technology Conference (2010)
13. Fraimis, I.G., Papoutsis, V.D., Kotpoulos, S.A.: A Decentralized Subchannel Allocation Scheme with Inter-cell Interference Coordination (ICIC) for Multi-Cell OFDMA Systems. In: IEEE Global Telecommunications Conference (2010)
14. 3GPP, R1-092303. Multi-cell PMI Coordination for downlink CoMP, InterDigital, June 29-July 3 (2009)
15. Qiang, L., Yang, Y., Shu, F., Gang, W.: Coordinated Beamforming in Downlink CoMP Transmission System. In: 5th International ICST Conference on Communications and Networking, China (2010)
16. Jang, U., Lee, K.Y., Cho, K.S., Ryu, W.: Transmit Beamforming based Inter-cell Interference and User Selection with CoMP. In: IEEE 72th Vehicular Technology Conference Fall (2010)
17. Castellanos, C.U., Calabrese, F.D., Pedersen, K.I., Rosa, C.: Uplink Interference Control in UTRAN LTE based on the Overload Indicator. In: IEEE 68th Vehicular Technology Conference (2008)
18. Zhang, G., Zhang, C., Zhang, J., Wei, G.: A Novel Uplink Interference Coordination Scheme Using High Interference Indicator. In: 72nd IEEE Vehicular Technology Conference Fall (2010)
19. Liu, W., Hu, C., Wei, D., Peng, M., Wang, W.: An Overload Indicator and High Interference Indicator Hybrid Scheme for Inter-Cell Interference Coordination in LTE System. In: 3rd IEEE International Conference on Broadband Network and Multimedia Technology, pp. 514–518 (2010)
20. Dahlman, E., Parkvall, S., Kkold, J.: 4G LTE/LTE-Advanced for Mobile Broadband. Academic Press, United Kingdom (2011)
21. Sklar, B.: Digital Communications: Fundamentals and Applications. Prentice Hall International Inc., New Jersey (2010)
22. Nam, Y., Liu, L., Wang, Y., Zhang, C., Cho, J., Han, J.: Cooperative Communication Technologies for LTE-Advanced. In: IEEE International Conference on Acoustics Speech and Signal Processing, pp. 5610–5613 (2010)

Experimental Study of Sensing Performance Metrics for Cognitive Radio Network Using Software Defined Radio Platform

M. Adib Sarijari, Rozeha A. Rashid, N. Fisal, M. Rozaini A. Rahim,
S.K.S. Yusof, and N. Hija Mahalin

Faculty of Electrical Engineering, Universiti Teknologi Malaysia
Johor, Malaysia
{adib_sairi,rozeha,Sheila,rozaini_pg,kamilah}@fke.utm.my,
nhija.m@gmail.com

Abstract. Cognitive Radio (CR) is a promising technology in wireless communication for an enhanced utilization of limited spectral resources. It allows unlicensed or cognitive users (CUs) to sense the spectral environment and access a channel exhibiting negligible activity of licensed or primary users (PUs). Hence, spectrum sensing is a crucial task for a CU to perform in an opportunistic spectrum access (OSA) based CR network to avoid harmful interference to PU. Two main performances metrics that are crucial in the design of spectrum sensing are the probability of false alarm (P_{fa}) and the probability of detection (P_d). These metrics are used to define the CR system quality of service (QoS). The threshold to decide on the presence of PU and the sensing time needed for the CR system are also determined based on these metrics. This paper presents the design of measurement methods to experimentally acquire the P_{fa} and P_d curves based on locally captured data to determine the value of the threshold and sensing time. The implementation, experimentation and measurement are done using GNU Radio and universal software defined radio peripheral (USRP) software defined radio (SDR) platform as the cognitive radio testbed. Spectrum sensing was done based on energy detection. Each of the energy based detection measurement is repeated 1000 times to obtain an accurate estimation of P_{fa} and P_d. The findings show that the target Quality of Sevice (QoS) of P_{fa} of 5% and P_d of 90% can be derived from the estimated sensing threshold of -39 dB and achieves a sensing time of 31.59 ms.

Keywords: Cognitive radio, software defined radio, spectrum sensing, probability of false alarm, probability of detection, opportunistic spectrum access.

1 Introduction

A recent spectrum occupancy measurement shows that a significant portion of the spectrum allocated to licensed services show little usage over time, with concentration on certain portions of the spectrum while a significant amount of the spectrum remains unutilized [1]. A new communication paradigm to exploit the existing wireless spectrum opportunistically is necessary to overcome limited available spectrum and inefficiency in spectrum utilization.

A. Abd Manaf et al. (Eds.): ICIEIS 2011, Part III, CCIS 253, pp. 666–677, 2011.

Originally introduced by Mitola [2], Cognitive Radio (CR) technology allows unlicensed or cognitive users (CUs) to take advantage of the spectrum holes by intelligently identifying and using them, and possibly releasing them when required by the primary users (PUs). Hence, it is a fundamental requirement that the CU performs spectrum sensing to detect the presence of PU signal and also locate unoccupied spectrum segments, the spectrum holes, as accurately and quickly as possible. The first hardware implementation of spectrum sensing is carried out by authors of [3] and [4]. Besides an energy detector based sensing, work on cyclostationary feature detector is also reported [5]. The experiment is carried out using Berkeley Emulation Engine 2 (BEE2). The work also presents the experimental design to measure the required sensing time for the Dynamic Spectrum Access (DSA) system based on the probability of false alarm (P_{fa}) and probability of detection (P_d). Two types of signal are taken into consideration; modulated signal and sine-wave pilot signals and the focus of the work is on low SNR condition. However, the methodology and steps in obtaining the curve of P_{fa} and P_d are not completely defined.

The flexibility of Software Defined Radio (SDR) makes it a well suited candidate to be the testbed for the implementation of cognitive features [6], [7]. SDR is a platform where all the signal manipulations and processing works in radio communication are done in software instead of hardware as shown in Figure 1. Therefore, signal will be processed in digital domain instead of in analog domain as in the conventional radio. The digitization work will be done by a device called the Analog to Digital Converter (ADC). As shown in this figure, the ADC process takes place after the Front End (FE) circuit. FE is used to down convert the signal to an Intermediate Frequency (IF) due to the limitation of the speed of current Commercially-of-The-Shelf (COTS) ADC and the processor to process the ADC output such as digital signal processing (DSP) processor or field programmable get array (FPGA). The digitized signal is passed to the baseband processor for further software-based processes such as demodulation, channel coding and source coding.

In this work, a software defined radio (SDR) platform called GNU radio and universal software defined radio peripheral (USRP) are used as the testbed for the spectrum sensing implementation and measurement. GNU Radio is an open source software toolkit which consists of a huge numbers of signals processing blocks library (i.e modulators, filters, amplifiers and etc). These signal processing blocks can be linked together for building and deploying the baseband part of the dedicated radio. USRP is an SDR hardware to link the baseband signal to the real world [8]. Its main function is to change the analog value of the spectrum to the digital domain and to change the digital domain signal to analog value. The hardware is able to cover frequencies up to 5.4GHz depending on the front-end used. In this work, the front-end RFX2400, which covers frequencies from 2.3GHz to 2.9GHz, is utilized.

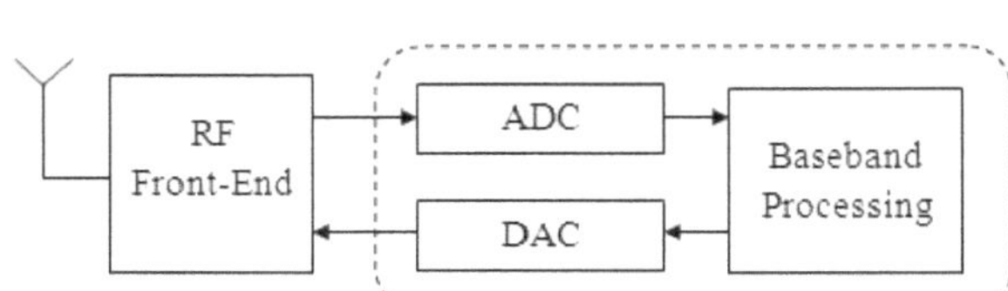

Fig. 1. Software Defined Radio Block Diagram

The paper is organized as follows: Section 2 presents a background on cognitive radio technology. While Section 3 defines channel sensing hypotheses and introduces the sensing performance metrics, the probabilities of detection and false alarm. Section 4 presents the measurement setup. The experimental results are discussed in Section 5. Finally, Section 6 provides conclusion and future works.

2 Cognitive Radio Technology

In [2], CR is defined as an intelligent wireless communication system that is aware and learns from its environment and adapts its internal states by making corresponding changes in certain operating parameters. The vital objective of the cognitive radio is to achieve the best accessible spectrum through cognitive capability and reconfigurability. In other words, CR also embodies awareness, intelligence, learning, adaptivity, reliability and efficiency. Cognitive cycle consists of three major steps as follows [1],[2],[9]:

a) Sensing of RF stimuli which involves the detection of spectrum holes to facilitate the estimation of channel state information and prediction of channel capacity for use by the transmitter.

b) Cognition/spectrum management which controls opportunistic spectrum access and capturing the best available spectrum to meet user communication requirements. Cognitive radios should decide on the best spectrum band to meet the Quality of Service (QoS) requirements over all available spectrum bands by managing functions such as optimal transmission rate control, traffic shaping and routing.

c) Actions to be taken can be in terms of re-configurable communication parameters such as transmission power, modulation and coding.

Those three tasks form a cognitive cycle as shown in Fig. 2.

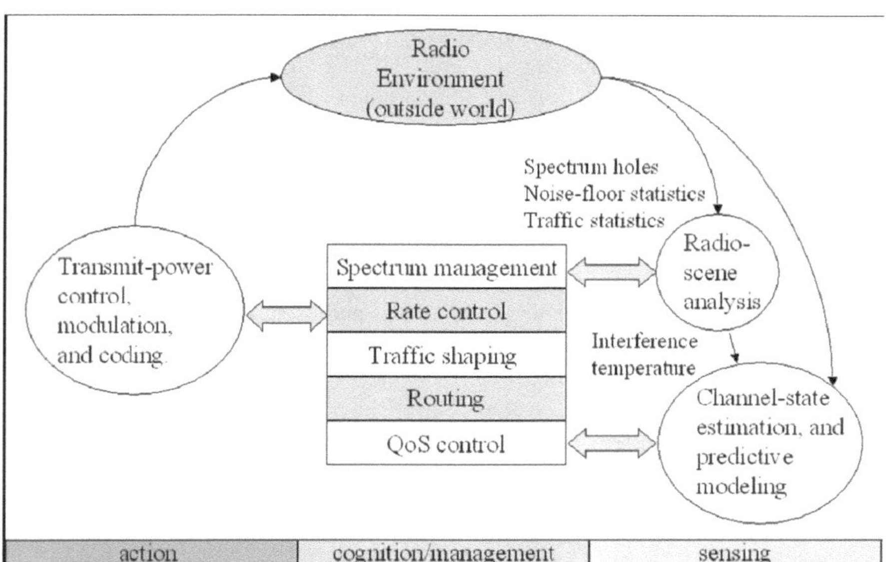

Fig. 2. Basic cognitive cycle [2]

This paper focuses on the energy detection based spectrum sensing, specifically on the measurement design for the determination of the spectrum sensing performance metrics for cognitive radio testbed. There are four performance metrics addressed in this design which is the threshold to detect the PU, the sensing time, the probability of detection and the probability of false alarm.

3 Spectrum Sensing Performance Metrics

The In a CR system where CUs are sensing the channel, the sampled received signal, $X[n]$ at the CU receiver will have two hypotheses as follows:

H_0: $X[n] = W[n]$ if PU is absent

$$H_0: X[n] = W[n] \qquad \text{if PU is absent} \tag{1}$$

where $n = 1, \ldots, N$; N is the number of samples and h is the gain of channel that is assumed to be 0 under hypothesis H_0 and 1 under hypothesis H_1. The noise $W[n]$ is assumed to be additive white Gaussian (AWGN) with zero mean and variance σ_w^2. $S[n]$ is the PU's signal and is assumed to be a random Gaussian process with zero mean and variance σ_x^2. Using energy detector [10], the decision based on Neyman-Pearson criterion will be

$$Y = \frac{1}{N}\sum_{n=1}^{N}(X[n])^2 \tag{2}$$

where Y is the output of the energy detector which serves as the test statistic. Taking γ as the threshold to decide whether signal is present or not, the performance metrics of the spectrum sensing can be characterized by a resulting pair of (P_{fa}, P_d) as the probabilities that the CU's sensing algorithm detects a PU under H_0 and H_1, respectively.

$$P_{fa} = P(Y > \gamma / H_0) \tag{3}$$

$$P_d = P(Y > \gamma / H_1) \tag{4}$$

As given in the equations above, P_{fa} is the probability of false alarm which is the probability of CU mistakenly detects the presence of PU when it is actually absent. While P_d is the probability detection which is the probability of CU correctly detects the presence of PU.

If the noise term is assumed to be circularly symmetric complex Gaussian, using central limit theorem, Gaussian distribution approximation for the probability density function (PDF) of Y can be derived from (3) and (4) [11];

$$P_{fa} = Q\left(\left(\frac{\gamma}{\sigma_w^2} - 1\right)\sqrt{N}\right) \tag{5}$$

$$P_d = Q\left(\left(\frac{\gamma}{\sigma_w^2} - SNR - 1\right)\sqrt{\frac{N}{2SNR + 1}}\right) \tag{6}$$

where signal-to-noise ratio (*SNR*) is taken as $\frac{|h|^2\sigma_x^2}{\sigma_w^2}$ and $Q(.)$ denotes the generalized Marcum Q-function. The challenge of the local spectrum sensing is to reliably decide on the two hypotheses to achieve high P_d for good protection of PU and low P_{fa} to provide satisfactory access for CUs. The determination of the remaining performance metrics; the threshold and sensing time, will be discussed in the following section.

4 Measurement Setup

The setup for the measurement on USRP and GNU Radio is designed as in Figure 3(a) and the block diagram of the setup is shown in Figure 3(b). Two USRP, one laptop and one personal computer (PC) were used. PC with USRP A acts as CU which will sense the spectrum while USRP B installed to the laptop acts as the PU. The daughter boards used in is RFX2400 which covers frequency from 2.3GHz to 2.9GHz. The frequency band used is ISM 2.4GHz band and each sensing will occupy 4MHz spectrum band.

In this work, the energy detector of CU, shown in Figure 4, is designed using 1024 FFT bin. *N*-number of samples is collected for each of the FFT bin. The *N* value is a variable and programmable. It is determined based on the preferred P_d. Each FFT bin is then averaged over *N* samples. The decision on the presence of PU is decided based logical-OR fusion of each average of 1024 FFT bin. The decision on the presence of PU is thus achieved if one or more bin from the 1024 FFT bin is higher than the predetermined threshold. The OR operation is chosen as it improves P_d which leads to higher protection of PU.

For PU radio, a GMSK modulated signal is generated at the center frequency, *fc* of 2.48GHz. PU signal is transmitted to measure the P_d of the platform.

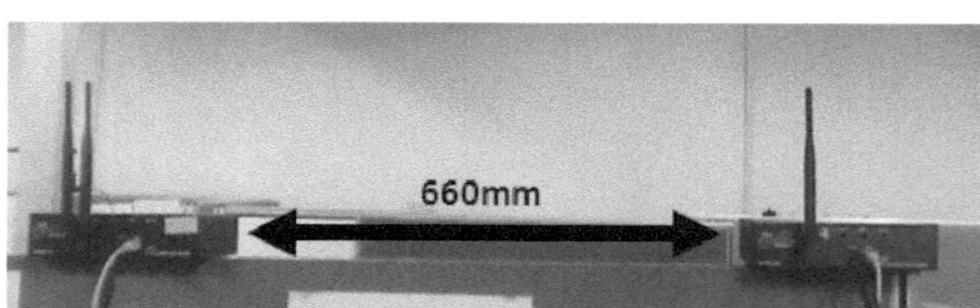

(a)

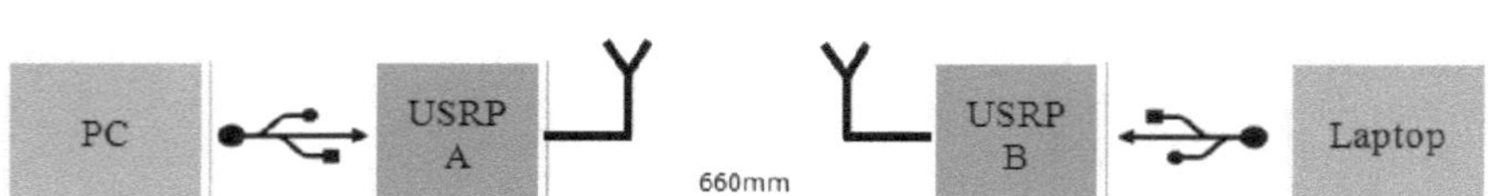

(b)

Fig. 3. (a). Spectrum Sensing Implementation Setup (b). Spectrum Sensing Implementation Block Diagram.

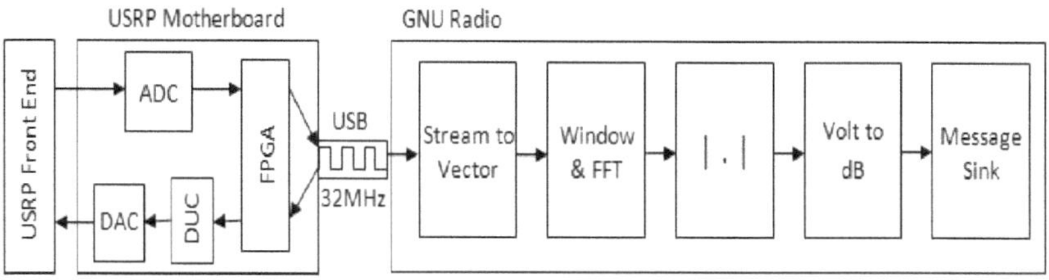

Fig. 4. GNU Radio Energy Detector Block Diagram

5 Experimental Results

This section discusses the sensing parameters such as the sensing threshold, probability of false alarm, probability of detection and the sensing time, which are all decided based upon locally measured data. The analysis on the captured data is used to assess the platform characteristics in terms of sensitivity and best performance in local environment.

5.1 Determining the Sensing Threshold

In the experiment to determine the P_{fa}, the measurement is carried out when there is no signal transmission from PU as shown in Figure 5. From this figure, the recorded noise spikes are in the range of -37.0dB and -41.0dB. Therefore, the threshold to decide the presence of PU can be set within this range. The spectrum analyzer reading is obtained from running the *usrp_fft.py* file from GNU Radio package.

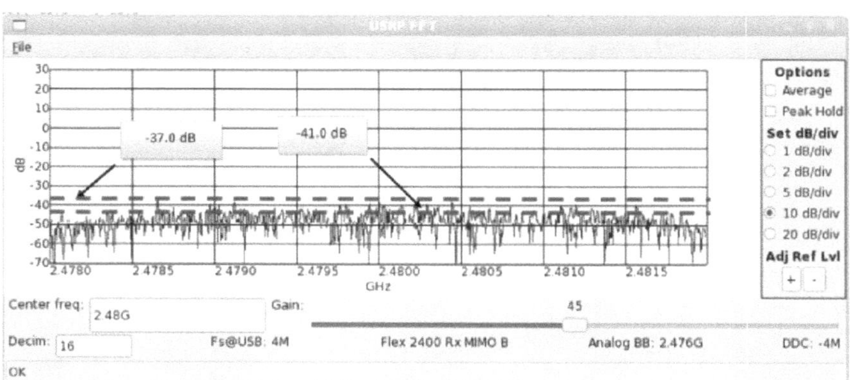

Fig. 5. Spectrum sensing in the absence of PU as observed using GNU Radio spectrum analyzer at 2.48GHz with 4MHz Bandwidth

The measurement result of Figure 5 is then used to obtain the P_{fa} curve of Figure 6 by varying the sensing threshold. This figure is further used to determine the optimum threshold in determining the presence of PU based on the targeted P_{fa}. For instance, if a target P_{fa} of 5% is chosen, the threshold curves that intersect with the P_{fa} value of

0.05 will be considered. It should be noted that higher number of samples size will cause longer sensing time to the CR system. In this work -39.0 dB is chosen as the sensing threshold to decide on the presence of PU for P_d measurement since it crosses P_{fa} value of 0.05 and hence, satisfies the desired P_{fa} of 5%.

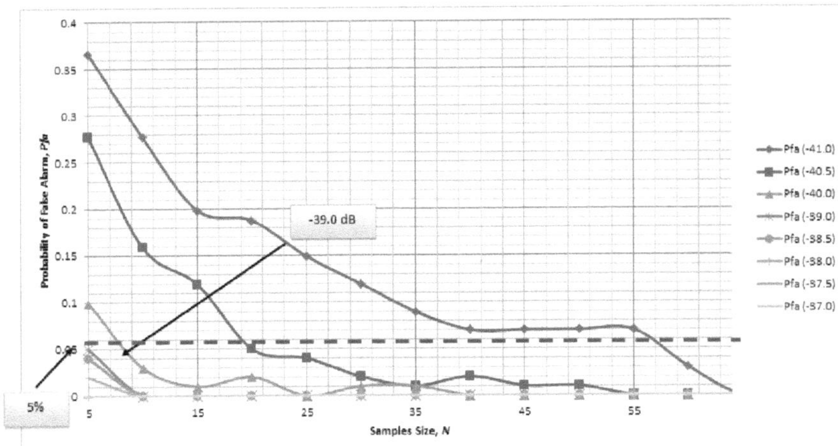

Fig. 6. Probability of False Alarm versus Sample Size

5.2 Determining the Probability of False Alarm

The measurement is done over an ISM 2.4GHz band and specifically centered at 2.48GHz. This channel is chosen since this frequency does not overlap with any local IEEE802.11 based access-points (AP) in the vicinity.

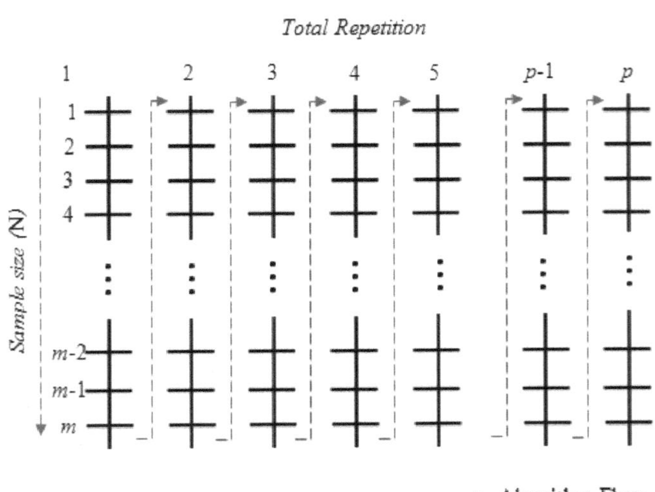

Fig. 7. Algorithm for P_{fa} measurement

Figure 7 illustrates the algorithm designed to collect the data in order to plot the P_{fa} against the sample size, N. As shown in this figure, the algorithm flows from the top to the bottom which represents the sample size, N and from the left to the rights which represent the total repetition. In this algorithm, m is the maximum measured sample size which in this work is equal to 64. This is due to the saturation of P_{fa} values for sample size larger than 64 as shown in Figure 8. p is the maximum repetition to estimate the value of the P_{fa} for each sample size and in this work, p is equal to 1000.

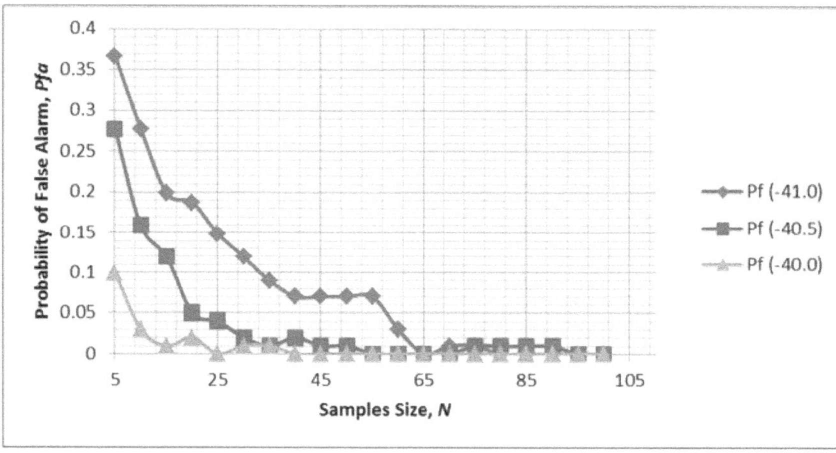

Fig. 8. The saturation of P_{fa} curve for N > 64

As shown in the flowchart of Figure 9, the algorithm begins by taking a reading on the energy value of the sensed signal by using the designed energy detector. Due to the FFT feature, the result of the energy detector is analyzed per sub-carrier basis. Each subcarrier is then averaged over the *sample size, N* by using (2).

The averaged subcarriers are compared with the threshold to decide the wrong detection of the PU in each sub-channel as indicated in (3). The results are then fused using the OR operation to obtain the decision using (7);

$$BinFuse(N) = OR\begin{Bmatrix} FFTBinAvrg_N(1), FFTBinAvrg_N(2), \ldots, \\ FFTBinAvrg_N(1024) \end{Bmatrix} \quad (7)$$

$BinFuse(N)$ is in Boolean in which value is either "1" or "0". The OR fusion means that if one or more subcarrier exceeds the power threshold, the channel is denoted as 1. The "1" notation indicates that the channel is occupied while "0" indicates the channel is free. The OR operation is used instead of averaging due to the possibility PU may be present in only a part of the 4MHz, i.e. 1MHz out of 4MHz. Therefore, if an average method is used, the remaining 3MHz where PU is absent will be dominant compared to the portion of frequency where PU is present. As such, the final result does not clearly show the presence of the PU.

If PU is detected, then a counter named $Pfa\_cnt(N)$ is increased by one as shown in (8).

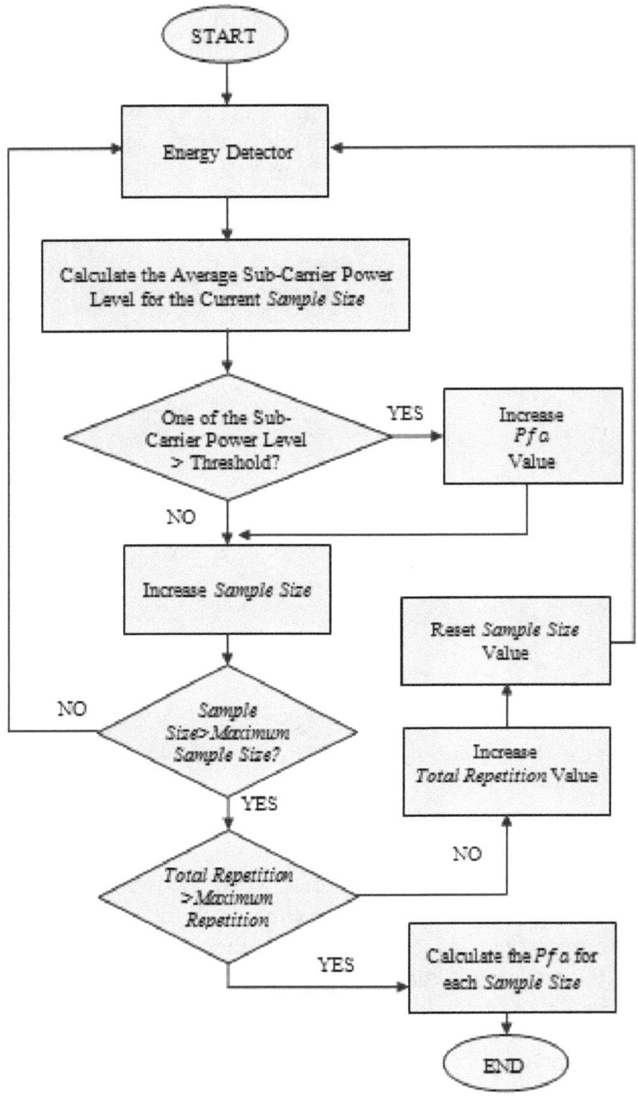

Fig. 9. Flowchart for *Pfa* Measurement Algorithm

$$Pfa\_cnt(N) = \begin{cases} Pfa_{cnt(N)} + 1, & BinFuse(N) = 1 \\ Pfa_{cnt(N)}, & BinFuse(N) = 0 \end{cases} \quad (8)$$

The measurement is repeated 1000 times. Finally, the value of P_{fa}, $Pfa\ (N)$ from the measurement is represented by number of times PU is detected in 1000 repetition of the measurement for each N. The value of P_{fa} is calculated in (9) and plotted in Figure 6:

$$Pfa(N) = \frac{Pfa_{cnt}(N)}{p} \quad (9)$$

In this work, a target P_{fa} of 5% is used for P_d measurement.

5.3 Determining the Probability of Detection

With the set P_{fa} of 5%, the measurement for probability of detection P_d is done by sweeping the signal level from -37.0dB to -39.0dB where the measurement is done when the PU signal is present, as shown in Figure 10. In this figure, it can be observed that PU is transmitting at center frequency of 2.48GHz with 1MHz bandwidth.

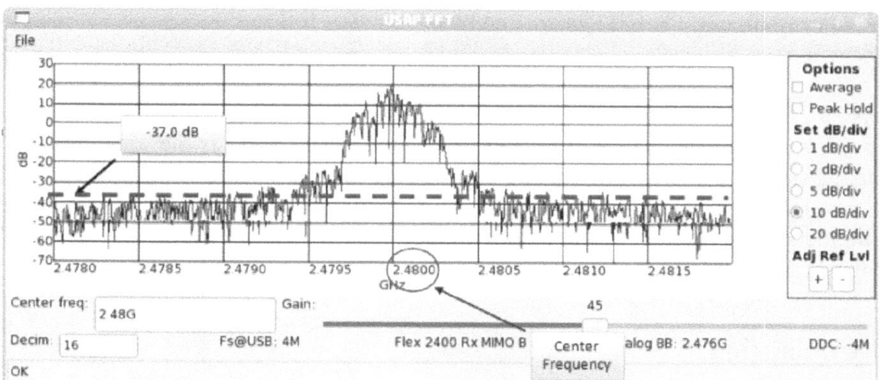

Fig. 10. Spectrum sensing in the presence of PU as observed using GNU Radio spectrum analyzer at 2.48GHz

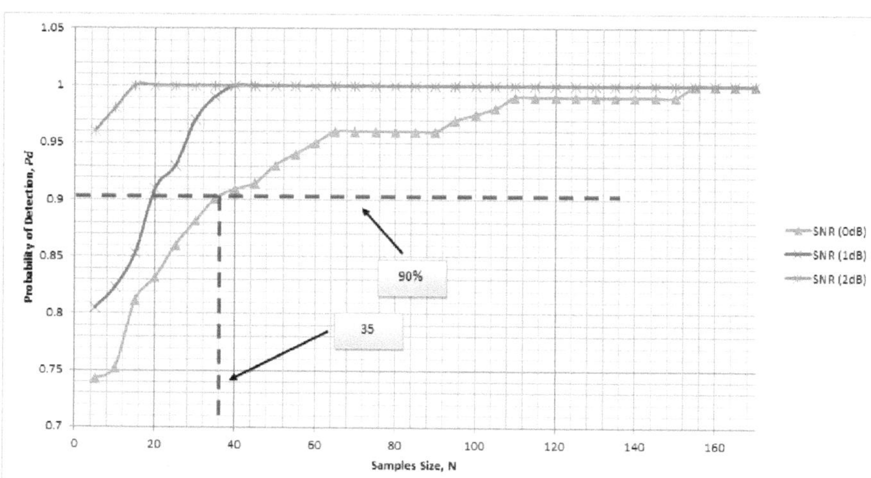

Fig. 11. Probability of Detection versus Sample Size

Similar to P_{fa} measurement, in order to accurately estimate the P_d, each detection measurement is repeated 1000 times. The obtained result is plotted in Figure 11. This graph is used to determine the required *sample size, N* for the desired P_d. At a predetermined noise threshold of -39.0dB, power received (Pr) of -39 dB, -38 dB and -37 dB are translated to Signal-to-Noise ratio (SNR) values of 0, 1 and 2 dB, respectively. A higher P_d leads to more *sample size* needed and hence, longer sensing time. Longer sensing time will reduce the data transmission time, and thus will result in a lower overall throughput. Since the experimental sensing performance closely matches that of the theoretical framework at P_d of 90% as reported in [12], the target Quality of Service (QoS) for P_d is set at the value.

5.4 Determining the Sensing Time

The sensing time of the CU system can be obtained as follows;

$$T_s = tN \tag{10}$$

where T_s is the sensing time, N is the number of samples required for the CU system to achieve the target P_d of 90%, which in this case is 35 and t is the time required to obtain a sample of the sensing result, namely, the sampling time. In this measurement, the sampling time is equal to 0.9025ms. This sampling time is obtained by using time stamping on the running designed energy detection system of Figure 4. Substituting all these values in (10) will give T_s equals to 31.59ms.

6 Conclusion

Many previous works produce results on sensing parameters based on simulation study. In this paper, we presented the measurement design to determine the sensing performance metrics of sensing threshold, probability of false alarm, probability of detection and sensing time using GNU Radio and USRP as the CR testbed. The analysis on the locally captured data is used to set the desired Quality of Service (QoS) for the system. A sensing threshold of -39 db satisfies the desired P_{fa} of 5% while a target P_d of 90% can be achieved by a sensing time of 31.59 ms. Future works include reducing the sensing time for better link utilization and throughput via bio-inspired algorithm and developing a proactive solution for CU's spectrum access based on past observations of sensing data.

Acknowledgment. The authors wish to express their gratitude to Ministry of Higher Education (MOHE), Malaysia and Research Management Center (RMC), Universiti Teknologi Malaysia for the financial support of this project under GUP research grant no: Q.J130000.7107.03J81.

References

1. Akyildiz, I.F., Lee, W.-Y., Vuran, M.C., Mohanty, S.: Next Generation/Dynamic Spectrum Access/Cognitive Radio Wireless Networks: A Survey. The International Journal of Computer and Telecommunications Networking 50, 2127–2159 (2006)

2. Mitola, J.: Software radios-survey, critical evaluation and future directions. In: IEEE National Telesystems Conference, May 19-20, pp. 13/15–13/23 (1992)
3. Cabric, D., Tkachenko, A., Brodersen, R.W.: Experimental Study of Spectrum Sensing based on Energy Detection and Network Cooperation. In: The First International Workshop on Technology and Policy for Accessing Spectrum. ACM International Conference Proceeding Series, vol. 222(12) (2006)
4. Cabric, D., Tkachenko, A., Brodersen, R.W.: Spectrum Sensing Measurements of Pilot, Energy, and Collaborative Detection. In: IEEE Military Communications Conference (MILCOM 2006), Washington, DC, pp. 1–7 (October 2006)
5. Cabric, D., Mishra, S.M., Brodersen, R.W.: Implementation Issues in Spectrum Sensing for Cognitive Radios. In: Asilomar Conference on Signals, Systems, and Computers, vol. 1, pp. 772–776 (November 2004)
6. Manicka, N.: GNU Radio Testbed, Thesis for Master of Science in Computer Science, University of Delaware (Spring 2007)
7. GNU Radio project, `http://gnuradio.org/redmine/wiki/gnuradio`
8. Matt Ettus, Universal software radio peripheral, `http://www.ettus.com`
9. Budiarjo, I., Lakshmanan, M.K., Nikookar, H.: Cognitive Radio Dynamic Access Technique. Wireless Pers Commun. 45, 293–324 (2008)
10. Rashid, R.A., et al.: Sensing Period Considerations in Fading Environment for Multimedia Delivery in Cognitive Ultra Wideband. In: International Conference on Signal and Image Processing Applications (ICSIPA 2009), Kuala Lumpur, November 18-19 (2009)
11. Poor, H.V.: An Introduction to signal detection and estimation, 2nd edn. Springer, New York (1994)
12. Rashid, R.A., Sarijari, M.A., Fisal, N., Lo, A.C.C., et al.: Spectrum Sensing Measurement using GNU Radio and USRP Software Defined Radio Platform. In: ICWMC 2011, Luxembourgh, Germany, June 19-24 (2011)

Development of TelG Mote for Wireless Biomedical Sensor Network (WBSN) Application

M. Rozaini A. Rahim, Rozeha A. Rashid, S.H.S. Ariffin, N. Fisal,
A. Hadi Fikri A. Hamid, M. Adib Sarijari, and Alias Mohd

Faculty of Electrical Engineering, Universiti Teknologi Malaysia,
Johor, Malaysia
mohd_rozaini@yahoo.com,
{rozeha,sharifah,Sheila,adib_sairi,alias}@fke.utm.my,
hadifikri@gmail.com

Abstract. Wireless Sensor Network (WSN) consists of sensor nodes that interact with each other to collectively monitor environmental or physical conditions at different location for the intended user. One of its potential deployments is in the form of Wireless Biomedical Sensor Network (WBSN) to measure physiological signals. The WBSN applications would allow the medical practitioners to continuously monitor and update the status of a patient remotely. This paper focuses on the development of a wireless sensor node platform for WBSN application which complies with IEEE 802.15.4 standard and operates in 2.4 GHz ISM (industrial, scientific and medical) band. The initial state of WBSN development is the design of the wireless sensor node called TelG. The main features of TelG include low power consumption, wearable, flexible and small size. It is then embedded with a self-built operating system called WiseOS to support customized operations.

Keywords: Wireless Biomedical Sensor Network, sensor node, continous monitoring and wireless sensor network.

1 Introduction

The recent development of high performance microprocessors and novel processing materials has stimulated great interest in the development of wireless sensor nodes for Wireless Biomedical Sensor Network (WBSN) application [1]. It allows physiological signals such as electroencephalography (EEG), electrocardiogram (ECG), blood pressure, glucose to be easily monitored wirelessly and attached to the patient's body. The wireless sensor nodes in WBSN application can be classified into several types, which are the swallowed capsule pill sensor, wired sensor with the wireless sensor node, portable sensors mounted on the surface of human body, implantable physiological sensor and nano-physiological sensors [2]. In this work, the wired sensor with the wireless sensor node will be used.

Some of the generic wireless sensor node platforms available have not been designed specifically for WBSN application but they are more on network research or environmental monitoring [3]. However, among these generic wireless sensor nodes, the Mica[4] and Telos[5] series have been used into WBSN application at Harvard

A. Abd Manaf et al. (Eds.): ICIEIS 2011, Part III, CCIS 253, pp. 678–688, 2011.

University as their first prototype for CodeBlue project [6-8]. In the CodeBlue project, this generic wireless sensor node has been connected to the pulse oximeter, electrocardiogram (EKG) and electromyography (EMG) sensor board to provide continuous monitoring. Another type is the Tmote Sky platform [9], where it is used to design a wireless ECG monitoring system [10].

There are a number of wireless sensor node platform purposely designed for WBSN application such as ECO[11], Body Sensor Network (BSN)[12], MASN[13], TELEMON[14], Wearable Patch ECG[15], zEEG[16], Ultra Low Power Node[17], Pluto[18], WBSN Node[19] and SHIMMER(Sensing Health with Intelligence, Modularity, Mobility, and Experimental Reusability) [20]. Most of these sensor nodes are used for ECG signal monitoring and ISM band as the frequency for transmission.

This paper focuses on the development of our own wireless sensor node for WBSN application named TelG mote. The design contributes specifically for home-based healthcare monitoring. Therefore, it adopts a holistic approach by addressing features that are convenient for home-use, such as wearability, low power and cost, reliability and multi-hop capability. The rest of the paper is organized as follows. Section 2 will describe briefly on the design of the TelG mote based on the requirement for biomedical application. The architecture of the TelG mote will be explained in section 3 while section 4 features the WiseOS operating system. Section 5 will discuss the results. Conclusion is drawn in Section 6.

2 WBSN Mote Design Requirement

Most of the existing WSN platforms in the market are designed for generic application and network research [21,22]. However, platform design and requirements of WBSN application are different from typical WSN application platform, although some subset of these requirements may be shared. TelG mote has been developed for WBSN application platform. As a WBSN platform, TelG mote must satisfy four design concepts such as wearability, low power and cost, reliability and multi-hop capability explained as follows.

Wearability. To achieve patient's comfort and continuous health monitoring, wireless platforms should be small and lightweight for the patient to carry.

Low Power and Cost. Low power is very important to expand node's lifetime where patient does not need to frequently change the battery. All components considered in TelG wireless sensor node design must consume minimal power, particularly for microcontroller, sensor and wireless modules.

Reliability. Reliability is a crucial element in the WBSN platform design. It must ensure the patient's data reliably reaches its destination. Some aspect to be considered is reliable wireless communication between nodes and efficient computation in each sensor node.

Multi-hop. WBSN platforms must be able to communicate through multi-hop to guarantee the data reaches the destination. Another benefit from multi-hop communication is it offers low power consumption. This is because long-distance transmission requires more power than a short one.

3 Telg Mote Architecture

Generally, the platform design architecture for WSN platforms is relatively similar with WBSN platforms. TelG mote architecture shown in Figure 1 consists of four major components listed as follows:

Processor. Core of the TelG mote.

Wireless Transceiver. Wireless link between neighbouring sensor nodes or intermediate nodes

Medical Sensor. Device for capturing physiological signal.

Power Supply. Power source for the TelG mote.

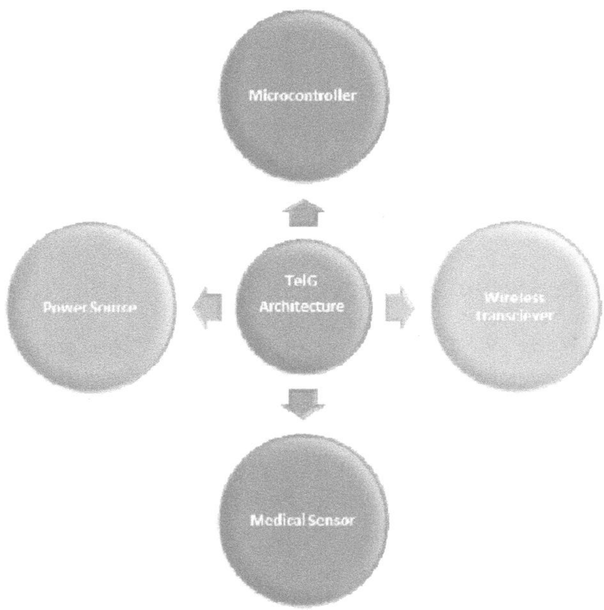

Fig. 1. TelG mote design architecture

3.1 Processor

Most of the WSN platforms are based on components-off-the-shelf (COTS) and the development of WSN depends extensively on the rapid advancement of micro processors. Unlike common Personal Computer (PC) applications, WBSN application requires much less processing power due to tight constraint on size and power consumption. Due to these reasons, WBSN platforms mainly use low power 8-bit microcontroller as its processor.

Table 1 shows the comparison between existing microcontrollers for wireless sensor nodes. ATmega644pv microcontroller was chosen as TelG mote microcontroller after evaluating existing product from Atmel, Motorola, and Microchip (refer to Table 1).

It is an 8-bit Harvard architecture with 16-bit address. It provides 32 8-bit general purposes registers and can operate at 1.8V to 5.5V for frequencies from 0 to 4 MHz and 2.7V to 5.5V for frequencies from 0 to 10MHz [23]. At 1MHz and 1.8V at ambient temperature, ATmega644pv provides 0.4mA active current, 0.1uA power-down mode, 0.6uA power-save mode and 32 kHz real-time clock (RTC) [23].

Table 1. Comparison between existing microcontrollers

Microcontroller	RAM (kB)	Flash (kB)	Active (mA)	Sleep (uA)
AT90LS8535	0.5	8	5	15
Mega128	4	128	8	20
Mega165/325/645	4	64	2.5	2
Atmega644pv	4	64	0.4	0.1
PIC Modern	4	60	2.2	1
80C51	2	60	15	3
HCS08	4	60	6.6	1
MSP430F14X	2	60	1.5	1
MSP430F16X	10	48	2	1

The TelG mote operates at 3.3V voltage supply, 7.3728MHz external clock at ambient temperature (25°C). The ATmega644pv provides 64K bytes of In-System Programmable Flash with Read-While-Write capabilities, 2K bytes EEPROM and 4K bytes of SRAM data memory. Larger RAM buffers will enable more sophisticated applications, for example video and image applications, to be implemented [22].

In order to achieve low power consumption, ATmega644pv only uses 4.9mA active current. Note that, active current only consumes two times less power compared to Mega128 used in MICAZ sensor node platform. Sleep mode is significant to provide low power consumption. ATmega644pv has six sleep modes including idle (1.8mA), ADC noise reduction, power-safe (0.62μA), power down (0.25μA), standby and extend standby. The time transition or wake-up time between entering and existing sleep mode is also significant for low power consumption. With a quick wake-up time, power consumption can be reduced. ATmega644pv provides 6 clock cycle for wake-up time. ATMEL offers two IC packages for ATmega644pv; DIP (Dual Line in Package) package and TQFP (Thin Quad Flat Pack) package. In this project, TQFP IC package is chosen to meet the requirement of smaller size sensor node platform.

Peripheral features of microcontroller also play a major role in deciding which microcontroller to choose from. In general, a microcontroller would support several common features such as timer, analog to digital converter (ADC), pulse width modulator, two-wire serial interface, serial USART and serial peripheral interface. These common features are important for the microcontroller to interact with its environment and for communication purposes. Atmega644pv in particular has two serial USART interfaces. Atmel family microcontrollers have several programming methods to choose from in order to program its flash memory. TelG sensor node platform is designed to be programmed using in-system programming (ISP) mode for easy usage.

3.2 Wireless Transceiver

The wireless transceiver is the most important part on a WBSN platform since it is the primary energy consumer. Today, there are many types of wireless transceivers with various features that exist in the market. In WBSN application, the selection criteria are low data rate, low power, short range and low complexity. IEEE802.15.4 wireless standard has been chosen for WBSN application after evaluating the characteristics of existing wireless standard [24].

XBee module from Digi is used on the wireless device. XBee module is an IEEE 802.15.4 compliant radio device based on CSMA-CA (channel sense multiple access) which will provide point to point, point to multipoint and also peer to peer communication. It is designed for low-latency and predictable communication timing applications [25].

Radio Frequency (RF) data rates for the XBee module can go up to 250Kbps and operates at 2.4GHz ISM (Industrial Scientific and Medical) frequency band. XBee module has a small form factor (2.438cm x 3.294cm). It has the power output of 1mW (+0dB) and capable of transmitting up to 30m indoor and 100m outdoor with the receiver sensitivity of -92dBm [25].

The XBee module has sixteen 5MHz channels ranging from 2.405 to 2.480 GHz, with 65,000 addressable network addresses for each channel. Since it employs IEEE802.15.4 standards, the data transmitted is in the form of packets where the maximum transmission unit (MTU) for each packet is 127 bytes. Each packet is acknowledged at the link layer in unicast mode providing best-effort-delivery except for broadcast mode. It is interesting to note that, the link layer standard required a coordinator in the network but XBee is designed to work even without a coordinator.

XBee uses serial USART as its interface. The host can be interfaced with XBee module with rates of up to 115.4Kbps. Since both the USART interface and operates at 3.3V and ATmega644PV (host) also operates at the same voltage level, XBee module can be connected directly without any voltage level circuit. One of the most appealing features of XBee module for application developers is its API Operation. The API provides an easy way for developers to issue a command to the module.

3.3 Medical Sensor

Medical sensors are used to measure physiological signal from the body. In the market, there are many medical sensors like ECG, EEG, SpO2 (oxygen saturation) and etc. Figure 2 shows the existing SpO2, ECG and CSN808 medical sensor modules in the market and these modules can be integrated with TelG sensor node platform.

The CSN808 board has the capability to sense ECG, (non-invasive blood pressure) NIBP, SpO2, pulse rate, respiration rate and temperature signal. This board works on a single low power of 6V and it is capable to sense three types of patient; adult, infant and neonate patient. It also has two channel temperature data and three channel ECG waveform including heart rate calculation and wave abnormality (ST) segment detection. In respiration rate sensing, CSN808 can calculate respiration rate and generate apnea alarm.

For the NIBP sensing, it has measurement modes from neonate to adult and measurement methods that include manual, automatic and continuous. Basically, most of the medical signal data processing is done by CSN808 and it sends data in packets. All the medical parameter detected by CSN808 can be extracted from that data packet because data packet transmission of CSN808 board uses serial transmission protocol and it is transmitted via RS232 interface. Data packet speed for CSN808 is 50 packets per second and consists of 25 bytes per packet.

Fig. 2. Medical Sensor Modules

3.4 Power

The heart of the wireless sensor node is the power supply. Power supply design (battery or solar) will give an impact to the size and the lifetime of the sensor node platform. Most of the sensor node depends on the design of the size of the power supply itself, regardless whether it is using dry battery or solar. Large battery size will generate higher capacity current and at the same times extends the life time of the sensor node.

To balance the tradeoff between size and life time, TelG wireless sensor node uses three pieces of AA batteries as its power supply. The AA battery is cheaper compared to existing power supply such as solar. The AA battery can generate 2890 mAh at 1.5 volt that can extend the life time of the sensor node between 4 and 6 month. The size of AA battery is smaller (14.5mm diameter and in cylindrical form) and lighter, hence, it is suitable for medical application for ease of mobility of the patient when wearing the device.

4 WiseOS Operating System

Almost every sensor node has its own operating system, either it is being ported from other sensor node platform or specifically designed for it. TelG mote is developed as a complete platform with its own operating system. For this purpose, WiseOS [26] is developed based on the TinyOS which is a popular operating system for sensor node. It supports modularity and concurrency based on event driven approach.

WiseOS is designed to implement TinyOS basic kernel. The WiseOS structure is fully written in C language and offers small footprint (RAM 2Kb, ROM 50b). In addition, it also enables a flexible and rapid prototyping of wireless sensor network applications and easy to use with small learning curve.

5 Results

TelG mote has been successfully developed. To determine the performance of TelG mote in terms of reliability and multi-hop capability, a simple experiment was conducted at the Digital Communication Lab, Faculty of Electrical Engineering, Universiti Teknologi Malaysia. Indoor environment is chosen because most of the WBSN systems focuses on indoor applications.

5.1 WBSN Node Platform

The first version of the TelG mote for WBSN application is shown in Figure 3. The size of TelG mote is 65mm x 54mm that includes one power LED (green) and four indicator LEDs in different colors (red, green, yellow and orange). The size of TelG mote is based on the medical sensor that is attached to the body which makes it a wearable sensor node. The small size and lightweight features are suitable for mobile as well as non-mobility patients.

Fig. 3. TelG Wireless sensor node platforms

The function of LEDs is for programming's debugging purposes. TelG mote is able to communicate with medical sensor either through USART port or ADC port. Two push buttons have been added to TelG mote; one is a reset button to reset the microcontroller and another button is for the user.

5.2 Low Power and Cost

TelG mote current consumption has been calculated by referring to the data sheet of selected components. The 3.3V voltage supply, 7.3728MHz external clock at ambient temperature (25°C) operating condition are used to determine the current consumption of the TelG mote. The current consumption of TelG mote is presented in Table 2. Based on Table 2, it shows that the consumed current when receiving is more than the current when transmitting. Interesting to note that the TelG mote feature has a lower microcontroller (MCU) wakeup time and idle current compared to TelosB (MSP430)[27]. TelG mote, estimated at only RM200 a piece, also costs lower than TelosB at RM 600 each. It also consumes less power due to the IEEE 802.15.4 wireless technology.

Table 2. Current Consumption of TelG mote

Operation	TelG
Voltage operation	3.3V
Standby mode	10.62 uA
Receive mode	54mA
Transmit mode	49mA
MCU idle	0.8mA
MCU active	4mA
MCU wakeup Time	0.8 us

5.3 Reliability and Multi-hop

Figure 4 shows the effect of distance to the packet reception rate (PRR) or probability of successful reception. Based on the figure 4, probability of successful reception between two neighbouring motes at distances below than 6 meters is 80%. This is due to the antenna used for TelG mote.

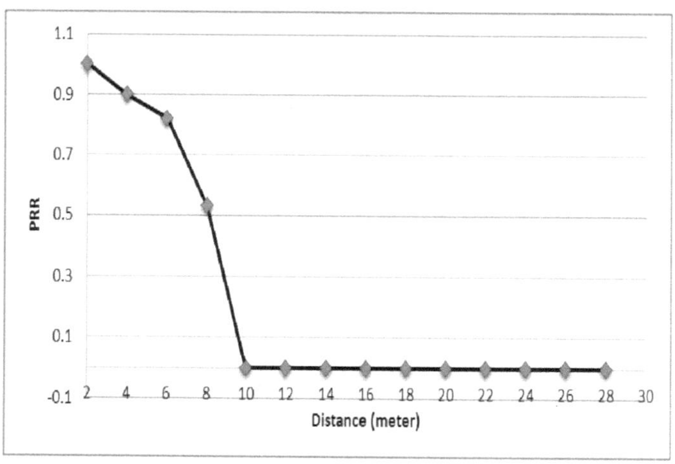

Fig. 4. Effect of distance to PRR

TelG mote can also communicate in single hop or multi-hop network. Figure 5 shows the effect of number of hops to end-to-end delay at 36 bytes packet size. The delay of a single hop can reach up to 15ms and end-to-end delay will increase around 15ms per hop.

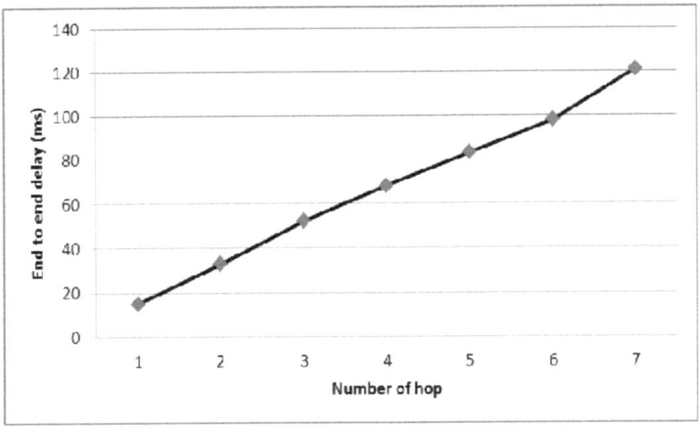

Fig. 5. Effect of number of hop to end-to-end delay

6 Conclusion

A new wireless sensor node platform for WBSN application called TelG mote has been developed. The platform offers enhanced technologies such as wearable, reliable, low power consumption, flexible and multi hop communication. TelG mote is developed to enable WBSN research and medical application's implementation. The main features of TelG mote is a health monitoring system that is small in size, energy and cost efficient, offers real-time data processing and multi-hop capability. Future works will include more deployment of the TelG mote in a real clinical environment to investigate its reliability and robustness and improving the design itself, hardware and software respectively.

Acknowledgment. The authors wish to express their gratitude to Ministry of Higher Education (MOHE), Malaysia and Research Management Center (RMC), Universiti Teknologi Malaysia for the financial support of this project under GUP research grant no: Q.J130000.7107.03J81.

References

1. Schwiebert, L., Gupta, S.K., Weinmann, J.: Research Challenges In Wireless Networks of Biomedical Sensor. In: MobiCom 2001: Proceedings of the 7th Annual International Conference on Mobile Computing and Networking, pp. 151–165. ACM, New York (2001)
2. Ren, H., Max, Q.-H., Meng, X.: Physiological Information Acquisition through Wireless Biomedical Sensor Networks. In: Proceedings of the 2005 IEEE International Conference on Information Acquisition, Hong Kong, Macau (2005)
3. Yang, G.-Z.: Conclusions and Future Outlook. In: Yang, G.-Z. (ed.) Body Sensor Networks, pp. 416–417. Springer, London (2006)
4. Hill, J.L., Culler, D.E.: Mica: A Wireless Platform for Deeply Embedded Networks. IEEE Micro. 22(6), 272–1732 (2002)

5. Polastre, J., Szewczyk, R., Culler, D.: Telos: enabling ultra-low power wireless research. In: IPSN 2005: Proceedings of the 4th International Symposium on Information Processing in Sensor Networks, p. 48. IEEE Press, Piscataway (2005)
6. Malan, D., Fulford-jones, T., Welsh, M., Moulton, S.: CodeBlue: An ad hoc sensor network infrastructure for emergency medical care. In: International Workshop on Wearable and Implantable Body Sensor Networks (2007)
7. Milenkovic, A., Otto, C., Jovanov, E.: Wireless sensor networks for personal health monitoring: Issues and an implementation. Computer Communications (Special issue: Wireless Sensor Networks: Performance, Reliability, Security, and Beyond) 29, 2521–2533 (2006)
8. Virone, G., Wood, A., Selavo, L., Cao, Q., Fang, L., Doan, T., He, Z., Stoleru, R., Lin, S., Stankovic, J.A.: A An Advanced Wireless Sensor Network for Health Monitoring. Unpublish note, Department of Computer Science, University of Virgina
9. Moteiv. Tmote Sky Zigbee-based WSN platform, `http://www.moteiv.com/`
10. Otto, C., Milenkovic, A., Sanders, C., Jovanov, E.: Final results from a pilot study with an implantable loop recorder to determine the etiology
11. Park, C., Chou, P.H.: An Ultra-Wearable, Wireless, Low Power ECG Monitoring System. In: Biomedical Circuits and Systems Conference, pp. 241–244 (November 2006)
12. Lo, B., Thiemjarus, S., King, R., Yang, G.Z.: Body sensor network - a wireless sensor platform for pervasive healthcare monitoring. In: Adjunct Proceedings of the 3rd International Conference on Pervasive Computing, pp. 77–80 (May 2005)
13. Hu, F., Jiang, M., Celentano, L., Xiao, Y.: Robust medical ad-hoc sensor networks (MASN) with wavelet-based ECG data mining. Ad Hoc Netw. 6(7), 986–1012 (2008)
14. Rotariu, C., Costin, H., Ciobotariu, R., Adochiei, F., Amariutei, I., Andruseac, G.: TELEMON - An Embedded Wireless Monitoring and Alert System for Homecare. In: XII Mediterranean Conference on Medical and Biological Engineering and Computing 2010, pp. 875–878. Springer, Heidelberg (2010)
15. Kew, H.-P., Jeong, D.-U.: Wearable Patch-type ECG using Ubiquitous Wireless Sensor Network for Healthcare Monitoring Application. In: ICIS 2009: Proceedings of the 2nd International Conference on Interaction Sciences, pp. 624–630. ACM, New York (2009)
16. Chen, H., Wu, W., Lee, J.: A WBAN-based real-time electroencephalogram monitoring system: design and implementation. Journal Medical System 34(3), 303–311 (2010)
17. Figueiredo, C.P., Cardona, J., Hoffmann, K.-P., Mendes, P.M.: Wearable and Ultra Low Power Wireless System for Physiological Monitoring. In: World Congress on Medical Physics and Biomedical Engineering, September 7-12, pp. 461–464. Springer, Heidelberg (2009)
18. Welsh, M., Chen, B., et al.: Sensor Network for Medical Care. In: SenSys 2005: Proceedings of the 3rd International Conference on Embedded Networked Sensor Systems, p. 314 (2005)
19. Chen, X., Meng, M.Q.H., Ren, H.: Design of Sensor Node Platform for Wireless Biomedical Sensor Networks. In: Engineering in Medicine and Biology Society 27th Annual International Conference, January 17-18, pp. 4662–4665. IEEE, Shanghai (2005)
20. Baker, C.R., Armijo, K., Belka, S., Benhabib, M., Bhargava, V., Burkhart, N., Der Minassians, A., Dervisoglu, G., Gutnik, L., Haick, M.B., Ho, C., Koplow, M., Mangold, J., Robinson, S., Rosa, M., Schwartz, M., Sims, C., Stoffregen, H., Waterbury, A., Leland, E.S., Pering, T., Wright, P.K.: Wireless Sensor Networks for Home Health Care. In: 21st International Conference on Advanced Information Networking and Applications Workshops, AINAW 2007, May 21-23, pp. 832–837. IEEE, Niagara Falls (2007)

21. Bischoff, R., Meyer, J., Feltrin, G.: Wireless Sensor Network Platforms. In: Boller, Chang, F.-K., Fujino, Y. (eds.) Encyclopedia of Structural Health Monitoring. John Wiley & Sons, Chichester (2009)
22. Hill, J., Horton, M., Kling, R., Krishnamurthy, L.: The Platforms Enabling Wireless Sensor Networks. Communication ACM 47(6), 41–46 (2004)
23. Atmel Corporation. 8-bit AVR Microcontroller with 16/32/64K Bytes In-System Programmable Flash ATmega644P/V. Data Sheet, Orchard Parkway San Jose 2008/2007
24. Ren, H., Meng, M.Q.-H., Chen, X.: Physiological Information Acquisition through Wireless Biomedical Sensor Networks. In: Proceedings of the 2005 IEEE International Conference on Information Acquisition, Hong Kong, Macau (2005)
25. Maxstream. XBee^{TM}XBee-PRO^{TM} OEM RF Modules. Lindon(UT): Product Manual (2006)
26. Rashid, R.A., Fisal, N., Hamid, A.H.A.: Wireless Multimedia Sensor Network Platform For Low Rate Image/Video Streaming. Jurnal Teknologi, 54(Sains & Kejuruteraan) Keluaran Khas, 1–12 (2011)
27. Crossbow Technology, Inc. TelosB Mote Platform, San Jose, California Datasheet (2004)

Delay-Based Loss Discrimination Mechanism for Congestion Control in Wireless Ad-Hoc Network

Adib M.Monzer Habbal and Suhaidi Hassan

InterNetWorks Research Group, School of Computing
University Utara Malaysia, Malaysia
{adib,suhaidi}@uum.edu.my

Abstract. Transmission Control Protocol (TCP) is the dominant protocol used in the Internet today. It was well designed to work over a wired network. However, TCP suffers from performance degradation in a wireless ad-hoc network. The main reason is that regular TCP misinterprets packet loss due to wireless channel error as network congestion and consequently reduces its sending rate,. In this paper, we propose a new end-to-end mechanism to support TCP discriminating congestion loss from none-congestion loss. The proposed mechanism is evaluated using simulation under different network topologies and varying PER levels; results demonstrate that the proposed scheme outperforms NewReno, in terms of throughput, by 30%.

Keywords: TCP, Wireless Ad-Hoc Network, Wireless Error Loss, Congestion.

1 Introduction

Wireless network can be broadly classified into infrastructure based network and ad-hoc network. Infrastructure based network is a collection of wired and wireless nodes that connect to each other depending on fixed infrastructure (i.e. base station or access point)[1]. While ad-hoc network is a group of wireless mobile devices that connect to each other using wireless channel, forming a temporary network without the aid of fixed infrastructure [2]. Thus, Nodes in ad-hoc network can act as end hosts or intermediary nodes.

Recently, ad-hoc network receives considerable attention due to its attractive properties of building a network on a fly with ease of deployment, speed of deployment and decreased dependency on infrastructure. Moreover, it is suited for use in a large variety of applications such as emergency services at a disaster site, military operations in a remote area, business meetings held in venues without network infra and sensor networks [3].

TCP, meanwhile, is a de-facto standard protocol that provides reliable, end-to-end, and connection-oriented data delivery over unreliable networks [4]. It is the dominant protocol used in the Internet today, since it is responsible for the transmission of around 90% of Internet traffic [5]. Therefore, it is very likely that TCP will also find its application in ad-hoc networks to ensure reliable end-to-end packet delivery and provide efficient bandwidth utilization.

A. Abd Manaf et al. (Eds.): ICIEIS 2011, Part III, CCIS 253, pp. 689–700, 2011.

TCP was well designed to work over a wired network where most packet loss occurs due to network congestion. It detects packet loss using retransmission time out (RTO) and triple duplicate acknowledgments (3 DupAcks); then it responds to it by adjusting the congestion window and RTO. However, wireless Ad-hoc network suffers from wireless error loss in addition to congestion loss, leading to poor performance of TCP because TCP treats all losses as congestion loss. Therefore, TCP requires a proper technique to discriminate the cause of packet loss.

In this study, we introduce a new end-to-end mechanism to improve TCP performance in wireless ad-hoc network. The proposed mechanism focuses on distinguishing congestion loss from none-congestion loss. Furthermore, it is implemented at the sender side only without any cooperation from the intermediate node or the lower layers.

The rest of the paper is organized as follows. Section two reviews the most related works. Section three describes the proposed mechanism in terms of design, implementation and accuracy. In Section four, simulation environment and performance metrics are introduced; then the simulation result is presented. Section five concludes the paper and discusses some possible extensions of our work.

2 Related Work

Literature has reported many studies and efforts to enhance TCP performance over wireless ad-hoc networks. Such techniques aiming to differentiate congestion loss from wireless error loss (none-congestion loss) are the point of focus for this section.

Wu and Chen developed jitter-based TCP (JTCP [6]) to adapt sending rates to the packets losses and jitter ratios (Jr). When the sender receives triple duplicate ACK or the retransmit timer expires, it compares the value of (Jr) with the inverse value of current congestion window size to distinguish the network congestion losses from wireless losses. When the Jr is less than {k/cwnd}, an inferred segment loss is regarded as a non-congestive loss. Otherwise, it is considered as a congestive loss. Here, k is a control parameter which should not be larger than cwnd. It has been shown that JTCP outperformed TCP Reno [7], TCP NewReno [8, 9], and TCPW [10] when the packet loss rate was at least 10 percent over a simulated wireless link. Nevertheless, it is ineffective to resolve a burst loss event by fast recovery upon a retransmission timer expiration since multiple segment losses may have occurred within the same congestion window [11]. As JTCP retransmits one segment for each timer expiration, this leads to the occurrence of several more timer expirations to recover the remaining segment losses in the same window, thereby causing substantial performance degradation. Besides, JTCP use extra information in the TCP header to store the sending and receiving timestamp.

Oliveira and Braun investigated the use of fuzzy logic theory for assisting the TCP error detection mechanism in MANET and introduced Fuzzy-based Error Detection Mechanism (FEDM) [12]. This approach relies on RTT mean and variants measurements. Simulation results have shown that the fuzzy engine may indeed distinguish congestion from channel error conditions, and consequently assist the TCP error detection. However, improvements are certainly possible as the model studied here is rather modest. For instance, independent fuzzy outputs for each of the evaluated conditions (congestion and medium error) could provide more flexibility in adjusting the engine. The membership functions can be optimized by using advanced learning/training techniques such as ANFIS, and self-adaptive setting models can render this approach very robust.

Fu et al. proposed the first multi-metrics end-to-end approach called ADTCP [13]. It identifies the presence of various network conditions, namely, congestion, disconnection, route change, and channel error. Upon each packet arrival at the receiver, receiver calculates four metrics value (inter-packet delay difference (IDD), short-term throughput (STT), Packet out-of-order Arrival (POR) and packet loss ratio (PLR)) and defines a value to be High or Low based on Relative Sample Density (RSD) technique, finally network state is estimated based on the rules listed in Table 1. The receiver passes state information to the sender in every outgoing ACK packet.

Table 1. Identification rules of network state, High:Top 30%; Low: Bottom 30%; '*': do not care

Heading level	IDD and STT	POR	PLR
Congestion	(High, Low)	*	
Route Change	Not (High, Low)	High	*
Channel Error	Not (High, Low)		High
Disconnection	Not (High, Low)	*	*
Normal		Default	

The sender maintains the most current state feedback received via these ACK packets and proceeds with normal TCP operation until a packet loss occur by either a retransmission timeout or a third duplicate ACK. The sender takes control actions according to the receiver's network state estimation. In case of congestion, the sender adopts same congestion control action as conventional TCP. When channel error is detected, the sender will retransmit the lost packet without slowing down. ADTCP provides flexibility for backward compatibility, also behaves TCP-friendly. It has become very well-known and has served as a basis for many later approaches. In real testbed, ADTCP show 30% throughput increase over Reno in case of weak channel. Yet, testbed showed 5% decrease in ADTCP throughput in clear channel due to its high computational cost. Nevertheless, ADTCP maintains a sample space to determine the level of each metric value (high or low); and using weight, it gives recent sample high value compared to old ones. However, sometime old value has negative influence and it is better to rebuild the sample space after loss recovered for eliminating the influence of the old case.

Previous researches present different approaches to distinguish congestion losses from wireless error losses based on one common ground; that is, delay (such as RTT, IDD, and Jitter) is a good loss indicator. However, more investigation is still needed in the performance of TCP over wireless ad-hoc network to overcome drawbacks which appeared in these works. In this paper, we propose Delay-Based Loss Discrimination mechanism (DBLD) for TCP congestion control over wireless ad-hoc network. DBLD is aimed to have the following key features:

a. Provide TCP sender with updated and accurate information about the network condition without interfering with the traditional TCP operation; Therefore, the sender can react appropriately.

b. Maintain TCP end-to-end semantic just like ADTCP. However, our mechanism is a sender based ONLY (i.e. no processing or data collection will be conducted at the receiver side). Therefore, DBLD is easier to be implemented in such a heterogeneous environment.
c. Use Delay as a loss indicator similar to previous works. But, ours applies simpler approach to identify network condition. Thus, DBLD is expected to reduce the complexity and computational costs posed in FEDM and ADTCP.
d. Achieve higher aggregate throughput.

3 Proposed DBLD Scheme

Traditional definition of congestion is a network overload in bottleneck node (i.e. buffer overflow). In wireless ad-hoc network, meanwhile, contention for access to the shared wireless channel offers the first sign of network overload or congestion. Furthermore, simulations show that link-layer contention induced packet drop dominates, while buffer overflow is almost never experienced by TCP flows in typical multihop wireless networks [14]. Thus, network overload becomes a phenomenon that occurs in an area rather than in a single node and it is still accompanied by increasing delay. Consequently, it is more accurate to calculate the delay along the forward and reverse paths to estimate the network overload. Therefore, our proposed mechanism uses RTT as a loss indicator. However, the following questions remain to be answered - How to calculate RTT samples and maintain TCP semantics? How to identify the RTT trend (evolution) based on the observed history of RTT samples? What is the suitable sample space size? How to answer these questions without posing extra overhead to TCP? We answer all these questions in the following sub-sections.

3.1 DBLD Design

RTT is defined in [15] as the time interval between sending a packet and receiving an acknowledgment for it (i.e. RTT measurements conflate delays along the forward and reverse paths). For example, let TSi denote the sending time of packet i, and TRi denote the receiving time of its Ack; then RTT may be expressed:

$$RTT = TRi - TSi \quad (1)$$

Accurate RTT estimation is necessary to identify changing network conditions. However, it may be difficult both in theory and in implementation. A solution to this issue is using TCP options proposed in RFC1323 [15], where the sender places a timestamp in each data packet, and the receiver reflects these time stamps back in ACK packets. Then a single subtract gives the sender an accurate RTT measurement for every ACK packet, see Eq.1.

The RTT values are collected by TCP sender and stored in a sample space (S). The size of S should be set appropriately. If it is too short, the observed samples are not enough to analyze network status; if it is too long, the observed samples may be outdated or not valid. Since conventional NewReno assumes a packet loss occurred upon receiving of 3 DupAcks, four Acks is enough to deduce packet loss event. Therefore, we assume that (S) with four RTT samples may help diagnose network conditions. We choose S size = 4.

Next, we should determine S contents that express the current network status. The standard TCP uses RTT samples to update the averaged RTT measurement only if the packet acknowledges some new data, (i.e., only if it advances the left edge of the send window). RTT value of any packet contains duplicate acknowledgement will be excluded in the calculation to avoid any fluctuation that may affect the accuracy of smooth RTT estimation. However, these values are very important to reflect the recent network condition. Therefore, the sample space will contain RTT1 of the latest new Ack, in addition to RTT2, RTT3, and RTT4 of the following 3 duplicate acknowledgements. Fig.1 shows sample space values.

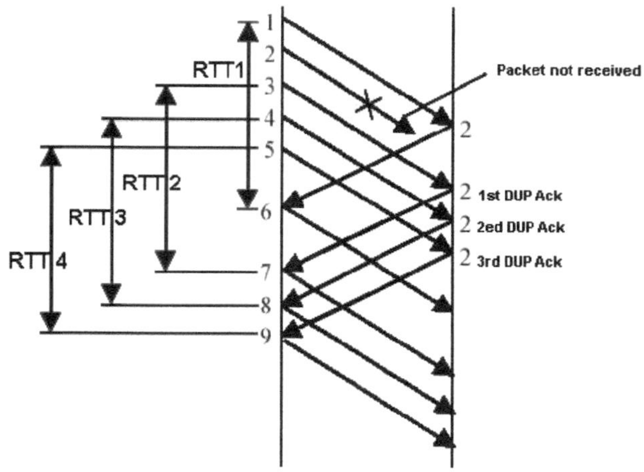

Fig. 1. DBLD Sample Space

Given the RTT samples, once 3 DupAcks is triggered the proposed mechanism will indicate the trend of RTT sample. If the trend is increasing; it indicates a sign of network congestion. Otherwise, the network is not congested, and it is a sign of wireless error. To capture this trend, we apply PairWise Comparison Test (PCT) on the RTT sample values, where each value in the sample space will be compared to the smooth RTT (SRTT) as follows:

$$PCT = \frac{\sum_{k=1}^{n=4} \mathrm{I}\,(\mathrm{RTTk} > SRTT)}{\mathrm{n} = 4} \quad (2)$$

Where I(X) is one if X holds (i.e., RTT sample is greater than SRTT), and zero otherwise. PCT takes a value in the range between [0,1] ; $0 \leq \mathrm{PCT} \leq 1$ 1. If there is an increasing trend, PCT approaches one. In the simulation, we choose PCT = 1.

3.2 DBLD Implementation

The proposed loss discrimination mechanism contains two main components, as follows:

i. Sender calculates monitoring metric values (RTT) for the latest new ACK received, and the following 3 duplicate acknowledgements, as illustrated in Fig.2.

```
UPON RECEIPT OF ACK:
If( RTT > SRTT)
      sum++;
```

Fig. 2. Pseudo code of collecting RTT sample

ii. When packet loss occurs due to 3 DupAcks, the sender will call PCT. If PCT value is equal to 1 then the RTT trend is increasing and it is a sign of network congestion. Therefore, fast retransmit and fast recovery will be invoked and congestion window will be reduced by 1/2. Otherwise, it is a wireless error loss; thus lost packet will be retransmitted immediately. In addition, congestion window should be adapted to the network situation. Since the existence of packet loss is a sign of network instability. We decide to set congestion window to 3*Cwnd/4. The reaction of the sender differs from traditional NewReno according to network conditions. The pseudo code in Fig.3 outlines the proposed mechanism and changes in TCP sender actions.

```
UPON 3rd DUPLICATE ACK:
If (PCT == 1)
      report congestion
      call TCP New-Reno fast retransmit and
      recovery (Cwnd = Cwnd/2)
else
      report wireless error
      retransmit the lost packet
      Cwnd = (3*Cwnd)/4
end if
sum = 0

PCT FUNCTION:
If ( sum / 4) ==1
      Return 1 // Increasing trend
else
      Return 0 //None-Increasing
```

Fig. 3. Pseudo code of the mechanism

3.3 Accuracy of DBLD

Proposing the use of an extra loss indicator should follow with increasing loss detection accuracy. In this section, we illustrate how our detection accuracy is better than standard/traditional one:

Assume two Hypotheses H_0 and H_1:

H_0: Congestion is absent (channel error is present), and
H_1: Congestion is present.

In addition, let event A denote that H_0 is selected and A^c denote that H_1 is selected. Based on these assumptions, False Alarm occurs due to choosing H_1 as cause of packet loss when H_0 is true (congestion loss is present when it is actually absent). Accordingly, the average probability of error is:

$$P[\text{Error}] = P[\text{False Alarm}] = P[\text{Error}|H_0]\ P[H_0] = P[A^c|H_0]\ P[H_0] \tag{3}$$

Our developed mechanism reduces this error as follows:

Let event B denote packet loss with increasing RTT trend and its complement B^c denote packet loss with none- increasing RTT trend. The result P[Error] is calculated as follows:

$$P[\text{Error}] = P[\text{False Alarm}] = P[\text{Error}|H_0]\ P[B|H_0]\ P[H_0] \tag{4}$$

Since probability, $0 < P[(B|H_0)] < 1$, is none-negligible, our mechanism achieves higher accuracy in terms of lower False Alarm.

3.4 Efficiency of DBLD

DBLD should be simple, flexible, and also computationally inexpensive. Thus, it has been designed to efficiently discriminate congestion loss from wireless error loss. Based on Fig.2 and Fig.3, it is clear that DBLD code needs O(1) for sample calculation, and O(1) for history maintenance. ADTCP code, in contrast, generates additional computational cost on the order of O(N) for each packet reception, and additional memory space of O(N) for sample. The same goes for FEDM. Therefore, DBLD is more efficient and this confirms our claim that DBLD will not increase complexity or computational cost.

4 Performance Evaluation

4.1 Network Environment Setup

We use the network simulator v2 (NS2) to perform the performance evaluation. We choose to keep most of the parameters of the simulations identical to those in [16], with a few exceptions. The following is a discussion of our simulation setup.

Table 2. Simulation Parameters

Parameters	Value
Routing Protocols	AODV
MAC Protocol	IEEE 802.11
PER	0% - 10%
Simulation Time	200 seconds
Simulation Topology	Chain & Grid
Packet Size	1000 bytes
Application Protocol	FTP
NS-2 version	2.34

To conduct our experiments, we consider a chain topology and grid topology as shown in Fig.4. All nodes are stationary and separated by 200m. The nodes communicate with identical, half-duplex wireless radios. The transmission range is set to 250m and the sensing range is set to approximately 550m. The data transmission and data packet size is set to 2Mbps and 1000bytes, respectively. Each simulation is run for 200 sec. The detailed information of the simulation model is stated in Table 2 below.

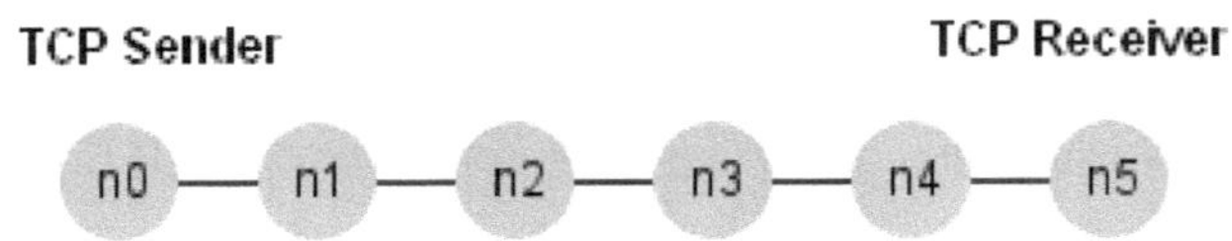

(a) Chain topology

(b) Grid topology

Fig. 4. Simulation topologies

4.2 Performance Metrics

We set up a single TCP connection between a chosen pair of sender and receiver nodes and measured the throughput over the lifetime of the connection. We use the total throughput received during simulation as the performance metric in this paper.

4.3 Result and Discussion

Chain Topology
It is quite common to have chain-like topologies in ad-hoc networks. Moreover, chain topology is the most resource-limited case that offers only one path so that its impact on TCP performance can be clearly observed. Therefore, the proposed DBLD scheme

is tested over 5-hop chain topology with varying PER ranging from 0% to 10%. The TCP throughput result under different PER is shown in Fig.5. The conventional NewReno is used as a reference of the performance bound while the other curve represents TCP with DBLD which is called TCP-DBLD.

Noticeably, with PER equal to 0; both TCPs receive the same throughput. When PER increases, TCP-DBLD achieves mildl improvement in throughput as compared to NewReno, with 4.4% increase in throughput for PER=0.02 and 7.4% for PER=0.04. The gap between TCP-DBLD and NewReno enlarges further and the improvement reaches the maximum value of 30% when PER = 0.06. Further increment of PER will produce a more noisy channel and collision probability will be high. Therefore, DBLD would not be able to contribute anymore, again both TCPs will get the same throughput for PER=0.08 and 0.1.

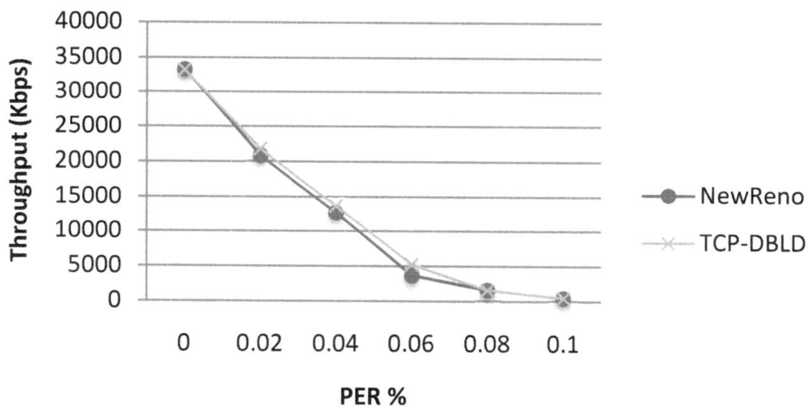

Fig. 5. Throughput in Chain Topology

TCP-DBLD behaves exactly like NewReno when PER does not exist or PER is high. This confirms our claim that DBLD will not interfere with the traditional TCP operation and only try to improve whenever it is possible. In case of PER=0, no improvement can be made. Hence, all losses are related to congestion and DBLD manage to accurately identify that. Additionally, when PER is high, the medium will become noisy and treat this case as congestion will be advised. On the other hand, It is worthwhile to point out that the main reason for the performance gain when PER equals to 0.02, 0.04 and 0.06 is due to the fact that DBLD mechanism provides accurate information about the network status (whether congested or not) and the cause of packet loss; therefore, TCP-DBLD takes appropriate action accordingly. Conventional NewReno, on the other hand treats any packet loss as congestion loss and reduces its transmission rate leading to degrade its performance.

Grid Topology

The grid topology has much more redundancy that provides alternative routes and back-up resources compared to chain topology. In this subsection, we have tested the proposed DBLD scheme over different scales of grid topology (5x5, 6x6, 7x7, and 8x8) with PER = 5% to see the possible performance improvement. Fig.6 shows the aggregate throughput of NewReno and TCP-DBLD over networks of the grid topology. For 5x5 grid, TCP-DBLD throughput is noticeably higher than NewReno. For 6x6 and 7x7, we observe a similar trend of the TCP throughput as that for 5x5 grid, with higher noticeable improvement over 7x7 grid. However, TCP-DBLD maintains the same throughput as NewReno over 8x8 grid. TCP-DBLD achieves 22% improvement over NewReno for 5x5, 16% improvement for 6x6, and 37% improvement for 7x7.

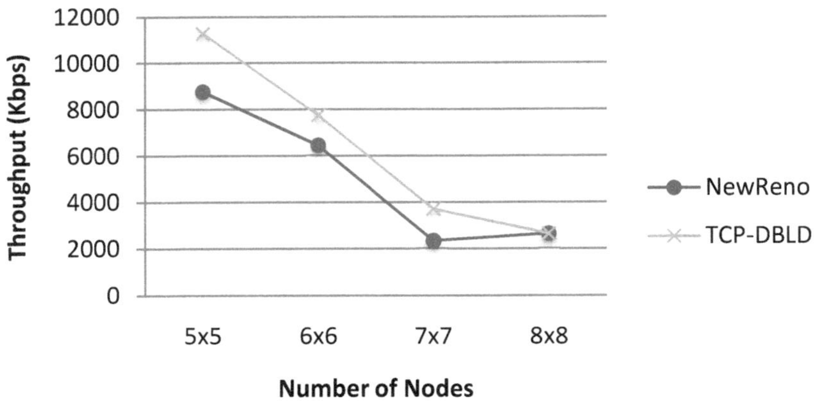

Fig. 6. Throughput in grid topology

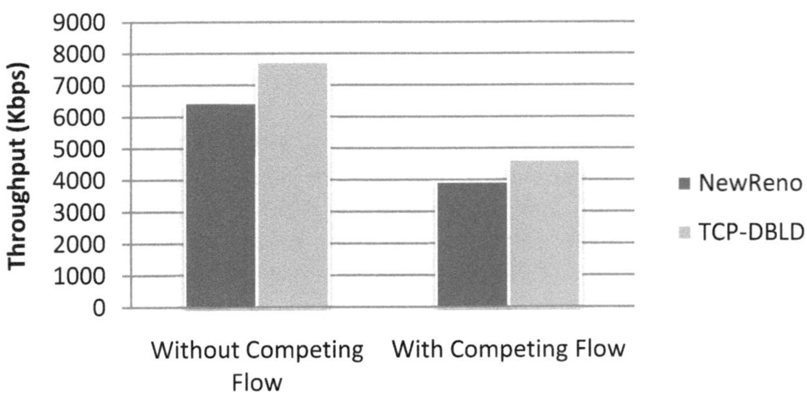

Fig. 7. Throughput in grid topology

Finally, in order to model a more realistic network environment, we consider a 6x6 grid topology with PER equal to 5% and the existence of more than one TCP traffic. The result is shown in Fig.7. Interestingly, TCP-DBLD achieves almost the same 16%

improvement over NewReno in the existence or the absence of competing flow. This means that TCP-DBLD is cabable of accurately distinguishing congestion losses from wireless error losses as compared to NewReno.

5 Conclusion and Future Works

In this paper, we propose a new end-to-end Delay-Based Loss Discrimination mechanism for TCP over a wireless ad-hoc network. The proposed mechanism focuses on differentiating congestion loss from wireless error loss using RTT as an indicator. The simulation results show that TCP-DBLD mechanism outperforms the conventional NewReno in terms of throughput. In the near future, we would like to continue investigating the performance of DBLD through further comparisons with other proposed mechanisms.

Acknowledgments. The authors would like to thank Prof. Madya Dr. Hasnah binti Ibrahim, Dr. Angela Amphawan, and Mr. Khuzairi bin Mohd Zaini for their useful comments on this paper.

References

[1] Stojmenovic, I.: Handbook Of Wireless Networks And Mobile Computing. John Wiley & Sons (2002)

[2] Sarkar, S.K., Basavaraju, T.G., Puttamadappa, C.: Ad Hoc Mobile Wireless Networks Principles, Protocols, and Applications: AUERBACH (2008)

[3] Boukerche, A.: Algorithms and Protocols for Wireless and Mobile Ad Hoc Networks. John Wiley & Sons (2009)

[4] Kurose, J., Ross, K.: Computer Networking: A Top-Down Approach Featuring the Internet, 5th edn. Addison-Wesley (2009)

[5] Mark, A., Aaron, F.: On the Effective Evaluation of TCP. SIGCOMM Comput. Commun. Rev. 29, 59–70 (1999)

[6] Wu, E.H.K., Mei-Zhen, C.: JTCP: Jitter-Based TCP For Heterogeneous Wireless Networks. IEEE Journal on Selected Areas in Communications 22, 757–766 (2004)

[7] Allman, M., Paxson, V., Stevens, W.: TCP Congestion Control, Request for Comments, RFC 2581, Network Working Group, Internet Engineering Task Force (1999)

[8] Parvez, N., Mahanti, A., Williamson, C.: An Analytic Throughput Model for TCP NewReno. IEEE/ACM Transactions on Networking PP, 1 (2009)

[9] Floyd, S., Henderson, T.: The NewReno Modification to TCP's Fast Recovery Algorithm. Request for Comments, RFC 2582, Network Working Group, Internet Engineering Task Force (1999)

[10] Claudio, C., Mario, G., Saverio, M., Sanadidi, M.Y., Ren, W.: TCP Westwood: End-To-End Congestion Control for Wired/Wireless Networks. Wireless Networks 8, 467–479 (2002)

[11] Ka-Cheong, L., Li, V.O.K.: Transmission Control Protocol (TCP) In Wireless Networks: Issues, Approaches, And Challenges. IEEE Communications Surveys & Tutorials 8, 64–79 (2006)

[12] de Oliveira, R., Braun, T.: A Delay-Based Approach Using Fuzzy Logic To Improve TCP Error Detection In Ad Hoc Networks. In: Wireless Communications and Networking Conference, WCNC 2004, vol. 3, pp. 1666–1671 (2004)
[13] Zhenghua, F., Greenstein, B., Xiaoqiao, M., Songwu, L.: Design And Implementation of a TCP-Friendly Transport Protocol for Ad Hoc Wireless Networks. In: Proceedings of the 10th IEEE International Conference on Network Protocols, pp. 216–225 (2002)
[14] Zhenghua, F., Haiyun, L., Zerfos, P., Songwu, L., Lixia, Z., Gerla, M.: The Impact of Multihop Wireless Channel on TCP Performance. IEEE Transactions on Mobile Computing 4, 209–221 (2005)
[15] Jacobson, V., Braden, R., Borman, D.: TCP Extensions for High Performance, Internet Engineering Task Force (IETF), RFC 1323 (May 1992)
[16] Josh, B., David, A.M., David, B.J., Yih-Chun, H., Jorjeta, J.: A Performance Comparison of Multi-Hop Wireless Ad Hoc Network Routing Protocols. In: Proceedings of the 4th annual ACM/IEEE International Conference on Mobile Computing and Networking Dallas, ACM, Texas (1998)

Cooperative Communication and Cognitive Radio (CR) Technology in LTE-Advanced

Faiz A. Saparudin, N. Fisal, Rozeha A. Rashid, Aimi S.A. Ghafar, and Siti M.M. Maharum

Center of Excellence in Telecommunication Technology,
Faculty of Electrical Engineering, Universiti Teknologi Malaysia,
Skudai, Johor, Malaysia
fasraf2@live.utm.my, {sheila,rozeha}@fke.utm.my,
{aimisyamimi,marwangi.maharum}@fkegraduate.utm.my

Abstract. Exponential increase in demands of wireless access over the years has led to rapid evolution for next generation wireless access technology. However, with scarce spectrum resource yet increasing bandwidth demand has become the main concern since this problem will hinder the evolution process and generally affects network performance. In this paper, by taking 3GPP (3rd Generation Partnership Project) LTE-Advanced (Long Term Evolution - Advanced) as a perfect specimen for 4G (fourth generation) standard candidate, we thoroughly investigate its key technologies thus providing overviews on network performance and efficiency improvement by implementing cooperative communication and cognitive radio (CR) technology.

Keywords: LTE-Advanced, Cognitive Radio, Cooperative Communication, Cooperative Relay.

1 Introduction

Increasing demands for wireless connection at higher throughput is the main motivation in the advancement of wireless technology. However, the limited radio spectrum resource that posed to be the key factor into supplying these demands has leads to its scarcity.

Research work in [1] has developed wireless access demand model. By assuming busiest market demands, the model shows that mobile broadband network capacity would reach bottleneck by mid-2013. Although the projection were estimates, it nevertheless shows that spectrum congestion will occur in the near future if no action are taken to efficiently utilize the spectrum and proportionally increase the capacity.

Thus, Cognitive Radio (CR) technology can be implemented as a way to avoid spectrum wastage and underutilization while maintaining overall system performance. CR technology also provides network environment awareness that will allow the system to self-manage and thus, will reduce manpower and operational expenses, respectively. Optimum spectrum utilization, reuse and management are essential especially in the next generation wireless communication system since it requires

A. Abd Manaf et al. (Eds.): ICIEIS 2011, Part III, CCIS 253, pp. 701–710, 2011.

higher bandwidth and more complex network topology (macrocells, microcells, femtocells etc.).

IMT-Advanced has been issued by ITU-R (International Telecommunication - Radiocommunication) as guidelines for the fourth generation wireless technology (4G) candidate. Although there are several candidates for the 4G system, the focus is on LTE - Advanced (Long Term Evolution Advanced) as proposed by 3GPP (3rd Generation Partnership Project). LTE-Advanced is the groundbreaking wireless access technology that will meet and most probably surpass IMT-Advanced requirements.

Since LTE-Advance is still at development stage, 3GPP has provided detailed information on LTE-Advanced which allow wide range of research and development for this technology. By taking this into account, LTE-Advanced is a perfect platform to further investigate for its need for deployment for the near future.

The main focus of this paper is exploring the technology components that are required in LTE-Advanced and the feasibility of using CR feature to improve LTE-Advanced system performance and efficiency in every possible way. In Section 2, we present a thorough description of proposed LTE-Advanced key technologies. While in Section 3, CR technology implementations to LTE-Advanced deployment will be discussed. Section 4 presents the performance assessment of cooperative communication. Finally, Section 5 concludes the paper.

2 LTE-Advanced Key Technology Components

Based on [2], ITU-R has thoroughly specified the requirements for next generation wireless technology by defining it in IMT-Advanced. Some of the key feature of IMT-Advanced are high quality mobile service, capability of interworking with radio access system and the most significant is peak data rate enhancement up to 1 Gbps for low mobility and 100 Mbps for high mobility. Since the former release of LTE (LTE release 8) is able to cater up to 300 Mbps for downlink and 75 Mbps for uplink, it does not satisfy the IMT-Advanced requirements and already considered as 3.9G, not 4G. Thus, in response of this, 3GPP has started research on LTE-Advanced as an evolution of LTE release 8 (LTE rel' 8) in order to meet the IMT-Advanced requirements. LTE-Advanced is targeted to capable of exploiting its former release technologies (i.e. UMTS, HSPA, LTE rel' 8) in ensuring backward compatibility and smooth transition. LTE-Advanced is also targeted to meet or even surpass the data rate of 1Gbps for downlink and 500Mbps for uplink. In order to achieve the performance specified by IMT-Advanced and to ensure ubiquitous communication network, several technology components for LTE-Advanced have been proposed. In the following subsection some of the technology components are presented.

2.1 Coordinated Multi-point Transmission (CoMP)

Severe performance degradation in term of spectrum efficiency, data rate and system throughput occur especially on cell edge due to loss and inter-cell interference (ICI). This will hinder ubiquitous system connectivity as envisioned in LTE-Advanced. Coordinated multi-point transmission (CoMP) has been proposed as the solution to mitigate cell-edge performance degradation and improve cell average throughput.

CoMP exploits inter-cell interference to its advantage by enabling information exchange between neighbouring cells and resource scheduling in term of time, frequency and space.

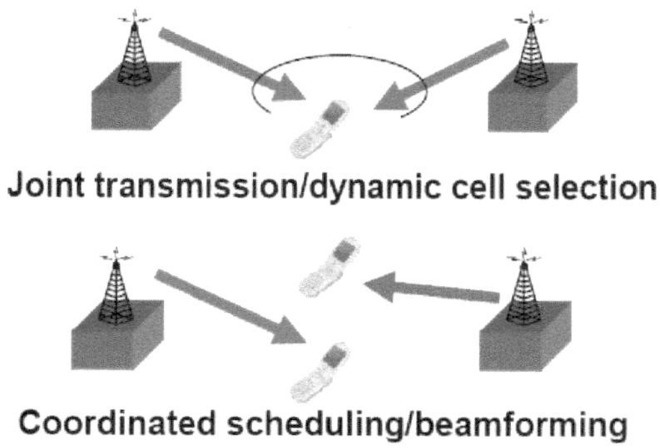

Fig. 1. Types of CoMP techniques proposed for LTE-Advanced

CoMP could be implemented in both uplink and downlink. As shown in Fig. 1, for downlink, CoMP is generally divided into two classes, Joint Processing (JP) and Coordinated Scheduling/Beamforming (CS/CB). JP operates by transmitting data from multiple cells simultaneously to single user equipment (UE). Joint transmission is performed by multiple cells mainly achieved by channel information based pre-coding algorithm [4]. JP also can be accomplished by dynamic cell selection where UE only receives transmission from the best selected cell based on signal power among neighbouring cells. In the other hand, CS/CB also has been considered for LTE-Advanced. CS/CB harnesses the beamforming and resource scheduling techniques to reduce inter-cell interference in order to improve especially in cell-edge region.

For uplink, multiple cell reception could be achieved by scheduling among the coordinated cells. Although CoMP techniques have some major challenges such as multi-cell synchronization and estimation, recent studies indicate that there are considerable increases in overall network performance. For example in [6], it is reported that median rate gain is increased by 50% and increase of fairness in field trial of uplink CoMP. The performance can be further increased with more advanced signal processing and joint detection algorithm.

2.2 Enhanced Multi-antenna Techniques

Spatial multiplexing and beamforming included in the multi-antenna technology has already been widely known as the key technology for LTE-Advanced. Spatial multiplexing of 8x8 MIMO for downlink and 4x4 MIMO for uplink has paved the way for LTE-Advanced to achieve targeted peak spectral efficiency of 30b/s/Hz for downlink and 15b/s/Hz for uplink. Open-loop and closed-loop spatial multiplexing has been studied for LTE-Advanced for which each technique has its own advantage and disadvantage. For open-loop spatial multiplexing, generally this technique provides straightforward approach in multiple antenna transmission. However, without information on the channel, detection complexity increases exponentially when the number of antenna increases. On the other hand, closed-loop spatial multiplexing utilizes reference signal (RS) where channel information feedback is provided to assist detection. 3GPP TSG Radio Access Network Working Group 1 (RAN WG1) which is responsible of studying radio layer 1 specification for LTE-Advanced has agreed that eight antennas transmission will be based on Demodulation RS (DM-RS) and Channel State Information RS (CSI-RS) [4]. Closed-loop spatial multiplexing suffers the setbacks of heavy overhead on the channel information feedback which is worse for fast moving environment.

Multi-user MIMO, considered for LTE-Advanced downlink, can provide higher degree of frequency domain scheduling, flexibility, and enhanced multi user interference suppression [3].

2.3 Carrier Aggregation

LTE rel'8 supports bandwidth of different size including 1.25MHz, 1.6MHz, 2.5MHz, 5MHz, 10MHz and 20MHz. The flexible spectrum allocation give the advantage of not just achieving peak data rate of 300Mbps, but also smooth transition from the earlier radio access technology (cdma2000, HSPA+ etc.).

Peak data rate of 1Gbps for LTE-Advanced requires high spectral efficiency and obviously wider bandwidth. LTE-Advanced has targeted to utilize bandwidth up to 100MHz while preserving backward compatibility with LTE rel'8. In order to do just that is by aggregation of LTE rel'8 bandwidth or so called "component carrier" (CC) on LTE-Advanced PHY layer. Carrier aggregation is done by concatenation of several LTE rel'8 compatible CC forming maximum LTE-Advanced bandwidth of 100MHz. As shown in Fig. 2, User equipment (UE) may receive a single CC or multiple CC simultaneously depending on UE capabilities, user requirements and needs.

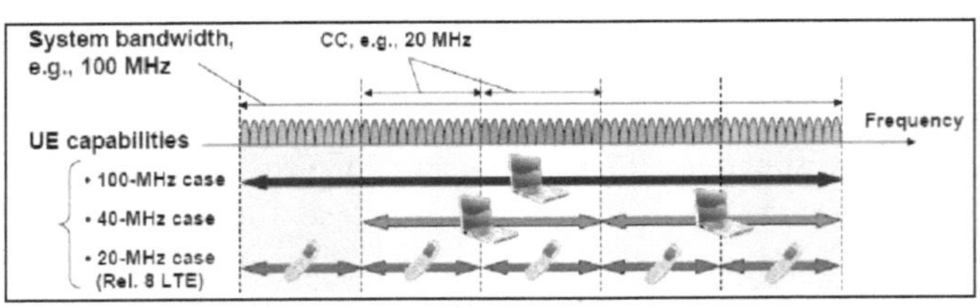

Fig. 2. Number of aggregated CC can be used depending on UE capabilities

However, with the increasing demands of wireless connectivity, spectrum congestion is inevitable and to find wide contiguous spectrum of up to 100MHz is seem improbable in the coming years. The possible solution to counter this problem is non-contiguous component carrier aggregation of different spectrum band are being studied. Intra-band and inter-band aggregation of CC in non-contiguous spectrum is shown in Fig. 3.

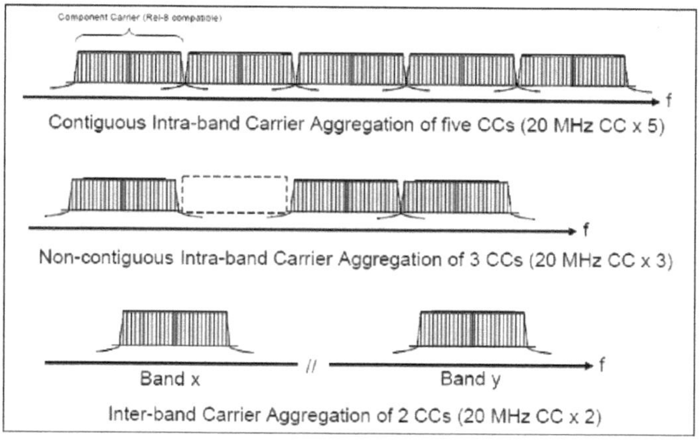

Fig. 3. Contiguous and non-contiguous spectrum aggregation of CC

2.4 Relay

LTE-Advanced envisioned ubiquitous network that provide highest possible data rate and performance while providing fair connectivity to its user. However, the wide spectrum proposed for LTE-Advanced contributes vast challenge in maintaining high throughput consistently at any location of the network.

Relaying is one of the techniques that have been considered as the solution for denser metropolitan environment because relay nodes (RN) increaser cell throughput and provide better coverage [19]. Apart from that, relaying also favored hassle free deployment especially for geographically unsuitable area for wired backhaul with LTE-Advanced base station, eNode B (eNB).

Generally, relay can be divided into Type-I and Type-II [11]. Based on Fig 4, Type-I relay is deployed outside the eNB coverage in order to provide better capacity for the user equipment (UE) especially at cell-edge. On the other hand, Type-II relay provides better quality-of-service (QoS) and link capacity within the eNB coverage.

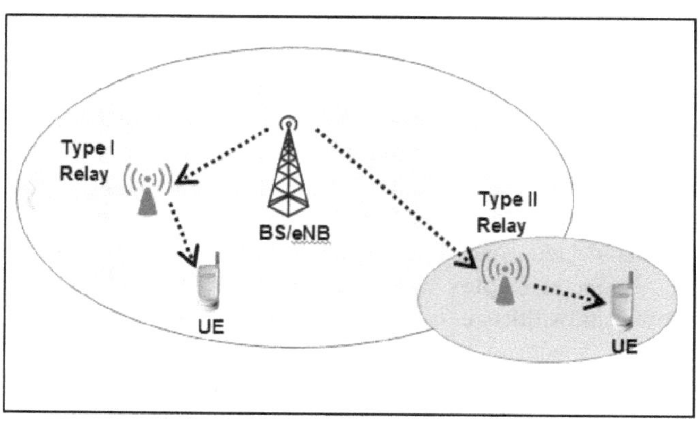

Fig. 4. Types of relay in typical deployment scenario

RN is responsible for not just simply to receive and retransmit modulated signals, but to decode and re-encode the signals before transmitting to the local UE without amplifying the noise. RN capabilities can be further expanded with the introduction of self-managing and cognitive feature which will be discussed in Section III.

3 CR Technology Implementation

The Cognitive Radio as defined in [7], is a type of radio in which communication systems are aware of their environment (may include location information) and internal states and can make decisions about their operating behaviors based on that information and predefined objectives. From the definition, we can deduce that CR consists of several features that include;

i. **Awareness:** Ability to sense and share information on its environment.
ii. **Adjustability:** Ability to respond to the environment by adjusting system parameter according to objective specified beforehand (modulation scheme, frequency, scheduling etc.)
iii. **Automatic:** Ability to work independently and autonomously without man-in-the-loop
iv. **Adaptability:** Ability to learn and adapt to the trend and increasing work efficiency in due time.

Hence, CR can be elaborated more by viewing into its practical implementations to wireless network, in this case, LTE-Advanced. In [8], CR technology was viewed to emerge within two main classes which are dynamic spectrum access (DSA) and self-X (X includes configure, monitor, diagnose, repair and optimize). These classes can clearly illustrate how CR will be implemented in LTE-Advanced.

In the following subsection, implementation of CR technology in LTE-Advanced and the need of cooperative communication will be discussed in several approaches and directions.

3.1 Cognitive Feature in LTE-Advanced Key Technology

From the overview of LTE-Advanced key technology presented in Section II, and based on [9], we can infer that cooperation and CR technology can be implemented from two main angles.

First is within the spectrum dimension. With cooperation of carrier frequencies in the spectrum, flexibility in occupying the spectrum can be increased hence increasing the system spectrum utilization and performance especially at higher bandwidth. Instead of rigid spectrum allocation, CR rearranges the spectrum so none of the precious resource is wasted. Since CR has the ability of sensing narrowband spectrum holes and LTE-Advanced employ aggregated LTE Rel'8 component carrier (which consist of narrow bandwidth), it is possible to re-allocate these carriers efficiently without leaving any spectrum holes. As in [10], CR sensing ability was seen as enabling technology in aggregating narrow band spectrum of different sizes.

Second, CR will enable intelligent cooperation within the LTE-Advanced network topology, mainly in two ways; (1) cooperation of the nodes in the same topological layer (homogeneous network) which increases efficiency especially at cell-edge and, (2) cooperation of the nodes in different topological layer (heterogeneous network) which can reduce inter-layer interference (e.g. between macrocells, microcells and femtocells).

Self-organizing network (SON) is one of the examples where cooperation within the network favors overall system performance. SON which includes self-configuration, self-optimization and self-healing, is an approach into employing CR self-X into the next generation wireless network, including LTE-Advanced.

3.2 CR Secondary User *(SU) Network*

Cognitive Radio technology has opened the doorway for secondary users (SU) to co-exist among primary users (PU). Although there are some who opposed the idea of opportunistic secondary user co-existence because it might be detrimental to the PU as mentioned in [8], the research on CR for SU network continues to grow in ensuring SU to stay "invisible" to PU while at the same time maintaining performance and QoS at an optimum level.

LTE-Advanced leads to diverse cell topological layer as to improve throughput and coverage. Macrocells, microcells and recently femtocells will have to coexist within the network. Femtocells or Home eNode Bs (HeNB) for LTE network are provided by mobile service provider to the end users for enhancing local network coverage such as home or office. HeNB deployments are uncoordinated and most probably financed by the users for their own home or office [18] almost resembles to Wi-Fi access points. Then, the users who subscribe to the service will clearly demand for exclusive access for their own HeNB. Thus, there will be limited number of dedicated users that are allowed to use these HeNB's as selected by the subscribers.

Here we can foresee that there will be such a waste of spectrum at a certain HeNB if not all of the dedicated users are not in use. Other users also could not occupy the spectral vacancies at that instance as it will interfere with dedicated users when they are suddenly in use.

Thus, we propose that CR secondary user concept can be employed in order to mitigate the problem in this scenario, as illustrated in Fig. 5. The concept indicates

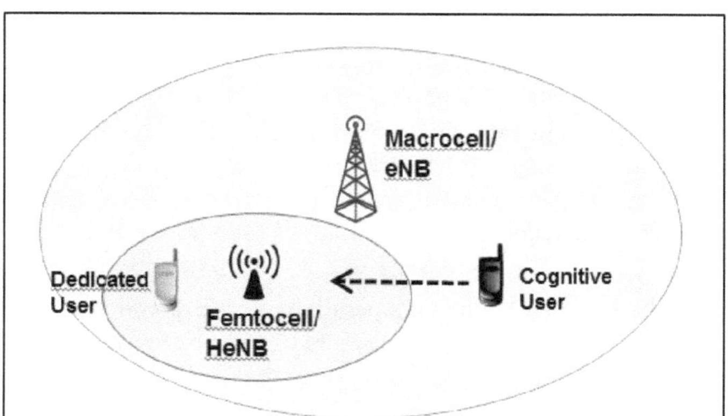

Fig. 5. CR user entering dedicated user femtocell coverage region

that PUs has the highest priority in occupying the spectrum and SUs are only allowed to occupy the spectrum in an opportunistic manner. Similarly, the selected dedicated users that have the priorities in using corresponding HeNB were seen as the PU while other users act as SUs. By adopting CR technology, user with CR feature (CR user) is now capable of accessing the HeNB.

Furthermore, CR users also should be able to enhance PUs performance by cooperative relaying. Based on Fig. 6, in a scenario when direct channel link between HeNB and PU (a_2) is weak, a CR user (CU) will cooperatively relay the data to the PU. This will increase the maximum achievable data rate of the PU in worst case primary link condition.

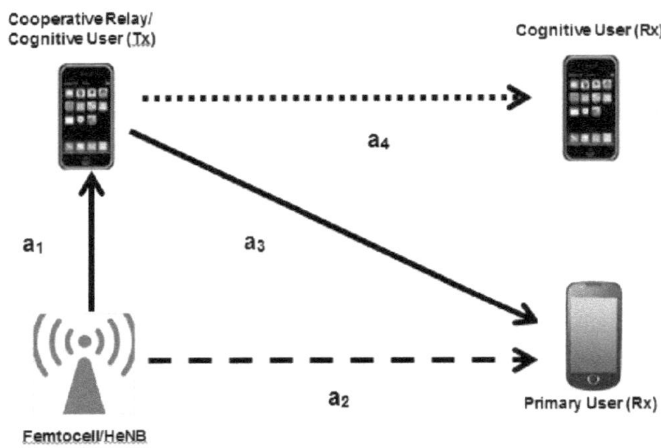

Fig. 6. Cooperative cognitive relay network setup

4 Performance Assessment

Cooperative communication has the potential in enhancing effectiveness of cognitive radio network. For example, apart from conventional direct point-to-point SU network, cognitive relaying has been proposed and studied [15]-[17]. Cognitive relay enables SUs to further expand their network and it allow SUs to transmit at lower power thus reduce possible interference to the PUs while at the same time increase PUs performance.

In order to assess the general network performance of cooperative cognitive relay, network setup as shown in Fig. 6 has been studied by assuming a_1, a_2 and a_3 as the path loss exponents, whereas a_1 and a_3 are the path through the cooperative relay and a_2 is the direct path to the receiver. Other included assumptions are:

i. The transmit power on HeNB is limited to 10W,
ii. Channel between HeNB and cooperative relay (a_1), cooperative relay and PU (a_3), and between cooperative relay and cognitive receiver (a_4) are strong,
iii. Channel between HeNB and PU (a_2) are weak.

Fig. 7 illustrates the achievable rate of PU and SU in variation of transmit power of the cognitive transmitter (α= 0.1 to α=1). The simulation showed that with only direct channel between HeNB to the PU, the achievable data rate is 0.0668Mb/s. However, with the cooperative relay strategy implementation, the maximum achievable data rate rise to 1.236Mb/s when the cognitive transmitter uses 90% of its transmit power to relay the primary data (1- α= 0.9) and the remaining 10% for cognitive secondary data (α=0.1).

In order for PU to achieve data rate up to 1.236Mb/s without the cooperative relay, HeNB would requires transmit power of 450W. This showed how significant is cooperative relaying in enhancing network performance and efficiency.

Thus, from the results we can infer that cooperative communications can significantly increase network performance in cognitive radio network.

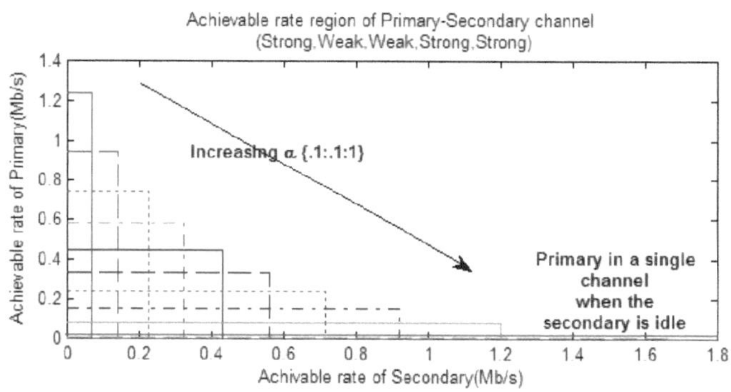

Fig. 7. Achievable data rate of PU and SU in variable cognitive transmitter power, α

5 Conclusion

By investigating every aspect of LTE-Advanced technology, CR is naturally required in many forms. CR technology implementations has been viewed not just as a tool to increase the capacity and performance for LTE-Advanced itself, but also as a techniques to allow secondary user to occupy in licensed LTE-Advanced band without causing harmful interference. Altogether, the ability of CR to sense and manage its environment (spectrum, geo-information, etc.) and resources (space, time and frequency) has favored LTE-Advanced by enhancing adaptability in almost every key technology including CoMP, spectrum aggregation and relay. Also, opportunistic SU network has been made possible by employing CR technology. Moreover, the introduction of cooperative communication will further enhance the network performance to a new level

Further studies can focus more on the novel way to exploit CR capabilities in order to opportunistically gain access in the LTE-Advanced band without causing detrimental effects on PUs performance while at the same time serving acceptable QoS to SUs

Acknowledgments. The authors would like to thanks the CoE in Telecommunication Technology Group for their support in realizing this research project. The work is financed by Zamalah/Institutional Scholarship provided by Universiti Teknologi Malaysia and the Ministry of Higher Education of Malaysia.

References

1. Rysavy Research, Mobile Broadband Capacity Constraints and the Need for Optimization (February 24, 2010)
2. ITU-R M.[IMT.TECH] - Requirements related to technical system performance for IMT-Advanced radio interface(s) (2008)
3. Mogensen, P.E., et al.: LTE-Advanced: The Path towards Gigabit/s in Wireless Mobile Communications. In: Wireless VITAE 2009, pp. 147–151 (2009)
4. Ning, W., Shaoqian, L., Gang, Y.: Joint Processing Precoding for Coordinated Multi-Point Transmission in LTE-A. ZTE Communications (2010)
5. 3GPP TSG RAN WG1 R1-090728 Further considerations on DL reference symbols for LTE-Advanced (February 2009)
6. Grieger, M.: Field Trial Results for a Coordinated Multi-Point (CoMP) Uplink in Cellular Systems. In: 2010 International ITG Workshop on Smart Antennas, pp. 46–51 (2010)
7. Venkatesha Prasad, R., Pawelczak, P., Hoffmeyer, J.A., Steven Berger, H.: Cognitive Functionality in Next Generation Wireless Networks: Standardization Efforts. IEEE Communication Magazine 46(4), 72–78
8. Buddhikot, M.M.: Cognitive Radio, DSA and Self-X: Towards Next Transformation in Cellular Networks. In: IEEE DySPAN 2010, pp. 1–5 (2010)
9. Guang, Y.: Cognitive Radio and Multi-Dimension Cooperative Communications. ZTE Communications 8(1) (March 2008)
10. Wang, W., Zhang, Z., Huang, A.: Spectrum Aggregation: Overview and Challenges. Macrothink Institute, Network Protocols and Algorithms 2(1) (2010)
11. 3GPP TR 36.814 V1.2.1, Further Advancements for EUTRA: Physical Layer Aspects, Tech. Spec.n Group Radio Access Network Rel. 9 (June 2009)
12. Abdelmonem, M., Ismail, M.H., El-Soudani, M.S., Nafie, M.: Coarse Spectrum Sensing for LTE Systems. In: 2010 IEEE 17th International Conference on Telecommunication, pp. 116–121 (2010)
13. Li, G.N., Yang, L., Zhang, N., Cui, K.: A New Primary User Sensing Approach based on LTE Wireless Sensor Networks. In: WiCOM 2009, pp. 1–4 (2009)
14. Parkvall, S., Dahlman, E., Furuskär, A., Jading, Y., Olsson, M., Wänstedt, S., Zangi, K.: LTE-Advanced – Evolving LTE towards IMT-Advanced. In: 2008 IEEE 68th Vehicular Technology Conference, pp. 1–4 (2008)
15. Luo, H., Zhang, Z., Chen, Y., Wang, W., Li, S.: Opportunistic Cognitive Relaying: A Win-Win Spectrum Sharing Scheme, Hindawi Publishing Corporation. EURASIP Journal on Wireless Communications and Networking 2010
16. Mao, X., Qiu, P.: Cognitive Relay. In: Future Generation Communication and Networking (FGCN 2007), pp. 264–269 (2007)
17. Song, C., Shiba, H., Shimamoto, S.: A Cognitive Relay Approach for Multi-hop Wireless Ad hoc Communication. In: ChinaCom 2008, pp. 1230–1234 (2008)
18. Rumney, M.: IMT-Advanced: 4G Wireless Takes Shape in an Olympic Year. Agilent Measurement Journal (September 1, 2008)
19. Yang, Y., Hu, H., Xu, J., Mao, G.: Relay Technologies for WiMAX and LTE-Advanced Mobile Systems. IEEE Communications Magazine (October 2009)

Erratum: Communications in Computer and Information Science: A New Scalable Anonymous Authentication Protocol for RFID

Mohammad Shirafkan, Naser Modiri, Mohammad Mansour Riahi Kashani, and Koosha Sadeghi Oskooyee

Islamic Azad University, North Tehran branch,
Department of Computer Engineering, Tehran, Iran
{Mohammadshirafkan,Nasermodiri}@yahoo.com,
{M_Riahi_Kashani,K_Sadeghi_Oskooyee}@iau-tnb.ac.ir

A. Abd Manaf et al. (Eds.): ICIEIS 2011, Part III, CCIS 253, pp. 639–653, 2011.

DOI 10.1007/978-3-642-25462-8_63

The paper "Communications in Computer and Information Science: A New Scalable Anonymous Authentication Protocol for RFID" authored by Mohammad Shirafkan, Naser Modiri, Mohammad Mansour Riahi Kashani, and Koosha Sadeghi Oskooyee, DOI 10.1007/978-3-642-25462-8_57, appearing on pages 639-653 of this publication has been retracted due to a severe case of plagiarism. It is a plagiarized version of the paper 'A Privacy-Friendly RFID Protocol Using Reusable Anonymous Tickets', authored by Mahdi Asadpour and Mohammad Torabi Dashti, published in the proceedings of the 10th IEEE International Conference on Trust, Security and Privacy in Computing and Communications (TrustCom 2011), DOI 10.1109/TrustCom.2011.29 and of the master thesis 'An Anonymous RFID Authentication Protocol and its Automated Analysis with OFMC' completed by Mahdi Asadpour at ETH Zurich.

The original online version for this chapter can be found at
http://dx.doi.org/10.1007/978-3-642-25462-8_57

Author Index